Mastering

Microsoft®

Exchange Server 2007 SP1

Mastering

Microsoft®
Exchange Server 2007
SP1

Jim McBee

WILEY

Wiley Publishing, Inc.

Acquisitions Editor: Agatha Kim
Development Editor: Stef Jones
Technical Editor: Brian Tirch
Production Editor: Eric Charbonneau
Copy Editor: Kim Cofer
Production Manager: Tim Tate
Vice President and Executive Group Publisher: Richard Swadley
Vice President and Publisher: Neil Edde
Book Designers: Maureen Forys and Judy Fung
Proofreader: Jen Larsen, Word One
Indexer: Ted Laux
Project Coordinator, Cover: Lynsey Stanford
Cover Designer: Ryan Sneed
Cover Image: © Pete Gardner / Digital Vision / Getty Images

Library of Congress Cataloging-in-Publication Data

McBee, Jim.
  Mastering Microsoft Exchange server 2007 SP1 / Jim McBee. — 2nd ed.
      p. cm.
  Includes bibliographical references and index.
  ISBN 978-0-470-41733-1 (paper/website : alk. paper)
  1. Microsoft Exchange server. 2. Client/server computing. 3. Electronic mail systems. I. Title.
QA76.9.C55M26387 2009
  004.692 — dc22
                              2008048403

Dear Reader,

Thank you for choosing *Mastering Microsoft Exchange Server 2007 SP1*. This book is part of a family of premium-quality Sybex books, all of which are written by outstanding authors who combine practical experience with a gift for teaching.

Sybex was founded in 1976. More than thirty years later, we're still committed to producing consistently exceptional books. With each of our titles we're working hard to set a new standard for the industry. From the paper we print on, to the authors we work with, our goal is to bring you the best books available.

I hope you see all that reflected in these pages. I'd be very interested to hear your comments and get your feedback on how we're doing. Feel free to let me know what you think about this or any other Sybex book by sending me an email at nedde@wiley.com, or if you think you've found a technical error in this book, please visit http://sybex.custhelp.com. Customer feedback is critical to our efforts at Sybex.

Best regards,

Neil Edde
Vice President and Publisher
Sybex, an Imprint of Wiley

To the memory of Elizabeth (Betty) Tucker McBee; the best mother a person could ever ask for. February 27, 1937–May 17, 2008.

Acknowledgments

Exchange Server 2007 has been out just over two years now and we are a year into the release of Service Pack 1. Almost a year ago, Agatha Kim (acquisitions editor at Wiley) and I began talking about how this book could be improved with a second edition. We looked carefully at what people had told us they liked as well as places that I felt like we could provide even more content.

Along the way, a lot of people have been involved in reviewing the content of this book. First and foremost is Devin Ganger (3Sharp); Devin jumped on board and developed the content for several chapters. Ben Craig, Simon Butler, Nathan Winters, and Ben Schorr also provided helpful content.

During the early development of the book and the first drafts of chapters, a number of Exchange gurus and administrators provided me with feedback on the book's outline, reviewed chapter content, or just answered my questions. These skilled people include William Lefkovics, Todd Hawkins, Paul Robichaux, John Fullbright, Chuck Swanson, Cynthia Wang, Desmond Lee, Josh Maher, Omar Drubi, Peter O'Dowd, Rich Matheisen, Glen Scales, Bob Christian, David Elfassy, Mark Watts, Andy Schan, Nick Gillott, Vlad Mazek, Rick Taylor, Konrad Sagala, Bob Lawler, Daniel Petri, Andy David, Missy Koslosky, Mark Arnold, Pavel Nagaev, Andy Webb, Bharat Suneja, Elizabeth Owusu, Damion Jones, and Siegfried Jagott. My hat is also off to the hundreds of people I have talked to at conferences and events over the past year who have given me ideas for topics and how things can be better explained.

As with any new product, often not much public information is available prior to its release. Many people at Microsoft patiently and carefully explained new concepts to me and answered questions. These good folks include Kevin Miller, Paul Bowden, David Espinoza, Scott Schnoll, Bharat Suneja, Ross Smith IV, KC Lemson, David Lemson, Jon Gollogly, Karena Lynch, Ben Winzenz, Tim McMichael, Nino Bilic, Melissa Travers, Harold Wong, and Evan Dodds.

I was also extremely lucky to be able to recommend a technical editor. The most experienced Exchange 2007 person I know outside of Microsoft is Brian Tirch. Since the Exchange 2007 beta 1 cycle, Brian has been running an Exchange 2007 organization with thousands of users.

This book gave me an opportunity to once again work with the great folks at Wiley. These include acquisitions editor Agatha Kim, development editor Stef Jones, production editor Eric Charbonneau, copy editor Kim Cofer, and proofreader Jen Larsen. Thanks to all of you for your guidance, sense of humor, and tolerance in the face of deadlines.

Thanks to everyone for all your help. Whatever errors of fact or judgment remain are mine and mine alone.

— *Jim McBee*

About the Author

Jim McBee, Honolulu, Hawaii, MCSE and MCT, is a consultant specializing in Exchange deployments and education and has worked for many Fortune 500 customers as well as the U.S. Department of Defense. He is the author of three editions of *Exchange Server 24/seven* and of *Microsoft Exchange Server 2003 Advanced Administration* and coauthor of *Mastering Microsoft Exchange Server 2007* and *Cabling: The Complete Guide to Network Wiring*, all from Sybex. Jim maintains a heavy speaking schedule at conferences around the world.

Contents at a Glance

Contents

Introduction

Mastering Microsoft Exchange Server 2007 SP1 is the latest in a successful series of Mastering Exchange Server books. Each of these books has had tens of thousands of readers learn the concepts of Exchange Server and helped Exchange administrators successfully support their Exchange systems better and more accurately.

I took a step back and looked at the previous editions of the book to try and figure out how much of the previous material was still relevant. I quickly realized that the book was going to have to be almost completely re-written because the entire administrative model of Exchange 2007 has changed. I was faced with the challenge of not only explaining a completely new management interface, but also the new Exchange Management Shell command-line interface, new server roles, and new features.

I started designing the first edition of this book almost a year before Exchange Server 2007 was to be released. Much of the book was written using Beta 2 code and consequently updated once the released version was ready. As soon as the book was released, I was already thinking about what I would like to add. Some of these things included feedback from readers, but these also included things I was learning as I was implementing Exchange Server 2007 and Exchange Server 2007 SP1. In writing this book, I had a few goals for both the book and the knowledge I wanted to impart to the reader:

♦ The book is designed to help you master the basics of Exchange Server 2007. I want you to get all of the basic skills necessary to install and manage an Exchange Server 2007 system.

♦ The skills and tasks covered in this book should be applicable to 80 percent of all organizations running Exchange Server.

♦ The book should educate not only "new to product" administrators, but those "new to version" administrators that are upgrading from a previous version.

♦ The book should introduce you to that 20 percent feature set that will only be applicable to certain types of organizations such as clustering and Unified Messaging.

Despite the fact that many things have changed in Exchange Server 2007, if you are upgrading from a previous version you will still be comfortable with the concepts and principles of operation. Exchange Server 5.5 was one of the most powerful, extensible, scalable, easy-to-use, and manageable electronic-messaging back-ends on the market. Exchange 2000 Server retained all of 5.5's best features and added new ones. Exchange Server 2003 went a step further, altering interfaces that didn't quite work in the 2000 flavor and adding some great new features.

When I started planning the second edition of this book, I needed to figure out what would change between the first edition and the second edition. I had a few goals that included incorporating reader feedback, discussing the improvements in Exchange Server 2007 Service Pack 1, discussing Windows Server 2008, and sharing some of the practical experience that I have gotten over the past two years. While much of the book is similar to the first edition, you will find new material in almost every chapter.

Microsoft listened to the advice of many of its customers, its internal consultants at Microsoft Consulting Services (MCS), Microsoft Certified Systems Engineers (MCSE), Most Valued Professionals (MVP), and Microsoft Certified Trainers (MCT) to find out what was missing from earlier versions of the product and what organization's needs were. Much of this work even started before Exchange Server 2003 was released. Some common requests, feedback, and complaints that customers frequently provided about earlier versions of Exchange Server included:

- Simplify the management interface and make it easier to script all Exchange management functions.

- Allow for local or remote replicas of Exchange databases.

- Provide better anti-spam capabilities and update anti-spam configuration data and signatures more frequently.

- Provide better security for mobile devices and make them easier to manage.

- Provide better integration with voicemail and faxing solutions.

- Make resource scheduling simpler, more powerful, and better integrated.

- Reduce the burden on help desks by enabling clients to be configured automatically.

Improvements to Exchange Server 2007

Improvements to Exchange Server 2007 are not to any single component of Exchange Server. For starters, the management interface was completely revamped. The new Exchange Management Console simplifies Exchange server administration with a totally redesigned interface that makes finding features and components much easier. The Exchange Management Shell provides a powerful alternative to the Exchange Management Console; all administrative tasks can be performed via the Exchange Management Shell including many advanced tasks that cannot be performed in the graphical user interface. All mail-enabled recipient administration (mailboxes, groups, and contacts) is now performed through the Exchange Management Console utility, not the Active Directory Users and Computers utility; needless to say this was a bit of a controversial decision. The Exchange 2000/2003 extensions for Active Directory Users and Computers no longer work reliably with Exchange Server 2007. Some features continue to work, but mail-enabled objects should not be created through Exchange System Manager and once they have been moved to Exchange 2007 servers they should not be managed using Exchange System Manager.

Another controversial decision was the decision to support only x64 processor architecture. Exchange Server 2007 requires Windows 2003 SP1 x64, Windows 2003 R2 x64, or Windows Server 2008 x64. The decision to support the x64 architecture was driven by the need for more RAM in larger organizations. Exchange Server 2007 has been tested heavily in environments with up to 32GB of RAM. More RAM dramatically improves disk I/O performance.

Exchange Server 2007's tight integration with Active Directory has not changed; almost all of the Exchange configuration data and recipient e-mail attributes are still stored in the Active Directory just as they were with Exchange 2000/2003. A popular misconception is that Exchange recipient configuration is no longer in the Active Directory because the recipient management utility is no longer Active Directory Users and Computers.

To simplify installation of Exchange Server 2007 and to make it easier for organizations that split server functions across multiple servers, the setup program allows you to chose which functions (called roles) the server supports. These roles include the Mailbox server, the Client Access server, the Hub Transport server, the Unified Messaging server, and the Edge Transport server. Additionally, during installation, a server can be configured as either an active cluster server or a passive cluster server. Allowing the installer to easily separate the functions of a server during installation makes setup simpler and makes a server more secure by only installing the components necessary for that server's functions.

One of the most interesting new feature sets for Exchange Server 2007 is the ability to replicate a database to another location on the same server. The replication is based on replicating the transaction logs; once it has been completely filled to another location, the logs are replayed to a backup copy of the database. Local continuous replication allows you to replicate a copy of the database to another location on the local server. Having an almost perfectly synchronized replicate allows you to very quickly recover from a database failure. Clustered continuous replication implementation allows you to keep a replicated copy of the databases from the active node on the passive node of the cluster.

Standby continuous replication (SCR) is one of the most exciting features included with Exchange Server 2007 Service Pack 1. SCR utilizes the Exchange 2007 replication technology to replicate databases to another mailbox server without the complexity of clustering. In the event of a complete outage on the first mailbox server, the database can be brought "live" on the server that hosts the replicated database.

Though features such as sender filtering, recipient filtering, sender ID, and real-time block list features have been retained, anti-spam capabilities have been improved with additional methods of connection filtering such as reputation filtering. An all-new version of the Intelligent Message Filter (IMF) is now included with Exchange Server 2007 and is called the content filter. Customers with Enterprise Client Access Licenses can get daily updates to the reputation filter and the content filter. Anti-spam components can be installed on the Hub Transport servers or they can be offloaded to dedicated Edge Transport servers in an organization's perimeter network. Enterprise Client Access Licenses allow an organization to use Microsoft's Forefront Security for Exchange (formerly Sybari Antigen).

If you ever wanted to have better control of messages "in transit," the re-designed message transport and transport rules will have you dancing on tables. All messages are delivered through a Hub Transport server role regardless of whether they are being delivered locally or remotely. Transport rules allow you to apply conditions to messages moving through the transport (such as sender/recipient, sender/recipient group memberships, message classification, and so on) and take an action on that message.

Calendaring and resource scheduling have been dramatically improved. The Free/Busy functions of earlier versions of Exchange have been completely replaced with a new web service. Resource mailboxes are now specific mailbox types rather than just a generic mailbox as with previous versions. The Calendar Concierge feature allows the administrator to configure automatic resource booking options.

Outlook Web Access is better than ever with a completely revamped interface that includes improved options, better scheduling integration, and the ability to manage mobile devices via the Outlook Web Access interface.

Another new web service is the Autodiscover service; the Autodiscover service works with Outlook 2007 and Windows Mobile 6 devices to enable Outlook to automatically be configured to connect to the correct Exchange resources regardless of whether the client is on the internal network or the external network.

An entirely new Exchange server function is the Unified Messaging server role; this server role integrates with your Voice over IP phone system or legacy PBX via VOIP gateway. This allows Exchange Server to handle your automated call routing, inbound voicemail, and inbound faxing. Exchange users can call in to the Unified Messaging server to retrieve their voice mail, have their e-mail read to them, listen to their calendar, or even move items around on their calendar.

With these and an impressive array of other features, Exchange Server 2007 can help your organization move smoothly and productively into the world of advanced, enhanced electronic messaging.

Windows Server 2008

Exchange Server 2007 Service Pack 1 can run on either Windows Server 2003 x64 or Windows Server 2008 x64. Many Information Technology organizations are now facing the same question. Which operating system should I use?

In most of the environments in which I work, Windows Server 2003 is still the de facto standard for any number of reasons. First and foremost, though, is that it is a known factor in the deployment; most of us have installed Windows Server 2003 many times by now, we are comfortable with it, and we know most everything we need to know to keep it running.

Windows Server 2008, on the other hand, has been released for less than a year. Most Exchange gurus I know have spent the past year or so getting up to speed on Exchange Server 2007 and less time with Windows Server 2008. When you get ready to deploy Exchange Server 2007, which operating system platform should you choose?

First, many medium and large organizations may actually have an information security policy or operational requirements that will prohibit you from deploying newer operating software until there is an officially sanctioned "build" or configuration. If you are in this boat, the decision has been made for you.

If not, though, you need to weigh your options and decide which one is right for you. Even though I know Windows Server 2003 much better, I tend to lean in the direction of Windows Server 2008 for a couple of reasons. Here are some factors that would influence me to choose Windows Server 2008:

◆ When I build a new application platform (such as for Exchange Server), I want to build it to last for three years. This means I don't want to have to install a new operating system or worry about upgrading the servers anytime in the next few years.

◆ Windows Server 2008 *is* the newest Microsoft operating system and it will become the predominant server operating system eventually.

◆ At some point in the next few years, Microsoft will announce that support for Windows Server 2003 will be more limited.

◆ When using technologies such as standby continuous replication or clustered continuous replication, the Mailbox servers involved must all be using the same version of the operating system.

What You Need to Run Exchange Server

Exchange Server 2007 is a complex product but the user interface has been completely revamped to be easier to administer Exchange. All of this complexity and parallel ease of use requires an industrial-strength computer. The minimum server requirement suggested here is for testing, learning about, and evaluating the product. It's also enough for a small, noncritical installation.

However, as I discuss in the book, when the server moves into critical production environments, where it will be accessed by large numbers of users, you'll need to beef up its hardware and add a number of fault-tolerant capabilities. On the client side, with the broad range of clients available for Exchange, the machines in most organizations should be more than adequate.

At a minimum, to test, learn about, and evaluate Exchange Server, you need the following:

♦ Microsoft Exchange Server 2007 Service Pack 1 and Windows Server 2003 SP1, Windows 2003 R2, or Windows Server 2008.

♦ An AMD Athlon x64 or Intel x64 compatible processor with 2GB of RAM and two 18GB disk drives. This allows you to complete exercises involving a single Exchange server.

♦ A minimum of three additional computers in the class just described. This allows you to complete exercises involving multiple computers in multiple administrative groups and Windows Server 2003 domains.

♦ Tape backup hardware or at least one independent disk drive for backup.

♦ A local area network (preferably connected to the Internet).

♦ At least one 800MHz Pentium III or 4 or equivalent computer with 256MB of memory running Windows XP Professional or Windows Vista for testing Outlook and other client-side functions.

During the development of this book, I used a combination of Dell Xeon-based servers, HP Athlon-based servers, and lots and lots of virtual machines using VMWare. During the development, I usually did not have access to 64-bit versions of VMWare so I used the 32-bit version of Exchange Server 2007 SP1 for testing. The 32-bit version of Exchange Server 2007 can be downloaded for evaluation, classroom, lab, and testing purposes, but it is not to be used in production.

How This Book Is Organized

This book is comprised of 26 chapters and an appendix, divided into seven broad topic areas. As you proceed through the book, you'll move from basic concepts to several increasingly complex levels of hands-on implementation.

This book won't work well for practitioners of the timeworn ritual of chapter hopping. Though some readers may benefit from reading one or two chapters, I recommend you read most of the book in order. Unless you already have considerable experience with these products, to get the maximum value out of this book, you need to track through the chapters in order. In later chapters, you will frequently find me referring to previous chapters to get more details on a specific topic.

One entirely new chapter in this book is Chapter 1, "Introduction to Messaging System Administration" this chapter was partially something that I had always wanted to write and partially based on reader feedback. Some readers that were new to managing an e-mail system felt like they did not know the basic concepts involved in managing an e-mail system. So I hope for new e-mail system administrators this chapter will give you more insight into managing an e-mail system.

If you are an Exchange 2000/2003 administrator and you are ready to get started with your migration, I recommend that you pay close attention to Part II, "Installing, Configuring, and Migrating" (Chapter 5, "Installing Exchange Server 2007," and Chapter 6, "Upgrading to Exchange Server 2007"). Though you should not read just these two chapters and then start your migration, these chapters will definitely send you on your way.

However, if you're in a hurry to get your hands dirty, start with Part III, "Basic Exchange Server 2007 Management; Chapter 7, "Administering Exchange Server 2007" will introduce you to the new Exchange Management Console and the new Exchange Management Shell, and Chapter 11, "Managing Recipients," will get you rolling on managing mail-enabled recipients. As long as you're not planning to put your quickie server into production immediately, there should be no harm done. Before going into production, though, I strongly suggest that you explore other parts of this book. Here's a guide to what's in each chapter.

Part 1: Understanding and Planning

This part of the book focuses on concepts and features of Microsoft's Windows Server 2003 and Exchange Server 2007 client/server electronic messaging system. It is designed to provide you with the underlying knowledge that you'll need when you tackle Windows and Exchange Server 2007 installation, administration, and management later in this book.

Chapter 1, "Introduction to Messaging Administration," is for those administrators that have been handed an Exchange organization but have never managed a previous version of Exchange or even another mail system. This will give you some of the basic information and background to help you get started managing Exchange Server and hopefully a little history and perspective.

Chapter 2, "Designing a New Exchange 2007 System," covers Windows Server 2003 and Exchange 2007 system planning and design, facilitating your initial use of these complex products in your organization. Other information includes factors to consider when planning a migration to Exchange Server 2007 from another version.

Chapter 3, "Introducing Exchange Server 2007," presents some basic information about Exchange Server 2007 products, helping you optimize the value of these products in your organization. This chapter introduces you to new features as well as features that are being de-emphasized in Exchange Server 2007.

Chapter 4, "Exchange Server 2007 Architecture," looks in some detail at the decision to move to the 64-bit architecture, as well as system requirements for running Exchange Server 2007. This chapter also discusses the Exchange Server 2007 dependencies on Windows 2003 or Windows 2008 and Active Directory.

Part 2: Installing, Configuring, and Migrating

Microsoft Exchange Server 2007 runs on top of Microsoft's Windows Server 2003 or Windows Server 2008. This part covers the installation of Exchange Server 2007. In previous versions of this book, I had also covered installation of Windows but I recommend you refer to a dedicated Windows reference such as *Mastering Windows Server 2003* by Mark Minasi (Sybex, 2003).

Chapter 5, "Installing Exchange Server 2007," provides the details on Exchange Server 2007 installation, server roles, disk configuration, and basic security.

Chapter 6, "Upgrading to Exchange Server 2007," covers migrating from Exchange 2000 or Exchange 2003 to Exchange Server 2007, including factors to consider before starting a migration and prerequisites. Also included in this chapter are recommendations for migration phases, co-existence, and reasons you would need to keep older Exchange servers in production.

Part 3: Basic Exchange Server 2007 Management

Attention shifts in this section to day-to-day Exchange Server operational tasks. Most of these tasks are carried out within the Exchange Management Console but some can only be performed through the Exchange Management Shell.

Chapter 7, "Administering Exchange Server 2007," covers many of the basic administrative changes to Exchange Server 2007, including the delegating permissions for users, using the Exchange Management Console, and an introduction to using the Exchange Management Shell.

Chapter 8, "Exchange Management Shell Primer," introduces you to some of the basics of Microsoft PowerShell and the Exchange Management Shell (EMS) extensions to PowerShell. Though most Exchange management tasks can be performed from the graphical user interface (GUI), even people who do not script or use the command prompt frequently will find the EMS an attractive and useful alternative to many GUI-based tasks.

Chapter 9, "Exchange Organization, Server, and Recipient Management," focuses on how to find the necessary configuration options for components that affect the entire organization, individual servers, or mail-enabled servers, as well as listing many of the Exchange Management Shell cmdlets. Much of this chapter is covered in more detail in other chapters, but this chapter will help both new Exchange administrators as well as those upgrading from previous versions when you need to find a particular option.

Chapter 10, "Imposing Limits," covers the different types of limits (mailbox sizes, message sizes, folder sizes, connector limits) that an administrator can apply in Exchange 2007 and how to apply them.

Chapter 11, "Managing Recipients," concentrates on the Recipients work center in the Exchange Management Console and on using it to administer and manage mail-enabled recipients. This includes mailbox-enabled users, resource mailbox management, mail-enabled groups, and mail-enabled contacts.

Chapter 12, "Managing Storage," discusses topics such as disk sizing from the perspective of disk space as well as the perspective of getting the I/O capacity right. Other topics include creating and managing databases and storage groups.

Chapter 13, "Managing Address Lists," covers the use of the default global address list, custom address lists, offline address books, and the distribution of offline address books.

Chapter 14, "Managing Mailbox Content," introduces the new messaging records management features of Exchange 2007, including creating managed custom folders, defining folder content settings, and configuring managed folder mailbox policies.

Chapter 15, "Managing Messages in Transit," introduces the new transport rule feature and how to implement this feature. This chapter also discusses message journaling.

Chapter 16, "Public Folder Administration," introduces management of public folders, the Exchange Public Folder Management Console (introduced in Exchange Server 2007 SP1), and the Exchange 2007 Exchange Management Shell cmdlets necessary to manage public folder properties. Additionally, this chapter covers using the Exchange 2003 System Manager console to manage public folder properties and the PFDAVAdmin utility from Microsoft.

Part 4: Exchange Server Reliability and Availability

If you ask your users what they expect most from you as the Exchange server administrator, they will probably tell you uninterrupted messaging service. Well, and maybe that you will answer your cell phone 24 × 7. In this part I discuss techniques for providing better availability for Exchange Server 2007 and for ensuring that you can recover in the event of a server failure or a disaster.

Chapter 17, "Reliability and Availability 101," introduces many of the concepts of providing better availability for Exchange Server 2007, including a lot of basic tips for ensuring that your server platform is reliable and stable. This chapter includes discussions of using Microsoft's Network Load Balancing utility and an introduction to clustering.

Chapter 18, "Implementing Replication Technologies," discusses the new replication features of Exchange Server 2007 including local continuous replication, clustered continuous replication, and standby continuous replication.

Chapter 19, "Backup and Disaster Recovery," includes discussions on developing a backup plan for your Exchange Server 2007 servers as well as backup procedures using the Windows Backup Utility. The chapter also covers restoring mailbox databases and restoring mailbox databases to recovery storage groups.

Part 5: Outlook

Exchange Server is a pretty nifty little gadget. But without clients, it's nothing more than fancy technology. Although this is a book on Exchange Server, the Outlook client merits some discussion. This section is devoted to that discussion.

Chapter 20, "Supporting Outlook 2007," takes an administrative perspective of the Outlook 2007 client, including features that are useful for the Exchange server administrator to be aware of. This chapter includes coverage of the new Autodiscover feature as well as how to set up Exchange Server to support Autodiscover.

Part 6: Connectivity

The Connectivity section of the book covers message delivery and Exchange client connectivity.

Chapter 21, "Delivering E-mail," concentrates on the Hub Transport and Edge Transport roles within an organization. This includes configuring a Hub Transport server to send and receive e-mail directly to and from the Internet or using the Edge Transport server role to provide anti-spam functions.

Chapter 22, "Getting to Know the Client Access Server Role," gives you a deep dive into how to implement the Client Access server in different types of environments, including using it to proxy and refer requests to remote sites and other Client Access servers. Additionally, this chapter provides a discussion and examples on how to use a certificate authority to request SSL certificates for web services.

Chapter 23, "Exchange Anywhere" addresses connectivity to the Exchange server from a variety of clients that might be used remotely, including using Outlook Web Access, Exchange ActiveSync, and Outlook Anywhere (RPC over HTTP). If you have POP3 or IMAP4 clients, this section also covers how to enable and configure these protocols on an Exchange Server 2007 Client Access server role.

Part 7: Security and Tracking Activities

The final section of this book revolves around security, auditing, and tracking, including improving security of each of the server roles, using the Exchange Best Practices Analyzer, enabling protocol logging, tracking messages, and using the Exchange Queue Viewer application.

Chapter 24, "Monitoring Performance," introduces some key concepts that are useful in determining if a server has performance issues. Additional topics include troubleshooting tools and useful analysis tools.

Chapter 25, "Securing Exchange Server," discusses the use of firewalls, hardening Exchange Server using the Security Configuration Wizard, and providing multiple layers of security for Exchange servers. This chapter also includes a discussion on publishing Outlook Web Access and other web applications using a reverse proxy server such as ISA Server.

Chapter 26, "Logging, Auditing, and Monitoring," wraps up my discussion of Exchange Server 2007 with logging, auditing, and monitoring topics. I feel particularly strongly that you should enable a fair degree of auditing and logging features in Exchange Server 2007 because this is frequently one of those things that you don't realize you need until after the fact. In this chapter, I also cover the use of the Queue Viewer and the Exchange Best Practices Analyzer.

Appendix: Cool Third-Party Applications for Exchange Server and Outlook Clients

This book's appendix takes you on a thrill ride through some of the many products that exist today to enhance and extend the reach of Exchange Server. Coverage includes applications and services that:

◆ Make Exchange Server installation and administration easier.

◆ Bring faxing and document management capabilities to Exchange servers.

◆ Improve upon the backup software built into Windows Server 2003/Exchange Server 2007 or third-party tools for Windows Server 2008.

◆ Provide near-line storage message archiving.

◆ Check for potential and actual internal and external security breaches.

◆ Guard Exchange servers and networks against virus attacks and spam messages.

◆ Provide messaging systems linking e-mail, telephone services, voice, and text.

◆ Improve workflow by using e-mail to connect users working on a common task.

Conventions Used in This Book

↩ The code continuation character is used on PowerShell commands to indicate that the line of text is part of a previous command line.

Remember, Exchange is designed to help your organization do what it does better, more efficiently, and with greater productivity. Have fun, be productive, and prosper!

Part 1

Understanding and Planning

In this part:

Chapter 1

Introduction to Messaging Administration

Congratulations! You may have just stepped into the most important job in your entire organization. No, not the CEO, the number one sales person, the janitor, the person that makes sure there is fresh coffee made, or even the one who prints out the monthly TPS reports. I'm talking about the person that keeps the e-mail system running.

Now, do I honestly believe the e-mail system is the most important component of an organization's information technology services? On a dollar-per-dollar basis, an organization's line-of-business applications (such as order entry, accounting, customer relationship management, shipping, billing, and others) are probably the most important types of applications when it comes to the actual value provided. However, e-mail is often one of the most visible services (if not the single most visible service) that IT professionals provide; most organizations have become dependent on "soft" information to run their business. As a result, users have in turn developed an attachment to e-mail that goes beyond the hard value of the information it contains. If there's a problem with e-mail, that affects users' confidence in their ability to do their jobs and their confidence in IT.

There is not much in this chapter that is specific to Exchange Server 2007, so an experienced e-mail administrator may want to proceed directly to Chapter 2, "Designing a New Exchange 2007 System" or Chapter 3, "Introducing Exchange Server 2007." However, everyone needs to start somewhere and if you are new to the job or need a refresher, this chapter is for you!

In this chapter, I attempt to provide a primer on some of the issues that you'll need to know in order to maximize the coverage of Exchange provided in the rest of the book. I hope that this chapter will serve as a good introduction to e-mail administration and prepare you to put Exchange Server 2007 in to the proper context.

In this chapter you learn about:

◆ The basics of e-mail

◆ Things every e-mail administrator should know

◆ A day in the life of the e-mail administrator

◆ E-mail protocols and services

◆ What Exchange Server is

Introducing E-mail

Okay, I agree that "Introducing E-mail" does seem like a pretty silly header, because most everyone within 50 miles of an Internet connection has an e-mail address. Does a simple concept such as sending text and attachments from one person to another really need an explanation? Well, no, but "What Does E-mail Do For Your Users, Or For Your Organization For That Matter?" is too long.

Sure, sending simple text e-mail and file attachments is the most basic function, but e-mail systems (the client and/or the server) may also perform the following important functions:

◆ Act as a personal information manager, providing storage for and access to personal calendars, personal contacts, to-do and task lists, personal journals, and chat histories.

◆ Provide the user with a single "point of entry" for multiple types of information such as voicemail, faxes, and electronic forms.

◆ Provide shared calendars, departmental contacts, and other shared information.

◆ Enable users to send faxes from their desktop to outside of their organization.

◆ Receive notifications of "work flow" processes such as finance/accounting activities, IT events (server status information), and more.

◆ Allow users to access their "e-mail data" through a variety of means including clients running on Windows computers, Apple computers, Unix systems, web browsers, and mobile phones.

◆ Perform records management and enable long-term storage of important information or information that must be archived.

These are just a few of the types of things that an e-mail system may provide to the end user either via the client interface or as a result of some function running on the server.

A Brief History of E-mail

If you're currently responsible for electronic messaging in your organization, no one has to tell you about the steadily expanding use of e-messaging. You know it's happening every time you check the storage space on your disk drives or need an additional tape to complete the backup of your mail server. This section discusses some of the aspects of electronic mail and the ever-changing nature of e-mail. Even experienced Exchange Server administrators may want to review this section to better understand how your users and requirements are evolving.

Over the past ten years, the number of e-mail addresses has grown significantly. The technology research company International Data Corporation (IDC) estimated that in 2002, the number of e-mailboxes worldwide was more than 500 million. As of 2006, the Radicati Group estimates that there are now more than 1.5 billion e-mail accounts worldwide, accounting for more than 135 billion e-mail messages per day.

SLOW INITIAL ADOPTION

I had my first e-mail box on a Digital Equipment Corporation (DEC) VAX/VMS system in 1980 and used e-mail continually through the 1980s. When I said "e-mail" my friends all said "e-what?" Early e-mail systems were looked at by organizations as a luxury or an option rather than an important part of an organization's daily work processes.

E-mail systems really began to take hold in the corporate world around 1988. More rapid adoption started in the mid 1990s. What happened to change these organizations' minds? Well, a few things:

- More and more organizations moved from mainframe-based systems to PC-based systems.

- Electronic information processing for even small and medium-sized businesses became more affordable.

- E-mail clients and e-mail servers included more and more features and capabilities that were attractive to users and management.

- The Internet served as an ideal way to link organizations together, and as more organizations became connected to the Internet people had more options for who they communicated with.

IMPROVING THE INTERFACE

Certainly e-mail systems have come a long, long way since the first mainframe and mini-computer systems from more than 30 years ago. Even the primitive text-based systems like cc:Mail, Microsoft Mail, WordPerfect Office, and Da Vinci eMail that first appeared on local area networks in the late 1980s are almost unrecognizable ancestors when compared with a modern system based on Exchange Server 2007 and Outlook 2007. Early e-mail clients were text-based and usually did not have any features other than the ability to read and send e-mail (no personal information management). Looking at an early version of Microsoft Mail (see Figure 1.1), it seems downright sparse.

FIGURE 1.1
Early e-mail clients had few features.

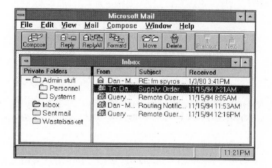

Modern e-mail clients are much more feature-rich than their predecessors. One interesting evolution is the features available when creating a message. New clients allow for the creation of much more complex e-mail messages than in the past. What does "more complex" mean? Well, take as an example the message shown in Figure 1.2. This Outlook 2007 message is formatted with fonts, a numbered list, a substantial message signature/disclaimer, and a corporate logo in the signature; all of this is formatted using HTML or rich text so that the message is viewable by any web-based mail system or HTML-compatible client. Finally, the message is digitally signed and authenticated with a digital signature.

Messages formatted with rich text or HTML, containing disclaimers and digital signatures, can help us to communicate more effectively. Therefore, organizations depend far more on e-mail today than they did even five years ago, and their users send even more mail than in the past.

In addition to regular e-mail messages, users are sending scheduling requests, contact items, forms-enabled e-mail messages, and more. Each of these increases the complexity of the messaging system and also an organization's dependency on it.

FIGURE 1.2

A typical modern e-mail message

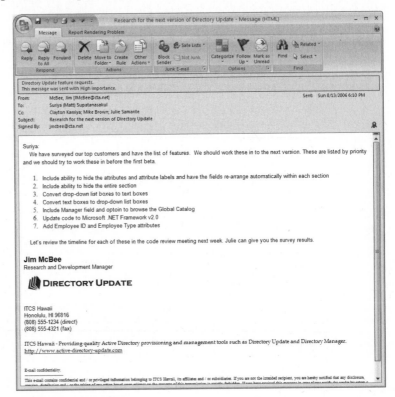

The message shown in Figure 1.2 it is 30KB in size, but has only a few hundred bytes of actual message content, including the recipient information.

Attachments

As if that weren't complex enough, many e-mail messages contain *attachments* — word-processing, spreadsheet, and other files that you can attach to messages. Using attachments is a simple way to move files to the people who need to see them. They also tend to gobble up disk space extremely fast!

Sure, you could send your files on disk or tell people where on the network they can find and download them. But e-mail attachments let you make the files available to others with a click of their mouse buttons. Recipients just double-click an icon and the attachment opens in the original application that produced it (always assuming your correspondent has access to an application or software compatible with the attachment). Using attachments offers the added advantage of putting the files and accompanying messages right in the faces of those who need to see them. This leaves less room for excuses such as "I couldn't find/open that network folder" or "The dog ate the disk."

As great as attachments can be, they have one real weakness: The minute an attachment leaves your Outbox, it's out-of-date. If you do further work on the original file, the work is not reflected in the copy that you sent to others. If someone then edits a copy of the attached file, it's totally out of sync with the original and all other copies. Getting everything synchronized again can involve tedious hours or days of manually comparing different versions and cutting and pasting them to create one master document.

Shared Files

Office 2003 and Office 2007 offer two neat ways to avoid this problem. First, they let you insert a link to a file. When you open the file, you're opening the file the link points to. If the file is changed, you see the changed file. Second, Office lets you attach a file to a message and set a shared folder where an updatable version of the file is stored. When the copy attached to the user's e-mail is updated, these updates can be incorporated into the shared copy of the file. This option allows broader access to the file than a link.

The use of portals such as Microsoft Office SharePoint Server is becoming increasingly commonplace in organizations as they look for better ways to store, find, and manage the data that their users are producing. As new versions of Outlook and Outlook Web Access offer better integration with SharePoint and provide an alternate to using e-mail for attachments, messaging administrators may start being able to reduce or even remove the impact of attachments in e-mail.

About Messaging Services

Electronic messaging is now far more than e-mail. Together, Exchange Server 2007 and its clients perform a variety of messaging-based functions. These include e-mail, message routing, scheduling, and support for several types of custom applications. Together these features are called messaging services.

How Messaging Services Are Used

Certainly, e-mail is a key feature of any messaging system, and the Outlook Calendar is far better than previous versions of Microsoft's appointment and meeting-scheduling software. Outlook 2007 together with Exchange 2007 introduces even more improvements. Figures 1.3 and 1.4 show the Outlook 2007 client Inbox and Calendar in action.

Figure 1.5 shows the new Outlook Web Access 2007 web browser client that you can use with Exchange Server 2007.

E-mail clients are exciting and sexy, but to get the most out of Exchange Server 2007, you need to throw away any preconceptions you have that messaging systems are only for e-mail and scheduling. The really exciting applications are not those that use simple e-mail or scheduling, but those that are based on the routing capabilities of messaging systems. These applications bring people and computers together for improved collaboration.

How Messaging Servers Work

At the core of any messaging system, you will find a common set of basic functions. These functions may be implemented in wildly different ways depending on the vendor or even the version of the product. Exchange Server has evolved dramatically over the past 13 years and its current architecture is almost nothing like the Exchange Server from 1996. Common components of most messaging systems include:

◆ A message transport system that moves messages from one place to another. Examples include the Simple Mail Transport Protocol (SMTP) or Remote Procedure Calls (RPCs).

◆ A message storage system that stores messages until a user can read or retrieve them. Messages may be stored in a client/server database, a shared file database, or even in individual files.

◆ A directory service that allows a user to look up information about the mail system's users such as a user's e-mail address.

◆ A client access interface on the server that allows the clients to get to their stored messages. This might include a Web interface, a client/server interface (such as RPCs), or the Post Office Protocol (POP).

◆ The client program that allows users to read their mail, send mail, and access the directory. This may include Outlook, Outlook Web Access, or iPhones.

FIGURE 1.3
The Outlook 2007 client Inbox

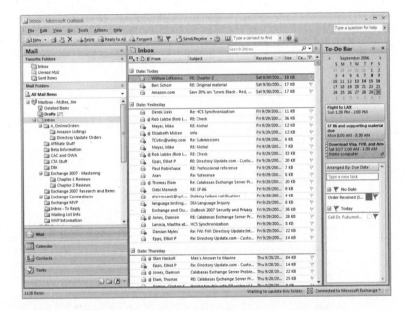

FIGURE 1.4
The Outlook 2007 client Calendar

FIGURE 1.5
Outlook Web Access web browser accesses mail stored on an Exchange Server 2007

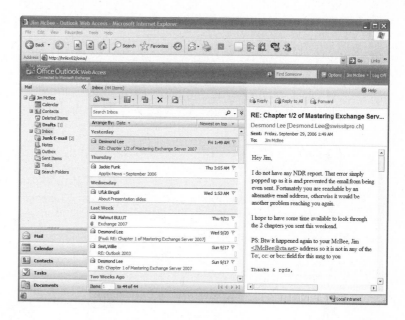

Working in tandem with real-time interactive technologies, electronic messaging systems have already produced a set of wildly imaginative business, entertainment, and educational applications with high payoff potential. All of this action, of course, accelerates the demand for electronic messaging capabilities and services.

Most organizations that deploy an e-mail system usually deploy additional components from their e-mail software vendor or third parties that extend the capabilities of the e-mail system or provide required services. These include:

◆ Message hygiene systems that help reduce the likelihood of a malicious or inappropriate message being delivered to a user

◆ Backup and disaster recovery solutions

◆ Message archival software to allow for the long-term retention and indexing of e-mail data

◆ Electronic forms routing software that may integrate with accounting, order entry, or other line-of-business applications

◆ Mail gateways to allow differing types of mobile phones to access the mail server such as BlackBerry devices or Palm-based mobile phones

◆ E-mail security systems that improve the security of e-mail data either while being transferred or while sitting in the user's mailbox

Application Networking Models

The technology industry has overused the term *client/server* to the point where it is almost meaningless. To put it simply, there are two kinds of networked applications: shared-file and client/server. The typical Exchange Server and Outlook deployment is a client/server messaging system and always has been. However, for people just getting involved in Exchange Server deployments, these concepts should be reviewed. It is also helpful to note that Exchange Server and Outlook are completely separate components. Although Outlook is the most popular (and feature-rich) client for Exchange Server, some organizations deploy Exchange Server entirely for Web or POP3 clients

SHARED-FILE APPLICATIONS

Early networked applications were all based on *shared-file* systems. The network shell that let you load your word processor from a network server also allowed you to read from and write to files stored on a server. At the time, this was the easiest and most natural way to grow networked applications.

Microsoft's first e-mail product, Mail for PC Networks, was a shared-file application. You ran a Windows, OS/2, DOS, or Macintosh client application, which sent and received messages by accessing files on a Microsoft Mail for PC Networks post office that resided on a network file server. The front-end application and your PC did all the work; the server was passive. Figure 1.6 shows a typical Microsoft Mail for PC Networks setup.

FIGURE 1.6

Microsoft Mail for PC Networks is a typical shared-file electronic messaging system.

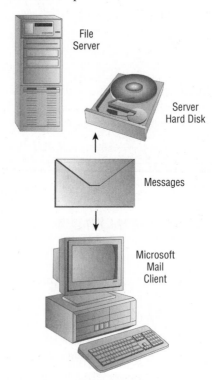

File Server

Server Hard Disk

Messages

Microsoft Mail Client

Easy as it was to deploy, this architecture leads to some serious problems in today's networked computing world:

◆ Changing the underlying structure of the server file system is difficult because you have to change both the server and the client.

◆ System security is always compromised because users must have read and write permissions for the whole server file system, which includes all other users' message files. Things are so bad that in some cases a naive or malicious user can actually destroy shared-file system databases.

◆ Network traffic is high because the client application must constantly access indexes and hunt around the server's file system for user messages.

◆ Because the user workstation writes directly to shared files, the server-based files can be destroyed if workstation hardware or software stops functioning for some unexpected reason.

◆ Often the client program would open these shared files and lock them for use. This frequently prevented important data files from being backed up.

Though they are still around (an Access database is a shared-file database, for example), shared-file applications are in decline. Sure, plenty of *legacy* (that is, out-of-date) applications will probably live on for the data-processing equivalent of eternity, but client/server systems have quickly supplanted the shared-file model. This is especially true in the world of electronic messaging.

CLIENT/SERVER APPLICATIONS

Though they have some limitations of their own, client/server applications overcome the shortcomings of shared-file apps. So today, networked applications increasingly are based on the client/server model. The server is an active partner in client/server applications. Clients tell servers what they want done using some common protocol, and if security requirements are met, servers do what they are asked.

Processes running on a server find and ship data to processes running on a client. When a client process sends data, a server receives it and writes it to server-based files. Server processes can do more than simply interact with client processes. For example, they can compact data files on the server or — as they do on Exchange Server — automatically reply to incoming messages to let people know, for instance, that you're going to be out of the office for a period of time.

A very simplified example of this is shown in Figure 1.7. In step 1, the client requests a specific e-mail message from the server. Then, in step 2, the server responds by opening the appropriate database, searching through the database, retrieving the message, and sending it back to the client in step 3. Although the database might be hundreds of gigabytes in size, this operation usually takes less than a second.

FIGURE 1.7
A simple client/server messaging system

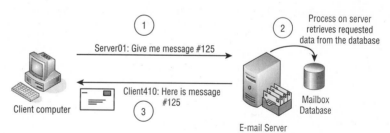

Client/server applications are strong in all the areas in which shared-file apps are weak:

◆ Changing the underlying structure of the server file system is easier than with shared-file systems because only the server processes access the file system.

◆ System security can be much tighter, again because only the server processes access the file system.

◆ Network traffic is lighter because all the work of searching and data access is done by the server, on the server.

◆ Because server processes are the only ones that access server data, breakdowns of user workstation hardware or software are less likely to spoil data. With appropriate transaction logging features, client/server systems can even protect against server hardware or software malfunctions.

As good as the client/server model is, it does have some general drawbacks. Client/server apps require more computing horsepower, especially on the server side. With Exchange, therefore, you should plan to start with very fast Pentium or better machines, lots of RAM, and plenty of hard disk and tape backup capacity — and expect to grow from there.

Client/server applications are more complex than shared-file apps. This is partly because of the nature of the client/server model and partly because client/server apps tend to be newer and thus filled with all kinds of great capabilities that you won't find in shared-file applications. Generally, you're safe in assuming that you'll need to devote more, and more sophisticated, human resources to managing a client/server application than to tending to a similar application based on shared files.

The good news is that Microsoft has done a lot to reduce the management load and to make it easier for someone who isn't a computer scientist to administer an Exchange system. I've looked at many client/server messaging systems, and I can say without any doubt that Exchange is absolutely the easiest to administer, even in its slightly more complex 2007 implementation. Exchange Server 2007 includes both a graphical user interface (GUI) and a management shell that organizes the processes of management very nicely. With these interfaces, you can do everything from adding users to assessing the health of your messaging system.

Things Every E-mail Administrator Should Know

The information in this section is something that I often find even my own e-mail administrators and help desk personnel are not aware of. Sometimes the most important skill any technology administrator has is not a specific knowledge of something, but generic knowledge that they can use to quickly find the right answer.

Finding Answers

This topic deserves special attention. One of my jobs is working in Tier 3 support for a large organization. The thing I respect the most about the administrators that actually run the system and handle the trouble tickets is if they have done their homework prior to coming to me with a problem.

Too often techies tend to make up an answer when they are not sure about something. Don't do that! When you are asked a question that you don't know the answer to, it is okay to say you don't know the answer. But follow that up by indicating that you will find the answer. Knowing the right resources (where to get answers) is therefore just as important as the technical knowledge it takes to implement the answer.

HELPFUL RESOURCES

Exchange has to be one of the most documented and discussed products (short of maybe Windows) that Microsoft produces. This means that most of the questions that I have about Exchange Server I can usually answer with the right Google search or looking in the right place. The most obvious place to start when you have a problem or a question is to perform an Internet search, but there are many other resources.

Exchange Server documentation   There is a world of information available to you out on the Internet, but let's start right on the local hard disk of your Exchange Server or anyplace you have installed the admin tools. Microsoft has done an excellent job of providing better and better documentation for Exchange Server over the past few years. The Exchange Server 2007 documentation is comprehensive and so readable you will wonder if it is really from Microsoft. Figure 1.8 shows an example of the Exchange 2007 documentation. Look for the following file: `C:\Program Files\Microsoft\Exchange Server\Bin\ExchHelp.chm` or run it from the Microsoft Exchange Server 2007 folder on the Start menu.

FIGURE 1.8

Viewing the Exchange 2007 documentation

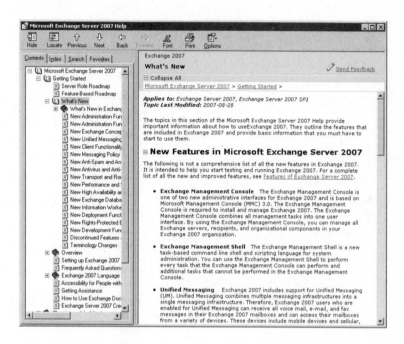

You can also download updated versions of the `ExchHelp.chm` from the following URL:

`http://technet.microsoft.com/en-us/exchange/bb330843.aspx?wt.svl=2007resources`

Exchange Server release notes   Another good resource for "I wish I had known that" types of things is the release notes. You should be able to find a link to the release notes here:

`C:\Program Files\Microsoft\Exchange Server\RelNotes.htm`

Exchange Server TechNet forums   If you have a question on which you have done your due diligence in searching and researching the problem, but you don't have an answer, it is time to ask the world. A good place to start is the Microsoft TechNet forums. You can find the Exchange server section here:

`http://forums.microsoft.com/technet/default.aspx?siteid=17`

When you post your question, please do not post a question like "Exchange is giving me an error." Post the exact error message and any error codes you are seeing. Also indicate, at minimum, what version of the software you are using (including service pack), the role of the server, and what operating system.

MSExchange.Org website   One of the best sites on the Internet for free, easy-to-access content about Exchange Server is `www.msexchange.org`. The articles are written by Exchange gurus from all over the world and are usually in the form of easy-to-read and easy-to-follow tutorials. There is also a forums section where you can post questions or read other people's questions.

CALLING FOR SUPPORT

If your system is down or your operations are seriously hindered and you don't have a clue what to do next, it is time to call in the big guns. Sure, you should do some Internet searches to try and resolve your problem, but Internet newsgroups and forums are not the place to get support for "business critical" issues.

Microsoft Product Support Services (PSS) is Microsoft's technical support organization. Its home page is `http://support.microsoft.com`. Professional support options (ranging from peer-to-peer support to telephone support) can be found at the following URL:

`http://support.microsoft.com/default.aspx?scid=fh;en-us;Prodoffer11a`

Telephone support is currently US$245 per incident for supporting during normal business hours; though this may seem expensive, believe me, when an Exchange server is down and the users are burning you in effigy in the company parking lot, $245 for business hours support is cheap.

When you call and get a support technician on the phone, don't be surprised or offended if he or she starts at the beginning and asks you a lot of elementary questions. They have to double-check everything you have done before they can look into more advanced problems. Once or twice, one of these basic questions has helped me locate a problem that I was convinced was more complicated than it really was.

I always encourage people to call PSS if they truly need assistance. But PSS engineers are not mind-readers, nor do they know every bit of Exchange code. You will do both yourself and the PSS engineer a big favor if you have all of your ducks in a row before you call. Do the following before you call:

◆ Attempt a graceful shutdown and restart of the server in question, if applicable.

◆ Perform a complete online backup if possible; if not, do a complete offline backup.

◆ Have a complete, documented history of everything you have done to solve the problem. At the first sign of trouble, you should start keeping a chronological log of the things you did to fix the problem.

◆ Find out if you are allowed to initiate support sessions with remote support personnel through a tool like Live Meeting or WebEx.

◆ Be at a telephone that is physically at the server's console, or be in a place where you can access the server remotely via the Remote Desktop Client. Your support call will be very brief if you cannot immediately begin checking things for the PSS engineer.

◆ Have the usernames and passwords that will provide you the right level of administrative access. If you don't have those, have someone nearby who can log you in.

◆ Save copies of the System and Application event logs. Be prepared to send these to PSS if requested.

◆ Download a copy of MPSReports (for more information see `http://exchangeorg.net /archive/2004/06/30/mpsreports-exchange-edition.aspx`) and run it on your Exchange server. Be prepared to send the resulting report to PSS if requested.

◆ Know the location of your most recent backup and how to access it when needed.

◆ Keep copies of all error messages. Don't paraphrase the message. Screen captures work great in this case. Pressing Alt+Print Scrn and pasting into a WordPad document works great, too. I usually create a document with screen captures along with notes of what I was doing when I saw each message.

Be patient; telephone support is a terribly difficult job. A little kindness, patience, and understanding on your part will most certainly be returned by the PSS engineer.

A Day in the Life of the E-mail Administrator

I know and work with a *lot* of e-mail administrators and I can honestly say that no two people have the same set of tasks required of them. Your CEO, Director of Information Technology, or even your supervisor is going to ask you to pull rabbits out of your hat, so don't expect each day to be the same as the last one. (And invest in some rabbits.) Keep up with your technology and supporting products so that you can be ready with answers or at the very least intelligent responses to questions.

DAILY ADMINISTRATIVE TASKS

So, what are some typical tasks that you may perform as part of your duties as an e-mail administrator? These tasks will really depend on the size of your organization, the number of administrators you have running your Exchange organization, and how administrative tasks are divided up.

◆ **Recipient management** is certainly the biggest day-to-day task involved with Exchange for medium and large organizations where there is lots of turn-over. Recipient management tasks may include:

    ◆ Assigning a mailbox to a user account

    ◆ Creating mail-enabled contacts

    ◆ Creating and managing mail groups

    ◆ Managing mail-enabled object properties such as users' phone numbers, assigning more e-mail addresses to a user, or adding/removing group members.

◆ **Basic monitoring tasks** to ensure that your Exchange servers are healthy and functioning properly:

    ◆ Checking queues for stalled messages

    ◆ Verifying that there is sufficient disk space for the databases and logs

    ◆ Making sure that the message hygiene system is functioning and up-to-date

    ◆ Running and verifying daily backups

    ◆ Reviewing the System and Application event logs for unusual activity, errors, or warnings

◆ **Daily troubleshooting tasks** include the following:

    ◆ Reviewing non-delivery report messages and figuring out why some mail your users are sending might not have been delivered.

    ◆ Looking up errors and warnings that show up in the Application and System event logs to determine if they are serious and warrant corrective action.

◆ **Security related tasks** are sometimes performed daily but others are performed only weekly or monthly:

- ◆ Looking at server and service up-times to ensure that servers are not rebooting unexpectedly.

- ◆ Reviewing the event logs for warnings that may indicate users are inappropriately accessing other users' data.

- ◆ Saving the Web and SMTP and connectivity logs.

◆ **E-mail client administration tasks** include the following:

- ◆ Helping users get Outlook connected and configured properly.

- ◆ Diagnosing problems Windows Mobile devices, BlackBerry devices, or iPhones.

COMMUNICATING WITH YOUR USERS

Communicating with your users is probably one of the most important things you do. Keeping your users informed and delivering good customer service is almost as important as delivering the IT service itself. Keeping users informed of full or partial service outages such as mobile or BlackBerry support or Web connectivity may not score any immediate points, but users appreciate honest, forthright information. Remember how you felt the last time you were waiting for an airplane to arrive that kept on being delayed and delayed and all the airline could do was be evasive?

PREPARING REPORTS

Maybe I have just worked in a large IT environment for too long now, but it seems to me that Information Technology is more and more about reports and metrics and less about delivering technological capabilities to the users. I am frequently asked to provide reports, statistics, and information on usage — not necessarily information on performance (how well the system performed for the users), but other types of metrics. Depending on your management, you may be asked to provide:

- ◆ Total number of mailboxes and mailbox sizes

- ◆ Top system users and top source/destination domains

- ◆ Anti-spam and message hygiene statistics

- ◆ Disk space usage and growth

- ◆ System availability reports indicating how much unscheduled downtime may have been experienced during a certain reporting period.

Exchange does not provide you with a way to easily access most of this data. The mailbox statistics can be generated using the Exchange Management Shell, but many of these will actually require a third-party reporting product.

Something that you can do to prepare for a reporting requirement is to ensure that you are keeping two to four weeks' worth of message tracking and protocol logs.

SCHEDULED DOWNTIME, PATCHES, AND SERVICE PACKS

No one likes downtime, whether it is scheduled or not. Management may actually be holding you to a specific service level agreement (SLA) that requires you to provide so many hours of up-time per month or to provide e-mail services during certain hours. Unscheduled downtime is anything that happens during your stated hours of operation that keeps users from accessing their e-mail.

Even a small organization can provide very good availability for its mail services, and without large investments in hardware. Good availability begins with the following:

◆ Server hardware should always be from a reputable vendor.

◆ Server hardware should be installed using the vendor recommended procedures.

◆ Once the server is in production it should not be used as a test-bed for other software.

Don't underestimate the importance of training and documentation. In general, the industry formula for providing better availability for any system is to spend more money to purchase redundant servers and build fail-over clusters. But often better training for IT personnel and a simple investment in system documentation as well as system policies and procedures can improve availability as well, and for less money. I once became involved in a system outage where an untrained operator accidentally brought down a 15,000 mailbox cluster simply because he had been asked to do a task he had never done before and there was no documentation on how to proceed. So keep in mind that documentation, training, and procedures are very important in improving up time.

Even the biggest fail-over clusters and most highly available systems need some scheduled downtime. Even if it is scheduled in the wee hours of the morning, undoubtedly someone somewhere somehow will need access when you are working on the system. Therefore, your scheduled downtime should be documented as part of your operational plans and your user community should know about these plans. The specific time window for maintenance should always be the same; for some organizations, this might be 6:30PM–10:30PM on Thursday once per month, whereas other organizations might schedule downtime 11:00PM until 4:00AM every Sunday.

The number one reason for downtime is to apply updates and fixes to the operating system or to the applications running on the server. Microsoft releases monthly updates for the Windows operating system and Windows components. Every few months, Microsoft releases roll-up (RU) fixes for Exchange Server 2007 that fix bugs or that may even add functionality.

Microsoft's updates are usually downloaded to your servers shortly after they are released. The server can download them directly from Microsoft or they can be downloaded from a Windows Software Update Service (WSUS) server inside your network. It is important that you make sure the Automatic Updates component of Windows Server is configured correctly. Figure 1.9 shows the Automatic Updates properties.

Configure the server with the option Download Updates For Me, But Let Me Choose When To Install Them. This is an important setting because if you choose the Automatic (Recommended) option, the server will automatically apply any update within a day or so of downloading the update. This is not a desirable result. Instead, you want the server to download the updates and notify you via the updates icon in the system tray.

FIGURE 1.9
Configuring automatic
updates

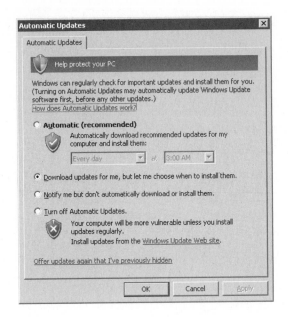

Tools You Should Know

Out of the box, Exchange Server is an excellent product, but sometimes the base software that you install can use some assistance. Some of these tools are actually installed with Exchange Server whereas other tools you may need to download.

PowerShell and the Exchange Management Shell   Even here in the very first chapter, I am extolling the virtues of the new management shell (or command line and scripting interface) for Windows called PowerShell. PowerShell enables some basic Windows management functions, such as managing event logs and services, to be performed via a command-line interface. This interface is simple to use and easy to learn, even for a GUI guy like me. The Exchange team has built the entire Exchange Server 2007 management interface as an extension to PowerShell. It is called the Exchange Management Shell (or EMS).

Though almost every chapter in this book will include at least some information about using the EMS to perform Exchange management tasks, I have dedicated all of Chapter 8, "Exchange Management Shell Primer," to helping you learn the EMS.

Exchange Management Shell test cmdlets   The Exchange Management Shell (EMS) has a series of command-line tools that are very useful for testing and diagnosing problems. These include tools for testing Outlook Web Access connectivity, Unified Messaging connectivity, Outlook connectivity, and even mail flow. They are installed when you install the Exchange Server 2007 Management Tools. For more information, at the EMS prompt type **Get-Help test***.

Exchange analyzers and troubleshooters   In the Exchange Management Console under the Toolbox section (shown in Figure 1.10) you can find a series of troubleshooting wizards and analyzation tools including the Exchange Best Practices Analyzer, the database troubleshooting wizard, and the performance troubleshooting wizard.

One of the most essential things that you can learn is how to use the Exchange Best Practices Analyzer to run Health Check reports and determine if there is something that might not be configured properly within your organization.

FIGURE 1.10

Viewing the Exchange Management Console Toolbox

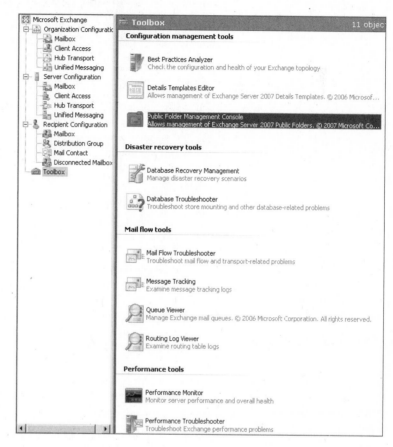

PFDAVAdmin Public Folder Management Tool   If your organization uses a lot of Exchange public folders, you may find that Exchange Public Folder Management Console is just not sufficient for managing permissions and propagating settings throughout the public folder tree. PFDAVAdmin is a powerful, free tool from Microsoft that is intended for advanced public folder property manipulation. You can download PFDAVAdmin from here:

`http://technet.microsoft.com/en-us/exchange/bb330849.aspx`

ADModify.NET   If you need to make bulk changes to Active Directory Objects such as users, groups, contacts, or even public folders, then you need ADModify.NET (shown in Figure 1.11). This powerful and free tool allows you to find and select objects from the Active Directory and then use a simple interface to modify one or more attributes of the selected objects. You can even use other attributes of that object to build a new attribute.

There are a few important things to note about ADModify. You must run it from your local hard disk, and the Microsoft .NET Framework v2.0 is required. Another important item to note is that it has an "undo" feature; you can back out a bulk change that you made if it turns out to be wrong. You can download ADModify from `http://www.codeplex.com/admodify`.

FIGURE 1.11
The main search screen
of ADModify.NET

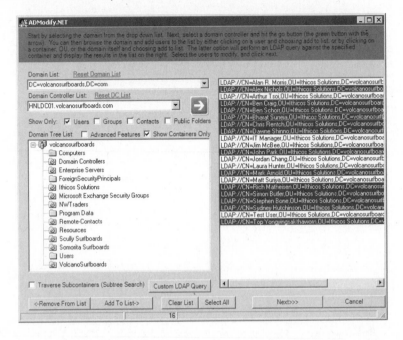

Quest ActiveRoles Management Shell for Active Directory   Quest Software is giving away one of the most useful add-in tools for Microsoft PowerShell that I have ever used. Its Management Shell for Active Directory allows you to manage users and groups using PowerShell even if you don't yet have Exchange Server 2007. I use this tool almost daily in organizations that have not yet migrated to Exchange Server 2007. You can download this free tool from Quest at:

`http://www.quest.com/powershell/activeroles-server.aspx`

PowerGUI   If you like the Quest ActiveRoles Management Shell, you will also like Power-GUI. PowerGUI is a graphical interface that "wraps itself" around PowerShell and allows you to see the results of PowerShell cmdlets. It will help you in writing scripts utilizing the Power-Shell and other extensions to PowerShell. A sample of PowerGUI is shown in Figure 1.12.

You can download PowerGUI from `http://powergui.org`.

Standards and Protocols

E-mail didn't just spring forth one day from the heads of the founders of the Internet fully formed and fully functional. Although few people fully appreciate it, the global e-mail system we take for granted every day is in a constant state of evolution. Countless numbers of systems participate in millions of daily connections, no two the same.

Every day, you and other people around the world effortlessly send and receive e-mail. By this point in time there have been hundreds, perhaps thousands, of e-mail clients and servers that have been, are being, and will be used, each with different design philosophies, features, and underlying programming languages.

FIGURE 1.12
Using the PowerGUI tool

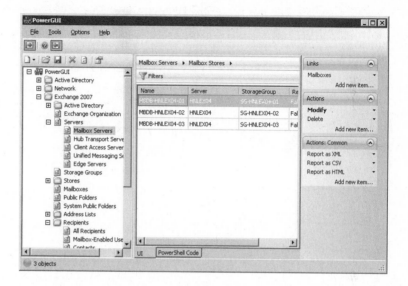

In order for these servers and clients to interoperate, there has to be at least some level of standardization. Although modern e-mail systems are overwhelmingly based on SMTP and a handful of related protocols and technologies, that wasn't always the case.

Components of an E-mail System

No matter the specifics of application and server, a handful of components and roles are involved in any e-mail transmission:

◆ The **mail user agent (MUA)** is the component that the user directly interacts with. If I were to use a postal metaphor, the MUA is roughly the equivalent of your local mailbox at the end of the driveway. Traditionally, the MUA has been a stand-alone client application such as Outlook; however, a web-based client such as Outlook Web Access also offers MUA functionality, even though it is a technically a server-side application.

◆ The **mail retrieval agent**, closely related to the MUA, is the component that handles retrieving messages from the main mail store. Depending on which protocols you are using, such as the Post Office Protocol (POP) or Internet Mailbox Access Protocol (IMAP), you can't just rely on new messages to be pushed to your MUA; something needs to pull them down for you. Typically, the MRA is not a separate component in modern systems, but a set of additional routines in the MUA that support message retrieval.

◆ If the MUA is the local mailbox, the **mail transport agent (MTA)** is the Post Office infrastructure connecting different towns and cities with each other. The MTA is responsible for accepting messages from other systems such as MUAs and MTAs, routing them, and ensuring their delivery on to their recipients. Messages typically travel though two

MTAs — the sender's and the recipient's (unless, of course, they share an MTA). In an Exchange 2007 system, the Hub Transport and Edge Transport roles fill the MTA role.

◆ Just as the MRA is a variant role often performed by the MUA, the **mail submission agent (MSA)** is a specialized form of the MTA. It's adapted to accept mail submissions from the MUA, introduce them into the mail flow, and handle any specialized processing that may be required. In Exchange 2007, this function is handled both in the Mailbox role as well as the Client Receive Connector on the Hub Transport role.

◆ What's missing from this picture? In this case, it's the equivalent of the local Post Office (or, if you prefer, the mail room in the big corporation) — the **mail delivery agent (MDA)** or **local delivery agent (LDA)**. Once the incoming message has been delivered to the proper collection of systems, the MDA/LDA is responsible for ensuring it's been put into the correct mailbox.

Each e-mail system can use a wide variety of solutions to implement these functions. Some applications, such as Exchange, incorporate all of these functions into a single end-to-end offering, whereas others provide just one piece of the puzzle, relying on other applications to provide the missing functionality. Even when using a complete solution, however, you can always mix and match pieces to provide functionality (such as using a third-party client for MUA functionality, or an edge mail appliance as an MTA to other mail systems). To ensure that these implementations work together, a series of standards have been developed over time.

Defining the Standards

When you have this many moving parts in a system — especially when they can be created, implemented, and configured by anyone — it helps if you define how the various parts work together. Although trying to create a true central authority for the Internet is a futile exercise, over the years the Internet community has evolved a method for describing, proposing, discussing, and documenting the various protocols that are in use across the world: a document known as the *Request For Comment*, or RFC.

RFCs began as informal memos among members of the academic teams that invented and programmed the hardware and software used to develop the Advanced Research Projects Agency Network (ARPANET), which was an early predecessor of the Internet. Whenever a team member wanted to suggest a new feature or protocol to the rest of the team, they'd write up an RFC describing their idea as a formal invitation for feedback. Over the years, as the ARPANET grew into the core of the Internet, RFCs expanded in scope to become more formal definitions and descriptions, sometimes retroactive.

Taken in total, the RFC archives provide a fascinating history of the Internet, although not all of the various technologies that have been used were documented through RFCs. Many of these alternatives, such as the X.400 standard for Message Handling Systems, were much more complicated and harder to implement than the systems described in the RFCs. In the end, the commercially developed X.400 standard and accompanying X.500 directory service protocols lost to SMTP, LDAP, and DNS. The latter protocols were all freely available in RFCs, allowing anyone with the time and interest to develop their own implementations.

RFCs are not static; they can contain errors or even just erroneous assumptions. As the world has changed, older RFCs are often updated, modified, or even superseded by newer RFCs. You can examine any of the RFCs online at `www.rfc-editor.org`. Table 1.1 summarizes some of the important mail transport RFCs.

TABLE 1.1:   Some of the Common RFCs Relating to SMTP

RFC	TITLE	DESCRIPTION
821	Simple Mail Transfer Protocol	Defines how clients and servers transmit messages to each other using a simple, text-based conversational model. Released in August 1982; modified by 974 and 1869 among others; obsoleted by 2821.
822	Standard for the Format of ARPA Internet Text Messages	Defines the format and some of the standard headers used in messages passed by SMTP. Released in August 1982; modified by 1123 among others; obsoleted by 2822.
974	Mail Routing and the Domain System	Introduces the MX record into DNS and explains how it affects mail routing to remote systems. Released in January 1986; obsoleted by 2821.
1123	Requirements for Internet Hosts — Application and Support	An attempt to codify best practices and identify (and fix) errata for a variety of protocols; Chapter 5 focuses on SMTP. Released in October 1989; updated by 5321.
1869	SMTP Service Extensions	Defines the EHLO mechanism for Extended SMTP (ESMTP), allowing new features to be easily added to SMTP without requiring a complete updated RFC. Critical for certain features we now take for granted, such as SMTP authentication, TLS support, and streamlined data transfers of binary messages. Released in November 1995; obsoleted by 2821.
2554	SMTP Service Extension for Authentication	One of the main SMTP extensions, used to allow clients and servers to provide authentication before message submission. Provided an alternative to an open relay configuration. Released in March 1999; obsoleted by 4954.
2821	Simple Mail Transfer Protocol	This update ties SMTP, Extended SMTP, and many of the updates and fixes into a single document. It was the operational standard for systems such as Exchange 2007. Released in April 2001; obsoleted by 5321.
2822	Internet Message Format	An update to 822, published as a companion to 2821. Released in April 2001; obsoleted by 5322.
4954	SMTP Service Extension for Authentication	Provides several minor updates to the existing SMTP AUTH mechanism. Released in July 2007.
5321	Simple Mail Transfer Protocol	The third release of SMTP, intended to be the standard for future messaging systems. Addresses several lingering operational prohibitions and loopholes that make it hard for messaging administrators to fight spam within strict RFC compatibility. Released in October 2008.
5322	Internet Message Format	An incremental update to the message format used by SMTP. Released in October 2008.

Part of what makes SMTP so relatively simple is that it isn't based on any complicated routing schemes; at its heart, it is a *store-and-forward* system. Once an SMTP system accepts responsibility for a message, it then attempts to deliver it to the next best hop that it knows about. An SMTP connection, in its simplest form, is easy to understand. It involves just two systems: the client, which opens the connection so that it can submit e-mail, and the server, which accepts inbound connections and determines if it can accept the message that has been submitted. This is what a typical session, sending a message from sender@client.tld to recipient@server.tld, would look like:

```
{The client connects to the server}
01 S: 220 smtp.server.tld ESMTP mail system ready
   C: HELO desktop.client.tld
   S: 250 Hello desktop.client.tld, I am glad to meet you
02 C: MAIL FROM:<sender@client.tld>
   S: 250 Sender ok
03 C: RCPT TO:<recipient@server.tld>
   S: 250 Recipient ok
04 C: DATA
   S: 354 End data with <CR><LF>.<CR><LF>
05 C: From: "Client Sender" <sender@client.tld>
   C: To: Another User <another@otherdomain.tld>
   C: Date: Wed, 22 Oct 2008 01:13:22 -0800
   C: Subject: Test message
06 C:
   C: Isn't SMTP easy?
07 C: .
   S: 250 Ok: queued as 918273645
08 C: QUIT
   S: 221 Bye
{The server closes the connection}
```

There are eight key points to note in this conversation:

1. The initial greeting from the server, combined with the HELO or EHLO ("hello") response from the client.

2. The client begins sending the *SMTP envelope* information that tells who the actual sender is. If the message is rejected or bounced, this envelope sender is the person who will receive the notification — not necessarily the person in the "From:" header.

3. The client continues the envelope by listing one or more recipients. Like the envelope sender, these recipients don't have to match the ones listed in the actual message. In fact, having an envelope recipient not listed in the message is precisely how Blind Carbon-Copy works.

4. The envelope is done; the client now begins submitting the actual message. Unless it uses modern SMTP extensions, this is just simple text.

5. First come the message headers. Note that these recipients don't match the ones in the envelope. Though these headers may be used for filtering, they won't be used for routing.

6. When the headers are finished, the client sends a blank line and continues with the message body starting on the next line.

7. When the message body is done, the client sends the *End of Data* sequence. The server now accepts or rejects the message; if the message is accepted, the server reports the associated queue information (much like a receipt).

8. The client indicates that it's finished with the connection. If it had another message to send to recipients on this system, it could reset this connection and reuse it for one or more following messages.

If the server were not the final destination for this message — perhaps it's just an edge mail system, handling all interaction with the Internet and performing message hygiene functions before routing accepted messages further into the organization — it would pass the system on to the next hop. Note that SMTP only handles message flow from the MUA through the MTA or MSA, and from one MTA to another MTA; it is not used to transfer messages to an MDA or LDA, or from the user's mailbox database back to the MUA or MRA.

DNS — Name Resolution

In the early days of the Internet, all of the hosts on the network were maintained in a single file called HOSTS. If you wanted to add a new computer to the Internet, you called up the guy who maintained the file and asked him to add your computer's name and IP address. Periodically, everyone on the Internet downloaded the latest version of the HOSTS file.

You can see how that would be a bit difficult today; the file would be huge, slow to search, and changing constantly. Plus it would require a massive team of people to maintain it. In 1984, a standard was proposed and adopted to allow name resolution by creating a hierarchical name space where different owners of the name space would be responsible for maintaining their own hosts. The pieces of the name space are called *domains*. Root servers would provide referrals to clients so that they could contact the correct servers that held the information. So, for example, I own a domain called somorita.com and I can control any hosts in that particular domain. The root servers on the Internet provide referrals to other servers on the Internet and point them to the servers that hold the somorita.com data.

As you may have guessed by now, I am talking about the Domain Name System (DNS); this is documented in RFC 1034. You may be wondering how DNS directly (or indirectly) affects mail servers, though. A full discussion of DNS can consume an entire book, but I wanted to discuss a few topics about which you should know some basic information.

Mail Exchanger (MX) records   The Mail Exchanger or MX record is the DNS entry for your domain that allows mail servers on the Internet to look up the host names of systems that accept mail for your domain. These DNS records point to public address (A) records or aliases (CNAMES) of the SMTP servers that accept mail for your organization; this may be your Hub Transport or Edge Transport server, a third-party message hygiene system, a simple SMTP relay server, or even a third-party managed provider. You can use the NSLOOKUP command to look up and validate MX records for your domain. Here is an example of looking up the servers that accept mail for apple.com:

```
nslookup -q=mx apple.com
Server:  dnsserver1.somorita.local
Address:  192.168.254.71

Non-authoritative answer:
apple.com    MX preference = 100, mail exchanger = mail-in3.apple.com
apple.com    MX preference = 10, mail exchanger = mail-in11.apple.com
```

```
apple.com    MX preference = 10, mail exchanger = mail-in12.apple.com
apple.com    MX preference = 20, mail exchanger = mail-in1.apple.com
apple.com    MX preference = 20, mail exchanger = mail-in2.apple.com
```

Notice in the MX records that the preference values are different for different records. Mail servers are always supposed to choose the record with the lowest preference value first and then only use the records with the higher preference values if the lower ones do not respond. If two or more records are equal, the sending mail server is supposed to load balance. For more information see http://en.wikipedia.org/wiki/MX_record.

Address records and aliases   Address records (also called A records) are DNS entries that point directly to an IP address. Aliases (also called CNAMES) point to other address records.

Pointer records   A pointer record (PTR) is not added specifically to your domain, but rather to a domain name that represents an IP subnet. All of these "domains" are found in DNS in the in-addr.arpa domain; PTR records allow clients to take the IP address of an Internet host and look up the name associated with the IP address. PTR records are usually created and managed by the owner of the IP subnet block, not the manager for a domain like somorita.com.

Sender Policy Framework   Sender Policy Framework (SPF) records are DNS records that help a receiving mail server determine whether or not the mail server that originally sent a message is authorized to send mail for that domain. SPF is often billed as an anti-spam system but it is better defined as an anti-spoofing system. For more information see www.openspf.org.

Service location records   Service location records (SRV) records are DNS records that help a client locate a specific server type that is provided for a domain. Active Directory publishes SRV records for a number of different services including the global catalog server, so there might be multiple global catalog SRV records for a particular domain. Another good example of the use of an SRV record is Outlook 2007 Service Pack 1 looking for Autodiscover services. For more information see http://en.wikipedia.org/wiki/SRV_record.

Split brain DNS   Split brain DNS systems are systems that (usually) have two different sets of DNS servers that host the same DNS server. Usually one set of DNS servers hosts the domain name for an internal network and is used to resolve the host names to internal IP addresses, while the other set is used to resolve IP addresses for hosts on the Internet. These are used when the organization's public and private domain name are the same and the organization does not want internal host information available to Internet users. For more information see http://msdn.microsoft.com/en-us/library/ms954396.aspx.

Accessing the Mailbox

As just mentioned, SMTP is designed for message transport — getting a message from one system to another. Once the message has been received and delivered to a mailbox store, there's one final hop that needs to happen — to the user's MUA. SMTP would be a poor protocol to handle this function, so the Internet community developed two common alternatives: POP3 and IMAP.

◆ **POP3**, the third version of the Post Office Protocol, is intended to be a simple, no-frills mailbox retrieval protocol. A POP3 client connects to the Mailbox server, provides the user's credentials, gets a list of messages that have arrived in the user's Inbox folder, and downloads one or more of them to the local client. POP3 is simple and lightweight to implement, ensuring that just about every e-mail client application supports it, but it has two main flaws in a traditional business setting:

1. It doesn't understand the concept of folders. POP3 will only pull messages from the Inbox; if you have server-side rules that move messages to alternate folders (or have moved them manually, perhaps through a web-based mail client), they will not be visible to POP3. Once messages have been downloaded to the MUA, they can of course be filed in any local folders.

2. By default, POP3 is designed to delete mail from the message store; it's really intended for situations where the mail store holds messages for a short time before the user picks them up. It wasn't designed to interact with a modern messaging system where the goal is to keep messages on the server, where they can be managed. Although you can configure most POP3-aware MUAs not to delete the server copy, this can cause other problems.

◆   **IMAP**, by contrast, was specifically designed to allow an MUA to interface with a message store that stays resident on the server. The current version of IMAP, 4.1, is a sophisticated protocol with many options. It easily handles folder hierarchies, local caching, and other high-end features required by heavy e-mail consumers. However, IMAP was designed with e-mail in mind; most IMAP clients do not synchronize calendar and contact information.

Both POP3 and IMAP are supported by Exchange 2007 out of the box, but they're not configured by default. Also, both require the users to have access to an SMTP server to submit any new messages or replies to; neither POP3 nor IMAP handles submitting new messages back from the MUA to the server. They're strictly *pull* protocols and require a *push* protocol like SMTP to ensure new messages get delivered.

POP3 CONNECTORS CONSIDERED HARMFUL

Back when local messaging systems were becoming common and high-end dedicated Internet links were rare and costly, companies that wanted to host their own mail server faced a choice: spend money to get a dedicated line and IP address to run their own SMTP service on the Internet, or get an ISP to handle and queue their incoming SMTP traffic for them. The queuing strategy was definitely more economical, but in order to work well, you needed to find an ISP that was technically savvy and supported the SMTP enhanced turn (ETRN) extension. In what I hope isn't too much of a surprise twist, these providers usually charged more for e-mail service.

As a result, some bright person decided to write a POP3 connector. The idea was simple: get my ISP to deliver all e-mail for my domain to a single POP3 mailbox. I can use a cheap POP3 dial-up account and a POP3 connector to download this e-mail and deliver it into my on-premises SMTP server, which will then send it on to the mailboxes of my users. At first glance, it's an ingenuous solution to a common problem.

However, POP3 connectors violate the basic underlying assumptions of SMTP. Once a message has been delivered to a mailbox at the ISP, it often loses the SMTP envelope information that helps route the message, especially in the case of a Blind Carbon-Copy recipient. It may have been subject to extra processing — or, more commonly, hasn't been put under any filtering at all. Now the POP3 connector must download the message and inject it back into the local SMTP server for any further filtering to happen, leaving the local SMTP server stuck with handling the bounces for any messages that it wouldn't have accepted (such as those to non-existent recipients or those that could have been easily filtered as spam before the message was accepted).

Proponents of POP3 connectors focus almost entirely on the cost and point out that there are solutions to each objection that people can make about connectors. They're typically right, to a point; any specific problem can be handled through a clever kludge or gimmick. Though they're quick to point out their own anecdotal evidence, what they don't say is that each of these gimmicks relies on you being lucky enough to have an ISP that does things in a way that the connector recognizes. Many of these "fixes" require the ISP to inject extra headers into the message that the connector will then strip right back out; these headers are non-standard and often proprietary, and ISP administrators are understandably not eager to implement these systems for a simple no-frills bargain POP3 account.

Most importantly, POP3 connectors can place extra burden not just on your ISP's system, but on your users and correspondents as well. Although SMTP was never intended to be an instantaneous way to transmit e-mail, it turns out that it's pretty darned efficient at doing just that, enough so that people now have the expectation that e-mail is received instantly. Anything that impairs this process is seen as a problem, whether or not it really is. POP3, by its nature, is a polling mechanism, and most ISPs that offer it intend users to poll their mailboxes no more than every 15 minutes. If your users believe they need to receive e-mail more frequently, your POP3 connector will have to poll your ISP's server more frequently in turn.

There are a handful of situations for which POP3 connectors are the right solution. In most deployments, however, they are just another case of penny wise, pound foolish; spending the small additional sum for a dedicated line (such as ADSL or business-grade cable modem) would have more than returned its value in increased speed and reliability.

Finding People and Services: Directory Services

One additional aspect to messaging systems is how they look up message senders and recipients. Early messaging systems used simple flat-file lookups — typically out of the same files that listed user accounts, such as the passwd files on a Unix system. Flat files get quickly unwieldy for a large number of users, though, so various systems began using alternatives:

◆ Sun's Unix variants offered the Network Information Services (NIS), which provided a shared directory service, including messaging aliases and delivery information, across hundreds or even thousands of hosts within an organization.

◆ Early versions of Windows NT offered the local SAM database — their equivalent of the Unix passwd file — as well as Windows NT domains. NT domains allowed multiple Windows machines to share the same user information, including e-mail addresses.

Other messaging systems often provided tight integration with a corresponding directory service. The X.400 messaging system required the corresponding X.500 directory service. Though the concept of X.500 was interesting and useful, it was far too complicated to implement for SMTP. However, many of the same constructs and architectural features went into the design of the Lightweight Directory Access Protocol (LDAP) service, which was described in a series of RFCs.

LDAP proved to be a good complement for messaging systems; almost all modern MUAs and MTAs provide the ability to look up contacts and users from an LDAP-based directory service. Microsoft's Active Directory, Novell's Novell Directory Service, and eDirectory products are direct adaptations and extensions of the LDAP standard. By using LDAP, a distributed mail system can efficiently route and process millions of messages with minimal administrative overhead. Exchange Server 2007 relies heavily upon Active Directory to do its work.

Messaging Application Programming Interface

The Messaging Application Programming Interface (MAPI) is a programming interface that allows a developer to more easily write an application that accesses e-mail or directory functions and services. Though often considered an industry standard, MAPI was actually developed by Microsoft in the early 1990s and the API set is published so that anyone can use it.

Outlook, for example, uses MAPI to access data on the Exchange server as well as accessing directory information from Active Directory. An underlying directory service provider and e-mail service provider allows MAPI to access these systems. Outlook includes an underlying service provider for Exchange server as well as a service provider that allows access to PST files and IMAP4/POP3 servers. Third parties have developed service providers that will allow Outlook to access other messaging systems such as Lotus Notes, HP OpenMail, Hotmail, and even Zimbra.

A number of variations and versions of MAPI have been released over the years as new messaging functionality has been developed. To communicate with a client/server messaging system such as Exchange server, MAPI relies on Remote Procedure Calls (RPCs) to transport MAPI requests and data between the client and the server.

Message Security

The SMTP protocol that allows us to easily send an e-mail to any e-mail server in the world is very simple, but it is also very insecure. Essentially, in order for my mail server to be able to send e-mail to, say, obama@whitehouse.gov, the server at whitehouse.gov needs to be able to accept the mail from me anonymously. If SMTP required authentication, whitehouse.gov would need to have a user account and password for anyone who was going to send them e-mail.

Due to the open nature of Internet mail, it is very easy for unscrupulous people to send unsolicited commercial e-mail (UCE), hereafter known as *spam*. It is also easy for mail to be spoofed so that it appears to come from a credible source (such as your bank) and encourages you to take an action such as logging on to a fake URL and providing your banking credentials; this is known as *phishing*.

It is easy for these unscrupulous people to send e-mails with malicious attachments that might spread a virus, load a program onto your computer that will further spread itself (such programs are called *worms*), load a program that will then generate spam to send to others (this is a *bot*), or load a monitoring or remote control program on your computer that a malicious hacker can then use. These viruses, worms, and Trojan horse–type programs are collectively known as *malware*.

Finally, e-mail is such an easy way to send information back and forth that your users may misuse use it by sending inappropriate information to their friends and colleagues. Inappropriate use of e-mail can open an organization up to bad publicity and even potential lawsuits, not to mention getting the senders and recipients into big trouble. See http://www.khon2.com/home/ticker/29852384.html for a good example of this.

Message Hygiene

Collectively, the science of scanning messages for inappropriate content is known as *message hygiene*. All mail systems today should include some type of message hygiene system that, at a minimum, protects against viruses and reduces the amount of spam that makes its way into the user's mailbox.

Out of the box, Exchange Server 2007 provides fairly decent protection against spam through the anti-spam components of the Edge Transport and Hub Transport servers. But you will need additional software for protection against viruses. Customers who have Enterprise Client Access Licenses (CAL) for all users can use Microsoft's Forefront Security for Exchange Server product (www.microsoft.com/forefront).

I discuss this issue in a bit more depth in Chapter 25, "Securing Exchange Server," but here are some basics of message hygiene security.

You may choose to implement your own message hygiene system, in which case you have your own servers performing the message hygiene functions. Figure 1.13 shows a multi-layer message hygiene system.

FIGURE 1.13

Implementing your own multi-layer message hygiene system

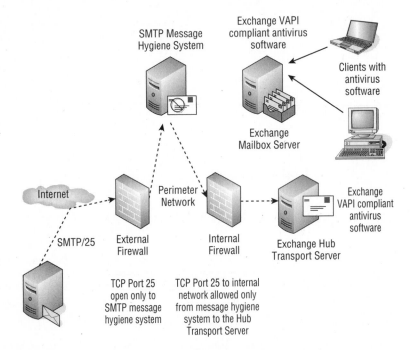

The message hygiene system in Figure 1.13 is a multi-layer system; this system has more than one place that may stop an e-mail-borne threat. Ideally, the majority of spam and malicious e-mail will be stopped by the message hygiene system in the perimeter network; this could be the Microsoft Exchange Edge Transport server or it could be one of the dozens of available SMTP-based message security systems available from third parties. The point of the hygiene system in the perimeter is to keep as much undesirable content as possible from reaching your production mail system and to protect the internal mail servers from possible attempts to compromise them.

Once a message is scanned in the perimeter network, it is then passed on to the Exchange servers on your internal network. There additional scanning takes place either when the message is moving through the message transport system or when the message is placed in the user's Inbox. Ideally, the scanning system (or scanning engine) on the inside of the network should be a different scanning engine from the one that is used on the perimeter.

The final layer of protection is implemented at the client. The client has a file and memory virus/malware scanner that looks at any content as it is opened, whether that content is in the user's Inbox or something downloaded from the Internet or something on a CD-ROM in the CD drive. Once again, ideally the software running on the client will be from a different vendor than the software running on the server. Running multiple types of scanning software improves the likelihood that newer threats will be stopped.

Some organizations decided that they don't want to have to maintain perimeter-based message hygiene systems so they use a third-party vendor that provides Internet-based scanning for them. These are usually known as managed providers and they have SMTP-based scanning systems that will scan messages coming to your mail system before they are delivered to your Exchange servers. Figure 1.14 shows an example of using a managed provider.

FIGURE 1.14
Using a managed provider

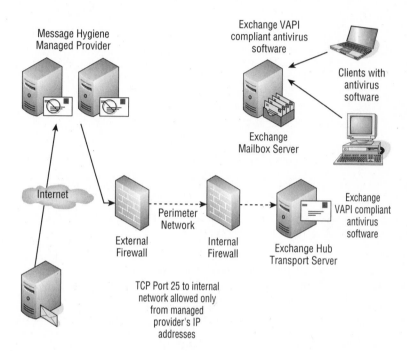

The additional cost of using a managed provider is offset by the fact that you don't have to maintain your own perimeter-based scanning system and that most malicious or unwanted e-mail content can be stopped prior to entering your network in the first place. Some third-party managed providers can also provide additional message security, disaster recovery, and message archival functions.

Approaches to Spam Protection

There are a lot of ways that your message hygiene system can determine if something is spam or is being sent by an unauthorized sender. Though each of these topics deserves in-depth treatment, my intent here is merely to familiarize you with the concepts.

Content inspection   The most common way that a message is determined to be spam or a phishing message is through content inspection. The software opens the message and looks for characteristics of spam messages, such as a message with nothing but a URL or image, messages that mention certain words or phrases, and so on. Based on the content, the software ranks the message with a number (usually called the Spam Confidence Level or SCL) from 0 to 9 with 0 being likely the message is not spam and 9 being very spammy. Internal messages are set to an SCL level of negative one (−1). The message transport can then be configured with your tolerance level for spam and can reject, delete, or quarantine messages with higher SCL values. Arguably, content inspection is considered the most accurate method of detecting spam.

Block lists   Block lists are lists that either you or a third party maintains. The lists contain IP addresses of known spammers, dial-up IP addresses, DHCP IP addresses, or IP addresses of systems that will allow spammers to send through. The third-party lists are often known as real-time block lists (RBLs) and are maintained (usually by volunteers).

Sender Protection Framework / Sender ID / Domain Keys   The Sender Protection Framework (SPF), now known as Sender ID, is an initiative backed by Microsoft that requires that all known senders on the Internet register the addresses of mail servers that will send mail on their behalf. The Domain Keys initiative (DKIM) is backed by Yahoo and requires that a sending system include a calculation in the header of each outgoing message that the receiving system then verifies. Both of these initiatives are more directly "anti-spoofing" systems than they are "anti-spam" systems, but they are useful in helping to ensure that messages really are coming from the stated sender — which can help reduce spam.

DNS Name and IP verification   Though Exchange Server cannot do some of these verifications, some SMTP systems will verify things such as whether or not your public IP address has a valid pointer (PTR) record and whether the DNS domain name you are using is valid. This can help reduce spam but also increases the probability of false positives. (A false positive occurs when the message hygiene mistakenly tags a legitimate message as spam and either quarantines, deletes, or rejects it.)

Sender inspection   Sender inspection or sender filtering is the least useful method of blocking spam because it requires maintaining lists of senders' SMTP addresses or lists of domains from which you will not accept inbound mail. The problem with this approach is that spammers usually do not use the same sender address twice.

Why Is My Mail Being Rejected?

Naturally, if you put a system in place that scans and possibly rejects e-mail based on the characteristics or the sender of the message, you are occasionally going to end up with false positives. These false positives will always be in the form of an important e-mail that is being sent to your CEO or one that she is waiting to receive. Take a look at the non-delivery report (NDR) shown in Figure 1.15; this message was rejected by the receiving mail system.

Exchange Server 2007's message transport system does a pretty good job of examining rejection codes and letting you know why a message was rejected, but you may still have to do some detective work. A remote mail system might reject mail from your users for a number of reasons:

◆   The public IP address from which you send mail is on a real-time block list (RBL) provider.

◆   Your public IP address is registered as a DHCP IP address on some RBLs; your Internet service provider (ISP) must correct this.

◆   You do not have Sender ID records registered in DNS for your public IP addresses, or the records are incorrect.

◆   The message has content that makes it look like spam such as suspicious words (mortgage, Viagra, enlargement, free) or the messages is very short (one sentence, for example).

◆   Your public IP address does not have a DNS PTR record; your ISP or the owner of the IP address must fix this.

◆ Your mail server is sending out the wrong mail domain name when it connects to a remote mail system. For example, your mail domain is somorita.com but it is saying your domain name is somorita.local.

FIGURE 1.15
Examining the report of a rejected message

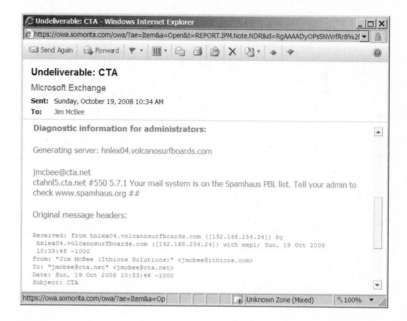

The Role of Storage

In medium-sized and large organizations, the Exchange administrator is usually not also responsible for storage. Many medium-sized and large organizations use specialized storage area networks (SANs) that require additional training to master. Storage is a massive topic and many books have been dedicated to discussing storage, but I feel it is important that you at least be able to speak the language of storage.

From the very beginning, messaging systems have had a give-and-take relationship with the underlying storage system. Even on systems that aren't designed to offer long-term storage for e-mail (such as ISP systems that offer only POP3 access), e-mail creates demands on storage:

◆ The transport (MTA) components must have space to queue messages that cannot be immediately transmitted to the remote system.

◆ The MDA component must be able to store incoming messages that have been delivered to a mailbox until users can retrieve them.

◆ The message store, in systems like Exchange, permits users to keep a copy of their mailbox data on central servers.

◆ As the server accepts, transmits, and processes e-mail, it keeps logs with varying levels of detail so administrators can troubleshoot and audit activities.

Though you'll have to wait for subsequent chapters to delve into the details of planning storage for Exchange, the following sections go over the broad categories of storage solutions that are used in modern systems.

Direct Attached Storage (DAS)

Direct attached storage (DAS) is the most common type of storage. DAS disks are usually internal disks or directly attached via cable. Just about every server, except for some high-end varieties, uses DAS at some level; typically, the operating system is on some DAS configuration. The main problem with DAS, historically, has been performance and capacity. To get around these problems, one can always just add more disks to the server. This gives you a configuration known as JBOD — Just a Box Of Disks.

Just a Box Of Disks (JBOD)

Although JBOD can usually give you the raw capacity you need, it has three flaws that render it unsuitable for most Exchange deployments:

♦ JBOD forces you to partition your data. Because each disk has a finite capacity, you can't store data on that disk if it is larger than the capacity. For example, if you have four 250GB drives, even though you have approximately one terabyte of storage in total, you have to break that up into separate 250GB partitions. Historically, this has caused some interesting design decisions in messaging systems that rely on file system–based storage.

♦ JBOD offers no performance benefits. Each disk is responsible for only one chunk of storage, so if that disk is already in use, subsequent I/O requests will have to wait for it to free up before they can go through. A single disk can thus become a bottleneck for the system, which can slow down mail for all of your users (not just those on the affected disk).

♦ JBOD offers no redundancy. If one of your disks dies, you're out of luck unless you can restore that data from backup. True, you haven't lost all of your data, but the one-quarter of your users who have just lost their e-mail are not likely to be comforted by that observation.

Luckily, some bright people came up with a great answer to JBOD: the Redundant Array of Inexpensive Disks, or RAID.

Redundant Array of Inexpensive Disks (RAID)

The basic premise behind RAID is to group the JBOD disks together in various configurations, allowing the computer (and applications) to see them as one very large disk device. These collections of disks are known as *arrays*; the arrays are presented to the operating system, partitioned, and formatted as if they were just regular disks. The common types of RAID configurations are shown in Table 1.2.

Note that several of these types of RAID arrays may be suitable for your Exchange server. Which one should you use? That question depends entirely on how many mailboxes your servers are holding, how they're used, and other types of business needs. Beware of anyone who tries to give hard and fast answers like, "Always use RAID-5 for Exchange database volumes." To determine the true answer, you need to go through a proper storage sizing process, find out what your I/O and capacity requirements are really going to be, think about your data recovery needs and service level agreements (SLAs), and then decide what storage configuration will meet those needs for you in a fashion you can afford. There are no magic bullets.

In every case, the RAID controller you use — the piece of hardware, plus drivers, that aggregates the individual disk volumes for you into a single pseudo-device that is presented to Windows — plays a key role. You can't just take a collection of disks, toss them into slots in your server, and go to town with RAID. You need to install extra drivers and management software, you need to take extra steps configuring your arrays before you can even use them in Windows, and you may even need to update your disaster recovery procedures to ensure that you can always recover data from drives in a RAID array. Generally, you'll need to test whether you can move drives in one array between two controllers, even those from the same manufacturer; not all controllers support all options. After your server has melted down and your SLA is fast approaching is not a good time to find out that you needed to carry a spare controller on hand.

TABLE 1.2:   RAID Configurations

RAID LEVEL	NAME	DESCRIPTION
None	Concatenated drives	Two or more disks are joined together in a contiguous data space. As one disk in the array is filled up, the data is carried over to the next disk. Though this solves the capacity problem and is easy to implement, it offers no performance or redundancy whatsoever, and makes it more likely that you're going to lose all of your data through a single disk failure, not less. These arrays are not suitable for use with Exchange.
RAID-0	Striped drives	Two or more disks have data split among them evenly. If you write a 1MB file to a two-disk RAID-0 array, half the data will be on one disk, half on the other. Each disk in the array can be written to (or read from) simultaneously, giving you a noticeable performance boost. However, if you lose one disk in the array, you lose all your data. These arrays are typically used for fast, large, temporary files, such as those in video editing. These arrays are not suitable for use with Exchange.
RAID-1	Mirrored drives	Typically done with two disks (although some vendors allow more), each disk receives a copy of all the data in the array. If you lose one disk, you've still got a copy of your data on the remaining disk; you can either move the data or plug in a replacement disk and rebuild the mirror. RAID-1 also gives a performance benefit; reads can be performed by either disk, because only writes need to be mirrored. However, RAID-1 can be one of the more costly configurations; to store 500GB of data, you'd need to buy two 500GB drives. These arrays are suitable for use with Exchange, depending on the type of data and the performance of the array.
RAID-5	Parity drive	Three or more disks have data split among them. However, one disk's worth of capacity is reserved for *parity checksum* data; this is a special calculated value that allows the RAID system to rebuild the missing data if one drive in the array fails. The parity data may be kept on one disk, or spread across all the disks in the array. If you had a four-disk 250GB RAID-5 array, you'd only have 750GB of usable space. RAID-5 arrays offer better performance than JBOD, but worse performance than other RAID configurations, especially on the write requests; the checksum must be calculated and the data + parity written to all the disks in the array. Also, if you lose one disk, the array goes into *degraded mode*, which means that even read operations will need to be recalculated and will be slower than normal. These arrays are suitable for use with Exchange, depending on the type of data and the performance of the array.

TABLE 1.2: RAID Configurations *(CONTINUED)*

RAID LEVEL	NAME	DESCRIPTION
RAID-6	Double parity drive	This RAID variant has become common only recently, and is designed to provide RAID-5 arrays the ability to survive the loss of two disks. Other than offering two-disk resiliency, base RAID-6 implementations offer mostly the same benefits and drawbacks as RAID-5. Some vendors have built custom implementations that attempt to solve the performance issues. These arrays are suitable for use with Exchange, depending on the type of data and the performance of the array.
RAID-10	Mirroring plus striping	A RAID-10 array is the most costly variant to implement because it uses mirroring. However, it also uses striping to deliver blistering performance, which makes it a great choice for high-end arrays that have to sustain a high-level of I/O. As a side bonus, it also increases your chances of surviving the loss of multiple disks in the array. There are two basic variants. RAID 0+1 takes two big stripe arrays and mirrors them together; RAID 1+0 takes a number of mirror pairs and stripes them together. Both variants have essentially the same performance, but 1+0 is preferred because it can be rebuilt more quickly and has far higher chances of surviving the loss of multiple disks. These arrays are suitable for use with Exchange, usually for highly loaded mailbox database volumes.

If you choose the DAS route (whether JBOD or RAID), you'll need to think about how you're going to house the physical disks. Modern server cases don't leave a lot of extra room for disks; this is especially true of rack mounted systems. Usually, this means you'll need some sort of external enclosure that hooks back into a physical bus on your server, such as SCSI or eSATA. Make sure to give these enclosures suitable power and cooling; hard drives pull a lot of power and return it all as heat. Also make sure that your drive backplanes (the physical connection point) and enclosures support *hot-swap* capability, where you can pull the drive and replace it without powering the system down. Keep a couple of spare drives and drive sleds on hand, too. You really don't want to have to schedule an outage of your Exchange server in order to replace a failed drive in a RAID-5 array, letting all of your users enjoy thrashed performance because the array is in degraded mode until the replacement drives arrive.

CHOOSING RAID CONTROLLERS

Beware! Not all kinds of RAID are created equal. Before you spend a lot of time trying to figure out which configuration to choose, you need to first think about your RAID controller. There are three kinds of them, and unlike RAID configurations, it's pretty easy to determine which kind you need for Exchange.

◆ **Software RAID** avoids the whole problem of having a RAID controller by performing all of the magic in the operating system software. If you convert your disk to dynamic volumes, you can do RAID-0, RAID-1, and RAID-5 natively in Windows 2003 and Windows 2008 without any extra hardware. However, Microsoft strongly recommends that you not do this with Exchange, and the Exchange community echoes that recommendation. It takes extra memory and processing power, and inevitably slows your disks down from what you could get with a simple investment in good hardware. You will also not be able to support higher levels of I/O load with this configuration, in my experience.

♦ **BIOS RAID** attempts to provide "cheap" RAID by putting some code for RAID in the RAID chipset, which is then placed either directly on the motherboard (common in workstation-grade and low-end server configurations) or on an inexpensive add-in card. The catch is that the card isn't really doing the RAID; it's again all happening in memory, this time in the associated Windows driver. If you're about to purchase a RAID controller card for a price that seems too good to be true, it's probably one of these cards. Although you can get Exchange to work with these, you can do so only with very low numbers of users. Otherwise, you'll quickly hit the limits these cards have and stress your storage system. Just avoid them; the time you save will more than make up for the up-front price savings.

♦ **Hardware RAID** is the only kind of RAID you should even be thinking about for your Exchange servers. This means good quality, high-end cards that come from reputable manufacturers that have taken the time to get the product on the Windows Hardware Compatibility List (HCL). These cards do a lot of the work for your system, removing the CPU overhead of parity calculations from the main processors, and they are worth every penny you pay for them. Better yet, they'll be able to handle the load your Exchange servers and users throw at them.

If you can't tell whether a given controller you're eyeing is BIOS or true hardware RAID, get help. Lots of forums and websites on the Internet will help you sort out which hardware to get and which to avoid. And while you're at it, spring a few extra bucks for good, reliable disks. Again, the time you save will be your own.

Network Attached Storage (NAS)

When early versions of Exchange Server came on the market, DAS was just the way you did things. As mailbox databases got larger and traffic levels rose, pretty soon people wanted to look for alternatives; DAS storage under Exchange 2000 and Exchange 2003 required a lot of disks, because they were optimized for the smaller disks that were on the market at the time.

One of the potential solutions people wanted to use was NAS devices. These machines — giant file servers — sit on the network and share out their disk storage. They range in price and configuration from small plug-in devices with fixed capacity to large installations with more configuration options than most luxury cars (and a price tag to match). Companies who bought these were using them to replace file servers, web server storage, SQL Server storage — why not Exchange?

For many years, Exchange Server wasn't compatible with NAS devices; Microsoft didn't support moving Exchange storage to NAS, and vociferously argued against the idea. In order to understand why, you have to understand the difference between file-level and block-level access.

When one network device shares storage with another device, it has two basic ways to do it.

♦ *File-level sharing* is the type of sharing we're used to any time somebody uses SMB/CIFS to create or mount a Windows file share; the client (the machine opening the file share) doesn't worry about how the files and folders are laid out on the physical disk, it just asks the server to perform certain operations on its behalf.

♦ With *block-level sharing*, the client computer is essentially presented with a raw device (the shared volume) that appears, thanks to the appropriate drivers, to be a locally attached drive. The client manipulates the raw disk blocks and file system just as it would on a physical disk; the server simply translates the client's view of the storage into the actual view.

Most NAS devices at the time, especially the inexpensive ones, only offered file-level sharing. Though you could (in theory) move the Exchange databases to NAS volumes, doing so created huge performance bottlenecks that would quickly overwhelm your system. This happened for two main reasons: network bandwidth and server latency. As it turns out, a Fast Ethernet 100Mbps network isn't nearly as fast as the physical bus connecting your drive controller and hard drives. On top of that, Exchange expects to have a fine level of control over when specific I/O operations go to disk; when you filter that all through file-level sharing, Exchange loses that control.

With all that said, Microsoft did finally provide a way for Exchange 2003 administrators to use NAS configurations. It required the following:

◆   Use of a HCL-certified Windows Storage Server 2003 storage device. You couldn't do it with just any random NAS server.

◆   Addition of the Windows Storage Server Feature Pack, installed on both the storage server and the Exchange server.

◆   Adequate network connectivity. The recommendation was for a dedicated Gigabit Ethernet segment between the storage server and the Exchange servers.

Apparently, despite all of the people asking for such a configuration, it didn't turn out to be a popular option, because NAS devices are no longer supported for Exchange Server 2007. Instead, the push is on reducing the overall I/O requirements so that DAS configurations become practical for small to midsize organizations.

Storage Area Networks (SAN)

The final type of network storage used with Exchange is SAN. The premise here is to move disks to dedicated storage units that can handle all the advanced features you need — high-end RAID configurations, hot-swap replacement, on-the-fly reconfiguration, rapid disk snapshots, tight integration with backup and restore solutions, and more. This helps consolidate the overhead of managing storage, often spread out on dozens of servers and applications (and their associated staff), into a single set of personnel. Then, dedicated network links connect these storage silos with the appropriate application servers.

Initially SAN solutions used fiber optic solutions to provide the necessary bandwidth for storage operations. As a result, these systems were incredibly expensive and were used only by organizations with deep pockets. Over time, however, many vendors have appeared offering SAN solutions that were increasingly affordable even for small companies. The main reason they've been able to do so is the iSCSI protocol; block-based file access routed over TCP/IP connections. Add iSCSI with ubiquitous Gigabit Ethernet hardware, and SAN deployments have become a lot more common.

Clustering is the other factor in the growth of Exchange/SAN deployments. Exchange 2003 supported clustered configurations, but they required the cluster nodes to have a shared storage solution. As a result, any organization that wanted to deploy an Exchange cluster needed some sort of SAN solution (apart from the handful of people who stuck with shared SCSI configurations). A SAN has a certain elegance to it; you simply create a virtual slice of drive space for Exchange (called a LUN, or *logical unit number*), use Fibre Channel or iSCSI (and corresponding drivers) to present it to the Exchange server, and away you go.

However, SAN solutions don't fix all problems, even with (usually because of) their price tag. Because SANs cost so much, there is often a strong drive to use the SAN for all storage and make full use of every last free block of space. Unfortunately, Exchange's I/O characteristics are very different than those of just about any other application, and few dedicated SAN administrators really know how to properly allocate disk space for Exchange:

◆ SAN administrators do not usually understand that total disk space is only one component of Exchange performance. For day-to-day operations, it is far more important to ensure enough I/O capacity. Traditionally, this is delivered by using lots of physical disks (commonly referred to as "spindles") to increase the amount of simultaneous read/write operations supported. It is important to make sure the SAN solution provides enough I/O capacity, not just free disk space, or Exchange will crawl.

◆ Even if you can convince them to configure LUNs spread across enough disks, SAN administrators immediately want to reclaim that wasted space. As a result, you end up sharing the same spindles between Exchange and some other application with its own performance curve, and then suddenly you have extremely noticeable but hard-to-diagnose performance issues with your Exchange servers. Shared spindles will kill Exchange.

◆ Although some SAN vendors have put a lot of time and effort into understanding Exchange and its I/O needs so that their salespeople and certified consultants can help you deploy Exchange on their products properly, not everyone does the same. Many vendors will shrug off performance concerns by telling you about their extensive write caching and how good write caching will smooth out any performance issues. They're true...up to a point. A cache can help isolate Exchange from effects of transient I/O events, but it won't help you come Monday morning when all your users are logging in and the SQL Server databases that share your spindles are churning through extra operations.

The moral of the story is simple: don't believe that you need to have a SAN. But if you do, get the best one you can afford. Make sure that your vendors know Exchange storage inside and out; if possible, get them to put you in contact with their on-staff Exchange specialists. Have them work with your SAN administrators to come up with a storage configuration that meets your real Exchange needs.

For more information on using SANs and sizing disks for Exchange Server, see the free eBook *The Shortcut Guide to Exchange Server 2007 Storage Systems* at `http://nexus.realtimepublishers.com/SGES2k7SS.htm`.

Compliance and Governance

Quite simply, today's legal system considers e-mail to be an official form of business communication just like written memos. This means that any type of legal requirement or legal action against your organization (regarding business records) will undoubtedly include e-mail. Unless you work in a specific vertical market such as healthcare or financials, the emergence of compliance and governance as topics of import to the messaging administrator is a relatively recent event. The difference between compliance and governance can be summarized simply:

> *Governance is the process of defining and enforcing policies, while compliance is the process of ensuring that you meet external requirements.*

However, both of these goals share a lot of common ground:

◆ They require thorough planning to implement, based on a detailed understanding of what behaviors are allowed, required, or forbidden.

◆ Though they require technical controls to ensure implementation, they are at heart about people and processes.

◆ They require effective monitoring in order to audit the effectiveness of the compliance and governance measures.

In short, they require all the same things you need in order to effectively manage your messaging data. As a result, there's a useful framework you can use to evaluate your compliance and governance needs: Discovery, Compliance, Archival, and Retention, also known as the DCAR framework.

DCAR recognizes four key pillars of activity, each historically viewed as a separate task for messaging administrators. However, all four pillars involve the same mechanisms, people, and policies; all four in fact are overlapping facets of messaging data management. These four pillars are described in the following list:

◆ **Discovery** is finding messages in the system quickly and accurately, whether for litigation, auditing, or other needs. It requires:

  ◆ Good storage design to handle the additional overhead of discovery actions.

  ◆ The accurate and thorough indexing of all messaging data that enters the Exchange organization through any means.

  ◆ Control over the ability of users to move data out of the messaging system through mechanisms such as personal folders (PSTs).

◆ **Compliance** is meeting all legal, regulatory, and governance requirements, whether derived from external or internal drivers. It requires:

  ◆ Clear guidance on which behaviors are allowed, required, or prohibited, as well as a clear description of which will be enforced through technical means.

  ◆ The means to enforce required behavior, prevent disallowed behavior, and audit for the success or failure of these means.

  ◆ The ability to control and view all messaging data that enters the Exchange organization through any means.

◆ **Archival** is the ability to preserve the messaging data that will be required for future operations, including governance tasks. It requires:

  ◆ Clear guidance on which data must be preserved and a clear description of procedural and technical measures will be used to enforce archival.

  ◆ The accurate and thorough indexing of all messaging data that enters the Exchange organization through any means.

  ◆ Control over the ability of users to move data out of the messaging system through mechanisms such as personal folders (PSTs).

◆ **Retention** is the ability to identify data that can be safely removed without adverse impact (whether immediate or delayed) to the business. It requires:

  ◆ Clear guidance on which data is safe to remove and a clear description of the time frames and technical measures that will be used to enforce removal.

  ◆ The accurate identification of all messaging data that enters the Exchange organization through any means.

◆ Control over the ability of users to move data out of the messaging system through mechanisms such as personal folders (PSTs).

If many of these requirements look the same, good; that emphasizes that these activities are all merely different parts of the same overall goal. You should be realizing that these activities are not things you do with your messaging system so much as they are activities that you perform *while managing* your messaging system. The distinction is subtle, but important; knowing your requirements helps make the difference between designing and deploying a system that can be easily adapted to meet your needs and one that you will constantly have to fight.

Many of these activities will require the addition of third-party solutions, even for Exchange 2007. What makes this space interesting is that a lot of these functions are now starting to be filled by hosted solutions, often at a competitive price.

WHERE JOURNALING FITS INTO DCAR

Journaling is a common technology that gets mentioned whenever compliance, archival, and discovery are discussed. However, I find that it often gets over-discussed. Journaling is not the end goal; it's simply a mechanism for getting data out of Exchange into some other system, which does what you're really wanting to do.

If journaling is a concern for you, you should stop and ask yourself why. What information are you trying to journal, and what do you want it for? I don't know a single Exchange administrator who has ever come up to me and said, "I want to journal my data." Instead, they say, "I need to archive my data and I have to use journaling to get it to my archival solution." Understanding why you need journaling will give you the ammunition you need to effectively design your Exchange organization. It will also help you identify when journaling may not be all that you need.

What Is Exchange Server?

In its very simplest form, Exchange Server provides the underlying infrastructure necessary to run a messaging system. Exchange Server provides the database to store e-mail data, the transport infrastructure to move the data from one place to another, and access points to access e-mail data via a number of different clients.

However, Exchange Server, when used with other clients such as Outlook or Outlook Web Access turn the "mailbox" into a point of storage for personal information management such as your calendar, contacts, task lists, and personal journal. Users can share some or all of this information in their own mailbox with other users on the message system and start to collaborate.

The Outlook and Outlook Web Access clients also provide access to public folders. Public folders look like regular mail folders in your mailbox, except that they are in an area where they can be shared by all users within the organization. A folder can have specialized forms associated with it to allow the sharing of contacts, calendar entries or even other specialized forms. Further, each public folder can be secured so that only certain users can view or modify data in that folder.

Exchange Server 2007's Unified Messaging server role further extends the functions of the Exchange Server in your organization by allowing your Exchange Server 2007 infrastructure to also act as your voicemail system and direct inbound faxes directly (and automatically) to the user's mailbox. Figure 1.16 shows a voice-mail message that arrived in a mailbox and can be checked via Outlook Web Access.

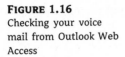

FIGURE 1.16
Checking your voice mail from Outlook Web Access

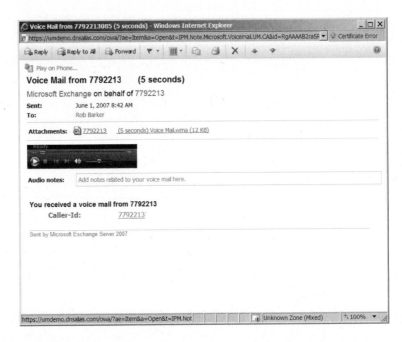

While integrated voicemail and faxing solutions are nothing new for Exchange customers, Microsoft is now providing these capabilities out of the box rather than having to rely on third-party products.

Microsoft has once again tightened the integration of collaborative tools with Office Communication Server 2007 and the Communicator client. OCS and the Communicator client can be used to integrate with Unified Messaging to provide notification of new voicemail and missed calls. Furthermore, Communicator can log chat and instant message conversation logs to a folder in the user's mailbox.

The capabilities of the client can be extended with third-party tools and forms routing software so that electronic forms can be routed through e-mail to users' desktops.

History of Exchange

The original version of Exchange Server that debuted in 1996 was called Exchange Server 4.0 because the previous version of Microsoft's e-mail offering was Microsoft Mail v3.2. However, Exchange Server 4.0 was nothing like MS Mail v3.2 in any way, shape, or form. Exchange Server v4.0 included client/server database technology, a much more comprehensive directory service, and built-in connectors for connectivity with the Internet (SMTP), as well as cc:Mail and Microsoft Mail.

Exchange continued to evolve with Exchange 5.0 and 5.5 as new capabilities such as improved Internet access, web-based e-mail, database engine optimizations, additional messaging connectors, and better scalability.

Exchange Server 2000 represented a big jump forward with even more scalability improvements, such as more databases on a single server. Exchange Server 2000 also moved from a dedicated directory service over to using Active Directory to store the Exchange configuration as well as recipient information. Internet connectivity and client interface improvements were also introduced in both Exchange 2000 as well as Exchange Server 2003.

Microsoft's Exchange Server products have played and will continue to play a key role in electronic messaging. Exchange Server 2007 is one of the most powerful, extensible, scalable, easy-to-use, and manageable electronic messaging back ends currently on the market. Combined with Microsoft's excellent Outlook clients, Internet-based clients from Microsoft and other vendors, mobile devices that use ActiveSync, and third-party or home-grown applications, Exchange Server 2007 can help your organization move smoothly and productively into the electronic messaging future.

The Universal Inbox

E-mail systems are converging with their voicemail and faxing cousins. The concept of unified messaging is nothing new to e-mail users. For at least the past 10 years, third-party vendors have included e-mail integration tools for voicemail and network faxing solutions. However, for most organizations, integrated voicemail and faxing solutions remain the exception rather than the rule. Exchange 2007 introduces integrated voice and fax solutions as part of the base product.

Organizations with IP-based telephone systems or telephone systems with an IP gateway can now easily integrate a user's voicemail and inbound faxing with the Exchange user's mailbox. The Exchange 2007 Unified Messaging server handles the interaction between an organization's telephone system and Exchange mailboxes. Inbound voicemail is transferred into the user's mailbox as a WMA file attachment; this message includes an Outlook form that allows the user to play the message. A short voicemail message may be anywhere from 40KB to 75KB in size, whereas longer voicemail messages may be 200KB to 500KB in size. One estimate that is frequently used for the size of a voicemail message is around 5KB per second of message.

Inbound faxes are transferred to the user's mailbox as messages containing an Outlook form with a Group IV TIFF attachment; a single-page fax can be as small as 25KB, whereas multipage faxes can easily be 200KB or larger. Incorporating third-party scanning and outbound faxing products (outbound faxing is not supported out of the box with Exchange 2007) can further increase the size of a mailbox.

With Outlook Voice Access, users can now dial in to the Exchange 2007 Unified Messaging server and access their mailbox, have e-mail read to them, have appointments read to them, and move or cancel appointments. If an appointment is changed, Outlook Voice Access will automatically notify attendees of scheduling changes; this is very useful if you are sitting in traffic on the freeway with nothing but your cell phone (using your headset of course)!

Inbound voicemail and inbound faxes will increase the demands on your Exchange server from the perspective of required disk space and possibly additional server hardware, though. This needs to be considered. Outlook Voice Access will increase the potential number of connections and usage of your Exchange mailbox servers and Unified Messaging servers.

Many Modes of Access

For years, the only point of access for one's e-mail system was to use a Windows, Macintosh, or Unix-based client and access the e-mail system directly. In the case of Outlook and Exchange, this access was originally in the form of a MAPI client directly against the Exchange server. As Exchange has evolved, POP3 and IMAP4 access has been included in the product, then web-based e-mail access, and finally mobile device access. Exchange Server 2007 supports additional technologies such as web services that can provide additional mechanisms for accessing data in mailboxes.

Outlook Web Access has evolved quickly and in Exchange 2007 bears almost no resemblance to the original version found in Exchange 5.0 in terms of features, functions, and the look of the interface.

Mobile device access was first provided to Exchange 2000 using Microsoft Mobile Information Server and then later included as part of Exchange 2003. Mobile device functionality has been further improved in Exchange 2007. Users are more frequently asking for integration of mobile devices with e-mail. The Radicati Group estimated that in 2006 there were 14 million wireless e-mail users but by 2010 that number will grow to 228 million. You can bet that your users will want to be included!

Unified Messaging and Outlook Voice Access now allow a user with nothing but a telephone to access his or her e-mail and calendar and even make changes via the telephone.

With all of these mechanisms for retrieving and sending e-mail, it is not unusual for users to be accessing their mailbox using more than one. In some cases, I have seen a single user accessing her mailbox from her desktop computer, her notebook computer (using RPC over HTTP), and her Windows Mobile device.

In medium and large organizations, the fact that users are now accessing their mailbox from more than one device and/or mechanism will affect not only hardware sizing but also, potentially, your licensing costs.

Architecture Overview

Understanding a bit about how Exchange Server works from an architectural perspective will help make you a better administrator. You don't have to be able to reproduce or write your own client/server messaging system, but it helps to know the basics.

EXCHANGE AS A CLIENT/SERVER MAIL SYSTEM

Since Exchange Server 4.0, Exchange has been a client/server messaging system. Remember back in Figure 1.7, how the client sends a request to the Exchange server, the Exchange server does the work, and then sends back only the response to the client? Well, that is how Exchange Server works; the mechanism that the Outlook client uses is the Messaging Application Programming Interface (MAPI); the data is sent using Remote Procedure Calls (RPCs). The underlying network infrastructure uses whatever the network transport is to move the RPC request from the client to the server. In years past, this might have been IPX/SPX or even NetBEUI, but it is very rare that you will find any network transport today other than TCP/IP. MAPI clients such as Outlook 2003 or 2007 directly access an Exchange Mailbox server using MAPI over RPCs, such as is shown in Figure 1.17.

The client/server architecture does not just stop at Outlook clients, though; Internet clients such as Outlook Web Access, Outlook Anywhere, POP3, IMAP4, Windows Mobile, and the iPhone all go through a "middle-ware" layer to get to their data. In the case of Exchange Server 2007, "web" access has been abstracted from the mail storage system and is run by a server role called the Client Access server. Figure 1.17 shows a simple diagram of how this works.

THE EXTENSIBLE STORAGE ENGINE (ESE)

The Exchange Server database uses a highly specialized database engine called the Extensible Storage Engine (ESE). Generically, you could say it is almost like SQL Server, but this is technically not true. It is a client/server database and is somewhat relational in nature, but it is designed to be a single-user database (the Exchange server itself is the only component that directly accesses the data). Further, the database has been highly tuned to store hierarchical data such as mailboxes, folders, messages, and attachments.

Without going into a lot of techno-babble on the database architecture, it is important that you understand the basics of what the database is doing. Figure 1.18 show conceptually what is happening with the ESE database as data is sent to the database. In step 1, an Outlook client sends data to the Exchange Server (the information store service), the information store service places this data in memory and then immediately writes the data out to the transaction log files associated with that database.

FIGURE 1.17
Client Access server architecture

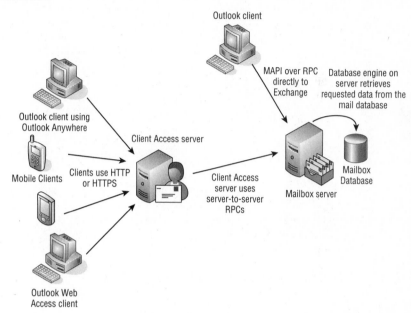

FIGURE 1.18
Exchange data and transaction logs

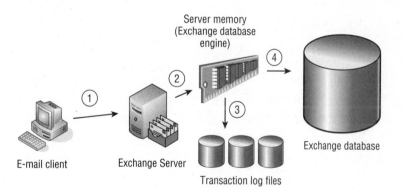

The transaction log that is always written to is the current transaction log for that particular database (e00.log for example). Each transaction log file is exactly 1MB in size, so when the transaction log is filled up, it is renamed to the next sequential number. For example, an old transaction log file might be named like this: e000004032.log.

The data is retained in RAM for some period of time (maybe 5 seconds or maybe 60 seconds) before it is then flushed to the database file. The actual period that data is retained in memory will depend on how much cache memory is available and how busy the server is. The important operation, though, is to make sure that as soon as the data is sent to the Exchange server it is immediately flushed to the transaction log files. If the server crashes before the data is written to the database file, the database engine (the information store service) will automatically "replay" the missing data by reading the transaction log files once the server is brought back up.

The transaction log files are important for a number of reasons. They are used by Microsoft replication technologies (as you learn in Chapter 18, "Implementing Replication Technologies") but they can also be used in disaster recovery. The transaction logs are not actually purged off the log disk until a full backup is run; therefore every transaction that occurred to a database (new data, modifications, moves, deletes) is stored in the logs. If you restore the last good backup to the server, Exchange server can replay and rebuild all of the missing transactions back in to the database — provided you have all the transactions since the last full backup.

EXCHANGE AND ACTIVE DIRECTORY

I could easily write two or three chapters on how Exchange Server interacts with the Active Directory, but the basics will have to do for now. Exchange Server relies on the Active Directory for information about its own configuration, user authentication, and e-mail specific properties for mail-enabled objects such as users, contacts, groups, and public folders. Look at Figure 1.19 to see some of the different types of interactions that occur between Exchange and the Active Directory. Because most of the Exchange configuration data for an Exchange server is stored in the Active Directory, all Exchange server roles must contact a domain controller to request its configuration data; this information is stored in a special partition of the Active Directory database called the configuration partition. The configuration partition is replicated to all domain controllers in the entire Active Directory forest.

FIGURE 1.19
Active Directory and
Exchange

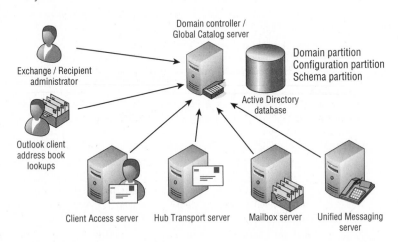

Each of the individual Exchange Server roles uses the Active Directory for different things. Following is a list of some of those functions:

Mailbox servers   Exchange Mailbox servers must query the Active Directory to authenticate users, enumerate permissions on mailboxes, look up individual mailbox limits, and determine which mailboxes are on a particular server.

Hub Transport servers   Exchange Hub Transport servers require access to global catalog servers in order to look up e-mail addressing information, home server information, distribution list membership information, and other data related to message routing.

Client Access servers   Exchange Client Access servers require access to the Active Directory to look up information about home servers for users, ActiveSync, and Outlook Web Access user restrictions.

Unified Messaging servers   Unified Messaging servers require access to the Active Directory in order to retrieve and play the user's personalized outgoing message as well as to retrieve e-mail address information so that voicemail and faxes can be delivered to the user.

Exchange management tools   The Exchange Server management tools must connect to the Active Directory in order to make configuration changes to Exchange server objects and to create, update, manage, or delete mail-enabled objects such as mailbox-enabled users or mail-enabled groups.

Outlook clients   Outlook clients require access to Active Directory global catalog servers in order to retrieve information about the global address lists as well as individual recipient information.

Controlling Mailbox Growth

As users have become more savvy and competent at using Outlook and the features of Exchange, and e-mail messages themselves have become more complex, the need for e-mail storage has grown. Back in the days of Exchange 4.0, an organization that gave its users a 25MB mailbox was considered generous. With Exchange 2003, a typical user's mailbox may have a storage limit of 300 to 500MB, with power users and VIPs requiring even more.

At TechEd 2006, Exchange gurus were tossing about the idea that in the future a default mailbox limit would be closer to 2GB as users start incorporating Unified Messaging features. We all see users with mailbox sizes in the gigabyte range, but is your organization prepared for a typical user with a 2GB message size limit? What sort of concerns will you face when your average user has 1 to 2GB of content (not just e-mail!) in his mailbox?

Certainly the need for more disk storage will be the first factor that organizations need to consider. However, disk storage is reasonably cheap, and many larger organizations that are supporting thousands of mailbox users on a single mailbox server already have more disk space than they can practically use. This is due to the fact that they require more disk spindles to accommodate the number of simultaneous I/Os per second (IOPS) that are required by a large number of users.

For more administrators with large amounts of mail storage, the primary concern they face is the ability to quickly and efficiently restore data in the event of a failure. These administrators are often faced with service level agreements that bind them to maximum restoration times. In even the most optimal circumstances, a 300GB mailbox database will take some time to restore from backup media!

Microsoft recommends that you do not allow an Exchange mailbox database to grow larger than 100GB unless you are implementing any of the new continuous replication technologies in Exchange 2007. If you use local continuous replication or clustered continuous replication to keep a copy of the database ready to use in case of database corruption, do not let the mailbox database grow to larger than 200GB. If you require more than 100–200GB of mailbox database storage, Exchange 2007 Standard Edition allows you to have up to 5 mailbox databases and Exchange 2007 Enterprise Edition allows you to have up to 50.

The solution in the past was to restrain the user community by preventing them from keeping all of the mail data that they might require on the mail server. This was done by imposing low mailbox limits, implementing message archival requirements, keeping deleted items for only a few days, and keeping deleted mailboxes for only a few days.

However, as Unified Messaging data now starts to arrive in a user's mailbox and users have additional mechanisms for accessing the data stored in their mailbox, keeping mail data around longer is going to be a demand and a requirement for your user community.

Personal Folders or PST Files

The Outlook personal folder or PST file can be the very bane of your existence. Outlook allows users to create a local database in which they can create folders and archive e-mail. Though this seems like a good feature on the surface, there are a few downsides:

◆ The data in PST files take up more space than the corresponding data on the server.

◆ The default location for a PST is the local portion of the user's profile; this means it is stored on the local hard disk of their computer and is not backed up.

◆ PST files can get corrupted much more easily than the data on the Exchange server.

◆ Performance when accessing PST files is not very good once a PST file is around 1GB or larger. And you should never allow a PST file to grow larger than 2GB even though Outlook 2003 and Outlook 2007 will allow you to do so.

◆ Once data is in a user's PST file, you, as the server administrator, have lost control of it. If you ever had to find all copies of a certain message, perhaps for a lawsuit, you would be out of luck.

E-Mail Archiving

Sometimes, managing a mail server seems like a constant race between Information Technology (IT) and users to keep users from letting their mailbox run out of space. Users are pack rats and generally want to keep everything. If there is an actual business reason for them to do so, then you should look at ways to expand your available storage to accommodate them.

However, as databases become larger and larger, the Exchange server will be more difficult to manage. You might start requiring hundreds and hundreds of gigabytes (or even terabytes) of storage for e-mail databases. Worse still, backups and data recovery take longer.

This is where e-mail archiving becomes useful. The last time I counted, there were more than 45 companies in the business of supplying e-mail archiving tools and services. Archiving products all have a lot of functions in common, including the ability to keep data long term in the e-mail archival, to allow the users to search for their own data, and to allow authorized users to search the entire archive.

If you look at how e-mail is archived, archive systems generally come in one of three flavors:

◆ Systems that depend on journaling to automatically forward every e-mail sent or received by specified users on to the archive system.

◆ Systems that perform a scheduled MAPI "crawl" of specified mailboxes, looking for messages that are eligible to be moved or copied to the archive.

◆ Systems that move data to the archive by copying the log files from the production mailbox servers and then replaying the logs in to the archive. This is called log shipping.

Each of these methods has its advantages and disadvantages with respect to storage, providing a complete archive, and performance overhead.

Messaging-Enabled Applications

Microsoft Office enables messaging in many word-processing and spreadsheet applications. For example, when you install the Outlook client on your computer, Microsoft's Office products such as Word and Excel are enabled for electronic messaging. Let's say you want to send a Word document. You can select the Routing Recipient option from the application's File ➢ Send To menu. An electronic routing slip pops up. You then add addresses to the slip from your Exchange address books or from your Outlook contacts, select the routing method you want to use, and set other attributes for the route. Finally, you add the routing slip to the document with a click of the Add Slip button and ship it off to others using options on the File ➢ Send To menu.

As you can see in Figure 1.20, a file can be routed either sequentially or all at once to each address you selected. Routing sequentially helps eliminate problems associated with multiple users editing the same file at the same time. With applications such as Microsoft Word that keep track of each person's comments and changes, once the document has been routed, the original author can read the comments and incorporate or not incorporate them as he sees fit.

FIGURE 1.20
Microsoft Word 2003 includes messaging-enabled functions for sending and routing.

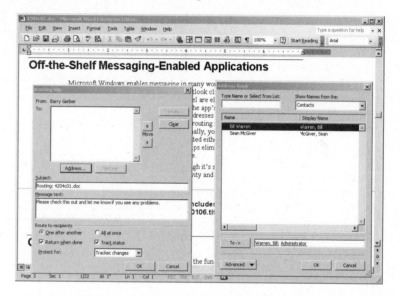

Although it's simple, application-based messaging can significantly improve user productivity and speed up a range of business processes.

Objects

Object insertion and linking further enhance the functionality of the Exchange messaging system. Take a close look at Figure 1.21. Yes, the message includes an Excel spreadsheet and chart. The person who sent the message simply selected Object from the Insert menu that appears on every Exchange message. Then he specified a file with an existing spreadsheet as the source of the object to be inserted into the message. The Outlook client then inserted the file into the message as an object.

The recipient can see the spreadsheet as a graphic image in the message, as shown in the figure. When the recipient double-clicks the graphic image, Excel is launched inside the message, and Excel's menus and toolbars replace those of the message (see Figure 1.22). In essence, the message becomes an Excel document.

The Excel spreadsheet is fully editable if Excel is available to the recipient. Without Excel, the recipient can only look at the spreadsheet in graphic image form. The graphic image changes when someone else edits the spreadsheet in Excel.

FIGURE 1.21
Object insertion makes
it easy to create
sophisticated
messaging-enabled
applications.

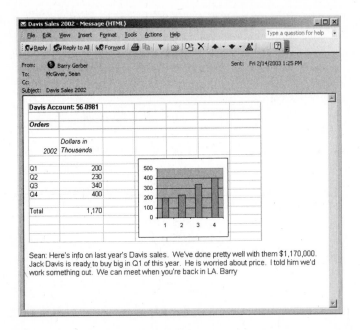

You can also insert in a message an object that is a link to a file that was created by an application such as Word or Excel. As with other kinds of object insertion, your recipient sees a graphic picture of the contents of the file and can edit the file by double-clicking the graphic picture. Links are a bit more flexible, because they allow users to work with files stored on a shared disk. With inserted objects, users work with a file embedded in the message itself.

Technically, this capability is provided not by the Exchange server, but by the Outlook client. However, OWA includes some of this same rich functionality, and the Exchange database and protocols are certainly built to support it, so many users consider it a feature of the Exchange system.

Public Folders

Public folders are for common access to messages and files. Files can be dragged from file-access interfaces, such as Windows Explorer, and dropped into public folders. The whole concept of public folders has many organizations in a quandary as they try to figure out the best place for these collaborative applications. Increasingly, applications that were once "best suited" for a public folder are now better suited for web pages or portals such as SharePoint workspaces. Although the whole concept of public folders is being deemphasized in Exchange 2007, this release continues to support public folders and many organizations will continue to find useful applications for public folders for the foreseeable future.

You can set up sorting rules for a public folder so that items in the folder are organized by a range of attributes, such as the name of the sender or creator of the item or the date that the item was placed in the folder. Items in a public folder can be sorted by conversation threads. Public folders can also contain applications built on existing products such as Word or Excel or built with Exchange or Outlook Forms Designer, client or server scripting, or the Exchange API set. You can use public folders to replace many of the maddening paper-based processes that abound in every organization.

FIGURE 1.22
Double-clicking an Excel spreadsheet object in a message enables Excel menus and toolbars.

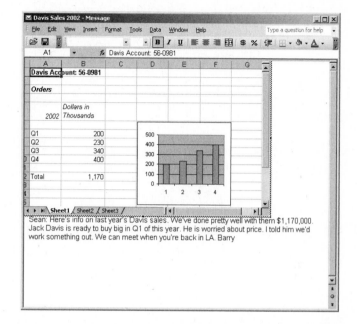

For easy access to items in a public folder, you can use a *folder link*. You can send a link to a folder in a message. When someone navigates to the folder and double-clicks a file, the file opens. Everyone who receives the message works with the same linked attachment, so everyone reads and can modify the same file. As with document routing, applications such as Microsoft Word can keep track of each person's changes to and comments on file contents. Of course, your users will have to learn to live with the fact that only one person can edit an application file at a time. Most modern end-user applications warn the user when someone else is using the file and if so allow the user to open a read-only copy of the file, which of course can't be edited.

Electronic Forms

Exchange Server 2007 continues to supports forms created with the Outlook Forms Designer (OFD). You can use OFD to build information-gathering forms containing a number of the bells and whistles that you're accustomed to in Windows applications. These include drop-down list boxes, check boxes, fill-in text forms, tab dialog controls, and radio buttons (see Figure 1.23).

OFD, which is easy enough for nontechnical types to use, includes a variety of messaging-oriented fields and actions. For example, you can choose to include a pread-dressed To field in a form so that users of the form can easily mail it off to the appropriate recipient. (The preaddressed To field for the form shown in Figure 1.23 is on the page with the tab marked Message, which is not visible in this figure.) When you've designed a form, you can make it available to all users or only to select users; users can access the completed form simply by selecting it while in an Outlook client.

FIGURE 1.23
Electronic forms turn messages into structured information-gathering tools.

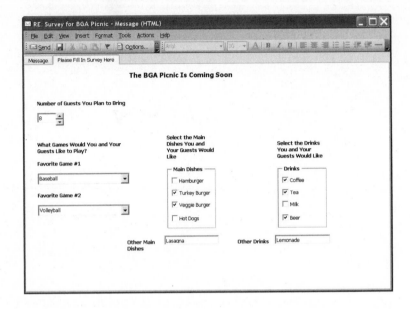

Summary

I hope that this chapter has given you some idea of what it is like to be an e-mail administrator and some of the things that you need to know. I have been using e-mail for almost 30 years and managing e-mail systems in one form or another for 20 years. I have watched how important e-mail has become to an organization over these past 20 years and I see how much organizations and users depend on their e-mail.

This gives me a source of pride to be able to provide such services to the users and to work in an area that is almost always changing with new technologies, features, and enhancements. As you now start your journey toward learning more about Microsoft Exchange Server 2007, I hope you too will find this as interesting and challenging as I do.

Chapter 2

Designing a New Exchange 2007 System

This topic comes early in the book because I feel it is important to keep your design goals (aka your end result) in mind as you are learning about a new software product or version of a software product.

Designing for 50 users is very different from designing for 50,000. The design process may involve a team of 25 people that represent IT, human resources, management, consultants, and the user community. Or it may just be you and your clipboard (oh, excuse me, your Tablet PC).

Deploying Exchange for the first time or migrating from a previous version of Exchange or another e-mail system involves careful planning. Many Exchange server deployments are slow or laden with problems because organizations don't take the time to properly gather and review all of the relevant information (especially factors affecting Exchange and Active Directory), and also don't take the time to carefully plan.

This chapter presents a step-by-step planning model based loosely on a process developed by Microsoft. Tracking these steps will help your organization decide where it wants to go with electronic messaging and how it can get there with Exchange. I can tell you from lots of experience that this process really works. I can usually gather the required information and generate a detailed first-draft plan, complete with a very convincing executive summary, in a month or so.

This chapter also offers practical information about the workings of Exchange Server 2007. You'll find detailed information about Exchange's network connection options: what they do and which networking topologies and protocols support them. This information is central to designing and implementing an Exchange system, and it's not found anywhere else in this book.

This chapter covers a lot of material. Just as you wouldn't try to implement a complex Exchange system in one day, you shouldn't try to plow through this chapter in one hour. Much of the information is more relevant to an organization deploying Exchange Server for the first time, but I hope that organizations that are upgrading from earlier versions will also find some useful information. If you are new to Exchange management and someone else designed your organization's Exchange infrastructure, this chapter may be of use to you when figuring out why some of the things are designed the way they are.

In this chapter, you learn to:

- ◆ Define migration goals
- ◆ Assign accountabilities for planning, design, and management

- ◆ Perform a needs assessment
- ◆ Plan your network configuration
- ◆ Roll out the plan

Defining Migration Goals

This may be the shortest section in the entire book, but I think it is one of the most important ones if you are migrating to Exchange Server 2007. Prior to installing or moving the first mailbox, replicating the first public folder, or even installing the first server, you need to decide up front what you expect to achieve with your migration and what your time frame should be for each of your achievements.

Determining the End State After Migration

Most importantly you need to figure out what your "end state" will be when you complete your deployment/migration. Factoring in all of the considerations that affect your organization and your messaging system is most important. Whether your system will be based on a single Exchange server in a single physical location or hundreds of Exchange servers spread out over multiple locations, you need to consider a number of design issues before implementation.

I usually find one of a small number of reasons that actually drive the decision to migrate to a new version of Exchange Server:

- ◆ Organization (or IT department) wants to be running the very latest version. These are usually the early adopters.

- ◆ Organization needs to upgrade in order to continue to run a product that is supported. If you fall in this category, you may still be running Exchange 5.0.

- ◆ A feature or set of features is available in the new version that will be of benefit to the organization's users or allow the IT department to deliver a higher quality of service.

- ◆ Upgrades to e-mail integrated applications require a later version of the mail server software.

- ◆ Servers are at the end of their life and it makes sense to upgrade to a newer version of the software when the servers are replaced.

The most common (in my experience) is the organization that sees a specific set of features in the newest version and that is their driving factor in moving forward. For medium sized and larger businesses, this is also one of the most problematic types of migration if goals are not clearly documented.

The reason this type of migration often has the most problems is that the organization wants to take all of the new features that are available and make them available to the users during the migration. For features such as local continuous replication, clustered continuous replication, or other "server-level" features, this may work just fine. These are implemented at the server level, can be engineered properly, and can be fully tested before the migration even starts.

However, features such as ActiveSync, Unified Messaging, remote document libraries via Outlook Web Access, or integration with rights management systems, may require additional training for your end users, additional documentation, and more resources from the IT department. Any features that require additional resources and that are not replacing an existing feature should be moved into a phase after the migration.

BEGIN WITH EXISTING FUNCTIONALITY

After planning, the initial phase of any migration should always be to maintain or replace existing functionality with similar functionality. Add new features only after the first phase is complete.

The first phase of the migration should always be to replace your existing functionality with similar functionality provided by the new version. Adding many new features to the migration process will be distracting and possibly take up valuable IT resources.

Define a schedule for your migration and which features and functionality will be made available during each phase of your migration. Once the schedule is defined and approved, stick to it. Don't let user requests (or demands) influence your decision to alter the migration plan unless there is a compelling business reason to do so. If you change your plan, make sure that you have the necessary resources to support the change.

I have helped to support many migrations over the past 20 years in which feature deployment was reprioritized on a weekly (or daily!) basis. Sometimes there is a specific business requirement to change the priorities, but often IT lets the users dictate how the migration progresses. A migration without focus or a specific plan will often take much longer to complete and in the end you will not be able to deliver the expected services to your users. Here are some tips when planning your migration:

♦ Determine what you want to achieve with the migration both near term and long term.

♦ Decide which features and functions will be used immediately and which will fall later in the process or after the migration has completed.

♦ Define milestones for specific pieces of your migration to be completed.

♦ Keep your focus on achieving your goals.

♦ Stick to your plan unless there is a specific business reason to deviate from it.

Taking an Inventory of Relevant Factors

Speaking from experience, most administrators think they have a pretty good idea of what they have running in their Exchange organization and how things are configured. Often, critical things are overlooked because no one took a step back and evaluated exactly what was running within the Exchange organization and what interaction the Exchange servers and clients have with additional software.

When you start any migration from one version of software to another, it is critical that you take a close look at your Exchange organization, what is running, and how Exchange may interact with things besides just Outlook.

EXCHANGE FEATURES IN USE

Documenting the Exchange features that you have currently in use might seem like a waste of time, but you will need to know this when it comes time to configure Exchange 2007 to replace your existing functionality with new features. Personal e-mail, calendars, contacts, and public folders are pretty obvious, but here are some additional examples:

♦ Conference room and equipment mailboxes

♦ Windows Mobile/ActiveSync devices

◆ Forms-based authentication/Outlook Web Access logon page

◆ Offline address books

◆ Mailbox management (Exchange 2000/2003 recipient policies)

◆ Mailbox and message size limits

◆ Server, mailbox database, and public folder database system policies

◆ Exchange 2003 anti-spam features

CLIENTS AND PROTOCOLS

Do you know every client type out there connecting to your Exchange server? I have been involved in a number of upgrades where the Exchange administrator was very surprised to find Outlook 98, Entourage, POP3 (Post Office Protocol version 3), and IMAP4 (Internet Message Access Protocol) clients. You might be surprised. Take a quick inventory of the e-mail clients that are deployed on your network. The Exchange 2000/2003 System Manager program allows you to add a Client Version column to the mailbox database's Logons container. From here, you can see the client versions that your users are using; an example of this is shown in Figure 2.1.

FIGURE 2.1
Viewing client versions using Exchange 2003 System Manager

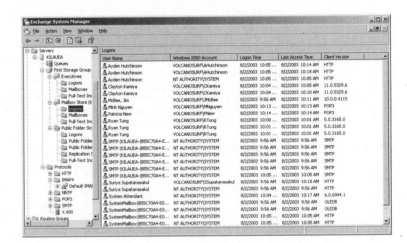

MAIL ROUTING AND MESSAGE HYGIENE

You need to know how mail flows within your organization and how the mail flow interacts with your organization's message hygiene system. If you are using third-party message hygiene systems (antivirus, anti-spam, and other types of content inspection or control), you should examine how these work and make sure you understand how you will interact with them in the future. Here is a list of things that you should be able to answer:

◆ Configuration and bridgehead servers for SMTP (Simple Mail Transfer Protocol) connectors

◆ How is outbound mail routing? Directly to the Internet via SMTP connectors using DNS (Domain Name System)? Or a smart host?

◆ Configuration and bridgehead servers for routing group connectors

◆ Inbound mail flow from the Internet; where do the MX (Mail Exchanger) records point? Directly to Exchange? A perimeter/DMZ system? An external service provider?

ACTIVE DIRECTORY

Exchange's dependency on Active Directory is tighter than it ever was before. Like Exchange 2000/2003, Exchange Server 2007 uses Active Directory as a common directory service for its configuration data, mail-enabled recipient information, and administrative permissions assignment. Exchange Server 2007 has taken that a step further and also depends on the Active Directory site architecture for message routing.

Exchange Server 2007 is a bit pickier on the Active Directory functional level and the version of Windows Server. There are a number of things relating to Active Directory that you should document. These include:

◆ Active Directory forest and domain functional level

◆ Names and locations of domain controllers

◆ Names and locations of global catalog servers

◆ Active Directory site architecture

◆ Active Directory site links and site link costs

◆ Which Active Directory sites currently have Exchange server located in them

◆ Mail-enabled group types in use: Universal? Global? Domain Local?

IN-HOUSE AND THIRD-PARTY SOFTWARE

One of the biggest mistakes organizations make when upgrading their messaging system to a new version of Exchange is that they don't do a full inventory of the software that is using the Exchange server and all of the third-party software that is in use. I have been involved in many upgrades where the organization could not finish the upgrade or got caught in the middle because it did not take into consideration all of the software that was being used. Here are some examples:

◆ Antivirus software

◆ Anti-spam software

◆ Fax server software

◆ Voicemail integration software

◆ Message archival software

◆ Photocopiers, fax machines, or scanners that integrate using Messaging Application Programming Interface (MAPI) or SMTP

◆ Compliance or discovery software

◆ In-house applications that use MAPI or SMTP

For each of these pieces of software, verify that it works with Exchange 2007 or that you have the budget to purchase updates. Verify that you will be able to have the updated software when you need it. Software such as your archival software may not need to be updated, but software such as Exchange-integrated antivirus almost always need to be upgraded when you upgrade Exchange to a new version.

DISK STORAGE

For you, disk storage may be as simple as adding more disks to an internal disk array or it may be as complex as having logical unit numbers (LUNs) allocated by your storage area network (SAN) engineer. Regardless, you want to make sure that whatever disk storage you plan to use will be sufficient.

◆ Ensure you have sufficient disk capacity not only for the data you expect to migrate but for future growth.

◆ If you will be upgrading operating systems (say from Windows 2000 to Windows 2003 or from Windows 2003 to Windows Server 2008), you need to verify that storage drivers, SAN management software, and even the SAN operating system are compatible with the versions of software you will be using.

◆ Ensure not only that the physical disk capacity meets your needs but also that the total disk I/O capacity does.

BACKUP AND DISASTER RECOVERY SOFTWARE

Like antivirus software, backup/restore software as well as other disaster recovery tools frequently needs to be updated when the Exchange or operating system Application Programming Interfaces (APIs) change or are updated. For the most part, software that works properly with Exchange 2003 seems to work fine with Exchange 2007, but you should always check with your vendor to make sure. If you run local backups on the Exchange servers, you will need to upgrade to a 64-bit version or an Exchange Server 2007–aware version. Some vendors have specifically released updated software that better integrates with Exchange 2007 and even the Windows PowerShell.

If you are using Snapshot technologies provided by your storage vendors or other third parties, again you should check with the vendor to make absolutely sure that all of the device drivers and management software works under Windows ×64 and Exchange Server 2007. This includes the software that does data restoration or mailbox-level access.

EXISTING HARDWARE

One of the biggest outcries that arose from the industry when Microsoft announced that Exchange 2007 would run under Windows ×64 only was that businesses would not be able to reuse their existing hardware. In my experience, if a platform has been in use for more than two or three years, the hardware is usually replaced anyway, so I don't find that a compelling argument — especially considering that most server-class hardware that has been sold since 2005 is already capable of running Windows Server 2003 ×64 or Windows Server 2008 ×64.

Some of your existing hardware can be reused in some cases; if the hardware supports the necessary minimum CPU and RAM requirements, you can reuse it. One way you can tell if your existing hardware and software supports the ×64 or EM64T CPU extensions is to run a nifty utility called CPU-Z (www.cpuid.com); this utility is shown in Figure 2.2.

Notice in Figure 2.2 that CPU-Z shows that the CPU supports the ×86-64 instructions. If this were an Intel CPU, EM64T would appear somewhere in the Instructions box.

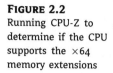

Figure 2.2
Running CPU-Z to determine if the CPU supports the ×64 memory extensions

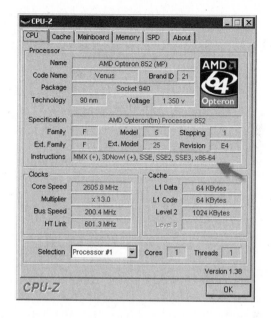

High-Level Steps for Planning a Deployment

This discussion builds upon a process presented by Microsoft in the Exchange documentation and other Microsoft publications, but it is far from a word-for-word regurgitation. Therefore, you should blame me — not Microsoft — if you encounter any problems from following the advice I give in this chapter. (And of course, if this stuff helps in any way, you should send the fruit baskets and such to me.)

Some of these steps include selecting an Active Directory architecture. Active Directory is widely deployed and thus some of these steps will probably be irrelevant for you. However, I hope you will find some relevance and useful information, so here, then, are the steps that I suggest you follow in designing your Exchange Server 2007 system:

1. Assign planning, design, and management responsibilities to staff.

2. Assess user needs.

3. Study your organization's geographic profile.

4. Assess your organization's network.

5. Establish naming conventions.

6. Select a Microsoft networking domain model.

7. Define your Active Directory site infrastructure.

8. Define administrative responsibilities.

9. Plan message routing links.

10. Plan servers and internal connections.

11. Plan connections to other systems.

12. Validate and optimize your design.

13. Deploy a test lab or a pilot project with a small group of users.

14. Roll out the plan.

These steps fit nicely into four categories:

◆ Delegating the planning, design, and management of your Exchange 2007 system

◆ Analyzing user and technical needs

◆ Dealing with the complex tasks involved in network planning

◆ Rolling out your Exchange system

As you go through this process, I strongly recommend that you and each of your team members take copious notes and that these notes be combined to form a journal that documents the process you took to arrive at your design decisions. This is often useful later when you need to figure out why you made certain decisions.

Now let's discuss each of the steps in more detail. The following sections fully describe all the tasks of designing and setting up an Exchange 2007 system and getting all the users up and running.

EXCHANGE DESIGN IS ITERATIVE, NOT LINEAR

Throughout this chapter, remember that designing an Exchange system is not a linear process but an iterative one. You'll find yourself coming back to each of the steps to gather new information, to reinterpret information that you've already gathered, and to collect even more information based on those reinterpretations. New information will likely lead to new questions, design changes, and further iterations. Even after you've fully implemented your Exchange Server 2007 system, you'll return to steps in the design process as problems arise or as your organization changes.

Within reason, the more iterations that you go through, the better your final design will be. But take care not to use iteration as a route to procrastination. Whatever you do, start running Exchange 2007 — if only in a limited test environment — as soon as you can.

Assigning Responsibility for Planning, Design, and Management

You need to ensure that two sets of specific responsibilities are assigned to staff. First, you have to assign a set of responsibilities related mostly to planning and design. Then you have to assign a second set of responsibilities that deal with ongoing management of key aspects of your Exchange Server 2007 system when it is in place.

Assigning Responsibilities for Planning and Design

Microsoft has identified 14 different roles that must be filled in planning, designing, and, to some extent, implementing and operating an Exchange Server system. That doesn't mean that you need 14 staff members to fill these roles, but it does mean that you need to assign each of these roles to a staff member. In a very large organization (tens of thousands of users), the people filling these roles will fill a large conference room, because each of these roles may well be assigned to a different staff member. If you're the only staff member responsible for Exchange, then you will hold most of these roles. Good luck! However the roles are assigned, the responsibilities for each of the roles must be covered.

Here's a list of the 14 roles and their related responsibilities:

Product manager. Sets objectives, coordinates schedules, manages external relationships, and sets the budget

Program manager. Has overall responsibility for Microsoft Exchange network design and implementation and specifies Exchange messaging system functional requirements

Exchange engineer. Determines technical configuration of all components of Exchange servers

Testing and QA engineer. Ensures that the Exchange messaging system conforms to functional requirements and corporate standards as well as planning acceptance or sign-off testing

Operations developer. Develops procedures, policies, and programs that monitor and control the Exchange network

Technical consultant. Provides consulting services and problem resolution for internal business units

Training developer. Develops training materials and documentation for end users and technical support personnel

Rollout planner. Determines the most efficient way to roll out Exchange servers and accompanying Windows servers, minimizes deployment costs, and promotes efficient implementation

Migration planner. Determines the work needed to migrate from an existing messaging system to Exchange Server 2007

Implementation manager. Manages the implementation of Exchange servers and associated components and the implementation of all of the plans made by all of the previous roles

End-user technical support technician. Provides end-user support for Exchange-related problems and questions

Messaging transport operations engineer. Maintains, operates, and repairs the Exchange server environment after installation

Marketing and consumer relations manager. Develops and carries out the Exchange rollout marketing program (product demonstrations, newsletters, pilot site coordination, and so on)

Financial controller. Monitors financial aspects of the project and tracks expenses against budget allocations

If you've ever implemented an information systems project, these roles are likely quite familiar to you, even if you've never thought specifically or in great detail about each of them. The key point here is that you're much more likely to successfully roll out your new Exchange Server 2007 system if you ensure that each of these 14 roles is properly filled. As we go through the planning and design process, think about these roles and how you might fill them.

Assigning Responsibilities for Day-to-Day Management

When your Exchange Server 2007 system has been implemented, you need to fill seven operational roles that support your system. Again, you might assign each of these roles to a separate person or combine and assign them to one or two people. These seven roles are listed here along with the responsibilities associated with them:

Recipient administrator/user manager. Administers mail-recipient aspects of Exchange Server 2007 and possibly account administration for Windows Server 2003 Active Directory, such as creation and management of recipients (Exchange mailboxes, distribution groups, and contacts)

Organizational administrator. Administers components of Exchange Server 2007 that affect all server roles throughout the entire organization, e-mail addressing rules, messaging records management, transport rules, and so on

Server administrator. Administers selected servers or groups of servers of the Exchange Server 2007 environment

Message routing manager. Administers the message routing infrastructure, including connectivity between Active Directory sites and messages sent to and received from the Internet

Message hygiene manager. Administers components of Exchange 2007 relating to message security, antivirus, anti-spam, content inspection, and transport rules

Public folder manager. Administers Exchange Server public folder hierarchy

Application development manager. Administers development of Exchange Server–related add-on applications

This list is based on a list of roles originally provided by Microsoft, though I have taken some liberties and separated server management roles, message hygiene, application development, and message routing into multiple categories.

As with the set of 14 roles described in the preceding section, as we go through the planning and design process, think about these operational roles and how you might fill them. If you think about your own experiences or your organization's needs, you might break down these roles into even more discrete operational responsibilities.

Performing a Needs Assessment

A needs assessment is a two-part process. First, you must understand the current state of affairs in some detail. Then, using your knowledge about what is currently in place, you must come up with an analysis of need that focuses on both keeping the best of what is and developing new approaches where required. You should perform needs assessments in each of these categories:

◆ Users

◆ Geography

◆ Data networks

You'll probably find that assessing user needs will be the most difficult because you're dealing almost exclusively with people and their perceptions of their needs and those of your organization. You should focus on the fact that, in addition to being an e-mail system, Exchange is a platform for a range of collaborative applications. You also should remember that user needs and wants have significant costs in time, money, and computer and network capacity.

A geographical needs assessment focuses on discovery of network components, servers, and users and the buildings, cities, states, and countries in which they are located. You need to know what kind of computing capacity, networking hardware, and software you have. Then you need to determine what, if any, changes must be made to ensure that everyone in your organization can participate in your Exchange system at a reasonably optimal level.

Exchange is nothing without quality network links from workstation to server and from server to server. Your network needs assessment should deal with three key issues:

1. Location and nature of your network connections

2. Bandwidth on your network

3. Network reliability

Assessing User Needs

Here you're interested in who needs what, when they need it, and how you'll provide it. You'll want to get a handle on the programming, software, hardware, management information services (MIS) systems, systems support, and training resources that will be required to satisfy user needs.

Remember that Exchange is an electronic messaging package, not just an e-mail product. Users might need specific electronic-messaging-enabled applications. Depending on what users have in mind, application development can be a real resource hog. Also remember that, in some cases, hardware and software might require new workstations, not just new servers.

Be prepared to give users a clear idea of what Exchange can do. You don't need to get technical with most users; just give them a view of Exchange from the end user's perspective. Take a look at Chapter 3, "Introducing Exchange Server 2007," and Chapter 4, "Exchange Server 2007 Architecture," to see how you might organize your presentation.

REMEMBER THE FUDGE FACTOR

Keep in mind that one of the biggest mistakes that most people make when implementing a system is to ignore or give only passing attention to the step of assessing user needs. Knowing as much as you can about what the users require up front means that you'll have an easier time during implementation. For example, imagine that you don't know from the get-go that your organization could benefit significantly from a particular custom-programmed electronic-messaging-enabled application. You go ahead and implement Exchange as an e-mail system with only the resources such an implementation requires. You get your Exchange system up and it's perking along just fine when, maybe three months later, some user comes up with this great idea for an electronic-messaging-enabled app. Boink! Suddenly you have to tell management that you need a few programmers and maybe more hardware to implement this idea that nobody thought of four or five months ago. I'll leave the rest to your imagination.

Regardless of what you find out in your user needs assessment, add a fudge factor in favor of more hardware and support personnel. Exchange has so many capabilities that you can be sure your users will find all kinds of ways to challenge whatever resources you make available. Depending on your users and their ability to get away with unplanned demands for resources, fudging by as much as 25 percent is reasonable. You can go with less fudge if your organization is particularly cost conscious and willing to adhere closely to plans.

Suffice it to say that a user needs assessment is the single most important part of the Exchange design process. Therefore, I'll cover it in more detail than the other Exchange design steps.

QUESTIONS TO ASK

You'll want to answer a number of questions during your user needs assessment. Here are the major ones:

◆ What kinds of users (for example, managers, salespeople, clerical staff, lawyers, doctors) does your organization have, and what do they think they want from the new Exchange system?

◆ What sorts of electronic messaging services are different groups of users likely to need (for example, e-mail, calendars and scheduling, public folders, specially designed applications)?

◆ Is integration with other collaborative applications such as SharePoint required?

◆ In addition to LAN access, will users need wireless LAN and/or WAN access to your Exchange system? Will this access have to be secure?

◆ Which specially designed applications can be developed by users, and which must be developed by MIS personnel?

◆ Do all users need every capability from day one, or can implementation be phased in, perhaps based on user groupings? If you are migrating from an existing messaging system, can you start by simply replacing the users' existing functionality and then adding more functionality at a later time?

◆ What client applications will be used by the users? Outlook MAPI clients? Outlook Anywhere (RPC over HTTP)? Outlook Web Access? Outlook Voice Access? POP3? IMAP4? Windows Mobile, iPhone, and other ActiveSync devices? Other mobile access technologies such as Blackberry and GoodMail?

◆ Is your organization affected by regulatory compliance such as laws that require specialized protection for some messages or mail retention for certain types of messages?

◆ What sorts of demands will users (or groups of users) put on your Exchange servers? Much of the information in this category can be used with Microsoft's Exchange server load simulation program to predict expected server load and project server hardware and networking requirements.

  ◆ How many mailboxes will you create per server?

  ◆ How many messages will the typical user send per day?

  ◆ How many messages will the typical user receive per day?

  ◆ How frequently will users send messages to others on their server? In their own site? In each of the sites in your organization? Outside your organization? (Be sure to break this down by the different kinds of external connections you'll have.)

  ◆ How often will users read messages in their mailboxes?

  ◆ How often will users read messages in public folders?

  ◆ How often will users move messages to personal folders stored locally and on the network?

◆ How often will users move messages to public folders?

◆ How big will the messages be? What percentage will be 1KB, 2KB, 4KB, 10KB, 40KB, 60KB, 80KB, 100KB, 200KB, and so on?

◆ What level of message delivery service will users want and need? This should be stated in hours or minutes between the time a message is sent and the time it is received. You'll need to specify this for both internal and external communications. Do you have a service level agreement that specifies expected response and message delivery times?

◆ What sorts of hardware and software resources (for example, computers, mobile phones, operating systems, Exchange client access licenses) will different groups of users need to implement Exchange on the client side?

◆ What kinds of training will be required for users or groups of users? Remember to consider training for administrators as well as training for anything that affects users.

◆ What sorts of IT department resources will be required to support user needs?

Studying Your Organization's Geographic Profile

You need a list of all the geographical locations in your organization. Here you should think not only in terms of cities, states, and countries, but also in-city and even in-building locations. Start at the top and work your way down. At this point, diagrams are important. Draw maps and building layouts.

This is the time to gather information on the workstations and servers you have in each location. You'll want to know how many run each of the different kinds of operating systems in your organization. Operating systems to watch for include these:

◆ Windows Server 2008

◆ Windows Server 2003

◆ Windows 2000 Server

◆ Windows 95/98/ME/2000/XP/Vista desktop operating systems

◆ Windows CE, Windows Mobile, and ActiveSync-enabled devices

◆ Apple Macintosh/Mac OS X

◆ Unix workstations by type of operating system

◆ Workstations used remotely

If you have hardware and software inventories for these machines, including CPU type, RAM, and free disk space, your job will be a lot easier. You can use all the information that you collect about workstations and servers to determine who's ready for Exchange and how many client access licenses you'll have to buy. Don't forget that you need to determine how many standard client access licenses you will need versus enterprise client access licenses.

As you gather information in other steps, begin to look at it in the context of your geographic profile. For example, you'll want to meld geographic information with what you find out about user needs and user groupings.

A number of tools are available that can scan computers on the network to make the inventory process much easier. Products like Microsoft System Center Configuration Manager or Altiris have built-in reporting. Utilities like `clusprep.exe` (Microsoft Cluster Configuration Validation Wizard) will do a system inventory. ClusPrep is available at the following URL:

```
http://www.microsoft.com/downloads/details.aspx?FamilyID=bf9eb3a7-fb91-4691-9c16-
553604265c31&DisplayLang=en
```

USER WORKSTATIONS: POWER PROMOTES PRODUCTIVITY

Most user workstations are underpowered. In most companies in which I have worked, we limp along for quite some time running substandard CPUs and not enough RAM. On older hardware, it may be all the computer can do to keep a word processor, a spreadsheet, and my e-mail software open at the same time. If I opened anything else, the machine started thrashing around so much between RAM and virtual memory that it slowed to a nearly useless crawl.

With a new system running Windows XP Pro or Windows Vista and with a dual core processor, fast hard disk, and 1GB to 2GB of RAM, I can run word-processing programs, spreadsheet programs, and Outlook together without wasting precious time to switch among them. And I still have plenty of horsepower left for all those tasks that I used to do with paper because I couldn't bring up the applications fast enough when I needed them. At will, I can now simultaneously open — and keep open — such apps as an accounting package and Microsoft Word, Excel, Project, and PowerPoint. With all that computer power, I'm also no longer reluctant to run other key programs — say, web browsers or Control Panel applets — at the drop of a hat.

Here's the bottom line: I've had my new system for less than a year. By my estimates, the productivity increase that I've experienced in that time has already paid back the cost of the system's purchase.

Maybe all your users don't need a dual core 3GHz Pentium system with Windows Vista and 2GB of RAM. However, as you start assessing user needs, don't let the dismal state of your organization's stable of workstations stop you and your users from reaching for the stars as you think about potential applications for Exchange.

Assessing Your Organization's Network

In this step, you just want to know what your network looks like now. This isn't the place to get into what kinds of networking you'll need; that comes later. You need to answer four key questions here:

◆ What's connected to what, and how? (Okay, if you're counting, that's two questions.)

◆ How much bandwidth do you have on each network?

◆ How reliable are your networks?

◆ What is the network latency between your outlying sites and your main data centers? Just because you have a fast link does not mean it has low latency. High-latency connections (greater than 100ms of lag time) will kill some Windows functions such as home folders, roaming profiles, and even Outlook connected "live" to the server.

WHAT'S CONNECTED TO WHAT, AND HOW?

Generally, in answering these questions, you should start at the top of your organization and work down to the domain or server level. For each link, name the following:

◆ Physical connection

◆ Networking topology

◆ Networking protocols running on the connection

For example, physical connection = local hardwire, networking topology = 100BaseT Ethernet, networking protocols = NetBEUI, TCP/IP, IPX/SPX. This information, especially when combined with the information you collected in steps 1, 2, and 3 in the section "Performing a Needs Assessment," will prove valuable as you start to plan for the Exchange connectivity that you'll need.

In looking at your organization's network, don't forget about connections to the outside world. Do you have connections to the Internet or trading partners?

HOW MUCH BANDWIDTH DO YOU HAVE ON EACH NETWORK?

Although bandwidth begins with network topology (type of connection), such as 100BaseT, T1, and DSL, it doesn't stop there. You need to know how much of your network topology's theoretical bandwidth is actually available.

TAKING ADVANTAGE OF CHEAP BANDWIDTH

Gigabit Ethernet is cheap. Most server class hardware comes with at least one if not two Gigabit Ethernet connections. Low-end Gigabit Ethernet switches are very reasonably priced. Your network backbone (domain controllers, file servers, Exchange servers) should all be connected to one another via switched Gigabit Ethernet.

To assess the actual bandwidth on each of your networks, you need some help from a network monitoring tool. If your networks are Windows 2003, you can try using the performance monitoring tools that come with the operating system to get a handle on traffic. For Windows 2000 and 2003, select Start Menu ➤ Programs ➤ Administrative Tools ➤ Performance. However, keep in mind that Microsoft's built-in tools will tell you only so much about the usage of your network. Consider third-party tools when doing network assessments.

What you want here is a chart that tells you, on average, how much of a network's bandwidth is available during each of the 24 hours in a day. You'll have to take several samples to get reliable data, but it's worth it. A warning light should go on in your head if you're already using more than, say, 60 to 70 percent of the available bandwidth on any network during daytime hours and you're not already running a heavy-duty messaging system such as Exchange. With that kind of scenario, you just might have to make some changes in the network before installing Exchange. I talk about those changes later; for now, be sure to collect this data on available bandwidth and incorporate it into your organizational maps.

How Reliable Are Your Networks?

Having a reliable network is an important issue. Increasingly in corporate America, there is strong pressure to centralize network servers. Centralization makes good economic sense. If all network servers are in one place, one set of staff members can support and monitor them, ensuring 24-hours-a-day, 7-days-a-week uptime.

Of course, 24/7 server availability is useless if the networks that people use to get to the servers are unreliable. I've seen this scenario play itself out in several organizations: They centralize the servers, the network fails, users can't get to their now mission-critical e-mail and other data, responsible IS planners are roundly criticized, and lower-level IS personnel are even more heavily criticized or fired. Grrr!

Assuring Availability

When contracting with wide area networking communications carriers, get a service level agreement that specifies exactly what level of availability they are providing you and what the cost to the provider is if they fail to meet those numbers. And keep in mind that 99.9 percent availability is still 8+ hours of downtime a year. If those 8 hours are in the middle of your business day, they will be noticed!

Here's the bottom line: Don't make your users work on unreliable networks. If your networks can't come close to matching the reliability of your servers, put the servers closer to their users. The little extra that it costs to manage decentralized servers is worth the access insurance that it buys. Sure, get those networks up to par, but don't risk your Exchange implementation on centralized servers before a reliable network is in place to support them.

Planning Your Network Configuration

Although it takes but a few words to say, planning your network configuration will take you on a long and winding road. The following sections cover some of the important parts of the planning process:

◆ Establishing naming conventions for objects in your Exchange server hierarchy

◆ Selecting a Microsoft networking domain model

◆ Defining administrative responsibilities

◆ Planning servers and internal connections to them

◆ Planning connections to other systems such as the Internet

◆ Validating and optimizing your design

You need to establish naming conventions for your Exchange organization, servers, connectors, and recipients. Some of these names depend on how you name Windows 2003 objects, whereas others have no dependency on the operating system. The Windows 2003 domain model that you choose will significantly affect how your Exchange servers interact, especially from a security standpoint.

Recipient, Organizational, and Server administrative permissions replace administrative group security in Exchange 2000/2003. How you set their boundaries depends heavily on how you want to parcel out responsibility for Exchange server management in your organization. Active Directory sites are now used as the boundary for local message routing instead of the routing group structure used in Exchange 2000/2003 and the server-to-server communication functionality of Exchange 5.5 sites.

The servers where you install Exchange 2007 must have adequate capacity; Chapter 4, "Exchange Server 2007 Architecture," reviewed some of the hardware requirements for Exchange Server 2007. Even if you plan for servers of very high capacity and even though Exchange 2007 allows lots of mailboxes on a server, you might want to consider distributing user mailboxes across multiple servers to increase performance. You also should consider setting user storage quotas to ensure adequate disk capacity over time. In addition, you should be sure that your servers are protected against low-level and catastrophic glitches by such things as fault-tolerant hardware, uninterruptible power supplies, and a reliable backup system. Finally, you should ensure that users have adequate bandwidth to access messages and other objects on your Exchange servers.

If you need to communicate with the Internet (and most organizations do), you will need to think about message hygiene (antivirus and anti-spam protection), perimeter network protection, how you allow SMTP mail in to your organization, and which Hub Transport server(s) will be responsible for sending and receiving Internet mail.

Finally, when key aspects of your Exchange system are in place, you need to test them to be sure that they work at all. Then you need to ensure that they work up to whatever performance and other standards you need to meet.

Okay, let's start our trip down that long and winding road.

Establishing Naming Conventions

Using naming conventions seems like such a small thing, but you will quickly change your mind if you work in an organization in which the server's IP address is easier and quicker to type (or remember!) than its name. Here you set some criteria for naming the key Exchange organizational components:

- Organization

  Note that the organization name is chosen when your first Exchange server is installed. Once it is set, it cannot be changed without removing all Exchange servers.

- Servers

- Storage groups and databases

- Recipients (including users, contacts, and distribution groups)

- Special recipients such as conference rooms and resources

- Exchange components

Your goal should be to establish a logical and consistent set of naming conventions that fit in well with your real-world organizational structure and culture.

NAMING THE ORGANIZATION AND SERVERS

Here's one easy and usually safe naming convention that you can use to name the organization and servers:

Organization   The master company name, for example, Ithicos Solutions. Names for the Exchange organizations can be up to 256 characters long, but I strongly suggest that you keep names to around 32 characters. Organization names should be less of a factor with Exchange 2007 because the organization name does not even appear in the Exchange Management Console.

Server You can use generic naming, such as, for example, EXCHANGE01, LAXEXMB01, LAXEXCA01, and so on.

Server names are set when you install Windows Server. You are allowed to use up to 63 characters, but you should limit them to 15 characters if pre–Windows 2000/XP clients will access them.

For most names, almost any character is permitted. However, I strongly suggest you use only the 26 uppercase and lowercase letters of the alphabet, the numerals 0 through 9, and the hyphen. Don't use spaces, underscores, or any accented letters.

When you begin to establish server names, if you are going to have more than one server in your organization, there are a few factors that you should take into consideration:

◆ The naming standard should be easy to remember.

◆ The naming standard should makes sense; yes it is fun to name servers after *X-Men* or *Battlestar Galactica* characters, but the naming makes absolutely no sense to anyone else.

◆ It should allow for some growth and scalability. Growth can be accomplished by including a couple of digits at the end of the name. Scalability can be accomplished by allowing for a portion of the name to identify a specific location if you have more than one location or think that you will in the future.

◆ The name should easily identify the server's function (mailbox server, domain controller, file server, and so on).

◆ In organizations with more than one location, the name should have a code that identifies the server's physical location. I am fond of airport codes or building numbers.

In an environment with more than a few servers, having some portion of the naming standard that helps to identify the role will quickly reduce frustration for everyone concerned. Table 2.1 shows some two-digit codes that can help to identify a server's role.

The codes in Table 2.1 are examples; you can expand on them or develop your own to meet your needs. Many organizations use three-digit codes to more accurately represent the function of a server.

Once you have role codes, you can begin to determine what the naming standard will look like. A favorite of mine includes a three-digit location code, followed by a server type code and a unique number; many organizations use the local airport code as the location code. Table 2.2 shows some examples of server names and how they would be decoded.

Naming Recipient Mailboxes

Even before you get to the point of assigning mailboxes, you should consider having a standard for creating and naming user accounts. Remember that the username (the pre–Windows 2000 name) must be unique for the entire domain. The user principal name (UPN) by default consists of the user's username and the forest root domain's DNS suffix; the UPN must be unique for the entire forest. Ideally, the username should also be unique across the entire forest. Some organizations will use the employee number (if applicable), whereas others randomly generate characters that are appended to the end of a username.

Username and Exchange Alias Can Differ

The username does not have to be the same as the Exchange alias; the Exchange alias is used (by default) to generate SMTP e-mail addresses for the mailboxes.

TABLE 2.1: Identifying Server Roles with Two-Digit Codes

SERVER FUNCTION	SERVER CODE
Mailbox	MB
Clustered mailbox	CM
Standby Continuous Replication target server	SC
Hub Transport	HT
Unified Messaging	UM
Client Access	CA
Edge Transport	ET
Combined functions	CF
Domain controller	DC
Cluster node	CN
File server	FS
Print server	PS
Web server	WB

TABLE 2.2: Examples of Server Names

SERVER NAME	EXPLANATION
LAXCN01	Los Angeles cluster node 01
LAXCN02	Los Angeles cluster node 02
LAXCM01	Los Angeles clustered Mailbox server 01
LAXHT01	Los Angeles Hub Transport 01
LAXCA01	Los Angeles Client Access 02
HNLCF01	Honolulu combined function server 01
SFOMB01	San Francisco Mailbox server 01
SFOCF01	San Francisco combined function server 01

You also need some criteria for naming mailboxes. There are four key names for each Exchange mailbox:

◆ First (Given Name)

◆ Last (Surname)

◆ Display

◆ Alias

Mailbox administrators create and modify these names in the Windows 2003 Active Directory Users and Computers Microsoft Management Console snap-in; the names can also be created or modified using the Exchange Management Console.

The first and last names are entered when the user's Windows 2003 login account is created. The display name is created from the first and last name (as well as the middle initial or name, if present). The alias name is created from the user's Windows 2003 logon name, which is entered when the user's Windows 2003 account is created.

The first and last names and the display name are Windows 2003 objects that are also used by Exchange. The alias is an Exchange object that is used in forming some Exchange e-mail addresses (for example, the user's Internet address). The Exchange alias should be unique, if possible, in order to avoid conflicts with other e-mail addresses that are created.

You can change the default rules for constructing mailbox names, and you can manually change these names. In Figure 2.3, you can see the first and last names as well as the display name for an Exchange 2007 mailbox in Active Directory Users and Computers, but this information can also be displayed and modified using the Exchange Management Console (EMC).

FIGURE 2.3

Display names are created using first and last names when a user account is created

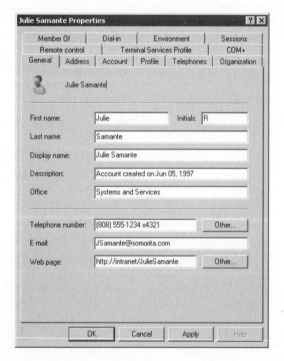

If you are wondering where the Exchange-specific Active Directory Users and Computers property pages are in Figure 2.3, they are no longer part of Exchange Server. All Exchange tasks are done with EMS or EMC.

Figure 2.4 shows the Exchange alias name for a user's mailbox; this information is only visible in the mailbox properties when using the Exchange Management Console. This is a big change for Exchange 2000/2003 administrators, who may be used to finding this information in Active Directory Users and Computers.

FIGURE 2.4

The alias name for an Exchange 2007 mailbox

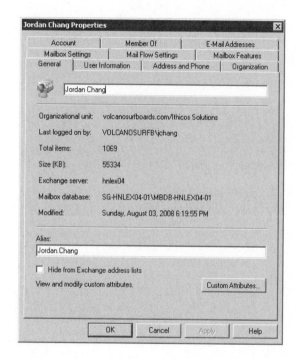

Display Names

Display names can be up to 256 characters long. They are only a convenience — they're not a part of the mailbox's e-mail address. However, they are the way in which Exchange users find the people they want to communicate with, so don't scrimp when setting them up.

The Outlook client global address list shows the display name for each mailbox (see Figure 2.5). You need to decide on a convention for display names. Display names will directly affect your users every day, so choose the naming standard carefully. This naming convention should account for potentially duplicate display names and allow for information in the display name that will let a user pick the correct name when there is, for example, more than one John Smith. You might even want to include department names or titles in display names so that users aren't faced with ambiguous selections, as they might be if they encountered a list of 25 recipients named John Smith. Options include *first-name-space-last-name* (as in John Smith) or *last-name-comma-space-first-name* (as in Smith, John). You may even opt for something fancier that includes the user's location, title, or department. The default is *first-name-space-last name*.

FIGURE 2.5

The Exchange client global address book shows each mailbox's display name

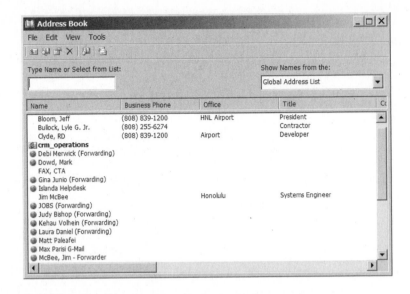

Practically speaking, display name lengths should be limited only by your users' willingness to read through lots of stuff to find the mailbox they're looking for. The length (and additional information in the display name) may also be affected by the size of the organization and how familiar your users are with their fellow e-mail recipients. Additional information in the display name (such as title or location) can make it a lot easier for users to determine that they are selecting the right mailbox from a list of thousands.

CONSIDER SECURITY WHEN CHOOSING DISPLAY NAMES

Display names are also included in messages going to the Internet, so be careful about including information that might be considered sensitive, such as job title.

Full-blown arguments have sprung up around the metaphysics of choosing display name conventions. I'll leave the decision to you, although I prefer the convention *Last_Name, First_Name* (as in Doe, Jane). In a larger organization, it is easier to find Jane Doe among a list of the Does than among a list of the Janes. If you are interested in some examples of how different display name standards would look, here are some ideas. Which of these would help you in preventing duplicate display names for your organizations?

Mark Watts	The default, first name and last name.
Elfassy, David	Last name and first name, commonly used and easy to follow.
Martha Lanoza at HQ (×54321)	Identifies first name and last name as well as the location and the user's telephone number extension.
Jones, Damion Mr. (SFO - Network Manager)	Includes location and title.

Craig, Benjamin GS-14 US Air Force	Pay grade and organization.
Maher, Joshua MAJ-US Army, Fort Irwin	Title, organization, and location.
Swanson, Chuck (Volcano Surfboards)	Includes company name (useful for mail going outside of your organization). This is also a useful standard when naming mail-enabled contacts because it allows your users to identify recipients outside of your company.
Tirch Brian CAPT N651 COMPACFLT	User's last name and first name without the comma. Includes the title, job code, and the department.

SOME DISPLAY NAME CHANGES REQUIRE EDITING ACTIVE DIRECTORY

Something as apparently simple as changing the default order of last and first name in display names isn't all that simple with Exchange 2007. In Exchange Server 5.5, you made the change in the Exchange Administrator program. With Windows Server 2003/Exchange Server 2007, you have to edit the Active Directory schema. Why? Display names aren't just for Exchange mailboxes anymore. They're also used whenever end users or system administrators go looking for a specific Windows 2003 user in Active Directory. That's why it's an Active Directory issue. Editing Active Directory is somewhat akin to editing the Windows Registry. It's not a job for amateurs, and it's a job that may be done by someone not directly involved in day-to-day Exchange Server 2007 management. In addition, the decision to change the display name default for an Active Directory namespace is no longer simply an Exchange Server issue. It's an organization-wide issue because these changes affect more than electronic messaging.

USING DIFFERENT DISPLAY NAMES FOR INTERNET MAIL

In some circumstances, it may be desirable to have a different display name used for mail that is sent to the Internet that is used for internal mail. Exchange and Active Directory provide a Simple Display Name attribute that you can edit via the Exchange Management Console or the Exchange Management Shell. You can enable this functionality on a per "remote domain" basis using the Set-RemoteDomain EMS cmdlet. See this article for more information: http://mostlyexchange .blogspot.com/2008/09/exchange-2007-and-simple-display-name.html.

Alias Names

For some messaging systems, the user's mailbox is identified by an alias name, which is part of the mailbox's address. Either Exchange itself or the gateway for the foreign mail system constructs an address using the alias. For other messaging systems, the mailbox name is constructed from other information.

Figure 2.6 shows the two addresses that Exchange built for a user by default for the Internet and for X.400. The Internet addresses use the Exchange alias Cheyne.Manolo. X.400 addresses do not use the alias. Instead, they use the full first and last name attributes of the user. Natively,

Exchange 2007 does not require the X.400 address but it is generated for backward compatibility with older e-mail systems.

FIGURE 2.6
Exchange Server uses the mailbox alias or the first and last names to construct e-mail addresses

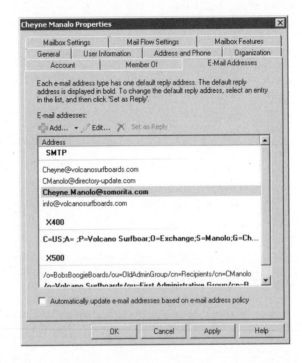

Aliases can be up to 63 characters long. That's too long, of course, because some people in foreign messaging systems will have to type in the alias as part of an electronic messaging address. Try to keep aliases short — 10 characters is long enough.

For some foreign messaging system addressing schemes, Exchange must remove illegal characters and shorten the alias to meet maximum character-length requirements. For example, underscores become question marks in X.400 addresses. You should do all you can to ensure that aliases are constructed using less-esoteric characters.

As with display naming, alias naming conventions are taken seriously, almost religiously. So don't be surprised if you have trouble deciding on one when you run them by "the committee."

ORGANIZATIONAL MAILBOXES OR ORGANIZATIONAL E-MAIL ADDRESSES

Companies are finding it increasingly useful to define mailboxes or e-mail addresses for job or organizational functions. Examples might include DNS.Manager@somorita.com or Software.Licensing@ somorita.com. See `http://mostlyexchange.blogspot.com/2008/09/organizational-mailboxes-or-smtp.html` for more information.

NAMING MAIL-ENABLED GROUPS

As simple as it sounds, many organizations spend hours or days debating and deciding their display name standard for mailboxes and then give no thought to naming their mail-enabled groups.

The thought actually comes once all of the mailboxes and mail-enabled groups have been created and they realize that groups are distributed throughout the global address list alphabetically just as the users are. There should be a naming standard for distribution group names just as there is with display names and alias names, and again, as with all naming standards, people can get pretty passionate about what they think is the best.

Mail-enabled groups are sorted using the group name attribute. This is configured either through Active Directory Users and Computers or through the EMC. Figure 2.7 shows the General property page of a mail-enabled group using the EMC; the group's display name is changed in the text box near the top of the property page.

FIGURE 2.7
Mail-enabled group properties as viewed through the Exchange Management Console

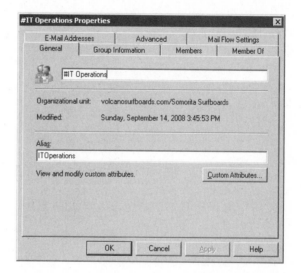

In Exchange 2007, all mail-enabled groups should be universal groups. Although this is not a hard and fast requirement, I strongly recommend doing so.

We all have our own preferences, but most Exchange administrators agree that there should be something in distribution group names that identifies them as mail-enabled distribution groups. Another possible idea is to include some character or character string that identifies and sorts all of the distribution groups together. Here are some examples:

- _Directory Update Sales Team

- $Everyone in Marketing

- DL - IT Help Desk

- zz Human Resources

This list illustrates three possible ways to name and sort mail-enabled groups. The first is to use a special character — such as the underscore (_), the dollar sign ($), the exclamation symbol (!), or the pound symbol (#). The advantage of these characters is that they will sort all of the mail-enabled groups to the top of the global address list. Another example is using the letters *DL* (for distribution list) in front of each mail-enabled group; this will keep all of the mail groups sorted together. Finally, you could use characters such as *zz*; this will put the mail-enabled groups together but place them all at the bottom of the global address list. The advantage of having them all at the bottom rather than at the top is that it is less likely that a user will accidentally select a group. For more information on sort orders, see the following article: `http://mostlyexchange.blogspot.com/2008/09/global-address-list-and-special.html`.

If users just need to see the groups in the global address list, they can also use the All Groups address list. The All Groups view shows only the objects in the directory that are mail-enabled groups. Note also in Figure 2.8 that I included a few of the common special characters so that you can see how they sort in the global address list.

FIGURE 2.8
The All Groups
address list

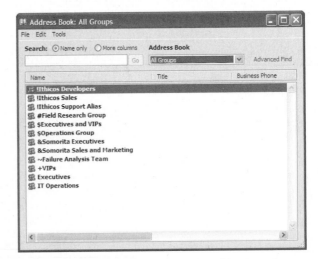

NAMING EXCHANGE COMPONENTS

Display names for mailboxes or groups affect the end user and therefore getting them right is a pretty important task. There are, however, a number of Exchange-related components or objects for which you should consider naming standards. Why? Because incorporating standards for Exchange objects will make *your* life and the lives of your fellow Exchange administrators easier.

The objects and components that I am alluding to are found in the Exchange Management Console or the Exchange Management Shell:

- Managed folder mailbox policies
- Offline address books
- Exchange ActiveSync mailbox policies
- Transport rules
- Edge subscriptions
- E-mail address policies
- Unified Messaging dial plans
- Unified Messaging policies
- Storage groups

◆ Send connectors

◆ Receive connectors

◆ Mailbox databases

In a small organization, naming conventions for policies and objects that are listed in the organization-wide and server configuration settings are not as necessary because you may have only a few of these. However, in a larger organization with many locations and possibly many groups of administrators, include in the name of each policy or object enough information to identify what the object does and who is responsible for it. For example, even a small organization can identify with the transport rules (shown in Figure 2.9). Once an organization has a dozen or more transport rules, it can be difficult to find the rule you need to edit.

FIGURE 2.9
Managing more than a few transport rules can become difficult

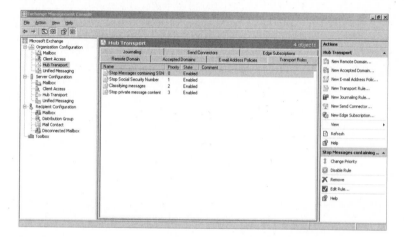

Imagine the difficulty that an organization with administrators in multiple organizations around the world would face when they have to find a specific transport rule that affects only a certain part of their user community.

Storage groups and mailbox databases are sets of objects that should have standardized names. This helps not only the person who must administer the mailbox servers but also the recipient/mailbox administrators. A clearly defined naming standard can help when creating mailboxes or assigning mailboxes. Figure 2.10 shows the Mailbox Settings screen for the New Mailbox Wizard; note the Storage Group and Mailbox Database fields.

In the naming standard I am using for the storage groups and mailbox database, I include MBDB for mailbox database or SG for storage group. The name also includes the name of the server on which the database or storage group is found and a unique number for that storage group or mailbox database. Here are some examples:

◆ SG-LAXMB01-01

◆ SG-NYCCM01-02

◆ Server1-SG1

◆ DB-LAXMB01-01

◆ DB-LAXMB01-02

◆ DB-LAXMB01-02

◆ Server1-SG1-DB1

FIGURE 2.10
Assigning a storage group and mailbox database to a new mailbox

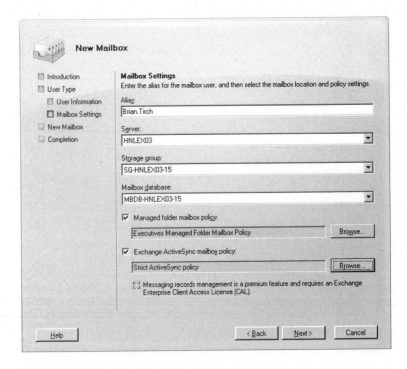

If you have already deployed some mailbox databases or storage groups, not to worry; you can easily rename them as you will find in later chapters. I recommend that you name the database file the same as the logical database. For example, the database DB-HNLEX03-01 would have a database file named DB-HNLEX03-01.EDB.

Selecting a Microsoft Active Directory Domain Model

Active Directory is widely deployed in organizations all over the world. This section may not be relevant to your organization because you may have a fully deployed Active Directory. However, even if you are a dedicated Exchange server administrator, understanding Active Directory is important and will make it easier for you to operate and troubleshoot Exchange.

As many different options for multiple trees and child domains as you may have (and may be tempted to use), I strongly urge you to consider a single domain mode whenever possible. This is by far the simplest to deploy and administer, and administrative permissions can still be delegated for individual resource and account management. Of course, if necessary, you can create a single root domain for your user accounts and create child domains (sub-domains) and control access to various network resources using this model.

Aside from certain security requirements, one of the main reasons for multi-domain Windows NT networks was the difficulty of building single domains that crossed lower-bandwidth links. Microsoft has outfitted Windows 2003 with such features as sites and site connectors to deal with this issue. Unless you must adhere to strong regulatory or security requirements, the single-root domain model really makes the most sense.

If it works for your organization, you can even use your Internet domain name for your Windows 2003 root domain. This simplifies Exchange server installation just a little, although you need to be especially careful to protect any internal resources that shouldn't be accessible on the Internet. If you want to use a separate DNS name for your Windows 2003 root domain, then by all means do so. This can also help to reduce confusion and make your DNS names a little easier to support. You can still use your Internet domain name for external Exchange messaging. I like this approach and use .local for Windows domain names and .com, .edu, and so on for Internet domain names.

Your Active Directory DNS names do not have to be the same as your Internet names and/or Internet SMTP addresses.

Defining Active Directory Sites

An Active Directory site is a collection of IP subnets that are all separated by reasonably high-speed connectivity. The definition of "high speed" is usually left up to the designer of the Active Directory, but I recommend that all of the subnets in a single Active Directory site have at least 10Mb Ethernet connectivity between each of the subnets in the site.

Since Windows 2000 was first released, Active Directory sites have been used to define replication paths between domain controllers and to help Windows clients find the closest domain controller when authenticating users. Exchange 2000/2003 servers used Active Directory sites to locate the domain controllers and global catalog servers that were closest to them on the network; they then used these domain controllers and global catalog servers for authentication, LDAP queries, and referring MAPI clients to global catalog servers.

In the past, administrators sometimes would not properly create all of the Active Directory sites for their organization or, worse, would not define all of the IP subnets properly. This would result in long login times and performance problems with Exchange because Exchange servers could be querying domain controllers and global catalog servers on the opposite side of the globe. An incorrect Active Directory site and subnet configuration is a mistake that you cannot afford to make with Exchange 2007. In addition to all of the performance problems that might occur with past versions, you may experience mail delivery failures because Exchange 2007 relies on the site architecture to properly deliver mail between Exchange servers in different sites.

TROUBLESHOOTING ACTIVE DIRECTORY SITE PROBLEMS

One simple way to check for Active Directory site problems is to check on each domain controller's Netlogon.log file found in the \windows\debug folder. If you see reports of clients logging in to that domain controller from undefined subnets, you know you have some subnets that are not fully defined with Active Directory.

If you have more than one network physical location that has domain controllers and Exchange servers, you need to get your site and subnet architecture clearly and accurately defined. You do this in the Active Directory Sites and Services management console (Figure 2.11). For each of your physical locations, you must define the IP subnets and associate those subnets with the correct Active Directory site.

FIGURE 2.11
Defining Active
Directory sites
and subnets

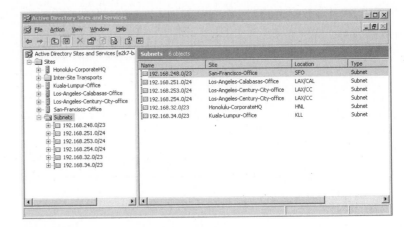

Exchange 2003 Administrative Group Boundaries

If you are planning to migrate from an Exchange 2000/2003 organization, you will retain the Exchange 2000/2003 administrative groups through the migration. If you are building a brand-new Exchange 2007 organization, you will not need to worry about administrative groups.

Administrative groups play a couple of roles in an Exchange 2000/2003 environment as well as an Exchange 2007 organization that is in the middle of a migration. First, they can be used to control administrative access to your Exchange 2000/2003 server environment. You can set permissions on an administrative group so that only certain users can manage the Exchange 2000/2003 servers and other objects in the group. In this way, you can parcel out responsibility for managing different sets of Exchange servers to different people.

The administrative group structure of your Exchange 2000/2003 environment will probably depend to some extent on the structure of your organization. If you want a particular group, such as a department, to manage its own Exchange server environment, you would create an administrative group, put the department's Exchange server(s) in the administrative group, and assign permissions to manage the group to the appropriate Windows 2003 users or group.

Once the first Exchange 2007 server is installed into an existing environment, a new Exchange administrative group is created that holds all of the Exchange 2007 servers regardless of the permissions necessary to manage them. This is called Exchange Administrative Group (FYDIBOHF23SPDLT); the text "FYDIBOHF23SPDLT" is a unique identifier is associated with the new administrative group name when the first Exchange 2007 server is installed to guarantee that the administrative group name is unique. The unique name for the Exchange Administrative Group (FYDIBOHF23SPDLT) administrative group's routing group is Exchange Routing Group (DWBGZMFD01QNBJR). These administrative group and routing group names are hard-coded and must not be changed.

SECRET CIPHERS

If you are curious about the unique identifiers DWBGZMFD01QNBJR and FYDIBOHF23SPDLT, I will let you in on a poorly kept secret. They are actually simple "shift" ciphers. Take each letter in the identifier FYDIBOHF23SPDLT and change it to the preceding letter in the alphabet and see what you get. Hint, *F* becomes *E*, *Y* becomes *X*, and so on. Conversely, with the DWBGZMFD01QNBJR identifier, take each letter in the identifier and change it to the next letter in the alphabet, so *D* becomes *E*, *W* becomes *X*. Try it and see what you get. If you are as big a fan of Exchange Server as I am, then I am sure you will agree.

Although the administrative groups do not show up in the Exchange 2007 Exchange Management Console, you can see them in the Exchange 2000/2003 Exchange System Manager console (see Figure 2.12).

FIGURE 2.12

Exchange System Manager after the first Exchange 2007 server is installed

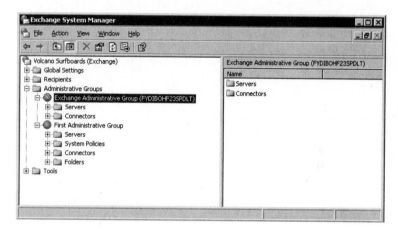

Exchange 2003 Routing Group Boundaries

In Exchange 2000/2003, the routing groups defined the physical separation of Exchange servers; this separation was usually determined based on slow, unreliable, or non-full-time links. When defining Exchange 2000/2003 routing group boundaries, you should keep a couple of things in mind. First, Exchange 2000/2003 routing groups and Microsoft network domains are related. Second, all the Exchange servers in a routing group should have certain networking capabilities.

Routing groups have been replaced by Active Directory sites in Exchange 2007, but an organization that is going to have interoperability between Exchange 2007 and Exchange 2000/2003 will continue to see routing groups in Exchange System Manager. When the first Exchange 2007 server is installed, a new administrative group and routing group is created that will allow interoperability between Exchange 2000/2003 servers and Exchange 2007. Figure 2.13 shows a new unique routing group that is created in the new Exchange 2007 specific administrative group. This routing group will hold all Exchange 2007 servers.

FIGURE 2.13

Exchange 2007 routing group container used for interoperability with Exchange 2000/2003

Planning Your Disk Space Requirements

Disk space is one of the requirements of Exchange that most often confuses people or is not configured properly. The disk space requirements for supporting the Exchange server itself are relatively straightforward. The disk volume on which Exchange Server 2007 is installed requires approximately 1.2GB of disk space; the system disk requires another 200MB of disk space. If the Exchange server is supporting the Unified Messaging server role, plan for an additional 500MB of disk space for each Unified Messaging language pack that will be installed.

The operating system disk should also have sufficient free disk space to allow a page file that is at least the amount of RAM plus 100MB. This is to allow Windows to dump the memory in the case of an operating system crash. Exchange servers that support larger numbers of mailboxes often have dedicated spindles or partitions just for the page file.

Figure 2.14 shows a conceptual diagram of an Exchange 2007 mailbox server that is designed to support 1,000 mailboxes. The following section explains the process I went through to estimate the storage required. In some cases, I picked a typical large drive size. Mailbox servers are by far the biggest consumers of disk storage, and this is something you must plan for. You must also be prepared for growth.

FIGURE 2.14
Disk configuration for an Exchange 2007 Mailbox server

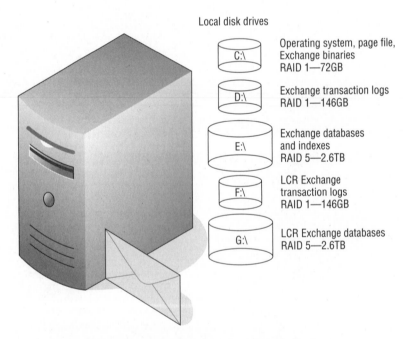

Local disk drives

C:\ Operating system, page file, Exchange binaries RAID 1—72GB

D:\ Exchange transaction logs RAID 1—146GB

E:\ Exchange databases and indexes RAID 5—2.6TB

F:\ LCR Exchange transaction logs RAID 1—146GB

G:\ LCR Exchange databases RAID 5—2.6TB

I have also taken into consideration the use of local continuous replication (LCR) in Figure 2.14 and thus have allocated disk space for it. Ideally, transaction logs and the operating system are on dedicated RAID-1 spindles and the databases are on dedicated RAID-5 or Raid 1+0 spindles. Even though I have labeled this figure as having local drives, you could deploy this same configuration using iSCSI or SAN disks. I estimated 72GB of space for the operating system, page file, and Exchange binaries, 146GB for the transaction log volume, and 2.6TB of space for the database volume.

Mailbox Server Storage

Exchange servers holding the Mailbox server role consume the most disk space. Exchange system designers often fall short in their designs by not allowing sufficient disk space for mail storage, transaction logs, and extra disk space. Often the disk space is not partitioned correctly, either. Here are some important points to keep in mind when planning your disk space requirements:

◆ Transaction log files should be on a separate set of physical disks (spindles) from their corresponding Exchange database files. RAID-1 or RAID-0+1 arrays provide better performance for transaction logs.

◆ Allow for at least 7 to 10 days' worth of transaction logs to be stored for each storage group. The estimated amount of transaction logs will vary dramatically from one organization to another, but a good starting point is about 5GB of transaction logs per day per 1,000 mailboxes. Tools like the Exchange storage calculator can be used to assist in disk space requirements. To get the Exchange storage calculator, visit this page: http://msexchangeteam.com/archive/2007/01/15/432207.aspx.

◆ Allow for 10 to 15 percent white space estimates in the maximum size of each of your database files.

◆ Allow for 10 to 15 percent deleted item and deleted mailbox retention space in each database file.

◆ When planning for local continuous replication, make sure the replicated transaction logs and backup copy of the databases are on separate physical disks from the source.

◆ Allocate enough free space on the disk so that you can always make a backup copy of your largest database and still have some free disk space. A good way to calculate this is to take 110 percent of the largest database you will support because that also allows you to defragment the database using ESEUTIL if necessary.

◆ Consider additional disk space for message tracking, message transport, HTTP protocol, POP3 protocol, and IMAP4 protocol log files.

◆ Always have recovery in mind and make sure you have enough disk space to be able to restore a database to a Recovery Storage Group.

So, to use some of these points when calculating necessary disk space, here is an example for a server that will support 1,000 mailboxes. Further, I am estimating that I will provide the typical user with a "prohibit send" size warning of 500MB and a "prohibit send and receive" limit of 600MB. In any organization of 1,000 users, you have to take in to consideration that 10 percent will qualify as some type of VIP that will be allowed more mail storage than a typical user; in this case, I will allow 100 VIP users to have a "prohibit send and receive" limit of 2GB.

This gives 540GB of mail storage requirements (600MB × 900 mailboxes) for the first 900 users plus another 200GB (2GB times 100 mailboxes) for the VIP users. This is a maximum amount of mail storage of 740GB. However, this estimate does not include estimates for deleted items in a user's mailbox and deleted mailboxes, so I want to add an additional overhead factor of about 15 percent, or about 111MB, plus an additional overhead factor of another 15 percent (another 111MB) for database "white space." The white space is the empty space that is found in the database at any given time.

So at any given time, for these 1,000 mailboxes, I can expect mail database storage (valid e-mail content, deleted data, and empty database space) to consume approximately 962GB, but because I like round numbers, I'll average that up to 1,000GB, or 1TB.

In this example, let's say that I have decided the maximum database size I want to be able to back up or restore is 100GB. This means that I need to split the users' mailboxes across 10 mailbox databases and storage groups.

For the transaction logs, I estimate that I will generate approximately 5GB of transaction logs per day. I should plan for enough disk space on the transaction log disk for at least 50GB of available disk space.

Next, because full-text indexing is enabled by default, I should allow enough disk space for the full-text index files. In this case, I will estimate that the full-text index files will consume a maximum of about 5 to 10 percent of the total size of the mail data, or approximately 100GB. If I combine the full-text index files on the same disk drive as the database files, I will require approximately 1.3TB of disk space.

Finally, on this server I am planning to implement local continuous replication, so I will need to plan for a separate set of spindles for the databases (1.3TB) and the transaction logs (50GB).

Anytime there is any doubt as to how much disk space you should include, it is usually a good idea to plan for more rather than less. Although disk space is reasonably inexpensive, unless you have sophisticated storage systems, adding additional disk space can be time consuming and costly from the perspective of effort and downtime.

Planning for Growth

Growth?! You may be saying to yourself, "I just gave the typical user a maximum mailbox size of 600MB and the VIPs a maximum size of 2GB! How can my users possibly need more mailbox space?" Predicting the amount of growth you may need in the future is a very difficult task. You may not be able to foresee new organizational requirements or that you might be influenced by future laws that require specific data retention periods.

In my experience, though, mailbox limits, regardless of how rigid you plan to be, are managed by exception and by need. In the preceding example, I calculated that I would need 1.3TB of disk space for my 1,000 mailboxes. Would I partition or create a disk of exactly that size? Probably not.

Instead of carving out exactly the amount of disk space you anticipate needing, add a "fluff factor" to your calculations. I recommend doubling the anticipated amount of storage you think you will require, but this is just a wild guess. In this example, though, I might anticipate using 2.6TB of disk space if I doubled my expected requirements. Here are some factors that you may want to consider when deciding how much growth you should expect for your mailbox servers:

◆ Average annual growth in the number of employees

◆ Acquisitions, mergers, or consolidations that are planned for the foreseeable future

◆ Addition of new mail-enabled applications such as Unified Messaging features or electronic forms routing

◆ Government regulations that require some types of corporate records (including e-mail) to be retained for a number of years

Conversely, there are potential things in your future that could actually reduce the amount of mailbox storage you require. Many organizations are now including message archival and long-term retention systems in their messaging systems. These systems archive older content out of a user's mailbox and move it to some type of external storage such as disk, storage area network (SAN), network attached storage (NAS), optical, or tape storage. The user can still access or search for archived content, but it no longer takes up space in your Exchange server mailbox databases.

Archive systems are great for organizations that must retain much of the information in their mailboxes but want to move it to external storage. However, depending on the system, you don't want to archive everything older than five days, because that may prevent the user from accessing it via Outlook Web Access or mobile devices. Further, once the content is archived and no longer residing in the user's mailbox, it will no longer be accessible from a user's desktop search engine such as the Google Desktop or the Windows Desktop search engine. So keeping a certain amount of content in the user's mailbox will always make sense.

Planning Servers and Internal Connections to Them

There's quite a bit to do in planning your servers and user links. You must decide what kinds of hardware to use for each of your Exchange servers. Then you need to think through some policies relating to storage. After that, you must figure out how to back up the servers. Then you need to make sure you've got adequate bandwidth on your local networks to keep Exchange happy; if you don't have it, you have to decide how to get it. Finally, before you go on to the next step in the Exchange design process, you must think about remote users and how you'll connect them to Exchange.

Designing Your Exchange Servers

The intricacies of Exchange Server design and fine-tuning could occupy a whole book; you'll have to experiment here. Fortunately, Microsoft doesn't leave you out in the cold when it comes to this experimentation. The company provides applications for testing the capacity of hardware you might use to run Exchange Server. These include the Exchange Server Jetstress, Exchange Load Generator, and Exchange Server Stress and Performance tools. Jetstress places load on your disk subsystem similar to an Exchange server load, and the Exchange Load Generator and the Exchange Server Stress and Performance tools test your server hardware (CPU, disk drives, RAM) and network capacity by simulating messaging loads on an Exchange 2007 server.

To begin your experimentation, install Windows Server 2003 and Exchange Server 2007. There are earlier versions of these tools (such as a tool called LoadSim) but I recommend you use the latest versions available from Microsoft. You can download these from `http://technet.microsoft.com/en-us/exchange/bb330849.aspx`.

DO NOT USE CAPACITY TESTING TOOLS IN PRODUCTION ENVIRONMENTS

Tools such as Load Generator, Stress and Performance, and Jetstress should never be run against production mail servers or in production environments.

Next, take out that set of user-demand numbers that you put together when you did your user needs assessment. Plug those numbers into the load generator, and run it against a reasonable Exchange server machine — say, a 3GHz Pentium 4 or Xeon machine with 2GB of memory and at least two 9GB SCSI/SAS hard drives. Don't run the load generator on your Exchange server. Instead, run it on a separate 1GHz or better Pentium-based Windows XP workstation with at least 1GB of memory. And don't try to simulate more than 200 users on one load generator machine. If you don't follow these guidelines, the load generator tools might not be capable of generating the loads that you've asked it to and you could be led to believe that your Exchange server hardware is adequate when it's not. If you need to simulate a large number of users make sure you have enough hardware to simulate the load.

In selecting servers for Exchange, my recommendation is to always go for the biggest guns that you can afford, commensurate with expected user loads. After working a while now with Windows Server 2003 and Exchange Server 2007, I have my own ideas about server sizing. A good machine would be a dual-core Intel Xeon or better computer with 4GB of random access memory (RAM) and a hardware RAID-5 disk capacity of at least 500GB. Such a computer should be capable of handling upwards of 200 average Exchange Server 2007 users, network bandwidth willing; however this configuration may not be suitable for all environments. A number of tools on the market are freely available from Microsoft to assist in server sizing.

In a busier environment, Exchange 2007 not only doesn't benefit from running on a domain controller, it actually suffers as it competes with Active Directory and other CPU/disk-intensive software that runs on a Windows Server 2003 domain controller.

If you had to gulp a few times after reading my recommendations for a production Exchange 2007 server, don't worry. You can get by with less horsepower, especially if you need to support fewer users.

If you do decide to go with less costly or less powerful hardware, I strongly suggest that you go with SCSI/SAS disk drives over Enhanced IDE drives or SATA drives. Enhanced IDE and SATA drives are nice and inexpensive, but for production Exchange servers, I prefer SCSI drives. They're fast and tend to be more reliable than IDE drives over the long haul. For best performance, choose ultra-wide SCSI drives.

When you're comfortable with the basic design of your servers, you need to plan for uninterruptible power supplies (UPSs). I consider a UPS to be part of a server, not an add-on. UPSs are cheap, given the peace of mind that they can bring. In spite of Windows Server 2003's and Exchange Server 2007's capability of recovering from most disastrous events, you don't want to tempt fate and risk damage to your organization's precious electronic messaging data. Get enough UPSs to serve the power needs of each server, and get a UPS that comes with software to gracefully shut down your servers if power stays off for an extended period. I talk more about UPSs in Chapter 17, "Reliability and Availability 101."

SERVER FAULT TOLERANCE

The more fault tolerance you can build into your Exchange Server hardware, the better you and your users will sleep at night. Almost nothing is worse than losing even one user's e-mail messages. Here are a few steps that you can take to improve server fault tolerance:

◆ Look for systems with error-correcting RAM memory.

◆ On the disk side, consider multiple SCSI controllers or RAID technologies implemented in hardware.

◆ Look for computers with two or more redundant power supplies.

◆ Buy computers that let you swap out failed RAID drives and power supplies without even bringing down your system (this capability is called *hot swap*).

◆ Consider Microsoft's Windows Server 2003/2008 Enterprise and Datacenter Server editions, which let you set up clusters of Windows/Exchange 2007 Mailbox servers that are able to continue serving users even if one cluster node fails.

◆ Use load-balancing services such as the Windows Load Balancing or the Cisco Local Director to provide higher availability for Client Access and Edge Transport servers.

◆ Install multiple Hub Transport servers in each Active Directory site that has Mailbox server roles for redundancy in message routing.

Setting Exchange Server Storage Policies

You need to start thinking now about how you'll manage user storage on each server. Storage management gives you more control over how much is stored on Exchange server disks, and it helps you remain within your server disk budget. You need to answer several disk management policy questions, including these:

◆ Do you want some or all of your users to store messages in personal folders on a workstation or networked disk drives instead of in their Exchange Server–based mailboxes? This is probably not a good idea and I recommend against using personal folders as a user's primary mail storage location because these are often not backed up.

◆ For those who will use their Exchange Server mailboxes, do you want to limit the amount of storage that they can use?

◆ Do you want to impose limits on the storage used by public folders?

◆ If you have public folders containing messages that lose value with time (for example, messages from Internet lists or Usenet news feeds), do you want Exchange to automatically delete messages from these folders based on message age?

◆ Will you implement Exchange Server's capability to save deleted messages for a designated period of time? This is a neat capability because users can recover messages that they accidentally deleted. However, all those "deleted" messages can take up lots of Exchange server disk space.

You can base your answers to most of these questions on the results of your user needs assessment, although you're bound to make adjustments as you pass through iterations of the design process. Also note that though it's tempting to force users to store messages in personal folders on local or networked disk drives to save space on the Exchange server disk, you then run the risk that key user messages won't get backed up. As the ever-present "they" say, "You pays your money and you takes your chances."

Planning disk storage is important enough that I had an entire section on planning your mailbox storage requirements and disk space. Later in Chapter 10, "Imposing Limits," I further this concept by dedicating an entire chapter to how you can impose storage limits and message size limits on your users.

Backing Up Your Exchange Servers

When you know what your Exchange servers and networks will look like, you can begin thinking about backing up your servers. You need to use backup software that is especially designed for Exchange's client/server-transaction-oriented architecture. Such software enables you to back up an Exchange server's information database without shutting down Exchange processes and thus closing off user access to the server. The software communicates with Exchange's information database service to ensure that the databases that it is responsible for are fully backed up. I talk more about the fine points of Exchange backup in Chapter 19, "Backup and Disaster Recovery."

Windows Server 2003's own backup program has add-ons to do a proper backup of Exchange servers though this capability does not work with Windows Server 2008. Windows 2003's volume snapshot capability is a great way to get a consistent image of a disk drive while applications such as Exchange are running and online. Other Windows Server 2003 backup vendors have released add-ons that can properly back up Exchange Server 2007. Third-party vendors can also support Windows 2003's volume snapshot capability. These products add better backup scheduling, easier-to-use logs, multiple-server backup from a single instance of the backup program, quicker and easier restore of backed-up data, and disaster recovery options.

Backups can be to tape or disk or, for greater reliability, to both. Volume snapshots are best and most quickly done to disk. Do backups to tape during off-hours when backup speed is less of an issue. Be sure to include both backup disk and backup tape in your hardware/software backup resources plans.

You can back up an Exchange server either locally or over the network. When you back it up over the network, you can run the backup from a Windows 2003 server or from an Exchange 2007 server. For Exchange servers with lots of disk space (200GB or more) and slow network links to potential backup servers (less than 100Mbps), I strongly suggest that you bypass the networked server backup option and do the backup locally on and from the Exchange server itself. You have to spend some money on a backup device and software for the Exchange server, but you'll get it back in available bandwidth and faster backups. Available bandwidth means that other network-dependent tasks — and there are lots of those on a Windows 2003/Exchange 2007 network — run faster. Faster backups mean shorter periods of that awful feeling you get when important data is not yet on tape.

If you have high-speed across-the-network backup systems, just make sure that the restoration of data can occur within your service level agreement. If you do not have a service level agreement, at least confirm that the restoration of data can occur in a time that your organization will consider reasonable. Remember restores from streaming media or from disk will take longer than backups; make sure tests are done to see if restore requirements can be met.

Whether you back up over the network or locally, don't skimp on backup hardware. You're going to *add* hard disk storage to your Exchange server, not take it away. Go for high-capacity 4mm, 8mm, digital linear tape (DLT), or linear tape-open (LTO) tape backup systems. Think about tape autoloaders, those neat gizmos that give one or more tape drives automatic access to anything from a few tapes to hundreds of them. If you choose to use disks in your backup strategy, use solid RAID disk-based backup systems, or if your organization has the resources and you need their special features, consider storage area networks with their sophisticated backup systems.

Don't forget those personal folders stored on user workstations. You have to decide who will be responsible for backing them up: Exchange staff, other MIS staff, or users themselves. The technology for centralized workstation backup is readily available. For example, agents for most third-party Windows Server backup products let you back up all or part of specific user workstations.

While you're at it, don't forget Windows Server backup. If you have Windows servers that don't support Exchange, you need to back them up too. You can back up a Windows server over the network, but if the servers have lots of disk space, consider the same local backup strategy that I suggested for Exchange servers. You can also consider a dedicated network just for backups. All you need is an extra Gigabit Ethernet adapter in each server and in your backup computer or computers and a gigabit hub.

Networking Your Exchange Users

When you have your server design down, you need to think about how to connect users to your Exchange servers. It's usually a no-brainer for local connections, although you want to be sure that you've got enough bandwidth to move the stuff that Exchange makes available to your users. For example, a message with a very simple embedded color screen capture is 855KB. The graphic looks impressive, and it lets you make a point that you never could have made without it. Still, you wouldn't want your recipients to get it over a 33.3Kbps or 56Kbps connection.

If you're concerned about LAN bandwidth, you can do a couple things. First, get rid of those slower networks. Dump 4Mbps Token Ring and Arcnet networks. Yes, they are still around. If you haven't already, you should be upgrading 10BaseT networks to Gigabit Ethernet. Second, segment your LANs to reduce the number of users on any segment. In this situation, you might even put multiple network adapters in your Exchange server, one for each segment or group of segments. And do take a look at faster networking technologies such as 100Mbps Ethernet or Gigabit Ethernet, those really neat networking switches that can replace routers and significantly improve network backbone performance, and the latest switched Fast Ethernet hubs that bring switching to workstation connectivity and are quite low in price these days. Yes, any of these options will cost your organization some bucks, but they're likely to be bucks well spent. Just as with user workstations, slow technologies don't get used and the benefits of the applications that you're trying to run on top of them are lost.

Don't forget remote Exchange users. Many users need to keep in touch when they're away from the office, whether at home or on the road. Remote users can connect to their Exchange servers by way of direct or RPC over HTTP links through an Internet service provider (ISP) using dial-up or home-based DSL or cable connections. And don't forget the Internet-based POP3, IMAP4, and web browser–based client options that are supported by Exchange Server. With their lighter-weight demands on workstation resources, they could be just what the doctor ordered for your remote users.

Ideally, users with lower bandwidth connections should be using Outlook 2003 or later and the Exchange local cache mode configuration. This will provide the best possible experience for the end user.

Validating and Optimizing Your Design

Validation means ensuring that you have a system that guarantees message delivery, integrity, and security. It also means making sure the system you designed is versatile enough to handle the range of documents, messaging formats, and applications that your organization needs. *Optimization* is a balancing act in which you try to build the fastest, most stable, and most reliable systems that you can while still meeting organizational requirements and keeping costs down.

Guaranteed Delivery

Guaranteed message delivery comes with reliable Windows 2003/2008 and Exchange 2007 servers and reliable internal and external networks. To increase the likelihood of guaranteed delivery, go for as much server fault tolerance and networking redundancy as your organization can afford. Use high-quality server and networking hardware and software inside your organization; buy outside networking services from stable, experienced, and well-established providers. Monitor the health of your networks, and be prepared to fix problems quickly. During the validation phase, send messages of all kinds through all your connections, and then check to see if they arrive intact. When problems arise, use Exchange's own message-tracking tools to catch up with wayward messages, and take advantage of Exchange's network- and system-monitoring tools to discover why a message didn't get through.

Reliability is only one side of guaranteed message delivery. You also need Exchange servers that are sufficiently fast and networks that have the bandwidth to move messages quickly enough to meet maximum delivery time parameters. If you specified that all messages should be delivered to all internal users within five minutes, for example, now's the time to see if your Exchange system is capable of performing up to spec. If not, you must either increase your permissible maximum delivery times or, depending on the source of the problem, come up with speedier servers or higher-bandwidth networks.

Message Integrity

Message integrity means that messages arrive in the same form as they were transmitted. Problems with message integrity can often be traced to mismatched binary message-part encoding and decoding. For example, a binary attachment to a message bound for the Internet is UUencoded by the sender, while the receiver expects MIME encoding. As you'll see later, there are lots of ways to set encoding parameters in Exchange to help avoid problems such as this.

Message Security

RSA encryption and public keys both work within a single Exchange organization and can be enabled to work across Exchange organizations. Exchange Server 2007 uses a number of Windows 2003–based security features to significantly enhance message security. For messages destined for foreign electronic messaging systems, Exchange Server implements a set of encryption and authentication standards: NTLM encryption, TLS encryption, SASL clear-text authentication, and Secure MIME (Multipurpose Internet Mail Encapsulation). (More on these topics comes in Chapter 25, "Securing Exchange Server.")

You can try to validate message security on your own or with the help of a certified electronic data processing auditor. If security is important to your organization, I strongly recommend the latter.

System Versatility

Exchange's internal message formatting, along with formatting available for Internet-bound mail, means that you are able to send documents of almost any type containing virtually anything from text to last night's Letterman show. But be sure to validate that everything you need is there and works.

Exchange Server is a very popular product, so plenty of Exchange-based applications are already available from third-party vendors; many more are in development. Keep your eyes open for the latest "killer" Exchange apps.

Optimization

When you've done everything to ensure guaranteed message delivery, message integrity, and security as well as system versatility, it's time for *optimization*. You optimize your design by checking out alternatives that might help improve your Exchange system.

Optimization can also focus on reducing costs without compromising the quality of your system. For example, you might want to come up with lower-cost options for connecting Exchange routing groups or for realizing network redundancy.

Rolling Out the Plan

The specifics of your rollout will depend on the plans you've made. There are some basic processes you have to attend to in a rollout. Many of these processes are people-oriented processes, not technically oriented processes. This section focuses on the former. *Rollout* doesn't mean dropping a whole Exchange system on your organization at once. It means making Exchange available to specific systems administrators and users according to a carefully thought-out schedule. You should also go through a testing phase with specific users. Rollout to your general user population needs to be geared to your assessment of user readiness, perhaps at the departmental or subde-partmental level. Rollout also must be deeply rooted in the capacity of systems and user support staff to handle the many issues that arise during implementation of a major new software product. And, in all of this, don't forget that without information technology commitment and support, it's highly unlikely that you'll be able to smoothly pull off a successful Exchange rollout.

Start in the right place.   You might start your rollout in the information technology (IT) department — maybe just with yourself, if you're part of IT. When you pick users, always start with users that will have the least impact until you are sure you have all the bugs worked out of your deployment. Keep management informed of the users that will be involved in the initial rollout. Next, you might move on to samples of users based on the groupings that you uncovered in your user needs assessment or an assessment of user readiness for the change you are about to drop on them. Remember, you've been working with Exchange and its clients for a while. IT support and users might have had little exposure to it. The change you are bringing will shake their world up more than it does yours. Then move steadily onward until all users are up and running in Exchange. The key is to get Exchange out to all users as quickly as possible without crashing your organization. (Here I am referring to your *real* organization, not your Exchange organization.)

Don't forget design during rollout.   Remember that rollout is an integral part of the Exchange design process. As you step through your implementation plans, be ready to change your design. If something doesn't work, change it now. Don't let things pile up to the point that change becomes virtually impossible. How you schedule your rollout relative to user need and readiness as well as MIS support capacity will determine how able you are to keep up with change orders.

Pay close attention to users.   Whether you're in a test or production rollout phase, be sure to keep your big shot and plain old users in the loop. Get them committed to Exchange. Let them know if and when they're going to see a new e-mail client. Show them the client, just so they can see how really easy it is to use to get basic work done. Explain to them how they can use the client you plan to provide both to do what they're already doing and to get other tasks done.

This is where user training comes in. You probably already know this, but user training is both essential and a major drain on resources. Spend lots of time planning user training. Think very carefully about the amount of time and dollars you're willing to devote to user training. Training is a very specialized activity. If you don't have enough training resources in-house, consider outsourcing user training. Know that some users will get it right away and some will come back again and again seeking answers to questions that were answered both in group training and one-on-one by user support personnel. Finally, remember that your Exchange rollout can be a great success technically, but if no one comes to the show, it will be considered a failure by your bosses or your clients and their bosses.

Stay close to IT staff.   Keep IT staff involved and informed as well. An Exchange installation and implementation is a big deal for an IT department. Over time, just about everyone in IT will get involved with Exchange. IT staff should understand and welcome Exchange, not see it as a threat to their jobs. Train IT personnel as data-processing colleagues rather than just end users. You don't have to tell everyone in IT everything there is to know about Exchange, but be sure to talk to them about both server and client basics from a more technical perspective.

Summary

Designing a new Exchange system is neither easy nor fast. You must complete several steps and then track back to ensure that you've taken each step's impact on other steps into account. Moving through this iterative process while covering each of the steps in painstaking detail ensures that your Exchange system will function pretty much as expected from the get-go and that costly redesign is kept to a minimum.

One of the most important steps is the allocation of responsibility for very specific stages of the design and implementation process. This should be the first step in the design process. It ensures that the right people with the right skills and knowledge are in place and that they are clearly in charge of and must account for their particular piece of the design puzzle.

Needs assessments are another key to effective Exchange system design. You must perform assessments of user need, the geographic distribution of your organization and its computing and networking resources, and your data network. Needs assessments focus not only on what new resources and ideas are required, but also on what can be preserved.

Exchange Server 2007 is a network-dependent, network-intensive system. You need to establish a consistent set of conventions for naming your Exchange organization, administrative groups, servers, and recipients. You must choose a Windows 2003 networking model that fits well with your organization's geographical distribution and business structures. You must define the boundaries of Exchange administrative groups, the administrative units you use in your Exchange organization. As with domain models, geographic distribution and business structures might be key to setting these boundaries. If required, you must define boundaries for Exchange routing groups and determine how your routing groups will communicate across wide area networks.

Next, you must design your Exchange servers, paying attention to performance, storage capacity, reliability, backup, and networking users. When you've designed your Exchange Server environment, you must deal with connecting your servers to other messaging systems, both public and private. Here you must select from among available Exchange connectors and gateways. As your Exchange network becomes a reality, you must ensure, through exhaustive testing, that everything works as planned and up to whatever performance, reliability, and other standards you must adhere to.

Finally, you need to develop a plan for rolling out your Exchange system when everything is ready and has been tested. You shouldn't expect everything to be perfect on first rollout. However, if you've adhered to the design steps laid out in this chapter, your rollout experience should be a fairly pleasant one.

The next chapter, "Introducing Exchange Server 2007," talks about Exchange Server 2007 installations. Chapter 4, "Exchange Server 2007 Architecture," talks about upgrading from Exchange Server 2000/2003 to Exchange Server 2007. Even if you don't need to do an upgrade, I encourage you to read Chapter 3. Thinking through the upgrade process will help you better understand the inner workings of Windows Server 2003 and Exchange Server 2007.

Chapter 3

Introducing Exchange Server 2007

Someone simply examining the product names Exchange Server 2003 and Exchange Server 2007 might not think there have been significant changes. Although moving from Exchange 2000 or Exchange 2003 to Exchange 2007 is not quite as significant as moving from Exchange 5.5 to Exchange 2000, Exchange Server 2007 does introduce enough new features and a major shift in the administration model that it must be considered a major release.

Exchange Server 2007 Service Pack 1 (SP1) has further improved on a lot of the shortcomings (perceived and actual) of Exchange 2007 as well as introducing new features that customers had been asking for. I discuss the new features of Exchange 2007 in this chapter as well as further improvements introduced in Service Pack 1.

This chapter covers the changes to Exchange 2007 not only to give experienced Exchange administrators the proper perspective on Exchange 2007, but also to educate newly minted Exchange administrators on just how powerful Exchange has become and on some of the new features.

In this chapter you learn to:

◆ Understand new features of Exchange 2007

◆ Know the features and functions being deemphasized or phased out

◆ Clear up some common points of confusion

Overview of Exchange Server 2007 and SP1

One of the most common misconceptions that even experienced Exchange administrators are making when approaching Microsoft Exchange Server 2007 is to assume it is a "point" release. It is too bad that Microsoft has moved away from a system that more objectively identifies the significance of the release, such as v4.0, v5.0, v5.5, and so on. Now the products are named without actually including major or minor versions.

During the year coming up to the initial release of Exchange 2007, experienced Exchange administrators have often made comments similar to this: "Exchange 2003 already has most of the features and functions that we need. How could it significantly be improved?" Clearly, Exchange 2007 offers a significant enough number of improvements that all Exchange administrators will see some of the advantages in upgrading. Many sessions have been attended at TechEd, seminars have been held, and literally hundreds of articles and blog entries have been written about Exchange 2007. Arguably, Exchange 2007 was the most anticipated (or dreaded!) release of Exchange Server ever. Certainly it was the most widely hyped. The improvements (along with the misconceptions about Exchange 2007) have been widely discussed.

Additional features were introduced in Exchange Server 2007 Service Pack 1 (SP1). A short list of these features includes simplified administration as well as improvements in e-mail life cycle management, scalability, the availability of services, improved recoverability, and security. Of course, organizations that are now deploying Windows Server 2008 are also excited that they can run Exchange Server 2007 (SP1 and later) on the newest version of the Microsoft operating system. Summarizing even a few of the new features in this brief introduction is difficult, but early adopters of Exchange 2007 have reported the following features to be some of the most popular and useful:

◆ Powerful message transport rules applied and enforced at the server

◆ Continuously replicated Exchange databases for both clustered servers and nonclustered servers

◆ Replication of mailbox database data to remove Exchange Server 2007 servers

◆ Vastly improved anti-spam features

◆ Customizable "over quota" and nondelivery messages

◆ Exchange Management Shell command line and scripting interface

◆ Transportable databases (databases that can be restored to a different server)

◆ Improved calendaring support via calendar concierge, the Availability service, and resource mailboxes

◆ Simplified permissions model and message routing

◆ Unified messaging technology that is now an integrated part of Exchange Server 2007

This list could go on for the entire chapter, but this gives you a taste of a few of the features that Exchange administrators as well as administrators from other messaging systems are getting excited about when they talk about Exchange 2007.

GET TO KNOW THE EXCHANGE MANAGEMENT SHELL (AND WEAR SUNSCREEN!)

To those of you who have been around the Internet long enough to remember the "Wear Sunscreen" e-mail that was supposedly the 1997 commencement address to MIT given by Kurt Vonnegut (but was in reality a column written by the *Chicago Sun Tribune*'s Mary Schmich), I give you "Learn the Management Shell":

GET TO KNOW THE EXCHANGE MANAGEMENT SHELL

If I could offer you one important tip when learning Exchange Server 2007, it would be that you should get to know the Exchange Management Shell. Sure, it looks intimidating and most everything you will ever need to do is in the Exchange Management Console. Many Exchange gurus out there will back me up on the value and usefulness of the new Exchange Management Shell whereas they might not agree with me on things such as real-time block lists, daily full backups, and keeping lots of free disk space available.

◆ Make regular Exchange data backups.

◆ Document.

◆ Don't believe everything you read from a vendor, their job is to sell you things.

- Don't put off maintenance that might affect your up-time.

- If you get in trouble, call for help sooner rather than later. A few hundred dollars for a phone call to your vendor or Microsoft Product Support Services is better than a few days of down-time.

- Share your knowledge and configuration information with co-workers.

- Accept certain inalienable truths: Disks will fail, servers will crash, users will complain, viruses will spread, and important messages will sometimes get caught in the spam filter.

- Get to know your users and communicate with them.

- SharePoint 2007 provides a good alternative for sharing many types of data you might find in public folder; get to know it.

- Make regular backups of your Active Directory.

- If a consultant is telling you something that you know in your gut is wrong, double check his work or run his recommendation by another colleague. Second opinions and another set of eyes are almost always helpful.

- Be careful with REGEDIT, ADSI Edit, and any advice you read on the Internet (or in books).

- But trust me on the Exchange Management Shell.

Features! Features! Get Your New Features Here!

Reviewing the impressive list of new features and enhancements to Exchange 2007, everyone can agree that there are at least a few features that anyone can use. Customers have been asking for some of these improvements for many years, and others are new features that most customers had not even realized that they needed.

Is there a "must move" feature? This is a question people have been asking me since Exchange Server 2007 was announced. For most of us, there is probably not a single feature that would drive an organization toward a migration to Exchange Server 2007. But when you combine a few features together, justifying a migration becomes very easy because the combination of features makes a compelling argument for an upgrade. However, for a few organizations, an important feature such as Unified Messaging or clustered continuous replication is the "single feature" that drives the upgrade.

The following sections review the new features and provide a summary of what each provides. Most of these features are discussed in more detail later in the book.

64-bit Architecture

For a long time, perhaps the most discussed (and perhaps the most controversial) enhancement to Exchange 2007 is that now Exchange 2007 Server uses 64-bit extensions. Now your production servers will have to have x64 architecture–based Intel Xeon and Pentium processors or AMD64 architecture–based AMD Opteron and Athlon processors.

Although many people are thrilled with this change in the architecture, there are, no doubt, folks screaming, "What!!!?? I have to buy new hardware just to upgrade?!" A good response to this concern is that on most any messaging system upgrade, the hardware is usually replaced anyway. Certainly this is true for hardware that has been in production for more than three or four years. And the good news is that most server-class hardware purchased at the end of 2005 or later probably already includes the x64 processor extensions. If you have existing hardware you want to use with Exchange 2007, confirm with your vendor that it will run Windows Server 2003 x64 or Windows Server 2008 x64.

32-BIT EXCHANGE ONLY FOR TEST ENVIRONMENTS

There is a 32-bit version of Exchange 2007, but it is not supported in production environments. Only 64-bit Exchange is supported in production.

Is the decision to move to the x64 memory architecture a bold move? Is the Exchange team forging the way to more robust applications? Well, to a certain degree, yes, but the move to the 64-bit architecture is more out of need than forging a bold, modern path. Anyone who has supported an older version of Exchange Server with a large number of mailboxes knows that Exchange is constrained by the amount of RAM that it can access and that Exchange significantly taxes the disk I/O system.

In order to provide additional features that organizations are now requiring, such as larger mailboxes, messaging records management features, improved message content security, transport rules, Unified Messaging integration, and improved journaling, Exchange Server clearly needs to be able to access more physical memory. With more RAM available, Exchange caching is more efficient and thus reduces the I/O requirements that are placed on the disk subsystem.

The bottom line? The x64 instruction set for processors means more RAM for applications.

If you are not sure whether your existing hardware supports the x64 extensions, you can check this in a number of ways, including confirming it with the hardware vendor. If the computer is already running Windows, you can get a handy little program called CPU-Z from www.cpuid.com. Figure 3.1 shows the CPU-Z program.

FIGURE 3.1
Using CPU-Z to identify
the CPU type

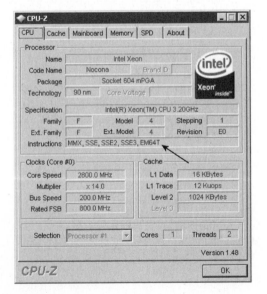

Notice in the Instructions line of CPU-Z that this particular chip supports EMT64T. This means this chip will support the x64 instruction sets. AMD processors will report that they support the x86-64 instruction set.

Exchange Management

Exchange Server management with Exchange 2007 becomes more and more complex as administrators try to make Exchange work within their organizations, particularly in larger organizations. Exchange 2000/2003 management of mail recipients was performed through the Active Directory Users and Computers console, and management of Exchange Server–related tasks and global recipient tasks is performed through the Exchange System Manager console. In Exchange 2007, all Exchange recipient administration tasks are now performed through the Exchange Management Console or the Exchange Management Shell.

Medium and large organizations usually develop specific needs to perform bulk changes to Exchange data, manage Exchange servers from the command line or scripts, and access or manipulate data stored in Exchange databases. Although making bulk changes or manipulating Exchange servers might seem like simple tasks (after all, Windows, Active Directory, and Exchange Server are all from the same company), the truth of the matter is that they're not.

Performing bulk recipient tasks such as creating multiple mailboxes, changing many e-mail addresses, and configuring bulk properties must be performed through an application programming interface (API) or scripting interface such as Active Directory Services Interface (ADSI). Management of Exchange server properties may also need to be performed through ADSI.

Manipulation of Exchange server operations such as mounting and dismounting of databases, queue management, diagnostics logging, and tracking log management has to be handled through a number of Exchange-related APIs such as Extended Messaging Application Programming Interface (MAPI), Lightweight Directory Access Protocol (LDAP), Web Distributed Authoring and Versioning (WebDAV), CDO for Exchange Management (CDOExM), Windows Management Instrumentation (WMI), Distributed Component Object Model (DCOM), Remote Procedure Calls (RPCs), and the Internet Information Server (IIS) management interface.

Finally, actually accessing or manipulating data stored in an Exchange database is also more complex than it might seem. A popular tool for Exchange 2003 administrators is the Exchange Merge (ExMerge) tool that allows data to be exported out of an Exchange mailbox and into a personal store (PST) file. Exchange Server 2007 SP1 introduced a new Exchange Management Shell function that allows the import and export of mailbox data to a PST file via the command line. However, this functionality requires that Outlook be installed on the machine on which you are running the import or export functions.

Actual manipulation of data in the mailbox databases could be accomplished through MAPI, Collaborative Data Objects (CDO), Exchange Object Linking and Embedding Database (ExOLEDB) functions, or Web Distributed Authoring and Versioning (WebDAV) functions. None of these methods is either simple or trivial for nonprogrammers. Anyone who has ever tried to dismount or mount a mailbox database using a script can attest to the programming complexity involved in such a simple task.

Clearly, for any organization that is interested in customized management of Exchange (small, medium, or large organizations), Exchange 2003 and earlier versions left a lot to be desired, and required tasks could often not even be performed due to their difficulty. In the minds of many experienced Exchange administrators, this was a gaping hole in the Exchange management architecture.

With Exchange 2007, the management interface has been completely rewritten from the ground up. All management operations related to Exchange management — whether they are performed against an Exchange server, Active Directory, the Registry, or the Internet Information Server (IIS) metabase — have been broken up in to unique tasks. All Exchange tasks can be performed from the Exchange Management Shell (command-line interface); a subset of these tasks can be performed from the Exchange Management Console graphical user interface. Anything that can be performed from the Exchange Management Console can be performed via the Exchange Management Shell; there are advanced administrative tasks that can be performed only from the Exchange Management Shell.

The Exchange Management Console (shown in Figure 3.2) has been completely redesigned to make it easier to use, to better organize Exchange management tasks, to reduce the complexity, and to make administrative tasks more discoverable.

FIGURE 3.2

The new and improved Exchange Management Console

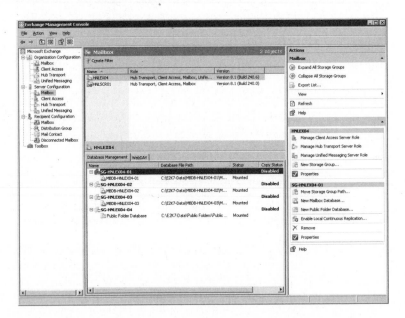

The new console is built on top of an entirely new scripting technology called PowerShell and a set of Exchange-specific extensions called the Exchange Management Shell. I go into more detail on the new management interface in Chapter 7, "Administering Exchange Server 2007."

Server Roles

In earlier versions of Exchange, once the Windows server was prepared to support Exchange, you simply installed an Exchange server. Then you would go about the process of customizing the Exchange configuration, configuring Internet Information Server, disabling unnecessary services, and preparing the server to assume the role you wanted it to assume, such as a mailbox server, a bridgehead server, Outlook Web Access front-end server, and so on.

Exchange 2007 officially introduces the concept of server roles at the point of setup. During the installation process, the setup program (Figure 3.3) asks the installer which roles the server will be performing.

FIGURE 3.3
Specifying server roles

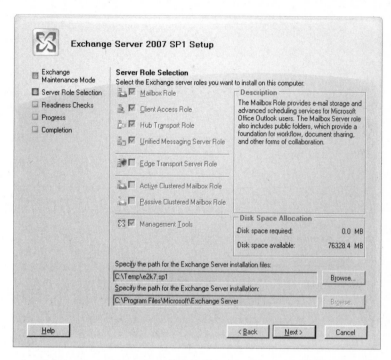

When running setup, if you choose a custom installation, you can specify the server roles by choosing from the following options:

Mailbox Role   Supports mailboxes and public folders.

Client Access Role   Supports functions such as Outlook Web Access, Outlook Anywhere (RPC over HTTP), Windows Mobile ActiveSync, POP3, and IMAP4, and supports web services such as Autodiscover, the Availability service, and calendar sharing.

Hub Transport Role   Supports message transport functions such as delivering mail locally (to other Exchange servers in the organization) or externally (to an SMTP smart host such as an Exchange Edge Transport server).

Unified Messaging Server Role   Supports delivery of inbound voicemail, inbound faxing, and Outlook Voice Access features.

Edge Transport Server Role   Supports separate anti-spam and antivirus functions for inbound and outbound messaging. The Edge Transport server is installed on a stand-alone machine usually in a perimeter network.

Active Clustered Mailbox Role   Configures a server to support clustering as an active node. Only the Mailbox server role can be clustered. Clustered servers can be configured as part of a single copy cluster (SCC) or a cluster continuous replication (CCR) cluster.

Passive Clustered Mailbox Role   Configures a server to support clustering as a passive node. Only the Mailbox server role can be clustered.

Once a role is selected, only the components necessary for that role are installed. This provides several benefits:

◆ Reduces the overhead on machines that are dedicated to a particular task (such as a Hub Transport server)

◆ Ensures that no unnecessary executables, DLLs, or services are installed

◆ Simplifies the creation of dedicated server roles

In a small organization with only one Exchange server, the same server may be assigned the Mailbox, Hub Transport, and Client Access server roles.

ABOUT THE STANDBY CONTINUOUS REPLICATION TARGET ROLE

Besides the roles listed in setup (Figure 3.3), you can also designate a Mailbox server as a standby continuous replication target server. However, this is done after the Mailbox server is completely installed.

Installer, Service Pack, and Patching Improvements

The setup program for Exchange 2000/2003 had some pretty serious annoyances; actually the whole process of getting a server up and running was pretty annoying. If a server did not meet the prerequisites, you had to close the setup program, fix the problem, and then restart the program. Once you got the release to manufacturing (RTM) or "gold" version installed you had to then install the most recent version of the Exchange service pack. Then, finally, you had to research all of the post–service pack critical fixes and apply those (sometimes in a specific order).

Microsoft has improved the setup process for Exchange Server 2007 and has simplified patching. Improvements have been made in four key areas:

◆ The Exchange Server 2007 setup program is good at finding missing prerequisites and will let you fix the missing prerequisite and then continue without starting over.

◆ The entire setup process can be performed from the command line using the setup.exe program and Exchange Management Shell cmdlets.

◆ Service packs are not released as a complete installation pack; all updates are built into the service pack and you can install directly from the latest service pack. No more installing the RTM version and then applying the latest service pack.

◆ Rollup releases are now released approximately once every two months. These releases contain a cumulative set of patches and critical fixes since the last service pack. So, rollup fix 4 (RU4) will contain *all* of the updates contained in RU3 plus the other fixes released since RU3 was released.

Now, all I have to do to get an Exchange Server completely built is to download the latest service pack, install Exchange Server 2007 from the service pack binaries, and then download the latest Exchange Server rollup fix and apply that fix. This greatly simplifies getting a server up and running *and* properly patched.

One thing I should note, though, is that if you get a rollup fix such as Exchange 2007 SP1 rollup fix 4 and then later you require an individual hot fix from Microsoft to fix a specific issue, you may need to uninstall the post rollup 4 hot fix prior to installing rollup fix 5. If you ever get a hot fix for Exchange 2007 to fix a specific issue, always ask the Microsoft product support person if you will have to uninstall it prior to applying the next rollup.

Improved Message and Content Control

All messaging system administrators can relate to challenges such as adequately managing the content that is stored on their mail servers, keeping business-essential information available when it is required, removing content that is no longer necessary, controlling the flow of messaging information, and preventing disclosure of information. If one or more of these challenges has been a problem for you, Exchange 2007 has solutions.

MESSAGING RECORDS MANAGEMENT

Messaging records management (early on referred to as e-mail life cycle management) introduces to Exchange 2007 a whole new concept in the control of messaging content. Messaging records management allows administrators to more closely control the life of message content (e-mail, faxes, voicemail, calendar entries, and so on) from the moment the information is created on the Exchange server until the point at which that information no longer has business or legal value. This helps the organization to maintain important records as long as necessary but discard unnecessary information in a timely fashion. Messaging records management settings are configured at the organization level so they will affect all Mailbox server roles.

To a certain extent, some of the features of messaging records management are distantly related to the Exchange 2000/2003 Mailbox Manager. Messaging records management has a number of components:

COMPONENT	FUNCTION
Managed default folders	Default folders are found when an Outlook 2007 MAPI client uses its mailbox, including Calendar, Contacts, Deleted Items, Inbox, Junk E-mail, Sent Items, RSS Feeds, and so on.
Managed custom folders	Managed custom folders are folders created by the Exchange server administrator for users who are included in a managed folder mailbox policy. Storage limits and managed content settings can be applied to these folders.
Managed folder mailbox policies	Managed folder policies define which folders are included in a particular policy. Managed folder mailbox policies are then assigned to mailboxes.
Managed content settings	Managed content settings define retention settings and message journaling features for content such as messages, faxes, and voicemail. You can configure message journaling based on a specific type of content or folder.

Once a user has been assigned to a managed folder mailbox policy, any additional custom folders that must be created in that user's mailbox will show up in the Managed Folders folder in the root of the user's mailbox, such as those shown in Figure 3.4.

Normally, content in these folders will be managed by the end users. Moving relevant content into these folders is their responsibility. In certain situations, managed content settings can accurately identify content types such as faxes or voicemail and can move those into the appropriate custom managed folders. Users can also build client-side rules that move content into their managed folders. Let's take a quick look at some of things that you can do with messaging records management:

♦ Control the length of time that message stay in users' folders, and the content types that appear there.

♦ Define additional folders within a user's folder that can be employed for message retention. Each custom folder can have its own retention policy.

♦ Automatically send copies of messages that users place in a managed folder to another e-mail address.

♦ Move messages from a specified folder based on content type (e-mail, contact, calendar, fax, voicemail, and so on) to another managed folder.

FIGURE 3.4
Managed folders assigned by the managed folder mailbox policy

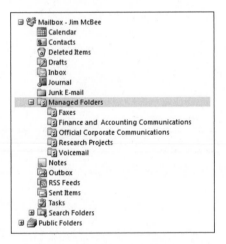

The first time you look at messaging records management, it is a bit confusing. It must be configured in several steps. The following list contains some of the steps:

♦ Create managed folder mailbox policies to define which default and custom folders will be managed.

♦ Assign the managed folder mailbox policy to one or more users.

A user is not required to have a managed folder mailbox policy. Only a single managed folder mailbox policy can be assigned to a user at one time.

♦ Create managed content settings for default folders (Inbox, Sent Items, and so on) to control the length of time that messages should remain in these folders and types of content that are allowed.

This step is optional.

♦ Create managed custom folders that will appear in the users' Managed Folders folder in their mailbox.

This step is optional.

◆ Create managed content settings for managed custom folders to control how content is managed or retained in the folders that will be created in the user's mailbox.

This step is optional.

One confusing point with respect to messaging records management is that on the surface it is documented as a premium feature of Exchange 2007 and thus requires an Enterprise Client Access License for each user who will have their mailbox managed by it. However, Microsoft makes an exception if you are using messaging records management features to simply clean up message items in the folders in the same way you would have used the Exchange 2000/2003 mailbox management feature.

MESSAGE TRANSPORT RULES

Message transport rules are quite similar to Outlook rules and are even created using a wizard similar to one used to create Outlook rules. However, message transport rules are quite a bit more powerful and are executed on the Hub Transport servers. Because all messages are processed by a Hub Transport server whether they are inbound, outbound, or designated for local delivery, you can build powerful policies to control the messages and data that flows within your organization. Transport rules can also be defined at your organization's perimeter by using an Edge Transport server.

All transport rules are defined globally, not on a per Hub Transport server basis. There is a practical limit of about 1,000 transport rules.

Although I cover a lot more about transport rules in Chapter 15, "Managing Messages in Transit," the following list gives you a taste of what you can do with transport rules and highlights some of the cool things you can do with them:

◆ Append disclaimers to outgoing messages

◆ Implement message journaling based on recipients, distribution lists, message classification, or message importance

◆ Prevent certain users or departments from sending e-mail to each other by creating an ethical wall (aka a Chinese wall)

◆ Intercept messages based on content or text patterns using regular expressions (REGEX) found in the message subject or message body

◆ Apply message classifications to messages based on sender or message content

◆ Take action on a message with a certain attachment or attachment type or an attachment size that exceeds a specified limit

◆ Examine and set message headers or remove data from the message header

◆ Redirect, drop, or bounce messages based on certain criteria

Every transport rule has three components: conditions, actions, and exceptions. The conditions specify under what conditions the rule applies, and the exceptions specify under what conditions it does not. The actions are the real interesting part of the transport rule, though. Figure 3.5 shows the Actions page of the Transport Rule Wizard; this dialog box has two parts. The first part is simply checking the actions to take, and the second part specifies more details about the action.

FIGURE 3.5
Examining a transport
rule

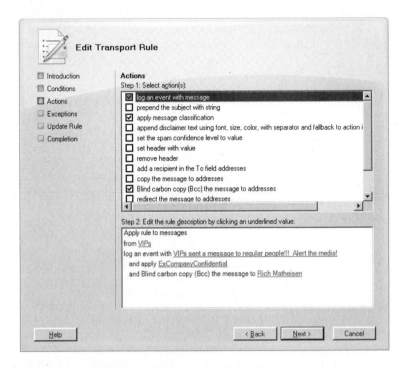

The steps I took before getting to the Actions page are as follows:

1. On the Conditions page, in Step 1, I selected a condition labeled From People.

2. Still on the Conditions page, in Step 2, I specified the list of people (or groups). Specifically, I selected the groups $Executives and VIPs as well as $Operations Group.

On the Actions page (shown in Figure 3.5), in the Step 1 box, I specified to Log An Event With Message, Apply Message Classification, and Blind Carbon Copy (BCC) The Message To Addresses options.

In the Step 2 box, I then specified the text of the event to log, the classification to apply, and to whom the BCC message should be sent.

PER-USER JOURNALING

Journaling a message is the process of keeping a message from one or more senders based on long-term storage, legal, regulatory, or human resources requirements. Exchange 2000/2003 essentially had one option for message journaling: Create an additional mailbox database and move any mailboxes that must be kept to that mailbox database. Exchange 2007 has introduced a lot of new options with respect to retaining messages:

◆ Messages can be retained based on folder or content type using managed content settings.

◆ Messages can be retained using transport rules by examining sender, recipient, message priority, message classification, or message content.

◆ Messages can also be retained by using transport rules to specify keeping only internal or only external messages.

◆ Messages can still be retained based on the journal settings on the mailbox database.

◆ Messages can be retained using a new hub transport feature called a journaling rule that allows messages to be retained based on a single sender or distribution group membership.

◆ Messages can be sent to an SMTP address that is external to the Exchange organization, such as a Microsoft Office SharePoint Server 2007 server or a third-party service provider.

Figure 3.6 shows an example of a transport rule that applies to the Executives group. Any mail sent to members of the Executives group has a copy of that message sent to the Executives Journal Mailbox. Though the journal rule shown in Figure 3.6 shows an internal Exchange mailbox in the Send Journal Reports To E-mail Address box, this could be any valid mail-enabled recipients including an external address.

FIGURE 3.6
Creating a journaling rule

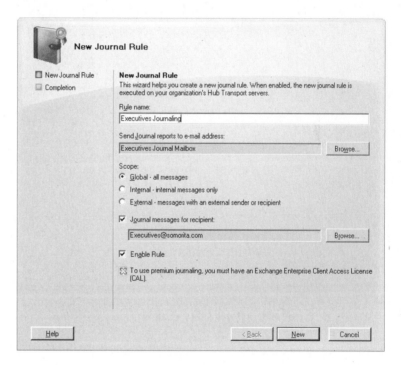

Journaling is a premium feature and thus requires an Exchange Server 2007 Enterprise Client Access License for each user that will have their mail journaled.

MESSAGE CLASSIFICATIONS

Organizations that send confidential, proprietary, or classified information via e-mail often implement message classification templates. However, these client-side templates display the message classification only for the sender and the recipients; in previous versions of Exchange there was nothing within the message transport that could take action on or evaluate a classified message.

Exchange 2007 allows a message to enforce rules based on the classification of a message, such as Do Not Forward, Partner Mail, Attachment Removed, Company Confidential, Company Internal, Attorney/Client Privilege, and customized classification levels. The sender can assign the classification using Outlook 2007, Outlook Web Access 2007, or message transport rules can assign a classification based on sender, recipient, message content, importance, and so on. Figure 3.7 shows an example of a message that is being composed in Outlook Web Access and has had the built-in Attorney/Client Privilege classification assigned to it; the classification text is shown just about the address list. The server administrator can create additional classifications and customize the text strings.

FIGURE 3.7
Classifying a message using Outlook Web Access

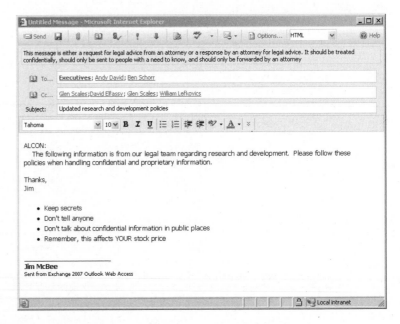

Content Storage Improvements

As mentioned earlier, e-mail systems have evolved not only in their complexity, but in the complexity (and size!) of the messages and mailbox content being sent and stored. Users' demands for improved searching and indexing of their mailboxes have stretched the limits of most server hardware. The following list includes some of the improvements with respect to data storage and recoverability:

◆ Support for recovering moved or deleted mailboxes using a recovery storage group

◆ Volume Shadow Copy restoration to recovery storage groups on alternate servers

◆ Lost log resilience that allows a database to be recovered even if the last few log files are missing

MAILBOX DATABASES

Even in a small or medium-sized organization, often mailbox size constraints are based solely on the ability to restore a certain amount of data given a specified maximum amount of time. To scale to larger mailboxes, the administrator must create more mailbox database and storage groups. However, even Exchange Server 2003 Enterprise Edition allowed a maximum of only 4 storage groups and 20 mailbox stores. (The *mailbox store* in Exchange 2000/2003 is called a *mailbox database* in Exchange 2007.)

In order to allow a server to scale to support larger mailbox sizes or more mailboxes, Exchange Server 2007 Enterprise Edition allows up to 50 storage groups and 50 mailbox databases. The mailbox databases can be configured in 50 separate storage groups or consolidated into as few as 10 storage groups of 5 databases each. Exchange Server 2007 Standard Edition supports a maximum of 5 storage groups and 5 databases. The recommendation from Microsoft is to scale outward on storage groups so that each database has its own transaction logs.

SMALLER TRANSACTION LOGS

Experienced Exchange 2000/2003 administrators will immediately recognize an Exchange transaction log because they are always 5,120KB in size. Exchange 2007 transaction logs, however, are quite a bit smaller — 1,024KB to be exact.

The transaction log files are smaller because Exchange 2007 has two new high-availability features called *local continuous replication* and *cluster continuous replication* that allow log files to be copied to another location and replayed into a backup copy of their corresponding database. Reducing the log file sizes ensures that data is copied more quickly to the standby location.

IMPROVED SEARCH FEATURES

Content indexing has been completely rewritten in Exchange 2007 so that it is far more efficient than in previous versions and is more closely integrated with the information store service. Improvements have been made so that the indexing process is throttled back during peak loads and does not affect client use of the Exchange server. By default, each mailbox database automatically has a full-text index associated with it. Messages are indexed upon arrival rather than on a fixed schedule; the index is up-to-date and immediately available to clients.

Full-text search capabilities are available from both Outlook clients as well as Outlook Web Access. Searches can be by word, phrase, or sentence. In addition to the message bodies, attachments such as Word documents, Excel spreadsheets, text files, and HTML files can be searched. Where previously the content index could consume between 20 and 40 percent of the size of the database, Exchange Server 2007 content indexing (enabled by default) usually consumes less than 5 percent of the database.

Improved High-Availability Features

One of the biggest enemies of high availability is slow restoration times. As mailbox databases get larger and larger, restore times get longer and longer. Often this is used as a rationale for limiting users' mailbox sizes to less than what they really need to do their jobs effectively.

As mentioned earlier, Exchange 2007 includes two new high-availability features called local continuous replication and cluster continuous replication. These features use a feature similar to the SQL Server log shipping technology. When a transaction log is completely filled, it is shipped (copied) to an alternate location and committed to a backup or standby copy of the database. By ensuring that there is always an up-to-date copy of the mailbox database online that is nearly complete and ready to be put into production, downtime due to a corrupted database can be greatly reduced.

CONTINUOUS REPLICATION BASICS

If I had to pick a single collection of features as the most compelling in Exchange Server 2007, the feature set would be the continuous replication features. This new technology supports three flavors of replication from the "active" data source to a passive data source.

Continuous replication comes in three flavors:

◆ For stand-alone mailbox servers, there is local continuous replication (LCR), which allows you to keep a replicated copy of one or more mailbox databases on the local server.

◆ If you want high-availability replication, there is cluster continuous replication (CCR), which keeps a replicated copy of the active databases on the passive node of the cluster.

◆ Exchange 2007 Service Pack 1 introduced standby continuous replication (SCR), which allows you to keep copies of one or more databases from one or more mailbox servers.

Unlike many tools from third-party vendors, which replicate data either at the disk block level or by taking snapshots of the disk and replication changes, Exchange continuous replication is similar to the SQL Server *log shipping* technology. This is considered a pull model. The active source Exchange database, logs, and database engine do not even realize they are being copied. The Microsoft Exchange Replication Service (`Microsoft.Exchange.Cluster.ReplayService.exe`) handles copying the logs and managing the passive databases.

Here are the steps involved in continuous replication:

1. Initially (for example, when continuous replication is set up or reconfigured) the current copy of the database is copied to the passive location; this is called *seeding*.

2. As an Exchange transaction log is filled up and renamed (that is, the E00.LOG file is filled and then renamed to E000000001.LOG), the renamed log file is copied to the passive location.

3. The replication service then verifies the log file and commits it to the passive copy of the database.

So the actual database file is not replicated at all, but it is kept in sync by copying the log files and replaying them.

You will probably understand this concept better with an illustration. Figure 3.8 shows how this process works. The Exchange database engine is run by the Microsoft Exchange information store; transactions fill up the current transaction log (E00.LOG). The transaction log file (E00.LOG) is renamed to the next available transaction log file name (in this case E0000000001.LOG). All of this is handled by the information store service.

FIGURE 3.8
Example of continuous replication

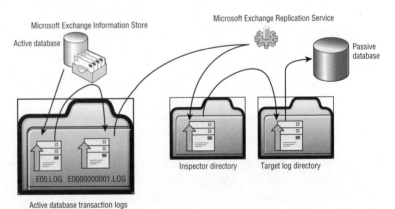

If continuous replication is enabled, the Microsoft Exchange Replication Service copies the E0000000001.LOG file to the Inspector directory. The location of the folder depends on the kind of continuous replication being used:

♦ **Local continuous replication:** The folder is on the local machine

♦ **Cluster continuous replication:** The folder is on a passive cluster node

♦ **Standby continuous replication:** The folder is on a remote mail server

The service verifies the checksum and signature of the log files in the Inspector directory to ensure they are not corrupted and that they are in the correct sequence. Once this is verified, the replication service copies the log file (E0000000001.LOG) to the target log file directory. The replication service then commits the transactions found in log file E0000000001.LOG to the passive copy of the database.

At any given time, the most out-of-sync the passive copy of the database is approximately 15 minutes old. This lag would be in the dead of night when there is absolutely no activity on the mailbox database. During a normal work day where users are actually using the database, the passive copy of the database will be no more than a few minutes behind.

If a database is dismounted or the information store service is stopped, the data is all committed to the active database and the log files are pulled over and replayed to the passive copy. If the administrator has to manually switch over to the passive copy of the database, the passive copy should be completely synchronized with the active copy of the database.

LOCAL CONTINUOUS REPLICATION

Local continuous replication (LCR) is one of the more interesting new features of Exchange 2007. It helps to ensure that an alternate copy of a mailbox database is maintained on the local server. This feature was at one time called *continuous backup*.

Keep in mind that local continuous replication is intended to allow for quicker database recovery in the event of database corruption. It is not intended at as a high-availability or resiliency solution.

The concept of LCR is illustrated in Figure 3.9. A backup copy of the production mailbox database is maintained on the local server. As the production database's transaction logs are completely filled, the transaction logs are copied to the backup location (step 1) and committed to the backup copy of the database (step 2).

In the event that the production database becomes corrupted, the administrator can switch from the production database to the backup copy of the database.

The following list describes some of the facts to keep in mind when considering LCR:

♦ LCR is designed to reduce restore time by keeping a copy of the database on the local server that can be brought into service in a very short period of time (a few minutes).

♦ Activation of a passive copy of the database is performed manually by the administrator.

♦ The LCR database must be stored on the local server.

♦ Each database that will be replicated must be in its own storage group.

♦ Plan to use separate logical units (LUNs) or physical disks for the LCR databases and transaction logs.

◆ Disk storage capacity will be double the requirements of a mailbox server without LCR if you replicate all mailbox databases.

◆ Replication will increase disk I/O capacity requirements by 125 to 150 percent and will place approximately an additional 20 percent CPU requirement on top of a standard mailbox server.

◆ Add an additional 1GB to 2GB of physical memory for servers that will use LCR.

◆ If you use snapshot backups, you can configure your disk snapshots to be done on the passive copies of the database. This can significantly improve performance for the active copies of the database during the snapshot period.

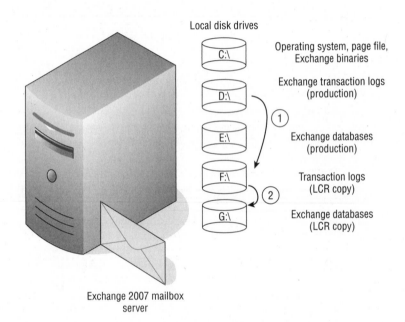

FIGURE 3.9
Local continuous replication

Local disk drives

Exchange 2007 mailbox server

CLUSTER CONTINUOUS REPLICATION

Cluster continuous replication (CCR) is a new high-availability feature of Exchange 2007. CCR introduces a whole new level of high availability and clustering to Exchange 2007. Unlike traditional single-copy clustering (SCC), in which there is only a single copy of the database, CCR has redundant hardware and a backup copy of the database. This backup copy of the database is kept current using replication technology similar to LCR. As transactions are committed to the production copy of a database, the log file is copied to the backup location and committed to the backup copy of the database.

CCR is implemented in the form of two-node, active-passive clustering. Quorum is maintained using a majority node set cluster; a third server acts as a "witness" by providing a file share on which the shared quorum database is located. The active node has one or more mailbox databases. The concept of CCR is illustrated in Figure 3.10.

As transactions are committed to the active node's databases and transaction logs, the transaction logs are shipped (copied) to the passive node (shown in step 1). Once the transaction log has been successfully copied to the passive node, the transactions in that log are committed to the corresponding database on the passive node (step 2). In the event of any type of failure on the active node, the passive node will automatically fail over and assume responsibility for the clustered mailbox server (formerly called an Exchange virtual server).

FIGURE 3.10
Cluster continuous replication

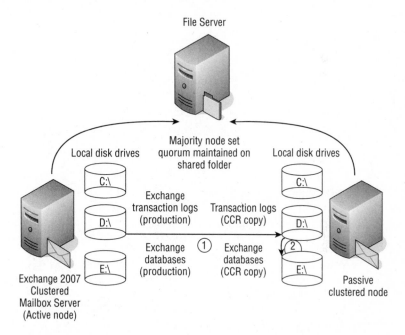

When you're running Windows 2003, the active and passive nodes must be on the same IP subnet, but Windows Server 2008 allows cluster nodes to be on different IP subnets. If an organization has virtual local area network (VLAN) capability, it can place the two nodes of a CCR cluster in separate locations.

Cluster continuous replication will help to reduce the "cost of entry" for organizations wishing to move to Exchange clustering because it eliminates the need for costly shared storage such as storage area networks (SANs). Data storage for CCR clusters can be located on direct attached storage (DAS) or on a SAN.

Keep in mind the following important points and tips when implementing CCR:

♦ Failover of the active clustered node is automatic, such as in the event of the failure of the server hardware.

♦ A single database failure will not induce an automatic failover.

♦ Data storage for CCR clusters can be located on DAS, or you can continue to use SAN storage. However, unlike traditional Exchange 2000/2003 clusters, the disks are not shared on the SAN. Each node of the cluster uses its own disks.

♦ Each database must be in its own storage group. If you need 10 mailbox databases, you must have 10 storage groups.

♦ The only Exchange server role that can live on a CCR cluster is the Mailbox server role. Hub Transport, Client Access, and Unified Messaging cannot be installed on a clustered server. This is by design and is intended to reduce the complexity of cluster and thus improve availability.

◆ If you want to put a public folder database in a CCR cluster, it can be the only instance of the public folder database in your organization. High availability of public folder data should be achieved by using multiple public folder servers; put replicas of the public folders on each public folder server.

◆ If an unplanned failover of the active clustered node occurs, the new active node will need to contact each of the Exchange 2007 Hub Transport servers in the site to make sure it has not missed any recently delivered e-mail messages.

STANDBY CONTINUOUS REPLICATION

Standby continuous replication (SCR) is one of the most valuable additions to Exchange 2007 Service Pack 1. It was one of the most commonly requested capabilities for Exchange customers. I frequently hear questions such as, "How do I provide remote recoverability for mailbox data?" or "How do I provide a standby solution short of implementing clustering?" Many third-party products that address these types of requests have been introduced to the market.

SCR FOR RESILIENCY AND CONTINGENCY, CCR FOR HIGH AVAILABILITY

I want to make something very clear. SCR is a resiliency or contingency solution; it does not provide *high availability* in the same way that CCR clustering provides high availability. Clustering-type high-availability solutions provide near immediate failover to a backup server (and data in the case of CCR); the failover is usually automatic and takes between two and ten minutes depending on the configuration. Clustering also implies little to no data loss.

In addition to providing high-availability and automatic failover solutions, clustering is useful in other ways. If you need to perform maintenance on an active node of the cluster, you simply move the Exchange services to a passive node of the cluster. Within a few minutes, all of the clients are right back at work and you can perform any necessary maintenance.

In contrast, the failover process involved in switching over to an SCR copy of a database is less trivial than it is for clustering and it is not automatic. You do not deploy this sort of solution for *high availability* requirements or the *we need to do maintenance on this server* requirements. You deploy it for situations where a server has failed permanently or where an entire site will become unavailable, such as in the case of a natural disaster. For this reason, I call it a resiliency or contingency solution, not a high availability solution. Setting expectations for features and functions will help you to do your job more easily.

SCR is implemented on an Exchange Server 2007 mailbox server and is configured to pull transaction logs from one or more Exchange Server 2007 mailbox servers. SCR can actually pull transaction logs from many Exchange Server 2007 mailbox servers in many different locations; the limiting factor will be whether you have enough bandwidth to pull transaction logs across the network to the SCR server. One other configuration point to keep in mind is that you are limited to a single database per storage group if you want to take advantage of the new replication technologies; however, that is okay because Exchange Server 2007 Enterprise Edition allows for up to 50 storage groups.

In the wild I have seen a few different implementations of SCR so far. These fall into several categories; the first of these, in Figure 3.11, shows how an organization would implement SCR if it is simply looking for resiliency of its mailbox data to a standby data center. The Exchange servers in Sydney and San Francisco are *combined function* servers, meaning that they implement multiple Exchange Server 2007 server roles. In this example, these servers each have the Mailbox, Hub Transport, and Client Access server roles.

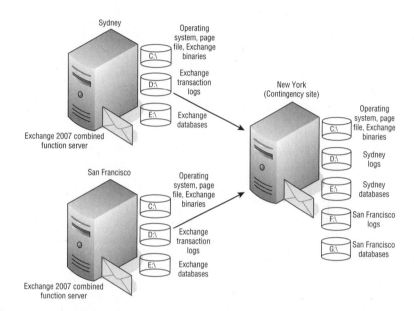

FIGURE 3.11
Basic standby continuous replication implementation

The third location is the contingency location in New York. This could be another of the company's offices or it could be a contingency site provider that offers the company rack space for a few servers. SCR is configured on a server in New York; initially the databases from Sydney and San Francisco are seeded onto a server in New York. Then SCR is configured to pull the committed transaction logs from the Sydney and San Francisco servers. SCR can be configured to immediately replay these logs to the passive copies of the database or wait a configured amount of time so that the passive copy is always a certain interval behind the active copy.

The setup shown in Figure 3.11 can be scaled so that Exchange servers at additional offices are replicated to New York. The limiting factor on the contingency server in New York will be the disk storage and I/O capacity as well as the maximum number of storage groups or storage databases that can be active on that server.

The server in New York is configured as a combined function server. If there is a failure at the San Francisco site, the administrator makes the decision to bring one or all of the San Francisco databases live on the New York server. The URL for Outlook Web Access would have to be pointed to the alternate server for users to access their mail. Outlook 2007 clients would automatically connect to the New York server after Active Directory has replicated the fact that the user's mailboxes in San Francisco are now on the New York server. The administrator would have to manually update Outlook 2003 and earlier clients.

For organizations that are concerned about both high availability and site resiliency, SCR can be combined with CCR. The source databases do not have to be on a stand-alone mailbox server; they can be on a clustered mailbox server. Figure 3.12 shows how an organization can combine a

CCR cluster in its main office (for high availability) with an SCR system in a remote office (for site resiliency).

FIGURE 3.12
Combined CCR and SCR implementation

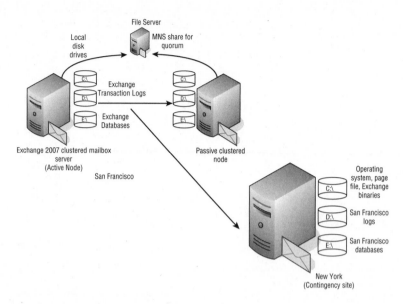

In this organization, the CCR cluster provides high availability in the event of hardware failure or in the event that the company needs to perform maintenance on one of the two nodes of the CCR cluster. The SCR system always pulls transaction logs from the active node of the cluster; it does not pull the logs from the passive node.

If there is ever a complete failure of the San Francisco site, the administrator must make the decision to perform the failover to the New York contingency site.

Schedulable and Internal/External Out-of-Office Messages

A very nice improvement from the user's perspective is the ability to schedule when out-of-office messages start and finish, and the ability to specify different out-of-office messages for internal users and external users. I did not really appreciate how helpful this would be until the first time I had to use the feature. Setting my out-of-office message at the end of the day before a trip is something I always forget to do. This feature allows me to set the schedule before I am frantically trying to get out of the office at the end of the day. This feature requires either Outlook Web Access 2007 or Outlook 2007 in order to manage. Figure 3.13 shows an example of the Out Of Office Assistant in Outlook Web Access.

When setting up an out-of-office message for external recipients, the user can specify whether the response goes only to senders whose address is in their Contacts folder or to any sender. Additional administrative control is now possible with OOF messages to restrict which domains an OOF message is sent to and disable some users' ability to configure OOF messages.

Improved Calendaring and Resource Management

Calendaring, resources, and out-of-office features were not as complete as most of today's sophisticated e-mail users require in earlier versions of Exchange and Outlook. Exchange 2007 and Outlook 2007 have improved each of these with new features and functions. For many of the calendaring and resource management features to work properly, Outlook 2007 is required and the Exchange 2007 Availability service must be configured on the Exchange Client Access servers.

FIGURE 3.13
Scheduling out-of-office messages for internal and external recipients

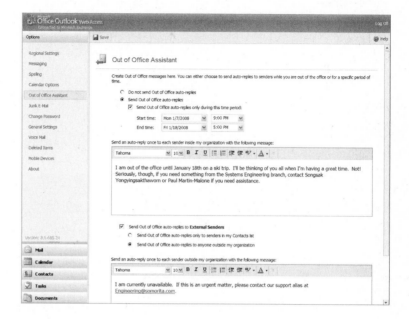

RESOURCE MANAGEMENT

One of the biggest hurdles that messaging system managers have had to overcome with Exchange is how to manage resource calendars. In earlier versions of Exchange, a resource calendar was nothing more than a mailbox whose calendar was shared to other users or a mailbox that had scripts or event sinks that allowed for automatic acceptance and processing of meeting requests for a particular resource. Exchange 2007 introduces the concept of resource mailboxes. At mailbox creation time (see Figure 3.14), the administrator designates the type of resource that is being created (room or equipment).

Custom properties such as room capacity or audiovisual capabilities can then be set on this resource. This information can be viewed within Outlook 2007 when a user is looking for a resource that suits particular requirements. The Resource Booking attendant provides features that control who can book a resource, for how long, and during which hours. The attendant also provides conflict information.

CALENDAR CONCIERGE

As users have become more sophisticated, their calendaring requirements have increased. The Calendar Concierge is a collection of features that allow for better management of user and resource mailboxes. The Exchange 2007 Calendar Assistant helps to keep out-of-date meeting requests from disturbing the user by ensuring that the user sees only the most recent meeting request. The Calendar Assistant also reduces the number of unnecessary messages relating to meeting requests, such as a Tentative response followed soon after by a Decline or Accept response. The user sees only the most recent message.

FIGURE 3.14
Resource type is designated when the mailbox is created.

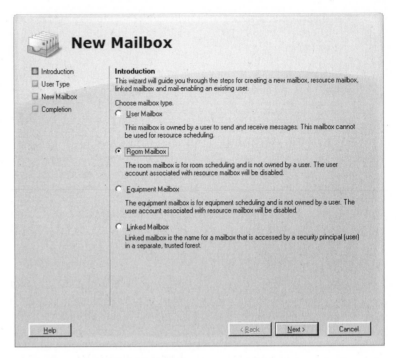

The Scheduling Assistant makes the process of scheduling a meeting using either Outlook 2007 or Outlook Web Access much simpler and recommends best meeting times based on requested attendees.

AVAILABILITY SERVICE

Earlier versions of Exchange used a system public folder for publishing a user's free/busy information. Periodically, the Outlook client had to connect to this public folder and update the user's free/busy times. Exchange 2007 introduces a new web service that runs on the Client Access server role and provides an interface to all users' free and busy times. Only Outlook 2007 clients are able to use this new web service, so the Availability service ensures that free and busy times published by older clients are accessible via the web service and free and busy times published by Outlook 2007 are available via the system public folder.

AUTODISCOVER

One of the most time-consuming things that an Exchange administrator has to do is to help configure Outlook clients to connect to the Exchange server. In the past, profiles had to be created via scripting or profile utilities. Exchange 2007 introduces a feature called Autodiscover that makes configuration of Outlook 2007 profiles much simpler. Once users provide their name and their e-mail address (see Figure 3.15), Outlook 2007 automatically discovers the correct server and updates the server if the mailbox moves (even if the original server is no longer online).

New and Improved Outlook Web Access

Those of us who gushed when we saw the Outlook Web Access interface in Exchange 2003 thought a web interface could not get much better. We were wrong. For Outlook Web Access in Exchange

2007, the Exchange team started over from scratch to build a much more functional interface than ever before. Here are some of the new features in Outlook Web Access 2007:

◆ Browse the global address list (GAL)

◆ Document access on internal file shares and Windows SharePoint services

◆ Manage and remotely wipe Windows mobile devices

◆ Improved meeting booking features

◆ Perform full-text searches on mailbox content

◆ Selectable message format (HTML or plain text) when composing a message

◆ Set out-of-office messages, define them as internal or external, and schedule when they start

◆ Manage voicemail features such as greeting, reset voicemail PIN, and turn on missed call notifications

FIGURE 3.15
Configuring Outlook 2007 to use Autodiscover

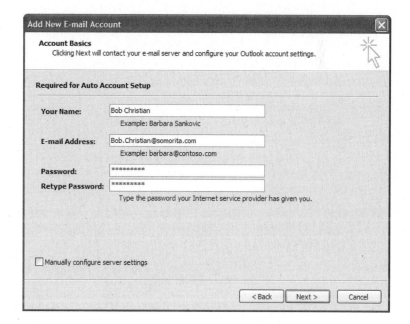

Edge Transport Services

The amount of spam and viruses that some organizations receive is staggering. Even small organizations are receiving tens of thousands of pieces of spam, dozens of viruses, and hundreds of thousands of dictionary spamming attacks each week. Some organizations estimate that as much as 90 percent of all inbound e-mail is spam or other unwanted content. Keeping as much of this unwanted content away from your Exchange servers as possible is important. A common practice for messaging administrators is to employ additional layers of message hygiene and security. The first layer is usually some type of appliance or third-party SMTP software package that is installed in the organization's perimeter network. The problem with these third-party utilities is that the administrator has to become an expert on an additional technology.

EDGE TRANSPORT IS NOT REQUIRED FOR EXCHANGE 2007

A common misconception about Exchange 2007 is that the Edge Transport role is required for Exchange 2007. This is not the case; you can continue to use your existing anti-spam/message hygiene system to front-end Exchange.

Microsoft's solution to this dilemma is the Edge Transport server. The Edge Transport server is a stand-alone message transport server that is managed using the Exchange Management Shell (EMS) and the same basic management console that is used to manage Exchange 2007. A server functioning in an Edge Transport should not be a member of the organization's internal Active Directory.

Functions such as transport rules are identical to those that run on an Exchange 2007 Hub Transport server. Content filtering (formerly referred to as the Intelligent Message Filter, or IMF) and Microsoft Forefront Security for Exchange are implemented on the Edge Transport server.

An example of how an organization might deploy an Edge Transport server is shown in Figure 3.16. Inbound e-mail is first delivered to the Edge Transport servers that are located in the organization's perimeter network where it is inspected by the content filter, Forefront Security for Exchange, and any message transport rules. The inbound message is then sent on to the internal Hub Transport servers. Additionally, the Exchange 2007 Hub Transport servers are configured to deliver mail leaving the organization to the Edge Transport servers rather than configuring them to deliver mail directly to the Internet.

FIGURE 3.16
Deploying an Edge
Transport server

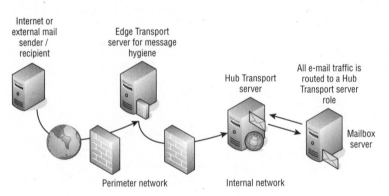

The Edge Transport server is a fully functional SMTP message hygiene system with many of the same features that are found in expensive message hygiene software packages and appliances. The following features are included:

◆ Per-user safe-sender lists are replicated from the user's mailbox out to the Edge Transport server.

◆ Recipient filtering is enabled when valid recipients are synchronized to the Edge Transport server's local Active Directory Application Mode (ADAM) database.

- Integrated Microsoft content filter is included for spam detection. Spam can be rejected, deleted, quarantined, or delivered to the user's Junk E-mail folder.

- Multiple message quarantines allow messages that are highly likely to be spam to be quarantined in the perimeter network while maintaining a separate quarantine inside the network for messages that are still tagged as spam but with a lower Spam Confidence Level (SCL).

- Microsoft Forefront Security for Exchange Server (formerly known as Antigen) is available for the Edge Transport server when Enterprise Client Access Licenses are used.

- Daily content filter and virus signature updates are available for organizations using Microsoft Forefront Security for Exchange Server.

- Real-time block lists (RBLs) and IP Reputation Service allow an IP address to be checked to see if it is a known source of spam. Reputation filters can be updated on a daily basis.

- Sender ID filters allow for the verification of the mail server that sent a message and whether it is allowed to send mail for the message sender.

- Sender reputation filters allow a sender to be temporarily placed on a block list based on characteristics of mail coming from that sender, such as message content, Sender ID verification, and sender behavior.

Unified Messaging

The concept of Unified Messaging means that information from multiple sources is all accessed in a single location. This concept is by no means a new one; third-party vendors have had fax and voicemail gateways for most major e-mail systems. The Exchange 2007 Unified Messaging server role represents Microsoft's entrance into this market. This feature can make users more efficient by providing a single location for inbound information; voicemails and faxes can be read via Outlook Web Access or Outlook. In addition, missed call information (someone who calls but does not leave a voicemail message) is sent to the user's mailbox.

An example of a voicemail that has been delivered to a user is shown in Figure 3.17. The form you see in the figure is in Outlook Web Access 2007. It includes a player control for playing the message via the PC speakers.

The form in Figure 3.17 also includes the ability to play the voice message on your desk phone. The Play On Phone option allows you to instruct the Unified Messaging server to call you at a specified extension (or optionally an external phone if the Unified Messaging dial-plan allows).

Further, users can call the Unified Messaging server via the telephone and listen to their voicemail, have their e-mail read to them, listen to their calendar, rearrange appointments, or look up someone in the global address book. Unified Messaging also allows the administrator to build a customized auto attendant for call routing. In my experience, a typical voicemail (using the default Windows Mobile codec) takes between 2KB and 3KB per second of message time. A higher quality codec can be used. However, with higher quality recordings come higher message sizes.

The Unified Messaging server role functions as just another Exchange server in your organization, but this role includes components that allow IP-based phone systems and IP/PBX (public branch exchange) gateways to interface directly with Exchange over the network. This is provided the IP phone system or IP/PBX can communicate using Session Initiated Protocol (SIP) over TCP or Real-Time Transport Protocol (RTP) for voice communication or T.38 protocol for real-time facsimile transport.

FIGURE 3.17

Viewing a voicemail message sent via Unified Messaging

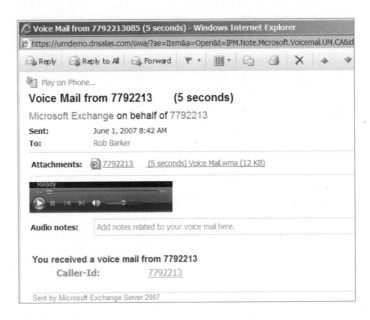

A LOOK AT THE UNIFIED MESSAGING MARKET

Not all voice and faxing systems support Unified Messaging "right out of the box." More and more vendors (such as Cisco and Mitel) are tweaking their voice over IP (VoIP) systems to talk directly to Exchange Server 2007 Unified Messaging, but you may still require a VoIP gateway of some type. Many traditional "hard wired" public branch exchanges (PBXs) will require a PBX-to-VoIP gateway, but even some VoIP systems will require a VoIP-to-VoIP gateway.

If you are like me, then you are more of a specialized network administrator. I have never managed a phone system in the past and am only slightly familiar with some of the phone terminology. I just assumed that VoIP was VoIP and that was that. Working with the folks who manage your telephone system will be a new and exciting experience. I was quite surprised to learn that there are more than 100 implementations of SIP out on the market.

As of 2007, Unified Messaging solutions have only about a 10 to 15 percent market penetration. That is, of course, depending on whose survey you read and how you define Unified Messaging. Some vendors define it as delivering a voicemail to a user's computer and allowing the user to play the voicemail over the PC speakers; this voicemail might have been delivered to the user's mailbox (on the server) or it might have been *pulled* by Outlook or another client application and stored in the user's PST file. Some vendors consider solely inbound faxing to be a unified messaging solution, though in my opinion that is not terribly unified.

Microsoft has decided to get into the Unified Messaging market for a number of different reasons:

◆ Unified Messaging has a fairly low market penetration thus far.

◆ Customers are often reluctant to deploy Unified Messaging solutions due to the complexity, administrative overhead, schema changes, client-side deployment requirements, and cost.

◆ Microsoft is determined to make its Unified Messaging implementation less expensive than competing products and much better integrated with Active Directory.

When the Exchange 2007 Unified Messaging role is integrated with an IP-based phone system or a PBX with an IP/PBX gateway, the following additional functions may be possible:

◆ Inbound voicemail is delivered directly to the user's mailbox.

◆ Inbound faxes are delivered directly to the user's mailbox.

 Microsoft's Unified Messaging implementation supports only inbound faxing. For a comprehensive faxing solution, I recommend you take a look at one of the many third-party faxing solutions.

◆ Users can call in to the phone system and have their e-mail read to them, listen to their schedule, or move appointments around on their schedule and notify attendees.

◆ Users can call in to the phone system and look up users from the global address list.

Outlook 2007 and Exchange Server 2007

The Autodiscover feature is one of a number of features and enhancements that are available only if you are both using the Outlook 2007 client and have your mailbox located on an Exchange Server 2007 server. Though this might not seem very fair, you have to keep in mind that sometimes a feature requires not only a client-side interface but also a server-side component to implement the feature. In general, when comparing client and server features, a mailbox must be on Exchange Server 2007 in order to use either the premium or light Outlook Web Access interfaces.

I am including some tables to help you figure out which of the new features are available to you depending on the clients you are using and the location of the user's mailbox. Table 3.1 shows the mail features that are available with the different Outlook and Exchange Server combinations.

Note that some features such as RSS feeds will show up via Outlook Web Access if they were pulled into the user's mailbox, but the user will not have an interface to see them properly.

Different calendaring features are available depending on the versions of Exchange Server and Outlook you are using. Table 3.2 shows the calendaring features and the server/client.

As you can see in Table 3.2, many of the new features of the calendaring interface require exclusively Outlook 2007, but a few nice improvements are available in that area via Outlook Web Access.

Next let's look at some of the new tasking features that are available. Table 3.3 shows the tasking features and which clients let you take advantage of them.

As you can see from Table 3.3, all of the tasking features require either Outlook 2007 or Outlook Web Access 2007 Premium; tasking features are not dependent on the mailbox server version. Next, let's look at the new out-of-office (OOF) features that are available. In my opinion, the new OOF features are some of the best in the new client interface. Table 3.4 shows the new out-of-office features and under what circumstances they can be used.

OOF?

In case you were wondering, though we use OOF to mean *out-of-office*, it originally stood for *out-of-facility*; this acronym originated at Microsoft in the pre-Exchange days when it used a Xenix-based (oh, the horror!) mail system.

Finally, there are some additional client/server features that your users may find useful. These are mostly with respect to security. Table 3.5 shows a list of these features and under what circumstances they may be used.

TABLE 3.1: Mail Features Available with Outlook Client and Exchange Server Combinations

FEATURE	O2K7/ E2K7	OWA 2007 PREMIUM	OWA 2007 LIGHT	OUTLOOK MOBILE	O2K7/ E2K3	O2K3/ E2K7
Attachment preview in reading pane	✓				✓	
View attachments as web page without client application		✓	✓			
Instant search across all Outlook items	✓	✓	✓	✓		
Better rules/removed 32KB rule limit	✓					
Native support for RSS feeds	✓				✓	
RFC 2822 support in-reply-to SMTP header for conversations	✓	✓	✓	✓	✓	✓
Message classifications	✓	✓				
Improved accessibility features for low-vision and blind users	✓		✓			
Color categories freely defined and assigned to any type of item	✓	✓			✓	

Windows Mobile and Improved Security

Windows Mobile and ActiveSync device support are certainly not new to Exchange Server 2007. Exchange Server 2003 had good support for Windows Mobile devices and you could even support mobile devices using Microsoft Mobile Information Server and Exchange 2000. Microsoft continues to improve the support and the manageability of mobile devices with newer versions of Windows Mobile, Exchange Server 2007 SP1, and updated versions of ActiveSync.

If you have supported Windows Mobile devices or other types of mobile devices, you realize how important centralized policies and security can be for your organization and your users. The latest versions of the Exchange ActiveSync (EAS) have been improved greatly over the years. The newest features can be assigned to users based on the ActiveSync policy that is assigned to the user. Figure 3.18 shows two of the advanced property pages.

Of course, you have to have the corresponding version of Windows Mobile that will take advantage of all of the newest features. Windows Mobile 5 with the Microsoft Security and Feature Pack (MSFP) uses EAS v2.5, Windows Mobile 6 uses EAS v12, and Windows Mobile 6.1 uses EAS v12.1. Table 3.6 shows a comparison of some features of various versions of EAS and the versions of Exchange Server.

TABLE 3.2: Calendaring Features Available with Outlook Client and Exchange Server Combinations

FEATURE	O2K7/ E2K7	OWA 2007 PREMIUM	OWA 2007 LIGHT	OUTLOOK MOBILE	O2K7/ E2K3	O2K3/ E2K7
Improved interface for booking meetings (Scheduling Assistant)	✓	✓	✓		✓	
Scheduling Assistant looks directly into a user's calendar instead of free/busy public folder	✓	✓	✓			
Improved resource picker interface with attributes such as room capacity	✓	✓	✓			
Add room as resource when you place in "To" field	✓	✓	✓			
Conference room resource settings configuration		✓	✓			
Multiple meeting updates collapsed, only latest one shown	✓	✓	✓	✓		✓
Meeting updates highlight updated fields	✓	✓	✓			
Updates with no time change apply automatically, no reply required	✓	✓	✓			
Dual time zone when scheduling a new meeting	✓				✓	
Notification of time change when dragging/dropping a meeting	✓				✓	
Calendar snapshots to share calendars with outside users	✓				✓	
Caching of other user's calendar data	✓				✓	
Two-way sync with team calendars in SharePoint	✓				✓	
Overlaying of multiple calendars in the same view	✓				✓	

TABLE 3.3: Tasking Features Available with Outlook Client and Exchange Server Combinations

FEATURE	O2K7/ E2K7	OWA 2007 PREMIUM	OWA 2007 LIGHT	OUTLOOK MOBILE	O2K7/ E2K3	O2K3/ E2K7
To-do bar with improved task information	✓	✓			✓	
Task information at the bottom of the calendar view	✓	✓			✓	
Assign a task by dragging into calendar	✓	✓			✓	
Flag message and assign task due date	✓	✓			✓	

TABLE 3.4: Out-of-Office Features Available with Outlook Client and Exchange Server Combinations

FEATURE	O2K7/ E2K7	OWA 2007 PREMIUM	OWA 2007 LIGHT	OUTLOOK MOBILE	O2K7/ E2K3	O2K3/ E2K7
Schedule OOF messages for future date/time	✓	✓	✓	✓		
Internal and external OOF messages	✓	✓	✓			
Send external OOF message only to contacts	✓	✓	✓			
OOF messages can include HTML formatting	✓	✓	✓	✓		

FIGURE 3.18
Examples of ActiveSync policies

TABLE 3.5: Additional Features Available with Outlook Client and Exchange Server Combinations

FEATURE	O2K7/ E2K7	OWA 2007 PREMIUM	OWA 2007 LIGHT	OUTLOOK MOBILE	O2K7/ E2K3	O2K3/ E2K7
Content policies for folders such as item retention, archive, and expiration	✓	✓	✓			
Outlook generates postmark for use with anti-spam systems	✓					✓
Warning for e-mail messages that appear to be phishing messages	✓	✓	✓			✓
End user has the ability to remotely wipe out mobile device		✓	✓			

Note that some of the advanced device configuration features requires the use of an Exchange Server 2007 Enterprise Client Access License (CAL) for the device. This does not mean that the Exchange 2007 server requires Enterprise Edition of Exchange Server, though.

If you are wondering where your iPhone and your BlackBerry devices fall in Table 3.6, the iPhone is an EAS v2.5 device. BlackBerries do not use ActiveSync; they rely on polices enforced from the BlackBerry Enterprise Server (BES).

New Programming Interfaces

Much of the underlying infrastructure of Exchange 2007 has been completely rewritten. As a result, many of the application programming interfaces (APIs) used to access Exchange data and to manage Exchange components have been replaced with new APIs.

EXCHANGE MANAGEMENT

Management of Exchange-related components and recipient objects is now performed with the new management API. All operations that can be performed have been defined as tasks. The management API provides access to all management functions via the Exchange Management Shell tasks, also known as cmdlets (pronounced "command-lets"). The Exchange Management Shell is a set of extensions for the Windows PowerShell. Exchange management functionality can be extended and accessed via managed code and custom scripts can integrate with and use .NET objects.

TRANSPORT AGENTS

All messages and message content traveling through the message transport system (on a Hub Transport server or an Edge Transport server) can be manipulated using transport agents. Transport agents are written using managed code. They replace Exchange 2000/2003 transport sinks.

TABLE 3.6: Exchange ActiveSync Features

Setting\ Restriction	E2K3 SP2 EAS v2.5	E2K7 EAS 12	E2K SP1 Standard CAL EAS v12.1	E2K7 SP1 Enterprise CAL EAS v12.1
Password Required	✓	✓	✓	✓
Min Password Length	✓	✓	✓	✓
Alphanumeric Device Password Complex	✓	✓	✓	✓
Inactivity Timeout	✓	✓	✓	✓
Max Failed Password Attempts	✓	✓	✓	✓
Policy Refresh Interval	✓	✓	✓	✓
Allow Non-provisionable Devices	✓	✓	✓	✓
Attachments Enabled		✓	✓	✓
Storage Card Encryption		✓	✓	✓
Password Recovery Enabled		✓	✓	✓
Allow Simple Device Password		✓	✓	✓
Max Attachment Size		✓	✓	✓
WSS Access Enabled		✓	✓	✓
UNC Access Enabled		✓	✓	✓
Password Expiration		✓	✓	✓
Password History		✓	✓	✓
Require Manual Sync When Roaming			✓	✓
Min Device Password Complex Characters			✓	✓
Max Calendar Age Filter			✓	✓
Allow HTML Email			✓	✓
Max Email Age Filter			✓	✓
Max Email Body Truncation Size			✓	✓
Max Email HTML Body Truncation Size			✓	✓

TABLE 3.6:   Exchange ActiveSync Features *(CONTINUED)*

SETTING\ RESTRICTION	E2K3 SP2 EAS v2.5	E2K7 EAS 12	E2K SP1 STANDARD CAL EAS v12.1	E2K7 SP1 ENTERPRISE CAL EAS v12.1
Require Signed SMIME Messages			✓	✓
Require Encrypted SMIME Messages			✓	✓
Require Signed SMIME Algorithm			✓	✓
Require Encryption SMIME Algorithm			✓	✓
Allow SMIME Encryption Algorithm Negotiation			✓	✓
Allow SMIME Soft Certs			✓	✓
Require Device Encryption			✓	✓
Allow Storage Card				✓
Allow Camera				✓
Allow Unsigned Applications				✓
Allow Unsigned Installation Packages				✓
Allow Wi-Fi				✓
Allow Text Messaging				✓
Allow POP/IMAP E-mail				✓
Allow Bluetooth				✓
Allow IrDA				✓
Allow Desktop Sync				✓
Allow Browser				✓
Allow Consumer E-mail				✓
Allow Remote Desktop				✓
Allow Internet Sharing				✓
Unapproved InROM Application List				✓
Approved Application List				✓

EXCHANGE MANAGED APIs

Exchange Managed APIs extend the Microsoft .NET Framework by providing classes and data structures that allow custom programs to access and manipulate different parts of e-mail message content. Functions include accessing MIME content; filtering e-mail body content; converting message content between plain-text, HTML, and RTF formats; and reading or writing calendar items.

WEB SERVICES

One of the most exciting new APIs is the Web Services API. Web Services allows developers to write applications that can remotely access mailboxes, folders, and message content. Many of the new Exchange services — such as the Autodiscover service, Availability service, and messaging records management — use the Web Services API. Services can be developed that can send notifications to client applications and provide synchronization of mailbox folders and items. The Web Services API provides these features:

◆ Ability to manage folders in a user mailbox, including creating, deleting, copying, changing, searching, viewing, and moving folders

◆ Ability to manage messages in a user mailbox, including creating, deleting, copying, changing, searching, viewing, moving, and sending messages as well as accessing message content

◆ Ability to enumerate distribution group memberships

Now, Where Did That Go?

As new and better functions and APIs have been introduced, naturally some functions are no longer emphasized or no longer supported. There has been a lot of confusion surrounding what will continue to be supported in Exchange 2007 and what will no longer work. The phrase "no longer supported" itself tends to also generate a lot of confusion. Some "no longer supported" functions may actually continue to work because they have not truly been removed. These functions and APIs fall into two unique categories: functions that have been deemphasized and functions that are no longer available.

Deemphasized Functions

When Microsoft says that in Exchange 2007 certain functions or APIs are no longer emphasized, this means that Microsoft will not continue to enhance these features. They will continue to be supported, and if there are bugs with these features, the bugs will be fixed. However, if something is being deemphasized, then the writing is on the wall; you should consider replacing your use of this technology with something else.

The following is a list of some of the APIs and functions that are being deemphasized:

◆ Public folders are still supported in Exchange 2007, but their use is being deemphasized as newer collaborative technologies have been introduced, such as SharePoint and other portal technologies.

◆ Collaborative Data Objects technologies such as CDOSYS, CDO 1.2.1, and CDOExM are being deemphasized. Applications using these APIs will continue to work but they should be rewritten using the Transport Agents API or Exchange Web Services API.

◆ Functions provided by Exchange WebDAV extensions are now provided by the Web Services API.

◆ The Exchange Object Linking and Embedding Database (ExOLEDB) API functionality is now provided via the Web Services API.

In addition, Microsoft is planning to continue support for public folders in future versions of Exchange, but you should not expect much new development around them.

Features No Longer Included

Some features and APIs have been completely removed from the Exchange 2007 product. If you require any of these features or APIs, you will need to keep an Exchange 2000 or Exchange 2003 server in operation:

◆ Exchange 5.5 interoperability is no longer available. You cannot install an Exchange 2007 server until your Exchange organization is in native Exchange 2000/2003 mode.

◆ Mail recipient management using the Active Directory Users and Computers console extensions no longer works. All recipient management must be performed through the Exchange Management Console. There are a few exceptions, of course, but using the Exchange Management Console or the Exchange Management Shell is preferred. This will also keep you from accidentally doing something that is not supported.

◆ Administrative groups are no longer available. All permissions delegation is handled either on a server-by-server basis or at the organization level.

◆ Outlook Mobile Access, the lightweight browser-based access for Wireless Access Protocol (WAP)-based mobile phones, is not available. Nor are Exchange ActiveSync Always Up-to-Date notifications.

◆ Non-MAPI public folder hierarchies are no longer available.

◆ Public folder access via Network News Transport Protocol (NNTP) and IMAP4 is no longer available.

◆ NNTP features have been cut from Exchange 2007 completely.

◆ Routing groups and routing group connectors are no longer required. In a native Exchange 2007 organization, the message routing topology is determined using the Active Directory sites in which the Exchange servers are located. Message delivery between Exchange 2007 servers in different Active Directory sites is handled automatically.

◆ Mailbox databases no longer have a streaming database file (STM file). All mail, regardless of its original source, is stored in the EDB database file.

◆ The Recipient Update Service functionality has been replaced. E-mail proxy addresses and address list membership is set on a mail recipient object at the time of creation. These can be updated from the Exchange Management Shell.

◆ X.400 connectors are no longer available. X.400 connectivity is no longer included with Exchange 2007; this functionality is available from a third party.

◆ ExMerge can no longer be run from the Exchange 2007 server console; it can continue to be run against Exchange 2007 mailboxes, but it must be run from a computer with Outlook installed.

◆ On two-node clusters, active-active clustering cannot be configured. Exchange 2007 requires active-passive clustering on two-node clusters.

◆ Transport event sinks no longer work. You must keep Exchange 2000/2003 Server for software that uses this functionality or update the code to use transport agents.

◆ Functionality for applications built from Workflow Designer and CDO for Workflow is not available. Applications built using these APIs should be replaced with applications built using Windows Workflow Services (WWS).

◆ Collaborative Data Objects for Exchange Management (CDOExM) is not available. Applications or scripts using CDOExM should be rewritten to use the new Exchange management APIs or Exchange Management Shell cmdlets.

◆ The Exchange Queue Viewer API has been cut from Exchange 2007. Applications that use this API should be rewritten using the new Exchange management APIs.

◆ Exchange Windows Management Instrumentation (WMI) classes have been discontinued. Applications that use Exchange WMI should be rewritten using the Exchange management APIs.

◆ The Exchange Event Service is no longer available. Applications should be rewritten to use the Web Services API instead.

◆ The Exchange Installable File System (ExIFS) is no longer available; this was commonly also referred to as the M: drive in Exchange 2000. This functionality can be duplicated writing applications using the Web Services API.

◆ The Exchange 2000/2003 Recipient Update Service (RUS) is no longer required to stamp mail-enabled objects with e-mail address and address list information. This information is now associated with mail-enabled objects when the object is created.

Clearing Up Some Confusion

I mentioned earlier that Exchange has certainly been hyped a lot during the design and beta testing process. This has generated a lot of buzz in the information technology (IT) industry, but this buzz has also generated a lot of confusion and some misinformation. I want to take this opportunity to clear up some of this confusion by answering some of the more common questions that have generated misconceptions about Exchange 2007.

Do I have to have three or four separate servers to run each of the server roles? A single server can host all four primary server roles (Mailbox, Client Access, Hub Transport, and Unified Messaging) except in the case of clustered mailbox servers. The Client Access, Hub Transport, and Unified Messaging server roles cannot be on the clustered mailbox server. The Edge Transport role must be installed on a separate server. The active clustered mailbox and passive clustered mailbox server roles must be on separate servers.

Is there a 32-bit version of Exchange? Yes, there is an evaluation, testing, and lab version of Exchange 2007 that is a 32-bit version. This version must not be used in production.

Is Microsoft Forefront Security for Exchange included with Exchange 2007? Forefront Security for Exchange (formerly known as Sybari Antigen) is included with Exchange 2007 if you have purchased Exchange Enterprise Client Access Licenses (CALs).

Is the Edge Transport server required?   No, Edge Transport servers are not required. You can use any third-party message hygiene system in your perimeter network or you can direct inbound and outbound mail through your Hub Transport servers or both.

Is Exchange 2007 using a SQL database for mailboxes and public folders?   Although there has been debate for years about using SQL Server for the Exchange databases, Exchange 2007 continues to use the Extensible Storage Engine (ESE), also known as the JET database engine.

Is Exchange Management Shell knowledge required? Do I have to learn scripting?   Most common administrative tasks can be performed through the Exchange Management Console graphical interface. Command-line management and scripting for Exchange 2007 has been greatly improved through the use of the Exchange Management Shell. Many tasks are simplified or more powerful through the Exchange Management Shell, but it is not necessary to learn scripting in order to start working with Exchange 2007. I strongly encourage you to get know many of the powerful features of the EMS as you get comfortable with Exchange 2007. A number of advanced administration tasks do not have a graphical user interface option.

What is happening with public folders?   The use of public folders with Exchange 2007 is still available and supported, but their use is being deemphasized as newer collaborative technologies such as websites and portals have become commonplace. I urge you to examine your public folder applications with an eye toward migrating them to systems such as Microsoft Office SharePoint Server 2007.

Is there still 32KB a limitation on folder rules?   For power users, the 32KB limit on the size of rules for a folder was a serious annoyance. This limit is no longer a constraint for Outlook 2007 users whose mailboxes are on an Exchange 2007 mailbox server; the default is 64KB, but this can be changed (increased or decreased) on a user-by-user basis.

Is local continuous replication (LCR) and cluster continuous replication (CCR) the same as mailbox replication?   LCR and CCR do not replicate individual mailboxes but rather an entire mailbox database. The administrator selects an entire storage group (which must contain only a single database); Exchange replicates the data to a backup copy of the mailbox database by copying the transaction logs as they are filled.

Do I need to use every Exchange 2007 server role to have a functional Exchange 2007 system?   In order to build a completely functional Exchange 2007 system, you need the Mailbox, Hub Transport, and Client Access server roles. These can all reside on the same physical server.

Can I run 32-bit applications with the 64-bit version of Exchange 2007?   Most 32-bit Windows applications will generally run on Windows 2003 x64, but applications that integrate with Exchange (such as message hygiene or backup applications) should be 64-bit.

Summary

For most organizations, no single feature of Exchange 2007 may justify an upgrade. However, once you start looking at a combined list of improvements to Exchange 2007, the upgrade or replacement of an existing messaging system is compelling. For many organizations, the new high-availability features such as LCR and CCR will be the most important, and for others, improvements in calendaring and Outlook Web Access will be.

All in all, this latest generation of Exchange Server packs a big punch and will be a welcome addition to any organization. The following is a short list of the features that I find the most compelling:

◆ Improved performance because of more available RAM

◆ The ability to support users' demands for larger mailboxes

◆ Improved high-availability functions such as CCR and LCR

◆ Unified Messaging integration

◆ Improved Outlook Web Access

◆ Automatic configuration of Outlook 2007 profiles

◆ Message transport rules and the Hub Transport role

Chapter 4

Exchange Server 2007 Architecture

What separates a good Exchange Server administrator or implementer from a great one? Well, certainly there are a lot of factors, including an eye for details, patience with users, and knowledge of Exchange. However, truly effective Exchange Server 2007 planning, deployment, administration, performance optimization, and troubleshooting depend at least partially on understanding what is going on behind the scenes. This includes knowledge of the Exchange Server architecture, installation options, database configuration, and server roles. Knowledge of the "inner workings" of Exchange Server can help you more quickly get to the source of a problem and it can help you when you need to grow your organization and provide additional services.

This chapter introduces you to some of the basics of Exchange Server architecture and how you can make some of the right decisions early in your Exchange Server deployments. Certainly understanding what Exchange Server 2007 requires of its underlying operating system is a good start. And it's important to understand the differences between Exchange Server 2007 editions and client access licenses so you can pick the edition with the features and scalability that your organization requires.

A lot of changes have occurred for Exchange 2007 from the perspective of architecture and the choices that are available to the Exchange designer, implementer, or administrator. Although a lot of these concepts were introduced in Chapter 1, this chapter goes in to more depth on the architectural changes.

In this chapter you learn to:

◆   Understand Exchange 2007 requirements

◆   Plan for disk space

◆   Manage the move to 64-bit Windows

Exchange Server 2007 Requirements

To properly support Exchange 2007, you need to make sure the hardware you are using meets certain minimum requirements. This is certainly true if you are expecting Exchange 2007 to perform as expected and you expect to run in an environment supported by Microsoft. The hardware and software requirements are a bit more complex than they were for previous generations of Exchange.

Hardware Requirements

In the past, Microsoft has made recommendations for hardware based on the absolute minimums required to run Exchange Server. Now, however, the recommendations are much more practical for real-world deployments. The goal is optimal performance, and the recommendations are now made with consideration for supporting applications that often run in concert with Exchange Server, such as antivirus, anti-spam, archiving, management, monitoring, and reporting software.

PROCESSORS

The requirement for 64-bit processors is the first big change for Exchange 2007. The processor should be at least 800MHz, though you will certainly benefit from processors faster than 2GHz and dual-core processors. The processor must be one of the following:

◆ Intel Xeon or Intel Pentium × 64 that supports the Intel Extended Memory 64 Technology (EM64 T)

◆ AMD Opteron or Athlon 64-bit processor that supports the AMD64 platform

The Intel Itanium IA64 processor family is not supported.

Table 4.1 shows the processor recommendations from Microsoft for different Exchange Server 2007 roles.

TABLE 4.1:   Processor Recommendations Based on Server Role

EXCHANGE 2007 SERVER ROLE	MINIMUM	RECOMMENDED	RECOMMENDED MAXIMUM
Edge Transport	1 × processor core	2 × processor cores	8 × processor cores
Hub Transport	1 × processor core	4 × processor cores	4 × processor cores
Client Access	1 × processor core	4 × processor cores	4 × processor cores
Unified Messaging	1 × processor core	4 × processor cores	4 × processor cores
Mailbox	1 × processor core	4 × processor cores	8 × processor cores
Multiple server roles (combinations of Hub Transport, Client Access, Unified Messaging, and Mailbox server roles)*	1 × processor core	4 × processor cores	4 × processor cores

*For more detailed information see http://technet.microsoft.com/en-us/library/aa998874.aspx.

You may have noticed in Table 4.1 that for some server roles, the maximum number of processors or processor cores is less than the maximum that Windows can actually support. Most all multithreaded applications will reach a point of diminishing returns when more processors are added, so it may not be worth it to add the maximum number of processors that Windows supports. When you have maxed out on the practical number of processors, the best move is to scale to additional servers that handle the same role.

In environments that scale past a few hundred mailboxes, certainly dual- or quad-processor systems will be put to good use. Organizations that deploy Exchange Server in a combination of roles to different physical machines will almost always benefit from a dual-processor or dual-core processor system.

PHYSICAL MEMORY

As mentioned previously, the advantage that Exchange 2007 really gets out of the 64-bit architecture is the ability to access more physical memory. Additional physical memory improves caching, reduces the disk I/O profile, and allows for the addition of more features.

Microsoft is recommending a minimum of 2GB of RAM in each Exchange 2007 server. This will, of course, depend on the roles that the server is supporting. Table 4.2 shows the minimum, recommended, and maximum memory for each of the server roles.

TABLE 4.2:   Minimum and Recommended RAM for Exchange Server 2007 Roles

SERVER ROLE	MINIMUM	RECOMMENDATION	MAXIMUM
Mailbox	2GB	4GB base memory plus per mailbox calculation	32GB
Hub Transport	2GB	1GB per CPU core	16GB
Client Access	2GB	2GB per CPU core	16GB
Unified Messaging	2GB	2GB minimum plus 1GB per CPU core	4GB
Edge Transport	2GB	1GB per CPU core	16GB
Multiple roles	4GB	8GB for combination Hub Transport, Client Access, and Unified Messaging plus the per-mailbox calculation*	8GB

*For more information see http://technet.microsoft.com/en-us/library/bb738124.aspx.

One important thing you may notice in Table 4.2 is that the maximum recommended RAM for a server that hosts multiple roles is 8GB. The assumption is that for servers that really required more than 8GB of RAM, you would start to segment the roles out to dedicated server roles rather than just piling on more RAM.

4GB BEST FOR MAILBOX ROLE

Though Microsoft's minimum RAM recommendation for any server hosting the Mailbox role is 2GB, I strongly recommend a minimum of 4GB.

Once you have calculated the minimum amount of RAM that you require for the server, if you are configuring a mailbox server, you will need to add some additional RAM for each mailbox. This will depend on your user community's estimated load profile. Table 4.3 shows the additional memory required based on the number of mailboxes supported. The user profiles are defined in Table 4.6, "User Profile, Mailbox Size, and Estimated IOPS for Exchange 2003," later in this chapter.

TABLE 4.3:   Additional Memory Factor for Mailbox Servers

USER PROFILE	MAILBOX MEMORY RECOMMENDATION
Light	Add 2MB per mailbox
Average	Add 3.5MB per mailbox
Heavy	Add 5MB per mailbox

So for example, a server handling a Mailbox server role should have 2GB of memory plus the additional RAM per mailbox shown in Table 4.3. If the Mailbox server is supporting 1,000 mailboxes and it is estimated that 500 of the users are average (1.75GB of RAM if assuming 3.5MB per mailbox) and 500 are heavy users (2.5GB of RAM if assuming 5MB per mailbox), the server should have about 6.3GB of RAM. For good measure, I would recommend going with 8GB of RAM so that there is additional RAM just in case it is required. Seasoned administrators of previous versions of Exchange will immediately notice that restrictions on usable physical memory no longer apply to Exchange 2007.

Remember that these RAM estimates are just that, estimates. Additional factors (message hygiene software, continuous replication, e-mail archiving, and so on) may require more or less RAM (usually more) than the calculations and recommendations here. For example, antivirus and anti-spam software on Mailbox servers can place a significant burden on RAM. Microsoft publishes a storage calculator that can be useful when estimating RAM requirements; see this page for more information:

```
http://msexchangeteam.com/archive/2007/07/05/445802.aspx
```

An alternate way to size memory for Mailbox servers is to estimate the amount of RAM required based on the number of storage groups. This method is calculated to ensure that each storage group (and mailbox database) that is in use is allocated sufficient memory for database caching. Table 4.4 shows the minimum memory recommendations based on storage groups.

If you calculate two different minimum recommendations for RAM, I strongly encourage you to use the larger of the two calculations. Up to 32GB, Exchange 2007 Mailbox servers will always benefit from additional performance. Of course, 32GB of RAM may not be required on a Mailbox server that is supporting only 200 mailboxes, so approach RAM sizing with a certain cautious exuberance.

OPTICAL MEDIA

Exchange Server 2007 ships only on DVD media. Although installing from a network share does work, it is generally a good idea to ensure that your servers have DVD drives available rather than CD-ROM drives. If your servers do not have DVD drives, you can still copy the Exchange software across the network or install from a network share folder.

FILE SYSTEM

The FAT and FAT32 file systems are not supported. All disks must be formatted using the NTFS file system.

DISK SPACE

Exchange Server 2007 is certainly not the first edition of Exchange for which administrators or designers have improperly estimated the amount of available disk space. More than a few times, I have seen administrators scrambling for more disk space, adding additional hard drives, moving databases and transaction logs around, or begging the SAN administrator for more disk space. This is so important, in fact, that an entire section is dedicated to this in Chapter 2, "Designing a New Exchange 2007 System."

TABLE 4.4:   Minimum RAM Recommendations Based on Storage Groups

NUMBER OF STORAGE GROUPS	MINIMUM RAM REQUIRED
1–4	2GB
5–48	4GB
9–12	5GB
13–16	6GB
17–20	7GB
21–24	8GB
25–28	9GB
29–32	10GB
33–36	11GB
37–40	12GB
41–44	13GB
45–38	14GB
49–50	15GB

For now, let's just leave the disk requirements at the utmost basics. I recommend that each system disk on an Exchange Server have at least 20GB of free disk space prior to the installation of Exchange 2007. The actual recommendation from Microsoft is 1.2GB disk space free and 200MB of free space on the system disk, but that is a bare minimum. The amount of disk space that each of the servers will actually require will depend on the server role, the number of users you support, mailbox limits, and leaving room to grow.

Operating System Requirements

There are a few requirements for the Windows Server operating system. Exchange Server 2007 SP1 will run on both Windows Server 2003 Service Pack 1 and Windows Server 2008.

Windows Server 2003 Requirements

For the release to manufacturing (RTM) version of Exchange 2007, the only version of Windows Server that can be used is the Windows Server 2003 × 64 SP1 (or later) or Windows Server 2003 × 64 R2 family. Windows 2003 with the Multilingual User Interface (MUI) pack can also be used. Exchange 2007 SP1 will also run on these versions of Windows Server.

Exchange 2007 can be installed on either the Standard Edition or the Enterprise Edition of Windows Server 2003. Windows 2003 Enterprise Edition is required if you will be installing clustered mailbox servers.

Though Microsoft recommends Windows 2003 SP1, I advise people to go ahead and use Windows Server 2003 SP2 or later.

The following list includes other requirements for preparing the Windows server to run Exchange 2007:

- Install the Microsoft .NET Framework v2.0.

- Install the Windows PowerShell. You can download the released version from:

  `http://www.microsoft.com/windowsserver2003/technologies/management/`
  `powershell/default.mspx`

- Install Microsoft Management Console 3.0. You can find more information and download links in Microsoft Knowledge Base article 907265, "MMC 3.0 update is available for Windows Server 2003 and for Windows XP."

Unlike with previous versions of Exchange, the Internet Information Server components Network News Transfer Protocol (NNTP) and Simple Mail Transfer Protocol (SMTP) should not be installed.

All additional applications that you run on an Exchange 2007 server should be 64-bit applications. Although Windows × 64 supports 32-bit applications in WOW64 emulation — provided the applications' kernel mode components are 64-bit — it remains to be seen whether mixing and matching 32-bit and 64-bit applications on an Exchange 2007 server is a good idea. Many of us still remember poorly performing and unstable 16-bit Windows applications that adversely affected Windows NT 4.0, so this may potentially be true with 32-bit Windows applications on Windows 64-bit.

The 64-bit versions of Windows support applications in WOW64 to support Exchange. The only requirement is that kernel mode components of those applications have to work, so those have to be × 64. The main application can be 32-bit running in WOW64. In my opinion, any third-party tools and utilities that run on an Exchange 2007 server should be 64-bit versions.

Windows Server 2008 Requirements

As of the release of Exchange Server 2007 Service Pack 1, Windows Server 2008 is supported. Unlike Windows Server 2003, which requires a number of updates and additional software to be downloaded, most everything that Exchange 2007 requires has shipped with Windows 2008. However, a lot of the components of Windows 2008 are not loaded by default so you may have to load or enable them.

Windows Server 2008 or not?

Should you more directly to Windows Server 2008 or stay with old reliable Windows Server 2003? In general, I think the benefits outweigh the downsides. For more information and my ongoing experiences, see the following blog posting:

`http://mostlyexchange.blogspot.com/2008/10/exchange-server-2007-on-windows-2008`
`.html`

Exchange Server 2007 SP1 will run on the × 64 versions of the following operating systems:

◆ Windows Server 2008

◆ Windows Server 2008 Enterprise

◆ Windows Server 2008 Datacenter

It will not run on the Web Server or Itanium-based systems versions of Windows 2008. Exchange 2007 will also not run on any server configured with just the server core components; this is because the .NET 2.0 Framework is required for Exchange 2007.

The following are the components that must be installed on Windows Server 2008:

◆ Active Directory management tools

◆ Windows PowerShell v1.0 (do NOT use the v2.0 betas unless authorized by Microsoft)

◆ IIS components (the components vary based on the server role)

◆ Windows failover clustering (if supporting CCR or SCC)

◆ Active Directory Lightweight Directory Services (if an Edge Transport server)

◆ Windows Media audio codecs

The simplest and quickest way to get all of the necessary components installed is to use the Server Manager command-line tool (`ServerManagerCMD`). Table 4.5 lists the commands and the server roles that require these components. Note that this table includes a few of my own recommendations such as installing the Active Directory remote management tools and the legacy web management tools on all servers. This is above and beyond Microsoft's baseline requirements.

The following link lists the installation requirements for Windows 2008:

```
http://technet.microsoft.com/en-us/library/bb691354(EXCHG.80).aspx
```

The Move to 64-Bit Architecture

The move to a 64-bit architecture has been a controversial decision on the part of Microsoft, but in my opinion this certainly makes a lot of sense. Additional accessible memory is the number one reason for moving to the 64-bit architecture. Exchange 2003 Server quickly becomes short on RAM available for caching and other Exchange operations. Microsoft could not add too many additional server-side features to Exchange 2007 without getting around this constraint.

Although the 32-bit architecture certainly leaves a lot of room to grow when fewer mailboxes per server are supported, servers with more mailboxes begin to hit limitations. Microsoft was faced with a decision to support both 32-bit and 64-bit versions of Exchange or to require everyone to move to the 64-bit version. Supporting two different processors' architectures for the same product is both more difficult and more costly than supporting a single version. This is certainly the case with Microsoft, but it is true to a certain degree for the customer as well. As third-party products are released, as fixes are released, and as customizations or tweaks are documented, there will be more possible choices for processors, editions, and operating systems and the customer's support responsibilities will become more difficult.

ROOM TO GROW

For servers supporting larger numbers of mailboxes, the Exchange team had clearly exceeded the limits of the 32-bit architecture with Exchange 2003. Adding additional server-side processes such as messaging records management, improved calendaring and scheduling, transport rules,

Unified Messaging services, integration with Windows Rights Management Services, and other new features would not have been possible without additional room to grow.

TABLE 4.5: Installing the Necessary Windows Server 2008 Components

SERVER ROLE	SERVER MANAGER COMMAND
All	ServerManagerCMD -I RSAT-ADDS
All	ServerManagerCmd -i PowerShell
All	ServerManagerCmd -i Web-Metabase
All	ServerManagerCmd -i Web-Lgcy-Mgmt-Console
Client Access and Mailbox	ServerManagerCmd -i Web-Server
Client Access and Mailbox	ServerManagerCmd -i Web-ISAPI-Ext
Client Access and Mailbox	ServerManagerCmd -i Web-Dyn-Compression
Client Access and Mailbox	ServerManagerCmd -i Web-Windows-Auth
Client Access and Mailbox	ServerManagerCmd -i Web-Digest-Auth
Client Access and Mailbox	ServerManagerCmd -i Web-Lgcy-Mgmt-Console
Client Access	ServerManagerCmd -i RPC-over-HTTP-proxy
Edge Transport	ServerManagerCmd -i ADLDS
Clustered Mailbox Server	ServerManagerCmd -i Failover-Clustering
Unified Messaging	ServerManagerCmd -i Desktop-Experience

IMPROVED CACHING AND REDUCED I/O PROFILES

Even on a server with only a few hundred mailboxes, Exchange Server 2000/2003 quickly reaches the maximum amount of RAM available for caching (1.2GB maximum). As more and more users vie for the same physical memory for caching, Exchange Server quickly becomes constrained by the amount of I/O (input/output) operations that the Exchange server's disk subsystem can support.

Hundreds of pages of material have been written on the concept of optimizing Exchange Server for maximizing performance by improving I/O performance with Exchange, and I certainly can't do the concept justice in just a few paragraphs, but understanding the basic input/output per second (IOPS) requirements of users is helpful. Microsoft and hardware vendors have done much research on I/O requirements based on the mailbox size and the average load that each user places on the server. Table 4.6 shows the estimated IOPS given a user type and an estimated mailbox size for Exchange 2003. IOPS requirements climb as the number of messages sent and received increases and as the mailbox size increases.

TABLE 4.6:   User Profile, Mailbox Size, and Estimated IOPS for Exchange 2003

USER TYPE	DATABASE VOLUME IOPS	MESSAGES SENT/RECEIVED PER DAY*	MAILBOX SIZE
Light	.5	5 sent/20 received	50MB
Average	.75	10 sent/40 received	100MB
Heavy	1.0	20 sent/80 received	200MB
Large	1.5	30 sent/120 received	500MB

Assumes average message size is approximately 50KB

For an Exchange 2003 server that is supporting 3,000 heavy mailbox users, the disk subsystem would have to support at least 3,000 IOPS. In order to meet this requirement, the disk subsystem may require too many additional disks; thus, the disk subsystem may have far more disk space than is actually necessary in order to support the IOPS profile. Failure to plan for sufficient IOPS capacity on the disk subsystem will significantly hurt performance.

The 64-bit architectural improvements to Exchange 2007 allow the operating system and Exchange Server 2007 to access more physical memory. With additional physical memory available for caching, disk I/O is significantly reduced. Microsoft estimates that I/O requirements are reduced by approximately 70 percent provided the Exchange 2007 server has the recommended amount of RAM. Table 4.7 shows the estimated IOPS requirements for Exchange 2007 Mailbox servers. Please keep in mind that these are estimates and may change over time. These numbers are also calculated when the Mailbox server is configured with more than the recommended amount of RAM.

TABLE 4.7:   User Profile, Mailbox Size, and Estimated IOPS for Exchange 2007

USER TYPE	DATABASE VOLUME IOPS	MESSAGES SENT/RECEIVED PER DAY*	MAILBOX SIZE
Light	.14	5 sent/20 received	50MB
Average	.20	10 sent/40 received	100MB
Heavy	.27	20 sent/80 received	200MB
Large	.41	30 sent/120 received	500MB

Assumes average message size is approximately 50KB

With this significant improvement in caching Exchange data, the Extensible Storage Engine (ESE) database engine needs to read and write from the disk less frequently and thus reduces the IOPS requirements. When the IOPS requirements are reduced, fewer disks are required to support the I/O load.

Active Directory and Exchange Server 2007

Active Directory is a grand repository for information about such objects as users, domains, computers, domain controllers, groups, contacts, and shared resources (such as files and printers). Active Directory lets you log in to very large domains and use resources across the domain with ease. All objects in Active Directory are protected by a security system based on Kerberos, an industry-standard secret-key encryption network authentication protocol developed at the Massachusetts Institute of Technology. (For more on Kerberos, see http://web.mit.edu/kerberos/www/.)

Windows Server controls who can see each object in Active Directory, what attributes each user can see, and what actions a user can perform on an object. The Windows Active Directory permissions model is richer and more complex under the hood than directory services permissions in earlier versions of Windows such as Windows NT 4, but it's quite easy to manage at the user interface level.

Exchange Depends on Active Directory

Exchange Server 2007, like Exchange 2000/2003, depends entirely on a healthy and functioning Active Directory and the availability of Domain Name System (DNS) services. In order for Exchange servers to properly locate domain controllers and global catalogs, DNS must accurately resolve domain controller and global catalog service location records and host information as well as information about Active Directory sites. Exchange must retrieve configuration and recipient information from Active Directory as well; if either DNS or Active Directory does not respond to an Exchange 2007 server's queries, clients will not be able to authenticate, address lookups will not occur, and e-mail will not flow.

Almost the entire Exchange 2007 configuration is stored in the Active Directory; this information is stored in a partition of the Active Directory called the Configuration partition. The Configuration partition (see Figure 4.1) is replicated to all domain controllers in the entire forest, not just the domain in which the Exchange server is installed.

FIGURE 4.1
Viewing the
Configuration partition
from ADSI Edit

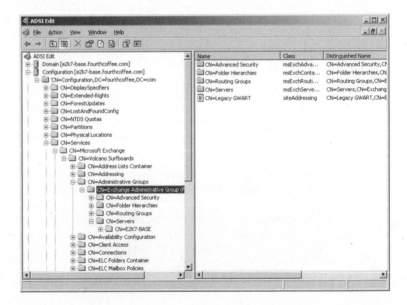

The information you see in Figure 4.1 represents the Exchange 2007 configuration as viewed using the Windows 2003 Support Tools utility ADSI Edit (ADSI stands for Active Directory Services Interface, which is an application programming interface for accessing Active Directory). This is a very primitive view of the Exchange configuration similar to the view that REGEDIT gives you of the Windows Registry. Actually configuring Exchange properties is much easier (and safer!) to do when you use the Exchange Management Console (EMC) or the EMS. You should only use ADSI Edit to manipulate your Exchange organization's configuration when you have specific guidance from Microsoft or a trustworthy source.

When an Exchange server starts running services such as the Microsoft Exchange System Attendant, the Microsoft Exchange Active Directory Topology service determines in which Active Directory site the Exchange server is located and then locates all domain controllers and global catalog servers in that site. Exchange Server then reads its configuration from Active Directory; this would include determining which roles that server supports, the mailbox databases to mount, and more.

When an Exchange 2007 Hub Transport server is routing messages to Exchange recipients, it must query a global catalog server in order to determine properties of the recipient such as proxy addresses, home mailbox server, and mailbox restrictions. Figure 4.2 shows the E-mail Addresses property page of a mailbox recipient; mail recipients are managed through the EMC.

FIGURE 4.2
E-mail Addresses
properties

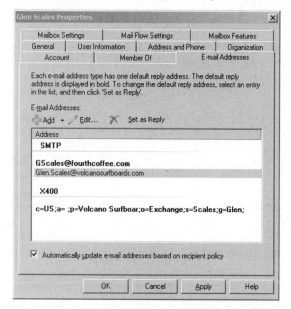

All recipient information is stored in the Active Directory, including information regarding e-mail addresses, home server, mailbox limits, message size limits, and so on. Exchange Server must retrieve this information from an Active Directory global catalog server. Exchange Server is dependent on the availability and health of domain controllers and global catalog servers; if Active Directory resources are not available, Exchange will not function.

Active Directory Site Membership

Exchange Server 2007 is an Active-Directory-site-aware application. Exchange 2007 uses Active Directory site information for a couple of purposes.

Exchange 2007 servers automatically learn the Active Directory topology and determine in which Active Directory site each Exchange 2007 server is located. Exchange Server uses the IP subnets to locate the sites; if the subnet information is incomplete or incorrect, Exchange Server will not be able to correctly determine site membership and mail may not be delivered properly.

Different Exchange Server 2007 server roles use the Active Directory site information in different ways:

- All Exchange 2007 server roles use the site architecture to locate domain controllers and global catalog servers closest to them from the network's perspective.

- Hub Transport servers determine the remote Hub Transport servers' names in other Active Directory sites to which they need to transmit messages intended for remote Mailbox servers.

- Mailbox servers determine which Hub Transport servers are in their own site so they can notify those servers that they have messages that must be transferred.

- Unified Messaging servers submit voicemail messages and faxes to Hub Transport servers in their own site for routing to Mailbox servers. Unified Messaging servers do not transfer voicemail and fax messages directly to a Mailbox server.

- Client Access servers look for site information in order to determine if they are located in the same Active Directory site mailboxes that they are being asked to provide access to. If not, the Client Access server refers the client to a Client Access server that is in the same site as the required Mailbox server.

- Exchange Server refers Outlook 2000, 2002, and 2003 clients to global catalog servers that are in the same site as the Exchange server for global address list lookups.

If there are weaknesses in your Active Directory site design, Exchange 2007 will certainly expose them. You should ensure that for Active Directory forests with more than one Active Directory site, subnets are properly defined and associated with the appropriate site. Specifically, Active Directory IP subnet information must be correct. If it's not, Exchange components might not function properly and messages might not be delivered.

Domain Controllers and Global Catalog Servers

The simplest way to describe the Exchange 2007 requirements for Active Directory is to say that all domain controllers should be running (at a minimum) Windows 2003 Service Pack 1 or later, each domain should be at Windows 2003 domain functional level, and the forest should be at Windows 2003 functional level. Although that is the best-case scenario, it might not be practical and it is not correct. The following are the actual minimum requirements for Windows 2003 domain controllers and Active Directory:

- Each Active Directory site that has Exchange 2007 servers must have at least one Windows 2003 Service Pack 1 or later global catalog server. For redundancy, an additional global catalog server should be available. The recommended ratio of Exchange servers to global catalog servers is based on the number of CPUs (and the CPU type); that ratio is 4 : 1 for DC/GC's using 32-bit processors and 8 : 1 for DC/GCs using × 64 processors. For each quad processor Exchange server, a single processor global catalog server should be available in the site, but that may not take into consideration redundancy requirements.

- Each domain that will host Exchange 2007 servers or mail-enabled recipients must be at a minimum Windows 2000 native functional level.

◆ If you are supporting the Exchange 2007 Outlook Web Access browsable global address list, you must use Windows 2003 Service Pack 1 or later global catalog servers.

◆ The schema master flexible single master of operations role must be hosted on a domain controller running Windows 2003 Service Pack 1 or later.

◆ If you have Exchange organizations in multiple forests and require forest-to-forest trusts, then all forests involved in forest-to-forest trusts must be at Windows 2003 forest functional mode.

TIPS FOR HEALTHY INTERACTION WITH ACTIVE DIRECTORY

Any experienced Exchange administrator will tell you that a healthy Active Directory goes a long way toward ensuring that Exchange servers are healthy and trouble free. I have learned a number of lessons (sometimes the hard way) over the years and can offer some useful tips for ensuring that Active Directory provides consistent and reliable directory services to Exchange.

◆ Even in small and medium-sized organizations, redundant domain controllers and global catalog servers help ensure higher availability.

◆ In large organizations, each Active Directory site that hosts Exchange servers should have at least two domain controllers that host the global catalog server role.

◆ In large organizations with many thousands of mailboxes, implementing dedicated domain controller/global catalog server sites that are exclusively for use by Exchange servers will ensure that Exchange does not interfere with Active Directory's other functions (such as authenticating users) and vice versa.

◆ All clients and member servers should have a primary DNS server and a secondary DNS server address configured.

◆ In large organizations, clients and member servers should have primary, secondary, and tertiary DNS server IP addresses configured.

◆ Either Windows 2003 32-bit or 64-bit can be used for domain controllers and global catalog servers, but if the Active Directory database (NTDS.DIT) exceeds 1GB, better performance will be achieved with 64-bit Windows 2003. For organizations with NTDS.DIT files larger than a few hundred megabytes, separating the database transaction logs to a RAID 1 volume array and the NTDS.DIT database file to a RAID 5 or RAID 1+0 array can also improve performance.

◆ Installing the DNS service on all domain controllers and using Active Directory–integrated DNS zones on all domain controllers in the forest will improve the reliability of DNS and therefore Active Directory. If you have more than two domain controllers/DNS servers in your organizations, all domain controllers and member servers should be configured with a primary DNS server, a secondary DNS server, and a tertiary DNS server.

Exchange Editions

When you plan to purchase Exchange 2007, you need to make sure you purchase the correct edition of Exchange Server and purchase the client access licenses to license the features that you will require. Table 4.8 lists some of the features that are included with Exchange 2007 Standard Edition and Enterprise Edition. Standard Edition can be used for Exchange server roles, however if more than five storage groups or mailbox databases are required or if you require clustered mailbox servers, then Enterprise Edition would only be required for the Mailbox servers.

TABLE 4.8: Exchange 2007 Standard Edition versus Enterprise Edition

FEATURE	STANDARD	ENTERPRISE
Maximum database size	16TB (unlimited)	16TB (unlimited)
Maximum number of storage groups	5	50
Supports Recovery Storage Group	✓	✓
Number of databases	5	50
Supports Client Access server role	✓	✓
Supports single-copy clustered mailbox servers		✓
Supports local continuous replication	✓	✓
Supports clustered continuous replication Mailbox servers		✓
Supports standby continuous replication	✓	✓
Supports Edge Transport role	✓	✓
Supports Hub Transport role	✓	✓
Supports local continuous replication	✓	✓
Supports Mailbox role	✓	✓
Supports Unified Messaging role	✓	✓

In the past, you only had a single option when purchasing Exchange Server client access licenses (CALs). Exchange 2007 introduces the Exchange Enterprise CAL and Exchange Standard CAL. Either can be used against either Exchange Server Enterprise Edition or Exchange Server Standard Edition. The choice for which CAL you require will depend on which premium features of Exchange Server 2007 you are going to require.

The Exchange Enterprise CAL adds features above and beyond the Exchange Standard CAL. The Exchange Standard CAL provides your users with the ability to use Exchange features such as accessing their mailbox from a MAPI client, Outlook Web Access, ActiveSync devices, and Outlook Anywhere (RPC over HTTP). The Exchange Enterprise CAL includes the following additional functions:

◆ Unified Messaging services

◆ Microsoft Forefront Security for Exchange Server

◆ Advanced compliance capabilities such as per-user and per-distribution group journaling

◆ Messaging records management features

◆ Anti-spam and antivirus protection using Microsoft Exchange Hosted Filtering Services as an external service provider

Standard client access licenses must be purchased for each mailbox that is accessed on your system. If you have users who use multiple devices (Outlook, Outlook Web Access, Windows Mobile, ActiveSync, Outlook Anywhere) to access their mailbox and their total percentage of time accessing their mailbox from their primary device is less than 80 percent, you must purchase an additional CAL for each user.

If you use Exchange Enterprise CALs for all of your users, you get to use all of the features available for Enterprise CALs. However, if you purchase Enterprise CALs only for a subset of your users requiring a feature such as Unified Messaging and Journaling and also choose to use Forefront Security for Exchange, the remainder of the users must be licensed separately for Forefront Security for Exchange.

Server Roles

The best way to think of Exchange 2007 server roles is to think of a server that has the necessary software and configuration to perform only a specific set of functions. This makes installing servers with dedicated functions much easier. Dedicated server roles are also more secure because only the necessary software is installed, thus reducing the attack surface.

The concept of server roles is not really new. In Exchange 2000/2003, to build a server for handling Internet messaging or inter-routing group messaging, you would install Exchange Server, flag the machine as a front-end server (optionally), and disable services such as the web service. To configure a machine as an Outlook Web Access or ActiveSync server, you would install Exchange, flag the Exchange server as a front-end server, and disable the information store and SMTP services. With Exchange 2007, the server roles are assigned when Setup is run.

Server Roles Overview

Exchange 2007 has made the assignment of specific server roles simpler by allowing the server roles to be designated at installation time. When you group together and install only the necessary services for a specific function, server installation is simpler and more secure and the server has less overhead. There are five basic server roles:

◆ Mailbox

◆ Client Access

◆ Hub Transport

◆ Unified Messaging

◆ Edge Transport

The Mailbox server role can be installed as a clustered mailbox server. In small and medium-sized organizations, a single physical server will usually host more than one server role except in the case of the Edge Transport role. Edge Transport must run on its own server.

MAILBOX SERVER ROLE

The Mailbox server role is responsible for mailbox and public folder databases and for allowing direct connectivity from MAPI/RPC clients. Clients such as Outlook 2003 or Outlook 2007 using MAPI/RPC will connect directly to the MAPI interface on the Mailbox server role. The Hub Transport and Client Access server roles are required for a fully functioning e-mail environment, but they do not necessarily have to be on the same physical server.

The Mailbox server role must exist on its own physical server if it is being installed as part of a clustered mailbox server environment. In that case, the Hub Transport, Client Access, and Unified

Messaging server roles must be on separate physical hardware. A server handling a mailbox server role will typically be configured with significantly more RAM, hard disk space, and processor capacity than the other server roles.

High-availability options for Mailbox servers include local continuous replication, single-copy clusters, and clustered continuous replication.

Local Continuous Replication

Local continuous replication (LCR) is a new technology for Exchange 2007. LCR is designed so that a production copy of a database can be synchronized and have a backup copy always ready to be put into production if the primary copy becomes corrupted; the administrator initiates the switch over to the backup copy of the database. LCR is configured storage group by storage group, and each storage group can have only a single database in it.

When a server is configured to support LCR, an additional set of local disks should be allocated for the LCR transaction logs and for the backup copy of the database. These disks can be directly attached to the server or attached via storage area network (SAN) or Internet small computer systems interface (iSCSI). As transaction logs are completely filled and closed on the production copy of the database, they are copied to the backup location and committed to the backup copy of the database.

Local continuous replication is resource intensive because transaction logs are being copied and replayed to backup copies of a database on the same server.

Clustered Continuous Replication

Clustered continuous replication (CCR) is also a new technology for Exchange Server 2007. This technology is similar to LCR in that as transaction logs are filled, they are copied to a backup location and committed to a backup (or passive) copy of the database. However, with CCR, the implementation is in the form of a two-node active-passive cluster. When Windows 2003 clustering services are used, both the active and passive nodes must reside on the same IP subnet. The backup location is on the passive node; the transaction log files are pulled to the passive node and committed to the database on the passive node.

If the primary node of the cluster fails, the passive node automatically comes online and takes over handling the clustered mailbox server. Unlike Microsoft's previous implementation of Exchange clustering (single-copy clusters), there is not a single copy of the database and transaction logs that is shared by all nodes of the cluster, however some small amount of data loss can occur depending on the type of failure.

Standby Continuous Replication

Standby continuous replication (SCR) allows you to have a replicated copy of a database on a remote mailbox server. This is different from CCR and an administrator must manually activate the standby copy if the primary copy fails. SCR should be considered a disaster recovery method, not high availability, because a number of manual steps are necessary to bring the database online.

Single-Copy Clusters

A single-copy cluster (SCC) is the same technology that existed in earlier versions of Exchange. An active node of the cluster owns shared disks (usually on a storage area network or on network attached storage, or NAS). The cluster can consist of from two to eight nodes, but there must always be at least one passive node. There is only a single copy of the database and transaction log files, and they are located on the shared storage.

If an active node of the cluster fails, one of the passive nodes will take ownership of the shared disks and database, mount the shared database, and start servicing clients for that particular clustered mailbox server (CMS); the CMS was known as an Exchange virtual server (EVS) in previous Exchange cluster implementations.

CLIENT ACCESS SERVER ROLE

The Client Access server is considered a middle-tier server; this server role handles communications between non-MAPI clients and the Mailbox server role. In order to have a fully functioning e-mail environment, the Client Access server role must be functioning. The following are some of the functions that the Client Access server role supports:

♦ Outlook Web Access clients

♦ ActiveSync-enabled mobile devices

♦ Outlook Anywhere (RPC over HTTP) clients

♦ POP3 and IMAP4 clients

♦ Offline Address Book Web distribution

♦ Web services such as Autodiscover and the Availability service

♦ Web Services that require access to user mailboxes

The Client Access server accepts connections from these clients via HTTP, POP3, or IMAP4 and then passes requests on to the Mailbox server via MAPI over RPC. Each Active Directory site that contains a Mailbox server role must also contain at least one Client Access server.

High-availability options for the Client Access server role include implementing some type of network load-balancing solution such as the Cisco Local Director or Windows Network Load Balancing. The Client Access role cannot be configured on a clustered mailbox server.

HUB TRANSPORT SERVER ROLE

The Hub Transport server role is responsible for all message delivery regardless of whether the message is being delivered from one mailbox to another in the same mailbox database, a Mailbox server in the same Active Directory site, a server in a remote Active Directory site, or outside of the organization. At least one Hub Transport server role is required in each Active Directory site that contains a Mailbox server.

For internal mail routing, Exchange Server 2007 will automatically load-balance and fail over if more than one Hub Transport server exists in an Active Directory site. For redundancy in inbound SMTP mail from outside the organization, you have a couple of options. If inbound mail is coming directly into the Hub Transport servers, multiple MX records or network load balancing are good solutions. If mail is coming into a perimeter network solution such as Edge Transport or a third-party SMTP gateway, configure these solutions to use multiple internal Hub Transport servers.

For smaller organizations with a single server Exchange implementation, the Hub Transport server can perform most of the message hygiene functions performed by the Edge Transport server role to connect Exchange to the outside world. However, separating message hygiene functions to a separate server role located on the perimeter network is more secure. Microsoft and other vendors offer spam filters that can be implemented at the client as well if they wish to offload this functionality to a third party, but client-side spam filtering means that the spam must first travel through your internal Exchange infrastructure.

UNIFIED MESSAGING ROLE

The Unified Messaging server role is considered a middle-tier system and is an entirely new concept for Exchange 2007. This server role integrates voicemail and inbound faxing with Exchange mailboxes. The Unified Messaging server requires an IP-based telephone switch or a traditional PBX-to-IP gateway (PBX stands for public branch exchange). The following functions are handled by the Unified Messaging server role:

◆ Provides voicemail for users of the IP-based phone system or through the PBX-to-IP gateway including voicemail greetings and options. Inbound voicemail is recorded as a WMA file and stored as a message in a user's Inbox.

◆ Accepts inbound faxes that are designated for specific mailboxes, converts the fax to a TIFF file, and stores that message in a user's Inbox.

◆ Allows users to dial in to the Unified Messaging server to retrieve voicemail, listen to e-mail messages, review their calendar, or change appointments.

◆ Provides voice menus and prompting call menus acting as an auto-attendant system.

EDGE TRANSPORT ROLE

The Edge Transport server role is an entirely new role. In the past, Exchange servers could be implemented as an additional tier of message hygiene protection. However, there are a number of reasons that you might not want to use Exchange servers as perimeter message hygiene systems:

◆ In order to process delivery reports, nondelivery reports, and address rewrites, the information store service must be running and the default mailbox database must be mounted.

◆ Placing an Exchange 2000/2003 server in the perimeter network requires many ports to be opened on the firewall from the perimeter network to the internal network.

◆ Allowing inbound e-mail directly to an Exchange server could jeopardize both Exchange and Active Directory.

For these reasons, a server role was developed that has many of the advantages of an Exchange 2007 server but can be made much more secure because it can run in the perimeter network as a stand-alone computer and does not require Active Directory membership. The following are some of the characteristics of the Edge Transport server role:

◆ The Edge Transport server role should be deployed in the perimeter network.

◆ It can be managed with Exchange Management Shell scripts and the Exchange Management Console in much the same way a regular Exchange server is managed.

◆ The only components required to run the Edge Transport role are the message transport system and an instance of the Active Directory Application Mode (ADAM) database.

◆ Features such as transport rules can be implemented in the perimeter network and provide message policy enforcement for messages entering or leaving the organization that is separate from that provided on the internal network.

◆ Connectivity between internal Hub Transport servers and Edge Transport servers can be authenticated and the data stream encrypted.

◆ The content filter functionality and other anti-spam and message security tools are built in, as is the ability to add third-party content filtering/message hygiene tools.

◆ Microsoft Forefront Security for Exchange Server can be employed on the Edge Transport server role for virus detection and quarantine.

For medium and large organizations, higher availability comes in the form of installing multiple Edge Transport servers and providing load balancing either using multiple DNS Mail Exchanger (MX) records, network load balancing, DNS round robin, or failover using multiple Internet connections.

Microsoft and Deployment Planning

Early in the Exchange 2007 life cycle, Microsoft defined some new terminologies, acronyms, and organization types that are used when designing and deploying an Exchange 2007 organization for businesses of different sizes. I felt it important to define these terms here so that there will be less confusion when reading both this book and the Microsoft documentation.

Using some of these terms, Microsoft has attempted to more clearly standardize design methodologies and approaches to deployment of Exchange in order to simplify Exchange operations.

The first of these terms is *Service Delivery Location* (SDL). The SDL is essentially the location of your servers. In a small organization, the SDL may be a secured and environmentally controlled closet within your own facility or it could be operated by a service provider or located at a co-location site. In a medium-sized or large organization, an SDL may be distributed through many data centers in dozens or hundreds of locations throughout the world or it could be a consolidated, centralized data center with hundreds of servers servicing clients worldwide.

This brings us to the location of the actual clients, or the *Client Service Location* (CSL). This is the location from which your clients access the services you are providing. In a small organization, the CSL may be on the same physical LAN as the SDL, whereas larger organizations may see the CSL span countries, continents, or the entire world.

To simplify deployment concepts, Microsoft has defined four types of organization models representing topologies in which Exchange 2007 may be deployed. These are the simple, standard, large, and complex organization types.

There is no exact formula for figuring out which organization type might describe your organization. The physical distribution of your user community, your organization's high-availability requirements, your organization's fault tolerance requirements, the volume of data that your users process, and other factors will all influence the organization model that you choose or a variation on these models that you choose to create yourself.

SIMPLE EXCHANGE ORGANIZATIONS

A simple Exchange organization is well suited for organizations that have fewer than 200 mailboxes. Please note that "200 mailboxes" is somewhat arbitrary because organizations with more or fewer mailboxes may fit in to this category depending on their user community, requirements, and messaging load.

The simple organization has a single Exchange 2007 server running on the same physical machine as the organization's domain controller. The Exchange 2007 server handles the Mailbox, Hub Transport, Client Access, and Unified Messaging roles.

The optional Edge Transport server role must still be on a separate physical server and should be located in the perimeter network.

In a simple Exchange organization, the users and the Exchange server are usually located in the same physical location, but that is not fixed rule. Even small organizations have telecommuters and users that access their organization using mobile technologies. Although the SDL is usually in the same location as the users, an emerging trend is for even small organizations to locate their server resources in a co-location site that provides Internet connectivity, power conditioning, backup power, air cooling, and physical security services. Another trend is to out-source the messaging functions entirely.

WINDOWS SMALL BUSINESS SERVER DEPLOYMENT

Organizations considering a single-server deployment that fits the simple Exchange organization model should consider a Microsoft Windows Small Business Server deployment. All of the compo-nents are tested together much more thoroughly (such as running Exchange Server on a domain controller).

Providing multiple layers of message hygiene and security for simple Exchange organiza-tions would come in the form of a reverse proxy to handle inbound HTTP requests and an Edge Transport server in the organization's perimeter network. Figure 4.3 shows a simple Exchange organization that is separated from the Internet using Microsoft Internet Security and Acceleration (ISA) Server and a perimeter network.

FIGURE 4.3
Protecting a simple
Exchange organization

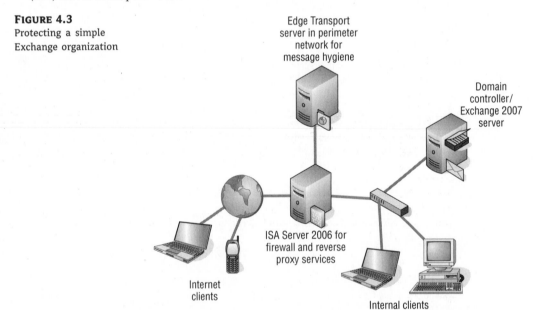

Microsoft also offers an additional service called Exchange Hosted Filtering that allows orga-nizations to direct their inbound mail to Microsoft's servers. The Hosted Filtering service inspects mail for viruses and spam and then passes the mail on to your servers. If you have purchased Enterprise client access licenses for all of your users, this service is included.

Inbound SMTP mail from the Internet is directed to the Edge Transport server, which is located in the perimeter/DMZ network. Inbound e-mail is inspected in the perimeter network for viruses or spam and message transport rules can enforce organizational policies on messages arriving from the Internet.

Inbound Outlook Web Access, ActiveSync, and Outlook RPC over HTTP connections termi-nate at the Microsoft ISA Server 2006 firewall; ISA Server acts as a reverse proxy, inspecting the inbound HTTP requests and then passing them on to the internal Exchange 2007 server's client access components.

STANDARD EXCHANGE ORGANIZATIONS

The standard Exchange model is by far the most common and flexible of the four Exchange server organization models. It will also be the organizational model most commonly found in organizations with from a few hundred to potentially tens of thousands of mailboxes. An organization will choose the standard Exchange model if any one of the following is true:

◆ Need to support more than approximately 200 mailboxes

◆ Require dedicated Exchange servers

◆ May need to split Exchange server roles among multiple physical servers

◆ Require dedicated domain controllers

◆ Need to support clustered mailbox servers

◆ Need to support more than one service delivery location (SDL)

◆ Require more scalability or infrastructure fault tolerance than the simple Exchange model can support

The standard Exchange organization is more scalable than the simple Exchange organization. Exchange servers are usually installed as member servers rather than on a domain controller. Exchange servers may span multiple Active Directory sites and server roles may be dedicated to specific physical servers rather than a single physical server. In this model, a single Active Directory forest is also required.

A standard Exchange organization with between a few hundred and a few thousand mailboxes might look like the one in Figure 4.4. In Figure 4.4, this organization has only a single SDL and requires high availability and redundancy. The Mailbox server is clustered to provide high availability for the mailbox databases, and the Client Access and Hub Transport roles are both installed on two physical servers. By combining these two roles on two servers, the organization can provide better availability for message transport and web clients.

The organization could scale to as many as five Active Directory sites with Exchange 2007 servers and multiple Internet access points but still be considered a standard organization. The number of mailboxes is somewhat less of a factor here than the organization's needs. A company that places greater importance on its messaging needs and availability will find itself with dedicated servers and Exchange servers installed as member servers. When designing an Exchange organization for a company that meets this profile, the administrator will have to take into consideration the business needs, budget constraints, and availability requirements of the organization.

LARGE EXCHANGE ORGANIZATIONS

Large Exchange organizations are the most scalable of the Exchange organizational models; they allow an Exchange organization to support tens of thousands or hundreds of thousands of mailboxes. A large Exchange organization can have the same characteristics a standard Exchange organization has plus the following:

◆ More than five Active Directory sites and multiple SDLs

◆ Multiple CSLs

◆ Multiple Active Directory domains within a single Active Directory forest

FIGURE 4.4
A standard Exchange
organization

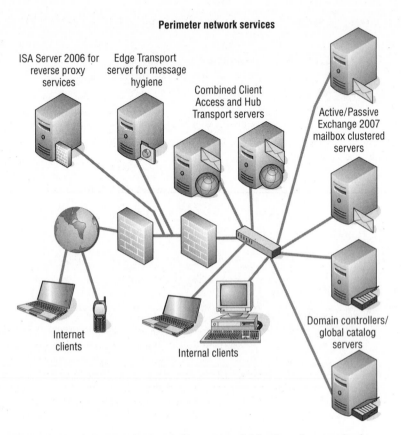

Although the large Exchange organization is certainly more scalable than the standard Exchange organization, the skills required to manage and build a standard Exchange organization do transfer upward to the large Exchange organization.

COMPLEX EXCHANGE ORGANIZATIONS

Complex Exchange 2007 organizations represent increasing complexity of Exchange 2007 in businesses that might have multiple Active Directory forests and resource forests or that host multiple companies within the same Exchange organization. In addition to the scalable features of a standard or large Exchange organization, the following are some of the characteristics of a complex organization:

◆ Multiple Active Directory forests with recipient replication using tools such as Microsoft Identity Integration Services (MIIS)/Identity Lifecycle Manager (ILM)

◆ Multiple-organization support or support for multiple subsidiaries or business units in a single Exchange organization

◆ Integration with external Exchange organizations such as when a new business unit has been acquired but not merged in to a single organization

◆ Public folders, free and busy information, or shared calendaring between multiple organizations all using Exchange Server 2007

Size is often not the determining factor when designing and deploying a complex Exchange organization. In some cases, due to business requirements, even an organization with fewer than 1,000 mailboxes may find itself requiring multiple forests or other situations that require a complex Exchange organizational design.

Combining or Splitting Server Roles

A common question with respect to Exchange 2007 and server roles is, When should server roles be split across multiple physical machines? With few exceptions, there is not a rule that says server roles should be split across multiple pieces of hardware. However, even for a smaller organization, the need for high availability will drive the need for multiple Exchange 2007 servers. The only server role that can be installed on a clustered mailbox server is the Mailbox role. This means an environment that requires clustering of the Mailbox server role will require the other server roles (Hub Transport and Client Access) to be located on separate physical server.

In a small environment, the Hub Transport and Client Access roles can exist on the same physical server. In a medium-sized environment that requires high availability of the Client Access and Hub Transport servers, two Windows servers could be installed and load-balanced. Both of those servers could then host the Client Access and Hub Transport server roles.

What are some other reasons multiple Exchange servers might be required? The justification for additional hardware will be different from one organization to the next and will often depend on the organization's size, but here are a few:

◆ Server load is too great for a single machine. For example, a server supporting 1,000 mailboxes may be using local continuous replication and thus have an IO profile that precludes having additional disk-intensive, processor-intensive, or Active Directory–intensive roles.

◆ Redundancy in message routing is required and thus multiple servers with the Hub Transport role are required.

◆ Redundancy when providing web services or Internet access to messaging data requires multiple Client Access servers.

◆ Simplifying server recovery and rebuilds may require placing different server roles on different physical servers.

Major Components

The services and components that you find on an Exchange 2007 server will vary depending on which roles are installed for that server. Figure 4.5 shows some of the Exchange 2007 services that are found in the Services console.

If you are an experienced Exchange 2000/2003 administrator, you will also find that many of the services and executables are not recognizable. Exchange 2000/2003 has fewer core components and they were all installed on any Exchange server that you built. The Exchange 2007 components are shown in Table 4.9.

Depending on the server's role(s), you will see many of these executables in the Windows Task Manager (shown in Figure 4.6). One frequently misunderstood service is the Microsoft Exchange Information Store service, or `store.exe`. By design this service will attempt to allocate as much physical memory as possible and hold that memory until other applications require the memory. At that time, the `store.exe` process will release memory. On a server with 32GB of physical memory, it may not be unusual to see this service using 80 to 90 percent of that RAM.

FIGURE 4.5
Common Exchange
Server 2007 services

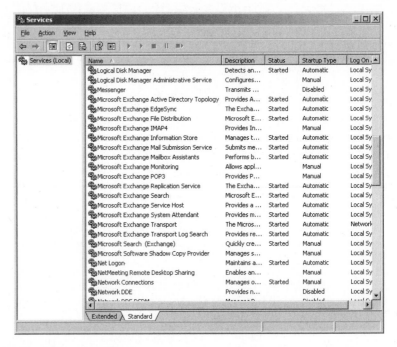

Databases and Database Sizing

Exchange 2007 includes a number of noteworthy improvements with respect to the Exchange mailbox and public folder databases. Although Exchange databases still use the Extensible Storage Engine (ESE), aka Jet database engine, rather than a SQL Server database, improvements allow greater scalability. The following are some of the changes that have been designed to improve scalability, improve performance, and make replication of data more feasible:

◆ The 64-bit version of the ESE database engine can access far more RAM for caching than previous versions.

◆ Each Exchange Server 2007 Enterprise Edition server supports up to 50 storage groups.

◆ Each Exchange Server 2007 Enterprise Edition server supports up to 50 databases.

◆ The database page size has been increased from 4KB (in previous editions) to 8KB in Exchange 2007 to improve read and write performance.

◆ Transaction log files are now 1MB in size rather than 5MB; this allows data to be replicated to a backup database location (in the case of LCR or CCR) much more quickly.

◆ The streaming database (STM) file found in previous versions of Exchange has been removed. Each Exchange database consists of a single EDB database file in which all content is stored.

I talked earlier about calculating the amount of disk space that you may require for Exchange Server 2007 mailbox servers. Chapter 1 reviewed the changing nature of e-mail and messaging technologies and emphasized that mail storage requirements are greater than ever. I always recommended planning for more disk space and e-mail capacity than you think you will require.

TABLE 4.9:   Exchange 2007 Components

SERVICE NAME/SHORT SERVICE NAME	EXECUTABLE NAME	FUNCTION
Microsoft Exchange Active Directory Topology /MSExchangeADTopology	`MSExchangeADT opologyService.exe`	Provides Exchange Server 2007 with Active Directory site, domain controller, and global catalog server information. This component is found on all Exchange 2007 server roles except the Edge Transport.
Microsoft Exchange ADAM/ADAM_MSExchange	`Dsamain.exe`	This is the ADAM instance that holds the Edge Transport server role's configuration, recipient information, safe sender lists, and blocked sender lists. This service is found only on the Edge Transport role.
Microsoft Exchange Anti-spam Update/MSExchange AntispamUpdate	`Microsoft.Exchange .AntispamUpdateSvc.exe`	This service provides updates for the content filter service. This service is found on the Edge Transport and Hub Transport server roles.
Microsoft Exchange Credential Service /EdgeCredentialSvc	`EdgeCredentialSvc.exe`	This service monitors credential changes for the ADAM database and updates the Edge Transport server. This service is found only on the Edge Transport server role.
Microsoft Exchange EdgeSync/ MSExchangeEdgeSync	`Microsoft.Exchange .EdgeSyncSvc.exe`	Handles synchronization of recipient and hub transport information to Edge Transport servers in the perimeter network. The EdgeSync process synchronizes to the Edge Transport server's ADAM database; the synchronization is a push synchronization from the Hub Transport role out to the Edge Transport server. This component is found on Exchange 2007 Hub Transport server roles.
Microsoft Exchange File Distribution/ MSExchangeFDS	`MSExchangeFDS.exe`	The File Distribution Service handles distribution of offline address books on Client Access servers and custom Unified Messaging prompts on UM servers. It is found on Exchange 2007 Client Access and Unified Messaging server roles.
Microsoft Exchange IMAP4/MSExchangeIMAP4	`Microsoft.Exc hange.Imap4Service.exe`	Provides IMAP4 client connectivity and is found on Exchange 2007 Client Access server roles. This service is set to manual by default and must be enabled to support IMAP4 clients.

TABLE 4.9: Exchange 2007 Components *(CONTINUED)*

SERVICE NAME/SHORT SERVICE NAME	EXECUTABLE NAME	FUNCTION
Microsoft Exchange Information Store/MSExchangeIS	Store.exe	The information store service runs the database engine and provides client access for MAPI clients as well as access to mailboxes for connections from Client Access and Hub Transport servers. This service is found only on Exchange 2007 servers with the Mailbox server role. This service also consumes the most RAM of any of the Exchange 2007 services.
Microsoft Exchange Mail Submission Service/MSExchange MailSubmission	MSExchangeMail-Submission.exe	Handles notifying Hub Transport servers that a message is waiting to be retrieved from a local database. This service attempts to distribute the message delivery load if multiple Hub Transport servers are found. This service is found on the Exchange 2007 Mailbox server role.
Microsoft Exchange Mailbox Assistants/MSExchange MailboxAssistants	Microsoft.Exchange .InfoWorker.Assistants .exe	The Mailbox Assistants service handles calendaring functionality such as Calendar Assistant, Resource Booking Assistant, Out-of-Office Assistant, and the Managed Folder Mailbox Assistant. This service is found only on Exchange 2007 Mailbox servers.
Microsoft Exchange Monitor-ing/MSExchangeMonitoring	Microsoft.Exchange .Monitoring.exe	Provides an interface for applications to use Exchange 2007 monitoring tasks. This service is found on all Exchange 2007 server roles.
Microsoft Exchange POP3/MSExchangePOP3	Microsoft.Exchange .Pop3Service.exe	Provides POP3 client connectivity and is found on Exchange 2007 Client Access server roles. This service is set to manual by default and must be enabled to support POP3 clients.
Microsoft Exchange Replication Service/MSExchangeRepl	Microsoft.Exchange .Cluster.ReplayService .exe	This service handles copying log files from their original location to the backup log location on Exchange 2007 Mailbox servers that have the local continuous replication or clustered continuous replication functions enabled. This service is found only on Exchange 2007 Mailbox server roles.

TABLE 4.9:   Exchange 2007 Components *(CONTINUED)*

SERVICE NAME/SHORT SERVICE NAME	EXECUTABLE NAME	FUNCTION
Microsoft Exchange Search Indexer/MSExchangeSearch	Microsoft.Exchange .Search.ExSearch.exe	The Microsoft Exchange Search Indexer provides content to the Microsoft Search (Exchange Server) service for full-text indexing. This service is found only on Mailbox server roles
Microsoft Exchange Service Host /MSExchangeServiceHost	Microsoft.Exchange .ServiceHost.exe	This service handles the configuration of RPC virtual directories and Registry information necessary to support Outlook Anywhere (RPC over HTTP). This service is found on Exchange Mailbox and Client Access server roles.
Microsoft Exchange Speech Engine/MSS	MSSService .SpeechService.exe	The Speech Engine service provides the speech processing capabilities that are used by Unified Messaging services. This service is found only on Unified Messaging server roles.
Microsoft Exchange System Attendant /MSExchangeSA	Mad.exe	This service provides monitoring and directory lookup services for Exchange server. This service is found only on Mailbox server roles.
Microsoft Exchange Transport/MSExchangeTransport	MSExchangeTransport .exe	This service provides the SMTP transport functions. Mail will not flow at all if this service is halted. This service is found on all Exchange 2007 Hub Transport and Edge Transport server roles.
Microsoft Exchange Transport Log Search/MSExchange TransportLogSearch	MSExchangeTransport LogSearch.exe	Provides the ability to search the Exchange message transport logs. This service is found on all Exchange 2007 Mailbox, Hub Transport, and Edge Transport server roles.
Microsoft Exchange Unified Messaging /MSExchangeUM	umservice.exe	The Unified Messaging service handles access to the user's mailbox via Outlook Voice Access, the creation of voicemail messages, and the creation of fax messages. This service is found only on the Unified Messaging server role.
Microsoft Search (Exchange)/ MSFTESQL-Exchange	Msftesql.exe	This Search service creates full-text indexes on mailbox content. This service is found only on the Exchange 2007 Mailbox server role.

TABLE 4.9: Exchange 2007 Components *(CONTINUED)*

SERVICE NAME/SHORT SERVICE NAME	EXECUTABLE NAME	FUNCTION
World Wide Web Publishing Service	svchost.exe/inetinfo	A component of Internet Information Services that is required on all Exchange 2007 Client Access server roles in order to provide access to web services. This service is required on Exchange 2007 Mailbox servers if you will be managing public folders using Exchange System Manager or PFDAVAdmin.

FIGURE 4.6
Exchange 2007 services in Task Manager

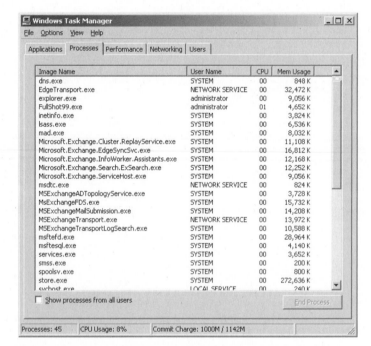

However, more e-mail storage means including in your Exchange server design a maximum size for each database. Why specify a maximum size for your database? As you saw earlier, specifying a maximum size gives you guidelines for distribution mailboxes and the maximum number of databases that your server must support. In general, there are a number of good reasons for limiting the maximum size of each database. Here are some thoughts and pointers on calculating maximum database size:

◆ Maximum database size when using streaming backups and restores should be around 50GB to 100GB.

◆ When using LCR as the primary database restoration mechanism, databases can be allowed to grow to 200GB.

♦ Always take into consideration the restoration time when calculating maximum database size and ensure that you can restore within a timeline specified by your service level agreement (SLA).

♦ Restoring from streaming tape backups can take significantly longer than restoring from backups on disk.

♦ Larger databases take longer for online maintenance procedures to run. Microsoft recommends online maintenance at least once every two weeks on each database for best performance.

One popular reason for limiting the size of a database or maximum mailbox sizes is the length of time it takes to restore a server. On one hand, this represents good planning, but often mail administrators wield that excuse like a sword in order to keep their user storage limits lower. An Exchange administrator commented once that "keeping mailboxes smaller is easier on us," meaning the IT department.

Storage limits and maximum mailbox sizes are all fine and good, but limits should not be set for the sake of IT. You should set limits that allow users to effectively do their jobs and to access the information they need to access, but you should also consider the needs of operations, archiving, and budgeting. Also keep in mind that the default mailbox limit for mailbox databases is 2GB unless you change it, so make sure when you create new mailboxes databases that you also configure the correct limits. See more about establishing limits in Chapter 10, "Imposing Limits."

Message Routing

In earlier versions of Exchange (2000 and 2003), if more than one physical or geographic location existed, the Exchange servers could be broken up based on their physical location. The architecture of message routing is based on routing groups. By placing Exchange servers in different routing groups, the administrator can control messaging traffic between those locations and can more accurately focus public folder connectivity by Outlook clients. In almost all situations, the servers located in routing groups correspond to the location of an Active Directory site, though not all Active Directory sites might actually have an Exchange server.

Exchange 2007 simplifies the management of the physical layout of Exchange by eliminating the need for routing groups and relying on the Active Directory site architecture instead. Servers with the Hub Transport role accept messages from Mailbox servers, determine the location of the destination mailbox database, and deliver the message to a Hub Transport server in the remote Active Directory site.

Message Routing and the Hub Transport Server

The Hub Transport server role is at the center of the message transport architecture. The Hub Transport server maintains Send and Receive connectors that are responsible for receiving mail from the Internet, sending mail to the Internet, sending mail to remote Hub Transport servers, and receiving mail from remote Hub Transport servers. All messages must be processed by the Hub Transport system regardless of whether they will be delivered to a local mailbox or a remote recipient.

In Exchange 2000/2003 there was the concept of SMTP virtual servers, which could either send or receive SMTP mail. In contrast, with Hub Transport, Send connectors are responsible for outbound SMTP mail only and Receive connectors are responsible for inbound mail only. One big advantage of this is separation of logging.

The message transport architecture and dependencies are illustrated in Figure 4.7.

FIGURE 4.7
Basics of the Hub
Transport architecture

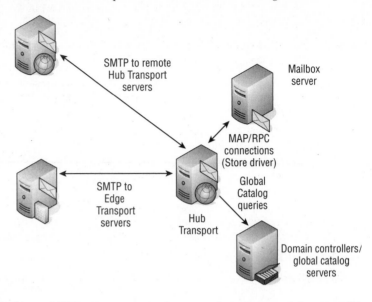

Messages enter the Exchange 2007 message transport system through one of three possible mechanisms:

◆ The Hub Transport via SMTP

◆ A Mailbox server's store driver via Remote Procedure Calls (RPCs)

◆ The file system's Pickup folder on the Hub Transport server

The Hub Transport relies on Active Directory for configuration, topology, and recipient information and thus must have access to domain controllers and global catalog servers.

Once a message is submitted to the Hub Transport system, it enters the message queuing system, where the message Categorizer reviews it and determines how to deliver it. There are five possible queues that can be found on a Hub Transport server:

◆ The *submission queue* is the queue in which messages are placed when they enter the Hub Transport server (via SMTP, store driver, or pickup folder). The categorizer processes the messages as they arrive in this queue. The submission queue is also called the categorizer queue or the submit queue.

◆ The *poison message queue* is the queue in which messages are placed if there is a problem that prevents the message from being categorized.

◆ The *unreachable domain queue* is the queue in which messages are placed if there is no route available.

◆ *Local delivery queues* are queues in which messages are placed if they are to be delivered to a Mailbox server in the same Active Directory site.

◆ *Remote delivery queues* are queues in which messages are placed to be delivered to remote Hub Transport servers or outside of the organization. The remote delivery queue is the only type of queue available on the Edge Transport server role.

The Categorizer component is the Hub Transport component that watches the submission queue. As messages arrive in the submission queue, the Categorizer picks them up and processes them. The following are some of the steps involved in message categorization:

◆ Expand any distribution lists, if applicable, by querying the global catalog.

◆ Resolve recipient addresses to determine which recipients are local, remote, or outside of the organization.

◆ Apply message transport rules to the message.

◆ Split the message into multiple parts if the message is going to local and remote recipients; this process is called bifurcation.

◆ Examine the message sender, recipients, header, body, and attachments and apply message transport rules that apply to the message.

◆ Convert the message to the appropriate message format (Summary-TNEF, MIME, or UUENCODE) depending on its destination.

◆ Determine the next "hop" for the message.

◆ Place the message in to appropriate local or remote delivery queue.

With a few exceptions, such as application transport rules, the Categorizer function has not changed from Exchange 2000/2003.

Message Transport Security

One of the intentions of the design of Exchange 2007 was to make messaging more secure. One of the outcomes of this was to ensure that message content is secured as it is being transmitted from one server to another. This includes authenticated connections and encrypting the data as it crosses the network. Figure 4.8 shows the possible places a message may be passed across the network and how protection is or may be implemented.

FIGURE 4.8
Security when messages are being transmitted

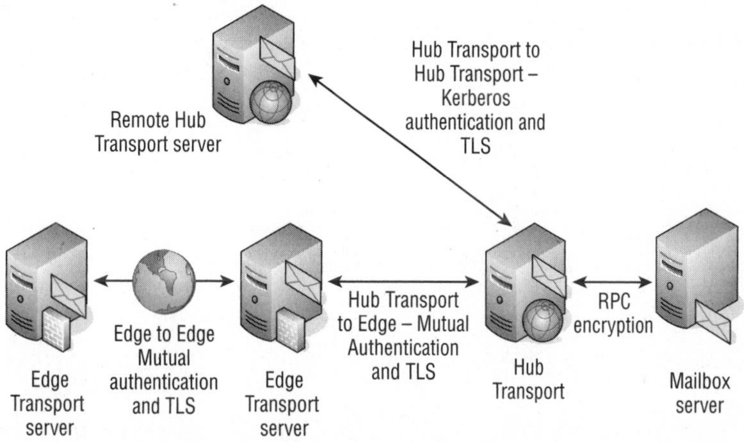

As messages are transmitted via MAPI over RPC between Mailbox servers and Hub Transport servers, RPC encryption is automatically used. When a message is transmitted from one Hub Transport server to another, the Hub Transport servers authenticate using Kerberos and the data stream is encrypted using Transport Layer Security (TLS). When messages are transmitted from a

Hub Transport server to an Edge Transport server, mutual authentication using certificates is used and messages can be encrypted using TLS. Optionally, an organization that is sending messages to another organization also using Edge Transport services can configure authenticated connections and TLS encryption to these remote organizations. Messaging security and Edge Transport are covered in more detail in Chapter 25, "Securing Exchange Server."

Inter Site Message Routing

In previous versions of Exchange, in order to deliver mail from one Exchange 2000/2003 routing group to another, a connector needed to be created (for example, Routing Group connector, SMTP connector, and X.400 connector). The Exchange 2007 equivalents of routing group connectors are SMTP Send and SMTP Receive connectors.

One feature that will surprise some Exchange 2000/2003 administrators is that, by default, Exchange 2007 Hub Transport servers will behave as if connectivity between them is a full mesh. In previous versions of Exchange, messages flowed only between Exchange servers with explicit routing group connectors.

Take, for example, the organization in Figure 4.9. This organization has four Active Directory sites. In three of them, there is a Mailbox server and a Hub Transport server.

FIGURE 4.9
Sample message routing architecture

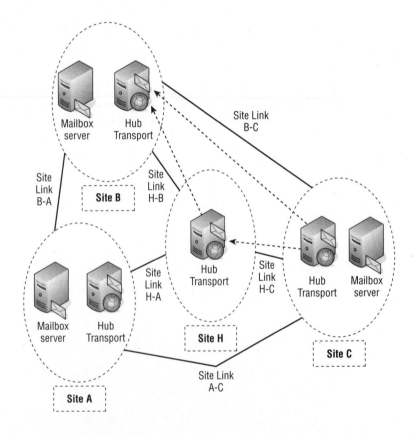

The Active Directory site link architecture defines the site links as shown in Table 4.10.

TABLE 4.10:   Sample Active Directory Site Links and Costs

LINK NAME	COST
Site Link H–A	1
Site Link H–B	1
Site Link H–C	2
Site Link A–C	100
Site Link A–B	100
Site Link B–C	100

Clearly, this Active Directory design intends for all replication to go through the "hub" site known as Site H. Thus, a logical assumption would be that messages would be routed using this site link cost architecture. However, if a message originates on a Mailbox server in Site C and is intended for a recipient in Site B, the Hub Transport server will always attempt to route the message directly first. If the direct path is not available, the message will be routed to the Hub Transport server in Site H. The site link costs are used to determine message routing paths only if the direct connection fails.

Summary

Microsoft Exchange Server 2007 continues to build on a solid history of messaging servers. Improvements in the architecture of Exchange 2007 allow for continued innovation, improvement, and scalability. The move to the 64-bit architecture is clearly needed to allow Exchange to be enhanced further and to reduce I/O requirements.

Server installation and configuration has been further enhanced and simplified by the introduction of server roles; the person who performs the Exchange Server installation chooses which components are necessary for a particular server's function.

Part 2

Installing, Configuring, and Migrating

In this part:

Chapter 5

Installing Exchange Server 2007

Now that you've had a chance to learn and absorb the theory behind the new Exchange 2007 architecture, you can get your hands dirty and get it installed in your organization.

In this chapter you learn to:

♦ Plan for installation

♦ Choose how to designate server roles

♦ Prepare your equipment

♦ Install Exchange Server 2007

♦ Perform post-installation tasks

Installation Overview

If you're familiar with Exchange 2003 or Exchange 2000, your first look at the Exchange 2007 installation process is going to be a mix of the familiar and the new. The look of the graphic-mode installer has completely changed; not only is it easier to navigate, but it actually gives you useful progress indicators as it works through its many complicated tasks and actions. This improvement alone is pretty good, but the ability to perform a full installation from the command line, while never leaving text mode, turns "pretty good" into "great."

Installing an Exchange 2007 server involves the following steps:

1. Choose your Exchange 2007 roles.

2. Prepare your Windows server.

3. Perform the installation, using either the graphic- or text-mode setup options.

4. Run through the post-installation checklists.

Listed out as a dry collection of steps, it sounds like a lot of work. It's actually pretty simple to do, and the new installation improvements allow you to automate a lot more of the work with a lot less effort than you could in previous versions of Exchange. Without further ado, let's get our hands dirty and get installing!

INSTALLING VERSUS UPGRADING

As you read through this chapter, you'll see that it presumes you're installing a brand-new Exchange 2007 organization rather than upgrading from an existing Exchange 2003 or Exchange 2000 organization. If you're looking to upgrade, you're going to want to read Chapter 6, "Upgrading to Exchange

Server 2007." Before you skip ahead, though, read through this chapter to master the mechanical steps of installing Exchange 2007. Chapter 6 doesn't cover them again but instead focuses on the specific issues you'll need to address in order to keep Exchange 2007 and your existing organization interoperating smoothly during your upgrade period.

Getting Started

Before we go any further, I think it is important to get a couple of things squared away. Microsoft has made some key improvements in both documentation and the installation process that you will want to know. This includes some improvements to the release notes, resources available to you, and suggestions for building a test lab.

Improvements to the Installation Process

Before you get the release-to-manufacturing (RTM or "gold disk") ready for installation, stop right in your tracks. As of this writing, Exchange Server 2007 Service Pack 1 has been released and a newer service pack may be available by the time you read this. Download the latest service pack and Exchange rollups — that is all you will need to install Exchange Server 2007.

But wait! What if you need Enterprise Edition instead of Standard Edition? It still does not matter! The actual "edition" that you are installing is based on the license key that you enter after the installation is complete. I cover that toward the end of this chapter.

So unlike previous versions of Exchange (or even most Microsoft products) where you install from the RTM CD (or DVD) and then apply the service pack, Exchange Server 2007 Service Pack 1 contains a complete set of installation binaries. Once you have installed Exchange Server 2007 from the Service Pack 1 installer, all you need is the most recent rollup fix for your particular version of Exchange.

Good Documentation: What a Concept!

The improvements in Exchange 2007 don't just stop at the technical. Shortly after the Exchange 2003 release, the folks on the Exchange product team realized that a lot of their customers needed the kind of documentation that only the product team could deliver and have since done their best to step up to the plate to deliver thorough, usable content that actually answers the questions and solves the problems faced by people just like you. By now, they've gotten it down to a fine art; as a result, the Exchange 2007 documentation is more complete and realistic than the documentation for any previous version of Exchange.

Books such as this can help fill in the gaps and give you a good objective view of how to use Exchange 2007. Vendor documentation (whether from Microsoft or someone else) tends to make assumptions about your environment that may not be valid in order to push you toward the most recently adopted set of best practices that may not have had time to filter out into the real world but have proven their worth. It may gloss over the pain points you're likely to hit even if you're following all of the official deployment advice. I, on the other hand, can tell you where those hidden assumptions are and how not meeting them will affect you. I can also explain the operations of Exchange so that you can judge whether a new best practice actually makes sense in your environment, and highlight where you're going to hit trouble even when you're doing everything right.

That said, the product documentation is still an invaluable reference that should be a core part of your Exchange toolkit. Best of all, the documentation is freely downloadable from the Microsoft website, and the installer gives you links directly to the applicable downloads, which Microsoft updates on a regular basis.

I recommend that you download the Exchange documentation, browse through it, and see what kind of material it covers. Note any topics that seem especially pertinent to your organization or to issues you think are likely to be a problem for you. Read through the sections that cover those topics and see whether they make sense; if they don't, put them aside for later. There will come a day when you will read back through those sections and suddenly realize that you understand what they are saying.

Are you back with me now? Great! It's time to sit down at (or connect to) your server and get busy installing Exchange 2007.

References and Resources

Before you start building the plan for your Exchange 2007 topology, you should be familiar with some resources that will impact your design and could alleviate a lot of stress down the road.

Exchange 2007 Release Notes   First and foremost, the Exchange 2007 Release Notes should make the top of your reading list (directly under this book). There you will find late-breaking caveats, bugs, and pointers from the Exchange development team that could greatly impact your migration day. You don't have to have the installation media in order to peruse the release notes. Just do a search for "Exchange 2007 Release Notes" on the Microsoft home page. Also keep in mind that support packs have their own sets of release notes that are required reading prior to applying the support packs. (I am assuming that you will be installing Exchange Server 2007 Service Pack 1 at a minimum.) You should read the release notes from the service pack as well.

READ THE RELEASE NOTES!

Even if you've decided you don't need to read the rest of the documentation, I urge you to at least read the single most critical piece of documentation: the release notes. You'll find them as a single HTML file in the installer directory, which will give you the location of the most current version of the release notes. These are required reading, because they'll tell you about any last-minute issues, workarounds, and bugs that may impact your deployment.

Microsoft Exchange Server TechCenter   The TechCenter online Exchange resource is dedicated to Exchange administrators looking for the latest documentation, downloads, and news without a lot of marketing fluff. You can find the TechCenter at http://technet.microsoft.com/en-us/exchange.

Exchange 2007 Planning & Architecture Guide   This guide is one of the more helpful pieces of documentation that Microsoft has put together on Exchange 2007. You can find it on the TechCenter here: www.microsoft.com/technet/prodtechnol/exchange/e2k7help/.

Microsoft Exchange Team blog   In recent years, Microsoft amended its Internet communication strategy to allow product teams to publish technical content in addition to sales and marketing materials. This significant paradigm shift has led to official Microsoft "blogs" that are managed by the designers, developers, and testers of its products. The Microsoft Exchange Team blog is full of fascinating tips, insights, and answers. It is updated on a regular basis. You can check out the blog at http://msexchangeteam.com/

Exchange newsgroups Lastly, if you are having a weird problem or seeing an error message you cannot figure out, consider that someone else might have seen that error in the past or had that same problem. Before you place your first call for paid tech support, it might be worth your while to check out the Exchange newsgroups that can be found on almost every search engine on the planet. My favorite entry point into newsgroups at the moment is `http://groups.google.com`.

Creating a Test Lab

If you have never installed Exchange Server 2007, I recommend performing a couple of "dry runs" so that you can get the kinks worked out of your process. I can't remember the number of times in the past that I have gotten a server or application configured and running, then started doing some testing, and decided that I could have done something better another way.

In this chapter, I am making the following assumptions:

◆ You are performing a "from scratch" installation.

◆ You have no Exchange servers in your organization.

◆ No updates have been made to your Active Directory, either from installing Exchange 2007 or from installing an earlier version of Exchange.

When building a "from scratch" lab, here are some things that you should be planning for:

◆ Isolate the test lab from your existing Active Directory; it should use its own Active Directory.
  Using a backup copy of your Active Directory in the test lab will allow you to test Exchange 2007 changes against your existing directory.

◆ Install all server roles that you will use in production and confirm that you can make each role behave as expected.

◆ Install all third-party software (backup software, message hygiene, software, archival software, and so on).

◆ Perform any customizations that you will perform to your production organization.

◆ If possible, duplicate (on a smaller scale) your storage and backup architecture.

◆ Test as much of the functionality as you possibly can, including basic messaging functions, Outlook 2007 Autodiscover, Outlook Web Access, continuous replication, clustering failovers, and so on.
  If you want to simulate a user load or simulate database activity on your new servers, you can use Microsoft tools such as Jetstress, the Exchange Load Generator, and Exchange Server Stress and Performance tool; you can find these at `http://technet.microsoft.com/en-us/exchange/bb330849.aspx`.

If you are nearing your starting point for your Exchange 2007 deployment, you may actually have the hardware that you will be using in production. This can provide you with a good opportunity for "burn in" of the new hardware, provided you are planning to completely wipe out the lab configuration (operating system and all disks) prior to installing them in production. But keep in mind that many organizations keep their test labs around after they deploy so that they can test changes, service packs, fixes, and new software additions.

SECURING YOUR TEST NETWORK

Isolate the network on which you run your test lab and use different usernames and passwords for admin accounts. This will help prevent "test" changes from accidentally being implemented in production.

As important as building a test lab is for ensuring a successful new deployment of Exchange 2007, it is even more critical in a migration. This is especially true in an intra-organization migration. I will come back and discuss test labs more in Chapter 6, "Upgrading to Exchange Server 2007," as well as discussing virtualization and imaging technologies.

Installation Prerequisites and Setting Goals

Do you have your server hardware racked and ready to go, and are you ready for installation? You can probably run into the computer room, insert the CD-ROM (well, DVD) in the server, and start installing. But before you do that, I hope I can save you some time and share with you some important prerequisites that you should complete (or at least know about) prior to getting started.

There is really nothing more annoying than running the Exchange Server setup program and finding out that some prerequisite has not been met. Some prerequisites are pretty easy to take care of, but others might take days or weeks. If you know about them, though, these are things that you take care of long before you actually install Exchange 2007.

Active Directory Requirements

One of the first things you need to plan to have taken care of is getting Active Directory squared away and ready to support Exchange Server 2007. One important factor that many people have discovered is that Exchange Server 2007 does not play nicely with Windows 2000 domain controllers; in fact, if the setup program even finds any in the same Active Directory site, it will fail. So you need to get Active Directory up to a minimum level.

Note that this list is my own list of recommendations. The official prerequisites may not be as stringent. Trust me though, these will get you through the migration with fewer problems and ensure that both Exchange and Active Directory are operating more cleanly. Some of these are things that I have found out the hard way, too:

♦ All domain controllers should be running Windows 2003 Service Pack 1 or later.

♦ All domains should be at Windows Server 2003 domain functional level.

♦ The forest should be at Windows Server 2003 forest functional level.

♦ If you have more than one physical location with domain controllers, define Active Directory sites and site links for replication.

♦ If you have more than one Active Directory site, define IP subnets and ensure that they are associated with the correct Active Directory site. If Exchange 2007 servers are on IP subnets that are not properly defined, you may have message routing problems.

♦ The Exchange organization must be set to native mode and all traces of Exchange 5.5 (site replication service or Active Directory Connector connection agreements) must be removed.

♦ Exchange 2000/2003 SMTP virtual servers should never have smart hosts configured. If you require smart host forwarding, you should be using an SMTP connector.

Preparing Active Directory Ahead of Time

Later in this chapter, I discuss using the Exchange 2007 setup.exe program options to customize your installation. Just like previous versions of Exchange Server, the setup.exe program allows you to perform the initial preparation of Active Directory (such as extending the schema and creating the necessary configuration containers) ahead of time. For some organizations, you may want to do this days or weeks before you actually install the first Exchange 2007 server.

BE SURE TO USE THE LATEST SETUP PROGRAM

You should use the setup.exe program from the latest Exchange 2007 service pack to prepare your Active Directory.

If you are running the Exchange 2007 preparation options from a Windows Server 2008, the server must have the Active Directory management tools installed. The quickest and easiest way to do this is to run this command:

```
ServerManagerCmd -i RSAT-ADDS
```

Several of the following preparation tasks assign permissions to forest-wide or domain objects. If you would like a detailed explanation of these permissions, visit the following website: http://technet.microsoft.com/en-us/library/bb310770(EXCHG.80).aspx

PREPARING A FOREST THAT ALREADY SUPPORTS EXCHANGE 2000/2003

If you are currently running Exchange 2000/2003, the first thing that you should do is to run setup.exe and prepare the forest to support the necessary permission interoperability between Exchange 2000/2003 and Exchange Server 2007. This also ensures that the Exchange 2000/2003 Recipient Update Service (RUS) continues to work properly after the forest is prepared for Exchange Server 2007. This is done with the /PrepareLegacyExchangePermissions switch and this must be done in each Active Directory domain that has Exchange-enabled recipients.

To prepare *all* domains in the forest, run the following command using a user account that is a member of the Enterprise Admins group:

```
setup.exe /PrepareLegacyExchangePermissions
```

If you want to run this command on a domain-by-domain basis, you can specify the following command and include the fully qualified domain name of the target domain. Here is an example that prepares the domain corp.volcano.com:

```
setup.exe /PrepareLegacyExchangePermissions:corp.volcano.com
```

For more information on this option, see the following web page: http://technet.microsoft.com/en-us/library/aa997914(EXCHG.80).aspx

EXTENDING THE SCHEMA

Exchange 2007 requires the Active Directory schema to have additional attributes and objects that even Exchange 2003 did not have. Therefore, the forest must be prepared. With Exchange 2000/2003, you did this with the /forestprep setup.exe option, but Exchange 2007 has a new setup option called /PrepareSchema. To extend the Active Directory schema, use a user account that is a member of the Schema Admins and Enterprise Admins Active Directory groups and run the following command:

```
setup.exe /PrepareSchema
```

Note that when you run this command, the Active Directory domain controller that holds the schema master role must be accessible. Ideally, you should run this from the same Active Directory site where the schema master resides.

Once the schema prep has completed, you will need to give the schema changes a chance to propagate through the forest's domain controllers. This may take anywhere from a few minutes to several days depending on your Active Directory architecture.

EXAMINING SCHEMA CHANGES

Curious about what changes are being made to the schema? Take a look at the LDF files in the \setup\data folder in the Exchange 2007 service pack installation files.

Visit the following link for more information about what the schema prep process is actually doing: http://technet.microsoft.com/en-us/library/aa997467(EXCHG.80).aspx

PREPARING THE ACTIVE DIRECTORY

After the schema is extended and replicated, the next step is to prepare the Active Directory with the necessary security groups and containers to support Exchange Server 2007. This is accomplished with the setup switch /prepareAD. This switch actually does quite a few different things to your Active Directory. These tasks include but are not limited to the following:

♦ Checks to see if the schema has been upgraded or extended to support Exchange Server 2007.

♦ Checks for the existence of the Exchange organization name container; if it does not exist, prompts for the organization name.

♦ Creates the necessary containers and objects in the Active Directory database configuration partition.

♦ Creates the Exchange Organization Administrators, Exchange Recipient Administrators, Exchange Servers, Exchange View-Only Administrators, Exchange Public Folder Administrators, and ExchangeLegacyInterop universal security groups in the Microsoft Exchange Security Groups organizational unit (OU) of the forest root domain.

♦ Adds the extended rights that are required for Exchange 2007.

♦ Creates an Exchange 2007–only administrative group called Exchange Administrative Group (FYDIBOHF23SPDLT) and the Exchange 2007–only routing group Exchange Routing Group (DWBGZMFD01QNBJR). These groups should never be renamed, nor should they ever contain Exchange 2000/2003 servers.

♦ Performs the /PrepareDomain steps for the domain in which the command was run.

Microsoft recommends that you run the /PrepareAD option from within the same Active Directory site as the Active Directory schema master. You must do this with a user account that is a member of Enterprise Admins. To prepare the Active Directory, run the following command:

```
setup.exe /PrepareAD
```

If you would like to read a more in-depth explanation of what the /PrepareAD process does, visit this web page: http://technet.microsoft.com/en-us/library/bb125224(EXCHG.80).aspx

PREPARING EACH DOMAIN

The final Active Directory preparation step is to prepare each Active Directory domain in the forest (at least the domains in which there will be Exchange 2007 servers or mail-enabled recipients) to support Exchange 2007.

If you have only one Active Directory domain in your forest, this step is unnecessary: the tasks to perform this have already been run by the /PrepareAD setup option. The Prepare AD process assigns the Exchange Servers and the Exchange Recipient Administrators universal security groups the required permissions to the domain.

You must be a member of the domain's Domain Admins group in order to run this command. Here is an example of the command necessary to prepare the corp.volcano.com domain:

```
setup.exe /PrepareDomain:corp.volcano.com
```

UPDATE BEFORE PREPARING DOMAINS

Make sure that all schema and Active Directory updates have replicated to the domain controllers in the specified domain prior to running /PrepareDomain.

If you would like to prepare all the domains in the forest at one time, you can run the following command (again, with an account that is a member of the Enterprise Admins group):

```
setup.exe /PrepareAllDomains
```

Selecting Server Roles

One of the most dramatic improvements you will immediately recognize when installing Exchange 2007 for the first time is the ability to select which "roles" you would like to install on your Exchange server. Microsoft first introduced the concept of roles in Exchange 2000 by allowing administrators to define whether Exchange was installed as a front-end or back-end server.

Exchange 2000/2003 front-end servers were intended to accept client requests and proxy them to the client's native back-end server for processing. Although this topology helps offload some of the back-end server's burden, it still requires a full installation of Exchange on both types of servers, leaving no granular control over which Exchange services are installed. With Exchange 2007 you now have the ability to separate the functions of your Exchange server, which allows your organization to dramatically increase Exchange's overall security, efficiency, and reliability. There are five roles you can choose to install on an Exchange 2007 server:

- Edge Transport role
- Client Access role

◆ Hub Transport role

◆ Mailbox role

◆ Unified Messaging role

Before you can reasonably expect to install Exchange 2007 on a server, you need to know what that server is going to be used for. As you remember from the section "Server Roles" in Chapter 3, "Introducing Exchange Server 2007," Exchange 2007 no longer installs the same set of binaries and services to every Exchange server (requiring you to then remove and shut down unnecessary features and services). Instead, it defines five separate roles: Edge Transport, Hub Transport, Client Access, Mailbox, and Unified Messaging.

Some of these roles are required in any organization, whereas others are optional. Others are required depending on how you plan to place your servers. Some roles can be co-located on the same physical server, whereas others must be stand-alone. You must factor a number of program dependencies, deployment best practices, and economic-driven compromises into your Exchange 2007 design. It can be overwhelming to untangle this web on your own.

REQUIRED EXCHANGE SERVER ROLES

If I have made most of the server roles sound optional, then I apologize. Sure, the Mailbox server role could be installed without any of the other server roles, but you would be left with an Exchange system that was relatively non-functional.

At a minimum, the following Exchange server roles are required for any Exchange 2007 organization to be functional.

MAILBOX SERVER ROLE

The Mailbox server role supports direct connectivity of Outlook MAPI clients for mailbox data and public folder data. A Mailbox server is required for e-mail data storage, public folders, and to act as a target for standby continuous replication.

HUB TRANSPORT SERVER ROLE

The Hub Transport server is responsible for all mail delivery within a single server, within an Active Directory site, between Exchange Hub Transport servers in different Active Directory sites, to external SMTP organizations, and from external SMTP organizations. This role is required. No e-mail gets delivered without the Hub Transport.

CLIENT ACCESS SERVER ROLE

The Client Access server role (or just CAS) is responsible for handling user access for Outlook Web Access, ActiveSync, POP3, and IMAP4 clients. The CAS server also handles services such as Autodiscover, Offline Address Book distribution (for Outlook 2007), free/busy information (for OWA and Outlook 2007), and other web services. Though some might argue that this is an optional server role, if you have Outlook 2007 clients or require other web services, it is not optional.

Instead of leaving you to guess, I offer the following discussions to help you determine which roles you need and where you need to place them. Although I can't account for every factor, I can help you sort out the ones that are driven by Exchange 2007 requirements and which ones are under your control.

SIZE OF USER BASE AFFECTS SERVER ROLE DEPLOYMENT

One of the key factors in determining which roles can be co-located, how many servers you need with a given role, and where to locate those servers is how many users you plan to support.

Edge Transport

If you're looking at using the Edge Transport role, you have a pretty easy deployment decision: it must be installed on its own physical server and cannot be co-located with any other role. Contrary to rumors floating around the Microsoft technical community, you will not be able to co-locate the Edge Transport role and Microsoft ISA Server 2006 on the same physical server as Exchange — at least not without pulling weird tricks using virtual servers, which would be less than secure and possibly take you outside the boundaries of Microsoft-supported configurations.

Why can't you install the Edge Transport role and ISA 2006 on the same server? Very simply, ISA 2006 cannot be installed on any 64-bit version of Windows Server — and if you remember, you can run your production Exchange 2007 servers only on x64 Windows Server 2003 or later. Microsoft may address this problem in future service packs, but at least for now, this is how it is.

32-BIT EXCHANGE 2007 VIOLATES LICENSING REQUIREMENTS

Don't try to fudge it by using the 32-bit version of Exchange 2007 on your Edge Transport server. That violates the licensing restrictions for Exchange and could end up costing you far more than buying a separate machine for ISA 2006 would. If that's not enough to dissuade you, the 32-bit version is a 120-day trial version; you'd have to rebuild your Edge Transport servers every four months. You also lose the automatic anti-spam definition updates (which aren't provided to 32-bit machines).

The real question is: Do you need to deploy the Edge Transport role? You are not required to have an Edge Transport server in your organization in order to successfully use Exchange 2007, but it offers a lot of advantages that the third-party anti-spam solutions don't. Remember that the Edge Transport role is specifically designed to be installed in your perimeter network, with no requirements for connectivity to Active Directory. In fact, Microsoft strongly recommends that you not join your Edge Transport servers to the same Active Directory forest (or forests, in a multi-forest organization) that your internal Exchange servers are joined to.

You can join the Edge Transport server to a management forest in your perimeter network or leave it as a stand-alone workgroup member and still get all of the new functionality without compromising your inner network security or driving your firewall administrator mad. The new Edge Subscription feature allows your Edge Transport servers to receive all of the necessary updates they need to fully protect your organization.

ABOUT THE PERIMETER NETWORK

The term *perimeter network* is Microsoft's preferred terminology for the network concept of the *DMZ*: a separate network segment that allows you to provide a degree of isolation between your protected internal servers and your servers (such as web servers or mail gateways) that need to accept incoming connections from untrusted hosts on the Internet. The two terms mean the same thing, but Microsoft is phasing out the use of DMZ in its documentation.

With legacy versions of Exchange, if you placed the servers directly in your perimeter network, you'd find that you had stepped directly into a nightmare of firewall configuration. Prior to 2007, all Exchange 2000 and 2003 servers were required to be full member servers in an Active Directory forest; in order to get them to work correctly in the perimeter, you had to poke so many holes in the firewall for the various protocols that you ended up with no real increase in protection. Though this was the recommended deployment for Exchange 2000 front-end servers for a time, Microsoft eventually started to recommend using a reverse proxy solution such as ISA Server in the perimeter network.

EDGE TRANSPORT DOES NOT PROVIDE REVERSE PROXY

The Edge Transport role is solely an SMTP message hygiene system; it does not provide any type of HTTP reverse proxy solution.

With the Edge Transport role, Exchange 2007 solves this problem the same way that it's solved by other edge mail router solutions, such as specialized messaging appliances or software mail applications such as Postfix, Sendmail, and Exim. These solutions place the Edge Transport server in the perimeter network without requiring it to have full access to Active Directory on the interior network. Like the other solutions, Edge is designed to do two things:

◆ Route SMTP traffic between your trusted Exchange servers and untrusted Internet hosts, using a best-practice perimeter network placement with full integration into your Exchange organization.

◆ Provide a "safe" platform for performing message hygiene functions (anti-spam, antivirus, and other forms of content inspection) in the perimeter network before your full Exchange servers (and Windows domain controllers) have to handle the extra load caused by unwanted message traffic. Edge Transport also sanitizes messages going out from your organization to the Internet so that you're not contributing pollution to the Internet.

An Edge server's main advantage is that it offers most, if not all, of the same message hygiene features you can find on other solutions — if not out of the box, then at least via add-ins that you can purchase or download from third-party vendors (or even develop yourself). And it does this while offering an unparalleled level of integration with your Exchange organization:

◆ Although the Edge server should never be joined to the same Active Directory forest as your Exchange organization, it can be joined to a separate management forest in your perimeter network if your perimeter is large enough to incur the overhead of an additional Active Directory deployment to secure and manage.

◆ The Edge Transport role requires a Hub Transport instance in your organization, both for SMTP routing and optionally for Edge Subscription configuration. This doesn't require additional hardware or installations because you have to have at least one Hub Transport instance anyway, but it may affect placement of your Hub Transport instances and Edge Transport servers to ensure good network connectivity between them.

◆ Using the Edge Subscription feature, your Hub Transport instances can be easily configured to automatically update your Edge Transport servers with the specific subset of data they need to effectively process incoming mail. Because this is a push process from Hub Transport instances to your Edge Transport servers, you don't need to open additional holes in your firewall (unlike mail router solutions that offer Exchange "integration" through LDAP lookups back into your domain controllers). Even though this step is not done as part of the install, you should consider it to be a required deployment step because you lose a lot of functionality (including the ability to manage your entire organization from inside the firewall) by not doing it.

◆ The Edge Transport server can be managed from within your organization using the Exchange Management Shell and the Exchange Management Console, just as you manage any other Exchange server. Again, this simplifies management and makes it easier to script bulk operations (although many of the common types of activities you might want to script are already automatically updated using Edge Subscriptions).

◆ The Edge Transport server comes with a host of existing anti-spam components out of the box. Though some of these components can also be deployed on a Hub Transport instance, many can't. See Chapter 21, "Delivering E-mail," for more details.

◆ An Edge Transport server easily integrates with the Microsoft Forefront Security for Exchange Server, a multi-engine malware scanner developed from the Antigen line of products that Microsoft acquired from Sybari.

◆ The Exchange 2007 organization can collect some of the per-user settings from user mailboxes, such as safe sender lists, and propagate them out to the Edge Transport server. This allows the Edge Transport server to intelligently accept and deny incoming messages based on who they're addressed to without requiring any additional work from the users or the Exchange administrators — a feature I have not seen in any other message gateway solution.

EDGE TRANSPORT WORKS WITH SMTP TRAFFIC ONLY

Do remember that the Edge Transport role is designed only for SMTP traffic. It does not handle any other protocols, such as client access protocols (for example, HTTP, POP3, IMAP, or MAPI). The Edge Transport role is purely for SMTP connections between your organization and mail servers out on the Internet. Also, Edge Transport cannot authenticate remote SMTP clients such as POP3 or IMAP4 users.

Client Access

If you only ever plan to have MAPI users connect to your Exchange mailboxes, you don't need to have a Client Access server in your Exchange organization.

WHY CLIENT ACCESS IS ABBREVIATED CAS

The Microsoft documentation refers to the Client Access role by the abbreviation CAS. How come the abbreviation for the Client Access role isn't CA? Easy: that acronym is already used to signify *certificate authority*, a key component of a public-key infrastructure. If you're using SSL or S/MIME, then you already deal with certificate authorities. Because it's common to deal with digital certificates and certificate authorities when configuring and managing Client Access servers, Microsoft avoided potential confusion by not reusing the acronym (in this case).

These days, however, it's the rare organization that offers only MAPI access to mailboxes. Although Outlook is the only full MAPI client that accesses Exchange mailboxes using MAPI Remote Procedure Calls (RPCs) protocol, it's not convenient or possible to use Outlook all the time:

◆ Microsoft's Entourage client for Mac OS X uses WebDAV (HTTP/HTTPS), as does Novell's Evolution client for Linux.

◆ Almost all other mail clients offer at least IMAP, POP3, or HTTP/HTTPS. Some of the more common mail clients out there are Apple Mail, Eudora, Mozilla Thunderbird; there are a vast number of others in use. Some clients will also offer NNTP access to Exchange public folders.

◆ Outlook Anywhere (the new name for RPC over HTTPS) uses HTTP or HTTPS.

◆ Exchange ActiveSync uses HTTP/HTTPS.

◆ Of course, Outlook Web Access uses HTTP/HTTPS.

NNTP No Longer Supported

Exchange 2007 no longer offers Network News Transport Protocol (NNTP) access, even if you implement public folders. You must use an Exchange 2000 or 2003 server in your organization to provide NNTP support if you wish to continue offering it. (NNTP access is outside the scope of this book.)

Clearly, if you have any need to offer HTTP, IMAP, or POP3 access to your users, you're going to need the Client Access role in your organization. Lest you be tempted to think of it as "just" a renamed front-end Exchange server, remember that the Client Access role does not offer the capability to handle SMTP. In the Exchange 2003 world, a front-end server still had the SMTP service running by default and would frequently be used as an SMTP bridgehead as well as a front-end server — to the point that many people became confused as to what exactly a front-end server was supposed to do! With Exchange 2007, the separation is very clear: the Client Access role handles client access protocols, and the Hub Transport role handles SMTP. If you need to put these roles onto separate machines, you can; if you need to combine them, you can.

Now you just need to know how many Client Access servers you need and where you need to locate them. At a minimum, keep the following rules of thumb in mind:

◆ You need at least one Client Access role in every site and domain in which you have Exchange Mailbox servers.

◆ The Client Access role needs to have good network connectivity (good available bandwidth and low latency, usually a 100Mbps Ethernet connection or better) with the Mailbox servers it serves.

◆ The Client Access role is required in order to allow any HTTP access to mailboxes, whether from internal clients or from outside of your organization.

◆ You may wish to have one set of Client Access servers handle external connections and another to service internal clients. The POP3 and IMAP protocols allow mailbox access only; they do not provide any way for the client to submit messages back to the server. These clients must use SMTP. As a result, you may wish to co-locate the Client Access and Hub Transport roles onto servers you use to handle external client access.

DON'T SET UP THE CAS ROLE IN THE PERIMETER NETWORK

Although you might think you can place the Client Access role in your perimeter network to deal with traffic coming from the Internet, suddenly you're back in the middle of the firewall configuration nightmare of trying to keep a member server in the perimeter. Instead, you should keep the Client Access role in your protected network and place an ISA 2006 server (or a Blue Coat appliance, a Linux Squid proxy server, or some other equivalent reverse proxy solution) in the perimeter to accept outside connections. Your firewall administrators will thank you. Also remember that with Exchange 2007, Microsoft does not support placing the Client Access role in the perimeter network. Getting this configuration to work securely means not only that you have a lot of extra work to do to secure your servers and connections, but also that you are risking going without full Microsoft product support when problems develop.

Hub Transport

Because all messages in an Exchange organization must travel through a server running the Hub Transport role, you must have at least one Hub Transport role in your organization. That's the easy part. Unless you have a small organization, though, you may want to have more than one Hub Transport role to avoid a single point of weakness.

HUB TRANSPORT HELPS WITH REGULATORY COMPLIANCE

If you think it's inefficient for Exchange 2007 to require all messages to be handled by the Hub Transport role, you need to consider the growing role of regulatory and policy compliance. This new architecture allows Exchange to easily inspect every single message and apply policies uniformly. See Chapter 15, "Managing Messages in Transit," for more details on the new transport rule and policy features.

Depending on the level of traffic that your Mailbox servers and network have to deal with, you may want to co-locate your Hub Transport and Mailbox roles on the same physical servers. Then again, you may want to have multiple Mailbox servers in each site, with only a pair of Hub Transport servers to provide the necessary message routing for the site. Regardless of where the roles are located, the Hub Transport and Mailbox roles communicate using MAPI RPCs.

As long as you meet the necessary minimum placement guidelines and take care to provide enough Hub Transport capacity close enough to your Mailbox servers to keep message traffic from getting caught in bottlenecks, you have an amazing degree of flexibility in how you actually deploy Hub Transport roles. Exchange 2007 servers running the Mailbox role will automatically discover the Hub Transport roles in your organization and attempt to use the ones in the same Active Directory site. If there are multiple Hub Transport instances in the site, the Mailbox servers will intelligently load-balance traffic among them without any extra effort on your part. If one of your Hub Transport instances becomes inaccessible, the Mailbox servers will automatically switch to another Hub Transport instance.

When deciding which physical servers to place the Hub Transport role on, keep in mind the following conditions:

◆ You need at least one Hub Transport role in every site and domain in which you have the Mailbox role. Servers running the Mailbox role can only connect to Hub Transport roles in the same site. If all of the Hub Transport instances in a site go down, Mailbox servers in that site will not be able to fail over to using a Hub Transport role in a neighboring site and all message traffic in the affected site will come to a grinding halt.

◆ If you co-locate the Hub Transport role with the Mailbox role, that Mailbox instance will always try to use the local Hub Transport instance before talking to other Hub Transport instances in the site. But this breaks the natural load-balancing behavior I mentioned previously. Load-balancing is a good reason to separate the Hub Transport and Mailbox roles in larger organizations or sites. Remember that you can't put the Hub Transport role on a cluster, so if you're going to deploy clustered Mailbox servers, you have to put the Hub Transport role on a separate server.

◆ The Hub Transport role needs to have good network connectivity with the Mailbox instances it serves.

◆ At least one Hub Transport instance is required to allow any SMTP access to your organization, whether from non-Exchange mail machines inside of your organization, from Edge Transport servers, or from some other mail routing solution that brings external mail into your organization.

◆ The Edge Transport role requires a Hub Transport instance in your organization, both for SMTP routing and optionally for Edge Subscription configuration. This really isn't a problem because you have to have at least one Hub Transport instance, but this will affect your design since you will want the Edge Transport and Hub Transport servers to have good network connectivity between them.

DON'T PUT HUB TRANSPORT IN THE PERIMETER NETWORK

If you're thinking about putting a Hub Transport instance in your perimeter network, don't. As with the Client Access role, you will go through a lot of effort to make it work, complicate your firewall configuration, and end up with an unsupported Exchange configuration. Use the Edge Transport role (recommended) or some other mail gateway solution instead.

Mailbox

Strictly speaking, you aren't required to have a single Mailbox server role in your organization. Of course, the resulting organization can have no mailboxes and is pretty darn pointless. Mailbox servers are the heart and soul of Exchange; as a result, you will probably spend more time installing and configuring the Mailbox role than any other.

Users have come to depend on the ubiquitous and near-instantaneous transmission of e-mail. Ten years ago, it was not uncommon to send an e-mail and know that it would be 10 to 15 minutes at a minimum before it was spooled off of the local mail server and out to the recipient. Today, that kind of delay is considered to be unacceptable unless there are special concerns regarding limited bandwidth or Internet connectivity. Even then, these types of concerns are considered the exception to the rule rather than the norm.

Modern e-mail users will start calling the help desk, or badgering the mail administrators, if they aren't receiving a steady stream of mail throughout the day. Imagine for a moment the reaction these same users are likely to have if they cannot access their Mailbox servers. Cached copies of their mailboxes in Outlook aren't going to cut it; the users are going to riot. It's not surprising, therefore, that a lot of money and time is spent ensuring the high availability of Mailbox servers. Because Outlook MAPI clients connect directly to the user's Mailbox server, the user is often the first to know if something's not right on the server.

In Exchange 2007, Microsoft tries to provide for high levels of availability for all of the server roles. The Mailbox role, however, is the only one that offers options for traditional clustering solutions, now called single copy clusters (SCCs). It also offers two new availability options: clustered continuous replication (CCR) and local continuous replication (LCR). These availability options are designed to keep the mailbox data available even if the server hardware fails, and are explained in more detail in Chapter 17, "Reliability and Availability 101." Because traditional clustering is only supported on the Mailbox role, you cannot co-locate other roles on a clustered mailbox server.

It should not be a surprise that the storage requirements for the Mailbox server role are potentially far more enormous than for the other roles. As a result, the disk configuration for your Mailbox instances is far more important than for any other role. Exchange 2000 and Exchange 2003 lived and died around their disk I/O requirements; Exchange 2007 still requires you to carefully plan, design, and test your disk subsystem, even with the I/O performance improvements provided by the 64-bit architecture.

When designing your Mailbox server roles, here are the relevant guidelines to keep in mind:

◆ All other factors being equal, the closer your users are to their Mailbox servers, the better. This is not to downplay the impact of Outlook cached mode and server consolidation, however, because most of the time not all other factors are equal.

◆ Other factors affecting Mailbox server deployment include but by no means are limited to the following:

  ◆ Overhead cost of the server hardware

  ◆ Level of hardware redundancy (the failure of a single power supply or disk controller can really ruin your day)

  ◆ Per-server power consumption

  ◆ Server room's cooling capacity

  ◆ Cost of disks

  ◆ Effects on backup and restore policies and SLAs

  ◆ Cost of training and maintaining administrative personnel

  ◆ Cost of software licensing

  ◆ Physical shelving and racking requirements

◆ If you're planning on doing single copy clustering, your Mailbox server hardware must be on Microsoft's Cluster Hardware Compatibility List. If you're going to do clustered continuous replication, however, your hardware only has to be on the Windows Hardware Compatibility List, which can be significantly cheaper.

◆ The Hub Transport role needs to have good network connectivity with the Mailbox instances it serves.

◆ If you co-locate the Hub Transport role with the Mailbox server role, that Mailbox role instance will always try to use the local Hub Transport instance before talking to other Hub Transport instances in the site. But this breaks the natural load-balancing behavior I mentioned previously. Load-balancing is a good reason to separate the Hub Transport and Mailbox server roles in larger organizations or sites. Remember that you can't put the Hub Transport server role on a cluster, so if you're going to deploy clustered Mailbox servers, you have to put the Hub Transport role on a separate server.

◆ The Mailbox role no longer uses the SMTP protocol to communicate with other Exchange servers in the organization. They use RPC to communicate with other roles in their site; all communications with servers in other sites take place through intermediary Hub Transport instances.

Unified Messaging

I'm not going to spend a lot of time talking about the Unified Messaging role because it requires an advanced set of equipment and skills to properly implement. If you're planning to deploy this role in your organization, you will require the services of experienced telephony personnel, whether in-house or contractors.

I've heard Microsoft personnel say that you can co-locate the Unified Messaging role on the same physical server as other roles as long as your organization is very small and there is plenty of extra capacity on your server. The catch though, is, determining what they mean by "very small." I have seen no specific guidance for determining how to size a Unified Messaging server and how to tell when it can safely coexist with some other server roles.

SEPARATE SERVER FOR UNIFIED MESSAGING RECOMMENDED

Unless you are hosting a handful of users — 30 or more — on a single Exchange 2007 server that is running other roles, I highly recommend that you consider buying a separate server to use for Unified Messaging. If e-mail is mission critical, voicemail is often as critical or more so. The cost of buying separate hardware and software licenses will more than pay for itself in the trouble you save by not having your single server overloaded on a constant basis, dropping both e-mail and voicemail. If you can't afford that cost, you probably need to rethink whether your organization will truly derive any benefit from the features the Unified Messaging role provides.

Combining Roles

There is no single, hard-and-fast rule that you can use to determine whether you can put all roles and all users on a single physical Exchange 2007 server. But here are some rough recommendations:

◆ If your organization is relatively small — say, you have less than a 15GB Exchange 2000 or 2003 Information Store and fewer than 200 users — you may opt to install all of your roles on a single powerful server.

◆ If you have fewer than 1,000 light users or 500 medium users, you may install all roles on a single powerful server.

◆ If you have only a few hundred users and no requirements for high availability or fault tolerance, a single server may be just fine.

However, there are some performance and security advantages to installing roles on multiple servers and caveats you should be aware of when co-locating the Mailbox role with any others:

◆ Though it can be co-located on the same server as the Mailbox role, the Unified Messaging role requires a great deal of resources. For this reason, I recommend using no more than 25 Unified Messaging mailboxes (enough for a small pilot program) on a server hosting both the Unified Messaging and Mailbox roles.

◆ The Mailbox role is the only one that can be clustered using Exchange's native clustering technologies. For this reason, if you plan on clustering your Exchange Mailbox roles, you cannot co-locate any other roles on the server hosting your Mailbox role.

EXCHANGE 2007 CLUSTERING SOLUTIONS ARE MORE AFFORDABLE

Those organizations that have found clustering to be cost or resource prohibitive in the past may find they're taking a second look at clustering with Exchange 2007. In the past, traditional clustering services were expensive because they required hardware on the Microsoft Cluster Hardware Compatibility List and Enterprise versions of Windows Server and Exchange. This type of clustering is still supported but is now called single copy clustering (SCC). Exchange 2007 introduced three more types of improved availability technologies: clustered continuous replication (CCR), local continuous replication (LCR), and standby continuous replication (SCR), each of which is discussed in further detail in Chapter 17. If you like, skip ahead and decide if these new clustering technologies are right for you, but be sure to come back!

◆ If a Hub Transport role is co-located on the same Exchange server as the Mailbox role, it will always use the locally installed Hub Transport service and only look for additional Hub Transport roles if the local Hub Transport service is not functioning. If you have multiple servers hosting the Hub Transport role and one of them fails, the Mailbox role will automatically fail over to all remaining servers hosting the Hub Transport role in the site.

◆ The Hub Transport role(s) in your Exchange organization are responsible for enforcing transport rules and journaling policies. As you build policies to meet regulatory requirements, you may find that a single Hub Transport role isn't sufficient to process all the mail in your organization.

◆ Because the Client Access role does not host SMTP services, you may find it advantageous to co-locate it on a server running the Hub Transport role so you can limit the number of hosts that have to be NATed (Network Address Translation) through your firewall.

◆ The Edge Transport Server role cannot be co-located with any other role.

Management Tools

There is a not-so-hidden sixth role in Exchange 2007: the Management Tools role, consisting of the Exchange Management Shell (EMS) and the Exchange Management Console (EMC). This role is the sole exception to the "no 32-bit Exchange 2007 on your production network" rule. You are allowed to install the 32-bit version of the Exchange management tools on your administrative workstation if you're still running the 32-bit version of Windows XP. In fact, Microsoft has provided the 32-bit version of the Exchange 2007 management tools as a separate download from its website. Visit the following URL for more information: `http://technet.microsoft.com/en-us/exchange/bb330843.aspx?wt.svl=2007resources`

Note that Microsoft does not support installing the Exchange management tools on the RTM version of Windows Vista. You must be using Windows Vista Service Pack 1. See Microsoft Knowledge Base article 931903 for more information.

Recommended Order of Installation

Now that you've decided which roles you're installing on your servers, in which order are you going to install them? If you're deploying a combined function server, you don't have to answer this question. When you have multiple physical servers, though, you need to figure out in what order you're going to deploy them. Which servers you deploy first is determined by what roles they have installed. The official Microsoft-recommended order is as follows:

1. Active Directory preparation

2. Edge Transport (optional)

3. Client Access

4. Hub Transport

5. Mailbox

6. Unified Messaging (optional)

Remember that *before* is a relative term; if you're combining the Client Access, Hub Transport, and Mailbox roles on one server, you're following the outlined order, even if it's the first Exchange server in the organization.

This installation order is good, but it is aimed at the organization upgrading from Exchange 2003 or 2000 to Exchange 2007. I really don't think it's the right fit for someone who is installing a brand-new Exchange 2007 organization. I recommend holding off on your Edge installation at least until after you've got a Hub Transport server in place, and possibly after you've got Mailbox servers up and running.

Why would I think that? There are a several reasons:

◆ The first is philosophical. Microsoft's order works from the outside layers of an organization into the crunchy nougat center. The preferred order of deployment for just about any software is to first establish the core functionality (in this case, the ability of your users to e-mail each other within your organization) and then go after the extras like Outlook Web Access, ActiveSync, Unified Messaging, and Edge Transport.

◆ If you recall, the Edge Transport role requires a Hub Transport role to talk to, both for SMTP and for the Edge Subscription feature to allow centralized provisioning and configuration. You aren't required to configure Edge Subscription, but then you lose nice functionality such as recipient filtering and per-user blocked/allowed sender lists — and you have to manage your Edge Transport server manually. Given my preferences, I'd rather install the Edge Transport server and be able to immediately configure the Edge Subscription as opposed to having to come back to it later.

◆ Finally, I tend to think that anyone who is installing Windows Server 2007 from scratch (as opposed to upgrading from a previous version of Exchange) is probably migrating from some other messaging system, whatever it may be. Sure, there are going to be new companies just getting started or existing companies transitioning from hosted e-mail scenarios, but the bulk of these "new" installations are already going to have an existing e-mail service. These companies probably already have some sort of messaging gateway or message hygiene system in place, and unless that's the major pain point driving their migration to Exchange 2007, they probably want to concentrate on getting users shifted over rather than fiddling with an Edge Transport server. Their existing spam appliance or Linux mail gateway is doing a fine enough job for the time being.

There's nothing wrong with Microsoft's recommended order of installation, and you won't be doing a bad thing by following it. Just be aware that it is a recommendation, not a rule; the installer won't refuse to install the HT role until it detects a CAS in the organization. If you have a good reason for altering the order to meet the needs of your organization, then by all means do it.

The two installation order guidelines that you definitely should follow are these:

◆ Install a Hub Transport instance in the site before you install your Mailbox instances. (You won't be able to test mail flow without a working Hub Transport instance in the site.)

◆ Wait to install the Unified Messaging role until everything else is installed and mostly working. (Unified Messaging is complicated enough to be worth giving it all your attention.)

Preparing the Windows Server

Before you actually install Exchange 2007 on your server, you have to make sure the chosen server is ready. I already covered the hardware and software requirements in previous chapters, but I'll quickly recap them here with an emphasis on the practical tasks ahead of you.

You'll need to consider the following aspects of your server before beginning the installation process:

◆ Operating system requirements

◆ Memory configuration

◆ Disk configuration

◆ Exchange prerequisites

Let's examine these in more detail.

Windows Server Basic Requirements

The following Windows operating system requirements must be met before beginning Exchange 2007 installation. Let's start with a few generic requirements first and then move on into requirements for Windows Server 2003 versus Windows Server 2008. Take a look at the following list and hopefully this will save you some time and keep you from spinning your wheels:

◆ Exchange Server 2007 is supported only on x64-based versions of Windows Server. The x86 version is provided only for your lab and testing purposes. Exchange Server does not run on Windows servers using the IA64 processor.

◆ Exchange Server 2007 does not run on the Web Server or Datacenter editions of Windows Server 2003.

◆ Exchange Server 2007 does not run on Windows Server 2008 server core installations.

◆ Unlike legacy versions of Exchange Server, the SMTP and NNTP components are not required (and, in fact, NNTP is not supported on Exchange 2007).

◆ Ensure that any other applications running on the server are meant for the same platform. Do not mix 32-bit and 64-bit applications on production Exchange 2007 servers; use only 64-bit add-ons and plug-ins. Remove unnecessary software.

◆ You should at least disable any server-level antivirus software on the server. I recommend that you remove it entirely; it competes with Exchange for memory and CPU, slows down disk access, and provides questionable value. If you must have antivirus software on the server, make sure it is configured to ignore all directories that Exchange uses — the binary install directory tree, transaction logs, mailbox databases, and queue databases.

◆ Disable any anti-spyware or anti-malware software you may have running, such as Windows Defender.

WINDOWS SERVER 2003 REQUIREMENTS

If you are planning to use Windows Server 2003, here are a few tips and requirements that you need to be aware of:

◆ Production servers should run Windows Server 2003 x64 Standard Edition or Enterprise Edition, or Windows Server 2003 x64 R2 Standard Edition or Enterprise Edition. Service Pack 2 with all updates is strongly recommended.

◆ Mailbox servers that will be clustered running on SCC or CCR clusters must run the Enterprise Edition of Windows Server 2003. Service Pack 1 is required, but I strongly recommend Service Pack 2.

◆ If the server you are installing will be hosting the Client Access server role, ensure that you have installed the IIS World Wide Web Service and the ASP.NET components. No other IIS components are required.

A few add-ons will be required depending on what is already installed on the Windows 2003 server:

Management Console Update   The Exchange Server 2007 management tools all require the Microsoft Management Console (MMC) v3.0 update for Windows Server 2003. If you are using Windows Server 2003 Service Pack 2, this update is included. Otherwise, you will need to download the updated MMC and install it prior to installing Exchange Server 2007. Visit the following web page for more information on this update: `http://support.microsoft.com/?kbid=907265`

Microsoft .NET Framework 2.0   Exchange Server 2007 and the management components require that Microsoft .NET Framework v2.0 be installed on Windows Server 2003. I recommend loading the latest .NET Framework package available. You can find this at the following web page: `http://go.microsoft.com/fwlink/?LinkId=107400`

Windows PowerShell v1.0   Exchange Server 2007 requires that Windows PowerShell v1.0 be installed on Windows Server 2003 regardless of which Windows service pack you are using. You can find the Windows PowerShell installer at the following URL: `http://support.microsoft.com/?kbid=926139`

After you have all of the required updates for Windows Server 2003 installed, I strongly recommend that you run another Microsoft Update pass to make sure you have the fixes and updates for everything you have installed.

DON'T UPGRADE POWERSHELL ON EXCHANGE SERVERS UNLESS INSTRUCTED

Resist the temptation to upgrade PowerShell on your Exchange servers (to get the benefits of these future upgrades) unless the release notes specifically say it is compatible with your deployed version of Exchange 2007, or unless you are instructed to upgrade by a future Exchange 2007 update. PowerShell is completely entwined with Exchange 2007 and an untested upgrade could break not only Exchange Server, but the Exchange installer as well.

MEETING WINDOWS SERVER 2008 REQUIREMENTS

Are you ready to take the plunge with Windows Server 2008? Many organizations are reluctant to deploy too many new technologies at the same time, and I frequently agree with this decision. However, if you are migrating from Exchange Server 2003 to Exchange Server 2007 and you will be able to keep Exchange Server 2003 in production during your pilot testing, this might be a good time to upgrade the operating system as well.

I'll be the first to admit that I am very weak on Windows Server 2008, though I worked with it quite a bit during the betas and I have deployed a number of Windows 2008 servers and Exchange Server 2007 running on Windows 2008. There are still the few sneaky things that are just different enough that it keeps me searching for a few minutes. All in all though, I am very enthusiastic about Windows Server 2008 and don't see any major roadblocks for most organizations.

Exchange Server 2007 Service Pack 1 requires one of the following x64 editions of Windows Server 2008:

◆ Windows Server 2008 Standard

◆ Windows Server 2008 Enterprise

◆ Windows Server 2008 Datacenter

When installing Exchange Server 2007 on Windows Server 2008, ensure that you are not using just the server core components and that you are using Exchange Server 2007 Service Pack 1.

WINDOWS SERVER 2003 OR WINDOWS SERVER 2008

If you are planning to use Windows Server 2008 in the reasonably near future (six months or so), consider deploying Windows Server 2008 sooner. There are a number of reasons that you may want to just go ahead and get it out of the way. Probably the most important of these is that you can't perform an in-place upgrade on a Windows Server 2003 with Exchange Server 2007; you must install a new operating system on a new server, then install Exchange, and then move the roles (or mailboxes) to the new server. To avoid disruption like this in the future, you may want to go ahead and deploy Windows Server 2008 now. See the following URL for more information: `http://msexchangeteam` `.com/archive/2007/10/04/447188.aspx`

When Windows Server 2008 is installed, only a minimum number of features and server roles are installed and configured. After you install the basic Windows Server operating system, you will need to then install the additional Windows Server 2008 roles and features. I have assembled a list of these in Table 5.1 along with the Exchange Server 2007 role the component is required for the ServerManagerCmd option name, and if it is considered a Windows Server 2008 role or feature.

TABLE 5.1: Windows 2008 Components Required for Exchange Server 2007

WINDOWS 2008 COMPONENT	EXCHANGE REQUIREMENT	ROLE OR FEATURE	SHORT NAME FOR SERVERMANAGERCMD
Active Directory Domain Services Tools	All roles	Feature	RSAT-ADDS
.NET Framework 3.0	All roles	Feature	PowerShell
RPC over HTTP proxy	CAS	Role	RPC-over-HTTP-proxy
Web Server	CAS, Mailbox	Role	Web-Server
Web Server ISAP extensions	CAS, Mailbox	Role	Web-ISAPI-Ext
Web Server Metabase	CAS, Mailbox	Role	Web-Metabase
Web Server legacy management console	CAS, Mailbox	Role	Web-Lgcy-Mgmt-Console
Web Server Basic Authentication	CAS, Mailbox	Role	Web-Basic-Auth
Web Server Digest Authentication	CAS	Role	Web-Digest-Auth
Web Server Windows Authentication	CAS, Mailbox	Role	Web-Windows-Auth
Web Server Dynamic Compression	CAS	Role	Web-Dyn-Compression
Active Directory Lightweight Directory Services	Edge	Role	ADLDS
Failover Clustering	Clustered mailbox server	Feature	Failover-Clustering
Desktop Experience	UM	Feature	Desktop-Experience

Some of the features or roles shown in Table 5.1 are installed using the Server Manager's Roles or Features option, whereas others are enabled once you have installed the feature. For example, let's say that I am going to install the Windows PowerShell feature. I would need to run the Server

Manager console (click Start ➤ Administrative Tools Server Manager) and then click the Add Features link on the right-hand side of the details pane of the console.

When I click Add Features, this launches the Select Features Wizard shown in Figure 5.1. I can scroll down and select the Windows PowerShell feature. Depending on the feature that I select, such as the Remote Admin tools, the wizard may need to install additional dependency components.

FIGURE 5.1
Using the Select Features Wizard to add a new feature

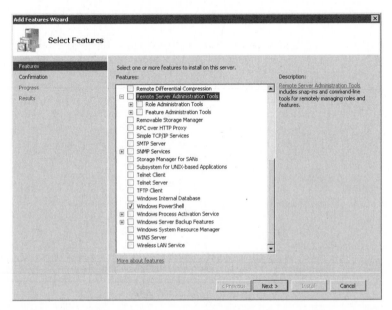

If you are getting to know Windows Server 2008, you may have already found the ServerManagerCmd program. This very useful tool allows you to install Windows Server 2008 roles and features from the command prompt. You just need to know the feature or role name. For example, if I wanted to install the IIS 7.0 web server, I would need to know its short name, `Web-Server`.

If you want to see a list of all the features and commands that you can install from the ServerManagerCmd program, at the command prompt, type the following command:

```
ServerManagerCmd -Query
```

This will generate a list that will show you the installed roles and features.

The first thing you need to install is the Active Directory Domain Services Tools (RSAT-ADDS). After you install that feature, you will need to reboot the server; you cannot proceed until you do so. Type this command:

```
ServerManagerCmd -Install RSAT-ADDS
```

Reboot the computer and log back on, because you have a few more services you need to install. At the command prompt, run the following ServerManagerCmd commands to install the additional components. (You do not have to reboot until all the commands have been run.) The following commands would be used if you were installing a combined function server:

```
ServerManagerCmd -Install PowerShell
ServerManagerCmd -Install Web-Server
```

```
ServerManagerCmd -Install Web-ISAPI-Ext
ServerManagerCmd -Install Web-Metabase
ServerManagerCmd -Install Web-Lgcy-Mgmt-Console
ServerManagerCmd -Install Web-Basic-Auth
ServerManagerCmd -Install Web-Digest-Auth
ServerManagerCmd -Install Web-Windows-Auth
ServerManagerCmd -Install Web-Dyn-Compression
```

Once these commands have been run, the server is now ready for Exchange Server 2007 to be installed.

Memory Configuration

The nice thing about running 64-bit Windows is that you don't have to worry about inserting arcane switches into your `boot.ini` configuration file, but memory configuration considerations do need to be addressed before beginning Exchange 2007 installation.

Specifically, ensure that you have the proper amount of RAM for your server's intended use and load. For Mailbox servers, the current official sizing guideline is to have at least 2GB base memory plus an additional 5MB per mailbox — though I recommend starting at 3GB to 4GB of base memory This ensures that you will have enough memory to cache the most frequently accessed items for all users on the server and get the full benefit of the switch to 64 bits.

FIND MORE RECOMMENDATIONS IN THE *PLANNING AND ARCHITECTURE* GUIDE

Because Microsoft will be updating the Exchange 2007 documentation on a regular basis, be sure to download and review the current specific recommendations made in the *Planning and Architecture* guide. This guide is available from the Microsoft Exchange 2007 TechNet website: www.microsoft .com/technet/prodtechnol/exchange/e2k7help/

Disk Configuration

The following disk configuration considerations should be addressed before beginning Exchange 2007 installation:

- All disk volumes used for Exchange must be NTFS formatted. No exceptions!

- Ensure that you have enough free disk space:

    - The system volume requires 200MB. This is above and beyond any necessary space for logs and program files (if you install Exchange on the system volume).

    - The system volume should allow Windows to create a page file that can hold a memory dump. This is the amount of physical RAM plus 100MB.

    - The disk volume you install Exchange on requires at least 1.2GB for the binaries.

    - If this server will hold the Unified Messaging role, allocate 500MB-plus for each Unified Messaging language pack that will be installed.

- Transaction log files should be on a separate set of physical disks (spindles) from their corresponding Exchange database files.

In Exchange 2007, the SMTP queue folders have been replaced by the queue database, which is an ESE database just like the message databases. As a result, you may need to provide extra spindles for the queue database and transaction logs on busy Edge Transport and Hub Transport servers.

◆ Allow for at least seven to ten days of transaction logs per storage group. One rule of thumb is 5GB of logs per day per 1,000 mailboxes.

◆ Allow for at least 10 to 15 percent white space estimates in the maximum size of each of your database files.

◆ Allow for 10 to 15 percent deleted item and deleted mailbox retention space in each mailbox database.

◆ LCR replica databases and transaction logs should be on separate physical disks from the originals.

◆ Leave sufficient free space on database disks to make an extra copy of your largest database without running out of space, such as when you're performing backups, recovering from backups, or performing troubleshooting and offline maintenance. One rule of thumb is 110 percent of the largest database you will support.

◆ Plan for full-text indexing to use around 10 percent of the total size of the mailbox database.

◆ Faster disks are always better than slower disks. The performance delta between 7,200RPM disks and 15,000RPM disks isn't even worth writing about.

◆ Try to use more reliable server-oriented disk technologies for your direct-attached storage, such as SAS and Ultra-SCSI over SATA or EIDE.

◆ Cap your maximum individual mailbox database size to allow you to back up and restore each database within the time limit specified by your service level agreement (SLA).

◆ Unlike with Exchange 2003, plan on creating one mailbox database per storage group. This improves your caching and gives you a separate set of transaction logs for each database, which means each database can truly be backed up (and restored) independently of the rest. If you plan on implementing SCR, CCR, or LCR, this is also a requirement. I recommend that you create additional databases in a storage group only when you've used up all of your available storage groups. Note, however, that this will increase the number of spindles you require to maintain proper I/O and offset the savings you gain from Exchange 2007's architecture.

DATABASE AND STORAGE GROUP LIMITS

Keep in mind the number of databases and storage groups you can have for your edition of Exchange 2007. Standard Edition restricts you to a maximum of five storage groups or databases, whereas Enterprise Edition gives you up to 50. So in Standard Edition, you could have a single storage group with five databases, two storage groups with some combination of five databases between them, or (best) five separate storage groups each with a single database.

Installing Exchange Server 2007

The time has come. You get to install Exchange 2007. But now you have to decide: graphic mode or text mode?

Graphic Installer

Most Exchange administrators are used to GUI setup wizards, and the Exchange 2007 installer (imaginatively named `setup.exe`) will be familiar territory, even if it has received a face-lift. When you run `setup.exe` without any command-line switches, you automatically start the installer as shown in Figure 5.2.

FIGURE 5.2
The Exchange 2007 setup GUI

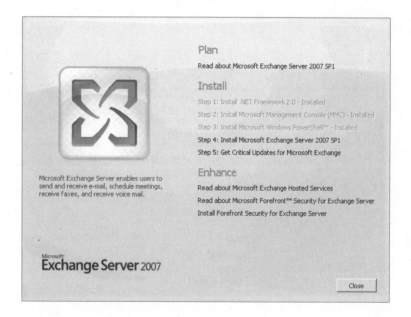

Notice in Figure 5.2 that the first three steps are already grayed out; this means that they have been completed and do not need to be performed.

When you select option 4 to install Exchange, the first screen you will see is the Introduction screen that welcomes you to the setup program and extols the virtues of Exchange Server 2007. Once you click Next, you will be taken into a typical setup process, including the display of the end user license agreement (EULA.) You must click the radio button next to I Accept The Terms In The License Agreement and click Next to proceed.

The next screen is the Error Reporting screen; from here you can specify whether this Exchange server is allowed to automatically send error reports to Microsoft. Though this might be a really helpful feature and may even sometimes help *you* get to the bottom of a problem, you should check to make sure it is okay to send crash dumps and error reports from your servers out to Microsoft. I recommend selecting No if you are not sure. Click Next to proceed to the Installation Type page of the installation wizard.

ABOUT THE EXCHANGE 2007 LICENSE

One thing you might notice is that the installer does not ask for a product key. When you install Exchange 2007, you have 30 days to enter a valid license key using Exchange Management Shell or the Exchange Management Console. The product key determines the actual edition of Exchange Server 2007 (Standard or Enterprise).

On the Installation Type screen, you will be asked whether you want a typical installation or a custom installation, as shown in Figure 5.3. The typical installation is suitable for a small, one-server Exchange organization; if you want to control which roles are placed on the server, you should select the custom installation.

FIGURE 5.3
Exchange 2007 setup options

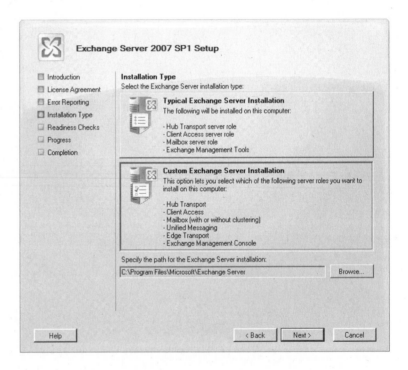

The Typical Exchange Server Installation selection on the Installation Type screen will automatically install a combined function server that supports the Mailbox, Hub Transport, and Client Access server roles. I always select Custom Exchange Server Installation just so I can see what is so customizable. Of course, if you require a more specialized installation you will also need to select the custom option.

If you are like me and selected the Custom Exchange Server Installation option, there's actually not a whole lot to customize: you are given a list of check boxes to select which roles you want to install, as show in Figure 5.4. Notice that some of them are mutually exclusive; if you check any role other than Edge Transport, the Edge Transport role will be grayed out and vice versa.

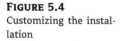

FIGURE 5.4
Customizing the installation

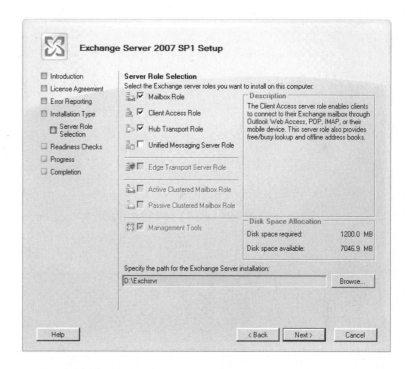

At this point, depending on what tasks you've already completed in your Exchange organization, you may be asked for further information:

◆ If this is the first Exchange server in the organization, you may be asked to provide the Exchange organization name.

◆ If this is the first Mailbox server in the organization, you will be asked if you will be supporting legacy clients (Outlook 2003 and earlier). If you select Yes, a public folder database is created.

◆ If setup detects an Exchange 2000/2003 organization and this is the first Exchange 2007 Hub Transport instance, you will be asked to select which existing Exchange 2003 SMTP bridgehead to use as your legacy routing server. This creates the necessary routing group connectors to ensure connectivity with the Exchange 2003 servers, which are in separate administrative groups and routing groups.

◆ If this is the first Exchange 2007 Mailbox instance in the organization, you are asked if you want to support legacy Outlook clients. If you choose not to support Outlook 2003 and previous, Exchange will not install a public folder database on the Mailbox server.

The decision to support legacy Outlook versions is not irreversible. You can manually create a public folder database and make the other minor changes necessary after installation has been completed. Finally, Exchange setup will perform the various tasks to complete installation. If you have the necessary privileges and setup does not detect the Exchange 2007 extensions to Active Directory, it will automatically perform the steps to configure Active Directory appropriately.

Otherwise it will fail with an error and you will have to rerun the installation using an account with the proper privileges.

Setup keeps track of the status of its various tasks and provides a detailed report of its progress. Figure 5.5 shows you all of the steps from a complete Exchange 2007 SP1 installation. Once you select Finish, setup will give you the option of immediately launching the EMC.

FIGURE 5.5

A successful Exchange 2007 installation

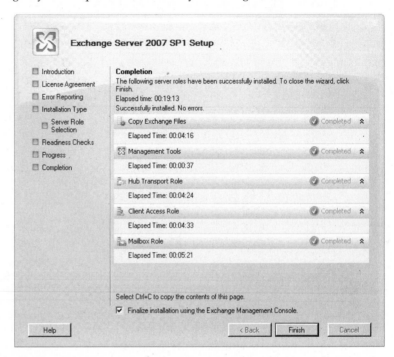

Command-Line Installer

For the first time, Exchange administrators finally have a first-class text-mode installer that can be used to completely install an Exchange organization without ever once kicking off a GUI or wizard. In fact, no matter whether you use setup in graphical or text mode, it will install over a special text-mode version of the installer exsetup that you can later use to modify the configuration of the server (such as adding or removing roles).

INSTALLING FOR THE FIRST TIME

When you initially install Exchange 2007 on a server, you need to run setup from the directory where you have the installation files. Here's an example of how easy it is to install a new Mailbox server instance into an existing Exchange 2007 organization:

```
setup /m:install /r:mb
Welcome to Microsoft Exchange Server 2007 Unattended Setup
Preparing Exchange Setup
    Copying Setup Files
    ........................ COMPLETED
```

```
The following Server Roles will be installed
    Management Tools
    Mailbox Role
Performing Microsoft Exchange Server Prerequisite Check
    Mailbox Role Checks
    ......................... COMPLETED
Configuring Microsoft Exchange Server
    Copying Exchange Files
    ......................... COMPLETED
    Mailbox Role
    ......................... COMPLETED
The Microsoft Exchange Server setup operation completed
    successfully.
```

That was almost understandable, wasn't it? Now, start thinking about how convenient it would be to install 5 (or 10, or 20, or more) Exchange 2007 servers into your organization using this method.

I'll go into more detail about the various options and switches you can give to setup in just a moment.

USING exsetup

In the previous examples, one of the tasks the Exchange installer performs is "copying Exchange files." Exchange is copying the necessary source files to the server's drive so that if you later decide you want to add a new role (or remove an existing one), you can do so from the local machine without requiring access to the installation media or a network share. After Exchange is installed, you now have a special copy of the installer, called exsetup.exe.

Other than the name, exsetup works just like setup; the list of setup options I go into later work the same for both setup and exsetup.

By default, exsetup is not placed in your PATH environment variable. It is located in the \bin subdirectory of the folder Exchange was installed to.

Because it is an executable, you can run it from the Start ➤ Run command, from cmd.exe, or from EMS. Here's an example of using exsetup to remove all installed roles from a server:

```
C:\Program Files\Microsoft\Exchange Server\Bin>exsetup
/mode:uninstall

Welcome to Microsoft Exchange Server 2007 Unattended Setup
The following Server Roles will be removed
        Hub Transport Role
        Mailbox Role
        Management Tools

Performing Microsoft Exchange Server Prerequisite Check

        Hub Transport Role Checks ...................... COMPLETED
        Mailbox Role Checks ...................... COMPLETED

Configuring Microsoft Exchange Server
```

```
       Hub Transport Server Role ........................ COMPLETED
       Mailbox Role ........................ COMPLETED
       Removing Exchange Files ........................ COMPLETED
```

The Microsoft Exchange Server setup operation completed
    successfully.

It's just as easy as installing!

WHY USE THE GUI?

One advantage that graphic-mode setup gives you is that if you're just trying to get Exchange installed
with minimal intervention, setup will mask a lot of the complexity for you. For example, if it determines that you haven't done the necessary Active Directory preparation, it will attempt to do it for
you. Though this may be nice for smaller organizations, the reality in larger organizations is that these
automatic steps may not be all you need to fully prepare your environment. By using text-mode setup
for these one-time options, you can take precisely the actions you want taken, and in the order and at
the time you want them taken.

SETUP OPTIONS

Both setup and exsetup look easy in the previous examples, but of course with an application as
complicated as Exchange 2007, there are always a few wrinkles that may keep things from being
as simple as we'd like. Let's take a closer look at the options available to us.

You can always see the complete set of setup and exsetup options by typing **setup /help** or
exsetup /help at the command prompt. Figure 5.6 shows an example of using the command line
to get exsetup help.

FIGURE 5.6
Getting help from
exsetup

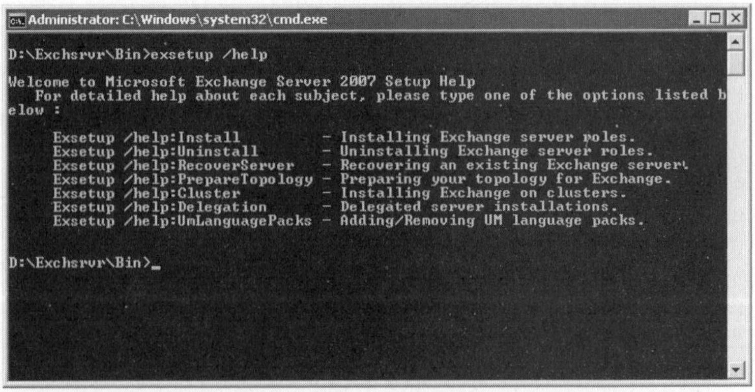

As you can see in Figure 5.6, more detailed help is available on each of the major setup
categories such as installation, removing exchange (Uninstall), performing disaster recovery
(RecoverServer), preparing the Active Directory topology (PrepareTopology), cluster setup,
delegated server installations (Delegation), and installing Unified Messaging language packs
(UmLanguagePacks).

Preparing Topology

Though we talked about this a bit previously in this chapter, here are once again the parameters that are used when manually preparing the organization for Exchange 2007:

/PrepareLegacyExchangePermissions or /pl When installing Exchange 2007 into an existing Exchange 2000/2003 organization, this performs the necessary permissions for coexistence.

/PrepareSchema or /ps This extends the Active Directory schema in the forest with the necessary Exchange 2007 additions.

/PrepareAD or /p This option is a useful shortcut for single-domain forests; it prepares Active Directory for Exchange 2007 by performing the /PrepareSchema option on the forest and /PrepareDomain on the local domain.

/PrepareDomain or /pd This parameter prepares the local domain for the Exchange 2007 by creating the necessary objects.

/PrepareDomain:<*domain FQDN*> or /pd:<*domain FQDN*> This parameter prepares the specified domain for the Exchange installation. This is useful for preparing specific domains in multi-domain Active Directory forests when not all domains need to be prepared.

/PrepareAllDomains or /pad This parameter prepares all domains in the forest for the Exchange installation.

Install and Uninstall

You've already seen examples of the install and uninstall modes. When you use these modes, the following switches are required. When multiple forms are listed, you can use any of them:

/mode or /m The /mode switch specifies the operation to perform: install, uninstall, or upgrade. Install is the default option.

/roles, /role or /r The /role switch specifies which server roles to install or uninstall. You can specify these roles or their abbreviations with the /role setup switch:

```
HubTransport, HT or H
ClientAccess, CA or C
Mailbox, MB or M
UnifiedMessaging, UM or U
EdgeTransport, ET or E
ManagementTools, MT or T
```

The following parameters are one-time options that are only required at specific points in the installation process:

/DoNotStartTransport Prevents the Edge Transport Service from being started during setup on Hub Transport and Edge Transport instances.

/EnableLegacyOutlook Specifies that legacy Outlook clients can connect to the Exchange 2007 servers. This parameter can only be specified during the first Exchange 2007 Mailbox role installation to an organization.

/LegacyRoutingServer When installing the first Hub Transport instance into an existing Exchange 2000/2003 organization, this allows you to specify which existing SMTP bridgehead server to route messages to (I talk more about this in Chapter 6, "Upgrading to Exchange Server 2007" and in Chapter 21, "Delivering E-mail").

/OrganizationName or /on   If the organization has not already been created, you must use the /OrganizationName option to specify the name of the Exchange organization.

The following advanced parameters provide extra control over specific role installs:

/AdamLdapPort   Tells setup to configure the Edge Active Directory Application Mode (ADAM) instance to use the specified port for LDAP connections.

/AdamSslPort   Tells setup to configure the Edge ADAM instance to use the specified port for SSL connections.

/AnswerFile or /af   Tells setup to use a pre-prepared answer file that contains advanced parameters to be used. The format for the answer file is Key = Value (see the setup help text for more details).

/DisableErrorReporting   I don't know why you'd want to use this, but if you want to disable error reporting, this is your option.

/NoSelfSignedCertificates   For the Client Access and Unified Messaging roles, this prevents setup from creating self-signed certificates for SSL/TLS sessions. By default, setup will create these certificates only if no other certificates are found (see Chapter 20, "Supporting Outlook 2007," for more details).

ADAM Is Now ADLDS

The Active Directory Application Mode (ADAM) feature is now known as Active Directory Lightweight Directory Services (ADLDS).

Delegated Installation Options

Once your administrators have performed the topology preparation and initial installations, you may want to enable other personnel in your organization to perform additional server installs, even if they don't have the correct permissions to modify Active Directory. This is especially useful when you want to delegate the installation of branch office Exchange servers to support personnel but don't want to have to grant them domain-wide permissions in Active Directory.

By using these options, you can pre-create and remove the necessary modifications for new servers in Active Directory, allowing personnel to perform the actual setup tasks:

/NewProvisionedServer:<*ServerName*> or /nprs:<*ServerName*>   This option creates a placeholder server object so that a delegated server admin can run the Exchange installation.

/RemoveProvisionedServer or /rprs   Use this option to remove the provisioned server object.

/ForeignForestFQDN   This option creates an additional set of the Exchange security groups in a separate forest.

/ServerAdmin or /sa   This optional parameter permits the delegation of setup rights. This parameter specifies the user or group that will be granted Server Administrator permissions. If you use this option, it can only be used with the /NewProvisionedServer switch.

Common Optional Parameters

The following parameters are optional and, in fact, can be used during almost every setup and exsetup operation if desired:

/DomainController or /dc This option instructs setup to use a specific DC for Active Directory reads and writes. You can specify the hostname in NetBIOS or FQDN format.

/SourceDir or /s This option specifies the path to the Exchange 2007 source files, whether on a network share or distributed media.

/TargetDir or /t Use this option to tell setup where to install the Exchange Server 2007 files on the local hard drive. By default, this location is %programfiles%\Microsoft\Exchange Server.

/UpdatesDir or /u Exchange updates stored in the directory specified by this option will be installed during setup.

Recovering a Server

Setup and exsetup provide a special mode to assist in the disaster recovery of an existing Exchange server. Using the /RecoverServer mode, setup will pull the server's configuration information from Active Directory rather than creating it as a new server.

Cluster

When you're creating clustered mailbox servers, things are a bit different. Setup and exsetup provide additional switches to add and remove clustered mailbox server instances. You would use these options when working with Mailbox servers that are using the Microsoft Clustering Service, which needs to be installed and configured before you install Exchange. See Chapter 17 for more details on using these setup options.

UM Language Packs

If the Unified Messaging role is installed on the server, you can use the following switches to add and remove Unified Messaging language packs:

/AddUmLanguagePack This switch adds the language packs for the specified cultures.

/RemoveUmLanguagePack This option removes the installed language packs.

Like other modes, these switches take the optional parameters /SourceDir and /UpdatesDir. Complete coverage of the Unified Messaging role is beyond the scope of this book, but here are a few examples:

◆ To add the German, French, and Japanese UM language packs from a network share, use this command:

```
Exsetup /AddUmLanguagePack:de-DE,fr-FR,ja-JP /s:\\myshare\langpacks
```

◆ To remove the German and French language packs, use this command:

```
Exsetup /RemoveUmLanguagePack:de-DE,fr-FR
```

You cannot add or remove the English (en-US) language pack; it is installed as part of the core UM role.

Performing Post-Installation Tasks

Exchange 2007 is installed, but your work isn't over. There are several post-installation tasks you have left to complete. For example, you might need to:

◆ Enter your Exchange Server Product Key. Without it you can only run the Exchange server for 120 days. Bear in mind, there is no activation key for the 32-bit "lab" version of Exchange.

◆ Run the Exchange Best Practices Analyzer. Because this utility is frequently updated, you should obtain the latest version from the ExBPA site at www.exbpa.com.

◆ Consider installing Microsoft Forefront Security or another form of antivirus software designed for Exchange 2007 on your Exchange servers that run the Hub Transport role.

◆ Configure the Client Access role to provide Offline Address Book functionality for your Outlook 2007 clients.

◆ Obtain an SSL certificate for your Client Access role.

◆ Configure ActiveSync on your Client Access role.

◆ Configure domain(s) for which you will accept mail.

◆ Configure an e-mail address policy to automatically generate e-mail addresses.

◆ Subscribe to the Edge Transport server (if you choose to use one).

◆ If not using an Edge Transport server, configure a Send connector and configure a Receive connector to accept anonymous connections.

◆ Create a default "Postmaster" mailbox.

Starting the Exchange Management Console

If you used setup's graphic mode to install Exchange, you were given the option to automatically start the EMC when the installation was complete. Otherwise, click Start ➤ All Programs ➤ Microsoft Exchange ➤ Exchange Management Console to launch the EMC.

When you first open the EMC, you see a screen much like that shown in Figure 5.7. It contains a list of tasks that you need to accomplish in order to finalize your deployment. This list may be longer or shorter depending on which roles you have in your organization. Each task is a hyperlink that will lead you to specific instructions on how to accomplish it.

There is also a tab in the EMC that shows you additional tasks you can perform to further improve the usability of your Exchange organization, such as configuring accepted domains. This is the End-to-End Scenario tab. You can see an example of this tab in Figure 5.8.

Defining the Exchange Server Edition

As I mentioned earlier in this chapter, the actual Exchange Server 2007 edition that you are running is determined when you enter the product key, not when you install the software. If you have any unlicensed servers in your organization, you will get a pop-up box each time you run the Exchange Management Console that reminds you that the servers are not yet licensed and how many days you have left. Figure 5.9 shows an example of this warning box.

Unlike some other Microsoft products, even if a server exceeds its evaluation period (120 days), it will continue to run. However, it will only allow for the creation of five databases. You should make sure that you license each of your servers with the proper product keys as soon as possible.

The decision you need to make, of course, is whether to use Enterprise or Standard Edition product keys. Most of the time, the Standard Edition product key will work just fine; here are some reasons you will need to use the Exchange Server 2007 Enterprise product key:

◆ The Mailbox server role will be part of a single copy cluster.

◆ The Mailbox server role will be part of a clustered continuous replication.

◆ The Mailbox server role will require more than five mailbox databases or storage groups.

FIGURE 5.7
Finalizing the deployment

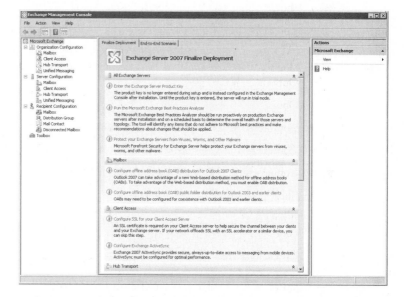

FIGURE 5.8
End-to-End Scenario tab of the EMC

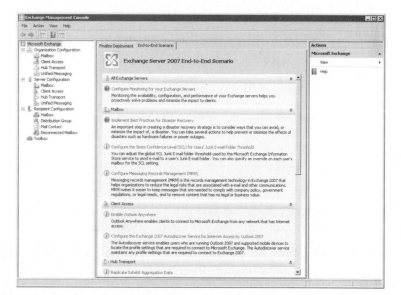

FIGURE 5.9
Unlicensed server warn-
ing box

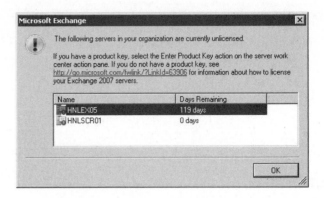

The preceding are pretty much the only scenarios that you will require Enterprise edition. Here are some configurations that still require *only* Standard Edition:

◆ Edge Transport, Hub Transport, or Client Access server role or combining Hub Transport and Client Access on the same machine.

◆ Unified Messaging server role.

◆ Mailbox servers that require five or fewer mailbox databases or storage groups that are in use at any time.

◆ Mailbox servers that will use local continuous replication or be a source/target for standby continuous replication. As long as the target only needs to have a maximum of five mailbox databases online at any time, it can be Standard Edition.

ENTER THE CORRECT PRODUCT KEY

Make sure you enter the right product key the first time. You cannot change from an Enterprise key to Standard key once you have entered the key.

To enter the license key, open the Exchange Management Console, navigate to the Servers container, and select the Enter Product Key link on the Actions pane. This launches a dialog box that allows you to enter the product key for this server.

If you are a command-line person, you can use the Exchange Management Shell (EMS) Set-ExchangeServer cmdlet to enter the product key. Here is an example of how you would enter the license key for server HNLEX05:

```
Set-ExchangeServer HNLEX05 -Productkey 12345-67890-54321-09876-12345
```

Once you have entered the product key, you need to stop the information store service and restart it in order for the update to take effect.

Delegating Permissions

One common post-setup task is the delegation of Exchange administrative permissions. By default, Exchange 2007 includes a number of predefined administrator roles that you can use as a basis for delegating management permissions among your staff. These built-in roles are as follows:

Exchange Organization Administrators   Users and groups assigned to this role have complete access to all Exchange properties and objects organization-wide. This is the highest level of permission in Exchange 2007.

Exchange Recipient Administrators   Users and groups assigned to this role can read all of the Domain Users containers in each Exchange-prepared domain in the Active Directory forest and have write access to the Exchange properties on all user objects in those containers. They can, in short, manage the Exchange properties of any recipient in an Exchange-prepared domain. Note that they do not have the underlying Active Directory permissions to create, manage, or delete the user objects, and if you do not run /PrepareAD for a given domain, they will have no Exchange-granted access to that domain.

Exchange Server Administrators   Users and groups assigned to this role are granted the ability to administer server-specific configuration items for the server this role is associated with. This role is granular on a server-by-server basis, allowing you to finely delegate administrative permissions without the use of administrative groups.

Exchange View-Only Administrators   Just what it says: users and groups assigned to this role get to peek at organization-wide configuration settings and Domain Users containers in Exchange-prepared domains, but they can't change any settings.

Exchange Public Folder Administrators   Members of this group can manage the public folder tree including setting limits on folders and managing replica lists.

CUSTOMIZING ADMINISTRATIVE PERMISSIONS

Some organizations may require more customized or granular permissions than the default Exchange Server 2007 groups provide. The Exchange Team has a good article on this at the following URL: http://msexchangeteam.com/archive/2006/11/03/430350.aspx.

You may have noticed that, by default, these permissions are set up to explicitly enforce a split-permission model between Active Directory and Exchange. This model helps medium-sized and large organizations enforce the difference between Active Directory administrators and Exchange administrators. All you need to do when you set up Exchange Server 2007 is to add your Exchange administrators to the right groups in Active Directory. These groups are found in the forest root domain under the Microsoft Exchange Security Groups OU; this OU and these groups are shown in Figure 5.10.

I cover permissions and delegation a bit more in Chapter 7, "Administering Exchange Server 2007."

IMPLICATIONS OF SPLIT-PERMISSION MODEL

The split-permission model has some subtle implications too. For example, the Exchange extensions to the Active Directory Users and Computers MMC snap-in are a thing of the past. In order to do any recipient management, you must use the Exchange tools.

FIGURE 5.10

Viewing the Exchange administrative groups in Active Directory Users and Computers

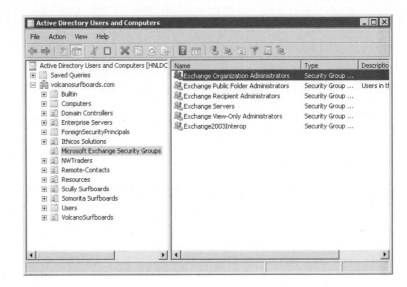

Summary

Installing Exchange 2007 may at first appear to be overwhelming. The proliferation of new server roles, combined with prerequisite software and hardware configuration, gives you a lot of options and details to keep track of. However, the new command-line installer gives you back a lot of power in managing your deployment. Your design work from the previous chapter combined with the detailed coverage and recommendations in this chapter will give you the specific guidance you need to easily determine which steps you need to take in which order.

If I had to reduce this chapter down to a single list of guidelines, here's what I'd want you to remember:

◆ Download and read the current Exchange 2007 documentation. Microsoft will be updating it on a regular basis to ensure that it stays fresh and incorporates the latest updates and real-world deployment feedback.

◆ Pay proper attention to sizing your servers.

◆ Text-mode setup is your friend.

◆ Do your Active Directory preparation before beginning to install server roles.

◆ You must have at least one Client Access server role and one Hub Transport server role per Active Directory site. These should be installed prior to the first Mailbox server role in that site.

◆ Don't install an Edge Transport server until you have a Hub Transport instance in your organization.

◆ Clusters must be dedicated to the Mailbox server role only.

◆ Wait to install the Unified Messaging server until you know everything else is working.

If you take your time and test your deployment plan thoroughly, you'll have a working Exchange 2007 installation in no time!

Chapter 6

Upgrading to Exchange Server 2007

With Exchange being the number one messaging system on the market, it's quite a solid bet that a lot of existing Exchange customers will be looking at upgrading. If you're reading this chapter, whether you turned to it directly or came here by way of the previous chapter, I'm guessing that you're one of those people. Many people have different expectations about what an upgrade consists of. We're used to *in-place upgrades* where we have an existing version of the software on the computer, run the installer, and end up with the new version of the software. Previous versions of Exchange have supported an in-place upgrade process for at least one previous version back, but the Exchange 2007 upgrade process doesn't.

As explained in previous chapters, the lack of support for 64-bit Windows in Exchange 2003 and the lack of support for 32-bit Windows in Exchange 2007 combine to make the upgrade process a bit more complicated. Life is not all gloom and doom, however, and this seeming complication will have its compensation in the end.

In this chapter you learn to:

◆ Choose between an upgrade and a migration

◆ Determine the factors you need to consider before doing your upgrade

◆ Understand the two Exchange 2007 upgrade strategies and how to tell where each is appropriate

◆ Coexist with legacy Exchange servers

◆ Perform an inter-organization migration

Upgrades versus Migrations

Before we go on, let me take a moment to clear up a matter of terminology and distinguish between *upgrading* and *migrating*.

Exchange 2000/2003 cannot be "upgraded" to Exchange 2007. You must perform a migration. The process of moving from Exchange 2000/2003 to Exchange Server 2007 is often referred to as an upgrade, but technically it is not. An upgrade occurs *in-place*; that is, it involves taking an existing server and installing the newer version of the software on *that* server. The server installation process then performs whatever changes it needs to convert the old software (and database) to the newest version.

IS IT A MIGRATION OR A TRANSITION?

If you start searching through the Microsoft documentation and then read books and articles on Exchange 2007 migration, you will see the term *transition* tossed around a lot. A transition is a type of migration that occurs when you install new Exchange servers in the same organization, the servers interoperate for some period of time, you move services and data over to the new servers, and then you shut down the old servers and remove them.

Most Exchange migrations are really transitions, because you usually install new servers and move the data over. However, I am using the term *migration* in a more generic sense.

Just to make things less straightforward, the Exchange 2007 documentation gives you two upgrade strategies:

◆ Upgrade your existing organization, which Microsoft calls a *transition*.

◆ Create a new organization and move your messaging data over. Unfortunately, Microsoft has chosen to call this *migration*. Be aware that this use of *migration* refers only to the act of moving your data between the two organizations!

To be consistent with Microsoft usage and minimize confusion, I'll use the term *upgrade* to refer to the process of moving from an existing Exchange 2000/2003 organization to Exchange 2007, no matter the strategy you use to get there. Actual migrations from messaging systems other than earlier versions of Exchange (or from Exchange 5.5) are outside the scope of this book.

When I need to refer to moving data between organizations, I'll explicitly say *migration strategy*. This helps me be clear and stay consistent with the excellent documentation provided for Exchange 2007.

Migration Overview

Again, Exchange 2000/2003 cannot be "upgraded" in-place to Exchange Server 2007; the services and data on Exchange 2000/2003 must be migrated or moved to Exchange Server 2007. There are a number of reasons for this:

◆ Exchange 2000/2003 runs only on Windows 2003 x32.

◆ Exchange Server 2007 runs only (in production) on Windows 2003 x64 or Windows Server 2008 x64.

◆ Exchange Server 2007 uses a single EDB file instead of the Exchange 2000/2003 EDB and STM files.

◆ Exchange Server 2007's message transport and Web access components are very different from those of Exchange 2003.

What you must do instead of an in-place upgrade is to install new Exchange Server 2007 servers into the existing Exchange organization. To the existing Exchange 2000/2003 servers, these new servers will appear like other Exchange 2000/2003 servers. Once you start installing new Exchange 2007 servers into the organization, you can start transitioning messaging services over to these new services. I go into this in more detail later.

MIGRATION TO NEW SERVER HARDWARE

Many organizations that are planning to replace Exchange 2000/2003 will just about be ready for an Exchange server hardware refresh. If you have new servers, here are the services that need to be transitioned, in roughly this order:

1. Transitioning Outlook Web Access, POP3, IMAP4, and Exchange ActiveSync to Exchange Server 2007 Client Access servers.

2. Messaging routing (Internet inbound/outbound) as well as routing between routing groups handled by Exchange Server 2007 Hub Transport servers.

3. Replicating public folders to Exchange Server 2007 Mailbox servers.

4. Moving mailboxes to Exchange Server 2007 Mailbox servers.

5. Transitioning anti-spam services to Edge Transport services (optional).

6. Deploying Unified Messaging and other new features.

LEAPFROG MIGRATION

If you just bought brand new Exchange Server hardware for your 2000/2003 servers, you are in more of a bind. You will still need at least one or two unused servers, but you can do a "leapfrog" migration to reuse existing hardware. Those steps might look like this:

1. Use a new server to deploy an Exchange 2007 Client Access server.

2. Redirect all Outlook Web Access, POP3, IMAP4, and ActiveSync clients to the new Client Access server.

3. Remove the Exchange 2000/2003 OWA server from production.

4. Rebuild the Exchange 2000/2003 OWA server as an Exchange Server 2007 Hub Transport server.

5. Redirect all Exchange 2000/2003 message routing functions from existing bridgehead server to new Exchange 2007 Hub Transport server.

6. Remove the Exchange 2000/2003 bridgehead server from production.

   Note that each Exchange 2000/2003 routing group must keep at least one bridgehead server functioning as long as that routing group has mailbox or public folder servers in it.

7. Rebuild the Exchange bridgehead server as an Exchange Server 2007 Mailbox server.

8. Move mailboxes to new Mailbox server role. Replicate public folders to new Mailbox server.

9. Remove public folder replicas from old Exchange 2000/2003 Mailbox server.

10. Remove old Exchange 2000/2003 Mailbox server from organization and use reuse the hardware as necessary.

Exchange 5.5 Migrations

I am still surprised at the number of questions that pop up in the newsgroups and Web support forums with respect to Exchange 5.5. I still know of a few organizations that run Exchange 5.5 on the theory that "it works so we don't want to replace it." One of the cosmic laws of software, though, is that sooner or later it must be upgraded. Exchange Server is no exception.

Unfortunately, there is no direct "migration" path from Exchange 5.5 to Exchange Server 2007. You have options, of course, but they are by no means simple or cheap.

If you have a small number of users and only one or two locations, you might consider "leapfrogging" through Exchange 2003. This means that you perform a migration to Exchange 2003 and then shortly thereafter perform another migration to Exchange Server 2007. This leapfrog process might be the smoothest transition for most of your users. It ensures that public folders, shortcuts, folder rules, permissions delegations, and Outlook profiles do not need to be modified. If you have the extra server hardware and you can use Exchange Server 2003 licenses temporarily, this is a good approach. However, it means that you must endure the pain of the Active Directory Connector (ADC) that synchronizes data between the Exchange 5.5 directory and the Active Directory; my stomach still tightens up when I think about configuring the ADC.

The other approach is to use a third-party migration utility such as the Quest Software Exchange Migration Wizard (www.quest.com). Although third-party tools usually represent a significant cost on your part, for larger organizations these utilities can ensure a smooth transition if you are migrating from Exchange 5.5 or performing an inter-organization migration.

AVOID HEADACHES — DON'T DEPLOY NEW FEATURES DURING MIGRATIONS

I have mentioned this before, but this bears repeating. Do not deploy new features of Exchange Server 2007 while you are still migrating mailboxes.

I know that you will be tempted to start using features such as messaging records management, Unified Messaging, improved Exchange ActiveSync features, per-mailbox journaling, or transport rules before the migration is finished. If there are features that you must deploy during your migration, just ensure that they will not interfere with your support of the users that are migrating.

The exception to this is features such as continuous replication that are deployed at the server level. These can be configured and tested before the first mailbox is ever moved.

My rule of thumb is to try to avoid deploying any feature that will require additional user support or training. These distract the help desk and the migration team from getting the migration completed in a timely fashion.

Considering Messaging Connectors

Another area for you to consider as you're getting ready to upgrade to Exchange 2007 is your connectors. In legacy Exchange organizations, you have four basic types of connectors: routing group connectors, SMTP connectors, X.400 connectors, and other foreign connectors to specialized messaging systems such as Lotus Notes and Novell GroupWise. In general, you'll want to treat these connectors in the following fashion:

Routing group connectors Routing group connectors still exist in Exchange 2007 but are meant solely as a means of interoperability with legacy Exchange servers. They will be naturally phased out as you convert your Exchange infrastructure over to Exchange 2007, decommission your legacy Exchange servers, and remove the legacy administrative and routing groups from your organization.

ABOUT LEGACY EXCHANGE SERVERS

I will use the phrase *legacy Exchange servers* in this chapter to refer to the existing Exchange 2000 Server and Exchange Server 2003 machines in your organization. This might cause a slight bit of cognitive dissonance for those of you used to thinking of Exchange 5.5 servers as legacy servers.

SMTP connectors   SMTP connectors provide connections to external SMTP-speaking systems and the Internet; they generally aren't used within legacy Exchange forests unless you have a multiple forest configuration. In Exchange 2007, connectors are divided into two types: Receive connectors, which are configured on a per-server basis, and Send connectors, which are configured and maintained throughout the organization.

As with the routing group connectors, these legacy SMTP connectors will be phased out as you move your message routing functions off of your legacy Exchange servers to your new Exchange 2007 Hub Transport and Edge Transport servers. I talk more about your routing and SMTP connector options, and tell you how to configure Exchange 2007 Hub Transport and Edge Transport SMTP connectivity to the Internet, in Chapter 18, "Implementing Replication Technologies."

X.400 connectors   X.400 connectors are finally gone in Exchange 2007. With the decline and fall of X.400 as a messaging standard, almost all of the X.400 connectors used in legacy Exchange organizations today are used to connect to the MTA service in Exchange 5.5 sites. Because you can't have Exchange 5.5 sites and servers in an organization with Exchange 2007, you'll need to get these sites and connectors removed before beginning your upgrade.

If you have a non-Exchange X.400 system that you connect to, you'll need to maintain your legacy Exchange server until you can arrange some sort of alternate connection supported natively by Exchange 2007.

Foreign connectors   Foreign connectors are dramatically different in Exchange 2007. The new foreign connectors don't try to implement a specific non-SMTP protocol; instead, they require you to define a drop directory on the Hub Transport server or network file share. When messages are routed through this connector, they will be written to the drop directory and the remote gateway software can then pick them up and process them appropriately.

If you're using the Exchange 2000 cc:Mail or MS Mail connectors, or the Exchange 2003 Group-Wise or Lotus Notes connectors can't transition to an SMTP connection, you'll need to keep the relevant legacy Exchange servers in your organization. (Of course, if you're still using cc:Mail or MS Mail, my only question to you is *why?*)

You'll need to consider your current routing topology, especially if you have a single routing group in your legacy organization. By default, legacy Exchange servers route messages directly out of their local SMTP virtual server. This default behavior means that, out of the box, Exchange 2000 Server and Exchange Server 2003 servers directly attempt to deliver external messages based on DNS MX record lookups instead of forwarding messages to bridgehead servers. For many small organizations, this behavior is acceptable, and as a result many Exchange administrators never get around to creating an SMTP connector and defining bridgehead servers for their organization.

When you install the first Exchange 2007 Hub Transport instance into your legacy Exchange organization, it creates its own routing group and associated routing group connector, as previously discussed. It also creates a default set of SMTP connectors that are enough to send and receive authenticated SMTP to/from other Exchange servers in the organization; the Send connector is configured with the default SMTP address space of *. You may suddenly find that your organization is unable to exchange mail with systems outside of your organization.

If this is the case, here's what's happened: You've failed to set an SMTP connector in your legacy Exchange organization. By installing your first Exchange 2007 Hub Transport instance, you've created a routable SMTP connector with the default address space. Your legacy Exchange servers do what they're supposed to do and allow this new SMTP connector configuration to override the SMTP virtual server configuration. Instead of attempting to send externally addressed messages directly to the MX host, the legacy Exchange servers send these messages through the brand-new routing group connector to your new Exchange 2007 Hub Transport server. Even better, the Hub Transport server only has the default connectors, which don't include the configuration necessary to allow unauthenticated traffic to and from the Internet; Exchange 2007 assumes that you'll be using the Edge Transport role to do that, and you'll have to configure it otherwise if you're not going to use the Edge Transport role. Now, all your outbound external mail starts to pile up in the Hub Transport server's queues.

Luckily, the fix for this situation is simple, and you even have three solutions from which to choose:

◆ Create an outbound SMTP Send connector on your Exchange 2007 Hub Transport server. This may be suboptimal in some instances, but if you're already using an external mail gateway, you can simply configure Exchange 2007 to pass outbound mail to the appropriate smarthost. I cover this option in detail later in Chapter 18.

◆ Deploy an Exchange 2007 Edge Transport server to handle your outbound traffic. If you're upgrading to Exchange 2007 to take advantage of its advanced message hygiene capabilities, I recommend this option; it gets your incoming and outgoing mail going through Exchange 2007 sooner rather than later. Again, I talk about this configuration in depth in Chapter 18.

◆ Create an SMTP connector with the default address space in your legacy Exchange organization before you begin installing Exchange 2007. This option has the advantage that it keeps mail flow in your organization going through a known and trusted set of bridgehead servers until you have your Hub Transport and Edge Transport servers configured and tested. If you have existing legacy Exchange servers configured with mail hygiene solutions, this is probably what you're going to want to select for the short term.

USING LEGACY EXCHANGE SERVERS AS BRIDGEHEADS DURING UPGRADE

Don't be afraid or hesitant to continue using your legacy Exchange servers as bridgeheads to the Internet while you're working your way through your Exchange 2007 upgrade. Although I firmly believe that configuring and troubleshooting message flow and routing is much easier with Exchange 2007, you still have a lot of material to learn and master as you begin to put Exchange 2007 into play. Choose your battles.

Legacy Exchange and Third-Party Services

Another factor you need to consider is whether you are using additional legacy Exchange services that are no longer present in Exchange 2007. I've already covered the case of the foreign connectors that are no longer part of Exchange 2007, but those aren't the only services and features you need to watch out for.

Previous versions of Exchange included several services that are now supplied by either Windows Server 2003 components or other Microsoft applications. If your organization depends on these, you'll need to keep the appropriate legacy servers around until you can migrate or upgrade the services off the Exchange servers.

Theses services include the following:

◆ Exchange 2000 Conferencing Server

◆ Exchange 2000 Instant Messaging Server

◆ Exchange 2000 Key Management Server

◆ Exchange 2000 Chat Server

If you are currently using these services and cannot (or will not) upgrade to Exchange 2007-compatible versions, you will need to leave the legacy Exchange servers hosting these services intact within your organization.

KEEPING LEGACY EXCHANGE SERVERS

If you are keeping legacy Exchange servers in your organization, do not forget to preserve the management consoles and tools necessary to administer the services.

You may also have third-party services that are essential to your organization. Examples of such services include, but by no means are limited to, the following:

◆ Message hygiene add-ins such as spam filters and virus scanners (both for transport and store).

◆ Fax services.

◆ Message discovery, compliance, archival, and retention solutions.

◆ Geo-clustering, mailbox snapshot, and other storage-related solutions.

◆ Transport event sinks, whether commercial or custom. A common event sink is a module to stamp disclaimers on all outbound e-mail.

◆ Conference room and shared resource booking management software.

◆ Mailbox database backup and restore agents.

Of course, there are many other possibilities. The point is that you need to ensure that these products are going to work with Exchange 2007. Some products may work directly with Exchange 2007 already, whereas others may require an upgrade of their own. In some cases, you may need to switch software packages if your current vendor's product isn't compatible with Exchange 2007 and you require that functionality.

There's always the possibility that you no longer need a given third-party package because new functionality in Exchange 2007 allows you to perform the same task natively.

Factors to Consider Before Upgrading

Are you ready to upgrade? Not so fast! Before you pull the trigger and pop the Exchange 2007 installation media into the drive, you need to consider a few factors. Let's take some time to go over them in more detail so that your upgrade is successful.

Prerequisites

Before you can begin upgrading your Exchange organization, you have to ensure that it meets the necessary prerequisites. I've gone over some of these already in previous chapters from the context of a fresh install of Exchange 2007, but let's look at them again, this time keeping in mind how your existing Exchange deployment may affect your ability to meet them.

HARDWARE AND OPERATING SYSTEM

For production use, you must have x64-compatible hardware — systems with one of the following types of processors:

- The Opteron processor line, made by AMD, found in high-end server hardware.

- Athlon 64 processors, also by AMD, meant for inexpensive servers and high-end workstations.

- Intel Xeon and Pentium line of processors with the Extended Memory 64 Technology (EM64T) extensions.

  The Xeon family is typically found in high-end servers, whereas the Pentiums are found in low-end servers and workstations.

The Intel Itanium processor line is not compatible with Exchange 2007. Unlike some other Microsoft restrictions, this isn't just a case of being an unsupported configuration; the Itanium processors are not compatible with the x64 specification and Exchange 2007 has not been compiled to run on the Itanium family of CPUs.

Nowadays, multi-core processors are increasingly common — both Intel and AMD. Although Windows recognizes multiple cores as separate processors when managing processes and threads, Microsoft licensing does not make a distinction between single-core and dual-core processors. This is to your benefit, because Exchange will certainly benefit from additional cores.

You can run Exchange 2007 on any of the following versions of Windows Server:

- Windows Server 2003 x64 Standard Edition with SP1 or later applied (I recommend that you use SP2)

- Windows Server 2003 x64 Enterprise Edition with SP1 or later applied (I recommend that you use SP2)

- Windows Server 2003 R2 x64 Standard Edition

- Windows Server 2003 R2 x64 Enterprise Edition

- Windows Server 2008

ECONOMIZING WITH WINDOWS SERVER 2003 STANDARD EDITION AND MULTI-CORE PROCESSORS

Windows Server 2003 Standard Edition limits you to a maximum of four CPUs. By making use of multi-core processors, you can still use the cheaper Standard Edition while maximizing your server's CPU power, which can be important for some server roles (or for servers that are hosting multiple roles).

Remember, though, that if you're planning on deploying clustered mailbox servers, you can't use Windows Server 2003 Standard Edition in clusters.

If you're one of the people using prerelease versions of Windows Longhorn Server (the code-name for the next generation of Windows Server), don't even think about trying to use it with Exchange 2007. You shouldn't be using prerelease versions of Windows in production (unless you're directed to by Microsoft as part of one of its early-adopter programs). However, bitter experience has taught the folks at Microsoft that even when they clearly tell people not to do something, someone out there will still try to do it, so Microsoft has made Exchange 2007 RTM incompatible with Windows 2008. Microsoft has, however, stated that Windows 2008 support is a part of Exchange 2007 SP1. You can't install Exchange 2007 on Windows 2008, nor can you have Windows 2008 domain controllers in any site that contains an Exchange 2007 server; you must be using Exchange Server 2007 SP1 or later.

When Microsoft first began releasing the requirements for Exchange 2007 deployments, no single revelation drew greater attention than the requirement for 64-bit hardware. Even now, many people insist that the lack of support for 32-bit hardware will dramatically increase the final cost of upgrades to Exchange 2007. Microsoft, though, makes the argument that most of the servers sold these days already have 64-bit support. Because the x64 hardware platform (initially introduced by AMD for its Opteron and Athlon 64 processors, then supported by Intel with the EM64T extensions to its Xeon and Pentium 4 processors) is backward compatible with 32-bit hardware and operating systems, many server manufacturers switched to offering 64-bit hardware regardless of which operating system their customers order.

This doesn't mean you're completely off the hook on the hardware front, however. Even if your current Exchange 2003 servers are running on 64-bit hardware, you can't just pop the Exchange 2007 DVD in and do an in-place upgrade. Why not?

- Previous versions of Exchange are all 32-bit only and can't be run on Windows Server 2003 x64. Note that this is not a matter of support; Exchange 2000 and 2003 simply will not run on 64-bit Windows — period, end of story.

- You can't upgrade from Windows Server 2003 x86 to Windows Server 2003 x64. You have to perform a clean install.

- You cannot upgrade a Windows Server 2003 server to Windows Server 2008 if Exchange Server 2007 is installed.

- You can't run the 32-bit version of Exchange 2007 in production. The 32-bit version is intended for testing and training and cannot be taken out of trial mode, which means that it will cease to operate after a set number of days.

This means that to reuse existing server hardware, you're going to have to have at least one spare server and be prepared to reinstall Windows and Exchange on your servers as you go.

I discuss this in more detail in the section "Transitioning Your Exchange Organization" later in this chapter.

ACTIVE DIRECTORY

Because Exchange 2007 continues to heavily depend on Active Directory, you need to take a good look at the domain controllers and global catalog servers in your Active Directory forest before starting the upgrade process.

Unlike Exchange 2003, which could use domain controllers running either Windows 2000 Server with the appropriate service pack or Windows Server 2003, Exchange 2007 requires that all of the following domain controllers be running Windows Server 2003 + SP1:

♦ The schema master domain controller. This is usually the first domain controller that you installed in the forest, unless you have moved the schema master flexible single master of operations (FSMO) role to another domain controller.

♦ At least one global catalog server in each Active Directory site in your forest where you will be installing an Exchange 2007 server.

My recommendation is to upgrade all your domain controllers to Windows Server 2003 + SP1, especially if you still have Windows 2000 Server domain controllers. The Active Directory improvements in Windows Server 2003 can vastly reduce the bandwidth required for Active Directory replication, and several Exchange 2007 features (such as address book browsing in OWA) rely on features in Windows Server 2003 SP1. By making sure you've upgraded all of your domain controllers, you increase the redundancy and resiliency of your Exchange/Active Directory integration.

CHECK THE HEALTH OF YOUR ACTIVE DIRECTORY SITE BEFORE UPGRADING

It is extremely important that Active Directory be healthy before you upgrade to Exchange 2007. Exchange 2007 relies directly on your Active Directory site structure for message routing information. In previous versions of Exchange, the Active Directory site design could become decoupled from the Exchange Server routing design.

Whether you upgrade all of your domain controllers or just the minimum number, you need to list all the domains in which you will either install Exchange 2007 or create Exchange 2007 recipient objects such as users, contacts, and mail-enabled groups. For each of these domains, ensure that the domain functional level is set to either the Windows 2000 native or the Windows 2003 native level. This ensures that you have no lingering Windows NT 4.0 servers acting as down-level domain controllers via the primary domain controller (PDC) emulator.

If you can't upgrade all of the domain controllers in your forest, I recommend at the very least upgrading all of the domain controllers in the sites and domains that will be hosting Exchange servers and recipient objects. Officially, you only need to have a single Windows Server 2003 SP1 global catalog server in each site, but Windows Server 2003 SP1 domain controllers offer many advantages to your organization above and beyond their benefits to Exchange Server 2007.

For Windows 2003 Active Directory forests, there is no direct requirement for the forest functional level as long as each domain that will be used for Exchange 2007 meets the per-domain requirements.

A few additional caveats exist:

◆ If you plan on using OWA and any of your domain controllers are using a non-English version of Windows, you will need to install the hotfix in Knowledge Base article 919166 on each non-English domain controller.

◆ DNS must be configured correctly. In addition, servers on which you plan to install Exchange 2007 cannot have a *disjoint namespace*; that is, the server's primary DNS suffix (set in the Computer Name tab of the computer's property sheet) must match the DNS name of the domain the server belongs to.

◆ You may want to use 64-bit Windows Server 2003 on your domain controllers for performance increases; however, this is not required.

◆ Assuming similar speeds and models of processor, you should still plan to meet the long-standing recommendation of a 4:1 or lower ratio of Exchange processors to global catalog processors in a given site. This helps ensure that global catalog lookups happen quickly enough to keep Exchange responding in a timely fashion.

◆ Avoid installing Exchange 2007 on a domain controller. Although this is technically possible, such a combined server is much less resilient to service outages or configuration changes and is much harder to restore in the event of a disaster. If you do go this route, you will have to uninstall Exchange if you ever want to demote the machine from being a domain controller; you cannot run `dcpromo` once Exchange is installed.

Exchange Version

The final prerequisite you must consider is what mode your legacy Exchange organization is in. By default, these versions of Exchange install in mixed mode even when you did not upgrade from Exchange 5.5. You must upgrade the organization to Exchange 2000 or 2003 native mode. Note that in order to do this, you must ensure the following points:

◆ No Exchange 5.5 servers remain in the organization.

◆ No legacy Exchange Site Replication Service (SRS) instances remain in the organization.

◆ No configured Connection Agreements in the Active Directory Connector (ADC) remain in the organization. In fact, if you still have the ADC in your organization and you have no more Exchange 5.5 servers or legacy Exchange SRS instances, remove the ADC from the organization.

Once you have verified that your Active Directory domains and forest and Exchange organization meet these prerequisites, you can begin the process of installing Exchange 2007 by preparing Active Directory as described in Chapter 4, "Exchange Server 2007 Architecture."

Setting the Legacy Routing Server Parameter

Chapter 5, "Installing Exchange Server 2007," briefly mentioned the /LegacyRoutingServer installation option. I will now cover more about why it exists and what problems it solves.

When you install Exchange 2007 into an existing legacy Exchange organization, you need to address some architectural differences. I said before that Exchange 2007 doesn't use administrative groups or routing groups, and that's almost completely true. Although Exchange 2007 servers don't make use of them, the legacy Exchange servers do require them; in a mixed organization, you're going to have the administrative groups and routing groups created for the older Exchange servers. So far, so good; the Exchange 2007 servers use the new Active Directory site-based architecture and the legacy Exchange servers use the administrative groups and routing groups. Under these conditions, everything is happy until the new Exchange 2007 server tries to interact with a legacy Exchange server.

To deal with this, the Exchange 2007 installer takes several actions to ensure compatibility with legacy Exchange servers:

◆ To facilitate communication with legacy Exchange servers, the Exchange 2007 installer creates a special administrative group the first time it is run in a legacy organization. All Exchange 2007 servers are placed into this special administrative group, which is named `Exchange Administrative Group (FYDIBOHF23SPDLT)`. The Exchange 2007 servers don't use this group, but it will show up, along with all of the Exchange 2007 servers, in the legacy Exchange System Manager.

◆ The installer also creates a special routing group for Exchange 2007 servers, named `Exchange Routing Group (DWBGZMFD01QNBJR)`. As with the administrative group, all Exchange 2007 servers are placed into this routing group, even though they use the native Exchange 2007 and Active Directory site-based routing mechanisms; the group and servers are visible in the legacy Exchange System Manager. The only purpose of this routing group is to force the legacy Exchange servers to use a routing group connector to communicate with Exchange 2007 servers.

◆ The installer also creates a universal security group named `ExchangeLegacyInterop` in Active Directory. Exchange 2007 servers use this group to determine which legacy servers are permitted to submit messages to the default SMTP Receive connectors on the Exchange 2007 Hub Transport instances. By default, these connectors require successful authentication and permit message submission only from legacy servers whose computer accounts are in this group, such as the legacy Exchange bridgehead server. I go into more detail in Chapter 21, "Delivering E-mail," about the various options for Hub Transport Receive connectors.

◆ When the first Exchange 2007 Hub Transport role is installed, the installer creates a two-way routing group connector between the Exchange 2007 routing group and a user-selected legacy Exchange bridgehead server. If you use the command-line installer, you use the `/LegacyRoutingServer` switch to specify which legacy Exchange server to use. You can add additional bridgehead servers to this routing group after the installation is complete, and I talk about that in more detail later in this chapter. As with the administrative and routing groups, this connector is visible in the legacy Exchange System Manager.

At first these changes may seem overwhelming, especially if your current Exchange organization consists of only one or two administrative and routing groups. The thought of adding another administrative group and routing group into the mix initially strikes many people as counter-intuitive; after all, the point of the move away from them is to simplify things, not clutter them up! Consider for a moment an organization that consists of the following elements:

◆ A single Active Directory forest and domain.

◆ Two sites, imaginatively named Site A and Site B.

◆ A domain controller and global catalog server in each site, for a total of four domain controllers.

◆ An Exchange 2003 organization, consisting of a separate administrative group and routing group for each site. For the sake of argument, we'll say that this administrative and routing group design is a legacy of an earlier upgrade from Exchange 5.5.

◆ Four Exchange 2003 servers in each site: two mailbox servers, a front-end server, and a bridgehead server. This makes a total of eight Exchange 2003 servers.

ABOUT EXCHANGE 2007 ADMINISTRATIVE AND ROUTING GROUPS

The names of the Exchange 2007 administrative and routing groups are designed to be unique, something that is not likely to be already present in any legacy organization. Do not rename these groups!

The Exchange 2007 administrative group and routing group are intended only for Exchange 2007 servers. Do not place legacy Exchange servers in these groups thinking that it will somehow improve interoperability or remove the need for the routing group connector. You will break mail flow because there is no other mechanism for translating between the legacy Exchange routing mechanism and the Exchange 2007 routing mechanism.

Now, this organization wants to install Exchange 2007. The goal is to end up with a total of six Exchange 2007 servers: one Mailbox instance, one Client Access instance, and one Hub Transport instance for each AD site. As shown in Figure 6.1, things certainly look messy while they're in the middle of their upgrade.

FIGURE 6.1
Logical structures present when Exchange 2007 coexists in a legacy organization

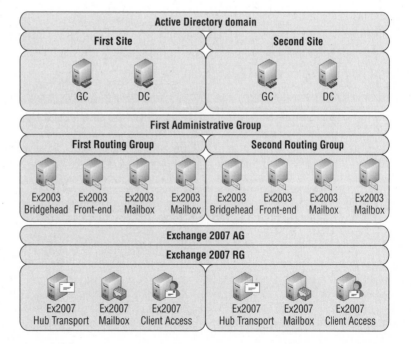

Very scary! They've got administrative groups, routing groups, and Active Directory structures all over the place. Even with at most a total of 18 servers to handle, tracking the multiple overlapping memberships gets ugly.

Ah, but when they've completed their upgrade, things are a lot calmer, as shown in Figure 6.2. They've got their two Active Directory sites, a single deprecated Exchange administrative group, and a single deprecated Exchange routing group.

FIGURE 6.2
Logical structures
simplified when only
Exchange 2007 remains

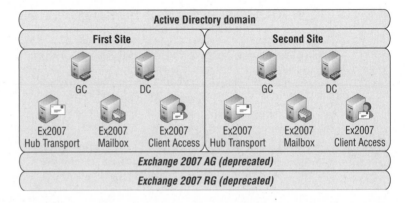

Once you've specified the legacy bridgehead server and successfully added the first Exchange 2007 Hub Transport instance into the organization, you can later configure the default routing group connector with additional legacy Exchange bridgehead servers or even create new routing group connectors to simplify the message routing paths in your organization. However, you're going to have to perform these tasks from the Exchange Management Shell; you won't see the legacy routing group connectors listed in the Exchange Management Console.

To see the existing legacy routing group connectors, use the Get-RoutingGroupConnector cmdlet. Its output is shown in Figure 6.3.

FIGURE 6.3
Output from the
Get-RoutingGroupConnector
cmdlet

To add a new legacy bridgehead to an existing legacy routing group connector, use the Set-RoutingGroupConnector cmdlet. Here is an example where I am adding Exchange 2003

servers hn1bh01.somorita.int and hn1bh02.somorita.int and Exchange 2007 servers hn1ht03.somorita.int and hn1ht04.somorita.int to a routing group connector called E2K7 to E2K3 RGC:

```
Set-RoutingGroupConnector -Name "E2K7 to E2K3 RGC"↵
-SourceTransportServers "hn1ht03.somorita.int",↵
"hn1ht04.somorita.int" -TargetTransportServers↵
 "hn1bh01.somorita.int", "hn1bh02.somorita.int"
```

This cmdlet ensures that the legacy servers are automatically added to the ExchangeLegacy-Interop security group so that SMTP authentication will take place and messages will flow properly.

To create a new routing group connector, use the New-RoutingGroupConnector cmdlet. Here is an example of creating a new routing group connector called E2K7 to Hawaii RG using the Exchange 2003 server hn1bh01.somorita.int and the Exchange 2007 server hn1ht01.somorita.net as bridgehead servers:

```
New-RoutingGroupConnector -Name "E2K7 to Hawaii RG"↵
-SourceTransportServers "hn1ht01.somorita.int"↵
-TargetTransportServers "hn1bh01.somorita.int"↵
-Cost 100 -Bidirectional $True -PublicFoldersEnabled $True
```

When you use the New-RoutingGroupConnector and Set-RoutingGroupConnector cmdlets to specify the TargetTransportServers and SourceTransportServers parameters, you need to specify all of the servers you wish to be bridgeheads for the connector. Each invocation of the cmdlet will overwrite the existing parameter.

Choosing Your Strategy

Now that you've considered the various factors that could affect your upgrade, you need to figure out which strategy you're going to use. As mentioned earlier, you have two main choices: *migration* or *transition*, as Microsoft calls them. Although neither option gives you the relative ease of the traditional in-place upgrade, each option has its own pros and cons. In the following sections, I review them briefly and then move on to a more in-depth discussion.

Comparing the Strategies

If you're like many readers, you probably have at least some preference for your upgrade strategy already in mind. Before you set that choice in stone, though, read through this section and see whether there are any surprises (good or bad) that might allow you to address some aspect of the upgrade that you hadn't previously considered. If, on the other hand, you're not really sure which strategy would be best for you, this section should help give you enough information to begin making a well-informed decision.

Let's start by taking a look at an overview of how the two strategies stack up. Table 6.1 lists several points of comparison between the migration and transition strategies.

For the most part, Table 6.1 speaks for itself; if any point requires more in-depth discussion, I address it properly during the detailed sections that follow.

TABLE 6.1:   Comparison of Exchange 2007 Upgrade Strategies

Point of Comparison	Migration Strategy	Transition Strategy
Tools	You will need a combination of free Microsoft tools to manage the multiple sets of data that need to be migrated (Active Directory user information and Exchange mailbox data at a minimum). These tools usually result in at least some minor information loss. Alternatively, you can spend extra money to purchase and use third-party tools.	You can use the built-in tools in Exchange 2007 and Windows Server to control all aspects of the transition, from building the new servers, reconfiguring Active Directory, or moving mailbox data.
Hardware	You will usually require a significant amount of new hardware. You may not need to have a complete spare set of replacement hardware, but you'll need enough to have the basic infrastructure of your new Exchange 2007 organization in place.	You can accomplish this strategy with a minimal amount of new hardware, typically no more than one or two extra servers, as long as your existing servers are 64-bit ready. Otherwise, you will need new hardware for your Exchange 2007 servers.
Active Directory and DNS	You must create a new Active Directory forest. Typically, this means that you cannot reuse the same AD and DNS domain names (although you will be able to share the same SMTP domain names).	You can make use of your existing Active Directory and DNS deployment; however, you will first need to upgrade your existing domain controllers and global catalogs to meet the prerequisites.
User accounts	You must migrate your user accounts to the new AD forest or re-create them.	Your users will be able to use their existing accounts without any changes.
Message routing	Your SMTP domains must be split between your legacy organization and your new organization; one of them must be configured to be non-authoritative and to route to the other. This configuration may need to change during the course of the migration. Additionally, you must set up explicit external SMTP connectors between the two organizations or play tricks with name resolution.	Your organization continues to be a single entity, with full knowledge of all authoritative domains shared among all Exchange servers. Message flow between organizations can be controlled by the simple addition of bridgehead servers to the default legacy routing group connector or the creation of additional legacy routing group connectors to meet the needs of your topology.

TABLE 6.1:   Comparison of Exchange 2007 Upgrade Strategies *(CONTINUED)*

POINT OF COMPARISON	MIGRATION STRATEGY	TRANSITION STRATEGY
Outlook profiles	You will need either to create new Outlook profiles (either manually or using the tools found in the matching version of the Microsoft Office Resource Kit) or use third-party tools to migrate them over to the new organization. This may cause loss of information.	As long as you keep the legacy mailbox servers up and running during an appropriate transition phase, Outlook will transparently update your users' profiles to their new mailbox server the first time they open it after their mailbox is moved to Exchange 2007.
Single-instance storage	Removing mailbox information from the organization to move it breaks single-instance storage. In order to preserve it, you'll need to look at buying third-party migration tools.	The mailbox movement tools included in Exchange 2007 will preserve single-instance storage as mailbox data is moved to the new Exchange 2007 servers and storage groups.

MIGRATING YOUR EXCHANGE ORGANIZATION

From the overview given in Table 6.1, it may seem as if I have a grudge against upgrading to Exchange 2007 by using the migration strategy. Although I have to admit it's not my favorite strategy, I'll hasten to say that migration offers many advantages that a transition upgrade doesn't offer:

◆ It is the only realistic way to consolidate two or more separate Exchange organizations into a single organization. This kind of consolidation can happen as the result of a major reorganization inside of one company or as the result of merger or acquisitions.

◆ It allows you to set up a *greenfield* (a term used to denote the ideal state of implementation) deployment of Exchange 2007. No matter how conscientious you are as an admin, any real network is the product of a number of design compromises. After a while, the weight of those compromises and workarounds add up; the design and structure of your network can reflect imperatives and inputs that no longer exist, or are no longer relevant, in your organization. It's nice to be able to wipe the slate clean, especially if that ends up being less work than trying to start with your current mess and clean it up.

◆ It permits you to move your Exchange servers out of your existing Active Directory forest and establish them in their own forest. If you're in an environment that separates administrative control between Active Directory and the Exchange organization, having a separate forest for Exchange can make it a lot easier to accomplish many of the day-to-day management tasks on your servers. (I don't know about you, but I'd much prefer to have control of the OU structure and Group Policy objects that affect my Exchange servers.) If the benefits of a multi-forest deployment outweigh the drawbacks, this configuration may actually improve the efficiency of the split between directory/account administration and Exchange administration.

◆ It gives you the chance to easily define new policies and procedures that apply equally to everyone, from account provisioning to server naming conventions. With the importance of regulatory compliance and strong internal IT controls and auditing rising on a daily basis, this can be a strong motivator.

◆ It allows you to perform additional configuration and testing of your new organization before you move the bulk of your live data and users to it. Being able to perform additional validation, perhaps with a pilot group of users, gives you additional confidence in the strength of your design and affords you extra opportunities to spot problems and correct them while you can.

◆ It gives you the ability to ensure that the new environment is properly locked down and secured. Exchange 2007 provides support for the Security Configuration Wizard, a new tool included with Windows Server 2003 SP1 and Windows Server 2003 R2 that permits administrators to easily and automatically harden and lock down servers based on what roles they play. When this tool is combined with the ability to define and configure a fresh set of Group Policy objects, a new organization can take advantage of security technologies and techniques that might be extremely difficult to deploy in your current environment while ensuring that your Exchange 2007 servers can still communicate with your legacy Exchange servers, your Active Directory infrastructure, and your users' machines.

Now that I've said that, I should point out that a migration strategy usually involves more work, more money, or both. Sometimes, though, it's what you have to do.

Take a look at what a migration might look like:

1. Deploy a new Active Directory forest and root domain, as well as any additional domains. These will probably be named something different from the domains in use in your current network so that you can operate in both environments (and your users can as well). You could be using this forest as an Exchange resource forest, or you could be moving all of your servers and desktops as well. Because migrations don't happen overnight, you'll probably need some sort of forest trust between your forests so that accounts and permissions will work properly while the migration is in progress. This step is outside the scope of this book.

2. Migrate a suitable set of user accounts to the new forest. Perhaps you're concentrating on one site at one time to minimize confusion; if so, you need to migrate each user account in the site to the corresponding site in the new Active Directory forest. Again, this step is outside the scope of this book.

3. Install Windows Server 2003 x64 SP1 (or, better, SP2) and Exchange 2007 SP 1 on a suitable number of 64-bit servers to form the core of your new Exchange 2007 organization. You don't need to have new servers for everything, but you usually need to have at least a site's worth of equipment on hand. You'll need to configure SMTP connectors between the two organizations, and you'll need to have some sort of directory synchronization going on between the two forests so that as users get moved into the new forest, each global address list (GAL) is properly updated to ensure that internal mail is delivered to the right Exchange organization. You'll probably need to configure public folder synchronization so that free-busy data is shared between the two organizations as well.

4. Move the mailbox data for the site from the legacy Exchange mailbox servers to the new Exchange 2007 mailbox servers. You'll need to update your users' Outlook profiles so that they can get to their mailboxes, and you'll need to ensure that the GAL information is

updated so that mail follows these users to their new mailbox servers. Once everything is working, you can remove the legacy Exchange servers from this site.

5. Don't forget that you may need to join your users' desktops, as well as any other Windows member servers (such as file/print, database, and web servers) to the new forest if it isn't being used exclusively as an Exchange resource forest. This step is outside the scope of this book.

6. Continue this process one site at a time until you've moved all of your user accounts and mailbox data into the Exchange 2007 organization and have decommissioned the remaining legacy Exchange servers.

Now you can see why I consider the migration strategy to be the labor-intensive route. You don't have the luxury of accepting your existing Active Directory structure and accounts. Though you can move message data over to a new organization, there's more effort involved in making sure users' profiles are properly updated; or you can rebuild your users' profiles and accept some data loss. If you're upgrading the desktop clients to Outlook 2007, you have the additional worry of whether you need to move the desktop machines into a new forest.

On the other hand, if you have an Active Directory deployment with serious structural problems (whether through years of accumulation or the results of previous mistakes), if you need to extract your Exchange servers into a separate Active Directory forest, or if there is some other reason transitioning your existing organization isn't going to work for you, then migration has a lot to offer.

Migrations require you to keep track of a lot of details and separate types of information. Though you can migrate all of the important information — mailboxes, public folders, global address list data — using the freely available Microsoft tools, you'll have a harder time migrating some of the smaller details that aren't mission critical but nonetheless can add up to a very negative user experience if omitted. If users' first experience on the new messaging system is having to reconfigure Outlook with all of their preferences, they're going to be less than happy about the experience. The cost of third-party migration tools may well prove to be a good investment that saves you time, reduces complexity, and gains you the goodwill of your users.

TRANSITIONING YOUR EXCHANGE ORGANIZATION

The process of transitioning your legacy Exchange organization to Exchange 2007 in many ways resembles the process required to upgrade from Exchange 5.5 to Exchange 2000 or Exchange 2003. If you have experience in that particular upgrade, relax; transitioning to Exchange 2007 is much easier. You're using Active Directory, so no directory upgrade or synchronization is required. You're not multiplying the number of organizational structures required, as the transition from Exchange 5.5 sites to Exchange 2000 administrative groups and routing groups did. You're not changing from the X.400-based MTA protocol to SMTP. All you're doing is moving mailboxes and public folder information, so it's easy. Well, as easy as these projects get.

Let's take a closer look at the average transition to Exchange 2007.

An Overview of Transition

Imagine that you have an Exchange 2003 organization that has eight mailbox servers, two front-end servers, and two bridgehead servers that handle all SMTP traffic with the Internet. For the sake of illustration, stipulate that all of your existing Exchange servers are already on 64-bit hardware; you have spares that you plan on using during the transition to keep your new hardware costs to a minimum.

In this organization, the transition process would look something like this:

1. Ensure that your organization meets all the prerequisites, including upgrading at least one Active Directory domain controller in each Active Directory site to Windows Server 2003 SP1 if they're not already at that level. You go ahead and run the Active Directory preparation to upgrade the forest schema with the Exchange 2007 extensions and to create the proper objects in the domains.

2. Install the first Exchange 2007 Client Access instance into your organization. Once it is configured, you can bring it into production use and decommission the first Exchange 2003 front-end server. You can then reuse this hardware to install the second Exchange 2007 Client Access instance and decommission the second Exchange 2003 front-end server.

3. Install the first Exchange 2007 Hub Transport instance into your organization. This instance could be on the same 64-bit machine as one of the Client Access instances (or as an intended Mailbox server) or on a separate machine; however, both the Client Access and Hub Transport roles need to exist before you install your first Exchange 2007 Mailbox instance. You also install an Exchange 2007 Edge Transport server on a separate machine. You configure the Edge Subscription connection between the Edge Transport server and the Hub Transport server and establish the Send connector. You can now remove the first Exchange 2003 bridgehead server.

4. Install the second Exchange 2007 Hub Transport instance. You can either install a second Edge Transport server or live with the existing one. Once the second Hub Transport instance (and second Edge Transport server, if deployed) is in production, you reconfigure your SMTP connectors so that your Edge Transport servers are now handling all external SMTP traffic. You then retire the second Exchange 2003 bridgehead server.

5. Install Windows Server 2003 x64 + SP1 or SP2 on your spare 64-bit mailbox server hardware. Install Exchange 2007 on it as the first Exchange 2007 Mailbox instance in the organization.

6. Move the mailboxes from the first Exchange 2003 mailbox server onto the first Exchange 2007 Mailbox server. Remove the first Exchange 2003 mailbox server from the organization.

7. Perform a clean install of Windows Server 2003 x64 + SP1 or SP2 on this server and then install the Exchange 2007 Mailbox instance. Move the mailboxes from the second Exchange 2007 server onto this new Mailbox instance.

8. Continue the process in Step 7 one server at a time until you have moved all mailboxes onto Exchange 2007 Mailbox instances and you have no remaining Exchange 2003 mailbox servers left in the organization. At this point, you will have the same number of spare servers you started with. If they are 64-bit machines, you can install some other Exchange 2007 role on them.

It sounds like a lot of work, but many people have favored this kind of approach even in previous upgrades to Exchange. It gives you the advantage of having a clean installation of Windows to work with and allows you to configure the operating system exactly the way you want it.

Order of Installation for Exchange 2007 Roles

Microsoft makes some specific recommendations on the order in which you should install the various roles. Technically, you can install your roles in any order you like. However, following Microsoft's recommendations allows you to minimize the deployment of new server hardware and get the most re-use value from your existing servers if that's a major consideration in your upgrade plans.

Microsoft's recommended order ensures that as each role is installed it can locate the prerequisite roles it depends on for proper function. You do not, however, need to install all instances of a particular role before beginning to deploy instances of the next role. You can always go back and install additional instances of any role as you scale up a site.

Client Access Servers

The Client Access role should be the first Exchange 2007 instance you install into a legacy Exchange organization. The reason for this is simple: once you actually have mailboxes on Exchange 2007 servers and your users attempt to access them using any protocol other than MAPI over RPC, you will need to have an Exchange 2007 Client Access instance to provide that protocol access. The Exchange 2007 Client Access role can also provide access to legacy Exchange mailboxes in much the same fashion that an Exchange 2003 front-end server provides access to both Exchange 2003 and Exchange 2000 mailbox servers. This allows you to switch client and web protocol access to Exchange 2007 and decommission your legacy front-end servers. In contrast, a legacy Exchange server cannot provide front-end or client protocol access to a server running a newer version of Exchange.

In smaller organizations, it is common to deploy the Client Access, Hub Transport, and Mailbox roles on the same physical server. In fact, this is the standard Exchange 2007 installation option when you use the GUI setup.

CLIENT ACCESS ROLE REQUIREMENTS AND BEST PRACTICES

Upgrading the front-end servers first has long been an Exchange best practice; even when applying service packs, you always want the front-end server running the most recent version of Exchange. Although the Client Access role isn't exactly the same thing as a front-end server, this rule of thumb still applies in Exchange 2007.

The Client Access role cannot be placed on clustered hardware. If you plan to use a clustered mailbox server configuration, you must place this role on a separate non-clustered machine (which can of course also run other roles such as Hub Transport).

When you are determining the number of Client Access instances you need, remember that you must have at least one Client Access instance in each Active Directory site where you will have an Exchange 2007 mailbox. Although any Client Access instance can answer an incoming request, if the requested resource is on a Mailbox server that is not in the same site as the initial Client Access instance, it will redirect the request to an available Client Access instance in the Mailbox server's Active Directory site.

This role is mandatory in an Exchange 2007 organization — unless you never plan on using any protocol to access your mailboxes other than Outlook in MAPI over RPC mode. If you use POP3, IMAP, or any of the HTTP-based protocols (OWA, Outlook Anywhere/RPC over HTTPS, or Exchange ActiveSync), you must have the Client Access role in your organization.

Hub Transport Servers

The Hub Transport role is the next logical role to install. Under the new Exchange 2007 architecture, Mailbox servers are no longer responsible for transporting messages directly. This task is now handled by the Hub Transport role. Likewise, all SMTP traffic with other routing groups and external systems is routed through Hub Transport instances. Even if you installed Exchange 2007 Mailbox servers first, they would literally be unable to communicate with any other Exchange servers until an Exchange 2007 Hub Transport instance was installed in the same site. If multiple Hub Transport instances are available in the same site, Exchange 2007 will automatically load-balance SMTP traffic across the available instances.

In smaller organizations, it is common to deploy the Client Access, Hub Transport, and Mailbox roles on the same physical server. In fact, this is the standard Exchange 2007 installation option when you use the GUI setup.

HUB TRANSPORT ROLE REQUIREMENTS AND BEST PRACTICES

If you are considering co-locating the Hub Transport role on the same physical server as the Mailbox role, remember that Mailbox instance will always attempt to use the Hub Transport instance that is on the same physical server and connect to other Hub Transport instances only if there is a problem. This can cause problems with the automatic load balancing in a site with multiple Mailbox servers.

The Hub Transport role cannot be placed on clustered hardware. If you plan to use a clustered mailbox server configuration, you must place the Hub Transport role on a separate machine (which can of course also run other roles).

When you are planning the number of Hub Transport instances you need, remember that you must have at least one Hub Transport instance in each Active Directory site where you will have an Exchange 2007 Mailbox server. As messages are routed to recipients in the organization, the Hub Transport instance that is processing the message looks up the mailbox data in Active Directory. If the mailbox is in the same site, the Hub Transport instance will directly pass the message along; if the recipient's mailbox is in a different site, the Hub Transport instance will transmit the message to an available Hub Transport instance in the recipient's Active Directory site.

The Hub Transport role is mandatory in an Exchange 2007 organization.

Mailbox Servers

After you have suitable Client Access and Hub Transport roles in a given site, you can begin deploying the Mailbox role. Until you have mailboxes hosted on Exchange 2007, the advanced features of Exchange 2007, such as Unified Messaging, cannot be used.

The Mailbox role is the only role that can be used in a clustered configuration.

When moving mailboxes to Exchange 2007 Mailbox servers, only use the Exchange 2007 Exchange Management Console Mailbox Move Wizard or the Exchange Management Shell Move-Mailbox cmdlet. In particular, do not use the wizard in legacy versions of Exchange or you could break the mailboxes.

The Mailbox role is mandatory in an Exchange 2007 organization. Well, I suppose that technically it's not — but if you're not going to have mailboxes, why bother to upgrade?

Edge Transport Servers

The Edge Transport server role can be deployed once you have a Hub Transport instance in your organization. Because the Edge Subscription process is initiated and controlled by Hub Transport instances, and Edge Transport servers should not be part of the same Active Directory forest as the rest of the Exchange organization, there are no requirements for site affinity.

The Edge Transport role must be placed on its own physical server and cannot be co-located with any other roles.

The Edge Transport role is designed to be placed in perimeter networks with limited connectivity to the internal network. Although there are no requirements for where you place the Edge Transport server, for best performance it should be placed so that it has a low-latency, high-bandwidth connection to the Internet, as well as one or more Hub Transport instances, through the appropriate firewalls.

Unified Messaging Servers

Although the Unified Messaging role is not within the scope of this book, I can make a few general observations about deploying it. This is probably the last role to deploy in your organization; it requires working Hub Transport and Mailbox instances in the organization; it also requires a Hub Transport instance to be placed in the same Active Directory site that the Unified Messaging server will be placed in. This Hub Transport instance will transmit messages created by the Unified Messaging server instance to recipient mailboxes in the organization.

Depending on the number of recipients and the hardware configuration, you can combine the Unified Messaging role with any (or all) of the Client Access, Hub Transport, or Mailbox roles on the same physical server.

The Unified Messaging role is, of course, optional.

For your users to make use of the UM functionality, you must have sufficient Enterprise Client Access Licenses (CALs) for those users.

Management Consoles

As you install Exchange 2007 on your servers, you may or may not wish to install the sixth role — the management tools. You can instead place the management tools role on a separate server or workstation and use it as a management console.

The management tools role is the only role that can be installed for production use with the 32-bit version of Exchange 2007. In other words, you can install it on existing management consoles. In fact, Microsoft makes the 32-bit version of these tools available as a separate download from its website.

You might want to install the Exchange 2007 management tools on the same machines your existing legacy Exchange management tools are on. If you do choose to use the 32-bit versions of the management tools, you will need to first install the 32-bit version of the Exchange 2007 prerequisites.

You cannot install the legacy Exchange System Manager on an Exchange 2007 server; legacy versions of Exchange are not supported on 64-bit Windows, and the IIS SMTP component required by the legacy System Manager would conflict with the Exchange 2007 SMTP stack.

So, under what conditions would you want to have the legacy System Manager on your Exchange 2007 management console?

♦ You still have existing legacy Exchange servers during the duration of your transition.

♦ You have legacy Exchange servers with features that are not supported in Exchange 2007. As long as you use these features, you will need to keep the legacy System Manager.

♦ You have public folders in your organization. Though you can manage them using the Exchange Management Shell, it is frankly easier to do it using the System Manager. If you have a large public folder infrastructure, I would say that keeping the System Manager is mandatory — unless, of course, you don't value your sanity.

> **ABOUT THE MOVE MAILBOX FEATURE**
>
> In legacy versions of Exchange, the creation of user accounts and provisioning of Exchange features all took place with extensions to the Active Directory Users and Computers MMC snap-in. In Exchange 2007, you can only use the management tools to provision existing users or create new mail-enabled objects. You may be tempted to continue using the Active Directory Users and Computers MMC snap-in to provision mailboxes and other recipients on your Exchange 2007 servers. However, these recipients are in "mixed mode" and cannot use most of the new Exchange 2007 features until you use the Exchange 2007 management tools to update them. When you move mailboxes to an Exchange 2007 Mailbox server using the Exchange 2007 Move Mailbox Wizard or Move-Mailbox cmdlet, the user object is automatically upgraded.

Coexistence

As you proceed with your Exchange 2007 upgrade, you will almost certainly have a period of time during which your Exchange 2007 servers will be required to coexist with legacy Exchange. During this time, there are several points you should consider:

◆ If you have multiple routing group connectors with legacy Exchange routing groups, especially so that there are multiple paths between a legacy Exchange routing group and the Exchange 2007 routing group, you must disable the propagation of link state routing. Link state routing is not used by Exchange 2007, but the presence of multiple paths can cause message routing loops in the legacy Exchange servers. The Exchange 2007 documentation contains instructions on performing this task under the topic "How to Suppress Link State Updates."

◆ Legacy Exchange servers use the X-EXCH50 SMTP extension to pass Exchange-specific properties with message data within the organization. Though Exchange 2007 no longer uses this connection, any routing group connectors created with legacy routing groups in the organization are automatically configured to support this extension. If you have a multiple-forest configuration where Exchange 2007 and legacy Exchange servers are communicating but in separate forests, you will need to enable this extension manually. The Exchange 2007 documentation contains instructions on performing this task under the topic "Configuring Cross-Forest Connectors."

◆ The Edge Transport role can be used as a smarthost for an Exchange 2003 organization without requiring the Active Directory preparation steps. However, because Edge Transport cannot synchronize with a legacy Exchange organization, you lose much of the advanced functionality that it offers.

◆ The UM role cannot offer services for recipients whose mailboxes are on legacy Exchange servers.

Performing an Inter-Organization Migration

If you have been digging through the Microsoft Exchange Server 2007 documentation, you may be a bit confused due to a slightly different use of terminology. Most of the rest of the world refers to moving to a new system of any type as a migration and that is why I keep using that word. Earlier in this chapter, I covered a migration type where you move existing services and data to Exchange

2007 servers from Exchange 2000/2003 servers in the same organization. This is what Microsoft officially refers to as a *transition*.

The last part of this chapter focuses on migrating from either an Exchange 2000 or 2003 organization into a new or separate Exchange 2007 organization. This type of migration is somewhat more difficult than an intra-organization migration, may be more disruptive for your users, and often leaves you with fewer options than a transition migration. However, you may be faced with an organizational configuration that leaves you no choice.

Is Inter-Organization Migration the Right Approach?

An inter-organization migration is quite a bit more complex for both the person handling the migration and also for the users. The "transition" migration is by far the simplest type of Exchange 2007 migration. Before you choose an inter-organization migration over a transition migration, you want to make sure you are choosing the right (and simplest) migration path.

Most organizations that are moving to Exchange Server 2007 will not need to perform an inter-organization migration. If the following checklist sounds like your organization, you will need to perform a "transition" organization:

♦ You have a single Active Directory forest and no resource forests.

♦ You are running Exchange 2000/2003.

♦ Your Exchange 2000/2003 organization is Active Directory.

Does this sound like you? If so, go back and read the first part of this chapter because performing a transition migration is what you are going to need to do. Because you already have Exchange 2000/2003 in your Active Directory, there is no need for the extra effort for an inter-organization.

So, who needs to perform an inter-organization migration? You might need to perform an inter-organization migration for a number of reasons. These include:

♦ You are consolidating one or more separate Exchange 2000/2003 organizations.

♦ You are moving Exchange resources from a resource forest into your accounts forest.

♦ You are moving from Exchange 5.5 to Exchange 2007.

♦ You are moving from a different messaging system to Exchange 2007.

If you have multiple organizations that you need to consolidate or some other type of migration, you really have no choice but to proceed down the inter-organization migration path. Proceeding down this path means different things to different organizations, but most of these inter-organizational migrations face a number of challenges. These include:

♦ Finding the tools necessary to perform the migration based on your needs.

♦ Moving mail data between two systems.

♦ Moving directory data between two systems.

♦ Maintaining directory synchronization and messaging between two systems during some period of inter-operability.

♦ Ensuring that e-mail flows correctly between the e-mail systems during the transition.

♦ Figuring out how and when to transition services such as public folders, MX records, mobile phones, and Web mail.

CHOOSING THE RIGHT TOOLS

When planning an inter-organization migration, it is important to pick the right tools to help you create accounts, move data, synchronize directories, create forwarders, and perform other migration tasks. Naturally, the most powerful and flexible of these tools are all provided by third parties rather than by Microsoft. However, Microsoft does provide some very basic tools that you can use to perform Exchange 2000/2003 to Exchange Server 2007 inter-organization migration.

Active Directory Migration Tool

If the user accounts have not yet been created or migrated into your target Active Directory, you should consider migrating the accounts from their original Active Directory rather than creating new user accounts. The Active Directory Migration Tool is a free tool from Microsoft that will help you migrate users, groups, and computers from one Windows domain or Active Directory to another. The big advantage of this tool is that it preserves the source domain's security identifier (SID) in the target account's SID history attribute and it preserves group membership.

You can download the Active Directory Migration Tool (ADMT) v3 from the Tools section of Microsoft's TechNet website at the following URL:

    http://technet.microsoft.com/en-us/windowsserver/bb405947.aspx

Move-Mailbox Cmdlet

The Exchange 2007 Move-Mailbox cmdlet has options that allow you to migrate mailbox data from a separate Exchange 2000/2003 organization and it will even create a disabled account for you if one does not exist. I cover this tool in more detail later in this chapter.

ExMerge and Import-Mailbox Cmdlet

If you have a small number of users (fewer than 50), you might opt to export all of their mail out from their old mail server using a tool like ExMerge (or even Outlook, yikes!) and then use the Exchange 2007 SP1 Import-Mailbox cmdlet to import mail data from these PST files into the user's new mailbox. This is a very basic solution, but it saves you from having to get to know Move-Mailbox and you still get to move your user's mail data. Keep in mind, though, that if you use this method you will lose things like folder rules and delegates that users have assigned to their folders.

Exchange 2003 Mail Migration Wizard

Exchange 2003 has an awesome migration utility called the Mail Migration Wizard that exports mail from Exchange 5.5, Exchange 2000, Exchange 2003, cc:Mail, Lotus Notes, and other mail systems. Exchange 2007 has no such tool, unfortunately. If you think you might need such functionality, you will need to install this tool on an Exchange 2003 server. If you are building a brand-new Exchange 2007 organization, you will need to install an Exchange 2003 server before you install your first Exchange 2007 server. Then you can migrate the mail temporarily to Exchange 2003 and move it on to Exchange 2007.

Third-Party Tools

If you have more than a few hundred users, a lot of public folder data, or very large mailboxes, or if you will need to maintain some level of interoperability between your old Exchange 2000/2003 system and your new Exchange 2007 system for a long period of time (longer than a few weeks), you should consider a third-party tool. These are often a really tough sell after an organization has invested a lot of money in a new mail system, but they can make your migration much easier and allow for better, long-term interoperability.

MAINTAINING INTEROPERABILITY

During either a true migration or a transition migration from one messaging system to another, the period of interoperability is always one of the biggest headaches. One of the first factors I always want to take into consideration when faced with an inter-organizational migration is developing a plan that will minimize the time during which the old system and the new system must coexist.

The transition type of migration is, of course, the simplest type if you are going to need two systems to coexist for some period of time. However, this is not always an option. If not, you need to figure out if you can perform an "instant" or light-switch migration, or if you need to have some period of interoperability.

Light-Switch Migrations

For a smaller number of users (fewer than 1,000 mailboxes, for example), I try to find a way to perform a "light-switch" migration. On Friday afternoon when the user leaves work, she is using the old system. On Monday morning when she returns to work, she is using the new system. This is a light-switch migration; from the user's perspective the transition occurs very quickly.

I like the "light-switch" migration strategy because it usually does not require you to perform any sort of destructive migration on the source system, and everything is migrated all at once. I have performed successful light-switch migrations for 20-user organizations all the way up to 1,500-user organizations. A number of factors will determine if a light-switch migration is possible in your organization. Here are some of the factors that I had to consider:

◆ Can all of the data be moved in a short period of time?

◆ Can users' Outlook clients, Outlook Web Access, and ActiveSync devices be directed or reconfigured to use the new servers effectively and accurately?

◆ Are there sufficient Help Desk and Information Technology resources to support the user community on "the morning after"?

◆ If new accounts have to be created for users, can the old passwords be synchronized or can new passwords be distributed to the users?

If you can properly support the light-switch migration, it is best for minimizing interoperability between two systems. Of course, the first goal has to be minimizing disruption for the user community, but a long transition between two mail systems can often be more disruptive if the interoperability issues are not properly addressed.

A lot of factors are involved in planning any inter-organization migration strategy, but here is a list of major factors and roughly the order in which they should be done:

◆ Deploy the new messaging system and test all components including inbound/outbound mail routing and Web components.

◆ Develop a plan for migrating Outlook profiles such as using Outlook 2007 Autodiscover or a script that creates a new profile.

◆ Create mailboxes and establish e-mail addresses that match the existing mailboxes on the source system.

◆ Move older data (mailboxes and public folders) if possible.

◆ Restrict user access to older mail system and start migration.

◆ Switch inbound e-mail to new mail system.

◆ Switch Outlook profiles to new servers.

◆ Switch over inbound HTTP/HTTPS access to mailboxes.

◆ Replicate public folder data.

◆ Move mailbox data; if using a third-party migration tool, try to replicate older mailbox data prior to migration day.

◆ Keep the old mail system up and running for a month or two just in case you need to retrieve something.

Interoperability Factors

In every migration I have been part of, I try to avoid keeping two mail systems operating in parallel for very long. Without the right tools, interoperability is a royal pain in the neck. That being said, you are probably wondering what some of the issues of interoperability are. Here is a partial list of some things you need to be concerned about and/or that your migration utilities should address:

◆ E-mail forwarding between domains should work seamlessly; e-mail should be delivered to the right location regardless of whether or not someone has been migrated.

◆ Directory/address book synchronization should work seamlessly; users should be able to continue to use the global address list and it should accurately reflect the correct address of the user.

◆ Mail distribution groups should continue to work properly regardless of where the member is located.

◆ Replying to e-mail messages that were migrated to the new system should still work.

◆ Public folder data and free/busy data should be synchronized between the two systems.

◆ You should have a plan that includes how to transition from one Web-based mail system and mobile device system to another.

◆ Your plan should include migrating users in groups or by department if possible.

◆ Your plan or migration utilities should also include a mechanism to migrate (or help the user to reproduce) rules, folder permissions, and mailbox delegate access.

Preparing for Migration

There are some things that you can do to get ready for your inter-organization migration; these will make things go more quickly for you. This includes gathering information about what you have to migrate as well as preparing for the actual steps of migration. Here is a partial list:

◆ Because you are migrating your users from an existing Exchange organization to a new Exchange 2007 organization, have all of the target systems' Exchange 2007 servers installed, tested, and ready to use prior to starting the migration.

◆ Document everything relevant about your source organization including connectors, e-mail flow, storage/message size limits, mail-enabled groups, Web access configuration (OWA, ActiveSync, IMAP4, POP3).

◆ Ensure that DNS name resolution between the two Active Directories is working correctly. You may need to configure conditional forwarders or zone transfers to achieve this.

◆ Ensure that WINS name resolution between all resources in both domains works properly. This may not be necessary, but it never hurts.

◆ Make sure there are no firewalls between the two systems; if there are, ensure that the necessary ports are open between the systems.

◆ Configure trust relationships between the two systems.

◆ Ensure that you have Domain Administrator and Exchange Administrator permissions in both the source and target systems.

◆ If you are planning to use the Active Directory Migration Tool (ADMT) to migrate user accounts, you must establish name resolution, a trust relationship, and admin accounts in both domains.

Moving Mailboxes Using the Move-Mailbox Feature

Exchange Server 2007 includes the new `Move-Mailbox` cmdlet, which can be used to move either mailboxes within an organization or between two different Exchange organizations. For inter-organization migrations, `Move-Mailbox` can be used whether the source server is running Exchange 2000/2003 or Exchange 2007; the target server must always be running Exchange 2007.

The `Move-Mailbox` cmdlet is a powerful tool with a lot of parameters and options. In this section, I focus just on its use when moving mail data between one Exchange organization and another. Keep in mind that one requirement for using the `Move-Mailbox` cmdlet is that the global catalog servers in both the source and target forest must be running Windows Server 2003 Service Pack 1 or later.

MIGRATING USER ACCOUNTS

When you use the `Move-Mailbox` cmdlet, if there is no user account for the mailbox that is about to be moved, `Move-Mailbox` can create a disabled account for that mailbox. However, that account will have none of the security credentials (such as the security identifier or the security group memberships) that it had in the source forest.

I strongly recommend that you find some method to migrate user accounts, security groups, and distribution groups prior to running `Move-Mailbox`. This will make the migration to the new forest and Exchange organization more seamless and easier for your users as well as yourself. Even a free tool such as the Active Directory Migration Tool v3 is powerful enough to help you to perform these tasks.

PERMISSIONS REQUIRED

When you are using `Move-Mailbox`, you need to have accounts in both the source and destination forests that will give you the necessary permissions to move mailbox data between the two organizations. Usually, the accounts you use for the source and target organizations will *not* be the same account; don't worry though, `Move-Mailbox` makes it easy to use to different accounts. In the source organization, you need the following:

◆ For Exchange 2000/2003 source servers, the account you are using must have been delegated the Exchange Administrator role for the organization or the administrative group in which the mailboxes are located.

◆ If the source server is an Exchange 2007 server, the account you are using must have the Exchange Recipient Administrator role.

◆ The account you are using must be a member of each Exchange server's local Administrator's group.

Naturally, in the target organization, the account you are using with Move-Mailbox must also have some special permissions:

◆ The account must be delegated the Exchange Recipient Administrator role in the target organization.

◆ The account must be delegated the Exchange Server Administrator role on the target server and be a member of the Exchange Mailbox server's local Administrators group.

Finally, regardless of the credentials that you are using for the source and target organizations, the account with which you are logged in to the Exchange server must be delegated the Exchange Server Administrator role for the server on which you are running Move-Mailbox.

MOVE-MAILBOX REQUIRED PARAMETERS

Let's start with the basic Move-Mailbox parameters that are required to move a mailbox from one organization to another, then move on to some "nice to have" options. I'll share some of these options and then some examples of how to use them.

-SourceForestCredentials The -SourceForestCredentials parameter allows you to set the username and password that will be used when connecting to the source Exchange 2000/2003/2007 server in the remote organization. When moving mailboxes between forests, this parameter is required. The input format for this parameter requires a specific security object format. I show an example of how to set this later in this chapter.

-TargetForestCredentials The -TargetForestCredentials parameter allows you to set the username and password that will be used when connecting to the target Exchange 2007 server. When moving mailboxes between forests, this parameter is optional unless you manually specify a target global catalog. The input format for this parameter requires a specific security object format. I show an example of how to set this later in this chapter.

-TargetDatabase The -TargetDatabase parameter allows you to specify the database to which the mailbox will be moved. This information is required, but if you do not include it in the Move-Mailbox command line you will be prompted for the target database name. The target mailbox database name can be in the format of -TargetDatabase "Mailbox Database", -TargetDatabase "ServerName\Mailbox Database", or -TargetDatabase "ServerName\First Storage Group\Mailbox Database". You must specify a target database name that is unique within the organization.

-GlobalCatalog The -GlobalCatalog parameter allows you to specify a global catalog server in the target forest that you can use. This parameter is optional unless you are specifying target credentials via the command line and then it is required. When specifying this parameter, you must use the fully qualified domain name of the global catalog server; here is an example: -GlobalCatalog hn1dc01.somorita.local.

-SourceForestGlobalCatalog The -SourceForestGlobalCatalog parameter is required and is used to specify a global catalog server in the source forest. You must be able to resolve this global catalog server using DNS. If you leave this parameter out, you cannot perform an inter-organization migration using Move-Mailbox.

-NTAccountOU The -NTAccountOU parameter is used to specify the OU in the target forest where an account should be created if no matching account is found. If the account already exists, the parameter is ignored and Move-Mailbox matches the source mailbox with the target account automatically. The target OU is specified as shown in this example:

-NTAccountOU "OU=Somorita,DC=somorita,DC=local"

A MOVE-MAILBOX EXAMPLE

Now that you know the basic parameters, let's take a look at how you would use these to perform a basic account migration. Here are the criteria for the migration:

◆ Source global catalog is duke.alohasurf.local

◆ Source user/mailbox is Brenda.Johnson

◆ Source credentials are Alohasurf\administrator

◆ Target credentials are VolcanoSurfb\Administrator

◆ Target mailbox database is HNLEX04\SG-HNLEX04-01\MBDB-HNLEX04-01

◆ Target OU is OU=Scully Surfboards,DC=volcanosurfboards,DC=com

The first thing you need to do is set the source and destination credentials. I mentioned earlier that you can't just specify the credentials in the command line because of the format that the `-SourceForestCredential` and `-TargetForestCredential` parameters are expecting the credentials to be in. But, you can use the PowerShell `Get-Credential` cmdlet to prompt you for each of these credentials and set them as a variable that you can use in the Move-Mailbox cmdlet. I am creating a variable called `$SourceUser` and will set that to the credentials of the source forest. Here is the cmdlet I would type:

```
$SourceUser = Get-Credential
```

When I type this cmdlet, I'm going to get a dialog box that prompts me for the username and password.

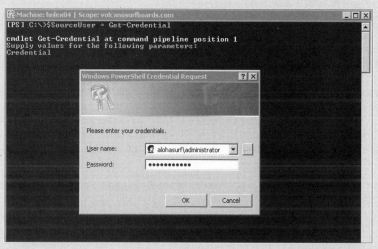

Once I enter the source forest's username and password and click OK, the dialog box goes away. I could then type `$SourceUser` and see the properties of that variable. Here is an example:

```
$SourceUser | FL
UserName : alohasurf\administrator
Password : System.Security.SecureString
```

I now need to repeat this process to set the $TargetUser variable; here is an example:

```
$TargetUser = Get-Credential
```

Once again, I will be prompted for credentials using the dialog box and this time I will provide the username and password for the target forest. I can now use these variables over and over again while I have this Exchange Management Shell (EMS) window open; if I close the window the variables will be cleared.

Now I am ready to actually move a user's mailbox. Here is an EMS command that will move Brenda Johnson's mailbox and create a disabled user account (if the account does not exist):

```
Move-Mailbox brenda.johnson -TargetDatabase MBDB-HNLEX04-01↵
 -SourceForestGlobalCatalog duke.alohasurf.local↵
 -NTAccountOU "OU=Scully Surfboards,DC=volcanosurfboards,dc=com"↵
 -SourceForestCredential $SourceUser
```

Notice that I left out the -GlobalCatalog and the -TargetForestCredential parameters. If I leave these out, the credentials of the currently logged-on user will be used. The EMS is going to prompt me to make sure that this is really what I want to do; once I confirm that I do want to move the mailbox, the move will actually begin. This particular mailbox was 19MB in size and it took approximately 5 minutes to move.

Once the Move-Mailbox is complete, you will get a report telling you about the move operation and how long it took to move. In the example shown in "A Move-Mailbox Example," Move-Mailbox created a disabled user account for me. Move-Mailbox will also synchronize as many of the source user account's attributes as it possibly can. This includes the display name, title, company, department, and phone number attributes. For example, Figure 6.4 shows Brenda Johnson's Organization property page from Active Directory Users and Computers in the target forest. The title, department, and company information was copied from the source account, but the manager attribute was not.

One interesting thing about the disabled account that Move-Mailbox creates is that it does not copy the user logon information. It generates a random username for the pre-Windows 2000 logon name and it does not set the UPN name as you can see in this screen capture.

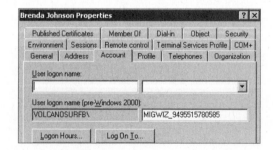

FIGURE 6.4
Many attributes from
the source account are
copied to the target
account

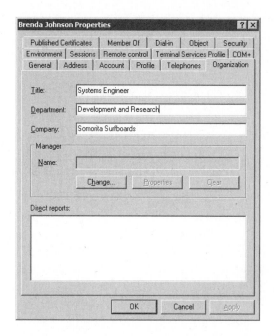

Another nice feature of the `Move-Mailbox` cmdlet when moving mailboxes from one organization to another is that the old e-mail addresses are preserved and the `legacyExchangeDN` attribute from the source user account is set as an X500 address on the target account. Notice in Figure 6.5 that Brenda Johnson's account has two X500 addresses. One of these addresses is from the Aloha Surf International Exchange organization; this was the `legacyExchangeDN` attribute for her mailbox in the source forest.

The `legacyExchangeDN` attribute from the source forest may seem like a pretty obscure parameter, but it serves an important function for mailboxes moved from one organization to another. This allows users that have been migrated to reply to e-mail that was sent to them prior to the migration and it allows them to use entries in their Outlook nickname cache (stored in the NK2 file) that they used prior to the migration.

MOVE-MAILBOX OPTIONAL PARAMETERS

`Move-Mailbox` has some parameters that can help you make your migration more efficient or allow you to move data prior to actually being ready to start the migration.

-AllowMerge   The -AllowMerge parameter is handy in situations where the mailbox already exists on the target system. You could use parameter if you are planning to move the majority of a user's mailbox a few days (or weeks) before the official migration. Then on migration day you could come back and use the -AllowMerge parameter and move the mailbox again in order to get anything that has changed since you last moved the mailbox. The -AllowMerge parameter can be used in either intra-organization or inter-organization mailbox moves.

-RetryTimeout   The -RetryTimeout parameter can be used to specify that the move mailbox operation should be terminated if it takes longer than the time that you specify. This is specified in hours, minutes, and seconds. Here is an example: -RetryTimeout 1:30:00.

FIGURE 6.5
Viewing the e-mail
addresses of a migrated
mailbox

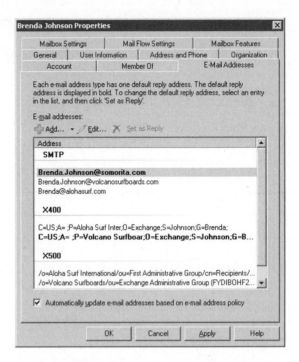

-SourceMailboxCleanupOptions   The -SourceMailboxCleanupOptions parameter speci-fies what to do once you have completed the mailbox move. One option you can use with this parameter is the DeleteSourceNTAccount option, which will delete the source account after the mailbox is moved. This is a dangerous option and I recommend against using it unless you are absolutely positive you will not need the old account or the mailbox anymore.

-ExcludeFolders   The -ExcludeFolders option lets you specify mailbox folders that should not be moved when the command is executed. For example, you would use this option if you did not want the Sent Items and Deleted Items to be moved: -ExcludeFolders "\Deleted Items", "\Sent Items".

-IncludeFolders   The -IncludeFolders option lets you specify only specific folders that you want to be moved. For example, if you only want to move the Inbox, Calendar, and Con-tacts folders, you would use this option: -IncludeFolders \Inbox, \Calendar, \Contacts.

-AttachmentFilenames   The -AttachmentFilenames option allows you to specify that only messages with specific attachments are moved. You can use wildcards with these parameters. For example, this will copy over just messages with DOC file attachments: -AttachmentFilenames *.doc.

-ContentKeywords   The -ContentKeywords option allows you to specify that only messages whose content has a specific keyword will be moved.

-SubjectKeywords   The -SubjectKeywords option allows you to specify that only messages whose subject line has specific keywords will be moved.

-RecipientKeywords The -RecipientKeywords option allows you to specify that only messages with specific keywords (or e-mail addresses) will be moved.

-SenderKeywords The -SenderKeywords option allows you to specify that only messages with specific senders will be moved.

Importing Data from PST

A nice new feature of Exchange Server 2007 Service Pack 1 is the addition of the Import-Mailbox cmdlet and the option to import data from a PST. There is a small limitation to this feature, though. It can only be run on a 32-bit version of the Management Tools and from a machine that has Outlook 2003 SP2 or later or Outlook 2007. If this is a feature that you are going to use, I recommend installing the 32-bit version of the Exchange Management Tools on your Windows XP workstation or Windows 2003 (32-bit version) server and install Office. You can download the 32-bit tools from Microsoft's website.

Before you begin trying to import PST data in to an existing mailbox, you need to make sure that you have the necessary permissions. By default, just because you are an Exchange Server Administrator does not mean you can import data. Use the Exchange Management Console or the EMS Add-MailboxPermission cmdlet to give your account permissions. Here is an example where I give user Rena.Dauria permission to user Grace.Tanaka's mailbox:

```
Add-MailboxPermission Grace.Tanaka -User Rena.Dauria -AccessRights FullAccess
```

One you have the necessary permissions to the mailbox and you have the 32-bit version of the Exchange management tools, you can import the PST file. Here is an example of importing a PST file called ARoberts.PST into the mailbox Andrew.Roberts:

```
Import-Mailbox Andrew.Roberts -PSTFolderPath c:\ARoberts.PST
```

You can also import just a specific date range of data into a user's folder using the Import-Mailbox cmdlet's -StartDate and -EndDate options. Here is another example:

```
Import-Mailbox Rena.Dauria -PSTFolderPath↵
    c:\RDauria.PST -StartDate 03/01/2006 -EndDate 03/01/2008
```

Summary

Upgrades to Exchange 2007 require you to think carefully about your current Exchange organization and to identify any potential trouble spots. You must be aware of how you plan to get from your current legacy organization to the final goal of an all-Exchange 2007 organization. Are you going to use a transition strategy and upgrade the organization from within, allowing legacy Exchange and Exchange 2007 to coexist side by side for a time, or are you going to pursue the migration strategy and re-create your Exchange 2007 organization from scratch?

Whichever strategy you use, you must be aware of any special roles, applications, and add-ons you are using that will not be compatible with Exchange 2007. Although you can allow these legacy servers to be part of the organization for a while, keeping legacy servers around indefinitely may create more problems than it solves.

Part 3

Basic Exchange Server 2007 Management

In this part:

Chapter 7

Administering Exchange Server 2007

The new Exchange 2007 administrative architecture is designed to be much more administrator friendly whether you prefer to work from the graphical user interface or from the command line. The Exchange Management Console has been greatly improved and the new Exchange Management Shell will keep command-line enthusiasts and Unix administrators very happy. If you are like me, you may find yourself happily going to the Exchange Management Shell to perform many tasks that you formerly would have used the GUI to perform.

In this chapter you learn to:

◆ Understand the new administrative architecture

◆ Use the Exchange Management Console

◆ Assign administrative permissions

◆ Perform basic tasks with the Exchange Management Shell

Understanding the New Administrative Architecture

Administrators of Exchange 2000/2003 in both small and large organizations always end up hearing the same complaints when it comes to managing an Exchange 2000/2003 organization. Maybe these are some of your beefs with Exchange 2000/2003 or maybe you have heard some of these common complaints:

◆ Finding the right object or configuration task within Exchange System Manager is difficult because the object or task is often buried many levels deep.

◆ The Exchange System Manager is poorly designed and often objects are found in the tree view and tree objects are found in the management pane.

◆ Management of Exchange servers and mail recipients through scripting is very difficult.

◆ Bulk management of recipient objects is difficult.

◆ There are too many different APIs for managing Exchange-related configuration data and mailbox data.

The Exchange 2003 administrative architecture has many shortcomings. The most noticeable is that automating or scripting most administrative tasks is difficult. An administrator may need to understand two or more scripting interfaces or Application Programming Interfaces (APIs), such as Active Directory Services Interface (ADSI), Collaborative Data Objects (CDOs), CDO for Exchange, CDO for Exchange Management, Exchange Windows Management Instrumentation (WMI) classes, and others.

Although the Exchange 2000/2003 Exchange System Manager (ESM) console (shown in Figure 7.1) is not the most difficult interface to use in the world, administrators frequently complain that it is difficult to actually find the objects that might need to be configured and the tasks that can be performed against each object.

FIGURE 7.1

Exchange System Manager console for Exchange 2000/2003

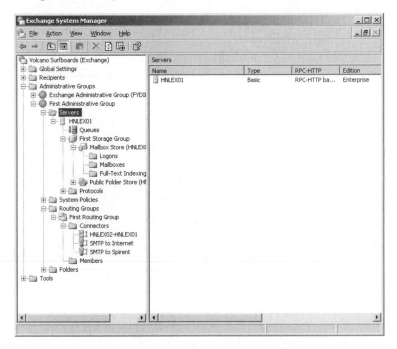

A common complaint among Exchange administrators is that the ESM interface objects are often buried seven or eight levels deep in the ESM hierarchy. Administrators also complain that leaf objects appear in the tree pane and tree objects appear in the results pane of the interface.

Whereas some of the configuration tasks are performed directly against the Active Directory and can be duplicated with an ADSI script, other tasks are performed against the Registry, Exchange components, the file system, or indirectly against Internet Information Server (IIS) components. Thus, many of the tasks that are performed in the ESM become extremely difficult to automate or script.

A better and more consistent interface for managing Exchange server objects, Exchange tasks, and mail recipients had to be developed. The management interface had to be capable of managing a combination of Active Directory objects (Exchange configuration and recipient information), Registry settings, file system components, IIS components, Windows services, and Exchange components. The new interface had to provide a consistent interface for managing Exchange and allow for easier scripting and command-line management.

About the same time that the Exchange team started working on a new management interface, the Windows team was designing a new shell and scripting interface for Windows. This shell (originally code-named Monad) is called the Windows PowerShell. PowerShell is a completely redesigned command-line interface (CLI) for Windows that may eventually replace the traditional command prompt that we are all used to.

The Exchange team decided to provide access to the Exchange management functions through the Windows PowerShell. All objects that would need to be manipulated by an Exchange server administrator (mailboxes, mailbox databases, distribution groups, and so on) were defined, and the actions that might be taken against these objects (enable, set, get, mount, test, and so on) were also defined.

From the objects that would need to be manipulated, and the actions that would need to be performed on these objects, a series of tasks (or actions) were defined. This is the underlying Exchange administrative model as shown in Figure 7.2.

FIGURE 7.2
Exchange 2007 administrative architecture

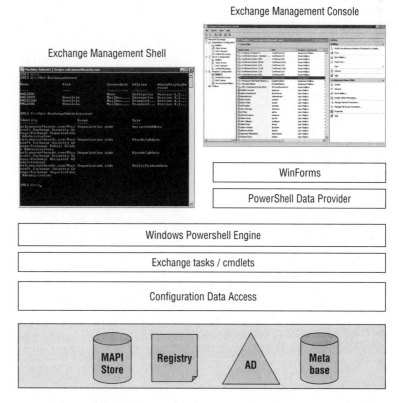

Exchange tasks are given access to differing types of data and components relating to Exchange through the Exchange Management API. These tasks, or cmdlets (pronounced "command-lets"), can be accessed via the Windows PowerShell and the Exchange Management Shell (EMS) or through the Exchange Management Console (EMC). The EMC interacts with the EMS tasks through the WinForms and PowerShell data providers. All of the EMS tasks are exposed as .NET classes and can also be accessed and used through applications written with the .NET Framework.

Installing the Administrative Tools

You will want to install the administrative tools on your desktop computer so that you do not have to be continually logging on to an Exchange server's console in order to administer Exchange Server 2007. If you are migrating, you may also want to provide access to manage Exchange 2000/2003 servers from desktop workstations. The catch is that the two management interfaces cannot be on the same machine.

EDGE TRANSPORT MUST BE MANAGED LOCALLY

All Exchange 2007 server roles can be managed remotely except the Edge Transport server role. The Edge Transport role must be managed from that server's console.

Installing the Exchange 2007 Management Tools

One of the nice things about Exchange 2007's setup program is that you can easily install all of the components necessary to manage Exchange Server 2007. That is the good news; the better news is that if you have the 32-bit version of Exchange 2007, you can install the Exchange management tools on Windows XP 32-bit or Windows 2003 32-bit. The Exchange management tools include the Exchange Management Shell, the Exchange Help file, the Exchange Best Practices Analyzer tool, and the Exchange Troubleshooting Assistant tool.

Just don't be tempted to install the 32-bit version of Exchange Server 2007 in production because the server components are intended only for testing, evaluation, training, and lab purposes and are not supported in production.

To start the installation, you will first need to meet some prerequisites. For each of the prerequisite pieces of software, there is a 32-bit and a 64-bit version, so the prerequisites depend on which version of Windows you are using:

1. If the workstation on which you are planning to install the Exchange 2007 management tools has the Exchange 2003 System Manager, remove it.

2. Ensure that the computer on which you are installing the Exchange management tools meets the following requirements:

   ◆ 512MB of RAM

   ◆ 1.0GHz processor or greater

   ◆ At least 500MB of free disk space

   ◆ Hard disk is formatted as NTFS

3. Install the IIS common files.

4. If it's not already installed, install the .NET Framework 2.0 and ensure that you have any updates and patches.

5. Install Microsoft Management Console (MMC) 3.0 if it's not already installed.

6. Install the Windows PowerShell, available at the following URL:

   ```
   http://www.microsoft.com/windowsserver2003/technologies/management
   /powershell/default.mspx
   ```

7. Once you have met the prerequisites, run the Exchange 2007 setup program.

8. On the Introduction screen of Exchange Server 2007 Setup Wizard, click Next.

9. Accept the license agreement and click Next.

10. Select Yes or No to error reporting and click Next.

11. On the Installation Type screen, select Custom Exchange Server Installation, specify the installation path if necessary, and click Next.

12. On the Server Role Selection screen (shown in Figure 7.3), select Management Tools and click Next.

13. Once the readiness checks have completed successfully, click Install.

14. Click Finish on the Completion screen.

FIGURE 7.3
Installing the Exchange 2007 Management Tools

Installing the Exchange 2003 Management Tools

Exchange 2003 management tools cannot be installed on an Exchange 2007 server. You must use the Exchange 2003 management tools from a computer other than your Exchange 2007 servers.

WHY INSTALL THE EXCHANGE 2003 MANAGEMENT TOOLS?

The Exchange 2003 management tools will be required for a couple of different reasons:

◆ If you are running Exchange 2000/2003 servers, you will need to manage those servers from the Exchange System Manager for Exchange 2000/2003.

◆ Even though Exchange 2007 Service Pack 1 includes public folder management support, there are still a few things you can do with the Exchange 2003 System Manager that you cannot do using the Exchange 2007 Management Console.

If you need to manage public folders through the ESM, any Exchange 2007 mailbox server that contains a public folder database must also have the World Wide Web Publishing Service installed. ESM uses the WebDAV interface to manage the public folder structure.

The Exchange 2003 management tools are 32-bit tools only, so you should install them only on Windows XP/2003 32-bit operating systems.

To install ESM on Windows 2003, here are the recommended prerequisites:

◆ Domain membership in the forest in which Exchange Server is installed

◆ Windows 2003 SP1 or later

◆ Internet Information Services (IIS) snap-in

◆ SMTP service (which can be disabled after installation)

◆ WWW Publishing Service (which can be disabled after installation)

◆ Windows Server 2003 Administration Tools Pack (`adminpak.msi`) is not a requirement for installation, but these tools are very helpful to have

To install the Exchange system management tools on Windows XP Professional, here are the recommended prerequisites:

◆ Windows XP Professional Service Pack 2

◆ Internet Information Services (IIS) snap-in

◆ Windows Server 2003 Administration Tools Pack

During installation, on the Component Selection screen (shown in Figure 7.4), ensure that the action type next to the Microsoft Exchange component is set to Custom and that the action type for the Microsoft Exchange System Management Tools component is set to Install.

FIGURE 7.4

Installing the Exchange 2003 system management tools

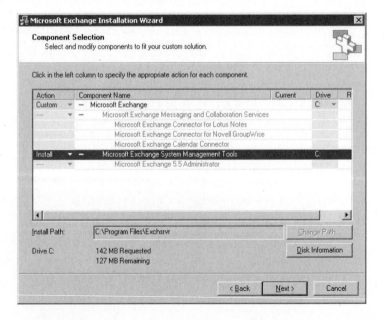

Once you have completed the installation, I recommend that you apply the latest Exchange 2003 service pack.

Exploring the Exchange Management Console

Now that you know how to install the Exchange 2007 management tools, let's take a look at the console layout, wizards, and new features. I think that you will be impressed once you have some time to get to know it. I am particularly impressed with the ease of use, how quickly you can find the exact tasks you need, and the ability to save your configuration.

There have been many improvements to reduce the complexity of the console tree, to make objects more discoverable, and to separate objects that can be configured from the tree and tree containers.

Console Layout

Let's start by taking a look at the console as a whole and then dissect it into its various components or parts. Figure 7.5 shows the EMC with the four major components, or panes.

FIGURE 7.5
Introducing the Exchange 2007 Management Console

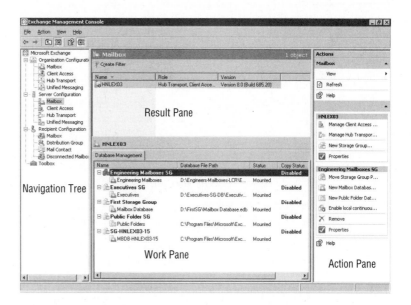

Notice that the default console is broken up into four separate sections, or panes. These are the navigation tree pane, the Work pane, the Results pane, and the Actions pane.

NAVIGATION TREE

The console navigation tree is one of the biggest improvements in the Exchange 2007 EMC. Unlike the Exchange 2003 System Manager, the EMC contains only static data and containers; there is no dynamic data and no objects that must be configured in the navigation tree. The EMC navigation tree is a maximum of only three levels deep and by default contains only four work centers. A view of just the navigation tree is shown in Figure 7.6.

FIGURE 7.6
Exchange Management
Console navigation tree

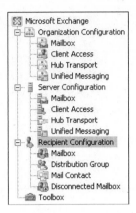

The work centers you see in Figure 7.6 show the different types of configuration data or operations that an administrator may be required to manage. Later in this chapter, you see how to break up the console so that an administrator can only see a particular work center. The Exchange 2007 work centers are as follows:

WORK CENTER	DESCRIPTION
Organization Configuration	Contains objects and properties related to the configuration of the entire Exchange 2007 organization. These objects and properties affect all servers and recipients.
Server Configuration	Contains the server objects that can be configured individually, such as mailbox databases, Outlook Web Access virtual directories, SMTP receive connectors, and Unified Messaging components.
Recipient Configuration	Contains the recipient data for all mail-enabled objects in the organization, including mail-enabled users, mail-enabled contacts, and mail-enabled groups. In Exchange 2000/2003, this information was managed through Active Directory Users and Computers.
Toolbox	A launching pad for additional tools or consoles, including the Exchange Best Practices Analyzer, the Queue Viewer, the Mail Flow Troubleshooter, and tools for database recovery management and message tracking.

Also note in Figure 7.6 that the Organization, Server, and Recipient Configuration work centers include containers that help to categorize the types of objects found in them.

RESULTS PANE

The Results pane of the EMC will be different depending on which work center object and subcontainer is highlighted in the navigation tree. For example, if you highlight the Recipient Configuration object in the tree, the Results pane will show all mail-enabled recipients (users, contacts, groups). A view of the entire Recipient Configuration container is shown in Figure 7.7.

However, the console layout will change and the scope of what is displayed in the Results pane will be different if you select the Mailbox subcontainer that is found under the Recipient Configuration object. Figure 7.8 shows the view of the Recipient Configuration Results pane when the Mailbox subcontainer is selected. As you would expect, the Results pane contains only user and resource mailboxes.

FIGURE 7.7
General view of the Recipient Configuration work center

Display Name	Alias	Recipient Type Details
!Ithicos Developers	!IthicosDevelopers	Mail-Enabled Universal Dis...
!Ithicos Sales	IthicosSales	Mail-Enabled Universal Dis...
!Ithicos Support Alias	IthicosSupport	Mail-Enabled Universal Dis...
#Everyone in Organiza...	EveryoneinOrganization	Dynamic Distribution Group
#Field Research Group	FieldResearchGroup	Mail-Enabled Universal Se...
$Everyone in Marketing	$EveryoneinMarketing	Dynamic Distribution Group
$Everyone in Sales	$EveryoneinSales	Dynamic Distribution Group
$Executives and VIPs	ExecutivesandVIPs	Mail-Enabled Universal Se...
$Operations Group	OperationsGroup	Mail-Enabled Universal Se...
&Somorita Executives	SomoritaExecutives	Mail-Enabled Universal Se...
&Somorita Sales and M...	SomoritaSalesandMarketing	Mail-Enabled Universal Se...
~All Ithicos Users	AllIthicosUsers	Dynamic Distribution Group
~Failure Analysis Team	FailureAnalysisTeam	Mail-Enabled Universal Dis...
+VIPs	VIPs	Mail-Enabled Universal Se...
Adelind Guiraud	aguiraud	User Mailbox
Adena Hawthorne	ahawthorne	User Mailbox
Administrator	Administrator	User Mailbox
Adri Duhem	aduhem	User Mailbox
Afton Mulot	amulot	User Mailbox
Aili Heatley	aheatley	User Mailbox
Ajoy Hertzog	ahertzog	User Mailbox
Al Shea	ashea	User Mailbox
Al Williams	AlWilliams	Mail Contact
Alan R. Morris	Alan.Moris	Mail User
Alanda Duignan	aduignan	User Mailbox
Aleen Arcuri	aarcuri	User Mailbox
Alek Callegari	acallegari	User Mailbox
Alex Nichols	Alex.Nichols	Mail User
Alidia Krieg	akrieg	User Mailbox
Alison Humber	ahumber	User Mailbox
Allianora Bielan	abielan	User Mailbox
Alparslan Michaelson	amichaelson	User Mailbox

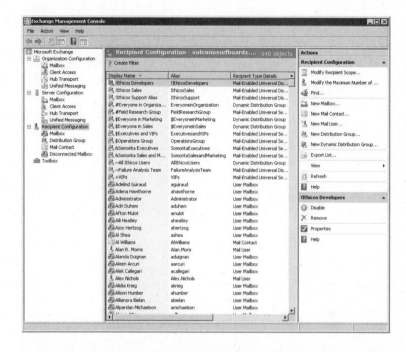

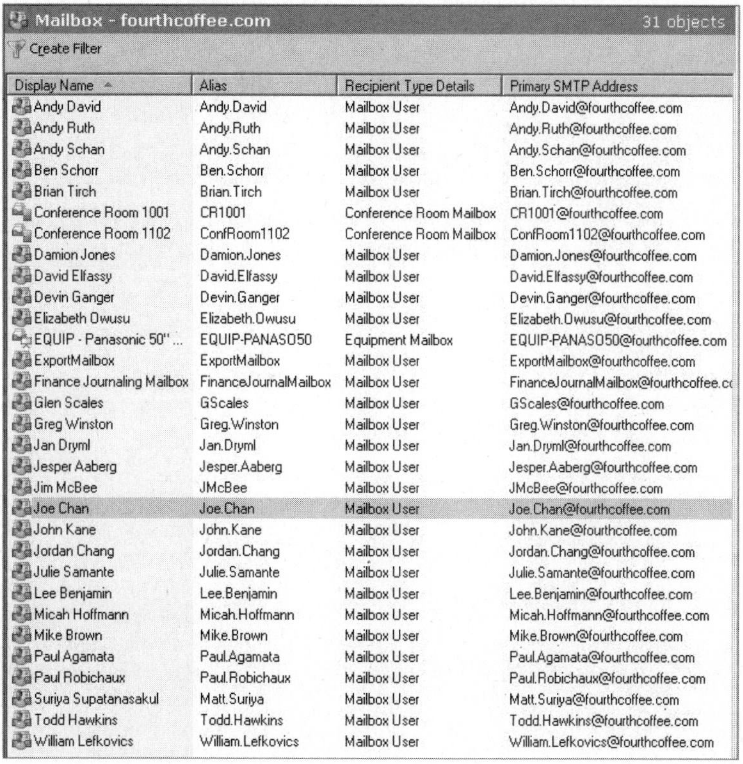

FIGURE 7.8
Mailbox-specific view of the Recipient Configuration work center

Display Name	Alias	Recipient Type Details	Primary SMTP Address
Andy David	Andy.David	Mailbox User	Andy.David@fourthcoffee.com
Andy Ruth	Andy.Ruth	Mailbox User	Andy.Ruth@fourthcoffee.com
Andy Schan	Andy.Schan	Mailbox User	Andy.Schan@fourthcoffee.com
Ben Schorr	Ben.Schorr	Mailbox User	Ben.Schorr@fourthcoffee.com
Brian Tirch	Brian.Tirch	Mailbox User	Brian.Tirch@fourthcoffee.com
Conference Room 1001	CR1001	Conference Room Mailbox	CR1001@fourthcoffee.com
Conference Room 1102	ConfRoom1102	Conference Room Mailbox	ConfRoom1102@fourthcoffee.com
Damion Jones	Damion.Jones	Mailbox User	Damion.Jones@fourthcoffee.com
David Elfassy	David.Elfassy	Mailbox User	David.Elfassy@fourthcoffee.com
Devin Ganger	Devin.Ganger	Mailbox User	Devin.Ganger@fourthcoffee.com
Elizabeth Owusu	Elizabeth.Owusu	Mailbox User	Elizabeth.Owusu@fourthcoffee.com
EQUIP - Panasonic 50" ...	EQUIP-PANASO50	Equipment Mailbox	EQUIP-PANASO50@fourthcoffee.com
ExportMailbox	ExportMailbox	Mailbox User	ExportMailbox@fourthcoffee.com
Finance Journaling Mailbox	FinanceJournalMailbox	Mailbox User	FinanceJournalMailbox@fourthcoffee.c
Glen Scales	GScales	Mailbox User	GScales@fourthcoffee.com
Greg Winston	Greg.Winston	Mailbox User	Greg.Winston@fourthcoffee.com
Jan Dryml	Jan.Dryml	Mailbox User	Jan.Dryml@fourthcoffee.com
Jesper Aaberg	Jesper.Aaberg	Mailbox User	Jesper.Aaberg@fourthcoffee.com
Jim McBee	JMcBee	Mailbox User	JMcBee@fourthcoffee.com
Joe Chan	Joe.Chan	Mailbox User	Joe.Chan@fourthcoffee.com
John Kane	John.Kane	Mailbox User	John.Kane@fourthcoffee.com
Jordan Chang	Jordan.Chang	Mailbox User	Jordan.Chang@fourthcoffee.com
Julie Samante	Julie.Samante	Mailbox User	Julie.Samante@fourthcoffee.com
Lee Benjamin	Lee.Benjamin	Mailbox User	Lee.Benjamin@fourthcoffee.com
Micah Hoffmann	Micah.Hoffmann	Mailbox User	Micah.Hoffmann@fourthcoffee.com
Mike Brown	Mike.Brown	Mailbox User	Mike.Brown@fourthcoffee.com
Paul Agamata	Paul.Agamata	Mailbox User	Paul.Agamata@fourthcoffee.com
Paul Robichaux	Paul.Robichaux	Mailbox User	Paul.Robichaux@fourthcoffee.com
Suriya Supatanasakul	Matt.Suriya	Mailbox User	Matt.Suriya@fourthcoffee.com
Todd Hawkins	Todd.Hawkins	Mailbox User	Todd.Hawkins@fourthcoffee.com
William Lefkovics	William.Lefkovics	Mailbox User	William.Lefkovics@fourthcoffee.com

You can further restrict the scope of what is displayed in the Results pane by applying a filter. At the very top of the Results pane is a Create Filter button; you can use this option to create expressions that define or restrict the scope of what is displayed in the Results pane. Though filters can be defined for any result in the Results pane, I am using the example once again of mail-enabled recipients. To create a filter, click the Create Filter button and the filter options will appear at the top of the Results pane.

The leftmost part of the filter defines the attribute on which you want to filter. Attributes on which you can build a filter include ActiveSync Mailbox Policy, Alias (Exchange alias), City, Company, Country/Region, Custom Attributes 1–15, Database (mailbox database), Department, Display Name, E-Mail Address, External E-mail Address, First Name, Last Name, Managed By, Mailbox Folder Mailbox Policy, Name, Office, Postal Code, Recipient Type Details, Server (home mailbox server), State or Province, UM Enabled, Unified Messaging Mailbox Policy, User Logon Name (pre-Windows 2000), and User Principal Name (UPN).

The middle option defines the operator for the attribute you are filtering; operators include Equals, Does Not Equal, Contains, Does Not Contain, Starts With, Ends With, Is Present, and Is Not Present. The actual operators you see will be based on the attribute on which you are building the filter.

Finally, the rightmost portion is where you enter the data for which you are building the filter. The following screen shot shows that I have created a filter that displays only mail-enabled users whose city is Honolulu. I can click the Add Expression button and add additional expressions to further filter the information that is displayed in the Results pane. In this example, I have further restricted the filter using two expressions so that it shows only recipients whose city is Honolulu and whose department is Viper Pilots.

Mailbox - fourthcoffee.com				6 objects
City	Equals	Honolulu		✕
Department	Equals	Viper Pilots		✕
Add Expression Remove Filter				Apply Filter

Display Name ▲	Alias	Recipient Type Details	Primary SMTP Address
Andy David	Andy.David	Mailbox User	Andy.David@fourthcoffee.com
Ben Schorr	Ben.Schorr	Mailbox User	Ben.Schorr@fourthcoffee.com
Damion Jones	Damion.Jones	Mailbox User	Damion.Jones@fourthcoffee.com
Elizabeth Owusu	Elizabeth.Owusu	Mailbox User	Elizabeth.Owusu@fourthcoffee.com
Glen Scales	GScales	Mailbox User	GScales@fourthcoffee.com
Jim McBee	JMcBee	Mailbox User	JMcBee@fourthcoffee.com

This filter will only be in effect for the Mailbox container because that is the subcontainer on which I created it; if I select the entire Recipient Configuration work center or the Distribution Group, Mail Contact, or Disconnected Mailbox subcontainers, the filter does not apply.

Certain types of attributes, such as the ActiveSync Mailbox Policy, Managed Folder Mailbox Policy, and the Unified Messaging Mailbox Policy, will include a Browse button that allows you to browse the directory for the specific policy for which you want to set the filter. When you choose the Recipient Type Details attribute, the last field is converted to a drop-down list and you can select the specific type of recipient you are looking for. The recipient types include Dynamic Distribution Group, User Mailbox, Legacy Mailbox (a mailbox located on Exchange 2000/2003), Linked

Mailbox, Shared Mailbox, Room Mailbox, Equipment Mailbox, Mail Contact, Mail User, Mail Universal Distribution Group, Mail Universal Security Group, and Mail Non-Universal Group.

WORK PANE

Some Results panes list objects that require more than just a single set of property pages. Objects such as Exchange servers have property pages, but also objects under the server, such as storage groups and mailbox databases. Server objects require an additional pane under the Results pane called the Work pane. In Figure 7.9, I have selected the Mailbox subcontainer found under the Server Configuration work center. Notice that there is a new pane below the Results pane; this is the Work pane.

FIGURE 7.9
Server objects include a Work pane.

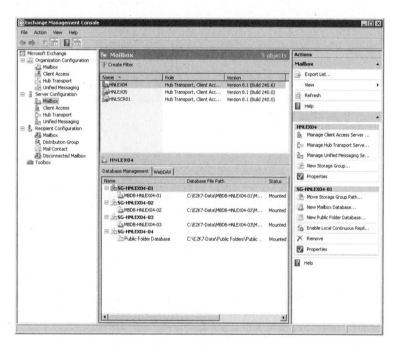

Because I have selected the Mailbox subcontainer, the Results pane lists only servers that hold the Mailbox server role. Because the Mailbox subcontainer is highlighted, the Work pane will have property pages (in this case, only one property page) related to mailbox server management. Notice that the Work pane has a Database Management property page that contains the storage groups for the highlighted server in the Results pane as well as the mailbox and public folder databases. Because the Mailbox subcontainer has been highlighted, you will see only the Mailbox-server-related properties in the Work pane.

If you select the Client Access subcontainer in the Server Configuration work center, the Work pane shows only the properties related to the Client Access server that you have selected in the Results pane. Figure 7.10 shows the Work pane if the Client Access subcontainer is selected.

ACTIONS PANE

The Actions pane is the most dynamic of the panes found in the Exchange Management Console. It is also arguably the biggest change found in the EMC interface. Any change of a selected object in the navigation tree, the Results pane, or the Work pane will change the Actions pane in one way or another. The Actions pane consists of the tasks or actions that are available for the selected object. As different objects are selected in the navigation tree, Results pane, or Work pane, the Actions pane will change. Microsoft added the Actions pane because Exchange administrators reported that they have difficulty finding out the available tasks for a particular object.

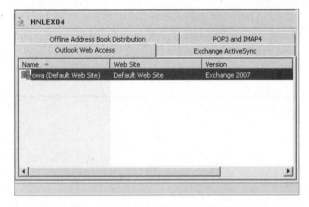

FIGURE 7.10
Work pane property pages and objects when the Client Access server subcontainer is selected

Figure 7.11 is a good example of the Actions pane. In this example, the Server Configuration's Mailbox subcontainer is selected, in the Results pane a mailbox server is selected, and in the Work pane, a storage group called SG-HNLEX04-01 is selected.

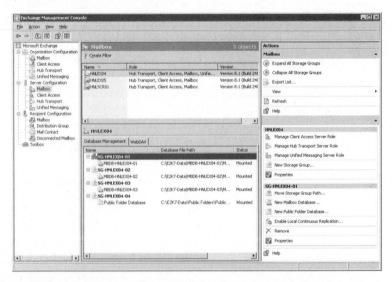

FIGURE 7.11
Corresponding actions available based on selected objects

Notice that the Actions pane has a Mailbox section, a section for the specific Exchange server that I am working on (HNLEX04), and a section for the storage group that I have selected (SG-HNLEX04-01). The actions that are available against the server (HNLEX04) are to view its properties, to create a new storage group, and to change the management view to another role (Manage Hub Transport Server Role, Manage Client Access Server Role, or Manage Unified Messaging Server Role). These actions are available because this server supports all three roles (Mailbox, Client Access, and Hub Transport).

Finally, the actions available in the SG-HNLEX04-01 section include moving the selected storage group's files, creating a new mailbox database, creating a new public folder database, enabling local continuous replication, removing the storage group, and viewing the storage group's properties.

The object SG-HNLEX04-01was also the most recent object selected in the interface, so the actions found in the Actions pane for this object will correspond with the actions found on the context (right-click) menu and on the Action pull-down menu.

One final example of Action menu tasks are the actions that are available when the Mailbox subcontainer under the Recipient Configuration navigation tree object is highlighted.

Figure 7.12 shows the Actions pane for the Mailbox subcontainer. Notice that the Actions pane has two sections; the first section shows the actions available for the Mailbox subcontainer. This includes modifying the maximum number of mailboxes returned, creating a new mailbox, and setting View options. Some nice new additions to the Exchange Management Console in Exchange Server 2007 Service Pack 1 include the ability to export a list of whatever is in the Results pane and a new Find interface.

FIGURE 7.12
Actions pane for
Recipient Configuration
Mailboxes subcontainer

The second section shows actions for a specific mailbox because I have selected the mailbox Mike Brown. From here, I can disable the mailbox, remove the mailbox from the account, move the mailbox to another database, enable Unified Messaging, or view the user and mailbox properties. Service Pack 1 also adds the ability to manage Send As and mailbox access permissions via the EMC. You may be wondering if this is the only information I will cover on recipient management. Don't worry; I just want you to become familiar with the console right now. Chapter 11, "Managing Recipients," covers recipient management in depth, including managing mailboxes, contacts, and groups.

Customizing the Exchange Management Console

The new Microsoft Management Console v3.0 is much more flexible and customizable than earlier versions. This means that you will be able to customize your Exchange Management Console even further and create specialized consoles for tasks such as recipient management.

There may be features or views of the EMC that you simply don't need in order to complete your daily tasks. Many of the console components (such as the tree, toolbar, status bar, and Actions pane) can be removed from the default view. From within your console, select View ➢ Customize to see the Customize View dialog box shown in Figure 7.13.

FIGURE 7.13
Customizing the components shown in the Exchange Management Console

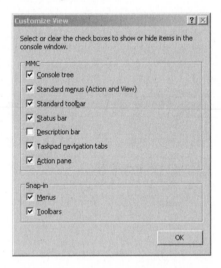

If you are creating a scaled-back EMC console for a junior or delegated administrator, restricting or removing some of the console features may be helpful in order to create a more simplified interface. From the Customize View dialog box, you can enable or disable the following components from the console view:

- The navigation (console) tree

- MMC-specific Action and View menus

- MMC-specific toolbars

- The MMC status bar

- The MMC description bar

- Taskpad navigation tabs (if creating taskpads)

◆ The Actions pane

◆ Exchange Management Console — specific menus

◆ Exchange Management Console — specific toolbars

For an experienced administrator, there will probably not be a need to restrict these features, but as you see in the following example, you can certainly make the console simpler by removing some of the unnecessary features.

CREATING A RECIPIENT MANAGEMENT CONSOLE

Even with earlier versions of the Microsoft Management Console (MMC), there was a lot of flexibility in creating and customizing the views that are available to the administrator. The Exchange 2007 EMC is even more customizable. Consoles can be scaled back and restricted so that only specific functions are available. In a medium-sized or large organization, an excellent example of this would be the need to create a management console that allows the user to manage only recipients.

In the following example, you create a console that allows the person using it to manage mailbox objects only. The end result of this customization is shown in the following graphic. I created a console that only shows the mailboxes for users in a specific OU and hides the console tree.

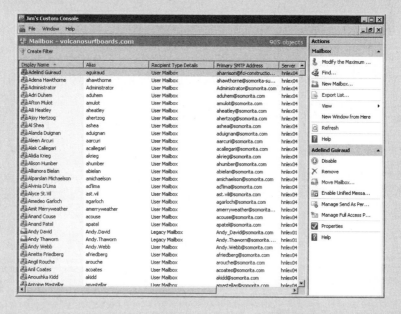

So, how did I scale back a full-blown EMC to just mailbox management features? It's pretty easy once you know of a few of the tricks. Follow these steps to create a customized MMC that can be used just for mailbox management. You can vary these steps to create other types of consoles, too.

1. Run mmc.exe to create an empty console window.

2. From the menu, select File ➢ Add/Remove Snap-in.

3. Click the Add button, scroll through the list of available snap-ins until you find Exchange Server 2007, and select it. Click Add, and then click Close.

4. Click the OK button.

5. In the console tree, expand the Microsoft Exchange Management Console and then expand the Recipient Configuration work center.

6. Right-click the Recipients Configuration container and choose Modify Recipient Scope to see the Recipient Scope dialog box. In the console shown in Figure 7.14, I had restricted the scope of the view to a single OU; you do this by selecting the View All Recipients In Specified Organizational Unit radio button and then specifying the domain name and OU name. This step will be optional if you do not need to filter by domain or OU.

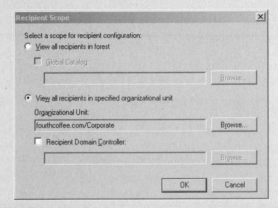

7. Right-click the Mailbox subcontainer under the Recipient Configuration work center and choose New Window From Here. This creates a window with just the mail-enabled recipients.

8. From the View menu, choose Add/Remove Columns, then remove Recipient Type Details from the Displayed columns list, because you know that everything in this list will be a mailbox. Add City and move it up to just under Alias. Click OK.

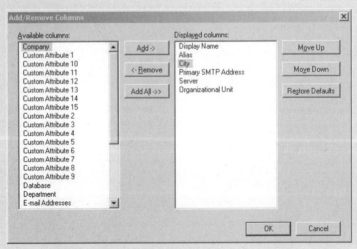

9. Now you can remove some of the unnecessary components of the console from the view. From the menu, select View ➤ Customize. This will display the Customize View dialog box. Ensure that the only check box that is enabled is the Action Pane check box; the rest of the console components are unnecessary for this specific console. Click OK when finished.

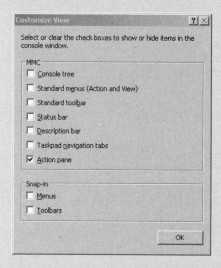

10. In the MMC, select File ➤ Options, and then in the Console Mode drop-down list, select User Mode — Limited Access, Single Window. Click OK.

11. In the MMC, select File ➤ Save As and give the MMC file a name such as MailboxRecipientManagement.msc.

12. If you have any other MMC windows open within the MMC you are creating, you will see a prompt that says, "You chose to display a single window interface when this console opens in user mode, but you have more than one window open. The user can view only the currently active window. Are you sure you want to display a single window interface when this console opens in user mode?" Simply answer Yes at this prompt.

Congratulations. You have just created a simplified EMC that will allow the user of this console to manage just mailbox recipients. You can use this MSC file from any computer on which the Exchange 2007 management tools have been installed, provided the user has been delegated the appropriate permissions to manage the user objects in Active Directory and has been delegated recipient administration permissions to Exchange 2007.

Toolbox Work Center

The Toolbox work center that is found in the Exchange 2007 EMC is a new concept for Exchange management tools. The Toolbox work center from a default installation of Exchange 2007 is shown in Figure 7.14.

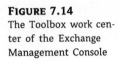

FIGURE 7.14
The Toolbox work center of the Exchange Management Console

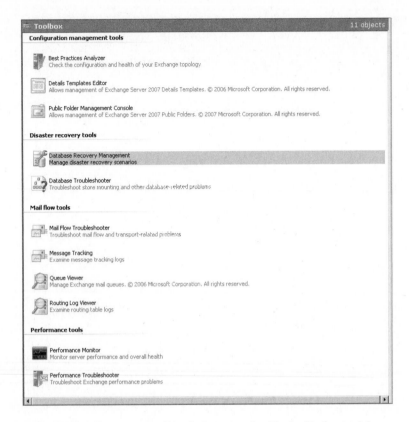

The tools that are found in the Toolbox are not directly integrated with the Exchange Management Console — rather the Toolbox provides links to these external tools. As new or updated tools are released by Microsoft, the Toolbox can be updated. The following tools are found in the Toolbox:

◆ The very popular Exchange Best Practices Analyzer (BPA) tool, which analyzes your Exchange configuration and makes recommendations for configuration and security improvements based on Microsoft and industry best practices.

◆ The Details Template Editor allows you to edit the details templates that users see when they view users, contacts, or groups from the Global Address List via Outlook.

◆ The Public Folder Management Console is new for Exchange Server 2007 Service Pack 1 and allows you to manage a limited set of public folder properties.

◆ The Database Recovery Management tool helps guide Exchange administrators through the process of performing disaster recoveries of various server roles including creating and managing a recovery storage group.

◆ The Database Troubleshooter tool helps an Exchange administrator determine why mailbox databases will not mount or why transaction log files will not replay.

◆ The Mail Flow Troubleshooter helps diagnose problems relating to messages being transferred between Mailbox, Hub Transport, and Edge Transport servers.

◆ The Message Tracking tool allows you to track a message's progress through an Exchange organization and see which Exchange components have processed the message.

◆ The Queue Viewer allows you to view the message queues on Hub Transport servers.

◆ The Routing Log Viewer allows you to open and view the routing table logs.

◆ The Performance Monitor tool is a Windows tool that helps analyze and troubleshoot Windows performance. When you launch the tool from the EMC Toolbox work center, it includes common performance counters related to Exchange servers.

◆ The Performance Troubleshooter tool analyzes a server and looks at common factors that could hurt performance, such as memory and disk configuration, and makes recommendations to improve them.

The Finalize Deployment Page

If you highlight the Microsoft Exchange portion of the EMC's navigation tree, two property pages appear in the Results pane. These are the Finalize Deployment and End-To-End Scenario pages; the Finalize Deployment page is shown in Figure 7.15.

FIGURE 7.15
Finalize Deployment tips in the Exchange Management Console

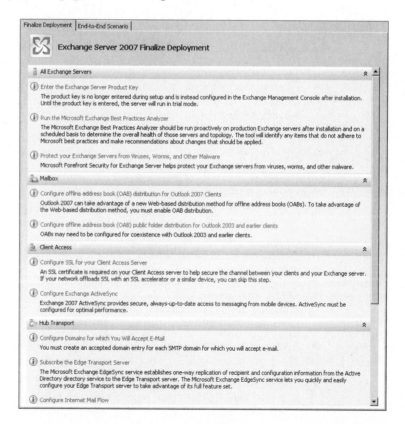

The information on the Finalize Deployment and End-To-End Scenario property pages provide links to tips and help on the topics shown. These tips and help topics are provided to give administrators quick reference to things they must commonly configure. For example, if you click the Create A Postmaster Mailbox task, the steps necessary to create a postmaster address are displayed.

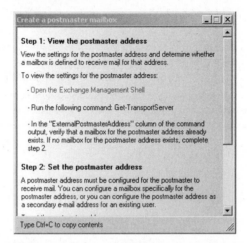

Here are some other tasks you'll find in the Finalize Deployment page. Not all of these are shown in Figure 7.15 so you will need to scroll down through the list to find others.

◆ Entering the Exchange Server product key. The product key is required to keep using the 32-bit evaluation edition longer than 120 days and it is required to use the Exchange Server 2007 Enterprise Edition features with the 64-bit version. See Chapter 5, "Installing Exchange Server 2007," for more information.

◆ Running the Exchange Best Practices Analyzer helps you to find potential configuration problems and tune your configuration to Microsoft's recommendations.

◆ Configuring offline address books for Outlook 2007 clients involves creating offline address book virtual directories on Client Access servers. This allows these clients to download the offline address book and use a local copy.

◆ Configuring offline address books for Outlook 2003 and earlier clients involves designating that the offline address books be created for older clients and replicated to public folder servers that are near the client computers.

◆ Configuring SSL for Client Access servers helps to secure Web client connectivity to Exchange. Each Client Access server includes a self-signed certificate, but these should be replaced with certificates that were signed by a trusted certificate authority.

◆ Configuring ActiveSync (including defining ActiveSync policies) is helpful if users will be using Windows Mobile– or ActiveSync-enabled devices.

◆ Configuring domains for which your Exchange organization will accept e-mail (creates an Accepted Domains list). This tells Exchange which domains are internal and which require you to relay mail.

◆ Subscribing the Edge Transport server to an EdgeSync subscription allows you to synchronize recipient, safe sender, and block sender lists to an Edge Transport server.

◆ Configuring Unified Messaging allows a user's mailbox to accept inbound faxing or inbound voice mail.

Wizards and Things

There have been a lot of additional improvements in the graphical user interface in an effort to make it more intuitive and easy to use. This includes making the wizards easier to use, providing indications that a wizard is working, showing problems where information is incorrect or missing, and giving the user the ability to view or block information.

Most wizards also include an option on most screens that allows you to type Ctrl+C and copy the contents of the wizards to the Clipboard. This is very useful if you need to quickly document what you are doing or if you need to paste this information into Notepad or some other editor. Most of the wizards also show the Exchange Management Shell command that was used to perform the task the wizard performed. You can use this information to create scripts and one-line commands for future use.

CONFIRMATION DIALOG BOXES

EMC wizards now include a confirmation page that allows administrators to confirm that the actions that they selected are really what they want to do. Figure 7.16 shows the confirmation screen for the Move Mailbox Wizard.

FIGURE 7.16
Confirmation screen for the Move Mailbox Wizard

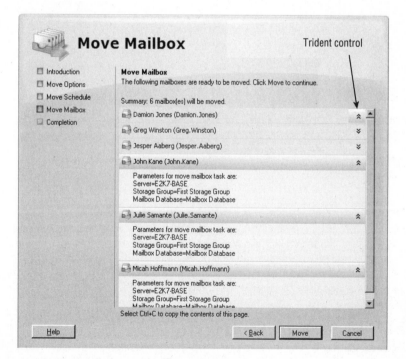

Confirmation dialog boxes and progress dialog boxes also include a new control called a trident control. I have included on Figure 7.16 a pointer to a trident control; they look like double v either facing upward or downward. By clicking these controls, you can expand the line for more information or collapse the line for less information.

PROGRESS DIALOG BOXES

Progress dialog boxes have been enhanced so that they give the administrator a better feel for "something is happening." Figure 7.17 shows the new progress dialog box for the Move Mailbox Wizard. Notice at the end of each of the status lines there is a trident control that allows you to display more information or to collapse each line so that less information is shown.

FIGURE 7.17
Move Mailbox Wizard
progress screen

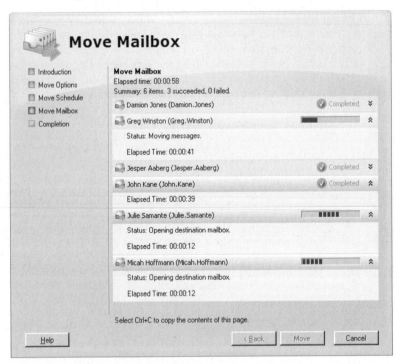

COMPLETION AND MANAGEMENT SHELL TASKS

If you are trying to learn the Exchange Management Shell (EMS) but find yourself continually having to look up how to do something, don't feel bad; you are not alone. The designers of the EMC wanted to help you along a little bit even when you're managing objects from the graphical user interface (GUI). When you run a wizard, the wizard's completion screen includes the EMS cmdlets required to complete the task that you just executed via the GUI.

An excellent example of this is the Move Mailbox Wizard that you have been looking at in previous screen captures. Figure 7.18 shows the Completion screen for the mailboxes that were moved.

Notice that the first mailbox that was moved *and* has a full completion report is the mailbox for Julie Samante; I collapsed the trident controls for the other mailboxes. The Completion dialog box includes the EMS command necessary to move Julie Samante's mailbox to another mailbox database. The Completion screen also gives you the option to type Ctrl+C and copy the text contents of the screen into the computer's Clipboard; you can then paste that text in to Notepad or some other program. Here you can see where I have copied the results of the command on the Completion screen so that I can reuse the command:

```
move-Mailbox "Julie Samante" -TargetDatabase:'CN=Mailbox Database,CN=First↵
    Storage Group,CN=InformationStore,CN=E2K7-BASE,CN=Servers,CN=Exchange↵
    Administrative Group (FYDIBOHF23SPDLT),CN=Administrative Groups,CN=Volcano↵
    Surfboards,CN=Microsoft Exchange,CN=Services,CN=Configuration,↵
    DC=fourthcoffee,DC=com'
```

FIGURE 7.18
Move Mailbox Wizard
Completion screen and
EMS cmdlets

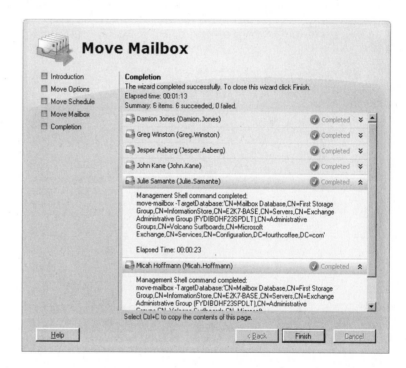

Although I am not quite ready to start teaching you the EMS cmdlets, I will tell you that this command was created using the absolute most unique name of the mailbox database. That is the distinguished name of the mailbox object. In this example, the distinguished name is as follows:

```
CN=Mailbox Database,CN=First Storage Group,CN=InformationStore,↵
    CN=E2K7-BASE,CN=Servers,CN=Exchange Administrative Group↵
    (FYDIBOHF23SPDLT),CN=Administrative Groups,CN = Volcano↵
    Surfboards,CN=Microsoft Exchange,CN=Services,CN=Configuration,↵
    DC=fourthcoffee,DC=com.
```

If there was only a single mailbox database called Mailbox Database in your entire organization, you could have moved Julie's mailbox by typing this:

```
Move-mailbox "Julie Samante" -TargetDatabase:"Mailbox Database"
```

However, the distinguished name of the mailbox store was used in order to guarantee uniqueness. As you start to learn the EMS, you will find there are usually multiple ways to accomplish the same task.

Schedule Dialog Boxes

The Move Mailbox Wizard also has a schedule option; the ability to schedule mailbox moves first came about in Exchange 2003, but since that time the wizard options have changed just a bit. Figure 7.19 shows the new schedule options. Now you can specify the start time and the maximum running time as opposed to the time at which the moves should stop if they are not completed. Anyone who has ever had to wait around until after hours to move mailboxes when running Exchange 2000 or Exchange 5.5 will tell you what a handy feature this is. Schedule your mailboxes to move and then go home!

FIGURE 7.19
The Move Schedule page of the Move Mailbox Wizard

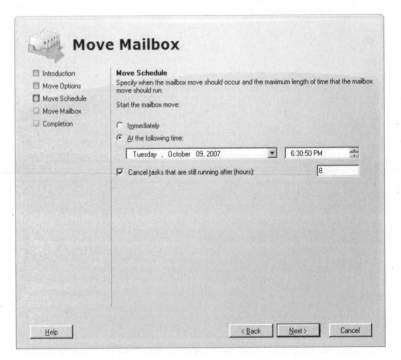

Error Notifications

Often when you are doing something in a graphical user interface, you get an error message but you can't quickly figure out where you made the error. The Exchange 2007 EMC helps to point you to the error more quickly not only by showing a pop-up error but also by including a warning icon next to the offending property.

In Figure 7.20, I am creating a mail-enabled contact. I tried to save the contact without first entering a valid external address; the EMC shows an error indicating that the proxy address cannot be empty, but also a small red and white exclamation point shows up next to the External E-Mail Address field. I have circled this exclamation point to make it a little more clear on the screen capture.

FIGURE 7.20
Improved error controls

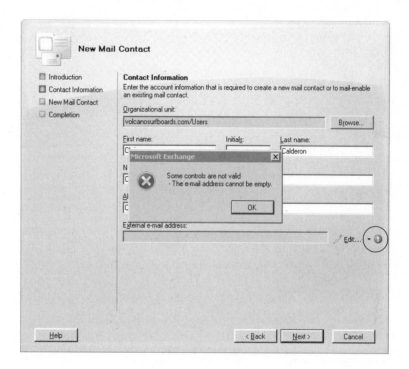

OBJECT PICKERS

When assigning a mailbox to an existing user or mail-enabling a universal group, you will use an object picker when you browse the Active Directory. In the simplest format, the object picker (shown in Figure 7.21) allows you to scroll through the list of user accounts in the Active Directory. Note that the object picker includes a Recipient Type Details column (User or Mailbox User), which may make the interface more difficult to use than it really needs to be by mixing up users who don't have mailboxes and those who already have mailboxes.

However, the object picker has some nice features. First, it automatically filters the list of users from the Active Directory so that only users without a mailbox or an e-mail address will appear. Second, you can enter part of the name for which you are searching in the Search box and click the Find Now button. If you do a little exploring, though, you will find an option under the View menu called Enable Column Filtering. Column filtering (also shown in Figure 7.21) allows you to specify a filter for any of the columns. The filter is similar to the Results pane filtering option; you can specify that the data in the column meets a certain criteria. The filter options are as follows:

- Column Contains
- Column Does Not Contain
- Column Starts With
- Column Ends With
- Column Is Exactly
- Column Is Not

FIGURE 7.21
Selecting objects from
Active Directory

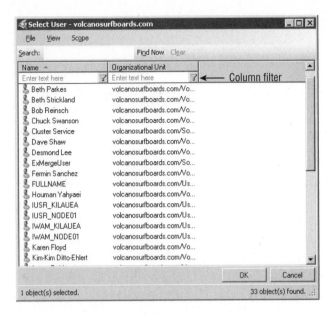

Delegating Administrative Permissions

In earlier versions of Exchange, administrative permissions were delegated via sites or administrative groups. If you are interoperating with Exchange 2000/2003, permissions for Exchange 2000/2003 administrative tasks will still be delegated via administrative groups. However, permission delegation has been simplified and made more flexible for Exchange 2007.

An important consideration to keep in mind is that having Exchange 2007 permissions does not automatically give you administrator permissions for Windows 2003 servers on which Exchange Server is operating, nor does it make you an Active Directory administrator.

Active Directory administrative permissions and Exchange 2007 administrative permissions are separated by design. This allows for more administrative flexibility.

Exchange 2007 Administrative Roles

Before looking at Exchange 2007 administrative roles, let's quickly review the Exchange 2000/2003 administrative roles. This will help administrators who are making the transition from Exchange 2000/2003 organizations to Exchange 2007 better understand the changes. Exchange 2003 offered three types of administrative roles, as shown in Table 7.1.

Although these worked well for some organizations, the roles could only be assigned to an entire administrative group or the entire organization. For medium-sized and large organizations where administrative tasks are sometimes very granular, the people assigned these roles may not necessarily have the specific permissions they need or they might have too many permissions. For example, if one group was responsible for managing all bridgehead servers and mail transport functions, the organization's bridgehead servers would have to all be in the same administrative group. If all servers (bridgehead, Outlook Web Access, and Mailbox servers) were in the same administrative groups, the management permissions would have to be assigned to all of the servers manually. Further, the administrative permissions for the organization and each administrative group had to be delegated once Exchange Server was installed.

TABLE 7.1:   Exchange 2003 Administrative Roles

ROLE	PERMISSIONS
Exchange View Only Administrator	Gives users or groups that have been assigned this role the ability to view the Exchange organization and server configuration. Mailbox administrators required this role in order to enumerate Exchange server names, storage groups, and mailbox database names.
Exchange Administrator	Gives users or groups that have been assigned this role the ability to manage (create/change/delete) Exchange objects at either the organization level or within a specific administrative group, depending on where the role was delegated.
Exchange Full Administrator	Gives users or groups all of the permissions that the Exchange Administrator role has but also the ability to change permissions on objects.

Exchange 2007 has improved the Exchange administrative model by defining five types of administrative roles:

Exchange Recipient Administrators   This role has the permissions to modify Exchange-related properties (e-mail addresses, home server, Client Access server, and Unified Messaging) of mail-enabled objects such as users, contacts, and groups. This role grants only read and write permissions to Exchange properties only for objects found in the Users container in each domain in which Exchange 2007 PrepareDomain has been run. For additional management permissions, an administrator would have to be delegated Active Directory permissions to manage objects in an OU, given membership in the Account Operators group, or be a member of Domain Admins. If a user or group is delegated the Exchange Recipient Administrator role, that user or group will have these permissions for the entire organization.

Exchange Server Administrators   This role can be delegated permissions to one or more individual Exchange 2007 servers regardless of the roles that server maintains. Someone with these permissions can manage any configuration data for that particular server, also has the Exchange View Only Administrator role, and will be made a member of the computer's local Administrators group. This role allows medium and large organizations to delegate permissions for Exchange management more precisely.

Exchange Organization Administrators   This role provides the permissions necessary to manage the organization-wide properties of Exchange 2007, including connectors, global settings, accepted e-mail domains, transport rules, Unified Messaging properties, ActiveSync policies, managed folders, and messaging records management policies. This role is by far the most powerful of the Exchange 2007 roles.

Exchange Public Folder Administrators   This role allows you to assign an administrator that can manage public folder properties such as limits and replicas. This group is new to Exchange Server 2007 SP1.

Exchange View-Only Administrators   This role allows administrators to view the Exchange configuration, but they cannot make any changes.

Most organizations will not need to do this, but these permissions can be delegated at the Organization Configuration level of the EMC navigation tree. Simply select the Organization

Configuration work center and choose the Add Delegate action; this will display the Add Delegate Wizard. In Figure 7.22, I am delegating the Exchange Server Administrator role for just a single Exchange server (called HNLEX05) to a group called Exchange Hub Transport Server Administrators.

FIGURE 7.22

Delegating Exchange 2007 administrative roles

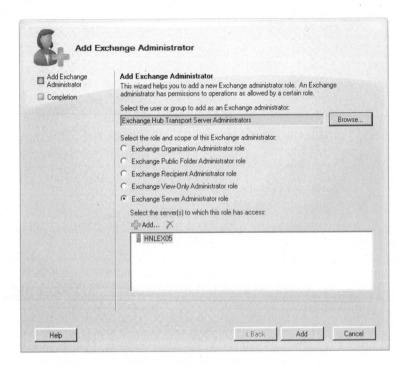

Exchange 2007 Built-In Administrative Groups

Now that I have explained the administrative roles that you *could* use to delegate permissions, I will tell you that you probably don't need to do any delegation yourself. For small or medium-sized organizations, you will probably not need to delegate additional roles for your users and groups. This is because when the first Exchange 2007 server is installed, some preconfigured groups are created for you. In most organizations, these groups will be sufficient for assigning the permissions you need for different types of administrators.

These universal security groups are created in an organizational unit (OU) called Microsoft Exchange Security Groups, which is found in the forest root domain. Figure 7.23 shows the Microsoft Exchange Security Groups organizational unit and the groups that are created in that container.

I recommend you use these built-in groups when assigning the necessary permissions to your administrators. The following are the built-in Windows security groups and the permissions they assign to their members:

◆ **Exchange Organization Administrators** provides members with the permissions necessary to manage all Exchange properties for the entire organization.

◆ **Exchange Recipient Administrators** provides members with the permissions necessary to manage mail-enabled objects (including assigning mailboxes to users and mail-enabling contacts and groups).

◆ **Exchange Public Folder Administrators** assigns members the ability to manage public folder properties. This group is new to Exchange Server 2007 SP1.

◆ **Exchange Servers** provides the permissions necessary for Exchange servers to interact with each other was well as with the Active Directory. Each Exchange 2007 server's computer account will automatically be assigned membership in this group. Administrators do not need to belong to this group.

◆ **Exchange View-Only Administrators** provides the permissions necessary to read Exchange configuration data from the Active Directory and read access to mail-enabled objects.

◆ **Exchange2003Interop** provides permissions necessary for interoperability with Exchange 2003. Administrators do not need to belong to this group.

FIGURE 7.23
Prebuilt Windows security groups for managing Exchange 2007

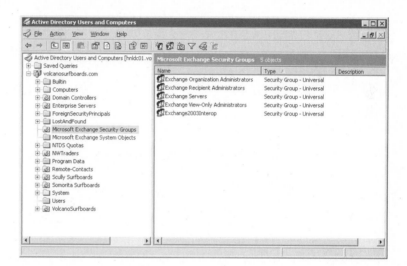

Summary

Exchange 2007 administration has definitely changed. Organizations that have become dependent on delegating mailbox administration through Active Directory Users and Computers will surely experience some growing pains as they transition their mail-recipient administrators back to the Exchange Management Console. To add insult to injury, the Exchange Management Console has been completely revamped and has a completely new look and feel.

That is the bad news. Well, not *really* bad news because the new Exchange Management Console is very intuitive and makes Exchange management much easier. The ability to create custom consoles that provide administrators with only the tasks necessary to do their jobs, such as managing mailboxes, will simplify mail recipient administration rather than make it more difficult.

After a few days of using the new Exchange 2007 administrative tools, you will wonder how you ever did your job without them.

Chapter 8

Exchange Management Shell Primer

The Exchange Management Shell is a set of Exchange-specific extensions to Microsoft's Power-Shell. In this section, I want to introduce you to both PowerShell and the EMS and to do so without overwhelming you. Introducing a concept like PowerShell or the EMS in just a few pages is difficult, but I hope to give you a basic idea of some of the capabilities and encourage you to learn more.

Is knowledge of the EMS required? Some administrators will manage their Exchange servers for years and rarely use the EMS, whereas others will use it daily. However, I think it is safe to say that at least limited knowledge of the EMS will be required by all administrators because some specialized configuration options can be set only from the EMS.

I hope that this chapter will provide you enough of an introduction to PowerShell so that you won't dread getting to know it.

In this chapter you learn to:

- ◆ Use PowerShell command syntax

- ◆ Understand object-oriented use of PowerShell

- ◆ Employ tips and tricks to get more out of PowerShell

- ◆ Get help with using PowerShell

Why Use PowerShell?

Based on discussions in Internet newsgroups, web forums, and classrooms about the decision to put the management architecture of Exchange 2007 on top of PowerShell, you would think that this was one of the most controversial decisions that Microsoft has ever made. Indeed, there has been enthusiastic debate (and name-calling) on both sides of the fence. Depending on whom you ask, some experienced Exchange administrators will tell you that the Exchange Management Shell (EMS) is the best improvement that has been introduced for Exchange 2007.

I have to admit, I have become one of the EMS's biggest supporters. All it took was spending a little bit of time with it and getting to know some of the basic functionality. The biggest fear that many administrators have is that they will have to learn not only some of the shell's commands (called cmdlets) but also a scripting language just to manage Exchange Server 2007.

The intent of the EMS is to provide a consistent interface for performing management tasks for Exchange 2007 servers, whether performing automation tasks, writing scripts, or extending the management capabilities. Tasks or operations that once required multiple programming APIs and hundreds of lines of scripting can now be accomplished in a single command. Single commands can be joined together — the output of one command can be piped to another command as input — to perform extremely powerful functions.

The base PowerShell provides more than 120 built-in cmdlets. In total, there are about 350 additional Exchange-related cmdlets that you can use in the EMS; the goal is to cover all Exchange-related administrative tasks. You will find cmdlets that manipulate other data in the Active Directory (such as cmdlets for managing user accounts) and control Exchange-related data in the Registry or Internet Information Services, but the cmdlets will only manipulate or manage data related to Exchange. The Exchange team is expecting other internal Microsoft teams such as the Active Directory or Internet Information Server team to provide their own extensions to the management shell.

There are a lot of very good reasons for Microsoft to create this management layer across all of its products. It provides a consistent management and scripting interface for all server products, develops a secure method for remote scripting, improves batching, and provides all administrators an easy way to automate and repeat anything you can do in the GUI.

Command Syntax

The problem with a lot of scripting languages and command shells is that as they get more complex and powerful, the command syntax gets more and more cryptic. PowerShell and the EMS seek to make using the command-line interface and scripting more intuitive. To this end, most of PowerShell and EMS cmdlets consist of two components, a verb and a noun.

JUST IN CASE

PowerShell cmdlets and the EMS extensions for PowerShell are case insensitive. That means that you can type everything in uppercase, everything in lowercase, or mix and match the case of the letters in your commands.

For readability and per suggestions from folks on the Exchange team at Microsoft, I am using Pascal casing in this book. When you use Pascal casing, the first character of each word is in uppercase; if the cmdlet has more than one word, the first letter in each word is in uppercase. All other letters in the cmdlet are in lowercase. So the cmdlet that is used to retrieve mailbox statistics is written as `Get-MailboxStatistics`.

Verbs and Nouns

The verb identifies the action that is being taken and the noun indicates the object on which the action is being taken. The verb always comes first and the verb and noun are separated by a hyphen such as `Get-Mailbox`. Table 8.1 shows some of the common verbs that are found when using the EMS; some of these are specific to the EMS, but most are generic to the Windows PowerShell.

TABLE 8.1:   Common EMS Cmdlet Verbs

VERB	DESCRIPTION
Get	Get is probably the most common verb that you will use. Get retrieves information about the specified object and outputs information about the object.
Set	Set is probably the second most common verb that you will use. Set allows you to update properties of the object specified in the noun.
New	New creates new instances of the object specified in the noun.
Enable	Enable activates or enables a configuration on the object specified, such as enabling an existing user account.
Remove	Remove deletes an instance of the object specified in the noun.
Disable	Disable disables or deactivates the object specified in the noun. An example of this is removing a mailbox from an existing user (but not deleting the user account).
Mount	Mount is used to mount an Exchange 2007 mailbox or public folder database.
Dismount	Dismount is used to dismount an Exchange 2007 mailbox or public folder database.
Move	Move can be used to move mailboxes to other mailbox databases.
Test	Test performs diagnostic tests against the object specified by the noun and the identity option.

The actual nouns that are used in conjunction with these verbs are too numerous to mention in even a few pages of text. Table 8.2 shows a list of some of the more common nouns; later in this chapter you learn how to use the online help to find more of the cmdlets that you need. The nouns in Table 8.2 can be used in conjunction with verbs such as the ones found in Table 8.1 to manipulate the properties of Exchange-related objects. However, not all verbs work with all nouns.

CMDLETS WORK ONLY WITHIN POWERSHELL

One important thing to keep in mind with cmdlets is that they are not individual executables, but rather .NET classes that are only accessible from within PowerShell and only if the Exchange extensions to PowerShell are loaded.

Help

There is a more detailed section near the end of this chapter titled "Getting Help"; however, as you start your journey into learning PowerShell and the EMS, you should know how to get quick and basic help. At any time you can use the Get-Help cmdlet to show what parameters any cmdlet takes. This is much like the man command on Linux systems:

```
Get-Help Get-Mailbox
```

TABLE 8.2: Common EMS Cmdlet Nouns

NOUN	DESCRIPTION
ActiveSyncMailboxPolicy	Properties of ActiveSync policies that can be assigned to a mailbox.
CASMailbox	Properties of a mailbox relating to client features such as OWA and MAPI.
ClientAccessServer	Properties specific to an Exchange Client Access server role.
DistributionGroup	Properties relating to mail-enabled distribution groups.
DynamicDistributionGroup	Properties relating to a dynamic distribution group.
EmailAddressPolicy	Properties relating to the policies that are used to define e-mail addresses.
ExchangeServer	Properties related to Exchange servers.
Mailbox	Properties related to user mailboxes.
MailboxDatabase	Properties related to mailbox databases.
MailboxServer	Properties specific to an Exchange Mailbox server role.
MailContact	Properties relating to mail-enabled contact objects.
MailPublicFolder	Properties relating to mail-enabled public folder objects.
MailUser	Properties relating to a user that has an e-mail address, but not a mailbox.
ReceiveConnector	Properties relating to Receive connectors.
SendConnector	Properties relating to Send connectors.
StorageGroup	Properties relating to storage groups.
TransportServer	Properties specific to an Exchange Hub Transport server role.
UMMailbox	Properties relating to Unified Messaging.
UMServer	Properties specific to an Exchange Unified Messaging server role.
User	Properties relating to user objects.

The Identity Parameter

For cmdlets that require input, usually the first parameter provided is the -Identity parameter. For example, if you want to retrieve information about a mailbox called Clayton Kamiya in the Corporate OU, you would type:

```
Get-Mailbox -Identity 'fourthcoffee.com/Corporate/Clayton Kamiya'
```

However, you will quickly find that the identity parameter is not required. And, if your aliases or account names are unique, even the domain and organizational unit information (OU) is not required. For example, this command would yield the exact same results:

```
Get-Mailbox 'fourthcoffee.com/Corporate/Clayton Kamiya'
```

As long as there is only one Clayton Kamiya in the Active Directory, you can even drop the domain and the OU name and this cmdlet will yield the exact same result:

```
Get-Mailbox 'Clayton Kamiya'
```

DO QUOTE ME

Anytime the identity you are using has a space in it, you must use quotes. Either single or double quotes will work as long as you are consistent.

The identity parameter is optional by design. As you will find shortly, the input can even be piped in from another cmdlet's output.

If you are not sure what input can be specified for the identity parameter, you can easily look up this information either in the Exchange online help or using the EMS command-line help (more on this later in this chapter). For now, let's look at one small piece of the Get-Mailbox help screen that shows the different values that can be used to identify a mailbox:

```
-Identity <MailboxIdParameter>
    The Identity parameter identifies the mailbox. You can use one
of the following values:
    * GUID
    * Distinguished name (DN)
    * Domain\Account
    * User principal name (UPN)
    * LegacyExchangeDN
    * SmtpAddress
    * Alias

    Required?                 false
    Position?                 1
    Default value
    Accept pipeline input?    True
    Accept wildcard characters? True
```

From here, you can see that the identity parameter will take the mailbox GUID, the user's distinguished name, the domain name and account, the UPN name, the legacy Exchange distinguished name, the SMTP address, or the Exchange alias.

Cmdlet Versus Command

You will notice me sometimes using "command" and sometimes using "cmdlet" when talking about PowerShell. There is a subtle difference:

◆ A cmdlet is the verb-noun combination that performs a specific task; it is the base PowerShell object that takes input, does something to it, and produces some output.

For example, `Get-Mailbox` is a cmdlet.

◆ A complete command is the cmdlet along with any necessary options that the task might require. The command necessary to retrieve information about a specific mailbox looks like this:

```
Get-Mailbox "Mark Watts"
```

PowerShell Versus Exchange Management Shell

When I talk about generic Windows PowerShell functions such as `Get-User` or `Get-Event`, I refer to those as PowerShell. The Exchange Management Shell (EMS) is a set of extensions or additional functions that are added to PowerShell. These include functions such the `Get-Mailbox` or `Mount-Database` functions that are specific to Exchange Server 2007. The Exchange Management Shell always includes the generic PowerShell function.

If you are running PowerShell and want to know what extensions are installed, you can use the `Get-PSSnapin` cmdlet like this:

```
Get-PSSnapin

Name        : Microsoft.PowerShell.Core
PSVersion   : 1.0
Description : This Windows PowerShell snap-in contains Windows
    PowerShell management cmdlets used to manage components of Windows
    PowerShell.

Name        : Microsoft.PowerShell.Host
PSVersion   : 1.0
Description : This Windows PowerShell snap-in contains cmdlets used
    by the Windows PowerShell host.

Name        : Microsoft.PowerShell.Management
PSVersion   : 1.0
Description : This Windows PowerShell snap-in contains management
    cmdlets used to manage Windows components.

Name        : Microsoft.PowerShell.Security
PSVersion   : 1.0
```

```
Description : This Windows PowerShell snap-in contains cmdlets to
    manage Windows PowerShell security.

Name        : Microsoft.PowerShell.Utility
PSVersion   : 1.0
Description : This Windows PowerShell snap-in contains utility cmdlets
    used to manipulate data.

Name        : Microsoft.Exchange.Management.PowerShell.Admin
PSVersion   : 1.0
Description : Admin Tasks for the Exchange Server
```

If you start the generic PowerShell, none of the Exchange Management Shell functionality will be available. This is because the shortcut to run PowerShell simply launches `PowerShell.exe`. The shortcut to run the Exchange Management Shell actually loads the Exchange Management Shell extensions and runs the `exchange.ps1` script to define/refine the environment a bit more.

You can load the EMS extensions for PowerShell by using the following command at the PowerShell prompt:

```
Add-PSSnapin -Name Microsoft.Exchange.Management.PowerShell.Support
Add-PSSnapin -Name Microsoft.Exchange.Management.PowerShell.Admin
```

This won't make a generic PowerShell command shell exactly like the Exchange Management Shell because the `exchange.ps1` script also needs to run. I generally recommend running the Exchange Management Shell from the Microsoft-installed shortcut on the menu but I wanted to give you an idea of what is happening "behind the scenes" that turns PowerShell into the Exchange Management Shell.

Cmdlet Parameters

PowerShell and EMS cmdlets also support a number of command-line parameters that are useful. Table 8.3 shows some of the parameters that cmdlets accept. Not all cmdlets will accept all of these parameters; these are usually optional, and, of course, some of these will not be relevant.

If you are piping output of one cmdlet into another, the parameters must be within the cmdlet that you want the parameter to affect.

Tab Completion

In order to be descriptive and helpful, some of the cmdlets are actually pretty long. Consider if you had to type `Get-DistributionGroupMember` several times! However, PowerShell includes a feature called Tab completion. If I type part of a command and then press the Tab key, PowerShell will complete the cmdlet with the first matching cmdlet it can find. For example, if I type `Get-Distri` and press Tab, PowerShell will automatically fill out `Get-DistributionGroup`. If I press Tab again, PowerShell will move on to the next matching cmdlet, or in this case `Get-DistributionGroupMember`.

The Tab completion feature also works for cmdlet parameters. If you type a cmdlet followed by a space and a hyphen, such as `Get-Mailbox -`, and then press Tab, you will cycle through all of the parameters for that particular cmdlet.

TABLE 8.3: PowerShell Cmdlet Parameters

PARAMETER	DESCRIPTION
-Identity	-Identity specifies a unique object on which the cmdlet is going to act. The -Identity parameter is a positional parameter, which means that it does not necessarily have to be on the command line; PowerShell will prompt you for the identity if it is not specified. As noted previously, in most cases you do not need to specify the -Identity parameter, just the unique object name.
-WhatIf	-WhatIf tells the cmdlet to simulate the action that the cmdlet would actually perform, but not actually make the change.
-Confirm	-Confirm asks the cmdlet to prompt for confirmation prior to starting the action. This option type is Boolean so you need to include either $True or $False. Some cmdlets (such as Move-Mailbox) ask for confirmation by default, so you could specify -Confirm:$false if you did not want the confirmation request to occur.
-Validate	-Validate will check the prerequisites of the cmdlet to verify that it will run correctly and let you know if the cmdlet will run successfully or not.
-Credential	-Credential allows you to specify alternate credentials when running a PowerShell command.
-DomainController	-DomainController allows you to specify the FQDN of a specific domain controller that you want to perform a PowerShell task against.
-ResultSize	The -ResultSize option allows you to specify a maximum number of results when working with Get- cmdlets.
-SortBy	The -SortBy option allows you to specify a sorting criteria when outputting data that is usually the result of a Get- cmdlet.
-Verbose	-Verbose instructs Get- cmdlets to return more information about the execution of the cmdlet.
-Debug	-Debug instructs the cmdlet to output more information and to proceed step by step through the process of performing a task. -Debug returns more information than a typical administrator needs to perform daily tasks.

Object Oriented

PowerShell is even more flexible because the output of commands is not text-based, but rather object-based. PowerShell uses an object model that is based on the Microsoft .NET Framework. PowerShell cmdlets accept and return structured data. Don't let the terms "object model" or "object oriented" scare you, though. This is really quite simple. For example, Figure 8.1 shows the output of the Get-Mailbox cmdlet.

FIGURE 8.1
Output of Get-Mailbox
cmdlet

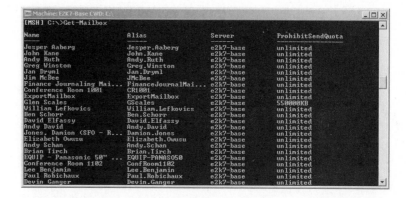

What you see on the screen is text to the user interface, but to PowerShell it is really a list of objects. You can manipulate the output to see the properties you want, filter the output, or pipe the output (the objects) to another cmdlet.

Filtering Output

In Figure 8.1, you can see that the cmdlet I used (Get-Mailbox) outputs every mailbox in the entire organization. There are a number of ways that you can filter or narrow the scope of the output that you are looking for from a specific cmdlet. In the case of Get-Mailbox and other cmdlets, you can specify just the identity of the mailbox that you are looking for.

PowerShell includes two options that can be used specifically for filtering the output. These are the Where-Object (or Where alias) and the Filter-Object (or Filter) objects. The Where clause can be used on most any cmdlet and the filter is applied at the client. The Filter clause is only available on a subset of the commands because this filter is applied by the server.

```
Get-Mailbox | Where-Object {$_.MaxSendSize -gt 25000000}
```

In the preceding command, the output of the Get-Mailbox cmdlet is piped to the Where clause, which filters the output. In this case, the output is any mailbox whose MaxSendSize parameter is greater than 25,000,000 bytes. Did you notice the portion of the Where statement $_.MaxSendSize? The $_ portion of this represents the object that is being piped to the Where-Object cmdlet and .MaxSendSize represents the MaxSendSize property of that object.

For non-programmers, this might seem a little difficult at first, but I promise it gets much easier as you go along. The operators are also simple to remember. Table 8.4 shows a list of common operators that can be used in clauses such as Where-Object or just the Where alias.

Formatting Output

If you look at the output of the Get-Mailbox cmdlet shown in Figure 8.1, you might be tempted to think that the output capabilities of PowerShell are limited, but this is far from the truth. The output shown in Figure 8.1 was the default output for the Get-Mailbox cmdlet. The programmer decided that the output should be in a formatted table with the name, alias, home server, and ProhibitSendQuota properties as columns. However, you can select on your own the properties you want by merely piping the output of the Get-Mailbox cmdlet to either the Format-Table (FT for short) or Select cmdlets:

```
Get-Mailbox | FT Name,ProhibitSendQuota,ProhibitSendReceiveQuota
```

TABLE 8.4: Shell Values and Operators

SHELL VALUE	OPERATOR	FUNCTION
-eq	Equals	The *object.property* value must match exactly the specified value.
-ne	Not equals	The *object.property* value must not match the specified value.
-gt	Greater than	-gt works when the *object.property* value is an integer.
-ge	Greater than or equal to	-ge works when the *object.property* value is an integer.
-lt	Less than	-lt works when the *object.property* value is an integer.
-le	Less than or equal to	-le works when the *object.property* value is an integer.
-like	Contains	-like is used when the *object.property* value is a text string. The matching string can either match exactly or contain wildcards (*) at the beginning or end of the string.
-notlike	Does not contain	-notlike is used when the *object.property* value is a text string and you want to see if the values do not match the string. The matching string can contain wildcards (*) at the beginning or end of the string.

Figure 8.2 shows the output of the preceding cmdlet.

The output of the Get-Mailbox cmdlet was directed to the Format-Table or FT cmdlet; the result was columns for the Name, ProhibitSendQuota and ProhibitSendReceiveQuota limits.

You may be wondering how you can learn all of the properties of an object. The default output of the Get-Mailbox cmdlet, for example, is probably not the most useful for your organization. I cover more on getting help in PowerShell and Exchange Management Shell later in this chapter, but here is a simple trick to see all of the properties of an object. Just direct the output of a Get- cmdlet to the Format-List (FL for short) cmdlet instead of the default Format-Table output.

When you direct the output of a cmdlet such as Get-Mailbox to the Format-List cmdlet, you will see ALL of the properties for that object. Figure 8.3 shows an example where I have directed the output of a Get-Mailbox cmdlet to the FL (Format-List) cmdlet.

The command I used is as follows:

```
Get-Mailbox "Clayton Kamiya" | Format-List
```

FIGURE 8.2
Formatting output to a
formatted table

FIGURE 8.3
Formatting output to a
formatted list

Directing Output to Other Cmdlets

You have already seen a couple of examples where I used the pipe symbol (|) to direct the output of one command to be the input of the next command, such as Get-Mailbox | FT. You can do this because PowerShell commands act on objects, not just text. Unlike other shells or scripting languages, you don't have to use string commands or variables to pass data from one command to another. The result is that you can use a single line to perform a query and complex task — something that might have required hundreds of lines of programming in the past.

One of my favorite examples would be making specific changes to a group of people's mailboxes. Let's say that you need to ensure that all executives in your organization should be able to send and receive a message that is up to 50MB in size rather than the default 10MB to which the system limits the user. Earlier I showed you how you could get the properties of the mailbox that you were interested in, such as the MaxSendSize and MaxReceiveSize properties.

First, let's use the Get-DistributionGroupMember cmdlet to retrieve the members of the Executives distribution group:

```
Get-DistributionGroupMember "Executives"
Name                                          RecipientType
----                                          -------------
Mark Watts                                    MailboxUser
David Elfassy                                 MailboxUser
Brian Tirch                                   MailboxUser
Paul Robichaux                                MailboxUser
Devin Ganger                                  MailboxUser
Julie Samante                                 MailboxUser
Todd Hawkins                                  MailboxUser
```

Remember that though you see the text listing of the group members, what is actually output are objects representing each of the members. So, now let's pipe the output of that cmdlet to the Set-Mailbox cmdlet and do some real work! To change the maximum incoming and outgoing message size for the members of the Executives group, you would type the following command:

```
Get-DistributionGroupMember "Executives" | Set-Mailbox MaxSendSize:50MB↵
-MaxReceiveSize:50MB
```

Notice that the Set-Mailbox cmdlet did not require any input because it will take as input the objects that are output from Get-DistributionGroupMember. When you run these two commands, there will be no output unless you have specified other options. But, you can easily check the results by requesting the membership of the Executives group, pipe that to the Get-Mailbox cmdlet, and then pipe that output to the Format-Table cmdlet, as shown here:

```
Get-DistributionGroupMember "Executives" | Get-Mailbox | Format-Table↵
    Name,MaxSendSize,MaxReceiveSize

Name                   MaxSendSize              MaxReceiveSize
----                   -----------              --------------
Mark Watts             50MB                     50MB
David Elfassy          50MB                     50MB
```

```
Brian Tirch              50MB               50MB
Paul Robichaux           50MB               50MB
Devin Ganger             50MB               50MB
Julie Samante            50MB               50MB
Todd Hawkins             50MB               50MB
```

Pretty cool, eh? After just a few minutes working with PowerShell and the EMS extensions, I hope that you will be as pleased with the ease of use as I am.

Tips and Tricks

Over the past three years of working with PowerShell and the Exchange Management Shell, I have learned a number of useful shortcuts, tips, tricks, and features of PowerShell that make it easier and more efficient to accomplish the task at hand. These include tricks for handling output of data, sending output to a file, sending e-mail from the shell, and debugging.

Managing Output

I want to start by talking about how to massage or manipulate the output of PowerShell and EMS cmdlets. In this section, I'm going to pick on the `Get-MailboxStatistics` cmdlet; I am using this cmdlet in my example because in my opinion its default output format is the least desirable of *all* of the EMS cmdlets. Whoever set the defaults for this cmdlet's output clearly expected the user to be proficient at manipulating the output. Here is an example of the `Get-MailboxStatistics` cmdlet's output without any additional parameters:

```
Get-MailboxStatistics

DisplayName                 ItemCount    StorageLimitStatus    LastLogonTime
-----------                 ---------    ------------------    -------------
Paleafei, Matt              4                  BelowLimit      8/9/2008 1:34:24 PM
Mike Brown                  306                BelowLimit      8/9/2008 1:34:00 PM
Simon Butler                2                  BelowLimit      8/9/2008 1:35:18 PM
Omar Droubi                 2                  BelowLimit      8/9/2008 1:34:00 PM
Clayton Kamiya              1063               BelowLimit      8/9/2008 1:33:31 PM
Rolly Perreaux              2                  BelowLimit      8/9/2008 1:34:55 PM
Brian Tirch                 2                  BelowLimit      8/9/2008 1:33:31 PM
Pavel Nagaev                1201                               8/9/2008 1:34:45 PM
Microsoft System Attendant  0                  BelowLimit      8/9/2008 1:36:36 PM
Andy Webb                   2                  BelowLimit      8/9/2008 1:33:31 PM
SystemMailbox{7B1D2E37-43}  402                BelowLimit      58-4A7D-
                                                               8195-CA208F521A18
```

Obviously this output is not very useful for most of us.

OUTPUT TO LISTS OR TABLES

Keep in mind that internally, when PowerShell is retrieving data, everything is treated as an object. However, when you are displaying something to the screen, you see just the textual information. Most cmdlets output data to a formatted table, but you can also output the data to a formatted list using the `Format-List` cmdlet or FL alias. Here is an example of piping a single mailbox's statistics to the `Format-List` cmdlet:

```
Get-MailboxStatistics "Clayton Kamiya" | Format-List

AssociatedItemCount     : 0
DeletedItemCount        : 0
DisconnectDate          :
DisplayName             : Clayton Kamiya
ItemCount               : 1063
LastLoggedOnUserAccount : VOLCANOSURFB\administrator
LastLogoffTime          : 8/9/2008 1:35:25 PM
LastLogonTime           : 8/9/2008 1:33:31 PM
LegacyDN                : /O=VOLCANO SURFBOARDS/OU=FIRST ADMINISTRATIVE
                          GROUP/CN=RECIPIENTS/CN=CKAMIYA
MailboxGuid             : 27757431-9cb2-4434-9547-443ebb9bd41e
ObjectClass             : Mailbox
StorageLimitStatus      : BelowLimit
TotalDeletedItemSize    : 0B
TotalItemSize           : 4190207B
Database                : HNLEX05\First Storage Group\Mailbox Database
ServerName              : HNLEX05
StorageGroupName        : First Storage Group
DatabaseName            : Mailbox Database
Identity                : 27757431-9cb2-4434-9547-443ebb9bd41e
IsValid                 : True
OriginatingServer       : hnlex05.volcanosurfboards.com
```

This example shows you all of the properties that can be displayed via the `Get-MailboxStastitics` cmdlet.

Following are the default results of filtering the command through the `Format-Table` or FT alias:

```
Get-MailboxStatistics "Clayton Kamiya" | FT

DisplayName              ItemCount   StorageLimitStatus   LastLogonTime
-----------              ---------   ------------------   -------------
Clayton Kamiya           1063               BelowLimit   8/9/2008 1:33:31 PM
```

However, the `Format-Table` and `Format-List` cmdlets allow you to specify which properties you want to see in the output list. Let's say that I want to see the user's name, item count, and total item size. Here's the command I would use:

```
Get-MailboxStatistics "Clayton Kamiya" | FT DisplayName,↵
ItemCount,TotalItemSize

DisplayName                                         ItemCount TotalItemSize
-----------                                         --------- -------------
Clayton Kamiya                                           1063 4190207B
```

There we go, that is a bit more useful. Not perfect, mind you, but the output format is getting better.

CONVERTING NUMBERS

In the previous example where I output user Clayton Kamiya's mailbox statistics, notice that his mailbox size is in bytes, not KB or MB. This makes the output just a bit less "readable" than I would like. Enter a PowerShell function that lets you apply an expression to the data that is being output to change how the data is displayed. Brace yourself, things are going to get a bit stickier. I will take a simple `Get-MailboxStatistics` command and keep adding additional formatting.

First, I want to give you a little background on the size properties that are used in the EMS and PowerShell. The properties that are designated to hold things like mailbox size and message size are defined as `ByteQuantifiedSize` properties. Essentially, this means that PowerShell knows this property represents byte data. Unfortunately, though, the output is always in just bytes. However, in the `Format-Table` cmdlet, instead of just putting in `TotalItemSize`, I can use an expression to manipulate the format of the output. This example specifies that I want the output to be converted to megabytes:

```
@{ expression={$_.TotalItemSize.Value.ToMB()}}
```

There is a bit of a catch to using this, so take a look at this example where I display the `TotalItemSize` of the mailbox in megabytes rather than in bytes:

```
Get-MailboxStatistics "Clayton Kamiya" | FT DisplayName,ItemCount,↵
@{expression={$_.TotalItemSize.Value.ToMB()}}
```

```
DisplayName                                    ItemCount .TotalItemSize.Value.To
                                                                            MB()

-----------                                    --------- -----------------------
Clayton Kamiya                                      1063                       3
```

Did you notice the column heading has changed to `.TotalItemSize.Value.To`? This is a bit of an inconvenient side effect of this feature, but there is a solution for changing the column heading to something more desirable and I'll show you that soon. For now, though, you may be wondering if you can change the output to something other than megabytes. Well, there are some other methods that you can use when working with `ByteQuantifiedSize` properties. These include:

PARAMETER	OUTPUT
ToBytes	Converts the data to a standard integer. This is useful when you are going to output to a CSV file that will be loaded into Excel.
ToKB	Kilobytes
ToMB	Megabytes
ToGB	Gigabytes
ToString	String
GetType	Displays the data type.

CHANGING COLUMN LABELS

In the last example, when I manipulated the data type to change the output from bytes to MB, the column header also got changed. However, I can change the label of the column heading pretty easily by using the Label parameter:

```
Get-MailboxStatistics "Clayton Kamiya" | FT DisplayName,ItemCount,↵
@{Label="Total Mailbox Size(MB)";expression={$_.TotalItemSize.Value.ToMB()}}

DisplayName                                    ItemCount    Total Mailbox Size(MB)
-----------                                    ---------    ----------------------
Clayton Kamiya                                      1063                         3
```

By adding the Label option, I can change the label that shows up on the column heading. This can make the output much more readable.

SORTING AND GROUPING OUTPUT

Any output can also be sorted based on any of the properties that you are going to display. If you are using the Format-Table command, you can also group the output by properties. First, let's go back and look at the original example where I am outputting all of the mailbox statistics for the local mailbox server. Let's say I am interested in sorting by the maximum mailbox size. To do so, I can pipe the output of Get-MailboxStatistics to the Sort-Object cmdlet. Here is an example:

```
Get-MailboxStatistics | Sort-Object TotalItemSize -Descending | FT DisplayName,↵
ItemCount,@{Label="Total Item size(KB)";expression={$_.TotalItemSize↵
.Value.ToKB()}}

DisplayName                                    ItemCount    Total Item Size(KB)
-----------                                    ---------    -------------------
Mike Brown                                          306                    5004
Clayton Kamiya                                     1063                    4091
SystemMailbox{7B1D2E37-...                          402                     360
Simon Butler                                          2                      12
Omar Droubi                                           2                      12
Brian Tirch                                           2                      12
Paleafei, Matt                                        4                      12
Andy Webb                                             2                      12
Rolly Perreaux                                        2                       7
Microsoft System Attendant                            0                       0
```

This example used the command Sort-Object TotalItemSize -Descending, but I could also have used the -Ascending option. There are several far more sophisticated examples in PowerShell help.

I can take this a step further when using the `Format-Table` cmdlet by adding a `-GroupBy` option. Here is an example where I am exporting this data and grouping it using the `StorageLimitStatus` property:

```
Get-MailboxStatistics | Sort-Object TotalItemSize -Descending | FT DisplayName,↩
ItemCount,@{Label="Total Item Size(KB)";expression={$_.TotalItemSize
.Value.ToKB()}}↩
-GroupBy StorageLimitStatus


   StorageLimitStatus: MailboxDisabled

DisplayName                                ItemCount      Total Item Size(KB)
-----------                                ---------      -------------------
Mike Brown                                       314                    21763


   StorageLimitStatus: ProhibitSend

DisplayName                                ItemCount      Total Item Size(KB)
-----------                                ---------      -------------------
Clayton Kamiya                                  1066                     5145


   StorageLimitStatus: BelowLimit

DisplayName                                ItemCount      Total Item Size(KB)
-----------                                ---------      -------------------
Omar Droubi                                        8                     1119
SystemMailbox{7B1D2E37-...                       402                      360
Andy Webb                                          6                      286
Simon Butler                                       2                       12
Brian Tirch                                        2                       12
Paleafei, Matt                                     4                       12
Rolly Perreaux                                     2                        7
Microsoft System Attendant                         0                        0
```

OUTPUT TO FILE

Outputting data to the screen is great, but it does not help you with reports. You can also output data to CSV and XML files. There are two cmdlets that make this easy to do:

◆ `Export-Csv` exports the data to a CSV file.

◆ `Export-Clixml` exports the data to an XML file.

Simply direct the output you want sent to a file and these cmdlets will take care of converting the data to the proper format. Let's take the same example I did previously where I want a report of all mailboxes and their `ProhibitSend` and `ProhibitSendAndReceive` limits. However, I cannot use the `Format-Table` cmdlet in this instance. I have to use the `Select-Object` or `Select` cmdlet to specify the output because I will be directing this to another cmdlet. Here is an example of the `Get-Mailbox` cmdlet when using the `Select` command:

```
Get-Mailbox | Select Name, ProhibitSendQuota, ProhibitSendReceiveQuota
```

The output of this cmdlet is shown here:

```
Name                  ProhibitSendQuota        ProhibitSendReceiveQuota
----                  -----------------        ------------------------
Missy Kosloksy             unlimited                   unlimited
Sueko Miura                unlimited                   unlimited
Daniel Petri               unlimited                   unlimited
Matt Paleafei              unlimited                   unlimited
Shawn Harbert               550000KB                    575000KB
Mike Brown                 unlimited                   unlimited
Dan Holme                  unlimited                   unlimited
Todd Hawkins               unlimited                   unlimited
Karen Floyd                unlimited                   unlimited
Jason Serino               unlimited                   unlimited
```

To direct this output to the `C:\report.csv` file, I simply pipe it to the `Export-Csv` cmdlet as shown here:

```
Get-Mailbox | Select name, prohibitsendquota, prohibitsendreceivequota |↵
    export-csv c:\report.csv
```

If you want to export the report to an XML file, simply use the `Export-Clixml` cmdlet instead of `Export-Csv`.

Finally, just like when working with the DOS prompt, you can redirect output of a command to a text file. To send the output of the `Get-Mailbox` to the file `c:\mailboxes.txt`, you would type:

```
Get-Mailbox > c:\mailboxes.txt
```

PUTTING IT ALL TOGETHER

Finally, I will leave you with one more example of `Get-MailboxStatistics` piping. Hopefully this will be an example that you can use in the future. I will do a report of the mailbox statistics using the `Get-MailboxStatistics` cmdlet and will narrow the focus of the output so that the system mailboxes are not included. Then I will export the mailbox statistics for a specific server. I will limit the output by using the `Where-Object` command, choose the properties to output using the `Select` command, and finally pipe that output to the `Export-Csv` cmdlet:

```
Get-MailboxStatistics -Server HNLEX04 | Where {$_.DisplayName -notlike↵
"System*"} | Sort-Object TotalItemSize -Descending | Select-Object↵
DisplayName,ItemCount,↵
@{Name="Total Item Size(KB)";expression={$_.TotalItemSize.Value.ToKB()}}↵
| Export-CSV c:\StorStats.csv
```

If you are thinking that this looks a bit sticky to implement, you are probably right. Getting this syntax together took me the better part of an afternoon and, arguably, you should be able to perform common tasks like exporting mailbox storage statistics from the GUI. However, on the bright side, now I have the command I need to run each time I want to generate this report; further, the knowledge to do this particular type of report within PowerShell carries over into many other tasks!

Running Scripts

PowerShell scripts are easy to build and to run, but there are a few things that you need to know to write your own scripts and/or to read others' scripts:

The file extension for a PowerShell script is .PS1.

You can't run the script from the source directory. You actually have to preface the script name with the path.

Let's say that I have a script called `c:\scripts\Report.ps1`. I can't just change it to the `c:\reports` directory and run `report.ps1`, so I would have to type `.\report.ps1`.

PowerShell (and scripts) use variables preceded with a $ symbol. You can set a variable within a script or just by typing it at the command line. The PowerShell variable is an object, so I can associate an object or an entire list of objects with a single variable.

For example, the following command associates the variable `$Matt` with the entire object for the user Matt Suriya:

```
$Matt = Get-User "Matt Suriya"
```

I could then use just specific properties of that object. For example, if I want to just output Matt's display name, I could type:

```
$Matt.DisplayName
```

Even better, I could then set Matt's display name to a variable called `$MattDisplayName` by doing this:

```
$MattDisplayName = $Matt.DisplayName
```

I can set a single variable to a lot of objects and then manipulate them all at once via a script. Here is an example where I set the `$AllUsers` variable to all of the users in the domain:

```
$AllUsers = Get-Users
```

Now here are some interesting things I can do with that variable. I could do a count of how many objects it contains like this:

```
$AllUsers.Count
944
```

Further, each of the 944 objects contained in the $AllUsers variable is treated as an item in an array, so I can retrieve individual ones, such as object number 939:

```
AllUsers[939] | FL samAccountName,DisplayName,WindowsEmailAddress,Phone,Office
```

```
SamAccountName        : Andrew.Roberts
DisplayName           : Andrew Roberts (Operations)
WindowsEmailAddress   : andrew.roberts@ithicos.com
Phone                 : 011-77-8484-4844
Office                : Tokyo
```

Though this is certainly not a comprehensive briefing on PowerShell scripting or variables, I hope it will give you a quick introduction to a few things that I found interesting and helpful when I got started.

SENDING E-MAIL FROM THE EXCHANGE MANAGEMENT SHELL

A nice feature that I stumbled across is the ability to use .NET libraries to send e-mail from within the Exchange Management Shell. I had thought this might be a "one-liner," but you need to set a number of properties in order to create and send an e-mail. So sending an e-mail really does require a script, albeit a simple one.

Props to Exchange MVP Neil Hobson for explaining this very well in the following article: http://www.msexchange.org/articles_tutorials/exchange-server-2007/managementadministration/getting-mailbox-statistics-exchange-2007.html.

Following is a script that takes advantage of the command I used earlier to generate a report to a CSV file along with a few bells and whistles:

```
#
#Script to send the Daily E-mail Report
#Script is based on script developed by Neil Hobson
#First, the administrator must change the mail message values in this section
$SMTPSenderAddress = "Daily.Reports@ithicos.com"
$SMTPRecipientAddress = "Matt.Suriya@ithicos.com"
#Set the Date using the uformat option of Get-Date cmdlet
$Today = Get-Date -uformat "%A %d %B, %Y"
#
$SMTPMessageSubject = "$Today - HLNEX04 Mailbox Usage Statistics"
$SMTPMessageBody = "Mailbox statistics for Exchange 2007 Server HNLEX04 for
    $Today are attached."
$SMTPServer = "hnlex04.volcanosurfboards.com"
#
#Run the daily statistics output to the C:\StorStats.CSV file
```

```
Get-MailboxStatistics -Server HNLEX04 | Where {$_.DisplayName -notlike
"System*"}↵
| Sort-Object TotalItemSize -Descending | Select-Object DisplayName,ItemCount,↵
@{Name="Total Item Size(KB)";expression={$_.TotalItemSize.Value.ToKB()}}
| Export-CSV c:\StorStats.csv
#
#Create the SMTP message object using the To, From, Subject, and Body previously
created
$SMTPMessage = New-Object System.Net.Mail.MailMessage $SMTPSenderAddress,↵
$SMTPRecipientAddress, $SMTPMessageSubject, $SMTPMessageBody
#
#Define the attachment C:\StorStats.CSV created by Get-MailboxStatistics
$Attachment = New-Object Net.Mail.Attachment("c:\storstats.csv")
#Add the attachment to the message
$SMTPMessage.Attachments.Add($Attachment)
#
#Send the message
$SMTPClient = New-Object System.Net.Mail.SMTPClient $SMTPServer
$SMTPClient.Send($SMTPMessage)
#
```

Running Scheduled PowerShell Scripts

Frequently PowerShell advocates will extol the virtues of creating simple PowerShell scripts (PS1 files) that you can schedule to perform routine tasks. I read quite a few articles and newsgroup postings about how easy this was to do. However, running the PS1 script using a scheduled task is a bit trickier. You can't just run a PS1 script from the DOS command prompt or the Task Scheduler. Before a PS1 script can be run, PowerShell has to be run, the Exchange Management Extensions have to be loaded, and then the script can be called.

The PowerShell executable (powershell.exe) is found in the C:\Windows\System32 \WindowsPowerShell\v1.0\ folder. The console file that tells PowerShell which snap-ins to load is the exshell.psc1 file. It is found (by default) at C:\Program Files\Microsoft\Exchange Server\Bin.

Finally, I need the name and the location of the script I am going to run, so let's say that is in c:\scripts\report.ps1. Rather than pasting all of this into the job scheduler, I'll just create a simple batch file that looks like this:

```
@echo off
cls
C:\Windows\System32\WindowsPowerShell\v1.0\PowerShell.exe↵
    -PSConsoleFile "C:\Program Files\Microsoft\Exchange↵
        Server\Bin\ExShell.psc1" -Command ". 'c:\scripts\report.ps1'"
```

Now I can test and schedule the batch file that I have written. Note that I am assuming the default locations for PowerShell and for the Exchange components.

Debugging and Troubleshooting from PowerShell

PowerShell has a lot of features that will help you to test your scripts as well as test one-line commands.

Set-PSDebug The cmdlet Set-PSDebug is designed to allow you to debug PowerShell scripts. To use this, add this command to your script: Set-PSDebug -Trace 1. This will allow you to examine each step of the script. You can enable more detailed trace logging by setting the trace level to 2: Set-PSDebug -Trace 2. If you add the -Step option to the command line, you will be prompted for each step. To turn off trace logging, use this command: Set-PSDebug -Off.

-WhatIf Most cmdlets support the -WhatIf option. If you add the -WhatIf option to the command line, the cmdlet will run and tell you what will happen without actually performing the task. This is useful for checking to make sure the command you are about to run will really do what you want.

-Confirm Most cmdlets support the -Confirm option and many cmdlets that perform more destructive types of options, such as those that begin with Remove-, Move-, Dismount-, Disable-, and Clear-, have the -Confirm option turned on by default. If this is turned on, the cmdlet will not proceed until you have confirmed it is okay to proceed. For cmdlets that confirm by default, you can include the -Confirm:$False option if you do not want to be prompted.

-ValidateOnly The -ValidateOnly option is a bit more powerful than -WhatIf. The -ValidateOnly option will perform all of the steps the cmdlet is specifying without actually making any changes and then will summarize what would have been done and if this would have caused any problems.

Getting Help

I have shown you a few simple, yet powerful examples of how to use PowerShell and the EMS. Once you dig in and start using the EMS you will need some references to help you figure out all of the syntax and properties of each of the cmdlets.

Exchange Server 2007 Help File

A great starting place for just reading about the cmdlets is in the Microsoft Exchange Server 2007 Help file. The help file documents explain how to do most common operations both through the graphical interface as well as through the EMS. Figure 8.4 shows the online help for how to create a new mailbox. After the procedures for creating the mailbox through the GUI are shown, you will also see the procedures for using the EMS.

After the example that is shown for creating the mailbox, you see a link to the New-Mailbox cmdlet that will take you to much more detailed information on that specific cmdlet. The New-Mailbox help topic (shown in Figure 8.5) will provide you with a great amount of detail about the use of the cmdlet. I strongly recommend you take advantage of the Exchange help file that is included with Exchange Server. In fact, you might want to even copy the file and save it to your workstation. The file name is ExchHelp.chm.

FIGURE 8.4
Referring to the online help for creating a new mailbox

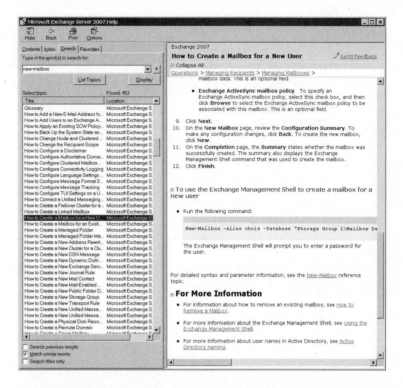

FIGURE 8.5
Online help for creating a new mailbox using the Exchange Management Shell

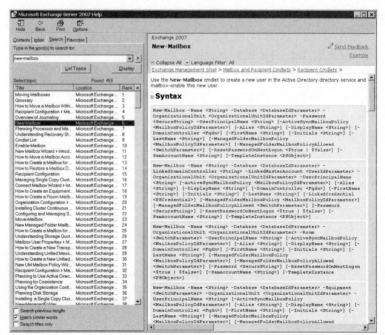

HELP FILES AND OTHER DOCUMENTATION UPDATED REGULARLY

I have noticed that Microsoft tends to update the help file more frequently than it updates the service packs. Visit the Exchange Server 2007 downloads site to make sure you have the latest help file at `http://technet.microsoft.com/en-us/exchange/bb330844.aspx`. The online documentation is updated even more frequently than the help file, so visit `http://technet.microsoft.com/en-us/library/bb124558.aspx` for the latest documentation.

Help from the Command Line

Information is also available on the cmdlets from within PowerShell. For a good starting point, you can just type the `help` command and this will give you a good overview of using PowerShell and how to get more help. I have summarized some of the other methods through which you can get help when working in PowerShell. Table 8.5 shows a list of some common methods of getting help on PowerShell and Exchange Management Shell cmdlets.

TABLE 8.5: Methods of Getting Help Within the EMS

ACTION	DESCRIPTION
Help	Provides generic PowerShell help information.
Help *Keyword*	Lists all cmdlets that contain the keyword. For example, if you want to find all cmdlets that work with mailboxes, you would type `help *Mailbox*`.
Get-Command *Keyword*	Lists all cmdlets and files (such as help files) that contain the keyword.
Get-Command	Lists all cmdlets (including all PowerShell extensions currently loaded such as the EMS cmdlets).
Get-ExCommand	Lists all Exchange cmdlets.
Get-PSCommand	Lists all PowerShell cmdlets.
Help *Cmdlet* or Get-Help *Cmdlet*	Lists online help for the specified cmdlet and pauses between each screen. Provides multiple views of the online help (such as detailed, full, examples, and default).
Cmdlet -?	Lists online help for the specified cmdlet.

When working with help within PowerShell, help topics are displayed based on the view of help that you request. In other words, I can't just type `Get-Help` and see everything about that cmdlet. The `Get-Help` cmdlet includes four possible views of help for each cmdlet. Table 8.6 explains the four primary views plus the parameters view.

TABLE 8.6:   Possible Output Views for the Get-Help Cmdlet

VIEW OPTION	EXPLANATION
Default	The default view lists the minimal information to describe the function of the cmdlet and show the syntax of the cmdlet.
Example	The example view includes a synopsis of the cmdlet and some examples of its usage.
Detailed	The detailed view shows more details on a cmdlet including parameters and parameter descriptions.
Full	The full view shows all the details available on a cmdlet, including a synopsis of the cmdlet, a detailed description of the cmdlet, parameter descriptions, parameter metadata, and examples.
Parameters	The parameters view allows you to specify a parameter and get help on the usage of just that particular parameter.

The Full option for Get-Help includes in its output each parameter's metadata. The metadata includes:

Required?	Is the parameter required? This is either true or false.
Position?	Specifies the position of the parameter. If the position is "named," the parameter name has to be included in the parameter list. Most parameters are named. However, the Identity parameter is "1," which means that it is always the first parameter and the -Identity tag is not required.
Default value	Specifies what a value will be for a parameter if nothing else is specified. For most parameters this is blank.
Accept pipeline input?	Specifies if the parameter will accept input that is piped in from another cmdlet. The value is either true or false.
Accept wildcard characters?	Specifies if the parameter accepts wildcard characters such as the asterisk or question mark character. This is either true or false.

Still not clear about what each view gives you? Perhaps Table 8.7 can shed some further light on the issue. This table shows you the different sections that are output when using each view option.

To use these parameters, you would use the following Get-Help cmdlet and the view option. For example, to see the example view for the Get-Mailbox, you would type:

```
Get-Help Get-Mailbox -Example
```

TABLE 8.7:   Information Output for Each Get-Help View

	DEFAULT VIEW	EXAMPLE VIEW	DETAILED VIEW	FULL VIEW
Synopsis	✓	✓	✓	✓
Detailed description	✓		✓	✓
Syntax	✓		✓	✓
Parameters			✓	✓
Parameter metadata				✓
Input type				✓
Return type				✓
Errors				✓
Notes				✓
Example		✓	✓	✓

I feel it is important for administrators to understand the available online help options, so let's look at a couple of more detailed examples for the Get-MailboxStatistics cmdlet. I am picking a cmdlet (Get-MailboxStatistics) that I feel is pretty representative of the EMS cmdlets but also does not have a huge amount of help information. First, let's look at the default view. (Although I have included the -Default option, it's not actually necessary because, well, it's the default.)

```
Get-Help Get-MailboxStatistics -Default

NAME
    Get-MailboxStatistics

SYNOPSIS
    Use the Get-MailboxStatistics cmdlet to obtain information about a
    mailbox, such as the size of the mailbox, the number of messages it
    contains, and the last time it was accessed.

SYNTAX
    Get-MailboxStatistics [-Identity <GeneralMailboxIdParameter>] [-
    DomainController <Fqdn>] [<CommonParameters>]

    Get-MailboxStatistics -Database <DatabaseIdParameter> [-
    DomainController <Fqdn>] [<CommonParameters>]

    Get-MailboxStatistics -Server <ServerIdParameter> [-
    DomainController <Fqdn>] [<CommonParameters>]
```

DETAILED DESCRIPTION
     To run the Get-MailboxStatistics cmdlet on a computer that has any
     server role installed, except the Edge Transport server role, you
     must log on by using a domain account that has the permissions
     assigned to the Exchange Server Administrators group. The account
     must also be a member of the local Administrators group on that computer.
      On Mailbox servers only, you can use the Get-MailboxStatistics
     cmdlet without parameters. In this case, the cmdlet will return the
     statistics for all mailboxes on all databases on the local server.

RELATED LINKS

REMARKS
     For more information, type: "get-help Get-MailboxStatistics -detailed".
     For technical information, type: "get-help Get-MailboxStatistics -full".

The default view (as you could have predicted from Table 8.7) includes the synopsis, syntax, and detailed description sections. Let's change our approach and look at the example view:

```
Get-Help Get-MailboxStatistics -Example
```

```
NAME
     Get-MailboxStatistics

SYNOPSIS
     Use the Get-MailboxStatistics cmdlet to obtain information about a
     mailbox, such as the size of the mailbox, the number of messages it
     contains, and the last time it was accessed.

     Get-MailboxStatistics
     Get-MailboxStatistics -Server MailboxServer01
     Get-MailboxStatistics -Identity contoso\chris
     Get-MailboxStatistics -Database "Mailbox Database"
     Get-MailboxStatistics | Where {$_.DisconnectDate -ne $null}
```

The example view does not have as much data, but a lot of techies learn by looking at examples so I find this view particularly useful. Next let's look at the detailed view; because this view includes the parameters, it will have quite a bit more information:

```
Get-Help Get-MailboxStatistics -Detailed
```

```
NAME
     Get-MailboxStatistics

SYNOPSIS
     Use the Get-MailboxStatistics cmdlet to obtain information about a
     mailbox, such as the size of the mailbox, the number of messages it
     contains, and the last time it was accessed.
```

SYNTAX
```
    Get-MailboxStatistics [-Identity <GeneralMailboxIdParameter>] [-
DomainController <Fqdn>] [<CommonParameters>]

    Get-MailboxStatistics -Database <DatabaseIdParameter> [-
DomainController <Fqdn>] [<CommonParameters>]

    Get-MailboxStatistics -Server <ServerIdParameter> [-
DomainController <Fqdn>] [<CommonParameters>]
```

DETAILED DESCRIPTION
   To run the Get-MailboxStatistics cmdlet on a computer that has any
server role installed, except the Edge Transport server role, you
must log on by using a domain account that has the permissions
assigned to the Exchange Server Administrators group. The account must
also be a member of the local Administrators group on that computer.
On Mailbox servers only, you can use the Get-MailboxStatistics
cmdlet without parameters. In this case, the cmdlet will return the
statistics for all mailboxes on all databases on the local server.

PARAMETERS
   -Database <DatabaseIdParameter>
      The Database parameter specifies the name of the mailbox
database. When you specify a value for the Database parameter, the
Exchange Management Shell returns statistics for all the mailboxes
on the database specified.
      You can use the following values:
      * Server\StorageGroup\Database
      * Server\Database
      * Database
      This parameter accepts pipeline input from the Get-
MailboxDatabase cmdlet.

   -Server <ServerIdParameter>
      The Server parameter specifies the server from which you want
to obtain mailbox statistics. You can use one of the following values:
      * Fully qualified domain name (FQDN)
      * NetBIOS name
      When you specify a value for the Server parameter, the command
returns statistics for all the mailboxes on all the databases,
including recovery databases, on the specified server. If you do not
specify this parameter, the command returns logon statistics for the
local server.
      This parameter accepts pipeline input from the Get-
ExchangeServer and Get-MailboxServer cmdlets.

```
-DomainController <Fqdn>
    To specify the fully qualified domain name (FQDN) of the
domain controller that retrieves data from the Active Directory directory
service, include the DomainController parameter in the command.

-Identity <GeneralMailboxIdParameter>
    The Identity parameter specifies a mailbox. When you specify a
value for the Identity parameter, the command looks up the mailbox
that is specified in the Identity parameter, connects to the server
where the mailbox resides, and returns the statistics for the
mailbox. You can use one of the following values:
    * GUID
    * Distinguished name (DN)
    * Domain\Account
    * User principal name (UPN)
    * Legacy Exchange DN
    * SmtpAddress
    * Alias
    This parameter accepts pipeline input from the Get-Mailbox cmdlet.

<CommonParameters>
    This cmdlet supports the common parameters: -Verbose, -Debug,
-ErrorAction, -ErrorVariable, and -OutVariable. For more
information, type, "get-help about_commonparameters".

Get-MailboxStatistics
Get-MailboxStatistics -Server MailboxServer01
Get-MailboxStatistics -Identity contoso\chris
Get-MailboxStatistics -Database "Mailbox Database"
Get-MailboxStatistics | Where {$_.DisconnectDate -ne $null}

REMARKS
    For more information, type: "get-help Get-MailboxStatistics -detailed".
    For technical information, type: "get-help Get-MailboxStatistics -full".
```

Naturally, the full view is going to contain a little bit more information than the detailed view. The full view includes the metadata for each parameter as well as examples:

```
Get-Help Get-MailboxStatistics -Full

NAME
    Get-MailboxStatistics

SYNOPSIS
    Use the Get-MailboxStatistics cmdlet to obtain information about a
    mailbox, such as the size of the mailbox, the number of messages it contains,
    and the last time it was accessed.
```

SYNTAX
    Get-MailboxStatistics [-Identity <GeneralMailboxIdParameter>] [-
    DomainController <Fqdn>] [<CommonParameters>]

    Get-MailboxStatistics -Database <DatabaseIdParameter> [-
    DomainController <Fqdn>] [<CommonParameters>]

    Get-MailboxStatistics -Server <ServerIdParameter> [-
    DomainController <Fqdn>] [<CommonParameters>]

DETAILED DESCRIPTION
    To run the Get-MailboxStatistics cmdlet on a computer that has any
    server role installed, except the Edge Transport server role, you
    must log on by using a domain account that has the permissions
    assigned to the Exchange Server Administrators group. The account
    must also be a member of the local Administrators group on that
    computer.
    On Mailbox servers only, you can use the Get-MailboxStatistics
    cmdlet without parameters. In this case, the cmdlet will return the
    statistics for all mailboxes on all databases on the local server.

PARAMETERS
    -Database <DatabaseIdParameter>
        The Database parameter specifies the name of the mailbox
    database. When you specify a value for the Database parameter, the
    Exchange Management Shell returns statistics for all the mailboxes
    on the database specified.
        You can use the following values:
        * Server\StorageGroup\Database
        * Server\Database
        * Database
        This parameter accepts pipeline input from the Get-
    MailboxDatabase cmdlet.

        Required?   true
        Position?   Named
        Default value
        Accept pipeline input?   True
        Accept wildcard characters? false

    -Server <ServerIdParameter>
        The Server parameter specifies the server from which you want
    to obtain mailbox statistics. You can use one of the following values:
        * Fully qualified domain name (FQDN)
        * NetBIOS name

When you specify a value for the Server parameter, the command returns statistics for all the mailboxes on all the databases, including recovery databases, on the specified server. If you do not specify this parameter, the command returns logon statistics for the local server.

This parameter accepts pipeline input from the Get-ExchangeServer and Get-MailboxServer cmdlets.

```
Required?                   true
Position?                   Named
Default value
Accept pipeline input?      True
Accept wildcard characters? false
```

-DomainController <Fqdn>

To specify the fully qualified domain name (FQDN) of the domain controller that retrieves data from the Active Directory directory service, include the DomainController parameter in the command.

```
Required?                   false
Position?                   Named
Default value
Accept pipeline input?      False
Accept wildcard characters? false
```

-Identity <GeneralMailboxIdParameter>

The Identity parameter specifies a mailbox. When you specify a value for the Identity parameter, the command looks up the mailbox that is specified in the Identity parameter, connects to the server where the mailbox resides, and returns the statistics for the mailbox. You can use one of the following values:
   * GUID
   * Distinguished name (DN)
   * Domain\Account
   * User principal name (UPN)
   * Legacy Exchange DN
   * SmtpAddress
   * Alias
This parameter accepts pipeline input from the Get-Mailbox cmdlet.

```
Required?                   false
Position?                   1
Default value
Accept pipeline input?      True
Accept wildcard characters? false
```

```
     <CommonParameters>
          This cmdlet supports the common parameters: -Verbose, -Debug,
     -ErrorAction, -ErrorVariable, and -OutVariable. For more
     information, type, "get-help about_commonparameters".

INPUT TYPE

RETURN TYPE

TERMINATING ERRORS
     (Category: )

     Type:
     Target Object Type:
     Suggested Action:

NON-TERMINATING ERRORS
     (Category: )

     Type:
     Target Object Type:
     Suggested Action:

     Get-MailboxStatistics
     Get-MailboxStatistics -Server MailboxServer01
     Get-MailboxStatistics -Identity contoso\chris
     Get-MailboxStatistics -Database "Mailbox Database"
     Get-MailboxStatistics | Where {$_.DisconnectDate -ne $null}

RELATED LINKS
```

Yes, that is a lot of text for examples of one cmdlet, but I hope that these examples will make it easier for you to quickly learn the capabilities of all cmdlets and how you can use them.

The EMS help system also gives you some options with respect to getting help on parameters. For example, here is an example if I want help on just the -Database parameter of the Get-MailboxStatistics cmdlet:

```
Get-Help Get-MailboxStatistics -Parameter Database

-Database <DatabaseIdParameter>
     The Database parameter specifies the name of the mailbox database.
     When you specify a value for the Database parameter, the Exchange
     Management Shell returns statistics for all the mailboxes on the
     database specified.
     You can use the following values:
     * Server\StorageGroup\Database
     * Server\Database
     * Database
```

This parameter accepts pipeline input from the Get-
MailboxDatabase cmdlet.

```
Required?                  true
Position?                  Named
Default value
Accept pipeline input?     True
Accept wildcard characters? false
```

The -Parameter option also accepts the asterisk (*) wildcard. Here is an example where I want
to see help on all of the parameters that contain SCLQuarantine:

```
Get-Help Set-Mailbox -Parameter *SCLQuarantine*
```

-SCLQuarantineEnabled <Nullable>
    The SCLQuarantineEnabled parameter specifies whether messages that
    meet the spam confidence level threshold specified by the
    SCLQuarantineThreshold parameter will be quarantined. If a message is
    quarantined, it is sent to the quarantine mailbox where the messaging
    administrator can review it. You can use the following values:
    * $true
    * $false
    * $null

```
Required?                  false
Position?                  Named
Default value              Null
Accept pipeline input?     False
Accept wildcard characters? false
```

-SCLQuarantineThreshold <Nullable>
    The SCLQuarantineThreshold parameter specifies the spam confidence
    level at which a message will be quarantined, if the
    SCLQuarantineEnabled parameter is set to $true.
    You must specify an integer between 0 and 9 inclusive.

```
Required?                  false
Position?                  Named
Default value              Null
Accept pipeline input?     False
Accept wildcard characters? False
```

Getting Tips

You may have noticed a useful tip each time you launched the Exchange Management Console.
Figure 8.6 shows the Tip of the Day text that you see each time you launch the EMS. There are
more than 70 of these tips.

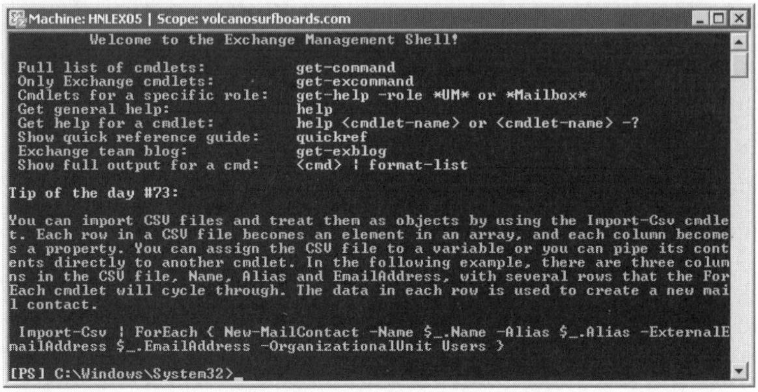

FIGURE 8.6
Viewing the Tip of the
Day

```
Machine: HNLEX05 | Scope: volcanosurfboards.com
            Welcome to the Exchange Management Shell!

Full list of cmdlets:           get-command
Only Exchange cmdlets:          get-excommand
Cmdlets for a specific role:    get-help -role *UM* or *Mailbox*
Get general help:               help
Get help for a cmdlet:          help <cmdlet-name> or <cmdlet-name> -?
Show quick reference guide:     quickref
Exchange team blog:             get-exblog
Show full output for a cmd:     <cmd> | format-list

Tip of the day #73:

You can import CSV files and treat them as objects by using the Import-Csv cmdle
t. Each row in a CSV file becomes an element in an array, and each column become
s a property. You can assign the CSV file to a variable or you can pipe its cont
ents directly to another cmdlet. In the following example, there are three colum
ns in the CSV file, Name, Alias and EmailAddress, with several rows that the For
Each cmdlet will cycle through. The data in each row is used to create a new mai
l contact.

 Import-Csv | ForEach { New-MailContact -Name $_.Name -Alias $_.Alias -ExternalE
mailAddress $_.EmailAddress -OrganizationalUnit Users }

[PS] C:\Windows\System32>
```

If you want to view additional tips, just type **Get-Tip** at the Exchange Management Shell prompt. You can also visit the following URL if you want to see more:

http://technet.microsoft.com/en-us/library/bb397216(EXCHG.80).aspx

You can even add your own tips if you don't mind editing an XML file; the tips for English are found in C:\program files\Microsoft\Exchange Server\bin\en\extips.xml.

CAN'T GET ENOUGH POWERSHELL

Early in the initial betas of Exchange 2007 (then known as Exchange 12), I was a shell-phobic. I griped and whined and complained each and every time I had to use the shell to do even the simplest task. I finally invested a few hours learning the basics of how to use the EMS and some of the basics of piping output of one cmdlet into another. Then I found that the online help had not only good documentation, but also examples! Finally, I found out how to use the help from the shell itself.

In just a few hours, I had gone from hating life with the shell to tolerating it. After seeing some examples and one-liners online and at TechEd, I was pretty much sold on the concept. When I actually had to start working with Exchange 2007 in production (rather than the lab), though, is when I finally became an EMS evangelist.

Third-party vendors are coming out with their own PowerShell extensions and I could not be happier. One of the most noteworthy extensions to PowerShell is Quest's ActiveRoles Management Shell for Active Directory (www.quest.com/powershell). I love this free extension for PowerShell and load it on my Exchange 2003 servers and Windows 2003 domain controllers.

Other noteworthy free add-ins and PowerShell sites include the PowerGUI (www.powergui.org), PoshConsole (www.codeplex.com/PoshConsole), as well as other PowerShell projects at Microsoft's CodePlex (www.codeplex.com). These extensions for PowerShell allow me to take advantage of my new-found knowledge of PowerShell to perform tasks other than just Exchange Server tasks and maintenance.

Summary

Microsoft Windows PowerShell and the Exchange Management Shell extensions may seem complex and intimidating at first, but it is nowhere near as complex as other command-line interfaces including other Windows CLIs. With just a few hours of practice, you will be using PowerShell and the EMS like an old pro.

After a few days of using the new Exchange 2007 administrative tools, you will wonder how you ever did your job without them. Each time I go back to working on an Exchange 2000/2003 system, I find myself longing for a migration so that I can use the new Exchange Management Shell.

Chapter 9

Exchange Organization, Server, and Recipient Management

The Exchange organization configuration information is stored in a number of different places. First and foremost, most of the Exchange configuration information is stored in the Active Directory's configuration partition, but you will also find Exchange-related configuration information in the Internet Information Server (IIS) metabase as well as the Windows Registry.

The administrative tools such as the Exchange Management Console (EMC) and the Exchange Management Shell (EMS) hide the complexity of accessing, viewing, and updating this configuration information.

Whether you are just getting started with Exchange Server as an e-mail platform or you are an experienced Exchange administrator, you may have a bit of trouble finding the right place to make a configuration change. Microsoft has tried hard to make the management interface simpler and more intuitive, but the fact remains that sometimes finding the right place to configure an object or a property is a little difficult.

This chapter should serve as an introduction to where the settings for different objects are located. You can find more information about configuring most of these in other places in the book.

In this chapter I hope to provide you with more insight into finding the right place to make configuration changes. For experienced Exchange 2000/2003 administrators, I provide some parallels to where you will find some of the configuration tasks that you used to perform in the Exchange System Manager.

In this chapter you learn to:

◆ Understand how the Active Directory stores configuration data

◆ Set Exchange organization-wide configurations

◆ Configure Exchange server by server

◆ Use tools for recipient management

Understanding the Active Directory Configuration Partition

Let's first take a quick look at where the configuration data is stored in the Active Directory. Most of the Exchange configuration is stored in the Active Directory configuration partition. The configuration partition is a piece of the Active Directory database that is replicated to all domain controllers in the entire forest. This partition stores information about Active Directory partitions, configuration, sites, display specifiers, and more.

When the first Exchange server is installed into an Active Directory forest, new configuration data is stored in this partition. The Exchange-related information is stored in the CN = Services, CN = Microsoft Exchange container. Figure 9.1 shows the Exchange organization container for Volcano Surfboards; this is revealed using the Windows 2003 support tool ADSI Edit.

FIGURE 9.1
Viewing the Exchange 2007 configuration data using ADSI Edit

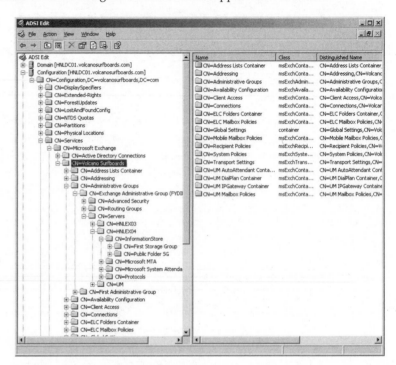

It is useful to know where the configuration data is located, but it is unusual to actually edit the information in the Active Directory configuration partition. The Exchange management tools organize and present the information you see in Figure 9.1 in a friendlier and more manageable format.

Managing Organization-Wide Configuration Parameters

Let's start with a view of the configuration options and parameters that affect the entire Exchange organization (every server and every object).

Parameters and objects found in the Organization Configuration work center affect every server and mail-enabled recipient in the entire organization.

For Exchange 2000/2003 administrators, these are the same types of things you would find under the Global Settings and Recipients containers in Exchange System Manager.

Setting the Junk E-mail Folder Threshold

You use the Get-OrganizationConfig and Set-OrganizationConfig cmdlets to view the organization configuration and set organization configuration parameters. For the organization configuration, there is one important parameter that will be of use to many administrators; this is the SCLJunkThreshold parameter. This is set by default to a spam confidence level (SCL) value of 4. The SCL scale measures the potential spamminess of a message on a scale of 1 to 9, with 1 not being spam and 9 being very likely spam. If messages are processed by the Content Filter (formerly known as the Microsoft Exchange Intelligent Message Filter) and are determined to have a value of 4 or higher, they will be placed in the user's Junk E-mail folder. Here is an example of how to view this information:

```
Get-OrganizationConfig | FL Name, SCLJunkThreshold

Name              : Volcano Surfboards
SCLJunkThreshold : 4
```

You can change the SCLJunkThreshold value using the following EMS command:

```
Set-OrganizationConfig -SCLJunkThreshold 5
```

Setting Message Size and Recipient Count Limit

Message sizes can be set in a lot of places; size limits can be configured for the entire organization, a specific connector, or an individual mailbox. However, to set them globally, you must set them from the EMS. The Get-TransportConfig and the Set-TransportConfig cmdlets have the -MaxReceiveSize, -MaxSendSize, and -MaxRecipientEnvelopeLimit parameters, which control the maximum incoming message size, the maximum outgoing message size, and the maximum number of recipients per message. Here is an example of using the EMS to view this information:

```
Get-TransportConfig | Format-List

ClearCategories              : True
GenerateCopyOfDSNFor         : {}
InternalSMTPServers          : {192.168.254.19, 192.168.254.102}
JournalingReportNdrTo        : Postmaster@volcanosurfboards.com
MaxDumpsterSizePerStorageGroup : 18MB
MaxDumpsterTime              : 05:00:00
MaxReceiveSize               : 25MB
MaxRecipientEnvelopeLimit    : 250
MaxSendSize                  : 35MB
TLSReceiveDomainSecureList   : {ithicos.com}
TLSSendDomainSecureList      : {ithicos.com}
VerifySecureSubmitEnabled    : False
VoicemailJournalingEnabled   : True
Xexch50Enabled               : True
```

All of these values can be changed using the Set-TransportConfig cmdlet. For more information, see Chapter 10, "Imposing Limits."

Configuring Administrative Roles and Permissions

When the first Exchange 2007 server is installed into the Active Directory forest, a container called Microsoft Exchange Security Groups (shown in Figure 9.2) is created in the root domain. These groups, also called *roles*, provide default levels of permission for carrying out various Exchange tasks.

FIGURE 9.2
Microsoft Exchange
Security Groups

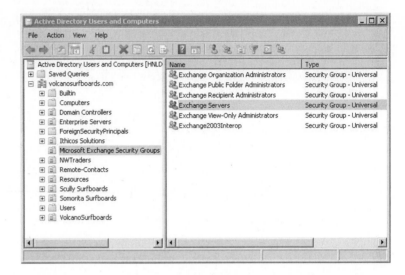

For most organizations, making a user a member of one of these groups will suffice when delegating the necessary permissions to manage the Exchange organization, Exchange recipients, or Exchange servers. But in larger organizations, custom permissions may need to be delegated or assigned based on the organization's requirements. Additional or custom permissions can be delegated using the EMC.

Figure 9.3 shows the EMC with the Organization Configuration work center selected and shows the default administrative roles that are created.

FIGURE 9.3
Using the Exchange
Management Console to
assign organization-wide
permissions

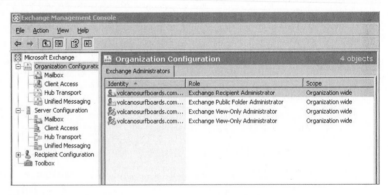

Exchange administrative permissions can also be viewed, assigned, and removed using the EMS cmdlets `Get-ExchangeAdministrator`, `Add-ExchangeAdministrator`, and `Remove-ExchangeAdministrator`.

You can find more information about administrative permissions in Chapter 7, "Administering Exchange Server 2007."

Configuring Messaging Records Management

Messaging records management combines a new set of features for Exchange Server 2007 with the Exchange 2000/2003 mailbox manager features. Messaging records management allows you to create custom folders in a user's mailbox and manage the content in both the default folders and

the custom folders. Management and configuration of messaging records management components is performed in the EMC under the Organization Configuration work center and under the
Mailbox subcontainer.

The Mailbox subcontainer of the Organization Configuration work center is shown in
Figure 9.4. The Managed Custom Folders tab in the Results pane allows you to create additional
managed custom folders and assign managed content settings to them.

FIGURE 9.4

Managing custom
folders

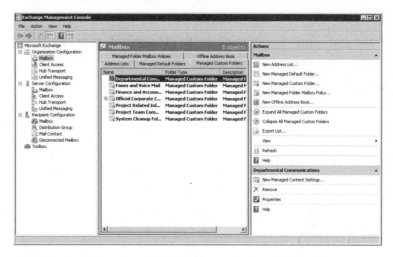

From the Managed Default Folders tab in the Results pane, you can assign managed content
settings to default folders such as the Inbox, Deleted Items, and Sent Items.

The final component of message records management (at least from the organization-wide
perspective) is the creation of managed folder mailbox policies. These policies specify which
folders are assigned to a mailbox. The mailbox is then assigned policies found on the Managed
Folder Mailbox Policies tab.

If you are inclined to manage messaging records management components from the command
line, here are some of the cmdlets you can use:

CMDLET	DESCRIPTION
Start-ManagedFolderAssistant	Starts the managed folder assistant on a Mailbox server.
Stop-ManagedFolderAssistant	Stops the managed folder assistant on a Mailbox server.
New-ManagedFolder	Creates a new managed custom or default folder.
New-ManagedFolderMailboxPolicy	Defines a new managed folder mailbox policy.
New-ManagedContentSettings	Creates a new managed content settings object in the specified managed folder.
Get-ManagedFolder	Retrieves a list of managed folders or the properties of an individual managed folder if it is specified in the command line.

CMDLET	DESCRIPTION
`Get-ManagedFolderMailboxPolicy`	Retrieves a list of managed folder mailbox policies or the properties of an individual managed folder mailbox policy if it is specified in the command line.
`Get-ManagedContentSettings`	Retrieves all of the managed content setting objects or the properties of an individual content settings object if it is specified.
`Set-ManagedFolder`	Sets the properties on a managed folder.
`Set-ManagedFolderMailboxPolicy`	Sets the properties on a managed folder mailbox policy.
`Set-ManagedContentSettings`	Sets the properties on a managed content settings object.
`Remove-ManagedFolder`	Removes an existing managed folder.
`Remove-ManagedFolderMailboxPolicy`	Removes a managed folder mailbox policy.
`Remove-ManagedContentSettings`	Removes a managed content settings object.

You can find more information about messaging records management in Chapter 14, "Managing Mailbox Content."

Managing Address Lists

A couple of different types of address lists can be created and managed in Exchange 2007. These include the custom address lists, offline address books, and global address lists.

Address lists were found in the Exchange 2000/2003 Exchange System Manager console under Recipients\All Address Lists and are also called custom address lists. Exchange 2007 includes the default address lists All Users, All Rooms, All Groups, and All Contacts. These address lists, as well as new ones, are managed from the Mailbox subfolder of the Organization Configuration work center. Figure 9.5 shows the Address Lists tab.

FIGURE 9.5
Address lists viewed
from the Exchange
Management Console

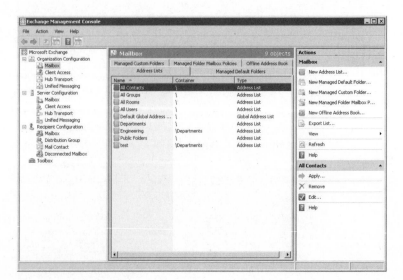

Offline address books are managed from the Offline Address Book tab in the Results pane of the Mailbox subfolder. Figure 9.6 shows the Offline Address Book tab.

FIGURE 9.6

Offline address book management in the Exchange Management Console

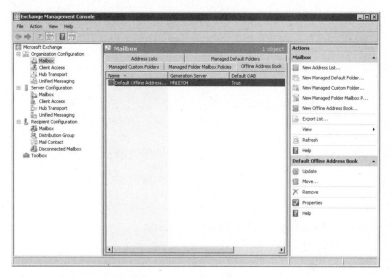

Global address list management is not configured from the Exchange Management Console but instead through the EMS. This is intentional because the Default Global Address List will be sufficient for most organizations. The following are the EMS cmdlets for managing custom address lists, offline address books, and global address lists:

CMDLET	DESCRIPTION
New-AddressList	Creates a new custom address list.
New-GlobalAddressList	Creates a new global address list.
New-OfflineAddressBook	Creates a new offline address book.
Get-AddressList	Retrieves a listing of the existing address lists or the properties of a specific address list.
Get-GlobalAddressList	Retrieves a listing of the existing global address lists or the properties of a specific global address list.
Get-OfflineAddressBook	Retrieves a listing of the existing offline address book or the properties of a specific offline address book.
Set-AddressList	Sets the properties of an existing address list.
Set-GlobalAddressList	Sets the properties of an existing global address list.
Set-OfflineAddressBook	Sets the properties of an existing offline address book.
Remove-AddressList	Removes an existing address list.
Remove-GlobalAddressList	Removes an existing global address list.
Remove-OfflineAddressBook	Removes an existing offline address book.
Update-AddressList	Updates the membership of an address list. Anytime address list membership criteria are changed, this should be run.

CMDLET	DESCRIPTION
Update-GlobalAddressList	Updates the membership of a global address list. Anytime global address list membership is changed, this should be run.
Update-OfflineAddressBook	Updates the offline address book information that is distributed to offline clients. This should be run on a regular basis.
Move-AddressList	Moves an address list from one address list container to another.
Move-OfflineAddressBook	Changes the offline address book generation server for an offline address book.

You can learn more information about creating and managing the different types of address lists in Chapter 13, "Managing Address Lists."

Setting ActiveSync Policies

Exchange 2007 allows you to support more than one ActiveSync policy for Windows Mobile devices. These are configured globally in the Client Access subcontainer of the Organization Configuration work center of the EMC. The Exchange ActiveSync Mailbox Policies tab is shown in Figure 9.7 with the General property page of one of the policies. (Exchange 2007 administrators will notice a few extra property pages — Sync Settings, Device, Advanced — when using Exchange Server 2007 SP1.) In Exchange 2003, you can find these settings under Global Settings\Mobile Services.

FIGURE 9.7
Managing ActiveSync mailbox policies using the Exchange Management Console

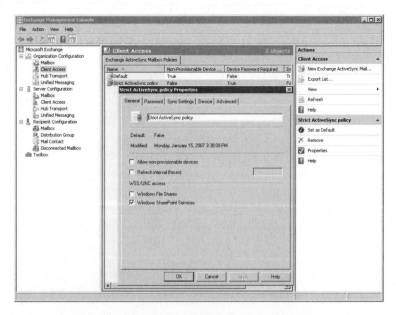

From an ActiveSync mailbox policy, you can define maximum attachment sizes, SharePoint and Windows file share access, password complexity, and device encryption requirements. Once a policy is defined, it must be assigned to the user accounts/mailboxes on which it must be enforced. The following is a list of EMS cmdlets that can be used to manage ActiveSync policies.

CMDLET	DESCRIPTION
New-ActiveSyncMailboxPolicy	Creates a new ActiveSync mailbox policy.
Remove-ActiveSyncMailboxPolicy	Deletes an existing ActiveSync mailbox policy.
Set-ActiveSyncMailboxPolicy	Sets the properties of the specified ActiveSync mailbox policy.
Get-ActiveSyncMailboxPolicy	Retrieves a list of ActiveSync mailbox policies or properties of an individual mailbox policy if the policy name is specified.

You can find more information about Exchange ActiveSync mailbox policies in Chapter 23, "Exchange Anywhere."

Removing or Wiping ActiveSync Devices

An ActiveSync device can be removed or disassociated from Exchange 2007 if the device is no longer used or it needs to be completely reset and rebuilt. You may also need to initiate a remote wipe of a device if the device is lost or stolen. You can use the following EMS cmdlets to manage these features:

CMDLET	DESCRIPTION
Get-ActiveSyncDeviceStatistics	Lists the statistics of a specific ActiveSync device when you specify the mailbox name that the device is synchronizing with.
Clear-ActiveSyncDevice	Initiates a remote wipe-out of the ActiveSync device the next time it connects to a Client Access server to synchronize.
Remove-ActiveSyncDevice	Removes an ActiveSync device partnership.
Test-ActiveSyncConnectity	Tests the ActiveSync synchronization for a specified mailbox.
Export-ActiveSyncLog	Parses the IIS HTTP logs for ActiveSync related information.

Managing Outbound Message Formats

When Exchange delivers a message to the Internet, it uses the format specified in the Remote Domains list. Different domains can use different outbound message formats, too. There is more to remote domain configuration than just message formats, though. A remote domain configuration includes:

◆ Out-of-office message types to be delivered

◆ Outbound message character sets

◆ Automatic reply, automatic forward, delivery report, and non-delivery report control

The default format is used for all outbound SMTP mail to all external domains and is configured in the Exchange Management Console Organization Configuration work center, under the Hub Transport section in the Remote Domains tab. The Remote Domains tab and the General property page of the default message format is shown in Figure 9.8. In Exchange 2000/2003, you can find this information in the Global Settings\Internet Message Defaults container.

FIGURE 9.8

Managing Internet message formats using the Exchange Management Console

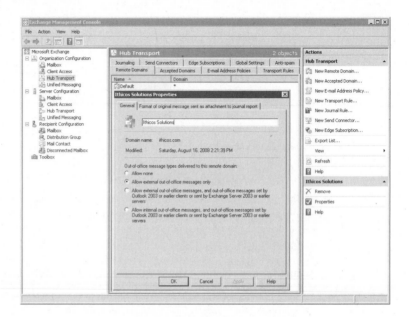

If you are inclined to manage these settings from the EMS, here are the EMS cmdlets for managing remote domain message formats:

CMDLET	DESCRIPTION
Get-RemoteDomain	Retrieves a list of existing remote domains or the properties of a specific remote domain object.
New-RemoteDomain	Creates a new remote domain object.
Set-RemoteDomain	Sets the properties of a remote domain object.
Remove-RemoteDomain	Deletes an existing remote domain object.

Configuring Accepted SMTP Domains

Exchange 2007 (like Exchange 2000/2003) must be configured with a list of SMTP domains that it will accept either as internal domains or as domains to be relayed to another SMTP system. In Exchange 2000/2003, this function was combined with recipient policies so that e-mail addresses could also be automatically generated if the policy applied to any recipients. In Exchange 2007, however, this function has been separated from recipient policies. Accepted domains are defined using the EMC by locating the Organization Configuration work center and viewing the Hub Transport subcontainer and the Accepted Domains tab. Figure 9.9 shows the Accepted Domains tab as well as the properties of one of the accepted domains.

FIGURE 9.9
Accepted Domains prop-
erties in the Exchange
Management Console

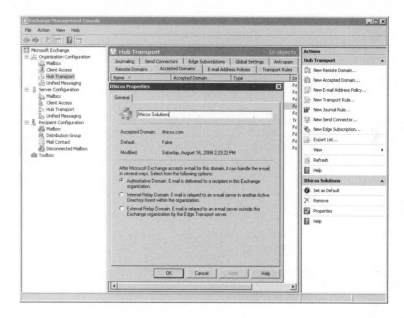

You can manage accepted domains using the EMS command shell also. The following are some of the relevant cmdlets:

CMDLET	DESCRIPTION
Get-AcceptedDomain	Retrieves a list of accepted domains or the properties of the specified accepted domain.
New-AcceptedDomain	Creates a new accepted domain.
Set-AcceptedDomain	Sets the accepted domain properties.
Remove-AcceptedDomain	Removes an accepted domain.

An accepted domain can be configured as one of the following three types:

◆ Authoritative domain — e-mail associated with this domain is always delivered to the internal Exchange organization

◆ Internal relay domain — a domain in which your Exchange organization has mail-enabled contacts

◆ External relay domain — a domain in which you relay all mail externally

You can learn more about configuring and using the accepted domains feature in Chapter 11, "Managing Recipients."

Generating and Assigning E-mail Addresses

E-mail address policies are responsible for generating e-mail addresses for mail-enabled recipients (mailboxes, groups, contacts, and so on). In Exchange 2000/2003, e-mail addresses were defined using a recipient policy. In Exchange 2000/2003, the recipient policy defined not only e-mail addresses that were generated for mail-enabled recipients but also which SMTP domains were accepted. In Exchange 2007, recipient policies and SMTP domain settings are separate.

Figure 9.10 shows the Edit E-mail Address Policy Wizard. To get there, select the Hub Transport subfolder and the E-mail Addresses Policies tab. The Edit E-mail Address Policy Wizard can be launched to create a new e-mail address policy or edit an existing one.

FIGURE 9.10
Editing an e-mail address policy using the Exchange Management Console

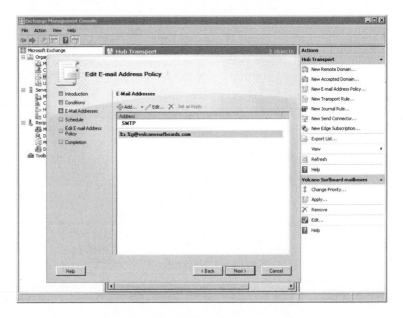

Once a policy is created, it must be applied to the mail-enabled objects. The policy is applied based on its conditions; conditions of a policy including recipients based on department name, company name, state, or a custom attribute. The administrator can apply the policy immediately after creation either by clicking the Apply button on the Actions pane or by running an EMS cmdlet. The following cmdlets apply to e-mail address policies:

CMDLET	DESCRIPTION
Get-EmailAddressPolicy	Retrieves a list of the e-mail address policies or the properties of a specified e-mail address policy.
Set-EmailAddressPolicy	Sets the properties of an e-mail address policy.
New-EmailAddressPolicy	Creates a new e-mail address policy.
Remove-EmailAddressPolicy	Removes an existing e-mail address policy.
Update-EmailAddressPolicy	Applies the policy based on the conditions specified when the policy was created. The policy must be applied before affected users can be assigned e-mail addresses that the policy specified.

You can learn more about creating and managing e-mail address policies by referring to Chapter 11, "Managing Recipients."

Managing Transport Rules

Transport rules are a new feature of Exchange 2007. They allow you to specify conditions under which a certain action will be applied to a message. An example of this would be applying an "Attorney / Client Privilege" classification label (the action) to any message sent by a member of the legal time group (the condition).

Transport rules are created and managed under the Transport Rules tab of the Hub Transport Rules pane (found under the Organization Configuration work center). Transport rules are edited and created using the Edit Transport Rule Wizard (see Figure 9.11).

FIGURE 9.11
Editing a transport rule using the Exchange Management Console

The following are the EMS cmdlets that can be used to create and manage transport rules:

CMDLET	DESCRIPTION
Get-TransportRule	Retrieves a list of transport rules or the properties of a specific transport rule.
Set-TransportRule	Sets the properties of a transport rule.
New-TransportRule	Creates a new transport rule.
Remove-TransportRule	Deletes a transport rule.
Disable-TransportRule	Disables a transport rule so that Hub Transport servers will not process that particular rule.
Enable-TransportRule	Enables a transport rule that was previously disabled.
Get-TransportRulePredicate	Lists the transport rule conditions.
Get-TransportRuleAction	Lists the transport rule actions.

I have devoted an entire chapter to creating, managing, and using transport rules. Please see Chapter 15, "Managing Messages in Transit."

Managing Journaling

Journaling is a feature that has been in Exchange since the Exchange 5.5 days. In previous versions of Exchange, though, you could only configure journaling for all mailboxes on an entire mailbox database. This feature still exists, of course, and can be used if that is the way you have configured journaling to work in your organization.

CONFIGURING JOURNALING FOR A MAILBOX DATABASE

You must locate the mailbox database that contains the mailboxes for which you want to keep journaled copies of sent and received e-mails. On the General property page (shown in Figure 9.12) of that mailbox database, you specify the journal recipient.

FIGURE 9.12
Configuring journaling for an entire mailbox database

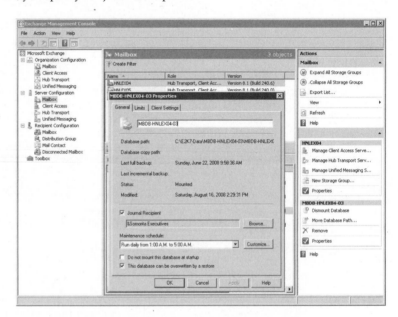

You can read more about properties of mailbox databases in Chapter 12, "Managing Storage."

JOURNALING VERSUS MESSAGE ARCHIVING

Don't confuse the concept of journaling with the concept of message archiving. Journaling allows you to save a copy of messages even before the user has seen them. Archiving usually happens at some point *after* the user may have opened the message (or maybe deleted it). Journaling is usually enabled for regulatory or compliance reasons. Some third-party message archiving systems now functionally combine the functions of journaling and archiving into a single product.

CONFIGURING JOURNALING ORGANIZATION-WIDE

Exchange 2007 introduced a couple of new approaches to journaling. You can now configure journaling with an organization-wide journaling feature found in the Journaling tab of the Organization Configuration work center's Hub Transport subcontainer. Figure 9.13 shows this tab and a journaling rule's General property page.

FIGURE 9.13
Creating a journaling rule

If you are so inclined, here are the EMS cmdlets you can use for managing journal rules:

CMDLET	DESCRIPTION
Get-JournalRule	Retrieves a list of journal rules or just the properties of a specified journal rule.
Set-JournalRule	Sets the properties of a journal rule.
New-JournalRule	Creates a new journal rule.
Remove-JournalRule	Deletes a journal rule.
Enable-JournalRule	Enables a journal rule that was disabled.
Disable-JournalRule	Disables the specified journal rule.

CONFIGURING JOURNALING THROUGH MESSAGING RECORDS MANAGEMENT

Journaling can also be achieved by creating transport rules that will forward a message to a journaling mailbox if certain conditions are met.

JOURNALING VIA MESSAGING RECORDS MANAGEMENT REQUIRES ACTION

If you use messaging records management to journal messages, this will allow you to journal messages based on user input. But something (the user, a managed folder mailbox policy, or a client-side rule) has to move the message to the folder from which journaling is performed.

Messaging records management introduces an additional way that messages can be journaled, though this feature requires user participation, so this approach can also be thought of as an archival or retention feature. On a managed content policy, you can configure the properties of a folder within a user's mailbox so that when a message is placed there, a copy of it is sent to a separate e-mail address. Figure 9.14 shows the Journaling property page of a managed custom folder.

FIGURE 9.14
Assigning journaling settings to a managed content setting

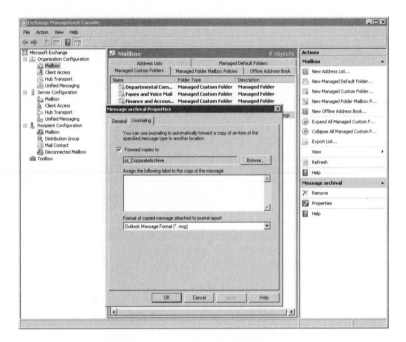

Managed content settings and messaging records management are discussed in more detail in Chapter 14, "Managing Mailbox Content."

Managing Outbound E-mail to External SMTP Domains

The Send connector is the component that you configure to send outbound SMTP mail to external SMTP domains. It is the equivalent of the Exchange 2000/2003 SMTP connector and is defined under the Organization Configuration work center of the EMC, and is found in the Hub Transport Results pane under the Send Connectors tab. One of the bigger differences (at least with respect to message transport) between Exchange 2000/2003 and Exchange 2007 is that Exchange 2007 will *not* send mail outside the organization without a Send connector (or an Edge Transport subscription).

The General properties of a Send connector as well as the Send Connectors tab are shown in Figure 9.15.

FIGURE 9.15
Properties of a Send connector as shown in the Exchange Management Console

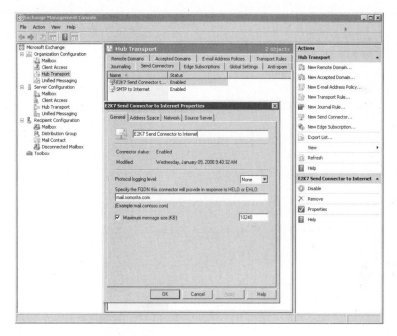

The EMS cmdlets necessary to create and manage a Send connector are as follows:

CMDLET	DESCRIPTION
Get-SendConnector	Retrieves a list of the existing Send connectors or properties of a specified Send connector.
Set-SendConnector	Sets Send connector properties.
New-SendConnector	Creates a new Send connector.
Remove-SendConnector	Deletes a Send connector.

For more information on connectivity and Send connectors, see Chapter 21, "Delivering E-mail."

Managing Edge Transport Subscriptions

Another new feature of Exchange Server 2007 is the Edge Transport server role. Although the Edge Transport role functions "similarly" to third-party SMTP message hygiene systems, one big difference is that the connection between the Edge Transport and the Hub Transport is authenticated and message transfer is encrypted.

In order to properly use the Edge Transport server role, you must configure an Edge Subscription that defines the authentication credentials. These are created and managed under the Edge Subscription tab of the Hub Transport Results pane. The New Edge Subscription Wizard is shown in Figure 9.16.

FIGURE 9.16
Creating a new Edge
Subscription using the
Exchange Management
Console

You might find a number of Edge Transport–related EMS cmdlets useful; these include the following:

CMDLET	DESCRIPTION
Get-EdgeSubscriptions	Lists the current Edge Subscriptions and their properties.
New-EdgeSubscription	Creates a new Edge Subscription.
Remove-EdgeSubscription	Deletes an Edge Subscription.
Start-EdgeSynchronization	Starts an immediate EdgeSync session.
Stop-EdgeSynchronization	Stops an EdgeSync session.
Test-EdgeSynchronization	Tests the specified Edge Transport server's subscription to ensure that the Edge Transport servers have current and accurate synchronized data.

To learn more about Edge Subscriptions, the Edge Transport server role, and anti-spam features, refer to Chapter 21, "Delivering E-mail."

Configuring Exchange Server Anti-Spam Features

There are a lot of possible ways to protect your organization from spam. You could have a managed provider that handles your spam services, or you could use a third-party appliance or software. You could use an Edge Transport server, or you could accept mail directly from the Internet to your Hub Transport servers.

If your Hub Transport servers are responsible for accepting mail directly from the Internet, you can install the anti-spam agents on the Hub Transport servers using the `Install-AntispamAgents.ps1` script. Figure 9.17 shows the Anti-spam tab for the organization-wide Hub Transport settings. You need to run the script on each Hub server on which you want to use the anti-spam agents.

FIGURE 9.17

Anti-spam configuration using the Exchange Management Console

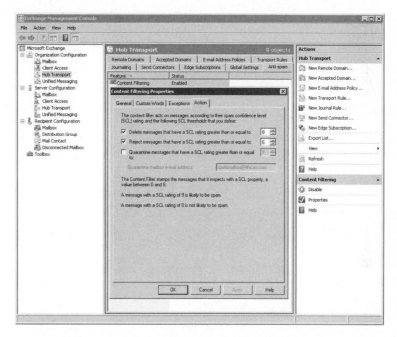

If you have been exploring the Exchange Management Console interface on your own, you may be surprised to see that Anti-spam tab. It is not there by default; you must run the `C:\Program Files\Microsoft\exchange server\scripts\Install-AntispamAgents.ps1` PowerShell script in order to install the necessary transport agents and to reveal this tab on the interface. Installing the anti-spam agent enables quite a few additional EMS cmdlets. These cmdlets will work on a Hub Transport server that has had the anti-spam agents installed and they will also work on an Edge Transport server:

CMDLET	DESCRIPTION
`Get-ContentFilterConfig`	Views the Content Filter configuration.
`Set-ConfigFilterConfig`	Sets the Content Filter configuration.
`Get-ContentFilterPhrase`	Views the Content Filter's list of phrases and words that are always considered spam or never considered spam.
`Set-ContentFilterPhrase`	Adds words or phrases to the Content Filter phrase list.
`Get-IPAllowListProvider`	Reviews the IP Allow List provider configuration.
`Set-IPAllowListProvider`	Sets the IP Allow List provider configuration.

CMDLET	DESCRIPTION
Add-IPAllowListProvider	Adds an IP Allow List provider.
Remove-IPAllowListProvider	Removes an IP Allow List provider.
Get-IPAllowListConfig	Views the IP Allow List configuration.
Set-IPAllowListConfig	Sets the IP Allow List configuration.
Get-IPAllowListEntry	Views the entries in the IP Allow List.
Add-IPAllowListEntry	Adds entries to the IP Allow List.
Remove-IPAllowListEntry	Removes an entry from the IP Allow List.
Test-IPAllowListProvider	Tests an IP Allow List provider.
Get-IPAllowListProvidersConfig	Views the configuration of the IP Allow List providers.
Set-IPAllowListProvidersConfig	Sets the configuration of the IP Allow List providers.
Test-IPBLockListProvider	Tests the specified IP Block List provider.
Get-IPBlockListConfig	Views the IP Block List configuration.
Set-IPBlockListConfig	Sets the IP Block List configuration.
Get-IPBlockListProvider	Views the IP Block List providers currently configured.
Set-IPBlockListProvider	Sets the configuration of an IP Block List provider.
Add-IPBlockListProvider	Adds a new IP Block List provider.
Remove-IPBlockListProvider	Removes an IP Block List provider.
Get-IPBlockListProvidersConfig	Views the configuration of an IP Block List provider.
Set-IPBlockListProvidersConfig	Sets the configuration of a specific IP Block List provider.
Add-IPBlockListEntry	Adds an IP address to the IP Block List.
Remove-IPBlockListEntry	Removes an IP address from the IP Block List.
Get-IPBlockListEntry	Views the IP Block List entries.
Get-RecipientFilterConfig	Views the Recipient Filter configuration.
Set-RecipientFitlerConfig	Sets the Recipient Filter configuration.
Get-SenderReputationConfig	Views the Sender Reputation configuration.
Set-SenderReputationConfig	Configures the Sender Reputation configuration.
Get-SenderIdConfig	Views the Sender ID configuration.

CMDLET	DESCRIPTION
Set-SenderIdConfig	Sets the Sender ID configuration.
Test-SenderId	Tests the Sender ID configuration.
Get-SenderFilterConfig	Views the Sender Filter configuration.
Set-SenderFilterConfig	Sets the Sender Filter configuration.
Disable-AntispamUpdates	Prevents the servers from downloading anti-spam system updates automatically.
Enable-AntispamUpdates	Enables automatic download and installation of anti-spam updates.
Get-AntispamUpdates	Views the configuration of the anti-spam updates system and retrieves updates.

For more information on using the Exchange 2007 anti-spam features and the Edge Transport server role, see Chapter 21, "Delivering E-mail."

Performing Server-by-Server Configuration

Now that you have looked at some of the configuration properties that you might need to use when configuring your Exchange Server 2007 organization, we'll shift gears and look at some of the things you can do for each server. The following sections focus on the properties and objects found within the Server Configuration work center of the Exchange Management Console.

Entering a Product Key

If you are using Exchange 2007 without entering a product key, you will be dutifully notified each time you run the Exchange Management Console. To enter the key, in the Results pane, select the server that needs a license key (this is the server with the small paper symbol and the blue and white exclamation mark icon). You should see the Enter Product Key task on the Actions pane. Figure 9.18 shows an example.

(Note that if you are looking at an unlicensed server using the 32-bit version of the Exchange Management Console, the Enter Product Key task will not appear on the Actions pane.)

You can also set the product key using the Set-ExchangeServer -ProductKey command.

Once an x64 server is licensed, the Enter Product Key task will no longer appear on the Actions pane.

EXCHANGE SERVER LICENSE CANNOT BE CHANGED

Make sure you are entering the right product key when you license an Exchange server. Once an Exchange server is licensed for a particular edition of Exchange, it cannot be changed.

Managing Server Properties

If you select each of the subcontainers under the Server Configuration work center, highlight a server in the Results pane, and then display the properties, you will see a slightly different set of property pages. However, if you highlight the Server Configuration container itself, all of the servers show up in the Results pane. If you display the properties of a server in the Results pane now, you will see all of the property pages for all of the server roles that are installed. Figure 9.19 shows the properties for an Exchange Server 2007 server that has all four server roles (Mailbox, Client Access, Hub Transport, and Unified Messaging) installed. Keep in mind that installing all four roles on a single server might be too much load for a medium-sized or large business.

FIGURE 9.18
The Exchange Management Console showing an unlicensed server

FIGURE 9.19
Properties of an Exchange 2007 server

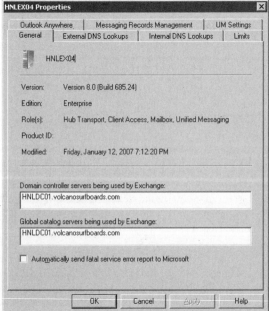

These properties are all viewed and set with different EMS cmdlets, depending on the server roles that are installed. The following are the cmdlets you would use for setting Exchange server properties:

CMDLET	DESCRIPTION
Get-ExchangeServer	Views Exchange server properties that are shared by all server roles.
Set-ExchangeServer	Sets Exchange server properties that are shared by all server roles.
Get-TransportServer	Lists the Hub Transport servers and views Hub Transport server properties.
Set-TransportServer	Sets Hub Transport server properties.
Get-MailboxServer	Lists all of the Mailbox servers and views Mailbox server properties.
Set-MailboxServer	Sets Mailbox server properties.
Get-ClientAccessServer	Lists all of the Client Access servers and views Client Access server properties.
Set-ClientAccessServer	Sets Client Access server properties.
Get-UMServer	Lists all of the Unified Messaging servers and views Unified Messaging server properties.
Set-UMServer	Sets Unified Messaging server properties.
Enable-UMServer	Enables a Unified Messaging server to process voicemail, faxes, and call routing.
Disable-UMServer	Disables a Unified Messaging server so that it will not process voicemail, faxes, or route calls.
Get-ClusteredMailboxServer	Retrieves a list of clustered Mailbox servers.
Move-ClusteredMailboxServer	Moves a clustered Mailbox server to a passive clustered node.
Start-ClusteredMailboxServer	Starts clustered Mailbox server services.
Stop-ClusteredMailboxServer	Stops clustered Mailbox server services.

Managing Mailbox and Public Folder Databases

If you highlight the Mailbox subcontainer of the Exchange Management Console, the Results pane will show you all servers that host the Mailbox server role. The Work pane (below the Results pane) will show you the storage groups, mailbox databases, and public folder databases. Figure 9.20 shows parts of the EMC that show the storage groups and databases.

FIGURE 9.20
Managing storage groups, mailbox databases, and public folder databases on a single server

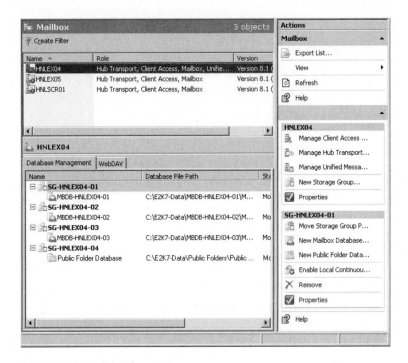

Quite a few tasks can be defined within this view of the EMC with respect to storage groups, mailbox databases, and public folder databases:

- Creating and deleting storage groups

- Creating and deleting mailbox and public folder databases

- Configuring or moving file locations for storage groups and databases

- Mounting or dismounting databases

- Configuring database maintenance schedules

- Enabling, suspending, and resuming local continuous replication

- Establishing storage limits for mailboxes and public folders supported on a particular database

- Configuring deleted item and deleted mailbox retention times

- Enabling mailbox database journaling

- Setting default public folder databases and offline address books

Likewise, there are also quite a few EMS cmdlets that can be used for managing storage groups, mailbox databases, and public folder databases. The cmdlets that are used to manage storage group properties are listed here:

CMDLET	DESCRIPTION
New-StorageGroup	Creates a new storage group.
Move-StorageGroup	Moves transaction logs or system files to another location.
Get-StorageGroup	Retrieves a list of storage groups or storage group properties.
Set-StorageGroup	Sets a storage group's properties.
Remove-StorageGroup	Deletes a storage group.
Enable-StorageGroupCopy	Enables local continuous replication for a storage group.
Disable-StorageGroupCopy	Disables local continuous replication for a storage group.
Suspend-StorageGroupCopy	Temporarily suspends local continuous replication.
Update-StorageGroupCopy	Instructs local continuous replication to re-establish local continuous replication.
Resume-StorageGroupCopy	Starts local continuous replication after it was previously suspended.
Restore-StorageGroupCopy	Switches the local continuous replication database for the production copy.
Get-StorageGroupCopyStatus	Views the status of local continuous replication.

If you are looking for additional information on creating and managing mailbox databases as well as managing local continuous replication, see Chapter 12, "Managing Storage."

Managing Client Access Server Properties

The Client Access server role has a lot of functions in an organization that is using Outlook 2007, Outlook Anywhere (RPC over HTTP), Outlook Web Access, or ActiveSync technologies. When you select the Client Access subcontainer of the Server Configuration work center, the Results pane shows the servers that host that particular server role. The Work pane shows tabs for Outlook Web Access, Exchange ActiveSync, POP and IMAC4, and Offline Address Book distribution. Figure 9.21 shows the Client Access subcontainer of the EMC.

Though some organizations may be able to use the default client access configuration of Exchange 2007, other organizations will need to perform some changes or do some customizing. You can configure the following options through the Client Access subcontainer:

◆ Enabling or disabling Outlook Anywhere

◆ Managing internal and external URLs for Outlook Web Access, offline address books, Outlook Anywhere, and Exchange ActiveSync

◆ Managing authentication options for Outlook Web Access

◆ Managing segmentation options for Outlook Web Access

◆ Managing POP3 and IMAP4 options

◆ Configuring file and SharePoint servers that can be accessed remotely by Outlook Web Access and ActiveSync users

The cmdlets that can be used to manage mailbox and public folder databases are:

CMDLET	DESCRIPTION
New-MailboxDatabase	Creates a new mailbox database.
Get-MailboxDatabase	Retrieves a list of mailbox databases or properties of mailbox databases.
Set-MailboxDatabase	Sets the properties of a mailbox database.
Remove-MailboxDatabase	Deletes a mailbox database.
Clean-MailboxDatabase	Disconnects mailboxes on the specified mailbox database if the mailbox has been deleted in the Active Directory.
New-PublicFolderDatabase	Creates a new public folder database.
Get-PublicFolderDatabase	Retrieves a list of public folder databases or public databases.
Set-PublicFolderDatabase	Sets the properties of a public folder database.
Remove-PublicFolderDatabase	Deletes a public folder database.
Mount-Database	Mounts the specified mailbox or public folder database.
Dismount-Database	Dismounts the specified pubic folder database.
Move-DatabasePath	Moves public folder or mailbox database files to another location.
Enable-DatabaseCopy	Enables local continuous replication for the specified database.

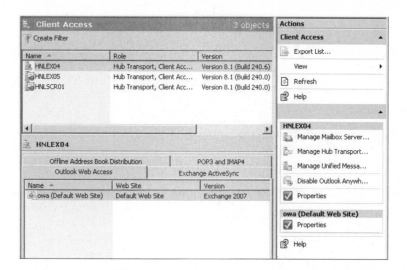

FIGURE 9.21
Managing Client Access
server properties

With this many possible Client Access server-related tasks, naturally there are a lot of EMS cmdlets. Some Exchange 2007 component settings cannot be managed through a graphical user interface, and so you must use the EMS. The following list includes some of the Client Access server role cmdlets:

CMDLET	DESCRIPTION
Get-OutlookAnywhere	Retrieves the Outlook Anywhere configuration.
Set-OutlookAnywhere	Sets the Outlook Anywhere configuration.
Enable-OutlookAnywhere	Enables Outlook Anywhere support for a Client Access server.
Disable-OutlookAnywhere	Disables Outlook Anywhere support for a Client Access server.
Get-OwaVirtualDirectory	Retrieves a list of the OWA virtual directories and the OWA virtual directory properties.
Set-OwaVirtualDirectory	Sets OWA virtual directory properties.
New-OwaVirtualDirectory	Creates a new OWA virtual directory.
Remove-OwaVirtualDirectory	Deletes an OWA virtual directory.
Test-OwaConnectivity	Tests OWA connectivity.
New-ActiveSyncVirtualDirectory	Creates a new Exchange ActiveSync virtual directory.
Set-ActiveSyncVirtualDirectory	Sets ActiveSync virtual directory properties.

CMDLET	DESCRIPTION
Get-ActiveSyncVirtualDirectory	Retrieves a list of the ActiveSync virtual directories and ActiveSync virtual directory properties.
Remove-ActiveSyncVirtualDirectory	Deletes an ActiveSync virtual directory.
Test-ActiveSyncConnectivity	Tests ActiveSync connectivity.
Export-ActiveSyncLog	Exports ActiveSync usage information from the IIS log files.
Get-OABVirtualDirectory	Retrieves offline address book virtual directory information and properties.
New-OABVirtualDirectory	Creates a new offline address book virtual directory.
Remove-OABVirtualDirectory	Deletes an offline address book virtual directory.
Set-OABVirtualDirectory	Sets the properties of an offline address book virtual directory.
Get-AutodiscoverVirtualDirectory	Retrieves a list of Autodiscover virtual directories and their properties.
Set-AutodiscoverVirtualDirectory	Sets Autodiscover virtual directory properties.
Remove-AutodiscoverVirtualDirectory	Deletes an Autodiscover virtual directory.
New-AutodiscoverVirtualDirectory	Creates a new Autodiscover virtual directory.
Get-POPSettings	Retrieves the POP3 configuration for a Client Access server.
Set-POPSettings	Sets the POP3 configuration.
Get-IMAPSettings	Retrieves the IMAP4 configuration for a Client Access server.
Set-IMAPSettings	Sets the IMAP4 configuration.

You can find more information about enabling Outlook Anywhere, Outlook Web Access, POP3, and IMAP4 in Chapter 23, "Exchange Anywhere."

Managing Receive Connectors

Receive connectors are defined for each Hub Transport server role in your organization. By default two Receive connectors are configured for each Hub Transport server — the Default Receive connector and the Client Receive connector. Inbound SMTP mail from the Edge Transport, a third-party message hygiene system, or directly from the Internet will be delivered to the Default Receive connector. You can see the Receive Connectors tab in the Work pane when you select the Hub Transport subcontainer of the Server Configuration work center in the EMC. The Default Receive connector Work pane is shown in Figure 9.22.

FIGURE 9.22
Managing Receive
connectors

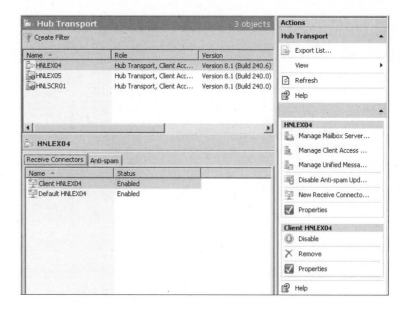

If you want to manage the Receive connectors from the EMS, here are the cmdlets you can use:

CMDLET	DESCRIPTION
Get-ReceiveConnector	Retrieves a list of Receive connectors and their properties.
Set-ReceiveConnector	Sets the properties of a Receive connector.
New-ReceiveConnector	Creates a new Receive connector.
Remove-ReceiveConnector	Deletes a Receive connector.

ACCEPTING INBOUND E-MAIL FROM THE INTERNET

One very common question on Internet newsgroups and forums is why Exchange 2007 will not accept inbound e-mail from the Internet. The Default Receive connector on the Hub Transport servers that will accept inbound e-mail from a third-party message hygiene system or directly from the Internet requires Anonymous users on its Permission Group property page to be enabled to receive mail from outside the organization.

You can find more information about managing Receive connectors as well as e-mail connectivity in Chapter 21, "Delivering E-mail."

Recipient Administration

Chapter 11, "Managing Recipients," goes into a lot more detail on recipient administration. For now, I want to introduce the Recipient Configuration work center of the Exchange Management Console and show you many of the recipient management cmdlets. Recipient management is most easily performed using the Recipient Configuration work center of the EMC (see Figure 9.23).

FIGURE 9.23
Managing Exchange
2007 recipients
using the Exchange
Management Console

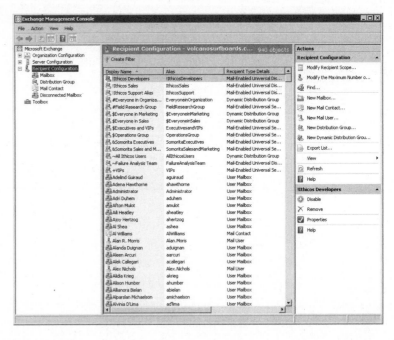

For many medium-sized and large businesses, the EMS will prove most useful for managing mail-enabled recipients. For that reason, I wanted to provide a fairly comprehensive list of the EMS cmdlets available. The following sections review the management of each type of recipient and provide you with a list of the EMS cmdlets that can be used for each.

MANAGE MAIL-ENABLED RECIPIENTS THROUGH EMC OR EMS

All mail-enabled recipient administration must be performed through the Exchange Management Console or the Exchange Management Shell. The Active Directory Users and Computers extensions for Exchange 2000/2003 do not work properly with Exchange Server 2007 recipients.

Mailbox Management

If you select the Mailboxes subcontainer of the Recipient Configuration work center of the EMC, you can see just the mailbox-enabled users in the organization. This could potentially be a pretty big list, so you can apply filters to narrow the scope of the list to just what you want to see. From here, you can select the properties of a single mailbox (see Figure 9.24).

The mailbox properties you see in Figure 9.24 include attributes of the user account that are not really Exchange-specific. For example, you can change information such as telephone numbers, department, web page, address, manager, and office location. You can perform quite a few tasks and actions against a mailbox, but not all of them can be performed via the graphical user interface. The following list includes some of these tasks:

◆ Managing user account attributes such as phone, address, and organization properties

◆ Moving mailboxes to another mailbox store (or even another Exchange organization)

- ◆ Assigning storage limits, messages size limits, recipient limits, and deleted item retention settings for a mailbox

- ◆ Defining message delivery restrictions and e-mail forwarding options

- ◆ Enabling web service features such as ActiveSync and Outlook Web Access as well as enabling or disabling MAPI connectivity

- ◆ Assigning ActiveSync and messaging records management policies to a mailbox

- ◆ Managing permissions that other users have to a mailbox

- ◆ Configuring Send As permissions to a mailbox

- ◆ Managing the ActiveSync devices associated with a mailbox

FIGURE 9.24
Managing a mailbox's properties using the Exchange Management Console

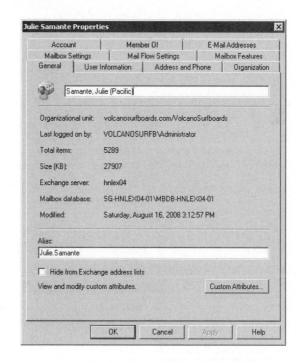

Here are the cmdlets that are used to manage mailboxes and user accounts:

CMDLET	DESCRIPTION
Get-User	Retrieves account information about a user in the Active Directory.
Set-User	Sets the properties of a user account.
Get-Mailbox	Retrieves mailboxes and properties of mailboxes.
Get-MailboxStatistics	Retrieves mailbox storage statistics for a mailbox database or a specified mailbox.

CMDLET	DESCRIPTION
Get-MailboxFolderStatistics	Retrieves mailbox folder statistics for a specified mailbox.
Get-MailboxCalendarSettings	Retrieves the Calendar Attendant settings for the specified mailbox.
Get-UMMailbox	Retrieves the Unified Messaging properties for the specified mailbox.
Get-CASMailbox	Retrieves the Client Access server properties for a specified mailbox.
Get-MailboxPermissions	Retrieves the permissions that are assigned or inherited for the specified mailbox.
Get-UMMailboxPIN	Retrieves a Unified Messaging PIN for the specified mailbox.
Move-Mailbox	Moves a mailbox from one mailbox database to another.
Connect-Mailbox	Reconnects an existing user account to a mailbox that was previously deleted.
Enable-UMMailbox	Enables a mailbox to support Unified Messaging.
Restore-Mailbox	Copies mailbox data from a recovery storage group to the production mailbox location.
Export-Mailbox	Exports mailbox content to an alternate location.
Remove-ActiveSyncDevice	Removes an ActiveSync device that is associated with the specified mailbox.
Clear-ActiveSyncDevice	Performs a remote wipeout of the specified ActiveSync device the next time it connects.
Get-ActiveSyncDeviceStatistics	Retrieves usage statistics and device information about the specified ActiveSync device.
New-Mailbox	Creates a new user account and mailbox.
Enable-Mailbox	Enables an existing user so that it has a mailbox.
Remove-Mailbox	Deletes the specified user account and mailbox.
Disable-Mailbox	Removes a mailbox from the specified user but does not delete the user account.
Set-Mailbox	Sets mailbox properties.
Set-UMMailbox	Sets Unified Messaging–related properties on a mailbox.
Set-CASMailbox	Sets Client Access server–related properties on a mailbox.
Add-MailboxPermission	Adds permissions to a mailbox.

CMDLET	DESCRIPTION
Remove-MailboxPermission	Removes permissions from a mailbox.
Set-UMMailboxPIN	Sets the Unified Messaging PIN for a mailbox.
Disable-UMMailbox	Disables a mailbox's UM features so that it no longer supports Unified Messaging.
New-MailUser	Creates a new user account and associates an external e-mail address with that user.
Get-ADPermission	Retrieves permissions associated with an Active Directory object.
Add-ADPermission	Sets Active Directory permissions on an object such as a mailbox-enabled user.
Remove-ADPermission	Removes Active Directory permissions from an object.
Enable-MailUser	Associates an external e-mail address with an existing user account.
Remove-MailUser	Removes a mail-enabled user account from the directory.
Disable-MailUser	Removes an external e-mail address that is associated with a user.
Get-MailUser	Retrieves a list of mail-enabled users or properties of mail-enabled users.
Set-MailUser	Sets properties of a mail-enabled user account.

Mail-Enabled Group Management

Mail-enabled groups are managed from the Distribution Group subcontainer of the Recipient Configuration work center. From here you can create new Active Directory groups, enable existing groups for mail, and edit the properties of existing groups. One of the more common tasks an administrator performs on mail-enabled groups is to add or remove members. Figure 9.25 shows the Members property page of a mail-enabled group.

Here is a list of tasks you may need to perform on mail-enabled groups:

◆ Managing group membership

◆ Configuring messaging restrictions such as maximum message size and who can send mail to a group

◆ Specifying if a group can receive anonymous messages

◆ Assigning additional SMTP addresses for a group

◆ Configuring an expansion server

◆ Configuring delivery report behavior

FIGURE 9.25
Managing the
membership of a
mail-enabled group

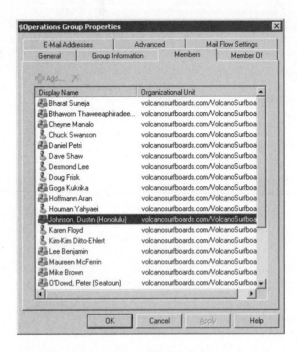

If you want to manage mail-enabled groups from the EMS, here are some of the cmdlets available:

CMDLET	DESCRIPTION
Set-Group	Manages the properties of a security or distribution group.
Get-Group	Retrieves a list of security and distribution groups (regardless of mail-enabled status) in the Active Directory.
Enable-DistributionGroup	Mail-enables an existing group in the Active Directory.
Disable-DistributionGroup	Disables the mail features of an existing group but does not delete it.
New-DistributionGroup	Creates a new group in the Active Directory and mail-enables it.
Remove-DistributionGroup	Deletes a mail-enabled group from the Active Directory.
Set-DistributionGroup	Sets the properties of a mail-enabled group.
Get-DistributionGroup	Retrieves a list of mail-enabled groups or the properties of specified mail-enabled groups.
Add-DistributionGroupMember	Adds a user to a mail-enabled group.

CMDLET	DESCRIPTION
Get-DistributionGroupMember	Retrieves the membership of a mail-enabled group.
Remove-DistributionGroupMember	Removes a member from a mail-enabled group.
New-DynamicDistributionGroup	Creates a new dynamic distribution group.
Set-DynamicDistributionGroup	Sets the properties of a dynamic distribution group.
Get-DynamicDistributionGroup	Retrieves a list of dynamic distribution groups or the properties of a specific dynamic distribution group.
Remove-DynamicDistributionGroup	Deletes a dynamic distribution group.

For more information on mail-enabled group management, see Chapter 11, "Managing Recipients."

Mail-Enabled Contact Management

Mail-enabled contacts appear in the Exchange global address list, but they do not need to be security principals. You can use the EMC to create and manage enabled contacts in the Mail Contacts subcontainer of the Recipient Configuration work center. Figure 9.26 shows the E-Mail Addresses property page of a mail-enabled contact. This page includes the e-mail addresses that will be accepted for this recipient as well as the external e-mail address of the recipient (the address to which the message will be forwarded).

FIGURE 9.26

Managing a
mail-enabled contact's
e-mail addresses

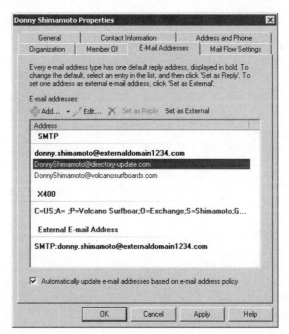

Mail-enabled contacts can be managed from the EMS as well as the EMC. Here are the EMS cmdlets you can use for managing mail-enabled contacts:

CMDLET	DESCRIPTION
Get-Contact	Retrieves the contacts from the Active Directory or retrieves the properties of specified contacts.
Set-Contact	Sets the properties of a contact in the Active Directory.
Enable-MailContact	Mail-enables an existing Active Directory contact.
Disable-MailContact	Disables the mail attributes for an Active Directory contact but does not delete the contact.
Remove-MailContact	Deletes a mail-enabled contact from the Active Directory.
Get-MailContact	Retrieves a list of the mail-enabled contacts in the Active Directory or the properties of specified contacts.
Set-MailContact	Sets the properties of a mail-enabled contact.

You can find more information on creating and managing mail-enabled contacts in Chapter 11, "Managing Recipients."

Public Folder Management

One thing that tends to confuse experienced Exchange 2000/2003 administrators is that in the RTM version of Exchange Server 2007 Microsoft did not provide a graphical user interface for managing public folders. This changed in Exchange Server 2007 Service Pack 1, but the Public Folder Management Console is still separate from the Exchange Management Console. To locate the Public Folder Management Console, use the Exchange Management Console and navigate to the Tools container; in that container you will find the Public Folder Management Console (shown in Figure 9.27).

FIGURE 9.27
Using the Public Folder
Management Console

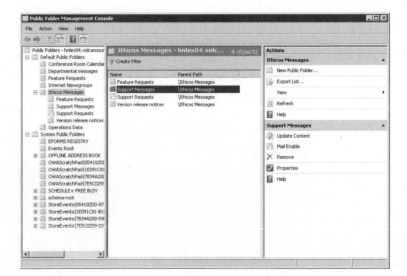

From the Public Folder Management Console, you can select the folder in the Results pane and manage things like replica lists and folder limits.

You still have a few things (such as managing permissions) that you can't do via the GUI. You can manage these features in the following ways:

◆ Keep a copy of the Exchange 2003 System Manager program running.

◆ Use the utility PFDAVAdmin.

◆ Use the Exchange Management Shell.

Here is a list of the EMS cmdlets that can be used to manage public folders:

CMDLET	DESCRIPTION
Remove-PublicFolderClientPermissions	Removes client permissions from a public folder.
Add-PublicFolderClientPermissions	Adds client permissions to a public folder.
Get-PublicFolderClientPermissions	Retrieves a list of client permissions for a public folder.
Get-PublicFolderAdministrativePermissions	Retrieves the public folder administrative permissions.
Add-PublicFolderAdministrativePermissions	Adds administrative permissions to a public folder.
Remove-PublicFolderAdministrativePermissions	Removes administrative permissions from a public folder.
New-PublicFolder	Creates a new public folder.
Remove-PublicFolder	Deletes a public folder.
Get-PublicFolder	Retrieves public folders or the properties of specified public folder properties.
Set-PublicFolder	Sets public folder properties.
Enable-MailPublicFolder	Mail-enables a public folder.
Disable-MailPublicFolder	Disables mail properties of a public folder.
Get-MailPublicFolder	Retrieves a list of mail-enabled public folders or properties of a mail-enabled public folder.
Set-MailPublicFolder	Sets mail-enabled public folder properties.
Update-PublicFolder	Forces an update of public folder content.
Update-PublicFolderHierarchy	Forces an update of the public folder hierarchy.
Get-PublicFolderStatistics	Retrieves public folder statistics.

You can find more information about public folder management in Chapter 16, "Public Folder Administration."

Summary

Even for experienced Exchange administrators, the new management interfaces can be a bit intimidating. It helps to know where to find the objects you need and the tasks that you most frequently perform.

This chapter reviewed where the configuration data is stored for Exchange Server; this is a special partition of the Active Directory called the configuration partition. The chapter also looked at the different work centers of the Exchange Management Console and the types of tasks that can be performed in each.

In the Organization Configuration work center, you perform configuration tasks that affect the entire organization. These objects found in the Organization Configuration work center have the potential to affect every server and mail recipient in the entire Exchange organization.

In the Server Configuration work center you can perform tasks that affect specific Exchange servers and server roles. Finally, the Recipient Configuration work center allows you to manage mail-enabled recipients (users, groups, contacts).

Chapter 10

Imposing Limits

Imposing limits on users and mailboxes seems like a strange topic to which to dedicate an entire chapter. This is an important topic because even in mature messaging environments (organizations that have had Exchange or some other client-server messaging system deployed for 10+ years), limits are often not imposed.

So why is this an important topic? Simple. You need to be configuring your organization for predictable operations. Every morning when you wake up and go to work, you need to have some assurances that, provided nothing terrible has happened, your mail system is in pretty much the same state it was in when you left it the day before. This not only helps with ongoing operations, it makes it easier to recognize when something has gone wrong.

Ensuring that your Exchange system is operating in a predictable fashion with respect to mailbox or message limitations means that you do not exceed your designed disk capacity and you don't flood your network connections with messages that are too large. Operating predictably certainly does not stop at mailbox limits, but for the purpose of this chapter, the scope is limited to just predicting disk space usage and network usage. This chapter discusses a number of different approaches to applying messaging system limits.

In this chapter you learn to:

- ◆ Understand typical limits
- ◆ Apply mailbox-by-mailbox mail storage limits
- ◆ Apply mailbox limits for an entire mailbox database
- ◆ Apply message size limits
- ◆ Apply limits to public folders

Why Limits Are Unpopular but Necessary

Mail administrators often cringe at the prospect of imposing limits on their users, certainly their VIP users. Imposing limits is a touchy subject, even with IT and company management, who may often feel that limits are necessary but should not apply to them.

As I mentioned, limits are important to maintaining predictable operations. Another important factor to consider is that limits help prevent abuse of the mail system, such as a user sending a message to the entire Everyone distribution group advertising his garage sale, or a user sending out a message with a 200MB attachment. (Don't laugh, I see this type of thing happen pretty regularly!)

Furthermore, more and more organizations are faced with state, provincial, or federal government regulations. For example, users may be required to keep historical information available, which would in turn affect the limits you impose on their mailboxes.

Failure to define and properly establish messaging system limits can have adverse or even catastrophic effects on your daily operations. This is very true of mailbox limits. More than a few Exchange administrators have come to work one morning only to discover that they are out of disk space on the database disk drive. Why? They were not on top of the mailbox growth and it caught them by surprise. Dealing with a server whose mailbox databases are dismounted because you are out of disk space is almost as difficult as facing management to explain why you are out of disk space and why you have to buy more.

HELPING MANAGEMENT UNDERSTAND LIMITS

The ultimate decision about limits and enforcement is usually "above our pay grade." Management has to understand why limits are necessary and what appropriate limits might be for your organization. Management must balance functionality, organizational requirements, availability, and, of course, system costs.

Regardless of what I may tell you are typical limits, you must find the right balance for your own organization. That balance may be far above or below the limits I recommend.

Although I certainly can't help you with your "political" issues, I can help you determine the right place to apply limits and maybe even suggest some appropriate limits.

Typical Limits

Way back in Chapter 3, "Introducing Exchange Server 2007," I talked some about the changing nature of e-mail and how message sizes and mailbox content has changed. Chapter 2, "Designing a New Exchange 2007 System," included a section called "Planning Your Disk Space Requirements." In that section, I took you through a planning exercise to figure out roughly how much disk space you will require given maximum mailbox sizes.

If your organization has not set mailbox limits or message size limits, your first challenge is to figure out what those actually need to be. If you currently have limits in place, you need to determine if they are effective.

Recommended Mailbox Storage Limits

Let's first look at mailbox storage limits. A question I am frequently asked is, "What is typical for the industry?"

Unfortunately, there is no set guideline for what "the industry" is doing with respect to mailbox limits. In the Exchange 2003 time frame, these limits are commonplace:

Issue warning	250MB
Prohibit send	275MB
Prohibit send and receive	300MB
Maximum outgoing message size	10MB (the default)
Maximum incoming message size	10MB (the default)

I have had individuals in some large corporations and European organizations report to me that the following limits are more commonplace. Notice that the message sizes are higher, but the mailbox limits are a bit lower:

Issue warning	150MB
Prohibit send	200MB
Prohibit send and receive	300MB
Maximum outgoing message size	20MB
Maximum incoming message size	20MB

Some organizations look at these limits and wish they could provide their users with that much mailbox space, whereas other organizations see these limits as clearly insufficient for their messaging needs.

Some of the new features of Exchange 2007 such as Unified Messaging have not yet been in use long enough to see any clearly defined mailbox size trends, but here are limits that I use for planning capacity for a typical organization:

Issue warning	500MB
Prohibit send	550MB
Prohibit send and receive	600MB
Maximum outgoing message size	10MB
Maximum incoming message size	10MB

These limits have to be carefully balanced with available disk space, backup and restore resources, and users' needs.

Regardless of what's standard, if your users require lots of mailbox space for official business reasons, you should find a way to support that requirement.

One large organization that I work with recently revised its mail limits shortly after migrating to Exchange Server 2007. The original limits were more like one of the ones I have just shown you, but now its limits are as follows:

Issue warning	25MB
Prohibit send	50MB
Prohibit send and receive	500MB
Maximum outgoing message size	5MB
Maximum incoming message size	5MB

A couple of things happened at this organization to make it so dramatically "dial down" its mail storage limits. The first is that the organization implemented e-mail archival and decided e-mail over 14 days old would be moved into the archive. The second was the implementation of SharePoint; with SharePoint, users are being strongly discouraged from sending one another attachments. Instead large files should always be posted to SharePoint.

As I mentioned in Chapter 3, Microsoft is driving home the point that a 2GB mailbox limit will become commonplace as organizations move to Exchange 2007. Indeed, the default Exchange 2007 mailbox database limits are as follows:

Issue warning	1,945MB
Prohibit send	2,048MB
Prohibit send and receive	2,355MB

This may be far higher than you want for your users. Although most of us would personally love to have a 2GB mailbox on our corporate mail server, there are a number of other factors that you should consider when setting mailbox limits.

Once you have evaluated some of these factors and decided that you need to raise your limits, you need to find a way to effectively increase your technological capacity to support these limits. This includes larger disks, faster backup/restore capabilities, and larger backup/restore capabilities, and it could include additional technologies such as archival solutions. The following list includes some of the factors you need to consider:

◆ Is there a business reason for giving users more mail storage? Consider the cost of users trying to find information that at one time was in their mailbox and is now gone.

◆ Evaluate your current limits (if you have them). Do your users have to delete/archive mail frequently in order to stay under their prescribed limit? Do they require e-mail that they have deleted or archived?

◆ Consider your VIPs, executives, and other heavy messaging users: Do they need more or less space than a typical user? A heavy messaging user may not necessarily be a VIP. In some organizations, the salespeople, engineers, architects, or paralegals may be the heaviest users of messaging technologies.

◆ Do you have an e-mail archival system in place that automatically moves older mail out of a user's folders or managed folders and stores that data in a long-term storage repository? Centralized repositories may actually reduce mailbox space requirements because data can be retained for much longer periods of time without actually impacting the mailbox database. However, retention periods for the content in a user's mailbox will still depend on allowing the user to access that data via Outlook, Outlook Web Access, Outlook using RPC over HTTP, or Windows Mobile devices. Depending on the archival system, older messages might not be accessible from all devices or locations, so this should be considered when planning for retention times.

◆ Basic mailbox content includes e-mail messages, appointments, contacts, tasks, and journaling information. What other technologies are you employing that would increase the average size of a mailbox?

  ◆ Integrated faxing? How many faxes would your users need to retain?

  ◆ Integrated voicemail? How many voicemail messages would your users need to retain?

  ◆ Forms routing and workflow? Would a historical record of forms processed (expense reports, purchase requests, travel approval, and so on) need to be retained by the sender as well as other people in the forms routing process?

◆ Are you faced with regulatory requirements that require the retention of certain types of information for a long period of time?

◆ Could larger mailbox sizes expose you to potential denial-of-service attacks where someone sends lots of large messages to your users until all mailboxes and possibly the database or transaction log disk are filled?

These are just some of the factors that may affect your decisions with respect to assigning mailbox limits.

Recommended Message Size Limits

Just when you think you are out of the woods with respect to this decision, you have another decision to make. What about message size limits?

ALTERNATIVE OPTIONS FOR LARGE FILE TRANSFERS

Is your maximum message too small? Some organizations are turning to companies like You SendIt (www.yousendit.com) for large file transfers.

The default message size limit for both incoming and outgoing messages is 10MB; this limit has not changed since Exchange 2003. This value is not just an arbitrary or nice round number; it is based on Microsoft's best practices and feedback from many customers. However, I often find this limit to be insufficient in environments where large attachments are used. Regardless of whether it is a good practice to send a 50MB file through e-mail, sometimes it is just not possible for users to easily transfer large attachments between organizations any other way.

If your organization requires the transfer of large files, always try to find an alterative such as using portals, websites, FTP servers, or instant messaging. If the files need to be transferred to other organizations, keep in mind that even if you raise your organization's outgoing message size limit, a remote organization might still be unable to receive messages as large as your users can send.

So what are some factors to take into consideration when planning for a maximum message size? This is not as clear-cut and easy to handle as mailbox size limits, but here are some things to think about:

◆ Do your users need to transmit large file attachments?

◆ Do you have a mechanism to prevent "large attachment" abuse? For example, you might want to prevent MPG, MOV, WMA, WMV, and MP3 files from being sent via e-mail, if those file types are considered inappropriate in your organization.

◆ Is there an alternative to sending or receiving large attachments? Some alternatives include:

  ◆ Allowing internal users to post content to a SharePoint portal page

  ◆ Using extranet pages

  ◆ Using intranet solutions

  ◆ Using instant messaging

  ◆ Providing external users with an alternative way to send you large files

◆ Providing remote users with a web page to upload files using a tool such as Blade Transfer Services (`http://www.blade.net.nz/BladeTransferServices.aspx`)

◆ Can large content be automatically compressed by some client-side utility, thus reducing attachment sizes?

◆ If large message sizes are allowed, can your network links and Internet connection handle the capacity?

Mailbox Storage Limits

Limiting the amount of content that is stored in a user's mailbox is pretty easy to do. In many respects, it is no different than handling limits was in Exchange 4.0. Limits can be applied to all mailboxes in a mailbox database, or the mailbox database limits can be overridden on a mailbox-by-mailbox basis.

One difference between Exchange 2000/2003 and Exchange 2007, though, is that Exchange 2007 does not include the concept of a mailbox store policy. The mailbox store policy allowed an administrator to apply limits to mailbox databases as a group rather than individually. In Exchange 2007, you will either have to apply limits manually or use Exchange Management Shell (EMS) tasks.

You will find a number of properties on a Limits property page of a mailbox database. Table 10.1 discusses these properties and what the options mean. If you have used earlier versions of Exchange, you are already familiar with these options and their effect on mailboxes.

Setting Mailbox Database Limits

Establishing limits on a mailbox database is a simple process. The settings are found on the Limits property page of each mailbox database. The Limits property page for the mailbox database named Viper Pilots is shown in Figure 10.1; the values are the defaults for a newly created mailbox database. Notice that the Prohibit Send And Receive At (KB) limit is 2,411,520KB (about 2.4GB!); this clearly reflects Microsoft's expectation that the typical user will require a great deal of mail content storage.

You can also set this limit using the EMS and the `Set-MailboxDatabase` cmdlet. For example, suppose you want to set the following limits on the Executives mailbox database:

Issue Warning	750MB
Prohibit Send	775MB
Prohibit Send and Receive	800MB

The following command will accomplish this:

```
Set-MailboxDatabase "Executives" -IssueWarningQuota:750MB↵
-ProhibitSendQuota:775MB -ProhibitSendReceiveQuota:800MB
```

Although this command will not output any results, you can confirm that the command was successful by using the `Get-MailboxDatabase` cmdlet. Another way to check this is to pipe the output to the `Format-List` cmdlet:

```
Get-MailboxDatabase "Executives" | Format-List Name, IssueWarningQuota,↵
ProhibitDendQuota,ProhibitSendReceiveQuota
```

```
Name                      : Executives
IssueWarningQuota         : 750MB
ProhibitSendQuota         : 775MB
ProhibitSendReceiveQuota : 800MB
```

TABLE 10.1:   Exchange Mailbox Database Limits

OPTION	EXPLANATION
Issue Warning At (KB)	Specifies the limit at which users are sent a warning e-mail message indicating that they are nearing their mail storage limit. The default is 1,991,680KB,
Prohibit Send At (KB)	Specifies the limit at which users are no longer able to send or reply to e-mail. User must reduce the amount of data in their mailbox before they can send new messages or reply to existing messages. The default is 2,097,152KB.
Prohibit Send and Receive At (KB)	Specifies the limit above which the mailbox will reject new mail as well as not allowing the user to send messages or reply to existing messages. The default is 2,411,520KB.
Warning Message Interval	Specifies the time of day when e-mail messages are sent to users that are over their Issue Warning At (KB) limit. By default this is done at 1:00AM., but it can be changed. (Be careful about selecting the Customize button; if you select an entire hour, the warning message will be sent four times that hour.)
Keep Deleted Items For (Days)	Specifies how long to keep an item once it has been emptied from the Deleted Items folder or has been hard-deleted. During this period, Outlook or Outlook Web Access users can recover items they deleted. When the specified time period is over, the message is permanently deleted and the space it consumed is reused. Deleted items are permanently purged during the online maintenance process. The default is 14 days.
Keep Deleted Mailboxes For (Days)	Specifies how long to keep a mailbox in a delete state before permanently deleting it. During this period, an administrator can reconnect a mailbox to an Active Directory user account that does not have a mailbox assigned to it. Once this limit has passed, deleted mailboxes cannot be recovered. Deleted mailboxes are permanently purged during the online maintenance process. The default is 30 days.
Do Not Permanently Delete Mailboxes and Items Until the Mailbox Database Has Been Backed Up	Tells the information store not to permanently delete an item or a mailbox even if it is past its retention time (as specified by Keep Deleted Mailboxes For (Days)) unless an online backup of the database has been made. Do not select this check box if you are performing offline backups, using a non-Exchange-aware backup, or performing backups only of the local continuous replication copy of the database. If you do, deleted items will never be purged from the database.

FIGURE 10.1
Default mailbox
database limits
properties

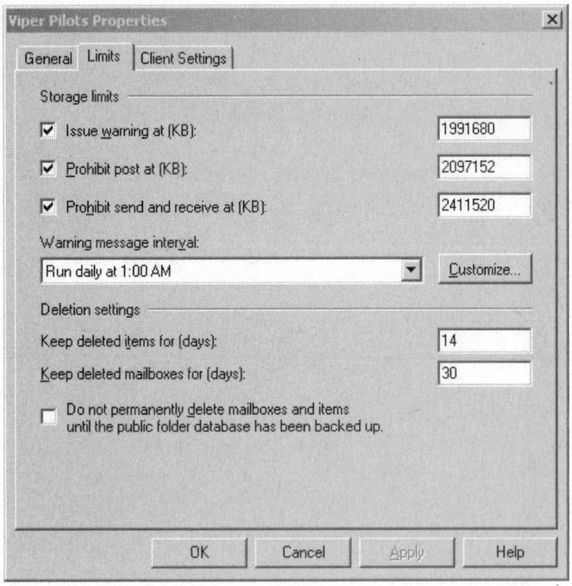

You can also output the data to the Format-Table cmdlet and view the same data in a slightly different format:

```
Get-MailboxDatabase "Executives" | Format-Table Name, IssueWarningQuota,↵
ProhibitDendQuota,ProhibitSendReceiveQuota
```

```
Name       IssueWarningQuota  ProhibitSendQuota  ProhibitSendReceiveQuota
----       -----------------  -----------------  ------------------------
Executives     750MB              775MB                  800MB
```

If you want to set default limits for an entire server, you can also use the EMS. First you need to generate a list of all of the mailbox databases on the desired server. For a server called E2K7-01, you can do this with the following command:

```
Get-MailboxDataase | Where {$_.Server -Like "E2K7-01"}
```

This command will output a list of objects. You can pipe those objects to the same Set-MailboxDatabase cmdlet I just showed you. The final command would look like this:

```
Get-MailboxDatabase | Where {$_.Server -Like "E2K7-01"} |↵
Set-MailboxDatabase -IssueWarningQuota:750MB -ProhibitSendQuota:775MB↵
-ProhibitSendReceiveQuota:800MB
```

RELATIVE QUOTA SIZING

Note that each limit must be higher than the one before it. The order is as follows:

```
IssueWarningQuota < ProhibitSendQuota < ProhibitSendReceiveQuota
```

If you make a mistake, the EMS in Exchange 2007 is smart enough to check these limits and warn you. Exchange 2007 will not even allow you to move a mailbox on to an Exchange 2007 server unless the limits are all ordered correctly. (By contrast, the Exchange 2003 extensions to Active Directory Users and Computers would allow you to set a smaller send quota than the warning quota.)

Here is an example of the warning message you receive when you accidentally set Prohibit-SendReceiveQuota smaller than IssueWarningQuota:

```
Set-MailboxDatabase "Executives" -IssueWarningQuota:750MB↵
-ProhibitSendQuota:775MB -ProhibitSendReceiveQuota:500MB
Set-MailboxDatabase : The value of property 'ProhibitSendQuota'
must be less than or equal to that of property
'ProhibitSendReceiveQuota'. ProhibitSendQuota:
'775MB', ProhibitSendReceiveQuota: '500MB'.
At line:1 char:20 + Set-MailboxDatabase <<<<
"Executives" -IssueWarningQuota:750MB -ProhibitSendQuota:775MB
-ProhibitSendReceiveQuota:500MB
```

Setting Mailbox-by-Mailbox Limits

By default, a mailbox's storage limits will be the same as the mailbox database limits. Individual mailbox size limits can be overridden on a mailbox-by-mailbox basis by using the Exchange Management Console. Locate the mailbox on which you want to apply limits in the Recipients work center, view the properties of the mailbox, select the Mailbox Settings property page, and double-click the Storage Quotas option. The Storage Quotas property page for an individual mailbox is shown in Figure 10.2.

FIGURE 10.2
Individual mailbox
storage quotas

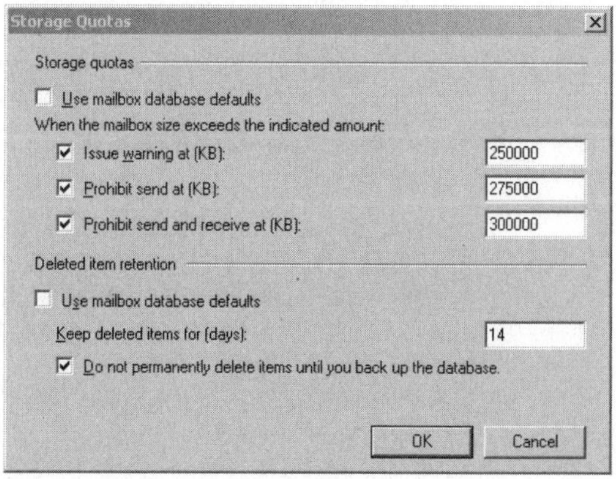

The storage quotas for an individual mailbox can also be set through the EMS by using the Set-Mailbox cmdlet. For example, if you want to use an EMS command to set the same limits shown in Figure 10.2 for a mailbox whose alias is Omar.Droubi, you would use the following cmdlet:

```
Set-Mailbox "Omar.Droubi" -UseDatabaseQuotaDefaults $False↵
-IssueWarningQuota:250000KB -ProhibitSendQuota:275000KB↵
-ProhibitSendReceiveQuota:300000KB
```

Note that the option -UseDatabaseQuotaDefaults must be set to $False, otherwise Exchange will not recognize that these limits have been overridden. This is the same as clearing the Use Mailbox Database Defaults check box in the user's Storage Quotas properties. (See Figure 10.2.)

This command will not output any results to the EMS, but you can check your work using the Get-Mailbox cmdlet. Because the names of all of the properties of the mailbox include the word *quota*, you can use the Select-Object (or just Select) cmdlet and a wildcard to specify the properties you are viewing. The command and the results are shown here:

```
Get-Mailbox Omar.Droubi | Select-Object Name,*quota*

Name                      : Omar Droubi
ProhibitSendQuota         : 275000KB
ProhibitSendReceiveQuota  : 300000KB
UseDatabaseQuotaDefaults  : False
IssueWarningQuota         : 250000KB
RulesQuota                : 64KB
```

Notice in this command that the mailbox size limits are set in KB rather than MB; bytes, KB, MB, or GB will work.

CONFIGURING MULTIPLE MAILBOX QUOTAS WITH THE EMS

It's probably going to take you longer to set a single mailbox storage quota using the EMS than it would using the EMC, but you can apply the skills you learn configuring a single mailbox to configure multiple mailboxes. Let's use the members of the executive team in an example. They are dispersed throughout many servers in the organization. They are, however, all members of a distribution group called Executives. You would use the Get-DistributionGroupMember cmdlet to retrieve all of the members of the Executives group and you would pipe that to the Set-Mailbox cmdlet. Here is an example:

```
Get-DistributionGroupMember "Executives" | Set-Mailbox↵
-UseDatabaseQuotaDefaults $False -IssueWarning:250000KB↵
-ProhibitSendQuota:275000KB -ProhibitSendReceiveQuota:300000KB
```

You can even run this command as a scheduled task to ensure that the members of Executives always have set the limits that you want them to have.

Message Size Limits

In most organizations, letting users send or receive messages with no limits on sizes can result in abuse of the messaging system. Before you know it, users might be sending 1GB MPEG files back and forth to one another. However, the other side of this equation is that there are actually situations in which large messages need to be sent in order to simplify file transfers.

You can limit large message transfers or prevent users from sending unauthorized large files in a number of ways. This includes applying global message size limits, limiting message sizes of typical users, limiting message sizes sent via send and receive connectors, and even stopping messages using transport rules.

Applying Global Message Size Limits

Exchange 2007 limits the maximum size of incoming and outgoing messages that a user can send to 10MB. This value has been determined based on analysis of many large customers' environments as well as best practices. You can change the global messaging limits via the Exchange Management Console by navigating to the Hub Transport subcontainer of the Organization Configuration container and then viewing the Global Settings tab in the Results pane. Under the Results pane is a Transport Settings object; its General property page is shown in Figure 10.3. This is a new GUI management option that was included with Exchange Server 2007 SP1.

FIGURE 10.3
Global message
transport properties

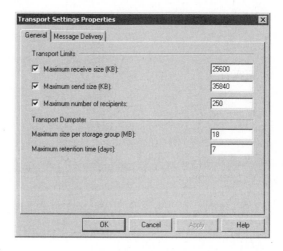

The global message transport values can also be viewed and set using the EMS cmdlet `Get-TransportConfig`. Here is the output of a `Get-TransportConfig` cmdlet with no parameters or formatting options:

```
Get-TransportConfig

ClearCategories            : True
GenerateCopyOfDSNFor       : {}
InternalSMTPServers        : {192.168.254.19, 192.168.254.102}
```

```
JournalingReportNdrTo            : <>
MaxDumpsterSizePerStorageGroup : 18MB
MaxDumpsterTime                  : 7.00:00:00
MaxReceiveSize                   : 10MB
MaxRecipientEnvelopeLimit        : 5000
MaxSendSize                      : 10MB
TLSReceiveDomainSecureList       : {}
TLSSendDomainSecureList          : {}
VerifySecureSubmitEnabled        : False
VoicemailJournalingEnabled       : True
Xexch50Enabled                   : True
```

You can use the `Set-TransportConfig` cmdlet to change these properties. Let's say that you want to change the default size of 10MB for inbound (`MaxReceiveSize`) and outbound (`MaxSendSize`) messages to 25MB; you would use the following cmdlet to do this:

```
Set-TransportConfig -MaxReceiveSize:25MB -MaxSendSize:25MB
```

Applying Message Size Limits Non-Globally

You can also limit the maximum message size sent or received by an individual mailbox, and you can change the limits for a group of mailboxes.

The easiest way to do this for a single mailbox is to use the EMC and locate the mailbox you wish to change in the Recipient Configuration work center. On the mailbox's Mail Flow Settings property page, you need to locate the Message Size Restrictions option, highlight that option, and click the Properties button. This will display the Message Size Restrictions dialog box shown in Figure 10.4.

In the example in Figure 10.4, this one user is limited to a maximum sending and receiving message size of 5MB. This is useful if you have to override the message size limits of a single mailbox.

In a larger organization, you may have large groups of people that require their limits be different than the global defaults. Once again, the EMS comes to the rescue.

Let's say that you have a mail-enabled group called Undergraduate Students and you want to override the default limits and restrict their maximum incoming and outgoing message sizes to 5MB. You need to use the `Get-DistributionGroupMember` cmdlet to retrieve the objects that are members of that particular distribution group. You will pipe the output of that cmdlet to the `Set-Mailbox` cmdlet. Here is an example that will accomplish this task:

```
Get-DistributionGroupMember "Undergraduate Students" | Set-Mailbox↵
-MaxSendSize:5MB -MaxReceiveSize:5MB
```

That was pretty simple to do! Now if one of your users attempts to send a message larger than the permitted size, he will receive a non-delivery report indicating that the message could not be delivered. An example of such a message is shown in Figure 10.5.

Restricting Internet Message Sizes

You might also want to restrict the size of messages that are sent to or received from the Internet. By default, your global default limits will be used for Internet-bound messages and messages received from the Internet. However, you can specify different message size restrictions on the connectors that are used to send and receive messages into your organization from outside of the organization. The maximum message sizes that a send or receive connector can process are not configurable through the EMC; you must use the EMS. For receive connectors that are used to accept inbound mail from the Internet, you can change the default limit (10MB) by using the `Set-ReceiveConnector` cmdlet.

FIGURE 10.4

Applying message size restrictions for a single mailbox

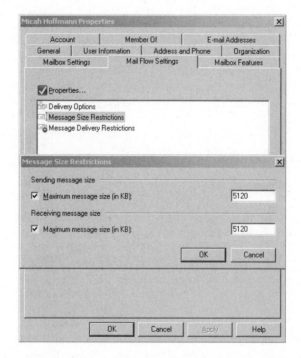

FIGURE 10.5

Non-delivery report indicating that a message is too large to be delivered

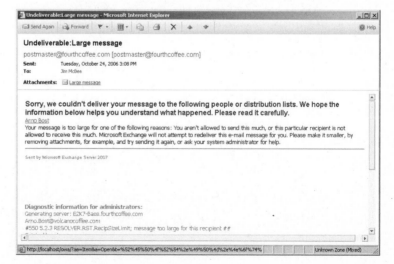

You can also use the `Get-ReceiveConnector` cmdlet to retrieve information about the receive connectors limits. Here is an example in which the receive connectors are enumerated:

```
Get-ReceiveConnector  | FT Name,*size*
Name                 MaxHeaderSize    MaxMessageSize    SizeEnabled
----                 -------------    --------------    -----------
Default HNLHT01      64KB             10MB              True
Client HNLHT01       64KB             10MB              True
```

To change the maximum message size (`MaxMessageSize`) property on the receive connector called Default HNLHT01, you would use the following command:

```
Set-ReceiveConnector "Default HNLHT01" -MaxMessageSize:5MB
```

You can change the send connector size limits (`MaxMessageSize`) in the exact same way using the `Set-SendConnector` cmdlet.

Though having the ability to tune the send and receive connectors is a good feature, if you have implemented additional SMTP message hygiene security using an SMTP gateway or the Exchange Edge Transport server, you should restrict inbound message sizes at that point instead. This will prevent messages that are larger than your Internet limits from even reaching the Exchange Hub Transport servers.

Limiting Maximum Attachment Sizes

I have not introduced transport rules yet in this book other than to mention that they exist and that they are applied by the Hub Transport server role. However, there is a condition that you can use on a transport rule that would be useful in catching messages with attachments larger than you will permit.

Let's consider as an example a situation in which an organization's information policy does not allow messages that are received from the Internet to have any single attachment larger than 5MB. You can define a transport rule that will catch these messages and drop them. Transport rules are found in the Transport Rule section of the Organization Configuration work center under the Hub Transport subcontainer.

When you launch the New Transport Rule Wizard, on the Conditions page (shown in Figure 10.6), you select two conditions. The first condition is "from users inside or outside the corporation" and the second is "when the size of any attachment is greater than or equal to limit."

Once these are selected and show up in the Step 2: Edit the Rule Description box, you need to ensure that the rule applies to messages sent from outside the corporation by clicking the value that looks like a hyperlink. This value defaults to Inside. You also need to click the attachment size value and change that to the maximum attachment size; the default value is 0KB.

After clicking Next on the Conditions page, you see the Actions page. You can then select the action(s) to take when the condition is met. These actions might include just dropping the message or returning an undeliverable report back to the sender informing them of the problem. An example of this is shown in Figure 10.7.

FIGURE 10.6
Defining a condition
that will reject messages
with attachments larger
than 5MB

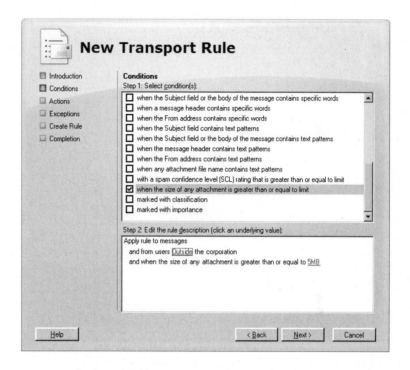

FIGURE 10.7
Defining an action to
send back a customized
report of undeliverable
mail message

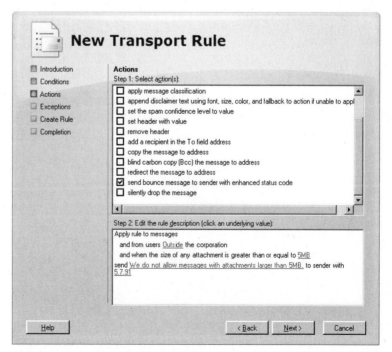

Recipient Limits

Another useful configuration property is the ability to restrict the maximum number of recipients per e-mail message. This helps to prevent misuse of the mail system. After all, the typical user in your organization probably does not need to send messages to all 100,000 users in your global address list, right?

Like Exchange 2003, by default Exchange 2007 restricts the maximum number of recipients to 5,000. That will include all recipients in the To, Cc, and Bcc lines of the message as well as the total number of members of distribution lists that are included in the address lines. So if a user addresses a message to a distribution group that has 5,001 members, the message will be returned with a non-delivery report. Figure 10.8 shows an example of the undeliverable report that was sent to a user who tried to send to a distribution group that has more members than the user is permitted to send to.

FIGURE 10.8
Report of undeliverable mail issued when recipient limit is reached

Setting a Global Recipient Limit

In most organizations (especially large ones), typical users probably do not need to send to 5,000 recipients. I recommend finding a more reasonable value that would apply globally (such as 50, 100, or 250) and then override the global recipient limit for users that would need to send to more than the global limit. If you want to view the current maximum recipients limit, here is an example:

```
Get-TransportConfig | Format-List MaxRecipientEnvelopeLimit

MaxRecipientEnvelopeLimit : 5000
```

To change the transport limit to 250, you would type this:

```
Set-TransportConfig -MaxRecipientEnvelopeLimit:250
```

Overriding a Global Recipient Limit

Once the global limit is set, you can override it on a mailbox-by-mailbox basis using the EMC. Locate the user's mailbox in the Recipient Configuration work center, display the properties of the mailbox, view the Mail Flow Settings property page, and double-click the Delivery Options selection to see the Delivery Options dialog box (shown in Figure 10.9). Enable the check box next to Maximum Recipients and then provide the maximum number of recipients in the text box.

FIGURE 10.9
Overriding the maximum number of recipients for a single mailbox

Once this value is overridden, this mailbox will be able to send messages to more recipients than the global default limit allows (if the global default is smaller) or fewer recipients than the global default limit allows (if the global default is larger).

If you need to do this in bulk, you can use the EMS. Like many other bulk operations that are applied to a group of objects, you need some method of finding these objects. In this example, assume you have a distribution group called E-Mail Entire Company. You will use the `Get-DistributionGroupMember` and the `Set-Mailbox` cmdlets to set a recipient limit on this group. The following command will set the `RecipientLimits` property of all members of the E-Mail Entire Company distribution group to 10,000:

```
Get-DistributionGroupMember "E-Mail Entire Company" |↵
Set-Mailbox -RecipientLimits:10000
```

That was pretty simple, wasn't it? Once you know just a few of the basic functions in the PowerShell and the EMS, you can start to do things that would have been very difficult in Exchange 2000/2003. You can even create a PowerShell script and schedule it to run periodically to ensure that the limit is always enforced.

Managed Folder Limits

Exchange 2007 introduces a new concept called managed folders. Managed folders allow the administrator to define retention policies for default folders such as Deleted Items, Inbox, and Journal as well as create custom folders for users. The users can use these folders to organize their mailboxes based on their organization's e-mail retention policies. Managed folders are covered in more detail in Chapter 14, "Managing Mailbox Content," when I cover messaging records management. However, there is a nice feature of managed folders that is useful when establishing limits.

There is a category of managed folders called Managed Custom Folders that consists of folders that the administrator can define and have automatically created (using a managed folder mailbox policy). The managed custom folders are found in the Mailbox subcontainer of the Organization Configuration work center under the Managed Custom Folders tab. The Managed Custom Folders tab of the results pane is shown in Figure 10.10.

FIGURE 10.10

The Managed Custom Folders tab of the results pane

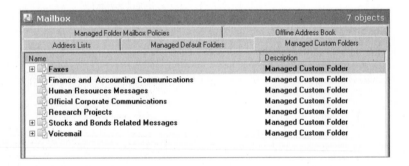

You can define the maximum amount of storage that a folder and all of its subfolders can have if the folder was created by a managed folder mailbox policy. However, the limit must be defined when the managed custom folder is created in the mailbox, so it must already exist in the policy when it is assigned to the mailbox. The administrator cannot change the limits on the policy once it is assigned.

Let's look at an example. Suppose you want to create a folder for faxes in the Managed Folders section of a user's mailbox. You will rely on the user to move faxes into this folder, but you want to make sure that the content of this folder (and all of its subfolders) never exceeds 50MB. When viewing the properties of the Faxes folder (shown in Figure 10.11), you can click the Storage Limit (KB) For This Folder And Its Subfolders check box and specify a maximum folder size.

If you are inclined to do things through the EMS, you could use the following EMS command to accomplish the same thing:

```
Set-ManagedFolder "Faxes" -StorageQuota:50MB
```

Public Folder Limits

Just as mailbox limits can help you to control growth of mailbox databases and prevent abuse, assigning limits to public folders can be equally important in controlling public folder growth. You can set a couple of different types of limits with respect to public folders. These include the default limits for the public folder database and individual folder limits.

FIGURE 10.11
Specifying a limit for a custom folder

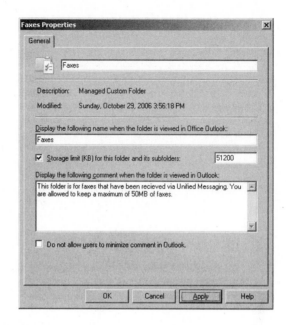

Defining Limits per Database

Each public folder database has default storage limits that affect all public folders that have a replica on it. The Public Folder Database Limits property page is shown in Figure 10.12. If you are an experienced Exchange 2000/2003 administrator, you may notice that there are default limits in Exchange 2007 where none existed previously.

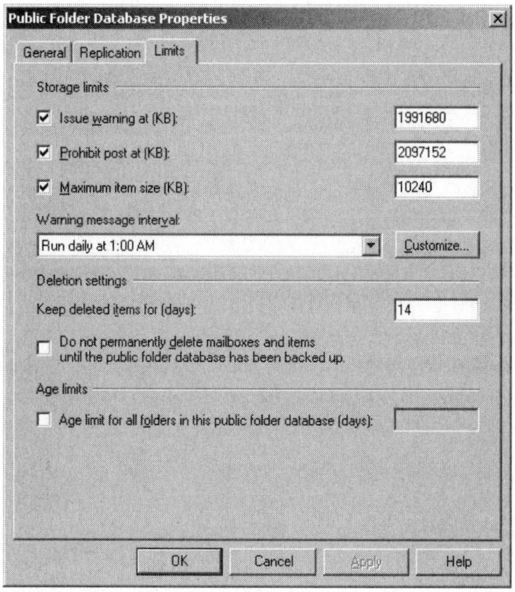

FIGURE 10.12
Default Public Folder Database Limits

The properties that are found on the Limits property page affect all public folder instances on the database. Table 10.2 describes these properties.

TABLE 10.2: Public Folder Database Limits Properties

PROPERTY	DESCRIPTION
Issue Warning At (KB)	Sends a warning message to the folder owner and folder contacts informing them that the folder has reached its storage limit. The default is 1,945MB.
Prohibit Post At (KB)	When the folder content exceeds this size, messages can no longer be delivered to this folder (if the folder is mail-enabled) and users cannot post to this folder. The default is 2GB.
Maximum Item Size (KB)	Specifies the largest message size that can be delivered to this folder (if mail-enabled) or the largest item that can be posted to this folder. The default is 10MB.
Keep Deleted Items For (Days)	Specifies the how long deleted folders will be retained before they are permanently purged. During this time, the folder owner can undelete items that were accidentally (or intentionally) deleted. The default interval is 14 days.

If you are fond of the EMC, you can retrieve this information from the PowerShell. In the following example, the public folder database is called Public Folder Database and the server is HNLEX02. The output of the Get-PublicFolderDatabase is being piped to the Format-List cmdlet:

```
Get-PublicFolderDatabase "HNLEX02\Public Folder Database" |↵
Format-List Name,MaxItemSize,IssueWarningQuota,ProhibitPostQuota,ItemRetention

Name                : Public Folder Database
MaxItemSize         : 10MB
IssueWarningQuota   : 1945MB
ProhibitPostQuota   : 2GB
ItemRetention       : 14.00:00:00
```

If you want to change one of these limits using the EMS (for example, you might set the MaxItemSize to 15MB), you would type this command:

```
Set-PublicFolderDatabase "HNLEX02\Public Folder Database"-MaxItemSize:15MB
```

Defining Folder-by-Folder Limits

You can also define folder-by-folder limits. These limits override the default limits specified on a public folder database. The Exchange 2007 Exchange Management Console provides a link to the Public Folder Management Console that will allow you to set some of the individual public folder properties such as message size. Figure 10.13 shows the Limits property page for a single folder shown in the Public Folder Management Console.

FIGURE 10.13

Viewing public folder storage quotas using the Public Folder Management Console

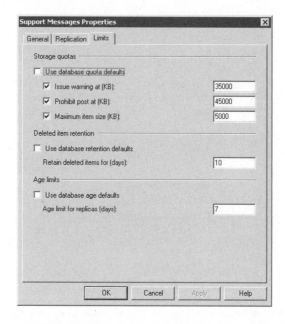

As you will find, there are still a few things that you cannot do using the Public Folder Management Console. If you want to define folder-by-folder limits using a GUI, you will have to have an Exchange 2003 System Manager console installed somewhere within your organization. Unfortunately, you cannot install the Exchange System Manager from Exchange 2003 on an Exchange 2007 server or any machine with the Exchange Management Console. See Chapter 5, "Installing Exchange Server 2007," for more information on installing and using the Exchange System Manager with Exchange 2007.

To manage individual public folder limits, you need to locate the Folders container in an Exchange administrative group. Once you have found the Folders container, you can browse the public folders, locate the folder you wish to set limits on, and display that folder's properties. Figure 10.14 shows the Limits property page of a folder called Research Documents. You will notice that the actual property page is almost identical to the Exchange 2007 Public Folder Management Console shown in Figure 10.13, but there are a few small differences.

Notice in Figure 10.14 that I have cleared the Use Public Store Defaults check box and have provided my own limits (Issue Warning, Prohibit Post, and Maximum Item Size) for this particular public folder.

If you do not have an Exchange System Manager console installed anywhere in your organization, you can still manage individual public folder properties using the Exchange Management Shell. For example, the following retrieves the properties of a public folder called Somorita Surfboards:

```
Get-Publicfolder "\Somorita Surfboards" | Format-List

AgeLimit                    : 30.00:00:00
EntryId                     : 000000001A447390AA6611CD9BC800AA002FC45A030037
```

```
C54B179C6AC547BE6A36965D18C96700000001C1690000
HasSubFolders                    : True
HiddenFromAddressListsEnabled    : True
LocalReplicaAgeLimit             :
MailEnabled                      : False
MaxItemSize                      : 4MB
Name    : Somorita Surfboards
ParentPath                       : \
PerUserReadStateEnabled          : True
PostStorageQuota                 : 65000KB
Replicas                         : {Public Folders, Public Folder Store (HNLEX01)}
ReplicationSchedule              : {}
RetainDeletedItemsFor            : 15.00:00:00
StorageQuota                     : 50000KB
UseDatabaseAgeDefaults           : False
UseDatabaseQuotaDefaults         : False
UseDatabaseReplicationSchedule   : True
UseDatabaseRetentionDefaults     : False
Identity                         : \Somorita Surfboards
IsValid                          : True
OriginatingServer                : hnlex03
```

FIGURE 10.14
Limits property page of
the Research Documents
folder

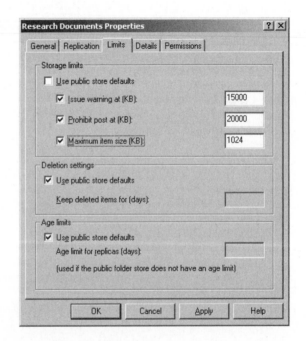

To set the prohibit post limit (`PostStorageQuota`) and the issue warning quota (`StorageQuota`) using the EMS, here is the command you would type:

```
Set-PublicFolder "\Somorita Surfboards" -PostStorageQuota:95MB -StorageQuota:80MB
```

Summary

When you start thinking about the number of places where you can define limits for an Exchange user, you'll see that there are quite a few. Planning for realistic and effective limits is important for your organization. Effectively limiting mailbox sizes, public folder sizes, and message sizes can help you to predict the growth of your mail storage requirements and prevent you from exceeding the storage you have available for Exchange content. Effective limits are an important part of proactive troubleshooting because they limit potential abuse of the mail system by preventing users from sending or receiving content that is too large.

## Chapter 11

Managing Recipients

Depending on the size of your organization, recipient management (handling the user accounts, groups, contacts, public folders, and other resources that can receive e-mail) may consume the vast majority of Exchange administration time. In a small organization, you may be responsible for every aspect of your Exchange server, including creating and managing recipients. In a larger organization with lots of changes, new users, and users leaving the organization, recipient administration will probably be handled by a person or team that is separate from the person that actually manages the Exchange Server infrastructure (message routing, backups, server maintenance, and so on).

This chapter discusses how to create and manage mail-enabled recipients. It also examines Exchange address lists and how e-mail addresses get defined.

In this chapter you learn to:

♦ Define e-mail address policies

♦ Establish mailboxes for user accounts

♦ Manage resource mailboxes

♦ Create mail-enabled groups

♦ Create mail-enabled contacts

♦ Manage resource mailboxes

Defining E-mail Addresses

Before I get in to the discussion of how to create mail-enabled users, groups, or contacts, I'll first discuss how these objects get their e-mail addresses. Those of you who are familiar with Exchange 2000/2003 probably remember that e-mail addresses were defined by a recipient policy. Once the recipient policy was defined, the Microsoft Exchange System Attendant's Recipient Update Service (RUS) would establish e-mail addresses for any mail-enabled recipient at some point in the future (hopefully just a minute or two).

This process is just a bit different in Exchange 2007. E-mail addresses are generated for the object at the time the mail-enabled recipient is created and they are generated by an Exchange Management Shell (EMS) task or the Exchange Management Console (EMC). Recipient policies from Exchange 2000/2003 have been broken up into two separate concepts:

♦ E-mail domains that your organization will accept mail for

♦ E-mail address policies for your users

For addresses that will be assigned to mailboxes on your Exchange 2007 servers, you define both an accepted domain and an e-mail address policy.

Accepted Domains

An accepted domain is an SMTP domain name (aka SMTP namespace) for which your Exchange 2007 servers will accept mail. The servers will either deliver the mail to Exchange 2007 mailboxes or relay it on to internal or external SMTP mail servers. If you are in the middle of a migration from Exchange 2000/2003, the accepted domains list will include the SMTP domains for your Exchange 2000/2003 mailboxes. Accepted domains must be defined for all e-mail addresses that will be routed into or by your Exchange 2007 servers.

Most small and medium-sized organizations will have only a single accepted domain.

SETTING UP AN ACCEPTED DOMAIN USING THE EMC

Accepted domains are found within the Organization Configuration work center under the Hub Transport subcontainer. When you choose the Accepted Domains tab in the Results pane, you will see a list of the accepted domains that have been defined for your organization, such as those shown in Figure 11.1.

FIGURE 11.1
List of accepted domains

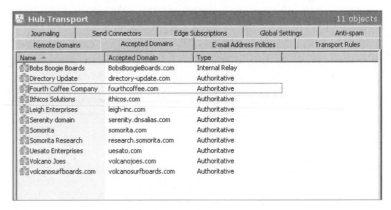

When Exchange 2007 is first installed, a single accepted domain is automatically created and given a name. This is the name of the Active Directory forest root domain; for many organizations this will not be correct because the naming convention for Active Directory domain names and SMTP domain names may be different. For example, your Active Directory name may be somorita.local whereas your public domain name for e-mail is somorita.com.

Accepted domains are simple to create and require little input. To create a new accepted domain using the EMC, click the New Accepted Domain task in the Actions pane to see the New Accepted Domain Wizard (shown in Figure 11.2). You only need to provide a descriptive name for the accepted domain, the SMTP domain name, and how messages for this domain should be treated when messages are accepted by Exchange 2007.

Keep in mind that you cannot change the domain name of an accepted domain once it is created. (You can change the domain type, however.)

SETTING UP AN ACCEPTED DOMAIN USING THE EMS

You can also manage accepted domains using the following EMS cmdlets:

◆ New-AcceptedDomain

◆ Set-AcceptedDomain

◆ Get-AcceptedDomain

◆ Remove-AcceptedDomain

FIGURE 11.2
Creating a new accepted domain

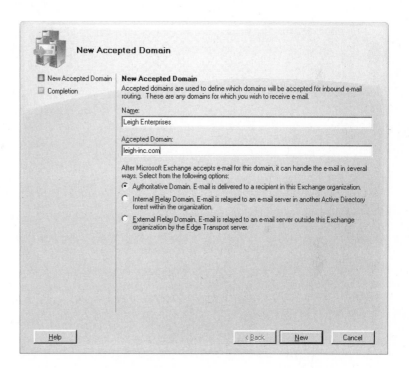

For example, to create the new accepted domain shown in Figure 11.2, I would use the following EMS command:

```
New-AcceptedDomain -Name "Leigh Enterprises" -DomainName "leigh-inc.com"↵
-DomainType "Authoritative"
```

ABOUT DOMAIN TYPES

One tricky thing about defining an accepted domain is that you must define how Exchange is to treat a message for it. You can choose from three types of domains when creating an accepted domain:

Authoritative domains   These are SMTP domains for which you accept the inbound message and deliver it to an internal mailbox within your Exchange organization.

Internal relay domains   These are SMTP domains for which your Exchange server will accept inbound SMTP mail. The Exchange server must have mail-enabled contacts that specify forwarding addresses for users in those domains. The Exchange server then relays the message onward to another internal mail system. Internal relay domains are used when two Exchange organizations are doing global address list synchronization.

External relay domains   These are SMTP domains for which your Exchange organization will accept inbound SMTP mail and then relay that mail onward to an external SMTP mail server, usually one that is outside of the organization's boundaries. If Edge Transport servers are used, the Edge Transport server handles external relay domains.

E-mail Address Policies

Exchange e-mail address policies are the configuration objects that are used by Exchange management tasks when new mail objects are created. Each policy's conditions are examined to see if the policy's conditions apply to the object that is being created; if the policy's conditions apply, the new mail-enabled object's e-mail address policies are generated based on the e-mail address generation rules.

Using the EMC, e-mail address policies are found in the Organization Configuration work center under the Hub Transport subcontainer. Once you have highlighted the Hub Transport subcontainer, select the E-mail Address Policies tab to see a list of the e-mail address policies in the organization. In Figure 11.3, I have only four e-mail address policies.

FIGURE 11.3
E-mail address policies for an Exchange 2007 organization

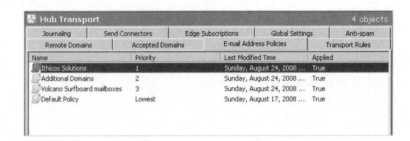

By default, a newly created Exchange 2007 organization has only a single e-mail address policy, called the default policy. The default policy is the lowest-priority policy and applies if no other policies above it apply. This is just like having multiple recipient policies in Exchange 2007.

CHANGING AN EXISTING POLICY

The e-mail address generation rule uses the object's Exchange alias and the domain name of the Active Directory forest root. Suppose you want to make two changes to the e-mail address policy:

- You want to change the SMTP domain name that is on the default policy to something else.

   For example, this is relevant when the default domain name for the Active Directory forest root is different from the public domain name used for SMTP and you need to fix this.

- You want all e-mail addresses to be generated using the first name, followed by a period, then the last name, and then the domain name.

First, you need to define an accepted domain. If the default accepted domain is not correct for your organization, you need to create a new accepted domain because Exchange 2007 does not allow you to change an accepted domain. Let's say that your Active Directory forest root is called fourthcoffee.com but your public SMTP domain is volcanocoffee.com. First, under the Accepted Domains tab of the Organization Configuration work center's Hub Transport subcontainer, create a new authoritative accepted domain for volcanocoffee.com.

Next, you need to change the default e-mail address policy so that it uses the new domain name and generates an address using the *firstname.lastname* format, such as josh.maher@volcanocoffee.com. Locate the default policy in the Organization Configuration work center (found under the Hub Transport subcontainer by clicking the E-mail Address Policies tab), highlight the default policy, and click the Edit task in the Actions pane. Click Next until you reach the E-mail Addresses page (shown in Figure 11.4).

FIGURE 11.4
E-mail address properties of an e-mail address policy

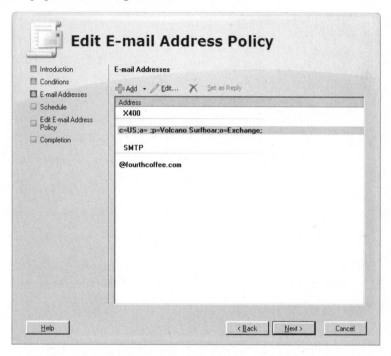

Notice in Figure 11.4 that the only e-mail address that is generated is `@fourthcoffee.com`. Highlight `@fourthcoffee.com` and click the Edit button to see the SMTP E-mail Address dialog box (shown in Figure 11.5). When you first see this box, the E-Mail Address Local Part check box is not checked. This means that the object's Exchange alias will be used when creating the SMTP address. You want to change that, so enable the E-Mail Address Local Part check box; once it's enabled, you will be able to select the First Name.Last Name (John.Smith) radio button.

Next, change the e-mail address domain found in the drop-down list at the bottom of the page. Once you have clicked OK in the SMTP E-mail Address dialog box, the e-mail address generation rules will have changed. The new rules are shown in Figure 11.6.

You have now modified the Default Policy and you need to click Next on the E-mail Addresses page to finish the modification. Next you will see the Schedule page of the wizard (see Figure 11.7). This might be a bit confusing at first because on the surface it doesn't seem like there is anything to schedule. However, remember that in Exchange 2000/2003, the Exchange Recipient Update Service (RUS) took care of adding SMTP addresses to mail-enabled objects. There is no equivalent for Exchange 2007 mail-enabled recipients. Thus, some process or task has to be kicked off that will do this. If you choose Immediately, this will kick off the `Update-EmailAddressPolicy` cmdlet with the `-Identity:'Default Policy'` option and immediately update any e-mail addresses.

If you don't choose Immediately, you have additional options:

◆ Do Not Apply skips the `Update-EmailAddressPolicy` cmdlet phase altogether. If you have just updated the default policy, you can always run the `Update-EmailAddressPolicy "Default Policy"` command from the EMS at a later point.

◆ At The Following Time allows you to schedule the `Update-EmailAddressPolicy` cmdlet to run later. This is useful if you know that it will have to update thousands of mail-enabled objects in your Active Directory and you don't want it affecting usage during the business day. This option, when selected, allows you to specify that the task be canceled if it is still running after a certain number of hours.

FIGURE 11.5
Changing how the SMTP address is generated

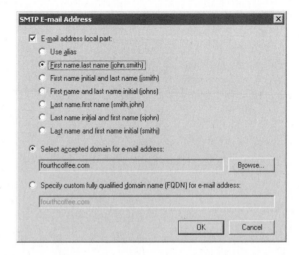

FIGURE 11.6
New e-mail address rules

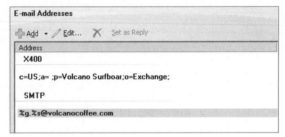

Of course, you can also create e-mail address policies using the EMS; the following is an example of an EMS command that would create an e-mail address policy for the domain ithicos.com:

```
New-EmailAddressPolicy -Name 'Ithicos Solutions' -IncludedRecipients↵
'MailboxUsers' -ConditionalCustomAttribute1 'test' -Priority '1'↵
-EnabledEmailAddressTemplates 'SMTP:%g.%s@ithicos.com'
```

One thing that I do want to point out is what happens to existing e-mail addresses once you change to a new default address. Figure 11.8 shows the E-Mail Addresses property page for the mailbox of a user whose address was updated; notice that this user has two e-mail addresses now. He has the old e-mail addresses `LBenjamin@directory-update.com` and `LBenjamin@fourthcoffee.com` and his newly created SMTP address `Lee.Benjamin@volcanocoffee.com`. The process of updating e-mail addresses never removes existing addresses; it creates the new address and makes it the Reply To address.

FIGURE 11.7
Scheduling an update to
the e-mail address policy

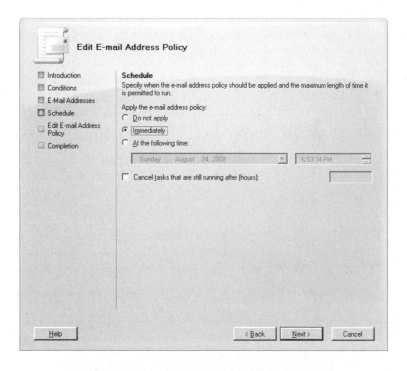

FIGURE 11.8
Newly created SMTP
address for an existing
user

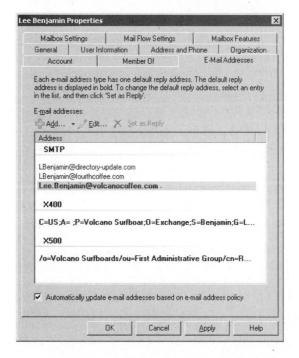

Although this example was done entirely in the graphical user interface, you could use the EMS to perform the same steps. The EMS cmdlets you would need to use to create, delete, modify, and update e-mail address policies are shown in Table 11.1.

TABLE 11.1:   EMS Cmdlets Used to Manipulate E-mail Address Policies

EMS CMDLET	DESCRIPTION
New-EmailAddressPolicy	Creates a new e-mail address policy.
Set-EmailAddressPolicy	Changes properties of the e-mail address policy specified.
Update-EmailAddressPolicy	Updates mail-enabled objects in the Active Directory if the conditions of the policy specified apply to those objects.
Get-EmailAddressPolicy	Retrieves a list of e-mail address policies and their properties.
Remove-EmailAddressPolicy	Deletes the specified e-mail address policy.

Finally, of course, if you want to see the e-mail addresses that have been applied to a mail-enabled object, you can also use an EMS cmdlet to retrieve that information. You would use Get-Mailbox, Get-MailContact, or Get-DistributionGroup. To retrieve the e-mail addresses for a mailbox whose alias is Julie.Samante, you could type the following command and see output similar to this:

```
Get-Mailbox "julie.samante" | Format-List DisplayName,EmailAddresses

DisplayName     : Julie Samante
EmailAddresses : {smtp:Julie.Samante@fourthcoffee.com,
SMTP:Julie.Samante@volcanocoffee.com}
```

CREATING A NEW E-MAIL ADDRESS POLICY

If you have a small or medium-sized organization, you probably support only a single SMTP domain for your users. However, even companies with a handful of mailboxes can sometimes require two or three SMTP domain names. Let's take as an example an organization that has two divisions, each of which requires its own unique SMTP addresses.

Previously, you changed the default policy for an organization so that all users would get an SMTP address of @volcanocoffee.com. Let's extend that example a bit further. Let's say that this organization has another division called Volcano Surfboards and its SMTP domain is @volcanosurfboards.com. Anyone whose company attribute in the Active Directory contains "Volcano Surfboards" should have an SMTP address of *firstname.lastname*@volcanosurfboards.com.

The first thing you need to do is define volcanosurfboards.com as an authoritative accepted domain. If you don't define the accepted domain, you cannot define the e-mail address policy.

Next, you want to create the e-mail address policy. In the EMC, select the Hub Transport subcontainer of the Organization Configuration work center, and then select the E-mail Address Policies tab in the Results pane.

To create a new e-mail address policy, click the New E-mail Address Policy task in the Actions pane. On the first page (see Figure 11.9) of the New E-Mail Address Policy Wizard, you will be prompted for the name of the policy and what type of objects this policy applies to.

FIGURE 11.9

Naming the e-mail address policy and defining the objects to which it applies

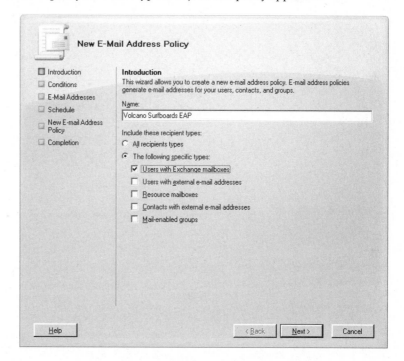

In this example, the policy is being created for the Volcano Surfboards company users and you want the policy to apply only to mailboxes, so you will provide that information on the screen shown in Figure 11.9. When you have provided this information, click Next to move on through the wizard.

The next screen, Conditions, is where you define the conditions under which this policy will be applied. There are two steps to the Conditions page. First, you need to narrow the scope to a specific condition, such as the State or Province attribute, Department attribute, or Company name attribute of the object. Second, you need to provide values for the attributes you have selected.

In this example, you want this policy to apply to anyone whose company name attribute contains Volcano Surfboards. Figure 11.10 shows the Conditions page after filling in the necessary information.

Once you select the condition Recipient Is In A Company, that option shows up in the Step 2 portion of the dialog as Users With Exchange Mailboxes In The *specified* Company(s). The word *specified* appears very much like a hyperlink; it is blue and underlined. If you click that link, a dialog box appears that allows you to edit or specify one or more company names. (See Figure 11.11.)

When you have entered the necessary company information (in this case, just a single company called Volcano Surfboards), you can click OK to close the Specify Company dialog box. You can verify that the conditions are defined correctly by clicking the Preview button on the Conditions page of the wizard. The Preview button displays the E-mail Address Policy Preview dialog box; you should see users with mailboxes and whose company name is Volcano Surfboards. This dialog box is shown in Figure 11.12.

FIGURE 11.10
Defining conditions for
an e-mail address policy

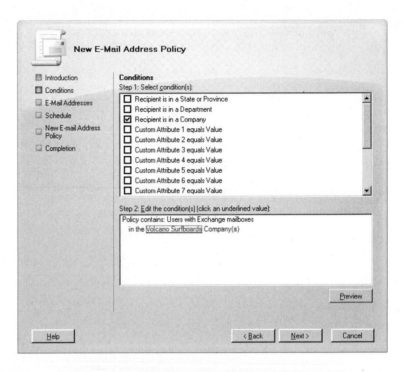

FIGURE 11.11
Specifying a company
name

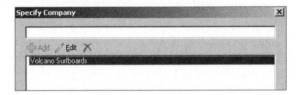

The Preview button is also helpful in confirming that attributes are being entered correctly in the Active Directory. Administrators may not recognize if everyone in a 10,000-user company exists in the Preview window, but hopefully it will give them an idea that the information is being entered correctly. In this case, if a user's company name does not contain exactly *Volcano Surfboards*, the policy conditions will not be met and the user's mailbox will have the e-mail addresses from the default policy.

The next step is to define the SMTP address or addresses that will be generated when the conditions of this policy apply. The default action for the Add button is to create a new SMTP address, but if you need to create a custom address, click the drop-down arrow to the left of the Add button to see a list that provides the option to create a Custom Address type. (See Figure 11.13.)

On the E-mail Addresses page, you need to click the Add button to create a new SMTP address. You will then see the SMTP E-mail Address dialog box; select the domain (in this example, volcanosurfboards.com) from the E-mail Address Domain drop-down list and click the First Name.Last Name (John.Smith) radio button option. (See Figure 11.14.)

If you have not yet created an accepted domain for volcanosurfboards.com, it will not show up in the drop-down list.

FIGURE 11.12
The E-mail Address Policy Preview dialog box helps to confirm that the policy conditions are correct.

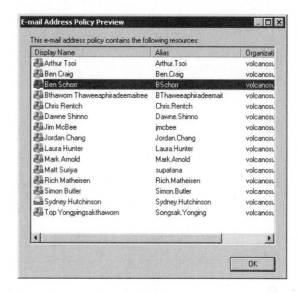

FIGURE 11.13
Adding a new SMTP address

FIGURE 11.14
Specifying the local part of an e-mail address

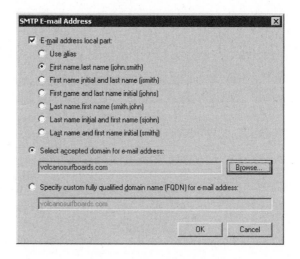

The next page of the New E-mail Address Policy Wizard is the Schedule page; if you want the addresses to appear immediately, you must click the Immediately radio button and click Next. If there are many thousands of addresses to be created, you may want to schedule the task to run during off-hours. Once you click Next on the Schedule page, you will see the Summary page. Here you can see the tasks that will be performed once you click the New button.

The final phase of e-mail address policy creation is the Completion page. Though no actual operations or input are required here (other than clicking the Finish button), this page is useful because it provides you with the cmdlets and commands that were used to perform this particular task. In the case of creating a new e-mail address policy, the task used two cmdlets (New-EmailAddressPolicy and Update-EmailAddressPolicy). The Completion page is shown in Figure 11.15.

FIGURE 11.15
Completion page of the New E-mail Address Policy Wizard

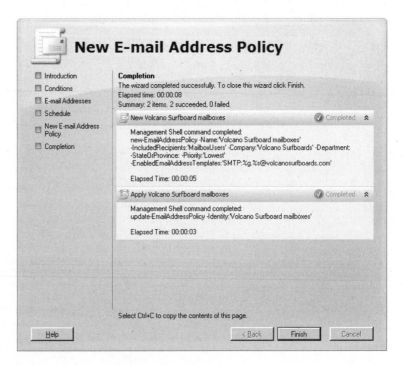

The EMS commands that were run to create the Volcano Surfboards EAP (e-mail address policy) and to update existing e-mail addresses were as follows:

```
New-EmailAddressPolicy -Name 'Volcano Surfboards EAP' -IncludedRecipients↵
'MailboxUsers' -ConditionalCompany 'Volcano Surfboards' -Priority '3'↵
-EnabledEmailAddressTemplates 'SMTP:%g.%s@volcanosurfboards.com'↵
Update-EmailAddressPolicy "Volcano Surfboards EAP"
```

Managing Mailboxes

In some organizations a single Exchange administrator is responsible for all management tasks, whereas in others the tasks are broken up across different levels of administrators. In medium-sized and large organizations, recipient management such as mailbox management is separated from other day-to-day Exchange administrative tasks. This is partially because mailbox management often falls into the category of user account administration and partially because mailbox administration in larger organizations is fairly time-consuming. Managing mailboxes involves the following tasks:

◆ Assigning mailboxes to users

◆ Updating Exchange-related properties of a user account

◆ Deleting mailboxes

◆ Creating and managing shared resources

◆ Moving mailboxes across different mailbox databases

The following sections cover how to accomplish these tasks. Although I mostly focus on using the EMC, I show you how to accomplish the same tasks using the EMS. There are certain tasks that you will only be able to accomplish using the EMS.

Managing User Mailboxes

This first section on mailbox management tackles the most common tasks: creating, managing, and deleting mailboxes associated with a real user account. Don't confuse user mailboxes with mailboxes that are associated with a resource such as a conference room or an overhead projector; user and resource mailboxes are almost identical, but I cover resource mailboxes later in this chapter.

The Exchange Management Console (EMC) allows you to associate a mailbox with an existing user in the Active Directory, or you can actually create the user account (if you have the necessary permissions).

The rules for mailbox ownership and associating an account with a mailbox have not changed since Exchange 2000. There are a couple of important things to keep in mind with respect to user account and mailbox management:

◆ A user account can own only a single mailbox.

◆ A user account can be given permissions to other mailboxes.

◆ Each mailbox must be associated with a user account that is in the same Active Directory forest as the Exchange server.

◆ A single user account from another Active Directory forest can own a mailbox, but a user account in the Exchange server's home forest must still exist and be associated with the mailbox.

Assigning a Mailbox to an Existing User Using the EMC

Let's start with a very common task, assigning a mailbox to an existing user. You may also hear this process referred to as "mailbox-enabling" a user or simply creating a mailbox. In this example, there is a user in the Active Directory whose account is Bharat.Suneja and his unique location is volcanosurfboards.com/IthicosSolutions/Bharat.Suneja. To assign this user a mailbox, you must use either the EMS or the EMC; remember that extensions for Active Directory Users and Computers from Exchange 2000/2003 do not work for Exchange 2007.

Launch the EMC and navigate to the Mailboxes subcontainer of the Recipient Configuration work center. From here, click the New Mailbox task on the Actions pane. This will launch the New Mailbox Wizard. The very first screen in this wizard (shown in Figure 11.16) introduces some entirely new concepts for administrators of previous versions of Exchange. This first screen asks you to define what type of mailbox you are creating.

FIGURE 11.16
Defining the type of mailbox to be created

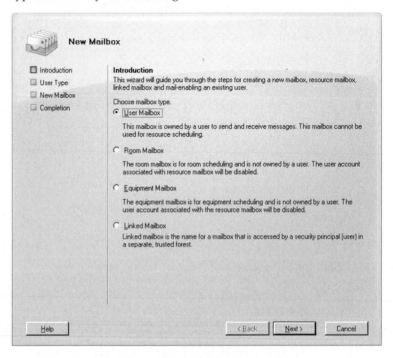

You have four possible choices for mailbox types; for all of them, there *must* be a user account in the same Active Directory in which the Exchange servers are located.

User Mailbox	Assigns a mailbox to an existing user account in the same Active Directory forest in which the Exchange server is located. This is the most common type of mailbox that most administrators will create.
Room Mailbox	Creates a disabled user account and assigns a mailbox to that user. The ResourceType property of the mailbox is set to Room, the RecipientTypeDetails property is set to ConferenceRoomMailbox, and the IsResource property is set to True.
Equipment Mailbox	Creates a disabled user account and assigns a mailbox to that user. The ResourceType property of that mailbox is set to Equipment, the RecipientTypeDetails property is set to EquipmentMailbox, and the IsResource property is set to True.
Linked Mailbox	Creates a disabled user account, assigns it a mailbox, and prompts the administrator to provide a user account in a separate, trusted forest. The account in the other forest is considered the owner of this mailbox and has the Associated External Account permissions to the mailbox. This is used in organizations that install Exchange in a resource forest.

In this first example, you are creating a simple mailbox-enabled user account, so you would choose the User Mailbox radio button and then click the Next button. On the next screen, you are asked whether you are creating a new user account or using an existing user account (Figure 11.17). Notice that you can include multiple user accounts; this feature was included with Exchange 2007 SP1.

When you select the Add button, you are presented with the Select User dialog box (Figure 11.18). From here, you can narrow down the scope of your search using the Search option. Note that only user accounts that are enabled and that do not have a mailbox will show up in this list.

After you select from the Active Directory a user that does not already have a mailbox assigned to it, the Mailbox Settings page allows you to define the mailbox database on which the mailbox will be hosted. Most of the information requested on the Mailbox Settings page (shown in Figure 11.19) will look familiar to Exchange 2000/2003 administrators.

FIGURE 11.17
User Type dialog box

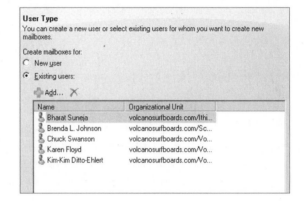

FIGURE 11.18
Select User dialog box

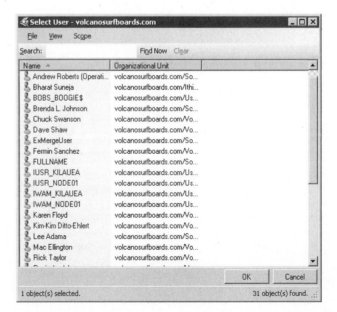

FIGURE 11.19
Assigning a mailbox to
a server, storage group,
and mailbox database

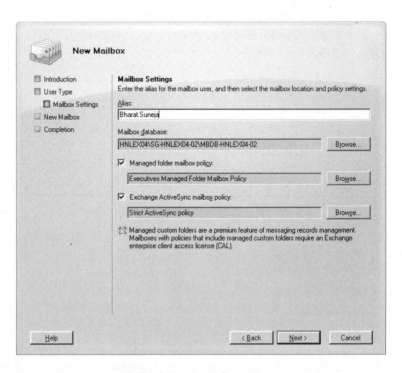

From the Mailbox Settings page, you specify the following information:

Alias
: The alias is used to generate the default SMTP addresses as well as other internal Exchange functions such as the legacy Exchange distinguished name. The alias defaults to be the same as the user account name, but it can be changed if you need it to conform to another standard.

Mailbox Database
: This browse list will consist of mailbox databases found in the organization.

Managed Folder Mailbox Policy
: The Managed Folder Mailbox Policy selection allows you to define which managed folder policy affects this particular mailbox. Once this has been assigned, the next time the messaging records management process is run, the managed folders specified by this policy will be created.

Exchange ActiveSync Mailbox Policy
: The Exchange ActiveSync mailbox policy defines the ActiveSync parameters for the user.

The next screen provides the configuration summary (Figure 11.20). Here you can review the configuration of the mailbox you are creating/assigning.

When you are convinced that the parameters for the mailbox you are creating are correct, you can click the New button. The EMC then launches an EMS cmdlet that actually enables the mailbox in the Active Directory. If you have selected a managed folder mailbox policy, you will see a warning dialog box that will remind you that clients prior to Outlook 2007 will not have all of the features available (Figure 11.21).

The last page of the wizard is the Completion page, which tells you if the operation was successful or not and shows you the EMS cmdlet and options that were used to perform the operation. Figure 11.22 shows the Completion page for the mailbox just created.

FIGURE 11.20
New Mailbox
Configuration Summary

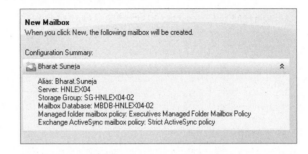

FIGURE 11.21
Managed folder mailbox
policy warning message

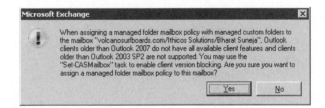

FIGURE 11.22
Successfully
completing the assign-
ment of a mailbox to an
existing user

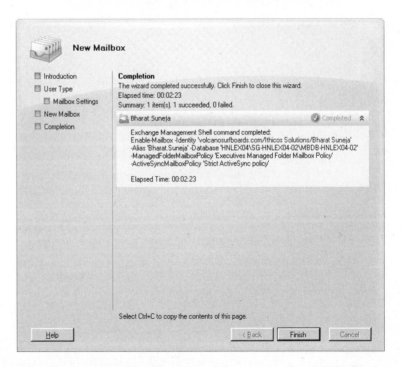

The Completion page also allows you to copy the output of the screen to the paste buffer so that you could then paste that output into a text editor. If you are just learning PowerShell and the

EMS, this makes it simple to learn what cmdlets do and how to use them. That is helpful if you want to mail-enable user accounts using the EMS.

ASSIGNING A MAILBOX TO A USER FROM THE EMS

In a larger organization, you will probably want to streamline or script the creation of new mailboxes and/or user accounts. The EMS allows you to do this easily. For now, though, let's look at the example you just completed from the EMC graphical user interface. You enabled a mailbox for an existing user, assigned that user a mailbox on the HNLEX04\SG-HNLEX04-02\MBDB-HNLEX04-02 mailbox database, assigned that user the Executives Managed Folder Mailbox Policy, and the Strict ActiveSync Policy. The exact cmdlet that was executed is as follows:

```
Enable-Mailbox -Identity 'volcanosurfboards.com/Ithicos Solutions/Bharat Suneja'↵
-Alias 'Bharat.Suneja' -Database 'HNLEX04\SG-HNLEX04-02\MBDB-HNLEX04-02'↵
-ManagedFolderMailboxPolicy 'Executives Managed Folder Mailbox Policy'↵
-ActiveSyncMailboxPolicy 'Strict ActiveSync policy'
```

The Exchange Management Console created this command and used object names to identify the user and the home mailbox database in very explicit terms. However, I want to show you another example and simplify it just a bit. In this case, you have another existing user whose account is Kevin.Miller and he is in the Volcanosurfb Active Directory domain. I will simplify this command as much as possible and here is the result:

```
Enable-Mailbox volcanosurfb\Kevin.Miller -Alias:Kevin.Miller -Database:Executives
```

Name	Alias	Server	ProhibitSendQuota
Kevin Miller	Kevin.Miller	HNLEX03	unlimited

This command works because there is only a single mailbox database in the entire organization called Executives.

ASSIGNING PERMISSIONS TO A MAILBOX USING THE EMS

On some occasions, you may need to assign a user the permission necessary to access another user's mailbox. This was easy enough to do in Exchange 2000/2003 using Active Directory Users and Computers. With Exchange 2007, you can perform the same task using the Manage Full Access Permission task on the Actions pane of the Exchange Management Console.

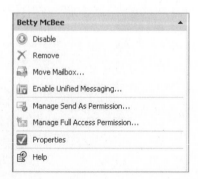

In Exchange 2007, there are two types of mailbox permissions:

◆ Full Access permission lets another user open the mailbox and view any message or folder within it.

◆ Send As permission lets another user send a message that appears to be coming from the user whose mailbox it is.

FULL ACCESS VERSUS SEND AS PERMISSION

Giving a user full access to another user's mailbox will allow the user to open the other user's mailbox and view any folder or message within the user's mailbox. However, if the user needs to be able to send a message as another user, full mailbox permission is not sufficient. Third-party products such as the Research In Motion Blackberry Enterprise Server's (BES) service account may require Receive As permissions to the mailboxes that it manages. And the BES service account must have Send As permissions on the Active Directory object. Receive As mailbox permissions can be added through the EMC or using the Add-MailboxPermission cmdlet. Send As permissions can be added through the EMC or using the Add-ADPermission cmdlet.

If you have been managing Exchange Server organizations for some time, you may remember a time when giving users full mailbox rights would allow them to see all the messages and folders as well as send messages as that mailbox. However, that changed with an Exchange Server 2003 post-Service Pack 2 hot fix. Now Send As permissions must be assigned separately.

Assigning Full Access Permission

To assign Full Access permissions, simply select the mailbox to which you want to add more permissions and click the Manage Full Access Permission task. This launches the Manage Full Access Permissions Wizard shown in Figure 11.23. In this example, I am adding user CKamiya and CEanes to the list of users that have full access for this mailbox.

FIGURE 11.23
Adding full mailbox access permissions

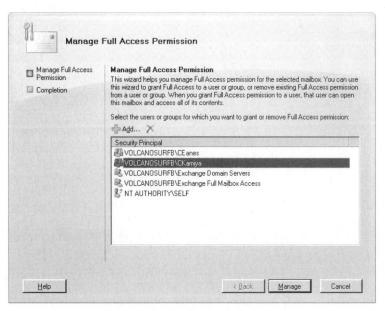

This could also be done using the EMS cmdlet `Add-MailboxPermission`. In this example, I am assigning user CKamiya permissions to access Betty McBee's mailbox:

```
Add-MailboxPermission Betty.McBee -User volcanosurfb\CKamiya -AccessRights
    FullAccess
```

Assigning Send As Permission

To assign Send As permissions, you need to run the Manage Send As Permission task on the Actions pane. Figure 11.24 shows the Manage Send As Permission Wizard; here I am assigning user PODowd the Send As permissions.

FIGURE 11.24
Assigning Send As permissions for a user

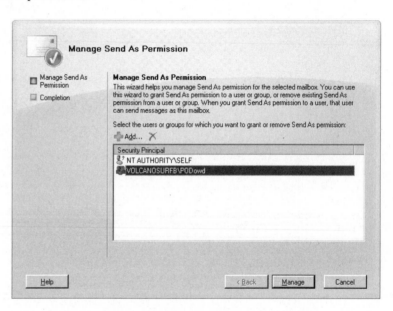

You can perform the same task using the EMS; here is an example of giving user volcanosurfb\PODowd Send As permissions to Betty McBee's mailbox:

```
Add-ADPermission 'CN=Betty McBee,OU=VolcanoSurfboards,DC=volcanosurfboards,DC↵
    =com' -User 'VOLCANOSURFB\PODowd' -ExtendedRights 'Send-as'
```

You can also remove the permissions you have assigned via the EMS with the following command:

```
Remove-ADPermission 'CN=Betty McBee,OU=VolcanoSurfboards,DC=volcanosurfboards,DC↵
    =com' -User 'VOLCANOSURFB\PODowd' -InheritanceType 'All' -ExtendedRights↵
'send-as' -ChildObjectTypes $null -InheritedObjectType $null -Properties $null
```

CREATING A NEW USER AND ASSIGNING A MAILBOX USING THE EMC

Previously, you saw that the EMC's New Mailbox Wizard would allow you to create a new user account at the same time you enable the mailbox. It is true that the new EMC has some rudimentary user creation and management tasks. On the User Type page of the New Mailbox Wizard, if you select the New User radio button and click Next, you are prompted for the user account information on a screen called the User Information screen (shown in Figure 11.25).

FIGURE 11.25

Creating a user account from the Exchange Management Console

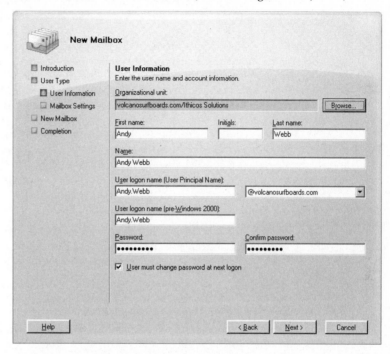

On the User Information screen, you provide some basic account information such as the first name, middle initials, last name, UPN name, pre–Windows 2000 account name, and the password. You must also specify the organizational unit (OU) in which the user account will be created, and, of course, you must have the Active Directory permissions necessary to create user accounts in that OU.

The rest of the wizard is exactly the same as if you were enabling a mailbox for an existing user. On the Completion page, though, you will notice some small differences in the cmdlet and the cmdlet's parameters. To create a user named Andy.Webb in the Ithicos Solutions OU and assign his mailbox to the MBDB-HNLEX04-01 mailbox database, here is the command that the EMC performed:

```
New-Mailbox -Name 'Andy Webb' -Alias 'Andy.Webb' -OrganizationalUnit↵
'volcanosurfboards.com/Ithicos Solutions' -UserPrincipalName
    'Andy.Webb@volcanosurfboards.com'↵
-SamAccountName 'Andy.Webb' -FirstName 'Andy' -Initials " -LastName 'Webb'↵
-Password 'System.Security.SecureString' -ResetPasswordOnNextLogon $true↵
-Database 'HNLEX04\SG-HNLEX04-01\MBDB-HNLEX04-01' -ManagedFolderMailboxPolicy↵
'Executives Managed Folder Mailbox Policy' -ActiveSyncMailboxPolicy↵
    'Strict ActiveSync policy'
```

Because the MBDB-HNLEX04-01 mailbox database is unique for the Exchange organization, you could shorten this command as follows if you are running it from the EMS:

```
New-Mailbox'Andy Webb' -Alias:'Andy.Webb'↵
-OrganizationalUnit:'volcanosurfboards.com/Ithicos Solutions'
```

```
-Database MBDB-HNLEX04-01'CN= -UserPrincipalName:'Andy.Webb@volcanosurfboards↵
.com' -SamAccountName:'Andy.Webb' -FirstName:'Andy' -Initials:" -LastName:'Webb'↵
-Password:'System.Security.SecureString' -ResetPasswordOnNextLogon:$True
```

When you include the -Password:'System.Security.SecureString' option, you are prompted to enter the password for the user; this helps prevent the password from being compromised. Notice that the cmdlet is not Enable-Mailbox as it was in the earlier section "Assigning a Mailbox to a User from the EMS." The Enable-Mailbox cmdlet is used to assign a mailbox to an existing user account. The cmdlet used here is the New-Mailbox; this cmdlet has options for creating the user account as well as enabling the mailbox. Notice there is an -OrganizationalUnit parameter that allows you to specify the domain and the OU name in canonical name format such as volcanosurfboards.com/IthicosSolutions.

The New-Mailbox cmdlet also has parameters for setting the password, pre–Windows 2000 account name, and UPN.

MANAGING USER AND MAILBOX PROPERTIES

Many of the user account properties that can be managed through the Active Directory Users and Computers console can now also be managed through the EMC or the EMS. Naturally, using the EMC is a little easier than using the command line, but the EMS is much more flexible and powerful once you learn how to use it.

Using the Exchange Management Console to Manage User and Mailbox Properties

Let's start with managing user and mailbox properties using the EMC. I want to take a look at a few of the things that you can do and some of the user property pages. Let's start by taking a look at the mailbox's General information property page shown in Figure 11.26. The General property page has some interesting information on it, including the user ID of the last person to access the mailbox, the mailbox size, the home Exchange server, and the mailbox database name.

On the General property page is also the Hide From Exchange Address Lists check box. This setting prevents the mailbox from appearing in address lists such as the global address list. The General property page also includes a Custom Attributes button that allows you to access all 15 custom attributes (aka extension attributes).

The field that is not clearly labeled is the Display Name field; this is the field that is next to the mailbox icon on the upper-left corner of the General property page. The display name is what users see in the global address list.

The next property page of interest is the E-Mail Addresses property page (shown in Figure 11.27). From the E-Mail Addresses property page, you can manage the SMTP addresses (and other address types) that are assigned to this particular mailbox. Notice in Figure 11.27 that this user has multiple SMTP addresses that can be used to send messages to this mailbox.

Regardless of how many e-mail addresses are assigned to this mailbox, when an Exchange user clicks the reply button to reply to a message sent to any of these addresses, the Set As Reply address is the one that is always used as the Reply To address. In Figure 11.27, this is the address shown in bold. This can be changed by selecting another address and clicking the Set As Reply button.

E-mail addresses are generated by an e-mail address policy, as discussed earlier in the chapter. If a policy that affects this mailbox is updated and reapplied, additional e-mail addresses will be created. If a policy that affects the default SMTP address is changed, the e-mail address policy can change a user's primary e-mail address. However, the user will retain the previous SMTP addresses. If you clear the Automatically Update E-mail Addresses Based On E-mail Address Policy check box, any changes to the e-mail address policy that affects this mailbox will not be made.

FIGURE 11.26
General information property page for a mailbox

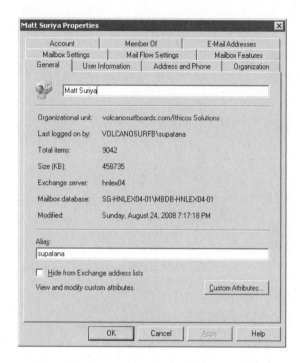

On the Mailbox Settings property page, there are two configuration items that are of interest. These are the Messaging Records Management and Storage Quotas options. These two sets of options are shown in Figure 11.28. Storage Quotas allow the administrator to override mailbox database limits.

The Messaging Records Management options allow you to specify the managed folder mailbox policy that affects this particular mailbox. In addition to defining which policy you use, you can specify an exception time (aka retention hold) during which no action will be taken on items in this mailbox that might ordinarily be deleted, archived, expired, or moved.

The Mail Flow Settings property page for the mailbox shows mailbox settings that most experienced Exchange administrators will already be familiar with. They are now just located in slightly different places. The properties found under the Mail Flow Settings property page are grouped into Delivery Options, Message Size Restrictions, and Message Delivery Restrictions sections. You merely need to highlight one of them and click the Properties button to see them.

The Delivery Options properties (shown in Figure 11.29) include a couple of important options. The first is the Send On Behalf permission; this allows anyone that has been assigned this permission to send a message on behalf of this user. For example, in Figure 11.29, user Matt Paleafei can now send a message on behalf of this mailbox. When the message arrives, it will say it is from Matt Paleafei on behalf of the specified mailbox. This implies, at least, a tacit authorization on the part of the mailbox owner that the message should have been sent by Matt Paleafei.

FIGURE 11.27
E-mail address
properties of a mailbox

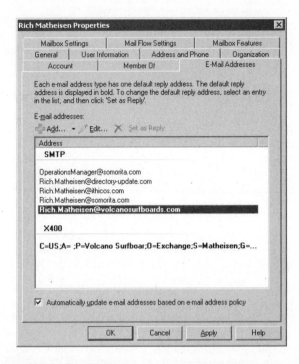

FIGURE 11.28
Storage Quotas and
Messaging Records
Management options
are found on the Mail-
box Settings property
page.

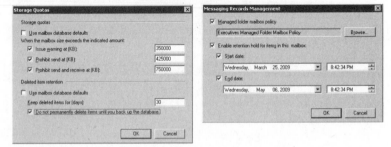

Also on the Delivery Options page is the option to deliver messages to an alternate recipient (aka forwarding address). The recipient that you specify must be a mailbox in your organization or a mail-enabled contact that you find within your global address list. If you select a mail-enabled contact that you have created in your global address list, this would let you forward all of this user's mail to an external mail system. That can be useful if someone has left the organization and wants to keep getting his or her mail. It could also be a disaster if that person has left your organization and gone to work for a competitor, so use this feature with caution.

If the Deliver Message To Both Forwarding Address And Mailbox check box is enabled, the message is delivered to both places. This is useful when "the boss" wants her assistant to receive all of her mail but she wants to see the mail as well.

Finally, the bottom part of the Delivery Options dialog box allows you to specify the maximum number of recipients to which this person can send a message. The global default is 5,000, but some organizations want to reduce this and then allow only the VIPs to send messages to large numbers of users.

FIGURE 11.29
A mailbox's delivery options

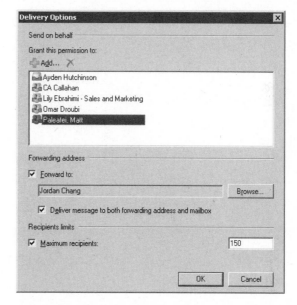

The Message Size Restrictions options allow you to specify the maximum size of messages the user can send or receive. If these are not specified, the user is limited by the global defaults or the connector defaults.

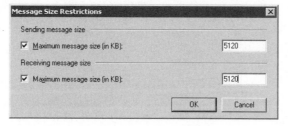

The final selection of settings found on the Mail Flow Settings property page is Message Delivery Restrictions. From the Message Delivery Restrictions options, you can restrict who is allowed to send mail to this particular mailbox. For example, if this is a VIP, you might want to restrict who can send to this mailbox to only a subset of users within the organization. Conversely, you could configure a mailbox to reject mail from a specific set of users. Figure 11.30 shows the Message Delivery Restrictions settings for a VIP's mailbox; the VIP wants to receive mail only from the other members of the $Executives And VIPs group, Matt Suriya and Matt Townley.

If you select the Require That All Senders Are Authenticated check box, this will cut down on the spam that mailbox receives, but it also means that no anonymous Internet mail will be received. By default, all mail received from the Internet is received anonymously.

If you have spent a lot of time troubleshooting non-delivery reports and error messages that your users have received in the past, you will be happy to hear that the Exchange team has worked hard to make the error messages more descriptive and helpful. In the case in which users send a message to someone they are not allowed to send to, they receive a non-delivery report message in return. Figure 11.31 shows an example.

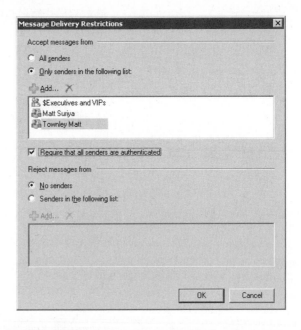

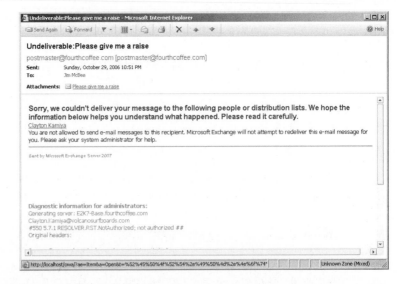

The final property page of interest to e-mail administrators is the Mailbox Features property page (shown in Figure 11.32). On this property page, you can enable or disable additional features of the mailbox such as Outlook Web Access, Exchange ActiveSync, Unified Messaging, MAPI access, POP3, and IMAP4.

FIGURE 11.32
Mailbox Features
property page

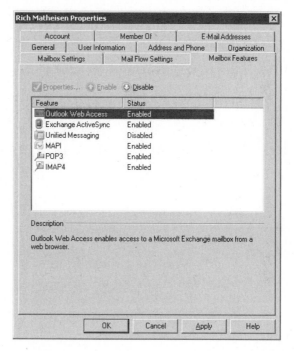

Some of these features can only be enabled or disabled, whereas others (such as the POP3 and IMAP4 features) have additional properties:

◆ The Exchange ActiveSync selection has a Properties option that allows you to configure the Exchange ActiveSync policy for this user.

◆ You can now disable MAPI clients.

◆ The Unified Messaging option allows you to specify the user's Unified Messaging properties if you have Unified Messaging server roles installed.

Using the Exchange Management Shell to Manage User Properties

You can also manage mailbox and user properties from the EMS. There are two cmdlets that you will need to know about in order to manage most of the properties. These are the `Set-User` and `Set-Mailbox` cmdlets. Let's start with the `Set-User` cmdlet and an example. Let's say that I want to update user Stan.Reimer's mobile phone number. I would type this:

```
Set-User Stan.Reimer -MobilePhone "(808) 555-1234"
```

The `Set-User` cmdlet has quite a few useful parameters. Table 11.2 lists many of these options. You can retrieve these from within the EMS by typing `Set-User -?` or `Help Set-User`.

TABLE 11.2:   Some Set-User Cmdlet Parameters

PARAMETER	FUNCTION
PostalCode	Sets the zip or postal code.
Manager	Sets the name of the user's manager; input value must be a distinguished name in canonical name format such as fourthcoffee.com/Corporate/Ben Craig.
DisplayName	Updates the user's display name, which appears in the global address list.
MobilePhone	Sets the mobile/cell phone number.
City	Sets the city or locality name.
FirstName	Specifies the given or first name.
LastName	Specifies the surname or last name.
Company	Sets the company name.
Department	Sets the department name.
Fax	Specifies the facsimile telephone number.
HomePhone	Sets the home phone number.
Phone	Sets the business phone number.
StateOrProvince	Sets the state or province.
StreetAddress	Sets the street address.
Title	Sets the title or job function.

You can retrieve the list of properties for Set-User by using the Get-User cmdlet, specifying a username, and then piping the output to the Format-List cmdlet. Here is an example:

```
Get-User vlad.mazek | Format-List
Id                  : fourthcoffee.com/Users/Vlad Mazek
IsValid             : True
Item                :
DistinguishedName   : CN=Vlad Mazek,CN=Users,DC=fourthcoffee,DC=com
Guid                : 08834c78-6fd7-4705-baed-54759df1dc26
Identity            : fourthcoffee.com/Users/Vlad Mazek
Name                : Vlad Mazek
ObjectCategory      : fourthcoffee.com/Configuration/Schema/Person
ObjectCategoryName  : user
ObjectClass         : {top, person, organizationalPerson, user}
ObjectState         : Unchanged
```

```
OriginatingServer     : E2K7-Base.fourthcoffee.com
Schema                : Microsoft.Exchange.Data.Directory.Management.UserSchema
WhenChanged           : 11/5/2006 6:34:21 AM
WhenCreated           : 11/5/2006 6:31:18 AM
SamAccountName        : Vlad.Mazek
Sid                   : S-1-5-21-313647035-3844660503-1830646060-1170
SidHistory            : {}
IsSecurityPrincipal   : True
UserPrincipalName     : Vlad.Mazek@fourthcoffee.com
Assistant             :
Company               : Own Web Now Corporation
Department            : Information Security
DirectReports         : {}
Fax                   : (808) 555-4300
HomePhone             : (808) 555-1022
Initials              :
FirstName             : Vlad
LastName              : Mazek
City                  : Honolulu
Manager               : fourthcoffee.com/Corporate/Andy Webb
MobilePhone           : (808) 555-4100
Office                : Honolulu
OtherFax              : {}
OtherHomePhone        : {}
Pager                 : (808) 555-4321
Phone                 : (808) 555-1234
PostalCode            : 96816
PostOfficeBox         : {}
StateOrProvince       : Hawaii
StreetAddress         : 7019 Kalakaua Avenue
                        Suite 2001
Title                 : Operations Manager
DisplayName           : Vlad Mazek
Notes                 : Created on Nov 5, 2006 per Mark Watts - Work Order BR-549
RecipientType         : MailboxUser
RecipientTypeDetails  : MailboxUser
SimpleDisplayName     : Vlad M
WebPage               : http://ownwebnow.com
```

SEEING NAMES AND VALUES WITH *FORMAT-LIST*

If you pipe the properties of an object to the Format-List (FL) cmdlet, this gives you a very handy way to see all of the property names as well as their current values.

Not only does the Get-User cmdlet allow you to view this information about a user account, it also allows you to see all of the property names. For example, if you did not know what the property name was for the State, you could look in the output listing and see that it is

-StateOrProvince. You could then change the user's state by typing the following EMS command:

```
Set-User vlad.mazek -StateOrProvince "Florida"
```

Using the Exchange Management Shell to Manage Mailbox Properties

The Set-User and the Get-User cmdlets helped me with non-Exchange-specific properties of a user account, but the Set-Mailbox and the Get-Mailbox cmdlets will help you to set the properties of a mail-enabled user account. In fact, you have already seen these cmdlets earlier in this book when I talked about setting mailbox storage limits. Let's take a quick look at some ways you can use these cmdlets. For example, if you want to change the user Cheyne.Manalo's rules quota, you would type this:

```
Set-Mailbox cheyne.manalo -RulesQuota:128KB
```

You can set a lot of properties through the EMS and the Set-Mailbox cmdlet. A few of the more useful ones are found in Table 11.3.

TABLE 11.3:   Some Set-Mailbox Properties

PARAMETER	FUNCTION
RulesQuota	Specifies the maximum amount of rules a user can have in a folder. Note that having more than 32KB of rules per folder requires the Outlook 2007 client.
SCLDeleteThreshold	Specifies the SCL (spam confidence level) value at and above which messages flagged as spam should be deleted.
SCLDeleteEnabled	Specifies if messages above the value of the SCLDeleteThreshold property should be deleted. There are additional SCL threshold options that are not listed in this table.
RecipientLimits	Specifies the maximum number of recipients per message that a user can send to.
EmailAddressPolicy Enabled	Specifies whether or not this mailbox should have its e-mail addresses updated by e-mail address policies.
MaxSendSize	Specifies the maximum size for messages that can be sent by this mailbox.
MaxReceiveSize	Specifies the maximum size for messages that can be received into this mailbox.
ForwardingAddress	Specifies an address to which mail sent to this mailbox will be forwarded. The value must be in canonical name format such as volcanosurfboards.com/Corporate/Mike Brown.
HiddenFromAddress ListsEnabled	If set to True, this mailbox will not appear in any of the Exchange address lists. The default is False.

TABLE 11.3:   Some Set-Mailbox Properties *(CONTINUED)*

PARAMETER	FUNCTION
CustomAttribute1	Specifies the value for Custom Attribute 1 (aka Extension Attribute 1). Fifteen custom attributes can be set through the EMS; simply change 1 to 2, 3, and so on.
ProhibitSendQuota	Specifies the mailbox size above which the user will not be able to send any new messages.
ProhibitSend ReceiveQuota	Specifies the mailbox size above which the mailbox will reject new mail and the user will not be able to send any messages.
IssueWarningQuota	Specifies the mailbox size above which users will receive a warning message indicating they are over their mailbox quota.
AntispamBypass Enabled	If set to True, this specifies that this mailbox should not have its mail filtered by the Exchange 2007 content filtering component on the Edge Transport or Hub Transport server. The default is False.
UseDatabaseQuota Defaults	If set to False, the mailbox uses the storage quotas set on the mailbox. If set to True (the default), the mailbox uses the mailbox storage quotas that are defined for the mailbox database on which the mailbox is located.

Table 11.3 shows you just a few of the parameters that can be used by the Set-Mailbox cmdlet or that can be viewed using the Get-Mailbox cmdlet. If you want to look up these parameters, from the EMS you can type Set-Mailbox -?, or you can type Help Set-Mailbox. As I showed you previously with Get-User, you can pipe the output for a mailbox to the Format-List (or FL) cmdlet and see all of the properties for that mailbox. Here is an example:

```
Get-Mailbox "Cheyne Manalo" | Format-List
Database                           : HNLEX03\First Storage Group\Mailbox Database
DeletedItemFlags                   : RetainUntilBackupOrCustomPeriod
UseDatabaseRetentionDefaults       : False
RetainDeletedItemsUntilBackup      : True
DeliverToMailboxAndForward         : True
RetentionHoldEnabled               : True
EndDateForRetentionHold            : 1/31/2007 2:01:32 PM
StartDateForRetentionHold          : 1/11/2007 2:01:32 PM
ManagedFolderMailboxPolicy         : Executives Managed Folder Mailbox Policy
ExchangeGuid                       : 5febe951-905a-4171-9b3b-d8bcfb8a728d
ExchangeSecurityDescriptor         : System.Security.AccessControl.
RawSecurityDescriptor
ExchangeUserAccountControl         : None
ExternalOofOptions                 : External
ForwardingAddress                  : volcanosurfboards.com/VolcanoSurfboards/
            To dd Hawkins
```

```
RetainDeletedItemsFor              : 30.00:00:00
IsMailboxEnabled                   : True
Languages                          : {}
OfflineAddressBook                 :
ProhibitSendQuota                  : 150000KB
ProhibitSendReceiveQuota           : 200000KB
ProtocolSettings                   : {HTTP§0§1§§§§§§, POP3§1§0§1§ISO-
8859-1§1§§§, IMAP4§0§1§4§ISO-8859-1§0§1§0§0}
RecipientLimits                    : 150
UserAccountControl                 : NormalAccount
IsResource                         : False
IsLinked                           : False
IsShared                           : False
LinkedMasterAccount                :
ResourceCapacity                   :
ResourceCustom                     : {}
ResourceType                       :
SamAccountName                     : CManalo
SCLDeleteThreshold                 :
SCLDeleteEnabled                   :
SCLRejectThreshold                 :
SCLRejectEnabled                   :
SCLQuarantineThreshold             :
SCLQuarantineEnabled               :
SCLJunkThreshold                   : 4
SCLJunkEnabled                     : True
AntispamBypassEnabled              : False
ServerLegacyDN                     : /o=Volcano Surfboards/ou=Exchange
    Administrative Group (FYDIBOHF23SPDLT)/cn=Configuration/cn=Servers/cn=HNLEX03
ServerName                         : hnlex03
UseDatabaseQuotaDefaults           : False
IssueWarningQuota                  : 125000KB
RulesQuota                         : 64KB
Office                             :
UserPrincipalName                  : CManalo@volcanosurfboards.com
UMEnabled                          : False
MaxSafeSenders                     :
MaxBlockedSenders                  :
Extensions                         : {}
AcceptMessagesOnlyFrom             : {}
AcceptMessagesOnlyFromDLMembers    : {}
AddressListMembership              : {Engineering, Default Global
Address List, All Users}
Alias                              : CManalo
OrganizationalUnit                 : volcanosurfboards.com/VolcanoSurfboards
CustomAttribute1                   : Angelina
```

```
CustomAttribute10            :
CustomAttribute11            :
CustomAttribute12            :
CustomAttribute13            :
CustomAttribute14            :
CustomAttribute15            :
CustomAttribute2             : Delta SkyMiles Member
CustomAttribute3             : 987654321
CustomAttribute4             : D.O.B. March 9, 1982
CustomAttribute5             :
CustomAttribute6             :
CustomAttribute7             :
CustomAttribute8             :
CustomAttribute9             :
DisplayName                  : Cheyne Manalo
EmailAddresses               : {smtp:Cheyne@volcanosurfboards.com,
    smtp:CManalo@directory-update.com,
X500:/o=Volcano Surfboards/ou=First Administrative Group/cn=Recipients/cn=CManalo,
    smtp:CManalo@research.somorita.com,
SMTP:CManalo@somorita.com, smtp:CManalo@volcanosurfboards.com}
GrantSendOnBehalfTo          : {Andy Webb, Bharat Suneja,
Bthaworn Thaweeaphiradeemaitree, Paul Moriguchi, Don Nguyen, Nathan Nakanishi}
HiddenFromAddressListsEnabled : False
LegacyExchangeDN             : /o=Volcano Surfboards/ou=First
Administrative Group/cn=Recipients/cn=CManalo
MaxSendSize                  : 20MB
MaxReceiveSize               : 10MB
PoliciesIncluded             : {}
PoliciesExcluded             : {{26491cfc-9e50-4857-861b-0cb8df22b5d7}}
EmailAddressPolicyEnabled    : False
PrimarySmtpAddress           : CManalo@somorita.com
RecipientType                : UserMailbox
RecipientTypeDetails         : UserMailbox
RejectMessagesFrom           : {Roberry Carter, Pavel Nagaev, Townley Matt}
RejectMessagesFromDLMembers  : {}
RequireSenderAuthenticationEnabled : False
SimpleDisplayName            :
UMDtmfMap                    : {}
WindowsEmailAddress          : CManalo@somorita.com
IsValid                      : True
OriginatingServer            : HNLDC01.volcanosurfboards.com
ExchangeVersion              : 0.1 (8.0.535.0)
Name                         : Cheyne Manalo
DistinguishedName            : CN=Cheyne Manalo,
OU=VolcanoSurfboards,DC=volcanosurfboards,DC=com
Identity                     : volcanosurfboards.com/VolcanoSurfboards/
```

```
Cheyne Manalo
Guid                      : 2565735d-c19b-4c88-9242-075eaa8e8fee
ObjectCategory            : volcanosurfboards.com/Configuration/
Schema/Person
ObjectClass               : {top, person, organizationalPerson, user}
WhenChanged               : 1/11/2009 2:06:16 PM
WhenCreated               : 12/12/2005 9:10:28 AM
```

When you look at these properties, please keep in mind that not all properties can be modified, even using the EMS. Many of these properties are system properties and are either created or managed by the system.

Managing Resource Mailboxes

Finally with Exchange 2007 and Outlook 2007, the client and the server know the different between a regular user mailbox and a resource mailbox. Exchange 2007 allows you to define two different types of resource mailboxes: room and equipment mailboxes. This section first looks at some of the basic features that allow you to define a resource mailbox and then shows you some of the more advanced features of Exchange 2007 and Outlook 2007, such as advanced calendaring.

To assign an administrator the permissions necessary to create, manage, and delete resource mailboxes, make that administrator a member of the Exchange Recipient Administrators group. This administrator will also require permissions to whichever Active Directory organizational unit will hold the disabled user accounts.

CREATING AND DEFINING RESOURCE MAILBOX PROPERTIES

Let's start with a simple example of defining a room resource mailbox. Let's say you want to create a conference room resource that will be called Conference Room 1103. Just as with creating a user account, you launch the New Mailbox Wizard, but on the Introduction page you choose the Room Mailbox radio button.

Everything else about creating a room mailbox resource is exactly the same as creating a user mailbox. If the user account does not yet exist in the Active Directory, specify that you are creating a new user, and then on the Mailbox Information page, provide the user account information (shown in Figure 11.33). Notice that the user is being created in an OU called Resources; that is an OU I created to hold resource user accounts.

Notice also in Figure 11.33 that I specified a first name and a last name. This is not really necessary, but I consider it a good practice. When you have completed the New Mailbox Wizard, a disabled user account is created. Right now, the resource user and the resource user's mailbox look almost identical to a regular user's mailbox. The icons are slightly different for the room and equipment mailboxes. The room mailbox icon includes a small door and the equipment mailbox includes a small projector screen. Here is an example of some resource mailbox listings; note that I have named all of these so that their display names start with the ~ (tilde) character. This ensures that they all sort together in the global address list.

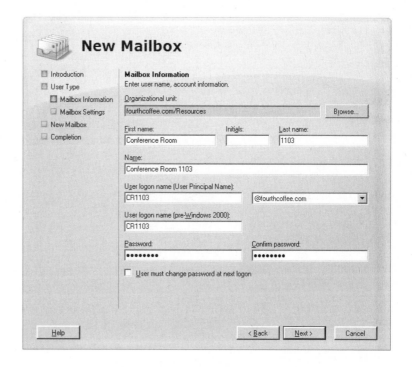

FIGURE 11.33
Defining user information for a conference room mailbox

But what really defines these as resources instead of just mailboxes? With Exchange 2007, some additional Active Directory attributes can be assigned to a user account that define a resource account as opposed to a regular mailbox. These attributes include the `RecipientType`, `RecipientTypeDetails`, `ResourceType`, `ResourceCapacity`, and `ResourceCustom` properties. Let's look at the resource-specific properties of the room resource I just created using the `Get-Mailbox` cmdlet. Here is the command and the output:

```
Get-Mailbox "conference room 1103" | Format-List Name,RecipientType,RecipientType↵
Details, ResourceType, ResourceCapacity, ResourceCustom
Name               : Conference Room 1103
```

```
RecipientType        : MailboxUser
RecipientTypeDetails : ConferenceRoomMailbox
ResourceType         : Room
ResourceCapacity     :
ResourceCustom       : {Room}
```

The following are the details of what you can expect to see for these properties when creating resource mailboxes:

◆ The `RecipientType` property for mailboxes (resource or regular) is always set to `MailboxUser`.

◆ The `RecipientTypeDetails` property will be set to either `ConferenceRoomMailbox` or `EquipmentMailbox`.

◆ The `ResourceType` property will be set to either `Room` or `Equipment`.

◆ The `ResourceCapacity` property is used to define room capacity (for example, the number of people that can sit in the room).

◆ The `ResourceCustom` property is used to define additional properties for this resource mailbox.

What these properties of the user account (and mailbox) do is set some features that define this mailbox as a resource mailbox. These special features enable Outlook 2007 and Outlook Web Access 2007 to recognize resource mailboxes and to differentiate a regular mailbox from an end user mailbox. Figure 11.34 shows the All Rooms view of the Outlook Web Access 2007 Address Book; this allows you to view just the conference room resources.

FIGURE 11.34
Viewing just the room resources in the Address Book using OWA

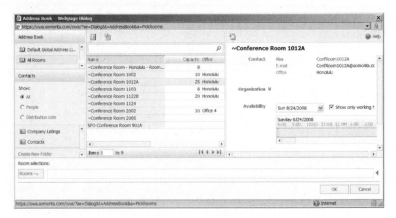

Enabling the client to separately view room resources makes choosing room resources simpler because it eliminates the necessity to browse the entire global address list.

DEFINING ADVANCED RESOURCE MAILBOX FEATURES

What you have seen so far with respect to resource mailboxes is not all that different from earlier versions of Exchange and Outlook. It's just that now you have the ability to better sort the address list. However, Exchange 2007 actually enables a few additional features on the mailbox that make it even easier to find the room resource you need. You probably noticed the properties `ResourceCapacity` and `ResourceCustom`. What good is scheduling a conference room if you can't schedule one that will hold all of the attendees? The `ResourceCapacity` property allows you to define in the Active Directory the capacity of a specific room resource.

Resource capacity is defined from the EMS using the `Set-Mailbox` cmdlet. Let's say you want to define the room capacity of Conference Room 1103 as 15 people. You would type this:

```
Set-Mailbox "Conference Room 1103" -ResourceCapacity 15
```

Before looking at how you would utilize this information, let's also look at the `ResourceCustom` property. What good is finding a conference room with a certain capacity if you can't find one with all of the tools or resources you need for a particular meeting? In many organizations, certain conference rooms are equipped with televisions, DVD players, and more. These things can be defined in the `ResourceCustom` property.

If you want to take advantage of this, the first thing you need to do is to define the types of properties in the property schema. Resource property schema properties are defined using the `Set-ResourceConfig` cmdlet, and you can view the current properties using the `Get-ResourceConfig` cmdlet. The property in which you are interested is the `ResourcePropertySchema`. Here is an example of retrieving the current value:

```
Get-ResourceConfig | Format-List Name,ResourcePropertySchema

Name                   : Resource Schema
ResourcePropertySchema : {Room/TV, Room/AV}
```

Each time you run the `Set-ResourceConfig` cmdlet, it replaces the existing value with the new value, so if you want to keep the existing properties, make sure you include the existing properties in the `Set-ResourceConfig` command line. Let's say, for example, that you want to define an additional type of resource property that some of the conference rooms have available. In this example, some of the conference rooms have massage chairs; to add an additional resource property of massage chair, you would type this command:

```
Set-ResourceConfig -ResourcePropertySchema ("Room/TV", "Room/AV", "Room↵
/MassageChairs")
```

Once the resource property schema includes a TV, A/V resources, and massage chairs, you can assign them as resources of a particular conference room. For room resource objects, you can do this on the Resource Information property page of the mailbox object. (See Figure 11.35.)

You can also set the custom resource properties via the EMS. For example, if Conference Room 1103 has TV and massage chair resources and a capacity of eight people, you would type this:

```
Set-Mailbox -Identity "Conference Room 1103" -ResourceCustom↵
   ("TV","MassageChairs") -ResourceCapacity 8
```

This sets both the custom resource properties and the resource capacity at the same time. If you want to verify this for this particular resource, you could type this:

```
Get-Mailbox "conference room 1103" | FL Name,*resource*

Name            : Conference Room 1103
IsResource      : True
```

```
ResourceCapacity  : 8
ResourceCustom    : {MassageChairs, TV, Room}
ResourceType      : Room
```

FIGURE 11.35
Custom resources in a
conference room

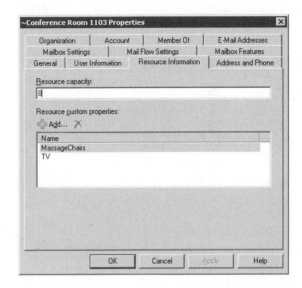

Note that the preceding example did not include the -Identity parameter in the Get-Mailbox options. This was intentional so that I could show you that it is optional; also note that the resource's display name, Conference Room 1103, is in lowercase. The cmdlets and the parameters are not usually case sensitive, either.

Once you have defined a resource with specific properties, such as the custom properties and the capacity, the properties will show up in Outlook and Outlook Web Access when you browse for room resources. Figure 11.36 shows the Select Rooms list box in Outlook 2007. Notice that the room capacity and the room's custom resources show up in this list.

FIGURE 11.36
Browsing for room
resources. Note the
Capacity and Description
columns.

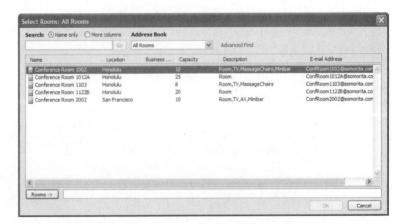

DEFINING RESOURCE SCHEDULING POLICIES

One of the more annoying things about creating resources in earlier versions of Exchange was that you had to be creative in figuring out a way to get a resource to automatically accept scheduled appointments. There were scripts, special procedures, and third-party tools that you could use to handle automatic booking, but often even a combination of tools and software did not meet your needs.

Exchange 2007 introduces a new way to define the features of a resource mailbox, including how a resource is automatically booked and who can book a particular resource. Options such as who can book a room or equipment resource, as well as time limits for booking the resource, are part of the resource's calendar scheduling policy.

These settings can be defined in one of two ways: using Outlook Web Access, or using the EMS.

Defining Resource Scheduling Policies Using Outlook Web Access

The simplest way to define a resource's calendar scheduling policy is to use Outlook Web Access. You must first enable the room resource mailbox account (because it will initially be created as a disabled user account), make sure you have the password, and then open the mailbox using Outlook Web Access. Once you have opened the mailbox in Outlook Web Access, click the Options button in the OWA interface, scroll down the options on the left pane, and choose the Resource Settings option. (This option does not appear for a regular mailbox.) The entire list of options is a little too big for one screen capture, so I am breaking it up into smaller screens so that I can describe each of the options; they are summarized for you in Table 11.4.

TABLE 11.4:   Resource Scheduling Parameters

FUNCTION	OWA SETTING	EMS CMDLET PARAMETERS
Process meeting requests automatically.	Automatically Process Meeting Requests and Cancellations	`-AutomateBooking` (default is `$False`).
Specify automatic processing options.		`-AutomateProcessing` Options: None – Disables all automatic processing. AutoUpdate – Requests automatically processed by the Calendar Attendant on the server AutoAccept – Requests automatically processed by the mailbox.
Do not show reminders for meetings in the resource mailbox.	Disable Reminders	`-DisableReminders` (Set to `$True` or `$False`)

TABLE 11.4: Resource Scheduling Parameters *(CONTINUED)*

FUNCTION	OWA SETTING	EMS CMDLET PARAMETERS
Specify a default reminder time for meeting requests.		-DefaultReminderTime
Specify from the present day the maximum booking window in which the resource can be booked. Default is 180 days.	Maximum Number of Days	-BookingWindowInDays
Specify if recurring meetings that continue to recur after maximum number of days will be rejected.		-EnforceSchedulingHorizon (Set to $True or $False)
Specify the maximum length of a meeting request. The default is 180 minutes.	Maximum Allowed Minutes	-MaximumDurationInMinutes
Specify that a resource can only be scheduled during working hours. These days and times are defined for each resource mailbox in the Calendar Options ➢ Calendar Work Week section of the OWA options.	Allow Scheduling Only During Working Hours	-ScheduleOnlyDuringWork Hours (Set to $True or $False)
Specify if conflicts should be allowed.	Allow Conflicts	-AllowConflicts (Set to $True or $False)
Specify if recurring meetings will be allowed.	Allow Recurring Meetings	-AllowRecurringMeetings
If conflicts are allowed, specify the maximum number of conflicts that can be scheduled before a meeting request will be declined.	Allow Up to This Number of Individual Conflicts	-MaximumConflictInstances
If the number of meeting requests (for recurring meetings) conflicting with already scheduled meetings exceeds this percentage, decline the meeting requests.	Allow Up to This Percentage of Individual Conflicts	-ConflictPercentageAllowed
Display pending meeting requests as free in the Free and Busy times.		-TentativePendingApproval (Set to $True or $False)

TABLE 11.4:   Resource Scheduling Parameters *(CONTINUED)*

FUNCTION	OWA SETTING	EMS CMDLET PARAMETERS
Specify that the resource mailbox send organizer information when a meeting request is declined due to a conflict.		-OrganizerInfo (Set to $True or $False)
Define a list of users and mail-enabled groups that can book this resource automatically if it is available. This booking is done by sending a meeting request message.	These Users Can Schedule Automatically If the Resource Is Available	-BookInPolicy (Specifies list of users or groups allowed to automatically book. The AllBookInPolicy option must be set to False.)
		-AllBookInPolicy (If true, allows everyone to automatically schedule meeting requests via a meeting request message.)
Define a list of users or mail-enabled groups that can manually submit a request to schedule the room resource if it is available. This booking is done by sending a meeting request message.	These Users Can Submit a Request for Manual Approval If the Resource Is Available	-RequestInPolicy (Specifies a list of users or groups that are allowed to send meeting requests for the resource delegate to approve or decline.)
		-AllRequestInPolicy (If set to True, meeting requests can be sent to this mailbox by anyone. If set to False, the list of users or groups specified by the -RequestInPolicy list determines who can send meeting requests to this resource.)
Define a list of users or mail-enabled groups that can automatically schedule a room resource if the resource is available and submit a request for manual approval if the resource is already booked. This booking is done by sending a meeting request message.	These Users Can Schedule Automatically If the Resource Is Available and Submit a Request for Manual Approval If the Resource Is Unavailable	-RequestOutOfPolicy (Specifies users or groups that can have their schedule requests automatically approved if the resource is available and have the request approved manually if there is a conflict. The -AllRequestOutOfPolicy option must be set to False for this option to work.)

TABLE 11.4: Resource Scheduling Parameters *(CONTINUED)*

FUNCTION	OWA SETTING	EMS CMDLET PARAMETERS
		-AllRequestOutOfPolicy (If set to True, meeting requests from everyone will be approved if the resource is available and sent to the resource mailbox delegate for approval if a conflict occurs.)
Send approval requests to resource mailbox delegates if they require approval.	Always Forward to Delegates	-ForwardRequestsTo Delegates
Accept schedule requests tentatively even if they require approval by the resource mailbox delegate.	Always Tentatively Accept These Requests	-AddNewRequestsTentatively
Accept schedule requests from senders outside of the Exchange organization.		-ProcessExternalMeeting Messages
Specify delegates of this resource.		-ResourceDelegates
Specify if organizer's name should be included on the meeting subject in the room resource mailbox.	Always Add Organizer Name to Meeting Subject	-AddOrganizerToSubject (Set to $True or $False)
Specify that the private flag is removed, if included, on accepted meetings.	Always Remove the Private Flag on Accepted Meeting	-RemovePrivateProperty (Set to $True or $False)
Specify if meeting request information should be included in the message when a declined message is returned to the user.	Include Detailed Information about Conflicting Messages in Response	-EnableResponseDetails (Set to $True or $False)
Specify if the organizer's name should be included in a message when a meeting request is declined.	Include Organizer's Name in Conflict Information	-AddOrganizerToSubject (Set to $True or $False)
Automatically delete e-mail messages that are sent to the resource mailbox.	Always Delete the Following When Sent to This Resource: E-mail Messages	-DeleteNonCalendarItems (Set to $True or $False)

TABLE 11.4:   Resource Scheduling Parameters *(CONTINUED)*

FUNCTION	OWA SETTING	EMS CMDLET PARAMETERS
Automatically delete attachments from e-mail messages sent to the resource mailbox.	Always Delete the Following When Sent to This Resource: Attachments from Meeting Requests	-DeleteAttachments (Set to $True or $False)
Automatically delete comments from meeting request messages.	Always Delete the Following When Sent to This Resource: Comments from Meeting Requests	-DeleteComments (Set to $True or $False)
Automatically delete subject of meeting requests.	Always Delete the Following When Sent to This Resource: Subject of Meeting Requests	-DeleteSubject (Set to $True or $False)

Figure 11.37 shows the Resource Scheduling Options section.

FIGURE 11.37
A resource mailbox's Resource Scheduling Options

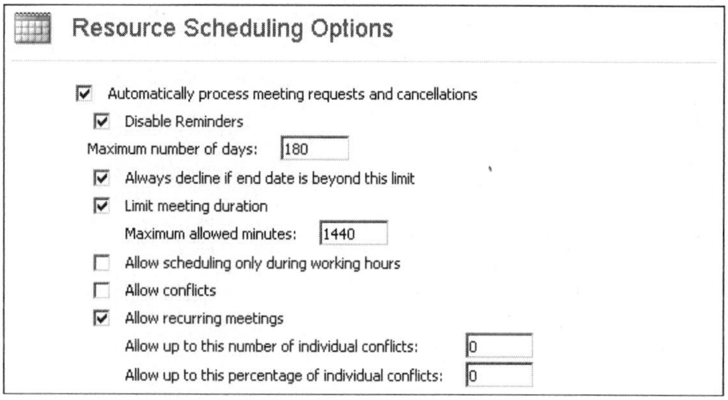

The Resource Scheduling Options section allows you to define some of the basics of how the resource will automatically accept schedule requests, whether or not it will accept recurring requests, whether or not it will even automatically process requests, and how to handle conflicting requests.

The next section in Resource Settings is Resource Scheduling Permissions; these are shown in Figure 11.38. By default, everyone is allowed to submit schedule requests to a resource and these request will be automatically processed based on the rules defined in the Resource Scheduling Options section.

Notice that in Figure 11.38, I have changed the auto-accept permissions for this room resource just a bit (after all, it does have massage chairs). This room can only be scheduled automatically by members of the Executives group; VIPs and user Mark Arnold can automatically schedule meetings for the resource *and* submit manual requests if the resource is unavailable. Note that permissions include whether or not manual requests are automatically sent to delegates of this resource.

FIGURE 11.38
Defining room resource
scheduling permissions

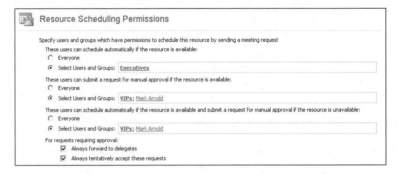

Delegates cannot be defined through this interface. Resource delegates must be defined using the EMS cmdlet Set-MailboxCalendarSettings. For example, if you want to assign user Simon.Butler as a delegate of this mailbox, you would type the following command:

```
Set-MailboxCalendarSettings "Conference Room 1103" -ResourceDelegates Simon.Bulter
```

The final two sections of Resource Scheduling are the Resource Privacy Options and Response Message sections; these are shown in Figure 11.39. Resource Privacy Options settings define how the automatic responses will format responses to meeting requests and if the original resource schedule request meeting will be deleted or not.

FIGURE 11.39
Resource Privacy
Options and Response
Message options

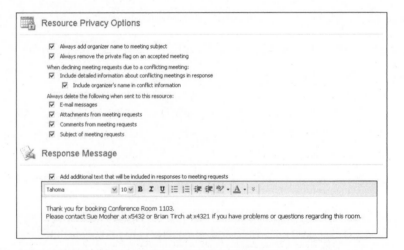

The Response Message section allows you to define a customized response that will be returned to users that request this resource. This can be useful in telling users who owns a particular resource or for sending back a reply as to the rules of usage for a resource.

Defining Resource Scheduling Policies Using the EMS

I mentioned that you could define the resource properties in two ways; the second way is using the Set-MailboxCalendarSettings cmdlet. Table 11.4, presented earlier in this chapter, describes the Outlook Web Access Resource Scheduling options and the corresponding parameters for the Set-MailboxCalendarSettings cmdlet. There will be EMS cmdlet parameters that are not available via the graphical user interface.

Now that you have seen the settings and how you can implement them using Outlook Web Access, let's take a look at them from the EMS using the Get-MailboxCalendarSettings cmdlet:

```
Get-MailboxCalendarSettings "Conference Room 1103" | FL
TestFields                       : {BookInPolicyRecipients, BookInPolicy,
RequestInPolicy, RequestOutOfPolicy, RequestInPolicyRecipients,
RequestOutOfPolicyRecipients}
AutomateProcessing               : AutoUpdate
AllowConflicts                   : False
BookingWindowInDays              : 180
MaximumDurationInMinutes         : 1440
AllowRecurringMeetings           : True
EnforceSchedulingHorizon         : True
ScheduleOnlyDuringWorkHours      : False
ConflictPercentageAllowed        : 0
MaximumConflictInstances         : 0
ForwardRequestsToDelegates       : True
DeleteAttachments                : True
DeleteComments                   : True
RemovePrivateProperty            : True
DeleteSubject                    : True
DisableReminders                 : True
AddOrganizerToSubject            : True
DeleteNonCalendarItems           : True
TentativePendingApproval         : True
EnableResponseDetails            : True
OrganizerInfo                    : True
ResourceDelegates                : {Simon Butler}
RequestOutOfPolicy               :
AllRequestOutOfPolicy            : False
BookInPolicy                     :
AllBookInPolicy                  : True
RequestInPolicy                  :
AllRequestInPolicy               : False
AddAdditionalResponse            : False
AdditionalResponse               :
RemoveOldMeetingMessages         : True
AddNewRequestsTentatively        : True
ProcessExternalMeetingMessages   : False
DefaultReminderTime              : 15
```

```
RemoveForwardedMeetingNotifications : False
Identity                            : volcanosurfboards.com/Users/
Conference Room 1103
```

CONFIGURING A RESOURCE BOOKING POLICY USING THE EMS

Using Outlook Web Access to manage your resource mailbox's resource booking policy options is pretty easy to do. For administrators that have only a handful of mailboxes, this is absolutely the best route to go. If, however, you have dozens of resource mailboxes that must be configured, using the Exchange Management Shell is the best way to go.

This section shows you some of the EMS cmdlets and parameters that will make your life a bit easier. First and foremost, let's look at how you can find all of the resource mailboxes in the entire organization. Remember that on a mailbox that is designated as a resource mailbox, there is a Boolean property called IsResource; if the mailbox is a resource mailbox, this property is set to True. You can use this to enumerate all of the resource mailboxes in the organization; here is an example of using the Get-Mailbox cmdlet to list mailboxes and the Where-Object (or just Where) cmdlet to filter and display only the mailboxes that are resource mailboxes:

```
Get-Mailbox | Where-Object {$_.IsResource -eq "True"}↵
| Format-Table Name,Alias,ResourceType
```

```
Name                     Alias               ResourceType
----                     -----               ------------
Conference Room 2002     ConfRoom2002                Room
Panasonic Flat Panel Pl... EquipPanaFlat1         Equipment
Conference Room 1002     ConfRoom1002                Room
Conference Room 1012A    ConfRoom1012A               Room
Conference Room 1122B    ConfRoom1122B               Room
Conference Room 1103     ConfRoom1103                Room
Conference Room 2005     ConfRoom2005                Room
Conference Room - Honol... ConfRoom2115              Room
Computer Projector 4     CompProjector4         Equipment
Conference Room 1124     ConfRoom1124                Room
Portable Minibar         PortableMinibar        Equipment
```

Let's say that you want to look at all of the resource booking properties for a particular resource; you would use the Get-MailboxCalendarSettings cmdlet. In the following listing, this is the conference room that was previously configured using Outlook Web Access:

```
Get-MailboxCalendarSettings "ConfRoom2115" | Format-List
```

```
AutomateProcessing         : AutoAccept
AllowConflicts             : False
BookingWindowInDays        : 180
MaximumDurationInMinutes   : 1440
AllowRecurringMeetings     : True
EnforceSchedulingHorizon   : True
ScheduleOnlyDuringWorkHours : False
```

```
ConflictPercentageAllowed          : 0
MaximumConflictInstances           : 0
ForwardRequestsToDelegates         : True
DeleteAttachments                  : True
DeleteComments                     : True
RemovePrivateProperty              : True
DeleteSubject                      : True
DisableReminders                   : True
AddOrganizerToSubject              : True
DeleteNonCalendarItems             : True
TentativePendingApproval           : True
EnableResponseDetails              : True
OrganizerInfo                      : True
ResourceDelegates                  : {}
RequestOutOfPolicy                 : {VIPs, Mark Arnold, Laura Hunter}
AllRequestOutOfPolicy              : False
BookInPolicy                       : {Somorita Executives}
AllBookInPolicy                    : False
RequestInPolicy                    : {Somorita Sales and Marketing}
AllRequestInPolicy                 : False
AddAdditionalResponse              : True
AdditionalResponse                 : <DIV><FONT face=Tahoma size=2>
You have booked Conference Room 2115 in the Honolulu Office
</FONT></DIV><DIV><FONT face=tahoma size=2>Please contact Sue Mosher
at x5462, Brian Tirch at x4821, or Chris Eanes at x4813 for more
information.</FONT></DIV><DIV><FONT face=tahoma size=2>Catering for
this room can be arranged through Julie Samante at x8821.</FONT></DIV>
RemoveOldMeetingMessages           : True
AddNewRequestsTentatively          : True
ProcessExternalMeetingMessages     : False
DefaultReminderTime                : 15
RemoveForwardedMeetingNotifications : False
Identity                           : volcanosurfboards.com/Resources/
Conference Room - Honolulu - Room 2115
```

AUTOMATIC PROCESSING: *AUTOUPDATE* VERSUS *AUTOACCEPT*

The property that actually enables the automatic processing of resource booking requests is the AutomateProcessing property. The default is AutoUpdate; if the automatic processing settings are set to AutoUpdate, the schedule requests are processed by the Calendar Attendant functions. This means that schedule requests are automatically placed on the calendar, but not within the boundaries of any policy. No automatic responses are sent out to the requester.

If the AutomateProcessing option is set to AutoAccept, this enables the Resource Booking Attendant features. Schedule requests for the resource are handled within the boundaries of the resource booking policy (who can request the resource, recurring requests, and so on). If a request is sent to this resource and is not within the limits set by the resource policy, a message is sent to the user that can provide additional information. To use the new booking attendant features, you need to set this option to AutoAccept.

Let's say that you want to configure another conference room resource mailbox so that it automatically accepts booking requests but only allows automatic processing for members of the Somorita Executives group. The following command will perform this task for the conference room whose alias is ConfRoom1002:

```
Set-MailboxCalendarSettings "ConfrRoom1002" -AutomateProcessing:AutoAccept↵
-BookInPolicy:("Somorita Executives")
```

If you wanted to enable automatic booking for all conference room resources in the entire organization and allow for the default booking policy (everyone can automatically schedule an available resource), you would use the Get-Mailbox, Where-Object, and Set-MailboxCalendarSettings cmdlets:

```
Get-Mailbox | Where-Object {$_.IsResource -eq "True"}↵
| Set-MailboxCalendarSettings -AutomateProcessing:AutoAccept
```

I mentioned earlier that if you want to configure delegates for a resource, they must be defined using the EMS cmdlet Set-MailboxCalendarSettings. For example, if you want to assign user Simon.Butler as a delegate of this mailbox, you would type the following command:

```
Set-MailboxCalendarSettings "Conference Room 1103" -ResourceDelegates Simon.↵
Bulter
```

SETTING READ PERMISSIONS ON A RESOURCE CALENDAR

Some organizations like to set read permissions to a resource calendar for all users so the users can see what is open; this has to be done from Outlook because the Set-MailboxCalendarSettings will not assign the necessary rights.

CONVERTING EXISTING RESOURCE MAILBOXES

If you are migrating from Exchange 2000 or 2003 to Exchange Server 2007 and you have a resource mailbox, even after you move the mailbox to an Exchange 2007 Mailbox server, it is still just a mailbox. The Exchange Server management tools are not smart enough to look at the name of a resource and "auto-magically" convert it to a resource mailbox if it looks like a resource mailbox. If you are migrating resource mailboxes to Exchange 2007 and you want the resources to be listed properly in the All Rooms address list and you want to use the resource booking features of Exchange 2007, you will need to do a few things:

1. Document all of the resource mailboxes in your organization.

2. Move the resource mailboxes to an Exchange 2007 Mailbox server.

3. Use the EMS to convert the mailbox to a resource mailbox.

4. Configure a resource booking policy for each resource.

The actual mechanics of converting the mailbox from a generic user mailbox to a resource mailbox are pretty simple. While the mailbox is located on Exchange 2000/2003, its recipient type is set to Legacy Mailbox; however, when it is moved to an Exchange 2007 Mailbox server, it is just a regular old, boring user mailbox. If you enable the user account and try to view the Resource Settings options in Outlook Web Access, you will not see that choice under Options.

Next, the mailbox needs to be converted to a resource mailbox. At the EMS prompt, use the `Set-Mailbox` cmdlet with the `-Type:Room` or `-Type:Equipment` option. Here is an example of converting a mailbox to a room resource mailbox:

```
Set-Mailbox "SFOConfRoom901A" -Type:Room
```

This is a pretty simple command, but the `Set-Mailbox` cmdlet did a number of things in the background that you did not even have to specify in the command-line options. Here is what actually got changed:

- The user account was disabled (yes, that is annoying, but that is what happens).
- The `IsResource` property was set to `True`.
- The `ResourceType` property was set to `Room` (or `Equipment` if you used that option).
- The `RecipientTypeDetails` property was set to `RoomMailbox`.
- The `AddressListMembership` property was updated to include membership in the All Rooms address list.
- The `AutomateProcessing` property was set to `AutoUpdate`, which is handled by the Calendar Attendant.

Moving Mailboxes

Moving mailboxes from one mailbox database to another is a pretty common task for most Exchange administrators. Often mailbox databases need to be "smoothed out" because too many large mailboxes are created on a single mailbox database. You may also need to decommission a server and thus move all of the mailboxes off of that server.

Mailboxes should usually be moved after a user's work hours. The mailbox can be moved while the user is working in it, but at the end of the move the user will be informed that he must close and reopen Outlook.

Consequently, I recommend that you move mailboxes during off-hours to minimize disruption to users; a user can leave Outlook open while the mailbox is being moved, though.

Mailbox move operations are certainly not instantaneous and can be quite lengthy depending on a number of factors, including bandwidth between servers, server speed, available RAM, and disk I/O. For typical servers on LAN-speed network segments, I estimate you can move from 500MB per hour to 1.5GB per hour. Your results may vary. Depending on your Active Directory infrastructure and replication times, Outlook Web Access users might not be able to reconnect to their mailboxes for up to 15 minutes because the home mailbox server attribute must replicate to all domain controllers.

As with all Exchange management tasks, you can perform move mailbox operations using the Exchange Management Console or the Exchange Management Shell.

MOVING MAILBOXES USING THE EXCHANGE MANAGEMENT CONSOLE

Mailboxes can be moved via the GUI using the Exchange Management Console (EMC). To move mailboxes using the EMC, open up the Recipient Configuration work center of the EMC and select the Mailboxes subcontainer. From within here, you can select one or more mailboxes and then select the Move Mailbox task from the Actions pane.

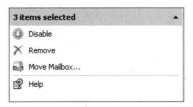

This launches the Move Mailbox Wizard. An experienced Exchange 2000/2003 administrator will recognize most of the options in the wizard. The most important is found on the Introduction page (see Figure 11.40). From the Introduction page you define the destination for the mailboxes you are about to move. This includes the server, storage group, and mailbox database; you must select the mailbox database from a browse list and this will automatically determine the correct server name and storage group name.

FIGURE 11.40
Defining the destination mailbox database

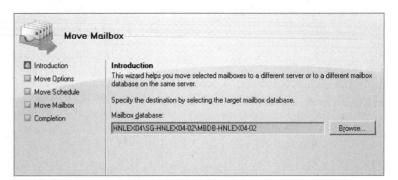

Once you have selected the destination mailbox database and clicked Next, the Move Options Wizard page is displayed. (See Figure 11.41.) On this screen you can specify whether or not to ignore corrupted messages. You can also manually specify a domain controller and global catalog server on this screen of the Move Mailbox Wizard.

Normally mailboxes don't have corrupted messages (otherwise your telephone will be ringing), but occasionally the properties of a message get corrupted. If a mailbox has more than the maximum number of corrupted messages specified, that particular mailbox will be skipped.

On the next page of the wizard are the Move Schedule options. From the Move Schedule page you can define whether the move operation starts immediately or at some point in the future. The Cancel Tasks That Are Still Running After (Hours) option allows you to specify that mailboxes that have not yet been moved after the number of hours specified will not be processed. In the options shown in the following screen shot, I have selected that mailbox moves will not start until 10:21 in the evening and will run for a maximum of 8 hours (if not completed prior to this).

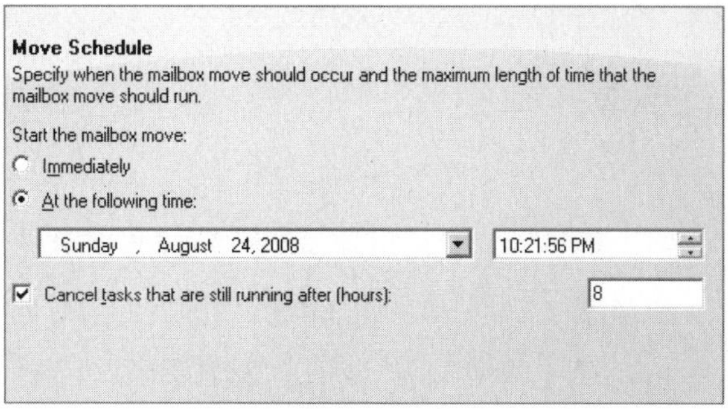

Move Schedule
Specify when the mailbox move should occur and the maximum length of time that the mailbox move should run.

Start the mailbox move:

○ Immediately

⦿ At the following time:

Sunday , August 24, 2008 ▾   10:21:56 PM ⇅

☑ Cancel tasks that are still running after (hours): 8

FIGURE 11.41
Options for moving a mailbox

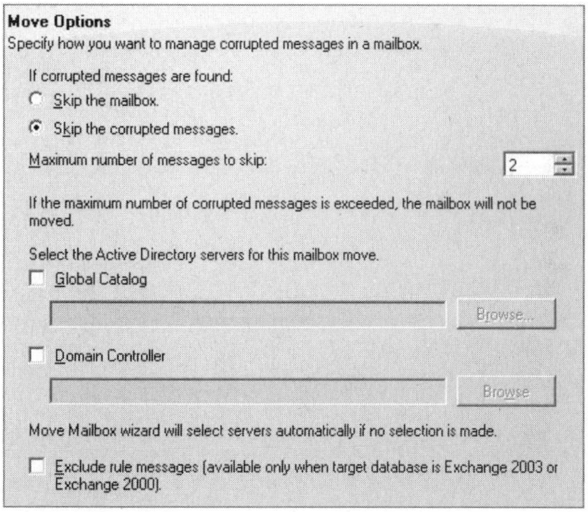

Move Options
Specify how you want to manage corrupted messages in a mailbox.

If corrupted messages are found:

○ Skip the mailbox.

⦿ Skip the corrupted messages.

Maximum number of messages to skip: 2 ⇅

If the maximum number of corrupted messages is exceeded, the mailbox will not be moved.

Select the Active Directory servers for this mailbox move.

☐ Global Catalog

[   ] Browse...

☐ Domain Controller

[   ] Browse...

Move Mailbox wizard will select servers automatically if no selection is made.

☐ Exclude rule messages (available only when target database is Exchange 2003 or Exchange 2000).

The next page is a confirmation page that allows you to review the mailboxes you are about to move as well as the destination server, storage group, and mailbox database. When you are confident you are moving all of the mailboxes you are supposed to move, you can click the Next button.

After you click the Next button, the move mailbox operation will begin. The move mailbox task will move up to four mailboxes simultaneously. When moving mailboxes using the GUI, you see animated status bars indicating that the operation is still in progress as well as the elapsed time. An example of this status information is shown in Figure 11.42, where you can see completed mailbox moves as well as mailbox moves that are still in progress.

After all of the mailboxes have been moved, the final screen shows you a summary of which mailboxes were moved, the total elapsed time, and any other relevant statistics. As with many other wizards in the EMC, the actual Exchange Management Shell (EMS) command that was necessary to move the mailbox is included in the report. In the following screen capture I have collapsed a few of the trident controls so that you can see more of the summary page. Notice for mailbox David Elfassy the EMS cmdlet `Move-Mailbox` and the parameters that were used to move the mailbox. (See Figure 11.43.)

If you want to keep a copy of the move mailbox report, you can use the Ctrl+C keyboard combination to copy the information on the Completion page to the Clipboard. When you are finished with the Completion page, just click Finish to close it.

FIGURE 11.42
Move Mailbox
operations

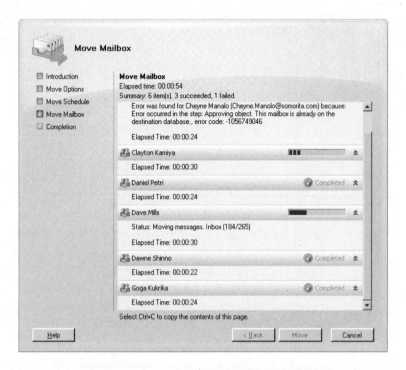

FIGURE 11.43
Move Mailbox
Completion report

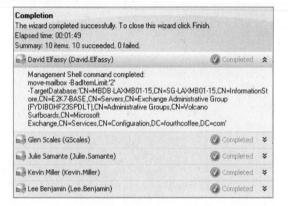

MOVING MAILBOXES USING THE EXCHANGE MANAGEMENT SHELL

I have just showed you how easy it is to move mailboxes using the EMC; you just select the mailbox you want to move and click Next through the wizard to specify any other options, and then the EMC generates the necessary cmdlet to move the mailbox or mailboxes selected. In the previous example, one of the mailboxes moved belonged to a user named David Elfassy. I decided that his mailbox should be moved to a mailbox database called MBDB-LAXMB01-15 in a storage group called SG-LAXMB01-15 and on a server called E2K7-BASE. The EMS generated the following command parameters for the `Move-Mailbox` cmdlet:

```
Move-Mailbox -BadItemLimit:'2' -TargetDatabase:'CN=MBDB-LAXMB01-15,↵
CN=SG-LAXMB01-15,CN=InformationStore,CN=E2K7-BASE,↵
CN=Servers,CN=Exchange Administrative Group (FYDIBOHF23SPDLT),↵
CN=Administrative Groups,CN=Volcano Surfboards,CN=Microsoft↵
Exchange,CN=Services,CN=Configuration,DC=fourthcoffee,DC=com'
```

Notice that the actual object to be moved was not included in the cmdlet; the way that the object information was passed to the `Move-Mailbox` cmdlet made this unnecessary. From the EMS, you can shorten this command quite a bit if the target database name (MBDB-LAXMB01-15) is unique across the organization. You could type the following and see the following output:

```
Move-Mailbox david.elfassy -TargetDatabase "mbdb-laxmb01-15"
Confirm
Are you sure you want to perform this action?
Moving mailbox: David Elfassy (David.Elfassy@volcanosurfboards.com) to
    Database:
E2K7-BASE\SG-LAXMB01-15\MBDB-LAXMB01-15. The operation can take a long time and the
mailbox will be inaccessible until the move is complete [Y] Yes  [A] Yes to All
[N] No  [L] No to All  [S] Suspend  [?] Help (default is "Y"): y
Identity                         : fourthcoffee.com/Corporate/David Elfassy
DistinguishedName                : CN=David Elfassy,OU=Corporate,
DC=fourthcoffee,DC=com
DisplayName                      : David Elfassy
Alias                            : David.Elfassy
LegacyExchangeDN                 : /o=Volcano Surfboards/ou=Exchange
Administrative Group (FYDIBOHF23SPDLT)/cn=Recipients/cn=David.Elfassy
PrimarySmtpAddress               : David.Elfassy@volcanosurfboards.com
SourceServer                     : E2K7-Base.fourthcoffee.com
SourceDatabase                   : E2K7-BASE\First Storage
    Group\Executives
SourceGlobalCatalog              : E2K7-Base.fourthcoffee.com
TargetGlobalCatalog              : E2K7-Base.fourthcoffee.com
TargetDomainController           : E2K7-Base.fourthcoffee.com
TargetMailbox                    :
TargetServer                     : E2K7-Base.fourthcoffee.com
TargetDatabase                   : E2K7-BASE\SG-LAXMB01-15\MBDB-LAXMB01-15
MailboxSize                      : 11KB
IsResourceMailbox                : False
SIDUsedInMatch                   :
SMTPProxies                      :
SourceManager                    :
SourceDirectReports              :
SourcePublicDelegates            :
```

```
SourcePublicDelegatesBL         :
MatchedTargetNTAccountDN        :
IsMatchedNTAccountMailboxEnabled :
MatchedContactsDNList           :
TargetNTAccountDNToCreate       :
TargetManager                   :
TargetDirectReports             :
TargetPublicDelegates           :
TargetPublicDelegatesBL         :
Options                         : Default
SourceForestCredential          :
TargetForestCredential          :
TargetFolder                    :
RsgMailboxGuid                  :
RsgMailboxLegacyExchangeDN      :
RsgMailboxDisplayName           :
RsgDatabaseGuid                 :
MoveType                        : IntraOrg
MoveStage                       : Completed
StartTime                       : 11/12/2006 4:02:41 PM
EndTime                         : 11/12/2006 4:03:03 PM
StatusCode                      : 0
StatusMessage                   : This mailbox has been moved to the
  target database.
```

If you wanted to include the bad item count, you could include the parameter -BadItemLimit:'2' in the command. Notice that this cmdlet asks you to confirm that you want the mailbox to be moved. To avoid the confirmation prompt, you can include in the command line -Confirm:$False and the cmdlet will not prompt you. So that command line would look like this:

```
Move-Mailbox david.elfassy -TargetDatabase "mbdb-1axmb01-15"↵
-Confirm:$False -BadItemLimit:"2"
```

A few other tricks may prove useful for you when you are using the Move-Mailbox cmdlet. Let's look at a couple of quick examples. In this first example, you want to move everyone that is a member of the Executives group to the mailbox database called Executives on the server E2K7MB01. You would type this command, which uses the Get-DistributionGroupMember cmdlet to enumerate the membership of the Executives group, and pipes that output to the Move-Mailbox cmdlet:

```
Get-DistributionGroupMember "Executives" | Move-Mailbox↵
-TargetDatabase "E2K7MB01\Executives" -Confirm:$False
```

Another useful set of cmdlets enumerates everyone whose mailbox is located on one mailbox database and then moves them to another database. You need to use the Get-Mailbox cmdlet and narrow down the scope of the search using the Where cmdlet so that you only output the objects for mailboxes located on a specific database:

```
Get-Mailbox | Where {$_.database -like "E2K7-Base\VIP\VIP Mailboxes"}↵
| Move-Mailbox -TargetDatabase "Executives" -Confirm:$False
```

With a little creativity, you can probably figure out a number of other ways to accomplish this task or tasks similar to this.

The EMC will move a maximum of four mailboxes at a time. However, the `Move-Mailbox` cmdlet has a -MaxThreads option that will allow you to set values as high as 30. This will allow `Move-Mailbox` to move more than four mailboxes at a time, provided your system can support the processor load, disk I/O load, and the increased network throughput. See `http://technet.microsoft.com/en-us/library/aa997599.aspx` for more information.

Retrieving Mailbox Statistics

Frequently Exchange mailbox administrators need to run a report and list the amount of storage that each mailbox is consuming. With previous versions of Exchange, this information was available via the GUI, but now it is available via the EMS cmdlet `Get-MailboxStatistics`. Here is an example of using this cmdlet without any parameters:

```
Get-MailboxStatistics

DisplayName                 ItemCount StorageLimitStatus  LastLogonTime
-----------                 --------- ------------------  -------------
Microsoft System Attendant  0         BelowLimit          11/11/2006 2:10:23 PM
Kevin Miller                6                             10/24/2006 2:40:31 AM
Suriya Supatanasakul        3                             10/24/2006 2:40:31 AM
Micah Hoffmann              2         BelowLimit          10/24/2006 2:42:06 AM
Andy David                  2         BelowLimit          10/24/2006 2:40:30 AM
Jenn Long                   10        BelowLimit          10/24/2006 2:40:31 AM
SystemMailbox{F4A7C474-FE   402       BelowLimit
E5-46EA-A886-C1D8393E27F}
```

Not a real attractive report, is it? And this report includes all mailboxes, including the system mailbox and system attendant mailboxes. If you don't use the -Server or -Database parameters, `Get-MailboxStatistics` will pull mailbox statistics only from the local server. I will show you how to exclude these from the report as well as provide more useful information. There are a few useful properties that are part of the objects that output when you use the `Get-MailboxStatistcs` cmdlet. These can be used to constrain the output that is sent to the screen (or a file) as well as the output if you redirect this information to a file. Table 11.5 shows some of the properties of the objects that are output when you use the `Get-MailboxStatistcs` cmdlet.

So, perhaps you only want to look at a mailbox report that includes the display name, total size of the mailbox, the total number of items, and the storage limit status. Further, you can also include the where clause and filter out any mailbox whose name contains the word *system*. The following example shows what this would look like:

```
Get-MailboxStatistics | where {$_.displayname -notlike "*System*"}↵
| FT displayname, @{expression={$_.totalitemsize.value.ToKB()};↵
width=20;label="Mailbox Size(kb)"},ItemCount,StorageLimitStatus

DisplayName     Mailbox Size(kb)    ItemCount StorageLimitStatus
-----------     ----------------    --------- ------------------

Lee Desmond          331221            1410    IssueWarning
EQUIP - Panas...         10               3    BelowLimit
Finance Journ...          3               1    BelowLimit
```

```
Elizabeth Owusu      958376      84325      MailboxDisabled
Damion Jones             10          3      BelowLimit
Andy Schan            21468       3112      BelowLimit
Paul Robichaux           5          2      BelowLimit
David Elfassy        183714       8713      ProhibitSend
Conference Ro...        375         72      BelowLimit
Andy Webb            539985      47444      IssueWarning
Manfred Estrada       83837        163      BelowLimit
Devin Ganger          7548         94      BelowLimit
```

TABLE 11.5:   Properties of Objects Output Using Get-MailboxStatistics

PROPERTY	DESCRIPTION
DisplayName	Name of the mailbox.
ItemCount	Total number of items stored in the entire mailbox.
TotalItemSize	Total size of all of the items in the mailbox except for items in the deleted item cache.
TotalDeletedItemsSize	Total size of items that are in the deleted item cache.
StorageLimitStatus	Status of the mailbox storage limits; the limits you may see are as follows:
	– BelowLimit – Mailbox is below all limits.
	– IssueWarning – Mailbox storage is above the issue warning limit.
	– ProhibitSend – Mailbox is above the prohibit send limit.
	– MailboxDisabled – Mailbox is over the prohibit send and receive limit.
Database	Name of the database on which the mailbox is located in the format of *ServerName\StorageGroupName\DatabaseName*, such as E2K7MB01\VIP SG\VIP Mailboxes.
ServerName	Name of the mailbox server.
LastLogoffTime	Date and time of the last time someone logged off of the mailbox.
LastLogonTime	Date and time of the last time someone logged on to the mailbox.
LastLoggedOnUserAccount	Domain name and username of the last person to access the mailbox.
DisconnectDate	Date and time when the mailbox was deleted or disconnected.

Did you notice that I threw in some new features of PowerShell? This includes taking the output and reformatting it using the Expression feature.

You can redirect the output to a text file using the > character and a filename:

```
Get-MailboxStatistics | where {$_.displayname -notlike "*System*"}↵
| FT displayname, @{expression={$_.totalitemsize.value.ToKB()};↵
width=20;label="Mailbox Size(kb)"},ItemCount,StorageLimitStatus↵
> c:\MailboxReport.txt
```

You could also pipe the output to either the Export-Csv or Export-Clixml cmdlet and send the data to a comma-separated value or XML file. Take a look at Chapter 8, "Exchange Management Shell Primer," for more detailed examples of how to "tune" the output of the Get-MailboxStatistics.

Deleting Mailboxes

Deleting mailboxes might not seem like such a complicated task until you look at the Actions pane once you have selected a mailbox in the Recipient Configuration work center. There are a couple of options with respect to deleting a mailbox, including simply disconnecting the mailbox from a user account, deleting both the account and the mailbox, and purging a previously deleted mailbox.

In the section of the Actions pane that reflects the mailbox that is currently selected in the Results pane, you will see both a Disable and a Remove option.

Both the Remove and the Disable options will delete the mailbox; it's just how they go about doing it that is the difference. The Disable option deletes the mailbox but not the user. The Remove option deletes both the mailbox and the user.

DELETING THE MAILBOX BUT NOT THE USER

If you choose the Disable option, the mailbox is disconnected from the user account but the user account remains in the Active Directory. This is the equivalent of using the EMS cmdlet Disable-Mailbox. For example, to remove a mailbox from an existing user, you could type this:

```
Disable-Mailbox Damion.Jones -Confirm $False
```

All this does is disconnect the mailbox from the user account; the user account remains in the Active Directory. After the deleted mailbox recovery time expires, the mailbox will be permanently removed from the mailbox database.

DELETING BOTH THE USER AND THE MAILBOX

If you choose the Remove option, the mailbox is disconnected from the user account *and* the user account is deleted from the Active Directory. You can also accomplish this from the EMS using the Remove-Mailbox cmdlet. Here is an example:

```
Remove-Mailbox Cheyne.Manalo
```

This command will prompt you to specify that you really want to remove the mailbox; you can avoid the confirmation prompt by including the -Confirm $False parameter. If you want to delete the mailbox and the account and prevent the mailbox from being recovered, you can include the -Permanent $True parameter. Here is another example that automatically confirms the deletion and permanently removes the mailbox:

```
Remove-Mailbox Jonathan.Long -Permanent:$True -Confirm $False
```

PERMANENTLY PURGING A MAILBOX

By default, after the deleted mailbox recovery time has expired, the mailbox will be permanently purged from the mailbox database. If you have already deleted the mailbox and want to permanently purge the mailbox from the mailbox database, you can also do that, but it requires two lines. The first line is going to set a variable ($Temp) that retrieves the mailbox object for a mailbox whose display name is Martha Lanoza. The second line uses that variable along with the MailboxGuid property of that mailbox to remove that mailbox from the VIP Mailboxes database. Here are the two commands that would need to be executed:

```
$Temp = Get-MailboxStatistics | Where {$_.DisplayName -eq 'Martha Lanoza'}
Remove-Mailbox -Database "VIP Mailboxes" -StoreMailboxIdentity $Temp.MailboxGuid
```

This example assumes there would only be a single mailbox whose display name is Martha Lanoza and that there is only a single mailbox database named VIP Mailboxes. With a little creativity, you can permanently purge mailboxes in other ways, but this is a very basic EMS method of doing this.

Reconnecting a Deleted Mailbox

Exchange Server allows you to "undelete" a mailbox that you may have accidentally disconnected from a user account. The simplest way to do this is to use the EMC, but you can also do it using the EMS.

RECONNECTING A MAILBOX USING THE EMC

In the Recipient Configuration work center you will find the Disconnected Mailbox subcontainer (shown in Figure 11.44).

Click the Connect to Server task in the Actions pane to see a mailbox listing; otherwise, deleted mailboxes may not show up in the Results pane.

The disconnected mailbox listing you see in Figure 11.44 is a list of the mailboxes on the mailbox server to which you are currently connected. You can view other mailbox servers by choosing the Connect to Server option in the Actions pane.

You could generate the same list using the Get-MailboxStatics command and filter based on viewing only objects whose DisconnectDate property contains data:

```
Get-MailboxStatistics | Where {$_.DisconnectDate -ne $null}↵
| Format-Table DisplayName,DisconnectDate
```

```
DisplayName          DisconnectDate
-----------          --------------
Micah Hoffmann       12/10/2006 3:13:37 AM
David Elfassy        12/02/2006 3:13:23 AM
Paul Agamata         11/25/2006 3:13:55 AM
Brian Tirch          11/20/2006 3:13:47 AM
Clayton Kamiya       11/16/2006 3:13:01 AM
```

FIGURE 11.44
Reconnecting mailboxes that have been deleted

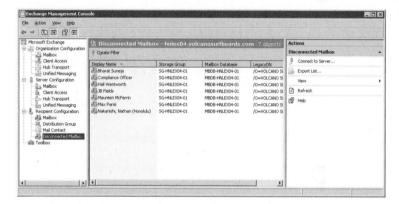

If you have removed one of these mailboxes from its user account accidentally, you can still reconnect it back to a user account. In the EMC's Disconnected Mailbox subcontainer, highlight the mailbox that you want to reconnect and choose the Connect task on the Actions pane. This will launch the Connect Mailbox Wizard (shown in Figure 11.45); the main page of the Connect Mailbox Wizard looks a lot like the main page of the New Mailbox Wizard.

FORCING A MAILBOX TO DISCONNECT

If a mailbox was deleted after the cleanup process has been run, it will not show up in the list of disconnected mailboxes. You may have to force Exchange to realize that the mailbox and its corresponding Active Directory user account have been disconnected. You can do this with the `Clean-MailboxDatabase` cmdlet.

From the Connect Mailbox Introduction screen you are asked what type of mailbox you are connecting. Choices include a user mailbox, room resource mailbox, equipment resource mailbox, and a linked mailbox.

Deleted mailboxes can only be connected to a user account that does not have a mailbox already associated with it.

On the Mailbox Settings page of the Connect Mailbox Wizard (shown in Figure 11.46), you must select the user account to which you want to connect this mailbox. The user account must not already have a mailbox associated with it. There are two different ways that you can locate the user account. If you choose the Matching User radio button and then click the Browse button, the EMC will make its "best guess" at finding the right user account in the Active Directory.

If you choose the Existing User radio button and then click the Browse button, you will be presented with a browse list of all users in the Active Directory. This list will include users that have been mailbox-enabled and those that do not have mailboxes. If you select a user that already has a mailbox, you will see an error message.

FIGURE 11.45
Starting the Connect
Mailbox Wizard

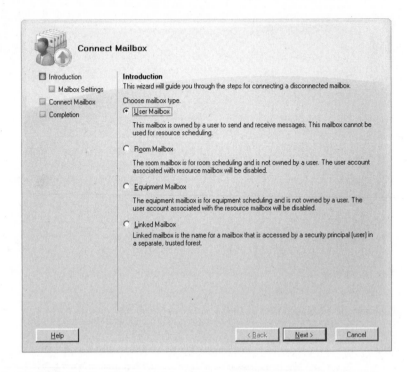

FIGURE 11.46
Mailbox Settings page
of the Connect Mailbox
Wizard

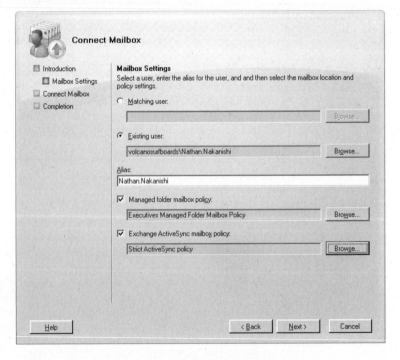

Regardless of whether you use the Matching User or the Existing User selection, the Exchange Alias value will be displayed and you can override it if necessary.

Note that you may also specify a managed folder mailbox policy and an ActiveSync policy for this mailbox. These can always be assigned later, but you have the option of reassigning them at the time when you are reconnecting the mailbox to the account. Remember that if you assign a managed folder mailbox policy you will be reminded that clients older than Outlook 2007 will not support all features of managed folder policies.

RECONNECTING A MAILBOX USING THE EMS

To reconnect a deleted mailbox using the EMS, you use the `Connect-Mailbox` cmdlet. This cmdlet takes as an identifier for the mailbox you are trying to connect to using the unique mailbox GUID, the display name, or the legacy Exchange distinguished name. The display name of the mailbox is by far the easiest to use. You also must provide the name of the database on which the mailbox is located and the user account to which you are connecting the account.

Before you do this, let's take a quick look at another iteration of the `Get-MailboxStatistics` cmdlet and how to enumerate the information you need to reconnect a mailbox. This output is displaying just the database name and the display name:

```
Get-MailboxStatistics | Where {$_.DisconnectDate -ne $null}↵
| Format-Table DisplayName,Database

DisplayName                    Database
-----------                    --------
Aran Hoffmann                  E2K7-BASE\VIPs SG\VIPs
Paul Agamata                   E2K7-BASE\Execs SG\Executives
Donny Shimamoto                E2K7-BASE\Execs SG\Executives
Clayton Kamiya                 E2K7-BASE\Execs SG\Executives
```

Let's say you have accidentally deleted user Clayton Kamiya's mailbox from the Executives mailbox database; this user also had a managed folder policy and an ActiveSync policy. To reconnect this user's mailbox to user account `volcanosurf\Clayton.Kamiya`, here is the command you would execute:

```
Connect-Mailbox "Clayton Kamiya" -Database:"Executives"↵
-User:"volcanosurf\Clayton.Kamiya" -Alias:"Clayton.Kamiya"↵
-MobileMailboxPolicy:"Standard User ActiveSync Policy"↵
-ManagedFolderMailboxPolicy:"All Employees"
```

In the previous section where I used the EMC to connect the mailbox back to the user, the `Connect-Mailbox` command was a bit more complex, but this is done to ensure uniqueness when a mailbox is being connected. Here is the command that was executed by the EMC:

```
Connect-Mailbox -Identity '5b6f9e40-aedf-4024-83a3-21a3b24997b1'↵
-Database 'hnlex04.volcanosurfboards.com\SG-HNLEX04-01\MBDB-HNLEX04-01'↵
-User 'volcanosurfboards\Nathan.Nakanishi' -Alias 'Nathan.Nakanishi'↵
-ManagedFolderMailboxPolicy 'Executives Managed Folder Mailbox Policy'↵
-ActiveSyncMailboxPolicy 'Strict ActiveSync policy'
```

Bulk Manipulation of Mailboxes Using the EMS

Probably the most useful feature of the PowerShell and the EMS is the ability to perform bulk manipulation of objects. Let's say I want to do something like turn off OWA for all users. This is set using the `Set-CASMailbox` cmdlet, not `Set-Mailbox`. I could do this with a one-liner, though, by retrieving a list of all mailboxes in the organization and then piping each mailbox to the `Set-CASMailbox` cmdlet. Here is one way to do this:

```
Get-Mailbox | Set-CASMailbox -OWAEnabled:$False
```

Does this look powerful? Does this look dangerous? I say yes on both counts. You can very easily do something you did not intend to do, so take great care when using the EMS if you are performing any type of bulk administration.

You are probably not interested in making mass changes to every mailbox or user account in your organization, at least not usually. That is why group membership comes in so handy. A few cmdlets are useful when it comes to using the membership of a group. The `Get-DistributionGroup` cmdlet will list all of the distribution groups in the organization, but it does not provide you with a membership list:

```
Get-DistributionGroup
```

Name	DisplayName	GroupType	PrimarySmtpAddress
$Operations Group	$Operations Group	Global, Security...	OperationsGroup@...
$Executives and ...	$Executives and ...	Global, Security...	ExecutivesandVIP...
DirectoryUpdateS...	!Directory Updat...	Universal	DirectoryUpdateS...
Executives	Executives	Universal	Executives@somor...
VIPs	VIPs	Universal, Secur...	VIPs@somorita.com
Somorita Executives	Somorita Executives	Universal, Secur...	SomoritaExecutiv...
Somorita Sales a...	Somorita Sales a...	Universal, Secur...	SomoritaSalesand...

To retrieve a list of objects that are members of a distribution group, you need the `Get-DistributionGroupMember` cmdlet. Here is the output (remember that this is not actually text within the PowerShell environment; these are unique objects that can be piped as input to another cmdlet):

```
Get-DistributionGroupMember "Executives"
```

Name	RecipientType
Goga Kukrika	UserMailbox
Pavel Nagaev	UserMailbox
Ryan Tung	UserMailbox
George Cue	UserMailbox
Chris Eanes	UserMailbox
Bthaworn Thaweeaphiradeemaitree	UserMailbox
Jason Sherry	UserMailbox

Do you remember a cmdlet I used to override the mailbox quotas for one mailbox? Well, let's expand on that and set that quota for all members of the Executives group. Here is an example:

```
Get-DistributionGroupMember "Executives" | Set-Mailbox↵
 -UseDatabaseQuotaDefaults:$False -IssueWarningQuota:200MB↵
 -ProhibitSendQuota:250MB -ProhibitSendReceiveQuota:300MB
```

This cmdlet retrieves the membership list for the Executives distribution group and then passes those objects as input to the `Set-Mailbox` cmdlet.

How about another common task? Let's say I need to move all of the mailboxes in the Executives group to a mailbox database called Executives. Here is the command to do that:

```
Get-DistributionGroupMember "Executives" | move-mailbox -BadItemLimit:2↵
 -TargetDatabase:Executives
```

I could extend that and move all mailboxes on a specific server by using the `-Server` option of the `Get-Mailbox` cmdlet to help me narrow my listing of mailboxes:

```
Get-Mailbox -Server:HNLEX04 | Move-Mailbox -TargetDatabase:HNLEX05\Executives
```

What if you only want to move the mailboxes on a specific database? Here is another example:

```
Get-Mailbox | Where {$_.database -like "HNLEX03\VIP\VIP Mailboxes"}↵
 | Move-Mailbox -TargetDatabase "HNLEX05\Executives" -Confirm:$False
```

With a little creativity, you can probably figure out a number of other ways to accomplish this or similar tasks.

Scripting Account Creation

In some organizations, many accounts are created at one time. The EMS and PowerShell give you the ability to automate this by reading the data in from a text or CSV file. Though you could probably automate the process if you created a really massive "one-liner," it is much easier to create a simple PowerShell script. First, let's look at a CSV input file of new user accounts:

```
Name,Database,OrganizationalUnit,UserPrincipalName
Saul Tigh,MB-DB1,colonialfleet.int/Military,Saul.Tigh@fleet.int
Helena Cain, MB-DB1,colonialfleet.int/Military,Helena.Cain@fleet.int
Felix Gaeta, MB-DB1,colonialfleet.int/Military,Felix.Gaeta@fleet.int
Tory Foster, MB-DB1,colonialfleet.int/Civilians,Tory.Foster@fleet.int
Tom Zarek,MB-DB1,colonialfleet.int/Civilians,Tom.Zarek@fleet.int
Samuel Anders,MB-DB1,colonialfleet.int/Civilians,Samuel.Anders@fleet.int
Hera Agathon,MB-DB1,colonialfleet.int/Civilians,Hera.Agathon@fleet.int
```

This CSV file has four columns; they represent the absolute minimum columns necessary to create an account and assign it a mailbox. Naturally, in real life you would have more columns (first name, last name, SAM account name, Exchange alias, and so on). Also, the OUs in the Active Directory must exist for these users.

Here is the script for creating these mailboxes:

```
# Read the c:\demo\newaccounts.txt file. The first line is the header line.
# Each additional line represents a user object.
# Read all of these in to the $Users variable.
$Users = Import-Csv C:\Demo\newaccounts.txt
# Output the contents of the $Users variable.
# This command is not necessary as it only outputs the list to the screen.
$Users

# Prompt the person running the script for a password.
# This password will be assigned to each user created.
$Password = Read-Host "Please enter a password for the users" -AsSecureString

# A simple Foreach loop to create the new users
# For each line in the $Users variable, run the New-Mailbox cmdlet.
# $User.Database represents the value of the Database field for the current user.
Foreach ($User in $Users) {
   New-Mailbox -Name $User.Name -Database $User.Database↵
-OrganizationalUnit $User.OrganizationalUnit -UserPrincipalName
$User.UserPrincipalName↵
--Password $Password
   }
```

Managing Mail-Enabled Groups

If your organization is like most organizations today, you make significant use of mail groups. You may refer to these as mail-enabled groups, distribution groups, or distribution lists. The official term for a mail group, though, is *mail-enabled group*. Like mail-enabled users, mail-enabled groups are Active Directory groups, but they have been assigned mail properties. Within the Active Directory, there are two basic types of groups:

Security groups These are groups that can be assigned permissions to resources or rights to perform certain tasks. Security groups can be mail-enabled and be used for addressing mail by Exchange Server recipients.

Distribution groups These are groups that are not security principals; they have no security identifier and thus cannot be assigned any rights or permissions. Distribution groups are intended for use with a mail system that integrates with the Active Directory, such as Exchange Server. There is a subset of distribution groups called a dynamic distribution group (DDG) but you will see these also referred to as a query-based distribution groups (QBDGs). A DDG's membership list is dynamic, based on some criteria the administrator defines.

When you create a new group using the Active Directory Users and Computers interface, you will also notice that you must provide a scope for the group in addition to defining the group type. (See Figure 11.47.)

All groups that will be utilized by Exchange 2007 must be set to the Universal scope. This tells the Active Directory that the membership list attribute for that group should be replicated to all global catalog servers in the organization. In previous versions of Exchange, you could mail-enable a global or domain local group. However, this could cause mail delivery problems in organizations that have multiple Active Directory domains.

FIGURE 11.47
Creating a new group in the Active Directory

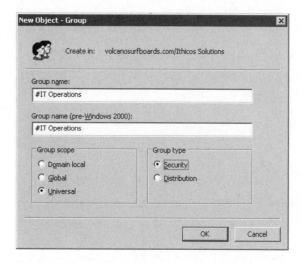

EXCHANGE 2007 AND GLOBAL OR DOMAIN LOCAL GROUPS

In Exchange 2007, by default, the only type of group that you can mail-enable using the Exchange Management Console is a universal group. However, if you have migrated from Exchange 2000/2003, you may have domain local or global groups that were mail-enabled previously. The recipient type for these groups is `MailEnabledNonUniversalGroup`. I recommend that you convert each of these domain local and global groups to a universal group. This will ensure that you do not have group expansion problems in multi-domain environments.

Creating and Managing Mail-Enabled Groups

Let's first go through the process of defining a mail-enabled group and look at the steps necessary to do so. Groups can be created or mail-enabled using the EMC and the EMS command shell. If you are inclined to use the EMC, groups have their own subcontainer called Distribution Group that is found under the Recipient Configuration container. Figure 11.48 shows an example of the Distribution Group container in the EMS.

An important consideration when creating group names is to create a standard for mail-enabled group display names. This will allow them to all be grouped together in the global address list. For example, in Figure 11.48, I have used special characters in front of the group names, mostly to illustrate how these will sort together in the global address list. Pick a standard that will work for your organization and that your users will be able to clearly understand.

USING THE EXCHANGE MANAGEMENT CONSOLE TO MANAGE GROUPS

The simplest way to create and manage mail-enabled groups is to use the EMC graphical interface. Previously, in the Active Directory, I created a group called IT Operations; the group's scope is universal and the type is a security group. However, just using Active Directory Users and Computers will not define any mail attributes.

FIGURE 11.48
Viewing the Distribution Group subcontainer

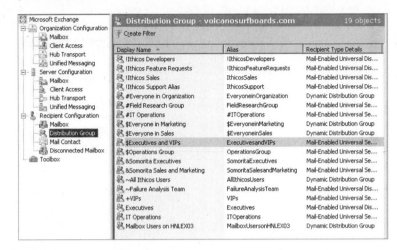

Creating Mail-Enabled Groups

To create a mail-enabled group, open the EMC, navigate to the Recipient Configuration work center, and find the Distribution Group subcontainer. Click the New Distribution Group task in the Actions pane to launch the New Distribution Group Wizard. The first screen in the wizard is the Introduction page, which prompts you to either create a new group or choose an existing group.

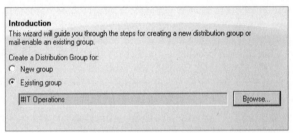

Because the group you want to mail-enable is already in the Active Directory, choose the Existing Group radio button and click the Browse button to locate and select the group. (See Figure 11.49.) The only group types that will appear in the Select Group dialog box will be universal groups that have not already been mail-enabled.

Once you have clicked Next on the Introduction page, the next page you see is the Group Information page (see Figure 11.50). The Group Information page will ask you to provide the display name for the group as well as the alias. By default, the alias is used to define the SMTP e-mail address for the group and should not have any spaces in it.

When you click Next on the Group Information page, you will see the confirmation page that allows you to verify the actions you are about to take. When you are sure that you have defined everything you need to define, you can click the New button and the group you have selected will be mail-enabled.

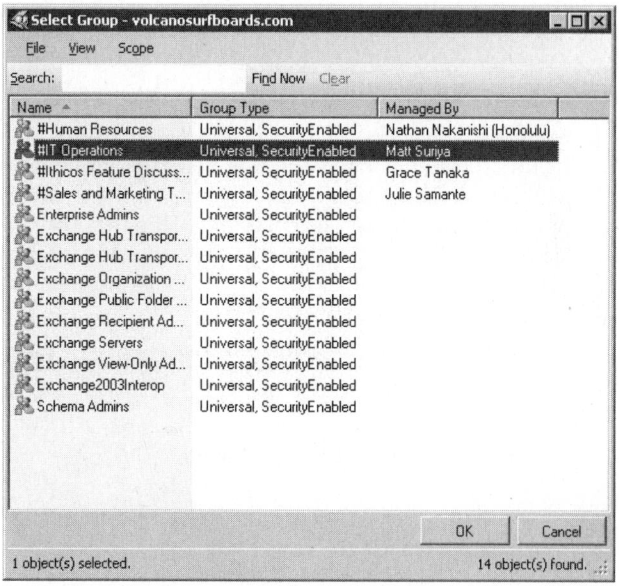

FIGURE 11.49
Selecting a group to mail-enable

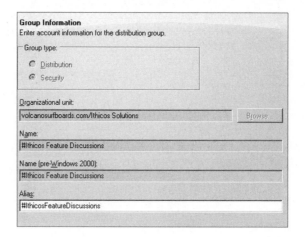

FIGURE 11.50
Entering information about the group

The resulting EMS command that performed the action is as follows:

```
Enable-DistributionGroup -Identity:'fourthcoffee.com/Corporate/IT Operations' ↵
-DisplayName:'IT Operations' -Alias:'IT_Operations'
```

The New Distribution Group Wizard can be used to create new mail-enabled groups as well as to mail-enable existing ones. If you choose to create a new group on the Introduction page, you must provide a few additional pieces of information on the Group Information page, including the group type (Distribution or Security), the OU in which the group will be created, the group's name, the group's pre–Windows 2000 name, the display name, and the alias. The EMS command that is executed uses the New-DistributionGroup cmdlet rather than the Enable-DistributionGroup cmdlet.

Managing Mail-Enabled Groups

You should be aware of some additional properties when you are creating mail-enabled groups. Let's start with the Mail Flow Settings property page. This page includes two components you can configure: Message Size Restrictions and Message Delivery Restrictions.

If you select the Message Size Restrictions option and click the Properties button, you will see the Message Size Restrictions dialog box. Notice that I have restricted the maximum message size for this particular group to 100KB; this can help prevent misuse of distribution groups or the accidental distribution of large files.

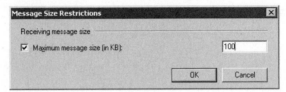

The Message Delivery Restrictions dialog box (shown in Figure 11.51) has a little more information. If you have looked at the message delivery restrictions for a single mailbox, you are already familiar with these settings and concepts. In the example in Figure 11.51, I have restricted who is allowed to send mail to this group. You can specify individuals and other groups. I recommend you always restrict who is allowed to send mail to large groups or groups that contain VIPs. This will help prevent accidents and keep unwanted mail content from your VIPs.

FIGURE 11.51
A distribution group's Message Delivery Restrictions dialog box

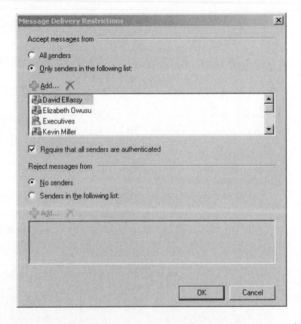

You may also notice the Require That All Senders Are Authenticated check box. For mail-enabled groups, this box is checked by default. I recommend that you keep it set this way;

after all, you probably don't want spammers or external salespeople to start sending mail to your Everyone@company.com or Executives@company.com addresses. However, you will have to uncheck this option if you have specific groups that need to receive e-mail from unauthenticated users.

The E-Mail Addresses property page (Figure 11.52) shows the e-mail addresses that can be used to address a message to the group. You can edit the existing addresses or add new ones.

FIGURE 11.52

E-mail address properties of a mail-enabled group

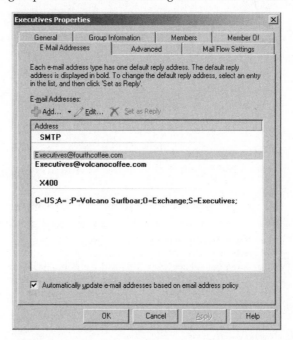

If a distribution list is used entirely within your organization, the Reply To address will not be particularly important. However, if you use lists both internally and externally, keep in mind that the Reply To address is the one that will be seen by people outside the organization. For example, if someone sends a message to your HelpDesk@company.com address and internal users reply to that message and courtesy copy (Cc) the distribution group, the original sender will see the Reply To address of the distribution group.

The final property page I want to take a look at is the Advanced property page. (See Figure 11.53.)

You should be aware of several properties on this page, and you should know what they may mean to your organization and users.

Simple Display Name   By default, when a message is sent from a recipient, the recipient's display name is included; in some organizations the display name can be quite long. Exchange also allows non-ASCII characters (Unicode characters) to be included in the display name. If you are connecting to older mail systems that do not support long display names or Unicode characters, you can include a simple display name that consists only of ASCII characters.

Expansion Server   Message *expansion* is the process of enumerating the members of a mail-enabled group and figuring out where each member is, either within your organization or externally. Expansion of large mail-enabled groups can be a pretty intensive process for a Hub Transport server as well as the Active Directory global catalog server that it is using.

FIGURE 11.53
Advanced properties of
a mail-enabled group

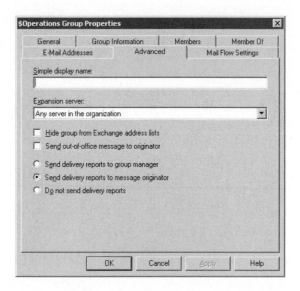

The Expansion Server drop-down list provides you with a listing of all of the Hub Transport servers in your organization. By default, Expansion Server is set to Any Server In The Organization. This means that the first Exchange Hub Transport server receiving the message is responsible either for expanding the mail-enabled group or for sending it on to another Hub Transport server. In some environments, you may want to manually specify which Hub Transport server handles expansion.

For example, if you have a mail-enabled group called Executives, and you know that all members of the Executives group are in the headquarters office, you could designate a Hub Transport server in the headquarters office to be responsible for expansion. But keep in mind that this solution provides no fault tolerance: if that Hub Transport server is down (or taken offline permanently), no other server would be available to handle expansion. I therefore recommend that you keep the default settings and allow Exchange to determine the appropriate place to expand the group's membership.

Hide Group from Exchange Address Lists   This check box (unchecked by default) allows you to prevent a mail-enabled group from being displayed in the address lists. This might be useful for specialized groups that are used just for mail distribution by an automated system or for users that know the SMTP address.

Send Out-of-Office Message To Originator   This check box allows you to specify whether an out-of-office message will be returned to the sender of a message if someone's out-of-office rule is enabled. This option is unchecked by default. For small or departmental mail-enabled groups, it might be useful to turn it on, but for large or company-wide distribution groups, you should probably leave this disabled.

Delivery Reports   If messages are not properly delivered to the intended recipients of a message sent to a mail-enabled group, you can control how the delivery reports are generated. There are three options:

◆   Send Delivery Reports To Group Manager will send the delivery reports to the person listed as the manager on the group's properties.

◆ Send Delivery Reports To Message Originator sends the delivery report back to the message sender.

◆ Do Not Send Delivery Reports prevents delivery reports from being sent to anyone.

Creating Dynamic Distribution Groups

Do you have a problem keeping your distribution groups up-to-date? Dynamic distribution groups (DDGs) may be the answer you have been looking for. Mail is sent to users in a DDG based on one or more criteria, such as organizational unit, city, or department. As a user's Active Directory properties are changed or updated, the DDG membership changes automatically.

DDGs are created a little differently than a regular mail-enabled group because you have to define the filter settings and the conditions of the group. In the Distribution Group subcontainer of the Recipient Configuration work center, you can launch the New Dynamic Distribution Group Wizard by clicking the New Dynamic Distribution Group task in the Actions pane. The Introduction page of the wizard shows some typical information required for creating a new group object. This page requires that you specify the organizational unit in which you want the object created, the display name (Name), and the Exchange alias of the group.

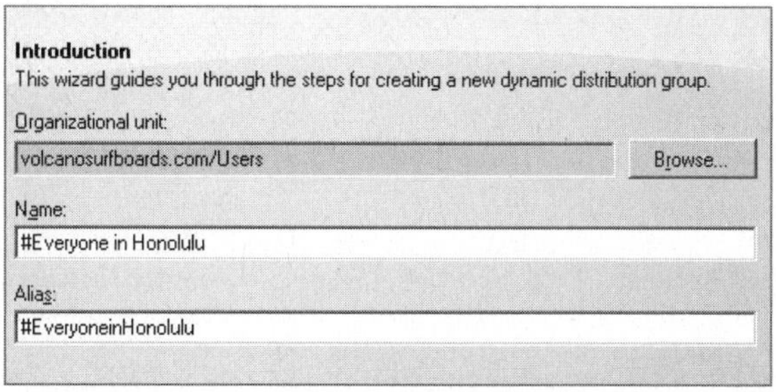

Once you have specified the information necessary on the Introduction page. The next page, Filter Settings (Figure 11.54), allows you to specify which recipient container (or the entire domain) you want to apply to the filter and which types of recipients that you want to display.

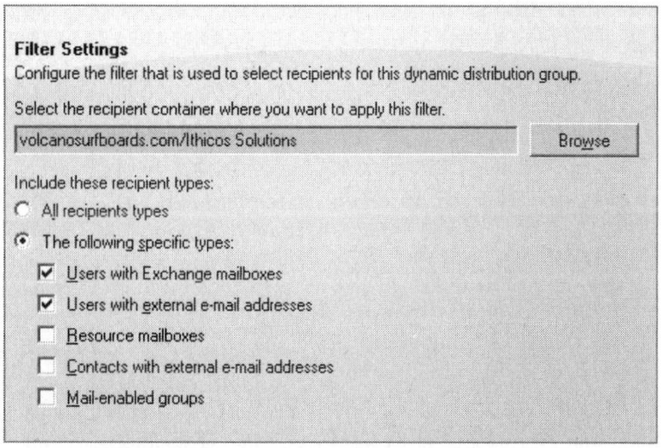

FIGURE 11.54
Filter Settings for a
dynamic distribution
group

The following recipient types can be included in the filter settings:

◆ All Recipients Types

◆ Users With Exchange Mailboxes (mailbox-enabled user accounts)

◆ Users With External E-mail Addresses (mail-enabled user accounts)

◆ Resource Mailboxes (room and equipment)

◆ Contacts With External E-mail Addresses

◆ Mail-enabled Groups

After selecting the recipient type and OU scope for the DDG and clicking Next, you will be able to further refine the scope of the group membership on the Conditions page. In the example shown in Figure 11.55, I have selected all users whose state or province is Hawaii.

FIGURE 11.55
Narrowing the membership of a dynamic distribution group

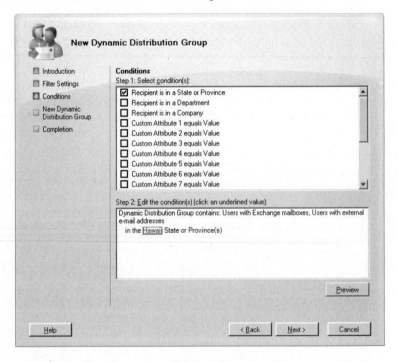

The Conditions page of the DDG allows you to specify the following attributes for inclusion in the DDG:

◆ State or province

◆ Department

◆ Company

◆ Custom attribute 1 through 15

Using DDGs will help emphasize the importance of having accurate and consistent information in the Active Directory. Looking back to the example in Figure 11.55, when the account was created, if there were users who misspelled their state name or used an abbreviation rather than spelling it out, the DDG would not include everyone I wanted it to include.

The Preview button on the Conditions property page is helpful in confirming that your scope and conditions are defined properly. By clicking this button, you will see the Dynamic Distribution Group Preview dialog box (Figure 11.56). From here, you should verify that the membership appears to be what you expected.

FIGURE 11.56

Previewing a dynamic distribution group

The next screen after the Conditions screen is the New Dynamic Distribution Group screen, where you confirm the configuration properties. When you are sure that the properties are correct, click the New button. As with most wizards in the EMC, the Completion screen will include the EMS command that was executed:

```
New-DynamicDistributionGroup -Name '#Everyone in Honolulu'↵
-IncludedRecipients 'MailboxUsers, MailUsers'↵
 -ConditionalStateOrProvince 'Hawaii'↵
 -OrganizationalUnit 'volcanosurfboards.com/Users'↵
 -Alias '#EveryoneinHonolulu'↵
 -RecipientContainer 'volcanosurfboards.com/Ithicos Solutions'
```

For existing DDGs, you can edit or redefine the conditions and the scope of the group on the Filter and Conditions property pages. Examples of these are shown in Figure 11.57.

USING THE EXCHANGE MANAGEMENT SHELL TO MANAGE GROUPS

If you are just getting started with Exchange 2007 and the EMS, managing groups is going to be a little tougher using the EMS than it will be if you use the EMC. However, I want to review the cmdlets that are available for managing and manipulating mail-enabled groups so that as you learn more about the EMS, you will have these cmdlets in your management arsenal. Table 11.6 lists the EMS cmdlets that you can use to manage groups and mail-enabled groups.

Creating Distribution Groups Using the EMS

For my purposes in this chapter, I am going to focus on only a few of the cmdlets listed in Table 11.6 and some of the more common properties that can be used with them. The best way to illustrate them is to use some examples. In the first example, let's say that you have a universal group in the Corporate OU in the Active Directory. The group is called Raptor Pilots. You want to set up this group as a distribution group.

FIGURE 11.57
Dynamic distribution group Filter and Conditions property pages

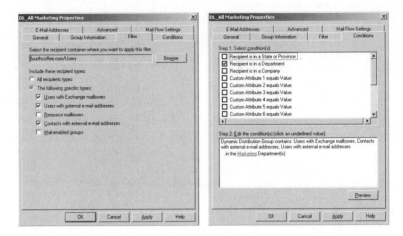

Because the group already exists in the Active Directory, you'll use the `Enable-Distribution Group` cmdlet. You need to assign the group an Exchange alias (the `-Alias` property) and you need to assign it a display name (`-DisplayName`). The following command would accomplish these tasks:

```
Enable-DistributionGroup "Raptor Pilots" -DisplayName:"Raptor Pilots"↵
-Alias:"raptorpilots"
```

If the group does not yet exist in the Active Directory and you wanted to create it in addition to mail-enabling it, you would use the `New-DistributionGroup` cmdlet. The following example creates the Raptor Pilots group in the Corporate OU; the `-OrganizationalUnit` property is required. The `-SamAccountName` property is also required if the group will be a security group:

```
New-DistributionGroup -Name:'Raptor Pilots' -Type:'Distribution'↵
-OrganizationalUnit:'fourthcoffee.com/Corporate'↵
-SamAccountName:'RaptorPilots' -DisplayName:'Raptor Pilots'↵
-Alias:'Raptor Pilots'
```

To add members to a group, you use the `Add-DistributionGroupMember` cmdlet. Conversely, you can use the `Remove-DistributionGroupMember` cmdlet to remove members. For example, if you want to add user Elizabeth.Owusu to the Raptor Pilots group, you would type the following command:

```
Add-DistributionGroupMember "Raptor Pilots" -Member "Elizabeth.Owusu"
```

To enumerate the members of a group, you use the `Get-DistributionListMember` cmdlet. Here is an example and the resulting output:

```
Get-DistributionGroupMember "Raptor Pilots"

Name                    RecipientType
----                    -------------
Jim McBee               UserMailbox
Elizabeth Owusu         UserMailbox
Clayton Kamiya          UserMailbox
```

TABLE 11.6:   EMS and PowerShell Cmdlets for Group Management

CMDLET	FUNCTION
Get-Group	Retrieves information about all Active Directory groups. This is a built-in PowerShell cmdlet; it is not added with the EMS.
Set-Group	Sets information about an Active Directory group; this will work for any Active Directory group, not just mail-enabled ones. This is a built-in PowerShell cmdlet; it is not added with the EMS.
Get-DistributionGroup	Retrieves information related to mail-enabled groups.
Set-DistributionGroup	Sets properties of mail-enabled groups.
New-DistributionGroup	Creates a new group in the Active Directory and mail-enables that group.
Enable-DistributionGroup	Mail-enables an existing group that was previously created in the Active Directory.
Disable-DistributionGroup	Removes mail attributes from a mail-enabled group but does not remove the group from the Active Directory.
Remove-DistributionGroup	Deletes the mail attributes of a mail-enabled group and removes the group from the Active Directory.
Get-DistributionGroup Member	Retrieves membership list information from a mail-enabled group.
Add-DistributionGroup Member	Adds members to a mail-enabled group.
Remove-DistributionGroup Member	Removes members from a mail-enabled group.
Get-DynamicDistribution Group	Retrieves information about a dynamic distribution group.
Set-DynamicDistribution Group	Sets properties for dynamic distribution groups.
New-DynamicDistribution Group	Creates a new dynamic distribution group.
Remove-DynamicDistribution Group	Removes mail properties from a dynamic distribution group and deletes the group from the Active Directory.

You can set many properties for a mail-enabled group, as you probably recall from seeing what you can set through the graphical user interface. To update the properties of a group from the EMS, you use the Set-DistributionGroup cmdlet. Table 11.7 lists some of the common properties that you can define for a mail-enabled group.

TABLE 11.7:   Common Mail-Enabled Group Properties

PROPERTY	FUNCTION
Alias	Sets the Exchange alias for the group. By default, the alias is used when SMTP addresses are generated.
CustomAttribute1 through CustomAttribute15	Sets 1 of the 15 custom attributes (aka extension attributes).
DisplayName	Sets the display name of the mail-enabled group; the display name is what is visible in address lists.
HiddenFromAddressLists Enabled	Sets whether or not the group will be displayed in address lists. The default is that the objects are visible. You can set this to $True and it will hide the lists.
MaxReceiveSize	Sets the maximum size message that can be sent to the group.

You can view the group's properties using the EMS cmdlet Get-DistributionGroup. This cmdlet lets you view the properties of the group. Many of these you can modify using the Set-DistributionGroup cmdlet. Here is how to view a mail-enabled universal group:

```
Get-DistributionGroup "Executives" | FL
GroupType                           : Universal
SamAccountName                      : Executives
ExpansionServer                     : /o=Volcano Surfboards/ou=Exchange
Administrative Group(FYDIBOHF23SPDLT)/cn=Configuration/cn=Servers/cn=HNLEX03
ReportToManagerEnabled              : False
ReportToOriginatorEnabled           : True
SendOofMessageToOriginatorEnabled   : False
AcceptMessagesOnlyFrom              : {}
AcceptMessagesOnlyFromDLMembers     : {}
AddressListMembership               : {Default Global Address List, All Groups}
Alias                               : Executives
OrganizationalUnit                  : volcanosurfboards.com/Users
CustomAttribute1                    :
CustomAttribute10                   :
CustomAttribute11                   :
CustomAttribute12                   :
CustomAttribute13                   :
CustomAttribute14                   :
CustomAttribute15                   :
CustomAttribute2                    :
CustomAttribute3                    :
CustomAttribute4                    :
CustomAttribute5                    :
CustomAttribute6                    :
CustomAttribute7                    :
```

```
CustomAttribute8              :
CustomAttribute9              :
DisplayName                   : Executives
EmailAddresses                :
    {smtp:Executives@volcanosurfboards.com,
     smtp:Executives@research.somorita.com,
  smtp:Executives@directory-update.com,
  X400:C=US;A= ;P=Volcano Surfboar;O=Exchange;S=Executives;,
   SMTP:Executives@somorita.com}
GrantSendOnBehalfTo           : {}
HiddenFromAddressListsEnabled : False
LegacyExchangeDN              : /o=Volcano Surfboards/ou=First  Administrative
Group/cn=Recipients/cn=Executives
MaxSendSize                   : unlimited
MaxReceiveSize                : unlimited
PoliciesIncluded              : {{5AB9DF03-4F43-491F-B77A-1D5DFD5E3410},
{26491CFC-9E50-4857-861B-0CB8DF22B5D7}}
PoliciesExcluded              : {}
EmailAddressPolicyEnabled     : True
PrimarySmtpAddress            : Executives@somorita.com
RecipientType                 : MailUniversalDistributionGroup
RecipientTypeDetails          : MailUniversalDistributionGroup
RejectMessagesFrom            : {}
RejectMessagesFromDLMembers   : {}
RequireSenderAuthenticationEnabled : False
SimpleDisplayName             :
UMDtmfMap                     : {}
WindowsEmailAddress           : Executives@somorita.com
IsValid                       : True
OriginatingServer             : HNLDC01.volcanosurfboards.com
ExchangeVersion               : 0.1 (8.0.535.0)
Name                          : Executives
DistinguishedName             : CN=Executives,CN=Users,
DC=volcanosurfboard,DC=com
Identity                      : volcanosurfboards.com/Users/Executives
Guid                          : 801ea663-4763-44f7-bb21-54a297918cf0
ObjectCategory                : volcanosurfboards.com/Configuration/Schema
/Group
ObjectClass                   : {top, group}
WhenChanged                   : 12/9/2006 12:41:21 PM
WhenCreated                   : 11/27/2006 8:38:44 AM
```

Finally, if you no longer need a group, you can use `Remove-Group` to get rid of it completely (including the group object in the Active Directory) or `Disable-Group` to simply remove the mail attributes from it.

Creating Dynamic Distribution Groups Using the EMS

Let's now look at an example where you create and manage a dynamic distribution group using the EMS. Let's say that you need to create a group called Everyone On The West Coast that consists only of mailbox-enabled users. You want to create the Active Directory object in the fourthcoffee.com domain and in the Corporate organizational unit. Further, let's say that the maximum receive size should be only 75KB.

To create this DDG, you would use the following cmdlet:

```
New-DynamicDistributionGroup -Name "Everyone on the West Coast"↵
  -IncludedRecipients 'MailboxUsers'↵
  -ConditionalStateOrProvince 'California, Oregon, Washington'↵
  -OrganizationalUnit 'fourthcoffee.com/Corporate'↵
  -Alias 'EveryoneOnWestCoast'↵
  -RecipientContainer 'fourthcoffee.com/Corporate'
```

After you get the group created, you use the Set-DynamicDistributionGroup cmdlet to update the maximum receive size:

```
New-DynamicDistributionGroup -Name "Everyone on the West Coast"↵
  -MaxReceiveSize 75KB
```

Dynamic distribution groups have a few additional property types that can be viewed using the EMS. Here is the output of the EMS and some of the additional properties that are found when using a dynamic distribution group:

```
Get-DynamicDistributionGroup "Everyone in Organization"↵
 | FL Name,*Recipient*,Conditional*
Name                        : Everyone in Organization
RecipientContainer          : volcanosurfboards.com/Somorita Surfboards
RecipientFilter             :
LdapRecipientFilter         : (&(!cn=SystemMailbox{*})
(& (mailnickname=*) ((&(objectCategory=person)(objectClass=user)(!(homeMDB=*))
(!(msExchHomeServerName=*)))(&(objectCategory=person)
(objectClass=user)((homeMDB=*)(msExchHomeServerName=*))) )))
IncludedRecipients          :
RecipientFilterType         : Legacy
RecipientType               : DynamicDistributionGroup
RecipientTypeDetails        : DynamicDistributionGroup
ConditionalDepartment       :
ConditionalCompany          :
ConditionalStateOrProvince  :
ConditionalCustomAttribute1 :
ConditionalCustomAttribute2 :
ConditionalCustomAttribute3 :
ConditionalCustomAttribute4 :
ConditionalCustomAttribute5 :
ConditionalCustomAttribute6 :
ConditionalCustomAttribute7 :
ConditionalCustomAttribute8 :
ConditionalCustomAttribute9 :
ConditionalCustomAttribute10 :
ConditionalCustomAttribute11 :
```

```
ConditionalCustomAttribute12 :
ConditionalCustomAttribute13 :
ConditionalCustomAttribute14 :
ConditionalCustomAttribute15 :
```

Converting Distribution Groups to Universal Groups

In previous versions of Exchange, you could create any type of group you wanted (domain local, global, or universal); however, in multi-domain environments, this could cause problems with distribution list expansion. If the Exchange server that performed the group expansion pointed to a domain controller from a domain that did not contain the membership list for a domain local or global group, the group would not be expanded and the message would not be delivered. Worse, the message sender might not get a notification that there was a problem.

For this reason, Microsoft is now recommending that all groups used with Exchange Server mail distribution be universal groups. If you create a domain local or global group using Active Directory Users and Computers and then try to mail-enable it using the Exchange Management Console, you will not even see the group in the list of available groups.

The group type can be changed using Active Directory Users and Computers, of course. On the General property page for the group (shown in Figure 11.58), simply select the Universal radio button and click OK to convert the group.

FIGURE 11.58
Converting a group to a universal group using Active Directory Users and Computers

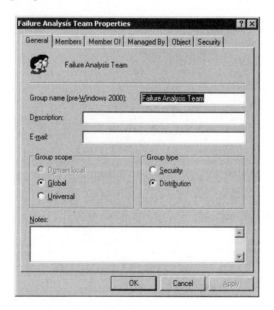

You can also convert the group to a universal group from the EMS.
You can convert groups one at time with the Set-Group cmdlet like this:

```
Set-Group "Operations Group" -Universal
```

However, one at a time is probably not the best use of your time. I recommend you convert all groups that are being used for mail distribution, but not necessarily your non-mail groups.

You can generate a list of just these groups with the `Get-DistributionGroup` cmdlet and a `Where-Object` filter; here is an example:

```
Get-DistributionGroup | Where {$_.RecipientType -eq "MailNonUniversalGroup"}
```

Name	DisplayName	GroupType	PrimarySmtpAddress
$Operations Group	$Operations Group	Global, Security...	OperationsGroup@...
$Executives and ...	$Executives and ...	Global, Security...	ExecutivesandVIP...
Field Research G...	Field Research G...	Global, Security...	FieldResearchGro...
Failure Analysis...	Failure Analysis...	Global	FailureAnalysisT...

This outputs a list of all groups that are mail-enabled and that are not universal groups. To convert them all at once is just a matter of piping this as input to the `Set-Group` cmdlet. Here is the command necessary to convert all of these groups to universal groups:

```
Get-DistributionGroup | Where {$_.RecipientType -eq "MailNonUniversalGroup"}↵
| Set-Group -Universal
```

Note that this command does not change whether the group is a security group or a distribution-only group.

Allowing End Users to Manage Group Membership

A very handy feature of Outlook is that when you locate a distribution group in the global address list and select its properties, if you have the right permissions, you can add and remove users, contacts, or groups from the group's membership. Figure 11.59 shows the Outlook interface that allows you to manage the membership of a mail-enabled group.

FIGURE 11.59
Managing group membership from within Outlook

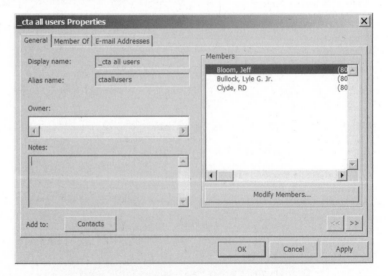

Note that only mail-enabled groups can have their membership managed by an Outlook client. This feature is not available for dynamic distribution groups.

In the EMC, a distribution group's Group Information property page (Figure 11.60) includes a Managed By field that allows you to set the "manager" of the group.

Disappointingly, this Managed By option does not allow the manager to manage the membership list. That takes is an extra step (or two). In Active Directory Users and Computers, locate the group and then display its properties. On the Managed By property page, you should see the option to define the manager and a Manager Can Update Membership List check box.

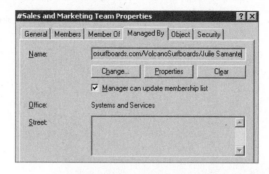

FIGURE 11.60
Group Information
property page

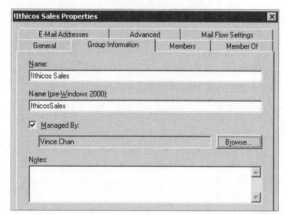

Essentially, when you select this check box, Active Directory Users and Computers adds an additional Active Directory permission that allows the manager to write to the members attribute of the group. Unfortunately, you can assign only a single manager for a group on this property page. However, with a little ingenuity, you can duplicate what Active Directory Users and Computers has done for additional managers. First you need to make sure the Advanced Features view is enabled so that the Security property page is visible.

To assign an additional manager permissions to edit the membership list, follow these steps:

1. Locate the distribution group in Active Directory Users and Computers and display its properties.

2. On the Security property page, click the Advanced button.

3. Click the Add button and select the user you want to manage this group.

4. On the Permissions Entry dialog box, select the Properties property page.

5. Scroll down the list of permissions and in the Allow column, select the Write Members permission (Figure 11.61).

6. Click OK three times.

FIGURE 11.61
Assigning additional managers for a distribution group

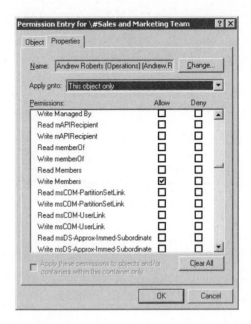

Managing Contacts

Many organizations like to have their users' frequently used contacts in their address lists rather than having users add them to their individual contacts folders. This is the intention of the *mail-enabled contact*, or what was called in Exchange 5.5 and earlier a custom recipient. Mail-enabled contacts appear in your organization's address lists, but these contacts direct e-mail to an external mail system. These external contacts' e-mail addresses are almost always SMTP, so I am going to limit my discussion to that type of contact.

In Exchange 2007, a contact object can be created in the Active Directory, but it will not be mail-enabled and thus will not appear in the Exchange address lists. This is different from Exchange 2000/2003, where you could mail-enable a contact using the Active Directory Users and Computers extensions.

Creating a contact object in the Active Directory is really simple and requires minimal information; you can simply create a new contact and specify the contact's name information. (See Figure 11.62.)

However, you may notice that there is no way to provide e-mail address information when you create a contact in the Active Directory. If you look at the contact's information (shown in Figure 11.63), you will see an e-mail property, but Exchange will not include the contact information in the address lists with just this information populated.

To properly mail-enable a contact for use with Exchange, you must use the EMC or the EMS tools.

Managing Mail-Enabled Contacts Using the EMC

Let's start by examining how you would create and manage a mail-enabled contact using the EMC. In the Recipient Configuration work center of the EMC you will find the Mail Contact subcontainer. If you highlight this container, you will see two new tasks on the Actions pane. These are the New Mail Contact and the New Mail User tasks.

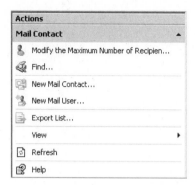

FIGURE 11.62
Creating a New
Contact Object in the
Active Directory

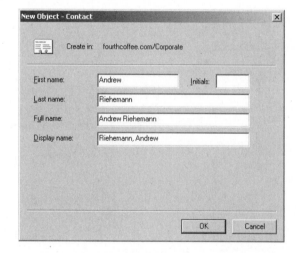

The mail contact is an object that appears in the Active Directory and Exchange address lists but is not a security principal. You cannot put the mail contact into any security groups and assign it any permissions because it does not have a security identifier. This type of contact is useful when you are enabling contacts that will appear in your address lists but never need any sort of permissions in your organization.

The mail user is a user account in your organization but not one for which you host a mailbox. For example, you might need to create a user account for an accounting auditor who will be working at one of your workstations for a few months. You want that person to appear in your Exchange address lists, but his mailbox is hosted somewhere else. This is also called a mail-enabled user. The easiest way to understand the difference between a mail-enabled user and a mailbox-enabled user is that you are *not* responsible for a mail-enabled user's e-mail storage, but you are responsible for a *mailbox*-enabled user's e-mail storage. The mailbox-enabled user is the type of mailbox I was covering earlier in this chapter.

Let's look at creating a mail-enabled contact. Simply click the New Mail Contact selection in the Actions pane to launch the New Mail Contact Wizard. The Introduction screen asks you if you want to create a new contact or mail-enable an existing contact in the Active Directory. In this example, you will mail-enable an existing contact, so choose the Existing Contact radio button and click the Browse button to locate this contact in the Active Directory. On the next page (the

Contact Information page shown in Figure 11.64), all you really have to provide is the external e-mail address. You cannot proceed if the object does not have an external e-mail address.

FIGURE 11.63
Contact information in the Active Directory

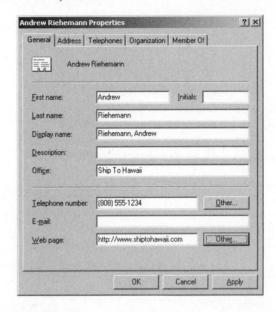

After you confirm that this is what you want to do, the Completion screen will show you the EMS command that was used to enable this object:

```
Enable-MailContact -Identity 'fourthcoffee.com/Corporate/Andrew Riehemann'↵
-ExternalEmailAddress 'SMTP:andrew.riehemann@externalorganization.com'↵
-Alias 'AndrewRiehemann'
```

Before we go on to look at the mail-related properties of a contact, let's look at the creation of a mail-enabled user. In a similar example, you already have created an existing user account in the Active Directory. You run the New Mail User Wizard and select an existing user. On the Mail Settings property page, all you need to specify is the External E-mail Address properties.

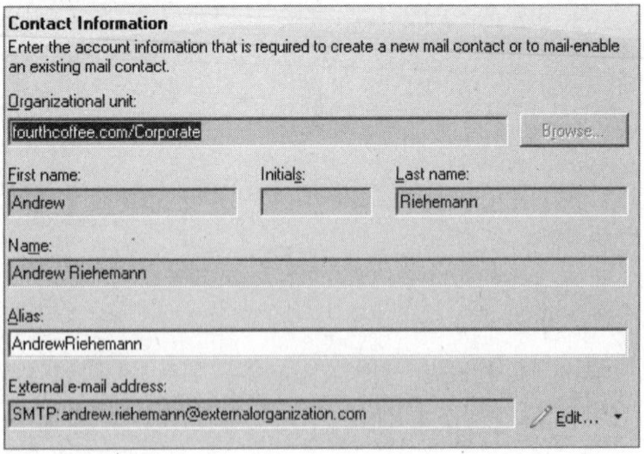

FIGURE 11.64
Creating a mail-enabled contact

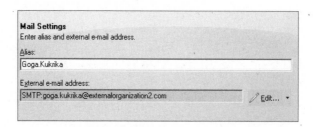

Once you confirm that the information is correct and complete the wizard, the Completion page will show the EMS command that was used to create the object:

```
Enable-MailUser -Identity 'fourthcoffee.com/Corporate/Goga Kukrika'↵
-Alias 'Goga.Kukrika'↵
-ExternalEmailAddress 'SMTP:goga.kukrika@externalorganization2.com'
```

With respect to the properties of a mail-enabled contact or a mail-enabled user, there is little that you have not already seen in this chapter, so I won't bore you with a lot of repetition. The General property page of the object does have something you may not have seen yet, though. Notice in Figure 11.65 that there is a Use MAPI Rich Text Format drop-down list.

FIGURE 11.65
Contact object's General properties

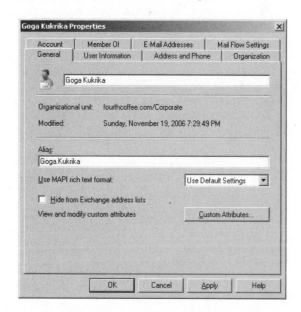

This setting determines whether the Exchange Hub Transport server will convert the message to a MIME or UUENCODE message when it leaves your organization. By default, all mail leaving your organization is converted into an Internet-standards-based format; this is almost always MIME. In some cases, this may strip out some formatting or features that users who use Word as their e-mail editor have put into the message. For just any old recipient on the Internet, this is fine because there is no guarantee that they have a mail client that can read those messages. However, if you know for sure that the recipient will have a mail reader that is capable of reading a rich-text-formatted message (Outlook, for example), then you can send the message to the recipient in that format. You have three possible settings in this drop-down list:

- Use Default Settings means that the message will be sent this way if the user specified in her address book that this recipient should receive mail in rich text format or if you have defined Remote Domains settings for your Hub Transport servers.

- Always means that regardless of the user's address book settings, the message will be sent to this recipient in rich text formatting.

- Never means that regardless of the user's address book settings, the message will always be converted to an Internet-standards message.

If someone sends a rich-text message and the recipient is not able to read it, the recipient will see attachments named `winmail.dat` or a MIME attachment called `application/tnef`. If you have specific remote organizations that need specific message formatting, the remote domains feature of Exchange Server allows you to specify formatting to be used for a specific SMTP domain. This can be found in the Organization Configuration under the Hub Transport subcontainer.

Managing Mail-Enabled Contacts Using the EMS

Once you get proficient at the EMC, as with many other tasks, you may want to try your hand at creating mail-enabled contacts or mail-enabled users from the EMS instead of the GUI. Table 11.8 shows the cmdlets that can be used to manipulate mail-enabled contacts and users.

The best way to learn how to use the EMS to create mail-enabled contacts and users is to look at some examples.

Let's say a user named Russ Kaufmann is a contractor that works in your company sometimes. He requires a desk and a company logon, so you have already created his Russ.Kaufmann account in the `forthcoffee.com` Active Directory; the account is in an OU called Corporate. You want Russ to appear in the address lists, but he should receive his e-mail at an external address: `Russ.Kaufmann@RussClusteringGuru.com`. Here is the command you would use to mail-enable his user account. In this example, you are using his common name attribute instead of his username:

```
Enable-MailUser "Russ Kaufmann" -Alias 'Russ.Kaufmann' ↵
-ExternalEmailAddress 'SMTP:Russ.Kaufmann@RussClusteringGuru.com'
```

Let's extend this example now to a mail-enabled contact. You have a contact that you want to appear in your address lists, but this contact does not need to be a security principal in your Active Directory. The contact does not yet exist, so you will create a mail-enabled contact in the Corporate OU for contact Rod Fournier whose external address will be `Rod.Fournier@RodClusteringGuru.com`:

```
New-MailContact -ExternalEmailAddress 'SMTP:Rod.Fournier@RodClusteringGuru.com' ↵
  -Name 'Rod Fournier' -Alias 'RodFournier' ↵
  -OrganizationalUnit 'fourthcoffee.com/Corporate' ↵
  -FirstName 'Rod' -Initials " -LastName 'Fournier'
```

When setting properties for the mail contact and mail user objects, there are some useful properties to know about. Table 11.9 shows some of the more common properties that these two object types share.

TABLE 11.8:   Exchange Management Shell Cmdlets for Mail-Enabled Contacts and Users

CMDLET	DESCRIPTION
New-MailContact	Creates a new contact in the Active Directory and mail-enables that contact.
Enable-MailContact	Mail-enables a previously existing contact.
Set-MailContact	Sets mail properties for a mail-enabled contact.
Get-MailContact	Retrieves properties of a mail-enabled contact.
Remove-MailContact	Removes the mail properties from a contact and deletes that contact from the Active Directory.
Disable-MailContact	Removes the mail properties from a contact.
New-MailUser	Creates a new user in the Active Directory and mail-enables that user.
Enable-MailUser	Mail-enables a previously existing user.
Set-MailUser	Sets mail properties for a mail-enabled user.
Get-MailUser	Retrieves properties of a mail-enabled user.
Remove-MailUser	Removes the mail properties from a user and deletes that user from the Active Directory.
Disable-MailUser	Removes the mail properties from a user.

TABLE 11.9:   Useful Properties of Mail Contact and Mail User Objects

PROPERTY	DESCRIPTION
Alias	Sets the object's Exchange alias.
CustomAttribute1 through CustomAttribute10	Sets custom attributes 1 through 10; these are also known as the extension attributes.
DisplayName	Sets the display name of the object.
ExternalEmailAddress	Sets the address that is to be used to deliver mail externally to the user or contact.
HiddenFromAddressLists Enabled	Specifies if the object is hidden from address lists or not. The default is $False, but it can be set to $True.
MaxSendSize	Sets the maximum size of a message that can be sent to this recipient.

Summary

Recipient management is one of the core functions of many Exchange administrators. Short of some daily monitoring and running your backups, recipient management will be the task that consumes most of your Exchange bandwidth. Day-to-day recipient management includes the following:

◆ Mailbox management

◆ Resource mailbox management

◆ Mail-enabled group management

◆ Contact management

As you get started with Exchange 2007, you will probably be more dependent on the Exchange Management Console for recipient management. Most of the tasks you will need to perform can be performed through the graphical user interface. As you get more comfortable with the GUI, though, I urge you to start learning more about the Exchange Management Shell. Combining some of the EMS cmdlets with PowerShell scripting capabilities can help to speed up many of the common tasks that you perform, such as bulk recipient creation and management.

Chapter 12

Managing Storage

If you break Exchange Server down into its three major functions, it provides a database engine, a message transport engine, and a method for accessing the data. Naturally, as Exchange administrators, we spend a lot of time thinking about the database — specifically, how many databases we should have, how big they should grow, and on which disk drives they should be placed.

Database sizing, database management, database creation, and backup management all end up taking a good percentage of our attention. We have to provide our users with the canvas on which they can spread their knowledge, or at the very least send around tacky humor.

This chapter covers some topics relating to the management of Exchange server data, databases, and storage groups, as well as disk capacity.

You learn to:

◆ Review storage requirements and constraints

◆ Understand disk size versus I/O capacity

◆ Create storage groups

◆ Create mailbox databases

Ruminations on Mail Storage

In this first section, I wanted to share some of my ruminations on mail storage. Plus, I had always wanted to use the word rumination in a sentence, so now I have fulfilled that goal. In this section, I wanted to talk about some of the factors that I take in to consideration when configuring e-mail storage, creating more databases, and asking for more disk capacity. (See Chapter 2, "Designing a New Exchange 2007 System," for additional information on planning disk space requirements.)

A common way to improve the scalability of Mailbox servers is to add storage groups and mailbox databases. Though this might not improve overall server performance or a user's perceived response time, it allows you to break up the amount of data you are storing and place it across multiple smaller mailbox databases. In turn, this allows you to support larger mailboxes. Keep in mind as you increase the number of mailboxes that each Mailbox server supports, increasing the amount of RAM will help improve performance and reduce the disk I/O profile.

When creating additional mailbox databases, you should plan to place each storage group's transaction logs on separate disk spindles from the database files. This can help improve performance (due to the nature of the I/O differences) as well as recoverability.

What's Keeping Me Up At Night?

Seriously, though, I spend quite a bit of time wondering if I have my storage configuration optimized. Think I'm still kidding? Well, ask yourself these questions about your own environment:

◆ Am I giving my users enough mailbox space to store enough historical information to do their jobs? Or (*shudder*) too much?

◆ Are users wasting mail storage on personal or non–work-related content such as MPG files of cats playing the piano (`http://www.youtube.com/watch?v=TZ860P4iTaM`)?

◆ Should I employ an e-mail archival system to move older content off the mailbox database and on to alternative storage? If I do, how much "recent" content should be left on the Exchange server versus moved out to the archive?

◆ Do I need to be keeping copies of certain types of messages (such as for regulatory, legal, or business reasons)?

FACTORS THAT AFFECT STORAGE

Wouldn't it be great if you could walk into your boss's office and ask for the budget to give every user a 20GB mailbox so they would never (well, not for a while at least) have to delete anything? Then you could create as many databases on your Exchange server as you could create before your fingers went numb and let the users go to town.

Unfortunately, we all have constraints within which we have to live; that goes for system administrators, end users, and our VIP users. So, thinking about adding more storage and allowing larger mailboxes or databases, what are some of the constraints that we face? Some of these are technological in nature and some are budgetary or political. I am hoping that you already know most of these and can skim right through them.

◆ Exchange Server 2007 Standard Edition supports a maximum of five mailbox databases/storage groups.

◆ Exchange Server 2007 Enterprise Edition supports a maximum of 50 mailbox databases/storage groups.

◆ Disks have a fixed I/O capacity; at some point with more data on a disk and more users trying to use that data, the disk will not be able to keep up with the read and write requests.

◆ The bigger a mailbox is, the longer it takes to back up and restore. For typical streaming backups of Exchange databases, the restore time will be twice as long as the backup time.

◆ Microsoft recommends a maximum Exchange database of no more than 100GB unless replication technology (such as LCR or CCR) is used. If LCR or CCR is used, the maximum database size should be no more than 200GB. But I am skeptical about increasing the database size to 200GB when using only SCR, because SCR is designed more for server recovery than for recovery of a single mailbox database.

◆ You need to plan for 7 to 10 days worth of transaction logs; a good starting point for estimating how much space transaction logs will consume is about 5GB of transaction logs for each 1,000 average users.

◆ You should assume that each database needs to contain 10% to 15% additional space for deleted items and for database white space.

Disk Size versus I/O Capacity

For a lot of Exchange Server administrators (myself included), the knowledge of and understanding of disk I/O capacity constraints came slowly. For some reason, I kept thinking that the disk technology far outperformed the database capacity. But as Exchange servers got more heavily loaded with more simultaneous users and larger databases, the demands on the disk got larger and larger. Now, not only do we have to factor in sufficient disk space to hold the amount of data we intend to store, but we have to make sure that the disk (or more accurately the disk subsystem) can support the expected I/O load.

Let's take a look at a quick example. Say you have an 18GB SCSI disk from the olden days; that disk may be able to support 100 reads and/or writes to the disk each second. That is not a big deal if you have 50 users, but what if you have 500 users? Can the disk subsystem service the I/O requests that those 500 users will put on it? If the disk system is not properly sized — both for capacity and for the required I/O load — then users will see performance problems.

This load is normally measured (and planned) in terms of the I/O per second profile of the users that will use the system. This is better known as IOPS (pronounced *eye-ops*.) The Exchange team at Microsoft has done a lot of research into the type of load that users place on an Exchange server; they have broken that down based on different types of users. Table 12.1 shows Microsoft's estimates for the I/O load that different types of users place on an Exchange 2007 server's disk subsystem; these numbers are much lower than they were for Exchange Server 2003 thanks to improved caching and additional available memory.

TABLE 12.1:   User Profile, Mailbox Size, and Estimated IOPS for Exchange 2007

USER TYPE	DATABASE VOLUME IOPS	MESSAGES SENT / RECEIVED PER DAY	MAILBOX SIZE*
Light	.14	20 sent/50 received	50MB
Average	.20	30 sent/75 received	100MB
Heavy	.27	40 sent/100 received	200MB
Large	.41	60 sent/150 received	500MB

These calculations do not consider additional overhead generated by BlackBerry devices, antivirus/antispam software, message archival, or other applications.

For a typical organization, I will use the Average value of .20 IOPS required for each user. However, you might want to use the Heavy value to ensure that you factor in enough "just in case" capacity.

There has been a lot of information written on IOPS and disk I/O capacity sizing and most of it is quite a bit more detailed than I can cover here. If you are interested in going into more depth on this concept, take a look at *The Shortcut Guide to Exchange Server 2007 Storage Systems* at:

    http://nexus.realtimepublishers.com/SGES2k7SS.htm

Adding More Mailbox Storage

In our worst-case scenario for how to estimate mailbox database size for a given configuration, I estimated that a single database could grow to 1.3TB in size. Although Exchange Server can technically support a database that large, it would take forever to back up, and worse, it would take forever to restore. Even if you are using snapshot technologies, if the snapshot backup software performs database verification, the verification would take far too long. So a database size of 1.3TB is just not practical.

Maximum Database Sizes

Microsoft recommends that you keep each mailbox database under about 100GB if you are not using any type of replication technology. If you are using local continuous replication (LCR), cluster continuous replication (CCR), or even standby continuous replication (SCR), you can consider allowing a maximum database size of 200GB.

I urge you to consider your existing environment when you think about these maximum sizes. Ultimately, you need to consider how much time it will take to restore one of these databases from a tape backup; if the absolute longest time you can take to restore a database from your backup media (for example a tape) is two hours, and your tape system restores at a rate of 30GB per hour, then the largest database size you should consider supporting is 30GB. A company's Recovery Time Objective/Recovery Point Objective (RTO/RPO) will most likely dictate recovery time and therefore will help you in calculating what your maximum database sizes should be.

Replication technologies such as LCR, CCR, and SCR allow you to maintain an up-to-date copy of a database ready to use in the event of a failure. Naturally, this can allow a much quicker recovery from a corrupted database or a failed server.

Determining the Number of Storage Groups and Databases

In Chapter 2, I worked on an example of the estimated storage requirements for an organization that supports 1,000 mailboxes. In that example, I estimated that the total database size (with all data) would be around 1.3TB of disk space. We have to divide up that number and figure out how many databases we need. Let's assume that we will use one of the replication technologies and that we have a backup and restore solution that will allow a 200MB database to be restored in a reasonable amount of time; in that case, we need a minimum of seven mailbox databases (1.3TB/200MB = 6.5).

STORAGE GROUPS AND EXCHANGE SERVER

For those of you who are new to Exchange Server, I want to take a moment and explain the concept of a *storage group*. A storage group is a collection of databases that all share a common set of transaction logs. As a transaction is written to a log file, it is serialized and identified so that the Exchange database engine (known as the Extensible Storage Engine, or ESE) knows to which database file the transaction belongs.

In Exchange 2000/2003/2007, a storage group can contain between one and five databases; these databases can be either a mailbox or a public folder database (one public folder database per server). However, there are guidelines that you may need to follow for performance or certain configurations. For example, if you implement cluster continuous replication or local continuous replication, you can have only one database per storage group. If you are coming from Exchange 2000 or even Exchange 2003, you may be planning to *fill up* each storage group with the maximum number of databases before creating the next storage group.

Exchange Server 2007 Standard Edition supports a maximum of 5 storage groups and a maximum of 5 databases. Enterprise Edition supports a maximum of 50 storage groups and 50 mailbox databases. If you own Enterprise Edition, you could create 10 storage groups that each hold 5 mailbox databases, but Microsoft's recommendation now — and mine — is that you create 1 storage group for each database.

There are two reasons for creating one database per storage group:

◆ The LCR, CCR, and SCR technologies support only one database per storage group. So if you plan to use any of those technologies (and I hope that you will), you must use one database per storage group.

◆ You can improve the overall performance of the database engine. Each storage group is configured with a 20MB checkpoint depth. This means that a maximum of 20MB of outstanding transactions can be written to the logs but not immediately committed to the database. If you have one mailbox database in a storage group, then that database's checkpoint depth is 20MB; however, if you have five mailbox databases a single storage group, each database's checkpoint depth is 4MB.

During busy periods of time, the ESE may have to write to the database more frequently if the transaction log depth per database is small. If each database has the full 20MB of transaction log depth available to it, the ESE can write data to the database in larger chunks, which is more efficient.

Allocating Disk Drives

The traditional logic for Exchange Server design was to place databases on a set of physical disk drives separate from the transaction log files. As Exchange 2000/2003 servers scaled upward to support thousands of mailboxes, administrators placed the transaction log files for each storage group on separate spindles (or physical disks) and placed the database files for each group on a different set of spindles.

Although placing different files on separate disks is pretty good advice, today many of us use Fiber Channel or iSCSI SANs to store our Exchange data. The SAN is usually some aggregation of a large number of disks in a RAID 4, RAID 5, RAID 0+1, or other redundant configuration. The person who manages the SAN (hereafter known as one of the SAN people) carves up the amount of storage you request from that large aggregation of disk space and assigns it to you as a logical unit (LUN) of disk space. You then configure your Windows server to connect to those LUNs across the iSCSI or Fiber Channel network (or fabric).

I was skeptical at first of putting Exchange databases on a *networked storage* device, but I have come to see the advantages for many medium and large organizations. The ability to combine large numbers of disks together into very large volumes and then allocate pieces of that large volume to the applications (such as Exchange) that need disk space can help reduce your storage costs and allow you take advantage of technologies such as snapshot backups and improved recoverability features. Further, because some of the storage is not physically connected to the server, a disaster that befalls the server hardware may not affect the storage system.

If you are a SAN user, you should ask your SAN people for two LUNs for each storage group. One LUN should be sized to hold a storage group's transaction log files and the other should be sized to hold that storage group's database — that is, of course, for a Mailbox server role. By putting one database on each LUN and one transaction log on each LUN, you ensure that the granularity of snapshot solutions is per database. Dedicating LUNs to specific tasks helps you isolate I/O for those tasks; you should avoid placing the data for other applications on those LUNs that would affect I/O.

For heavily used Hub Transport server roles, you might also want to put the Hub Transport server database and log files on a SAN; the transport database and the log files should each go on their own LUN.

Those of you who think about disks and disk performance may be wondering about all of those LUNs being carved out of the same logical disk. If your SAN is improperly sized and without enough spindles, performance can be a problem. A properly engineered SAN solution should provide enough total I/O capacity for all of the LUNs and the applications that will use those LUNs to function correctly.

Managing Storage Groups

Creating a new storage group is a simple process in either the Exchange Management Console (EMC) or the Exchange Management Shell (EMS). Storage groups for each Mailbox server role are created and managed from the EMC within the Mailbox subcontainer of the Server Configuration work center. Figure 12.1 shows the Mailbox subcontainer of the Server Configuration work center along with the Database Management work pane.

FIGURE 12.1
Managing storage groups and mailbox databases using the Exchange Management Console

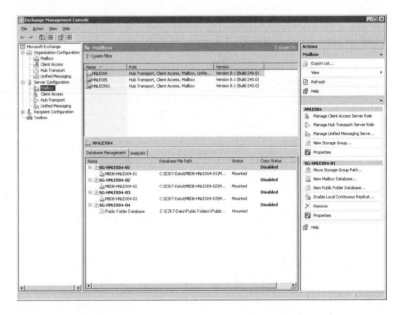

All EMC-based storage group, mailbox database, and public folder database management is performed through the Database Management pane. However, the Database Management pane is shown below the Results pane only if you have selected the Mailbox subcontainer. The Actions pane on the right side of the EMC interface gives you access to the following storage group management tasks:

◆ Creating a new storage group

◆ Moving existing storage group files (the action is called Move Storage Group Path)

◆ Creating a database (mailbox or public folder) within the storage group

◆ Enabling local continuous replication

You can also retrieve a list of storage groups using the `Get-StorageGroup` EMS cmdlet. Here is an example:

```
Get-StorageGroup
```

Name	Server	Replicated	Recovery
SG-HNLEX04-01	HNLEX04	None	False
SG-HNLEX04-04	HNLEX04	None	False
SG-HNLEX04-02	HNLEX04	None	False
First Storage Group	HNLSCR01	None	False
SG-HNLEX04-03	HNLEX04	None	False
Public Folder SG	HNLSCR01	None	False
First Storage Group	HNLEX05	None	False

I could have narrowed the scope of that query using the `Where` cmdlet or the `-Server` cmdlet to list only the storage groups from a specific server. Here are two examples that list only the storage groups on server HNLEX04:

```
Get-StorageGroup -Server HNLEX04
Get-StorageGroup | Where {$_.Server -eq ''HNLEX04''}
```

To create a new storage group, choose the New Storage Group task from the Actions pane to run the New Storage Group Wizard. The wizard is quite simple and has only two pages; the New Storage Group page (shown in Figure 12.2) prompts for the name of the storage group, the path to the transaction log files, and the path to the system files.

You can also enable local continuous replication when you create the storage group, but we will come back and do that later. Notice also in Figure 12.2 that we are selecting the default location for the transaction logs and system files. We will come back and move them later.

When you click the New button on the New Storage Group Wizard, the task is executed and the new storage group is created; the EMS cmdlet that is executed is the `New-StorageGroup` cmdlet. The Completion page shows the EMS command that was executed to create this storage group:

```
New-StorageGroup -Server 'HNLEX03' -Name 'Executives SG' -LogFolderPath↵
'C:\Program Files\Microsoft\Exchange Server\Mailbox\Executives SG'
-SystemFolderPath↵
'C:\Program Files\Microsoft\Exchange Server\Mailbox\Executives SG'
```

Now that the storage group is created, the first thing you should do is move the transaction log and system files to an alternate path to help optimize your Exchange Server's disk I/O performance. This can also be accomplished via the EMC or the EMS. In the EMC, you just need to select the storage group you want to move and then choose the Move Storage Group Path task from the Actions pane. The Introduction page of the Move Storage Group Path task is shown in Figure 12.3.

FIGURE 12.2
Creating a new storage group using the Exchange Management Console

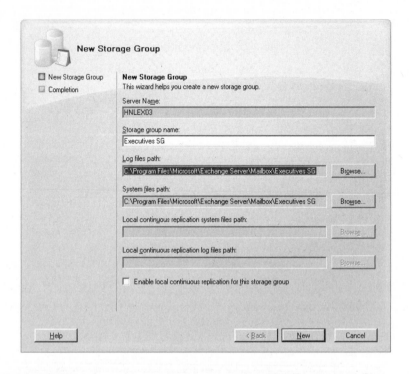

FIGURE 12.3
Moving a storage group's transaction logs and system files

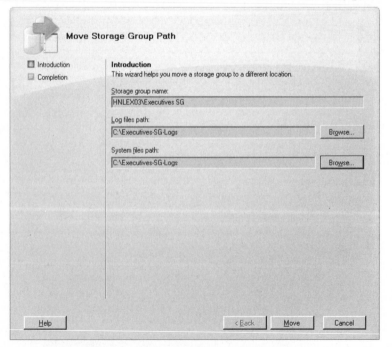

The only information that is required to move the storage group is the new location of the log files path and/or the system files path. When you click the Move button, the task is executed. The EMS cmdlet `Move-StorageGroupPath` sets the storage group's path *and* moves the existing system and/or log files. The following command was executed:

```
Move-StorageGroupPath -Identity 'HNLEX03\Executives SG'↵
-LogFolderPath 'C:\Executives-SG-Logs' -SystemFolderPath 'C:\Executives-SG-Logs'
```

However, if no mailbox databases have been created and mounted in the storage group, there will be no system or transaction log files. The wizard will tell you if it does not find any files. In that case, you would need to run a slightly modified version of the cmdlet because the files do not need to be moved. You would need to include the -`ConfigurationOnly` switch in the command line. I have also included -`Confirm:$False` so I don't see the message that there are no files to be moved:

```
Move-StorageGroupPath 'HNLEX03\Executives SG' -LogFolderPath
'C:\Executives-SG-Logs'↵
-SystemFolderPath 'C:\Executives-SG-Logs' -ConfigurationOnly -Confirm:$False
```

You can view the properties of the storage group by selecting it in the Database Management work pane and then selecting its Properties task on the Actions pane. (There may be two Properties tasks on the Actions pane — one for the server and one for the storage group. In that case, select the one in the storage group portion of the pane.)

The storage group properties are shown in Figure 12.4. From here you can change the storage group's display name or enable circular logging. Circular logging tells the Exchange database engine not to keep more than a few of the previous transaction log files. Enabling circular logging will prevent up-to-the minute recoverability of databases from a restore because there will not be enough transaction logs available after the most recent backup.

FIGURE 12.4
Viewing a storage
group's properties

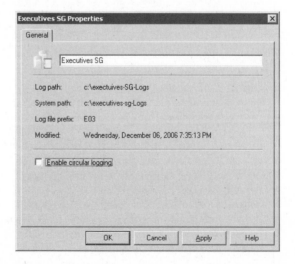

The storage group's properties also include the transaction log path, the system files path, the log file prefix, and the date on which the storage group was last modified. The log file prefix is used when creating log files for this storage group; this is a system-assigned value and cannot be changed. In the case of the storage group shown in Figure 12.4, the log file prefix is E03; a sample log filename would look like this: E03000011A0.log.

You can also retrieve the storage group's properties using the Get-StorageGroup cmdlet. The following example shows all of the properties of the Executives SG storage group:

```
Get-StorageGroup 'Executives SG' | FL

LogFolderPath             : c:\executives-SG-Logs
SystemFolderPath          : c:\executives-sg-Logs
CircularLoggingEnabled    : False
ZeroDatabasePages         : False
LogFilePrefix             : E03
LogFileSize               : 1024
RecoveryEnabled           : True
OnlineDefragEnabled       : True
IndexCheckingEnabled      : True
EventLogSourceID          : MSExchangeIS
LogCheckpointDepth        : 20971520
CommitDefault             : False
DatabaseExtensionSize     : 256
PageFragment              : 8
PageTempDBMinimum         : 0
Server                    : HNLEX03
ServerName                : HNLEX03
CopyLogFolderPath         :
CopySystemFolderPath      :
Recovery                  : False
Name                      : Executives SG
Replicated                : None
HasLocalCopy              : False
MinAdminVersion           : -2147453113
AdminDisplayName          :
ExchangeVersion           : 0.1 (8.0.535.0)
DistinguishedName         : CN=Executives
    SG,CN=InformationStore,CN=HNLEX03,CN=Servers,
CN=Exchange Administrative Group (FYDIBOHF23SPDLT),
CN=Administrative Groups,CN=Volcano Surfboards,
CN=Microsoft Exchange,CN=Services,CN=Configuration,
DC=volcanosurfboards,DC=com
Identity                  : HNLEX03\Executives SG
Guid                      : 772e9d5a-0b82-4cdc-867b-8922ed55215f
ObjectCategory            : volcanosurfboards.com/Configuration/
Schema/ms-Exch-Storage-Group
ObjectClass               : {top, container, msExchStorageGroup}
```

```
WhenChanged              : 12/6/2006 7:35:13 PM
WhenCreated              : 12/6/2006 7:13:46 PM
OriginatingServer        : HNLDC01.volcanosurfboards.com
IsValid                  : True
```

Many of these values can be changed by the Set-StorageGroup cmdlet. If you want to enable circular logging, you would type this command:

```
Set-StorageGroup 'Executives SG' -CircularLoggingEnabled:$True
```

Managing Mailbox Databases

Now that you have created a storage group, you can create a new database in it. Although both Exchange Server 2007 Standard Edition and Enterprise Edition allow up to five mailbox databases in a storage group, the examples here will be limited to a single mailbox database per storage group. This is the Microsoft recommendation, and one mailbox database per storage group is also a requirement of local continuous replication and continuous copy replication.

Viewing Mailbox Databases

You can view the current mailbox database for each server using the EMC, or you can use the Get-MailboxDatabase cmdlet to list all of the mailbox databases in the entire organization:

```
Get-MailboxDatabase
```

Name	Server	StorageGroup	Recovery
MBDB-HNLEX04-01	HNLEX04	SG-HNLEX04-01	False
MBDB-HNLEX04-02	HNLEX04	SG-HNLEX04-02	False
Mailbox Database	HNLSCR01	First Storage Group	False
MBDB-HNLEX04-03	HNLEX04	SG-HNLEX04-03	False
Mailbox Database	HNLEX05	First Storage Group	False

Of course, you can narrow the scope of this output to just a specific server or a specific storage group using the Where-Object cmdlet (well, just the Where alias) or the -Server option. Here are some examples:

```
Get-MailboxDatabase -Server HNLEX03
Get-MailboxDatabase | Where {$_.Server -eq "HNLEX03"}
Get-MailboxDatabase | Where {$_.StorageGroupName -eq "Executives SG"}
```

Creating Mailbox Databases

To create a new mailbox database, highlight the storage group in which you want the mailbox database to be created and select the New Mailbox Database task from the Actions pane. This launches the New Mailbox Database Wizard that is shown in Figure 12.5. All that is required to create a new mailbox database is to provide the name; the path will automatically be completed and the database's EDB file will be put in the same path as the transaction logs.

FIGURE 12.5
Creating a new mailbox database using the Exchange Management Console

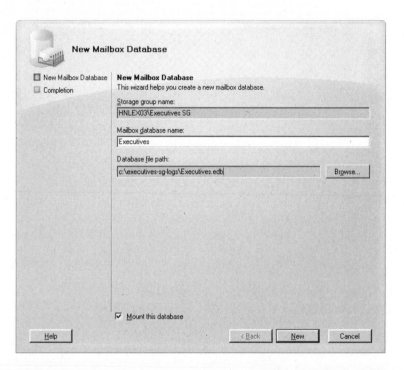

STANDARDIZE DATABASE NAMES

When creating a new mailbox database, name the database something that is standardized and descriptive. Making sure the filename matches the display name of the database will ensure that it is easier to manage.

Normally, you would click the Browse button and select a correct location for the mailbox database now, but I will show you how to move the mailbox database in the next section.

EXCHANGE 2007 USES EDB, NOT STM

Exchange 2000/2003 administrators may notice that the database has only an EDB file. Exchange 2007 does not have an STM file; each Exchange 2007 database consists of a single EDB file.

The wizard creates the configuration for the database and then mounts the database. This will initialize a new empty database file. The resulting commands are as follows; the New-MailboxDatabase cmdlet is used in the command to create the database and the Mount-Database cmdlet is used in the command to mount the database:

```
New-MailboxDatabase -StorageGroup 'CN=Executives SG,CN=InformationStore,↵
CN=HNLEX03,CN=Servers,CN=Exchange Administrative Group (FYDIBOHF23SPDLT),↵
CN=Administrative Groups,CN=Volcano Surfboards,
```

```
CN=Microsoft Exchange,↵
CN=Services,CN=Configuration,DC=volcanosurfboards,DC=com'↵
-Name 'Executives' -EdbFilePath 'c:\executives-sg-logs\Executives.edb'

Mount-Database -Identity 'CN=Executives,CN=Executives SG,CN=InformationStore,↵
CN=HNLEX03,CN=Servers,CN=Exchange Administrative Group (FYDIBOHF23SPDLT),↵
CN=Administrative Groups,CN=Volcano Surfboards,CN=Microsoft Exchange,↵
CN=Services,CN=Configuration,DC=volcanosurfboards,DC=com'
```

Notice that when the database was created, the distinguished name of the storage group was used. However, if the storage group and database names were unique, you could also specify these commands this way:

```
New-MailboxDatabase -StorageGroup 'Executives SG' -Name 'Executives'↵
-EdbFilePath 'c:\executives-sg-logs\Executives.edb'

Mount-Database 'Executives'
```

Moving a Mailbox Database

I created the database in the default path so I could illustrate the process of moving it. Using the EMC, you can move the database by choosing the Move Database Path task in the Actions pane. The only thing that needs to be provided in the Move Database Path Wizard is the new location of the database file.

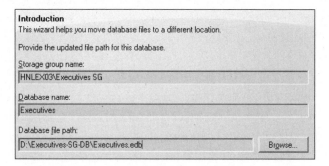

When you specify that you are about to move the database, you are warned that the database will be dismounted while the files are being copied and that it will be inaccessible.

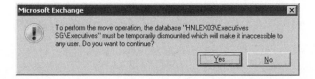

The amount of time that it takes to move the database file will depend both on the size of the database file and the speed of the disk subsystem. Once the file is moved, the Completion page of the Move Database Path Wizard will show the EMS command that was used to move the database file. Here is an example:

```
Move-DatabasePath -Identity 'HNLEX03\Executives SG\Executives' ↵
    -EdbFilePath 'D:\Executives-SG-DB\Executives.edb'
```

Properties of a Mailbox Database

Now let's look at some of the properties of a mailbox database. Figure 12.6 shows the General property tab of the mailbox database property page. At the top is the display name of the mailbox database. From here, you can rename the database if you need to conform to a new database naming standard. The path to the database is shown, but you cannot change the path here; you must use the Move-MailboxDatabase cmdlet or the Move Database Path task. The database copy path is set when you configure local continuous replication.

FIGURE 12.6
General property page of
a mailbox database

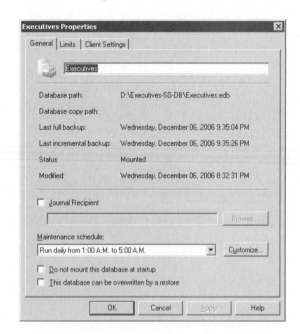

There is a lot of dynamic information on the General property page of a mailbox database as well. This includes:

◆ Last Full Backup indicates the last time a full or normal backup was run using an Exchange API–based backup solution. Transaction logs would have also been purged at that time.

◆ Last Incremental Backup indicates the last time an incremental backup was run. This backup type will back up the storage group's transaction logs and then it purges them.

◆ Status indicates if the database is mounted or dismounted.

◆ Modified shows the date and time the database properties in Active Directory were last changed.

This information (including the dynamic information) can be retrieved using the -Status option of the Get-MailboxDatabase cmdlet.

```
Get-MailboxDatabase MBDB-HNLEX04-01 -Status | FL Name,*last*,Mounted

Name                          : MBDB-HNLEX04-01
SnapshotLastFullBackup        : False
SnapshotLastIncrementalBackup :
SnapshotLastDifferentialBackup :
SnapshotLastCopyBackup        :
LastFullBackup                : 6/22/2008 9:45:47 AM
LastIncrementalBackup         :
LastDifferentialBackup        :
LastCopyBackup                :
Mounted                       : True
```

The Journal Recipient option allows you to specify a journaling recipient for all mailboxes located on this mailbox database. If this is enabled, a copy of any message or delivery receipt sent or received by a mailbox on this system will be sent to the journal mailbox.

The Maintenance Schedule drop-down list (and its Customize button) allows you to schedule online maintenance for this particular database. Online maintenance includes purging deleted items permanently from the mailbox database, purging deleted mailboxes permanently from the database, verifying that mailboxes on the database are all connected to an Active Directory account, cleaning up unused folder views, and rearranging white space. Online maintenance must be completed periodically, otherwise the database will become less and less efficient and the database file will continue to grow because the deleted items and mailboxes will never be completely purged.

The Do Not Mount This Database At Startup check box allows the administrator to prevent the database from being mounted after the information store service is restarted. This might be useful when the administrator wants to make the mailbox databases available one or two at a time rather than all at once.

The This Database Can Be Overwritten By A Restore check box is used when you must restore a database file from an offline backup. An offline backup occurs when the database file itself is backed up, for example, when making a file copy of the database file. This check box has no effect when restoring from an online backup.

The next tab on a mailbox database property page is the Limits property page. We looked at different ways to establish limits on mailbox database in Chapter 10, "Imposing Limits," but let's do a quick review here (see Figure 12.7).

The Storage Limits section allows you to specify the amount of storage that the mailbox is allowed to have. What you see in Figure 12.7 are the storage limit defaults. Administrators used to previous versions of Exchange will be surprised to learn that newly created mailbox databases have defaults. *Everyone* will be surprised to see the actual default values:

◆ Issue Warning At (KB) is set to 1,991,680KB. When a mailbox reaches this limit, users will receive an e-mail message informing them that they have reached a limit on their mailbox and they should clean up some data in it.

◆ Prohibit Send At (KB) is set to 2,097,152KB. Once the mailbox hits this limit, the user will be unable to send new messages or reply to existing messages. Both Outlook and Outlook

Web Access will inform the users if they try to send a message while they are over this limit.

◆ Prohibit Send and Receive At (KB) is set to 2,411,520KB. When a mailbox exceeds this limit, the mailbox is closed or disabled. Even though the user can access the mailbox, the server will not allow the user to send new messages or reply to existing messages. In addition, the mailbox will not receive any incoming mail from other Exchange users or from outside of the organization.

FIGURE 12.7
Setting limits on a mailbox database

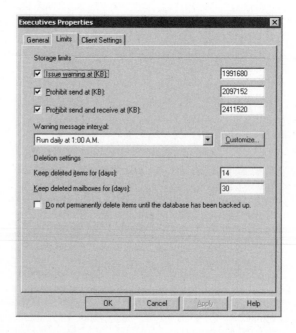

Outlook Web Access has a neat new feature that will inform users of how close they are to their limit or if they are over their limit. Simply move your mouse pointer over the top of the mailbox in the folder listing pane of Outlook Web Access and you will see a pop-up box similar to one of the ones shown in Figure 12.8.

FIGURE 12.8
Size limit messages in Outlook Web Access

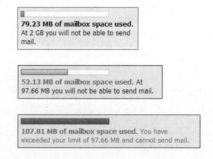

The limit that you see in the messages is the Prohibit Send At (KB) limit, not the Prohibit Send And Receive At (KB) limit.

The Warning Message Interval drop-down list determines the interval at which Exchange generates a warning message informing users that they are over their Issue Warning limit. By default, this is sent once daily at 1:00AM local time. You can customize this to another time, but be careful. The Schedule dialog box (shown in Figure 12.9) has a detail view option of either 1 hour or 15 minutes.

FIGURE 12.9
Using the Schedule dialog box

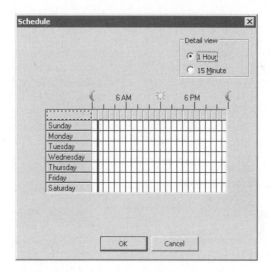

When using any schedule box that has both a 1 hour view and a 15 minute view, switch to the 15 minute view to set a schedule. If you select an entire hour, then whatever process you are scheduling will run four times per hour. In this case, if you select an entire hour, a warning message will be sent to all mailboxes over their warning limit four times per hour. The users would *not* be amused. An example of the warning message is shown in Figure 12.10.

FIGURE 12.10
Warning message users receive when their mailbox exceeds the Prohibit Send At (KB) limit

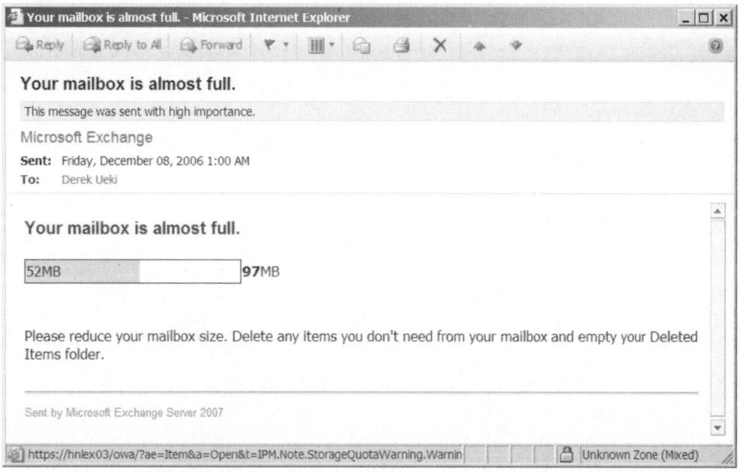

The Deletion Settings section of the Limits tab allows you to configure how long the server will retain deleted items for this mailbox and how long the server will retain a mailbox once it is deleted. The Keep Deleted Items For (Days) option specifies how many days the Exchange server will keep items that have been deleted either from the Deleted Items folder or via a hard delete (Shift + Delete) from another folder. Once a message has been in the deleted item cache for longer than this period (14 days by default for Exchange 2007), the user will no longer be able to retrieve the message using the Outlook Recover Deleted Items feature.

The Keep Deleted Mailboxes For (Days) option specifies how long the mailbox database will keep a deleted mailbox before it is permanently purged. The default is 30 days and that is reasonable for most organizations. A mailbox that has been deleted but not purged can be recovered using the EMC's Disconnected Mailbox feature or via the EMS `Connect-Mailbox` cmdlet.

The Do Not Permanently Delete Items Until The Database Has Been Backed Up check box tells the server that it should not permanently purge an item or a mailbox until the mailbox database has been backed up. This ensures that a copy of the deleted item or deleted mailbox could be recovered from backup media if necessary.

The Client Settings tab of a mailbox database (shown in Figure 12.11) allows the administrator to specify two configuration settings that affect the mailboxes on this database. The first is the Default Public Folder Database setting; this field contains the name of the public folder database that MAPI clients should connect to first when retrieving information about public folder hierarchy or content.

FIGURE 12.11
Client Settings
properties of a mailbox
database

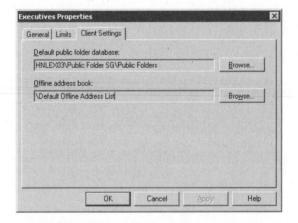

The Offline Address Book setting affects clients that work in offline mode or local cache mode. Here you specify which offline address book (OAB) a MAPI client should download. The default OAB contains the default global address list and is sufficient for most small- and medium-sized businesses.

The properties you have just examined using the graphical user interface can also be examined using the `Get-MailboxDatabase` cmdlet. The following example retrieves mailbox database properties and sends them to a formatted list:

```
Get-MailboxDatabase 'Executives' | FL
JournalRecipient            :
MailboxRetention            : 30.00:00:00
OfflineAddressBook          : \Default Offline Address List
OriginalDatabase            :
PublicFolderDatabase        : HNLEX03\Public Folder SG\Public Folders
```

```
ProhibitSendReceiveQuota    : 2355MB
Recovery                    : False
ProhibitSendQuota           : 2GB
IndexEnabled                : True
AdministrativeGroup         : Exchange Administrative Group (FYDIBOHF23SPDLT)
AllowFileRestore            : False
BackupInProgress            :
CopyEdbFilePath             :
DatabaseCreated             : True
Description                 :
EdbFilePath                 : D:\Executives-SG-DB\Executives.edb
ExchangeLegacyDN            : /o=Volcano Surfboards/ou=Exchange Administrative
  Group (FYDIBOHF23SPDLT)/cn=Configuration/cn=Servers
/cn=HNLEX03/cn=Microsoft Private MDB
HasLocalCopy                : False
DeletedItemRetention        : 14.00:00:00
LastFullBackup              :
LastIncrementalBackup       :
MaintenanceSchedule         : {Sun.1:00 AM-Sun.5:00 AM, Mon.1:00 AM-Mon.5:00AM,
Tue.1:00 AM-Tue.5:00 AM, Wed.1:00 AM-Wed.5:00 AM, Thu.1:00 AM-Thu.5:00 AM,
Fri.1:00 AM-Fri.5:00 AM, Sat.1:00 AM-Sat.5:00 AM}
MountAtStartup              : True
Mounted                     :
Organization                : Volcano Surfboards
QuotaNotificationSchedule   : {Sun.1:00 AM-Sun.1:15 AM, Mon.1:00 AM-Mon.1:15AM,
Tue.1:00 AM-Tue.1:15 AM, Wed.1:00 AM-Wed.1:15 AM, Thu.1:00 AM-Thu.1:15 AM,
Fri.1:00 AM-Fri.1:15 AM, Sat.1:00 AM-Sat.1:15 AM}
RetainDeletedItemsUntilBackup : False
Server: HNLEX03
ServerName                  : HNLEX03
StorageGroup                : HNLEX03\Executives SG
StorageGroupName            : Executives SG
IssueWarningQuota           : 1945MB
EventHistoryRetentionPeriod : 7.00:00:00
Name   : Executives
MinAdminVersion             : -2147453113
AdminDisplayName            : Executives
ExchangeVersion             : 0.1 (8.0.535.0)
DistinguishedName           : CN=Executives,CN=Executives SG,
CN=InformationStore,CN=HNLEX03,CN=Servers,CN=Exchange
Administrative Group (FYDIBOHF23SPDLT),CN=Administrative Groups,
CN=Volcano Surfboards,CN=Microsoft Exchange,CN=Services,
CN=Configuration,DC=volcanosurfboards,DC=com
Identity                    : HNLEX03\Executives SG\Executives
Guid                        : 99c3570b-d19b-493b-aec6-4da1b2c3bbb3
ObjectCategory              : volcanosurfboards.com/Configuration/Schema/
ms-Exch-Private-MDB
ObjectClass                 : {top, msExchMDB, msExchPrivateMDB}
```

```
WhenChanged            : 12/6/2006 8:32:31 PM
WhenCreated            : 12/6/2006 8:27:15 PM
OriginatingServer      : HNLDC01.volcanosurfboards.com
IsValid                : True
```

Some of these properties can be changed through the EMS using the Set-MailboxDatabase cmdlet. For example, to change the Prohibit Send At (KB) quota to 100MB, you would type this:

```
Set-MailboxDatabase 'Executives' -ProhibitSendQuota:100MB
```

Not all of the properties that you see in the output of the Get-MailboxDatabase cmdlet can be changed, of course. Some of them are system properties. The mailbox database location must be changed using the Move-MailboxDatabase cmdlet.

Summary

Scaling upward and outward is a necessary evil for organizations with more than a few hundred users. Though a single machine can easily support all the necessary server roles for a few hundred mailboxes, if it is not properly configured, it may experience performance problems. Recognizing potential performance bottleneck points and how to correct them is an essential skill for Exchange administrators. Properly sizing Exchange databases and storage groups is an important task for the Exchange administrator.

As more mailboxes are supported on a single Exchange Mailbox server, scaling the server upward to support more storage is also an important configuration item. Creating more storage groups and mailbox databases will help you to support larger mailboxes and more data while preventing any single database from growing too large.

Chapter 13

Managing Address Lists

Over the past 20 years, LAN-based and host-based e-mail systems have become more complex and have offered more and more features. One of the features that has become indispensable is an address book of recipients to which you might commonly send mail. The address book provides you with a view into the mail system's directory service database. In an Exchange environment, this address book is referred to as the *global address list* (GAL) and the directory service is the Active Directory.

In most cases, the global address list is a comprehensive listing of all mail-enabled objects in your Active Directory. Most user mailboxes, resource mailboxes, mail-enabled users, mail-enabled contacts, and mail-enabled groups will appear in the GAL. If you have mail-enabled public folders that are not hidden, they will also appear in the GAL. However, there are system objects (such as system mailboxes) as well as hidden objects that will not appear in the global address list.

For mobile users or users who work offline, you can build a subset of the information in the main GAL that can be more easily downloaded and viewed offline. These are called *offline address books*.

In many small- and medium-sized businesses — and even some large organizations — the default listing of the GAL, the default address lists, and the default offline address book will prove to be sufficient. However, other organizations may find a need to customize these.

In this chapter you learn to:

◆ Define additional global address lists

◆ Create custom address lists

◆ Customize offline address books

Viewing the Global Address List

Exchange clients view the GAL using a number of different mechanisms. The most common methods to view information in the Exchange GAL are using an Outlook MAPI client and Outlook Web Access. You can also view the GAL via Windows Mobile devices, BlackBerries, or even via an iPhone. Probably the least commonly used method is a direct LDAP query.

For many organizations, the GAL is used not only for addressing e-mail but for looking up information about other users in the organization, such as address, title, and telephone numbers. Figure 13.1 shows the Outlook 2007 address book when viewing the GAL.

FIGURE 13.1
Viewing the global
address list

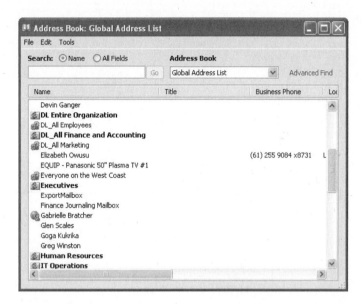

Note that the GAL shown in Figure 13.1 is probably not very useful for the organization's company white pages or company directory. There is not much additional information on the mailboxes and contacts; even the title and business phone number are missing for most mail-enabled objects.

CHANGES TO THE GAL MIGHT BE DELAYED

Any changes you make, such adding a new address list or creating new global address lists, will not appear until users close their mail client and re-open it. Because these objects are all stored in the Active Directory, waiting for the Active Directory to replicate to all global catalog servers may also slow the availability of new address lists. Outlook clients in local cache mode may experience longer delays since they download the offline address book only once per day.

Managing Global Address Lists

The global address list, by its very definition, is a list of all mail-enabled objects in the entire directory (in this case, the Active Directory). You can create multiple global address lists for your organization, but your users see only one. They cannot pick and choose which GAL they see in Outlook or Outlook Web Access.

Most small and medium-sized businesses will never need more than the default global address list. In fact, organizations with tens of thousands of mailboxes often never need more than a single GAL. So why is there a feature that lets you create more than one GAL? An organization might need more than one GAL for a couple of reasons:

◆ The Exchange organization is hosting more than one company or subsidiary, but users only need to see a subset of the entire organization.

◆ The Exchange organization is a hosting environment that runs many companies, but users in each company should see only the other users in their company.

Creating Global Address Lists

Creating multiple global address lists and defining the permissions for them is a little beyond the job scope for the typical reader of this book, but I want to cover some of the basics nonetheless. If you are sure you do not need custom GALs, you can safely skip this section of the chapter.

DETERMINING WHICH GAL A USER WILL SEE

A user will never see more than one global address list at a time or even be offered a choice of which GAL to look at. So now you may be asking, if there are multiple global address lists in a single Exchange organization and if users cannot select which one they are viewing, then how do you use them? The client (Outlook or Outlook Web Access) selects which GAL you see based on one of three criteria, applied in this order:

1. The GAL to which the user has permissions is selected first.

2. If the user has permissions to more than one GAL, the GAL to which the user is a member is selected.

3. If the user has permissions to more than one GAL and is a member of more than one GAL, the largest GAL is selected.

EMS CMDLETS FOR MANAGING GALs

You create and manage GALs entirely through the EMS. Therefore, you should be aware of the EMS cmdlets that manipulate GAL objects. If you have been studying the EMS cmdlets in much detail, you probably already know the verb portion of the cmdlet and just need the noun. Table 13.1 shows the cmdlets that are used to manage GAL objects.

TABLE 13.1:   Cmdlets Used to Manage Global Address List Objects

CMDLET	EXPLANATION
New-GlobalAddressList	Creates a new global address list object
Get-GlobalAddressList	Retrieves a list of GAL objects or properties of a specific GAL
Set-GlobalAddressList	Sets properties of existing GAL objects
Update-GlobalAddressList	Updates recipients in the Active Directory so that they appear in this GAL if applicable
Remove-GlobalAddressList	Deletes a GAL object

If you want to retrieve a list of all the GAL objects, you can use `Get-GlobalAddressList` and see these results:

```
Get-GlobalAddressList | Format-Table Name
Name
----
Default Global Address List
```

The real meat and potatoes of the GAL is the query, or filter, that is used to construct the membership list. A couple of properties of GAL objects allow you to define the query that is used to construct the list. You can define a custom LDAP query, a recipient filter, or address list conditional properties. One conditional property of a GAL is the `ConditionalCompany` property. Let's do the `Get-GlobalAddressList` query again, but this time include these properties in a formatted list:

```
Get-GlobalAddressList | Format-List Name,RecipientFilter,LdapRecipientFilter,↵
ConditionalCompany
```

```
Name                : Default Global Address List
RecipientFilter     : (Alias -ne $null -and (ObjectClass -eq `user` -or
   ObjectClass -eq `contact` -or ObjectClass -eq `msExchSystemMailbox`
-or ObjectClass -eq `msExchDynamicDistributionList`
-or ObjectClass -eq `group` -or ObjectClass -eq `publicFolder`))
LdapRecipientFilter : (&(mailNickname=*)(|(objectClass=user)(objectClass=contact)
(objectClass=msExchSystemMailbox)(objectClass=msExchDynamicDistributionList)
(objectClass=group)(objectClass=publicFolder)))
ConditionalCompany  :
```

First notice that the `ConditionalCompany` property was empty for this particular GAL. The `LdapRecipientFilter` property contains the filter that would be used if this GAL was being used by an Exchange 2000/2003 Recipient Update Service. It maps to the Active Directory attribute `purportedSearch`. The `RecipientFilter` property is used by Exchange 2007 to apply membership to address lists; for you Active Directory fanatics out there, this property maps to the `msExchQueryFilter` attribute of the GAL object.

Let's take apart that `RecipientFilter` before we go any further and see what listing it is really generating. Inside the inner set of parentheses, notice that the filter applies to any type of `ObjectClass` that is equal to (-eq) user, contact, system mailbox, dynamic distribution list, group, or public folder. This is almost every type of object in the domain, right? The filter narrows it down a little further by saying that the `Alias` property (the Exchange alias) must not be null. This means that the objects in question must be mail-enabled. Got all of that? Don't worry if it is a little fuzzy; creating multiple GALs is a very advanced topic and requires some practice. But understanding some of the basics of how the address lists are defined, scoped, or restricted can help you in other areas of Exchange Server 2007.

Let's use an example now to further illustrate the concepts and practices of implementing more than one GAL. In this example, my company has just purchased a new company (Scully Surfboards) and has moved all of their mailboxes over to our organization's Exchange servers. However, the users from the company we just purchased are a little finicky and don't like seeing *anyone* in their global address list but their own little branch of the company. Granted, we could just give them their own Active Directory and Exchange server, but that might be a waste of hardware, software, and human resources. So we will create a GAL called Scully Surfboards. Here is the command:

```
New-GlobalAddressList -Name "Scully Surfboards"
```

All this command does is create a new GAL called Scully Surfboards; we did not even use any of the `RecipientFilter` or conditional filter properties. Let's say that we want anyone whose company name attribute is equal to Scully Surfboards to be in this GAL. We need to modify this GAL using the `Set-GlobalAddressList` cmdlet. The cmdlet needs to set the `-ConditionalCompany` property and it needs to set the `-IncludedRecipients` property. Because this list will *only* contain mailbox-enabled users, the `-IncludedRecipients` property only needs to have `MailboxUsers`. The following command will accomplish this:

```
Set-GlobalAddressList "Scully Surfboards" -ConditionalCompany "Scully↵
Surfboards" -IncludedRecipients "MailboxUsers"
```

Now let's take a look at some of the properties that were created for this new GAL object.

```
Get-GlobalAddressList "Scully Surfboards" | Format-List Name,RecipientFilter,↵
LdapRecipientFilter,RecipientFilterApplied,IncludedRecipients,ConditionalCompany

Name                   : Scully Surfboards
RecipientFilter        : (RecipientType -eq `UserMailbox´ -and Company
-eq Scully Surfboards´)
LdapRecipientFilter    : (&(objectClass=user)(objectCategory=person)
(mailNickname=*)(msExchHomeServerName=*)(company=Scully Surfboards))
RecipientFilterApplied : False
IncludedRecipients     : MailboxUsers
ConditionalCompany     : {Scully Surfboards}
```

Notice that the `RecipientFilter` and `LdapRecipientFilter` properties were automatically generated even though we used a "pre-canned" filter.

Applying Global Address Lists to Mail Objects

In the previous example, I created a new GAL called Scully Surfboards. In an Exchange 2000/2003 environment, eventually anyone whose company name was equal to Scully Surfboards appears in this GAL. That was because there was a process called the Recipient Update Service (RUS) that took care of little housekeeping tasks like adding recipients to address lists. Many people who are new to Exchange may think that this sort of thing just magically happens, but there has to be some "back end" process that actually handles this.

Anyone who has fought RUS problems with earlier versions of Exchange will be happy to know that the RUS is no longer responsible for this task. Actually, the RUS has been retired from Exchange active duty permanently. When a new mailbox-enabled user is created by the Exchange Management Console, the cmdlet that creates the user evaluates each of the address lists available. The `RecipientFilter` and `LdapRecipientFilter` properties of an address list are examined to determine if the user being created should be included in that particular address list. If the user should be included in the address list, that user's `showInAddressBook` attribute in Active Directory will include that particular address list name.

Intuitively, you might think that each time an address list is displayed, the query or filter is simply executed once again. It turns out that enumerating members of an address list is much more efficient if the address list information is stored with the mail-enabled object. Figure 13.2 shows the `showInAddressBook` attribute for a newly created mailbox-enabled user whose company attribute contained Scully Surfboards; the object was viewed using the ADSI Edit utility.

FIGURE 13.2
Viewing a mail-enabled
object's showInAddress-
Book attribute

The value was stored in this attribute as the distinguished name of the GAL; in this example that name is as follows:

```
CN=Scully Surfboards,CN=All Global Address Lists,CN=Address Lists↵
    Container,CN=Volcano Surfboards,CN=Microsoft Exchange,CN=Services,↵
CN=Configuration,DC=volcanosurfboards,DC=com
```

That takes care of mail-enabled recipients that are created *after* the GAL is created. But what about mail-enabled recipients that are already in the Active Directory or ones whose company name is changed after they are created? This is the job of the `Update-GlobalAddressList` cmdlet. If you know that the GAL is out-of-date or not showing everyone it should, here is how you can update it:

```
Update-GlobalAddressList "Scully Surfboards"
```

If you wanted to update all of your recipients and all of the GAL objects, you could run these two cmdlets:

```
Get-GlobalAddressList | Update-GlobalAddressList
```

In an earlier EMS cmdlet, I showed you the properties of the Scully Surfboards address list. This included a property called `RecipientFilterApplied`. This property was set to `False`. Once you actually use the `Update-GlobalAddressList` to apply this address list to recipients, this will change to `True`. Here is an example:

```
Get-GlobalAddressList "Scully Surfboards" | FL Name,RecipientFilterApplied
Name                    : Scully Surfboards
RecipientFilterApplied : True
```

However, `RecipientFilterApplied` automatically goes back to `False` if you make any changes to any of its properties.

Applying Permissions to Global Address Lists

Thus far I have created a global address list called Scully Surfboards and made sure that anyone whose company name attribute is equal to Scully Surfboards will be included in it. However, when users who are included in that address list log on to Outlook or Outlook Web Access, they are going to be sorely disappointed because they will still see the default global address list. Why is that? I have not yet changed the permissions on the default global address list, so the client continues to choose that one because it is the largest.

Let's now expand the example just a bit so that you can restrict who has permissions to which address lists. You need to do this with Active Directory security groups, and to do it right you need to create two security groups. You will define a group called View the Big GAL and a group called View the Scully Surfboards GAL. You will add the appropriate users to each security group; if a user is a member of both security groups, he will see the largest of the two GALs when he uses Outlook.

The easiest way to edit the permissions on the GAL objects is to use the ADSI Edit utility from the Windows 2003 Support Tools. You will need to open ADSI Edit, browse down through the Configuration partition to Services, Microsoft Exchange, *Organization Name*, Address Lists Container, and All Global Address Lists. This is shown in Figure 13.3.

FIGURE 13.3
Using ADSI Edit to manage the permissions on a global address list

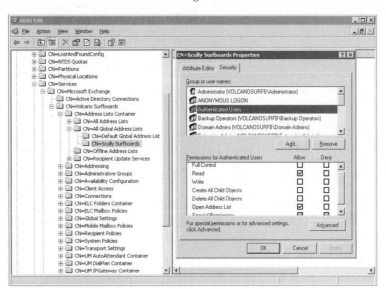

In Figure 13.3, you are looking at the Security properties of the Scully Surfboards GAL object. Notice that Authenticated Users has the Read and Open Address List permissions. Clear the Read and Open Address List check boxes in the Allow column for Authenticated Users; don't check the Deny permissions because that will override the permissions you are about to assign. Now add the View the Scully Surfboards GAL group to this list and assign that group Read and Open Address List permissions in the Allow column.

Now you need to do the same thing to the default global address list group; you must add the View the Big GAL group and allow that group Read and Open Address List permissions and you must clear the Read and Open Address List permissions from the Authenticated Users group.

This may seem like a bit of hassle to set up, but once you have started down this configuration path, it is easy to add additional GALs and to assign them permissions in the same way.

One potential stumbling block that you will have to cross when you are creating multiple global address lists is that, by default, the global address list allows authenticated users to access it. You must clear the Allow permissions for the Authenticated Users group; this will ensure that users do not see the default GAL in Outlook.

Managing Subsets of the Global Address List

In an organization with hundreds, thousands, or tens of thousands of mail-enabled objects in its default global address list or custom global address lists, actually finding someone or sorting based on a certain criterion (such as department) can be overwhelming. Unlike multiple global address lists (which may be of use only in very specific circumstances), subsets of the address list containing only part of the organization's users can help users in even small or medium-sized organizations find or sort parts of the global address list.

Address lists are a great way to allow users to view a subset of the global address list such as their own department or users in their own city.

The function of an address list is to help users narrow the scope of the recipients in the GAL so that they see a subset of their entire address book. For example, a user might want to view everyone in a specific department, state, or company. The user chooses which of these address lists he wants to view from within the Outlook address book. Figure 13.4 shows the Outlook address book and the drop-down list that exposes the address lists available.

FIGURE 13.4
Viewing the available address lists from within Outlook

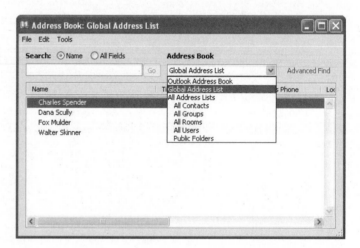

Available address lists can be viewed and managed using the EMC or via the EMS. In the EMC, they are found in the Organization Configuration work center under the Mailbox subcontainer. Figure 13.5 shows the Address Lists container and the Actions pane from the Organization Configuration work center.

FIGURE 13.5
Viewing the address lists using the Exchange Management Console

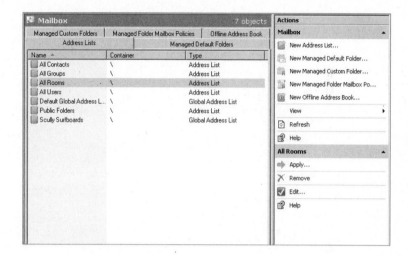

Default Specific Address Lists in Exchange 2007

Figure 13.4 showed the specific address lists that are created by default for Exchange 2007. They have very simple filters and can be helpful for your users in basic ways, but if you find them unnecessary, you can always delete them and create more useful address lists. Table 13.2 lists the default address lists and what they contain.

TABLE 13.2:   Address Lists Built Into Exchange 2007

LIST NAME	EXPLANATION
All Contacts	All mail-enabled contact objects and mail-enabled users
All Groups	All mail-enabled groups and dynamic distribution groups
All Rooms	All conference room resource mailboxes
All Users	All mailbox-enabled users

EMS Cmdlets for Address Lists

As you have probably guessed by now, you can also enumerate the address lists using the Get-AddressList cmdlet. In this chapter, you are going to stick mostly to the EMC when creating and managing address lists. However, so that you have these cmdlets in your arsenal, I am including the address list cmdlets in Table 13.3; you will find that the nouns in these cmdlets are almost identical to the ones used for managing global address lists.

TABLE 13.3:   EMS Cmdlets for Manipulating Address Lists

CMDLET	EXPLANATION
New-AddressList	Creates a new address list
Set-AddressList	Sets address list properties
Get-AddressList	Retrieves address lists
Move-AddressList	Moves an address list from one container to another
Update-AddressList	Updates recipients of the specified address list so that they are now shown in the specified address list
Remove-AddressList	Deletes an address list from the directory

CREATING CUSTOM ADDRESS LISTS

Let's go through a simple example of creating a couple of new address lists. In this example, users want to be able to sort and view the global address list based on departments within the company.

STEP 1: CREATE AN ADDRESS LIST CONTAINER

The first thing you need to do is to create an empty address list container. Launch the New Address List Wizard, and the Introduction screen prompts you for the types of recipients. Specify a name for the address list and select None as the type of recipients to include.

In this example, you are creating a root container for address lists called Departments.

Introduction

This wizard allows you to create a new address list. Address lists display a subset of recipients in an organization based on properties of the recipient.

Name:

Departments

Container:

\

Browse

Include these recipient types:

◉ None

◯ All recipients types

When this task runs, the following command is used:

```
New-AddressList -Name `Departments´ -Container `\´ -IncludedRecipients `None´
```

STEP 2: CREATE AN ADDRESS LIST

Once you have a Departments container in the root of the address lists, you want to create an address list inside the container and specify that it should contain only people from a certain department.

Run the New Address List Wizard once again. This time on the Introduction page, you can specify that it should contain All Recipient Types or you can choose specific recipient types (mailbox-enabled users, mail-enabled users, mail-enabled contacts, and so on).

Select the container in which you want this address list to reside.

This address list will contain mailboxes from the Engineering department, so you want this list to appear under the Departments container previously created.

STEP 3: SET CONDITIONS FOR THE ADDRESS LIST

Next you find the Conditions screen. Setting the conditions for an address list is much like setting the conditions or filter for a dynamic distribution group. For this example, select the Recipient Is In A Department check box in Step 1. In Step 2, you must click the underlined text and specify the department name.

STEP 4: SCHEDULE WHEN TO POPULATE THE ADDRESS LIST

The next screen of the New Address List Wizard is the Schedule screen. Earlier in this chapter, I talked about the fact that address lists are not generated "on-the-fly" each time you want to see who is a member. Each mail-enabled object has an attribute in Active Directory that indicates which address lists they should be shown in; this multi-valued attribute is called the showInAddressBook attribute. Address lists get populated in this attribute for each object that matches the query by some process. In the case of global address lists, this process is kicked off by the Update-GlobalAddressList cmdlet; for address lists, this process is kicked off by the Update-AddressList cmdlet.

The Schedule page asks you when this should process be kicked off. Ideally, you run it immediately, but if you know that the address list is very large (say thousands of mail-enabled objects), you might want to defer the process until a quieter period for your network.

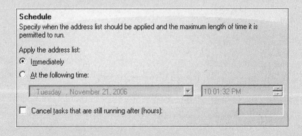

STEP 5: VIEW THE SUMMARY AND EXECUTE THE COMMAND

The next screen is merely confirming what will be applied or performed when you click the New button. It is confirming the following information: A new address list called Engineering will be created in the \Departments container. This address list will contain all types of mail-enabled recipients whose department is equal to Engineering.

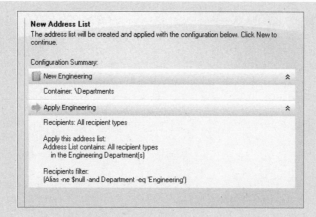

When you click the New button, two commands are actually executed. The first creates the specified address list. The second updates any recipients that meet the conditions of the address list:

```
New-AddressList -Name `Engineering´ -Container `\Departments´ ↵
-IncludedRecipients `AllRecipients´ -ConditionalDepartment 'Engineering'

Update-AddressList -Identity '\Departments\Engineering'
```

The result of this operation is that when you view the global address list in Outlook or Outlook Web Access, there is a new Engineering address list, which shows only the members of the Engineering department.

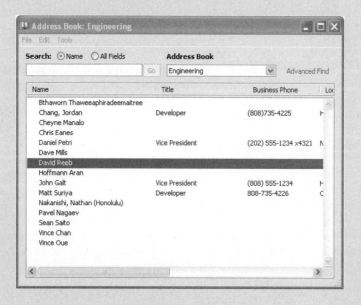

If you want to view information about the address list created in "Creating Custom Address Lists," you can use the `Get-AddressList` cmdlet to retrieve it. The following lines show some of the properties of the newly created address list. I have intentionally cut out some of the lines to shorten the amount of text I am showing you here. If you try this yourself, you will see more properties.

```
Get-AddressList "Engineering" | FL
Container                    : \Departments
DisplayName                  : Engineering
Name : Engineering
RecipientFilter              : (Alias -ne $null -and Department
     -eq `Engineering´)
LdapRecipientFilter          : (&(mailNickname=*)(department=Engineering))
LastUpdatedRecipientFilter   : (Alias -ne $null -and Department -eq `
     Engineering´)
RecipientFilterApplied       : True
IncludedRecipients           : AllRecipients
ConditionalDepartment        : {Engineering}
ConditionalCompany           : {}
ConditionalStateOrProvince   : {}
ConditionalCustomAttribute1  :
ConditionalCustomAttribute2  :
ConditionalCustomAttribute3  :
RecipientFilterType          : Precanned
IsValid                      : True
OriginatingServer            : HNLDC01.volcanosurfboards.com
DistinguishedName            : CN=Engineering,CN=Departments,CN=All Address Lists,
CN=Address Lists Container,CN=Volcano Surfboards,CN=Microsoft Exchange,
CN=Services,CN=Configuration,DC=volcanosurfboards,DC=com
Identity                     : \Departments\Engineering
```

If a user account is mailbox-enabled and the department is equal to Engineering, it will automatically be included in the Engineering address list. However, if an account is mailbox-enabled and then the department attribute is later changed to Engineering, you need to run the `Update-AddressList` cmdlet. In this case, the command would be as follows:

```
Update-AddressList "Engineering"
```

You could also run the following cmdlet and update all of the address lists in the organization:

```
Get-AddressList | Update-AddressList
```

If you have a large global address list, take great care in running the `Update-AddressList` cmdlet, because it will take up system resources while the update process is running both on the system running the command and on the domain controller it is using. However, if there are a lot of changes within your organization that cause changes to attributes that are conditions of address lists, you might want to schedule those cmdlets to run every night.

Choosing a Preferred Address List

A fairly common question among users is whether they can view a specific address list rather than the global address list. Many users prefer to see only the users in their particular department, for example. Users can set their own default address lists:

1. Launch the address book and choose Tools ➢ Options.

2. The Addressing page (shown in Figure 13.6) has a drop-down list option called Show This Address List First; from here you can select any available address list.

FIGURE 13.6
Changing the default address list

If an address list does not appear for a user, the user may need to close Outlook and reopen it. If the user is working in local cache mode, she may need to download the latest offline address book or wait for the newest offline address book to be generated.

EXCHANGE 2000/2003 ADDRESS LISTS MUST BE UPGRADED

If you are migrating from Exchange 2000/2003 and you have address lists that you created with one of those versions, they must be upgraded. As a matter of fact, you cannot even edit a legacy address list without upgrading the list; you will get an error message.

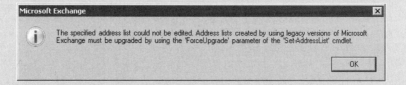

To fix this error, you need to run the Set-AddressList EMS cmdlet and update the scope of the filter. You need to include the -ForceUpgrade $True option.

Managing Offline Address Books

The offline address book allows users to work in Outlook even while disconnected from the Exchange server and retain access to the organization's address lists. The administrator of the Exchange organization can define what is contained in an offline address book. All versions of Outlook have the ability to download an offline address book even though the format and the method of distribution has changed over the years.

Outlook 2003 and earlier clients retrieve their offline address book (OAB) files from a system public folder called OFFLINE ADDRESS BOOK. In the OFFLINE ADDRESS BOOK folder structure, there are subfolders for different versions of Outlook.

Starting with Outlook 2007, the Outlook client can download the OAB files from either the OFFLINE ADDRESS BOOK public folder or a Web Service distribution point on an Exchange Client Access server.

With a default installation of Exchange 2007, a default offline address book is automatically created. You can manage it or create additional offline address books using the Exchange Management Console. The Mailbox subcontainer of the Organization Configuration work center includes an Offline Address Book tab in the results pane; this is shown in Figure 13.7.

FIGURE 13.7
Managing offline address books using the Exchange Management Console

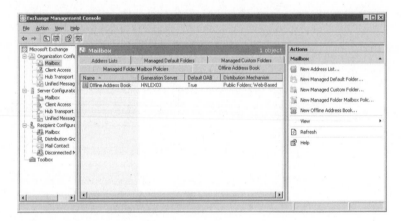

Managing the Default Offline Address Book

YOU DON'T NEED TO EDIT THE DEFAULT OFFLINE ADDRESS BOOK

In most cases and organizations, the default offline address book will be sufficient. Even an organization with tens of thousands of users can fit compactly into offline address book files. Unless you have a very specific need for assigning users an offline address book that is different than your global address list, you probably do not need to make changes to address lists included with the default offline address book.

The default offline address book includes the organization's default global address list. You can modify the address lists that are contained in the default offline address book on the Address Lists property page (see Figure 13.8).

FIGURE 13.8
Configuring the address
lists that an offline
address book contains

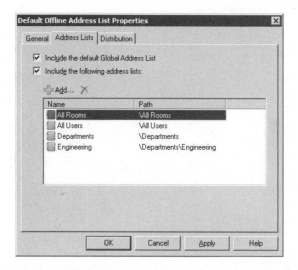

The Include The Default Global Address List check box configures the offline address book to include the entire global address list. You can also check the Include The Following Address Lists check box and add additional address lists that should be included in the offline address book.

The Distribution property page (shown in Figure 13.9) allows you to configure which clients and offline address book versions you are going to support. For each of the older Outlook versions, a public folder is created. In a large organization, you would want to ensure that those folders are replicated to public folder servers in each major location in your network.

FIGURE 13.9
Offline address book
Distribution properties

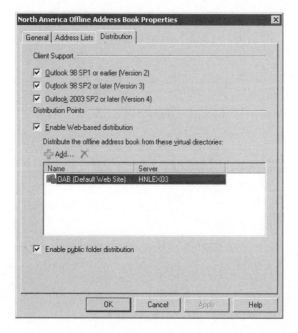

The Distribution Points section allows you to specify whether you will be distributing the offline address book via a public folder. Public folder distribution of the offline address books is required for Outlook 2003 and earlier clients. You do this by ensuring that the Enable Public Folder Distribution check box is checked.

For Outlook 2007 clients, you can click the Enable Web-Based Distribution check box and provide OAB paths. Outlook 2007 clients locate the Web distribution points using the Autodiscover service. In a larger organization with more than one Active Directory site that contains Exchange servers, an Exchange Client Access server role in each site should be configured to host an OAB virtual directory, and then that path should be included in the list of virtual directories that host each offline address book.

The OAB virtual directory paths are defined on each Client Access server role in the Server Configuration work center under the Client Access subcontainer. For each Client Access server role, there is a Offline Address Book Distribution property page in the work pane. Here you will find the OAB virtual directory; by default you will see the one for the default website (shown in Figure 13.10).

FIGURE 13.10
OAB virtual directory for the default website

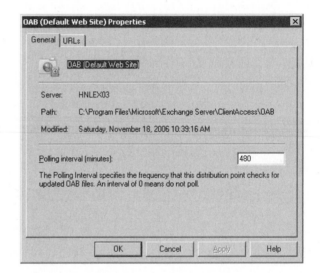

There is not really a lot you can configure for the OAB virtual directory. On the General property page, you can configure the polling interval for that particular virtual directory. The polling interval specifies how often the Client Access server will check for updated OAB files. The default is every 480 minutes, but in between automatic polling times, you can force the OAB files to be updated using the `Update-FileDistributionService` cmdlet. To update the OAB files on server HNLEX03, you would type this:

```
Update-FileDistributionService HNLEX03 -Type "OAB"
```

The URLs property page allows you to configure the internal and external URLs that the clients use to connect to the OAB distribution points.

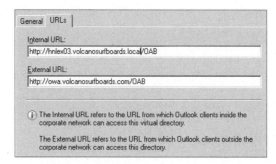

CREATING AN OFFLINE ADDRESS BOOK

In this example, you are going to assign certain users a smaller offline address book. You don't want them to see the entire global address list, but rather just the Engineering department. This type of scenario might be useful in a hosting environment or if your company has multiple subsidiaries or business units hosted in a single Exchange organization.

The easiest way to create a new offline address book is using the EMC:

1. Simply choose the New Offline Address Book task from the Actions pane to see the New Offline Address Book Wizard.

2. On the Introduction page, you must define the name of the offline address book, the server that will be responsible for rebuilding it, if it should contain the default global address list, and if it should contain additional address lists. In this case, you want the Engineering Department OAB to include only the Engineering address list.

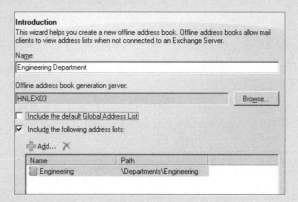

3. When you click Next, you see the Distribution Points page, in which you define whether you want to distribute the OAB via OAB virtual directories on the Client Access servers (Outlook 2007 only), via a public folder (Outlook 2007 and earlier), or both. If you select Enable Web-Based Distribution, make sure you include an OAB virtual directory on a Client Access server in each Active Directory site.

4. When you click New, the EMC creates the necessary EMS command to generate the new OAB and executes the command. Here is the command that was executed to generate this OAB:

```
New-OfflineAddressBook -Name `Engineering Department`↵
-Server `HNLEX03` -AddressLists `\Departments\Engineering`↵
-PublicFolderDistributionEnabled $true -VirtualDirectories↵
`HNLEX03\OAB (Default Web Site)`
```

Note that unless you specify otherwise, all Outlook versions are supported when the offline address book is created.

Defining Offline Address Book Generation Schedules

By default, the content in an offline address book public folder is generated once per day (at 5:00 AM local time). For an organization with tens of thousands of mail-enabled objects in its address lists, this can be pretty CPU intensive for the server doing the generation. The update schedule is defined on the General property page of each offline address book; this property page is shown in Figure 13.11.

I wanted to broach this subject because Outlook 2003 or 2007 in local cache mode only downloads the address book approximately once every 24 hours. If you create new mail-enabled objects or make changes to existing objects at 9:00 AM, for example, those changes will not be incorporated into the offline address book until the next day. The client then might not download the changes for another day. This delay often raises support questions.

In organizations with less than 5,000 mail-enabled objects, I recommend that you rebuild your offline address book two or three times per day. This increases the likelihood that new changes will be downloaded more quickly to clients that are in local cache mode. For larger organizations, you have to balance the load that the rebuild places on your Exchange servers and global catalog servers against the importance of having more up-to-date information.

Assigning Offline Address Books

By default, all users are assigned the default offline address book. Address books are assigned based on the mailbox database on which the user's mailbox is located. You can view or change this setting on the Client Settings property page. To change the offline address book that the users whose mailboxes are on this database use, click the Browse button next to the Offline Address Book box and select the correct OAB.

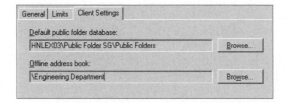

FIGURE 13.11
General property page of an offline address book

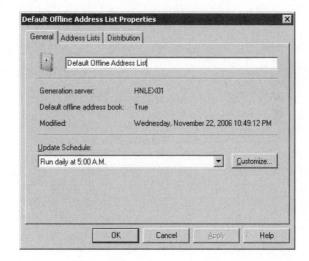

You could have used the following EMS command to accomplish the same thing:

```
Set-MailboxDatabase "Engineering Mailboxes"↵
-OfflineAddressBook "Engineering Department"
```

Managing Offline Address Books Using the Exchange Management Shell

A number of EMS cmdlets are used for managing offline address books. Though OAB management is not something that you do every day, knowledge of these cmdlets may come in handy, so I decided to include them. Table 13.4 contains the EMS cmdlets for use with OABs.

I have intentionally kept the information about using the EMS to manage offline address books fairly light in this book because most of the common tasks can easily be accomplished using the EMC. Good online help is available for these cmdlets, though, if you decide you want to be brave and experiment with the EMS when creating or managing OABs.

TABLE 13.4: Exchange Management Shell Cmdlets Used to Manage Offline Address Books

CMDLET	EXPLANATION
New-OfflineAddressBook	Creates a new offline address book
Set-OfflineAddressBook	Sets the properties of an existing offline address book
Get-OfflineAddressBook	Retrieves a list of offline address books or the individual properties a specified offline address book
Update-OfflineAddressBook	Updates the offline address book contents for public-folder-based OABs
Update-FileDistributionService	Updates the offline address book content for web-based offline address book clients
Remove-OfflineAddressBook	Deletes an offline address book
New-OABVirtualDirectory	Creates a new OAB virtual directory on a Client Access server
Set-OABVirtualDirectory	Sets the properties on an existing OAB virtual directory
Get-OABVirtualDirectory	Retrieves a list offline address book virtual directories or the properties of one or more OAB virtual directories
Remove-OABVirtualDirectory	Deletes an OAB virtual directory

Summary

Managing address lists is a task that usually occurs when you are initially rolling out your Exchange organization. Indeed, creating multiple global address lists is something the typical Exchange administrator never has to do. Creating multiple Exchange global address lists is a more common task within organizations with hundreds of thousands of users or organizations that provide hosting services to multiple companies or their own organization's subsidiaries.

Address lists provide users with a useful way to sort or view only a subset of the global address list information. As you learn more about how your user community works and what their needs are, you may find that additional address lists are a good addition at any point in your Exchange deployment.

Finally, offline address books are another component that you typically do not manage on a day-to-day basis. These are the sort of Exchange components that you "set and forget"; once they are configured, you usually do not need to make too many changes. Just make sure when you configure them that you understand the delay that some users may experience in seeing new changes to the address lists.

Chapter 14

Managing Mailbox Content

The need to control mailbox content and size is often due to limited disk space for mailbox databases but it may also be due to company security policies, electronic discover (eDiscovery) requirements, or for regulatory compliance. Over the years, a lot of solutions for managing mailbox and folder content have come and gone.

Seasoned Exchange Server administrators are probably familiar with the Exchange 2000/2003 Mailbox Manager function or may even be familiar with the Exchange 5.5 Mailbox Cleanup Agent. These tools gave the administrator some control over how long content was kept in a user's mailbox folder. The administrator could configure these tools to delete information in a mailbox if it was older than the specified number of days or larger than a specified size.

Many organizations are now employing archival solutions that will remove content from users' mailboxes and store it on long-term storage such as tape, optical, network attached storage (NAS), or storage area networks (SANs). In some cases, archival solutions are put in place merely to reduce the size of the Exchange databases but still allow users long-term access to their old mail data. In other cases, an organization is required to keep certain types of message content such as financial data, official company communications, and healthcare-related data.

Mailbox archiving has raised new issues and challenges for not only the Exchange administrator but for management and users as well. Some types of messages may need to be retained for long periods of time, but not necessarily one copy of each message in each mailbox. There has to be some method of determining which messages should be retained or archived and sometimes that task may fall on the user.

Organizations that are concerned about meeting regulatory requirements with respect to message archiving and long-term retention of certain types of messages may also be interested in keeping a journaled copy of messages.

This chapter covers some of the new messaging records management features of Exchange 2007, and how to reproduce some of the Exchange 2000/2003 Mailbox Manager functions.

In this chapter you learn to:

◆ Understand the basics of messaging records management

◆ Manage default folders

◆ Create and manage custom folders

◆ Assign managed folder mailbox policies

◆ Configure Exchange 2007 servers to support messaging records management

Understanding the Basics of Messaging Records Management

Before diving into how you would actually set up and implement messaging records management, let's discuss some of the basics. This includes some possible usage scenarios, what the user would see, and the basics of getting started.

First and foremost, let's get some terminology out of the way. Messaging records management encompasses management of e-mail content "at rest." This means that you are managing the content while it is sitting in a folder within someone's mailbox. Don't get this concept confused with transport rules, which are discussed in more detail in Chapter 15, "Managing Messages in Transit." Also, if you see or hear the term *e-mail lifecycle management*, remember that this term was used during the Exchange 2007 beta testing process; the correct term is *messaging records management*.

MESSAGING RECORDS MANAGEMENT AND LICENSING

There has been a lot of confusion regarding the licensing requirements for the messaging records management features of Exchange Server 2007. In general, this feature is considered an Enterprise feature and thus requires an Exchange Enterprise client access license (CAL) for each user that will be "managed."

However, there are exceptions. Any feature that you could have used the Exchange 2000/2003 Mailbox Manager feature to perform can be used with Exchange Server 2007 with only a standard client access license. This includes automatically deleting folder content or moving folder content to a System Cleanup folder or the Deleted Items folder.

User Participation

It is important to keep in mind that messaging records management does not include "important message pixie dust." A popular misconception is that content that should be retained will automatically be moved to the appropriate managed folder. Messages do not get organized automatically. Users must participate in messaging records management by moving their relevant content into the appropriate managed folders.

There are two different perspectives on what we can implement with messaging records management. There are certain things that we can do without the users' intervention, such as purging mail in their existing folders or moving mail to a message archive.

However, the real mission of messaging records management is to get the user to participate in the process. We can use the messaging records management process to create custom folders in the user's mailbox, but it is up to the user to determine which types of messages belong in which folder.

Figure 14.1 shows a set of custom folders that were created inside a folder called Managed Folders. These are called managed custom folders.

The administrator decides what the managed custom folder names will be and assigns a managed folder mailbox policy to the mailbox to ensure that the folders are created. There are additional things that the administrator can do with these folders, but for now we will stick with the basics.

FIGURE 14.1
Custom managed folders created by a managed folder mailbox policy

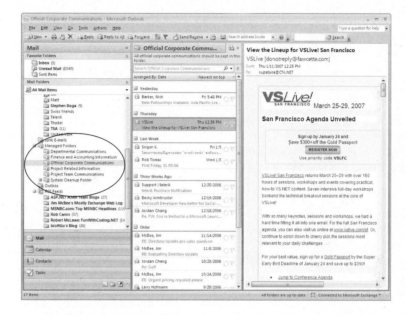

The users are trained to categorize their mailbox content based on the folders you make available to them. This will allow the administrator to then purge folders such as the Inbox or Sent Items every 60, 90, or 180 days without worrying about purging important information. You can specifically archive the data that you find in Managed Folders or you can leave it on the server for a longer period of time based on the users' needs or the organization's requirements.

The most important thing to realize is that, as I mentioned previously, the user must participate in the process.

Possible Scenarios

After you finish reading this chapter, you will probably find a lot of potentially useful scenarios for messaging records management. This is true even if your organization does not perform mailbox archiving or has to deal with regulatory compliance. So, what are some possible uses for messaging records management?

◆ Creating custom folders that are used by users to categorize or organize information that must be retained

◆ Defining content settings that purge certain types of content from either custom folders or the default folders

◆ Defining for managed custom folders content settings that automatically journal specified content types (or all content types) that are moved into the folder

◆ Defining content settings for managed default folders

◆ Defining maximum folder sizes for managed custom folders

◆ Using managed content settings to expire items in a folder so they are eligible for archiving

These are just a few of the possible uses for messaging records management.

Getting Started with Messaging Records Management

Messaging records management folders, content settings, and policies can be defined in the Exchange Management Console (EMC) or the Exchange Management Shell (EMS). For most of the actions I will be describing, I will show you the EMC interface and follow up with EMS commands as necessary.

The messaging records management content settings, policies, and folders are found in the Organization Configuration work center of the EMC under the Mailbox subcontainer. This work center is shown in Figure 14.2. You can see the Managed Default Folders tab in the results pane.

FIGURE 14.2
Viewing the messaging records management components in the Exchange Management Console

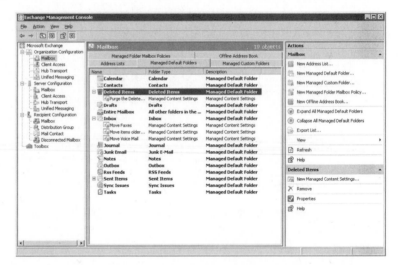

You cannot set up messaging records management using a single dialog box or wizard. A couple of steps are involved in getting started. I go into more detail later in the chapter on how to do each of these steps, but let's start with a basic outline of how you would get started with a policy:

1. Create managed custom folders (if applicable).

2. Define managed content settings for the managed custom folders.

3. Optionally create managed content settings for default folders.

4. Create managed folder mailbox policies that include managed custom folders and/or managed default folders.

5. Assign the managed folder mailbox polices to users.

6. Configure the mailbox servers to run the Managed Folder Assistant on a schedule.

Managing Default Folders

Let's start by talking about a mailbox's default folders; these are the folders that the Outlook client automatically creates the first time the mailbox is accessed. The default folders list is found under the Managed Default Folders tab in the results pane shown in Figure 14.2.

List of Default Folders

The Managed Default Folder list is static; you cannot create additional default folders either through the EMC or the EMS. The following is a list of the folders that are considered default folders:

- Calendar
- Contacts
- Deleted Items
- Drafts
- Entire Mailbox
- Inbox
- Journal
- Junk E-mail
- Notes
- Outbox
- Rss Feeds
- Sent Items
- Sync Issues
- Tasks

Depending on the client version you are using, you may not see all of these folders. For example, if you have never opened your mailbox using the Outlook 2007 client, you will not see the Rss Feeds folder in your mailbox.

Creating Managed Content Settings

Though you cannot define new default folders, you can manage the content in the existing folders. Managed content settings can be defined for each folder (and also for the entire mailbox). In many ways, the managed content settings work the same way that they did in the Exchange 2000/2003 Mailbox Manager.

When creating a managed content setting, you must define what type of content it will be affecting; this means that you specify the message type. Table 14.1 shows the message types that you can define for managed content settings; this table includes the `MessageClass` property that would be used when creating managed content settings via the EMS and the `New-ManagedContentSettings` cmdlet.

TABLE 14.1: Message Types for Managed Content Settings

MESSAGE TYPE	MESSAGECLASS	EXPLANATION
All Message Content	*	All content types in the folder
Calendar Items	IPM.Appointment	Entries found on a calendar
Contacts	IPM.Contact	Contact items
Documents	IPM.Document	Message content that has been set as a document
Faxes	IPM.Note.Microsoft.Fax	Faxes generated by the Exchange 2007 Unified Messaging server role or compatible applications
Journal Items	IPM.Activity	Journal items
Meeting Requests, Responses, and Cancellations	IPM.Schedule	Schedule requests, responses to schedule requests, cancellations, and so on
Missed Calls	IPM.Note.Microsoft.Missed.Voice	Notices of telephone calls missed when using Exchange 2007 Unified Messaging
Notes	IPM.StickyNote	Note items usually found in the Outlook Notes folder
OCS Communicator conversation	IPM.Note.Microsoft.Conversation	Logs conversations generated by Office Communication Server's Communicator client
OCS Communicator Phone device call log	IPM.Note.Microsoft.Conversation.Voice	Call log messages that are generated when using Office Communication Server phone devices.
Posts	IPM.Post	Post item types usually used for public folders
RSS Items	IPM.Post.RSS	RSS feed data in the Outlook 2007 client RSS Feeds folder
Tasks	IPM.Task	Task items
Voice Mail	IPM.Note.Microsoft.Voicemail	Voicemail messages generated by the Exchange 2007 Unified Messaging server or equivalent software

You can optionally specify a retention period for items that meet the conditions of the message content setting. The retention period is specified in days and the retention period starts from one of two points:

◆ The When Delivered, End Date For Calendar And Recurring Tasks selection allows you to specify that the starting point for the retention cycle is when the message arrives in the mailbox. Alternately, if the item is a calendar entry or recurring task, the retention cycle starts at the end date of the item.

◆ The When Item Is Moved To The Folder selection specifies that the retention date starts when the item is first placed into the folder.

Once the retention period expires, you have to take an action on any items that meet your criteria. Table 14.2 shows a list of the possible actions you can take on an item at the end of the retention period. The table also includes the RetentionAction value that would be used if you were creating managed content settings from the EMS instead of the EMC.

TABLE 14.2:   Actions That Can Be Taken on Items at the End of the Retention Period

ACTION	RetentionAction	EXPLANATION
Move to the Deleted Items Folder	MoveToDeletedItems	Moves the item to the Deleted Items folder; this setting is not valid if you are trying to create a managed content setting in the Deleted Items folder.
Move to a Managed Custom Folder	MoveToFolder	Moves the item to a managed custom folder that you specify.
Delete and Allow Recovery	DeleteAndAllowRecovery	Deletes the item, but allows a user to undelete the item before the item is removed from the deleted item cache.
Permanently Delete	PermanentlyDelete	Deletes the item and does not allow it to be recovered from the deleted item cache.
Mark as Past Retention Limit	MarkAsPastRetentionLimit	Marks the item as past the retention limit but takes no further action. At this point, message archival software could take over and archive just the messages that are past their retention limit.

An additional option you have available when you are creating a managed content setting is to automatically journal a copy of the message to a mailbox or external location. You look at an example of journaling using the managed content settings later in this chapter.

If you want to use the EMS to see the managed content settings that you have created, here is an example of using the `Get-ManagedContentSettings` cmdlet:

```
Get-ManagedContentSettings

Name                      MessageClass              ManagedFolderName
----                      ------------              -----------------
Message archival          *                         Official Corporate
   Com...
Purge the Deleted Item ... *                        Deleted Items
Move items older than  ... *                        Inbox
Move items older than  ... *                        Sent Items
Move Faxes                IPM.Note.Microsoft.Fax*   Inbox
Move Voice Mail           IPM.Note.Microsoft.Voi..  Inbox
```

There are a number of cmdlets that you can use from within the EMS to create or manipulate managed content settings. These are shown in Table 14.3.

TABLE 14.3: Exchange Management Shell Cmdlets for Manipulating Managed Content Settings

CMDLET	EXPLANATION
New-ManagedContentSettings	Creates a new managed content setting
Set-ManagedContentSettings	Changes the properties of an existing managed content setting object
Get-ManagedContentSettings	Retrieves managed content settings
Remove-ManagedContentSettings	Deletes a managed content setting object

Let's now look at some practical examples of managed content settings.

KEEPING THE DELETED ITEMS FOLDER CLEAN

One pet peeve of many Exchange administrators I know is that users will delete messages from their Inbox or Sent Items folder, but never actually empty the Deleted Items folder. It is not uncommon to find hundreds of megabytes of message content in a user's Deleted Items folder. In the following example, you set up conditions on the Deleted Items folder so that nothing older than 14 days is kept in the Deleted Items folder but users can recover the deleted message from the deleted item cache after you empty their Deleted Items folder.

To do this through the EMC, locate the Deleted Items folder in the Managed Default Folder list and select it. On the Actions pane, select New Managed Content Settings, which will launch the New Managed Content Settings Wizard (shown in Figure 14.3). On the Introduction screen of the wizard, you specify the name of the managed content settings item, the type of message content it will apply to (in this case, all message content), the length of retention, when the retention period starts, and the action to take.

FIGURE 14.3

Configuring a managed content setting to delete items that have been in the Deleted Items folder longer than 14 days

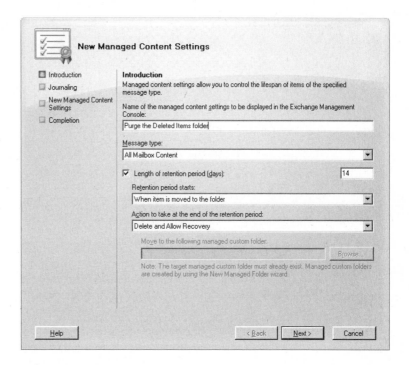

If you want to delete an item from a folder after a specified number of days, choose the one of the two following options from the Retention Period Starts drop-down list:

◆ When Item Is Moved To The Folder

There is a bug in the release to manufacturing (RTM) version of Exchange that may prevent items from being deleted if you choose the When Item Is Moved To The Folder option. Be aware of this if you are an early adopter, but the issue has been fixed in E2K7 SP1.

◆ When Delivered, End Date For Calendar And Recurring Tasks

Because you are working on a default folder, not a custom folder, the option to specify a managed custom folder is not available. Once you click Next, you move to the Journaling page in the wizard, but you do not need anything from that page for this particular managed content setting. The New Managed Content Settings page allows you to review what you are about to configure and then you click New. Like most EMC wizards, the Completion screen will include the EMS command that was actually executed to complete this task. The following is the EMS command that was necessary to define this managed content setting:

```
New-ManagedContentSettings -Name `Purge the Deleted Items folder´↩
-FolderName `Deleted Items´ -RetentionAction `DeleteAndAllowRecovery´↩
-AddressForJournaling $null -AgeLimitForRetention `14.00:00:00´↩
-JournalingEnabled $false -MessageFormatForJournaling `UseTnef´↩
-RetentionEnabled $true -LabelForJournaling `` -MessageClass `*´↩
-MoveToDestinationFolder $null -TriggerForRetention `WhenMoved´
```

Note that although you have defined the managed content setting to this particular folder, it will not yet apply to anyone's mailbox, nor will any server actually enforce this content setting. The managed folder mailbox policies and scheduling the Managed Folder Assistant are covered later in this chapter.

MOVING CONTENT TO AN ALTERNATE LOCATION

A good use of managed content settings is to move content to an alternate location. In this example, you see how to mimic one of the functions of the Exchange 2000/2003 Mailbox Manager. It had the ability to move mail that was nearly ready to be deleted from the system in to a System Cleanup folder. Mail could then be purged from the System Cleanup folder after it had been in that folder for a specified number of days.

You are going to create a managed content setting that moves all items in the Inbox folder into a System Cleanup Folder.

Before you carry out the instructions in this example, you should create a managed custom folder called System Cleanup Folder:

1. Locate and select the Inbox in the Managed Default Folder list. Then on the Actions pane, select New Managed Content Settings, which will launch the New Managed Content Settings Wizard.

2. Specify a retention period of 180 days, specify that the action to take is Move To A Managed Custom Folder, and then in the section labeled Move To The Following Managed Custom Folder, select System Cleanup Folder.

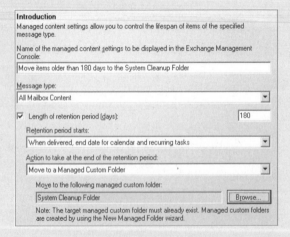

The EMS command that created this managed content setting is very similar to the one used to purge the Deleted Items folder:

```
New-ManagedContentSettings -Name `Move items older than 180 days↵
to the System Cleanup Folder' -FolderName `Inbox'↵
 -RetentionAction `MoveToFolder' -AddressForJournaling $null↵
 -AgeLimitForRetention `180.00:00:00' -JournalingEnabled $false↵
 -MessageFormatForJournaling `UseTnef' -RetentionEnabled $true↵
 -LabelForJournaling `' -MessageClass `*'↵
```

```
    -MoveToDestinationFolder `System Cleanup Folder`↵
    -TriggerForRetention `WhenDelivered`
```

If you now wanted to move items in the Sent Items folder that are older than 180 days into the System Cleanup Folder, you could do so by making a single modification to the managed content settings. The only change that is required is to the -FolderName parameter; its value must be changed to 'Sent Items':

```
 New-ManagedContentSettings -Name `Move items older than 180 days↵
   to the System Cleanup Folder` -FolderName `Sent Items`↵
   -RetentionAction `MoveToFolder` -AddressForJournaling $null↵
   -AgeLimitForRetention `180.00:00:00` -MessageClass `*`↵
   -MoveToDestinationFolder `System Cleanup Folder`↵
   -TriggerForRetention `WhenDelivered`
```

Because you did not require the journaling settings, you can remove those from the New-ManagedContentSettings command line.

Creating and Managing Custom Folders

Managed custom folders are folders that you define as the administrator and then assign to users' mailboxes. As you saw in Figure 14.1, the managed custom folders are created in the user's mailbox in the Managed Folders folder. Creating a managed custom folder is very simple. While you are viewing the Managed Custom Folders tab, simply click the New Managed Custom Folder task in the Actions pane. Figure 14.4 shows the New Managed Custom Folder Wizard.

This wizard has only two pages. The Introduction page asks that you provide a name for the folder, the display name that is shown in Outlook, and a comment that is shown in Outlook. Optionally, you can specify a storage quota option (a maximum amount of data that the managed custom folder can contain). The EMS command that was used to generate this managed custom folder is as follows:

```
 New-ManagedFolder -Name `Project Team Communications`↵
  -FolderName `Project Team Communications` -StorageQuota `25000KB`↵
  -Comment `Place information in this folder related to your internal↵
  project time communications.  This information will be retained in↵
  your mailbox for 360 days from the date it was originally moved to↵
  this folder.`
```

The command that you enter for the folder is useful in helping users to know what the folder is supposed to be for. This comment will be displayed at the top of the listing of messages in the folder if you are using Outlook 2007. (See Figure 14.5.) This information is not displayed with earlier versions.

The storage quota option is useful if you are planning to restrict content for each of the managed folders. Once users reach the storage quota maximum for this folder, the folder name will turn red and users will see a dialog box informing them that their mailbox needs to be cleaned up. This dialog box (shown in Figure 14.6) is displayed only if you are using Outlook 2007 as the client.

FIGURE 14.4
Creating a new managed
custom folder

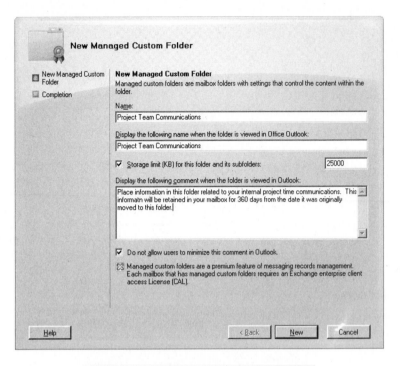

FIGURE 14.5
Comment text for a
custom folder

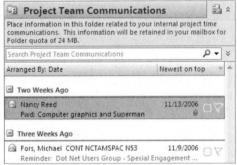

The only problem with the dialog box shown in Figure 14.6 is that it does not tell the user which folder is over its limit.

The Get-ManagedFolder cmdlet allows you to retrieve a list of both the managed custom folders and the default folders:

```
Get-ManagedFolder | Format-Table Name,Description

Name                              Description
----                              -----------
Calendar                          ManagedDefaultFolder
Contacts                          ManagedDefaultFolder
Deleted Items                     ManagedDefaultFolder
Drafts                            ManagedDefaultFolder
Inbox                             ManagedDefaultFolder
```

Junk Email	ManagedDefaultFolder
Journal	ManagedDefaultFolder
Notes	ManagedDefaultFolder
Outbox	ManagedDefaultFolder
Sent Items	ManagedDefaultFolder
Tasks	ManagedDefaultFolder
Entire Mailbox	ManagedDefaultFolder
Rss Feeds	ManagedDefaultFolder
Sync Issues	ManagedDefaultFolder
Official Corporate Communications	ManagedCustomFolder
Project Related Information	ManagedCustomFolder
Finance and Accounting Information	ManagedCustomFolder
Departmental Communications	ManagedCustomFolder
System Cleanup Folder	ManagedCustomFolder
Project Team Communications	ManagedCustomFolder

FIGURE 14.6
Users are prompted to
clean up their mailbox
if a managed custom
folder is over its size
limit.

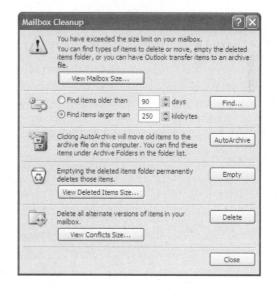

If you are a fan of the EMS, Table 14.4 shows the cmdlets that can be used for creating and
managing managed custom folders.

TABLE 14.4:   Managed Folder Exchange Management Shell Cmdlets

CMDLET	EXPLANATION
New-ManagedFolder	Creates a new managed custom folder
Set-ManagedFolder	Sets properties for an existing managed custom folder
Get-ManagedFolder	Retrieves a list of the managed folders in the organization
Remove-ManagedFolder	Deletes a managed custom folder

Managed Folder Mailbox Policies

Creating managed custom folders and defining managed content settings are just part of the equation when implementing messaging records management. Now you actually have to assign those managed folders to mailboxes. You assign folders to mailboxes with the managed folder mailbox policy. Once you have created a managed folder mailbox policy, you can assign the policy to one or more mailboxes.

ONE MANAGED FOLDER POLICY PER MAILBOX

A mailbox can have only one managed folder policy assigned to it.

Creating Managed Folder Mailbox Policies

Managed folder mailbox policies are found in the Mailboxes subcontainer of the Organization Configuration work center. You find them under the Managed Folder Mailbox Policies (yes, say that three times fast!) tab; by default there are no managed folder mailbox policies. In a small organization, you may need only a single managed folder mailbox policy, whereas larger organizations may have many policies. The policies assign different managed folders or managed content settings to different users based on their departments, job functions, or company division.

A managed folder mailbox policy has very few properties. When you launch the New Managed Folder Mailbox Policy Wizard, you are asked to provide a name for the policy, and you must provide the folders (both custom and default) that will be managed by this policy. Figure 14.7 shows the New Mailbox Policy page of this wizard.

FIGURE 14.7
Creating a managed folder mailbox policy

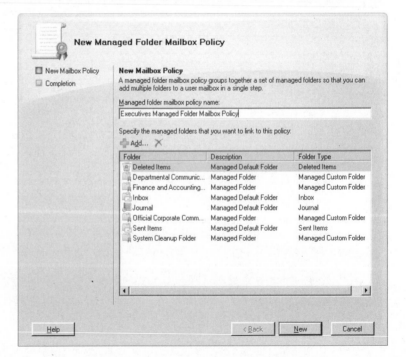

Note that the folders linked with this policy include both custom and default folders. A folder can be linked with more than one policy. The resulting EMS command that is executed to create this policy is as follows:

```
New-ManagedFolderMailboxPolicy -Name `Executives Managed Folder Mailbox Policy'↵
-ManagedFolderLinks `Inbox',`Finance and Accounting Information',↵
'Official Corporate Communications','Deleted Items','Departmental↵
    Communications', `Sent Items',`Journal','System Cleanup Folder'
```

Assigning Managed Folder Mailbox Policies to Users

After a managed folder mailbox policy is defined, the next step is to assign it to a user. You can do this in one of two ways. You can assign the policy to a user during account creation; Figure 14.8 shows the Mailbox Settings page of the New Mailbox Wizard. You can check the Managed Folder Mailbox Policy check box and then browse for a listing of available managed folder mailbox policies in the organization.

FIGURE 14.8
Assigning a managed folder mailbox policy at account creation

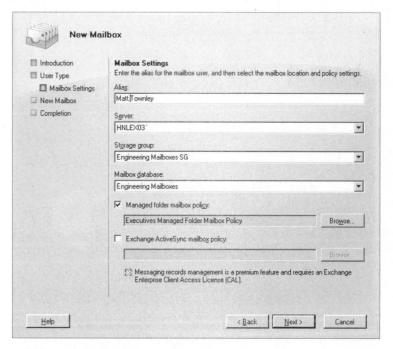

If your organization is supporting Outlook 2003 or earlier clients, you will see a warning message informing you that not all of the managed folder features may be available to the user. This dialog box appears whenever you assign a managed folder mailbox policy to a user account.

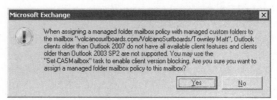

If you are using the Exchange Management Shell, you will notice an additional option in the `Enable-Mailbox` or `New-Mailbox` command line. This option is `-ManagedFolderMailboxPolicy` and it sets the `ManagedFolderMailboxPolicy` property on the mailbox. Here is an example of an EMS command that would enable a mailbox and set the managed folder mailbox policy:

```
Enable-Mailbox `volcanosurfboards.com/VolcanoSurfboards/Townley Matt´ ↵
-Alias `Matt.Townley´ -Database `Engineering Mailboxes´ ↵
-ManagedFolderMailboxPolicy `Executives Managed Folder Mailbox Policy´
```

If someone created an account without defining the managed folder mailbox policy, you can assign a policy to the account using the EMC. Locate the mailbox in the Recipient Configuration work center, display the mailbox's properties, go to the Mailbox Settings property page, select Messaging Records Management, and click the Properties button. This will display the Messaging Records Management properties for that mailbox (see Figure 14.9).

FIGURE 14.9
Messaging Records
Management Properties
of a mailbox

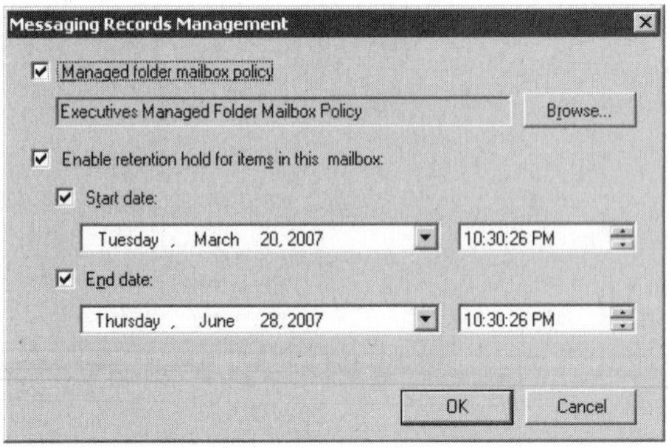

From the Messaging Records Management properties, you can define which managed folder mailbox policy is assigned, and you can optionally specify a period of time during which the policy does not apply to the particular mailbox.

If the mailbox already exists, you can assign the policy using the EMS. For example, if you want to assign user Supatana to the Executives Managed Folder Mailbox Policy, you would type the following EMS cmdlet:

```
Set-Mailbox "Supatana" -ManagedFolderMailboxPolicy "Executives Managed
Folder Mailbox Policy"
```

Actually, if you know that you have to assign a group of mailboxes to a specific policy, it is much easier to do using the EMS. For example, if you want to assign everyone in the Executives group to a managed folder mailbox policy, you can use a single EMS command to accomplish this. Before I show you the command, let's take apart the pieces.

First you want to enumerate the objects that are members of the Executives distribution group. You would use the `Get-DistributionGroupMember` cmdlet. Here is what that would look like:

```
Get-DistributionGroupMember "Executives"
Name                                  RecipientType
----                                  -------------
Saso Erdeljanov                       UserMailbox
```

```
Jordan Chang                        UserMailbox
Don Nguyen                          UserMailbox
Goga Kukrika                        UserMailbox
Pavel Nagaev                        UserMailbox
George Cue                          UserMailbox
Julie Samante                       UserMailbox
Chris Eanes                         UserMailbox
Bthaworn Thaweeaphiradeemaitree     UserMailbox
Cheyne Manalo                       UserMailbox
Jason Sherry                        UserMailbox
Konrad Sagala                       UserMailbox
```

Remember that when you retrieve information using the PowerShell, what is actually output is the objects; you can pipe those objects to other cmdlets. You want to pipe this command to the Set-Mailbox cmdlet in order to assign the ManagedFolderMailboxPolicy property:

```
Get-DistributionGroupMember "Executives" | Set-Mailbox↵
-ManagedFolderMailboxPolicy "Executives Managed Folder Mailbox Policy"
```

Another useful thing you can do from the EMS is to list the mailboxes that are already assigned to a particular policy. You just need to implement the Where cmdlet and filter only the objects whose ManagedFolderMailboxPolicy property starts with Default. Here is an example:

```
Get-Mailbox | Where {$_.ManagedFolderMailboxPolicy -like "*Default*"}↵
| Format-Table Name,Managed*
```

```
Name                        ManagedFolderMailboxPolicy
----                        --------------------------
Nathan Nakanishi            Default Managed Folder Mailbox Policy
Lily Ebrahimi               Default Managed Folder Mailbox Policy
Aran Hoffmann               Default Managed Folder Mailbox Policy
Ryan Tung                   Default Managed Folder Mailbox Policy
```

Enabling Messaging Records Management on the Mailbox Server

The final piece of enabling messaging records management is to configure the mailbox servers to actually schedule and run the Managed Folder Assistant. Managed custom folders do not get created, nor do the content settings get enforced, unless the Managed Folder Assistant is run. Each Exchange server that has the Mailbox role assigned to it has a Messaging Records Management property page. From this property page, you can define a schedule on which the Managed Folder Assistant runs.

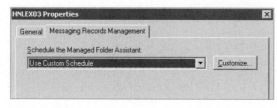

When you click the Customize button, you are presented with a schedule dialog box (see Figure 14.10). The Detail View radio buttons allow you to specify if you are looking at the schedule in 15-minute increments or 1-hour increments.

FIGURE 14.10
Schedule dialog box for the Managed Folder Assistant

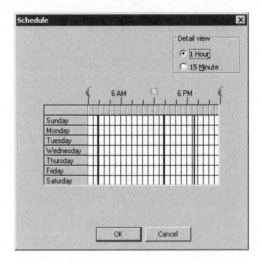

As with other schedule dialog boxes that have a 1-hour view and a 15-minute view, be very careful when selecting a schedule. (If you use the 1-hour view and select an entire hour block, the Managed Folder Assistant will run four times per hour.) I recommend that you select the 15-minute view and then schedule times in 15-minute intervals. Further, unless you have a business requirement to run the Managed Folder Assistant more frequently, I recommend that you schedule it to run no more than two or three times per day.

If you want to kick off the Managed Folder Assistant manually, there is a cmdlet that lets you do this: the Start-ManagedFolderAssistant cmdlet. It will create any custom folders that need to be created and manage any folder content that is now eligible to be managed by messaging records management. This cmdlet is useful to know if you have just assigned a new policy to a group of users and want to make sure that any custom folders that need to be created are created immediately.

If you run Start-ManagedFolderAssistant from the EMS on a mailbox server, no parameters are necessary. However, if you want to run it on a remote mailbox server, you would type this (substituting the name of your server):

```
Start-ManagedFolderAssistant hnlex03
```

You can also run the Managed Folder Assistant against a specific mailbox, as in this example:

```
Start-ManagedFolderAssistant -Mailbox Suriya.Supatanasakul
```

Summary

Messaging records management starts with some of the features found in the Exchange 2000/2003 Mailbox Manager, such as the ability to automatically delete older content found in users' mailboxes, and then extends them further to make Exchange 2007 more friendly in environments that have third-party message archival systems as well as organizations that are required to follow government or organizational regulations.

Managed custom folders allow the administrator to specify folders in each user's mailbox that can be used for organizing and categorizing official or unofficial communications. User participation is a key factor in ensuring that these folders are successful.

The managed content setting feature allows administrators to actually control, move, and delete the content that is found in either the default Exchange folders or the managed custom folders that the administrator has created.

Chapter 15

Managing Messages in Transit

As you may have noticed by now, in spite of the extra features it offers, Exchange provides messaging as its core functionality. Messaging systems have been part of the business environment for years — long enough for the novelty of electronic messaging to wear off and for it to become a staple of the office. E-mail is now ubiquitous; right or wrong, your users think of it in the same class as utilities such as electricity or telephone. Because of this perception, the majority of messaging administrators must now deal with issues such as regulatory compliance that once were the province of a only few types of businesses.

Legacy versions of Exchange were not equipped with the tools and technology to allow administrators to effectively deal with these sorts of issues out of the box. Electronic discovery, regulatory compliance, long-term message data archival, and effective retention policies — the basic Exchange architecture was designed without these needs in mind. But in today's business world, they are very real problems that some administrators may face. The solution has traditionally been the implementation of expensive, complicated, third-party software suites.

When setting the design goals for Exchange 2007, Microsoft wanted to ensure that it was better adapted for modern needs and problems. Wisely, the product team didn't try to become compliance experts and bake every possible needed feature into the product; if they had, we'd be seeing the first delivery sometime around 2014. Instead, they concentrated on building in key features and providing a framework for third parties to continue to develop and test Exchange 2007–compatible solutions.

This chapter covers three of the key changes in Exchange 2007 that, though not being full-featured compliance solutions, will make it much easier for you and third-party applications to manage archival, compliance, retention, and discovery activities.

In this chapter you learn to:

- ◆ Understand Exchange Server 2007 transport architecture

- ◆ Manage message classifications

- ◆ Deploy transport rules

- ◆ Set up message journaling

Introducing the New Exchange 2007 Transport Architecture

In all versions of Exchange from 4.0 through 2003, the message database was an integral part of the message routing and transport architecture. This is in large part because of its use of the MAPI protocol, in which the client's main point of contact with the messaging system is the MAPI session to the user's mailbox server. This store-centric architecture made it possible for Exchange to perform certain tasks very quickly and efficiently, but also made it more difficult to consistently perform certain types of tasks on *all* e-mail messages (inbound, outbound, and internal) necessary to meet regulatory requirements. The new role-based architecture in Exchange 2007 is a direct answer to many of these difficulties.

To illustrate the problem, take the common requirement in many businesses of ensuring that messaging policies are applied to all messages in the organization. In older versions of Exchange, if you send a message to another user whose mailbox is on the same server your mailbox is on, the message never passes through a transport component. As a result, the code for the message store becomes more complex in order to apply policies at this level, third-party developers have to find ways to hook into this process, and the mailbox server runs more and more code that has nothing to do with the basic task a mailbox server is supposed to handle (which is storing and retrieving messages in the most efficient manner possible).

In contrast, the new distinction in Exchange 2007 between transport servers (two different kinds, in fact: Hub Transport (HT) and Edge Transport) and mailbox servers permits the mailbox servers to run only the code that deals with storage and disk I/O. If a message is submitted for delivery, the mailbox server doesn't have to try to figure out exactly what to do with it; instead, it hands the message off to a local HT role in the site. The HT server can figure out which policies apply, which recipients need to get a copy of it, and whether any special actions need to be taken. All messages are now handled consistently, the code is cleaner and more efficient, and third-party applications have a well-defined set of interfaces to hook into without having to account for a ton of screwy, special edge cases.

ALL MESSAGES PASS THROUGH HUB TRANSPORT

Yes, you read that correctly. Every single message you send in Exchange passes through a Hub Transport server, even when you're sending it to another mailbox in your storage database. Although this might seem inefficient at first glance, the reality is that the resulting benefits make this a great design change.

This chapter covers three new capabilities in Exchange 2007 in detail:

◆ *Message classifications* are annotations to an e-mail message that mark it as belonging to a designated category of information that Exchange and Outlook may need to treat in a special fashion. These annotations are exposed as properties of the message, allowing clients to display them visually for the users as well as permitting them to be exposed to the rules engine for automated processing. As an example, all messages with certain keywords can be classified as being confidential.

◆ *Transport rules* are server-side rules that allow you to create and apply messaging policies throughout the entire Exchange Server 2007 organization. They come in two varieties: Hub Transport rules, which are intended to be used for compliance enforcement and policy application activities, and Edge Transport rules, which are designed to help protect your organization from viruses and other external threats.

◆ *Message journaling* is the process of capturing complete copies and histories of specified messages within your organization. Journaled message reports are generated and sent to specified recipients, which can be within the Exchange organization or some external entity. Journaling may not be exciting or useful by itself, but it's one of the main ways to get messaging data into an external archival system.

Setting Up Message Classifications

At their heart, message classifications are simply labels that are set on certain messages. These labels in turn allow other software such as Outlook and Outlook Web Access (OWA) to display a visual warning for the user and, optionally, take special action when processing the message with mailbox rules.

Message classifications consist of three properties:

◆ The *display name* determines how the classification is to be displayed in the client user interface and is scanned by the mailbox rules engine.

◆ The *sender description* allows the client interface to tell the sender the purpose of this classification if it isn't clear from the display name alone.

◆ The *recipient description* allows the client interface to tell the recipient the purpose of this classification.

Figure 15.1 illustrates how Outlook 2007 displays a message classification on a message by means of the additional colored field directly above the To line. The text of this message classification states, "R + D Internal Only — This message may contain confidential Ithicos Solutions confidential Research and Development information. Do not forward to external parties without department lead approval."

FIGURE 15.1
A message classification displayed in Outlook 2007

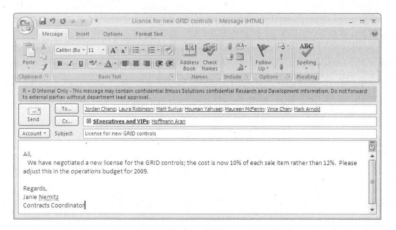

For Outlook end users, this classification was simple to add — all they needed to do was to select the Permissions button and choose from a list of valid classifications.

The same classification labels are also included (automatically) with Outlook Web Access. Figure 15.3 shows a user selecting a classification to apply to a message he is sending in OWA.

Out of the box, Exchange 2007 comes with four message classifications: A/C Privileged, Attachment Removed, Company Confidential, and Company Internal. By default, these classifications are informational only; no associated rules enforce them, and their purpose is simply to display text to recipients. You can modify these default classifications, and create new ones, to suit your business needs, such as the message classifications shown in Figure 15.2. No GUI exists for creating and managing classifications; you must use the Exchange Management Shell (EMS). However, once they are created, you can use the GUI Transport Rule Wizard (covered later in this chapter in the section "Creating New Rules with the Exchange Management Console") to apply them using transport rules.

FIGURE 15.2
A list of message classifications

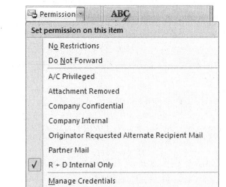

FIGURE 15.3
Applying a message classification in OWA

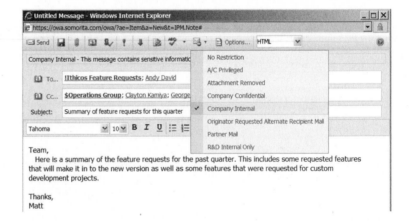

In addition to the basic classification properties, you can optionally set some other properties:

◆ You can specify the precedence, which determines the order that a given classification is applied to a message if multiple classifications are set. You have nine values (Highest, Higher, High, MediumHigh, Medium, MediumLow, Low, Lower, and Lowest) from which to choose.

◆ You can specify whether a given classification should be retained on the message if it is forwarded or replied to; some classifications, such as Attachment Removed, would make little sense when applied to a forwarded copy of a message or to its replies.

◆ You can create localized versions of message classifications if you are working in a multilingual organization.

CONTROLLING MESSAGE CLASSIFICATIONS IN OWA AND OUTLOOK 2007

By default, OWA supports the display and manual selection of message classifications. To use them in Outlook 2007, you must manually deploy them, which is covered in "Deploying Message Classifications" later in this chapter. Advanced users can control permissions on message classifications and thus restrict the use of some classifications to a subset of users. See the Exchange 2007 help topic "Deploying Message Classifications" for instructions if you need this capability.

Modifying and Creating Message Classifications

To create new classifications or customize the properties of existing classifications, you must use the Get-MessageClassification and Set-MessageClassification cmdlets in the Exchange Management Shell.

Get-MessageClassification　This cmdlet shows you the existing message classifications in your organization:

```
Get-MessageClassification
```

Set-MessageClassification　This cmdlet modifies the properties of an existing classification. The following example takes an existing classification named NewMC, sets its precedence to High, and sets the RetainClassificationEnabled property so that the classification will be retained across forwards and replies:

```
Set-MessageClassification -Identity NewMC -DisplayPrecedence High↵
-RetainClassificationEnabled $True
```

New-MessageClassification　This cmdlet creates a new message classification in your organization, configuring it on your Exchange 2007 servers and registering it in the Active Directory:

```
New-MessageClassification -Name "RandDInternal" -DisplayName "R+D
   Internal Only"↵
-RecipientDescription "This message may contain confidential and/or↵
 proprietary information.  If you have received this message in error, please↵
 delete it."  -SenderDescription "This message may contain confidential↵
 Ithicos Solutions confidential R and D information. Do not forward to
   external parties without department lead approval."
```

LOCALIZING THE TEXT OF YOUR MESSAGE CLASSIFICATIONS

If you need to create localized versions of your new classification, see the Exchange 2007 help topic "How to Create Localized Versions of Message Classifications" for instructions.

Deploying Message Classifications

When you create or modify classifications, they are automatically visible to OWA users. In what is a particularly painful oversight, the same is not true for Outlook 2007 users. If you want your Outlook 2007 users to benefit from message classifications, you have two tasks to complete:

1. Export the message classifications from Exchange 2007 to an XML file.
2. Configure Outlook 2007 to use the XML file that contains the classification information.

These steps must be performed every time you add new classifications or modify display properties of existing classifications. Just to make it even more annoying, these tasks are completely manual.

The following sections cover these steps in greater detail.

EXPORTING CLASSIFICATIONS FROM EXCHANGE

If you're looking for an EMS cmdlet to export all of your classifications, stop. You have to use EMS, but no built-in cmdlet exists to perform this task. Here's how to do it:

1. Navigate to the Scripts subdirectory of the folder you installed Exchange 2007 to (by default, this folder is located at: `C:\Program Files\Microsoft\Exchange Server\Scripts`).

   Microsoft has provided several useful and complex EMS scripts in this folder; the one you want is named `Export-OutlookClassification.ps1`. Though you can use the `Export-OutlookClassification.ps1` script to export a single classification, you will probably want to export all classifications and configure Outlook to use them.

2. To export all of the classifications to a file called `c:\Classifications.XML`, type the following command:

   ```
   & 'C:\Program Files\Microsoft\Exchange Server\Scripts\Export-↵
   OutlookClassification.ps1' > c:\Classifications.xml
   ```

OUT-OF-SYNC CLASSIFICATIONS

If the XML file that Outlook uses is out of sync with the actual classifications specified on the Exchange server, Outlook will not display the classifications that are missing from the file. It will, however, retain them if they can be retained, and they will still be on the messages (and can be viewed in OWA). Once the file is updated, they will become visible to the user.

IMPORTING CLASSIFICATIONS IN OUTLOOK

This task has two parts: creating the necessary Registry entries and copying over the XML file you just created in the previous step. Once you've created the Registry settings on a given client, you don't need to keep setting them when you update the classifications XML file.

Copying the XML File

Copying the file over is simple; you can do it manually, via a batch script, or through your existing desktop management solution. If you are going to be changing the classifications on a regular basis, you might want to think about configuring some sort of automated deployment system to minimize the need for manual involvement. For example, you might consider the use of a logon script to ensure that the latest copy of the classifications XML file is pushed out to your clients. If you've deployed Microsoft Systems Management Server (or some third-party equivalent) in your environment, you can also use that mechanism.

Outlook reads the file in when it starts, so if the file is updated while Outlook is open, it will not use the updated information until it is next restarted.

Creating the Registry Entries

The following Registry key and values must be created on all Outlook 2007 computers whose users have mailboxes on Exchange 2007 servers and who are going to be sending message classifications.

Until these Registry entries are created, classifications will not be displayed in Outlook, even though they exist on messages.

In the `HKCU\Software\Microsoft\Office\12.0\Common` key, first create a new key named `Policy`. Within this new key, create the following values:

```
"AdminClassificationPath"=text:"C:\Path\To\Filename.xml"
"EnableClassifications"=dword:00000001
"TrustClassifications"=dword:00000001
```

You should set the values of these keys accordingly:

◆ `AdminClassificationPath` is the full path and filename of the XML file you copied from the export process. Though this path can be on a network share, that might cause problems for laptop users or other users who lose network connectivity. The file is small, so there's no harm in copying it to the local hard drive.

◆ `EnableClassifications` allows you to toggle whether message classifications are read and honored in Outlook 2007 on a per-user basis. The value of 1 enables classifications, and the value of 0 disables them.

◆ `TrustClassifications` allows you to toggle whether Outlook actually trusts classifications on messages that are sent to users on legacy Exchange mailbox servers. The value of 1 enables trust, 0 disables it. Microsoft recommends that you enable this value only for mailboxes on Exchange 2007 servers.

DEPLOYING MESSAGE CLASSIFICATION USING THE OFFICE INSTALLER

The Office 2007 Customization Tool, now part of the Office installer, allows you to specify additional Registry keys that will be installed when Office is installed on a machine. If you want to ensure that message classification support is universally deployed and supported in your organization, you might want to include these Registry settings in your configuration when creating your installation scripts.

Setting Up Transport Rules

The two flavors of transport rules (Edge Transport and Hub Transport rules) in Exchange 2007 give you the ability to define and automatically enforce messaging policies within your organization. In Exchange 2007, transport rules are enforced on the Hub Transport and Edge Transport roles. You can use transport rules to append disclaimers to messages, search messages for certain types of content, apply ethical walls, append classifications, insert text into a message, and more.

You can create and manage transport rules in both the Exchange Management Console and the Exchange Management Shell. In the EMC, transport rules are found under the Organization Configuration properties and under the Hub Transport subcontainer as shown in Figure 15.4.

Although you use the same processes to create and manage the rules on both roles, the actual actions you can take, and the way the rules are stored, are different. Transport rules are very similar to mailbox rules, but they are applied at the server level to all traffic that goes through that server.

Like mailbox rules, transport rules have three parts:

◆ *Conditions* identify the message properties that trigger the application of the rule to a given message. If you define no conditions, the rule will apply to all messages.

◆ *Exceptions* identify message properties that exempt a given message from being processed by the rule even if it matches the defined conditions. Exceptions, like conditions, are optional.

◆ *Actions* modify the properties or delivery of messages that match the conditions without matching the exceptions defined by the rule. In a given rule, there must be at least one action, and you can have multiple actions.

FIGURE 15.4
Locating the Hub Transport rules in the Exchange Management Console

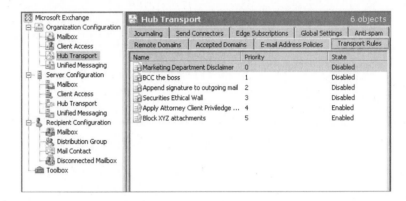

Transport rules on a Hub Transport server are defined and stored in the Active Directory; each Hub Transport server in the organization sees the entire set of defined rules and attempts to match them against all messages. This allows you to define a single, consistent set of message policies throughout your organization. You can define a total of 1,000 transport rules in your organization. That may seem like a lot, but in large enterprises, you often need hundreds of transport rules to fully define the automated policy restrictions required.

TRANSPORT RULES AND SERVER DESIGN DECISIONS

The number of messages per hour and the number of transport rules will affect your design decisions regarding the amount of RAM and number of processors that are on the Hub Transport servers. An organization that sends 2,000 messages per hour and has 10 transport rules will need far less computing power (and fewer Hub Transport servers in each site) than an organization that sends 10,000 messages per hour and has a few hundred transport rules.

Because rules are stored in the Active Directory, modifications to your transport rules are subject to your normal AD replication. Depending on your site topology, it may take some time before your current changes replicate fully throughout your organization.

LEGACY EXCHANGE SERVERS DO NOT SUPPORT TRANSPORT RULES

If you have legacy Exchange servers in your organization, they will not make use of your transport rules. If acting as bridgeheads, these servers may represent a significant loophole in your messaging policy enforcement. Likewise, legacy Exchange mailbox servers do not pass all messages through a Hub Transport server, so you may notice that some policies are not applied consistently until all mailboxes are on Exchange 2007 servers.

In contrast, transport rules for Edge Transport servers are defined on a per-server basis and stored in the local ADAM database on the Edge Transport server. Thus, though you have no replication delays to worry about, you do have to manually maintain a consistent set of rules on your Edge Transport servers or you'll find you have some interesting discrepancies to track down at a later date.

If you have multiple Edge Transport servers, I recommend creating an EMS script to manage your transport rule configurations. Not only can you easily reuse this script on each Edge Transport server to maintain consistency, but the script makes for great documentation on what your current configuration is.

Selecting Conditions and Exceptions

Because conditions and exceptions are both involved in identifying whether a given message should be processed by the rule, it should be no surprise that they give you the same set of options. Which options you get depends on whether you're creating the rule on a Hub Transport or Edge Transport server. The Exchange 2007 help files contain detailed descriptions of how each of these conditions and exceptions are defined and applied, but the following discussion should help you get an idea of what types of selection criteria you have available at your fingertips.

HUB TRANSPORT CONDITIONS AND EXCEPTIONS

The conditions of the rule define the circumstances under which the rule will apply. Figure 15.5 shows the Conditions page of the Edit Transport Rule Wizard and some of the conditions that can be applied to the rule.

You can select the following transport rule conditions on Hub Transport servers:

◆ From people

◆ From a member of distribution list

◆ From users inside or outside the organization

◆ Sent to people

◆ Sent to a member of distribution list

◆ Sent to users inside or outside the organization

◆ Between members of distribution list and distribution list

◆ When any of the recipients in the To field is people

◆ When any of the recipients in the To field is a member of distribution list

◆ When any of the recipients in the Cc field is people

◆ When any of the recipients in the Cc field is a member of distribution list

◆ When any of the recipients in the To or Cc fields are people

◆ When any of the recipients in the To or Cc fields is a member of distribution list

◆ When the Subject field contains specific words

◆ When the Subject field or the body of the message contains specific words

◆ When a message header contains specific words

◆ When the From address contains specific words

◆ When the Subject field contains text patterns

- When the Subject field or the body of the message contains text patterns

- When the message header contains text patterns

- When the From address contains text patterns

- When any attachment file name contains text patterns

- With a spam confidence level (SCL) rating that is greater than or equal to limit

- When the size of any attachment is greater than or equal to limit

- Marked with classification

- Marked with importance

FIGURE 15.5
Transport rule condi-
tions

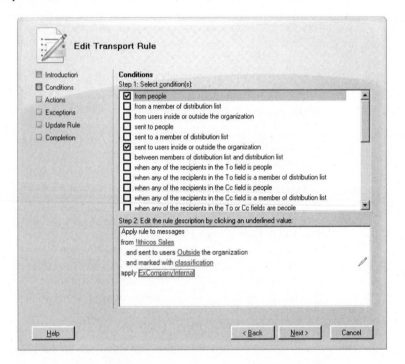

EDGE TRANSPORT CONDITIONS AND EXCEPTIONS

When creating a transport rule on an Edge Transport server role, you can define the following conditions:

- When the Subject field contains specific words

- When the Subject field or the body of the message contains specific words

- When a message header contains specific words

- When the From address contains specific words

- When any recipient address contains specific words

- When the Subject field contains text patterns

- When the Subject field or the body of the message contains text patterns

- When the message header contains text patterns

- When the From address contains text patterns

- When text patterns in any of recipient address match a transport rule

- With a spam confidence level (SCL) rating that is greater than or equal to limit

- When the size of any attachment is greater than or equal to limit

- From users inside or outside the organization

SPECIFYING TEXT PATTERNS WITH REGULAR EXPRESSIONS

Several conditions and exceptions allow you to specify text patterns, which Exchange will then attempt to match against the specified fields. These patterns are known as regular expressions; see the Exchange 2007 help topic "Regular Expressions in Transport Rules" for more details and examples.

Selecting Actions

As with conditions and exceptions, your choice of possible actions depends on whether you're creating the rule on a Hub Transport server or an Edge Transport server. The Exchange 2007 help files contain detailed descriptions of how each of these actions is defined and applied.

HUB TRANSPORT ACTIONS

The actions of the transport rule specify what the rule will do to the message (or what it will do *about* the message). Figure 15.6 shows the Actions page of the Edit Transport Rule Wizard.

You can select the following actions on Hub Transport servers:

- Log an event with message

- Prepend the subject with string

- Apply message classification

- Append disclaimer text using font, size, color, with separator, and fallback to action if unable to apply

- Set the spam confidence level to value

- Set header with value

- Remove header

- Add a recipient in the To field addresses

- Copy message to addresses

- Blind copy (Bcc) the message to addresses

- Redirect message to addresses

- Send bounce message to sender with enhanced status code

- Silently drop the message

FIGURE 15.6

Viewing the Actions page of the Edit Transport Rule Wizard

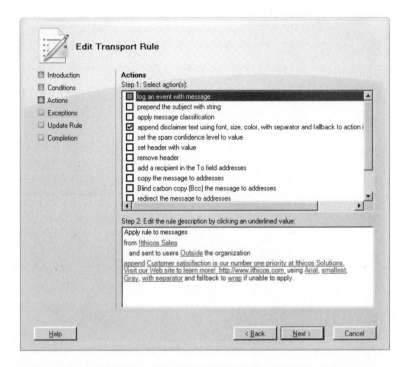

EDGE TRANSPORT ACTIONS

You can select the following actions on Edge Transport servers:

♦ Log an event with message

♦ Prepend the subject with string

♦ Set the spam confidence level to value

♦ Set header with value

♦ Remove header

♦ Add a recipient in the To field addresses

♦ Copy the message to addresses

♦ Blind carbon copy (Bcc) the message to addresses

◆ Drop connection

◆ Redirect the message to addresses

◆ Put message in quarantine

◆ Reject the message with status code and response

◆ Silently drop the message

Creating New Rules with the Exchange Management Console

To create a new transport rule on your HT servers using the EMC, launch the EMC. Navigate to Exchange Organization ➤ Organization Configuration ➤ Hub Transport in the left-hand pane, then select the Transport Rules tab in the middle pane. Click the New Transport Rule task in the pane on the right to start the New Transport Rule Wizard.

Figure 15.7 shows the Introduction screen of the wizard. Here you provide the name and optional description of the new rule, as well as select whether the rule will be enabled once it is created. The Name field is required. I recommend using the Comment field liberally — otherwise, after you have 50 transport rules you will begin to lose track of what each one does without digging through the rule itself. Click Next to continue once you have configured a name and comment.

FIGURE 15.7
New Transport Rule Wizard Introduction page

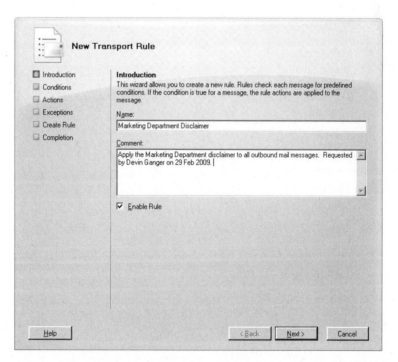

Figure 15.5 (shown previously) shows the Conditions page of the wizard. The default condition is Apply Rule To Messages (there is no checkbox for this), which will match all messages. If you want to narrow down which messages will be affected, select the check boxes of one or more conditions; they will be added to the lower text field.

To fill in the values of the conditions, click the underlined blue text fields and select the results from the selection dialog boxes that are opened. Once you are satisfied with the selections, click OK to close the selection dialogs. Click Next to continue.

Figure 15.6 (also shown previously) shows the Actions page of the Edit Transport Rule Wizard. There are no default actions. Select the check boxes of one or more actions; they will be added to the lower text field.

Figure 15.8 shows the Exceptions screen; essentially this is the same set of conditions that you find on the Conditions page. Unlike the Conditions page, though, there are no default exceptions. Exceptions allow you to specify the conditions under which the transport rule will *not* apply. If you want to create an exception, select the check boxes of one or more exceptions; they will be added to the lower text field.

FIGURE 15.8

New Transport Rule Wizard Exceptions screen

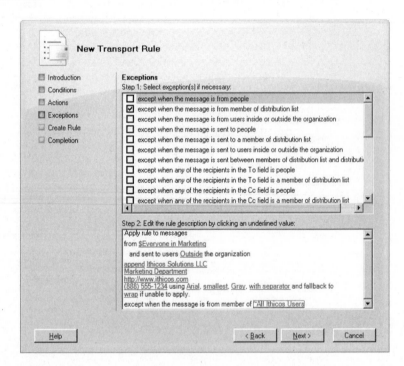

Figure 15.9 shows the Create Rule screen. This screen gives you a summary of the rule that will be created. In Figure 15.9, you can see a rule I have created that applies a disclaimer to all messages sent to external recipients (users outside the organization) but that will not apply if the message is sent to the mail group &Somorita Sales And Marketing. If you are happy with the mail group, click New to create the rule.

The transport rule is now created in the Active Directory and will be replicated to all domain controllers in your organization and thus applied by all Hub Transport servers in your organization. The results of the operation, including the EMS command line used to create the rule, will be shown on the Completion screen, as shown in Figure 15.10.

FIGURE 15.9
New Transport Rule
Wizard Create Rule
screen

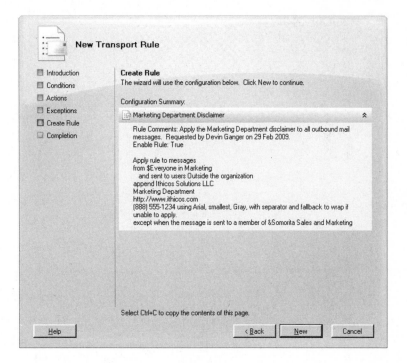

New Transport Rule

☑ Introduction
☑ Conditions
☑ Actions
☑ Exceptions
☑ Create Rule
☐ Completion

Create Rule
The wizard will use the configuration below. Click New to continue.

Configuration Summary:

📄 Marketing Department Disclaimer　　　　　　　　　　　　　　　　⊗

Rule Comments: Apply the Marketing Department disclaimer to all outbound mail messages. Requested by Devin Ganger on 29 Feb 2009.
Enable Rule: True

Apply rule to messages
from $Everyone in Marketing
　and sent to users Outside the organization
append Ithicos Solutions LLC
Marketing Department
http://www.ithicos.com
(888) 555-1234 using Arial, smallest, Gray, with separator and fallback to wrap if
unable to apply.
except when the message is sent to a member of &Somorita Sales and Marketing

Select Ctrl+C to copy the contents of this page.

[Help]　　　　　　　　　　　　[< Back]　[New]　[Cancel]

CREATING A NEW EDGE TRANSPORT RULE

To create a new transport rule on your Edge Transport server using the EMC, launch the EMC on your ET server. Follow the same steps as for creating a new HT transport rule.

Here is the Exchange Management Shell command that was generated to create this new transport rule:

```
New-TransportRule -Name 'Marketing Department Disclaimer' -Comments 'Apply the↵
Marketing Department disclaimer to all outbound mail messages.  Requested by↵
 Devin Ganger on 29 Feb 2009. ' -Conditions
   'Microsoft.Exchange.MessagingPolicies.Rules.Tasks.FromPredicate',↵
'Microsoft.Exchange.MessagingPolicies.Rules.Tasks.SentToScopePredicate'
   -Actions↵
'Microsoft.Exchange.MessagingPolicies.Rules.Tasks.ApplyDisclaimerAction'
   -Exceptions↵
 'Microsoft.Exchange.MessagingPolicies.Rules.Tasks.SentToMemberOfPredicate'↵
-Enabled $true -Priority '0'
```

FIGURE 15.10
New Transport Rule
Wizard Completion
screen

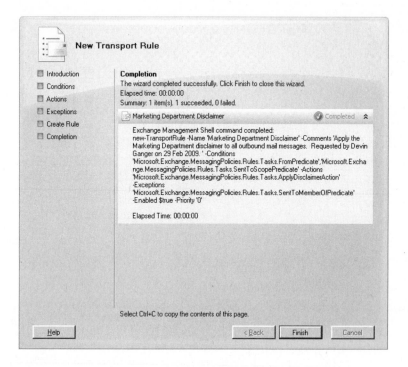

Creating New Rules with the Exchange Management Shell

The following Exchange Management Shell commands let you add, change, remove, enable, or disable transport rules that are used by the Transport Rules agent on a Hub Transport server or an Edge Transport server:

Get-TransportRule   This cmdlet shows you the existing transport rules in your organization (if run on an HT server) or Edge server (if run on an ET server):

```
Get-TransportRule
```

Enable-TransportRule   This cmdlet sets an existing transport rule as enabled, which means it will be applied to messages:

```
Enable-TransportRule -Identity MyTransportRule
```

Disable-TransportRule   This cmdlet sets an existing transport rule as disabled, which means that it will still be present in the configuration but will not be applied to messages:

```
Disable-TransportRule -Identity MyTransportRule
```

The Disable-TransportRule cmdlet is useful for troubleshooting problems with transport rules. You can also disable ALL transport rules with this command:

```
Get-TransportRule | Disable-TransportRule
```

Remove-TransportRule   This cmdlet allows you to delete an existing transport rule:

```
Remove-TransportRule -Identity TransportRuleToDelete
```

Set-TransportRule   This cmdlet allows you to modify the parameters of an existing transport rule:

```
$Condition = Get-TransportRulePredicate FromMemberOf↵
$Condition.Addresses = @((Get-DistributionGroup "Sales Group"))
Set-TransportRule -Identity FromSales -Condition @($condition)
```

To make this cmdlet manageable, I made use of variables to create the condition *from a member of the distribution list* and fill its Addresses property with the *Sales Group* distribution list. I then passed the variable into the **Set-TransportRule** cmdlet, modifying the condition of the *FromSales* rule.

New-TransportRule   This cmdlet allows you to create a new transport rule. Creating a new rule from the EMS is beyond the scope of this book, but it follows the same principles as the **Set-TransportRule** example. From the EMS, issue the following command for a full description of the cmdlet, including examples:

```
Help New-TransportRule -full
```

You may have noticed in the previous examples of creating or editing a transport rule that when you reference the actions or the conditions, you have to use the object names. You can retrieve a list of the actions by using the **Get-TransportRuleAction** cmdlet and a list of the conditions using the **Get-TransportRulePredicate** cmdlet.

Introducing Journaling

A lot of people confuse *journaling*, which is the process of capturing a set of communications for future use, with *archiving*, which is the practice of removing less frequently accessed or older message data from the message store in favor of a secondary storage location.

◆   *Archiving* is all about getting stuff — usually older and bulkier messages and attachments — out of your mailboxes, so you can reduce the performance hit on your comparatively expensive mailbox server storage systems and reduce your backup windows.

Archival solutions are outside the scope of this book; Exchange 2007 offers no native archiving abilities.

◆   *Journaling* is record keeping; you're defining a set of users whose traffic you must keep track of, and Exchange dutifully captures faithful copies of every message they send or receive.

As stated before, journaling is one of the main strategies that compliance and archival vendors use to get messaging data into their solutions.

Although you may not have any explicit applicable regulatory language that forces you to implement journaling, journaling can still be one of the easier ways to meet what requirements you do have. As compliance becomes more of an issue, the ability to quickly and easily put your hands on complete and accurate records of messaging communications will become critical.

Legacy Exchange offered rudimentary journaling; Exchange 2003 offered envelope journaling, which finally captured sufficient information to be of general use. The base journaling mechanism used by Exchange 2007 is also envelope journaling, which captures all recipient information (even Bcc: headers and forwards). However, you have two options for journaling:

◆ *Standard journaling* (aka per-mailbox database journaling) uses the Journaling agent on Hub Transport servers to journal all messages sent to and from recipients and senders whose mailboxes are homed on specified mailbox databases.

You configure standard journaling on the General property page of a mailbox database such as the one shown in Figure 15.11.

◆ *Premium journaling* (aka per-recipient journaling) also uses the Journaling agent on Hub Transport servers, but it's more granular. It offers you the ability to design journaling rules for groups or even specific users if need be.

You must have an Exchange Enterprise Client Access License (CAL) to use premium journaling.

FIGURE 15.11

Implementing standard journaling on a mailbox database

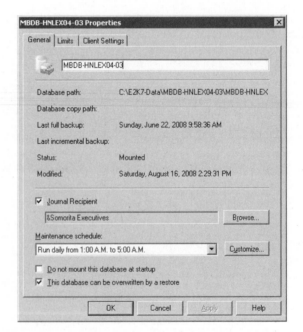

Implementing Journaling

The Journaling agent, present on your Hub Transport servers, is responsible for detecting whether a given message falls under your journaling rules. When you use standard journaling, you enable it for an entire mailbox database. Any messages sent to or by recipients whose mailboxes are located on a journal-enabled database will be detected by the Journaling agent and copies will be sent to a designated *journal recipient*. This journal recipient can be another recipient in the Exchange organization — if it is an Exchange mailbox it must be dedicated to the purpose — or an SMTP address on another messaging system.

WHY USE AN EXTERNAL JOURNAL RECIPIENT?

Journaling to an external recipient may seem like a crazy idea at first blush. However, this allows Exchange 2007 to be used with compliance and archival solutions that are not part of the Exchange organization or even with hosted solution providers.

If you use an external journal recipient, you should ensure that your SMTP transport connections to the external system are fully secure and authenticated. Exchange 2007 supports the use of the Transport Layer Security (TLS) protocol; see Chapter 21, "Delivering E-mail," for details on how to configure TLS connections to specific domains and how to enable SMTP authentication.

When you use premium journaling, you create journal rules that define a subset of the recipients in your organization. Premium journaling rules are stored in the Active Directory and propagated to all Hub Transport servers, depending on the normal AD replication mechanism. The Journaling agent on the Hub Transport server detects that the rule matches a given message and again sends a copy of the message to the journal recipient. Premium journaling rules are found on the Hub Transport subcontainer of the Organization Configuration in the Exchange Management Console. An example of this is shown in Figure 15.12.

FIGURE 15.12
Locating the journaling rules in the Exchange Management Console

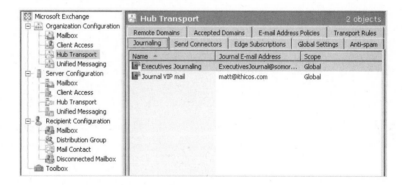

Journaling rules can have three scopes, which helps the Journaling agent decide whether or not it needs to examine a given message:

- The Internal scope matches messages where all senders and recipients are members of the Exchange organization.

- The External scope matches messages where at least one sender or recipient is an external entity.

- The Global scope matches all messages, even those that may have already been matched by the other scopes.

To create a new journaling rule, run the New Journal Rule Wizard found on the Actions pane. In Figure 15.13, I am creating a new journal rule that will journal messages sent to or from the VIPs mail group whether the messages is internal or external.

This same operation could have been performed using the Exchange Management Shell and the following command:

```
New-JournalRule -Name 'Journal VIP mail' -JournalEmailAddress↵
'volcanosurfboards.com/Users/zz_VIP Mail Archive' -Scope 'Global'↵
-Enabled $True -Recipient 'VIPs@somorita.com'
```

FIGURE 15.13
Creating a new journaling rule

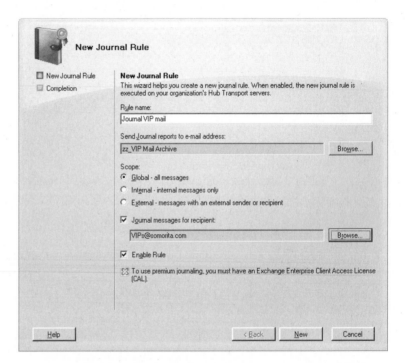

To guard against the loss of journaling reports in the event of trouble within your Exchange organization, you can designate an *alternate journaling mailbox*. This mailbox will receive any non-delivery reports that are issued if your journaling recipient cannot be delivered to. Unfortunately, you can configure only a single alternate mailbox for your entire organization. Not only can this cause performance and mailbox size issues, but your local regulations may prevent you from mixing multiple types of journal information in one mailbox.

Reading Journal Reports

The journaling process creates a special Exchange message known as the *journal report*. This message is essentially a wrapper that contains a summary of the original message properties. It also contains a pristine copy of the original message that generated the report, neatly attached to the journal report. An example of a journaled report is shown in Figure 15.14. Notice on the Message tab that you have the information about the message; the actual message is on the other tab.

FIGURE 15.14

An example of a journaled message

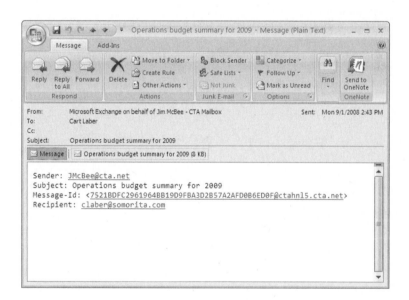

The journal reports are designed to be human and machine readable, allowing you to automate processing of journal reports via a third-party application as well as perform manual checks on the data.

Table 15.1 shows the fields that Exchange 2007 places in the journal report.

Depending on your routing topology and journal rule configuration, you may receive multiple journal reports for a given message. This is not an error; it reflects the fact that any given Hub Transport server may not have a complete view of the organization, depending on AD replication, recipient caching, and other factors.

TABLE 15.1:   Exchange 2007 Journal Report Fields

FIELD	WHAT IT CONTAINS
To	The SMTP address of a recipient in the To header or the SMTP envelope recipient. If the message was sent through a distribution list, this field contains the Expanded field. If the message was forwarded, this field contains the Forwarded field.
Cc	The SMTP address of a recipient in the Cc header or the SMTP envelope recipient. If the message was sent through a distribution list, this field contains the Expanded field. If the message was forwarded, this field contains the Forwarded field.
Bcc	The SMTP address of a recipient in the Bcc header or the SMTP envelope recipient. If the message was sent through a distribution list, this field contains the Expanded field. If the message was forwarded, this field contains the Forwarded field.
Recipient	The SMTP address of a recipient who is not a member of the Exchange 2007 organization, such as Internet recipients or recipients on legacy Exchange servers.
Sender	The sender's SMTP address, found either in the From or Sender header of the message.
On Behalf Of	The relevant SMTP address if the Send On Behalf Of feature was used.
Subject	The Subject header.
Message-ID	The internal Exchange Message-ID.

Summary

The new message transport architecture of Exchange 2007 provides a wide variety of new capabilities that can make your job easier. Although these new features are not going to be complete compliance solutions for any but the smallest of organizations, they provide a consistent, manageable way to establish controls across your organization.

Message classifications provide a way to visibly tag selected messages and show that they require specific treatment. On their own, they're merely advisory, but combined with transport rules and mailbox rules, they can become powerful selection criteria for managing messages and ensuring policy compliance. The catch is that although they work out of the box with OWA, using them with Outlook 2007 requires you to get your hands dirty copying files and adding Registry entries.

Transport rules give you a powerful, centralized method for creating automated policy enforcement in your environment. You can create rules on both Hub Transport and Edge Transport servers, although they serve slightly different purposes.

Journaling is still around and better than ever in Exchange 2007. In addition to journaling to mailboxes within the organization, you can now designate external recipients to send reports to. Standard journaling enables journaling on a per-database basis, whereas premium journaling allows you to create journaling rules targeted to specific groups or even individual users.

Chapter 16

Public Folder Administration

For many companies, public folders are a major part of their Exchange Server deployments. Public folders are a powerful way to share knowledge and data throughout your organization, and they've been a staple of Exchange Server. They are a great way to share content and information with many users, and because they can be mail-enabled, they can also be an easy way for third-party application developers to hook into Exchange. All you have to do is use the MAPI libraries to connect to Exchange as a user with permissions to the specified public folder and you've got the ability to send and receive messages — and share them with multiple users — without having to do a lot of coding.

With respect to public folder support, Microsoft has made a number of nice improvements in Exchange Server 2007 and also in Service Pack 1. The new EMS cmdlets for handling public folders are definitely worth the price of admission, and the lack of built-in GUI functions are offset by a tool known as PFDAVAdmin.

In this chapter you learn to:

◆ Understand how public folders are supported in Exchange 2007

◆ Manage public folders

◆ Understand and choose public folder management tools

◆ Work with the public folder hierarchy

◆ Manage replication

Understanding Public Folder Support in Exchange 2007

Despite the rumors of their demise, public folders are alive and well, and in some ways they're even better in Exchange 2007 than they ever have been. Exchange Server 2007 addresses a number of common complaints. Public folder management was a weakness in previous versions of Exchange Server for the following reasons:

◆ There were few freely available command-line tools for managing public folders and public folder databases.

◆ Bulk management of public folders in the legacy Exchange System Manager had limited functionality.

◆ There was no easy way to export or import properties, permissions, or other settings from one public folder or server to another.

◆ The public folder replica and replication information displayed by the legacy System Manager was often incomplete, misleading, or just plain wrong.

When Microsoft announced it was "deemphasizing" support for public folders in Exchange Server 2007, a lot of Exchange administrators immediately got worried. What was the future of public folders? Would Exchange Server 2007 continue to support them? If not, what would the migration path look like?

Unfortunately, Microsoft's announcement has caused a lot of worry and confusion. Combined with the lack of any GUI public folder management tools in the initial release of Exchange 2007, the announcement led a lot of people to the conclusion that you just can't do public folders anymore. If you've got a large public folder deployment in your organization, this is obviously an area of concern for you.

Happily, Microsoft has clarified its position on public folder support. Public folders are still fully supported in Exchange Server 2007 (and will be through 2016) and probably even beyond that point. However, Exchange Server 2007 is the first version to provide support for Microsoft Windows SharePoint Services integration as an alternative method of seamlessly sharing data within your organization and making it available to Outlook 2007 and Outlook Web Access (OWA) users.

In the meantime, you can go forward with your Exchange 2007 migration secure in the knowledge that you will be able to continue using your public folder infrastructure. You can continue to use the Exchange 2003 System Manager console to create, manage, and delete public folders, or you can use the functionality built into Exchange 2007.

PUBLIC FOLDERS, COLLABORATION, AND "THE FUTURE"

Customers and students frequently ask me if they should continue to support public folders. Note that this is my opinion and does not represent any official position by any company or organization. Though I really can't do much with SharePoint other than spell it, I can see the writing on the wall. SharePoint is the future of collaborative solutions in a Microsoft world.

Exchange Server public folders can still do some things that it is hard (or impossible) to do with SharePoint. One such task is easily replicating content from one location to another and making it transparent to the end user. Still, the collaborative and information sharing capabilities of SharePoint certainly seem to outweigh those of Exchange Server in most respects.

Now is the time to start looking to the future; especially if you have thousands (or tens of thousands) of public folders. If you are starting to deploy SharePoint, look at each of your public folders (and public folders that are being requested for future use) and decide if SharePoint is a better platform. Companies such as Quest Software even have migration tools that will help you move data and applications from public folders to SharePoint.

Understanding Native Exchange 2007 Support

The Exchange Management Console (EMC) offers minimal support for public folders. A new Public Folder Management Console will provide you some basic functionality for managing public folder properties. However, Exchange 2007 provides the bulk of its built-in support via Exchange Management Shell (EMS) cmdlets. Don't worry; they're not difficult to use, even if you're not a script or command-line guru.

Before I show you how to use the new public folder cmdlets, though, I'll cover exactly what you can do in the EMC. Be warned that it isn't much: you can create and delete public folder databases on your mailbox servers and manage the basic properties of these databases. The new Public Folder Management Console provides some basic capabilities for viewing the public folder hierarchy, adding or deleting public folders, setting folder properties, or viewing and managing replication.

During the installation of your first mailbox server, you will be asked if the server will support legacy Outlook clients. If you answer yes to this question, the setup process automatically creates a public folder database on that server. If you answer no, the server will not have a public folder database. You can still create a new public folder database on that server, however. You can also use the /EnableLegacyOutlook setup switch if you want the public folder database to be created automatically when you're using the command-line setup.

Additional Exchange 2007 servers that you install with the Mailbox server role will *not* include a public folder database. You will need to create these databases wherever you need public folder replicas.

Public Folder Features in Several Versions of Exchange

For the most part, public folders on Exchange Server 2007 servers are fully supported just as they were in Exchange 2000/2003. However, there are a few missing features that you need to be aware of. Some of these features have been added back in Exchange Server 2007 Service Pack 1:

◆ The Exchange Installable File System (ExIFS) that allowed you to access the public folders from a drive letter no longer exists in Exchange Server 2007 and SP1.

◆ Only the MAPI public folder tree (the default public folder tree) is available on Exchange 2007 and SP1. This is the public folder tree that is accessible from Outlook clients. Exchange 2000/2003 general-purpose public folder trees are not available.

◆ Public folder access is only available via Outlook Web Access when running Exchange Server 2007 SP1 or later.

◆ The graphical user interface for managing public folders was missing in Exchange Server 2007 RTM but has been added in Service Pack 1.

◆ For new Exchange installations, you must specify during the first server setup that you want to support legacy Exchange clients (meaning Outlook 2003 and earlier), otherwise the first public folder database is not created.

◆ The public folder database is not created automatically on additional Mailbox servers you install. You should create a storage group and public folder database on the Mailbox servers on which you want to place a public folder database.

DATABASE VERSUS STORE

As you may have figured out already, we now, once again, refer to Exchange 2007 databases as *databases* rather than *stores*; this is just a change of terminology, so don't get too stressed about it. I always liked *database* better anyway.

Public Folder Limitations

If you have been using public folders for years, you are probably already aware of these limitations. If so, you can probably skip this section. My intent here is to make sure you understand that public folders are not necessarily a "fix all" solution for information sharing. Public folders have the following limitations:

◆ Although you can store files in public folders, Exchange is not really designed to be a file repository, so you shouldn't use your public folders to store gigabytes and gigabytes of files or messages with file attachments.

◆ High availability and redundancy of public folder content is achieved by creating additional replicas of public folder content on other public folder databases.

◆ Microsoft discourages you from putting public folder databases on cluster continuous replication Mailbox servers. High availability should be achieved with public replicas. The only exception to this rule is if you have only a single Mailbox server (on the CCR cluster) in your organization.

◆ All user accounts must be mail enabled in order to be assigned client permissions to any public folder.

◆ If permissions such as the ability to create root-level public folders are not controlled, the public folder infrastructure could get out of control. It is not common to see older Exchange organizations with dozens or even hundreds of root-level public folders.

◆ IMAP and POP users cannot access public folders.

Moving the Public Folder Hierarchy to Exchange 2007

If you are migrating from Exchange 2000/2003 to Exchange Server 2007 and you are planning to continue to use public folders, there is one important step you should take care of sooner rather than later. You need to move the public folder hierarchy from the Exchange 2000/2003 administrative group into the Exchange Server 2007 administrative group. Notice in Figure 16.1 that there is a Folders container under First Administrative Group; this is where the public folder hierarchy is currently held.

FIGURE 16.1
Default location for the public folder hierarchy

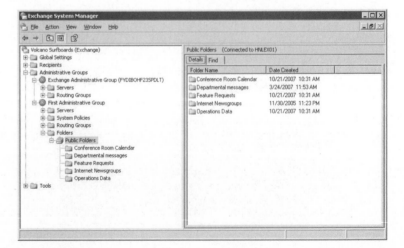

Though Exchange Server does not really care which administrative group the hierarchy is located in, Outlook clients will break if you delete the administrative group without first moving the hierarchy. I have heard of several instances where someone removed all of their legacy Exchange 2000/2003 servers and then removed the administrative group that held the public folder hierarchy. As a result, Outlook 2003 and earlier clients could no longer access the public folders and they could no longer access system folders such as the Free/Busy folders and the offline address book.

DON'T DELETE ADMINISTRATIVE GROUPS WHEN MOVING THE PUBLIC FOLDER HIERARCHY

Do *not* delete the Exchange 2000/2003 administrative groups without moving the public folder hierarchy. To be on the safe side, you should just leave the old admin groups in place; you will not see them in the Exchange Server 2007 admin tools and it doesn't hurt anything to leave them there after all of your Exchange 2000/2003 servers are removed.

I strongly recommend that you move the public folder hierarchy to the Exchange 2007 administrative group — Exchange Administrative Group (FYDIBOHF23SPDLT) — as soon as you get Exchange Server 2007 running in your organization. Follow these steps to move the public folder hierarchy:

1. Using the Exchange 2000/2003 System Manager, expand the Administrative Groups container, right-click the Exchange Administrative Group (FYDIBOHF23SPDLT), and choose New ➢ Public Folders Container.

2. Expand the Exchange 2000/2003 administrative group that holds the public folder hierarchy (in the example shown in Figure 16.1, that would be First Administrative Group).

3. Open the Folders container and drag the Public Folders container to the new Folders container in the Exchange Administrative Group (FYDIBOHF23SPDLT) container. When you release the mouse button, the public folder hierarchy will be moved to the new public folder container.

4. Don't forget to create the public folder databases and replicate the public folder and system folder content to Exchange Server 2007.

Managing Public Folder Databases

As I mentioned earlier, public folder databases are not created by default on Exchange Server 2007 Mailbox servers. When you set up the first Mailbox server in the organization, you can include a public folder database by specifying that the server will support legacy Exchange clients. You must create additional public folder databases manually.

Creating Public Folder Databases

One big change from Exchange 2000/2003 is that all mailbox servers back then automatically had a public server database created on them in the First Storage Group. This is no longer the case; if the public folder database is created automatically, it is found in the Second Storage Group.

An Exchange 2007 Mailbox server can hold only a single public folder database.

If you need to create a public folder database manually on additional mailbox servers in your organization, I recommend that you create an additional storage group. To meet the requirements for local continuous replication and cluster continuous replication, each storage group must have a single database in it. Further, some server configurations (such as cluster continuous replication [CCR] servers) should not have a public folder database on the server.

Microsoft recommends that, with CCR, there shouldn't be a public folder database on the cluster unless the cluster contains the only public folder database in the organization.

CREATING A STORAGE GROUP FOR A PUBLIC FOLDER DATABASE

If you need a new public folder database on a server that does not have one already, you must first create a storage group to hold the public folder database. This is most easily done by following these steps to create a new storage group:

1. Open the Exchange 2007 Management Console and navigate to the Servers subcontainer under the Server Configuration work center.

2. In the Results pane, select the server on which you want to create the new storage group and click the New Storage Group task from the Actions pane.

3. In the New Storage Group Wizard, specify the name of the storage group and the path for the log files and the system files.

4. When you have completed the information, click New to create the storage group. You can review the Completion screen once the task is completed and then click Finish.

The Completion screen includes the results and the EMS command that was generated to create the new storage group. The following example EMS command creates a storage group called Public Folder SG on the server HNLSCR01. The log and system files are placed in C:\PFSG:

```
New-StorageGroup -Server 'HNLSCR01' -Name 'Public Folder SG'↵
-LogFolderPath 'C:\PFSG' -SystemFolderPath 'C:\PFSG'
```

SETTING PROPERTIES OF A STORAGE GROUP

Storage groups have only a few settable properties. Figure 16.2 shows the properties of a newly created storage group. From this screen you can rename the storage group or enable circular logging. The option to zero out deleted database pages still exists but must be set using the Set-StorageGroup cmdlet.

FIGURE 16.2
Properties of a storage group

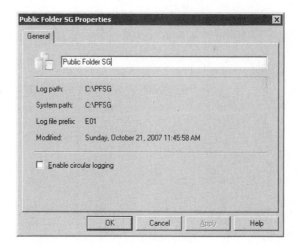

Additional EMS tasks that may be relevant to the storage group are the same as for any storage group. Table 16.1 contains a list of storage-group-related EMS cmdlets.

TABLE 16.1: EMS Cmdlets for Storage Groups

CMDLET	FUNCTION
Get-StorageGroup	Retrieves information about a specific storage group or all storage groups
Move-StorageGroup	Moves the storage group files to another location
New-StorageGroup	Creates a new storage group
Set-StorageGroup	Sets the properties of a storage group

CREATING A PUBLIC FOLDER DATABASE

Now that you have a storage group to hold your public folder database, you can create the database. This is performed most easily using the Exchange Management Console (EMC), but you can use the EMS as well.

CREATING THE DATABASE USING THE EMC

Follow these steps to create the public folder database using the EMC:

1. Using the EMC, navigate to the storage group you have created for the public folder database; this will be found in the Database Management work pane.

2. Run the New Public Folder Database Wizard by either right-clicking the storage group or choosing the task from the Actions pane.

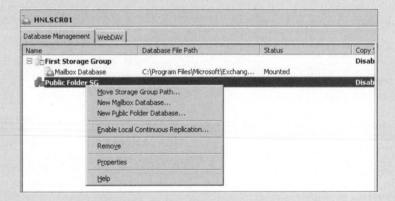

3. In the New Public Folder Database Wizard, enter the name of the public folder database and make sure that you specify a valid path in the Database File Path textbox.

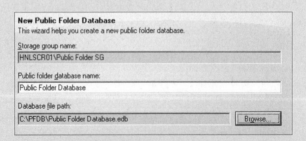

4. Once you have provided the necessary information, click the New button; you can then review the tasks that were performed on the Completion page. When you are finished, click Finish to close the wizard.

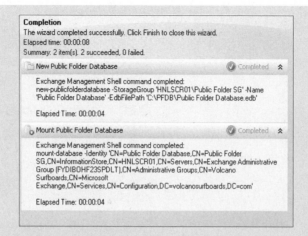

Completion
The wizard completed successfully. Click Finish to close this wizard.
Elapsed time: 00:00:08
Summary: 2 item(s). 2 succeeded, 0 failed.

New Public Folder Database ✓ Completed ⌃

Exchange Management Shell command completed:
new-publicfolderdatabase -StorageGroup 'HNLSCR01\Public Folder SG' -Name
'Public Folder Database' -EdbFilePath 'C:\PFDB\Public Folder Database.edb'

Elapsed Time: 00:00:04

Mount Public Folder Database ✓ Completed ⌃

Exchange Management Shell command completed:
mount-database -Identity 'CN=Public Folder Database,CN=Public Folder
SG,CN=InformationStore,CN=HNLSCR01,CN=Servers,CN=Exchange Administrative
Group (FYDIBOHF23SPDLT),CN=Administrative Groups,CN=Volcano
Surfboards,CN=Microsoft
Exchange,CN=Services,CN=Configuration,DC=volcanosurfboards,DC=com'

Elapsed Time: 00:00:04

CREATING THE DATABASE USING THE EMS

The Completion page of the wizard also includes the EMS commands that were generated for the task you ran. The following is the command that was necessary to create the public folder database in the Public Folder SG storage group on server HNLSCR01 and specify that the database is located in the C:\PFDB:

```
New-PublicFolderDatabase -StorageGroup 'HNLSCR01\Public Folder SG'↵
-Name 'Public Folder Database' -EdbFilePath 'C:\PFDB\Public Folder Database.edb'
```

In addition, because the database was to be mounted at startup, the following command could be used:

```
Mount-Database -Identity 'CN=Public Folder Database,CN=Public Folder SG,↵
  CN=InformationStore,CN=HNLSCR01,CN=Servers,CN=Exchange Administrative↵
  Group (FYDIBOHF23SPDLT) ,CN=Administrative Groups,↵
  CN=Volcano Surfboards,CN=Microsoft Exchange,CN=Services,CN=Configuration,↵
  DC=volcanosurfboards,DC=com'
```

This Mount-Database command is a bit long because it includes the distinguished name of the database. This guarantees that the cmdlet is mounting a unique database, but there are simpler commands that will achieve the same result. Here are two examples:

```
Mount-Database "Public Folder Database"
Mount-Database "HNLSCR1\Public Folder SG\Public Folder Database"
```

Note that the task might not mount the database due to replication delays in the Active Directory; if the cmdlet connects to one domain controller to make the changes and Exchange Server is connected to another domain controller for its configuration, you may have to mount the database manually. In this case, the Mount-Database cmdlet may display a message that Exchange Server 2007 can't mount a database that it does not even know exists yet.

Managing Public Folder Database Properties

Now that you have a public folder database created, let's look at the properties of that database that you can manage using the EMC as well as the EMS. We'll start with the EMC and look at some of the properties you can set. Figure 16.3 shows the general properties of a newly created public folder database.

FIGURE 16.3

General properties of an Exchange 2007 public folder database

From the General property page, you can change the display name (logical name) of the public folder database (the first field in Figure 16.3), define the online maintenance window, specify if the database should be mounted at startup, and specify whether or not the database can be overwritten by a restore from backup.

You also view some statistical information about the public folder database such as the database path, the local continuous replication path (called the Database Copy Path in the Properties window), the date of the last full backup, the date of the last incremental backup, the status of the database, and the last time the database's properties were modified.

On the Replication property page of the public folder database, you can specify the replication schedule (the default is Always), the Replicate Always Interval (the default is 15 minutes), and the maximum replication message size.

The Limits property page allows you to set some of the same types of information for public folders that you can set for mailboxes. Figure 16.4 shows the Limits property page for this newly created public folder database. These settings will affect any newly created folder on this particular public folder database.

There are some important things you should take note of on the Limits property page. Specifically, look at the Issue Warning At and Prohibit Post At limits for each folder. By default, a warning will be issued for each folder once it exceeds 1,945MB (1,991,680KB) and users won't be able to post messages after the folder's size exceeds 2,048MB (2,097,152KB). Yes, you are reading that correctly, that is in MB! The maximum item size is 10MB (10,240KB). This can, of course, be overridden on a folder-by-folder basis.

FIGURE 16.4

Default limits for an Exchange 2007 public folder database

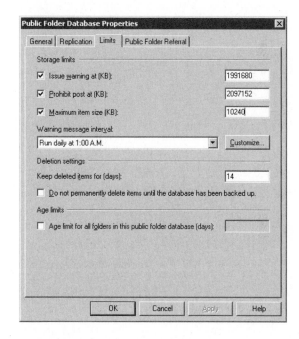

The Warning Message Interval option specifies the time of day that over-the-limit warning messages are generated and e-mailed to public folder contacts and owners.

Deleted items are retained for 14 days; during this time the folder owner can undelete items (or folders) that were inadvertently deleted. You can tell Exchange to keep deleted items after the expiration interval by clicking Do Not Permanently Delete Items Until The Database Has Been Backed Up.

Finally, the Age Limits property instructs the database to delete any item in any folder on this database that exceeds the age limit. This is useful if you want to age out older content, but it is probably more useful to apply this on a folder-by-folder basis.

The Public Folder Referral property page (Figure 16.5) shows how to enable a feature that was first introduced in Exchange 2003. By default, when an Outlook client connects to its *home* public folder database, if the public folder it requires is not on that particular database, it is given a referral to another public folder server. The referral list has all public folders that contain a replica of the required folder and is sorted and gives preference to public folder servers in the local administrative group (not routing group).

In Exchange 2007, the referral list is generated based on the Active Directory site that the public folder replicas are located in and is sorted based on the site cost. This may not be desirable for public folder connectivity, so you can specify a custom list and a cost value that should be used to sort the list of public folder servers.

FIGURE 16.5
Public folder referral
properties

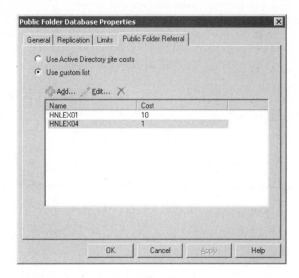

REMEMBER TO UPDATE REFERRAL LISTS

One of the common problems that occurs from manually setting a list of servers to which referrals should be generated is that, over time, servers are removed from service and no one remembers to update this list. If you manually specify servers, don't forget to update the list as servers and databases are updated.

All of the properties of public folder databases can be managed from the Exchange Management Shell. Table 16.2 contains a list of EMS cmdlets that can be used to manage public folder databases.

TABLE 16.2:   EMS Cmdlets for Public Folder Databases

CMDLET	FUNCTION
New-PublicFolderDatabase	Creates a new public folder database
Set-PublicFolderDatabase	Sets properties of a public folder database
Get-PublicFolderDatabase	Retrieves a list of public folder databases and their properties
Remove-PublicFolderDatabase	Deletes a public folder database

Defining the Default Public Folder Server

How public folders are accessed depends on the client version. By default, Outlook 2007 and Outlook Web Access clients use the new Exchange 2007 web services to determine the location of a public folder. Previous versions of Outlook will first look for a public folder on the user's public folder database, which might or might not be the same Exchange server where the user's mailbox is located. The default public folder database is configured on the Client Settings property page of the Properties dialog box for a mailbox database (see Figure 16.6).

FIGURE 16.6
The default public folder database property of the mailbox database

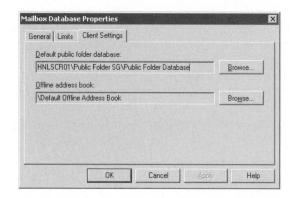

If a specific public folder doesn't exist in the default public folder database, the client is directed to a server where the public folder resides. As you can imagine, when many public folders are accessed over a lower-bandwidth network, server and network loads can get pretty heavy as users access public folders on one or a limited number of Exchange servers. If you need to, you can replicate folders on one Exchange server to other Exchange servers.

Defining Public Folder Administrators

In a small or medium-sized organization, one or two administrators are going to be responsible for all Exchange Server administrative tasks, including managing the public folders. However, in very large organizations, you may need to delegate the public folder administration tasks to a different person or group. Exchange Server 2007 SP1 automatically creates a group in the Microsoft Exchange Security Groups OU called Exchange Public Folder Administrators. Members of this group can manage the Exchange public folder attributes in the public folder and perform public folder operations, including these tasks:

◆ Creating public folders

◆ Creating top-level public folders

◆ Modifying public folder permissions

◆ Modifying public folder administrative permissions

◆ Modifying public folder properties such as content expiration times, storage limits, and deleted item retention time

◆ Modifying public folder replica lists

◆ Mounting and dismounting public folder databases

Though I recommend using the built-in groups for assigning administrative permissions anytime you can, you can also use the Add Exchange Administrator Wizard found on the Organization Configuration object. Figure 16.7 shows how you can use this wizard to delegate administrative permissions to a user or group.

FIGURE 16.7
Delegating a user the
Exchange Public Folder
Administrator role

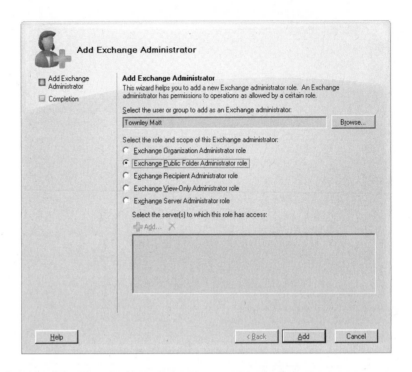

Managing Public Folders

When you start working with public folders, setting permissions, creating replicas, and setting folder limits, you will find a number of different tools available to you. As a matter of fact, you may need a couple of different tools to accomplish everything you need to accomplish. For example, you might need the Exchange 2007 Public Folder Management Console to create a folder and to mail-enable it (assign it an e-mail address) and then Outlook would be required to set permissions on the folder.

Using the Exchange 2007 Public Folder Management Console

Exchange Server 2007 Service Pack 1 includes a new console called the Public Folder Management Console; you can find it in the Toolbox work center of the Exchange Management Console. When you first launch this console, it will select an Exchange 2007 server with a public folder database, but you can change that if the server that is automatically selected is not convenient. Figure 16.8 shows the new SP1 Exchange Public Folder Management Console.

You will notice that the Public Folder Management Console looks a lot like the Exchange Management Console. The left side of the console shows the console tree; this area is only for viewing the public and system folders. You cannot manipulate any folder properties in the tree view. This was very confusing for me when I was learning this console: I kept *right-clicking* folders in the Tree pane.

In the Results pane in the middle, you can see the public folders within the part of the public folder tree that you currently have selected. If you plan to manage any properties of a public folder, you must select that folder here in the Results pane. For example, I currently have the

Departmental Messages folder highlighted. I can manage it by choosing Properties from the Actions pane (or just right-clicking and selecting Properties).

FIGURE 16.8
Exchange Public Folder
Management Console

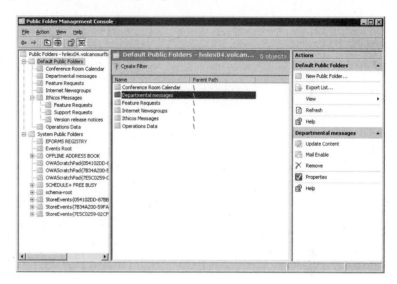

VIEWING THE PROPERTIES OF A PUBLIC FOLDER

Figure 16.9 shows the General properties of the Departmental Messages folder.

FIGURE 16.9
Viewing a public folder's
General property page

The General property page shows the display name, path, total items, size, public folder database, and the date the folder's properties were last modified. In an environment with more than one public folder server, this information will not always be accurate, though. In some cases, the General property page displays "Not available on this server." This means you are looking at a public folder database that does not have a local replica of this particular folder.

Next is the Replication property page, which shows you the servers and public folder databases where you can find a replica (copy) of this particular public folder. The Replication property page for the Departmental Messages folder is shown in Figure 16.10; this folder has two replicas.

FIGURE 16.10
Viewing the replicas of a public folder

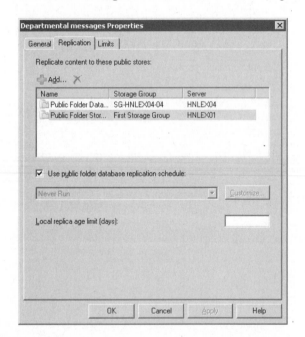

Earlier in this chapter, I showed you how you can specify a global default for limits for a particular public folder database. The Limits property page (shown in Figure 16.11) on an individual public folder allows you to override this per-database limit. Notice that by default the folder will use the limits set for it on its public folder database, but you can override that.

ADDITIONAL MANAGEMENT TASKS

You may have noticed two additional tasks in the Actions pane. The first is the Update Content task. If you click this task, Exchange will attempt to synchronize any missing or added content in this folder to other replicas.

The second task is the Mail Enable task. Just as in earlier versions of Exchange, a public folder can have an e-mail address. By default, public folders are no longer configured with an e-mail address. However, you can mail-enable a folder so it shows up in your global address list and has an e-mail address.

FIGURE 16.11

Viewing the limits of a specific public folder

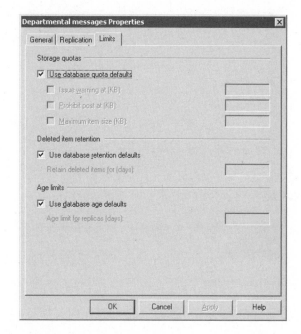

Suppose I select a folder called Support Requests in the Results pane and then click the Mail Enable task. This action automatically mail-enables the folder so that it shows up in the Exchange address lists; now the folder has some new property pages. One of the new property pages (Exchange General) is shown in Figure 16.12.

On the Exchange General property page, you can see the Exchange alias (which is used to generate the SMTP addresses as well as the display name) and the simple display name. You can also access the custom attributes. If you don't want the public folder to show up in the address lists, ensure that you check the Hide From Exchange Address List check box.

On the E-Mail Addresses property page (shown in Figure 16.13), you can see and edit the e-mail addresses that are assigned to the folder's Active Directory object.

Anyone can now send e-mail to this folder from outside of the organization by addressing mail to `support_requests@directory-update.com`. One important thing to note is that the default permissions on a folder include allowing the Anonymous user to contribute to a folder. If you remove this permission, the folder will not accept e-mail from outside of your organization.

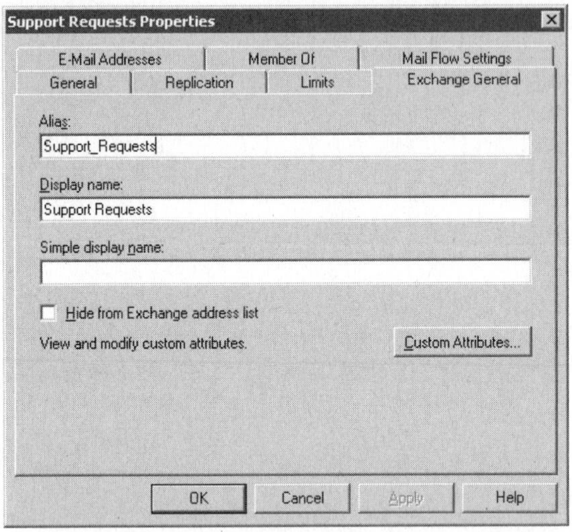

FIGURE 16.12
Viewing the Exchange
General property page of
a public folder

FIGURE 16.13
E-mail addresses for a
mail-enabled folder

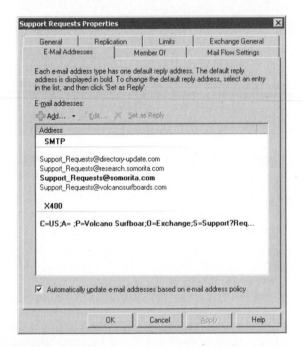

Understanding Public Folder Replication

In Figure 16.10, you saw the replica list of the public folder. This list controls which servers have a replica of a particular public folder. Why would you want to replicate public folders? Well, this depends on the size of your organization, but I can think of four reasons:

◆ You need to balance public folder access loads on your Exchange servers. Having all of your users connect to a single server for all of their public folder access can quickly result in an overwhelmed server if you have a large number of users or if you have heavy public folder usage.

◆ You have an Exchange server or group of Exchange servers separated from other servers in your organization by low-bandwidth links. In that case, you may be better off having limited replication traffic over your links and allowing users to connect to local replicas, keeping their traffic on the LAN.

◆ Public folder replication is essential when you're planning to remove an Exchange server from your organization (like all those Exchange 2003 servers you're migrating away from). If the server you're removing hosts the only replica for a set of public folders and you don't want to lose those folders, you must replicate them to another Exchange server in your organization.

◆ Additional replicas act as a fault-tolerance mechanism as well, but this should not replace regular backups.

Using the Exchange Management Shell to Manage Public Folders

One of the capabilities in Exchange Server 2007 is the inclusion of the Exchange Management Shell and the ability to manage public folders from the command line. Command-line management of public folders is a feature that has been sorely missing from previous versions of Exchange Server.

ABOUT TYPING LONG LINES IN THE EMS

In some of the following examples, you'll see lines terminated by a ↵ character. This character tells you that this is supposed to represent a single command line. You can also use the backtick (`` ` ``) character if you want to continue typing on the next line. PowerShell uses the backtick character for line termination; it tells the shell that the logical line of input will be continued on the next physical line. This allows you to break up long lines for display and still ensure that they work correctly when you enter them.

PERFORMING GENERAL PUBLIC FOLDER TASKS

These cmdlets apply to the entire public folder hierarchy at once and provide broad control of your public folder infrastructure:

Get-PublicFolderStatistics This cmdlet provides a detailed set of statistics about the public folder hierarchy on a given server:

```
Get-PublicFolderStatistics -Server "MBX01"
```

If the -Server parameter is not specified, the cmdlet will default to displaying the statistics on the local server.

Resume-PublicFolderReplication This cmdlet re-enables all public folder content replication when it has been suspended:

```
Resume-PublicFolderReplication
```

Suspend-PublicFolderReplication This cmdlet suspends all public folder content replication:

```
Suspend-PublicFolderReplication
```

Update-PublicFolderHierarchy This cmdlet starts the content synchronization process for the public folder hierarchy on the specified server:

```
Update-PublicFolderHierarchy -Server "MBX01"
```

MANIPULATING INDIVIDUAL PUBLIC FOLDERS

These cmdlets are designed to work with a specific public folder:

Get-PublicFolder This cmdlet retrieves the properties for the specified public folder. If you don't name a public folder by specifying a value for the -Identity property, it will default to the root public folder:

```
Get-PublicFolder -Identity "\Jobs\Posted" -Server "MBX01"
```

By default, the Get-PublicFolder cmdlet returns the values for only a single folder. The -Recurse switch changes the behavior to report on all subfolders as well:

```
Get-PublicFolder -Recurse
```

If you need to see system folders, you'll need to set the -Identity property to a value beginning with the string \NON_IPM_SUBTREE.

```
Get-PublicFolder -Identity \NON_IPM_SUBTREE -Recurse
```

New-PublicFolder This cmdlet creates a new public folder. The -Path property is required and provides the name and location of the new public folder:

```
New-PublicFolder -Name New -Path "\Jobs" -Server "MBX01"
```

Remove-PublicFolder This cmdlet deletes a public folder. The -Path property is required and provides the name and location of the public folder to be deleted:

```
Remove-PublicFolder -Path "\Jobs\Old" -Server "MBX01"
```

By default, the Remove-PublicFolder cmdlet removes only the named public folder. The -Recurse switch will delete all subfolders as well, which is handy for removing an entire group of folders at once.

Set-PublicFolder This cmdlet allows you to set most of the properties for the named public folder, such as limits, replicas, replication schedules, and more:

```
Set-PublicFolder -Identity "\Jobs\Posted" -Server "MBX01"
```

You cannot use the Set-PublicFolder cmdlet to mail-enable a public folder or to change its mail-related attributes. See the next section, "Manipulating Public Folder Mail Attributes," for the cmdlets to use for these tasks.

Update-PublicFolder   This cmdlet starts the content synchronization process for the named public folder. The -Identity property is required:

```
Update-PublicFolder -Identity "\Jobs\Posted"
```

MANIPULATING PUBLIC FOLDER MAIL ATTRIBUTES

These cmdlets are designed to work with a specific public folder and modify the attributes it receives when it is mail-enabled:

Disable-MailPublicFolder   This cmdlet takes an existing mail-enabled public folder and renders it mail-disabled (what a great term!):

```
Disable-MailPublicFolder -Identity "\Jobs\New"
```

Enable-MailPublicFolder   This cmdlet takes an existing public folder and renders it mail-enabled. The optional -HiddenFromAddressListsEnabled switch allows you to hide the folder from your address lists:

```
Enable-MailPublicFolder -Identity "\Jobs\New"  -HiddenFromAddressListsEnabled↵
   $true -Server "MBX01"
```

You set the mail-related attributes separately using the Set-MailPublicFolder cmdlet.

Get-MailPublicFolder   This cmdlet retrieves the mail-related properties for the specified public folder. If you don't name a public folder by specifying a value for the -Identity property, it will default to the root public folder:

```
Get-MailPublicFolder -Identity "\Jobs\Old" -Server "MBX01"
```

Set-MailPublicFolder   This cmdlet allows you to set the mail-related properties for the named public folder, such as alias, e-mail addresses, send and receive sizes, permitted and prohibited senders, and so on:

```
Set-MailPublicFolder -Identity "\Jobs\Posted" " -Alias PostedJobs↵
   -PrimarySmtpAddress "Jobs@Ithicos.com"
```

Once you have set the mail-related attributes for a public folder, you must still mail-enable it using the Enable-MailPublicFolder cmdlet.

MANAGING PUBLIC FOLDER DATABASES

These cmdlets allow you to manage the public folder databases:

Get-PublicFolderDatabase   This cmdlet provides the functionality used by the EMC and allows you to view the properties of existing public folder databases:

```
Get-PublicFolderDatabase -Server "MBX01"
```

This cmdlet takes one of three parameters: -Identity, -Server, or -StorageGroup. The parameters are not compatible with each other. Use only one of the three to narrow down your selection.

New-PublicFolderDatabase   This cmdlet allows you to create a new public folder database.

You can see the New-PublicFolderDatabase cmdlet in action by using the EMC to create a new database; it will show you the exact syntax it used with the cmdlet.

Remove-PublicFolderDatabase   This cmdlet deletes an existing public folder database from the active configuration of the server:

```
Remove-PublicFolderDatabase ' -Identity "Public Folder Database"
```

The corresponding EDB file is not deleted by the Remove-PublicFolderDatabase cmdlet; you have to manually remove it from the hard drive.

Set-PublicFolderDatabase   This cmdlet provides the underlying functionality used by the EMC to update the properties of existing public folder databases:

```
Set-PublicFolderDatabase -Identity "Public Folder Database"↵
-Name "New and Improved PF Database"
```

MANAGING PUBLIC FOLDER PERMISSIONS

These cmdlets allow you to modify and monitor the permissions on your public folders. Administrative and client permissions are handled through two separate sets of nouns. The Exchange 2007 documentation contains the list of specific permissions that you can apply.

Add-PublicFolderAdministrativePermission   This cmdlet lets you add an administrative permission entry to a given public folder:

```
Add-PublicFolderAdministrativePermission -User 'Jim' - Identity "\Jobs\Posted"↵
 -AccessRights "ViewInformationStore, AdministerInformationStore"
```

You can specify a single access right or list multiple rights at once using the syntax shown in the example for the Add-PublicFolderAdministrativePermission cmdlet.

Add-PublicFolderClientPermission   This cmdlet lets you add a client permission entry to a given public folder:

```
Add-PublicFolderClientPermission -User Makoto.Suzuki↵
 -Identity "\Jobs\Posted" -AccessRights CreateItems
```

You can specify a single access right or list multiple rights at once using the syntax shown in the example for the Add-PublicFolderAdministrativePermission cmdlet.

Get-PublicFolderAdministrativePermission   This cmdlet lets you view the administrative permission entries on a given public folder:

```
Get-PublicFolderAdministrativePermission  -Identity "\Jobs\Posted"
```

Get-PublicFolderClientPermission   This cmdlet lets you view the client permission entries on a given public folder:

```
Get-PublicFolderClientPermission  -Identity "\Jobs\Posted"
```

Remove-PublicFolderAdministrativePermission This cmdlet lets you remove an administrative permission entry from a given public folder:

```
Remove-PublicFolderAdministrativePermission -User Lyle.Bullock↵
-Identity "\Jobs\Posted" -AccessRights ViewInformationStore
```

You can specify a single access right or list multiple rights at once using the syntax shown in the Remove-PublicFolderAdministrativePermission example.

Remove-PublicFolderClientPermission This cmdlet lets you remove a client permission entry from a given public folder:

```
Remove-PublicFolderClientPermission -User Nathan.Peters↵
-Identity "\Jobs\Posted" -AccessRights CreateItems
```

You can specify a single access right or list multiple rights at once using the syntax shown in the Remove-PublicFolderAdministrativePermission example.

USING ADDITIONAL SCRIPTS FOR COMPLICATED TASKS

Although the cmdlets described in the preceding sections are certainly great for single folder operations, performing common operations on entire groups of folders starts getting sticky. Because most of us aren't scripting gurus, Exchange 2007 provides some example EMS scripts that allow you to perform more complicated server and management tasks that affect groups of folders:

◆ AddReplicaToPFRecursive.ps1 adds the specified server to the replica list for a given public folder and all folders underneath it.

◆ AddUsersToPFRecursive.ps1 allows you to grant user permissions to a folder and all folders beneath it.

◆ MoveAllReplicas.ps1 finds and replaces a server in the replica list of all public folders, including system folders.

◆ RemoveReplicaFromPFRecursive.ps1 removes the specified server from the replica list for a given public folder and all folders underneath it.

◆ ReplaceReplicaOnPFRecursive.ps1 finds and replaces a server in the replica list of a given public folder as well as all subfolders.

◆ ReplaceUserPermissionOnPFRecursive.ps1 finds and replaces one user in the permissions on a given public folder and all its subfolders with a second user; the original user permissions are not retained.

◆ ReplaceUserWithUserOnPFRecursive.ps1 copies one user's access permissions on a given public folder and all its subfolders to a second user while retaining permissions for the first user; it's confusingly named.

◆ RemoveReplicaFromPFRecursive.ps1 removes the given user's access permissions from the given public folder and all its subfolders.

You can find these scripts in the Scripts subfolder of the Exchange 2007 installation folder. Note that with the default Windows PowerShell configuration, you just can't click on these scripts and run them; you must invoke them from within the EMS, usually by navigating to the folder and calling them explicitly.

Using Outlook to Create a Public Folder

Exchange public folders can also be created by mailbox-enabled users in their e-mail clients. Here's how you create a public folder using the Outlook client:

1. Open Outlook and make sure the folder list is displayed.

2. Double-click Public Folders in the folder list, or click the plus icon just in front of Public Folders. Notice that the plus sign becomes a minus sign when a folder is expanded to show the folders within it.

   You've now expanded the top-level folder for public folders, which contains two subfolders: Favorites and All Public Folders.

3. Expand the All Public Folders folder and you'll see that it has at least one subfolder: Internet Newsgroups. If your organization uses public folders, you probably have at least one other subfolder here as well.

USING A FAVORITES LIST FOR FREQUENTLY USED FOLDERS

If your Exchange organization has a large number of public folders, you can drag the ones that you use a lot to your Favorites subfolder. This makes them easier to find. Folders in the Favorites folder are also the only ones that are available when you work offline without a connection to your Exchange server. Only public folders that are in your Favorites folder will be downloaded when working in local cache mode.

---

4. Right-click All Public Folders, select a child folder, and select New Folder from the menu that pops up. This brings up the Create New Folder dialog box (see Figure 16.14).

FIGURE 16.14
Naming a new folder

5. Enter a name for the folder; I've given mine the name Custom Development

   Note that the folder will hold two different kinds of items:

♦ E-mail items are messages.

♦ Posted items contain a subject and text. You can post an item in a folder designed to hold posts without having to deal with messaging attributes such as whom the item is sent to. To post an item, click the down arrow near the New icon on the main Outlook window and select Post In This Folder from the drop-down menu.

6. When you're done creating your folder, click OK.

If you're told that you don't have sufficient permissions to create the folder, you need to assign those permissions using one of the other Exchange public folder management tools. If you have Exchange administrative permissions, you can make this change yourself.

The new public folder now shows up under the All Public Folders hierarchy. If you can't see the full name of your new folder, make the Folder List pane a little wider.

7. To set additional properties for your folder, right-click your new folder and select Properties from the pop-up menu.

The Properties dialog box for the folder is shown in Figure 16.15.

FIGURE 16.15
The Outlook client's
Properties dialog box
for a public folder

I'm not going to spend a lot of time with this dialog box. Among other things, mailbox owners use public folder Properties dialog boxes to do the following:

♦ Add a description for other mailbox owners who access the folder.

♦ Make the folder available on the Internet.

♦ Set up a default view of the folder, including grouping by such things as the subject or sender.

◆ Set up some administrative rules on folder characteristics, access, and such.

◆ Set permissions for using the folder.

Using the Exchange 2003 System Manager

In Exchange 5.5, you could only create public folders using an e-mail client. You couldn't create one in the Administrator program. The Exchange 2003 System Manager program lets you create public folders as an Exchange administrator. Although Exchange Server 2007 Service Pack 1 offers a new Public Folder Management Console, it is still lacking some of the graphical user interface features that you may require for public folder management including managing folder permissions, setting administrative permissions, and easily propagating new settings to all folders under a root folder.

REQUIREMENTS FOR USING EXCHANGE 2003 SYSTEM MANAGER WITH EXCHANGE 2007

To use the Exchange Server 2003 System Manager, the Exchange 2007 server must have the Web server component of IIS installed and it must support WebDAV.

MANAGING FOLDER PROPERTIES USING THE EXCHANGE 2003 SYSTEM MANAGER

Launch the System Manager, expand the Administrative Groups node, expand the desired administrative group, and expand the Folders node. Right-click the Public Folders container and select New ➤ Public Folder from the pop-up menu to bring up the new public folder Properties dialog box. Let's take a look at the key property pages on this dialog box.

CREATE PUBLIC FOLDERS IN THE Folders\Public Folders CONTAINER

You should create folders in the Folders\Public Folders container, not in the public folder database. The public folder database holds created folders. Seems simple, but if I had a dollar for every time I wrongly went to the public folder database to create a new public folder, well, I'd at least be on the beach in Hawaii right now.

General Property Page

You use the General property page to name your folder and enter a description. The Path field shows where the folder is located in the Public Folder hierarchy after it has been created. If Maintain Per-User Read And Unread Information For This Folder is selected, each user will see items in the folder that they have read in non-bold text. If this option is not selected, all items show in bold text for all users whether or not they have been read.

Replication Property Page

This is a very important property page because it is used to manage replication of folders between this server and other Exchange servers. Replication enables you to put copies of the same folder on multiple Exchange servers. It is very useful either for local load balancing or to limit wide area network traffic and improve performance by placing copies of folders in routing groups at geographically distant sites.

Limits Property Page

You've seen limits property pages before. Let's look at each of the three types of limits on this page:

Storage Limits   As with mailboxes, you can set thresholds at which warnings are sent and posting to the folder is prohibited. You can also set a maximum posted-item size. If you want, you can choose to use the default storage limits settings for the public folder database where the folder resides.

Deletion Setting   As with mailboxes, you can set the maximum number of days that a deleted item will be kept for recovery before being totally deleted. If you deselect the Use Database Retention Defaults check box, you can enter a number of days that deleted items should be retained. If you don't want items retained at all, set the number of days to 0.

Age Limits   This is the number of days that an item in the folder lives before being deleted. This is a very useful tool for controlling storage usage.

SECURITY SETTINGS FOR PUBLIC FOLDERS

In some earlier versions of Exchange, the Windows group Everyone had rights by default to create folders in the Public Folders container. This right extended to both top-level folders (folders within and, thus, just below the Public Folders container) and subfolders within top-level folders. This is addressed in Exchange Server 2007 and the Everyone group does not have this right.

If you want to change the permissions for the Everyone group, right-click the Public Folders container and select Properties. Use the Security tab in the Public Folders Properties dialog box to add or remove users and groups or their rights in the Public Folders container.

Take extra caution when providing large numbers of users with permissions to create root-level public folders; you may end up with hundreds of root-level public folders that were created without any sort of oversight or planning.

Even if you don't want to change the Exchange Server 2007 default, I strongly recommend that you take a look at the Security tab. Many of the permissions on it are specific to public folders and are therefore quite different from the permissions for other types of Exchange recipients.

ACCESSING PUBLIC FOLDERS USING THE EXCHANGE 2003 SYSTEM MANAGER

You can still create and manage public folders using the Exchange 2003 System Manager; although the EMS is relatively easy to use, many administrators who use it infrequently will be more comfortable using a graphical interface, at least at first. For the most part, public folder management is straightforward in multi-server Exchange Server environments. However, there's a trick to choosing the right public folder database (store).

Look at Figures 16.16 and 16.17, which show the public folders on the two servers HNLEX01 and HNLEX04, an Exchange 2003 server and an Exchange 2007 server, respectively.

First, notice that HNLEX01 (the Exchange 2003 server) has many public folders that don't exist on HNLEX04 (the Exchange 2007 server). This should demonstrate that by default the Public Folders container on each Exchange server contains only those folders that have replicas located in that store. So far, this is simple and makes sense; ready for the curveball?

FIGURE 16.16
Public folders on
HNLEX01, an Exchange
2003 server

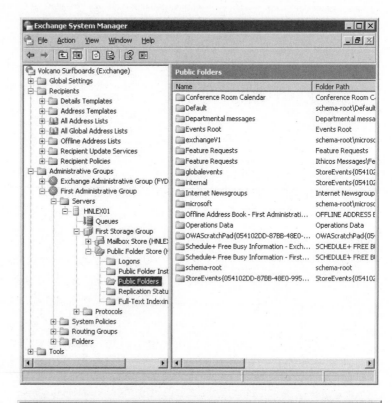

FIGURE 16.17
Public folders on
HNLEX04, an Exchange
2007 server

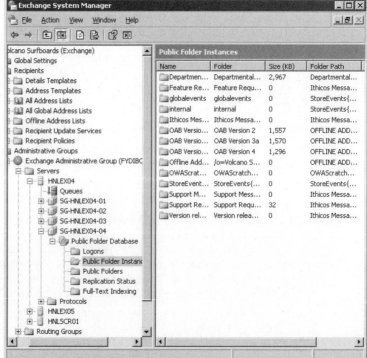

Say that I want to create a new public folder on HNLEX04. First, I need to locate the Public Folders container that holds the default public folder tree for my organization. I've selected that container in Figure 16.18.

FIGURE 16.18
The default public folder
tree container

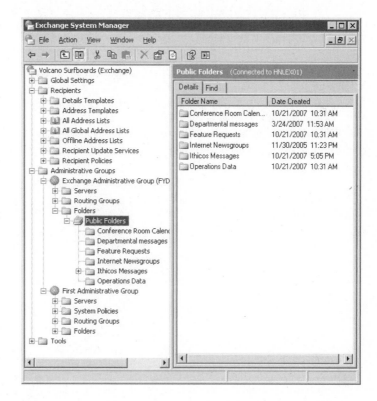

To ensure that I'm working with the right public folder database, I need to right-click the Public Folders container, select Connect To from the menu, select the appropriate public folder database from the Select a Public Folder Database dialog box, and click OK. See Figure 16.19.

FIGURE 16.19
Choosing a public folder
database

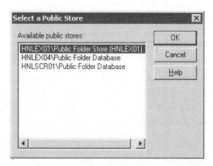

Now I know that I'm working on the correct public folder database, and I can graphically manage and create public folders on my Exchange 2007 server to my heart's content.

> **FINDING THE RIGHT PUBLIC FOLDER DATABASE**
>
> The folders that are displayed in the Public Folders container don't tell you whether you're connected to the correct public folder database. This display is based on the organization-wide public folder hierarchy, so you see all public folders in your organization regardless of what server they are stored on in the Public Folders container.

While you've still got legacy Exchange servers in your organization, you can control management access to the default public folder tree by moving that tree to an administrative group other than the one in which the tree was originally created. You should aim to move the public folder tree into the Exchange 2007 administrative group.

To do this, you must create a new Folders container in the desired administrative group and then drag and drop the default public folder tree into the new Folders container. See Figure 16.20 for an example of this being done on HNLEX01, an Exchange 2007 mailbox server in my organization.

FIGURE 16.20
Creating a new Public Folders container on an Exchange 2007 server

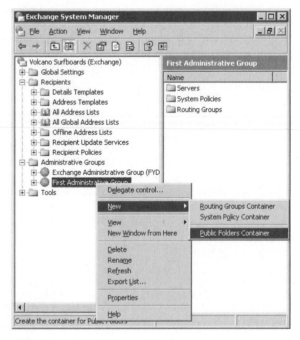

For example, say I've dragged my default public folders tree from its default location to the Exchange 2007 administrative group and created a new Public Folders container just for public folder management. Delegated administrators can both view and change the properties of all public folders in the tree and create new folders in the tree. I've delegated control over the administrative group Public Folders Management to a new Windows 2003 security group, PFAdmins; members of this group includes only those users I want to be able to manage the public folders in my organization. I then modify the management permissions for the Public Folders container to only allow management functions to members of the PFAdmins group.

After these changes the managers of the Exchange 2003 Los Angeles and New York administrative groups who are also members of the new security group will have full control over the public folders in their administrative groups. Managers of the Los Angeles and New York administrative groups who aren't also members of the PFAdmins security group can no longer create new public folders. That's because administrative creation of public folders can be done only on the default public folders tree, to which they no longer have access.

Using the Public Folder DAV Administrator Tool

It is really unfortunate that the initial release of Exchange 2007 provides no GUI for public folder management. Though the EMS cmdlets are very functional, it can take some time to master using them; in the meantime, you still have public folders to administer.

Happily, Microsoft has an outstanding freely available GUI tool, the Public Folder DAV (Distributed Authoring and Versioning) Administrator (PFDAVAdmin.exe). PFDAVAdmin is a .NET application that uses WebDAV instead of MAPI to access the public folder database.

PFDAVADMIN AND "DEEMPHASIZED" WEBDAV

You might now be wondering if using PFDAVAdmin is a good idea, given its reliance on WebDAV. In Exchange 2007 support for the WebDAV protocol is "deemphasized," meaning that Microsoft doesn't promise it will be around for the next major version of Exchange. But it's still here in Exchange 2007 — and it allows you to use this wonderful management tool.

PFDAVAdmin requires the .NET Framework version 1.1 to be installed, which means you must maintain multiple versions of the .NET Framework on your management servers and workstations. Though this is not a big deal, I strongly recommend that you run PFDAVAdmin from your workstation rather than trying to run it from the Exchange server.

PFDAVAdmin (shown in Figure 16.21) is a wonderfully flexible tool. At first glance, it seems to give you the ability to manage public folder permissions using a GUI that is close to the legacy Exchange System Manager.

In addition to querying and setting permissions, you can add, replace, and remove individual access control entries (ACEs) across a set of folders without having to wholesale replace the access control lists (ACLs) in question. PFDAVAdmin will also notify you when an ACL is damaged or in noncanonical order (meaning that the ACEs aren't properly ordered) and allow you to fix these problems on more than one folder at once.

How ACEs Get Out of Order

Administrators who made use of the Installable File System (IFS) — otherwise known as the M: drive — in Exchange 2000 and 2003 would often use the Windows Explorer permission tool to modify permissions on public folders. Unfortunately, this usually causes ACEs to get written in the wrong order, causing all sorts of subtle problems. PFDAVAdmin is the easy way to fix them, if you've got to deal with them — and you don't have to wait until you've got Exchange 2007 in your organization to do it! Luckily, Exchange 2007 makes the IFS go away, so once you fix the problems, they're not likely to come back.

FIGURE 16.21
Using the PFDAVAdmin tool

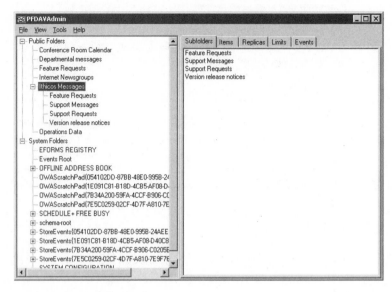

You can also use PFDAVAdmin to do the following:

◆ Perform bulk operations on folder properties. In addition, you can do bulk search and removal operations of per-item permissions.

◆ Apply changes to your list of replicas to a folder and all subfolders without overwriting each folder's replica list (that is, add or remove specific server entries without making each folder's replica list an exact copy of your starting point).

◆ Export folder permissions on folders, public folder databases, and mailbox databases.

◆ Export and import public folder replica lists.

Microsoft makes PFDAVAdmin freely available through the Microsoft Exchange tools download website at the following URL:

```
http://www.microsoft.com/downloads/details.aspx?FamilyId=635BE792-D8AD-49E3-
ADA4-E2422C0AB424
```

USING LEGACY EXCHANGE PUBLIC FOLDER TOOLS

There are a couple of additional tools that Exchange administrators have used throughout the years. Although they work with legacy Exchange servers, many of them are not certified for use with Exchange 2003 (let alone Exchange 2007). However, you can still use them as long as you have legacy Exchange public folder servers in your organization. There are two in particular I'd like to mention:

◆ The PFAdmin tool (PFAdmin.exe) is a command-line tool for common administrative tasks. With it you can manage ACLs, manage replicas, and re-home folders. If you happen to have old product CDs lying around, you can find a copy of this tool on the BackOffice Resource Kit (BORK) 4.5 CD.

◆ The PFInfo tool (PFInfo.exe) is a GUI tool that provides reporting on a server's folder replicas and associated permissions. The output of this tool can even be used as input to PFAdmin, allowing you to provide a level of consistency across multiple servers.

Though you might be tempted to use PFAdmin and PFInfo in your Exchange 2007 organization (especially if you're already using them), I recommend that you finally retire these tools *before* retiring your legacy Exchange public folder servers. The most compelling reason to use these tools with legacy Exchange servers was to provide the missing command-line and scripting capability for public folder management, and now that Exchange 2007 includes the EMS, you should really put the effort into mastering the public folder cmdlets it provides.

There is one additional legacy tool you might find of value. The Public Folder Migration Tool (PFMigrate.wsf) is a Visual Basic script that was introduced in the Exchange Server 2003 Deployment Tools (ExDeploy). This script was designed for one purpose: to provide a simple interface for performing bulk public folder replica transfers from Exchange 5.5 servers to Exchange 2003 servers. However, because it can handle cross-administrative group replica transfers, PFMigrate can be used to move replicas to Exchange 2007 servers. The script is downloadable from the Microsoft website as part of the latest versions of the Exchange Server 2003 ExDeploy tools.

Working with the Public Folder Hierarchy

You can create public folders in any available public folder database on any Exchange mailbox server. By default, public folder databases are not created on Exchange 2007 mailbox servers unless you specify that the server will be used with clients running Outlook 2003 and earlier. When you create a new public folder database on an Exchange 2007 mailbox server, you can create a new storage group for it or place it in a storage group that already has one or more mailbox databases in it.

A public folder hierarchy, or public folder tree, is a list of public folders and their subfolders that are stored in the default public folder database on the Exchange servers in an Exchange organization. The hierarchy also includes the name of the server on which a copy of each folder resides. Because the hierarchy exists in Active Directory as a separate object, it does not contain any of the actual items in your various public folders. There is one organization-wide public folder hierarchy object, although in previous versions of Exchange, you could create additional public folder trees that were not visible through the Public Folder object in Outlook but could be accessed through other methods, such as NNTP. (Note that you can't provide NNTP access to public folders from Exchange 2007 servers.)

You cannot create non-visible public folder trees using the management tools in Exchange 2007; you will need to continue using the Exchange 2003 System Manager if you need to create these objects.

Replicating Public Folders

In a single Exchange server environment, the hierarchy exists and is stored on the Exchange server. In an environment with multiple public folder databases, each Exchange server that has a public folder database has a copy of the public folder hierarchy. Exchange servers work together to ensure that each Exchange server in an administrative group has an up-to-date copy of the public folder hierarchy. This process, called *public folder hierarchy replication*, is automatic. In Exchange 2000 and Exchange 2003, there were certain limitations with this process when replication crossed administrative and routing group boundaries. Once you've fully migrated to Exchange 2007, these limitations will be a thing of the past; all Exchange 2007 servers are in a single separate administrative group that has been created for backward compatibility with Exchange 2000 and Exchange 2003 servers in the organization.

The Exchange 2003 System Manager uses the public folder hierarchy to appropriately display public folder objects in various containers and to retrieve information about public folders, whether that information is stored in the hierarchy or on the server where the public folder physically resides. E-mail clients such as Outlook and OWA use the hierarchy to display a list of public folders available on all servers in the organization and to access items in a specific folder. Security limits associated with a given public folder, of course, limit the actual access granted to administrators and users.

The public folder hierarchy also includes what are called *system folders*, such as the Schedule+Free Busy folder. I talk about it and the other system folders later in this chapter.

How public folders are accessed depends on the client version. By default, Outlook 2007 and Outlook Web Access clients use the new Exchange 2007 web services to determine the location of a public folder. Previous versions of Outlook will first look for a public folder on the user's public folder database, which might or might not be on the same Exchange server where the user's mailbox is located. The default public folder database is configured on the General property page of the Properties dialog box for a mailbox database (see Figure 16.22).

FIGURE 16.22
The Default Public Folder Database property of the mailbox database

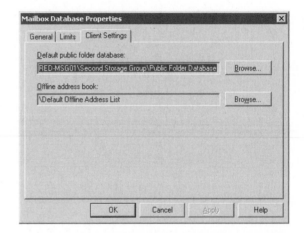

If a specific public folder doesn't exist in the default public folder database, the client is directed to a server where the public folder resides. As you can imagine, when many public folders are accessed over a lower-bandwidth network, server and network loads can get pretty heavy as users access public folders on one or a limited number of Exchange servers. If you need to, you can replicate folders on one Exchange server to other Exchange servers.

Configuring Public Folder Replication

Technically, all copies of a public folder, including the one on the Exchange server where the folder was originally created, are called *replicas*. There's good reason for this. After a folder has been replicated, users will place items into it via the replica on their own default public folders server or on the nearest server as calculated using connector costs. So no replica of the folder can be considered a master copy. The replicas of a folder update each other on a regular basis, reinforcing the idea that there is no master copy.

You can set up replication of a public folder on either the server that will provide the folder or the server that will hold the new replica of the public folder. To replicate a folder, follow these steps:

1. Open the Exchange Server 2007 Public Folder Management Console and expand the Default Public Folders container. You may need to navigate through the public folder tree if you want to manage the replica configuration of a child folder.

2. Select the public folder you want in the Results pane and select Properties from the Actions pane to see the properties of the public folder. Select the Replication property page. Click Add to open the Select Public Folder Database dialog box. In Figure 16.23, things are set up so that the content replicates on server HNLEX04.

FIGURE 16.23
Setting up replication of a public folder

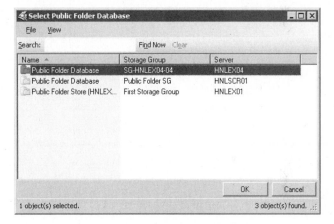

3. Clicking OK in the Select Public Folder Database dialog box adds HNLEX04 to the list of public folder databases to which the folder's contents will be replicated. You can see this in Figure 16.24. (The folder being replicated is called Feature Requests.)

FIGURE 16.24
The Replication Properties dialog box of the Feature Requests folder, showing the locations of the folder's replicas

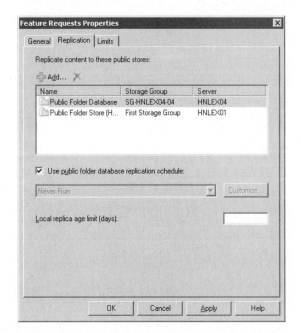

Let's look quickly at some of the other properties that you can set on the Replication property page. You can set the public folder database replication schedule. Depending on the importance of the contents of the folder and the available network bandwidth, you can accept the default Always Run, select other options from the drop-down list, or create your own custom schedule for replication of this folder. In order to set a schedule, you must clear the Use Public Folder Database Replication Schedule check box.

The Local Replica Age Limit (Days) option allows you to specify the maximum age that an item will be retained in a particular replica of the folder. Once the item reaches that age, Exchange Server will automatically remove it.

REPLICATING SYSTEM FOLDERS

The legacy Exchange systems use a special type of public folder to hold information used by Exchange servers and their clients. To see the system folders, expand the System Public Folders container in the Exchange Public Folders Management Console.

Some of these folders must be replicated to assure smooth functioning of your Exchange system. One of these is the Schedule+Free Busy folder, which holds calendar information for every mailbox in the administrative group.

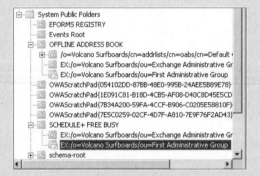

If this folder isn't available to other mailbox servers, users will not be able to schedule meetings while looking at the free/busy times for people they want to invite. This folder's absence can also cause some Outlook clients to issue regular and very annoying warnings about not being able to find free/busy information.

Ensure that at the very least the free/busy folder is visible across administrative groups, and if that's going to be a problem, consider replicating it. Do remember, though, that Exchange 2007 no longer requires system public folders to handle free/busy information for users on Exchange 2007 mailbox servers when dealing with newer clients (Outlook 2007 and above).

Be careful about most of the other system folders. Unless you know what you're doing, let the system replicate them.

Managing Public Folder Permissions

You can manage folder permissions in one of two ways. The simplest is just to use Outlook; navigate to the public folder, right click to display its properties, and select the Permissions property page (shown in Figure 16.25).

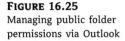

FIGURE 16.25
Managing public folder
permissions via Outlook

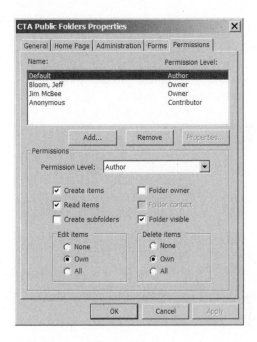

Of course, when you are using Outlook, your user account must be one of the owners of the folder. Otherwise the Permissions property page will not be displayed. What you see on the Permissions property page are the permissions that the groups (mail-enabled groups) or users will have to the folder.

You can use the Permissions property page to assign specific folder access rights to Exchange users and distribution groups, who can then work with a public folder using their Outlook clients. For emphasis, let me restate what I just said in a somewhat different form: *You grant public folder access permissions to Exchange recipients, not to Windows 2003 users and groups.* Once access to a public folder is granted, Exchange recipients access the folder in their Outlook client while connected to their mailbox.

For a graphic reinforcement of this point, click Add in the Permissions box to start adding a new user or group that will have access to this public folder. This action opens a dialog box that looks very much like the Outlook Address Book that you use to select recipients to send a message to. You do not see the dialog box that you use to select Windows 2003 users and groups. (Click Cancel to get out of the Add Users dialog box.)

Because I created the public folder in Exchange System Manager while logged in as the domain administrator, Administrator is given the role of Owner. The owner of a public folder has complete control over the folder.

If a user has the correct permissions on a public folder, that user can change access permissions on the folder for other users. Permissions on a public folder can be modified in two places:

◆ From within the Outlook client using the Permissions property page for a public folder

◆ Using the Client Permissions dialog box that is available in Exchange System Manager

Which of these you use depends on your security rights. If you are an Exchange user with no extraordinary permissions who is an owner of a public folder, you manage permissions for the folder in Outlook using the Permissions property page for a public folder. If you're an Exchange administrative user, you can change permissions on any public folder using the Client Permissions dialog box.

There is a group named Default that includes all Exchange recipients not separately added to the Name list box. When the folder is created, this group is automatically given the default role of Author. Authors can edit and delete only their own folder items, and they don't own the folder and can't create subfolders.

To make assigning permissions easier, Microsoft has come up with several interesting roles. Each role has a specific combination of permissions to the folder. The roles include Owner, Publishing Editor, Editor, Publishing Author, Author, Nonediting Author, Reviewer, Contributor, and Custom — each with a different combination of client permissions.

I should also note that you can use the PFDAVAdmin tool to assign permissions as well as to fix permissions that might be broken. The PFDAVAdmin tool's Permissions dialog box (shown in Figure 16.26) allows for much more detailed viewing and editing of permissions but is quite obviously not an end-user tool.

FIGURE 16.26
Changing permissions
using PFDAVAdmin

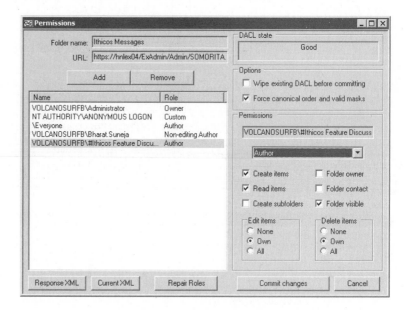

Summary

If you're coming new to Exchange 2007 or don't have a lot of investment in public folders in your current Exchange organization, you probably haven't been too worried about the rumors of the demise of public folders in Exchange 2007. These rumors are fortunately not true; public folders are still supported in Exchange, even if the out-of-the-box management options aren't all that we could hope for.

By concentrating its effort on providing solid support for public folder management in the Exchange Management Shell, Microsoft has finally provided the missing command-line management interface that can simplify dealing with one-off public folder management tasks.

These cmdlets also make it easy to do large-scale scripted and bulk management operations. The new Exchange Public Folder Management Console will also help you when managing public folders, though it does lack some key functionality.

The lack of a full featured public folder management tool, however, is offset by Microsoft's continued development and support of the PFDAVAdmin tool, which provides a familiar interface for those who are used to the legacy Exchange System Manager. However, it also gives you a lot more power, providing sophisticated bulk operations and import/export capabilities that make managing large public folder deployments smoother. While you still have legacy servers in your organization, you can continue using the legacy Exchange 2003 System Manager to manage your public folder replicas.

Part 4

Exchange Server Reliability and Availability

In this part:

Chapter 17

Reliability and Availability 101

Picking a single most important responsibility for an Exchange server administrator is tough to do. Arguably, I would have to say that the biggest responsibility is actually a tie between making sure your company's information is backed up and making sure you are providing access to that information when a user requires it.

If you attend any Windows or networking conferences, the disaster recovery and high-availability sessions are always the ones that are standing room only. Apparently, then, providing good availability and having the ability to recover from a serious outage are universally thought of as important.

This chapter covers steps that you need to take in order to provide your users with better availability. As you will quickly learn, a lot of the things you need to do to improve the availability of Exchange are common sense and technologies that you already understand.

Experienced Exchange server administrators and consultants will tell you that some of the most important things that you do to improve availability are all procedural rather than technical. They will also tell you that much of the unplanned downtime they have been exposed to has been due to something really simple that no one thought of.

In this chapter you learn to:

- ◆ Understand the basics of high availability

- ◆ Build redundancy and fault tolerance

- ◆ Know when to implement clustering

High Availability Starts with the Basics

Too often when a consultant sets foot in a new organization that is having availability problems, the consultant starts talking about clustering, load balancing, storage area networks, replication technologies, and so on. Everyone in the room has that "deer in the headlights" look in their eyes, but all of those new technologies sure sound great!

Unfortunately, availability problems are frequently related to "people and process" rather than being technical problems. Poor documentation, insufficient training, lack of procedures, and improper preparation for supporting Exchange are the most frequent causes of downtime.

> **RELIABILITY FIRST**
>
> In general, focusing on making sure that your operating system is stable, Exchange is properly installed, and the server hardware is very reliable will help you achieve better availability than going for a "high tech" solution. I am not saying that "high tech" solutions such as clustering are not good solutions, but you should ensure that your platform is stable before investigating them. Even the best technical solution can become very unstable if the personnel managing the system are not properly trained.

Reliability vs. Availability

No one likes to have unplanned downtime, even if it is just for a few minutes because you need to reboot a server. An hour of unscheduled downtime in the middle of the business day is the sort of thing that users will remember for the next year. Consequently, a lot of organizations avoid unplanned downtime, even if they might be able to do something during the off-hours.

Nevertheless, it is not wise to sacrifice the reliability of your system just to make your availability numbers look good. In general, an hour of unplanned downtime to fix an impending problem is much more acceptable than an entire day of downtime if the impending problem actually causes a crash.

Some of the tasks that might need to be performed sooner than your scheduled maintenance window include replacing disk drive that is running in a degraded state or swapping out a failed power supply.

Good reliability helps you sleep at night. Good availability helps you keep your job.

Scheduled Maintenance

People don't often think about high availability and scheduled downtime at the same time. However, there will always be maintenance tasks that require some scheduled downtime. When planning your weekly or monthly operations schedule, you need to make sure that you have a window available for maintenance. This window of time should be published to your user community and they should expect that the system may be unavailable during those times.

Scheduled downtime may be a hard sell in your organization. This is especially true if you have users who work around the clock. Still, you can make a compelling argument for this downtime window if you think about all the things you might need to do during your scheduled downtime:

◆ Performing server reboots

◆ Applying configuration changes

◆ Installing service packs and critical updates

◆ Updating firmware and the FlashBIOS

◆ Performing database maintenance such enabling or managing LCR databases

◆ Replacing power supplies, disks, UPS batteries, or RAID controller batteries

◆ Reconfiguring IP addressing or networking equipment

◆ Addressing environmental issues such as air conditioning, UPS, power, and the security system

Granted, not every organization needs a weekly maintenance window, but you should ask for it anyway. You don't have to use the maintenance window if you have no maintenance to perform.

When scheduling the window, take into consideration staffing concerns. After all, if you schedule maintenance once per week, someone knowledgeable has to be available during that time to perform the work.

Finally, when planning your scheduled downtime windows, make sure downtime during these windows does not count against your "nines."

The Quest for Nines

No respectable discussion about improving service availability is complete without a definition of *nines*. Everyone is familiar with the quest to achieve 99.999 percent availability. This is a measure of the time that you are providing services (in this case, e-mail services) in comparison with the time you have stated you will provide e-mail services.

If you ask your users how many "nines" you should be providing, they are undoubtedly going to tell you that you should be operating at 99.999 percent availability. What does that mean? Let's assume that you are expected to provide e-mail services 365 days per year, 24 hours per day, 7 days per week. Here is a breakdown of several "nine" values and the actual amount of unplanned downtime you could actually have to achieve them:

99.999%	About 5.3 minutes
99.99%	About 53 minutes
99.9%	About 8.7 hours
99.7%	About 1 day
99%	About 3.7 days

Providing "five nines" is pretty hard to do; one server reboot during the business day and you have exceeded your maximum permissible downtime for the entire year. Even providing 99.99 percent availability is a hard target to meet, though not unrealistic if you have designed into your system redundancy, fault tolerance, and high-availability solutions.

If you were to plot on a graph the cost to implement a system on the Y-axis and the desired nines on the X-axis, you will find that the cost climbs considerably as you approach (or pass) 99.999 percent availability.

For organizations that are having availability problems, I typically recommend that you first target somewhere between 99.7 and 99.9 percent availability. With good procedures, scheduled maintenance windows, hardware, and properly configured software, you can easily meet this goal even without clustering.

The Process Is Just as Important as the Technology

Some of us are just techies at heart, but information technology is more than just providing technology to our user communities. We must take into consideration a lot of other factors besides the technology, including budget, customer service, availability, documentation, responsibility, and change control. The process of running and managing information technology is becoming just as important as the technology itself.

With respect to Exchange Server, I recommend that you document and indoctrinate a number of things into your organization. These include creating documentation, processes, and procedures for the following:

◆ Daily and weekly maintenance

◆ Keeping documentation up-to-date

◆ Security review and audit procedures

◆ Change management and configuration control procedures

◆ Service pack and update procedures

◆ Escalation procedures and who is responsible for making decisions

◆ Information technology acceptable use and ethics policies

Building a Reliable Platform

Recommending that you build a reliable platform for Exchange may seem a bit obvious. After all, everyone wants a reliable platform. My recommendations are meant to help you make sure that your hardware and software platform is as reliable and stable as possible.

Don't skimp.   First and foremost, when you are choosing server hardware, don't skimp when it comes to choosing the hardware you will use to support your organization's e-mail servers. You may not need the "BMW 525i" of servers, but at the very least you should be planning to buy a reliable "Honda Civic" type server. Maybe the analogy is not very good, but the point is that you need a server from a major vendor. The server hardware should have a warranty and hardware support options for replacing failed components.

Purchase components from the server vendor.   When you choose components for your server (such as additional RAM, disks, disk controllers, tape devices, and so on), you should purchase these components from your server vendor. This ensures that anything that you put inside that server's case is going to be supported by the vendor. This also helps to ensure that the hardware and software integrates.

Make sure components are compatible.   When choosing server hardware and components, make sure all components are on the Windows Server 2003 x64 or Windows Server 2008 x64 Hardware Compatibility List. This is especially true if you are planning to implement clustering, volume shadow copy backups, storage area networks, or iSCSI storage. You can view the catalog of Windows Server–tested products at www.windowsservercatalog.com.

Install the latest updates.   As you unbox your shiny new x64-capable server, remember that it has probably been sitting on a shelf in a warehouse for a few months or longer before it made it to your door. This means that it may well be a little out-of-date. The vendor's setup CDs are going to be out-of-date and the Windows Server 2003 R2 CD-ROM is going to have out-of-date device drivers. There are a few things I recommend you do:

◆ Download the latest server setup CD from your hardware vendor. Use this CD to install Windows onto the server.

◆ Download any firmware and FlashBIOS updates that are relevant to the server's motherboard, backplane, network adapters, disk controllers, and so on.

◆ Confirm that you have the latest device drivers for additional hardware on your system. This includes network adapters, disk controllers, tape devices, host bus adapters, and so on.

◆ When formatting hard disks, use a 64KB allocation unit size.

◆ Confirm that you have the correct versions of any third-party software that you will be using, such as antivirus software, backup software, and storage area network (SAN) or storage management software.

◆ Apply all service packs and critical updates that are available before putting the server into production.

Set up your hardware with care. When setting up your hardware, following these procedures will minimize downtime:

◆ If your server has dual-power supplies, connect each power supply to a different UPS.

◆ As you are building your server, make sure that you have all the components you need and that they are ready to be put into production. When you bring a server online for users, you want to know for sure that you don't need to come back in a few weeks and install additional software or hardware.

◆ Label everything that you might need to quickly identify in the features, including things like the server name (both the front of and back of the rack), network cables, and even device IDs for disk drives.

Fault Tolerance vs. High Availability

You have probably heard as many explanations of what fault tolerance and high availability mean as I have. Over the years, these two terms have been squashed together so many times that even knowledgeable people use them interchangeably. However, there is a distinct difference between fault tolerance and high availability.

FAULT TOLERANCE

Fault-tolerance features or components enable a system to offer error-free, nonstop availability in the event of a failure. Examples include mirrored disks or striping with parity volumes as well as uninterruptible power supplies (UPSs) and redundant power supplies. If a component that has fault tolerance fails, the system continues to operate without any sort of interruption in service.

The bottom line is that implementing fault tolerance for individual components such as disks, power supplies, and UPS systems is reasonably cost effective. However, implementing full-fledged fault-tolerance solutions for an entire complex application such as Exchange is very costly.

Clustering is not a fault tolerance solution; clustering does not prevent an outage due to a fault from occurring. Clustering helps to ensure that you recover service more quickly.

HIGH AVAILABILITY

High-availability solutions are things that you do in order to provide better availability for a specific service. Implementing fault tolerance is one of these things. However, although high-availability solutions promise "better" availability through the use of technologies such as clustering and replication, they do not offer uninterrupted service or complete tolerance from faults.

Complexity vs. Supportability

Do not install anything that you are not prepared to support yourself or for which you don't have someone on standby on the other end of a telephone ready to support you. I frequently see companies that have put into production high-availability solutions, failover solutions, backup software, or procedures that are beyond their ability to support. A good example of this is a company whose vendor convinced it to install a SAN-based replication solution and a customized failover script. However, no one within the customer's organization had any experience with the SAN or the replication software or even knowledge of how the failover script worked.

No high-availability solution comes without ongoing costs. This cost may be in the form of training, additional personnel, consultant fees, or ongoing maintenance.

I don't want to discourage you from seeking solutions that will meet your needs, but approach these solutions with realistic expectations of what they will require to support. Keep these tips in mind:

- Practice simplicity in any system you build or design. Even when the system is complex, keep the components and procedures as simple as possible.

- For any solution that you implement, ask yourself how difficult it would be to explain it for someone else to manage.

- Document everything!

Outlook Local Cached Mode and Perceived Downtime

If a server crashes in the woods, but no one is around to hear it, was there truly downtime? Downtime and outages are a matter of perception. If no one was affected, then no one will be calling the help desk to complain. For Outlook 2003 and 2007 users, Microsoft has included a feature that allows Outlook to keep a complete copy of the mailbox cached on the local hard disk.

By default, Outlook 2003 and 2007 enable cached Exchange mode (see Figure 17.1), but in some older Outlook profiles this feature may have been turned off.

This setting won't help you with server reliability, but it can help with the user perception of those annoying little outages such as network problems or server reboots.

An Exchange server administrator can set a parameter on a user's mailbox that requires the use of cached mode. This is done using the `Set-CASMailbox` cmdlet. For example, if you want to require that Outlook 2003 or Outlook 2007 must be in cached Exchange mode for a certain user's mailbox, you would use this command:

```
Set-CASMailbox "Henrik.Walther" -MAPIBlockOutlookNonCachedMode $True
```

Building Redundancy

Redundant computing and networking systems can be an easy, though not always inexpensive, route to Exchange server reliability and availability. Automatic failover from a nonfunctional to a functional component is best. Even if you have to bring your system down for a short time to replace a component, you'll be a hero to your users if you can do it with minimal or no data loss.

In addition to eliminating or sharply reducing downtime, redundant systems can help you avoid the pain of standard or disaster-based Exchange server recovery.

FIGURE 17.1
Ensuring that cached Exchange mode is enabled

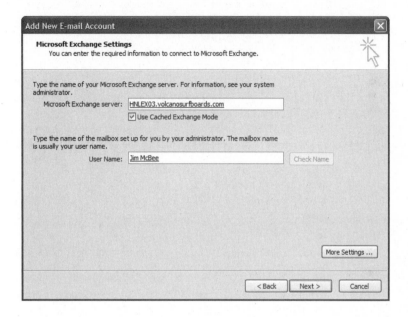

System redundancy is a complex matter. It's mostly about hardware, though a good deal of software, especially operating system software, can be involved. This section deals with two areas that are essential to redundant systems: server redundancy and network redundancy.

Server Redundancy

The following sections discuss two basic kinds of server redundancy:

◆ Intraserver redundancy

◆ Interserver redundancy

Intraserver redundancy is all about how redundant components are installed in a single server. *Interserver redundancy* involves multiple servers that, in some form or other, mirror each other. The goal with either kind of redundancy is for good components or servers to replace bad ones as quickly as possible. Automatic replacement is highly desirable.

INTRASERVER REDUNDANCY

When you think redundancy in a server, you think about storage, power, cooling, network adapters, and CPUs. Redundant disk storage and power components are the most readily available in today's servers. Tape storage has lagged behind disk storage in the area of redundancy, but it is available. Redundant cooling fans have been around for some time. Historically, Intel has not offered good support for redundant CPUs. However, the company now provides hardware for this purpose, and that hardware is finding its way into production servers.

Let's look at each aspect of server redundancy in more detail.

Redundant Storage

Redundant disk storage relies on a collection of disks to which data is written in such a way that all data continues to be available even if one of the disk drives fails. The popular acronym for this sort of setup is RAID, which stands for Redundant Array of Independent Disks.

There are several levels of RAID, one of which is not redundant. These are certainly not the only ones you will find in storage technologies. Many vendors create proprietary implementations in order to get better performance or redundancy. Here's a quick look at a few of the more common levels of RAID:

RAID 0   Raid 0 is also called *striping*. When data must be written to a RAID 0 disk array, the data is split into parts and each part of the data is written (striped) to a different drive in the array. RAID 0 is not redundant, but it provides the highest performance because each byte of data is written in parallel fashion, not sequentially, and there is no delay while parity data is calculated.

RAID 0 requires a minimum of two disk drives of approximately equal size.

I don't recommend implementing RAID 0 by itself in production because it provides no fault tolerance. RAID 0 is included here because RAID 0 strategies are used in another RAID design that I discuss later.

RAID 1   In RAID 1, all data on a drive is mirrored to a second drive. This provides the highest reliability. Write performance is fairly slow because data must be written to two drives. Read performance can be enhanced if both drives are used when data is accessed. RAID 1 is implemented using a pair of disks. Mirroring requires considerably more disk storage than RAID 5.

RAID 0 + 1   As with RAID 0, data is striped across each drive in the array. However, the array is mirrored to one or more parallel arrays. This provides the highest reliability and performance and has even higher disk storage requirements than RAID 1.

RAID 5   Data to be written to disk is broken up into multiple blocks. Part of the data is striped to each drive in the array. However, writes include parity information that allows any data to be recovered from the remaining drives if a drive fails. RAID 5 is reliable, though performance is slower. With RAID 5, you must have at least three disks, and you lose the equivalent of one disk in total GB of storage. You can recover from losing one disk in a RAID 5 array. For example, a RAID 5 array of three 36GB drives gives you 72GB, not 108GB of storage. This is more efficient than RAID 1 or 0 + 1, which both require a disk for each drive mirrored, but write performance is about one-third of RAID 0 + 1 and read performance is about one-half of RAID 0 + 1.

So, which RAID level is right for you? RAID 0 + 1 is nice, but I reserve it for organizations with really demanding performance requirements such as servers with high I/O per second requirements and who don't mind buying double the amount of disk space they require. You compromise some with RAID 5, but it's the best price-performance-reliability option.

It should be clear how RAID works from a general redundancy/reliability perspective. Now you're probably wondering how it works to assure high availability. The answer is pretty simple. With a properly set up RAID 1, 0 + 1, or 5 system, you simply replace a failed drive and the system automatically rebuilds itself. It's best practice to make sure you have spare drives that can be used to immediately replace a failed drive. If you are running RAID 5 you can recover from the loss of one disk, but if you lose a second disk before replacing that disk, you will lose the data. If the system is properly configured, you can actually replace the drive while your server keeps running and supporting users. If your RAID system is really highly neat, you set up hot spares that are automatically used should a disk drive fail. A lot of this depends on the vendor of the RAID controller and whether or not the controller allows automatic rebuilds and hot spares.

If RAID sounds like a good idea but you're worrying about costs, consider this: For most mainstream server vendors, adding a RAID controller option and a few hundred gigabytes of usable storage will increase the cost of the server by only a few thousand dollars. Figure out what a few hours (or days) of downtime and possibly a few days of lost e-mail data would cost and I think you'll conclude that the peace of mind that comes with redundant server hardware is worth the extra cost.

HARDWARE-BASED RAID HAS THE BEST PERFORMANCE

For the best performance, be sure to use a RAID solution that is implemented in hardware on a RAID adapter. Limited software-based RAID is available in Windows Server 2003, but you're not going to be happy with the speed of such an implementation.

RAID solutions don't necessarily have to be implemented inside a server. There is one very viable, if expensive, RAID solution that connects to your server or servers via a very high-throughput link. The technology is called a *storage area network* (SAN). SAN devices connect to servers using fiber-optic cable, or Ethernet in the case of iSCSI. You can connect multiple servers to a SAN. Each server is connected to the SAN through one or more very high-speed switches. This provides excellent throughput between the SAN and each server. Backups also benefit from the SAN's high levels of performance. Tape units are available that connect directly to SAN fiber switches.

SANs include fairly complex storage and management software. Support is not a trivial matter, though support requirements are reduced somewhat because data can be consolidated onto one device. Minimal SAN implementations are measured in terabytes (TB) of storage. Five TB is not unusual for such an implementation. At this writing, because of their costs and complexity, SANs are being promoted by vendors for really high-end storage capacity and performance requirements. Microsoft takes the same position regarding running Exchange on SANs.

Generally, if you're going to implement a SAN solution, you'll do it in a clustered server environment. For more on server clustering, see the section "Interserver Redundancy" later in this chapter.

LESS EXPENSIVE ALTERNATIVES TO SAN

If SANs are too rich for your blood, take comfort; there are alternatives. You can buy lower-throughput, lower-capacity, external RAID, or iSCSI storage systems that attach to your server or servers using sufficiently high-speed links to support an Exchange environment. Vendors such as Network Appliance (www.netapp.com), LeftHand Networks (www.lefthandnetworks.com), Compaq (www.hp.com), and Dell (www.dell.com) offer this hardware.

If you've been tempted by network attached storage (NAS) solutions, forget it. Exchange databases must reside on a disk that is directly attached to the server. Through their switches, SANs are attached to the servers they support. NAS devices are not. It is no different than if you tried to configure a mailbox or public folder database on a disk residing on another server on your network. It doesn't work.

However, if you are looking at iSCSI solutions, those are now supported.

Tape backup devices are available based on Redundant Array of Independent Tapes (RAIT) technology. Like RAID disk units, RAIT tape backup systems either mirror tapes one to one or stripe data across multiple tapes. As with disks, multitape striping can improve backup and restore performance as well as provide protection against the loss of a tape. Obviously, RAIT technology includes multiple tape drives. It is almost always implemented with tape library hardware so that tapes can be changed automatically, based on the requirements of backup software.

Redundant Power Supplies

Redundant power supplies are fairly standard in higher-end servers. Dell, IBM, and HP server-class hardware all include an additional power supply for a small incremental cost. Each power supply has its own power cord and runs all of the time. In fact, both power supplies provide power to the server at all times. Because either power supply is high enough in wattage to support the entire computer, if one power supply fails, the other is fully capable of running the computer. As with storage, system monitoring software lets you know when a power supply component has failed.

Many higher-end servers offer more than two redundant power supplies. These are designed for higher levels of system availability. They add relatively little to the cost of a server and are worth it.

Ideally, each power supply should be plugged into a different circuit. That way, the other circuit or circuits will still be there if the breaker trips on one circuit. I urge organizations that have high-availability requirements like hospitals to go a step further and ensure that one of the power supplies is plugged into an emergency circuit that is backed up by the organization's diesel-powered standby electricity-generating system. And, of course, each circuit should be plugged into an uninterruptible power supply (UPS).

Large-scale data centers will often implement two backup generators, two completely separate power grids, and two different sets of UPSs. Each server has a power supply connected to one grid and the other power supply is connected to the other.

Compaq, now a part of Hewlett Packard, offers another form of power redundancy, redundant voltage regulator modules (VRMs). In some environments, it's fine to have multiple power supplies, but if the power to your server isn't properly regulated because the computer's VRM has totally or partially failed, you'd be better off if the power had just failed.

Redundant Cooling

Modern CPUs, RAM, and power supplies produce a lot of heat. Internal cooling fans are supposed to pull this heat out of a computer's innards and into the surrounding atmosphere. If a fan fails, components can heat to a point where they stop working or permanently fail. Redundant cooling fans help prevent this nightmare scenario. In most systems, there is an extra fan that is always running. Monitoring software lets you know when a fan fails. The system is set up so that the remaining fans can support the server until you are able to replace the failed fan.

One-for-one redundant fans are becoming more and more available. With these, each fan in a system is shadowed by an always-running matching fan. When a fan fails, monitoring software lets you know so you can replace it.

Redundant CPUs

As I mentioned earlier, redundancy has not been a strong point of Intel CPUs. Mainframe and specialty mini-computer manufacturers have offered such redundancy for years. Pushed by customers and large companies such as Microsoft, Intel now has a standard for implementation of redundant CPUs.

Each CPU lives on its own plug-in board. Each CPU has its own mirror CPU. Mirroring happens at extremely high speed. When one CPU board detects problems in the other CPU, it shuts down the CPU and takes over the task of running the server. Intel claims that these transitions are transparent to users.

System monitoring software lets you know that a CPU has been shut down. You can use management software to assess the downed CPU to see if the crash was soft (CPU is still okay and can be brought back online) or hard (time to replace the CPU board). If the board needs replacing, you can do it while the computer is running. This is another victory for hot-swappable components and high system reliability and availability.

Intel is marketing this technology for extremely high-reliability devices such as telecommunications networking. However, I expect that it will quickly find its way into most higher-end corporate server systems.

ABOUT ECC AND REGISTERED MEMORY

Although they don't fall into the category of redundancy because they don't use backup hardware, error-correcting code (ECC) memory and registered memory deserve brief mention here. ECC memory includes parity information that allows it to correct a single bit error in 8 bits of memory. It can also detect, but not correct, an error in 2 bits per byte. Higher-end servers use special algorithms to correct full 8-bit errors. Registered memory includes registers where data is held for one clock cycle before being moved onto the motherboard. This very brief delay allows for more reliable high-speed data access.

Uninterruptible Power Supplies

In most installations around in the world, the uninterruptible power supply (UPS) is a standard part of the installation. In its simplest form, the UPS is an enclosure with batteries and some power outlets connected to the batteries. During normal operations, the UPS will keep the batteries fully charged and allow the server to pull its power from the commercial power source. In the event of a power failure or a brownout, the batteries kick in and keep supplying power to the server.

I see a few things that people do wrong constantly. One of the biggest mistakes people make is that they do not plan for sufficient capacity. Consequently, the UPS is overloaded and cannot provide power to everything connected to it. Here are a few tips:

◆ Always buy more UPS capacity than you think you are going to need.

◆ Plan for at least 15 minutes of battery capacity at maximum load.

◆ Don't forget other things that may end up plugged into the UPS, such as monitors, external tape devices, and external storage systems.

◆ Make sure that network infrastructure hardware is protected by a UPS; this includes routers, switches, and SAN and NAS equipment.

◆ UPS batteries need to be replaced. Replace batteries based on the manufacturer's schedule.

◆ Power calculators can assist in determining the amount of Amps required.

INTERSERVER REDUNDANCY

Interserver redundancy is all about synchronizing a set of servers so that server failures result in little or no downtime. A number of third-party solutions are available that provide some synchronizing services, but Microsoft's Windows clustering does the most sophisticated and comprehensive job of cross-server synchronization. I'm going to focus on this product. I'll also spend a bit of time on redundant SMTP hosts using a simple DNS trick.

Mailbox Server Redundancy

To provide higher availability for mailbox access, you should consider implementing Exchange server clustering. The Enterprise and Datacenter editions of Windows Server 2003 include clustering capabilities. Interserver redundancy clustering is supported by the Microsoft Cluster Service (MSCS). MSCS supports clusters using up to eight servers or nodes. The clustered servers present themselves to clients as a single server. A server in a cluster uses ultra-high-speed internode connections and very fast, hardware-based algorithms to determine if a fellow server has failed. If a server fails, another server in the cluster can take over for it with minimal interruption in user access. It takes between two and five minutes for a high-capacity Exchange server cluster with a heavy load (around 5,000 users) to recover from a failure. With resilient e-mail clients such as Outlook 2003 or Outlook 2007, client-server reconnections are transparent to users.

I take a closer look at clustering Exchange servers later in this chapter in the "Introduction to Clustering" section.

Redundant Inbound Mail Routing

Larger organizations will want to provide some redundancy for their inbound mail from the Internet. Redundant inbound messaging starts with at least two SMTP servers. Figure 17.2 shows two Exchange 2007 Edge Transport servers in the organization's perimeter (DMZ) network. This could just as easily be any type of SMTP mail system located in the perimeter network. If Edge Transport servers are not used, then these servers could be on the internal network and they could be Exchange 2007 Hub Transport servers.

FIGURE 17.2
Redundant inbound mail routing

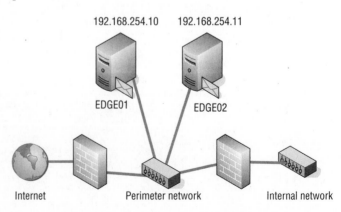

Server EDGE01 has an IP address of 192.168.254.10 and server EDGE02 has an IP address of 192.168.254.11. I will pretend that these are the public IP addresses. The most common way to provide redundancy for inbound mail is to use DNS and Mail Exchanger (MX) records. Here is a sample of the MX records that would provide inbound mail routing for a domain called somorita.com:

```
somorita.com      IN    MX    10    edge01.somorita.com

somorita.com      IN    MX    10    edge02.somorita.com

edge01            IN    A           192.168.254.10

edge02            IN    A           192.168.254.11
```

That number 10 in the MX record is called a priority value. Most mail servers will automatically load-balance between these two servers when they send mail. I could change one of the MX record's priorities to something higher and mail would always be routed to the lower-priority MX record. It doesn't matter what you set the higher value to as long as it is higher. You can have as many MX records for an Internet domain as you want. Just be sure each points to a different server.

Another method of providing higher redundancy and high availability for inbound SMTP servers is to use some type of load balancing. I talk more about that later in this chapter in the "Network Load Balancing" section.

Neither Network Load Balancing nor multiple MX records provides complete fault tolerance for inbound mail routing. They provide better availability, but if an Edge Transport server fails while a message is being delivered to your organization, the message transfer will fail. However, the sending server will reestablish a connection and automatically use the other Edge Transport server either because of the additional MX records or because network load balancing directs the SMTP client to the other server.

Redundant Internal Mail Routing

Internal mail routing is handled by the Exchange 2007 Hub Transport server role. If the Hub Transport role is on a separate physical server from the Mailbox server role, then all mail delivery — whether on the local Mailbox server, another Mailbox server in the same Active Directory site, or a Mailbox server in a remote Active Directory site — must be routed through the Hub Transport server role. If the Mailbox server role and the Hub Transport server role are on the same physical machine, the local Hub Transport server role takes care of messaging routing.

In a larger environment where server roles are all split, the best way to achieve redundancy in message routing is to install at least two servers that host the Hub Transport server role in each Active Directory site. Figure 17.3 shows a sample network with two Active Directory sites. Each Active Directory site has two servers with the Hub Transport role installed.

Exchange 2007 will automatically load-balance among the Hub Transport servers that it's using within your organization. If a server fails and an alternate Hub Transport server is available within the Active Directory site, Exchange will start using the other Hub Transport server.

Redundant Outbound Mail

Within your Exchange organization, all mail delivery is handled by the Hub Transport server role. This is also true for e-mail that is destined for outside sources, such as Internet domains. Outbound mail is delivered using Send connectors and/or using Edge Subscriptions to Edge Transport servers located in your perimeter network. Figure 17.3 includes two Edge Transport servers located in the perimeter network. To achieve redundancy in outbound mail routing, you would need to create Edge Subscriptions for the Edge Transport servers and define a Send connector that will deliver mail to the Edge Transport servers.

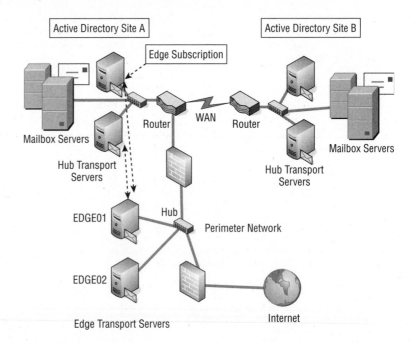

FIGURE 17.3
Improving redundancy with multiple Hub Transport servers

Again, this solution is not a completely fault-tolerant solution but rather a high-availability solution. If an Edge Transport or Hub Transport server fails during message routing or transmission, Exchange will attempt to deliver messages through an alternate path.

Client Access and Unified Messaging Redundancy

The Client Access server role and the Unified Messaging server role can both be made more available by implementing multiple servers supporting these roles in the same Active Directory site and then implementing some type of load-balancing solution.

Figure 17.4 shows an example of how you could provide higher availability for Client Access and Unified Messaging server roles. In this figure, the physical servers host both roles. Load balancing between the two physical servers will provide users with connectivity to the least busy server at the time that they need to connect. Load balancing will also direct users to the remaining server if the first server fails.

Notice in Figure 17.4 that load-balanced ISA servers are included in the perimeter network. This allows you to securely publish Exchange 2007 web services such as Outlook Web Access, Outlook Anywhere, ActiveSync, and the Availability service. The ISA servers act as reverse proxy servers and handle the initial inbound HTTP/HTTPS connection from Internet clients.

Load-balancing a Client Access or Unified Messaging server provides higher availability, but it does not provide complete fault tolerance. If the Exchange server fails, any active connections on that server will be terminated and the user (or VOIP call) will be terminated and the connection will have to be reestablished.

FIGURE 17.4
Implementing load balancing for Client Access and Unified Messaging servers

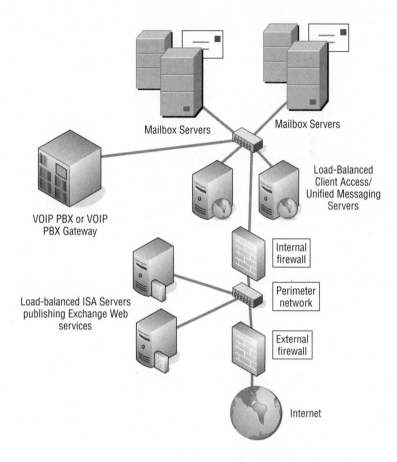

Network Load Balancing

I have mentioned load balancing a few times in this chapter as a mechanism for improving availability for certain types of server roles or functions. Load balancing works well in situations where you have multiple servers (two or more) that can handle the same type of request. This includes web servers and SMTP mail servers. In the case of something like a web server, the assumption is that a copy of the website is located on all of the servers that are being load-balanced.

BENEFITS OF USING LOAD BALANCING WITH EXCHANGE

In the case of Exchange, you can use load balancing to help provide better availability to the following server roles:

- Client Access servers

- Hub Transport servers (for inbound e-mail from the Internet or POP3/IMAP4 clients)

- Edge Transport servers

- Unified Messaging servers

SMTP servers that provide inbound STMP connectivity from outside of your organization — such as the Edge Transport or Hub Transport servers — are best served by providing load balancing via multiple DNS Mail Exchanger (MX) records.

Load balancing does not work for mailbox servers because the mailbox is only accessible from one server at a time, even when the servers are clustered. If you set up load balancing for Hub Transport, Unified Messaging, or Client Access servers, this only provides higher availability for the client access point; the actual mailbox data must still have a high availability solution such as clustering.

A number of solutions are on the market for load balancing, including Cisco's Local Director appliance (www.cisco.com) and F5's BIG-IP (www.f5.com) appliance. Microsoft includes a built-in load-balancing tool with Windows Server 2003 called Network Load Balancing (NLB). You will often hear NLB people refer to NLB as a clustering technology; indeed, even the Microsoft Windows Server 2003 documentation refers to the feature as NLB clustering.

VERIFY BEFORE ADDING TO CLUSTER

Prior to actually setting up load balancing for the first time, you always want to ensure that each node or host works independently before you put it into a load-balanced cluster. This will save you a lot of troubleshooting time.

SETTING UP A LOAD BALANCING SOLUTION

Let's take a quick look at load balancing from a conceptual point of view and apply those concepts to an Exchange example. Figure 17.5 shows an example of load balancing where I want to provide higher availability for my Client Access servers. In this example, there are two Windows Server 2003 servers that are hosting the Exchange 2007 Client Access role and they are load-balanced using the Windows Network Load Balancing tool.

FIGURE 17.5
Implementing Network
Load Balancing

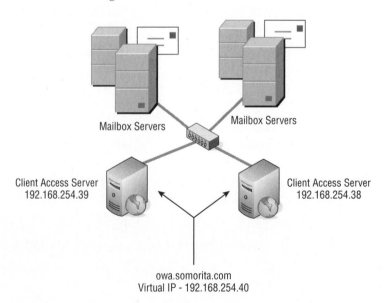

Mailbox Servers

Mailbox Servers

Client Access Server
192.168.254.39

Client Access Server
192.168.254.38

owa.somorita.com
Virtual IP - 192.168.254.40

Each Windows server is assigned its own unique IP address, but all servers must be on the same IP subnet. These IP addresses are 192.168.254.38 and 192.168.254.39. The "cluster" IP address will be 192.168.254.40. I will create a DNS record called `owa.somorita.com` that will be mapped to 192.168.254.40. I will ask my Outlook Web Access, Outlook Anywhere, and ActiveSync clients to use this FQDN. The load-balanced IP address must be on the same IP subnet as the hosts.

As connections attempts are made to the IP address 192.168.254.40, the two hosts communicate with each other and decide which host should accept the connection. The connection will be accepted by one of the two hosts and that connection is maintained until the client disconnects or the host is shut down. The entire process is transparent to the end user.

DNS ROUND ROBIN FOR LOAD BALANCING

One option you will frequently hear people talk about when running more than one web server is to use DNS round robin. With DNS round robin, you configure a single hostname with multiple IP addresses. The DNS server rotates IP addresses it gives out. Though this works reasonably well, the client may change IP addresses after the DNS cache lifetime expires and that will break an SSL session.

Setting up an NLB cluster using the Windows Server 2003 Network Load Balancing Manager is pretty straightforward. In my example, I am setting up two servers into an NLB cluster. In this case it is best to run the NLB Manager from the console of one of the two servers. Follow these steps:

1. Log on to the console of one of the servers as a member of the local Administrators group and then launch the Network Load Balancing Manager program from the Administrative Tools folder.

   The console should show no NLB clusters.

2. From the Cluster menu, choose New to get to the Cluster Parameters screen (shown in Figure 17.6).

FIGURE 17.6
Creating a new NLB cluster

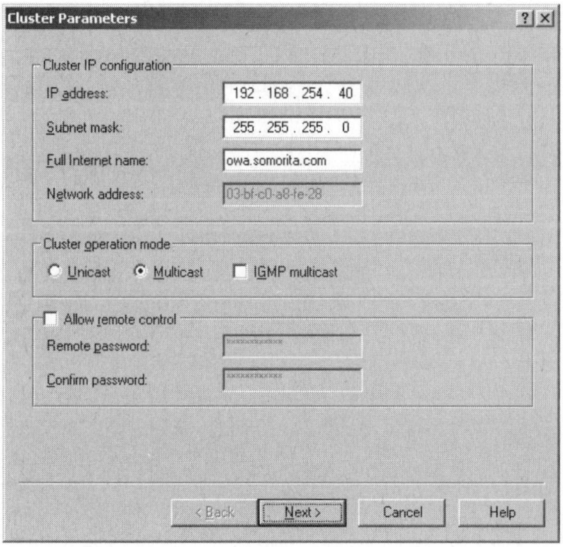

3. In the IP address and subnet mask fields, enter the "cluster" IP address and subnet mask, not the IP address and subnet mask of the individual node. In this example, I am using 192.168.254.40.

4. The Full Internet Name box is usually optional, but it is a good idea to enter here the name that the clients will be using when they connect to this NLB cluster.

5. Finally, in the Cluster Operation Mode section, depending on your network, either Unicast or Multicast should work, but I recommend using multicast mode. When you have finished with this screen, click the Next button.

6. The following screen is the Cluster IP Addresses screen, which allows you to add additional cluster IP addresses. In most cases, this is not necessary, so you can click Next again.

7. The next screen is the Port Rules dialog box. Because you are not going to change anything on this screen, you can click Next.

   Port rules allow you to configure the actual TCP or UDP ports to which the NLB cluster will respond. For example, you might configure a rule that says the cluster only services TCP port 80 or 443 if you wanted to provide Network Load Balancing clustering for just web applications. The default screen is shown in Figure 17.7.

FIGURE 17.7
Defining port rules for a Network Load Balancing cluster

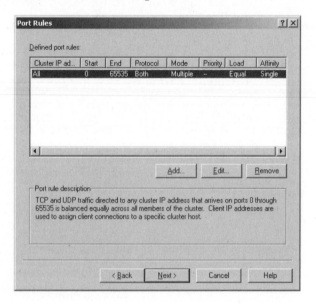

In the default configuration, all ports are used with the cluster, and for simplicity's sake you should leave it this way. Notice in Figure 17.7 that the protocol column is set to Both (meaning TCP and UDP) and the port range is 0 to 65535. You might want to lock down the port range to only the ports you need, such as TCP port 443.

8. In the Connect dialog box, when creating a new NLB cluster, there should be no interfaces or host information listed by default. In the Host box, type the IP address of the first host that will be joining the cluster and click Connect.

   This will initiate a connection to the host you specify and list the network adapters that can be configured to join the cluster; this is shown in Figure 17.8.

FIGURE 17.8

Adding a host to the Network Load Balancing cluster

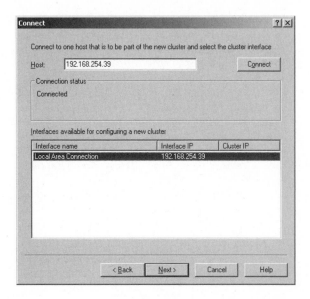

9. Select the network adapter to which you want to bind NLB and click Next.

10. The following screen is the Host Parameters dialog box (shown in Figure 17.9). Here you have three tasks: Specify a priority for the adapter (each host needs a unique priority), confirm the IP address and subnet mask of the host you are adding to the NLB cluster, and select the initial state of the host. I recommend that you always select Started as the default state so that you don't have to remember to start each node of the cluster manually after a reboot.

11. When you have finished configuring the host parameters, you can click the Finish button.

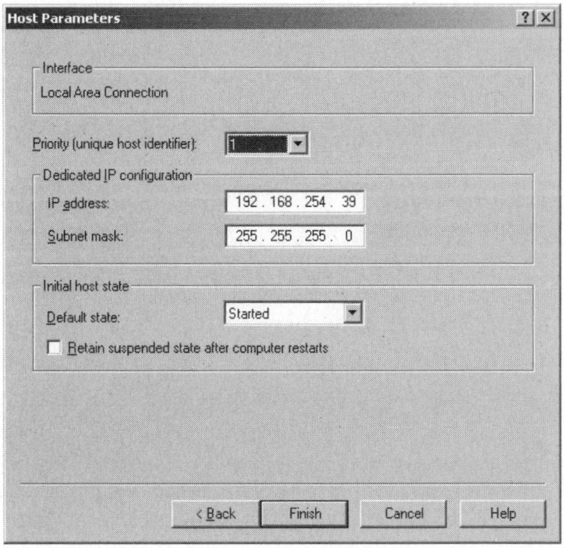

FIGURE 17.9

Confirming host parameters for a member of a Network Load Balancing cluster

Host Parameters	? X

Interface
Local Area Connection

Priority (unique host identifier): 1

Dedicated IP configuration

IP address: 192 . 168 . 254 . 39

Subnet mask: 255 . 255 . 255 . 0

Initial host state

Default state: Started

☐ Retain suspended state after computer restarts

< Back | Finish | Cancel | Help

The configuration change for this particular node of the NLB cluster will begin. If you are connected to the server via the Remote Desktop Connection client, you may be disconnected because the network will be stopped and restarted.

In some instances, I have seen a situation in which configuring NLB leaves a node in an inconsistent state that must be manually reconfigured from the console. Though this is rare, if the server is remote, it is always a good idea to have someone available onsite who can log on to the server console and fix the problem. Or you could have some type of out-of-band server management tool available.

When you have configured the first node into the NLB cluster, you can add additional nodes. In the NLB Manager, connect to the existing cluster (if you are not already connected) and right-click the cluster name. From the pop-up menu, select Add Host to Cluster. This takes you through another wizard that allows you to add a new node to the NLB cluster. When you have finally added all of the nodes, the NLB Manager (shown in Figure 17.10) will show you the status of the cluster and all of the nodes.

FIGURE 17.10
Examining the status of the Network Load Balancing cluster

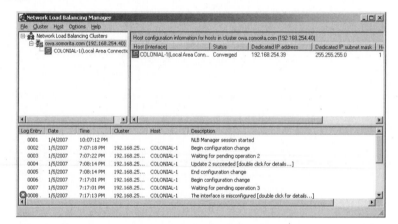

Network Redundancy

The concepts that apply to server redundancy also apply to network redundancy. There are network adapters, switches, bridges, and routers that support intra-device redundancy. Of course, as you learned with Exchange connectors, redundancy doesn't mean much if redundant devices are connected to the same physical network.

You can achieve network interface card (NIC) redundancy by using what is called *NIC teaming*. With teaming, two or more NICs are treated by your server and the outside world as a single adapter with a single IP address. For fault tolerance, you connect each NIC to a separate layer 2 MAC address-based switch. All switches must be able to physically communicate with each other; that is, they must be in the same layer 2 domain and they must support NIC teaming. All the network cards work together to send and receive data. If one NIC fails, the others keep on chugging away doing their job and you are notified of the failure. You need Windows Server 2003 or Windows Server 2008–based software from your NIC vendor to pull this off. Dell, HP, IBM, and others offer this software and compatible NICs.

Beyond the switch, you can use routers with redundant components. Cisco Systems (www.cisco.com) makes a number of these. Cisco also offers some nice inter-device redundancy routing options. They can get expensive, so if you want redundant physical connections to the Internet or other remote corporate sites, you need to factor in their cost.

If you use an ISP, you should pick one with sophisticated networking capabilities. Maybe you can't afford multiple redundant links to the Internet, but your ISP should have them. Look for ISPs that use the kinds of routers discussed in the previous paragraph.

Supporting Infrastructure Redundancy

Exchange servers depend heavily on the ability to access domain controllers and global catalog servers. Exchange must locate these resources on the network using DNS. For this reason, it is imperative that any organization with more than one domain controller make sure that more than one domain controller is configured as a global catalog server.

Microsoft's "formula" for determining how many domain controllers/global catalog (DC/GC) servers are required to support Exchange is one x86-based DC/GC CPU core for each four Exchange CPU cores or one x64-based DC/GC CPU core for each eight Exchange CPU cores. So an organization supporting 750 users on a single-dual processor Exchange server would require only a single DC/GC. This obviously would provide no redundancy. Plus, this formula is assuming dedicated DC/GCs for Exchange.

I recommend an alternate formula that is a little more complex, but more effective:

◆ Start with the minimum number of DC/GCs you require for basic directory services and authentication functions within your network. For an organization with 750 users, I would recommend two DC/GCs.

◆ Add additional DC/GCs based on Microsoft's formula for calculating the additional DC/GCs required to support Exchange.

Using this formula, a 750-user, single Exchange server network would have a minimum of three DC/GCs. You should follow this formula for any physical location that has an Exchange server. Any physical location that has an Exchange server should also have a minimum of two DC/GCs.

I also recommend using the Windows Server 2003 DNS server and ensuring that the Active Directory DNS zones are configured as Active Directory–integrated zones. All DC/GCs on the network should have the Windows Server 2003 DNS service installed. The DNS zone should be configured to replicate to all DNS servers in the entire forest (not just the domain).

All Exchange servers should be configured to use at least two DNS servers for name resolution. On networks with more than two DNS servers, you should configure a primary, secondary, and tertiary DNS server. You can do this on the Advanced TCP/IP Settings property page (see Figure 17.11).

In the example in Figure 17.11, the server has been configured with a primary and a secondary DNS server; these are the DNS servers in the local Active Directory site. The third DNS server is in a remote site. This would be queried only if the local DNS servers could not return a response to a query.

Introduction to Clustering

Conceptually, clustering is fairly simple to describe. A cluster is a collection of computers that work together to provide a single service. In some implementations of a cluster, multiple nodes all share the workload; the Windows Server 2003 Network Load Balancing feature is an example. In other implementations, one node provides the actual service (this is called the active node) and another node is waiting to take over that service if the first node fails (this is the passive node). An example of this is how Exchange 2007 mailbox servers are clustered.

FIGURE 17.11
Configuring more than
two DNS servers for a
Windows server

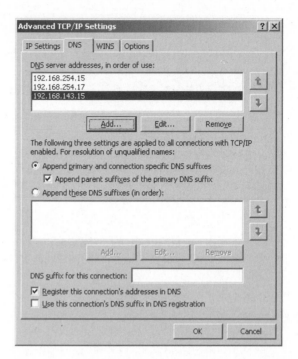

Clustering is certainly nothing new. Microsoft has supported Exchange clustering since the Exchange 5.5 days, but other vendors, such as Digital Equipment Corporation (now part of HP), Tandem (now part of HP), IBM, and others, have supported clustering technologies for the past 25 years.

The purpose of clustering varies somewhat, but almost always one of the primary intentions is to have a mechanism to provide a higher level of availability. Network Load Balancing not only provides higher availability for the services it offers, it can also allow you to scale further and support more clients.

REPLICATION TECHNOLOGIES

Exchange Server 2007 has available some new replication technologies, including local continuous replication (LCR) and standby continuous replication (SCR) features. I talk more about these in Chapter 18, "Replication Technologies."

In the following sections, I want to introduce you to the clustering concepts supported by Exchange 2007 Mailbox server roles and familiarize you with some of the advantages and disadvantages of these types of clustering. If these technologies sound like "the next step" for your organization, then I encourage you to read further though the Microsoft website and white papers for implementation details. Full implementation details of mailbox clustering are beyond the scope of this book.

Is Clustering the Next Step?

When organizations are considering implementing Exchange clusters, the reason is that they want to achieve higher availability for their e-mail services. The most important question that should be asked, though, is whether clustering is the next step toward higher availability.

Carefully look at all of the reasons that you have had unscheduled downtime over the past year or two. Determine the root cause for each of these downtime incidents. For each of these, ask yourself if redundant hardware or redundant copies of the database would have spared you that downtime. You may be surprised at what you find. Many organizations find that clustering would solve almost none of their unscheduled downtime problems.

Next, examine the additional costs involved in implementing clusters. These costs include hardware, software, storage, consulting, and training. You need to know whether these additional costs can be justified based on the amount of downtime that you have had versus the level of availability you require.

Clustering: The Good, the Bad, and the Ugly

I certainly don't want to discourage anyone from implementing Exchange clustering. If the technology is right for your organization and it will provide you with value, then certainly you should be seriously considering clustering your important Exchange 2007 mailbox servers. In the next sections, I give you my opinion of the good, bad, and ugly points of clustering.

THE GOOD

Many people who implement Exchange clustering become raving fans of the technology and would have the word *clustering* tattooed on their foreheads if their spouses or significant others would allow it. Let's look at a few of the high points and selling points for implementing a cluster:

◆ It increases availability by bringing failed mailbox servers back online sooner.

◆ It increases your ability to meet service level agreements.

◆ It reduces scheduled downtime windows for mailbox servers.

◆ Clustered continuous replication allows for replicated copies of mailbox data.

◆ It provides automatic failover of Exchange mailbox services.

◆ Failover times are usually under five minutes in duration.

◆ A failover can be invisible to desktop users of Outlook in cached Exchange mode.

THE BAD

Naturally, there are a few points that are going to count against clustering when you begin planning or implementing a clustered environment:

◆ Exchange 2007 only supports clustering the Mailbox server role, and no other roles can be installed on the server.

◆ There may be additional software costs (Windows and Exchange server licenses are required for the passive node; Enterprise Edition of Windows and Exchange are required).

◆ Single copy clusters require shared storage such as storage area networks (SANs) regardless of whether iSCSI- or Fibre Channel-attached shared storage is used. This can significantly increase costs.

◆ Some third-party software (backup, message hygiene, and so on) is not supported on clustered nodes.

◆ Additional expertise is required to manage clustering technologies and shared storage.

◆ Some typical management functions (such as stopping and starting a service) are different on clusters than they are on typical Windows servers.

The Ugly

Why the "ugly" category? Well, the "bad" category is all technology and cost. These are things that as information technology professionals, I can address through budgeting and training. However, "the ugly" rears its head at the management layer. Often clustering technologies are sold to senior management by salespeople. The technical implementation and requirements get a little fuzzy at this layer.

◆ When clustering is "sold" to management, expectations are often very high for what can be delivered. Management often views clustering as "magic" or the "answer to all our problems."

◆ Failover times are usually between two and five minutes, but sometimes longer. The perception is often that failover is always instantaneous.

◆ Exchange clustering does not protect an organization from power failures, network infrastructure failures, Active Directory problems, DNS problems, and so on.

◆ Additional expertise and training are required to support the additional complexity. Often this is in the form of consultants and classes. This is a factor that management often does not hear about.

Overcoming the Bad and the Ugly

Both the bad and ugly aspects of clustering can be overcome. The most important factor is to separate fact from fiction and hype in all of your management discussions, briefings, presentations, and documentation. Don't oversell the technology or feed the perception that Exchange clustering is actually "magic e-mail pixie dust." A lot of us get caught in the "gee it will be *so* great to have this new technology" frenzy that we are afraid to present all of the facts for fear we will lose our funding.

Balance and tone down the enthusiasm of salespeople, vendors, and senior management by presenting a realistic view of clustering features, functions, and benefits.

The Intimidation Factor

One interesting factor of implementing a cluster is the intimidation factor. Junior or inexperienced administrators often look at clustering technology as a black box. Though they may have been trained to manage Windows servers, they are not trained in clustering.

Interestingly enough, this can function as a factor for improving availability. Quite a bit of downtime that I have come in contact with has been the result of junior administrators taking action without enough knowledge and making a situation worse. Frequently, though, with clusters, the junior administrator will leave them alone and wait for someone with more clustering experience.

Single Copy Clusters

In Exchange 2000/2003, I just referred to mailbox clusters as an Exchange cluster. However, in Exchange 2007, there are two different approaches to implementing clustering. The first is a single copy cluster (SCC), which is identical to an Exchange 2000/2003 cluster. In this case, the "single copy" part of the name refers to the fact that there is only a single copy of each Exchange 2007 mailbox or public folder database. The database resides on some type of shared storage array.

With single copy clusters, there can be between two and eight nodes in the cluster. At any given time, at least one node is in the passive role and is ready to assume responsibility for a clustered mailbox server.

TERMINOLOGY UPDATE

If you used Exchange 2000/2003 in a clustered environment, then you are used to the term *Exchange virtual server* (EVS). This term has been replaced by *clustered mailbox server* (CMS).

Figure 17.12 shows a simple illustration of a two-node active-passive cluster. In this diagram, both the active node (NODE01) and the passive node (NODE02) are connected to the shared storage system. NODE01 owns the clustered mailbox server's name (EXCHANGE01), the clustered mailbox server's IP address (192.168.254.10), the shared disks (F:\ and G:\), and the other Exchange server resources such as the system attendant and the information store services.

FIGURE 17.12
Simple two-node clustered mailbox server

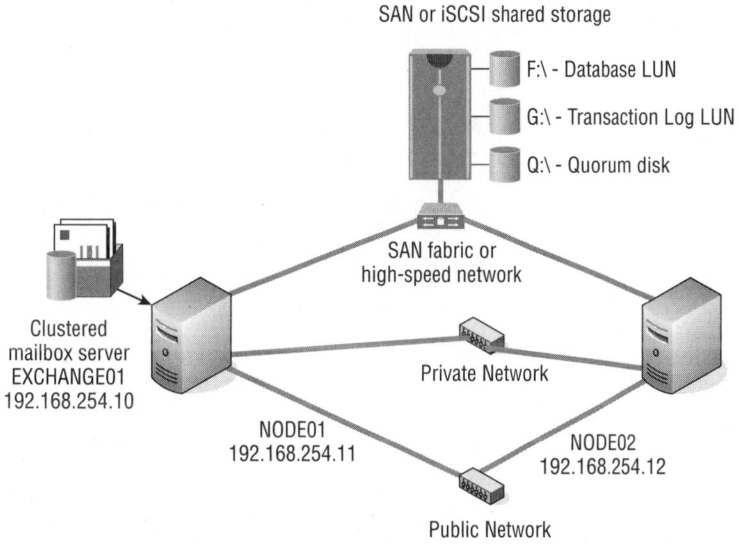

Take note of the clustered mailbox server's name, EXCHANGE01. This name is part of a clustered resource and is not permanently assigned to any physical node in the cluster. This name, EXCHANGE01, is the name that Outlook clients use when connecting to the Exchange server.

All of the nodes in a single copy cluster are connected to both a public network and a private network. The private network is used for the cluster heartbeat. The heartbeat is what the nodes in the cluster use to determine if the other nodes are still alive and healthy. One of the two nodes will also own the cluster name and cluster IP address, though these are not shown in Figure 17.12. The same node that owns the generic cluster resources also owns the Q:\ drive resource, or the quorum disk. The quorum disk holds the cluster database and information about which node in the cluster owns each clustered resource. This helps to keep a passive node from taking over a resource that is owned (and in use) by an active node of the cluster.

If anything about physical NODE01 or the services running on it fails, this will initiate what is known as a *failover*. A failover occurs when the passive node in the cluster determines that something is not working properly on the active node. The resources necessary to bring the clustered mailbox server online are taken over by the other node. So, in the example shown in Figure 17.12, NODE02 would assume control of the shared disks, the Exchange clustered mailbox server name, the clustered mailbox server IP address, and the Exchange services. The failover takes as long as necessary to mount the shared disks and then to start the Exchange services and mount the databases found on the shared disks. Depending on how busy the server was at failure, up to 20MB worth of outstanding transactions for each storage group may have to be committed to the database.

Clustered Continuous Replication Clusters

Clustered continuous replication (CCR) is a new technology to Exchange 2007. CCR clusters use many of the same principles as single copy clusters, but without the requirement of shared storage. Instead, as log files are filled up on the active node of the cluster, the passive node copies those log files over and commits them to a backup copy of the database that resides on the passive node. CCR clusters are always two-node clusters. One node is always the active node and one node is always the passive node.

Figure 17.13 shows a simple CCR configuration. In this diagram, both the active and passive nodes have local storage. This storage could conceivably be on a SAN or iSCSI storage system, but the storage would not be shared between the two nodes. The only thing that is actually shared is a shared folder on a third server. The file share on the third server contains information that is used in the event that the two nodes cannot communicate over the private network. This helps to ensure that a failover does not occur due to the loss of the private network. This cluster type is called a majority node set. In Figure 17.13, the witness file share is a file server, but it could just as easily be one of the Client Access or Hub Transport server roles.

As transaction logs are filled and committed to the disk on the active node, they are copied to the passive node. A service on the passive node then commits those transactions to the backup copy of the databases.

In the event of a failure of the active node, the passive node will mount the databases and roll forward any transaction logs that have not yet been committed. It will then assume the role of the production Exchange server (in this case EXCHANGE01).

Though I really like CCR clustering, there are a few positive and negative points you should be aware of when deciding to use this technology:

◆ The database on the passive node may not be completely synchronized with the active node. It might be a minute or two behind the active node (depending on activity levels and replication delays). The transport dumpster on the Hub Transport servers helps to minimize loss of mail items; however, it does not prevent loss of data such as calendar changes.

◆ The hardware on the active node and the passive node does not need to be identical, but it should be comparable with respect to CPU, memory, network, and disk capacity.

◆ Databases are replicated on a storage-group-by-storage-group basis and you can have only one database per storage group in a CCR environment.

◆ CCR clusters reduce the complexity of Exchange mailbox server clustering somewhat because they do not require shared storage.

◆ CCR clusters can increase administrative complexity if the passive node of the cluster becomes out of sync with the active node. This may happen if log files are not being copied to the passive node.

◆ CCR clusters do not scale as well as SCC clusters. For example, a four-node SCC cluster could support three active Exchange nodes. To support three active clustered mailbox servers using CCR, you would need six servers.

FIGURE 17.13
Simple clustered continuous replication configuration

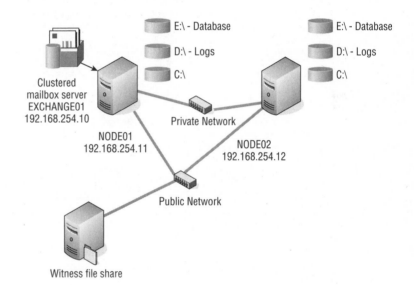

Summary

In this chapter, I talked about some of the most important things you do as an Exchange administrator — that is, doing everything you can to provide higher availability for your messaging services.

An important part of providing higher availability is to ensure that you have the ability to perform proper and required maintenance during a time window that does not count against your availability numbers. Scheduled maintenance is important for ensuring the reliability and security of your Exchange environment. Don't sacrifice reliability for availability.

When looking at ways to improve your availability, you should look at the causes of any unscheduled downtime. Study what you need to do to eliminate or prevent those from happening in the future. This may include providing additional fault-tolerance components in your Exchange environment, such as redundant disks, redundant power supplies, and uninterruptible power supplies.

You can improve availability of services such as Client Access, Unified Messaging, Hub Transport, and Edge Transport server roles by implementing Network Load Balancing to balance the load between multiple servers that host the same server role and direct clients to a working server in the event one of the servers fails.

Clustering technologies can help you work toward higher availability for your mailbox servers. Single copy clusters work in much the same way as previous versions of Exchange did when cluster technology was implemented. Clustered continuous replication clusters are a new breed of clustered mailbox servers that provide redundancy not only for the physical server, but also for the databases.

In the next chapter, I go into more detail on the local continuous replication (LCR) and standby continuous replication technologies (SCR) and in Chapter 19, I cover one of the other most important tasks that you perform as an Exchange administrator. This is a task that you must do daily: performing and verifying backups of your data and any other information necessary to recover a server in the event of a disaster.

Chapter 18

Implementing Replication Technologies

If I had to pick a single collection of features that are the most compelling in Exchange Server 2007, the feature set would be the continuous replication features. This new technology supports three flavors of replication from an "active" data source to a passive data source. Understanding how these types of replication work and how you can use them to your advantage will help you to determine which of them are right for you.

Continuous replication comes in three flavors. For stand-alone Mailbox servers, there is local continuous replication (LCR), which allows you to keep a replicated copy of one or more mailbox databases on the local server. LCR provides you with the capability to very quickly restore a database from backup in the event of database corruption.

If you want high-availability replication, there is cluster continuous replication (CCR), which keeps a replicated copy of the active databases on the passive node of the cluster. CCR combines the best of active/passive clustering with replication; the active node of the cluster has the "production" databases but the passive node has a replicated copy that is almost 100% in sync. In the event of a failure of the active node, the passive node will take over automatically.

Exchange 2007 Service Pack 1 introduced standby continuous replication (SCR), which allows you to keep copies of one or more databases from one or more mailbox servers. SCR allows you to replicate copies of one (or more) databases to a remote Exchange Server 2007 Mailbox server. In the event of a failure, the administrator can redirect users to the remote server and users can go back to work very quickly.

My primary goal in this chapter is to get you familiar with how the replication technologies work and how you can implement LCR and SCR.

In this chapter you learn to:

- ◆ Understand continuous replication

- ◆ Implement local continuous replication

- ◆ Implement standby continuous replication

Basics of Continuous Replication

Understanding the basics of how the replication technology will help you to plan the best way to use it in your environment.

REPLICATION, STORAGE GROUP, DATABASE, AND FOLDER NAMES

Since my NetWare 2.0 days, I have been a big fan of naming standards and I suggested some of these in Chapter 2, "Designing a New Exchange 2007 System." As the number of servers, mailboxes, and databases within some organizations have grown, I have also advocated a naming standard for mailbox database names. Storage area networks now make it easy for a server to own (intentionally or accidentally) disks (aka logical units, or LUNs) that might belong to another node. Thus naming databases and labeling disk volumes properly become more important. And with databases (and folders) being replicated to other servers in your organization, it is even more important to make sure that folders are named in a standard and consistent way.

Though this may not seem like a relevant topic for a high availability or replication chapter, as you learn more about shared SAN storage and SCR it will begin to make perfect sense.

STANDARDIZING STORAGE GROUP AND DATABASE NAMES

Storage groups and mailbox databases are sets of objects that should have standardized names. This helps not only the person who must administer the mailbox servers but also the recipient/mailbox administrators. A clearly defined naming standard can help when creating mailboxes or assigning mailboxes.

In my naming standard for the storage groups and the mailbox database, I include MBDB for mailbox database and SG for storage group. The name also includes the name of the server on which the database or storage group is found, and a unique number for that storage group or mailbox database. Here are some examples:

    SG-LAXMB01-01

    SG-NYCCM01-02

    MDB-LAXMB01-01

    MDB-LAXMB01-02

    MDB-LAXMB01-02

With just a glance, you can tell which Mailbox server the database belongs to. This will also help a lot when working with the Exchange Management Shell, because you won't have to type the entire "path" (*server name\storage group\database*) when referencing a mailbox database. This system helps to ensure that each database in your entire organization has a unique name rather than just something like Mailbox Database. If you have already deployed some mailbox databases or storage groups, not to worry; you can easily rename them.

In addition, I recommend that you name the database file the same as the logical database. For example, the database MBDB-HNLEX03-01 would have a database file named MBDB-HNLEX03-01.EDB.

STANDARDIZING DRIVE LETTER AND FOLDER NAMING

If you built a single copy cluster (SCC) in the past, you already know that all nodes of the cluster need to see the disks with the same drive letters. However, with the advent of SCR, you also need to have consistent drive letters and folder names.

SCR requires that the target drive letter and path for databases and transaction logs be the same as the source. So if your transaction logs are on D:\E2K7-Logs and your database is on E:\E2K7-Data, the SCR target server must have the same drive letters available *and* the folder names that are created automatically will be the same. If you have only a single database in your organization, this issue might not be a big deal, but I'm betting that you want a bit more flexibility. If you will have multiple source servers that use SCR to replicate to a single SCR target, it is probably a good idea to use mount points on the D: and E: drives for the source servers. That reduces the number of drive letters you have to match up between the source and the target SCR servers. (Mount points allow you to collect many LUNs or disks from many sources but use very few drive letters.)

For example, on the source servers, you might have a drive letter and folder called D:\E2K7-Logs and one called E:\E2K7-Data. However, for the databases, the folders might represent mount points and be named as such:

E:\E2K7-Data\MDB-LAXMB01-01

E:\E2K7-Data\MDB-LAXMB01-02

E:\E2K7-Data\MDB-LAXMB01-03

In this example, if the server with these mount points is then replicated with SCR to a target server with a single, very large E: drive, all of the folders would be unique under the target's E:\E2K7-Data folder.

How Continuous Replication Works

Unlike many tools from third-party vendors, which replicate data at either the disk block level or by taking snapshots of the disk and replication changes, Exchange continuous replication is more similar to the SQL Server *log shipping* technology. This is considered a *pull* model. The active Exchange database, logs, and database engine do not even realize they are being copied. The Microsoft Exchange Replication Service (Microsoft.Exchange.Cluster.ReplayService.exe) handles copying the logs and managing the passive databases.

Initially (as when continuous replication is set up or reconfigured) the current copy of the database is copied to the passive location; this is called *seeding*. As an Exchange transaction log is filled up and renamed (that is, when the E00.LOG file is filled and then renamed to E000000001.LOG), the renamed log file is then copied to the passive location. The replication service then verifies the log file and commits it to the passive copy of the database. So the actual database file is not replicated at all, but it is kept in sync by copying the log files and replaying them.

You will probably understand this concept better with an illustration. Figure 18.1 shows an example of how this process works. The Exchange database engine is run by the Microsoft

Exchange Information Store; transactions fill up the current transaction log (E00.LOG). When full, the transaction log file (E00.LOG) is renamed to the next available transaction log file name (in this case E0000000001.LOG). All of this is handled by the Information Store service.

FIGURE 18.1
How continuous
replication works

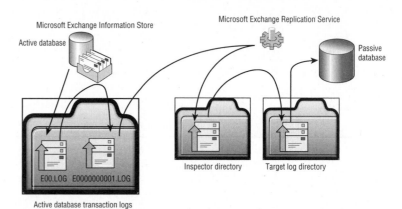

Active database transaction logs

If continuous replication is enabled, the Microsoft Exchange Replication Service copies the E0000000001.LOG file to the Inspector directory. This folder may be on the local machine (in the case of local continuous replication), a passive cluster node (in the case of cluster continuous replication), or a remote mail server (in the case of standby continuous replication).

The service verifies the checksum and signature of the log files in the Inspector directory to ensure that they are not corrupted and that they are in the correct sequence. Once this is verified, the replication service copies the log file (E0000000001.LOG) to the target log file directory. Transactions found in log file E0000000001.LOG are committed to the passive copy of the database.

At any given time, the passive copy of the database will be no more than 15 minutes out of sync with the active database. A 15-minute lag would occur in the dead of night when there is absolutely no activity on the mailbox database. During a normal work day where users are actually using the database, the passive copy of the database will be no more than a few minutes behind.

If a database is dismounted or the information store service is stopped, the data is all committed to the active database and then passed over to the passive copy. If the administrator has to manually switch over to the passive copy of the database, the passive copy should be automatically synchronized with the active copy of the database.

Local Continuous Replication

For even a small organization, local continuous replication (LCR) is one of the most interesting new features of Exchange 2007. LCR helps to ensure that an alternate copy of a mailbox database is maintained on the local server. This feature was at one time called *continuous backup*. The concept of LCR is illustrated in Figure 18.2. A backup copy of the production mailbox database is maintained on the local server. As the transaction logs of the production database are completely filled, the transaction logs are copied to the backup location (step 1) and committed to the backup copy of the database (step 2).

In the event that the production database becomes corrupted, the administrator can switch from the production database to the backup copy of the database. Here are some important points and tips to remember with respect to local continuous replication:

◆ LCR is designed to reduce restore time by keeping a copy of the database on the local server that can be brought into service in a very short period of time (a few minutes).

◆ Activation of a passive copy of the database is performed manually by the administrator.

◆ The LCR database must be stored on the local server.

◆ Each database that will be replicated must be in its own storage group.

◆ Plan to use separate logical units (LUNs) or physical disks for the LCR databases and transaction logs.

◆ Disk storage capacity will be double the requirements of a mailbox server without LCR if you replicate all mailbox databases.

◆ Replication will increase disk I/O capacity requirements by 125 to 150 percent.

◆ Add an additional 1GB to 2GB of physical memory for servers that will use LCR.

◆ Factor in an additional 20 percent CPU capacity on top of a standard mailbox server.

◆ If you use snapshot backups, you can configure your disk snapshots to be done on the passive copies of the database. This can significantly improve performance for the active copies of the database during the snapshot period.

FIGURE 18.2
Local continuous replication

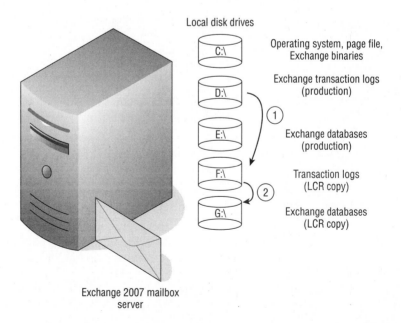

Local disk drives

C:\ — Operating system, page file, Exchange binaries

D:\ — Exchange transaction logs (production)

E:\ — Exchange databases (production)

F:\ — Transaction logs (LCR copy)

G:\ — Exchange databases (LCR copy)

Exchange 2007 mailbox server

Cluster Continuous Replication

Cluster continuous replication (CCR) is another interesting new feature of Exchange 2007. A thorough and in-depth discussion of CCR would consume several chapters and is beyond the scope of this book, but I hope this will serve as a good introduction to CCR. CCR introduces a whole new level of high availability and clustering. Unlike traditional single copy clustering (SCC) in which there is only a single copy of the database, CCR not only has redundant hardware but a backup copy of the database. This backup copy of the database is kept current using replication technology similar to LCR. As transactions are committed to the production copy of a database, the log file is copied to the backup location and committed to the backup copy of the database.

CCR is implemented in the form of two-node, active-passive clustering. Quorum is maintained using a majority node set cluster; a third server acts as a witness by providing a file share on which the shared quorum database is located. The active node has one or more mailbox databases. The concept of CCR is illustrated in Figure 18.3. As transactions are committed to the active node's databases and transaction logs, the transaction logs are shipped (copied) to the passive node (shown in step 1).

FIGURE 18.3
Clustered continuous replication

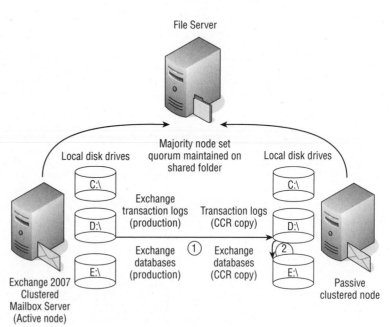

When the transaction log has been successfully copied to the passive node, the transactions in that log are committed to the corresponding database on the passive node (step 2). In the event of any type of failure on the active node, the passive node will automatically fail over and assume responsibility for the Clustered Mailbox Server (formerly called an Exchange Virtual Server).

When running Windows 2003, the active and passive nodes must be on the same IP subnet; however, if you are using Windows Server 2008, you can have clustered nodes on different subnets. If an organization has VLAN capability, it can conceivably place two nodes of a Windows 2003 CCR cluster in separate locations.

Cluster continuous replication will help to reduce the "cost of entry" for organizations wishing to move to Exchange clustering, because it eliminates the need for costly and complex shared storage such as storage area networks (SANs). Keep in mind the following important points and tips when implementing CCR:

◆ Failover of the active clustered node is automatic, such as in the event of the failure of the server hardware.

◆ A single database failure will not induce an automatic failover.

◆ Data storage for CCR clusters can be located on direct attached storage (DAS) or you can continue to use SAN storage. However, unlike traditional Exchange 2000/2003 clusters, the disks are not shared on the SAN. Each node of the cluster uses its own disks.

◆ Each database must be in its own storage group. If you need 10 mailbox databases, you must have 10 storage groups.

◆ The only Exchange server role that can live on a CCR cluster is the Mailbox server role. Hub Transport, Client Access, and Unified Messaging cannot be installed on a clustered server. This is by design and is intended to reduce the complexity of cluster and thus improve availability.

◆ If you want to put a public folder database in a CCR cluster, it must be the only instance of the public folder database in your organization. High availability of public folder data should be implemented using multiple public folder servers and multiple replicas of public folder data, not using CCR.

◆ If an unplanned failover of the active clustered node occurs, the new active node will need to contact each of the Exchange 2007 Hub Transport servers in the site to make sure it has not missed any recently delivered e-mail messages. CCR will request missing messages from the Hub Transport server's transport dumpster. By default, the transport dumpster will hold up to 18MB of messages for each storage group.

Standby Continuous Replication

Short of maybe some fixes to the management interface, standby continuous replication (SCR) is the most valuable addition to Exchange 2007 Service Pack 1. This is one of the most commonly requested capabilities for Exchange customers. I frequently hear questions such as, "How do I provide remote recoverability for mailbox data?" or "How do I provide a standby solution short of implementing clustering?" Many third-party products have been introduced to the market that address these types of requests.

SCR IS FOR RESILIENCY OR CONTINGENCY, NOT HIGH AVAILABILITY

I want to make something very clear. SCR is a resiliency or contingency solution; it does not provide *high availability* in the same way that CCR clustering provides high availability. Clustering-type high availability solutions provide near immediate failover to a backup server (and data, in the case of CCR); the failover is usually automatic and takes between two and ten minutes depending on the configuration. Clustering also implies little to no data loss.

In addition to providing high availability and automatic failover solutions, clustering is useful in other ways. If you need to perform maintenance on an active node of the cluster, you simply move the Exchange services to a passive node of the cluster. Within a few minutes, all of the clients are right back at work and you can perform any necessary maintenance.

> The failover involved in switching over to an SCR copy of a database is less trivial than it is for cluster-ing and it is not automatic. You do not deploy this sort of solution for *high availability* requirements or *we need to do maintenance on this node* requirements. You deploy it for situations where a server has failed permanently or where an entire site will become unavailable, such as in the case of a natural disaster. For this reason, I call it a resiliency or contingency solution, not a high availability solution. Setting expectations for features and functions will help you to do your job more easily.

Let's look at standby continuous replication for Exchange Server 2007 Service Pack 1. SCR is implemented on an Exchange Server 2007 mailbox server and is configured to pull transaction logs from one or more Exchange Server 2007 mailbox servers. SCR can actually pull transaction logs from many Exchange Server 2007 mailbox servers in many different locations; the limiting factor will be whether or not you have enough bandwidth to pull transaction logs across the network to the SCR server. One other configuration point to keep in mind is that you are limited to a single database per storage group if you want to take advantage of the new replication technologies; however, that is okay because Exchange Server 2007 Enterprise Edition allows for up to 50 storage groups.

In the wild I have seen a few different designs and implementations of SCR so far. These fall into a few categories; the first of these, in Figure 18.4, shows how an organization would imple-ment SCR if it is simply looking for resiliency of its mailbox data to a standby data center. The Exchange servers in Sydney and San Francisco are *combined function* servers, meaning that they implement multiple Exchange Server 2007 server roles. In this example, these servers each have the Mailbox, Hub Transport, and Client Access server roles.

FIGURE 18.4
Standby continuous replication implementation to a contingency site

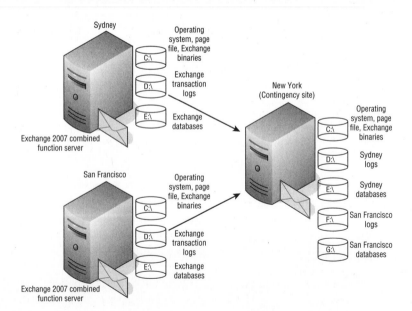

The third location is the contingency location in New York. This could be another of the company's offices or it could be a contingency site provider that provides the company rack space for a few servers. SCR is configured on a server in New York; initially the databases from Sydney and San Francisco are seeded onto a server in New York. Then SCR is configured to pull the committed transaction logs from the Sydney and San Francisco servers. SCR can be configured to immediately replay these logs to the passive copies of the database or wait a configured amount of time so that the passive copy is always a certain interval behind the active copy.

The SCR solution shown in Figure 18.4 can be scaled so that Exchange servers at additional offices are replicated to New York. The limiting factor on the contingency server in New York will be the disk storage and I/O capacity as well as the maximum number of storage groups or storage databases that can be active on that server.

The server in New York is configured as a combined function server. If there is a failure of the San Francisco site, the administrator makes the decision to bring one or all of the San Francisco databases live on the New York server. The URL for Outlook Web Access would have to be pointed to the alternate server. Outlook 2007 clients would automatically connect to the New York server after Active Directory has replicated the fact that the users' mailboxes in San Francisco are now on the New York server. The administrator would have to manually update Outlook 2003 and earlier clients.

For organizations that are concerned about both high availability and site resiliency, SCR can be combined with CCR. The source databases do not have to be on a stand-alone mailbox server; they can be on a clustered mailbox server. Figure 18.5 shows how an organization can combine a CCR cluster in its main office (for high availability) with an SCR system in a remote office that provides site resiliency.

FIGURE 18.5
Standby continuous replication when implemented with cluster continuous replication

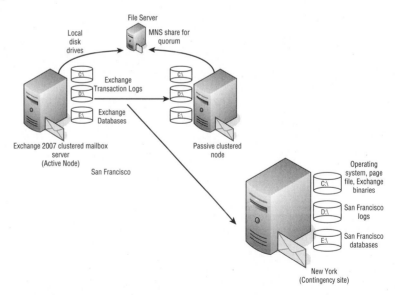

In this organization, the CCR cluster provides high availability in the event of hardware failure or in the event that the company needs to perform maintenance on one of the two nodes of the

CCR cluster. The SCR system always pulls transaction logs from the active node of the cluster; it does not pull the logs from the passive node.

If there is ever a complete failure of the San Francisco site, the administrator must make the decision to perform the failover to the New York contingency site.

Implementing and Managing Local Continuous Replication

Local continuous replication (LCR) is another one of the more promising features of Exchange 2007. The key point of LCR is to allow you to have a nearly completely replicated copy of the current database on the local server. In a situation where the production database is no longer functioning, the administrator can quickly switch from the production database to the LCR database.

LCR is enabled on a per-storage-group basis and the storage group cannot have more than one mailbox or public folder database. When first enabled, LCR creates a seeded copy of the current database; at the point of creation, the LCR database that was seeded will be the same as the production database. As transactions are committed to the production database, the transaction logs are filled. When a transaction log fills up, LCR copies the transaction log file to the LCR transaction log location for that particular storage group. The log is then replayed into the LCR copy of the database; Microsoft calls the LCR database the *passive* copy of the database. At any given time, the LCR database should be within one transaction log of being completely synchronized. If the database is dismounted, the LCR database becomes fully synchronized.

LCR and the Exchange Database Transaction Log

Local continuous replication is one of the reasons that the Exchange database transaction log file size was reduced from 5MB to 1MB. This ensures that transactions are copied and committed to the LCR database more quickly.

The advantage of LCR is that it reduces the time necessary to restore a database from backup to practically no time at all. You can safely support larger and larger database sizes and still maintain good recoverability and good recovery times. However, supporting LCR is not a license to have 5TB mailbox databases; you still have to worry about a situation in which you might have to completely rebuild the server, the entire disk subsystem, or reseed the LCR copy of the database. Databases must be backed up to an alternate media, even if you have LCR copies. Further, the database size should not be so large that online maintenance cannot be completed at least once every week.

Microsoft recommends mailbox databases of no more than 100GB without LCR and mailbox databases of up to 200GB with LCR.

Maintain Backups to Alternate Media!

Local continuous replication provides you with a locally backed-up copy of databases. If the entire server fails or must be rebuilt, you still have to restore data from an alternate media. Keep this in mind when planning for database sizes. Also, using LCR does not excuse you from performing regular backups to alternate media.

One additional possible advantage to using LCR is that you can streamline your backup process. Streaming backups and Volume Shadow Copy Service (VSS) backups of production databases can adversely affect performance during the backup windows. Backup windows have to be precisely calculated in order to ensure that online maintenance is completed at least once a week for each database.

An alternate backup approach for Exchange is to use LCR to keep a completely synchronized copy of the production database and then use a VSS backup of the LCR database. As long as the LCR copy of the database is not on the same spindles as the production database, the VSS backup should not noticeably affect the I/O on the production database disk.

Requirements for Local Continuous Replication

You need to plan for some requirements when you implement LCR. These include ensuring that you have adequate server capacity and that your storage groups are configured properly. Here are some tips:

♦ LCR will generally increase CPU and memory capacity on a server by at least 30 to 40 percent. Do not implement LCR on a server that is already on the verge of developing performance problems. Move mailboxes or server roles to another server to lighten the load on the Mailbox server on which you plan to enable LCR.

♦ For the best level of recoverability and performance, LCR databases and transaction logs should not be on the same physical disks or logical units (LUNs if you using a SAN) as the production databases and logs.

♦ Sufficient disk capacity must exist for LCR databases and transaction logs. If you have 500GB of available disk space for the production databases, you need the same amount for your LCR database. The disks that host the LCR databases and transaction logs should have the same I/O capacity as the production databases.

♦ On heavily loaded Mailbox servers, you may run out of drive letter capacity when adding LCR databases and transaction logs. Volume mount points can be used in this instance.

♦ Each storage group can have no more than one mailbox or public folder database.

♦ The LCR solution for organizations with more than one public folder database is to use public folder replication. If you have only one public folder in the entire Exchange organization, you can use LCR replication for the public folder database.

♦ It is more efficient to start using LCR immediately after you create a storage group and mailbox database. Enabling LCR for an existing storage group and database will take longer if the database file size is large.

If you can't meet the prerequisites for LCR, you should improve the capacity of your server resources and configuration before you start. If a server is not configured with the proper capacity for LCR, performance problems will get worse.

Configuring Local Continuous Replication

Configuring LCR is pretty simple and it can be done via the Exchange Management Console (EMC) or the Exchange Management Shell (EMS). I will take you through a configuration of LCR using the EMC and then cover the necessary EMS steps to accomplish the same tasks.

To enable a storage group to use LCR via the EMC, you can use a wizard. Follow these steps:

1. In the EMC, locate the storage group under the Mailbox subcontainer in the Server Configuration work center.

2. Highlight the server name in the Results pane and then locate the storage group in the Work pane.

3. Select the Enable Local Continuous Replication task in the Actions pane; this runs the Enable Storage Group Local Continuous Replication Wizard. The Introduction page of this wizard is shown in Figure 18.6.

FIGURE 18.6
Enable Storage Group Local Continuous Replication Wizard

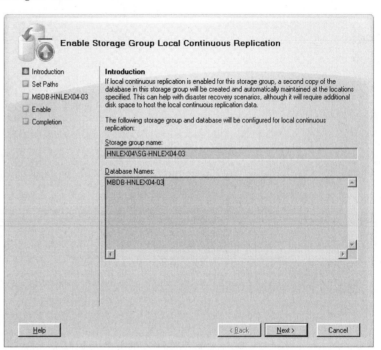

4. On the Introduction page of the wizard, you just confirm the storage group name and confirm that there is only a single database in the storage group. (The database list is labeled "Database Names," but the wizard will stop you later if the storage group has more than one database.)

5. Just as with creating a storage group, you must define the location of the transaction log files and the system files. On the Set Paths page (shown in Figure 18.7), you must specify the LCR paths for the transaction logs and system files. Ideally, these paths should not be on the same physical disk as the original transaction logs, the original database, and the LCR database.

   Figure 18.8 shows the MBDB-HNLEX04-03 database page of the Enable Storage Group Local Continuous Replication Wizard. This page is unique to the database contained in the storage group you have selected and thus its name will depend on the database that appears in the Database Name field.

FIGURE 18.7
Specifying LCR paths
for transaction logs
and system paths

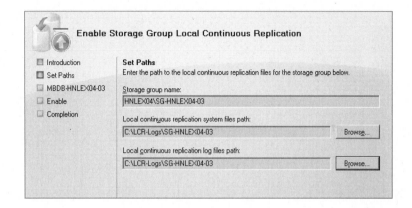

FIGURE 18.8
Specifying a path for
the LCR database

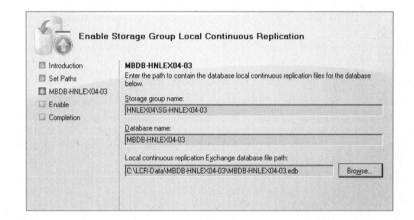

6. On the MBDB-HNLEX04-03 page shown in Figure 18.7, the only thing you can specify is the location of the LCR database. Ideally, like the LCR path for the system and transaction log files, this path should not be on the same physical disk as the original database and transaction log files, or the disk containing the LCR transaction log and system files.

The Enable page of the wizard simply shows the configuration summary of what tasks are about to be performed.

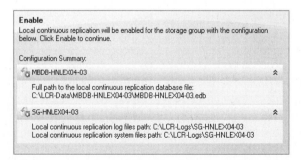

LCR INTRODUCES PERFORMANCE OVERHEAD

If you are using LCR, keep in mind that you will be more than doubling your disk I/O overhead. For each production database you maintain, there will be an LCR copy *of* that database as well as the LCR copy *for* that database. Plus the transaction logs from the production location are copied to the LCR location.

I strongly encourage anyone using LCR to make sure that the LCR databases are on separate spindles to reduce the possibility of severe performance issues.

Once you click the Enable button on the Enable page, the `Enable-DatabaseCopy` and `Enable-StorageGroup` copy cmdlets establish LCR for this storage group and database. The following are the commands that were actually executed by the wizard for this example:

```
Enable-DatabaseCopy -Identity 'HNLEX04\SG-HNLEX04-03\MBDB-HNLEX04-03' ↵
-CopyEdbFilePath 'C:\LCR-Data\MBDB-HNLEX04-03\MBDB-HNLEX04-03.edb'

Enable-StorageGroupCopy -Identity 'HNLEX04\SG-HNLEX04-03' ↵
-CopyLogFolderPath 'C:\LCR-Logs\SG-HNLEX04-03' ↵
-CopySystemFolderPath 'C:\LCR-Logs\SG-HNLEX04-03'
```

Notice that the `Enable-StorageGroupCopy` command used the server and storage group name to identify the storage group; this is a change from Exchange 2007 RTM, where the distinguished name was used.

To help you disseminate and decode what was done, here is a summary of the configuration parameters used to enable LCR for the storage group and database:

Storage group name	SG-HNLEX04-03
Database name	MBDB-HNLEX04-03
LCR transaction logs path	C:\LCR-Logs\SG-HNLEX04-03\
LCR system files path	C:\LCR-Logs\SG-HNLEX04-03\
LCR database path	C:\LCR-Data\MBDB-HNLEX04-03\

Managing Local Continuous Replication

Once LCR is enabled for a storage group, you may need to perform a few management tasks. Management tasks for LCR include checking the health of a storage group's replication, suspending replication, resuming replication, and resynchronizing (aka *reseeding*) the entire database.

HEALTH CHECKS

Once storage group replication is enabled, you can confirm that it is working in a number of different ways. The first way is just to look at the listing of storage groups and database names in the Work pane. Notice for the SG-HNLEX04-03 storage group that the value in the Copy Status column is Healthy.

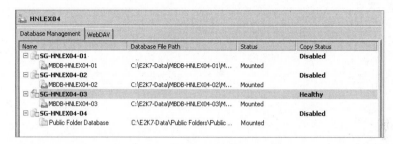

Here are the possible status values you may see in the Copy Status column (or in the SummaryCopyStatus property when you use the EMS cmdlet):

◆ *Healthy* means that LCR is working normally and data is replicating and being committed to the LCR copy of the database.

◆ *Disabled* means that LCR is not configured.

◆ *Suspended* means that an operator has temporarily stopped replication.

◆ *Seeding* means that the production database is being copied to the LCR location.

◆ *Failed* means that something has failed during the replication process and there may be problems with the configuration, logs, or database. Consult the event logs.

◆ *Not Supported* means that the current configuration does not support or allow LCR.

Viewing the same information using the EMS and the Get-StorageGroup cmdlet will yield this listing:

```
Get-StorageGroup
Name                    Server          Replicated      Recovery
----                    ------          ----------      --------
SG-HNLEX04-01           HNLEX04         None            False
SG-HNLEX04-04           HNLEX04         None            False
SG-HNLEX04-02           HNLEX04         None            False
First Storage Group     HNLSCR01        None            False
SG-HNLEX04-03           HNLEX04         Local           False
```

Notice that the Replicated column in this listing shows storage group SG-HNLEX04-03 as being replicated locally.

Using the EMS cmdlet Get-StorageGroupCopyStatus, you can retrieve more useful and detailed information about the LCR status of a particular storage group. Here is an example:

```
Get-StorageGroupCopyStatus "SG-HNLEX04-03" | FL

Identity                : HNLEX04\SG-HNLEX04-03
StorageGroupName        : SG-HNLEX04-03
SummaryCopyStatus       : Healthy
```

```
NotSupported                      : False
NotConfigured                     : False
Disabled                          : False
ServiceDown                       : False
Failed                            : False
Initializing                      : False
Resynchronizing                   : False
Seeding                           : False
Suspend                           : False
CCRTargetNode                     :
FailedMessage                     :
SuspendComment                    :
CopyQueueLength                   : 0
ReplayQueueLength                 : 0
LatestAvailableLogTime            : 9/3/2007 5:10:00 AM
LastCopyNotificationedLogTime     : 9/3/2007 5:10:00 AM
LastCopiedLogTime                 : 9/3/2007 5:10:00 AM
LastInspectedLogTime              : 9/3/2007 5:10:00 AM
LastReplayedLogTime               : 9/3/2007 5:10:00 AM
LastLogGenerated                  : 31
LastLogCopyNotified               : 31
LastLogCopied                     : 31
LastLogInspected                  : 31
LastLogReplayed                   : 31
LatestFullBackupTime              :
LatestIncrementalBackupTime       :
SnapshotBackup                    :
IsValid                           : True
ObjectState                       : Unchanged
DumpsterServersNotAvailable       :
DumpsterStatistics                :
```

SUSPENDING AND RESUMING REPLICATION

There is really not much that you need to do to an LCR database once it is replicating. If you have to do maintenance on the disk on which LCR is running or if you want to stop all replication, you can highlight the storage group that is running LCR and click Suspend Local Continuous Replication in the Actions pane. When you choose to suspend LCR, you are prompted for comment. Simply type the reason you are suspending LCR and click Yes.

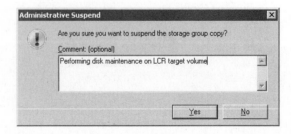

To resume LCR on the storage group, select the storage group and click Resume Local Continuous Replication in the Actions pane. You will be prompted to confirm that this is what you want to do and you will see the comment describing the reason that LCR was suspended previously.

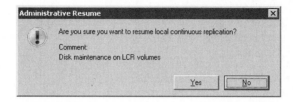

You can accomplish the same thing using the Suspend-StorageGroupCopy and Resume-StorageGroupCopy cmdlets:

```
Suspend-StorageGroupCopy "SG-HNLEX04-03" -SuspendComment "LCR disk maintenance↵
on December 12" -Confirm:$False
```

Once LCR is suspended, you can confirm it also using the Get-StorageGroupCopyStatus cmdlet, as you can see in this example:

```
Get-StorageGroupCopyStatus "SG-HNLEX04-03" | Format-List↵
Identity,StorageGroupName,SummaryCopyStatus,Suspend,SuspendComment

Identity           : HNLEX04\SG-HNLEX04-03
StorageGroupName   : SG-HNLEX04-03
SummaryCopyStatus  : Suspended
Suspend            : True
SuspendComment     : Performing disk maintenance on LCR target volume
```

The application event log will contain event ID 2083 from the MSExchangeRepl service indicating that replication for the storage group has been suspended; this is shown in Figure 18.9.

REPLAYING LOGS AFTER A SUSPENSION

If you suspend LCR during busy times for your server, expect to have a lot of logs that need to be replayed when you resume LCR.

When you are ready to resume LCR for that storage group, you can use the Resume-StorageGroup Copy cmdlet:

```
Resume-StorageGroupCopy "SG-HNLEX04-03"
```

The Resume-StorageGroupCopy cmdlet starts the log files copying and replaying once again and it clears the SuspendComment property. For a brief period of time (it seems until new transaction logs are copied over to the LCR target), the SummaryCopyStatus property both in the EMS and in the EMC will say *Initializing*. Here is an example of resuming the copy and retrieving the status shortly after the copy has been restarted:

```
Resume-StorageGroupCopy "SG-Hnlex04-03"

Get-StorageGroupCopyStatus "SG-HNLEX04-03" | Format-List↵
Identity,StorageGroupName,SummaryCopyStatus,Suspend,SuspendComment

Identity          : HNLEX04\SG-HNLEX04-03
StorageGroupName  : SG-HNLEX04-03
SummaryCopyStatus : Initializing
Suspend           : False
SuspendComment    :
```

FIGURE 18.9

Event ID indicating that replication for a storage group has been suspended

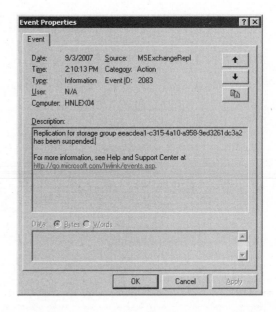

When LCR is restarted, you will see the following event information in the application event log:

```
Event Type:      Information
Event Source:    MSExchangeRepl
Event Category:  Action
Event ID:        2084
Date:            9/3/2007
Time:            2:19:33 PM
User:            N/A
Computer:        HNLEX04
Description:
Replication for storage group eeacdea1-c315-4a10-a958-9ed3261dc3a2 has
  been resumed.
```

You will also see events in the event log indicating that the log files have started copying (event ID 2114) and log files have started replaying (event ID 2115). These are normal and expected:

```
Event Type:        Information
Event Source:      MSExchangeRepl
Event Category:    Service
Event ID:          2114
Date:              9/3/2007
Time:              2:23:49 PM
User:              N/A
Computer:          HNLEX04
Description:
The replication instance for storage group SG-HNLEX04-03 has started
copying logfiles. The first logfile copied was generation 32.
```

```
Event Type:        Information
Event Source:      MSExchangeRepl
Event Category:    Service
Event ID:          2115
Date:              12/11/2006
Time:              8:05:08 AM
Computer:          HNLEX04
Description:
The replication instance for storage group SG-HNLEX04-03
has started replaying logfiles. Logfiles up to generation 33
have been replayed.
```

RESYNCHRONIZING LOCAL CONTINUOUS REPLICATION

Under some circumstances, it may become necessary to resynchronize the database or to manually resume replication. This operation is also called *reseeding*. You may need to reseed in the following conditions:

◆ You created an LCR database before the original database was created.

◆ You have performed an offline defragmentation of the original database.

◆ The LCR database gets deleted.

◆ The LCR database becomes corrupted.

In Exchange 2007 SP1, you can force the database to resynchronize via the EMC or via the EMS cmdlet `Update-StorageGroupCopy`. Using the EMC, select the storage group that needs to be updated and then run the Update Storage Copy task on the Actions pane. This launches the Update Storage Group Copy Wizard, shown in Figure 18.10.

Notice in Figure 18.10 that I have told the wizard to delete the existing log files; this will also delete the existing database and reseed it. Once I click Next and then confirm the configuration summary, the wizard will suspend the storage group copy (`Suspend-StorageGroupCopy`) and then run the `Update-StorageGroupCopy` cmdlet; this cmdlet will delete the existing log files, checkpoint file, and database file; reseed the database; and start copying the log files again.

FIGURE 18.10
Updating the storage
group copy

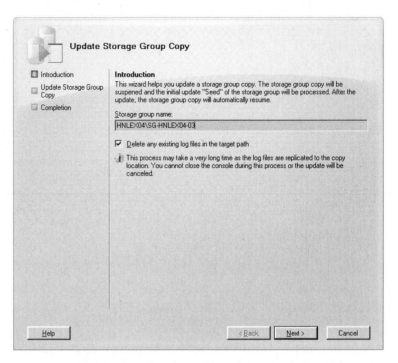

You can, of course, do all of this manually. You would need to suspend the storage group
copy and then run the Update-StorageGroupCopy cmdlet. Prior to running this cmdlet, you
should suspend LCR for the storage group that you are working on and then delete the LCR files
(database and transaction log files) unless you are planning to use the -DeleteExistingFiles
parameter. Here is an example:

```
Suspend-StorageGroupCopy 'HNLEX04\SG-HNLEX04-03'↵
-SuspendComment "Suspending to update database files"

Update-StorageGroupCopy "SG-HNLEX04-03" -DeleteExistingFiles↵
-Confirm:$False

Confirm
Continuous replication seeding found an obsolete checkpoint
'C:\LCR-Logs\SG-HNLEX04-03\E03.chk' file for storage group copy
'SG-HNLEX04-03'. The checkpoint file will be deleted, and then the
database will be seeded if you confirm now.
[Y] Yes  [A] Yes to All  [N] No  [L] No to All  [S] Suspend  [?] Help
(default is "Y"):y

Confirm
Continuous replication seeding found an existing target database
```

```
'C:\LCR-Data\MBDB-HNLEX04-03\MBDB-HNLEX04-03.edb' for storage group
copy 'SG-HNLEX04-03'. This target database will be deleted, before
seeding starts, if you confirm.
[Y] Yes [A] Yes to All [N] No [L] No to All [S] Suspend [?] Help
(default is "Y"):y
```

The reseeding operation can take a fairly significant amount of time if the production database is large, but the EMS will show you a progress bar.

Remember that it is making a copy of the production database. If you do this when the load on the Exchange server is typical, you may affect your end users' response times when they are using the server. I recommend that you perform this operation during off-hours or periods of low usage.

Recovery Using Local Continuous Replication

The reason you put LCR into operation in the first place is so you can quickly bring online a backup copy of the database. You would only need to do this if the production database has become corrupted. Database corruption is a tough topic to address in just a few lines, but I should state clearly here that as long as the production database is not on the same disk as the transaction logs, the LCR transaction logs, and the LCR copy of the database, the corruption should not extend to the LCR copy of the database.

How will you know that your production database is corrupted? I can think of a few situations:

◆ Normal or full backups of the production database fail.

◆ Online backups of the database using Exchange-aware backup software will perform a page-by-page check of the database as it backs it up. If a page-level error is detected, the backup halts, and the error is logged both to the backup log and to the application event log.

◆ Corruption is detected during normal operations (for example, if the database engine reads a page of data that is corrupted). Exchange confirms that the page in the database is bad and logs an event to the Event Viewer (see Figure 18.11).

◆ The database will not mount or reports errors when you try to mount it.

FIGURE 18.11
Errors found when
Exchange Server reads
a corrupted page from
the database

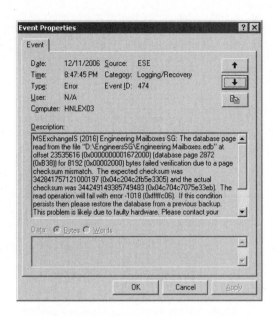

Monitoring for potential errors in your production databases is something you should do regularly, or you should configure your monitoring system to monitor for specific errors in either the application event log (such as the one shown in Figure 18.11) or the backup logs, such as the one shown here:

```
Backup started on 12/11/2006 at 8:47 PM.
The 'Microsoft Information Store' returned 'Error returned from an
ESE function call (d).
' from a call to 'HrESEBackupRead()' additional data '-'The 'Microsoft
 Information Store' returned 'Error returned from an ESE function call
 (d).
' from a call to 'HrESEBackupRead()' additional data '-'
The operation was ended.
Backup completed on 12/11/2006 at 8:47 PM.
Directories: 0
```

Note in the case of the error shown in Figure 18.11 that the database was mounted and functioning. The error did not interfere with the normal functioning of the database but was rather a single page in the database that could not be read properly. This error was probably due to the disk subsystem, device driver, or firmware. It is unlikely that the problem would extend to the LCR copy of the database.

If you realize that your production database is corrupted, you can manually switch the LCR database into production. You do this using the `Restore-StorageGroupCopy` cmdlet. Before I show you an example, let's look at the current location of the live database and logs as well as the locations of the LCR files. Here are two quick ways to retrieve this information using the EMS and the corresponding results:

```
Get-StorageGroup "Engineering Mailboxes SG" | FL name,*path*

Name               : Engineering Mailboxes SG
LogFolderPath      : D:\EngineersSG
```

```
SystemFolderPath     : D:\EngineersSG
CopyLogFolderPath    : E:\EngineersSG-LCR
CopySystemFolderPath : E:\EngineersSG-LCR

Get-MailboxDatabase "Engineering Mailboxes" | FL name,*path*

Name            : Engineering Mailboxes
CopyEdbFilePath : G:\Engineers-Mailboxes-LCR\Engineering Mailboxes.edb
EdbFilePath     : F:\EngineersSG\Engineering Mailboxes.edb
```

There are two steps to switching over to using an LCR database instead of the original production database:

1. The production database must be dismounted.

2. The LCR database/log locations are swapped out.

There are two approaches to swapping out the database. The first (and desired) approach is to copy the LCR database to the production database location. Here is an example:

```
Dismount-Database "engineering mailboxes" -Confirm:$False
Restore-StorageGroupCopy "Engineering Mailboxes SG"
      Base name: e02
      Log file: D:\EngineersSG\E0200000774.log
      Csv file: E:\EngineersSG-LCR\IgnoredLogs\q5cfbb2m.koe

      Base name: e02
      Log file: E:\EngineersSG-LCR\E0200000774.log
      Csv file: E:\EngineersSG-LCR\IgnoredLogs\5p52d1ni.kxz

Integrity check passed for log file: E:\EngineersSG-LCR\inspector\E0200000775.log
Integrity check passed for log file: E:\EngineersSG-LCR\inspector\E0200000776.log
Integrity check passed for log file: E:\EngineersSG-LCR\inspector\E0200000777.log
Integrity check passed for log file: E:\EngineersSG-LCR\inspector\E0200000778.log
Integrity check passed for log file: E:\EngineersSG-LCR\inspector\E0200000779.log
Integrity check passed for log file: E:\EngineersSG-LCR\inspector\E02.log
WARNING: Restore-StorageGroupCopy on Engineering Mailboxes SG was successful.
All logs were successfully copied.
```

Once this process is executed, you must manually copy the LCR database into the production location. You can do this by just copying the files, or, if the paths are the same but the drive letters are unique, you could simply reassign the drive letters. For example, if the production database is on D:\EngineeringMailboxes and the LCR database is on F:\EngineeringMailboxes, you could simply tell the server that the D: drive is now the F: drive. The advantage to this approach is that the documented locations of all of the database and storage group files remain the same. The downside to this is that the *only* Exchange data that could be on the D: and E: drives in this example would be that one database that is being swapped out.

The other way to swap out the database files is simply to swap out the locations; you do this with the Restore-StorageGroupCopy cmdlet and the -ReplaceLocations option. Here is an example:

```
Restore-StorageGroupCopy "Engineering Mailboxes SG" -ReplaceLocations
      Base name: e02
```

```
Log file: D:\EngineersSG\E020000001F.log
Csv file: E:\EngineersSG-LCR\IgnoredLogs\raobyk4o.lqt

Base name: e02
Log file: E:\EngineersSG-LCR\E020000001F.log
Csv file: E:\EngineersSG-LCR\IgnoredLogs\hosrmoec.5v1
```

```
Integrity check passed for log file: E:\EngineersSG-LCR\inspector\E02.log
WARNING: The Restore-StorageGroupCopy operation for storage group copy
Engineering Mailboxes SG was successful, and production paths
were updated. All logs were successfully copied.
```

The database can now be remounted, but it is now in use in a different location. You can confirm this with the `Get-StorageGroup` and the `Get-MailboxDatabase` cmdlets. Notice also that LCR has been disabled for this storage group after the `Restore-StorageGroupCopy` cmdlet was run:

```
Get-StorageGroup "Engineering Mailboxes SG" | FL Name,*path*,HasLocalCopy

Name                 : Engineering Mailboxes SG
LogFolderPath        : E:\EngineersSG-LCR
SystemFolderPath     : E:\EngineersSG-LCR
CopyLogFolderPath    :
CopySystemFolderPath :
HasLocalCopy         : False
```

```
Get-MailboxDatabase "Engineering Mailboxes" |↵
  fl Name,HasLocalCopy,*path*

Name            : Engineering Mailboxes
HasLocalCopy    : False
CopyEdbFilePath :
EdbFilePath     : G:\Engineers-Mailboxes-LCR\Engineering Mailboxes.edb
```

KEEP DOCUMENTATION UPDATED WITH LATEST LCR LOCATIONS

The Microsoft online documentation makes a very good point that if you use the — ReplaceLocations parameter, you should make an effort to update your documentation to reflect the new database location or move the database back to the original location. Otherwise, your documentation will be out-of-date and other administrators may be confused as to why the production databases are in folders that have *LCR* in their name.

Implementing and Managing Standby Continuous Replication

Standby continuous replication (SCR) is not only one of the most anticipated features of Exchange 2007 SP1, it is also my favorite. SCR can be implemented in a number of different configurations depending on your organization's requirements. I felt that it was important to cover SCR in more depth than I covered clustering technologies such as SCC or CCR, because it will be of more use to many different organizations.

Standby Continuous Replication Basics

I'll start with the basics of SCR and define some of the concepts, terms, limitations, and possible ways to implement SCR. I covered some of this in Chapter 3, "Introducing Exchange Server 2007," but I want to go into more depth here so that you can better understand what configuration you want to use. I was surprised to learn the number of possible configuration options and recovery options and I think you will be, too.

SCR is configured at the storage group level, not for an entire Exchange server. Let's start with Figure 18.12 and look at some of the components of SCR.

FIGURE 18.12

Basics of standby continuous replication

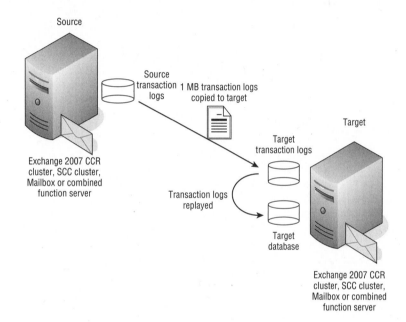

The *source* is any storage group on any Exchange Server 2007 Mailbox server; this storage group server could be a dedicated Mailbox server, a combined function server, a CCR cluster, or an SCC cluster. You can pick and choose which storage groups that you want replicated to a remote SCR target.

The *target* can be any Exchange 2007 SP1 server that has the Mailbox server role installed on it; this can include a dedicated Mailbox server, a combined function server, a CCR cluster, or an SCC cluster. If you plan to replicate storage groups to a remote CCR or SCC cluster, the cluster service and Mailbox server roles can be installed, but the cluster cannot have an active clustered mailbox server on it.

The target server can be Exchange Server 2007 Standard Edition or Enterprise Edition; however, if the Exchange server will host more than five mailbox databases (regardless of the number of source storage groups), Enterprise Edition must be used.

Once you configure a storage group to have a standby server, Exchange will create in the target Exchange server *seed* copies of the database in the source storage group. This can be time-consuming if your database is already a few gigabytes or larger, or if the source and the target are on different sides of a WAN link.

Once the seeding is complete, the Microsoft Exchange Replication Service on the target server will copy transaction logs from the source storage group, confirm that the transaction logs are correct, and then replay them into the database. There is a built-in replay lag time of 24 hours and 50 logs, so transactions are not committed to the target database right away. Exchange 2007 changes the size of the transaction log from 5MB (in the Exchange 2003 and earlier days) to 1MB. This ensures that transaction logs are copied more quickly; in periods of no messaging activity, a transaction log is still generated (even empty) once every 15 minutes.

STANDBY CONTINUOUS REPLICATION AND WINDOWS SERVER VERSIONS

An important tip to keep in mind when implementing standby continuous replication is that all SCR target servers must be running the same operating system as the source server. This is not a problem if you are standardized so that you are using only Windows Server 2003 or Windows Server 2008, but not both. However, if you have a mix of Windows Server 2003 and Windows Server 2008, then an SCR source server on Windows Server 2008 can only use other Windows Server 2008 servers as SCR targets.

Replicating, Verifying, and Replaying Data

Earlier in this chapter I discussed the basics about continuous replication (see "How Continuous Replication Works"). Let's take our knowledge of how transaction logs are copied and then committed and apply it to a real-world example. The following is the output of the `Get-StorageGroupCopyStatus` command for a storage group that is configured for LCR. I checked in the active log location's folder and found that the current log file was `E0300000030.LOG`; the same log file was found in the LCR log location.

```
Get-StorageGroupCopyStatus "SG-HNLEX04-03" | FL Identity,*log*

Identity                     : HNLEX04\SG-HNLEX04-03
LatestAvailableLogTime       : 9/3/2007 4:35:20 PM
LastCopyNotificationedLogTime : 9/3/2007 4:35:20 PM
LastCopiedLogTime            : 9/3/2007 4:35:20 PM
LastInspectedLogTime         : 9/3/2007 4:35:20 PM
LastReplayedLogTime          : 9/3/2007 4:35:20 PM
LastLogGenerated             : 48
LastLogCopyNotified          : 48
LastLogCopied                : 48
LastLogInspected             : 48
LastLogReplayed              : 48
```

According to `Get-StorageGroupCopyStatus`, the last log generated, copied, inspected, *and* replayed was log 48 (that is in decimal), and the most recent log file I found was `E0300000030.LOG` (which is 48 in decimal). So I'm comfortable in knowing that the log file has been copied over and that the data is safely committed into the SCR copy of the database.

Deployment Scenarios

Several possible scenarios are available to you for deploying SCR. Figure 18.13 shows a common scenario in which the storage groups on the server in Honolulu are configured to replicate to the server in San Francisco. However, the server in San Francisco is also supporting local mailbox databases.

FIGURE 18.13
Simple SCR deployment

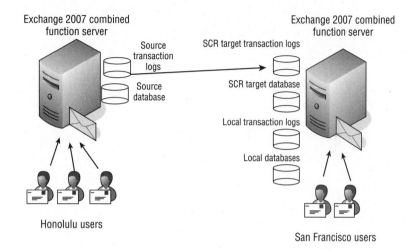

A common variant on this configuration is when a dedicated server is placed in San Francisco and only the storage groups from the Honolulu server are replicated to a remote server.

With SCR, you'll get a better return out of your extra server hardware because a single SCR target can accommodate storage groups from multiple SCR sources. Figure 18.14 shows an SCR target server that is accommodating storage groups from multiple Exchange 2007 storage group sources.

FIGURE 18.14
Directing a multiple sources to a single SCR target

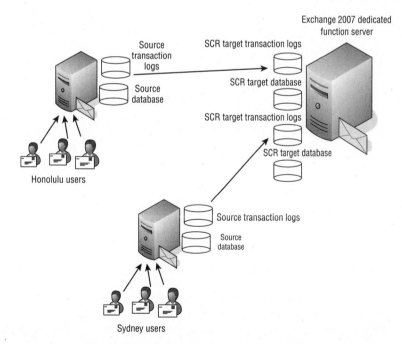

If you are already clustering your Mailbox servers, you can provide additional site resiliency with an option such as the one shown in Figure 18.15. In this type of configuration, a CCR cluster exists in the Honolulu office; both nodes of the cluster are in that local office. The storage groups on the CCR cluster are replicated to a Mailbox server in the San Francisco office.

FIGURE 18.15
Adding additional resiliency for an existing CCR cluster

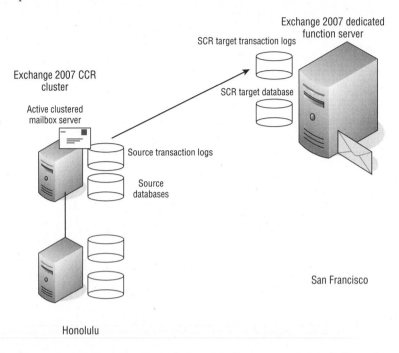

The SCR target in San Francisco can be either a stand-alone Mailbox server that is dedicated to SCR or a standby cluster with no active nodes.

Enabling Standby Continuous Replication

Unlike LCR, SCR can be enabled only by using EMS cmdlets; that is the bad news. However, the good news is that you use existing cmdlets and all of the setup work on the SCR target is done for you automatically. There's only one thing to keep in mind. Remember when I talked about folders and drive letters in the "Basics of Continuous Replication" section of this chapter? Well, if you have a folder on your SCR source called D:\E2K7-Data, then there *must* be a D: drive on the SCR target. A folder will be created called \E2K7-Data on the D: drive.

Actually enabling storage groups for SCR is even easier that you might think. You use the Enable-StorageGroupCopy cmdlet with the -StandbyMachine option. Here is an example for enabling storage group SG-HNLEX04-03 for SCR replication on a machine called HNLSCR01:

```
Enable-StorageGroupCopy SG-HNLEX04-03 -StandbyMachine HNLSCR01
```

That's it! Yes, it was that easy. There are a few new options for Enable-StorageGroupCopy and Update-StorageGroupCopy that are specific to SCR, though:

-StandbyMachine   This option is a multi-valued property you use to specify one or more Exchange 2007 Mailbox servers that serve as SCR targets for a particular storage group.

-ReplayLagTime   This option specifies the amount of time the SCR target waits before it replays a transaction log into an SCR copy of the database. By default, it waits 24 hours or 50 logs, whichever comes first. You can drop this value to as low as 0, but Exchange 2007 will always wait for 50 logs to accumulate before it replays a log. This parameter is formatted as *Days.Hours:Minutes:Seconds* (for example, if I want to drop the time to 15 minutes, I would type -ReplayLagTime 0.0:15:00). This can be configured only when you are using the Enable-StorageGroupCopy cmdlet.

-TruncationLagTime   This option allows you to specify the amount of time that the replication service waits before truncating transaction logs that have been replayed into the SCR target of the database. This can be configured only when you're using the Enable-StorageGroupCopy cmdlet.

-SeedingPostponed   This option allows you to specify that you do not want the seeding process to occur right away.

Well, okay, it was not quite *that* easy. Enabling a storage group for SCR can be somewhat easy if the databases are new and all of the transaction logs that have been created for the database still exist. However, a database that has been in production for quite some time will yield a slightly different result. Here is another example:

```
Enable-StorageGroupCopy SG-HNLEX04-03 -StandbyMachine HNLSCR01↵
-ReplayLagTime 0.0:15:00
WARNING: SG-HNLEX04-03 copy is enabled but seeding is needed for the copy.
The storage group copy is temporaily suspended. Please resume the copy after
seeding the database.
```

In this particular example, SCR was enabled for storage group SG-HNLEX04-03, but the seeding did not take place. Replication is suspended until the database is seeded. I can confirm this with the Get-StorageGroupCopyStatus cmdlet such as in the following example:

```
Get-StorageGroupCopyStatus SG-HNLEX04-03 -StandbyMachine HNLSCR01↵
| FL Name,SummaryCopyStatus


Name                      SummaryCopyStatus
SG-HNLEX04-03             Suspended
```

In this case, I need to use the Update-StorageGroupCopy cmdlet to force the seeding. You might think you could run this from any server in your environment, but you actually have to run it from the SCR target system. In this particular example, I need to do this from an EMS prompt on server HNLSCR01. The following image shows an example, including the progress bar that shows the seeding taking place. Note that because the storage group I am using as a source for seeding is on a different server, I have to use the server name and the storage group name.

Monitoring Standby Continuous Replication

Monitoring the health of SCR is important; after all, you are going to rely on SCR to be part of your recovery. You have a few options available when it comes to monitoring SCR; you can use the Get-StorageGroupCopyStatus cmdlet or you can use the Test-ReplicationHealth cmdlet.

USING *GET-STORAGEGROUPCOPYSTATUS*

A few pages back in the ''Replicating, Verifying, and Replaying Data'' section, I showed you how you can use the Get-StorageGroupCopyStatus command to retrieve the statistics for a storage group. However, to retrieve the statistics for a particular SCR target, you must specify the -StandbyMachine option so that the cmdlet knows the SCR target for which it must retrieve the statistics:

```
Get-StorageGroupCopyStatus SG-HNLEX04-03 -StandbyMachine HNLSCR01↵
| FL Identity,*status*,*log*,*length*
```

```
Identity                        : HNLEX04\SG-HNLEX04-03
SummaryCopyStatus               : Healthy
LatestAvailableLogTime          : 11/18/2007 4:17:05 PM
LastCopyNotificationedLogTime   : 11/18/2007 4:17:05 PM
LastCopiedLogTime               : 11/18/2007 4:17:05 PM
LastInspectedLogTime            : 11/18/2007 4:17:05 PM
LastReplayedLogTime             :
LastLogGenerated                : 1513
LastLogCopyNotified             : 1513
LastLogCopied                   : 1513
LastLogInspected                : 1513
LastLogReplayed                 : 1484
CopyQueueLength                 : 0
ReplayQueueLength               : 29
```

Notice that the current log file generation is 1513 (the most recent log on the SCR target is E03000005E9.LOG), but the last log that was replayed was 1484. This is because of the SCR replay latency (24 hours by default).

With LCR or CCR, at any given time, the most out-of-sync the passive copy of the database will be is approximately 15 minutes. This lag would be in the dead of night when there is absolutely no activity on the mailbox database. During a normal workday when users are actually using the database, the passive copy of the database will be no more than a few minutes behind.

However, with SCR, the copy of the database is always held back by either 24 hours or 50 transaction logs; this is to ensure that any type of logical corruption that might occur to the production copy of the database does not get replicated and committed to the target database.

If a database is dismounted or the information store service is stopped, the data is all committed to the active database and then the log files are copied to the passive location and replayed. If the administrator has to manually switch over to the passive copy of the database, the passive copy should be completely synchronized with the active copy of the database.

Notice also in the preceding EMS output of the `Get-StorageGroupCopyStatus` cmdlet that the `SummaryCopyStatus` is `Healthy`. This is, of course, what you want to see. There are several possible status values that you might see in this property:

- *Healthy* indicates that everything is working properly, logs are being copied, and logs are being replayed.

- *Disabled* indicates that the specific Exchange server specified in the `-StandbyTarget` parameter is not configured as an SCR target.

- *Not supported* indicates that something in the current configuration does not allow SCR to be configured.

- *Seeding* indicates that database seeding is taking place.

- *Initializing* indicates that the SCR target is restarting but is not currently copying logs. If all is normal, this usually happens when the SCR target has just rebooted and it has not yet started copying and replying logs.

- *Service down* indicates that the SCR target system's Microsoft Exchange Replication Service is stopped or not responding.

- *Synchronizing* indicates that the system is in the middle of copying over any remaining logs after the administrator has initiated a switch-over to make the SCR target live.

- *Failed* indicates that something serious has gone wrong between the SCR source and the SCR target. This might happen if something happens to the source server's database or log files. An offline defragmentation on the SCR source could cause this to occur.

USING *TEST-REPLICATIONHEALTH*

The `Test-ReplicationHealth` cmdlet was added to Exchange Server 2007 in Service Pack 1. This new cmdlet helps you perform replication health checks for not only SCR, but also CCR and LCR replication configurations. You must run this cmdlet from the server on which you want to test the replication health; in the case of SCR, you must run this cmdlet on the SCR target machine. Here is the default output on a server that is functioning as an SCR target:

```
Test-ReplicationHealth

Server          Check                Result      Error
------          -----                ------      -----
HNLSCR01        ReplayService        Passed
HNLSCR01        SGCopySuspended      Passed
HNLSCR01        SGCopyFailed         Passed
HNLSCR01        SGInitializing       Passed
HNLSCR01        SGCopyQueueLength    Passed
HNLSCR01        SGReplayQueueLength  Passed
HNLSCR01        SGStandbyReplayLag   Passed
```

When you run `Test-ReplicationHealth`, the cmdlet performs a number of different checks to ensure that replication is working properly. Some of these checks are specific to the type of replication you are performing (such as LCR, CCR, or SCR).

Examples of Recovery Using an SCR Target

The recovery options that are available to you in an SCR scenario will depend on a number of factors, including your existing configuration on both the source and the target. The following scenarios are based on people who are ready for early adoptions of Exchange 2007 SP1 and SCR:

Database portability recovery.   If the SCR target hosts production mailbox databases for other users as well as hosting SCR targets from remote mailbox servers, your only option for recovery will be to mount the SCR copy of the database as one of the local databases on the SCR target and then point the users' mailboxes to the new server. For example, let's say that mailbox database MBDB-HNLEX04-03 was on server HNLEX04 before, but it must be brought online on server SFOEX01. Then the database would be mounted and users would be reconfigured so that their home mailbox server was SFOEX01.

Dedicated recovery server.   If you have chosen to replicate *all* of a source server's storage groups to the SCR target, and if the SCR target has only that one source server's storage groups, you can rebuild the target server using the `Setup /RecoverServer` option. For example, all of server HNLEX04's storage groups are replicated to server SFOSCR01, then if HNLEX04 is permanently down, you could run `Setup /RecoverServer` and rebuild server SFOSCR01 as server HNLEX04. Rebuilding a stand-alone server can be a bit tricky because the original server must have Exchange Server running in order to be an SCR target, but when you need to switch over you must remove Exchange Server and re-install it using the `Setup /RecoverServer` setup option.

Cluster server recovery.   For the past few years, I have been helping customers design high-availability solutions using Exchange clustering. Since the release of Exchange 2007, I have been a big fan of CCR clusters for providing high availability, but I have never felt that CCR is a good *site-resiliency* solution. I have had either to use third-party products to replicate the database or to replicate snapshots of the database and then have methods of activating the mailboxes in the remote location. Trust me, none of this was very simple.

The new design I now recommend to organizations that want high availability as well as site resiliency is the one previously shown in Figure 18.15. The CCR cluster in the primary location hosts all of the storage groups that would be replicated to an SCR target in another location. The SCR target must be a passive node of the remote cluster. If there is ever a failure, the remote SCR target can be brought online with database portability recovery features or it can be brought online with the `Setup /RecoverCms` command. However, keep in mind that if you ever have to use the `/RecoverCms` option, the original entire cluster must be down.

Summary

I say with all sincerity that I believe one of the most important tasks that an Exchange administrator or an Exchange system engineer performs is to ensure the best possible reliability and availability for e-mail. Even without tools that help you provide higher availability, administrators should take their jobs seriously by getting the right training for their job, building their servers to be as reliable as possible, and ensuring that their configuration remains solid.

Exchange 2007 has introduced new technologies that help us to ensure even better reliability. Local continuous replication, while not technically a high-availability technology, is a technology that allows you to restore service more quickly in the event of a database becoming corrupted. With cluster continuous replication, you can automatically fail over to a replicated copy of the production databases and provide the best possible availability.

Perhaps the most promising feature of Exchange 2007 Service Pack 1, though, is standby continuous replication, which allows you to keep one or more replicas of one storage group on a server or all storage groups on a server. These replicas can be in the local site and/or in remote sites to provide site resiliency.

Chapter 19

Backup and Disaster Recovery

In Chapter 17, "Reliability and Availability 101," I talked about some of the most important things an Exchange administrator does on a daily basis. At the top of the list (well, very nearly the top) is ensuring that you provide good availability to your user community. However, at the *very* top of the list is providing good recoverability.

If you do a Google search for "disaster recovery" or "backup software" for Exchange, you will end up with literally more than a million possible hits. Many of them will be discussing third-party software products, tools, utilities, and hardware technology that help you to perform backups of your Exchange data.

Although many good products on the market can assist you in recovering from any number of problems with Exchange, I recommend that you evaluate these products against your recovery requirements rather than simply looking at the bells and whistles of the software.

There are far too many backup software packages for me to provide you with procedures for each, so I will be using the standard Windows Backup utility in my instructions. Many of the concepts and skills you learn simply using the Windows Backup utility will carry over to other backup products. There is, of course, a big catch when using the Windows Server 2003 Backup utility: it works only with Windows 2003.

This chapter not only provides you with procedures for backing up and restoring Exchange databases, it helps you to develop backup procedures that are sufficient for your organization.

In this chapter you learn to:

- ◆ Plan for the best possible recoverability
- ◆ Use the Windows Backup utility to back up Exchange
- ◆ Understand backup options when using Windows Server 2008
- ◆ Restore Exchange data to the recovery storage group
- ◆ Restore a corrupted database
- ◆ Develop a disaster recovery strategy

Providing Good Recoverability

A wise technology curmudgeon once said, "Don't create a backup plan, create a restore plan." That is good advice. Administrators will typically look at the data on a server and select the data that they think they need to back up. A better approach is to back up the data that you need to restore and back it up frequently so you will not lose more data than you can afford to lose.

What Does Good Recoverability Mean?

Simply put, providing good recoverability means that you have available the information necessary to meet your organization's recovery objectives. This means that you are backing up everything you might need to restore and that you have procedures in place to ensure that you are you are able to restore the information that you need to restore. Here are some important requirements of a good recoverability plan:

- You have documentation necessary to recover every server role.

- You have analyzed the information necessary to perform a complete recovery of each Exchange server role.

- You perform regular backups of all data.

- Your backups allow you to meet your recovery point objectives.

- Your backups allow you to meet your recovery time objectives.

- You perform periodic verifications to ensure that you can restore data even if you are simply restoring to a recovery storage group.

- Your transaction logs are available if you need to restore the last full backup.

RECOVERY POINT OBJECTIVES

The term *recovery point objective* (RPO) defines the time to which you are able to recover data when measured from the point at which you lost data. The RPO could be the previous day's backup or it could be a specific number of hours. If a traditional tape backup solution were your only method of recovery, the RPO would be a long period of time. If you specify that your RPO is the previous day's backup, a catastrophic failure of your Exchange server's storage system could cause you to lose up to 24 hours worth of data. Depending on the type of data that you are backing up or restoring, that can be a lot of critical data, especially for an e-mail system that is being updated continually. If you specify that the RPO is a fixed number of hours (such as six hours), you must perform some type of backup every six hours.

Determining your RPO and the maximum amount of acceptable data loss is important when it comes to planning your backup capacity and backup schedules. There are technologies that can help you to reduce the RPO for your organization by ensuring that you reduce the likelihood of a failure or that you keep your databases and transaction logs more highly available:

- Implementing local continuous replication (LCR) or clustered continuous replication (CCR)

- Storing databases and transaction logs on SAN- or iSCSI-based storage systems that are not affected by failure of an Exchange server

- Using SAN-based replication solutions that can keep replicated copies of databases and transaction logs

Of course, a simple solution to reduce your RPO is to perform more frequent backups of your data.

RECOVERY TIME OBJECTIVES

The *recovery time objective* (RTO) is the targeted amount of time it takes you to restore service for a particular application. Depending on the type of outage you experience, you may have different types of RTOs. An RTO for a single failed database might be 30 minutes, whereas recovery of an entire failed server might be eight hours.

For Exchange, there are two types of recoveries that you should consider:

◆ In a dial-tone restore, messaging services are restored quickly, but actual Exchange data is restored at some point in the future (hopefully the very near future).

◆ In the second type, the entire messaging system (messaging services plus data) is restored at the same time.

Defining and understanding your RTO can help you decide if your current processes, backup hardware, and backup software are sufficient. Factors that might cause you not to meet your RTO include:

◆ Having too much data to restore in a short period of time

◆ Slow restore hardware

◆ Personnel who do not fully understand the restoration procedures

---

IMPROVING RESTORATION TIMES

An organization that I work with had an issue with one of its Exchange Mailbox servers; the issue was hardware related and much of the recovery time was waiting on the hardware to be fixed. The bottom line for management was that recovery took nearly 20 hours. Due to pressure from management as a result of this incident, a number of steps were taken to reduce the RTO. These included:

◆ Installing an e-mail archiving system that held archived e-mail older than two months. This reduced the size of the production Mailbox server databases by nearly 80 percent.

◆ Switching from a streaming backup to a snapshot based backup/restore system.

◆ Moving the databases and transaction logs to an external disk storage system.

◆ Keeping an extra server in stock that could be used for disaster recovery.

INFORMATION NECESSARY FOR RECOVERY

Probably the worst possible thing that can happen to an Exchange server is a complete server failure involving the operating system and data disks. This type of failure would require not only rebuilding the operating system, but reinstalling Exchange, reconfiguring any customizations that have been made to the system, and restoring the data. This type of recovery is called a *bare metal restore*.

If any one of your Exchange servers completely or partially failed, would you have the information necessary to rebuild it? First and foremost, the Active Directory data must be available, because that is where much of the Exchange server configuration is located. Medium and large businesses should always have multiple Active Directory domain controllers, and the domain controllers and Exchange servers should run on separate hardware. Even a small business can simplify recovery by ensuring that Exchange Server is not installed on Active Directory domain controllers.

There is, of course, other important information that you will need in order to recover a server. Here is a list of the documentation that you should collect to simplify recovery:

◆ Server disk configuration (drive letters, capacity, LUN configuration if applicable)

◆ Backups of certificates used for SSL (including private keys)

◆ OWA, Autodiscover, ActiveSync, and other web services virtual directory configurations

◆ Security customizations such as configuration files created by the Security Configuration Wizard

◆ Any custom scripts that you have created

BUILDING A CRASH CART

One of the first things that usually happens when even the most skilled IT department realizes that they have to do a server recovery is the "where is that?" syndrome. This naturally occurring phenomena is a result of no one knowing where to find things that are needed right away. Too frequently, CD-ROMs and DVD ROMs disappear, product keys get lost (or they are in a mailbox that is on the server that is down), and operating system setup CDs must be downloaded and burned again.

I recommend building a disaster recovery kit or a crash cart for each type of server that you support. This can be something as simple as a three-ring binder that contains the following:

◆ Escalation procedures, such as who makes the decision to restore

◆ Contact list, including cell phone numbers for IT management and a notification list of people who should be told about an outage

◆ Server hardware, Windows, and Exchange documentation

◆ Product keys, activation codes, and license key disks

◆ Windows operating system and service pack CD-ROMs

◆ Hardware vendor CD-ROMs (such as a CD-ROM used to run setup for a particular piece of hardware)

◆ Exchange Server 2007 DVD

◆ CD or floppy disk drive with the device drivers that are currently in use on the server

◆ Third-party CD-ROMs such as antivirus software and backup software

◆ Anything else that is critical to the server being rebuilt

Once you have built this kit, set it aside and do not loan any of the contents to anyone. If you have a shrink-wrap machine, it might be a good idea to shrink-wrap the binder so that no one is tempted to borrow anything. As the system is updated, new vendor CDs become available, service packs are released, and so on, remember to keep your crash cart up-to-date.

TESTING BACKUPS

Everyone who writes about backups always warns you to test your backups. Don't let the monotony of repetition lead you to ignore this warning. As many have said, a backup is useless if you can't restore from it. I recommend testing backups when you first set them up and then again whenever you change anything — from server software and hardware to backup hardware and software. Try to restore to hardware that is as much like the hardware on your real server as possible, though sometimes it is also a good idea to restore to really different hardware just to be sure you can handle some diversity.

A number of system managers tell me that they just don't have the time to test backups. Actually, they usually use the past tense, as in, "I just didn't have time to test my backups." And this is usually in response to calls from clients in the middle of a serious outage (aka resumé-producing event). These are usually administrators who have drifted far up the Exchange creek (crashed server) and now find themselves without a paddle (backup).

What can I say? If you really don't have time to test backups, tell your boss and ask for more resources, or work with the boss to prioritize the tasks you have. While you're talking with the boss, be sure to add that without backup tests, you can't guarantee you'll be able to bring e-mail back up in case of a hardware or software failure. You can also use this argument when requesting the kinds of redundant hardware discussed in Chapter 17, "Reliability and Availability 101." If nothing else comes of these discussions, you will have at least set your boss's expectations at a more realistic level should all or part of all heck break loose.

Understanding Online Backups

The Exchange database file structure is a pretty complex thing. At the most basic level, the database is organized in a modified "b-tree" structure. All data is stored in 8KB pages; each page consists of a "next page" pointer, a "previous page" pointer, a checksum, and some data. If any of these pieces of the page becomes corrupted, the database itself could be in serious jeopardy.

The Exchange database is also pretty smart; in the header of the database there is information about the database, including the last time the database was mounted, the last full backup, and the last incremental backup. You can retrieve some of this information using the EMS cmdlet `Get-MailboxDatabase`, but remember that you need to use the -Status option in the command line. Here is an example:

```
Get-MailboxDatabase "MBDB-HNLEX04-01" -status | FL  name,*database*,*backup*

Name                            : MBDB-HNLEX04-01
OriginalDatabase                :
PublicFolderDatabase            : HNLEX04\SG-HNLEX04-04\Public
   Folder Database
DatabaseCreated                 : True
BackupInProgress                : False
SnapshotLastFullBackup          : False
SnapshotLastIncrementalBackup   : False
SnapshotLastDifferentialBackup  :
SnapshotLastCopyBackup          :
LastFullBackup                  : 10/12/2008 8:23:35 AM
LastIncrementalBackup           : 10/12/2008 10:31:07 AM
LastDifferentialBackup          :
LastCopyBackup                  :
RetainDeletedItemsUntilBackup   : False
```

You can also retrieve this information using the ESEUTIL.EXE utility, but using this utility requires that the database be dismounted. The following output is part of the output generated when I used the command `eseutil.exe /mh mbdb-hnlex04-01.edb`:

```
  Last Consistent: (0x10DA,8,E9)  10/12/2008 08:43:48
      Last Attach: (0x10AB,9,86)  10/07/2008 17:56:24
      Last Detach: (0x10DA,8,E9)  10/12/2008 08:43:48
             Dbid: 1
    Log Signature: Create time:09/01/2007 20:40:08 Rand:625118265 Computer:
       OS Version: (5.2.3790 SP 2)
```

```
Previous Full Backup:
        Log Gen: 4309-4310 (0x10d5-0x10d6)
          Mark: (0x10D6,8,16)
          Mark: 10/12/2008 08:28:21

Previous Incremental Backup:
        Log Gen: 1621-4312 (0x655-0x10d8)
          Mark: (0x10D9,8,16)
          Mark: 10/12/2008 10:31:09
```

There are essentially four approaches or methods that you take when you need to backup an Exchange database. Just keep in mind that whichever backup type you choose to use, it must be compatible with Exchange Server 2007.

Backups that are not Exchange aware   This backup type makes a backup of the actual file (or possibly the disk blocks, in the case of some hardware solutions). If you use standard tape backup software and attempt to back up the Exchange database files, you won't succeed unless you dismount the database files or stop the information store service.

Some third-party backup systems have open-file agents that can back up the Exchange database file even when it is in use. These should not be used with Exchange Server under any condition unless they have been approved by Microsoft for use with Exchange. These types of backups do not purge the transaction log files once the backup is completed, nor do they mark the backup as completed in the header of the database.

Streaming backup   The streaming backup method *uses the Exchange APIs* to perform the backup. This backup type does not back up the actual database file but rather requests the database one page at a time. As the Exchange database engine is reading each page of the database, it verifies the next page and previous page pointers, reads the data, and ensures that the checksum is correct. If the backup process detects corruption in the database, the backup halts. This is a feature of Exchange that is designed to help prevent you from continually making backups of corrupted data.

However, if the backup completes successfully, you know that the database has no problems with corrupted pages. Once the database has been successfully backed up, the transaction logs are backed up and then purged.

Volume Shadow Copy Service (VSS) backup   A VSS backup usually works in conjunction with third-party hardware and software. A VSS backup backs up the data at the disk level by taking a "snapshot" of the disk and backing up all disk blocks that have changed since the last snapshot. The VSS backup approach will always require quite a bit of disk space; usually the snapshots consume just a bit more than the actual data. The advantage of a VSS backup system is that it is much faster than streaming backups. If the VSS backup is compatible with Exchange, it will verify that the database is not corrupted and purge the transaction logs just like a streaming backup.

Mailbox-level or brick-level backup   This type is supported by a number of third-party vendors. These backups use MAPI client software and back up each mailbox message by message and folder by folder. The advantage of these is that you can restore a single folder or single message without having to restore an entire database. However, with brick-level backups, there are often problems getting the backup client to work properly and they usually take at least three to four times longer to back up a mailbox database than a streaming backup takes. I do not recommend brick-level backups.

These are four basic types of Exchange backups. Undoubtedly, though, you will also come across some specialized or vendor-specific solutions. Though many of these solutions will have some merit, ultimately you should consider a solution that you know will allow you to recover the data you need to recover. If you choose a specialized backup and recovery solution, ensure that the vendor offers good support and that you are able to contact its support department when necessary.

What Can Go Wrong?

Anything that *can* go wrong *will* go wrong. Pessimists make good system administrators — at least pessimists that prepare for any possible contingency. When you are making plans for system backups, think about each type of restore, outage, or disaster that might occur within your organization and how you can mitigate those risks. I am going to discuss most of these in more detail, but here is list of possible issues that would require administrator intervention:

Deleted message or folder   Users can recover their own deleted items or folders using the Recover Deleted Items feature of Outlook or Outlook Web Access. The only requirement is that the Recover Deleted Items cache is enabled for the mailbox database. By default, deleted items and folders are retained for 14 days. If a message or folder cannot be retrieved, the administrator can always restore the database on which the mailbox resides to a recovery storage group.

Deleted mailboxes   Accidents do sometimes happen; user accounts and mailboxes can accidentally be deleted. By default, a deleted mailbox can be reconnected to a user account (that does not have a mailbox) for 30 days after it was deleted.

Corrupted databases   Rarely, an Exchange database can become corrupted. If you are using local continuous replication (LCR), you can swap out the production database for the LCR database. If you are using clustered continuous replication (CCR), you can move the clustered mailbox server to the passive node of the database and start using the CCR copy of the database. If you are not using either LCR or CCR, you will need to restore the database from the last complete backup.

Server failure   The worst case failure situation is when the entire server fails. If you have not clustered the server (in the case of a Mailbox server role) or provided a high-availability solution such as network load balancing for Client Access, Hub Transport, Unified Messaging, or Edge Transport server roles, you will need to rebuild the server (possibly from scratch) in order to restore the messaging services the server is providing.

Running Backups

In my opinion, the most important daily task that an Exchange administrator performs is running and verifying backups. Many administrators will probably take exception to this, but I firmly believe backups are essential. The ability to provide recoverability from alternate media (such as a tape or replicated snapshot) will be of paramount importance if you ever experience a complete server failure. I think your users will agree with me that a few hours of outage, queues backing up, or ActiveSync not working counts as a minimal disruption compared with the prospect of losing everything in their mailbox.

Exchange Backup Types

There are essentially four different types of backup that can run against an Exchange 2007 database. These backup types are all considered streaming backups and are performed against production databases, not against LCR or CCR copies of databases. You should pick one or more of these backup types based on the frequency of backup, backup capacity, and restoration requirements.

Full backup The full backup is by far the simplest to perform, and it's the simplest to restore from. A full backup of an Exchange mailbox database, public folder database, or storage group backs up the entire database file and all transaction logs associated with the database and storage group. The database is requested page by page and each page is verified to ensure that the checksum and page pointers are correct. Once this backup is complete, the transaction logs that were backed up are purged by the information store. You should be running full backups at least once per week; if you have the backup capacity and backup windows available, you should run full backups each night.

Differential backup Differential backups back up only the transaction logs associated with a storage group. This means that the actual data being backed up consists of only the changes that have been performed against a database since the last full backup. The database file is not backed up, nor are the transaction logs purged after the backup is completed. If you are performing incremental backups several days in a row, the amount of transaction logs backed up each time will continue to increase. The differential backup allows for simpler restoration if you are not performing nightly backups. When using differential backups, a restore only involves restoring the last full backup and the last differential backup.

Incremental backup Incremental backups back up only the transaction logs associated with a storage group. Once the transaction logs have been backed up, they are purged. Incremental backups back up only the changes to the database since the last full backup or the last incremental backup was run. If you are performing a weekly full backup and then daily incremental backups, a full restore will require all of the incremental backups since the last full backup was performed. The difference between a differential and incremental backup is slight; the database transaction logs are purged after an incremental whereas they are not after a differential backup.

Copy backup A copy backup is almost identical to a full backup. The entire selected database is backed up as well as the transaction logs, but the transaction logs are not purged after the backup. Purging transaction logs helps free up disk space on the transaction log disk; if you are running copy backups without full backups, you may find the transaction log disks filling up.

Backup Frequency, Schedules, and Rotation

Regardless of how much high-availability technology you have deployed, ultimately you need to have offline copies of your Exchange data. Redundant disks, clustering, and even replication solutions do not excuse you from performing regular backups.

Some organizations back up once per day (risking the loss of up to 24 hours of data) and use the same tape media (or target backup destination) all the time (risking media failure). Some fairly common questions that organizations that are deploying Exchange need to ask are: how often should we back up, when should we back up, and how long should we keep the backup media?

BACKUP FREQUENCY

The frequency of the backup will be determined partially on your backup capacity, partially on your system capacity, and partially on your recovery point objective. A recovery point objective of six hours means that you must perform some type of backup once every six hours.

Each time a backup is executed, a certain amount of system resources (CPU, network, disk, memory) is used to run the backup. The impact can be reduced by ensuring that backups that are run during normal work hours run as quickly as possible; you can do this by using incremental or differential backups.

You can also decrease the overhead that a backup takes by using LCR to replicate the databases to an alternate disk drive and then performing VSS backups of the LCR databases.

BACKUP SCHEDULE

Backups should be scheduled during periods of reduced activity on the server. For a typical business that supports users within a single time zone, the server is most busy supporting user activity from 7:00AM until approximately 6:00PM. You can schedule your backup operations outside of these hours. However, you should ensure that the online backup of each database does not interfere with the online maintenance period for that database. By default, this is daily from 1:00AM until 5:00AM, but this can be modified on the General property page of each mailbox or pubic folder database. Figure 19.1 shows the General property page and the Maintenance Schedule drop-down list.

FIGURE 19.1
The default online maintenance time for a database is 1:00AM until 5:00AM

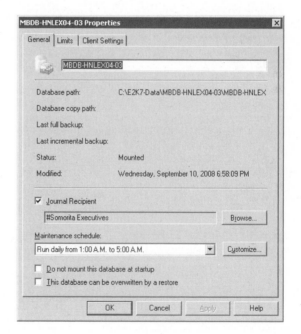

ONLINE MAINTENANCE AND ONLINE BACKUPS

If an online backup of a database starts while online maintenance is running, online maintenance will halt. Microsoft recommends that online maintenance complete on each database once every two weeks, but I recommend that it complete successfully at least once every few days. Once a database gets behind in its maintenance tasks, it takes much longer to complete the maintenance tasks.

You should periodically verify that online maintenance is completing for each database. Although a number of events show up in the Application event log indicating online maintenance is occurring, the event that you should look for to indicate that maintenance has completed on a database is from the extensible storage engine (ESE) and is event ID 701; this indicates that the online defragmentation pass has completed for a particular database.

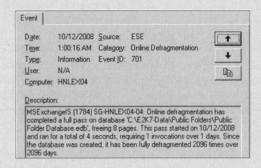

The online defragmentation operation for the database is the last online maintenance task that runs during online maintenance.

In general, I recommend starting online backups of the Exchange database between 8:00PM and 10:00PM. This gives the online backup time to complete so that online maintenance can be run. You can also reschedule online maintenance to run at another time.

If you have a tight recovery point objective, you should consider running multiple backups each day. For example, if your recovery point objective is six hours, you should consider running a full backup that completes at midnight and differential backups at 6:00AM, noon, and 6:00PM. Though recovery from a full backup and existing transaction logs is usually possible, it requires you to have all the transaction logs available since the last full backup.

Backup Media Rotation

Having implemented a backup strategy that lets you rotate tapes off site, you should be sure the rotation happens. Also, you should buy a fireproof, magnetic-media storage safe and keep all other backups onsite in that safe. A fireproof safe for paper does not protect magnetic media. Temperature and humidity control requirements for magnetic media are higher than for paper.

As I have implied throughout this chapter, you can make an initial backup to tape or disk. If you choose to do initial backups to disk, here are a few precautions you might want to consider:

◆ Don't back up to the disk that contains what you're backing up. You can't recover the disk if the backup is blown away when the disk is blown away.

◆ Immediately back up to tape whatever you backed up to disk. Even if your backup is on a different disk, it will do you no good if that disk fails.

◆ Rotate and store these tapes just as you would initial backups to tape. You can no more afford to lose these tapes than your initial backups to tape.

How long should you keep your backups? The ultimate answer to this question depends on whether or not you are compelled by either a law or a company policy regarding data retention.

Some organizations have policies or are compelled by law to be able to restore data from five or more years in the past, whereas other organizations may not wish to restore past two weeks.

VSS BACKUPS AND BACKUP ROTATION

As VSS has become more and more popular, I have seen fewer media rotation plans. This is because there really is not alternate "media" in place for VSS backups. The point of VSS backups is that the snapshots of your data are right there on the disk with the production data. A snapshot can be very quickly restored back in to production, if necessary.

This process allows you to recover data very quickly, which is a major advantage and selling point for VSS backups. However, there is no "external" storage for a VSS backup. Some third-party backup and storage systems allow you to mirror the snapshot to remote storage for the purposes of disaster recovery and this works quite well.

By law or by company policy, you may be required to keep data available to be restored for several years. If you are moving to VSS-type solutions, verify the retention policies that govern your organization to ensure you remain in compliance with your internal data retention or backup policies as well as government regulations that may affect your industry.

One possible solution is to rely on your e-mail archiving system (if you have one) for long-term data-retention compliance. Another is to periodically perform tape backups of Exchange data strictly for the purpose of meeting retention policies — but ensure that you perform the backups often enough to meet your organization's stated requirements.

Tape retention policies are, unfortunately, only partly related to technical issues. For legal reasons, some organizations must retain data, including e-mail data, for extended periods. Other organizations, to avoid the legal hassles associated with the subpoenaing of data, choose to dump their backups almost as quickly as they are created; this strategy may get you in a lot of trouble if that data is ever required.

For the system administrator, there is only one issue. Your users need to understand the implications for data recovery of whatever retention schedule is implemented. If legal niceties aren't an issue in your organization, I recommend that you retain daily backups for the last two weeks and one weekly full backup for up to a month or even up to a year, depending on your level of comfort.

In larger or publicly held organizations, you should consult with someone who is responsible for data retention and/or regulatory compliance. I have a basic tape rotation schedule I recommend that provides the operation for very good recoverability for a year's worth of historical data, but as time passes by the exact date that you can recover is less specific. Table 19.1 shows how to label a series of tapes for this rotation schedule.

Naturally, this backup rotation is very simple and assumes that you perform full backups nightly and only Monday through Friday, but it can be adopted for your needs.

Another backup method that is becoming popular is to use the Windows Backup utility and back up to a BKF file rather than to tape and then to keep the two most recent backups on the server's local disk. The advantage of this method is that it is very quick to restore a recent backup file. However, if you use this method, you should save the BKF files on a different Windows disk volume than the one on which the transaction logs or databases are located, and you should make backup copies of the BKF files to tape as part of your normal backup procedures.

TABLE 19.1:   Sample Exchange Backup Rotation Schedule

TAPE LABEL	PURPOSE OR USAGE
Monday - Even	Tape used on Monday if the day of the week is even
Monday - Odd	Tape used on Monday if the day of the week is odd
Tuesday - Even	Tape used on Tuesday if the day of the week is even
Tuesday - Odd	Tape used on Tuesday if the day of the week is odd
Wednesday - Even	Tape used on Wednesday if the day of the week is even
Wednesday - Odd	Tape used on Wednesday if the day of the week is odd
Thursday - Even	Tape used on Thursday if the day of the week is even
Thursday - Odd	Tape used on Thursday if the day of the week is odd
Friday - 1	Tape used on first Friday of the month
Friday - 2	Tape used on second Friday of the month
Friday - 3	Tape used on third Friday of the month
Friday - 4	Tape used on fourth Friday of the month
Friday - 5	Tape used on fifth Friday of the month
January–December	Create one tape for each month of the year. Use this tape on or about the first of the month as a long-term archive.

Using Windows Backup to Run Exchange Backups

Many third-party software utilities are available that include an Exchange agent capable of performing online backups of Exchange databases. In the examples for this chapter, I am going to use the Windows 2003 Backup utility rather than one of the third-party utilities. Note that this will not work for Windows Server 2008. Let's go through an exercise of backing up the Exchange databases to a backup (BKF) file for a server.

PERFORMING A WINDOWS BACKUP

To run a Windows Backup, launch the Windows Backup utility (ntbackup.exe), switch to the Backup tab, and navigate through the tree to the Microsoft Exchange Server container. An example of this is shown in Figure 19.2; in this example, I have checked the entire Microsoft Information Store object, which will include all storage groups and databases.

If you select a specific storage group in the tree, you can view the mailbox or public folder databases in that storage group in the right-hand pane of the Windows Backup utility. In

Figure 19.2, the entry in the Backup Media Or File Name box is `C:\January27-Full-When Backup.bkf` (the name is not completely visible in the box) — I am backing up to a disk file rather than to a tape. Do not select System State in the directory listing tree if you are also backing up Exchange databases. System state backups should be performed separately.

FIGURE 19.2

Selecting the Microsoft Information Store object for backup

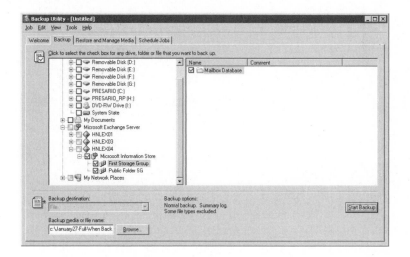

When you click the Start Backup button, you are presented with the Backup Job Information dialog box. From this box, you must give the backup set a description and specify if you are overwriting the existing backup media. Be careful about appending to an existing backup file; if this is not what you intended to do, the backup file may grow until you run out of disk space. The description is important when you get ready to perform a restore of a database, so make sure the Backup Description and the If The Media Is Overwritten, Use This Label To Identify The Media boxes both include descriptive text.

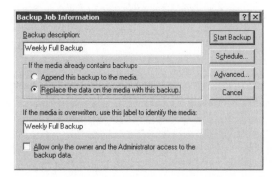

If you click the Advanced button in the Backup Job Information dialog box, you will see the Advanced Backup Options dialog box. Almost everything on this dialog box is irrelevant for

Exchange backups except for the Backup Type drop-down list. For Exchange backups, you can select Normal, Copy, Incremental, or Differential from the Backup Type drop-down list. There is a Daily selection in this drop-down list, but it has no function for Exchange.

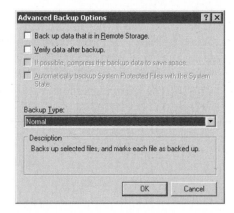

The Schedule button in the Backup Job Information dialog box allows you to define a schedule for this backup to run. If you click the Schedule button, the first thing you have to do is to save the current backup selections to a backup selection script file (BKS). This file will be used when the ntbackup.exe program is executed by the Windows Task Scheduler service.

You must also provide a service account and password under which the scheduled job will run. The user account that you specify must have the right to log on as a service and it must have the rights to run backups on the Exchange server. Once you have specified a service account, you see the Schedule Data tab of the Scheduled Job Options dialog box and are prompted for the job name of the scheduled task.

By default, the job is scheduled to run immediately, but you can click the Properties button on the Schedule Data property page and view the Schedule settings. In the following example, I have scheduled this backup job to run every Friday evening at 8:00PM.

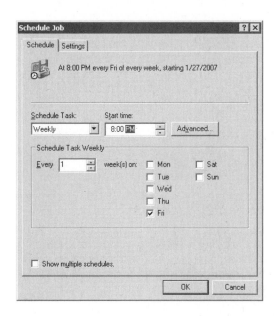

This wizard will schedule a command to run at the time you specify and under the security context of the account you specified. Here is the command line for the weekly backup job that I just scheduled:

```
C:\Windows\system32\ntbackup.exe backup "@C:\Documents and↵
Settings\Administrator.VOLCANOSURFB\Local Settings\Application↵
Data\Microsoft\Windows NT\NTBackup\data\WeeklyFullBackup.bks" /n↵
"Weekly Full Backup" /d "Weekly Full Backup" /n "Weekly Full Backup"↵
/v:no /r:no /rs:no /hc:off /m normal /j "Weekly Full Backup" /l:s↵
/f "c:\January27-Full-Backup.bkf"
```

Once you save the scheduled task data, you can see the scheduled jobs in Control Panel ➢ Scheduled Tasks. An example is shown in Figure 19.3. From this dialog box, you can also right-click any of these tasks and choose Run to start the job immediately.

FIGURE 19.3
Viewing scheduled backups in the Scheduled Tasks control panel

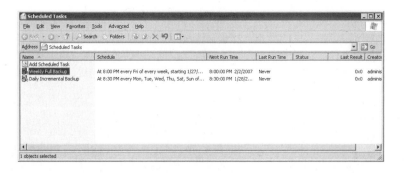

PERFORMING REMOTE BACKUPS

The Windows 2003 Backup utility and third-party backup utilities can back up Exchange Server 2007 running on remote Windows Server 2003, but after Service Pack 1 was released, an additional limitation was put in place. On each server you want to back up remotely using a streaming backup, you must enable this via the Registry.

Browse to the following Registry key:

```
HKLM\System\CurrentControlSetServices\MSExchangeIS\ParametersSystem
```

Locate or create a `REG_DWORD` value called `Enable Remote Streaming Backup` and set this value to 1. This will enable remote streaming backups for this Exchange server.

Verifying Exchange Backups

The best way to verify a backup is to confirm that it restores properly. You certainly don't have time to do that every day, but I recommend that every few months you select a database and restore it to a recovery storage group just for practice.

However, you should do some quick verification tasks as part of your daily operations. The first is to examine the backup program's log of the backup. This serves a couple of purposes, not the least of which is finding possible errors. Figure 19.4 shows the backup log from the Windows Backup utility for a backup of a mailbox and public folder database.

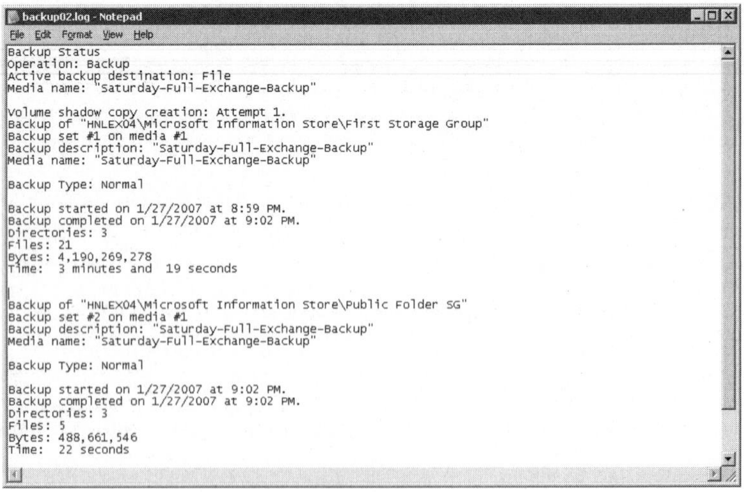


```
Backup Status
Operation: Backup
Active backup destination: File
Media name: "Saturday-Full-Exchange-Backup"

Volume shadow copy creation: Attempt 1.
Backup of "HNLEX04\Microsoft Information Store\First Storage Group"
Backup set #1 on media #1
Backup description: "Saturday-Full-Exchange-Backup"
Media name: "Saturday-Full-Exchange-Backup"

Backup Type: Normal

Backup started on 1/27/2007 at 8:59 PM.
Backup completed on 1/27/2007 at 9:02 PM.
Directories: 3
Files: 21
Bytes: 4,190,269,278
Time:  3 minutes and  19 seconds


Backup of "HNLEX04\Microsoft Information Store\Public Folder SG"
Backup set #2 on media #1
Backup description: "Saturday-Full-Exchange-Backup"
Media name: "Saturday-Full-Exchange-Backup"

Backup Type: Normal

Backup started on 1/27/2007 at 9:02 PM.
Backup completed on 1/27/2007 at 9:02 PM.
Directories: 3
Files: 5
Bytes: 488,661,546
Time:  22 seconds
```

FIGURE 19.4
Sample backup log

There are a few things you should note from this backup report:

- The backup report contains no error messages or warnings. This should help you to sleep better.
- The backup report indicates that what you wanted to back up (the First Storage Group storage groups and the Public Folder SG) was backed up.
- The amount of data that was backed up corresponds with the amount of data that you believe should be backed up.

◆ And finally, you can see the amount of time the backup took versus the amount of data. In this example, the mailbox database was 4GB and it took just over three minutes to back up. That is about 1.3GB per minute. That is not really great backup throughput, but sufficient for a low-end test system.

The final place you should check for information about backups is the Windows Application event log. Figure 19.5 shows the Application event log immediately after an online backup. The source column shows ntbackup, ESE BACKUP, and ESE-related events that are all part of the backup process.

FIGURE 19.5

Event viewer showing backup-related events

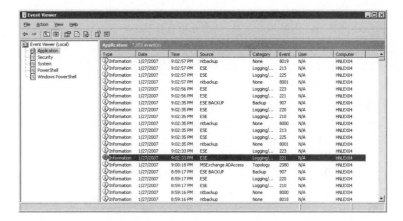

As you scan through the log entries created by the backup process, you will find that many of these events are just informational, such as an event that lets you know the backup program is starting or has completed. Events from the source ntbackup are reports of this kind, and events from ESE and ESE BACKUP are reporting on the actual Exchange backup process being used.

There are two events, though, that you should watch for and you should see for each database that you are backing up. You will see these events for any streaming backup of an Exchange database regardless of which database you are using. These events are from the ESE source and are event IDs 220 and 221. They are shown side by side in Figure 19.6. Event ID 220 indicates that the backup of a specific database (named in the Description field) is now beginning, and event ID 221 indicates that the backup of that specific database has completed. The actual text of the event says "Ending the backup of the file," but it means that the backup was successful.

After all of the Exchange databases in a selected storage group are backed up, you will see events indicating that the transaction logs for a particular storage group are being backed up and then purged. This is another indication that all of the databases in a particular storage group have been backed up successfully. Figure 19.7 shows ESE events 223 and 224. Event ID 223 shows you the transaction logs that are being backed up for the storage group specified in the Description field.

Event ID 224 indicates that the backup logs have been backed up and they are now being purged. Both event ID 223 and 224 are good events because they indicate successful operations. Table 19.2 shows the ESE and ESE BACKUP event IDs that you look for during an online backup. Usually to completely understand what is being backed up, you will need to read the Description field to see what database, transaction log, or storage group is affected.

FIGURE 19.6
Important ESE backup events

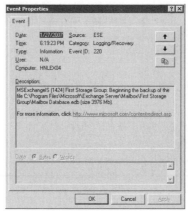

FIGURE 19.7
ESE backup events related to transaction logs

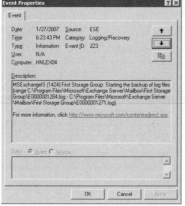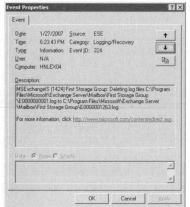

You can also view the backup status of individual databases using the Exchange Management Console or the Exchange Management Shell. In Figure 19.1, earlier in this chapter, I showed that you can see the last time an incremental or differential backup was performed on a mailbox database. You can also use the EMS cmdlet `Get-MailboxDatabase` and the `-Status` option to retrieve database status information. Here is an example:

```
Get-MailboxDatabase "HNLEX04\Mailbox Database" -Status |↵
Format-List Name,Server,*backup*,Mounted
Name                            : Mailbox Database
Server                          : HNLEX04
BackupInProgress                : False
LastFullBackup                  : 1/27/2007 8:59:17 PM
LastIncrementalBackup           : 1/28/2007 1:06:22 PM
RetainDeletedItemsUntilBackup   : False
Mounted                         : True
```

TABLE 19.2:   Exchange Database Engine Backup Events

EVENT ID	SOURCE	DESCRIPTION
210	ESE	Indicates that a full backup of a specified storage group is beginning.
211	ESE	Indicates that an incremental or differential backup of the specified storage group is starting.
220	ESE	Indicates that a backup of a specified database is starting.
907	ESE BACKUP	Indicates that the backup data transfer method is shared memory.
221	ESE	Indicates that a backup of the specified database is completed.
223	ESE	Indicates that backup of specified transaction logs is starting.
224	ESE	Indicates that transaction logs for the specified storage group are being purged after successful backup.
213	ESE	Indicates that backup of specified storage group (databases and transaction logs) has completed.

Backup Options for Windows Server 2008

Many Exchange Server administrators who were fond of the Windows Backup utility (myself included) were thrown for a bit of a loop when we installed Exchange Server 2007 SP1 on Windows Server 2008. We found that there was no local backup utility to back up Exchange Server. (There is, of course, a Windows Server 2008 backup utility.)

Exchange Server provides a series of APIs for a backup vendor to use when performing a streaming backup so that they can request the database one page at a time. Those APIs still exist in Exchange Server 2007, but the underlying Windows 2008 Backup utility does not take advantage of them.

One difference between Exchange Server 2007 SP1 on Windows Server 2008 and Exchange Server running as part of the Windows Small Business Server (SBS) 2008 bundle is that with SBS this backup capability is included and the Windows Backup utility will be able to perform streaming backups.

The ability to perform a remote streaming backup using the Windows Backup utility has also been removed. I have performed remote backups of Exchange Server 2007 on Windows Server 2008 using the Windows Backup utility on Windows Server 2003, but this generates errors and the backup does not complete properly, so I recommend you find a supported solution.

My analysis of this removal of built-in backup support is that Microsoft would like to drive many Windows Backup users toward its new Microsoft System Center Data Protection Manager (DPM) solution. Microsoft states that you have two options for backing up Exchange Server 2007 on Windows Server 2008:

◆ Acquire a third-party backup utility that can perform local and/or remote streaming backups of Exchange Server. For third-party utilities that perform remote backups, the utility must have an agent that runs on each remote server.

◆ Use a third-party VSS-based backup application that performs database snapshots and that is Exchange Server 2007–aware. The VSS-based utility must be able not only to perform the backup of the data but also to verify the integrity of the database.

See the Exchange Team's blog for more information at the following URL:

`http://msexchangeteam.com/archive/2008/03/05/448338.aspx`

Recovering Mailboxes and Items in Mailboxes

Although a deleted item or mailbox is not exactly a national emergency, the user who is being affected may think it is pretty darn important. Recovering quickly from even simple problems like a deleted message or a deleted mailbox is important for good relations with your user community.

Recovering Deleted Items

When users delete an item from their mailbox, the item is moved to the Deleted Items folder. When the item is deleted from the Deleted Items folder, it is moved into the deleted items cache, where it is kept for the Keep Deleted Items retention period. By default, this is configured at 14 days for each mailbox database; this is configured for the entire mailbox database on the mailbox database's Limits property page (shown in Figure 19.8).

FIGURE 19.8
Limits property page for a mailbox database

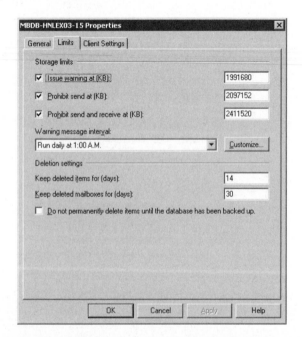

Once the Keep Deleted Items period has expired, the item is permanently deleted during the mailbox database's online maintenance process.

A user can retrieve something from the deleted item cache using Outlook by selecting the Deleted Items folder and then choosing Tools ➢ Recover Deleted Items. This will launch the Recover Deleted Items From dialog box (see Figure 19.9); from here you can select the item you want to recover and then click the Recover Selected Items button on the toolbar. This is the button that has an envelope icon with a small blue arrow on top of it.

FIGURE 19.9
Recovering a deleted item

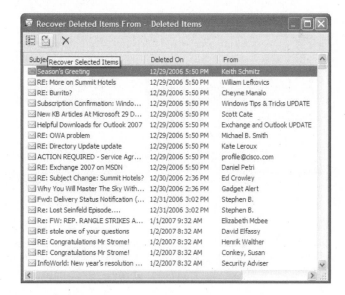

Once the item is recovered, it will be restored to the Deleted Items folder. If the user is in Outlook cached Exchange mode, the item may take a minute or two to reappear locally.

There is also a type of delete called a *hard delete*, in which a message bypasses the Deleted Items folder. This can happen when the user highlights the message and presses Shift+Delete. A hard delete can also occur if a user downloads messages using a POP3 or IMAP4 client and then deletes them from the server. When a hard delete is used, you cannot restore the message from the Deleted Items folder. You have to restore it from the folder from which the message was deleted.

If the user hard-deleted the message from his Inbox, the Tools ➢ Recover Deleted Items menu choice is not available by default in Outlook 2003 and earlier. To make it available, you can use a little Registry trick. On the client computer, locate the following Registry key:

```
HKLM\SOFTWARE\Microsoft\Exchange\Client\Options
```

In this key, create a REG_DWORD value called `DumpsterAlwaysOn` and set it to 1. Restart Outlook and the Tools ➢ Recover Deleted Items menu choice should now be available.

If the item cannot be recovered using one of these methods, the only other choice available to the administrator may be to perform a recovery to a recovery storage group and restore the mail data that way.

Recovering Deleted Mailboxes

Occasionally after a mailbox is deleted, someone comes to the IT department and says that they need it back. This might be because the user did not really leave or there might be something important in the mailbox that must be recovered. By default, each mailbox database is configured with a deleted mailbox recovery time of 30 days. This is configured on the Limits property page (shown previously in Figure 19.8) in the Keep Deleted Mailboxes For (Days) property.

A mailbox can be recovered and reconnected to a user account, as long as that account does not have a mailbox assigned to it already. Mailboxes are reconnected using the Disconnected Mailbox subcontainer of the Recipient Configuration work center in the EMC. When you select this container, you then click the Connect to Server task in the Actions pane to specify the mailbox server on which the deleted mailbox exists.

Figure 19.10 shows the Disconnected Mailbox subcontainer and a list of deleted mailboxes in the Results pane. To reconnect a deleted mailbox, highlight the mailbox and choose the Connect task from the Actions pane.

FIGURE 19.10
Reconnecting a deleted mailbox

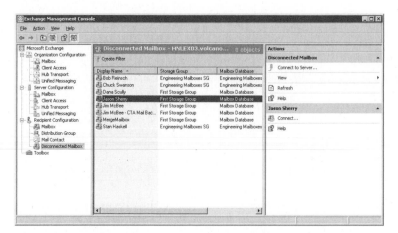

When you choose Connect, you will be taken through the Connect Mailbox Wizard. This is very similar to the wizard that runs when you create a mailbox. The Introduction screen asks if this is a user, room, equipment, or linked mailbox. The Mailbox Settings page allows you to specify the user account to which you are reconnecting the mailbox as well as the Exchange alias, the managed folder mailbox policy, and the Exchange ActiveSync policy. The Mailbox Settings page of the wizard is shown in Figure 19.11.

The mailbox reconnection could also have been done from the EMS using the Connect-Mailbox cmdlet. You need to retrieve the mailbox's unique GUID, though. This can be retrieved using the Get-MailboxStatistics cmdlet. Here is an example using the Connect-Mailbox cmdlet:

```
Connect-Mailbox -Identity 'e0b25cd9-b6b6-4214-9a1f-e0e1ddbea257'↵
-Database 'HNLEX03.volcanosurfboards.com\First Storage Group\Mailbox Database'↵
-User 'volcanosurfboards\Bob.Reinsch' -Alias 'Bob.Reinsch'↵
-ManagedFolderMailboxPolicy 'Executives Managed Folder Mailbox Policy'↵
-ActiveSyncMailboxPolicy 'Strict ActiveSync policy'
```

FIGURE 19.11
Specifying the user account to which the mailbox will be connected

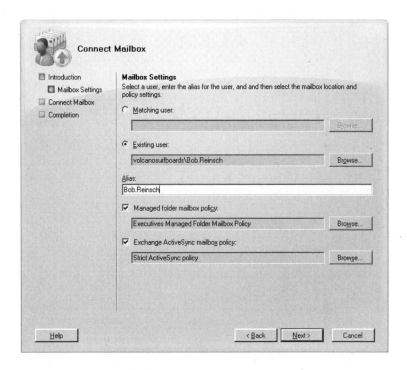

Restoring an Exchange Database

Restoring an Exchange Server 2007 database is not a terribly difficult process once you understand a few basic rules. This section goes through the restoration process using the Windows 2003 Backup utility and restores the default mailbox database (called Mailbox Database). You might need to restore a database from backup if the production database has become corrupted, if the disk holding the database has become corrupted, or if the entire server failed. Note that this process and the steps involved will vary greatly depending on the backup software that you use.

Let's take as an example a situation in which a mailbox database needs to be restored. The first thing you need to know is what the backup schedule is and what tapes are available. In this example, you perform a nightly full backup and then an incremental backup at noon each day. The problem that requires the restoration occurs on Tuesday at 3:00 in the afternoon. In this example, you also will also assume that you have all of the transaction log files that have been created since the last incremental backup.

Put together a checklist of things you want to do prior to starting this restoration of the database named Mailbox Database:

1. Ensure that there is sufficient disk space for the database to be restored.

2. Ensure that there is sufficient disk space for the temporary files.

3. Find the backup media for the Monday night full backup and the Tuesday noon incremental backup.

4. Dismount the mailbox store if mounted.

   If there is a current database file in the database folder, I recommend that you rename it just in case you need it in the future.

5. Verify that there is not a recovery storage group somewhere in the organization that has this particular database configured. If there is, the database will be restored to the recovery storage group, not the production location.

Because you are using the Windows Backup utility, you will run that program and then select the Restore and Manage Media tab. Then, in the left pane of the Backup utility, you must find the backup media and set you wish to restore. The first set you need to restore is the full backup set from Monday night. Figure 19.12 shows the Windows Backup utility and the selected information to be restored. Notice that both the Mailbox Database and the Log Files selections have been chosen from the Monday Night - Full Backup set.

FIGURE 19.12
Restoring the database named Mailbox Database and associated log files

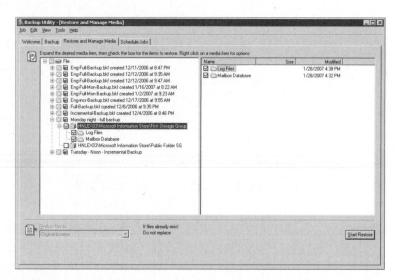

When you have finished selecting the mailbox database and transaction log files, click the Start Restore button. You are presented with the Check Backup File Location dialog box because you are restoring from a BKF file instead of a tape. If the correct file is not specified, you can click the Browse button and locate the correct BKF file.

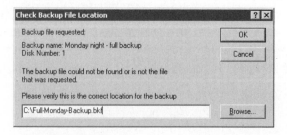

Next the Restoring Database Store dialog box appears, where you can direct the restore to an alternate server and specify the temporary file location for the restored log files. The transaction log files will not be restored to the production transaction log location. Take note of the temporary location for the log and patch files because you will need it again when you restore the incremental backup files.

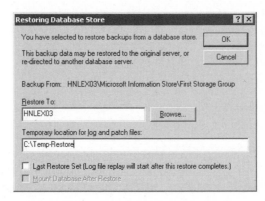

Notice the check boxes on the bottom of the Restoring Database Store dialog box. These are labeled "Last Restore Set (Log File Replay Will Start After This Restore Completes)" and "Mount Database After Restore." Because you have another restore set to go after this restore, you want to leave these check boxes cleared.

The restore process is shown on the Restore Progress information screen. It may take a while depending on the size of the database. Generally, restoring from tape will take twice as long as the backup took, so you should factor that into your restore estimates.

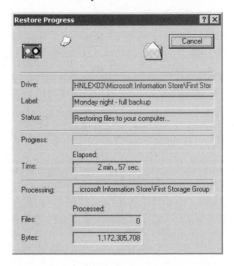

During and after this restore, there will not be much of interest in either the Application event log or the backup log. The Windows Backup utility's log only has some information about the storage group name to which the restore was performed and the amount of data. An example is shown here:

```
-----------------------------------------------
Restore Status
Operation: Restore
Backup of "HNLEX03\Microsoft Information Store\First Storage Group",
 Restored to"HNLEX03\Microsoft Information Store\First Storage Group"
Backup set #1 on media #1
Backup description: "Monday night - full backup"
Restore started on 1/28/2007 at 4:59 PM.
Restore completed on 1/28/2007 at 5:08 PM.
Directories: 3
Files: 20
Bytes: 3,648,996,564
Time:  8 minutes and 30 seconds
-----------------------------------------------
```

Once this backup completes, you have to repeat the process. Except this time, you select the incremental backup that was made on Tuesday at noon. This backup set will only have log files because it was an incremental backup.

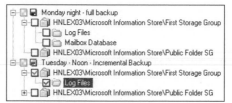

When you click the Start Restore button, you will need to provide the same path to the log files and backup files. In the Restoring Database Store dialog box, you want to make sure that the Last Restore Set (Log File Replay Will Start After This Restore Completes) and the Mount Database After Restore check boxes are checked. This will automatically start the transaction log replay process.

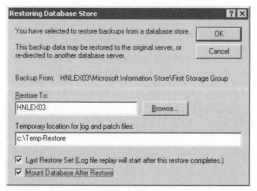

When the restore process begins, it will run much quicker than the full restore did because all it will be doing is restoring the transaction logs since the previous night.

Once the restore is complete, the Application event log will begin to get interesting. Figure 19.13 shows event ID 204. This event indicates that the transaction log replay is beginning and that the process will start with the log files restored from tape (the log files from the full backup and then the incremental backup) that are found in the temporary restore directory.

FIGURE 19.13
Restore process starts replaying log files

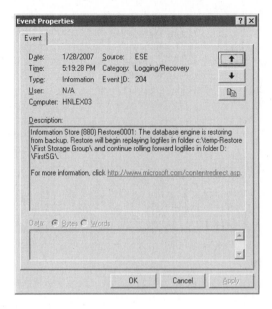

The log files found in the temporary restore folder will get the database restored up through the incremental backup that occurred at noon on Tuesday. However, in this example, you have all of the transactions that have occurred up through the time you had to restore the database. So the transaction replay (rolling forward) will continue in the production transaction log folder. Figure 19.14 shows event ID 301, which shows the current transaction log that is being replayed. The figure shows that the most recent transaction log (E00.LOG) is being replayed.

FIGURE 19.14
Replaying a transaction log

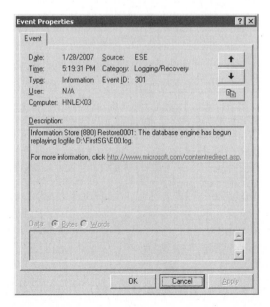

Using the Recovery Storage Group

One of the nicest additions to Exchange 2003 was the recovery storage group feature; this feature allows an administrator to create the recovery storage group (RSG) and add existing mailbox databases to the list of mailbox databases that can be restored to the RSG. When an Exchange-aware backup utility attempts to restore one of the databases in the RSG, the database is restored to the RSG rather than to the production location. This feature is also supported on Exchange 2007 Mailbox servers, but there is no graphical user interface for creating the RSG and adding mailbox databases to it.

Note that the recovery storage group can only be used when restoring mailbox databases, not public folder databases.

RSG management in the release-to-manufacturing version of Exchange 2007 is handled from within the EMS or from within the Exchange Database Recovery Management Wizard in the Toolbox work center. Here are some important points about RSGs to keep in mind:

◆ Restoring an RSG does not interfere with normal Exchange operations.

◆ An RSG can be restored to any Exchange 2007 Mailbox server, not just the server on which it originally existed.

◆ RSGs can be used to restore a mailbox from a previous backup so that a mailbox, folder, or item can be recovered.

◆ RSGs can be used to verify the integrity of backups without building a recovery system.

Preparing to Use a Recovery Storage Group

Before you use an RSG, there are a few things that you should consider and prepare. This includes ensuring that you have sufficient disk space and that you understand the limitations of the RSG.

You can create only one RSG on an Exchange 2007 Mailbox server. This RSG can contain Exchange 2007 mailbox databases from any storage group on any server in the entire organization, but at any one time an RSG can contain only mailbox databases from one original storage group. Exchange 2003 mailbox databases are not supported.

The Exchange 2007 Mailbox server on which you create the RSG must have a disk volume with sufficient disk space to support the database(s) to be restored and the transaction logs, and to allow creation of temporary files that might be necessary during the restore. When you create the RSG, you must specify the path for the transaction logs and system files; these cannot be changed later.

A mailbox database that is restored to the RSG cannot be accessed by end users, from Outlook, or from Outlook Web Access. The mailbox data can be retrieved only by using the `Restore-Mailbox` cmdlet.

Databases in an RSG cannot be mounted automatically, they do not have online maintenance performed on them, message records management policies do not apply, neither LCR nor CCR applies to them, and they cannot be backed up.

Restoring a Mailbox Database to a Recovery Storage Group

Let's go through a sample recovery of a mailbox database using an RSG and the Exchange Database Recovery Management tool. In this example, a user has deleted something really important from his mailbox and he did so at 10:00 Tuesday morning. For whatever reason, you are unable to undelete the item. For this restore, you will use the previous night's (Monday's) full backup. You don't need the noon incremental backup because by that time the user had deleted the message. The LCR or CCR copies of the database would not do any good either because they are up-to-date copies of the production database. So you need to restore the Monday night backup to a recovery storage group.

The first step now is to create an RSG and put the mailbox database into it. Though you can do this from the EMS, it is much simpler from the Exchange Database Recovery Management tool. From the Toolbox work center, launch the Exchange Database Recovery Management tool and it will start through the Troubleshooting Assistant. Like most tools based on the Troubleshooting Assistant, you need to first go to the Welcome screen and provide a label to identify your activity, the Exchange server name, and a domain controller name.

Enter Server and User Information

Enter an identifying label for this activity: `Recovering Mike Brown's mailbox`

☐ Perform analysis of raw data files (ignore server and credentials entries below)

Exchange server name (required): `hnlex04`

Domain controller name (required): `HNLDC01`

When you have entered this information, at the bottom of the screen click Next.

The first screen that really tells you that you are managing databases is the Select One Of The Following Tasks screen. In the Manage Recovery Storage Group section, click the Create A Recovery Storage Group link.

Manage Recovery Storage Group
Select one of the tasks below to manage the recovery storage group.

➡ Create a recovery storage group

From the Select The Storage Group To Link With The Recovery Storage Group, select the storage group that holds the database you want to restore. In this case, it will be the SG-HNLEX04-01.

Select the Storage Group to Link with the Recovery Storage Group

Server name: hnlex04

```
SG-HNLEX04-01
SG-HNLEX04-02
SG-HNLEX04-03
SG-HNLEX04-04
```

The recovery storage group is linked to an existing storage group. Only databases from the linked storage group can be mounted in the recovery storage group.

◀ Previous   ▶ Next

When you click Next, you are taken to the Create The Recovery Storage Group screen (shown in Figure 19.15) where you provide the name for the RSG as well as paths for the transaction logs, system path, and checkpoint file. The wizard will make some recommendations based on the original paths but you can change that by clicking the Browse buttons to select a new location for the files. Just make sure that the locations you are selecting for the RSG will have enough disk space to support the restored database. When you're finished filling out the Create The Recovery Storage Group screen, click the Create The Recovery Storage Group link at the bottom of the page.

FIGURE 19.15
Specifying the paths for the recovery storage group

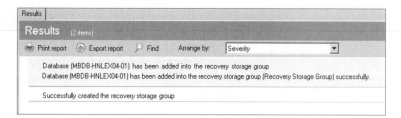

On the Create The Recovery Storage Group Result screen, you can verify that the RSG has been created and the database named Mailbox Database has been assigned to this RSG.

Once you have returned to the Tasks Center screen of the Troubleshooting Assistant, you can manage the RSG and the databases you have restored. Figure 19.16 shows the Select One Of The Following Tasks screen.

Before you can do anything else, though, you need to restore the database to the RSG. The good news now is that the procedure is exactly the same for restoring to the RSG as it is if you are restoring to the production location of the database. The backup software does not have to be told anything new. Select the database you want to restore, and because there is an RSG that holds that database, the Exchange information store service will automatically put the database in the RSG. This means that you do not need to interfere with the production database at all.

The preceding tasks in the wizard can be accomplished from the EMS, although if you create and manage RSGs infrequently you will probably want to stick to the wizard. To perform the recovery from the EMS, you would need to create a storage group whose type is an RSG. Here is an example:

```
New-StorageGroup -Name "Recovery Storage Group" -Server HNLEX03↵
-LogFolderPath C:\RSG -SystemFolderPath C:\RSG -Recovery
```

FIGURE 19.16
Recovery storage group
management tasks

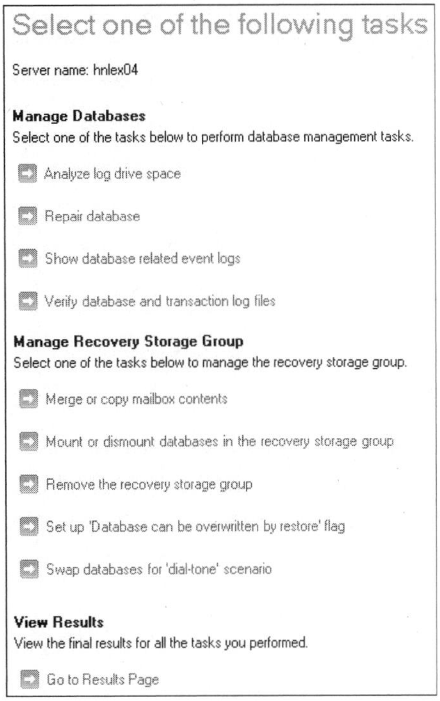

Select one of the following tasks

Server name: hnlex04

Manage Databases
Select one of the tasks below to perform database management tasks.

- Analyze log drive space

- Repair database

- Show database related event logs

- Verify database and transaction log files

Manage Recovery Storage Group
Select one of the tasks below to manage the recovery storage group.

- Merge or copy mailbox contents

- Mount or dismount databases in the recovery storage group

- Remove the recovery storage group

- Set up 'Database can be overwritten by restore' flag

- Swap databases for 'dial-tone' scenario

View Results
View the final results for all the tasks you performed.

- Go to Results Page

Next you need to assign the mailbox database to the RSG you have just created. Use the database name of the production database that you are restoring:

```
New-MailboxDatabase -MailboxDatabaseToRecover "Mailbox Database"↵
-StorageGroup "HNLEX03\Recovery Storage Group" -EDBFilePath C:\RSG
```

Next, you need to set this database so that you can allow the file to be restored. You would use this cmdlet:

```
Set-MailboxDatabase "HNLEX03\Recovery Storage Group\Mailbox Database"↵
-AllowFileRestore
```

Finally, after you restore the mailbox database, you will need to mount it. The command to do that would be as follows:

```
Mount-Database "HNLEX03\Recovery Storage Group\Mailbox Database"
```

Recovering Information from a Recovery Storage Group

As mentioned earlier, you cannot access an RSG from either Outlook or Outlook Web Access, so you need to use either the `Recover-Mailbox` EMS cmdlet or the Disaster Recovery Management tool. You restored the appropriate backup to the Exchange server and now you can use the Mount Or Dismount Databases In The Recovery Storage Group task shown previously in Figure 19.16.

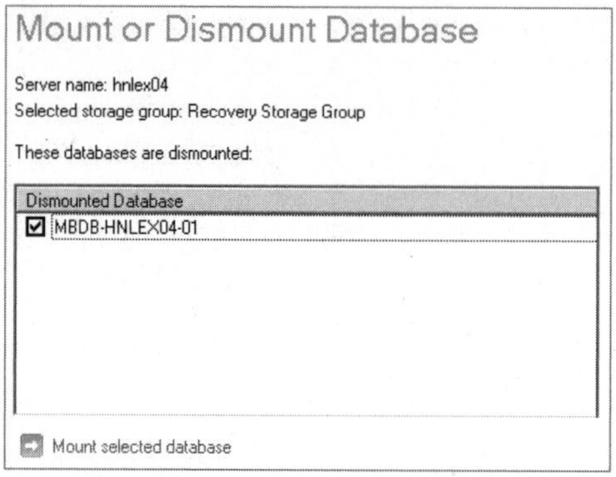

Once the database is mounted, you can copy or merge data back into the user's mailbox. From the Select One Of The Following Tasks screen, choose the Merge Or Copy Mailbox Contents link and on the next page click the Gather Merge Information link. On the Select Merge Options page, click the Show Advanced Options link so that you can see more detailed information about mailbox matching, date range filters, subject filter, and the start and end filter dates. An example is shown in Figure 19.17.

FIGURE 19.17
Selecting merge options

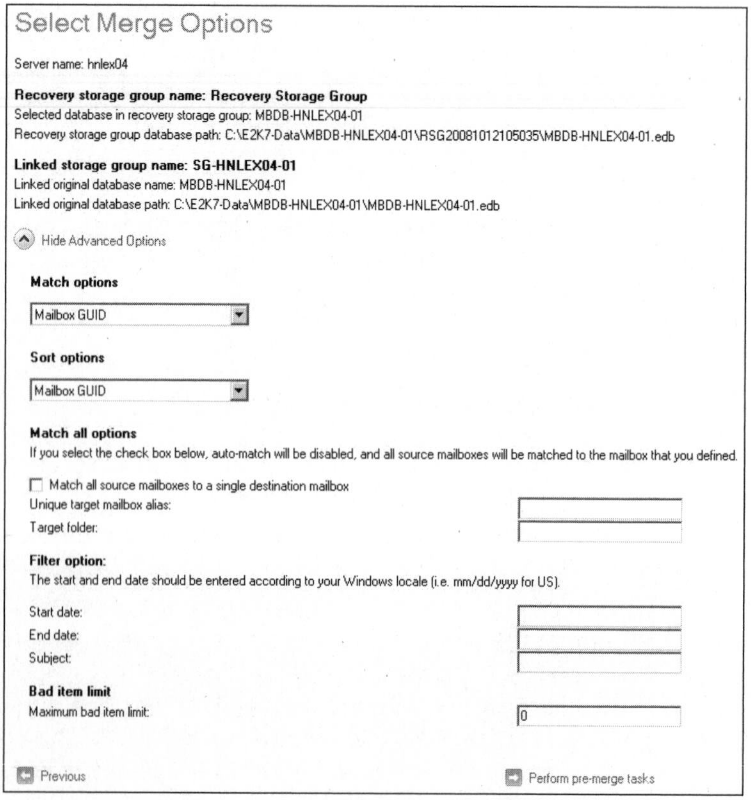

If you are planning to merge data from the RSG database into the production database, the most accurate way to match up a mailbox in the RSG database with one in the production database is to use the mailbox's GUID.

Notice also in Figure 19.17 that if you select the Match All Source Mailboxes To A Destination Mailbox check box, you can specify the alias of a mailbox to which you want *all* of the data copied. This is useful if you don't want to merge the data back into the original mailbox. When you have made your selections on the Select Merge Options screen, the next step is to click the Perform Pre-Merge Tasks link.

The next screen is the Select Mailboxes To Copy Or Merge screen; this is shown in Figure 19.18. From here, you can select the mailboxes that were found in the recovery storage group whose data you want copied or merged into the target mailbox. In this example, select the user who deleted the important message and absolutely has to get it back.

FIGURE 19.18
Selecting the mailboxes to be merged

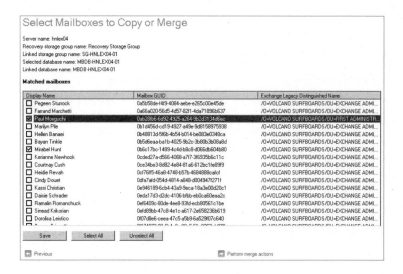

After selecting the mailboxes to merge or copy, click the Perform Merge Actions link to start the merge.

You could also have accomplished the same thing with the `Restore-Mailbox` EMS cmdlet but with more options, such as restoring only items in a certain date range. Here is an example of restoring a single mailbox and only items between 1/25/07 and 1/28/07. In this instance, you are restoring the data to a folder in the user's own mailbox, called Recovered Data:

```
Restore-Mailbox "Russ Kaufmann" -RSGDatabase "Recovery Storage↵
Group\Mailbox Database" -StartDate "01/25/07" -EndDate "01/28/07"↵
-TargetFolder "Recovered Data" -RSGMailbox "russ kaufmann"
Confirm
Are you sure you want to perform this action?
Recovering mailbox content from the mailbox 'Russ Kaufmann' in the recovery
database 'HNLEX03\Recovery Storage Group\Mailbox Database' into the mailbox for
'Russ Kaufmann (Russ.Kaufmann\somorita.com)'. The operation can take a long
time.
[Y] Yes [A] Yes to All [N] No [L] No to All [S] Suspend [?] Help
```

```
(default is "Y")                    :y
Identity                            : volcanosurfboards.com/VolcanoSurfboards/
Russ Kaufmann
DistinguishedName                   : CN=Russ Kaufmann,
OU=VolcanoSurfboards,DC=volcanosurfboards,DC=com
DisplayName                         : Russ Kaufmann
Alias                               : Russ.Kaufmann
LegacyExchangeDN                    : /o=Volcano Surfboards/ou=Exchange
Administrative Group (FYDIBOHF23SPDLT)/cn=Recipients/cn=Russ.Kaufmann
PrimarySmtpAddress                  : Russ.Kaufmann\commatsomorita.com
SourceServer                        : HNLEX03.volcanosurfboards.com
SourceDatabase                      : HNLEX03\Recovery Storage Group\Mailbox Database
SourceGlobalCatalog                 : HNLDC01
SourceDomainController              :
TargetGlobalCatalog: HNLDC01
TargetDomainController              :
TargetMailbox                       : volcanosurfboards.com/VolcanoSurfboards/
Russ Kaufmann
TargetServer                        : HNLEX03.volcanosurfboards.com
TargetDatabase                      : HNLEX03\First Storage Group\Mailbox Database
MailboxSize                         : 9868B
IsResourceMailbox                   : False
SIDUsedInMatch                      :
SMTPProxies                         :
SourceManager                       :
SourceDirectReports                 :
SourcePublicDelegates               :
SourcePublicDelegatesBL             :
SourceAltRecipient                  :
SourceAltRecipientBL                :
SourceDeliverAndRedirect            :
MatchedTargetNTAccountDN            :
IsMatchedNTAccountMailboxEnabled    :
MatchedContactsDNList               :
TargetNTAccountDNToCreate           :
TargetManager                       :
TargetDirectReports                 :
TargetPublicDelegates               :
TargetPublicDelegatesBL             :
TargetAltRecipient                  :
TargetAltRecipientBL                :
TargetDeliverAndRedirect            :
Options                             : Default
SourceForestCredential              :
TargetForestCredential              :
TargetFolder                        : \Recovered Data\Recovered Data
- Russ Kaufmann - 1/28/2007 10:02:34 PM
RsgMailboxGuid                      : dfafe65a-4dcf-45e8-812f-60736cd11216
```

```
RsgMailboxLegacyExchangeDN       : /O=VOLCANO SURFBOARDS/OU=EXCHANGE
ADMINISTRATIVE GROUP (FYDIBOHF23SPDLT)/CN=RECIPIENTS/CN=RUSS.KAUFMANN
RsgMailboxDisplayName            : Russ Kaufmann
RsgDatabaseGuid                  : cde8e7e1-03f7-465b-a705-80a399c64e9a
MoveType                         : Restore
MoveStage                        : Completed
StartTime                        : 1/28/2007 10:02:39 PM
EndTime                          : 1/28/2007 10:02:42 PM
StatusCode                       : 0
StatusMessage                 : This mailbox in the recovery storage group database
    has been restored to the target usermailbox.
```

The result of this is that a folder is created in user Russ Kaufmann's mailbox that has everything from 1/25/07 through 1/28/07. This is shown in Figure 19.19. At this point, the help desk can now assist the user in copying back into the correct folder the very important message that got deleted.

FIGURE 19.19
The Recovered Data folder structure is created.

Cleaning Up After Using a Recovery Storage Group

Restoring data from a backup to a Recovery Storage Group is simple; because the RSG has been created and the appropriate database has been assigned to the RSG, *any* backup utility that supports the Exchange APIs will be able to restore to the RSG. Exchange Server handles restoring the data to the right place. And as long as an RSG exists that contains the database you want to restore, the database will be restored to the RSG, not to the production location.

People often miss the simplicity of this and try to make it more complicated; I know that I did. They expect that Registry keys need to be set or that the backup utility will provide a "RSG restore location" or something. It is not that difficult at all.

However, one thing that does throw people is that once the database is restored to the RSG and the necessary data has been extracted, they fail to actually get rid of the RSG and the database that is mounted in the RSG. This is bad for several reasons; the smallest of these reasons is that you are taking up additional disk space and additional memory to support this mounted database.

The reason that might come back to haunt you, though, is if the RSG and the database remain and then at some point later you need to perform a disaster recovery and restore the *entire* database to the production location. Remember: The restore process will always restore to the RSG, not to the production database.

So when you finish using the RSG, make sure that you dismount the RSG database and remove both it and the RSG. You can do this by dismounting the database in the RSG and then using the Remove The Recovery Storage Group task on the main tasks screen. This takes you through a quick wizard that will remove the database and the RSG for you.

Remove the Recovery Storage Group

Server name: hnlex04

Recovery storage group name: Recovery Storage Group

These databases are dismounted:

MBDB-HNLEX04-01

⬅ Previous   ➡ Remove the recovery storage group

DON'T FORGET TO DELETE THE RSG DATABASE AND LOG FILES

The Remove The Recovery Storage Group task does not delete the RSG database and log files. You must do this manually.

Recovering from Disasters

From a hardware and software perspective, I have already talked about at least 90 percent of the disaster recovery puzzle. If you're an Exchange system administrator and you've protected your servers with redundant hardware, especially interserver redundant hardware, or you can restore any crashed Exchange server under your management, you've pretty much got it made. If you also have to worry about Windows 2003 and you can bring a domain controller or stand-alone server back from the dead with VSS or Automatic Server Recovery (ASR) backups or even clunky, more traditional streaming backups, you're in a good place, too.

All too often the term *disaster recovery* is misused in our industry to mean something as simple as restoring a database. In the big picture, this is not a disaster for most organizations. In this section, I want to talk more about real disasters and disaster recovery.

Disaster recovery adds another dimension to the reliability and availability picture. You have to deal with simultaneous multisystem unavailability, up to and including the sudden disappearance of all or a major part of your server, storage, workstation, and networking systems. The cause of such a disaster can be anything from a terrorist attack to an earthquake, from a building fire to a major power outage or lightning strike.

Disaster recovery isn't fun to think about. There are so many variables, including the potential for astronomical costs, that it's easy to either go bonkers or avoid even thinking about the whole thing. The best way to calm yourself and your boss when disaster recovery rears its ugly head is by building and living by a set of best-possible, cost-realistic strategies that specify what you'll do to avoid disasters and the actions you'll take if disaster strikes.

Disaster Recovery Strategies

Shopping for a disaster recovery solution is a lot like buying a new car. Car salespeople will frequently urge you not to worry about price and just test-drive the car you really want. Before you know it, you have spent a lot of time looking at your ideal car even though you know you can't afford it.

Suppose you take this approach to disaster recovery. You call in a company that specializes in disaster recovery and before you know it, you've got a proposal for a multimillion-dollar solution. The solution, by the way, is usually quite impressive. If only you could afford it.

The first thing you need to consider when developing a disaster recovery strategy is what your organization does and how a disaster might affect what it does. If e-mail and related Exchange services are central to your organization's operation and bottom line, you need a very aggressive disaster recovery strategy. If your organization could do without e-mail for a few days, then a less aggressive strategy should be acceptable.

In building your disaster recovery strategy, don't be driven by unrealistic assessments of the importance of e-mail. And don't take a seat on the curb in discussions about the role of e-mail in your organization. You live with Exchange. You know what users are doing with e-mail, and you hear user complaints when your Exchange system isn't available. Your goal must be to drive e-mail disaster recovery deliberation toward a solution that you are comfortable with — the checkbooks, egos, or misperceptions of your bosses notwithstanding. As strategies are considered, you need to make sure your management clearly understands the limits of each. This is not just to protect yourself, but to set realistic management expectations from the get-go.

PIGGYBACKING E-MAIL ON EXISTING DISASTER RECOVERY STRATEGIES

Unless e-mail is all your organization does, there should be a disaster recovery strategy for other IT functionality. Adding e-mail to an existing strategy can be a relatively inexpensive option. But don't piggyback if you know the strategy won't work for e-mail. I have been in situations where e-mail was both more and less important than other IT functions. Management loved it when I told them that e-mail required a less aggressive disaster recovery strategy. They hated it when I pressed for a more aggressive (more expensive) strategy for e-mail.

I am going to discuss five disaster recovery strategies, from the fanciest and most costly to the more mundane and reasonably priced. Remember that most of these strategies can be implemented either in-house or by a third party. Don't write off outsourcing for disaster recovery. For some organizations, it is a good, cost-effective option.

Here are the disaster recovery strategies covered in this section:

- ◆ Offsite replication of an entire system, such as CCR solutions
- ◆ Offsite replication of servers, workstations, disk storage, backup hardware, software, and data
- ◆ Onsite replication of an entire system, such as CCR solutions
- ◆ Onsite replication of servers, disk storage, backup hardware, software, and data
- ◆ Onsite presence of spare servers, disk storage, and backup hardware

For many organizations, a combination of these strategies makes the most sense. Disasters come in all flavors and intensities. Sometimes they require the aggressive solutions of offsite full-system replication. Sometimes a less aggressive strategy is all that's required. The key is to understand the various disaster recovery strategies and pick the ones that best serve your organization.

KNOW THE REST OF YOUR PLAN, TOO

Keep in mind as you read through the discussion of disaster recovery strategies that a strategy is not a plan — it is only one part of a plan. Once you've selected the strategy or strategies that work for your organization, you should develop a written plan that provides specifics. You need to specify your strategy in detail and provide step-by-step, up-to-date instructions for recovering after a disaster. You also need clear and up-to-date documentation for your hardware systems and the software running on them. And, once you've completed your disaster recovery plan, make sure paper and electronic copies are available offsite. The best-laid plans have no value if you can't find a copy when you need it.

OFFSITE REPLICATION OF AN ENTIRE SYSTEM

Any location that is prone to natural disasters should consider their recovery strategy or their contingency of operations strategy keeping in mind that their main location may no longer be operable. Hurricane Katrina and two California earthquakes are examples in recent memory where it was not "business as usual" after a disaster. For example, in the Los Angeles basin, any recovery strategy has to take into account the possibility of earthquake-related collapsing buildings and fractured WAN infrastructure. For those clients who need to operate without missing a beat and who can afford it, offsite replication of their entire system, including up-to-the-minute replication of data, is the right answer.

Solutions such as remote Exchange servers that use standby continuous replication (SCR) can help fill this requirement, but remember that these remote "standby" data centers must have domain controllers, Client Access servers, Hub Transport servers, and Internet connectivity to resume business. The idea is that the minute a production system takes a major hit, the offsite system becomes the production system. Appropriate IT and other staff go to the offsite location and begin doing their thing. Though the transition is never going to be totally transparent, with networking switchovers and the loss of last-minute data to deal with, a total offsite strategy can get an organization up and running quickly. One addendum to this strategy is to actually use the disaster site to conduct the organization's business. Staff at each site performs a portion of all or some of the IT and other business tasks of the organization. When disaster strikes, required personnel are already at the disaster recovery site and able to keep the organization running until reinforcements arrive.

As you can imagine, this sort of disaster recovery strategy is very, very expensive. It's for banks and other financial institutions, really big hospitals, and other corporate giants that both need this sort of quick recovery capability and can afford to put it in place. However, even small businesses that depend on transactions or communications from all over the world may benefit from implementing this strategy on a small scale. Part of my own business is almost entirely e-mail and eCommerce based, and we would be at a standstill if we had no e-mail for a day, week, or month. I am sure that our customers would have gone someplace else after a month.

None of my clients has placed their system in one of those bunkers built into a mountain in Colorado that you might have read about or seen in the movies. However, they have implemented less aggressive strategies where a replicated system is set up in a nearby structure and data is kept up-to-date, though not up to the minute, using tape backups. Often the offsite location is in a single-story building, which is less likely to be seriously damaged in an earthquake. They still have to worry about potential damage and loss of WAN infrastructure, but it's quite okay if these folks can back up within a day or so and not within minutes or hours of a disaster. So this strategy is fine for them.

OFFSITE REPLICATION OF SERVERS, WORKSTATIONS, DISK STORAGE, BACKUP HARDWARE, NETWORKS, RELATED SOFTWARE, AND DATA

The major difference between this strategy and offsite replication of data is that you don't replicate your entire production system offsite. You replicate just enough of the system to get your organization back up and running in a reasonable time. In this disaster recovery scenario, you replicate hardware and operating system and applications software as required. However, you don't necessarily replicate data. You plan to recover data from backups shortly after a disaster strikes. You also don't necessarily replicate WAN links.

If you need to replicate data or even your entire disk storage system, consider the SAN systems discussed earlier in this chapter in the "Understanding Online Backups" section. Using capabilities built into SAN systems, and the Windows Server 2003 cluster service, you can replicate the data on one SAN to another SAN. Such replication is fairly quick and well suited to disaster recovery strategies where data needs to be readily available after a disaster strikes.

Instead of going with a third-party product, you may choose to implement a Windows 2003 cluster and an Exchange Server 2007 clustered continuous replication solution. CCR does not require costly storage and third-party replication tools because the ability to replicate an Exchange database is built into the product.

This disaster recovery strategy works if your organization can stand up to a few days of downtime. You and other IT staff need to be ready to scramble to get things running, but you don't have the staff expense and other costs associated with trying to build a full mirror of your production system.

ONSITE REPLICATION OF AN ENTIRE SYSTEM

This strategy is the same as offsite replication, except your replicated disaster recovery system exists in close physical proximity to your production system. This is a pretty fancy strategy, especially if you also have an offsite replication of your entire system. However, if you need to get up and running after a major system failure, onsite full-system replication might be the only answer.

Windows Server 2003 and 2008 cluster services can play a major role here and in the next two strategies. Because your system is onsite, you can use the very high-speed, server-to-server, server-to-storage, and server-to network links that make clustering such a great server and storage replication solution. It won't solve all of your replication problems, but it takes care of major components in the replication equation.

Even without implementing a full-blown clustering solution, Exchange Server 2007 replication technologies such as SCR (discussed in Chapter 18, "Implementing Replication Technologies") can provide the right solution.

Onsite Replication of Servers, Disk Storage, Backup Hardware, Networks, Related Software, and Data

As I am sure you've gathered, this strategy is an onsite version of the second disaster recovery strategy I discussed. It can provide the tools you need to meet the operating requirements of your organization. Windows Server 2003 cluster services and clustered continuous replication can make this strategy much easier to implement.

Onsite Presence of Spare Server, Disk Storage, Backup and Network Hardware, Software, and Data

Under this strategy, you have spares at hand, but they're not kept up-to-date by replication. Rather, you activate spares when a disaster requires.

Like so much of the discussion of disaster recovery strategies, this one brings to mind earlier discussions of server recovery in non-disaster situations. I hope, as we come to the end of this relatively brief treatment of disaster recovery strategies, that you begin to synthesize the content of this chapter into a coherent view of the Exchange Server 2007 reliability and availability continuum.

Summary

Providing users with reliable and available Exchange Server services is a complex task. You have to combine redundant hardware with a whole range of backup and recovery strategies and, in case the unusual should happen, disaster recovery strategies.

Hardware redundancy and mastery of backup and recovery strategies takes you a long way down the path to high server reliability and availability. It also gives you a leg up as you enter the complex world of disaster recovery. Disaster recovery strategies depend significantly on hardware redundancy and Windows and Exchange Server backup and recovery strategies.

Good disaster recovery strategies and plans are based on a careful balance between organizational needs and the resources required to meet those needs. E-mail disaster recovery needs might or might not be met by an organization's non-e-mail disaster recovery strategies. When disaster recovery strategies are considered, it's most important that bosses and managers understand the benefits and disadvantages of each strategy. Whatever strategy or set of strategies is chosen, bosses and managers must have a clear set of expectations regarding what can be recovered in what time frame.

Disaster recovery strategies can range from complex and costly offsite replications of entire systems to the onsite presence of spare pieces of hardware. The mechanics of a recovery after a disaster are the easiest things to specify and carry out. Maintaining the presence of mind required to pull off a disaster recovery is not so easy, but it's just as important.

Part 5

Outlook

In this part:

## Chapter 20

Supporting Outlook 2007

Though this book is about Exchange Server 2007, briefly visiting the topic of installing and supporting Outlook with Exchange Server 2007 is a good use of our time. Outlook Web Access as well as POP3 and IMAP4 clients may be popular in some places, but the Outlook client is king of the hill. This is because Outlook offers the widest range of features and takes advantage of most Exchange Server functions.

Outlook 2007 introduces a number of new features, including several that are of particular interest to Exchange administrators and that your users might ask you about, such as the To-Do Bar and RSS feeds. This chapter isn't intended to be a comprehensive review of Outlook 2007. For more in-depth information about Outlook 2007, you should see *Microsoft Outlook 2007 Bible* (Wiley, 2007).

In this chapter you learn to:

- ◆ Install Outlook

- ◆ Know the new interface

- ◆ Send mail, use instant search, and synchronize

- ◆ Use Outlook to manage your time and book appointments

- ◆ Understand Outlook 2007 and Exchange Server Autodiscover features

Installing Outlook 2007

The Office 2007 installation routine has been completely rewritten from the ground up. Now the Local Installation Source (LIS) is the standard method of installation; a fully compressed source is copied to the workstation on installation, and the installation is carried out from there. This makes the installation faster and more robust. When service packs or updates are issued in the future, there is no longer any need to provide the installation media (presuming you didn't remove the compressed LIS files after installation) because all the installation files are still right there on the workstation hard drive.

With previous versions, doing a customized deployment often meant either walking around and touching all of your workstations or using multiple tools to create customizations and "transforms" that you would apply to your installation.

Office 2007 has a single tool that lets you customize all of the settings in the product in one move. Its output is an XML file called `config.xml`, which you place in the \Updates folder and it will be automatically applied during setup.

I don't have time to go through every possible deployment scenario, so I'll go through the most basic one in this chapter to get you started.

System Requirements

Outlook 2007, like the rest of the Office 2007 suite, requires the following:

◆ Windows XP Service Pack 2 or newer for the client operating system

◆ At least 2GB of hard drive space

◆ At least 256MB of RAM

   In reality, of course, running Windows XP, much less Office 2007, in 256MB of RAM is not a very satisfying way to work, so I recommend a bare minimum of 512MB of RAM; really, you should aim for 1GB or more if you can.

   Especially if you're running Vista you'll want the 1GB of RAM, and to get the benefits of Vista's Aero interface, you'll want a video card with at least 128MB of memory on board.

◆ Exchange 2000 or later

   Because you're reading a book about Exchange 2007, it probably isn't necessary to mention that Outlook 2007 is not supported by Exchange versions prior to Exchange 2000. It's time to finally migrate off those old Exchange 5.5 servers if you still have any in use.

Administrative Install

In Office 2003 you performed your base installation by running `setup /A` and actually doing an install to a share on a server that would serve as your base for client installs. In Office 2007, you simply copy the contents of the Office CD to a network share. Done.

SHARING VERSUS COPYING

Why wouldn't you just share the CD instead of copying it to a network drive? Actually, you can. . .if you don't intend to do any customizations and you're okay with an "out of the box" install of Office, and your users are okay with being prompted for product keys and other installation information. Most deployments will want to enter that information for the users, however, and an install from the hard drive will perform better than an install from the CD.

Once you've completed that step, copy any product updates you might have into the `\Updates` folder of the installation share you've created.

Languages

Office 2007 is designed to be language neutral — that means that the core application files are not specific to any language and adding additional languages is as simple as copying any language packs you want to the installation point and answering no if asked to overwrite duplicate setup files.

Being language independent has several advantages over previous versions:

◆ It's easy to add additional languages. Just copy in the language packs.

◆ You don't have to have any language you don't want, including English.

◆ Updates are much smaller. In past versions, the core files, and their related updates, were larger because they included the English (typically) language files. In 2007, updates to the core files don't have to include any language features.

◆ Installation files are much smaller. In previous versions, if you wanted to install English and Japanese you needed two complete sets of the installation files. In Outlook 2007, the language-neutral core files don't have to be duplicated, which can save a considerable amount of space.

Customization

In previous versions of Office, you needed to use a number of different tools to customize your installation. Those tools have all been rolled into a single tool for customizing Office and Outlook 2007 — the unimaginatively named Office Customization Tool (OCT).

The OCT lets you configure your Office settings ahead of time and will create a setup customizations file called an MSP file that you simply place in the \Updates folder of your installation share. When you run setup on the clients, it will automatically apply whatever changes and customizations you've made.

To run the OCT, type setup /admin in the installation directory.

The OCT has four sections — setup, features, additional content, and Outlook — and each section has several pages of options.

Setup   The setup section includes the primary options for setting up the application, including installation location, organization name, product key, and licensing. Outlook 2007 can't coexist with previous versions of Outlook and the setup routine will uninstall all previous versions of Office by default. The setup section gives you the option to tell setup to leave certain installed applications (but not Outlook!) alone.

Features   The features section lets you specify which Office features should be installed and which should not be installed as well as set options like which features should be installed on first use. Keep in mind that, thanks to the Local Installation Source, if you set a feature to install on first use, it will be available to install when the user needs it, even if the user doesn't have the original media or is disconnected from your network. The Local Installation Source provides the install files needed to complete the installation on demand.

Additional Content   The additional content section is where you can specify files you'd like to add to or remove from the workstation, or any custom Registry entries you'd like to create or remove. This section also lets you specify any shortcuts you'd like to create on the user's machine.

Outlook   Outlook has its own section in the OCT. In the Outlook section you can customize the user's default profile, use an existing profile, or create a new one. If you lock down the computers so that the users don't have administrative rights, the profile settings you make on installation cannot be changed by the users. In this section, you can add additional accounts, such as POP3 or IMAP accounts, to the user's profile and even configure their send/receive groups if you like.

Client Deployment

At the client side, installation is as simple as running setup.exe from the workstation. That can be done manually by the end user or administrator, via a log-in script, or with any number of other utilities, such as Microsoft Systems Management Server, Altiris, and ScriptLogic. If you've used the OCT and correctly placed your MSP file, the setup routine will proceed without asking the end user for any input.

MIGRATING FROM OTHER MAIL CLIENTS

Some organizations may have need to migrate data from mail clients other than Outlook. Outlook 2007 does include a number of converters, but they cannot be automatically run during installation. Each user will have to migrate their data individually.

If you want to install other Office products, you need only copy those files from the CD to the same installation point. Be sure to answer no when prompted to overwrite duplicate setup files.

Autodiscover

Configuring Outlook 2007 is easier than in any previous version. If you're logged in to an authenticated domain account, Outlook 2007 can look up your user record in Active Directory and automatically enter your alias and e-mail server.

Outlook 2007 has the ability, under certain circumstances, to automatically configure itself to connect to an information service and set up the profile with little or no input from the user. In order to enable this capability for your clients, you have to enable Autodiscover on an Exchange 2007 server that has the Client Access (CAS) server role installed.

Note that if you want to enable Autodiscover on the server, you will have to use the Exchange Management Shell to do so — it can't be enabled from the Exchange Management Console.

For more information about configuring Autodiscover on the server, please see the section "Configuring Autodiscover" later in this chapter.

Autodiscover works for Outlook 2007 clients within your LAN as well as Outlook 2007 clients who will use RPC over HTTP, which Microsoft now calls Outlook Anywhere. Outlook Anywhere allows mobile users to connect Outlook 2007 to their Exchange server via regular HTTP protocol without having to connect to a virtual private network first. Essentially it tunnels RPC packets (the basic mechanism for Outlook/Exchange communication) over the HTTP protocol. Outlook 2007 can also usually autoconfigure your POP or IMAP account settings if you give it your e-mail address and password.

The Outlook 2007 User Interface

Outlook 2007's user interface is not dramatically different from Outlook 2003. Unlike the rest of the Office 2007 suite (except for OneNote and InfoPath), Outlook 2007 has not completely gone to the new Ribbon interface. The main Outlook window, known as the *explorer window*, still features the old menu bar/toolbar interface that you are familiar with. The *inspector windows* — the windows you get when you open a specific Outlook item — do have the new Ribbon.

One change to the Office 2007 user interface is the introduction of *skins*. Your users can choose among the traditional blue skin, a new clean silver one, and an ominous black one. To change the color scheme, follow these steps:

1. Click the New button as if to create a new item (or just start one of the Ribbon-enabled Office applications like Word or Excel).

2. Click the Office button at the top left of the application.

3. Click the Options button for your application.

4. On the first screen of the Options settings you should see a list box for color scheme.

Figure 20.1 shows setting the color scheme to silver.

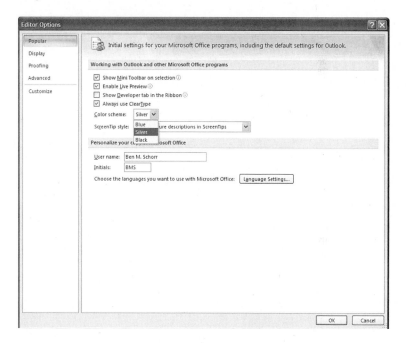

Be aware that any change you make will change the color scheme for the entire Office 2007 suite. Once you've changed the scheme, you can close the new item inspector window without saving it.

Inbox

The Inbox is the default delivery point for incoming communications. Traditionally this has meant e-mail, but increasingly firms are deploying *unified messaging*, which means that in addition to e-mail, your Inbox may contain voicemail and faxes.

Along the left side of the main Inbox screen you will see the now-familiar Navigation Pane, as shown in Figure 20.2. You use the Navigation Pane in Outlook 2007 to switch among the major categories such as Inbox, Calendar, or Contacts. At the top of the Navigation Pane you'll see the Favorite Folders section where users can place folders they access frequently to make them easier to find.

To the right of the Navigation Pane is the item list, which is, again, essentially the same as the pane that you are familiar with in Outlook 2003. One major difference, however, is the search box at the top of the item list. This is your quick interface to Outlook 2007's Instant Search capability (see the section "Finding Items and More with Instant Search" later in this chapter for more information). Typing in that field will cause Outlook to initiate a search of the current folder.

On the far right side of the screen you'll see the most significant difference in the Outlook 2007 interface: the To-Do Bar. The To-Do Bar gives users access to their upcoming appointments as well as their task list and e-mail messages flagged for follow-up. For a little more exploration of the To-Do Bar, see the section ''Managing Your Time with Outlook'' later in this chapter.

FIGURE 20.2

The Inbox in Outlook 2007

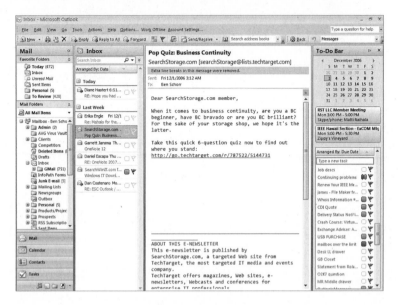

To maximize your screen real estate, you can minimize both the Navigation Pane and the To-Do Bar by clicking the double-arrows at the top of the respective window.

Editor

If you want to create or edit an item in Outlook, you'll need to use the editor. In Figure 20.3, you can see the new item editor, which, unlike the Outlook explorer screen, does get the new Ribbon interface. If it looks a lot like Word 2007 to you, there's a good reason for that — it *is* Word 2007. The user can no longer choose between using the Outlook or Word editors — there is no more Outlook editor. All users will use the Word editor, and they have it even if they don't have Word installed because Outlook ships with a special stripped-down version of Word that comes as a Dynamic-Link Library (DLL). This means that users will gain a number of advanced formatting features, including the ability to use WordArt, tables or charts, and the full set of Word styles.

Calendar

The Outlook calendar enables users to keep track of their schedules. The Calendar folder has undergone a few UI changes, shown in Figure 20.4, that your users will probably enjoy. You can open multiple calendars at the same time, as you could in Outlook 2003, simply by checking the appropriate box in the Navigation Pane. In the 2007 version, however, you can now overlay the calendars on top of each other by clicking the Overlay arrow that appears on the tab of the other calendars.

Adding the calendar of another user in your company is a simple matter. Simply click the Open A Shared Calendar link in the Navigation Pane and type the alias of the user whose calendar you want to open. If that user has granted you permissions to access his calendar, this process will add that user to your Navigation Pane as an additional calendar. Viewing that user's calendar thereafter is a simple matter of checking the box next to his name.

FIGURE 20.3

The Word editor is the only editor in Outlook 2007

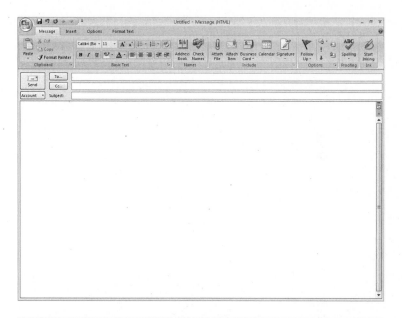

FIGURE 20.4

The calendar keeps you on schedule

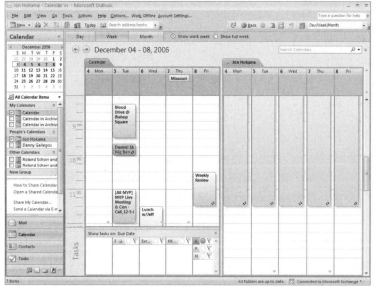

One of the problems with the way the Tasks folder has traditionally been used is that users have wanted to display their tasks on the calendar day that they were due instead of in a separate list off to the side of the screen. To achieve that they have often entered their tasks right onto the calendar, either as appointment items or as all-day appointments. That isn't really the way the calendar was intended to be used, however, and it highlighted a weakness in the way task items were presented. In Outlook 2007, tasks are displayed in a bar located beneath the calendar so that the tasks due on a certain date line up nicely with the calendar date. That makes it easier to see which tasks are due when.

Contacts

The Contacts folder is where you can save contact information for the people you interact with most. The most notable difference in the Contacts folder of Outlook 2007 is the new Business Card view, as shown in Figure 20.5. You'll notice that the To-Do Bar persists in the Contacts folder as well.

FIGURE 20.5
The Business Card view of your Contacts folder

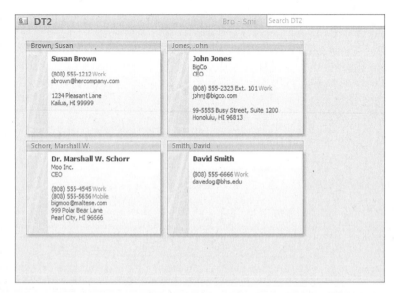

Tasks

The Tasks folder has some useful new views, perhaps the best of them being the To-Do List view, which gives you a rich view of your tasks and follow-up items complete with a reading pane that allows you to view an item without having to open it (see Figure 20.6).

New E-mail Features in Outlook 2007

E-mail has become perhaps the most ubiquitous computing task in business. I don't have to tell you it's mission critical — you know that. In fact, it's important enough that you bought a book about Exchange Server. I don't have enough pages in this book for a comprehensive review of e-mail, but the following sections highlight a few e-mail features of the Outlook 2007 client that I think are important.

Out-of-Office Assistant

Outlook 2007 has an improved Out-of-Office Assistant, which now lets you set different out-of-office messages for internal and external users. This is handy if you want to give a rich set of information to internal users but don't want to share all of that with users outside of your organization.

Also, your users can now schedule their out-of-office messages ahead of time so that they will start on a particular day and stop on another day. Gone are the days when they remembered on the flight that they forgot to turn it on. Gone are the days when you had to remind them at noon that people were still getting out-of-office messages about their recently completed vacation.

FIGURE 20.6
The Tasks folder helps
you get things done

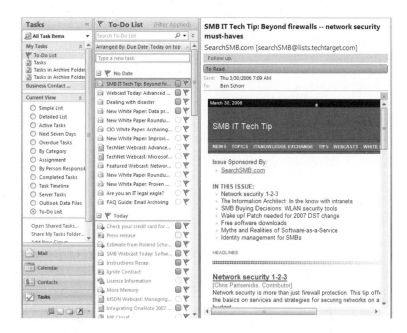

Mailbox Full

If the user's mailbox fills up to the point where Exchange is going to prevent messages from being sent to that mailbox, the submission of a new message will now fail on the client side instead of the server side. That means that the message the user was trying to send will stay in his Outbox on the client side until the recipient's mailbox can be cleaned up enough to allow the user to receive messages again.

Mailbox Cleanup

That brings us to mailbox cleanup. On the Tools menu, the users will find the Mailbox Cleanup tool, which gives them a single dialog box (shown in Figure 20.7) from which they can perform a number of useful cleanup tasks:

Mailbox Size   Gives users an easy way to see how large their mailbox is and which folders are the largest.

Find   Purpose-built find tools to help the user quickly find messages older than a certain age or larger than a certain size.

ABOUT THE LARGE MAIL SEARCH FOLDER

The Large Mail search folder is also a useful tool for keeping mailbox size down. I find that most users don't realize that they may have messages with gigantic attachments filling up their mailboxes. Either deleting the messages or moving the attachments to the file system and then removing the attachment from the message can dramatically reduce total mailbox size.

AutoArchive   One button for the user to initiate an AutoArchive. This can be one of the easiest and most effective ways to reduce mailbox size.

Empty Deleted Items   How many users have you seen with thousands of items in their Deleted Items folder?

AUTOMATICALLY ARCHIVING THE DELETED ITEMS FOLDER

If you have users who can't seem to remember to empty their Deleted Items folders and who don't want Deleted Items emptied for them automatically on shutdown, consider turning AutoArchive on for the Deleted Items folder and setting it to permanently delete items older than a couple of weeks.

Delete Conflicts   When a synchronization error occurs, Outlook keeps a copy of items found in conflict. Over time those items can add up, and they do count against the mailbox quota. Here is a quick tool to see how big of a problem it is and a convenient way to clean them out quickly.

FIGURE 20.7
The Mailbox Cleanup tool helps keep your user mailboxes under quota

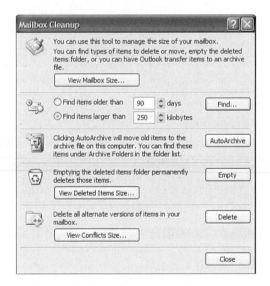

Recover Deleted Items

In Outlook 2003 with Exchange 2003, you could enable Deleted Items Recovery, which meant you could recover any items that you deleted and then emptied from your Deleted Items folder (within the specified time limit). A well-kept secret was that you could actually enable recovery from any folder with a registry hack. In Outlook 2007, Deleted Items Recovery is enabled for all folders by default. The users need only to select the folder they want to recover and then click Tools ➤ Recover Deleted Items.

RSS Feeds

For more than a decade, various forms of "push" technology have been tried. The notion of being able to push content, especially time-sensitive content like breaking news, to end users is a powerful one. In the past couple of years, a new technology has evolved that is the most promising (and least proprietary) solution so far. Really Simple Syndication (RSS) specifies how a website or content provider can publish content to an Internet site. A software application called an RSS reader or newsreader can connect to that site on a scheduled basis (hourly or sometimes even more often) and check for new or updated content. If there is some, the RSS reader will automatically download that content and present it to the end user. Think of it like a magazine, where new articles just appear as they are published. Not surprisingly, RSS is flourishing — nearly every site that updates content regularly, like news sites or blogs, is now publishing one or more RSS feeds.

Outlook 2007 integrates an RSS reader into the main product right out of the box. Now you can subscribe to your favorite RSS feeds, and even synchronize your feeds with Internet Explorer 7, and have those RSS items delivered to Outlook where they can appear right alongside your e-mail items.

CREATING A SEARCH FOLDER FOR SPECIFIC CONTENT

A popular technique for dealing with multiple mail folders and RSS feeds is to create a Search folder that consolidates all messages received on a certain subject, including RSS articles. This gives the user a single view with which to deal with all new items.

To subscribe to an RSS feed in Outlook, simply copy the URL for the RSS feed, choose Tools ➢ Account Settings ➢ RSS Feeds in Outlook, click New, and paste the URL into the provided field as I have in Figure 20.8. Outlook will connect to that feed, get its default settings, and then start downloading articles from it. By default, Outlook will put that RSS feed into its own new folder under the RSS Feeds main folder.

FIGURE 20.8
Adding an RSS feed to
Outlook 2007

Rules Wizard

The Rules Wizard is a useful tool that has evolved along with Outlook. With the wizard, users can create custom rules that automate message processing, automatically moving messages to subfolders or taking other actions based upon criteria they specify such as message sender or content.

32KB RULES LIMIT GONE

If your users extensively employ the Rules Wizard, they've probably run into the problem of Outlook informing them that they've hit the limit on how many rules they can have. That limit was never really placed on the number of rules but rather on the total size of those rules, and since Exchange 5.0, it has been limited to 32KB. A single really enormous rule could trigger that limit, but more often it was several dozen large rules that did it.

Why 32KB? Because the entire collection of a user's rules had to be able to fit within a remote procedure call (RPC) and the maximum allowable RPC buffer is 32KB.

Outlook 2003 was a little worse than its predecessors in this regard because Outlook 2003 rules used Unicode, which requires more space. Most users would hit the limit at around 20 rules in Outlook 2003. Since Outlook 2000, you could force all of your rules to be client-side rules, which got you around the limitation but required the Outlook client to be running in order for the rules to fire.

Exchange 2007 raises the rules limit to a default of 64KB, but the administrator can customize it up to 256KB for each individual mailbox.

The default rules quota of 64KB can be changed to any size up to 256KB using the Exchange 2007 Exchange Management Shell (EMS) cmdlet `Set-Mailbox`. For example, to set user Bob.Lawler's mailbox to a rule limit of 128KB, you would type the following EMS command:

```
Set-Mailbox Bob.Lawler -RulesQuota 128KB
```

You could use the EMS to set the rules quota for an entire department by using one cmdlet (`Get-DistributionGroupMember`) to retrieve the names in a particular department (such as the sales department) and piping the output of that cmdlet to the `Set-Mailbox` cmdlet. Here is an example:

```
Get-DistributionGroupMember "Sales Department" | Set-Mailbox -RulesQuota 128KB
```

Finding Items and More with Instant Search

If you used Outlook 2003 (or earlier), you probably had the experience of typing something in the search tool and then watching the little magnifying glass rotate around and around and around for quite a long time before finally bringing your results. With Outlook 2007, Microsoft has integrated the Windows Desktop Search (WDS) technology so that WDS is constantly indexing your Outlook items in the background. You'll be prompted to install WDS when you install Office 2007. This means when you type a search term in the new search box (see Figure 20.9), Outlook returns the results almost immediately. In fact, you can perform what is called a *type-ahead search* in which you start to type your search string and Outlook presents you with a list of results almost immediately. As you continue to type, the results list will narrow further until you complete the string.

FIGURE 20.9
Instant Search helps you find your items

You can search the current folder or perform an All Items search that will search across all the folders of a specified type. That means you can find contacts, notes, e-mail messages, and more that contain the term you're looking for in a matter of seconds.

If you're having problems with the index — for example, if content you know exists doesn't get returned by a search — you may need to try rebuilding the index. Here are the steps to do so:

1. Right-click the Windows Desktop Search icon on the system tray.

2. Select Windows Desktop Search Options.

3. Click Advanced.

4. Click Rebuild.

Keep in mind that a full rebuild of the index can take quite a while. Depending upon how many items you have and how fast your computer is, it could be on the magnitude of hours to get the index fully rebuilt and usable.

Synchronizing with SharePoint

One of the strengths of technology in a corporate setting is in enabling collaboration among coworkers or departments. Microsoft's premier solution in collaboration technology today is called SharePoint, and it is a collection of technologies, built on Windows, that let administrators easily create browser-based portals for users to collaborate, share documents, create and maintain lists, and perform a number of other tasks. One of the strengths of SharePoint is that not only can it be used on an intranet, it can also be published to an extranet.

One of the significant frustrations that users and administrators had with previous versions of Outlook and SharePoint revolved around linking lists like contacts or calendars. You could access a SharePoint contacts list, for example, using Outlook 2003; you could even synchronize it and access it offline. What you couldn't do was edit any of those contact items in Outlook or have any additions synchronize back to the SharePoint server. The same was true for calendars as well, of course. Because it required extra steps to go back to the SharePoint site to make any edits, a lot of users simply skipped it and didn't make the best use of the SharePoint/Outlook connection.

With Outlook 2007 and SharePoint 2007, now you can do two-way synchronization so that you can edit those calendars, contacts, or other lists in Outlook and have the changes reflected in SharePoint. As an Exchange administrator, you should be aware of the capabilities that SharePoint 2007 brings to the table because, increasingly, things you are in the habit of doing with Exchange public folders can (and will) be done with SharePoint lists instead.

Managing Your Time with Outlook

Outlook 2007 makes some significant upgrades to the way users manage time and projects. One of the most noticeable new features is the To-Do Bar (shown on the right of Figure 20.10), which integrates users' tasks, e-mails flagged for follow-up, and Calendar items into their Inbox. The To-Do Bar replaces the task pane that users of earlier versions of Outlook were familiar with. In previous versions, the Tasks folder tended to be underused because users didn't like having to switch to the Tasks folder (or use the task pane in Calendar) in order to view their To-Do list. The To-Do Bar gives you a quick and accessible view of your To-Do list and upcoming appointments right from within the Inbox or most of the other folders.

FIGURE 20.10

The To-Do Bar helps to keep you on task

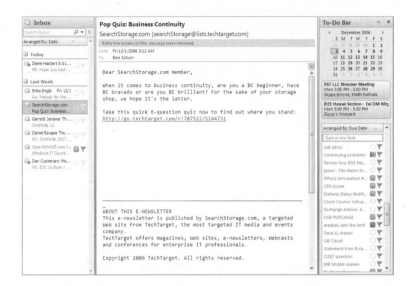

Adding a task is as simple as clicking the field at the top of the tasks list on the To-Do Bar and typing the subject of your task there. When you press Enter, it will automatically be assigned to today's tasks.

If you'd like to add more information to the task, change the due date or priority, or assign it to somebody else, just click the task to open it from the To-Do Bar and the item inspector will open and let you make your edits.

When you complete the task, just single-click the flag on the right of the task item on the To-Do Bar and it will be marked complete and removed from the To-Do Bar (but it's still in your Tasks folder, just marked complete).

If you need to remove a task or other item from the To-Do Bar, just right-click the item and choose Delete from the pop-up menu that appears.

Categories and Follow-Up Settings

Outlook 2007 also changes the way that Quick Flags are used. In Outlook 2003, Quick Flags gave you seven user-definable colors that you could use to quickly and broadly categorize e-mail items for follow-up. Outlook 2007 removes the distinct colors and replaces them with the categories feature, which now assigns a color to each category. The result is one less form of categorization — no need for a follow-up flag *and* a category — and a great many more colors rather than just the seven in Outlook 2003. Outlook 2007 also adds the ability to specify when the item should be followed up and then places that for-follow-up item on the To-Do Bar as if it were a task. This blurring of e-mail items and tasks is a powerful tool for facilitating user productivity.

FLAGGING A CONTACT ITEM

A lot of users don't realize that you can flag a contact item for follow-up. In Outlook 2007, that means it will appear on your To-Do Bar along with your tasks and other follow-up items. It's a handy way to be reminded that you need to contact a person. To flag a contact, while the contact item is open, click the Follow Up button on the Ribbon and select when you'd like to follow up. The flag isn't extremely obvious in the Contacts view (it just adds the "Follow Up: Tomorrow" field to the folder view), but this feature is best used with the To-Do Bar, which is a much more intuitive interface.

In Outlook 2003 and earlier versions, the categories were stored in the Registry, which made things difficult for users who used multiple computers and wanted consistent categories. With Outlook 2007, the categories (and their associated colors) are stored in the default data store, which means that they go wherever the user's data store does.

Calendaring and Scheduling

Outlook 2003 significantly improved the scheduling capabilities of the client, and Outlook 2007 builds upon those capabilities. Meeting organizers now cannot change the time or location of a meeting or cancel it without sending an update to all of the attendees. The organizer can change the notes or reminder time without an update going out, however.

NetMeeting and Microsoft Exchange Conferencing No Longer Supported

Don't expect to use Outlook 2007 to schedule NetMeeting events anymore. Neither NetMeeting nor Microsoft Exchange Conferencing is supported by Microsoft anymore. This functionality has moved to Microsoft Office Live Meeting.

Configuring Resource Mailboxes

If you have an Exchange server, you probably also have resources that you want to be able to schedule, such as conference rooms, audio/visual equipment, and maybe demonstration gear to take on the road. With Outlook and Exchange, you can create mailboxes for those resources; they will then have their own calendars that will accept reservation requests from your users and maintain a "free/busy" status that the users can use to determine whether they are available.

Exchange 2007's resource mailboxes are handled somewhat differently from the resource mailboxes in Exchange 2003 and earlier. In Exchange 2007, there are extensions made to the AD schema to uniquely identify resource mailboxes. I recommend creating a new organizational unit (OU) for resources so that regular users and resources don't get lumped together in the Active Directory.

Creating a resource mailbox is not unlike creating any other kind of mailbox:

1. Start the Exchange Management Console.

2. Click Recipient Configuration.

3. In the Actions pane, click New Mailbox. The New Mailbox Wizard will start to walk you through the process.

4. On the Introduction page, select Room Mailbox and click Next.

5. On the User Type page, select New User and click Next.

The wizard will then prompt you for the standard account information, username, alias, and so forth.

After you've created the mailbox, you could stop there, but usually you'll want to configure the resource mailbox to automatically process meeting requests for your users. To do that, follow these steps:

1. Go to a workstation that has Outlook installed.

2. Log in with the resource account.

3. Create an Outlook profile for that resource mailbox.

4. Once you've logged in to the resource mailbox with Outlook, choose Tools ≻ Calendar Options and click the Resource Scheduling button.

5. On the resulting dialog box you can configure the resource scheduling options.

For more information about creating and managing resource mailboxes, see Chapter 11, "Managing Recipients."

Using Outlook 2007 and Autodiscover

Exchange 2007 introduces a new feature called Autodiscover that Outlook 2007 and later clients can take advantage of. Autodiscover is a web service that resides on the Exchange 2007 Client Access server role. The popular notion of Autodiscover is that it helps Outlook 2007 to automatically locate an Exchange 2007 server and that is correct. However, Autodiscover actually helps Outlook locate a number of different types of Exchange resources, including these:

◆ User's home mailbox server

◆ Outlook Anywhere URL

◆ URL (internal or external) for the offline address book

◆ URL (internal or external) for Unified Messaging

◆ URL (internal or external) for Availability service

When users launch Outlook 2007 for the first time, they are prompted for some basic information (e-mail address or domain/username and password). Outlook 2007 contacts the Autodiscover web service and looks up information such as the home mailbox server, display name, and URLs for Outlook features such as free/busy information and the offline address book. If this information is changed, the Outlook client gets updated information (including the home mailbox server name) from the Autodiscover service.

SPECIFY DEFAULT SMTP ADDRESS FOR AUTODISCOVER

When users specify their e-mail address, they should use their default SMTP address. Autodiscover may not work for additional SMTP addresses.

Internal vs. External Autodiscover

Outlook 2007 uses two different approaches to locate an Autodiscover site and determine the necessary information.

INTERNAL AUTODISCOVER

The first approach is used when the Windows computer is a member of the Active Directory forest in which the Exchange server exists. Figure 20.11 shows the process that Outlook uses to locate resources. In this example, the computer on which Outlook 2007 is installed is a member of the Active Directory forest. This is considered the service process for internal clients.

FIGURE 20.11
Autodiscover when a client is member of the Active Directory

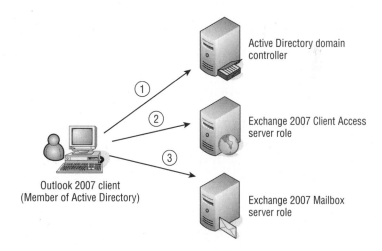

1. Active Directory domain controller

2. Exchange 2007 Client Access server role

3. Exchange 2007 Mailbox server role

Outlook 2007 client
(Member of Active Directory)

In step 1 in Figure 20.11, Outlook is launched for the first time and there is not yet an Outlook profile for the user account. Outlook contacts the Active Directory to find a service connection point (SCP). A service connection point is an Active Directory object that can be used to publish and locate network services. The SCP object will provide Outlook with the fully qualified domain names of Client Access servers; Outlook contacts a Client Access server in its local Active Directory site.

In step 2, the Outlook 2007 client queries the Client Access server to retrieve the user's home server. The username and domain name are used to locate the user's home mailbox server. Outlook also retrieves information about the location of the Availability service and the distribution points for the offline address book. From this information, the Outlook profile is created.

In step 3, Outlook is able to connect to the user's home Exchange server.

EXTERNAL AUTODISCOVER

If the desktop client is not a member of the Active Directory or is outside of the corporate network and cannot contact a domain controller, Outlook 2007 uses a different approach. This is the Autodiscover service process for external access. In this approach, DNS is used to locate the Autodiscover service. Figure 20.12 shows an example of how the Autodiscover service is located for an external client. In this example, users must provide their e-mail address because it cannot be provided for them using their Active Directory user account.

FIGURE 20.12
External Autodiscover
location process

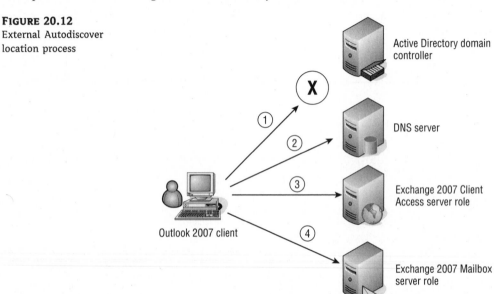

In step 1, Outlook tries to contact an Active Directory domain controller (if the client is a member of the Active Directory). If Active Directory cannot be located or the computer is not a member of the Active Directory, the user is presented with the Add New E-mail Account dialog box shown in Figure 20.13. From this dialog box, users must enter their primary SMTP address, their name, and their account password. The e-mail address is important because the SMTP domain name is used in step 2.

In step 2, the Outlook 2007 client performs a DNS query and uses the SMTP domain name. In this example, the domain name is somorita.com. Outlook will use the following URLs to try to connect in order to locate the Autodiscover server:

```
https://somorita.com/autodiscover/autodiscover.xml
https://autodiscover.somorita.com/autodiscover/autodiscover.xml
```

These URLs will need to be resolvable in DNS and accessible from outside your network for external clients. If you will use the DNS approach for "external" clients on your inside network, you will want to make sure that one of these two URLs is resolvable using your internal DNS.

The Client Access server that hosts either of the Autodiscover URLs will then return the Outlook Anywhere information necessary to configure Outlook 2007 as well as external URL locations for the Availability service and the offline address book distribution point.

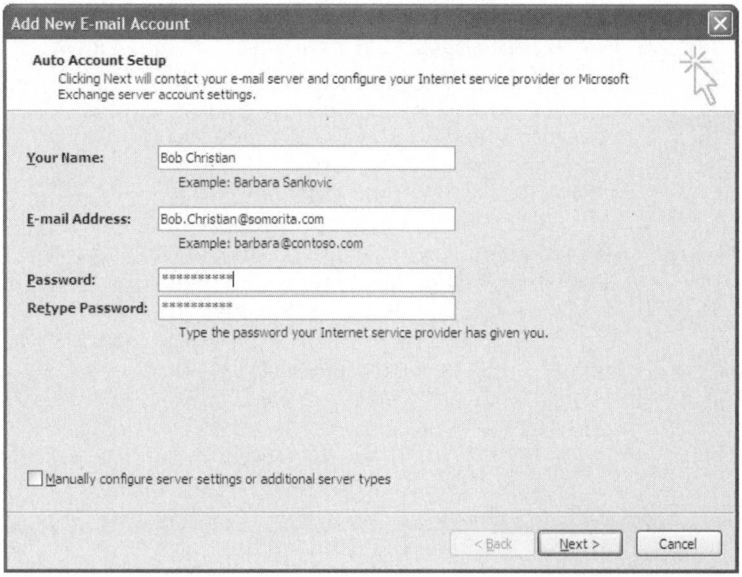

FIGURE 20.13
Providing Outlook
with your information
manually

Outlook 2007 SP1 introduced the ability to use a DNS service location (SRV) record to locate the correct Autodiscover URL. See this site for more information:

```
http://exchange-genie.blogspot.com/2007/07/autodiscover-ad-attribute.html
```

Configuring Autodiscover

When an Exchange 2007 Client Access server is installed, an SCP record is created in Active Directory for it. This includes the internal Outlook Anywhere settings, the internal URL for the offline address book, and the internal URL for Exchange web services. However, depending on your environment, there may be additional configuration settings that you need to perform, if, for example, you needed to enable Outlook Anywhere (formerly RPC over HTTP) or define external URLs for other web services.

CONFIGURING AUTODISCOVER VIRTUAL DIRECTORIES

An Autodiscover virtual directory is automatically created on each Exchange 2007 Client Access server. The only way to configure this is through the Exchange Management Shell. The Get-AutoDiscoverVirtualDirectory cmdlet can let you view the Autodiscover virtual directories. Here is an example:

```
Get-AutodiscoverVirtualDirectory

Name : Autodiscover (Default Web Site)
InternalAuthenticationMethods : {Basic, Ntlm}
ExternalAuthenticationMethods : {Basic, Ntlm}
BasicAuthentication           : True
DigestAuthentication          : False
```

```
WindowsAuthentication        : True
MetabasePath     : IIS://HNLEX03.volcanosurfboards.com/W3SVC/1/
ROOT/Autodiscover
Path : C:\Program Files\
Microsoft\Exchange Server\ClientAccess\
Autodiscover
Server           : HNLEX03
InternalUrl      :
ExternalUrl      :
AdminDisplayName :
ExchangeVersion  : 0.1 (8.0.535.0)
DistinguishedName              : CN=Autodiscover (Default Web Site),
CN=HTTP,CN=Protocols,CN=HNLEX03,CN=Servers,CN=Exchange Administrative
Group (FYDIBOHF23SPDLT),CN=Administrative Groups,CN=Volcano Surfboards,
CN=Microsoft Exchange,CN=Services,CN=Configuration,DC=volcanosurfboards,DC=com
Identity         : HNLEX03\Autodiscover (Default Web Site)
Guid : 4ec07bc6-2e2a-4877-8d66-9626325a6666
ObjectCategory   : volcanosurfboards.com/Configuration/Schema/
        'ms-Exch-Auto-Discover-
Virtual-Directory
ObjectClass      : {top, msExchVirtualDirectory,
 msExchAutoDiscoverVirtualDirectory}
WhenChanged      : 12/22/2006 9:10:00 PM
WhenCreated      : 12/22/2006 9:10:00 PM
OriginatingServer              : HNLDC01.volcanosurfboards.com
IsValid          : True
```

If you want to set the external URL for Autodiscover, here is the command:

```
Set-AutodiscoverVirtualDirectory "HNLEX03\Autodiscover (Default Web Site)"↵
-ExternalUrl "https://owa.somorita.com"
```

CONFIGURING OUTLOOK ANYWHERE AND AUTODISCOVER

By default, Outlook Anywhere is not enabled on the Client Access servers. To enable Outlook Anywhere, locate each Client Access server in the Server Configuration work center in the Exchange Management Console (EMC) and select the Enable Outlook Anywhere task on the Actions pane. This launches a wizard that prompts you for the external hostname and the type of authentication and gives you the option to use SSL offloading. (See Figure 20.14.)

If you are using network load balancing, the external hostname will be the fully qualified domain name that the clients will use externally. When you have completed the information required by the wizard, you can click the Enable Outlook Anywhere button.

Optionally, you could enable Outlook Anywhere using the `Enable-OutlookAnywhere` cmdlet. Here is an example:

```
Enable-OutlookAnywhere -Server 'HNLEX03' -ExternalHostname 'owa.somorita.com'↵
-ExternalAuthenticationMethod 'Basic' -SSLOffloading $false
```

Once Outlook Anywhere is enabled, you can select the properties of the Client Access server and view the Outlook Anywhere properties of that particular Client Access server. An example is shown in Figure 20.15.

FIGURE 20.14
Enable Outlook
Anywhere Wizard

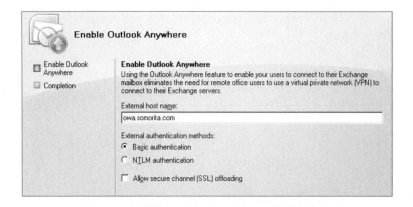

FIGURE 20.15
Configuring the external
hostname for Outlook
Anywhere

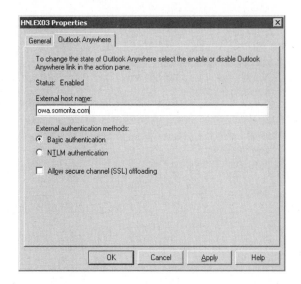

You can retrieve the same information (and more) using the Get-OutlookAnywhere cmdlet; here is an example:

```
Get-OutlookAnywhere

SSLOffloading              : False
ExternalHostname           : owa.somorita.com
ExternalAuthenticationMethod : Basic
MetabasePath               : IIS://HNLEX03.volcanosurfboards.com/
W3SVC/1/ROOT/Rpc
Path: C:\WINDOWS\System32\RpcProxy
Server                     : HNLEX03
AdminDisplayName           :
ExchangeVersion : 0.1 (8.0.535.0)
Name: Rpc (Default Web Site)
DistinguishedName          : CN=Rpc (Default Web Site),CN=HTTP,
CN=Protocols,CN=HNLEX03,CN=Servers,CN=Exchange AdministrativeGroup
```

```
(FYDIBOHF23SPDLT),CN=Administrative Groups,CN=Volcano Surfboards,
CN=Microsoft Exchange,CN=Services,CN=Configuration,DC=volcanosurfboards,DC=com
Identity                    : HNLEX03\Rpc (Default Web Site)
Guid: 3f68d1ed-90ae-4778-aa23-88919b5a3284
ObjectCategory              : volcanosurfboards.com/Configuration/Schema/
ms-Exch-Rpc-Http-Virtual-Directory
ObjectClass                 : {top, msExchVirtualDirectory,
 msExchRpcHttpVirtualDirectory}
WhenChanged                 : 1/8/2007 6:24:32 PM
WhenCreated                 : 1/8/2007 6:24:32 PM
OriginatingServer           : HNLDC01.volcanosurfboards.com
IsValid                     : True
```

When configuring the external hostname for Outlook Anywhere, remember that this is the URL that will be referred to external Outlook 2007 clients when Autodiscover is used.

OFFLINE ADDRESS BOOKS AND AUTODISCOVER

The offline address book distribution points by default contain only the internal URL used to locate them. You can set these using the graphical user interface by selecting the properties of the offline address book virtual directory in the Exchange Management Console. The URLs property page of the default OAB virtual directory for a Client Access server is shown in Figure 20.16.

FIGURE 20.16
Setting the external URL
for offline address book
distribution

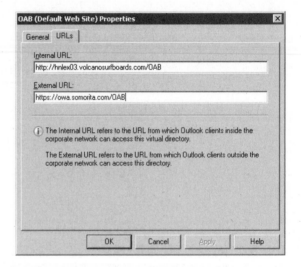

You can also set this parameter using the EMS cmdlet Set-OABVirtualDirectory. Here is an example:

```
Set-OABVirtualDirectory "hnlex03\OAB (Default Web Site)"↵
-ExternalURL https://owa.somorita.com/OAB -RequireSSL:$True
```

You can view the configuration of the offline address book virtual directory using the Get-OABVirtualDirectory cmdlet. Here is an example:

```
Get-OabVirtualDirectory | Format-List

Name : OAB (Default Web Site)
PollInterval                   : 480
OfflineAddressBooks            : {}
RequireSSL                     : True
MetabasePath                   : IIS://HNLEX03.volcanosurfboards.com/W3SVC/1/ROOT/
OAB
Path                      : C:\Program Files\
Microsoft\Exchange Server\ClientAccess\OAB
Server                    : HNLEX03
InternalUrl       : http://hnlex03.volcanosurfboards.com/OAB
InternalAuthenticationMethods : {WindowsIntegrated}
ExternalUrl       : https://owa.somorita.com/OAB
ExternalAuthenticationMethods : {WindowsIntegrated}
AdminDisplayName               :
ExchangeVersion                : 0.1 (8.0.535.0)
DistinguishedName              : CN=OAB (Default Web Site),
CN=HTTP,CN=Protocols, CN=HNLEX03,CN=Servers,CN=Exchange Administrative
Group (FYDIBOHF23SPDLT),CN=Administrative Groups,CN=Volcano Surfboards,
CN=Microsoft Exchange,CN=Services,CN=Configuration,DC=volcanosurfboards,DC=com
Identity                  : HNLEX03\OAB (Default Web Site)
Guid : f54b7b26-640e-4359-b845-02c2d995dd44
ObjectCategory            : volcanosurfboards.com/Configuration/Schema/
ms-Exch-OAB-Virtual-Directory
ObjectClass               : {top, msExchVirtualDirectory,
msExchOABVirtualDirectory}
WhenChanged               : 1/8/2007 7:17:58 PM
WhenCreated               : 12/22/2006 9:09:56 PM
OriginatingServer         : HNLDC01.volcanosurfboards.com
IsValid                   : True
```

CONFIGURING WEB SERVICES AND AUTODISCOVER

If remote or external clients will need access to custom web services, you should configure the external URL for web services. This can only be done via the EMS. The following cmdlet is an example for setting the external URL for a Client Access server:

```
Set-WebServicesVirtualDirectory "hnlex03\EWS (Default web site)"↵
-ExternalUrl https://owa.somorita.com/EWS/Exchange.asmx -BasicAuthentication:$True
```

To check the configuration of the Web Services virtual directory, you can use the Get-WebServicesVirtualDirectory cmdlet:

```
Get-WebServicesVirtualDirectory
Name : EWS (Default Web Site)
InternalAuthenticationMethods : {Basic, Ntlm}
ExternalAuthenticationMethods : {Basic, Ntlm}
BasicAuthentication            : True
DigestAuthentication           : False
WindowsAuthentication          : True
MetabasePath                   : IIS://HNLEX03.volcanosurfboards.com/W3SVC/1/
ROOT/EWS
Path          : C:\Program Files\Microsoft\Exchange Server\ClientAccess\
exchweb\EWS
Server                         : HNLEX03
InternalUrl    : https://hnlex03.volcanosurfboards.com/
EWS/Exchange.asmx
ExternalUrl                    : https://owa.somorita.com/EWS/Exchange.asmx
AdminDisplayName               :
ExchangeVersion  : 0.1 (8.0.535.0)
DistinguishedName              : CN=EWS (Default Web Site),CN=HTTP,
CN=Protocols, CN=HNLEX03,CN=Servers,CN=Exchange Administrative Group
(FYDIBOHF23SPDLT),CN=Administrative Groups,CN=Volcano Surfboards,
CN=Microsoft Exchange,CN=Services,CN=Configuration,DC=volcanosurfboards,DC=com
Identity                       : HNLEX03\EWS (Default Web Site)
Guid : b5cd3ea1-42c1-42b0-87db-35072316cf6a
ObjectCategory                 : volcanosurfboards.com/Configuration/Schema/
ms-Exch-Web-Services-Virtual-Directory
ObjectClass                    : {top, msExchVirtualDirectory, msExchWebServices
        VirtualDirectory}
WhenChanged                    : 1/8/2007 7:07:25 PM
WhenCreated                    : 12/22/2006 9:10:12 PM
OriginatingServer              : HNLDC01.volcanosurfboards.com
IsValid                        : True
```

AUTODISCOVER AND SECURE SOCKETS LAYER

If you have tried to deploy both internal and external URLs already, then you are already wondering how Secure Sockets Layer is supposed to work if the FQDN of the internal location is different than the external FQDN. After all, if certificates are requested you usually only provide one name in the certificate signing request. There is a workaround, however, that allows you to have more than one DNS domain name for a Client Access server. To do this, you have to use the New-ExchangeCertificate cmdlet. The command line is fairly involved; here is an example:

```
New-ExchangeCertificate -generaterequest↵
-subjectname "dc=com,dc=volcanosurfboards,o=Volcano Surfboards,↵
cn=owa.somorita.com"↵
-domainname HNLEX03,HNLEX03.volcanosurfboards.com,owa.somorita.com,↵
autodiscover.somorita.com -path c:\certrequest-HNLEX03.txt
```

This cmdlet creates a certificate request with multiple hostnames. In this case, the hostnames include `owa.somorita.com`, `autodiscover.somorita.com`, `hnlex03`, and `hnlex03.volcanosurf-boards.com`.

I can take the contents of this file and get a certificate signed and issued by a trusted certificate authority, or I could sign it myself using Windows Certificate Server. The result will be a file (in this case, `certnew.cer`) that is returned to me from the certification authority. Here is an example of using the `Import-ExchangeCertificate` cmdlet to import the signed certificate into the certificate store:

```
Import-ExchangeCertificate -path c:\certnew.cer -friendlyname "HNLEX03 Cert"
```

If you are used to creating certificate requests using the Internet Information Services Manager console, there is a new step you may not be familiar with. The `Import-ExchangeCertificate` cmdlet imports the certificate into the computer's personal certificate store, but it does not assign it to the default website. You will need to follow these steps to associate the certificate with the default website:

1. Run the Internet Information Server Manager console.

2. Open the Web Sites container, right-click Default Web Site, and select Properties.

3. Select the Directory Security property page.

4. Click the Server Certificate button and click Next.

5. Select the Assign An Existing Certificate radio button and click Next.

6. In the Select a Certificate list, select the certificate you have just imported using the `Import-ExchangeCertificate` cmdlet. When you have selected the certificate, click Next. (See Figure 20.17.)

7. Confirm that port 443 is the SSL port. This is usually the case. Click Next.

8. On the Certificate Summary page (see Figure 20.18), you can see some of the details of the certificate. When you are ready, click Next and then click Finish.

FIGURE 20.17
Selecting an imported certificate

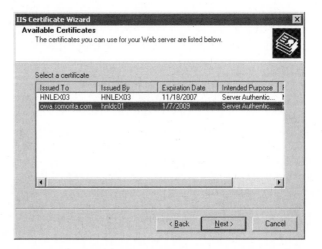

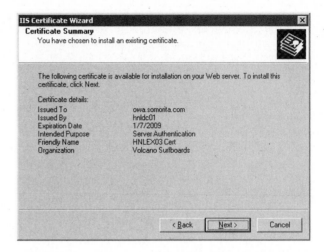

Congratulations. The certificate is now installed and associated with the default website. On the Directory Security property page, you can click the View Certificate button to see more details about the certificate. On the Details property page, if you scroll down to Subject Alternative Name in the Field column (see Figure 20.19), you will see the additional names you have specified for the certificate.

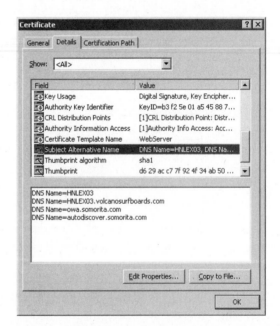

In the example just shown, the internal names of the server were HNLEX03 and HNLEX03.volcanosurfboards.com. The external names were owa.somorita.com and autodiscover.somorita.com.

> **CONFUSED BY CERTIFICATES?**
>
> Are certificates in Exchange Server 2007 just a bit confusing? Don't feel left out if you feel that way — many people do. I re-visit the certificates topic again in Chapter 22, "Getting to Know the Client Access Server Role."

Summary

Outlook 2007 is a pretty user-friendly electronic-messaging client with lots of bells and whistles, such as task and calendaring capabilities and contacts. When Outlook 2007 is installed properly on a server, a user can easily install Outlook on a workstation and begin using it without having to respond to a single installation query.

Creating, composing, and reading Outlook messages are very straightforward tasks. The Outlook address book, which can include Exchange mailboxes, distribution groups, contacts, and public folders, simplifies the e-mail addressing process. As with managing messages, basic public folder creation and management is an easy task, most of which can be done right in the Outlook client.

Among other things, Outlook profiles allow a single user to access a range of mail accounts with ease. Each user may have one or more Outlook profiles. When creating an Outlook profile, you can choose to access messaging services such as Exchange Server and Internet mail servers. You can also include personal folders and specific kinds of address books in a profile. By selecting a profile when Outlook 2007 starts, you choose which set of messaging services and other features will be available during your Outlook session.

The Outlook 2007 menu structure is complex, and unlike most of the other applications in the suite, it doesn't benefit much from the new Ribbon UI, but it's familiar to most users and easy to use when you're clear on what certain menu items do. Exchange Server 2007 brings several significant enhancements to the Outlook 2007 menu structure. One of these enables an Outlook user to recover items that were accidentally deleted (including items hard-deleted from folders).

The Exchange service Autodiscover features should reduce the support burden for Outlook 2007 users by reducing the number of calls to the help desk and the confusion surrounding getting an initial Outlook profile configured when users first start using a new desktop computer.

Part 6

Connectivity

In this part:

Chapter 21

Delivering E-mail

Exchange Server's primary purpose in life is to send, receive, and store messages. Sure, it stores contacts, calendar information, and tasks, but delivering e-mail messages is its life's purpose. In previous versions of Exchange, messages that were to be delivered locally (to a user whose mailbox was on your mailbox database or another database on the same server) never actually left that particular server. That all changes in Exchange Server 2007.

The new Hub Transport server role is now responsible for moving messages from one mailbox to another. All messages must now pass through the Hub Transport server role. No matter where your messages come from, they have to travel through a Hub Transport server before delivery to your mailbox, even if the message comes from the same storage group, in the same Exchange database, or from the mailbox right next door. This lightens the transport load on the Mailbox server role and centralizes transport to a single server role.

Exchange 2007 lets you do a lot with a message while it is in transit (see Chapter 15, "Managing Messages in Transit," for more information).

This chapter discusses message transfer from both the internal message routing perspective and the perspective of messages that are sent to/received from the Internet and how to reduce the amount of spam you receive.

In this chapter you learn to:

◆ Understand improvements in Exchange Server 2007 message transport

◆ Track message routing within the organization

◆ Deploy an Edge Transport server

Transport Improvements in Exchange Server 2007

Before we delve into how internal e-mail routing works, it's worth noting a few of the many improvements Exchange 2007 delivers in comparison to earlier versions of Exchange.

Prior to Exchange 2007, all messages were processed by the same server that connected MAPI clients, managed the information store, and hosted Outlook Web Access. This all-in-one approach worked well for many years, but it couldn't scale with the growing needs of organizations that had become increasingly dependent on their messaging systems. To remedy this, Microsoft has abstracted all message processing and delivery functions into the Hub Transport server role. As discussed in Chapter 4, "Exchange Server 2007 Architecture," the Hub Transport server role processes all messages regardless of their source or destination — even if they're in the same mailbox database, in the same storage group, or on the same server. At first blush, this may seem inefficient in comparison to routing in previous versions of Exchange. But, when you take into account new features like message classification, transport rules, and journaling, it makes sense for the Hub Transport server to offload some of the Mailbox server role's burden.

The Hub Transport server role can share a server with any other server role, except for clustered mailbox servers and Edge Transport servers. This means that if a Mailbox server does not also host the Hub Transport server, then the entire message is transferred to the Hub Transport server via Remote Procedure Calls (RPCs), then categorized, and finally routed to the appropriate location. This is true even if that location is the same mailbox database from which the message originated. This is one of the reasons that it is so critical to have a Hub Transport server in each Active Directory site that contains a Mailbox server.

SENDING ALL E-MAIL THROUGH HUB TRANSPORT: WASTE OR EFFICIENCY?

On first glance, having every e-mail message that is sent travel via RPC through the Hub Transport server role (whether that role is on the same Windows server or a different server) and back to the Mailbox server role seems like a waste of processor cycles and network bandwidth.

But think about a couple of the design goals of Exchange Server 2007. One of these is to abstract message transport functions out of the Mailbox server completely. All messages should be processed exactly the same way. As long as there are any types of transport functions being run by the Mailbox server role, this goal cannot be met.

Second, the new message transport architecture needs to be able to treat all messages equally when processing transport rules and other transport agents. Otherwise, transport rules would apply only to server-to-server messages. By having the entire message sent through the Hub Transport server, you can apply rules or functions not only to the message header, but also to the entire message body and attachments.

Exchange 2007 also introduces some significant changes to routing topology. Looking back to earlier versions of Exchange, administrators used *routing groups* (called *sites* in Exchange 5.5) to build their e-mail routing systems. Routing groups allowed organizations to engineer a message transport solution unique to their topology, but they were often superfluous to another underlying architecture: Active Directory (AD). Exchange 2007 leverages your existing infrastructure by defining an AD site as the natural boundary for an e-mail routing domain. As long as your AD topology is correctly designed, Exchange will automatically discover the most efficient way to route e-mail.

Many Exchange administrators were puzzled by the fact that Exchange 2000 and 2003 depended on Internet Information Server (IIS) for SMTP services. Happily, Exchange 2007 replaced IIS virtual SMTP servers with Send and Receive connectors for establishing SMTP connections — all of which is managed from within the Exchange Management Console (or Shell). This means you no longer need to install IIS on an Exchange 2007 server in order to perform e-mail routing.

Exchange 2007 improves upon the idea of a legacy Exchange 2000 or 2003 front-end server by introducing the Edge Transport server role. This hardened Exchange server's purpose is to accept and deliver Internet e-mail and perform *message hygiene* functions (such as anti-spam, content filtering, and antivirus) on messages before they enter the internal network.

The Edge Transport server is separated from the rest of the Exchange server roles because it does not communicate directly with Active Directory but utilizes an ADAM directory database that is stored local to the server. The Edge Transport server role was designed to exist in a perimeter network/demilitarized zone (DMZ) segregated from the internal network. Both the Edge Transport and the Hub Transport servers facilitate transport in an Exchange organization.

Unlike a front-end server, an Edge Transport server does not require connectivity to your internal AD infrastructure in order to route e-mail and only requires minimal ports be opened between your DMZ and internal networks (Hub Transport server or servers).

Message Routing within the Organization

I'll start with a bit of review about how Exchange 2007 delivers messages within a single organization. I covered this in Chapter 4, "Exchange Server 2007 Architecture," but I want to ensure that you properly understand it. The message routing architecture is sufficiently different from earlier versions of Exchange 2000/2003 that it deserves additional mention.

You should understand a couple of important points about the basics of Exchange 2007 message routing:

◆ All messages must go through the Hub Transport server role.

◆ The Active Directory site architecture is used as a boundary for message routing.

◆ All Active Directory sites that contain a Mailbox server must also have a Hub Transport server and a Client Access server.

One of the nice features of Exchange Server 2007 is that as long as your Active Directory site architecture has been properly configured, you will not need to worry about message routing architecture design.

Basics of Exchange Message Routing

In previous versions of Exchange, the message routing architecture was based on a structure that was defined by the administrator. For example, in Exchange 2000/2003, the message routing architecture was defined by a collection of servers separated by full-time and reasonably good available bandwidth. This collection of servers is called a *routing group*. Prior to Exchange 2000, all servers were grouped together into a single collection of servers called a *site*.

In Exchange 2000/2003, the administrator could define the routing groups and move servers between routing groups based on their message routing requirements. Messages were then delivered between routing groups using some type of connector. The most common connector for routing groups is a connector called the *routing group connector* (RGC), which uses SMTP to deliver messages.

Exchange 2007 changes this by relying on the Active Directory site architecture rather than requiring administrators to create a separate routing infrastructure for their organization. Figure 21.1 shows a simple Active Directory site topology that consists of three Active Directory sites.

In Figure 21.1, each Active Directory site has a Mailbox server and a Hub Transport server. The Hub Transport server will always attempt a direct delivery of a message to a Hub Transport server in a remote Active Directory site even if that remote Active Directory site does not have an Active Directory site link directly to it. If you are still running any Exchange 2000/2003 servers, though, they retain their routing group architecture and have routing group connectors to the Exchange 2007 Hub Transport servers.

By default, Exchange Server 2007 Hub Transport servers always attempt to directly deliver a message to a remote Hub Transport server (in another Active Directory site). This feature ensures the quickest and most direct delivery of e-mail messages to remote sites. The Hub Transport ignores the Active

Directory site link costs (and possibly your underlying network topology) and performs direct delivery.

However, some organizations may have a requirement that all e-mail be delivered through a "hub" site. This is still possible by modifying the behavior of the Hub Transport delivery mechanism using the Set-AdSite Exchange Management Shell cmdlet. You must do two things to make this functionality work:

1. Enable the hub site functionality using a command similar to this:

   ```
   Set-AdSite SiteName -HubSiteEnable $True
   ```

2. Ensure that the Active Directory site link costs truly represent a "least cost" route from your remote sites to the hub site.

Microsoft recommends that you implement hub site routing only if your network topology requires it, such as due to having a firewall between all of the remote sites.

FIGURE 21.1
Sample Active Directory
site infrastructure

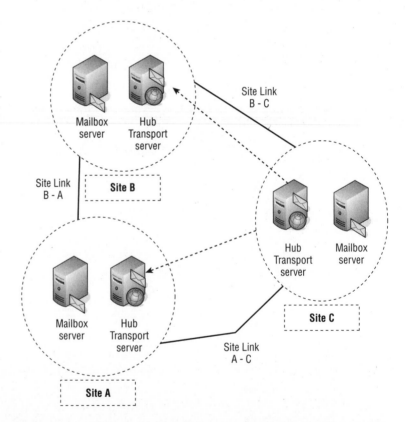

The Hub Transport server role is at the center of the message routing architecture for messages being delivered internally as well as messages leaving the organization. All messages are processed by the Hub Transport server role regardless of whether they are being delivered locally or remotely. Figure 21.2 shows an example of the Hub Transport sitting at the center of the message delivery universe.

FIGURE 21.2
The Hub Transport is at the center of all message delivery

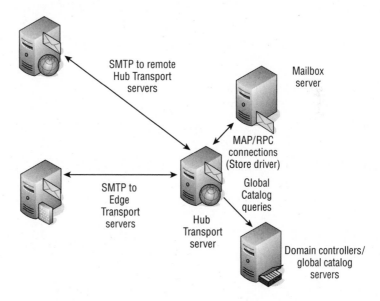

SMTP to remote Hub Transport servers

Mailbox server

MAP/RPC connections (Store driver)

SMTP to Edge Transport servers

Global Catalog queries

Hub Transport server

Domain controllers/ global catalog servers

The Hub Transport server role handles categorization, rule processing, transport-level journaling, and delivery for mail that is intended for local delivery and Mailbox servers in the same Active Directory site. The Hub Transport server uses the messaging API (MAPI) and RPCs to commute with the Mailbox server role. If a message is to be delivered to a Mailbox server in a remote Active Directory site, the Hub Transport server delivers the message via SMTP; the remote Hub Transport server then delivers the message to the local Mailbox server via RPC.

The Exchange Server 2007 Hub Transport server handles the message categorization. Essentially, the Categorizer is the component that figures out where the message is going next. Messages arrive in the submission queue, and the Categorizer picks up the message and processes it. The following are some of the steps involved in message categorization:

◆ Expand any distribution lists, if applicable, by querying the global catalog.

◆ Resolve recipient addresses to determine which recipients are local, remote, or outside of the organization.

◆ Apply message transport rules to the message.

◆ Split the message into multiple parts if the message is going to both local and remote recipients; this process is called *bifurcation*.

◆ Examine the message sender, recipients, message header, body, and attachments and apply message transport rules that apply to that message.

◆ Convert the message to the appropriate message format (Summary-TNEF, MIME, or UUENCODE) depending on the destination of the message.

◆ Determine the next "hop" for the message.

◆ Place the message into appropriate local or remote delivery queue.

With a few exceptions, such as application transport rules, the Categorizer function has not changed from Exchange 2000/2003.

As messages are moved within your organization's infrastructure, they are protected with different types of encryption. The encryption used is either RPC encryption or Transport Layer Security (TLS) encryption. Figure 21.3 shows different paths the message may take and how it is encrypted. I showed this in Chapter 2, "Designing a New Exchange 2007 System," but I wanted to review them here.

FIGURE 21.3
Messages are encrypted during transit

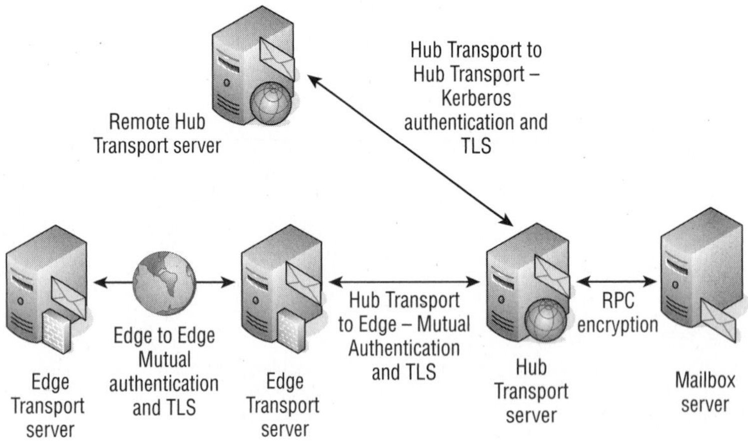

As messages are transmitted via MAPI over RPC between Mailbox servers and Hub Transport servers, RPC encryption is automatically used. When a message is transmitted from one Hub Transport server to another, the Hub Transport servers transport the message using SMTP, they authenticate using Kerberos, and the data stream is encrypted using TLS. When messages are transmitted from a Hub Transport server to an Edge Transport server, SMTP is used for message transfer, mutual authentication using certificates is used for authentication, and messages can be encrypted using TLS. Optionally, an organization that is sending messages to another organization also using Edge Transport services can configure authenticated connections and TLS encryption to these remote organizations.

Send and Receive Connectors

In Exchange 2000/2003, each Exchange server had one or more SMTP virtual servers. These SMTP virtual servers received inbound mail from other servers, from outside of the organization, or from POP3/IMAP4 clients. The SMTP virtual server could be configured to host an SMTP connector for delivering messages to external SMTP hosts or it could host a routing group connector (RGC) for delivering messages to remote Exchange 2000/2003 routing groups.

Exchange Server 2007 has replaced the SMTP virtual servers and SMTP connectors with Send connectors and Receive connectors.

RECEIVE CONNECTORS

The Receive connector is the point where inbound SMTP mail is received on the Hub Transport server. Receive connectors do not deliver outbound mail (unlike the Exchange 2000/2003 SMTP virtual server). Each Hub Transport server automatically has two Receive connectors. These are the Default connector and the Client connector. Figure 21.4 shows the Exchange Management

Console and the Server Configuration work center. In the Hub Transport subcontainer, you can see each server that hosts the Hub Transport role. The Receive connectors for server HNLEX04 are shown.

FIGURE 21.4

Receive connectors for an Exchange 2007 server

The properties of the Client HNLEX04 Receive connector are shown in Figure 21.4, specifically the Network property page of the Receive connector. Notice that the Client Receive connector listens on port number 587, not port 25. The Client Receive connector is intended for receiving mail from non-MAPI clients such as POP3 and IMAP4 clients. You would, of course, have to change the non-MAPI client's outbound SMTP port in order to use this connector.

The Default Receive connector is used to receive inbound SMTP mail from other Exchange 2007 Hub Transport servers in the organization. In Figure 21.5, the Permission Groups properties of the Default HNLEX04 Receive connector are shown. These are the default permissions for the Default Receive connector.

Notice that the Default Receive connector does not accept connections from anonymous users. This means that you cannot use it to receive e-mail from the Internet even though the Receive connector is listening on port 25. I'll come back to this later when I cover receiving e-mail from the outside.

You can also view the properties of a Receive connector using the `Get-ReceiveConnector` cmdlet. Here is an example that displays all the properties of the Default HNLEX04 Receive connector:

```
Get-ReceiveConnector "Default HNLEX04" | FL

AuthMechanism              : Tls, Integrated, BasicAuth,
```

```
    BasicAuthRequireTLS, ExchangeServer
Banner                             :
BinaryMimeEnabled                  : True
Bindings                           : {0.0.0.0:25}
ChunkingEnabled                    : True
DefaultDomain                      :
DeliveryStatusNotificationEnabled  : True
EightBitMimeEnabled                : True
DomainSecureEnabled                : False
EnhancedStatusCodesEnabled         : True
Fqdn            : HNLEX03.volcanosurfboards.com
Comment                            :
Enabled                            : True
ConnectionTimeout                  : 00:10:00
ConnectionInactivityTimeout        : 00:05:00
MessageRateLimit                   : unlimited
MaxInboundConnection               : 5000
MaxInboundConnectionPerSource      : unlimited
MaxInboundConnectionPercentagePerSource : 100
MaxHeaderSize                      : 64KB
MaxHopCount                        : 30
MaxLocalHopCount                   : 3
MaxLogonFailures                   : 3
MaxMessageSize: 10MB
MaxProtocolErrors                  : 5
MaxRecipientsPerMessage            : 5000
PermissionGroups                   : ExchangeUsers, ExchangeServers,
    ExchangeLegacyServers
PipeliningEnabled                  : True
ProtocolLoggingLevel               : Verbose
RemoteIPRanges: {0.0.0.0-255.255.255.255}
RequireEHLODomain                  : False
RequireTLS                         : False
Server                             : HNLEX04
SizeEnabled                        : EnabledWithoutValue
TarpitInterval                     : 00:00:05
AdminDisplayName                   :
ExchangeVersion                    : 0.1 (8.0.535.0)
Name                               : Default HNLEX05
DistinguishedName                  : CN=Default HNLEX04,CN=SMTP
  Receive Connectors,CN=Protocols,CN=HNLEX04,CN=Servers,CN=Exchange
Administrative Group (FYDIBOHF23SPDLT),CN=Administrative
Groups,CN=Volcano Surfboards,CN=Microsoft
Exchange,CN=Services,CN=Configuration,DC=volcanosurfboards,DC=com
Identity                           : HNLEX04\Default HNLEX03
Guid                               : 42364fae-4383-4eac-a6dd-2e8e7b2a2a08
ObjectCategory: volcanosurfboards.com/Configuration/
    Schema/ms-Exch-Smtp-Receive-Connector
ObjectClass                        : {top, msExchSmtpReceiveConnector}
```

```
WhenChanged               : 12/27/2006 9:13:54 AM
WhenCreated               : 11/18/2006 10:36:04 AM
OriginatingServer         : HNLDC01.volcanosurfboards.com
IsValid                   : True
```

FIGURE 21.5
Default Receive
connector permissions

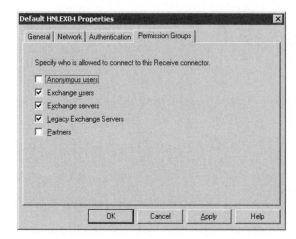

With few exceptions, you will usually not need to create additional Receive connectors, nor will you need to make many changes to the existing Receive connectors that are used internally.

SEND CONNECTORS

Although Receive connectors are configured for each server, Send connectors are organizational connectors that you can assign to a number of different Hub Transport servers. Each server also has an implicit Send connector, but that connector is used only for transferring mail to other Hub Transport servers. The implicit Send connector does not show up either in the Exchange Management Console (EMC) or when you use the Exchange Management Shell (EMS), and there are no properties that can be set for the implicit Send connector. Send connectors are managed in the EMC under the Hub Transport subcontainer of the Organization Configuration work center. Figure 21.6 shows the Source Server properties for a connector called E2K7 Connector To Internet.

Figure 21.6 shows the Source Server properties of a Send connector. The Source Server property page is where you designate which Hub Transport servers will deliver messages for this particular Send connector. When you assign more than one Hub Transport server as a source server, the outbound messaging load will be load-balanced among the source servers. You can view the properties of this Send connector also using the EMS cmdlet `Get-SendConnector`; here is an example:

```
Get-SendConnector "E2K7 Send Connector to Internet" | FL

AddressSpaces             : {smtp:*;1}
AuthenticationCredential  :
Comment                   :
ConnectedDomains          : {}
```

```
ConnectionInactivityTimeOut  : 00:10:00
DNSRoutingEnabled            : False
DomainSecureEnabled          : False
Enabled                      : True
ForceHELO                    : False
Fqdn                         : mail.somorita.com
HomeMTA                      : Microsoft MTA
HomeMtaServerId              : HNLEX04
Identity                     : E2K7 Send Connector to Internet
IgnoreSTARTTLS               : False
IsScopedConnector            : False
IsSmtpConnector              : True
LinkedReceiveConnector       :
MaxMessageSize               : 10MB
Name                         : E2K7 Send Connector to Internet
Port                         : 25
ProtocolLoggingLevel         : None
RequireTLS                   : False
SmartHostAuthMechanism       : None
SmartHosts                   : {smtp-server.relay-isp.com}
SmartHostsString             : smtp-server.relay-isp.com
SourceIPAddress              : 0.0.0.0
SourceRoutingGroup           : Exchange Routing Group (DWBGZMFD01QNBJR)
SourceTransportServers       : {HNLEX04}
UseExternalDNSServersEnabled : False
```

FIGURE 21.6
Managing Send
connectors

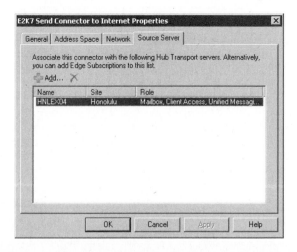

Because Exchange Server 2007 does not have a default SMTP connector for outbound mail, you will need to create at least one Send connector. Most organizations will need to create only a single Send connector; this connector will be used to send mail to the Internet, to an Edge Transport server, or to an SMTP smarthost system that will deliver mail to the Internet on behalf of the Exchange server.

CREATING A SEND CONNECTOR

This section goes through an example of creating a Send connector that will be responsible for sending mail to the Internet. In the Hub Transport subcontainer of the Organization Configuration work center, make sure the Send Connectors tab is highlighted, and then click the New Send Connector task on the Actions pane. This launches the New SMTP Send Connector Wizard shown in Figure 21.7. On the Introduction page, you must provide the name of the connector and specify the intended use of the connector.

FIGURE 21.7

Introduction page of the New SMTP Send Connector Wizard

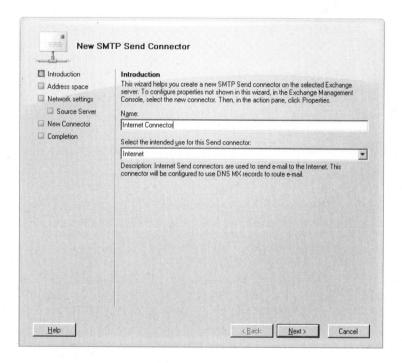

The wizard will allow you to create four types (intended use options) of Send connectors, but these are just predefined configurations and you can always change the properties of the connector you create later. The four types of Send connectors you can create are as follows:

◆ The Custom Send connector type allows you to manually configure all of the configuration settings at some point after the connector is created.

◆ The Internal Send connector type allows you to configure a connector that connects to other Hub Transport servers in your organization. Because all internal mail routing is automatic, you will usually not need to create an internal Send connector.

◆ The Internet Send connector type is used to send mail to the Internet using DNS MX records.

◆ The Partner Send connector type creates a connector that will be used to send mail to specific Internet domains and will use certificate authentication and TLS encryption.

On the Address Space page of the wizard, you can specify the SMTP domains to which this Send connector will deliver e-mail. Because this connector is going to send mail to the Internet, use an address space of * for this example. The * address space means all SMTP addresses that are not explicitly defined on another connector.

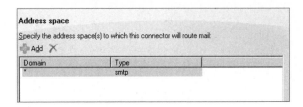

On the Network Settings property page, you can configure Smart Host if you want mail to be delivered to another SMTP host for external delivery, such as with an Edge Transport server, or you can specify Use Domain Name System (DNS) "MX" Records to Route Mail Automatically. If you use DNS for mail delivery, this Send connector will be responsible for all outbound mail delivery.

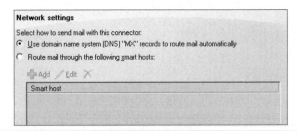

The Source Server page allows you to specify the Hub Transport servers that will deliver mail for this Send connector. If you have more than one Hub Transport server, I recommend you use additional Hub Transport servers for redundancy.

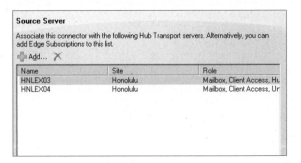

Once you click the New button on the New Connector page, the EMC will execute the command necessary to create the new Send connector. The following is the EMS command that was executed:

```
New-SendConnector -Name 'Internet Connector' -Usage 'Internet'↵
-AddressSpaces 'smtp:*;1' -DNSRoutingEnabled $true↵
-UseExternalDNSServersEnabled $false -SourceTransportServers 'HNLEX03','HNLEX04'
```

Once you have created the connector, you should make one additional configuration option. On the General property page (shown in Figure 21.8) of the Send connector, enter the public name of the FQDN for this server, such as mail.somorita.com.

FIGURE 21.8

General properties of a
Send connector

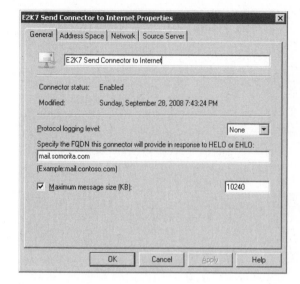

This is the name that the Send connector uses in the EHLO or HELO command when it connects to a remote SMTP system. If you don't specify an FQDN for the connector to use, the connector will use the default FQDN for the server. Often this is an internal name that is not recognized on the Internet. Some Internet hosts will reject a connection if the name cannot be resolved.

Connectivity to Exchange 2000/2003

When you install Exchange 2007 in an existing Exchange 2003 organization, to allow coexistence and facilitate routing, setup creates an administrative group, a routing group, and a Windows security group for backward compatibility. (In a native Exchange 2007 organization, routing group connectors are not used. They are necessary only when interoperating with Exchange 2000/2003.) These groups are as follows:

◆ Setup creates an administrative group for the Exchange 2007 servers to be housed in. This administrative group is called Exchange Administrative Group (FYDIBOHF23SPDLT). All Exchange 2007 servers will be in this administrative group; do not move them out of this administrative group.

◆ Setup creates a routing group called Exchange Routing Group (DWBGZMFD01QNBJR). All Exchange 2007 servers will be in this routing group and you must not move them out of this routing group.

◆ Setup creates an Active Directory universal security group called ExchangeLegacyInterop. The ExchangeLegacyInterop group has permissions that allow Exchange 2003 and Exchange 2007 servers to send messages between each other.

The new administrative and routing groups are not visible within the Exchange 2007 Management Console, but you can see them using the Exchange 2000/2003 System Manager console (see Figure 21.9).

FIGURE 21.9
Viewing the Exchange 2007 administrative and routing group

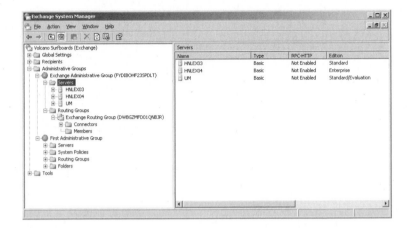

If you are installing Exchange Server 2007 into an existing Exchange 2000/2003 environment, during the installation of the first Exchange 2007 Hub Transport server role, you are prompted for an Exchange 2000/2003 server to use as a bridgehead. The setup program will create a routing group connector from the Exchange Routing Group (DWBGZMFD01QNBJR) routing group to the specified server in the remote routing group.

ADDING MORE BRIDGEHEAD SERVERS

Only the first Hub Transport server is set up as a bridgehead server to Exchange Server 2003; you must use the Set-RoutingGroupConnector cmdlet to add additional bridgeheads.

For example, say an organization has two routing groups, the New York Routing Group and the San Francisco Routing group. Each routing group has two Exchange 2003 servers that function as bridgehead servers for the routing group connector that connects the New York and San Francisco routing groups, as illustrated in Figure 21.10.

When the first Exchange 2007 server is installed, the Exchange Routing Group (DWBGZMFD01QNBJR) is created and the setup program prompts the installer for a remote Exchange 2003 server to use as a bridgehead. In this example, I am choosing one of the servers in the San Francisco routing group.

The setup program creates a routing group connector from the Exchange 2007 routing group to the San Francisco routing group. A single local bridgehead and a single remote bridgehead are defined. An identical routing group connector is created from the San Francisco routing group to the Exchange 2007 routing group. Figure 21.11 shows the properties of one of these routing group connectors using the Exchange 2003 System Manager console.

If you have multiple routing groups and multiple bridgehead servers, you will want to correct a couple of issues. First, there is no redundancy between the Exchange 2003 servers and the Exchange 2007 servers. If either the Hub Transport server or the Exchange 2003 bridgehead server that is being used for the routing group connector fails, messaging between the Exchange 2003 and Exchange 2007 mailboxes will halt.

FIGURE 21.10
Message routing between Exchange 2003 and Exchange 2007

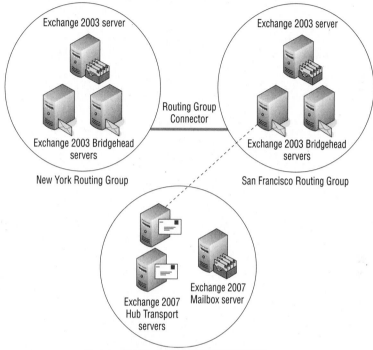

FIGURE 21.11
Properties of a routing group connector as viewed from Exchange 2003 System Manager

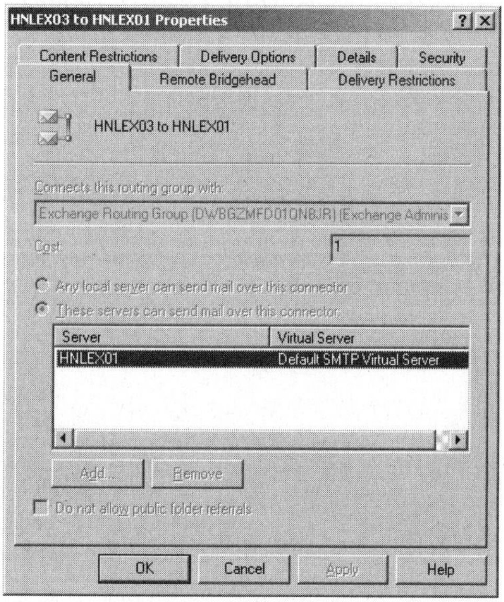

Second, you will want to verify that all messages from New York to the Exchange 2007 Mailbox servers (and vice versa) will be sent through the San Francisco Exchange 2003 bridgehead servers.

Routing group connectors between Exchange 2007 and Exchange 2003 cannot be modified using the Exchange 2000/2003 System Manager console or the Exchange 2007 Exchange Management Console. Therefore, you need to correct both of these issues using the Exchange Management Shell and the routing group cmdlets. Table 21.1 lists the most useful cmdlets for managing routing groups between Exchange 2000/2003 and Exchange 2007.

TABLE 21.1:   Cmdlets for Managing Routing Groups Between Exchange 2000/2003 and Exchange 2007

CMDLET	DESCRIPTION
Get-RoutingGroupConnector	Retrieves the routing group connectors or properties of specified connectors
New-RoutingGroupConnector	Creates a new routing group connector
Remove-RoutingGroupConnector	Deletes a routing group connector
Set-RoutingGroupConnector	Sets the properties of a routing group connector

Because this is all done from the EMS, let's start with some basics. Here is an example of using the Get-RoutingGroupConnector with no parameters to retrieve a list of the routing group connectors:

```
Get-RoutingGroupConnector
Name                   SourceRoutingGroup          TargetRoutingGroup
----                   ------------------          ------------------
HNLEX03 to HNLEX01     Exchange Routing Group...   First Routing Group
HNLEX03 to HNLEX01     First Routing Group         Exchange Routing Group
```

The SourceRoutingGroup and TargetRoutingGroup columns have been truncated to fit better into the page in case you were wondering where the full name of the Exchange 2007 routing group is. Here is an example of retrieving all the properties of the HNLEX03:

```
Get-RoutingGroupConnector "HNLEX03 to HNLEX01" | FL

TargetRoutingGroup          : Exchange Routing Group (DWBGZMFD01QNBJR)
Cost                        : 1
TargetTransportServers      : {HNLEX03}
ExchangeLegacyDN            : /o=Volcano Surfboards/ou=First
Administrative Group/cn=Configuration/cn=Connections/cn=HNLEX03 to HNLEX01
PublicFolderReferralsEnabled : True
SourceRoutingGroup          : First Routing Group
SourceTransportServers      : {HNLEX01}
HomeMTA                     : Microsoft MTA
HomeMtaServerId             : HNLEX01
MinAdminVersion             : -2147453113
```

```
AdminDisplayName           :
ExchangeVersion            : 0.1 (8.0.535.0)
Name                       : HNLEX03 to HNLEX01
DistinguishedName          : CN=HNLEX03 to HNLEX01,
CN=Connections,CN=First Routing Group,CN=Routing
Groups,CN=First Administrative Group,CN=Administrative
Groups,CN=Volcano Surfboards,CN=Microsoft
Exchange,CN=Services,CN=Configuration,DC=volcanosurfboards,DC=com
Identity                   : HNLEX03 to HNLEX01
Guid: 4445126d-f275-4f5e-9934-d0048591a59a
ObjectCategory             : volcanosurfboards.com/Configuration/Schema/
ms-Exch-Routing-Group-Connector
ObjectClass                : {top, msExchConnector, msExchRoutingGroupConnector}
WhenChanged                : 11/19/2006 6:38:35 PM
WhenCreated                : 11/19/2006 6:38:35 PM
OriginatingServer          : HNLDC01.volcanosurfboards.com
IsValid                    : True
```

If you wanted to add HNLEX04 as an additional target bridgehead server, you would use the `Set-RoutingGroupConnector` cmdlet. But this is going to be a bit tricky because the display names of the routing group connectors are identical. You need to retrieve just the connector that connects from the Exchange 2000/2003 routing group to the Exchange 2007 routing group. Here is an example using the `Where-Object` cmdlet:

```
Get-RoutingGroupConnector | Where-Object {$_.TargetRoutingGroup -eq↵
"Exchange Routing Group (DWBGZMFD01QNBJR)"}
Name                SourceRoutingGroup       TargetRoutingGroup
----                ------------------       ------------------
HNLEX03 to HNLEX01    First Routing Group      Exchange Routing Group
```

You can pipe the results of that cmdlet to the `Set-RoutingGroupConnector` cmdlet. Here is an example:

```
Get-RoutingGroupConnector | Where $_.TargetRoutingGroup -eq↵
"Exchange Routing Group (DWBGZMFD01QNBJR)"} | Set-RoutingGroupConnector↵
-TargetTransportServers HNLEX03,HNLEX04
```

Now you can verify that this change has been made. Here a command that will list the relevant properties of that routing group connector:

```
Get-RoutingGroupConnector | Where {$_.TargetRoutingGroup -eq↵
"Exchange Routing Group (DWBGZMFD01QNBJR)"}↵
| FL Name,TargetRoutingGroup,SourceRoutingGroup,*transport*
Name                 : HNLEX03 to HNLEX01
TargetRoutingGroup   : Exchange Routing Group (DWBGZMFD01QNBJR)
SourceRoutingGroup   : First Routing Group
TargetTransportServers : {HNLEX04, HNLEX03}
SourceTransportServers : {HNLEX01}
```

Supporting Internet E-mail

Most organizations have the ability to send and receive Internet mail. This section covers configuring Exchange Server 2007 to send and receive Internet mail as well as implementing anti-spam protection. Outbound e-mail is actually pretty simple to configure and support because all you need to do is create a Send connector, which was discussed earlier in this chapter.

Inbound e-mail is another matter. You can choose from a number of different configurations or topologies to configure your Receive connectors based on security and message hygiene requirements. Depending on your needs and requirements, you can use one of the following:

◆ E-mail is sent directly to the Exchange 2007 Hub Transport server.

◆ E-mail is sent to the Edge Transport server, which performs anti-spam and antivirus inspections and then passes the message on to a Hub Transport server.

◆ E-mail is first sent to third-party software or a third-party appliance for message hygiene functions and then forwarded on to a Hub Transport server.

◆ E-mail is first sent to third-party software or a third-party appliance for message hygiene functions, then to an Edge Transport server for additional message hygiene functions, and then finally on to the an Exchange 2007 Hub Transport server.

◆ E-mail is sent to a managed provider such as MessageOne or Microsoft Exchange Hosted Security where message hygiene, archival, and other security functions are performed. Then the e-mail is sent to the organization's Exchange 2007 Hub Transport servers.

I could actually come up with a number of additional permutations and possibilities for message security and message hygiene functions. Actually, I could fill up a couple of chapters of material on message hygiene, messaging security, and possible configurations. However, I'll keep this simple and explain the topic more conceptually.

First I will explain how to allow Exchange 2007 to receive e-mail directly from the Internet, and then talk about the use of the Edge Transport server.

Configuring Exchange to Receive Internet Mail

In this section, I cover the fairly simple task of allowing one or more Exchange 2007 Hub Transport servers to receive mail from any Internet sender. Figure 21.12 illustrates this configuration. Both the external and internal firewalls allow SMTP traffic sent over TCP port 25 from any Internet host to be sent directly to the Exchange 2007 Hub Transport server.

The Default Receive connector accepts the messages directly from Internet hosts once you have modified the Permission Groups properties. Many organizations use this type of configuration successfully, but remember that this violates the concept of multilayer security because all content is delivered directly to the Hub Transport server role. You must employ some type of message hygiene function on the Hub Transport server to protect your organization from viruses and spam. Antivirus solutions are discussed in Chapter 25, "Security and Tracking Activities."

By default, the Exchange 2007 anti-spam agents are not available on a Hub Transport server. However, you can enable the anti-spam agents on a Hub Transport server using the Install-AntispamAgents.ps1 script in the \Program Files\Microsoft\Exchange Server\Scripts folder. Once the agents are installed, either reboot the Exchange server or restart the Microsoft Exchange Transport service. You can restart the service using the Exchange Management Shell with the following command:

```
Restart-Service msexchangetransport
```

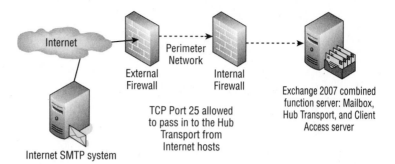

Once the anti-spam agents are installed, management of the anti-spam agents on a Hub Transport is almost identical to managing them on an Edge Transport server. I discuss these later in this chapter.

I mentioned this previously, but I want to make sure that you allow anonymous users to connect to the Receive connector that is exposed to the Internet. If you forget this step, you will end up spending a lot of time troubleshooting why your Exchange server is rejecting e-mail from the Internet. On the Permission Groups properties (shown in Figure 21.13) of the Default Receive connector, make sure that you have checked the Anonymous Users check box.

FIGURE 21.13
Allowing a Receive
connector to receive
mail from the Internet

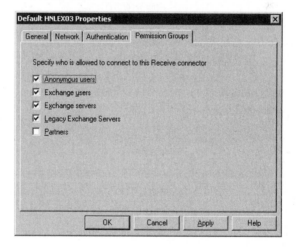

By default, your Exchange 2007 servers will only accept e-mail destined to the Windows Active Directory DNS domain that the server was a member of. In order to accept e-mail intended for your external SMTP domain, you will need to create a new accepted domain. This was discussed in Chapter 11, "Managing Recipients," but I thought it was important enough to reiterate here.

An accepted domain is a domain for which your Exchange organization can accept e-mail. You will need an accepted domain configuration for each domain for which your Exchange servers will accept e-mail. The accepted domain is the FQDN after the @ symbol in your e-mail address.

NON-DELIVERY MESSAGE FOR LACK OF ACCEPTED DOMAIN

If you fail to create an accepted domain for the e-mail domains for which you accept mail, people who send e-mail directly to your users will probably get an NDR with the error "550 5.7.1 Unable to relay."

Let's go through a quick example. Accepted domains are created in the Hub Transport sub-container of the Organization Configuration work center. You see the list of accepted domains on the Accepted Domains tab in the Results pane. In this example, you support users whose e-mail domain is `volcanocoffee.com`, so you can accept inbound mail intended for that domain. You should choose the New Accepted Domain task on the Actions pane to launch the New Accepted Domain Wizard (shown in Figure 21.14).

FIGURE 21.14
Creating a new accepted domain

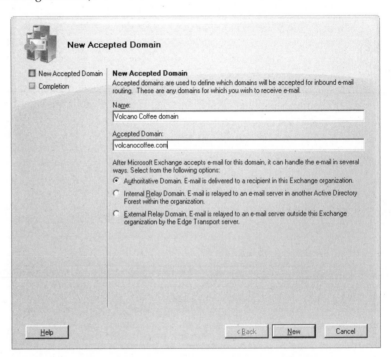

You must specify a name for the accepted domain along with its DNS domain name. Because the e-mail addresses will all belong to internal mailboxes (this is the usual configuration), select the Authoritative Domain radio button, and then click New to create the new accepted domain. (For more information on authoritative, internal relay, and external relay domains, see Chapter 11.)

Using Edge Transport Services

Implementing an additional layer of protection for your e-mail servers is always a good idea. This is certainly not a new concept for medium and large organizations. Even 10 years or more in the past, organizations frequently would put an SMTP server in their perimeter network and configure the SMTP in the perimeter network to accept their inbound mail and then relay the mail into an internal mail server. Usually this was a hardened Unix system that performed only SMTP mail relay functions.

As viruses became more prevalent, these systems began to include virus-scanning functions. As spam became more and more of a problem, these systems were configured to filter or quarantine messages suspected of being spam. This concept of inspecting mail before it arrives on the mail server has spawned a whole cottage industry of service providers, appliance vendors, and third-party software.

Performing this initial inspection could be important for a number of reasons:

♦ It filters the unwanted content arriving on your network before it reaches internal mail servers.

♦ It reduces the load on mailbox and internal mail transport servers by keeping unwanted content off of them.

♦ It provides an additional layer of protection against spam or viruses.

♦ It filters the mail as closely as possible to the originating source.

♦ It prevents Internet hosts from directly accessing the internal Exchange servers.

Microsoft decided shortly after the release of Exchange Server 2003 that the Exchange server platform was not the best place for preliminary virus and spam inspection. Neither was it a good idea to put any Active Directory member server in the perimeter network. After all, an Exchange server is a member of the Active Directory and requires connectivity to other Exchange servers as well as the Active Directory domain controllers and global catalog servers. To build an Exchange 2000/2003 server for handling just message transfer, a number of unnecessary components had to be installed. The information store service even had to remain running. If this server were compromised, the entire network could be exposed.

The Edge Transport server was developed with minimal messaging functionality but with a certain amount of "knowledge" of your internal recipients and infrastructure. Essentially, it is nothing more than a message transport engine that allows for the plug-in of additional components such as transport rules, anti-spam agents, and antivirus software. Edge Transport does not communicate directly with or require Active Directory; instead, Edge Transport uses the Microsoft Active Directory Application Mode (ADAM) (in Windows Server 2008 ADAM is now known as Active Directory Lightweight Directory Services or just AD LDS) database for its configuration. The Hub Transport server runs a feature called Microsoft Exchange EdgeSync that pushes configuration data, recipient information, and safe sender lists. The EdgeSync process replicates the following data from the internal Active Directory to the ADAM database:

♦ A list of the valid SMTP addresses for the Active Directory, including mailbox-enabled users, mail-enabled users, mail-enabled contacts, mail-enabled groups, and mail-enabled public folders

♦ The list of internal accepted domains

♦ The list of remote domains

♦ Configured message classifications

♦ Safe and blocked sender lists for each user

♦ Internal Send connector configuration

Edge Transport rules are based on SMTP addresses, not Active Directory objects — but you can use the SMTP addresses of mail-enabled groups. For the most part, the Edge Transport rules are a subset of hub rules — the exception is quarantine, which is available only on the edge, because it is intended for spam.

As an added advantage, the Edge Transport server is managed using the same management tools (the Exchange Management Console, Exchange Management Shell, Queue Viewer, Best Practices Analyzer, and so on) you use to manage other Exchange 2007 server roles, so there is no steep learning curve associated with deploying the Edge Transport server role.

To maximize the security benefits, I recommend that the Edge Transport server be deployed in your perimeter network such as is shown in Figure 21.15. Figure 21.15 takes a slightly modified version of the implementation shown in Figure 21.12. The organization's DNS MX record directs inbound e-mail to the Edge Transport server that is located in the perimeter network.

FIGURE 21.15
Deploying an Exchange
Edge Transport server

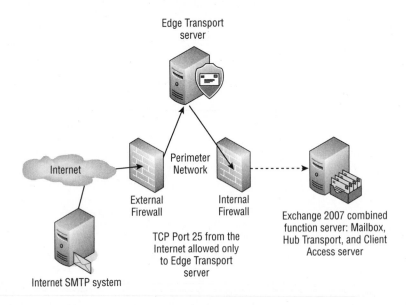

The Edge Transport server performs anti-spam and antivirus functions and then passes messages on to an internal Hub Transport server. The firewall is configured so that TCP port 25 inbound from the Internet is allowed only to the Edge Transport server. Likewise, the internal firewall only allows inbound TCP port 25 from the Edge Transport server in the perimeter network and only to the Hub Transport server on the internal network.

The Edge Transport server has specific anti-spam transport agents installed that handle different types of filtering, analysis, and transport rules. Table 21.2 shows the transport agents that are installed on an Edge Transport server. All the transport agents are installed and enabled by default.

SETTING UP THE EDGE TRANSPORT

This section goes through a sample configuration of the Edge Transport server and the Hub Transport server, as illustrated in Figure 21.16. The internal firewall must first be configured to allow certain types of inbound and outbound connectivity between the internal network and the perimeter network. Specifically, connectivity is required between the Edge Transport server and the Hub Transport server. I have kept this example really simple; you would need to scale this for additional Hub Transport servers and Edge Transport servers.

This setup has the following requirements:

◆ The Edge Transport server must be able to send SMTP (TCP port 25) to the Hub Transport server.

◆ The Hub Transport server should be able to send SMTP to the Edge Transport server if the Edge Transport server will be used for outbound mail.

◆ The Hub Transport server must also be able to communicate using the ports designated for LDAP synchronization to the ADAM database.

◆ These are either TCP port 50389 for regular LDAP or TCP port 50636 for secure LDAP. You will usually use port 50389 unless you have configured ADAM on the Edge Transport to use SSL.

TABLE 21.2:   Edge Transport Server Transport Agents

AGENT	FEATURES PROVIDED
Address Rewriting Inbound agent	Messaging policy and compliance
Address Rewriting Outbound agent	Messaging policy and compliance
Attachment Filter agent	Anti-spam and antivirus
Connection Filter agent	Anti-spam and antivirus
Content Filter agent	Anti-spam and antivirus
Edge Rule agent	Messaging policy and compliance
Protocol Analysis agent	Anti-spam and antivirus
Recipient Filter agent	Anti-spam and antivirus
Sender Filter agent	Anti-spam and antivirus
Sender ID agent	Anti-spam and antivirus

FIGURE 21.16
Simple Edge Transport deployment

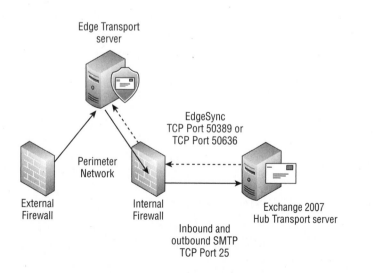

You might need to open additional ports through the internal firewall and to the Edge Transport server if you want to use the Remote Desktop Connection (RDP) client to manage the Edge Transport server remotely. The RDP client uses TCP port 3389.

To configure simple mail flow between an Edge Transport server and a Hub Transport server, you could just configure the necessary Send and Receive connectors, but you would not be receiving the full benefits of the Edge Transport role. To do so, you need to configure Edge Synchronization (EdgeSync). This process involves five basic steps:

1. Perform prerequisite checks and configuration settings.

2. Create an Edge Subscription file on the Edge Transport server.

3. Copy the Edge Subscription file to the Hub Transport server.

4. Import the Edge Subscription file and create a Send connector for the Edge Subscription.

5. Start the Microsoft Exchange EdgeSync service on the Hub Transport server (if it's not already started).

You should perform all of these steps within 24 hours because the bootstrap account that is created with the Edge Subscription file is only good for 24 hours from the time it was created.

The Edge Subscription that you are creating will work for all existing Hub Transport servers at the time you create it. However, if you add additional Hub Transport servers into the Active Directory site, you must create a new Edge Subscription for each Hub Transport server that will communicate with the Edge Transport.

Configuring EdgeSync

Let's go through the preconfiguration checklist and make sure you are ready to configure EdgeSync. Here is a list of tasks you should perform:

◆ Confirm that DNS name resolution between the Hub Transport and the Edge Transport works. In some cases, you may need to create HOSTS files for the two systems if the internal Hub Transport server is not resolvable in DNS by the Edge Transport server and vice versa.

◆ Ensure that the necessary ports on the firewall are opened.

◆ Configure the accepted domains and remote domains for your organization (on the internal Exchange 2007 servers).

◆ Define the internal SMTP servers so that Sender ID knows which servers are internal to your organization and the connection filters know not to reject connections from your internal IP addresses.

The internal SMTP servers must be configured using the EMS cmdlet `Set-TransportConfig`. In the following example, the internal mail servers are defined as having the IP addresses 192.168.254.102 and 192.168.254.19:

```
Set-TransportConfig -InternalSMTPServers 192.168.254.102,192.168.254.19
```

Next you need to switch to the console of the Edge Transport server and create the Edge Subscription file. The following command creates a new EdgeSync subscription file called `EdgeSync.xml`. Note that the confirmation message mentions a couple of the prerequisites:

```
New-EdgeSubscription -FileName "c:\EdgeSync.xml"

Confirm
Creating an Edge Subscription makes the configuration of this Edge
Transport server ready to be managed via EdgeSync. Any of the
following types of objects that were created manually will be deleted:
accepted domains; message classifications; remote domains; and Send
connectors. Also, the InternalSMTPServers list of the TransportConfig
object will be overwritten during the synchronization process. The
Exchange Management Shell tasks that manage those types of objects will
be locked out on this Edge Transport server. You must manage those
objects from inside the organization and allow EdgeSync to update the
Edge Transport server. EdgeSync requires that this Edge Transport
server is able to resolve the fully qualified domain names (FQDN) of
the Hub Transport servers in the Active Directory site to which the
Edge Transport server is being subscribed. Those Hub Transport servers
must be able to resolve the FQDN of this Edge Transport server. You
should complete the Edge Subscription inside the organization in the
next "1440" minutes before the bootstrap account expires.
[Y] Yes  [A] Yes to All  [N] No  [L] No to All  [S] Suspend  [?] Help
(default is "Y"):y
```

READY THE SNEAKERNET: TRANSFERRING THE *EDGESYNC.XML* FILE

One of the things that Exchange administrators are often not prepared for is that they must transfer the `edgesync.xml` file from the Edge Transport server to the Hub Transport server. Have a floppy disk or a USB thumb drive handy when you generate this file at the Edge Transport server.

The file that is created is shown in Figure 21.17. Take special note of the `<EdgeServerFQDN>` XML tag. This value will be used by the Hub Transport server when it must transmit data (SMTP data or EdgeSync replication data) to the Edge Transport server, so this FQDN must be resolvable by the Hub Transport server.

Other content you will find in the EdgeSync subscription file includes the Edge server's certificate, the username, and password information that the Hub Transport server will use when authenticating to the Edge Transport server and vice versa.

You need to transport this `EdgeSync.xml` file to the Hub Transport server now. If all file sharing ports between the perimeter and the internal network are locked down, you may have to use a USB drive, CD-ROM, or a floppy disk (oh, the horror). Once you have the EdgeSync subscription file on the Hub Transport server, you can import the file into the Exchange 2007 organization.

In the Organization Configuration work center of the Exchange Management Console, open the Hub Transport subcontainer and select the Edge Subscriptions tab. To import the new EdgeSync subscription file, choose the New Edge Subscription task from the Actions pane. This launches the New Edge Subscription Wizard (shown in Figure 21.18).

FIGURE 21.17

The result of the New-EdgeSubscription command

FIGURE 21.18

Creating a new Edge Subscription for the Hub Transport server

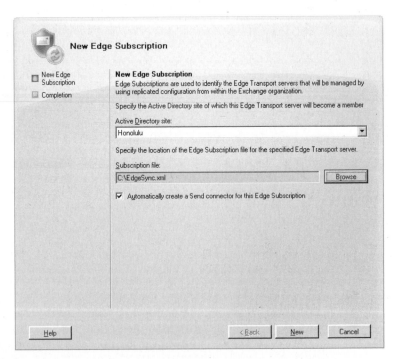

You must specify the Active Directory site that this Edge Transport server will be a member of. I recommend that you allow the New Edge Subscription Wizard to create the necessary Send connector to be used with the Edge Transport server. When you are ready, click the New button. The Completion page will remind you to verify firewall connectivity and name resolution.

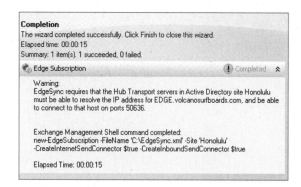

Completion
The wizard completed successfully. Click Finish to close this wizard.
Elapsed time: 00:00:15
Summary: 1 item(s). 1 succeeded, 0 failed.

Edge Subscription   (!) Completed ⌃

Warning:
EdgeSync requires that the Hub Transport servers in Active Directory site Honolulu
must be able to resolve the IP address for EDGE.volcanosurfboards.com, and be able
to connect to that host on ports 50636.

Exchange Management Shell command completed:
new-EdgeSubscription -FileName 'C:\EdgeSync.xml' -Site 'Honolulu'
-CreateInternetSendConnector $true -CreateInboundSendConnector $true

Elapsed Time: 00:00:15

The Edge Synchronization process should start almost immediately and will synchronize configuration data once every hour afterward. Recipient information will be synchronized once every four hours. You can force the synchronization to run by running the EMS cmdlet `Start-EdgeSynchronization` with no parameters.

If you want to include your user's safe sender list in the synchronization, you should also schedule the `Update-SafeList` cmdlet to run periodically (usually once per day is fine). This command should run on the Hub Transport server. Here is an example that will update the safe sender lists for all users so that they are pushed to the Edge Transport via the Edge Sync process:

```
Get-Mailbox | Update-SafeList
```

If you have more than 1,000 recipients in your organization, you will need to tell `Get-Mailbox` to return more than the default 1,000 recipients. You can use this command instead.

```
Get-Mailbox -ResultSize Unlimited | Update-SafeList
```

Confirming That EdgeSync Is Running

Once you have started Edge Synchronization, you can perform a few tasks to confirm that the data is synchronizing to the ADAM database on the Edge Transport server. The first, of course, is to check the Application event log on the Hub Transport server that is running EdgeSync. Event ID 1000 from source MSExchange EdgeSync indicates that synchronization has completed successfully. Figure 21.19 shows this event.

Annoyingly, the times listed in the Description field of Event ID 1000 are in GMT rather than in local time. The actual event time displays in local time, but the time in the description is different, so keep that in mind if you are troubleshooting.

In addition, you can verify that the configuration data has been transferred over to the Edge Transport server's ADAM database by looking in the Exchange Management Console on the Edge Transport server. Figure 21.20 shows the Exchange Management Console and the Edge Transport work center. In the Accepted Domains tab in the Work pane for server EDGE, you can see the accepted domains that were transferred from the Exchange 2007 organization.

Any objects or properties that have synchronized from the internal Exchange Server 2007 organization (such as accepted domains, remote domains, Send connectors) should not be managed on the Edge Transport server. These objects and properties should be managed on the internal Exchange Server 2007 organization; they will be replicated to the Edge Transport server automatically.

FIGURE 21.19
Viewing successful EdgeSync information

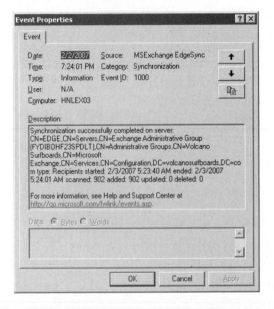

FIGURE 21.20
Viewing the accepted domains that have synchronized to an Exchange 2007 Edge Transport server

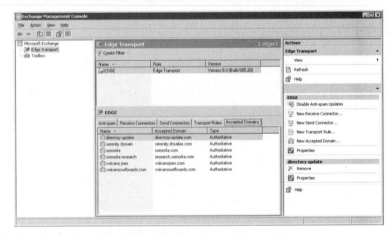

MANAGING EDGE TRANSPORT SERVERS

Note that the Edge Transport's management console cannot be accessed remotely. You must manage Edge Transport servers from their console or using Remote Desktop Connection.

Configuring the Edge Transport Server to Fight Spam

You now have an Edge Transport server running and synchronizing with the internal Exchange Server 2007 system and the Active Directory. Out of the box, many of the anti-spam agents are enabled and configured; the configuration is usually targeted toward a typical organization. You can make some tweaks to ensure that your organization is effectively filtering spam. You can find the anti-spam features of the Edge Transport server on the Anti-Spam tab, as shown in Figure 21.21.

FIGURE 21.21

Customizing anti-spam features of an Edge Transport server

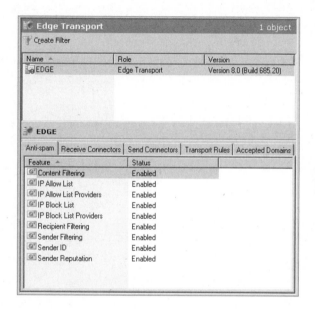

You can see the different anti-spam configuration options you can configure for the Exchange 2007 Edge Transport server. It is also helpful to note that the same anti-spam configuration options will be available for your Exchange Server 2007 organization if you have run the `Install-AntispamAgents.ps1` script on your Hub Transport servers.

Content Filtering

Content Filtering is a new feature in Exchange Server 2007 that was formerly known as the Intelligent Message Filter. The content filter examines the message's content based on keyword analysis, message size, and other factors and assigns the message a spam confidence level (SCL) ranking. This ranking is from 0 to 9. A message with a ranking of 0 is the least likely to be spam and a message with an SCL of 9 is very likely to be spam. Based on the SCL value of the message, you have several actions you can take (see Figure 21.22).

You can take three possible actions, ranked in order of severity:

1. Delete messages that meet or exceed a specific SCL threshold. This is the most drastic of actions. The sender is not notified that this has occurred, and you can't later evaluate whether the message really was spam.

2. Reject messages that meet or exceed a specific SCL threshold. The Exchange server analyzes the message and kicks it back to the sender with text indicating that the message was rejected because it looks like spam.

3. Quarantine messages that meet or exceed a specific SCL threshold. Any messages with the specified SCL value or higher will be sent to an SMTP address where you can then analyze them to determine if they are truly spam or not.

FIGURE 21.22
The Action property page of the Content Filtering object

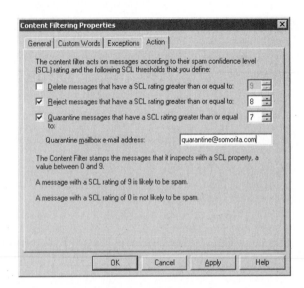

You can activate none, one, two, or all three of the actions, but the SCL values must progress downward in accordance with the severity of the action. For example, you could set a reject value of 8 or higher and a quarantine value of 7 or higher. In that case, any messages with an SCL value of 8 or 9 will be rejected; messages with an SCL value of 7 will be sent to the quarantine e-mail address. However, you cannot set a quarantine value of 9 but then delete everything with an SCL value greater than or equal to 7.

On the inside of your Exchange organization, a global value called the SCL Junk Threshold is set to 8 by default. This instructs the information store to place any messages with a spam confidence level of 8 or higher into the user's Junk E-mail folder. Users can then review their Junk E-mail folder to determine whether a message was truly spam. However, if you set the quarantine value on the Edge Transport server to 7, then only messages with an SCL value of 6 or less will reach the Junk E-mail folder.

You can safely drop the SCL value to 5 or 6. To lower the Junk E-mail threshold for all users, on one of the Exchange Server 2007 servers in your organization, type this command:

```
Set-OrganizationConfig -SCLJunkThreshold 6
```

You can view the organization configuration using the Get-OrganizationConfig cmdlet.

In some cases, a specific user may need a different set of SCL values than the Edge Transport server provides. The values the Edge Transport server provides can be customized on a user-by-user basis. In the following command, I have disabled the quarantine and reject parameters for a particular user, and I have specified that this user's Junk E-mail threshold is 4:

```
Set-Mailbox "Matt Paleafei" -SCLRejectEnabled $False -SCLQuarantineEnabled $False↵
  -SCLJunkThreshold 4 -SCLJunkEnabled $True
```

You can view the resulting configuration for the mailbox with the `Get-Mailbox` cmdlet. Here is an example:

```
Get-Mailbox "Matt Paleafei" | FL Name,*scl*

Name                    : Matt Paleafei
SCLDeleteThreshold      :
SCLDeleteEnabled        :
SCLRejectThreshold      : 7
SCLRejectEnabled        : False
SCLQuarantineThreshold  : 9
SCLQuarantineEnabled    : False
SCLJunkThreshold        : 4
SCLJunkEnabled          : True
```

On the Exceptions property page of the Content Filtering properties, you can configure the SMTP addresses of the internal recipients to which you do not want to apply the content filter. This can be useful when managing a mailbox that is so important you never want any of its messages to be filtered.

The Custom Words property page of the Content Filtering object enables some interesting features (see Figure 21.23). You can enable two types of word lists. If the message contains words in the first list, even if the message appears to be spam, the message is accepted. If the words in the second list are contained in a message, the message is blocked unless it contains words from the first list.

The list with words and phrases that are always accepted can be particularly useful if legitimate messages to your company will frequently contain a particular word or phrase that might otherwise be filtered.

IP Block and Allow Lists

The IP Block List and IP Allow List features allow you to specify individual IP addresses, subnets, or entire ranges of IP addresses from which you will not accept or will always accept mail, respectively. Figure 21.24 shows the interface for the IP Block List, but the interface for the IP Allow List is identical.

In the foreground of Figure 21.24, you can see the interface for adding a single IP address. A nice feature of this interface is that you can specify that you always want to block an IP address, subnet, or address range or that you want to automatically unblock the address after a date and time.

IP Block and IP Allow Providers

An IP block list provider is better known as a *real-time block list* (RBL) provider. This is a service that keeps track of known sources of spam, open relays, open proxies, IP addresses used by dial-up connections, and IP addresses used by DHCP ranges. These are all frequent sources of spam. Conversely, an IP allow list provider is a service provider that maintains a list of IP addresses that are likely not to send spam.

FIGURE 21.23
Configuring custom words for the content filter

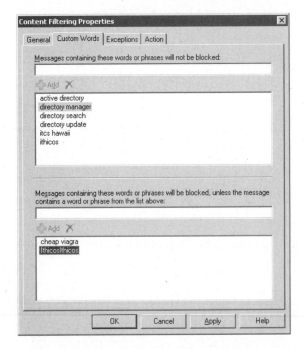

FIGURE 21.24
Configuring an IP Block List entry

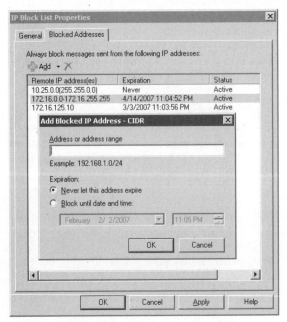

The most common configuration is an IP block list provider. When an SMTP client connects to your Edge Transport server, the Edge Transport server issues a DNS query using the reverse format of the IP address along with the DNS suffix of the block list provider. For example, if an SMTP client at IP address 192.168.254.10 connects to an Edge Transport server, it will issue the DNS query 10.254.168.192.sbl-xbl.spamhaus.org if it is configured to use the Spamhaus SBL-XBL list.

USING IP BLOCK LIST PROVIDERS

I am a big fan of block list providers (also known as real-time block lists) and I encourage my customers to use them. On average, a typical block list such as the Spamhaus ZEN list will help you cut in half or more the amount of spam that you receive.

In one particular situation, I used the Exchange Server's performance monitoring tools to determine how many messages per day the Exchange Server content filter considered a spam confidence level of 7 or higher. This particular organization was receiving nearly 40,000 messages per day that had an SCL of 7 or higher.

After enabling the IP block list provider to use the zen.spamhaus.org block list, the average daily count of messages with an SCL of 7 or higher dropped to 16,000. The messages identified by the RBL as spam were dropped at the Hub Transport and were not transferred. This saved on bandwidth as well as Hub Transport processing capacity.

If the IP address is not on the Spamhaus block list, the DNS query will return a "host not found" message. However, if the entry is on a block list, the DNS query will return an IP address such as 127.0.0.1, 127.0.0.2, and so on. The different return codes have different meanings for different providers.

Figure 21.25 shows the IP Block List Providers properties; in this figure, three block list providers have been configured.

FIGURE 21.25

Viewing the current IP block list providers

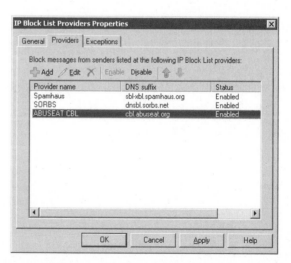

If you click the Add button, you can add RBL providers (there are none configured by default). Figure 21.26 shows part of the Add IP Block List Provider dialog box and the custom error messages screen. The information that is required in the Add IP Block List Provider dialog box is a name for the provider and the DNS suffix or the lookup domain. You get the DNS suffix from the block list provider.

FIGURE 21.26

Adding a new IP block list provider

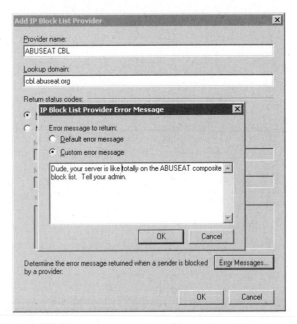

When you add a new IP block list provider, you can also configure it so that it responds only to certain error codes. This could be useful, for example, if the provider returns different error codes for different types of hosts and you only want to block mail for certain error codes.

For each block list provider, you can configure a custom error message. This can be useful for administrators whose systems may be on a block list. I recommend configuring a message that would be helpful for the administrator of a system from which you are rejecting mail.

The Exceptions property page is useful if you want to specify SMTP addresses to which the RBL blocking should not apply.

A lot of RBL providers are available on the Internet, and almost all are free. Some of these providers are pretty accurate, and some are not. Some are more aggressive than others. The more aggressive RBLs will often block entire IP subnets or entire IP ranges from regions of the world. Other IP block lists make it difficult to remove your IP address if you get on their list. Table 21.3 lists some of the RBLs I recommend using. I usually recommend choosing two RBLs; in the table they are in order of preference. My preference is to choose less aggressive RBLs and also use other filtering technologies such as content filtering or sender reputation.

Recipient Filtering

When recipient filtering is enabled, the Edge Transport is configured to reject mail intended for any SMTP address that is not found in the Active Directory or to reject mail intended for specific SMTP addresses. This will reduce a lot of the garbage messages that your Exchange server accepts and then has to issue a non-delivery report for. Figure 21.27 shows the Blocked Recipients list for the Recipient Filtering object.

I recommend that you check the Block Messages Sent To Recipients Not Listed In The Global Address List check box. This will help reduce the burden placed on your system by zombie networks of spammers. However, by recommending that you enable this check box, I am assuming that you have EdgeSync enabled and that all valid SMTP addresses are replicated to the Edge Transport server's local ADAM database.

TABLE 21.3:   Recommended IP Block List Providers

PROVIDER	PROVIDER'S WEBSITE	PROVIDER'S DNS SUFFIX
Spamhaus	www.spamhaus.org	zen.spamhaus.org
ABUSEAT CBL	cbl.abuseat.org	cbl.abuseat.org
SORBS	www.sorbs.net	dnsbl.sorbs.net
Spamcop	www.spamcop.net	bl.spamcop.net

FIGURE 21.27
Configuring recipient filtering

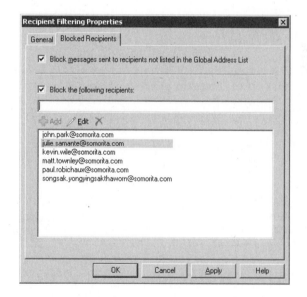

If you are performing recipient filtering, newly created mailboxes may have their mail rejected by the Edge Transport server until the replication runs again. You can force the synchronization after new mailboxes are created by running the Start-EdgeSynchronization cmdlet. Or just make sure that the users do not give anyone their e-mail address for at least four hours after the account is created.

Sender Filtering

Sender filtering is one of the oldest anti-spam features in Exchange; it is probably also the least effective. The premise is that you provide a list of SMTP addresses or domains that should not be able to send your users e-mail. The problem is that most spammers don't use the same e-mail address twice, so this is less than completely effective. Figure 21.28 shows the Blocked Senders property page of the Sender Filtering object.

FIGURE 21.28

Configuring sender filtering

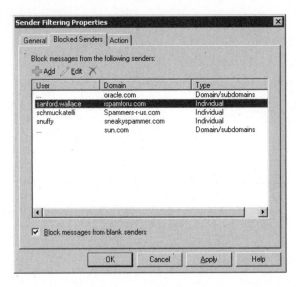

You can block individual senders and you can block all senders in a specific domain. One interesting anti-spam technique that some organizations employ is to put their own domain in this list. This prevents those spam messages that claim to be from one of your own recipients. However, if you do that on an internal Hub Transport server, make sure that it is not being used for POP3, IMAP4, or other clients that use SMTP to send mail internally.

Another interesting anti-spam technique that blocks a few pieces of mail is the check box Block Messages From Blank Senders. If a message does not have a sender (and it should), then this rejects the message.

The interface is a little different than in previous versions of Exchange Server. When you add or edit blocked senders, you have the option of adding an individual user or an entire domain and subdomains.

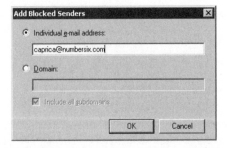

On the Action property page of the Sender Filtering object, you can specify what action to take. You can either reject the message entirely or stamp the message with a blocked sender and allow it on through. If you stamp the message as being from a blocked sender, the content filter will rank it as spam.

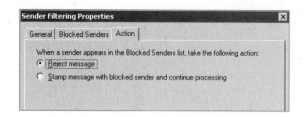

Sender ID

Contrary to popular misconception, Sender ID is not an anti-spam technology but an anti-spoofing technology. Quite simply, each organization on the Internet that sends e-mail should register a sender protection framework (SPF) record in their public DNS server. This SPF record contains a list of the servers authorized to send mail on behalf of their domain.

When a server receives a message from a particular domain, it analyzes the message to determine the actual sender and determines which server sent it. If the message originated from an authorized server, it is probably not being spoofed. If it is accepted from a server that is not in the DNS SPF record, the message might be from a spoofed sender.

On the Action property page of the Sender ID object, you can specify which action to take. Figure 21.29 shows the Action property page. You can reject the message, delete the message, or accept it for further processing by the content filter.

FIGURE 21.29
Configuring a Sender ID
action

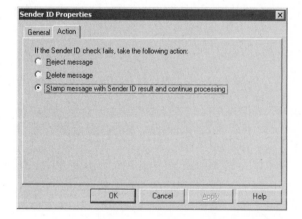

The problem with Sender ID is that fewer than 15 percent of all domains on the Internet have an SPF record, at least by my estimates. And frequently an organization's SPF records get out-of-date and are therefore wrong. The only thing worse than not having an SPF record is having one that is wrong. Therefore, it is impractical to reject or delete messages that fail the Sender ID test. You should keep this setting configured to Stamp Message With Sender ID Result And Continue Processing.

Sender Reputation

Sender reputation is the most promising feature of Exchange 2007 when it comes to reducing the amount of spam you receive. This is because much of the spam that is received today is sent by 'bot or zombie networks. Spammers have joined forces with virus writers; the virus writers have written malware that infects hundreds of thousands of users' computers. Periodically, these computers check with the spammer and download a new batch of spam. Blocking a single IP address becomes impractical because the spammers have so many of these computers all over the Internet. However, these zombie networks are usually not using correct SMTP commands and are not RFC compliant. A lot of spammers also use SMTP proxies by sending messages through a proxy on the Internet.

Sender reputation allows Exchange to analyze the connections that are coming in to an Edge Transport server and look for things such as the number of protocol errors, invalid delivery attempts, and the number of messages from the same sender. These can be used to determine if a specific IP address is sending spam. On the Action property page of the Sender Reputation object (shown in Figure 21.30), you can specify the Sender Reputation Level Block Threshold value; this is a value from 0 to 9 that is used to block senders that exceed a certain "suspicious" threshold.

FIGURE 21.30
Configuring the sender reputation level block threshold

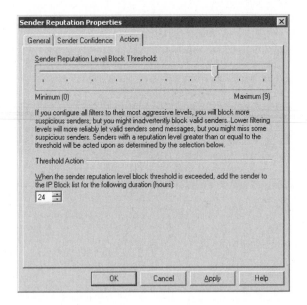

The default for the SRL block threshold is 9, but I recommend scaling it back to a slightly less aggressive value of 7 or 8 and then monitoring it to see if a lot of spam still gets through. If so, you can increase it slightly, but keep in mind that as you get more aggressive with this value, the possibility of valid connections getting rejected becomes higher.

The Threshold Action section allows you to specify how long a sender is retained on an IP block list once the sender has been determined to be suspicious. The default is 24 hours and I recommend that you keep that value.

Exchange can test for open proxies and determine if the source of a connection is an open proxy that is probably being used to send spam. On the Sender Confidence property page (Figure 21.31), you can enable the open proxy test. If a connecting SMTP client is determined to be an open proxy, it will be added to the IP block list for the time specified on the Action property page.

FIGURE 21.31
Configuring the sender reputation filter to perform an open proxy test

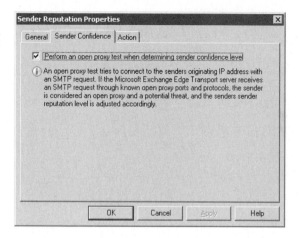

CONFIGURING THE EDGE TRANSPORT SERVER TO ENFORCE ORGANIZATION POLICIES

The Edge Transport server has a transport rules feature just as the Exchange 2007 Hub Transport server does. You may find this useful if there are certain types of organizational policies that you wish to enforce on messages that are arriving on the Edge Transport server and before they are delivered on to the Exchange 2007 Hub Transport server. I discussed transport rules in more detail in Chapter 15, "Managing Messages in Transit."

To illustrate the use of transport rules on the Edge Transport server, let's go through an example that enforces a policy of blocking outbound messages that contain certain confidential words and phrases. Here are the requirements:

1. All messages being sent to a user outside of the organization should have this transport rule applied to them.

2. If the message subject or body contains the words *confidential*, *secret formula*, or *secret recipe*, we want to take action on the message.

3. If the message meets the criteria, an error should be recorded in the event log, the message should be dropped, and a copy of the message should be sent to the company audit alias.

For this example it is assumed that the Edge Transport server is used to relay outbound messages to the Internet as well as to accept inbound messages. This example could also apply to transport rules used inside the organization.

In the Actions pane, select the New Transport Rule task to launch the New Transport Rule Wizard. On the Introduction page (shown in Figure 21.32), provide a descriptive name for the policy as well as an accurate description of the function of the transport rule. When finished, click Next to move on to the next page of the wizard.

On the Conditions page, specify the conditions of the transport rule. For this rule, two conditions must be met: the message must be from a user inside the organization and there must be specific words in the message body or subject. First check the condition When The Subject Field Or The Message Body Of The Message Contains Specific Words; this will add that condition to the Step 2 portion of the wizard page. From here you need to click the specific word's link so that you can use the Specify Words dialog box. In the Specify Words dialog box, you can add or remove words and phrases that are part of the condition.

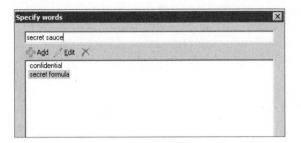

FIGURE 21.32
Introduction page of
the New Transport Rule
Wizard

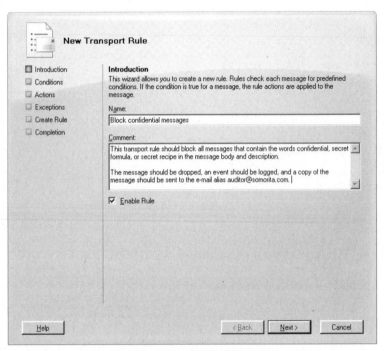

When finished, click the OK button to close the Specify Words dialog box. You now need to select the second condition. Select the From Users Inside Or Outside The Organization check box. This adds that selection to the Step 2 portion of the wizard page. The default is from users inside the organization, but you could change this by clicking the Inside link to see the Select Scope dialog box.

The finished product for the Conditions page looks like Figure 21.33. You can see the conditions selected on the top part of the wizard page (the Step 1 section) and the additional information that was specified for the conditions (Step 2), such as the words to search for and the fact that it applies to message sent by users inside the organization.

FIGURE 21.33
Conditions page of the
transport rule

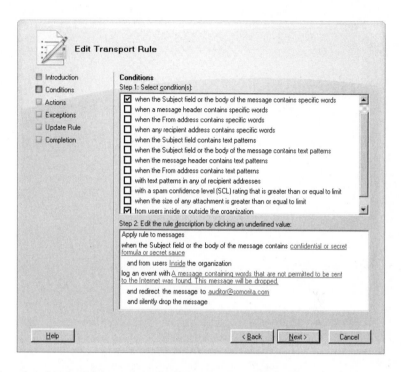

The next page of the wizard is the Actions page. On this page, you specify what you want to do if you find a message that meets the conditions you set on the Conditions page. First, you select the Log An Event With Message action; this adds a message link to the Step 2 section of the page. You click the message link to see the Specify Event Message dialog box. Here you enter the information you want entered in the event log.

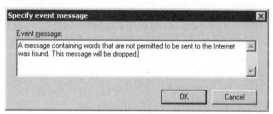

Next you select the Redirect The Message To Address check box and then click the addresses link that is now in Step 2 of the wizard page. This will display the Specify Recipients dialog box. Here you need to add the SMTP address `auditor@somorita.com`.

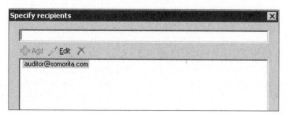

After you add the e-mail address to the Specify Recipients dialog box, click OK and then check the Silently Drop The Message check box. There is nothing else you need to do for this particular action. Figure 21.34 shows the finished product for the Actions property page.

FIGURE 21.34
The Actions page of the New Transport Rule Wizard

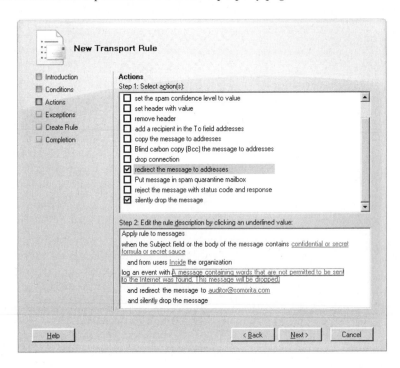

You can now click Next to see the Exceptions page of the wizard. The Exceptions page allows you to add exceptions to this particular rule. In this example there are none, so you can click Next to move on to the Create Rule configuration summary. From here, you can click the New button to create the new rule.

Summary

One of the primary functions of an Exchange server is to send and receive messages. That job is the function of the Hub Transport server role. Once you start sending messages between more than one Exchange server, you must understand how Exchange Server 2007 uses your existing Active Directory infrastructure to route messages between Hub Transport and Mailbox servers.

Once you open your Exchange servers to receive e-mail from the Internet, you also have to contend with spam and viruses. Exchange Server 2007 introduced the concept of the Edge Transport server role, which helps in the fight against unwanted message content.

The next few chapters cover some additional topics that should be helpful to you when managing your message routing infrastructure. Chapter 25, "Securing Exchange Server," discusses concepts that include providing multilayer virus protection and hardening the Windows Server platform. Chapter 26, "Logging, Auditing, and Monitoring," includes topics such as enabling protocol logging for debugging and tracking purposes as well as using the Exchange Server 2007 queue management features.

Chapter 22

Getting to Know the
Client Access Server Role

Although most of the components in Exchange Server 2007 have undergone a pretty serious change, few components have been as dramatically overhauled as the Exchange Server 2003 front-end server. The front-end server role has been replaced by the Client Access server role and this role is no longer optional.

The Client Access server role is involved in almost all methods of Exchange 2007 mailbox access, including Outlook Web Access (OWA), IMAP/POP3, Exchange Active Sync, and Outlook Anywhere (formerly RPC over HTTP). The only access method in which it isn't directly involved is the standard Exchange MAPI over RPC connection. As you will see, even for this method of connection, the Client Access server is still involved indirectly via Autodiscover and the provisioning of the offline address books and Free/Busy information. This is all part of Microsoft's plan to abstract all transport and data access functions out of the information store and away from the Mailbox server role.

The Exchange 2007 Client Access server implements new ways to access the offline address book and access Free/Busy information. These services are available only from Outlook 2007 and Outlook Web Access 2007 clients. Legacy clients such as Outlook 2003 make use of the public folder access methods used in Exchange 2003.

The Client Access server also provides functionality for Unified Messaging by enabling the pin reset and play-on-phone features. In addition, it is where Exchange Web Services are provided. The Exchange Web Services form the basis of the Autodiscover feature used by Outlook 2007 to automatically configure Outlook profiles and will become the standard method for programmatic access to data in Exchange going forward.

This chapter introduces the new features of the Client Access server role and shows you the steps required to get the most out of them.

In this chapter you learn to:

- ◆ Understand hardware and software requirements for the Client Access server role
- ◆ Position the Client Access server in your LAN
- ◆ Set up the Autodiscover service
- ◆ Understand the new features of the Availability service
- ◆ Generate SAN certificates

Hardware and Software Requirements for the Client Access Server Role

Since Exchange Server 2000/2003, the concepts of how the front-end server works have changed significantly with the introduction of the Client Access server. The hardware requirements and deployment options have also changed. Topics such as proxying and redirection were not something you had to worry about in earlier versions of Exchange.

Client Access Server Operating System Requirements

When I talk about clients, people are sometimes confused about which version of Exchange is required for a particular task. Therefore, I think it is worth clarifying the software requirements of the Client Access server role. The Client Access server role is absolutely fine running on the Standard Edition of Exchange Server 2007, Windows Server 2003, and Windows Server 2008. This is the case even when you want to use Network Load Balancing (NLB) to load-balance the Client Access role or improve availability. There is no need to use the Enterprise Edition of either Exchange or Windows Server to use NLB.

Client Access Server Hardware Recommendations

One of the first considerations when planning for your installation of the Client Access server role is what hardware to use. As you can see from the introduction, the Client Access server actually has a lot of work to deal with. Alongside all the services mentioned earlier, there are considerable changes to the way both Outlook Web Access and message access is provided, which adds further load to the Client Access server.

OWA in Exchange 2003 was rendered on the Mailbox server with the front-end server simply proxying the connection. This has changed in Exchange 2007. Now all the rendering is done on the Client Access server. In addition, whereas Exchange 2003 used to make use of the STM file to store Internet format messages, Exchange 2007 now performs all message conversion for non-MAPI clients on the Client Access server. These architecture changes were implemented to remove the load from the Mailbox server (assuming you are running the roles on separate boxes) to help enable Exchange to scale better.

So what does this mean in terms of hardware? Well, the Client Access server makes heavy use of CPU, RAM, and network resources. Disk access is typically not heavy. The recommendations and requirements are as follows:

- As with all versions of Exchange 2007 installed in a production environment, an x64-capable processor is required.

- Only one CPU core is required, but Microsoft recommends that four CPU cores be assigned to a Client Access server.

- Only limited benefit will be gained by adding more than four cores.

Memory is the second part of the hardware question to consider:

- The minimum recommendation is 2GB of RAM.

- In general, servers should be sized with 2GB for each CPU core up to a maximum of 16GB.

  The usage of CPU and RAM by the Client Access server role is closely related, and you will find that both increase together.

The last of the three areas is networking. The Client Access server role puts heavy use on the network, and ensuring that there are no delays is especially important if servicing clients from multiple sites. Therefore, I recommend providing Gigabit Ethernet where possible.

In my experience, a Client Access server with a single dual-core CPU, 4GB of RAM, and Gigabit Ethernet can support all but the heaviest of loads.

Finally, before leaving this section, it is worth noting that, in general, you should aim to provide one Client Access server CPU core for every four Mailbox server CPU cores.

Positioning the Client Access Server in Your LAN

After you complete your design for the hardware on which the Client Access server role will run, the next step to consider is the positioning of the Client Access server role in your LAN.

The first principle is that every Active Directory site hosting a Mailbox server requires a Client Access server.

Exchange 2000/2003 supported (although it was not recommended) placing your Exchange front-end server in your DMZ to isolate it slightly from your internal LAN. In Exchange 2007, this scenario has changed. Placing the Client Access server in your DMZ/perimeter network is no longer supported in part because the Client Access server uses Remote Procedure Calls (RPCs) to connect to the Mailbox server role. There are several reasons for this change. First, processes on the Client Access server have very high-level access to your Exchange organization. Second, the number of ports you must open to provide Active Directory access for your Client Access server leaves a rather large hole for potential attack.

REVERSE PROXY RECOMMENDED

You can either publish a Client Access server directly to Internet clients or you can use a reverse proxy to provide an additional layer of protection. I strongly urge you to put your Client Access servers on your internal network and use a reverse proxy to publish the servers to the Internet.

So what are you expected to do? Well, the recommendation is to place the Client Access server role on your internal LAN and then proxy connections to it using a reverse proxy server like ISA 2006. This gives you many benefits, not the least of which is that the only thing being exposed directly to Internet traffic is the proxy/firewall — which is designed specifically for that exposure. When using ISA, you also get the benefit of pre-authentication, which ensures that only authenticated traffic gets through to your internal LAN. On top of this, because ISA inspects all inbound connection requests to ensure they are valid, it makes things even more secure by closely checking all traffic to your Client Access server boxes for potential HTML exploits and nonstandard HTML requests before passing it through to your LAN.

Client Access Server Proxying

Let's take a more detailed look at how providing remote access works and, specifically, how your placement of Client Access servers and Internet connections affects what happens.

First, remember that front-end servers in Exchange 2003 simply proxied requests to back-end servers using HTTP, but Client Access servers now perform a lot of the processing themselves (like Outlook Web Access rendering) and, instead of talking HTTP to the Mailbox servers, they now talk encrypted RPC.

If you have a single Active Directory site (Site A) with Exchange servers in it, you have a fairly simple scenario, as shown in Figure 22.1. You would provide remote access via the reverse proxy mentioned earlier to either a single Client Access server or a pool of load-balanced servers. This scenario is simple for all types of clients and works very much like Exchange 2003 worked.

FIGURE 22.1
A simple single site
Exchange setup

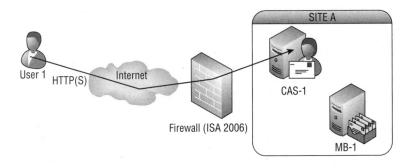

So what about when you introduce another Active Directory site (Site B) with Mailbox and Client Access servers? It depends! If you still provide remote access via the original Site A (in other words, a central point), your users will request access to their data from the Client Access server in Site A. At this point, the Client Access server in Site A will look up in Active Directory the details for the connecting user (User 2) and may find that their mailbox is actually hosted on a Mailbox server in Site B (MB-2).

SOME LIMITATIONS OF PROXYING

Proxying only works between the requesting Client Access server and a Client Access server in the site of the Mailbox server. If firewalls are in place that prevent this traffic, proxying won't negotiate a hop-to-hop route via another site where there is connectivity.

Proxying occurs for Outlook Web Access and Exchange ActiveSync but not for IMAP or POP3. For these you must connect to a Client Access server in the same Active Directory site as your mailbox.

Proxying works only for virtual directories configured to support integrated authentication, which means if you want forms-based authentication (FBA) to be used internally, you will need to configure separate Outlook Web Access virtual directories for internal use. You have to do this anyway if you use ISA and FBA to publish Outlook Web Access, because ISA requires that only it processes FBA and that the published OWA site uses basic authentication.

At this point, the Client Access server in Site A (CAS-1) will contact a Client Access server in Site B (CAS-2) via HTTPS and then proxy the users' request to it. The CAS-2 gets the info from the Mailbox server and passes it back to the CAS-1, again via HTTPS, and from there the info is passed back to the client. Note in Figure 22.2 that the cross-site traffic is via HTTPS rather than RPC. HTTPS is used because Microsoft found early on during the testing phase of Exchange 2007 design that running the RPC traffic across sites caused performance problems and unreliable connectivity.

FIGURE 22.2
CAS proxy with a single
Internet connection

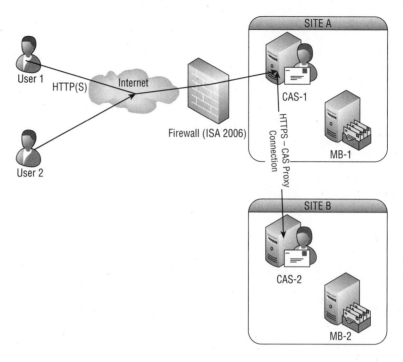

A few differences exist between Outlook Web Access and Exchange ActiveSync proxying. To better explain this, I will introduce some parameters that affect proxying. The InternalURL and ExternalURL parameters can be specified on Web-accessible virtual directories such as Outlook Web Access, Offline Address Book, Autodiscover, Exchange ActiveSync, Unified Messaging, and Exchange Web Services. Each of these virtual directories has a URLs property page that allows you to configure the internal and external URLs.

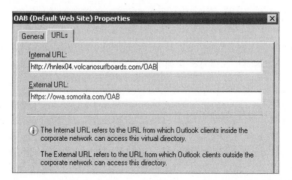

The InternalURL and ExternalURL parameters let you specify different URLs for Client Access server access. The InternalURL parameter is set by default on installation and is what the default self-signed certificate (see the section "Certificates" later in this chapter) uses for its principal name. If you are configuring a Client Access server only for internal access (either by internal clients or via another Client Access server proxying request), you should set the ExternalURL parameter to $Null for the virtual directories listed here:

◆ Outlook Web Access

◆ Offline Address Book

◆ Unified Messaging

◆ Exchange Web Services

◆ Exchange ActiveSync

You can clear the directories using either the GUI or the Exchange Management Shell (EMS). Here is an example of using the EMS to set the default OWA virtual directory's ExternalURL parameter to a null value:

```
Set-OwaVirtualDirectory "owa (Default Web Site)" -ExternalURL:$Null
```

When a Client Access server is externally accessible, the ExternalURL parameter should be configured with the URL used to access the service — for example, https://webmail.domain.com/owa.

So how do these parameters affect proxying? For Exchange ActiveSync it works as follows:

1. The Client Access server in Site A (CAS-1) locates a Client Access server in the same Active Directory site as the user's Mailbox server (Site B) and determines whether the Client Access server has the InternalURL property configured and is using Integrated Windows authentication. If so, the user is proxied to the Client Access server specified by the InternalURL property.

2. If the InternalURL is not correct or Integrated Windows authentication is not configured, the request is rejected and an error code is returned to the mobile device.

3. If the Client Access server in Site B (CAS-2) has the ExternalURL property configured on the Microsoft-Server-ActiveSync virtual directory, an HTTP error code 451 will be returned.

4. When proxying Outlook Web Access requests, the Client Access server in Site A (CAS-1) determines whether the Client Access server in Site B (CAS-2) has the InternalURL property configured. CAS-1 then determines whether the ExternalURL is specified. If so, the user is redirected to the server that is specified by the ExternalURL property.

5. If the ExternalURL is not specified, the CAS-1 in Site A will proxy the user's request to the CAS-2 in Site B.

The reason for this difference in behavior is that Outlook Web Access is browser based and supports redirection. Exchange ActiveSync, based around a different architecture, doesn't support redirection, although a future version of Windows Mobile might include this feature.

Client Redirection

Redirection occurs when you set up multiple Client Access servers in different Active Directory sites and define each server with the ExternalURL. In this case, if users connect to a Client Access server that's not in their Active Directory site, they will be presented with a page that includes a link to the correct Client Access server in their Active Directory site (see Figure 22.3). Note that redirection is not automatic — the user is prompted with a URL to click.

FIGURE 22.3
The Outlook Web Access redirection page

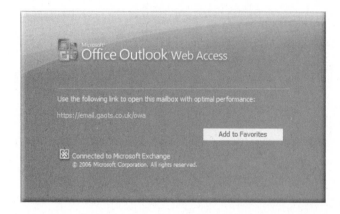

So you might be thinking, How is redirection used? Well, because of the performance issues I mentioned earlier, it is sensible to prevent a large amount of proxying; therefore, Microsoft recommends that we run our Exchange environments with separate name spaces for different geographical regions where the main Mailbox servers are hosted — for example `https://owa.europe.domain.com` and `https://owa.usa.domain.com`. Redirection would occur if someone with a U.S.-hosted mailbox connected to the Europe OWA URL.

Interoperability with Exchange 2003

Now let's look at what happens with client access when you move from an Exchange 2000/2003 organization to an Exchange 2007 one.

As part of the transition, the Exchange 2007 Client Access server role is the first that should be installed. It should be used to replace Exchange 2003 front-end servers. The Exchange 2007 Client Access server retains the old `/Exchange`, `/Public`, and `/ExchWeb` virtual directories required to support access to mailboxes on legacy Exchange servers.

This access follows the same model as in Exchange 2000/2003. Even if the Client Access server and the Exchange 2000/2003 back-end server are in different Active Directory sites, the connection is proxied directly to the back-end server via HTTP rather than via a Client Access server in the site in which the back-end server is located.

As for Client Access to Client Access servers, you must fulfill authentication prerequisites if you want proxying to work. The authentication method should be Integrated authentication, and forms-based authentication must be disabled. You must also make sure that `-RedirectToOptimalOWAServer` is set to `$True`, which can be done with the following Exchange Management Shell cmdlet:

```
Set-OwaVirtualDirectory "owa (default web site)" -RedirectToOptimalOWAServer $True
```

This command tells the OWA virtual directory to proxy requests to the appropriate site.

Services Provided by the Client Access Server

Before moving on to actual configuration and management of the Client Access server, I want to take some time to explain in more detail the services that are actually provided.

The Autodiscover Service

As mentioned in the chapter introduction, the Exchange 2007 Client Access server role brings with it a lot of new functionality. One of the most noticeable features, as far as a user or desktop administrator is concerned, is autoconfiguration of Outlook 2007 profiles. This at last provides a way to get users up and running very easily on a new machine without using scripts, running Custom Installation Wizard installs, or relying on users to set up their own account (which is always dangerous!). Now all users have to do when connected to the domain is click Next a few times because Outlook picks up all the relevant info from the account they logged in with. If not connected to the domain, users are simply asked to enter their e-mail address and password. (Note that users must specify their primary address; otherwise, Autodiscover may not work.)

The service that provides this leap forward is the Autodiscover service. On top of profile configuration, this service also provides information to Outlook 2007 about the URL for downloading the offline address book, URLs for UM and Outlook Anywhere, and finally, the URL for the Exchange Web Services which, among other things, provides availability information.

WINDOWS MOBILE 6.1 SUPPORTS EXCHANGE ACTIVESYNC AUTODISCOVER CONFIGURATION

Originally, Windows Mobile 6 was planned to support Autodiscover for configuring the devices for Exchange ActiveSync. Unfortunately, this feature didn't make it into Windows Mobile 6, but it arrived in Windows Mobile 6.1.

Autodiscover works in two different ways, depending on whether the client is on the internal LAN and a member of the forest where the mailbox is held, or external to the LAN.

INTERNAL AUTODISCOVER

The Autodiscover process is different depending on whether or not the computer is in an Active Directory. The method used when Autodiscover is used on a client within the LAN is described here and shown in Figure 22.4.

1. When Outlook is launched, it checks to see if a profile exists. If there is none, it automatically fills in the user's e-mail address and password from Active Directory.

2. Outlook then searches Active Directory for a Service Configuration Point (SCP), which is a method of publishing information about services in Active Directory. The location of the SCP in Active Directory is shown in Figure 22.5.

   The information published in the SCP will give Outlook the FQDN of the servers hosting the Autodiscover service (the Client Access servers).

3. Outlook queries the Client Access server.

4. The server prepares an XML file specifically for the user.

5. This XML file is downloaded by the Outlook client, which applies the settings and connects the users to their mailbox.

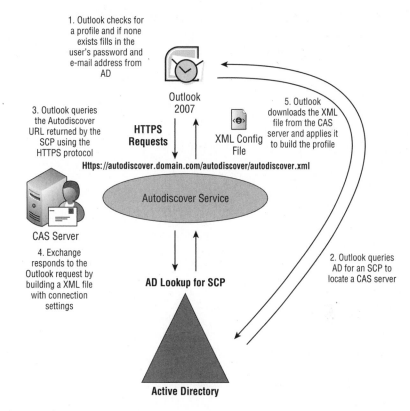

FIGURE 22.4
The Autodiscover process on the LAN

1. Outlook checks for a profile and if none exists fills in the user's password and e-mail address from AD

3. Outlook queries the Autodiscover URL returned by the SCP using the HTTPS protocol

Outlook 2007

HTTPS Requests

XML Config File

5. Outlook downloads the XML file from the CAS server and applies it to build the profile

Https://autodiscover.domain.com/autodiscover/autodiscover.xml

CAS Server

Autodiscover Service

4. Exchange responds to the Outlook request by building a XML file with connection settings

2. Outlook queries AD for an SCP to locate a CAS server

AD Lookup for SCP

Active Directory

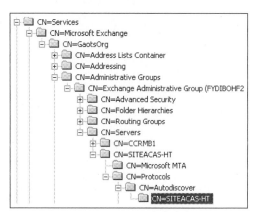

FIGURE 22.5
The location of the SCP as seen from Active Directory Sites and Services

```
CN=Services
  CN=Microsoft Exchange
    CN=GaotsOrg
      CN=Address Lists Container
      CN=Addressing
      CN=Administrative Groups
        CN=Exchange Administrative Group (FYDIBOHF2
          CN=Advanced Security
          CN=Folder Hierarchies
          CN=Routing Groups
          CN=Servers
            CN=CCRMB1
            CN=SITEACAS-HT
              CN=Microsoft MTA
              CN=Protocols
                CN=Autodiscover
                  CN=SITEACAS-HT
```

EXTERNAL AUTODISCOVER

If the user is outside the Active Directory forest (for example, on a machine that is not domain joined) or on a machine that is outside the LAN, the internal Autodiscover process fails at Step 2 of the preceding process, the stage of attempting to locate the SCP. In this case, Outlook uses the following process, which is also shown in Figure 22.6.

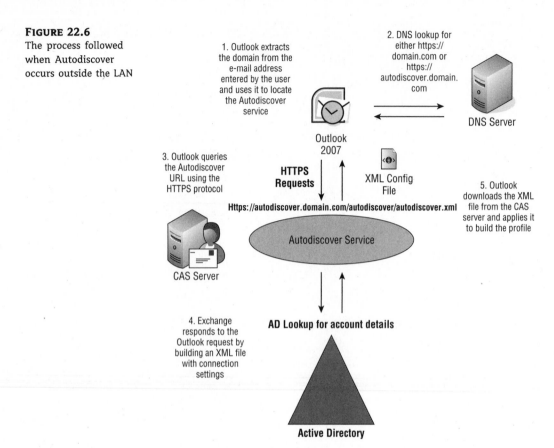

FIGURE 22.6
The process followed
when Autodiscover
occurs outside the LAN

1. Outlook extracts
the domain from the
e-mail address
entered by the user
and uses it to locate
the Autodiscover
service

2. DNS lookup for
either https://
domain.com or
https://
autodiscover.domain.
com

DNS Server

Outlook
2007

3. Outlook queries
the Autodiscover
URL using the
HTTPS protocol

**HTTPS
Requests**

XML Config
File

5. Outlook
downloads the XML
file from the CAS
server and applies it
to build the profile

Https://autodiscover.domain.com/autodiscover/autodiscover.xml

Autodiscover Service

CAS Server

4. Exchange
responds to the
Outlook request by
building an XML file
with connection
settings

AD Lookup for account details

Active Directory

To find a Client Access server that can provide Autodiscover functions externally, the Outlook client will try to connect to one of these two URLs (where the domain is somorita.com):

```
https://somorita.com/autodiscover/autodiscover.xml
https://autodiscover.somorita.com/autodiscover/autodiscover.xml
```

For more information on this process, see the following URL:

```
http://technet.microsoft.com/en-us/library/bb332063.aspx#OutlookAndAD
```

Here are the steps that Outlook goes through to automatically configure the Outlook profile:

1. Outlook first prompts the user to enter his name, password, and e-mail address instead of getting the user info from the logged-on user and connecting to the SCP to locate a Client Access server.

2. Outlook then makes use of data from the e-mail address entered by the user. It takes the section after the @ sign and does a DNS lookup.

3. First it makes an attempt to connect to `https://somorita.com/autodiscover` `/autodiscover.xml`. If this fails, an attempt is made to connect to `https://autodiscover` `.somorita.com/autodiscover/autodiscover.xml`.

   If both attempts fail, Outlook attempts to connect using HTTP. Therefore, for the Autodiscover process to work correctly, one of the URLs must be resolvable both externally and, if using non-domain-joined machines on the LAN, internally.

4. Once the connection has been made, the process continues in the same way as for internal connections, with Exchange creating a specific XML file containing the relevant details for the user based on the credentials entered in Step 1.

5. Outlook then downloads the XML file and uses it to build the profile.

   Note that Outlook 2007 Service Pack 1 clients will also check DNS to see if there is a service location (SRV) record for autodiscovery.

AUTODISCOVER PROCESS AND CONFIGURATION

Having outlined the processes involved, take a look at the configuration that can be carried out for the Autodiscover service. First, here's the actual XML that is passed to the client:

```xml
<?xml version="1.0" encoding="utf-8"?>
<Autodiscover xmlns="http://schemas.microsoft.com/exchange/autodiscover/
    responseschema/2006">
<Response xmlns="http://schemas.microsoft.com/exchange/autodiscover/outlook/
responseschema/2006a">
  <User>
    <DisplayName>Nathan Winters</DisplayName>
    <LegacyDN>/o=OEXCH015/ou=Exchange Administrative Group (FYDIBOHF23SPDLT)
/cn=Recipients/cn=nathan_nwinters</LegacyDN>
    <DeploymentId>996755d4-d79d-4cf9-94ba-fb91ec8877f8</DeploymentId>
  </User>
  <Account>
    <AccountType>email</AccountType>
    <Action>settings</Action>
    <Protocol>
      <Type>EXCH</Type>
      <Server>EXVMBX015-3.exch015.msoutlookonline.net</Server>
      <ServerDN>/o=OEXCH015/ou=Exchange Administrative Group (FYDIBOHF23SPDLT)
/cn=Configuration/cn=Servers/cn=EXVMBX015-3</ServerDN>
      <ServerVersion>720082AD</ServerVersion>
      <MdbDN>/o=OEXCH015/ou=Exchange Administrative Group (FYDIBOHF23SPDLT)
/cn=Configuration/cn=Servers/cn=EXVMBX015-3/cn=Microsoft Private MDB</MdbDN>
<ASUrl>https://owa015.msoutlookonline.net/EWS/Exchange.asmx</ASUrl>
<OOFUrl>https://owa015.msoutlookonline.net/EWS/Exchange.asmx</OOFUrl>
  <UMUrl>https://owa015.msoutlookonline.net/UnifiedMessaging/Service.asmx</UMUrl>
        <OABUrl>Public Folder</OABUrl>
    </Protocol>
```

```
      <Protocol>
        <Type>EXPR</Type>
        <Server>owa015.msoutlookonline.net</Server>
        <SSL>On</SSL>
        <AuthPackage>Basic</AuthPackage>
        <OABUrl>Public Folder</OABUrl>
      </Protocol>
      <Protocol>
        <Type>WEB</Type>
        <External>
          <OWAUrl AuthenticationMethod="Fba">https://owa015.msoutlookonline.net/owa
</OWAUrl>
          <Internal>
            <OWAUrl AuthenticationMethod="Basic, Fba">
https://owa015.msoutlookonline.net/owa</OWAUrl>
            <Protocol>
              <Type>EXCH</Type>
<ASUrl>https://owa015.msoutlookonline.net/EWS/Exchange.asmx</ASUrl>
            </Protocol>
          </Internal>
        </External>
      </Protocol>
    </Account>
</Response></Autodiscover>
```

As you can see, a fair amount of information is included, in particular the URLs for the main services. So where does this information come from and how is it set?

As I mentioned earlier, when the Client Access server is installed, a virtual directory called Autodiscover is created in the IIS default website. It is from here that the configuration file is downloaded by the Outlook 2007 client. What you might be wondering is how you tell Autodiscover which URLs to give out. This is where we come back to the parameters from earlier: InternalURL and ExternalURL.

If the client is configured to use RPC (that is, MAPI), the Autodiscover service provides information about the internal URL. Once Outlook Anywhere (RPC over HTTP) is configured, the information is taken from the ExternalURL parameter.

It is therefore important to configure the ExternalURL values for the following virtual directories:

◆ WebServicesVirtualDirectory — EWS (Default Web Site)

◆ UMVirtualDirectory — UnifiedMessaging (Default Web Site)

◆ OABVirtualDirectory — OAB (Default Web Site)

You can configure the ExternalURL parameters for these virtual directories either from the GUI (Exchange Management Console) or from the EMS prompt; using the EMS, you would use the following commands:

```
Set-WebServicesVirtualDirectory -Identity "EX-01\EWS (Default Web Site)"↩
-ExternalUrl "https://mail.northwind.co.uk/EWS/Exchange.asmx"
```

```
Set-UMVirtualDirectory -Identity "EX-01\UnifiedMessaging (Default Web Site)"↵
 -ExternalUrl "https://mail.northwind.co.uk/UnifiedMessaging/Service.asmx"
Set-OABVirtualDirectory -Identity "EX-01\OAB (Default Web Site)"↵
 -externalurl "https://mail.northwind.co.uk/OAB"
```

The `ExternalURL` parameter for the Outlook Anywhere service is not set up on the virtual directory because it is configured as part of the setup process for Outlook Anywhere.

ADVANCED AUTODISCOVER SCENARIOS

Having considered the basic setup of the Autodiscover service, here are a few more advanced scenarios to look at.

Highly Distributed Network

The first scenario is what to do when you have a highly distributed network. We looked at how Exchange can proxy information between Client Access servers and discussed how, in some situations, it is necessary to have multiple Client Access servers accessible to the Internet using different URLs for different locations. In this type of situation, you will need to make some Autodiscover changes.

You can configure Autodiscover for Site Affinity, which allows you to specify preferred Active Directory sites. These preferred sites connect a client to a particular instance of the Autodiscover service. You need this setup when you have Active Directory sites connected by low bandwidth links and it helps prevent intranet WAN congestion. The configuration code looks like this:

```
Set-ClientAccessServer -Identity "ServerName" -AutodiscoverServiceInternalURI↵
 "https://internalsitename/autodiscover/autodiscover.xml"↵
 AutodiscoverSiteScope "SiteName"
```

Trusted Active Directory Forest

The second scenario is how to configure the Autodiscover service to work with a trusted Active Directory forest. This situation could arise if you use an Exchange resource forest. In this case, you must export the information about the SCP from the forest where Exchange is hosted (the source) and import it into the forest where users are held (the target). You do this as follows:

1. On an Exchange 2007 Client Access server in the source forest, run the following command:

   ```
   $a = Get-Credential
   ```

2. You are prompted to enter the credentials that will allow the import into the target forest. The credentials are saved to a variable named *a*.

3. On the same Client Access server, run the following command:

   ```
   Export-AutoDiscoverConfig -TargetForestDomainController <StringofDCname>↵
    -TargetForestCredentials $a
   ```

TESTING AUTODISCOVER AND EXCHANGE WEB SERVICES

Finally, here's how you test and view AutoConfiguration settings in Outlook:

1. With Outlook open, hold down Ctrl and click the Outlook icon in the system tray.

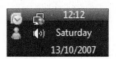

2. Select the Test E-mail AutoConfiguration option.

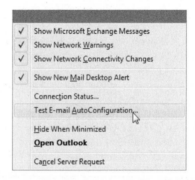

3. You will be presented with a dialog box, shown in Figure 22.7, where you can enter the e-mail address and password for your user.

Outlook will perform the same steps as it would during Autodiscover and present the results in the lower pane.

FIGURE 22.7
The Test E-mail Auto-Configuration window showing Autodiscover results

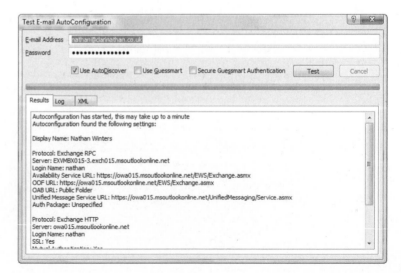

The Availability Service

Let's move on and look at the other functions that Exchange Web Services provides, in particular the Availability service. The Availability service, like the Autodiscover service, is a web service. Also like Autodiscover, it is installed by default as part of the Client Access server role. It takes care of the following Exchange functions:

◆ Retrieves live Free/Busy information for mailboxes on Exchange 2007

◆ Retrieves live Free/Busy information from other Exchange 2007 forests

◆ Retrieves published Free/Busy information from public folders (for legacy mailboxes or for mailboxes using legacy Outlook clients)

◆ Views attendee working hours

◆ Shows meeting time suggestions

The key functions in the preceding list are the live Free/Busy parts! Yes, for the first time in Exchange, you can get real-time information about a user's calendar. Before you get too excited, you should know that this is only possible with Outlook 2007 or Outlook Web Access 2007 clients. Any earlier clients have to make do with the old Schedule+ Free/Busy system public folder method, which is one of the reasons you are asked whether you have any legacy clients when you're installing Exchange. Table 22.1 shows the combinations of server and client along with the outcome the different options have on which method of Free/Busy access is used.

TABLE 22.1:   Clients and Free/Busy Access Methods

CLIENT	LOGGED-IN MAILBOX	TARGET MAILBOX	F/B RETRIEVAL
Outlook 2007	Exchange 2007	Exchange 2007	Availability service reads Free/Busy from the target mailbox.
Outlook 2007	Exchange 2007	Exchange 2003	Availability service makes HTTP connection to the /public virtual directory of Exchange 2003 mailbox.
Outlook 2003	Exchange 2007	Exchange 2007	Legacy behavior: Looks up Free/Busy in local Schedule+ public folders
Outlook 2003	Exchange 2007	Exchange 2003	Legacy behavior: Looks up Free/Busy in local Schedule+ public folders.
OWA 2007	Exchange 2007	Exchange 2007	Calls Availability Service API, which reads Free/Busy from the target mailbox
OWA 2007	Exchange 2007	Exchange 2003	Calls Availability service API, which makes HTTP connection to the /public virtual directory of the Exchange 2003 mailbox.
Any	Exchange 2003	Exchange 2007	Legacy behavior: Looks up Free/Busy in local Schedule+ public folders.

Here's how the Availability service works:

1. The Outlook client locates the Availability service URL using Autodiscover. The client then connects to the URL (on the Client Access server) given by Autodiscover.

2. If the target mailbox is in another Active Directory site, the Client Access server will make an HTTPS connection to the target Client Access server. The target Client Access server will obtain the Free/Busy information by communicating, using MAPI, with the Mailbox server and will then send the information back to the source Client Access server, which passes it on to the client.

3. If the target mailbox is in the same Active Directory site, the Client Access server will communicate with the Mailbox server (via MAPI) and obtain the Free/Busy information. The source Client Access server will then provide the data back to the Outlook 2007/Outlook Web Access 2007 client.

The Availability Web Service enables some other great functionality. When coupled with the Outlook 2007 scheduling assistant, it provides suggested meeting times and Exchange suggests the time when all users and resources are available. It also allows users to share their calendar information in more granular ways. For each target person or group, users can choose one of four levels of sharing on the property page for their calendar, as shown in Figure 22.8.

FIGURE 22.8
Specifying the level of detail viewable by Free/Busy lookups

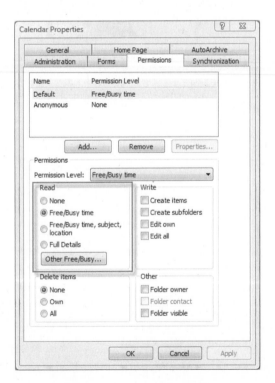

In the Permissions tab of the Calendar Properties, users can control the following settings:

◆ Whether items can be deleted or modified

◆ Item and detail visibility, such as the subject of a meeting, location, and meeting time

◆ How Free/Busy information is published

Finally, the Availability service provides the ability to configure cross-forest, and therefore cross-Exchange organization, lookups for user availability. For more information about this particular feature, see the following site:

`http://technet.microsoft.com/en-us/library/bb125182.aspx`

Offline Address List Distribution

Before moving on, I want to cover one last feature that has changed in Exchange 2007: offline address list distribution. Like Free/Busy information, in previous versions of Exchange, the offline address book (as it was then known) was distributed via public folders. This has changed in keeping with all the other new web services in Exchange 2007. The offline address list is now distributed, at least for Outlook 2007, from a web share.

Because the offline address list is still generated by the System Attendant service on the Mailbox server, you may wonder how the Client Access server does the distribution. Well, in Exchange 2007, there is a new service called the Microsoft Exchange File Distribution Service (ExchangeFDS), which runs on the Client Access server. Its job is to pick up the files left by the System Attendant service on the Mailbox server in the share \\MBXServ\ExchangeOAB and copy them to the local web directory (`https://serverFQDN/oab`) on the Client Access server.

One thing to note when setting up the offline address list is that, by default, the distribution share is not configured for HTTPS. You can rectify this problem when you configure its external access by using the following command:

```
Set-OABVirtualDirectory -Identity "EX-01\OAB (Default Web Site)"↵
 -ExternalURL "https://mail.northwind.co.uk/OAB" -RequireSSL:$true
```

For some excellent troubleshooting information about offline address list distribution, look at the following website:

`http://blogs.msdn.com/dgoldman/archive/tags/Offline+Address+Book+Related/`
`    default.aspx`

Certificates

In previous versions of Exchange, the use of certificates was very simple. By default there were none installed, so if you wanted to use one, you requested a certificate with the principal name of your external access URL and installed it on the default website. This gave you secure access to OWA and RPC over HTTP. In Exchange 2007, things are somewhat different. In an effort to ensure that out-of-the-box Exchange 2007 secures traffic, there is now installed by default a self-signed certificate, which is used for SMTP, POP3, IMAP4, and Outlook Web Access (IIS).

In "The Autodiscover Service" section earlier in this chapter, you learned that Autodiscover requires single virtual directories — for example /autodiscover and /oab — to be accessed by different names internally and externally and that both access methods require the use of SSL. For those of you used to SSL certificates, this presents a problem: the URL entered when creating the certificate must be the one used for access. So how can this work, as you now need one certificate to provide for two or more names?

When you take a look at the default certificate you will hopefully notice some important details. Figure 22.9 shows the certification path details; in this case the certificate is self-signed.

FIGURE 22.9
The Certificate detail window showing the Certificate Path

Figure 22.10 shows that the certificate makes use of the Subject Alternative Name field to provide more than just the single URL.

So what does this mean to you? Well, it means that if you try to access Exchange from a box that is either not on your domain/forest or try accessing it from over the Internet, you will get the familiar *you do not trust the provider of this certificate* errors.

Machines joined to your domain don't return an error about the untrusted certificate because they can see a Service Discovery Record, created in Active Directory by setup, which Outlook considers trustworthy.

You might think, therefore, that to get around these trust issues you would go into IIS Administrator, remove the existing certificate, and replace it with one you have purchased as you would in Exchange 2003. Unfortunately, this would lead to a whole lot more errors! In particular, when connecting Outlook 2007 clients, you would get an error message that one of the names on the certificate doesn't equal the hostname of the Client Access server. This is because Outlook 2007 tries to connect to the hostname of the Client Access server.

FIGURE 22.10
The Subject Alternative
Name field of the default
certificate

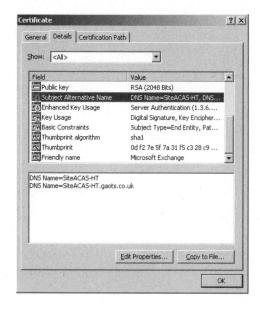

CERTIFICATES WITH SUBJECT ALTERNATIVE NAMES (SANs)

So what are these Subject Alternative Names (SANs) and what are they used for? By default, the SANs are as follows:

◆ Hostname

◆ Domain name

◆ FQDN

◆ Autodiscover.domainname.com

The SANs support secure access to Outlook Web Access, Exchange ActiveSync, Autodiscover, and Outlook Anywhere (when enabled) without the need for multiple certificates that would require multiple IP addresses and websites to be created on Client Access servers.

TIPS ABOUT SAN CERTIFICATES

Certificates that support Subject Alternate Names are also referred to as Unified Communications Certificates. To find certificate authorities that will issue this type of certificate, search the Internet for "Subject Alternate Name" or "Unified Communications Certificates". You can also view the info at the following site: http://support.microsoft.com/kb/929395.

When specifying the common name for a certificate, you should use the name that will most frequently be used from the Internet, such as mail.somorita.com or owa.ithicos.com.

You can use the same domain name for the internal and external domain as long as you have your DNS set up correctly.

Now you need to know where and how you can get one of these SAN certificates. You can get them either from yourself (self-signed) or from a third-party certificate authority like Comodo, DigiCert, and Entrust. One thing to bear in mind is that these certificates are somewhat new and therefore more expensive and a little harder to get hold of; not all third-party certificate authorities will issue you one. Check with the certificate authority you are planning to use.

Use the following steps to get a SAN certificate:

1. First, decide on the external name for your e-mail access (in this case, `email.domain.com`).

2. Next, open the Exchange Management Shell and generate your certificate request using a command like the following (substituting your domain names):

   ```
   New-ExchangeCertificate -GenerateRequest -DomainName email.domain.com, ↵
      autodiscover.domain.com,hostname,internaldomain.com, ↵
      hostname.internaldomain.com -FriendlyName "Exchange SAN cert" ↵
      -PrivateKeyExportable:$true -path c:\ExchSANcert.txt
   ```

   Make sure that the first domain you enter is the external one that you will use for Outlook Anywhere and Outlook Web Access. This domain goes into the common name field of the certificate and is required by Outlook Anywhere.

3. After running the command, you will have a text file in the path specified, which you should submit to your certificate authority (be that your internal one or a certificate authority like DigiCert or VeriSign).

4. Once you receive the certificate back, you need to import it using the following command:

   ```
   Import-ExchangeCertificate -Path c:\certificate.cer
   ```

5. When you run the `Import-ExchangeCertificate` command, the output will contain a `ThumbPrint`, which is what you will use to refer to the certificate in future commands. Make a note of it.

6. Enable the certificate by using the following command, which will enable use for all Exchange services:

   ```
   Enable-ExchangeCertificate -ThumbPrint Value -Services "IIS,SMTP,IMAP,POP"
   ```

When you check the SAN field after you configure your new certificate, you will see all the entries you specified, as shown in Figure 22.11.

GETTING A LITTLE HELP GENERATING SAN CERTIFICATES

Quite frankly, Microsoft should be a bit embarrassed by the whole SAN certificate debacle. Certainly there have been a lot of good blog postings and articles written since the Exchange Server 2007 was released, but the initial support for SAN certificates by certificate authorities was sorely lacking and it seemed as if most people were not prepared to support SAN certificates. I personally had never heard of a SAN certificate before working with the Exchange Server 2007 beta code.

A lot of early (and current!) adopters muddled through finding a certificate authority that would support a SAN certificate, getting the SAN certificates generated, and installing them with the right Client Access or Hub Transport components.

FIGURE 22.11
The SAN entries for a certificate

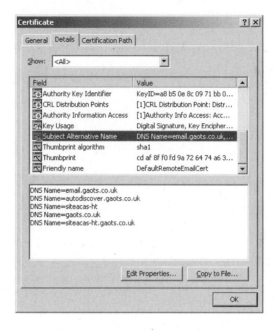

Following are some good resources for learning more about SAN certificate generation and installation:

◆ The Exchange Team has a good blog posting on the lessons learned when generating SAN certificates:

   http://msexchangeteam.com/archive/2007/02/19/435472.aspx

◆ Henrik Walther has a good article that steps you through the process when generating SAN certificates that must be supported by mobile devices:

   http://www.msexchange.org/articles_tutorials/exchange-server-2007/
      mobility-client-access/securing-exchange-2007-client-access-
      server-3rd-party-san-certificate.html

◆ Nathan Winters (who helped author this chapter) has a good blog entry that reiterates these concepts:

   http://www.mmmug.co.uk/blogs/nweb/archive/2008/01/17/1958.aspx

Possibly the best help of all, though, came from certificate authority DigiCert. This is in the form of a really great Web interface that prompts you for the information about the certificate as shown in Figure 22.12.

When you click the Generate button, the wizard will generate the Exchange 2007 Management Shell `New-ExchangeCertificate` cmdlet syntax you need to issue that particular certificate request. All you need to do is to copy that EMS command, paste it in to the EMS, and run it to generate the certificate request.

FIGURE 22.12
Generating a certificate request command using the DigiCert wizard

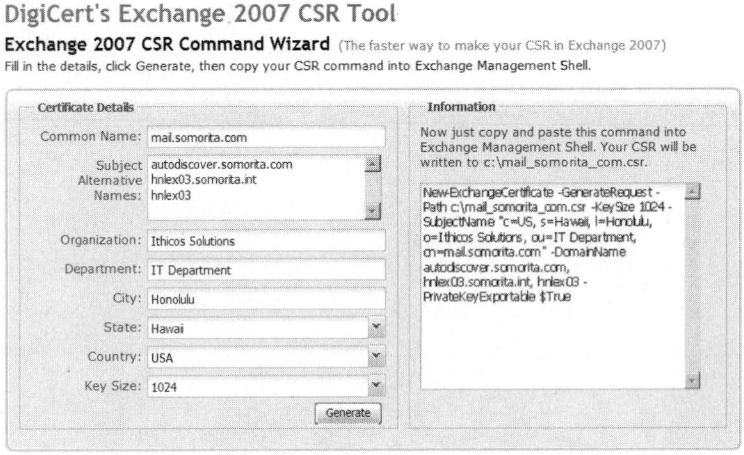

So given that these SAN certificates are quite expensive and may not be available from your usual provider, I can suggest some areas where you can do things differently. First, I should say that the simplest method is described in the preceding section. What follows is a method to save a little money, but it is certainly not simple!

CREATING SELF-SIGNED SAN CERTIFICATES

1. As in the simple scenario discussed earlier, you continue to make use of the default website for access to Autodiscover and Outlook Anywhere and for internal access to Outlook Web Access with forms-based authentication (FBA). You then add a new IP address to the server and create a new website, as shown in Figures 22.13 and 22.14, ensuring that the second IP address of the server is used for external access to OWA.

2. After configuring the new website, use the EMS to add a new OWA virtual directory as follows:

```
New-OwaVirtualDirectory -OwaVersion "Exchange2007" -Name "owa"↵
-WebSiteName "ExternalOWA"
```

The virtual directory is shown in Figure 22.15.

FIGURE 22.13
The TCP/IP setting
page after adding a
second IP address

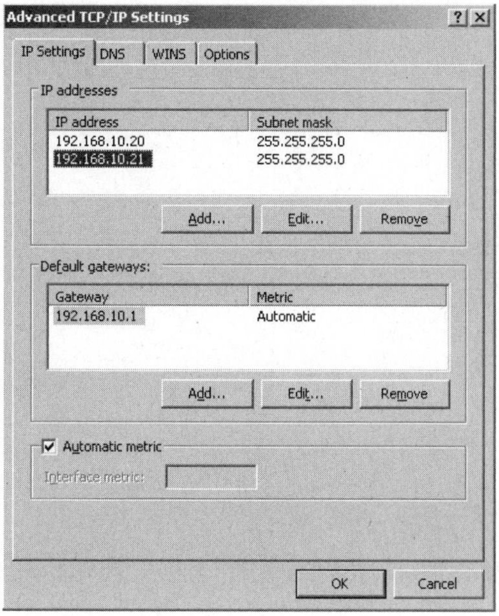

FIGURE 22.14
Creating a new web-
site to use the new
IP address

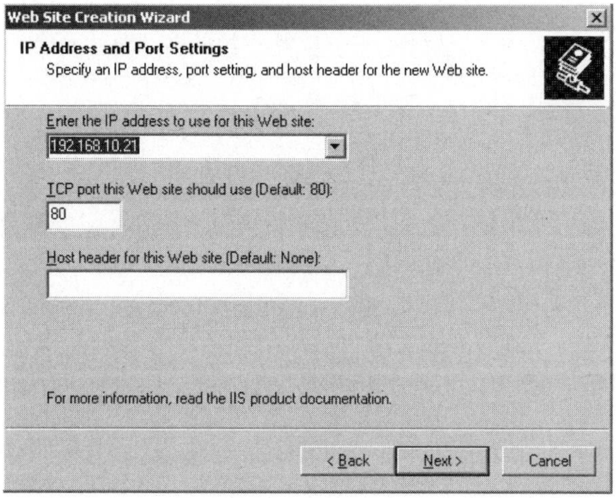

FIGURE 22.15
The new website and
virtual directory in
IIS Manager

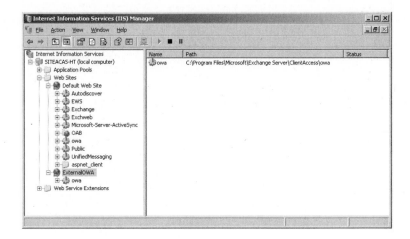

3. Set the ExternalURL parameter as follows:

```
Set-OwaVirtualDirectory -Identity "owa (ExternalOWA)" -InternalURL↵
https://email.gaots.co.uk/owa -ExternalURL https://email.gaots.co.uk/owa
```

4. Request and install a new certificate for the website using the Web Server Certificate Wizard on the new website.

5. Set the authentication mode in the Exchange Management Console; if you require a logon form, select the Use Forms-based Authentication option and then specify the logon credentials option such as Domain\User Name, User Principal Name (UPN), or User Name Only as shown in Figure 22.16.

FIGURE 22.16
Selecting the authen-
tication method in
Exchange Management
Console

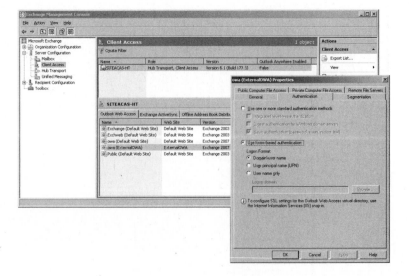

I suggest this method because it lets you use a self-signed certificate, which is free, for the default website. You can then set up any number of SANs you want. You still have to purchase a certificate for the external OWA website, but you only need the standard type that you purchased previously for Exchange 2000 and 2003.

Another reason for following this setup is that it may be required anyway. When ISA 2006 is used to publish Outlook Web Access, forms-based authentication must be provided by ISA. Therefore, you must set authentication to Basic on the published Outlook Web Access virtual directory. If you still want internal clients to use forms-based authentication and therefore get the nice splash screen login (not to mention it's more secure), you need a different Outlook Web Access site for internal users.

This setup does have certain limitations. First, you must ensure that your certificate authority (CA) is trusted on all clients that will access the default website (Autodiscover, Outlook Anywhere, and Internal Outlook Web Access). As long as these machines are domain joined, you can use Group Policy to ensure that your root certificate authority is trusted.

But you may have a problem if you want non-domain-joined machines connecting externally using Autodiscover and Outlook Anywhere. In my experience, laptop machines are generally domain joined and people are discouraged (prevented) from connecting home PCs to the corporate e-mail system for obvious reasons, so in many cases this is not a big problem.

One other inconvenience is that you will have to place the certificate authority certificates on mobile devices if you want them to use this method of access. Again, this is a simple provisioning task; however, you can also set up a second Exchange ActiveSync virtual directory in the website that was created for external access to Outlook Web Access.

So as you can see, this method involves a little more work and has a few caveats. However, it does facilitate cheaper certificates and the use of forms-based authentication for Outlook Web Access both internally and externally in conjunction with ISA 2006.

Summary

This chapter should give you a good understanding of the new features that Exchange 2007 uses to provide client access. The Client Access server role is one of the most complex in Exchange 2007, with a huge number of settings that can be configured. One key area to understand thoroughly before beginning your deployments is Autodiscover, which is the service that holds together so many of the Client Access server features. The new Outlook Web Access and Exchange ActiveSync features provide a superb platform for client access to Exchange, one that users will be productive using and administrators will find convenient to manage.

Chapter 23

Exchange Anywhere

E-mail has become what most businesses consider their most critical application, and as such, users demand access to their e-mail around the clock, wherever they may be. Throughout the versions of Exchange, the remote access options have improved, with each version offering more. The remote capabilities of Exchange allow users to have access to their mailbox from almost anywhere in the world. They have allowed the hosting industry to expand rapidly. Users no longer need to be co-located with the e-mail server to have full access and the full functionality that Exchange can offer.

Exchange 2007 builds on the enhancements that Exchange 2003 introduced. Outlook Web Access just gets better with every version of Exchange. RPC over HTTPS gets a new name (long overdue) and is now known as Outlook Anywhere. ActiveSync has also been enhanced, but some features will require the next version of Windows Mobile 6.1. Exchange 2007 also continues to provide access using more traditional methods, the old favorites POP3 and IMAP.

When considering what remote access options to offer your user community, you do need to consider security requirements as well. E-mail can often contain sensitive information, and without a secure deployment can actually put your network at risk. Fortunately, it is possible to secure all of the remote access methods to e-mail, a process that protects your network without compromising functionality. Securing access to e-mail using Exchange is discussed in Chapter 25, "Securing Exchange Server" and all techniques discussed in this chapter should be considered along with the security needs of your organization.

In this chapter you learn to:

- ◆ Understand Client capabilities

- ◆ Implement Outlook Web Access

- ◆ Implement ActiveSync and Windows Mobile devices

- ◆ Use Outlook Anywhere

- ◆ Support POP3 and IMAP4 clients

Exchange Server 2007 and Client Features

Do I need Outlook 2003 or Outlook 2007 to take advantage of Autodiscover? Will Windows Mobile 6.x give me the ability to better lock down mobile devices? The questions could go on and on. A couple of fairly common questions that administrators (and even end users) ask are:

- ◆ What type of client do I need to be using to get some features?

- ◆ Is there a specific minimum version required of a particular client type?

Outlook 2007 Features

The Autodiscover feature is one of a number of features available only if you are using the Outlook 2007 client and have your mailbox located on an Exchange 2007 server. The new client-side rules limit also requires both Outlook 2007 and Exchange 2007. Though this might not seem very fair, you have to keep in mind that sometimes not only a client-side interface but also a server-side component is required to implement the feature.

EXCHANGE SERVER 2007 REQUIRED FOR OUTLOOK WEB ACCESS

When comparing client and server features, it's important to note that a mailbox must be on Exchange Server 2007 in order to use either the premium or light Outlook Web Access interfaces.

I am including some tables to help you figure out which of the new features are available to you, depending on the clients you are using and the location of the user's mailbox. Table 23.1 shows the mail features that are available with the different Outlook and Exchange server combinations.

Note that some features, such as RSS feeds, will show up via Outlook Web Access if they were pulled into the user's mailbox, but the user will not have an interface to see them properly.

Table 23.2 shows the calendaring features available with different server/client combinations.

As you can see in Table 23.2, many of the new features of the calendaring interface work only with Outlook 2007, but a few nice improvements are available via Outlook Web Access.

Next let's look at some of the new tasking features. Table 23.3 shows the tasking features and which clients let you take advantage of them.

As you can see from Table 23.3, all of the tasking features require either Outlook 2007 or Outlook Web Access 2007 Premium; tasking features are not dependent on the mailbox server version.

In my opinion, the new out-of-office (OOF) features are some of the best in the new client interface. Table 23.4 shows the new out-of-office features and the circumstances under which they can be used.

OOF?

In case you were wondering why we use OOF to mean *out-of-office*, it originally stood for *out-of-facility*; this acronym originated at Microsoft in the pre-Exchange days when it used a Xenix-based mail system.

Finally, there are some additional client/server features that your users may find useful. These are mostly security-related features. Table 23.5 shows these features and the circumstances under which they may be used.

Windows Mobile and Improved Security

Windows Mobile and ActiveSync device support are certainly not new to Exchange Server 2007. Exchange Server 2003 had good support for Windows Mobile devices, and you could even support mobile devices using Microsoft Mobile Information Server and Exchange 2000. Microsoft continues to improve the support and the manageability of mobile devices with newer versions of Windows Mobile, Exchange Server 2007 SP1, and updated versions of ActiveSync.

TABLE 23.1: Mail Features Available with Outlook Client and Exchange Server Combinations

FEATURE	O2K7/ E2K7	OWA 2007 PREMIUM	OWA 2007 LIGHT	OUTLOOK MOBILE	O2K7/ E2K3	O2K3/ E2K7
Attachment preview in reading pane	✓				✓	
View attachments as web page without client application		✓	✓			
Instant search across all Outlook items	✓	✓	✓	✓		
Better rules; 32KB rule limit removed	✓					
Native support for RSS feeds	✓				✓	
RFC 2822 support for in-reply-to SMTP header for conversations	✓	✓	✓	✓	✓	✓
Message classifications	✓	✓				
Improved accessibility features for low-vision and blind users	✓		✓			
Color categories freely defined and assigned to any type of item	✓	✓			✓	

TABLE 23.2: Calendaring Features Available with Outlook Client and Exchange Server Combinations

FEATURE	O2K7/ E2K7	OWA 2007 PREMIUM	OWA 2007 LIGHT	OUTLOOK MOBILE	O2K7/ E2K3	O2K3/ E2K7
Improved interface for booking meetings (Scheduling Assistant)	✓	✓	✓		✓	
Scheduling Assistant looks directly into a user's calendar instead of free/busy public folder	✓	✓	✓			

TABLE 23.2: Calendaring Features Available with Outlook Client and Exchange Server Combinations *(CONTINUED)*

FEATURE	O2K7/ E2K7	OWA 2007 PREMIUM	OWA 2007 LIGHT	OUTLOOK MOBILE	O2K7/ E2K3	O2K3/ E2K7
Improved resource picker interface with attributes such as room capacity	✓	✓	✓			
Add room as resource when you place in the "To" field	✓	✓	✓			
Conference room resource settings configuration		✓	✓			
Multiple meeting updates collapsed, only latest one shown	✓	✓	✓	✓		✓
Meeting updates highlight updated fields	✓	✓	✓			
Updates with no time change apply automatically, no reply required	✓	✓	✓			
Dual time zone when scheduling a new meeting	✓				✓	
Notification of time change when dragging/dropping a meeting	✓				✓	
Calendar snapshots to share calendars with outside users	✓				✓	
Caching of other users' calendar data	✓				✓	
Two-way sync with team calendars in SharePoint	✓				✓	
Overlaying of multiple calendars in the same view	✓				✓	

TABLE 23.3: Tasking Features Available with Outlook Client and Exchange Server Combinations

FEATURE	O2K7/ E2K7	OWA 2007 PREMIUM	OWA 2007 LIGHT	OUTLOOK MOBILE	O2K7/ E2K3	O2K3/ E2K7
To-Do Bar with improved task information	✓	✓			✓	
Task information at the bottom of the calendar view	✓	✓			✓	
Assign a task by dragging into calendar	✓	✓			✓	
Flag message and assign task due date	✓	✓			✓	

TABLE 23.4: Out-of-Office Features Available with Outlook Client and Exchange Server Combinations

FEATURE	O2K7/ E2K7	OWA 2007 PREMIUM	OWA 2007 LIGHT	OUTLOOK MOBILE	O2K7/ E2K3	O2K3/ E2K7
Schedule OOF messages for future date/time	✓	✓	✓	✓		
Internal and external OOF messages	✓	✓	✓			
Send external OOF message only to contacts	✓	✓	✓			
OOF messages can include HTML formatting	✓	✓	✓	✓		

If you have supported Windows Mobile devices or other types of mobile devices in the past, you realize how important centralized policies and security can be for your organization and your users. The latest versions of the Exchange ActiveSync (EAS) have improved greatly over the years. The newest features can be assigned based on a user's ActiveSync policy. Figure 23.1 shows the Device property page, which includes the options for enabling or disabling features such as a mobile device's WiFi interface, camera, removable storage, Bluetooth, and synchronization options.

Figure 23.2 shows the Advanced tab of the ActiveSync Policy Properties, which allows you to specify allowed or blocked applications, filenames, and other software features of the mobile device.

Of course, you must have the corresponding version of Windows Mobile to take advantage of all of the newest features. Windows Mobile 5 with the Microsoft Security and Feature Pack

(MSFP) uses EAS v2.5, Windows Mobile 6 uses EAS v12, and Windows Mobile 6.1 uses EAS v12.1. Table 23.6 shows a comparison of the features available with various versions of EAS and versions of Exchange Server.

TABLE 23.5: Additional Features Available with Outlook Client and Exchange Server Combinations

FEATURE	O2K7/ E2K7	OWA 2007 PREMIUM	OWA 2007 LIGHT	OUTLOOK MOBILE	O2K7/ E2K3	O2K3/ E2K7
Content policies for folders such as item retention, archive, and expiration	✓	✓	✓			
Outlook generates postmark for use with anti-spam systems	✓				✓	
Warning for e-mail messages that appear to be phishing messages	✓	✓	✓		✓	
End user has the ability to remotely wipe out mobile device		✓	✓			

FIGURE 23.1
ActiveSync device policies

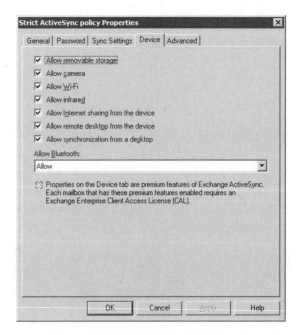

FIGURE 23.2
ActiveSync advanced
policies

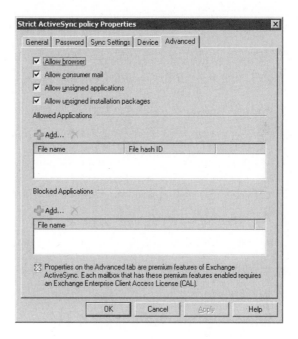

TABLE 23.6: Exchange ActiveSync Features

SETTING/ SETTING/RESTRICTION	E2K3 SP2 / EAS v2.5	E2K7 / EAS v12	E2K SP1 / STANDARD CAL / EAS v12.1	E2K7 SP1 ENTERPRISE CAL / EAS v12.1
Password Required	✓	✓	✓	✓
Min Password Length	✓	✓	✓	✓
Alphanumeric Password	✓	✓	✓	✓
Inactivity Timeout	✓	✓	✓	✓
Max Failed Password Attempts	✓	✓	✓	✓
Policy Refresh Interval	✓	✓	✓	✓
Allow Non-provisionable Devices	✓	✓	✓	✓
Attachments Enabled		✓	✓	✓
Storage Card Encryption		✓	✓	✓

TABLE 23.6:   Exchange ActiveSync Features *(CONTINUED)*

SETTING/ SETTING/RESTRICTION	E2K3 SP2 / EAS v2.5	E2K7 / EAS v12	E2K SP1 / STANDARD CAL / EAS v12.1	E2K7 SP1 ENTERPRISE CAL / EAS v12.1
Password Recovery Enabled		✓	✓	✓
Allow Simple Device Password		✓	✓	✓
Max Attachment Size		✓	✓	✓
WSS Access Enabled		✓	✓	✓
UNC Access Enabled		✓	✓	✓
Password Expiration		✓	✓	✓
Password History		✓	✓	✓
Require Manual Sync When Roaming			✓	✓
Min Device Pwd Complex Characters			✓	✓
Max Calendar Age Filter			✓	✓
Allow HTML E-mail			✓	✓
Max E-mail Age Filter			✓	✓
Max E-mail Body Truncation Size			✓	✓
Max E-mail HTML Body Truncation Size			✓	✓
Require Signed SMIME Messages			✓	✓
Require Encrypted SMIME Messages			✓	✓
Require Signed SMIME Algorithm			✓	✓
Require Encryption SMIME Algorithm			✓	✓

TABLE 23.6:   Exchange ActiveSync Features *(CONTINUED)*

SETTING/ SETTING/RESTRICTION	E2K3 SP2 / EAS v2.5	E2K7 / EAS v12	E2K SP1 / STANDARD CAL / EAS v12.1	E2K7 SP1 ENTERPRISE CAL / EAS v12.1
Allow SMIME Encryption Algorithm Negotiation			✓	✓
Allow SMIME Soft Certs			✓	✓
Require Device Encryption			✓	✓
Allow Storage Card				✓
Allow Camera				✓
Allow Unsigned Applications				✓
Allow Unsigned Installation Packages				✓
Allow Wi-Fi				✓
Allow Text Messaging				✓
Allow POP/IMAP E-mail				✓
Allow Bluetooth				✓
Allow IrDA				✓
Allow Desktop Sync				✓
Allow Browser				✓
Allow Consumer E-mail				✓
Allow Remote Desktop				✓
Allow Internet Sharing				✓
Unapproved InROM Application List				✓
Approved Application List				✓

Note that some of the advanced device configuration features require the use of an Exchange Server 2007 Enterprise Client Access License (CAL) for the device. The Enterprise Edition of Exchange Server 2007 is not required, though.

---

iPhone Support and ActiveSync

I know you are dying to ask, so go ahead... Can the president of the company use her iPhone with Exchange Server 2007?

In my own opinion, the iPhone is an awesome little consumer device; it is probably the slickest consumer device on the market by a long stretch. The first version of the iPhone could only communicate with the Exchange Server using IMAP4. However for the iPhone 2.0 software, Apple licensed the ActiveSync software from Microsoft. I saw the iPhone drive one company's migration from Lotus Notes to Exchange Server 2007.

The iPhone 2.0 software will actually use Autodiscover to try and locate the iPhone, but the full Exchange ActiveSync v12.1 feature set (shown in Table 23.6) is not available via the iPhone. The device management features for the iPhone are more equivalent to those of EAS v2.5.

Here are two good references for setting up the iPhone to sync with the Exchange server using ActiveSync:

```
http://support.kerio.com/index.php?_m=knowledgebase&_a
=viewarticle&kbarticleid=489
```

```
http://blog.fosketts.net/2008/07/10/how-to-set-up-iphone-exchange-activesync/
```

Using Outlook Web Access

Outlook Web Access (OWA) is one of the biggest selling points of Exchange, and it simply gets better with every new version. Though I consider myself a dedicated Outlook user, for the better part of most days I use Outlook Web Access. It is one of the most complex Web applications available, and it offers significant levels of customization while retaining a familiar Outlook-like interface, allowing end users to quickly get to grips with it as an interface for their e-mail. From the very moment you access the forms-based login page, you know that you are using something exceptional. Figure 23.3 shows the default forms-based authentication login page, which can be customized to your company look and feel if required.

From the logon page, users can select a radio button that indicates whether they are using a public or shared computer or a private computer. If they are using a private computer, their inactivity time-out is 8 hours, but if they select the radio button that indicates they are using a public computer, the inactivity time-out is 15 minutes. This can help improve security by automatically disconnecting inactive users from their mailbox. The time-outs can be configured on a per-server basis via a Registry change.

The first time end users log in to OWA, they get the chance to set their location and language (see Figure 23.4). This avoids the problems with previous versions of OWA using the location information of the machine being used.

Once you are logged in, the interface is very familiar. Anyone who has used Outlook or OWA on Exchange 2003 will feel comfortable quickly. You have full access to your mailbox, including all folders, contacts, tasks, and notes, as you would expect. Figure 23.5 shows the full OWA interface.

FIGURE 23.3
Outlook Web Access
logon form

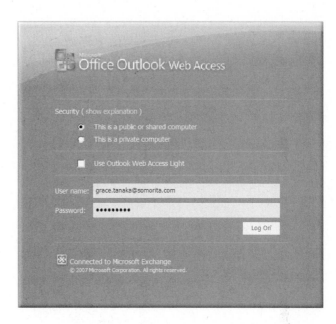

FIGURE 23.4
Setting the location and
language options

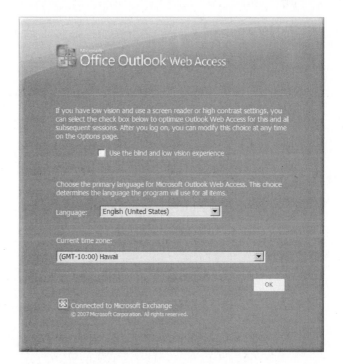

FIGURE 23.5
Exchange 2007 Outlook
Web Access interface

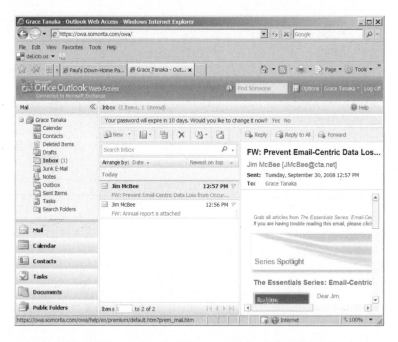

New in this version is the ability to open another Exchange 2007 mailbox directly from the interface simply by selecting the box in the upper-right corner where your name appears. You are prompted for the name of the other mailbox (provided you have permissions for it).

The list of options has grown considerably, giving you more control over how OWA works for you, displays messages, and works with other users. You can access options by clicking the Options button on the upper-right portion of the OWA interface. Figure 23.6 shows the Options pane and the message options.

There are also options that allow your users to control their Windows Mobile handhelds. With a supported handset, they can wipe the device or recover their password. With Exchange Server 2003 this was only possible through the optional tool Mobile Admin. Administrators can disable this functionality if required and also have control over the device from the server. An example of this feature is shown in Figure 23.7.

Exchange 2007 introduced more control over your Out-of-Office message, allowing you to have one message for known people and another message for everyone else. Outlook Web Access provides an interface for the two message types through the Options pane. Figure 23.8 shows the Out-of-Office Assistant features that users can access through the OWA Options interface. Notice a few new Out-of-Office features, including the ability to schedule when the auto-replies are sent, an option for sending a separate Out-of-Office reply to external senders, and the ability to specify whether external senders must exist in your Contacts folder.

FIGURE 23.6
Editing Outlook Web
Access user options

FIGURE 23.7
Managing end-user
mobile devices via OWA

FIGURE 23.8
Setting Out-of-Office
options through Outlook
Web Access

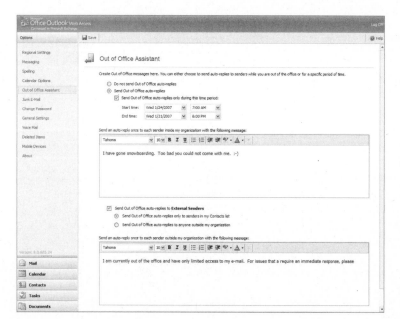

The option to change your network password through OWA is now built in (Exchange 2003 required manual configuration of this feature). Network password control can be turned off as well, should that be required.

If you wish to support password changes for Exchange 2003 mailboxes, the virtual directories will need to be added to the Client Access servers as before. The built-in password change feature is for Exchange 2007 mailboxes only.

Access to attached files has been improved. A new WebReady feature allows access to common file types such as Microsoft Word documents even if the application is not installed on the machine being used to access OWA. A new feature for OWA called Document Access allows access to SharePoint sites and document libraries on your network through the OWA interface.

As with Exchange 2003, the interface that you see for Outlook Web Access depends on the version of Exchange that your mailbox is located on. Therefore, although all users can see the new Exchange 2007 login screen, if their mailbox is on Exchange 2003, they will get OWA for Exchange 2003, not Exchange 2007.

Outlook Web Access is handled by an Exchange 2007 server that has the Client Access server (CAS) role installed. The CAS role replaces the front-end server functionality from previous versions of Exchange.

One of the new features I find useful in Outlook Web Access is the enhanced address book access. If you click the small Address Book icon next to the Find Someone box, you are presented with the Address Book dialog box (shown in Figure 23.9) divided into three columns.

FIGURE 23.9
Using the Outlook Web Access address book feature

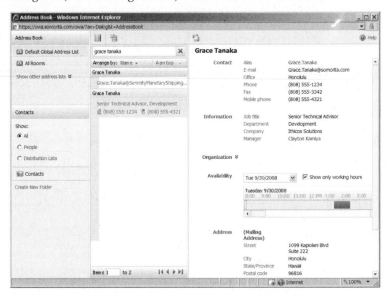

The first column lets you select what types of addresses you can see. The second column lists the users in the global address list. The third column (which can be turned off) shows you their availability that day as well as their address book details. Therefore, you could use this feature to see whether the person you want to call is in a meeting, out of the office, and so on.

Configuring Outlook Web Access

Outlook Web Access is enabled by default, so you don't have to do anything special to enable the feature. However, you do have control over what the end user can do with Outlook Web Access. Most of the Exchange 2007 Outlook Web Access options are enabled on a per-server basis.

Performing Configuration via the Exchange Management Console

To configure the server via the Exchange Management Console (EMC), you need to select the server you want to configure in the Server Configuration work center. In the lower pane, you will see the directories configured on the server. Right-click OWA and choose Properties.

Authentication

The Authentication tab allows you to enable or disable forms-based authentication (FBA) and change how much information the end user needs to put in when using FBA. In a single-domain model, you can set a default domain so that end users just need to enter their username and password in the logon form. Figure 23.10 shows the Authentication property page of the OWA virtual directory.

FIGURE 23.10
Configuring Outlook Web Access authentication options

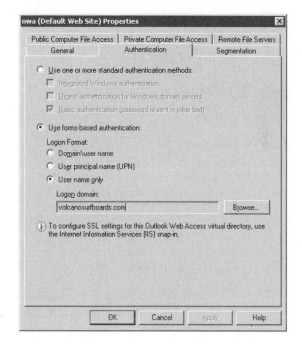

Note that a virtual directory can have only one authentication option; if you have some users who want Integrated Windows Authentication and some users who want forms-based authentication, you need to create two different OWA virtual directories.

Segmentation

The Segmentation tab allows you to enable and disable features in OWA (see Figure 23.11). This can include user management of their handheld device, whether they can change their network password through OWA, access to folders, and other options.

By default, all options are enabled. The following options can be disabled:

◆ You can disable Exchange ActiveSync integration, which allows the user to manage their Windows Mobile-or ActiveSync-enabled devices.

◆ You can hide all address lists (by disabling All Address Lists) instead of just the global address lists.

◆ You can hide the Calendar, Contacts, Journal, Tasks, and Search folders features.

◆ You can disable Junk E-mail filtering features.

◆ You can require that users use the basic client rather than the premium client.

◆ You can disable e-mail signatures.

◆ You can disable spell checking features.

◆ You can disable the ability to change themes.

◆ You can disable the change password feature.

◆ You can disable Unified Messaging integration.

◆ You can disable rules access.

◆ You can disable public folder access.

◆ You can disable S/MIME support.

◆ You can disable recover deleted items.

FIGURE 23.11
Configuring
Outlook Web Access
segmentation

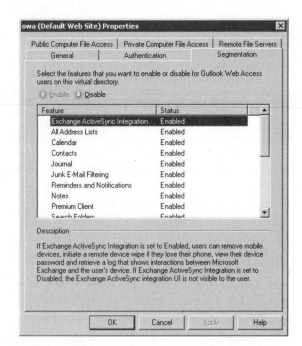

Public and Private File Access

Public and private file access allows you to specify the types of files that users can access if they have selected a public/shared computer (default) or a private computer on the OWA logon page. The Public Computer File Access and Private Computer File Access tabs allow you to control access to files — either files attached to e-mail messages or files from Remote File Access — and are identical as far as the options that are available to you. This includes the new WebReady document viewing options, which allow users to view documents for common file types such as Microsoft Word without having the application installed on their machine. Figure 23.12 shows the Private Computer File Access property page.

FIGURE 23.12

Configuring private computer file access

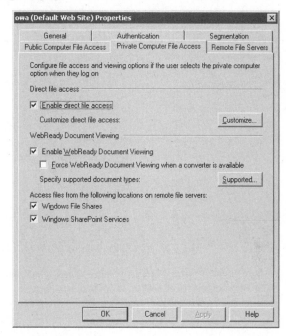

If you click the Customize button on the Private Computer File Access property page, you can configure direct file access, which allows you to force end users to save certain types of documents to their local machine before access is granted. You can also block access to file types altogether. These options were previously available in the OWA Admin Tool for Exchange 2003 but now can be managed via the Exchange Management Console; this can be managed on the direct file access dialog box (shown in Figure 23.13).

FIGURE 23.13

Direct File Access Settings dialog box

Remote File Servers

The Remote File Servers property page (shown in Figure 23.14) controls access to documents and SharePoint on remote servers through OWA.

I discuss remote file access later in this chapter in the "Configuring Document Access" section.

FIGURE 23.14
Configuring Outlook
Web Access for remote
file server support

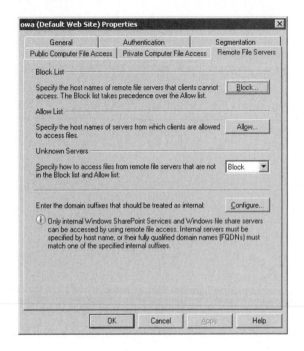

SIMPLIFYING THE OWA URL

If the server that the end users are accessing is a dedicated Exchange Client Access server, you can simplify the URL so that users don't need to add /owa at the end of the address. For example, the user can type `https://owa.somorita.com` rather than `http://owa.somorita.com/owa`. You do this via a simple change through Internet Information Server (IIS) Manager:

1. Open IIS Manager, and open the website that has OWA enabled on it.

2. Right-click the website container and choose Properties.

3. Click the Home Directory property page. Select the option A Redirection To A URL. This will enable the option Redirect To. Enter in the box the URL to which you want to redirect users that connect to the default website. In Figure 23.15, I am redirecting the user to `https://owa.somorita.com/owa`.

4. Select the check box labeled A Directory Below URL Entered.

5. Click OK.

This technique works for most any Web application, not just Exchange Server's virtual directories. Note that in a mixed environment, you should use the legacy /exchange virtual directory, because /owa will not allow access to Exchange 2003 mailboxes.

FIGURE 23.15
Redirecting the default
website to the OWA
virtual directory

Using Outlook Web Access in Larger Organizations

With the changes in Exchange routing in Exchange 2007, the location of the Client Access server becomes more important. The simple rule now is that each Active Directory site that has a Mailbox server also needs a Client Access server. That also means OWA, which is one of the functions of the Client Access server role. With the removal of Exchange's own routing capability (via routing groups in Exchange 2003 and 2000), Exchange 2007 now uses AD sites for routing.

However, you are not limited to a single Client Access server. You can have more than one. In some sites, where there is heavy remote access, you may want to look at having more than one CAS and then using load balancing and the Availability service to ensure that the servers are used to their fullest. If you have more than one Client Access server or more than one Active Directory site in which you have Client Access servers, please go back and read Chapter 22, "Getting to Know the Client Access Server Role."

Enabling Document Access

Document Access is a new feature of Outlook Web Access that allows users of OWA to access Windows file shares and SharePoint Services sites through the OWA interface. Although the feature is enabled by default, no SharePoint sites or internal file shares are configured.

You will want to carefully consider whether to enable this feature for your servers, because the level of access control may not be enough for many sites. You should look at what can be accessed through this process before allowing it to be used by the end users.

The feature can be enabled on a per-server or per-user basis, allowing the administrator to control who can and cannot access the resources.

You can also control whether it is enabled depending on the selection of a public or private computer on the login screen. However, because you don't know where these computers are located, this level of control is limited at best. As soon as users figure out that choosing a different option allows the use of different features, they will select the option with the features they want to use wherever they are.

You can grant access to Windows file servers only on a per-server basis. Therefore, if a server hosts a number of shares, all of those shares will be available. One way around this limitation is to use a domain distributed file system (DFS) system. However, this involves adding the DNS name of your Active Directory forest root domain to the list of shares, which may expose or bring undue attention to other elements of the domain, such as the netlogon share.

CONFIGURING DOCUMENT ACCESS

You configure Document Access as part of the Outlook Web Access feature set, either via the Exchange Management Console or through the `Set-OwaVirtualDirectory` command.

WHEN CHANGES TO DOCUMENT ACCESS TAKE EFFECT

Changes to document access and segmentation take effect after 60 minutes of inactivity for users already logged in or when a user logs in. If you want to force the changes to take effect, you need to run the `IISReset /Noforce` command on the Client Access server.

Exchange Management Console

You can use the Exchange Management Console to configure the document access options. Because it is part of Outlook Web Access, you configure the options on the OWA virtual directory. To access this directory, open EMC and then open the Server Configuration work center. Select the server you want to configure. In the list of directories in the lower pane, select the OWA directory that you want to change, and then choose Properties in the Actions pane to the right.

Access to remote file and SharePoint servers is enabled or disabled on the two file access tabs. In each one, you will see the options to enable access toward the bottom.

To grant or block access, select the Remote File Access tab. When configuring file server access, note that the block list overrides the allow list. When entering the server name, enter just the name — such as HNLFS01. Do not enter \HNLFS01.

You don't have to enter the fully qualified name for file servers because the list of domain suffixes controls that. However, if you do enter a server name with its fully qualified domain name (for example, HNLFS01.somorita.int), then somorita.int needs to be in the list of internal domain suffixes.

If you are granting access to a domain DFS, you need to add the domain to the list of allowed servers and the list of internal DFS suffixes. You can define them in the list of suffixes that are treated internally (see Figure 23.16).

If there is no dot in the URL, the URL is treated as internal. If there is a dot in the URL, it is treated as internal only if the domain suffix is in the internal sites list.

Exchange Management Shell Commands

To use the Exchange Management Shell to enable access to Windows file shares (UNC paths) for end users who have selected the Public Computer option on the login screen, use the following command:

```
Set-OwaVirtualDirectory -Identity "owa (default web site)"↵
-UNCAccessOnPublicComputersEnabled $true
```

FIGURE 23.16
Configuring internal
domain names

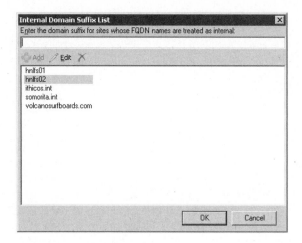

For SharePoint access, the command is almost identical:

```
Set-OwaVirtualDirectory -Identity "owa (default web site)"↵
 -WSSAccessOnPublicComputersEnabled $true
```

For private computers, the command is the same as except the word `Private` is used instead of `Public`:

```
Set-OwaVirtualDirectory -Identity "owa (default web site)"↵
 -UNCAccessonPrivateComputersEnabled $true
```

By default, all servers are blocked; therefore, to grant access you must add servers to the list. To allow access to servers hnlfs01 and hnlfs02 you would use the following command:

```
Set-OwaVirtualDirectory -Identity "owa (default web site)↵
 -RemoteDocumentsAllowedServers hnlfs01,hnlfs02
```

To allow access to a DFS share, the command would be almost the same:

```
Set-OwaVirtualDirectory -Identity "owa (default web site)↵
 -RemoteDocumentsAllowedServers somorita.int
```

When it comes to blocking servers, you have a number of options. The first option is to set all servers not listed as blocked, which is the default. The second option is to allow access to all servers except the ones explicitly blocked. Depending on your environment, both options may be of benefit. However, remember that you have to set the options on each CAS server.

To block a specific server (for example, hnlfs04), use the following command:

```
Set-OwaVirtualDirectory -Identity "owa (default web site)"↵
 -RemoteDocumentsBlockedServers hnlfs04
```

To set the default action for servers not listed, use the following command:

```
Set-OwaVirtualDirectory -Identity "owa (default web site)"↵
 -RemoteDocumentsActionForUnknownServers Allow
```

Replace `Allow` with `Block` to block access, as in this example:

```
Set-OwaVirtualDirectory -Identity "owa (default web site)"↵
 -RemoteDocumentsActionForUnknownServers Block
```

Using Outlook Anywhere

Outlook Anywhere is the new name for RPC over HTTP. Wrapping all the RPC traffic that Outlook requires into a single HTTP traffic stream allows Outlook to connect to your Exchange server over the Internet, through your own firewall and any firewall on the client side, without having to open a large number of ports.

If Outlook Anywhere is deployed with an SSL certificate, you only have to open a single port, 443. If you have deployed an SSL certificate to secure OWA and Exchange ActiveSync, you can use the same certificate for Outlook Anywhere.

With careful network configuration using a split DNS system, you can also use Outlook Anywhere inside your own firewall, allowing mobile clients to come and go on your network without having to reconfigure their machines. When successfully deployed, it should be totally transparent to the end user.

To use Outlook Anywhere, the client OS needs to be Windows XP Service Pack 2 or higher with Outlook 2003 or later installed. As with Outlook Web Access, Outlook Anywhere requires a server with the Client Access role installed.

TIPS FOR SETTING UP OUTLOOK ANYWHERE

Outlook Anywhere should be run over an SSL-secured connection. This ensures that the username and password information passes over the Internet encrypted. Although the dialog boxes in Outlook make it seem that you can run the feature without SSL, in practice, trying to get it to run without SSL is complex.

When setting up Outlook Anywhere for the first time, if possible, configure your network so that the name on your SSL certificate works both inside and outside the firewall. Then get everything to work inside first. This ensures that any firewall problems are not causing a connection failure.

SETTING UP A SPLIT DNS SYSTEM

Split DNS (aka Split Brain DNS) describes a configuration in which you have two DNS servers that deliver different results to a DNS query, depending on which DNS server is used. This can be useful when you want your clients to use the same DNS domain name whether they are inside your network or on the Internet. You can use Split DNS to deploy a single name for Outlook Anywhere, Outlook

Web Access, or any other web service that is accessible both internally and externally. Setting up a Split DNS system is simple, but it does take some care:

1. Establish what services are being accessed externally using your external domain name. This will probably include your website and possibly an FTP site. If you have access to the DNS records, take a look at what hosts are configured for your domain name. Make a note of any that are not configured to point to resources inside your network.

2. Create a new DNS zone on your internal DNS servers with a name that matches your external domain name. You may already have one if your Active Directory domain uses your external domain name. In this new zone, add your external hosts with their external IP addresses.

3. Add your internal hosts to the DNS zone.

4. Once the zone has been set up, replicate it to other internal DNS zones.

5. To test the system, drop into a command prompt and ping www.*yourdomain*.com (where *yourdomain* is the external domain name). You should get a response back from the external IP address where your website is hosted.

6. Next, ping mail.*yourdomain*.com (where mail.*yourdomain*.com is an internal host — the Exchange server, for example). You should get a response back from the Exchange server's internal IP address.

Any failures, such as the wrong IP address or unknown host errors, mean that the DNS zone isn't set correctly.

Configuring Exchange for Outlook Anywhere

Configuration of Outlook Anywhere is quite straightforward — a nice change from how it worked in Exchange 2003, which required a number of Registry changes to the Exchange server and domain controller if you were not using a front-end/back-end scenario. Outlook Anywhere is enabled on a per-server basis.

1. Set up a trusted SSL certificate.

   I discuss SSL certificate use in Chapter 25, "Securing Exchange Server." However, remember that for this feature to work correctly, the certificate needs to be trusted by the client. Outlook cannot cope with any SSL certificate prompts.

2. Install the RPC Proxy component.

   Before you make any changes to Exchange, the RPC Proxy component needs to be installed. You will find this in Add/Remove Programs, Add/Remove Windows Components. The option is under Network Components. After the component is installed, a reboot should not be required.

3. Enable Outlook Anywhere on Exchange Server.

   As with all components in Exchange 2007, you can enable the Outlook Anywhere option using the Exchange Management Console or the Management Shell.

CONFIGURING OUTLOOK ANYWHERE USING THE EMS

To configure Outlook Anywhere using the EMS, use a command similar to this one:

```
Enable-OutlookAnywhere -Server:'HNLEX04' -ExternalHostName:'owa.somorita.com' ↵
  -DefaultAuthenticationMethod:'Basic' -SSLOffloading:$false
```

In the preceding command, HNLEX04 is the real name of the server and owa.somorita.com is the name by which the server is known on the Internet and the name used in your SSL certificate.

The `Enable-OutlookAnywhere` cmdlet option `IISAuthenticationMethods` allows you to adjust the authentication type that is supported by the server. In a change from Exchange 2003, you can use either `Basic` or `Integrated`, but not both.

SSL offloading is a process where the SSL certificate is held elsewhere — for example, on another proxy server or appliance. If you do not have SSL managed elsewhere, be sure to use `-SSLOffloading:$false` in the command; otherwise the feature will fail to work correctly.

For more information on the `Enable-OutlookAnywhere` cmdlet, see the following website:

```
http://technet.microsoft.com/en-us/library/bb124993(EXCHG.80).aspx
```

CONFIGURING OUTLOOK ANYWHERE USING THE EMC

If you want to configure Outlook Anywhere using the Exchange Management Console, follow these steps:

1. First, open the console, expand Server Configuration work center, and open the Client Access subcontainer.

2. Select the server on which you want to enable Outlook Anywhere. In the Actions pane on the right, select Enable Outlook Anywhere.

3. The Enable Outlook Anywhere Wizard (shown in Figure 23.17) appears. Enter the external name that the clients will be using to access the server — this should match your SSL certificate.

4. Select your authentication method. I suggest starting with Basic.

Once configured, the options for Outlook Anywhere can be changed by selecting the server under Client Access and choosing Properties. An additional tab will be seen for Outlook Anywhere configuration.

Configuring the Outlook Client for Outlook Anywhere

On Outlook 2007, you can configure Outlook Anywhere via the Autodiscover service or manually. You must configure Outlook 2003 manually. Versions of Outlook prior to 2003 do not support Outlook Anywhere.

In all cases, you must have Outlook installed on a machine running Windows XP Service Pack 2 or higher. You can use any version of Windows XP, including Home and Media Center. For Vista also, any version may be used, not just the business editions.

If the host machine is not a member of the domain or forest that Exchange is installed in, you will need to take extra care with configuring the client.

AUTOMATICALLY CONFIGURING THE OUTLOOK CLIENT FOR OUTLOOK ANYWHERE (OUTLOOK 2007 ONLY)

You can automatically configure Outlook Anywhere by using the Autodiscover service of Exchange 2007, which is available only with Outlook 2007. If you are using Outlook 2003, you will need to manually configure the client.

FIGURE 23.17

Enabling Outlook Anywhere using the Exchange Management Console

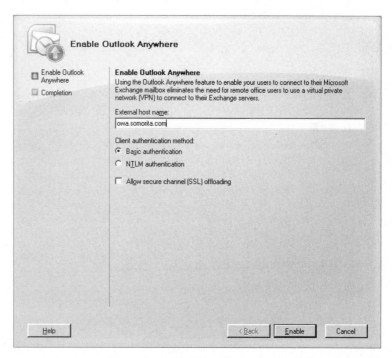

However, if this is your first time with Outlook Anywhere, you should manually configure it to begin with, and then move to Autodiscover configuration once you have a working deployment. I discuss Autodiscover setup and configuration in Chapter 20, "Supporting Outlook 2007."

TEST THE SSL CERTIFICATE BEFORE CONFIGURING OUTLOOK CLIENTS

Test the SSL certificate before you try configuring any Outlook client. Open Internet Explorer, and browse to `https://mail.domain.com/rpc` (where `mail.domain.com` is the name on your SSL certificate). If you get an SSL certificate prompt, the client will fail to connect correctly.

MANUALLY CONFIGURING THE OUTLOOK CLIENT FOR OUTLOOK ANYWHERE: LAN-BASED OR DOMAIN CLIENTS (OUTLOOK 2003 AND LATER)

If you just enabled Outlook Anywhere, I recommend that you carry out your initial testing and configuration of the client manually. This will allow you to troubleshoot the process and configuration. Once it is working correctly, you can use the settings with Autodiscover for Outlook 2007. Outlook 2003 users will need to continue to use the manual setup process, described here. If you have configured Outlook 2003 to use RPC over HTTP with Exchange 2003 in the past, you'll see that the process is identical. Outlook 2007 just changes some of the labels.

Carry out your first configuration inside the network using a machine that is part of the domain. By doing the initial setup inside, you can be sure that everything is working correctly. Once you have a working connection, you can move outside of your LAN and then your domain to confirm connectivity. Follow these steps:

1. Configure Outlook in the usual way, and confirm that it is connecting to the Exchange server correctly.

2. Open the Property page for the account. This varies with the version of Outlook. In Outlook 2003, choose Tools ➢ Email Accounts ➢ View or Change Existing E-mail Accounts, and then click Next. Choose Change to access the account settings.

3. Click the More Settings button, which is in the lower-right corner. Click the Connection tab.

4. Enable the option Connect To Microsoft Exchange Using HTTP, which is under Outlook Anywhere (Outlook 2007) or Exchange over the Internet (Outlook 2003). Then click the Exchange Proxy Settings button.

5. Complete the boxes to match your environment. You use only the hostname when entering addresses; no directory name is required.

6. Make sure that the entry in the first box, Use This URL To Connect To My Proxy Server For Exchange, matches the name on your SSL certificate.

7. Enable both Connect Using SSL Only and Only Connect To Proxy Servers That Have This Principal Name In Their Certificate (Outlook 2007) or Mutually Authenticate The Session When Connecting With SSL (Outlook 2003).

8. Finally, set the authentication settings to match what you set on the Exchange server when enabling Outlook Anywhere.

9. Click Apply and OK to get out of each box, and restart Outlook.

10. Confirm whether Outlook is making a connection to the Exchange server using HTTPS. You have two ways to do this:

    ◆ Close Outlook completely; consider using Task Manager to ensure that it has closed because it isn't unusual for another application — such as the ActiveSync desktop client and the BlackBerry desktop manager — to keep Outlook running. Then choose Start ➢ Run, type **outlook.exe /rpcdiag**, and press Enter. Outlook will start normally, but it will also include an additional diagnostics box. This will show the connection method being used. All connections should show HTTPS, as in Figure 23.18.

◆ The diagnostics box can also be started once Outlook is running. While holding down the Ctrl key, right-click the Outlook icon in the system tray next to your clock. On the menu, you will see an additional item, Connection Status. Select that and the diagnostics box will open.

FIGURE 23.18
Viewing the connection statistics

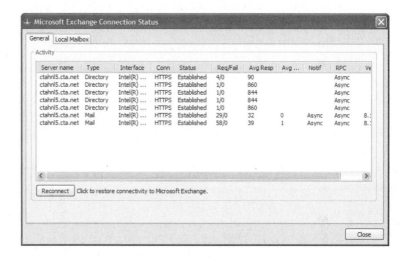

That Connection Status box is also useful if you are troubleshooting a conventional TCP/IP Outlook connection because it can show you which domain controller Outlook is connecting to.

MANUALLY CONFIGURING THE OUTLOOK CLIENT FOR OUTLOOK ANYWHERE: EXTERNAL CLIENTS THAT ARE NOT MEMBERS OF THE DOMAIN (OUTLOOK 2003 AND LATER)

Outlook Anywhere makes it possible for a client machine that is not part of your Windows domain to connect to Exchange and have the full feature set of an Exchange client available to them. This is what hosted Exchange companies do.

However, if Outlook is not on the same network as the Exchange server, getting it to use Outlook Anywhere can be a little fiddly. Ideally, your clients should be using Outlook 2007 because this allows you to use the Autodiscover service to configure Outlook automatically. However, if your end users are using Outlook 2003 as a client, manual configuration is the only option.

Before you begin, make sure that the feature is working internally with a domain member by following the instructions earlier in this chapter (in the section "Configuring the Outlook Client for Outlook Anywhere") for configuring a client on the domain and network. If you have not verified that the feature is working beforehand, troubleshooting any problems becomes a lot more difficult.

The configuration process for machines that are outside of the firewall is almost identical to the process for those that are inside:

1. Configure Outlook as you would ordinarily, including entering the Exchange server's real name, not the external name from the certificate. However, *do not* click the Check Name button because the name check process will fail. Instead, click More Settings. You will get a prompt about the Exchange server being unavailable. Accept that. Then you will see another box prompting you to check the name again. Click Cancel to clear that message. That should open the More Settings dialog box. Click the Connection tab.

2. This step is identical to the setup process on the LAN. Enable the option Connect To Microsoft Exchange Using HTTP, which is under Outlook Anywhere (Outlook 2007) or Exchange over the Internet (Outlook 2003). Then click the Exchange Proxy Settings button.

3. Fill in the boxes to match your environment. In this case, the speed options don't really apply because you want to always use HTTP, so enable both options. With the authentication, choose the same one you selected when enabling the service on the Exchange server.

4. After configuring the settings, click OK or Apply to close the windows until you get back to the Check Name dialog box. Click Check Name. Outlook will now prompt you for credentials. Enter the credentials in the format of *domain\username* and then the password.

    For example, if your domain name was e2007 and your username was bob.smith, you would enter **e2007\bob.smith**. Don't bother with the Remember My Password option at this time. Once authentication is successful, the server name and username should be underlined.

5. Click Next and Finish to close the Account Setup Wizard.

You can now start Outlook as usual. Because the computer is not a member of the domain, you will need to authenticate to the domain that Exchange is located in, so you will get a username and password prompt. This will happen each time Outlook is started and cannot be avoided.

For password maintenance of end users connecting to Exchange in this way, suggest that they change their password through Outlook Web Access.

After ensuring that Outlook Anywhere is working correctly, you need to ensure that the relevant port is open on your firewall. If you are using SSL, only port 443 is required — no other special changes are required.

Refer to Chapter 25 for more information on setting your firewall to work with Outlook Anywhere and other Exchange features.

Windows Mobile and ActiveSync

Currently two ActiveSync applications are available from Microsoft.

◆ The traditional ActiveSync is an application that is installed on the desktop machine and allows synchronization through Outlook.

◆ With Exchange 2003, Microsoft introduced Exchange ActiveSync (EAS), which allows synchronization directly to the Exchange server over a network or Internet connection. This was initially on-demand sync but Exchange 2003 Service Pack 2 enabled the "push e-mail" feature using HTTP or HTTPS. Push e-mail enables e-mail to be synchronized with the device as new messages arrive; when a message arrives in the user's Inbox, the Exchange server notifies connected mobile devices that a new message must be synchronized to the device.

Exchange 2007 takes EAS and has further enhanced it, although to take full advantage of the new features in EAS, you need to be using Windows Mobile 6.1.

Exchange ActiveSync was available with Windows Mobile 2003 but really became popular only with Windows Mobile 2005. To use the push technology, you need to have a device with the Messaging and Security Feature Pack (MSFP) installed. This is not available as a separate download but will be part of a software update from the handset supplier.

Both Microsoft Messaging and Security Feature Pack updates for mobile devices and Windows Mobile 6 updates must be obtained from the device vendor or the cell phone provider, not Microsoft.

If you have purchased a device since approximately June 2006, it almost certainly will come with a version of Windows Mobile 5.0 with MSFP. Many devices that run Windows Mobile 5 can be upgraded to the MSFP version and even some devices can be upgraded to Windows Mobile 6 or 6.1. You must check with the vendor from which you got the device, though.

How Can You Tell Whether Your Device Has the MSFP?

You can identify whether your handset has the MSFP update in two ways. In both cases you need to look at the version information. You can find this in Settings ➢ System under the About applet.

You need to look at the version information. (See Figure 23.19.) You will see a string that is something like OS 5.1.195 (Build 14847.2.0.0). With some handsets, the build number says Messaging and Security Feature Pack. If that is the case, you know for sure. If yours does not, then you need to look at the build number. The key element is the last three digits. To have the MSFP installed, it needs to be 2.0.0 or higher. Build 2.0.0 was the first build to have the MSFP update.

FIGURE 23.19
Checking for MSFP

Windows Mobile Emulator Software

The screen captures in this chapter were created using a Windows Mobile 5.0 emulator and are presuming that you are using a Windows Mobile-based device with at least that version of the software. You can find instructions for the older versions of Windows Mobile on Microsoft's website as well as emulators for Windows Mobile 6.0 and 6.1.

As an administrator, you will want to test Windows Mobile for yourself; however, getting a hold of a device with the relevant software may be difficult. Microsoft has released an emulator for Windows Mobile, which was originally designed for developer use but is now available as a stand-alone product. You can install this onto your workstation and connect to the Exchange server over your network. At the time of writing, you can download the emulator from this site:

```
http://www.microsoft.com/downloads/details.aspx?FamilyId=3D6F581E-C093-4B15-
AB0C-A2CE5BFFDB47&displaylang=en
```

Configuring Exchange to Support ActiveSync

Exchange ActiveSync (EAS) should be enabled by default from the standard installation of the Client Access server role. You can confirm whether this is the case by checking for the presence of a number of elements in IIS Manager. In the IIS Manager under Default Web Site (see Figure 23.20), check to see whether the virtual directory Microsoft-Server-ActiveSync exists.

FIGURE 23.20
Checking for Exchange ActiveSync in the IIS Manager

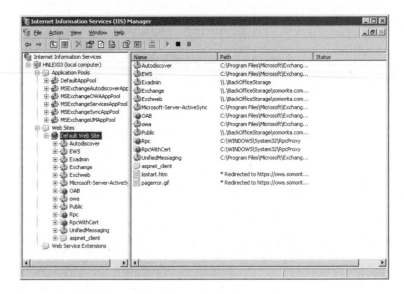

You can also check the Exchange-related application pools. For example, right-click the MSExchangeSyncAppPool application pool. If Start is available, EAS is not running. Choose Start to enable the application pool.

You can do additional configuration of ActiveSync through the Exchange Management Console. Under Server Configuration, choose the Exchange ActiveSync tab. Right-click the virtual directory listed and choose Properties. You'll see three tabs. The first tab, General, allows you to set the internal and external URL for ActiveSync. The second tab, Authentication, allows you to control authentication, including whether to use client certificates. The third tab, Remote File Servers, allows you to control remote file server access. This is identical in operation to remote file server access through Outlook Web Access but is not available with the current versions of Windows Mobile.

For Exchange Management Shell configuration, you use two cmdlets:

◆ The cmdlet `New-ActiveSyncVirtualDirectory` allows you to create a new virtual directory for another website on the same server.

◆ The cmdlet `Set-ActiveSyncVirtualDirectory` allows you to change settings for the ActiveSync virtual directory. This includes settings not available to you through the Exchange Management Console. The following command will enable basic authentication on a server named EXCHANGE01:

```
Set-ActiveSyncVirtualDirectory -Identity "EXCHANGE01\microsoft-server↵
-activesync" -BasicAuthEnabled:$true
```

Defining and Assigning an ActiveSync Policy

An ActiveSync policy allows you to define certain settings for mobile devices. With Exchange 2003, the policy applied to all devices, or there were exceptions for certain users. The level of control was very low. You can now have different settings for different users, allowing you more control over the devices — possibly depending on their job function.

DEFINING AN ACTIVESYNC POLICY

ActiveSync policies apply across your Exchange organization, so they are set in the Organization Configuration work center in the Client Access subcontainer. The policy is divided into two main areas: access and password.

The General property page (shown in Figure 23.21) is for access-related settings. You can define whether basic settings such as the configuration refresh interval, access to UNC and WSS servers, and non-provisionable devices can be configured.

Non-provisionable devices are devices that do not support the Autodiscover service. Most sites will need to enable non-provisionable devices, at least initially until all user devices are using a version of Windows Mobile that supports provisioning via Autodiscover.

The Password property page (shown in Figure 23.22) is for the password policy. The settings on this tab are fairly self-explanatory. If you want to be able to take advantage of the remote wipe features, you need to require a password. If you do not, when you attempt to wipe the device, end users will be asked to allow enforcement of a password policy. By saying no, they can maintain access to the device. Allow Simple Password is a policy that allows the end user to set a password such as 1234. If you have policies regarding secure passwords, you may not want to enable that option.

You can have more than one ActiveSync policy; to create another one, select New ActiveSync Policy from the Actions pane in the Exchange Management Console, or run the cmdlet New-ActiveSyncPolicy with the required parameters.

FIGURE 23.21
Viewing the General properties of an ActiveSync policy

FIGURE 23.22
Viewing the Password requirements in an ActiveSync policy

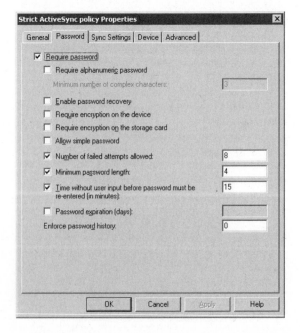

VIEWING OTHER TABS OF THE ACTIVESYNC POLICY PROPERTIES PAGE

The Exchange Server 2007 Service Pack 1 Device tab is shown in Figure 23.1 and the Advanced tab is shown in Figure 23.2, earlier in this chapter.

This command will create a new policy called Sales, with Device Password enabled:

```
New-ActiveSyncMailboxPolicy -Name: "Sales" -DevicePasswordEnabled:$true
```

ASSIGNING AN ACTIVESYNC POLICY

You can assign a policy to an individual user or to multiple users at the same time.

Assigning a Policy to a Single User Using the EMC

To assign a policy to a single user through the Exchange Management Console, follow these steps:

1. Open up the Recipient Configuration work center and select Mailbox.

2. Find the user that you want to assign the policy to, and select Properties from the Actions pane.

3. Click the Mailbox Features tab and choose Exchange ActiveSync, and then click Properties.

4. Enable the Apply An Exchange ActiveSync Policy option, and click Browse to choose the policy. Then click OK/Apply as required to close the user properties.

Assigning a Policy to Multiple Users Using the EMS

To assign policies to multiple users at the same time, you need to use the Exchange Management Shell using the `Set-CASMailbox` command. For example, to set the policy `Sales` on user `David.Sengupta`, you would run the following command:

```
Set-CASMailbox David.Sengupta -ActiveSyncMailboxPolicy↵
(Get-ActiveSyncMailboxPolicy "Sales").Identity
```

If you want to assign a policy to all users, which may be a good way to start off, you have to use a combination of commands. This command will set the policy Default Policy on all users:

```
Get-Mailbox | Set-CASMailbox -ActiveSyncMailboxPolicy↵
(Get-ActiveSyncMailboxPolicy "Default Policy").Identity
```

Configuring a Windows Mobile Device

This section guides you through configuring a Windows Mobile device. These instructions and screen shots were created using the Windows Mobile 5.0 emulator, which is running build 2.0.0. Therefore, you may find that a few screens on your device look slightly different than what is shown here. The entries are identical, so it should be easy enough to adapt to the later versions of Windows Mobile that are released after this book is published.

To configure your device to sync with Exchange, follow these steps:

1. Select ActiveSync from Programs. If this is the first time you have configured ActiveSync, you should simply select the text "set up your device to sync with it." If you already have ActiveSync configured to synchronize with a desktop, you can change the settings from the menu, or use ActiveSync on the desktop to configure synchronization with a server.

2. You will be asked for the server address. This needs to be the external name of the Exchange server — for example, `mail.domain.com`. If you are going to use SSL, the name needs to match what is on the certificate. The certificate also needs to be trusted by the device (either because you are using a commercial certificate that has a root certificate in the device or because you have imported the root or client certificate into the device in advance).

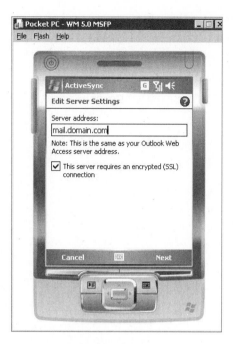

3. Enter the username, password, and domain for the account that is being used. If you want to sync automatically, you will need to save the password.

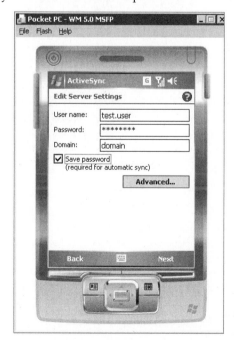

PASSWORD CAUTIONS

Saving your password is a security risk, and it could also cause your account to be locked out if you change your password. When changing your Windows password, remember to change the password on the device as well.

4. Whether you want to set the advanced settings is up to you. Advanced settings deal with item conflict (default is Replace The Item On My Device) and event logging (default is None).

5. On the last screen, you can set what is synchronized over the server connection. Most users will be configuring all four options (Inbox, Calendar, Contacts, and Tasks). You cannot sync the Notes folder over the air, so if you are using the Notes feature in Outlook, you will need to continue to use the desktop ActiveSync as well.

6. You can adjust how much is synchronized for some of the types, such as Calendar and E-mail. Select the type and choose Settings to adjust. Calendar allows you to change how much of your calendar is synchronized. E-Mail allows you to change how much old e-mail is synchronized and whether attachments come across.

7. Press Finish. The device will attempt to sync for the first time. If there is a lot of e-mail to come across, you should have the device connected to the network via USB ActiveSync for that first sync.

Managing a Windows Mobile Device

At some point one of your users will lose their device, or you will need to wipe it. Management of the Windows Mobile devices is now built in to Exchange. You can manage the devices in three ways:

◆ The end user can manage it through Outlook Web Access.

◆ You can manage it through the EMC.

◆ You can manage it through the EMS.

End User Management Through Outlook Web Access

By default, end users can manage their device through Outlook Web Access. Administrators can turn off this option if they want. However, if you have lots of remote users, you may want to enable this feature so that users can wipe a device as soon as they realize that they lost it. Mobile device management is within Options of OWA (shown previously in Figure 23.7) once the user has logged in.

Administrator Management Through the EMC

You can manage the device through the Exchange Management Console by right-clicking the user in the Recipients Configuration work center and choosing Manage Mobile Device. (This option appears only if a mobile device is associated with the user's mailbox.) This runs the Manage Mobile Device Wizard (shown in Figure 23.23).

FIGURE 23.23
Manage Mobile Device Wizard

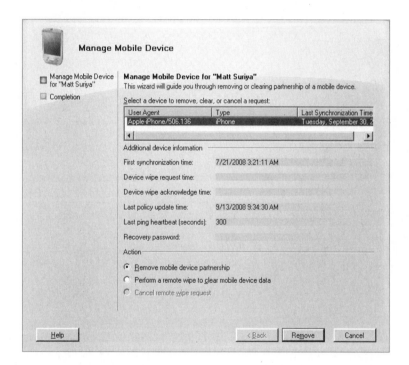

You can configure a mailbox so that only a single mobile device is allowed to connect to that mailbox. You must first sync the device and get the device ID for the permitted device. Then you can use the Set-CASMailbox cmdlet. Here is an example:

```
Set-CASMailbox -identity StefJ -ActiveSyncAllowedDeviceIDs <deviceID>
```

To wipe the device, click the action labeled Perform A Remote Wipe To Clear Mobile Device Data and then click Clear. You can go back into this screen to confirm that the wipe has taken place.

Administrator Management Through the EMS

You can manage mobile devices through the Exchange Management Shell. A series of commands will allow you to wipe a device. To wipe the device through the EMC, you need to perform the following steps:

1. The first step is to get the identity of the device. To get the identity of the device that is used by user Chuck.Swanson, run the following command:

   ```
   Get-ActiveSyncDeviceStatistics -Mailbox Chuck.Swanson | FL Identity
   ```

2. After you have the device ID, you can send the wipe command. To wipe a device with the ID of WM_Chuck.Swanson11, use this command:

   ```
   Clear-ActiveSyncDevice -Identity WM_chuck.swanson11
   ```

3. To confirm that the wipe was successful, use the following command:

   ```
   Get-ActiveSyncDeviceStatistics -Mailbox Chuck.Swanson
   ```

If the wipe was successful, you should see date and time information in the output including in the DeviceWipeSentTime, DeviceWipeRequestTime, and DeviceWipeAckTime properties.

Supporting POP3 and IMAP4 Clients

IMAP4 and POP3 are probably the most basic e-mail protocols in use. With SMTP, they are the most straightforward of the e-mail delivery mechanisms, and virtually every e-mail server available supports them. However, they do have their drawbacks, particularly when used with Exchange.

For example, if you collect your e-mail with POP3 from your Exchange mailbox, all e-mail in the mailbox will be marked as read whether or not the message has actually been read on the client.

The other major issue with POP3 is that it is designed to remove the e-mail from the server and store it locally. It is very easy to make an error in configuration and remove all of the e-mail from the server. Although there are options to leave e-mail on the server, it's easy to overlook them.

Things are a little better with IMAP4 because the e-mail is actually stored on the server. However, you still are limited on the functionality from Exchange compared to the full Outlook client or Outlook Web Access.

As such, POP3/IMAP4 access should be the last access protocol of choice, and where possible you should not be supporting it. However, in some environments, such as academic environments, POP3 and IMAP4 clients are very popular and must still be supported.

In Service Pack 1, Microsoft added support to configure the POP3 and IMAP4 protocols using the Exchange Management Console. You can, of course, configure them using the Exchange Management Shell as well.

Configuration of SMTP for use by POP3/IMAP4 clients can be carried out using the Exchange Management Console. However, you may want to look at deploying TLS/SMTP (see Chapter 25, "Securing Exchange Server") because the standard port 25 is often blocked for accessing remote SMTP servers from home user type connections, meaning the POP3/IMAP4 clients will be unable to send e-mail through your server.

POP3 AND IMAP4 DON'T SUPPORT COMPLIANCE

Because of the nature of the POP3 and IMAP4 protocols, keeping a copy of messages for compliance reasons is almost impossible. The end user could send the message through another SMTP server, leaving no trace of the message on your server.

If you need to track e-mail messages for compliance reasons, you should look at using a MAPI connection such as Outlook Web Access or Outlook Anywhere.

Configuring Exchange to Support POP3 and IMAP4 Clients

Configuring Exchange Server 2007 to support POP3 or IMAP4 clients requires a couple of steps. These include enabling the services and configuring the Client Access servers to support these protocols.

ENABLING THE SERVICES

Before clients can connect to the POP3 or IMAP4 services, the services must be enabled and started because they are set to start manually. You can enable POP3 and IMAP4 in two ways. As with Exchange 2003, you can change the service in the Services console (shown in Figure 23.24) from Disabled to Automatic and then start the service.

FIGURE 23.24
Using the Services console to configure the POP3 service

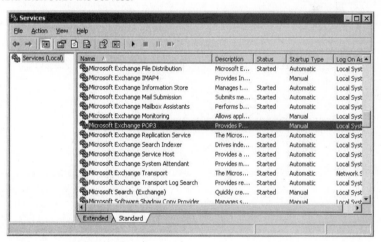

You can also enable the services through the Exchange Management Shell. To enable POP3, use the following command:

```
Set-Service msExchangePOP3 -startuptype automatic
```

Once it's enabled, you need to start the service:

```
Start-Service -service msExchangePOP3
```

For IMAP, the procedure is almost identical:

```
Set-Service msExchangeIMAP4 -startuptype automatic
```

To start the service, use the following command:

```
Start-Service msExchangeIMAP4
```

CONFIGURING POP3 AND IMAP4: SERVER

Once you have enabled the services, you can configure them through the Exchange Management Console or the Exchange Management Shell. The default settings may be suitable for you. Each Client Access server has its own POP3 and IMAP4 configuration settings; these are found on the Work pane when viewing the properties of a Client Access server (see Figure 23.25).

FIGURE 23.25
Locating the Client Access server's POP3 and IMAP4 configuration settings

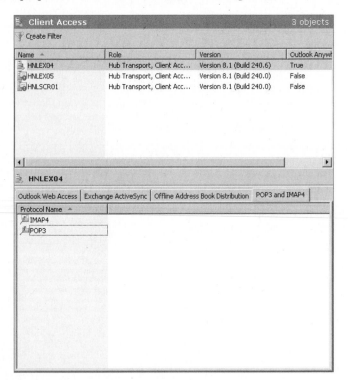

The POP3 and IMAP4 options mostly have the same settings (though a few settings and options might be slightly different). The options for the POP3 and IMAP4 service include:

◆ Binding information for IP addresses and ports on which the service can be used

◆ Authentication options, including allowing plain text or requiring secure logon from the client

◆ Connection limits and timeout settings

◆ Message body formats and calendar request URL or iCalendar options

Some of these options (the Retrieval properties) can be seen in Figure 23.26.

FIGURE 23.26

Viewing the IMAP4 service's Retrieval Settings tab

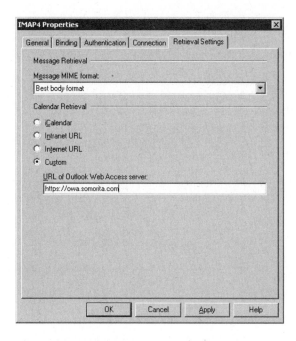

You can check the current settings or change the settings using the following EMS cmdlets:

◆ POP3: Get-PopSettings / Set-PopSettings

◆ IMAP4: Get-ImapSettings / Set-ImapSettings

Here is an example of viewing the IMAP4 service settings using the Get-ImapSettings cmdlet:

```
Get-ImapSettings | FL

ProtocolName                       : IMAP4
Name                               : 1
MaxCommandSize                     : 10240
ShowHiddenFoldersEnabled           : False
UnencryptedOrTLSBindings           : {0.0.0.0:143}
SSLBindings                        : {0.0.0.0:993}
X509CertificateName                : owa.somorita.com
Banner                             : Microsoft Exchange Server 2007 IMAP4 service ready
LoginType                          : SecureLogin
AuthenticatedConnectionTimeout     : 00:30:00
PreAuthenticatedConnectionTimeout  : 00:01:00
MaxConnections                     : 2000
MaxConnectionFromSingleIP          : 2000
MaxConnectionsPerUser              : 16
MessageRetrievalMimeFormat         : BestBodyFormat
ProxyTargetPort                    : 143
```

```
CalendarItemRetrievalOption      : iCalendar
OwaServerUrl                     :
EnableExactRFC822Size            : False
AdminDisplayName                 :
ExchangeVersion                  : 0.1 (8.0.535.0)
DistinguishedName                : CN=1,CN=IMAP4,CN=Protocols,CN=HNLEX04,
    CN=Servers, CN=Exchange Administrative Group (FYDIBOHF23SPDLT),
    CN=Administrative Groups, CN=Volcano Surfboards,CN=Microsoft Exchange,
    CN=Services,CN=Configuration, DC=volcanosurfboa
                                   rds,DC=com
Identity                         : HNLEX04\1
Guid                             : e0aa80b7-fdba-4175-b97f-6b3c4a0da0e8
ObjectCategory                   : volcanosurfboards.com/Configuration/Schema/ms-Exch-
    Protocol-Cfg-IMAP-Server
    ObjectClass                    : {top, protocolCfg, protocolCfgIMAP,
    protocolCfgIMAPServer}
WhenChanged                      : 12/9/2007 2:39:44 PM
WhenCreated                      : 1/11/2007 11:33:19 PM
OriginatingServer                : HNLDC01.volcanosurfboards.com
IsValid                          : True
```

CONFIGURING POP3 AND IMAP4: MAILBOXES

By default, all user accounts are enabled for POP3 and IMAP4 access. You may want to review the accounts and disable that functionality for those users who will not be accessing Exchange using POP3 or IMAP4. You do this using the Set-CASMailbox command.

For example, to disable POP3 for a user nick.gillott@somorita.com, use the following command:

```
Set-CASMailbox -Identity nick.gillott@somorita.com -POPEnabled:$False
```

You can view the status of the mailboxes simply by entering the command Get-CASMailbox, which will display all mailboxes in the Exchange organization and whether or not they are enabled.

CONFIGURING A RECEIVE CONNECTOR FOR USE WITH POP3 AND IMAP4

POP3/IMAP clients need to have an SMTP connector to send their outbound e-mail through. For Exchange 2007, that means a Receive connector must be configured to accept their messages and allow them to be relayed through the server to the clients.

There should already be a connector configured that is suitable for use, which is called Client *servername*. You can see this through the Exchange Management Console or by the Exchange Management Shell command Get-ReceiveConnector.

Very little configuration of this default connector should be required. Note that this connector is configured to use port 587, which is the TLS port. It uses the certificate that is installed on the Exchange server during installation. If you intend to have clients relay e-mail through the server on this port, you need to either import the certificate to their machine so that it is trusted or replace the certificate with one from a trusted CA.

If you want to use the standard TCP port 25 to relay e-mail, you need to review the configuration of the server connector.

In all cases, basic authentication needs to be enabled on the connector because it is the only type of authentication that SMTP clients support. You can also use basic authentication, requiring TLS.

More information is available on Receive connectors in Chapter 21, "Delivering E-mail."

Configuring a POP3 or IMAP4 Client

You will no doubt be familiar with the configuration of POP3/IMAP clients and SMTP. For Exchange, it is almost the same as any Internet e-mail account you may have configured.

For the server address of the POP3, IMAP, and SMTP servers, you should use a hostname. Although you can use an IP address, if you ever need to change the IP address of the server, it is far easier to change a single DNS entry than to try to get many users to update their e-mail client configuration.

What you use for your hostnames is up to you — as long as they resolve correctly on the Internet. You may already have a hostname setup that points to your Exchange server used for MX records. If so, you could use the same hostname in the account settings. Alternatively, if you think that you might change the configuration in the future so that the servers are different, you may want to use pop3.domain.com, imap.domain.com, and smtp.domain.com, having them all point at the same IP address. If you need to change them later on, simply adjust the DNS records.

If you are using TLS/SSL for account access, ensure that you change the port setting in the e-mail client to use the alternative port. This is often found in the advanced settings.

Finally, you need to enter credentials. For Exchange, these credentials need to be in a specific format:

◆ For POP3 and IMAP access, it is in the format of *domain\username\alias*.

◆ For SMTP access, it is in the format of *domain\username*.

◆ In both cases, you can also use the UPN, *username@domain.local*.

The choice of authentication format is up to you and what you think will be easiest to support. I suggest deciding on one format and then sticking to it so that it is easier to write documentation and help guides while maintaining some consistency.

Summary

Access to e-mail away from the desktop is now very important to most users. Exchange 2007 provides more options than ever before for that access. End users now have full access to their e-mail wherever and whenever they need it, and the security of the network is maintained.

Providing the necessary remote options for your users is important. This chapter covered a couple of different ways that you can provide access to Exchange from anywhere.

Outlook Web Access provides much of the same functionality that you would get sitting at your desk and using regular Outlook, but through a Web browser. Exchange Server 2007 OWA has once again been improved to provide the user with more functionality than ever before.

For users who need a full-featured e-mail client even while traveling, Exchange Server 2007 provides Outlook Anywhere. Outlook Anywhere allows Outlook 2003 and Outlook 2007 clients to connect to their Exchange server using RPC over HTTP or RPC over HTTPS and synchronize their e-mail without the complexity involved in connecting multiple RPC ports through your company firewall. All that is necessary is port 80 or port 443 (recommended).

Windows Mobile and ActiveSync users can be provided with access to their mailbox from their mobile device. They can synchronize their mailbox from anywhere they can get a cell phone or WiFi signal.

Finally, although in some organizations POP3 and IMAP4 clients have been replaced completely by Web-browser-based clients or Outlook, many organizations still use POP3 and IMAP. Exchange continues to support these clients.

Part 7

Security and Tracking Activities

In this part:

Chapter 24

Monitoring Performance

Under what circumstances should you add an Exchange server? How do you know whether you need an additional Active Directory global catalog server? When should you add mailbox servers to a remote Active Directory site? When should you create more storage groups? Or mailbox databases? How many mailboxes should be located on a single mailbox database?

These are all questions that affect your Exchange 2007 design, deployment, and even day-to-day operations. If you don't provide sufficient resources, the Exchange organization will not operate as effectively as it should. Sometimes the decision points for adding more servers or creating new databases are clearly defined based on your organization's requirements. Other times, however, the decision matrix for expanding your Exchange Server environment is not always cut-and-dried.

Performance monitoring has always been a little bit art and a little bit science. Granted, if you can evaluate all of the factors involved then you can probably turn it in to a complete science, but sometimes just a bit of creativity is required.

In this chapter you learn to:

- ◆ Decide when to grow

- ◆ Understand performance monitoring basics

- ◆ Effectively use important performance monitoring counters

Deciding When to Grow

Do you have clear guidance that tells you when you should expand, add servers, or add capacity? Sometimes your gut instinct just tells you that it is time. But is that something you can take to your boss?

If you are lucky, you can back up your request for a new server, more RAM, or more capacity with tangible evidence. This chapter discusses both the tangible and intangible factors that may influence the need to expand your Exchange organization.

When you are trying to increase your budget, nothing impresses your boss more than having hard numbers or company policies to back up your requests (well, unless you have a PowerPoint presentation with lots of colorful clipart). And you may even be surprised to learn just what you can assign hard-core values to.

Organizational Requirements

The first factors discussed actually involve organizational requirements. A number of organizational requirements may affect the number of servers, segmenting Exchange server roles, and their physical placement. As you have probably already guessed, high availability and fault tolerance requirements will certainly increase the number of servers required. Here are some factors that will increase the number of Exchange 2007 servers that you will require:

◆ Clustering always requires at least two servers for the Mailbox server role; one server is the active mailbox server and one server is the passive server. This includes shared copy clusters as well as clustered continuous replication clusters.

◆ Other server roles cannot be installed on a clustered mailbox server. This means that other roles, such as Hub Transport, Client Access, or Unified Messaging servers, must be placed on separate physical machines.

◆ Fault tolerance for internal message routing is achieved with multiple Hub Transport servers in each Active Directory site in which you have Exchange Mailbox servers. Exchange 2007 will automatically load-balance among multiple Hub Transport servers in the same Active Directory site.

◆ Fault tolerance or higher availability for server roles such as Client Access or Unified Messaging is achieved with multiple servers using a load-balancing technology.

◆ You can also use DNS round robin, but that is not recommended. Round robin DNS queries can generate client problems because clients may have the IP address of one Client Access server for a few minutes, but when their DNS cache expires they may get a different Client Access server. This can break SSL sessions and other Microsoft .NET applications.

◆ Each Active Directory site that contains a Mailbox server must have the Hub Transport and Client Access server roles deployed. If the Unified Messaging server role is used, the Active Directory site must have a Unified Messaging server installed.

◆ When sizing Active Directory domain controllers running on x32 operating systems, for each four CPU cores worth of Exchange server, you should have at least one dedicated Active Directory domain controller/global catalog server core. If the domain controllers are running x64 operating systems, include at least one domain controller CPU core for each eight Exchange server cores.

◆ Using Edge Transport services always requires an additional Windows server. Providing fault tolerance for Edge Transport server roles means installing at least two Edge Transport server roles. It is recommended that the Edge Transport servers be installed in your organization's perimeter or DMZ network.

◆ Large organizations will often create a dedicated Active Directory site containing domain controllers and global catalog servers. These servers are then used exclusively by Exchange servers. This way Exchange does not interfere with domain controllers that are handling user and computer authentication and vice versa.

Network Infrastructure Requirements

Let's not forget about supporting network infrastructure services. In a small organization, a single machine hosting a Windows domain controller, global catalog server, and DNS server will be sufficient. However, if your organization is supporting more than a few hundred mailboxes, the requirements for more supporting infrastructure components will increase as well. Here are some factors that may increase the number of network infrastructure services your organization requires:

◆ Some organizations split their DNS servers on to servers or appliances that are separate from the servers that support Active Directory. Though I normally recommend using the Windows 2003 DNS server running on a domain controller, if you choose to move DNS to another system, you should make sure that you have redundancy and that all Windows servers are configured with a primary and secondary DNS server. If you want to use the Active Directory-integrated DNS zone feature of the Windows 2003 DNS server, the DNS server must be running on a domain controller.

◆ The generic recommendation for the number of x32 domain controllers and global catalog servers is one domain controller CPU core for each four Exchange CPU cores. The generic recommendation for x64 domain controllers is one domain controller CPU core for eight Exchange CPU cores. This does not take into consideration fault tolerance for the domain controllers, so in organizations with more than 500 mailboxes, I recommend at least one redundant domain controller. That domain controller should also be configured as a global catalog server.

◆ If fault tolerance is specified in your Exchange design, it should also be specified in your Active Directory design. This means each Active Directory site that contains an Exchange mailbox server (and consequently Hub Transport and Client Access server roles) should contain two domain controller/global catalog servers.

◆ Remember that Outlook 2000 and later clients also use global catalog servers for global address list lookups. This means that Outlook clients will directly communicate with global catalog servers.

Recoverability Requirements

Another factor that I consider a tangible factor when designing an Exchange 2007 system is recoverability and meeting service-level agreements. As you learned in Chapter 19, "Backup and Disaster Recovery," there are many types of outages and many approaches to recovering from them. Your Active Directory and Exchange designs may be subject to meeting a specific service-level agreement that includes a statement defining recovery time for different types of outages:

◆ The simpler a server's configuration is, the more quickly you can rebuild it if you have to perform a bare metal restore. Bare metal restores usually require that you start over with the server build and redo everything from the operating system on up to the application and all customization that has been done to the server. Although small organizations (under 500) may not be able to segment server roles onto dedicated server hardware, for large organizations this certainly can help reduce the complexity of the server. Reduced server configuration complexity assists in speeding recovery.

◆ The local continuous replication (LCR) feature of Exchange 2007 is one of its most promising features with respect to improving recoverability times. LCR allows you to keep an almost completely synchronized copy of the database ready to put into production in case the live copy of the database becomes corrupted. At a bare minimum, this feature will require twice as much disk space (if you replicate all of your databases) as you had originally planned for. Naturally, there is additional disk I/O and memory overhead associated with keeping a synchronized copy of the database, so if you are using LCR you may not be able to support as many mailboxes on one mailbox server.

◆ The time it takes to restore a mailbox database from backup is directly proportional to the size of the database. Larger databases mean longer restoration times in the event of a single database corruption or failure. Creating more databases with fewer mailboxes can help reduce recovery time. Exchange Server 2007 Standard Edition provides you with up to 5 mailbox databases and Exchange Server 2007 Enterprise Edition provides you with up to 50. I recommend that no single database exceed 100GB in a non-LCR environment and 200GB in an LCR environment.

◆ Potential speed of data restoration may affect the sizing of your servers. Calculate the amount of data that you will be hosting on any given mailbox server and then calculate how long it will take you to restore that data in a worst-case scenario. Is that acceptable in your environment?

Performance Monitoring Recommendations

Do you remember those hard numbers and graphs that prove to your boss that you have exceeded your current computing capacity? Nothing beats performance monitoring tools and reports for visually providing tangible evidence that you are exceeding your capacity. You look at these in more detail later in this chapter, but for now here are some ways that you can use performance monitoring to locate bottlenecks that would indicate insufficient resources:

◆ Performance monitoring may indicate insufficient hardware resources such as memory or disk I/O capacity on existing servers.

◆ When querying a domain controller or global catalog, performance monitoring may pinpoint bottlenecks that indicate either a performance problem or an overloaded domain controller/global catalog.

Designing for Political Realities

The final tangible factor in sizing servers and choosing hardware is the eighth layer of the OSI model; this is the political layer. We all frequently joke about our jobs being part politics, but in many organizations this is a reality. Here are some factors that might require a political design decision rather than a technical design decision:

◆ Satellite or regional offices might require their own Exchange server hardware even in the face of consolidation.

◆ Executives or some divisions of an organization might expect to be on isolated server hardware.

◆ A department might believe that having their mail on a server with everyone else is not secure enough.

Even within a large IT organization, IT politics may drive the Exchange server design to the point that the Domain Admins and Enterprise Admins for the user's Active Directory don't "trust" the Exchange server admins. This usually results in the build-out of a "resource" forest just for Exchange Server. This means that all mailboxes are created with a disabled user account in the resource forest and "linked" to the accounts forest.

Monitoring Performance

Using the Windows performance monitoring tools with Exchange Server is a topic that could easily cover an entire chapter or even two. In this chapter, I cover some basic performance monitoring counters and EMS cmdlets that can help you in determining whether you have performance problems.

Performance Degradation

If all we had to worry about was measuring performance and planning for server capacity, our jobs would be much easier. In your server design, capacity planning, and analysis, you have a number of additional factors to consider:

◆ Consolidated servers (multiple roles on a single server) can contribute to degraded server performance. On a server that supports more than 500 mailboxes as well as other functions, such as Hub Transport and Client Access server roles, you should ensure that transaction logs, message databases, and message queues are all on separate physical disk drives.

◆ Local continuous replication (LCR) will significantly increase the I/O requirements for Mailbox servers. LCR databases and transaction logs must be on separate physical disks to ensure that performance does not suffer.

◆ LCR will place a significant burden on the server's CPU — by some estimates, as much as 40 percent additional burden if all databases have an LCR copy. Consider this when calculating CPU capacity and the number of mailboxes that a single server can support.

◆ Antivirus software configured to perform real-time scans of mailbox databases using the Exchange Antivirus API can use significant amounts of RAM and CPU capacity.

◆ Antivirus applications on Hub Transport servers can also use quite a bit of RAM and consume some of the CPU resources.

◆ Transport rules are executed for every message that passes through a Hub Transport server. The more transport rules that are processed, the more CPU and memory overhead will be consumed by the Hub Transport server. In an organization with more than 100 transport rules, consider segmenting the Hub Transport role to its own physical hardware and ensuring that the disk I/O capacity for the Hub Transport server is sufficient for the I/O load that the Extensible Storage Engine (ESE) database requires.

◆ Backup applications use a significant amount of resources during the backup process. Streaming backup applications use a lot of disk I/O time when backing up data in mailbox databases. Volume shadow copy backups of production databases will also impact perceived response time for users who are working during the backups. You should perform streaming backups during the off-hours or implement LCR and then perform volume shadow copy backups of the LCR databases rather than the production databases.

◆ Implementing Secure Sockets Layer (SSL) on Client Access servers is essential for providing better security for Web applications such as Outlook Anywhere, Outlook Web Access, and ActiveSync. However, SSL will introduce approximately a 25 percent CPU overhead on the Client Access server.

◆ EdgeSync can place a larger load on a Hub Transport server if it is run frequently. EdgeSync requires internal connectivity to both Active Directory and mailbox servers.

◆ Running scheduled tasks such as updating address lists and e-mail address lists can generate additional disk utilization as well as CPU activity and Active Directory queries.

◆ Third-party e-mail archiving products can significantly increase the I/O load that the server is experiencing when the products are crawling the database for information to copy or move into their archive.

◆ Third-party mobile solutions like BlackBerry Enterprise Server (BES) can increase I/O significantly.

Exchange Management Shell Cmdlets for Performance Monitoring

Exchange 2007 has a few cmdlets that are useful when testing or measuring potential performance problems.

Test-MAPIConnectivity

The Test-MAPIConnectivity cmdlet allows you to test MAPI connectivity to a mailbox you specify. For example, if you want to test MAPI connectivity for a mailbox named Suriya.Supatanasakul, you would type this:

```
Test-MAPIConnectivity Suriya.Supatanasakul
```

MailboxServer	Database	Result	Latency(MS)	Error
HNLEX03	Mailbox Database	Success	20	

The mailbox test will access the database on which the mailbox is located and then access the mailbox. The output tells you whether or not that test was successful in accessing the mailbox and how much latency was measured. The latency should usually be less than 200 milliseconds. Higher latencies could indicate that there is a network problem or that the server is not responding to RPC requests quickly enough.

If you do not specify a mailbox name, the cmdlet will access all of the system mailboxes on the local server and report latency for each of those mailbox databases:

```
Test-MAPIConnectivity
```

MailboxServer	Database	Result	Latency(MS)	Error
HNLEX03	Engineering Mail	Success	58	
HNLEX03	Mailbox Database	Success	18	

Test-Mailflow

The Test-Mailflow cmdlet measures server response time. Without any parameters, the Test-Mailflow cmdlet will send mail to the local system mailbox:

```
Test-Mailflow
```

TestMailflowResult	MessageLatencyTime	IsRemoteTest
Success	00:00:01.6388565	False

The `MessageLatencyTime` column indicates (in hours, minutes, and seconds) how long it took to deliver a message. When mail is sent within an Active Directory site (or within a server), this should take no longer than 2 or 3 seconds. By sending a test message (to a system mailbox by default), the `Test-Mailflow` cmdlet tests not only the Mailbox server's responsiveness, but also how well the Hub Transport server is responding, and the efficiency of Active Directory queries. Each of these can be a bottleneck when a message is sent.

You can specify a source server and a target server using the `-TargetMailboxServer` parameter. Here is an example:

```
Test-Mailflow hnlex01 -TargetMailboxServer hnlex03

TestMailflowResult    MessageLatencyTime    IsRemoteTest
-----------------     ------------------    ------------
Success               00:00:02.8396133          True
```

For tests that indicate a message latency time of greater than 3 to 5 seconds within the same Active Directory site, or greater than 10 seconds between Active Directory sites, you should begin to look for potential bottlenecks. These might include:

◆ Insufficient Hub Transport server capacity

◆ Low system resources (low memory, not enough disk I/O capacity) on the mailbox server

◆ Bottlenecks when Active Directory is queried

Test-OwaConnectivity

If you want to test the responsiveness of Outlook Web Access, the `Test-OwaConnectivity` cmdlet can prove useful. However, that cmdlet requires you to create a Client Access server (CAS) test user. The `New-TestCasConnectivityUser.ps1` script (included with the Exchange 2007 scripts) will create this user for you.

PERFORMANCE MONITORING AS A WORK OF ART

There is a lot more to performance monitoring than just adding a few counters to a chart or report and then making some conclusions based on what you see. Getting an accurate picture of the performance and bottlenecks is something between a science and an art form. Before jumping into the actual mechanics of performance monitoring, I would like to cover just a few basic and important tips:

◆ When monitoring, take averages over a period of hours (usually during the busiest part of the day).

◆ Avoid the temptation to make load-balancing decisions based on looking at a small snapshot of performance. Spikes or lulls in usage will not represent your average performance.

◆ Don't run performance monitoring against a server you have just rebooted. Sometimes a server may take a few days to settle into a typical performance profile.

◆ Always develop a performance baseline for a system so that you know what counter values are "normal" for a particular usage profile. Remember, though, that "normal" will change over time as usage increases, more features are used, or more users are added to the system.

Using the System Monitor

Now let's look at some of the basics of using the System Monitor application and what you can find when you use the Performance Monitor console and the System Monitor object. Figure 24.1 shows the Add Counters dialog box from the System Monitor tool. Counters are the meat and potatoes of what you are looking for when you use the System Monitor tool in the Performance Monitor console. Let's look a little more closely at this interface.

FIGURE 24.1
Adding counters to the System Monitor tool

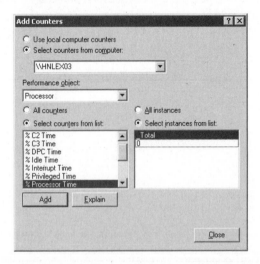

At the top of the Add Counters interface is the option to specify which computer you are actually looking at. You can either specify the local computer or you can monitor another computer across the network. This means you don't actually have to be sitting on the console of the computer you want to monitor.

The Performance Object drop-down list allows you to select a specific performance object or category. Different software components will add additional performance monitor objects to a server. Exchange Server 2007 server roles will also add performance objects. This explains why you will see different performance objects on different servers.

Some performance objects have multiple instances. A good example is the Processor object. You will have a _Total instance that represents all of the processes combined and you will have individual processor numbers (starting from 0). This means that you could monitor the performance of an individual CPU on a multiprocessor system.

Finally, we get to the counters list. The counters are what actually provide us with data about the components of Windows and Exchange. In Figure 24.1, you see that the performance object that is selected is the Processor object; possible counters for that particular object include the percentage of idle time (% Idle Time), the percentage of time the CPU is running privileged threads (% Privileged Time), and the percentage of time the processor is doing real work (% Processor Time). Each object will have unique counters. Some of these counters report actual, measured data and others (such as the processor counters) may report on data measured in a percentage (0 to 100).

When performance monitor data is displayed, there are two views you'll find useful. The first, and most commonly used, is the chart view (see Figure 24.2).

The chart view is best for spotting trends; by default it provides only 100 seconds of historical information, but the sample interval can be changed in the General tab of the System Monitor

Properties page (shown in Figure 24.3). If you are trying to gather information over a period of time (say, for an entire morning), you would definitely want to change the sample interval. For example, if you wanted the chart to include three hours worth of information, you would change the sample interval to about 77 seconds.

FIGURE 24.2
Using the chart view of the System Monitor

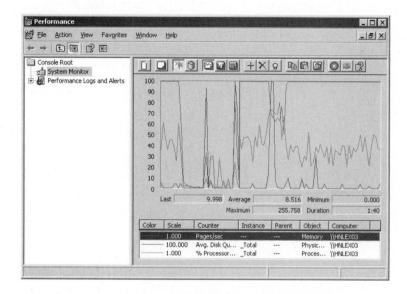

FIGURE 24.3
Changing System Monitor properties

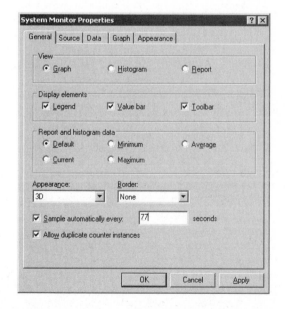

The Performance Monitor console can also record activity over a period of time using the Counter Logs feature. You can schedule the Performance Monitor to start at a specific time (such as 8:30 in the morning), record the objects and counters you desire, and then stop at a specific time. You can then use the recorded Performance Monitor counters to review activity in a chart (or report) over time.

The report view of the System Monitor is not as spiffy-looking as the chart view, but it provides you with a much easier way to look at actual numbers as opposed to trends. If the data source you are viewing is current activity, the values shown on the report view will be the average of the previous recorded value and the current recorded value. If the data source is a previously recorded log file, the report view shows you the average over the life span of the log file.

The System Monitor view in Figure 24.4 shows the report view. When looking at live data, the report view is helpful for looking at a specific piece of information at a certain point in time. But remember that when you're looking at performance statistics and analyzing bottlenecks, a particular point in time is not as useful as looking at averages over a period of time, such as when the server is busiest.

FIGURE 24.4

Using the report view of System Monitor

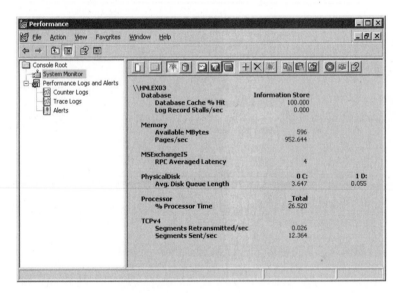

The report view is most helpful in seeing information that is static or that does not change much over time.

Locating Bottlenecks

Once you get the hang of using Performance Monitor, you will be impressed with the level of detail that you can examine on a Windows system and just what you can uncover. One interesting example of this is using the System Monitor's chart view to locate bottlenecks. (Remember those snazzy graphics you need for your boss.)

System bottlenecks may mask themselves as other performance problems, so you have to be quite careful about the conclusions that you reach. For example, a Mailbox server that is low on memory may be paging to disk heavily. If you are not evaluating all of the necessary performance objects, you might think that the problem was a disk bottleneck. In that case, you would want to check the available RAM and the page file usage.

When looking at the amount of memory that the store.exe process consumes, keep in mind that it is a performance feature that enables the program to consume high levels of RAM and use it for database caching. The `Store.exe` process will use this RAM as long as it is not required by another application.

In Figure 24.5, though, the System Monitor is clearly showing a disk bottleneck. Users on this particular server are complaining of slow mail delivery and Outlook errors. The `E:\` drive of this server is where the databases are hosted. The chart shows that the Disk Transfers/sec are averaging just under 680 transfers per second.

FIGURE 24.5

Examining a disk bottleneck in a System Monitor chart

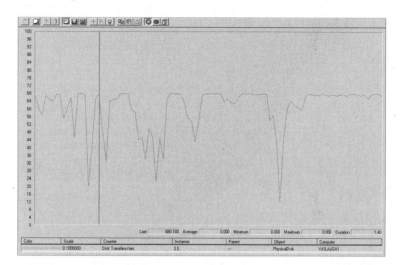

Bottlenecks are not always quite so obvious, but this gives you an idea of how powerful this tool can be. In the example in Figure 24.5, the disk I/O capacity of the `E:\` drive simply was not great enough to provide the I/O per second (IOPS) for the total number of simultaneous users that would use the server.

Keep in mind that different Exchange Server 2007 server roles use server resources (hardware) differently. For example, a Mailbox server uses a *lot* of RAM, disk I/O, and processor capacity. A Client Access server, on the other hand, relies more on processor capacity and to a lesser degree memory. A Hub Transport server relies on processor capacity (especially if there are a lot of transport or journaling rules) and uses a certain amount of RAM.

Performance Monitor Counters

As mentioned earlier, a full discussion of performance monitoring and Exchange 2007 could consume several chapters. Indeed, once Exchange 2007 is installed on a server (depending on the roles selected), nearly 70 different Performance Monitor objects are created; that says nothing of the actual counters and instances of each of these objects!

This section looks at some of the counters that may help you to understand when a server has exceeded its capacity. Let's start with some basic operating system objects and counters; these are pretty universal when it comes to performance monitoring, so you may have seen them before. The recommendations that I am making for minimum or maximum thresholds are based on my own experiences and may not agree with "official" Microsoft documentation. Some of the basic operating system counters are shown in Table 24.1. These can help you decide if you need to add more capacity to an existing server or to add an additional server.

TABLE 24.1: Operating System Performance Counters and Recommended Thresholds

OBJECT/COUNTER	RECOMMENDED VALUES
Processor/%Processor Time	This is the total percentage of time that the server's CPU is doing useful work (as opposed to idle threads). Examine this counter over a period of typical usage rather than worrying about spikes in activity. The average value of %Processor Time should usually be less than 70%. If CPU activity is excessive, examine other counters to make sure the server does not need memory or additional disk capacity before deciding you need additional CPU capacity. If the server is truly CPU bound, the solution may be to move some Exchange roles or mailboxes to an additional Mailbox server. If a server does appear to have a CPU bottleneck, you can use the Processor object's %Processor Time counter to isolate which process is using the most CPU time; for this counter, select the process instances you are interested in monitoring.
Memory/Available MBytes	Shows the total amount of unused RAM. All versions of Exchange Server love physical memory. Exchange Server 2007 can consume just about as much memory as you can throw at it. This additional memory will improve performance by allowing more and more data to be cached in RAM, thus reducing dependencies on disk I/O. If you see the Available MBytes counter reporting that there is less than 10% of the total amount of RAM available, you should consider adding additional RAM.
Memory/Pages/Sec	The Pages/sec counter indicates the number of times per second that Windows goes to the page file to store or retrieve information that is in virtual memory. Paging can harm performance because disk access is significantly slower than RAM access. Specific maximum recommended paging values for the Pages/sec counter may vary widely depending on who is making the recommendation. In general, I consider sustained values of more than 10 pages/sec to be excessive. Additional physical RAM is usually the answer to reducing paging, though faster hard disks to support the page file may also provide better throughput for paging.
TCPv4/Segments Retransmitted/Sec	This counter shows the number of TCP segments that have had to be retransmitted each second. If you find that the value of this counter is greater than 5% of the total TCPv4/Segments Sent/Sec counter, you may have network problems such as congested routers or switching problems. Either of these things can cause dropped or lost packets. Always check your network card configurations to make sure they are connected and make sure your network drivers are up-to-date, but this problem is almost always related to the physical infrastructure of your network.
Database/Database Cache % Hits	This is an Exchange Server-specific counter for the ESE database engine that tells you what percentage of disk requests are serviced from cache rather than from the disk. This value should be as high as possible (greater than 95%). The lower the value, the more of a disk I/O burden Exchange places on the disk subsystem. Increasing the available RAM on a server can improve the Database Cache % Hits ratio.

TABLE 24.1: Operating System Performance Counters and Recommended Thresholds *(CONTINUED)*

OBJECT/COUNTER	RECOMMENDED VALUES
Database/Log Record Stalls/Sec	This is an Exchange Server-specific counter for the ESE database engine that tells you if the ESE database engine is having to wait because the log buffers are full. Increasing the log buffer size may correct this, or you can increase the amount of memory in the server. Increasing the memory may reduce the number of I/O operations that are necessary. If the server has sufficient memory, improving the speed of the disk subsystem may be the next move. Moving transaction log files to dedicated spindles can help, as can increasing the I/O capacity of the disks that are used by the transaction logs. On servers that are hosting multiple server roles, moving roles that are disk intensive (such as the Mailbox and Hub Transport roles) to different servers can reduce the I/O load on the disk subsystem.
LogicalDisk/%Disk Time	This counter reports how busy the disk is performing read and write operations. This counter should be monitored over a period of typical activity. This value should not exceed 75% average utilization. If disk usage is excessive, adding physical memory or additional disk I/O capacity can help, as can moving data or transaction logs off to other physical disks.
LogicalDisk/Avg. Disk Queue Length	The average disk queue length is the number of requests waiting in the disk queue either to be written to the disk or to be read from the disk. This is another value that should be monitored over a period of average activity rather than looking at a single point in time. The value should not be more than 2 over a sustained period of activity. Larger values may indicate that the disk subsystem is not able to keep up with the disk I/O requirements. If disk usage is excessive, adding physical memory or additional disk I/O capacity can help, as can moving data or transaction logs off to other physical disks.
MSExchangeIS/RPC Averaged Latency	The RPC Averaged Latency counter reports the latency of remote procedure calls that are serviced by the information store. The value is the average latency of the last 1,024 RPC packets; the value displayed is in milliseconds. In general, it should not exceed 50 milliseconds. Insufficient server resources can often cause this value to be too high, but a high value is more frequently due to network problems.
MSExchangeIS/RPC Requests	The RPC Requests counter reports the number of remote procedure call requests that are currently being serviced by the information store. The information store can service a maximum of 100 requests and this value should usually not exceed 30 requests. Insufficient Exchange Server resources (either memory or I/O capacity) usually contribute to the server's accumulating RPC requests. If RPC requests are not being serviced in a timely manner, the RPC Averaged Latency counter value will also increase.

TABLE 24.1: Operating System Performance Counters and Recommended Thresholds *(CONTINUED)*

Object/Counter	Recommended Values
Network Interface/Bytes Total/Sec	Bytes Total Per Second indicates the total data transfer rate of the network adapter. For 100MB network adapters, this value should be below approximately 6MB/second. For 1GB network adapters, this value should be below 60MB/second. Higher values may indicate that the network is a bottleneck or the server is under too much load. Installing additional servers and moving mailboxes or server roles may alleviate this condition. Upgrade to 1GB adapters and switches for the network segment that hosts the Exchange servers with only 100MB network adapters. Additional network adapters can also alleviate performance problems by locating clients on one network segment and Active Directory resources on a different network segment.
MSExchange ADAccess Domain Controllers/LDAP Read Time	LDAP Read Time is the time (in milliseconds) that it takes to send an LDAP query and receive a response. For this counter, there are multiple instances (each a separate domain controller). The value of this counter should stay below 50ms on average. If it is higher on a sustained basis, you have a domain controller bottleneck. Adding additional domain controllers, adding memory to existing domain controllers, or replacing 32-bit Windows domain controllers with 64-bit domain controllers may help. Of course, poor network performance can also cause this counter to be high; local domain controllers are always preferred to domain controllers in another Active Directory site.
MSExchange ADAccess Domain Controllers/LDAP Search Time	LDAP Search Time is the amount of time (in milliseconds) that it takes to send an LDAP search to a domain controller and then receive a response. Performance characteristics for this counter are the same as for LDAP Read Time.

Though I can't easily come up with performance counters that will help you in every situation, the ones in Table 24.1 are generic enough to help you get started and to help you in deciding if you have a specific type of bottleneck.

Helpful Performance Tools

Microsoft provides a couple of tools for you "right out of the box" with Exchange Server 2007. Frequently, these tools can help you narrow down the root cause of a specific problem or help you find a problem that you did not even know that you had.

I want to provide a strong word of caution, though. These tools will make recommendations based on a set of default measurement values or Microsoft's recommended best practices. These may not be the best recommendations for your environment — so review each recommendation with a critical eye. These tools may make recommendations but that does not mean you should blindly adjust system settings.

In this section, I show you the Exchange Best Practices Analyzer and the Exchange Performance Troubleshooter. I decided not to go in to a whole lot of detail because these tools are not only easy to use, but you really should sit down and run them yourself to get a feel for the options and what you can discern from these tools.

Exchange Best Practices Analyzer

One of the most popular tools that Microsoft has ever released for free (and certainly one of the most popular tools the Exchange Team has ever provided) is the Exchange Best Practices Analyzer (ExBPA). The tool even has its own website (`www.exbpa.com`).

I recommend you run the ExBPA every two or three months even if you have no obvious problems.

The ExBPA downloads an updated configuration file when you run it so that it has the latest recommendations, configurations, and threshold information each time it runs. Microsoft updates this configuration file periodically based on recommendations from the Exchange Team, Microsoft Consulting Services, and Microsoft Customer Support Services.

The ExBPA can be downloaded from the ExBPA website or you can run it from the Best Practices Analyzer link in the Exchange Management Console's Toolbox container. Running a best practices report is quite simple:

1. On startup, the ExBPA will ask you if you want to check for updates. You should always check for updates and download the newest configuration files if they are available.

2. After the update check, the next screen will ask you to Select Options For A New Scan. Select this link.

3. On the Connect To Active Directory page, specify the name of a domain controller that is in the same site that you are in, and click the Connect To The Active Directory Server link.

4. On the Start A New Best Practices Scan, you need to provide some options including a name for this scan, the servers that you want to scan, and the type of scan to perform. The default is a Health Check (see Figure 24.6) and that is the one I recommend you run.

5. When you have selected the scan type and provided a name, click the Start Scanning link.

FIGURE 24.6
Using ExBPA to perform a Health Check

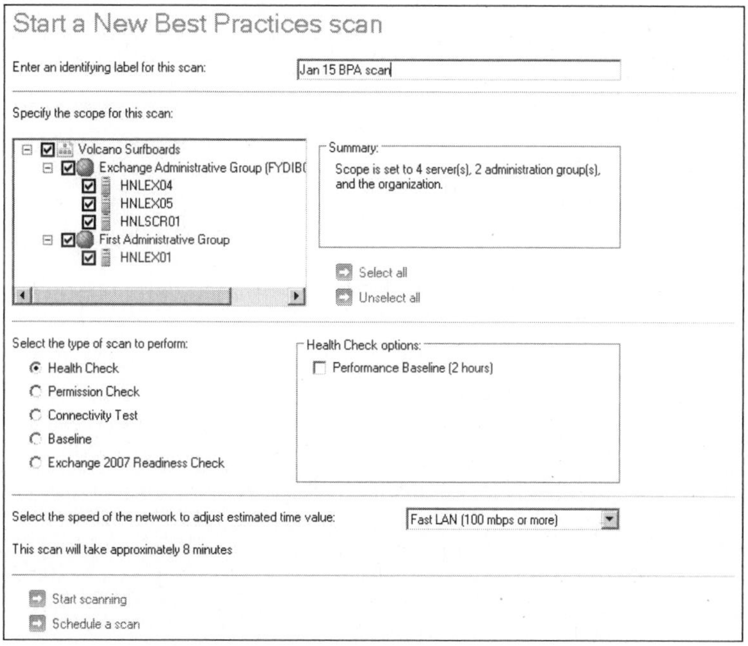

Start a New Best Practices scan

Enter an identifying label for this scan:
Jan 15 BPA scan

Specify the scope for this scan:

- Volcano Surfboards
  - Exchange Administrative Group (FYDIB(
    - HNLEX04
    - HNLEX05
    - HNLSCR01
  - First Administrative Group
    - HNLEX01

Summary:
Scope is set to 4 server(s), 2 administration group(s), and the organization.

Select all
Unselect all

Select the type of scan to perform:
- Health Check
- Permission Check
- Connectivity Test
- Baseline
- Exchange 2007 Readiness Check

Health Check options:
- Performance Baseline (2 hours)

Select the speed of the network to adjust estimated time value:
Fast LAN (100 mbps or more)

This scan will take approximately 8 minutes

Start scanning
Schedule a scan

Depending on the number of servers you have selected and your network architecture, the ExBPA Health Check scan may take between a few minutes and a few hours. Once it is complete, you can click the View A Report Of This Best Practices Scan link. A sample report is shown in Figure 24.7.

FIGURE 24.7
Viewing an ExBPA Health Check report

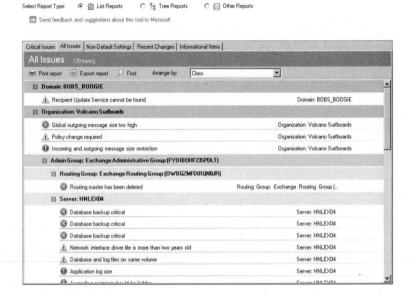

Exchange Performance Troubleshooter

The Exchange Performance Troubleshooter is one of the tools available in the Exchange Management Toolbox and is part of the Exchange Troubleshooting Assistant tool, which also includes the Database Troubleshooter, Database Recovery Management, and Mail Flow Troubleshooter. The Exchange Performance Troubleshooter tool gathers information about the Exchange server and performs analysis based on some preset thresholds.

When you run the ExPTA, it asks for some basic information about your environment (domain controller and Exchange server name) and asks you about some of the symptoms that you may be experiencing. Then it gathers some information about system performance including the following:

◆ RPC counters

◆ Server health

◆ Disk drive, database, and transaction log configuration

◆ LDAP performance statistics

◆ Network usage

◆ Queue health

When the Performance Troubleshooter is complete, it will present you a report that allows you to view the results of its analysis. An example of this is shown in Figure 24.8.

FIGURE 24.8

Viewing the results of the Exchange Performance Troubleshooter

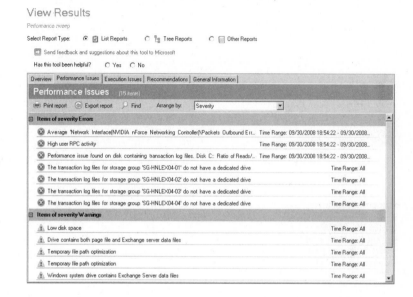

Summary

For many of us, performance monitoring is just part of our basic job responsibilities. We run servers that are over-tasked and under-configured or whose usage has just scaled beyond what we ever expected. Performance monitoring gives us the ability to provide quantifiable reasons why we are experiencing problems and how we can go about resolving them — including more hardware.

Scaling upward and outward is a necessary evil for organizations with more than a few hundred users. Though a single machine can easily support all the necessary server roles for a few hundred mailboxes, if it is not properly configured, it may experience performance problems. Recognizing potential performance bottleneck points and how to correct them is an essential skill for Exchange administrators.

Microsoft provides some excellent troubleshooting tools with Windows and Exchange Server. You should make an effort to get to know some of the features that you can use not only in the Performance Monitor console, but also the Exchange Best Practices Analyzer and the Exchange Performance Troubleshooter.

Chapter 25

Securing Exchange Server

Regardless of whether your Exchange servers are accessed by users on a local area network, whether your users receive e-mail from the Internet, or whether you are providing web services such as Outlook Web Access, ActiveSync, and Outlook Anywhere to Internet users, you need to keep security in mind. You'll be surprised how easy it is to make Exchange Server 2007 reasonably secure.

During setup, the person who installs Exchange Server chooses the specific Exchange server roles that a particular server will host. Only the software necessary to support the chosen roles is actually installed. This is in contrast to the installation process for Exchange 2000/2003; most Exchange services had to be installed and then the installer would need to later disable services that were not necessary. An Exchange Server 2007 server that is hosting only the Mailbox role will not have unnecessary services installed and running.

This chapter covers many of the common steps you can easily perform to ensure that your Exchange server is as secure as possible without breaking your budget. It also covers firewalls, perimeter networks, reverse proxies, and SMTP relays, all of which will help you to solidify your security and help you to sleep more soundly at night.

In this chapter you learn to:

- ◆ Understand security basics
- ◆ Use the Security Configuration Wizard
- ◆ Implement Secure Sockets Layer (SSL) with Exchange
- ◆ Set up message hygiene and multilayer security
- ◆ Deploy reverse proxy to protect web services

Understanding Exchange Server Security Basics

When you are planning the procedures, technology, and precautions that you will implement to ensure better security for your Exchange Server infrastructure, you should aim for a goal that I refer to as being "reasonably secure." I am not talking about locking up your servers tighter than the gold storage at Fort Knox, but I do mean taking the precautions and implementing the technology to make your organization "at least" as secure as the other companies in your own industry. This will mean something entirely different to a small business that has no confidential or proprietary data in its mail system than it will to, for example, a health care provider.

Starting with the Obvious

Anyone experienced in fighting unauthorized intruders will tell you that malicious hackers usually attempt an attack by looking for the "low-hanging fruit." They look for known vulnerabilities and a weak defensive perimeter. So let's start with the more obvious security precautions and procedures. Many readers will look at this list and think it is painfully simple, but I find many organizations still miss the most basic points when securing their Exchange systems and even their networks.

◆ Your internal network should always be protected by a firewall. More on this later in this chapter in the section called "Protecting Your Firewall." Physical server security is almost as important as firewall security. Ensure that servers are physically secured and in an environmentally controlled place. Backup media should be physically secured.

◆ No unnecessary Windows services, third-party software, or beta software should be installed on any Exchange server.

◆ Keep all operating systems and application software (Exchange included) up-to-date. You should plan to apply server-side critical security patches and updates within 4 to 6 weeks of release. In most situations, service packs should be applied within 8 to 12 weeks of release, after verifying that no incompatibilities exist with current software or hardware.

◆ Administrator accounts (both local and domain) should be renamed and should have complex passwords assigned. The guest account should be disabled.

◆ Limit the membership of the Administrators and Power Users groups to only absolutely necessary users. Limit the membership in Domain Admins, Enterprise Admins, and the domain's Administrators groups.

◆ Auditing and logging should be enabled on all Exchange servers. You can find more information on security logging and protocol logs in Chapter 26, "Logging, Auditing, and Monitoring."

◆ Server administration at the server console should be restricted to tasks that absolutely must be done "at the server." All other admin tasks (managing users, performing backups, and so on) should be performed remotely.

◆ Administrative and operator accounts should not have mailboxes. Practice separation of administrative responsibilities from day-to-day tasks such as using e-mail, word processing applications, and so on.

◆ Do not install e-mail client software on your servers and do not use your servers to surf the Internet.

◆ Internet connectivity for servers should be blocked or severely limited. You may need to configure your servers to get Microsoft Updates or antivirus signature updates, but in that case the servers should *only* be allowed to go to those Internet update sites.

◆ Outbound SMTP (TCP port 25) should only be allowed from specific, authorized mail server hosts.

Thinking About Intruders

Almost all discussions of security, malicious hackers, and protecting your information infrastructure focus on protecting resources from being compromised from outside. Though that will yield useful precautions and information for consideration, security violations do not always come from outside of your firewall. Employees and users from business partners may also be a source of data theft, data compromise, information leaks, and other security events. With that in mind, here are a few tips to consider:

◆ Enable mailbox logon diagnostic logging so that if necessary you can review who has accessed each mailbox.

◆ Network connections between business partners must be properly firewalled and audited. This not only protects your own information, it ensures accountability on the part of your own employees. Business partners should be provided with access to only the specific resources they require and nothing more. This is also true of resources that your own employees may need from your partner.

◆ Practice the principle of least permissions not only for administrators but also for users. Security group membership must be audited regularly to ensure that users do not have excessive rights and permissions.

Understanding Message Security Types

Messaging security can actually mean a lot of different things to different people. So let's quickly review the different types of security involved:

Operating system and Exchange Server software security   Securing and protecting the operating system and the Exchange Server applications (services) is probably what most people think about when they think about Exchange Server security. And that is what much of this chapter discusses. This encompasses ensuring that the attack surface of the operating system and Exchange services has been minimized. We do this by employing firewalls, operating system/application updates, good physical security, and solid administrative procedures.

The security of e-mail data in transit   Protecting e-mail data while the data is in transit usually involves some type of network encryption. This could be Secure Sockets Layer (SSL)/Transport Layer Security (TLS) or IP security (IPSec). We protect data in transit if we are concerned about the physical layer of our network (or the networks on which e-mail traffic crosses) being compromised and allowing someone to perform protocol analysis. The Outlook client can implement built-in encryption and encrypt message traffic between the client and a Mailbox server. Implementing HTTPS on Client Access servers ensures that web clients (such as Outlook Web Access, Windows Mobile ActiveSync, or Outlook Anywhere) transmit data securely.

The security of e-mail data at rest   Most of the time, e-mail data is at rest. E-mail is in the sender's Sent Items box, in a message queue, or in the recipient's Inbox. The message data may be moved into an archival system or copied out to a personal folder (PST) file. Protecting e-mail data at rest involves encrypting the data so that only authorized recipients can open a message. Technologies that can provide message encryption include Secure Multipurpose Internet Mail Extensions (S/MIME) and enterprise rights management (ERM) or digital rights management (DRM) technologies.

Protecting Your Firewall

The Internet can be a dangerous place, harboring worms, 'bots, malicious hackers, script kiddies, and reality TV streaming video. Organizations that own public IP addresses often see dozens of attacks or probes against those IP addresses every day; these probes are often just someone (via an automated program) looking for a known vulnerability that they can exploit. Some organizations see attacks directed against their resources from a malicious hacker who is intentionally trying to do the organization or its data harm.

Something has to provide a layer of protection against these types of attacks. The firewall is a device that sits between an external network (an untrusted network) and a private or trusted network. In medium and larger organizations, actual management of the organization's firewall is outside of the e-mail administrator's area of responsibility. Oftentimes even in small organizations the firewall is managed by someone else. However, as an e-mail administrator, you are responsible for setting up your servers to receive SMTP mail from the Internet, send SMTP mail to the Internet, and possibly receive inbound traffic from HTTP/HTTPS clients. So you need to be able to converse effectively with the people who will provide the necessary access. If this is all "old hat" to you, then please skip on to the next section.

Figure 25.1 shows a simple Exchange 2007 deployment that is protected by a firewall. This organization is protected by an external firewall and an internal firewall. The network that sits between them is the perimeter network or the demilitarized zone (DMZ) network. The perimeter network is intended for servers that you must protect to some degree, but you do not want the traffic intended for those servers to be coming directly into your internal network. In this diagram, I am showing two separate firewalls, but this is a conceptual diagram. Some organizations will have both an internal firewall and an external firewall, whereas others will have a single firewall that provides internal, external, and perimeter network ports.

FIGURE 25.1
Typical firewall deployment protecting Exchange Server 2007

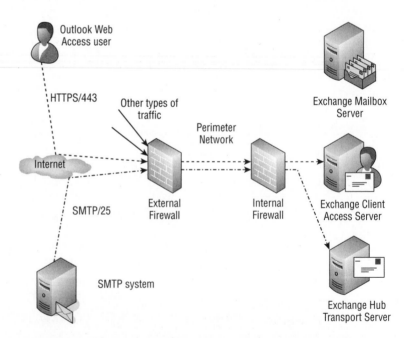

In this deployment, inbound SMTP (TCP port 25) mail from the Internet hits the firewall. The external firewall sees that TCP port 25 is permitted, but only for certain internal IP addresses. The inbound SMTP traffic is then directed to the internal firewall, where possibly a second set of restrictions or access lists (often called rules or an access control list) is consulted. The internal firewall allows inbound SMTP, but only to the Exchange 2007 Hub Transport server.

The same would happen for inbound HTTPS traffic (TCP port 443) that comes from Outlook Web Access, Windows Mobile ActiveSync clients, and Outlook Anywhere clients. The external and internal firewalls determine that TCP port 443 is permitted, but only to the internal Exchange 2007 Client Access server.

DON'T PUT CLIENT ACCESS AND HUB TRANSPORT ROLES IN PERIMETER NETWORK

A very common question is whether or not the Exchange Client Access and Hub Transport server roles should be placed in the perimeter network. No, the Hub Transport and Client Access server roles should not be placed in the perimeter network. Neither Microsoft nor any reputable Exchange expert will advise you to do this. If you are advised to do this, get a second opinion. If you do this and then call Microsoft for help, you will be informed that this is not a supported configuration.

Any other type of traffic that hits the firewall would not be allowed even to the perimeter network. Figure 25.1 showed a very simple example; most organizations' firewall configurations are far more complex. You may also be publishing more than one or two applications.

Table 25.1 shows some of the typical ports that may be required on different Exchange server roles.

TABLE 25.1:   Typical Ports Required by Exchange Applications

APPLICATION	PORT	EXCHANGE SERVER ROLE
SMTP	25	Hub Transport server
SMTP w/TLS	25	Hub Transport server
HTTP	80	Client Access server
POP3	110	Client Access server
IMAP4	143	Client Access server
HTTPS (HTTP with SSL)	443	Client Access server
Secure SMTP for clients	587	Hub Transport server
POP3 with SSL	995	Client Access server
IMAP4 with SSL	993	Client Access server

Although Table 25.1 does list some ports that are not encrypted (such as HTTP, POP3, and IMAP4), I do not recommend that these ports be opened. I recommend all Internet applications use SSL ports to protect logon credentials and data. IMAP and POP clients that require an SMTP server should use the Hub Transport's Client Receive connector for secure SMTP connectivity. I have intentionally left out LDAP ports because this would require that LDAP be opened to Active Directory domain controllers or global catalog servers; I do not recommend exposing any Active Directory services directly to the Internet.

Provided your Windows and Exchange servers are up-to-date on patches and you have taken reasonable measures to lock down your server configuration, the configuration shown in Figure 25.1 should provide reasonably good security. However, I will discuss the use of SMTP relay hosts (and the use of the Edge Transport server role) as well as reverse proxy servers to provide even better security for Exchange servers that are exposed to the Internet.

Using the Security Configuration Wizard

Microsoft includes a tool with Windows Server 2003 Service Pack 1 and Windows Server 2003 R2 called the Security Configuration Wizard (SCW). This tool includes templates for different types of server roles; the wizard asks you about the server roles, network security settings, and services that should be running on the server. The wizard then disables unnecessary services and helps to lock down or harden the server.

The SCW is a very powerful Windows tool that is helpful in ensuring that your servers are secured to the best point possible. However, if you do not configure the policy correctly or if you do not take into consideration the roles that the server is supporting or the software that the server is supporting, you will break something.

You might have wondered if the SCW includes templates for Exchange 2007 roles. It does not include Exchange Server 2007 templates, but it does include Exchange 2000/2003 templates and this is a source of confusion. You should not attempt to use the built-in SCW Exchange 2000/2003 templates. There is a procedure for updating a server's templates with Exchange 2007-ready templates.

The SCW has a "rollback" feature that will prove very useful when you're tuning your server's security configuration. If you have a plain-vanilla installation of Exchange with no additional software or options, the defaults will all work fine. In other situations, though, some fine-tuning may be required.

Preparing the Security Configuration Wizard for Exchange 2007

Exchange 2007 includes two files that you can use to register the necessary templates and settings for the SCW so that it recognizes Exchange Server 2007 roles and requirements:

- `Exchange2007.xml` includes the necessary configuration and extensions to register an Exchange Server 2007 Mailbox, Hub Transport, Client Access, Unified Messaging, or clustered mailbox server role with the Security Configuration Wizard.

- `Exchange2007Edge.xml` includes the necessary configuration and extensions to register an Exchange Server 2007 Edge Transport server role with the Security Configuration Wizard.

These files are found (by default) in the `C:\Program Files\Microsoft\Exchange Server\scripts` folder. To register a Mailbox, Hub Transport, Client Access, Unified Messaging, or clustered mailbox server with the SCW, change to the scripts folder and use the following command:

```
scwcmd register /kbname:"Ex2007KB" /kbfile:"Exchange2007.xml"
```

To register the SCW extensions for an Exchange 2007 Edge Transport server role, change to the scripts folder and use this command:

```
scwcmd register /kbname:"Ex2007KB" /kbfile:"Exchange2007Edge.xml"
```

Using the Security Configuration Wizard

The Security Configuration Wizard is pretty simple to use. You can find a shortcut to the SCW in the Administrative Tools folder. Do not run this tool on an Exchange 2007 server until you have registered the Exchange 2007 extensions, though. In order to run the SCW, you must be a member of the server's local Administrators group. When you launch the SCW, the first screen just introduces you to the SCW. Once you click Next, you are taken to the Configuration Action screen. Here you are prompted to select the action you want to perform as shown in Figure 25.2.

FIGURE 25.2
Selecting an SCW configuration action

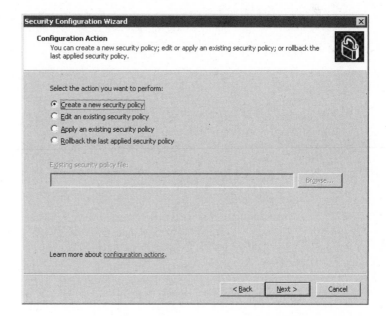

You can choose four possible actions from the Configuration Action page of the wizard:

◆ Create A New Security Policy will walk you through the wizard and create a new set of security policy settings. This is the step you choose when you run the SCW for the first time.

◆ Edit An Existing Security Policy lets you make adjustments to a policy you have previously created.

◆ Apply An Existing Security Policy lets you apply or re-apply a policy you have previously created.

◆ Rollback The Last Applied Security Policy allows you to undo security settings you have recently applied. This is very, very helpful if you have applied a policy that breaks something.

If you are not sure about a specific setting when running the SCW, it is best to take the defaults or recommended settings.

For this example, select Create A New Security Policy. On the next page of the wizard, you specify a server to use for defining the baseline of the security policy you are going to create.

This can be another server on your network or it can be the local server. You must have administrative permissions on the server that you are selecting. When you click Next, the SCW will analyze the current security settings and it will give you an opportunity to view the configuration database. The configuration database will show you all of the options and server roles that are currently available and known to the SCW. You can view the configuration database to verify that it knows about Exchange 2007 server roles. Click Next until you come to the Select Server Roles page of the wizard. From the page shown in Figure 25.3, you can see the server roles that the SCW has detected.

FIGURE 25.3

Selecting the installed server roles

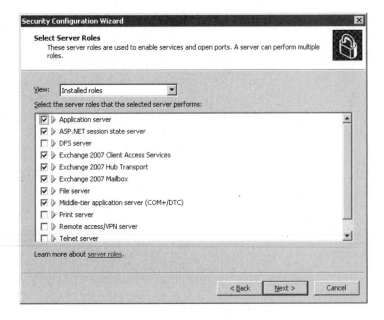

If the View drop-down box shows that Installed Roles is selected, you will see the roles that the SCW detected on the server. From here, you can clear check boxes next to server roles that are unnecessary on this particular server. In this example, the server originally had the Print Server role, but notice in the screen shot that the Print Server check box is cleared. When the policy is applied, the Print Spooler service will be disabled. This means that this machine will not be able to use either locally installed printers or shared printers. Though this may be an inconvenience, there is rarely a need to print from a server that is dedicated to some specific Exchange Server function.

The next page of the wizard is the Select Client Features page. This page shows you the services and software that are used by client applications. In Figure 25.4 you can see client-side services such as the DHCP Client, the DNS Registration Client, the Automatic Update Client, and more.

Take care not to disable a service that you may need to support Exchange. It is deceptively easy to break something important, such as domain membership or DNS lookups.

The Select Administration And Other Options page shows you the components that are used to manage a server and provide other networking services. For example, the Browser and the Browse Master services are in this list. For an Exchange 2007 server, these options will be cleared, which means this server will not participate in the My Network Places feature of Windows. Though browser functionality is not required for Exchange Server or Exchange clients, other software might require it, so review the list shown in Figure 25.5 carefully.

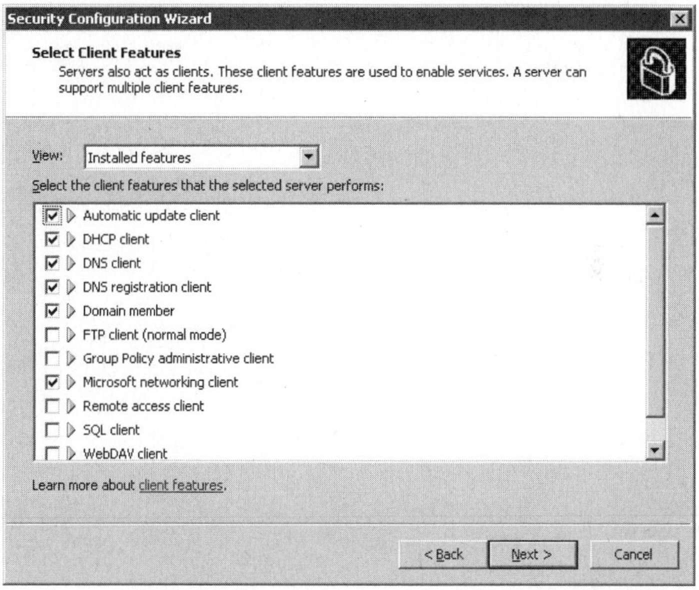

FIGURE 25.4
Selecting client features

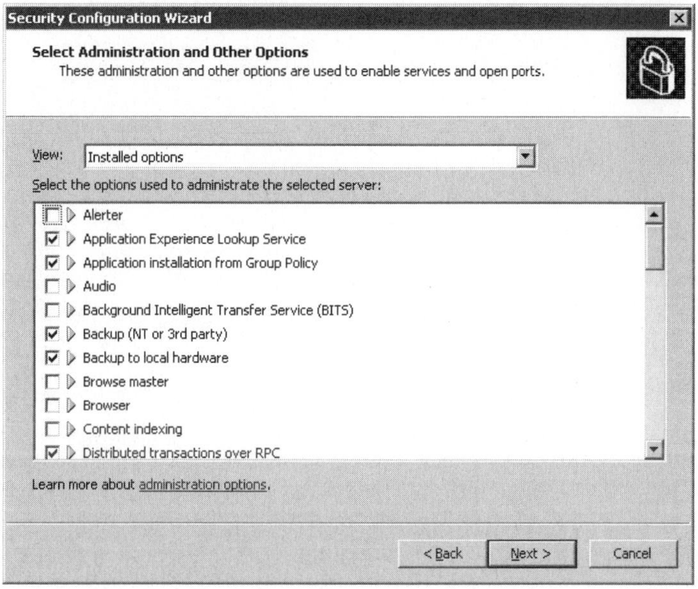

FIGURE 25.5
Reviewing the administration and other options in the SCW

The SCW determines which options are most likely required to administer an Exchange 2007 server, but it is important to realize that some fine-tuning may be necessary. The next screen of the wizard is the Select Additional Services page; here you can select additional software that is not defined in the SCW extensions. When you get to the Handling Unspecified Services page, you are presented with options to disable services that are not defined or leave them alone.

Unless you are sure you know that disabling services will not affect the required functionality of the Exchange server, I recommend you choose the Do Not Change The Startup Mode Of The Service option.

The Confirm Service Changes page of the SCW (shown in Figure 25.6) allows you to view the current state of the service and what will be changed once you implement this particular SCW setting. By default, only the services that are affected by the SCW are listed.

FIGURE 25.6
Reviewing the SCW changes prior to updating the server's configuration

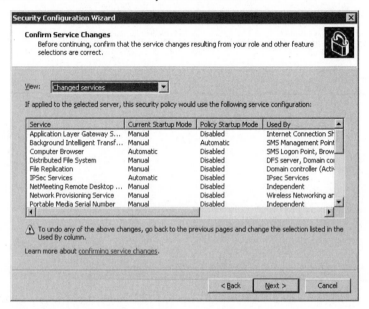

Review the list of services that will be modified and ensure that no critical services that you require are going to be disabled. When you are sure that everything meets your requirements, click Next to move on to the network security section of the wizard. This section is optional, but you may want to consider running it if you want to tighten down the ports being used on the network. On the first screen of the network security portion of the SCW, you can select the Skip This Section check box and skip the network security section all together.

When you have finished selecting the applications that are allowed to listen on network ports, you are asked to confirm the port changes as shown in Figure 25.7.

The next section is the Registry section of the SCW. This title is a little misleading because what the SCW is configuring or locking down is specifically Windows configuration settings that can help reduce the possibility of attacks such as password cracking and protocol attacks. The actual Registry settings that are affected in this section are in the `HKLM\System\CurrentControlSet\LanManServer\Parameters` key and the `HKLM\System\CurrentcontrolSet\Control\LSA` key. You can skip this section also.

The Require SMB Security Signatures property page allows you to specify that server message block (SMB) signing is required for all SMB traffic; this will generate slightly more CPU load and it will prevent clients older than Windows NT 4 SP6 from connecting to file or printer shares. However, this can reduce the possibility of a man-in-the-middle type of attack in which a user's session is hijacked.

The Outbound Authentication Methods wizard page allows you to configure the types of authentication that can be used when connecting to a remote server. By default, Domain Accounts authentication is the only method selected; this means that all computers to which you connect from this server must be domain members.

On the Outbound Authentication Using Domain Accounts wizard page, you can specify the types of operating systems you will be connecting to. The default is that all remote operating systems will be Windows NT 4 (or compatible) or later. Depending on the configuration on the Outbound Authentication Using Local Accounts page, you may also see the Inbound Authentication Methods wizard page, which allows you to configure the LAN Manager/NTLM authentication level. Finally, on the Registry Settings Summary screen in Figure 25.8, you can verify the types of changes that are about to be made.

FIGURE 25.7
Confirming inbound port configuration

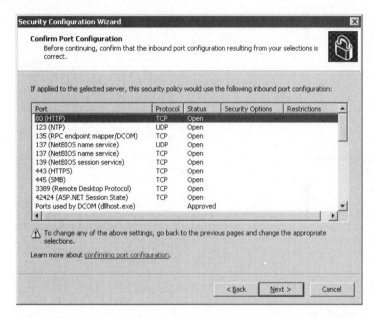

FIGURE 25.8
Reviewing Registry changes

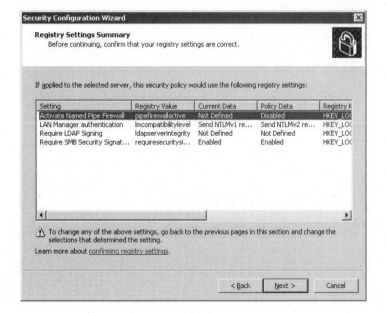

The next section is the System Audit Policy section, used to enable auditing settings. These are the same auditing settings that you can enable in the local security policy or via a group policy object (GPO). You can disable auditing, audit only successful events, or audit both success and failures.

The Audit Policy Summary page of the wizard shown in Figure 25.9 allows you to confirm which settings you are making.

FIGURE 25.9

Reviewing audit policy changes

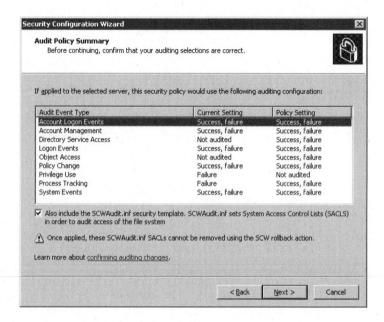

In the Internet Information Services section, you specify that web service extensions are enabled and which virtual directories will be allowed. Much of the configuration that you perform on the Internet Information Services section is similar to using the Microsoft IIS Lock Down tool. Unless you are running additional web applications on your Exchange servers, I recommend taking the defaults.

The IIS Settings Summary page shows you the current settings and the changes that will be made. (See Figure 25.10.)

Finally, on the Security Policy File Name page, you are at the point that you are ready to save your security policy. Enter a name for your security policy file and provide a description. One of the really nice features of the SCW is that you can click the View Security Policy button and view all of the settings of your security policy. Figure 25.11 shows an example. The SCW Viewer will also let you print out the security policy if you like to keep hard copy records of your configuration.

Once you save the policy, the next page of the wizard will ask you if you want to apply the security policy now or apply it later. You may also need to reboot the server after the policy changes have been applied.

I recommend creating and testing a security policy prior to putting a server into production so that you don't have to worry about rebooting during working hours. You can always save your policy and apply it later.

FIGURE 25.10
Reviewing IIS configuration changes

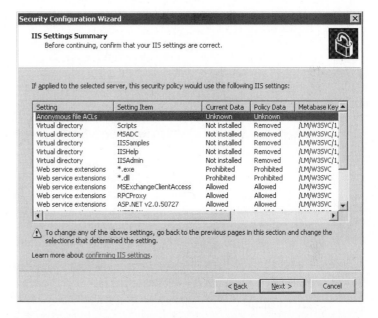

FIGURE 25.11
Viewing your security policy

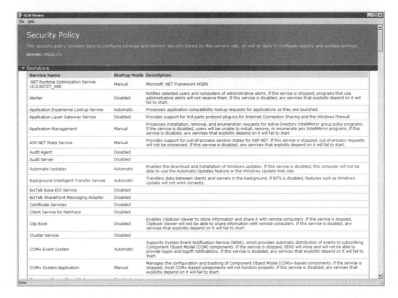

Using Secure Sockets Layer (SSL) with Exchange

Secure Sockets Layer (SSL) is the foundation for almost all network-layer protection of Exchange data in Exchange Server 2007. SSL is a technology that allows a network client and a server to negotiate an encryption key that is used as a session key to encrypt data sent between the client and the server. The client requests the server's certificate (which will become important here shortly) and uses the server's public key to initially exchange an encryption key.

Although the technology was designed for use with the HTTP protocol, it can be adapted to be used with almost any protocol, including SMTP, POP3, and IMAP4. It should be noted that the actual technology that is used with SMTP is Transport Layer Security (TLS), which is the Internet standardized version of SSL.

Using Self-Signed Certificates and Exchange 2007

A certificate is automatically installed on all Exchange Server 2007 Hub Transport and Client Access servers so they can use SSL or TLS. This certificate is a self-signed certificate that is generated automatically by the installation process. The self-signed certificate allows Outlook Web Access clients to use HTTPS web services and it allows Hub Transport servers to use TLS.

You might think this is all well and good, but self-signed certificates are problematic for a few reasons. First, when users connect to an Outlook Web Access site that is using a self-signed certificate, they see a web browser error like the one shown in Figure 25.12.

FIGURE 25.12
Connecting to a website with an untrusted certificate

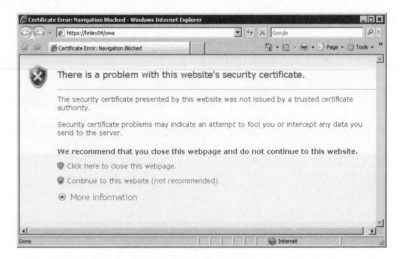

Though users can simply click Continue To This Website (Not Recommended) and proceed to Outlook Web Access and SSL will work, I strongly discourage any organization from allowing end users to do this. Getting users in the habit of ignoring security warnings is never a good thing.

The second problem will occur with Outlook 2007 when the client connects to the Autodiscover, Availability, and offline address book virtual directories. Figure 25.13 shows the error that may be displayed if the client does not trust the server's certificate.

Outlook Anywhere clients may not work if they don't trust the certificate authority that signed the certificate on the Hub Transport server. Remote SMTP servers that attempt to initiate TLS to Exchange 2007 Hub Transport servers may also not transmit mail if they do not trust the Hub Transport server's certificate.

Requesting and Installing Certificates for Exchange Server 2007

Chapter 22, "Getting to Know the Client Access Server Role," contains a pretty thorough review of certificates and requesting certificates. But I felt it was important to reiterate this topic again. This topic is especially important because there has been a lot of confusion regarding certificates and Exchange Server 2007.

When planning an Exchange deployment that includes the use of SSL or TLS, you need to ensure that certificates that are used by Hub Transport servers and Client Access servers are properly trusted. Let's look at the general properties of a self-signed certificate used for an Exchange server. This property page is shown in Figure 25.14.

FIGURE 25.13

A security warning of an untrusted certificate

FIGURE 25.14

Viewing a certificate's general properties

Trusted certificates have three characteristics:

◆ The date range for the certificate includes the current date. This is the Valid From information.

◆ The FQDN that the server was issued to matches the name that the client used to connect to the server. This is the Issued To information.

◆ The issuer of the certificate is a certificate authority that is trusted by the local computer. This is the Issued By information.

The reason the self-signed certificate is invalid is that the issuer is not one of the trusted certificate authorities. You need to get a certificate that has been issued by a trusted certificate authority. This can be one of many third-party certificate authorities or it could be your own internal certificate server. If you use an internal certificate server, you still have to distribute your certificate server's certificate to all clients that will use certificates issued by that server.

WINDOWS TRUSTED CERTIFICATE AUTHORITIES

For a list of certificate authorities that are trusted by Windows by default, see the Microsoft Root Certificate Program Members list at the following URL:

`http://msdn.microsoft.com/en-us/library/ms995347.aspx`

For simplicity's sake, I recommend using a third party's certificate server. Though an annual fee is usually involved, this is the simplest approach and ensures that clients do not receive security warnings or errors.

With simple websites and with Exchange 2000/2003, generating a certificate request was pretty basic. All you needed to do was to generate the request and use the FQDN that the users would be using to connect to your site. Then you sent the certificate request to the certificate authority to be signed.

Exchange 2007 Client Access servers use different URLs for internal and external clients. This is not only because of Outlook Web Access, but also due to Autodiscover, the Availability service, offline address books, and other web services that may be associated with the default website in IIS. Let's take as an example a server that hosts the Hub Transport and Client Access server roles for an organization. It may be referred to by a number of different names under different circumstances. The server's name is HNLEX04, the Active Directory DNS name is volcanosurfboards.int, and the public domain name is somorita.com. The following hostnames and fully qualified domain names may be used against this server:

◆ `hnlex04`

◆ `hnlex04.volcanosurfboards.int`

◆ `mail.somorita.com` (by remote web clients)

◆ `autodiscover.somorita.com` (by remote Autodiscover clients)

You might think that you need multiple virtual web servers in order to support all of these different names, but that is not the case thanks to a feature of X.509v3 certificates called a *subject alternative name*. This feature allows for multiple hostnames and DNS domain names to be associated with a single web server. However, you cannot use the Internet Information Services

Manager to generate a certificate request. You must use the Exchange 2007 Exchange Management Shell (EMS) cmdlet `New-ExchangeCertificate` to generate the request. Let's do an example that requests a certificate with the following information:

Organization name	Somorita Surfboards
Organizational unit	IT Department
FQDN domain name	`mail.somorita.com`

Additional names	`hnlex04,`
	`hnlex04.volcanosurfboards.int,`
	`autodiscover.somorita.com`

Certificate request filename	`C:\CertReq.txt`

On the console of server `hnlex04`, you must type the following command to generate the certificate request file. Below the command is the output of the certificate request generation:

```
New-ExchangeCertificate -GenerateRequest -SubjectName↵
"ou=IT Department,o=Somorita Surfboards, cn=mail.somorita.com" -domainname↵
hnlex04,hnlex04.volcanosurfboards.int,autodiscover.somorita.com"↵
-path c:\CertReq.txt
Thumbprint      Services   Subject
----------      --------   -------
5BDE878D6A6D34DE6462557F785B19D424642D42  .....    CN=mail.somorita.com, O...
```

The certificate request file (`CertReq.txt`) is not exactly a beauty-come-hither. As a matter of fact, it is in a format that almost no one but a certification authority could love. Figure 25.15 shows the text of the certificate signing request.

The text that you see in Figure 25.15 is actually a base64 encoded request of the information that you created using the `New-ExchangeCertificate` cmdlet. You will need to take this text and give it to the certification authority; usually this is done by copying the CSR text and pasting it in to a text box on the certificate authority's website, as shown in Figure 25.16.

Depending on the certificate authority, you may get a signed certificate back immediately (especially if you have an account) or you may have to wait a few hours or even days for verification to take place. Ultimately, you will download a certificate file or the CA will e-mail the file to you. You need to save this to a file on to the server's local file system (`hnlex04`, in this example) and use the EMS cmdlet `Import-ExchangeCertificate` to import the certificate into the machine's certificate store.

The following example is importing a newly generated certificate into the machine's certificate store. The certificate filename is `WebServices.cer` and will be assigned the friendly name of HNLEX04 Web Services Certificate. Here is an example:

```
Import-ExchangeCertificate -path c:\WebServices.cer↵
-FriendlyName "HNLEX04 Web Services Certificate"

Thumbprint      Services   Subject
----------      --------   -------
A171D0FA13E121AA553A83A4BDDC7BE830CB8034  .....    CN=mail.somorita.com, O...
```

FIGURE 25.15
The text of a certificate signing request

FIGURE 25.16
Pasting the certificate signing request into a text box on a certificate authority's website

This imports the certificate into the certificate store, but it does not enable the certificate. You now have to use the `Enable-ExchangeCertificate` cmdlet to associate the certificate with IIS (or other Internet services). Notice the thumbprint attribute; this will come in handy. Here is the command to enable the certificate for use with web services (IIS) as well as SMTP, POP3, and IMAP4:

```
Enable-ExchangeCertificate -Thumbprint↵
A171D0FA13E121AA553A83A4BDDC7BE830CB8034 -Services "IIS,POP,IMAP,SMTP"
```

If you don't remember the thumbprint, you can use the `Get-ExchangeCertificate` cmdlet to retrieve it for you. Here is an example:

```
Get-ExchangeCertificate | Where-Object {$_.Subject -like *mail.somorita.com*"}↵
| Format-List


AccessRules          : {System.Security.AccessControl.CryptoKeyAccessRule,
System.Security.AccessControl.CryptoKeyAccessRule}
CertificateDomains : {mail.somorita.com, hnlex04, hnlex04.volcanosurfboards.int,
autodiscover.somorita.com}
HasPrivateKey        : True
IsSelfSigned         : False
Issuer: CN=hnldc01, DC=volcanosurfboards, DC=com
NotAfter             : 1/22/2009 7:08:17 PM
NotBefore            : 1/23/2007 7:08:17 PM
PublicKeySize        : 2048
SerialNumber         : 5334E5FC000000000009
Status               : Valid
Subject              : CN=mail.somorita.com, OU=IT Department,
O=Somorita Surfboards
Thumbprint           : A171D0FA13E121AA553A83A4BDDC7BE830CB8034
```

Implementing a Message Hygiene System

An important component of your overall Exchange design is properly implementing a message hygiene system. *Message hygiene* is an all-encompassing term that covers antivirus and anti-spam technology. The anti-spam components of Exchange 2007 are discussed in Chapter 21, "Delivering E-mail"; in this chapter I want to cover some of the best practices associated with the anti-spam components.

Choosing an Antivirus System

At least 10 antivirus software packages are available on the market that work with Exchange 2007 or that are in development to work with Exchange 2007:

- ◆ Symantec Mail Security for Microsoft Exchange (www.symantec.com)

- ◆ Trend ScanMail for Microsoft Exchange (www.trendmicro.com)

- ◆ GFI MailSecurity for Exchange (www.gfi.com)

- ◆ eTrust InnoculateIT for Exchange (www.ca.com)

- F-Secure Antivirus for Exchange (`www.f-secure.com`)

- Proland Protector Plus Antivirus for Exchange (`www.pspl.com`)

- Kaspersky Security for Exchange Server (`www.kaspersky.com`)

- McAfee GroupShield for Exchange (`www.mcafee.com`)

- Sophos PureMessage for Exchange (`www.sophos.com`)

- Microsoft Forefront Security for Exchange (`www.microsoft.com`)

If you have purchased Exchange Server Enterprise Client Access Licenses and you have a Microsoft Software Assurance agreement, this includes licenses to use Microsoft Forefront Security for Exchange Server, so the decision as to which software package to use may have already been made for you. However, if you are in the process of evaluating Exchange-aware antivirus software, here are points to consider:

- The software should use the Exchange antivirus APIs (AVAPI) when scanning the information store as well as scanning the messages in the message transport system.

- The software should use a different scanning engine technology and virus signature definitions than the client software on your perimeter network or client workstations uses.

- Consider software that uses more than one scanning engine technology and signature database.

- The software should be able to have updates scheduled at least once every hour. The updates should be applied automatically.

- In organizations with more than one Exchange server, look for software that can be centrally configured and managed.

- Consider software that can be configured with features such as file attachment blocking, customizable notification messages, and reporting features.

- The software should offer automatic mail database scanning, scheduled scanning, and manual scanning, as well as the ability to turn off automatic scanning altogether.

Blocking File Attachments

If you talk to any administrator that has ever survived a serious virus outbreak, you will hear about several common causes of the virus or worm outbreak:

- E-mail was not being scanned for viruses.

- Viruses were downloaded to a user's desktop via an external mail system such as Yahoo! or Hotmail.

- Virus signatures were out-of-date or not yet available.

- Virus payload came into the network via a file attachment type that was not being blocked.

I hope you are planning to remedy the first bullet point by ensuring that all e-mail content is scanned as it enters your organization. The second bullet point can best be remedied by ensuring that all clients on your network have adequate virus protection installed. Virus signatures being out-of-date or not yet available, as well as viruses arriving via attachments that were allowed (when they should not have been), are something you can do something about on the e-mail server. In this section, I want to review some potentially dangerous attachment types that you should consider blocking.

Table 25.2 shows a list of commonly suspected attachment types that many administrators block using their antivirus software.

TABLE 25.2: Common Attachment Types That Might Be Dangerous

ATTACHMENT TYPES	ATTACHMENT DESCRIPTION
BAT	DOS/Windows batch file
CMD	Windows command file
COM	DOS command file
EXE	Executable program
JS	JavaScript file
MSI	Windows installer file
PIF	Program information file for 16-bit application
SCR	Screensaver executable
SHS	Shell scrap objects
VB	VBScript file
VBS	VBScript file
WSC	Windows script component file

Everyone knows about script files and executables, but there are a lot of other ways that hostile content can make its way onto your network. A long time ago, Microsoft published a list of attachments called Level-1 attachments that could conceivably transport a program or a script that could then be executed by a user or, even worse, executed automatically when a user opened a message. Outlook 2000 Service Pack 3 and later as well as Outlook Web Access won't even allow a user to open or save these file types, but remember that not all users use these applications. Many administrators block Level-1 attachments so that they are stripped off of a message completely. The complete list of Microsoft Level-1 attachments is shown in Table 25.3.

TABLE 25.3: Microsoft Level-1 Attachment Types

ATTACHMENT TYPES	ATTACHMENT DESCRIPTION
ADE	Microsoft Access project extension
ADP	Microsoft Access project

TABLE 25.3: Microsoft Level-1 Attachment Types *(CONTINUED)*

ATTACHMENT TYPES	ATTACHMENT DESCRIPTION
APP	Microsoft Visual FoxPro application
ASP	Active server page
ASX	Windows media audio or video shortcut
BAS	Visual Basic class module or a BASIC program
BAT	DOS/Windows batch file
CER	Security certificate
CHM	Compiled HTML help file
CMD	Windows command files
COM	DOS command file
CPL	Control Panel extension
CRT	Security certificate
CSH	KornShell script file
EXE	Executable programs
FXP	Microsoft Visual FoxPro compiled program
HLP	Windows help file
HTA	HTML program
INF	Windows setup information file
INS	Internet naming service
ISP	Internet communication settings
JS	JavaScript
JS	JScript script file
JSE	JScript encoded script file
KSH	KornShell script file
LNK	Link or shortcut file
MDA	Microsoft Access add-in program

TABLE 25.3:   Microsoft Level-1 Attachment Types *(CONTINUED)*

ATTACHMENT TYPES	ATTACHMENT DESCRIPTION
MDB	Microsoft Access program
MDE	Microsoft Access MDE database
MDT	Microsoft Access workgroup
MDW	Microsoft Access workgroup
MDZ	Microsoft Access wizard program
MSC	Windows console definition
MSI	Windows installer files
MSI	Windows installer package
MSP	Windows installer patch
MST	Windows installer transform file
OPS	Office preferences file
PCD	Photo CD image
PIF	Program information file for 16-bit application
PIF	Shortcut to MS-DOS program
PRF	Microsoft Outlook profile setting
PRG	Microsoft Visual FoxPro program
PST	Microsoft Outlook Personal Folders file
REG	Registration entries
SCF	Windows Explorer command
SCR	Screensaver executables
SCT	Windows Script Component
SHB	Shell scrap object
SHS	Shell scrap object
TMP	Temporary file

TABLE 25.3:   Microsoft Level-1 Attachment Types *(CONTINUED)*

ATTACHMENT TYPES	ATTACHMENT DESCRIPTION
URL	Internet shortcut
VB	VBScript file
VBE	VBScript encoded script file
VBS	VBScript file
VBS	Visual Basic Script file
VSMACROS	Visual Studio.NET macro project file
VSS	Visio shapes and Visio stencils file
VST	Visio template file
VSW	Visio workspace
WS	Windows script file
WSC	Windows script component
WSF	Windows script file
WSH	Windows script host settings file

Implementing Multiple Layers of Protection

A particular virus may sneak into your e-mail system because a signature has not yet been released for it. You can help mitigate this risk by checking for updates to signatures hourly, but an antivirus software vendor might take anywhere from a few hours to a few days to release signatures after learning about a new threat.

The likelihood that you will catch all viruses with a single scanning engine is pretty good, but additional scanning engines and additional layers of scanning can be even more effective. Multiple layers of protection are always a good precaution. Let's look at a couple of different approaches for doing this. In our definition of multiple layers of e-mail protection, the following should always be implemented:

- E-mail should be scanned in at least two different places.

- Multiple scanning engines, signature databases, or scanning technologies should be implemented. Don't be afraid to use more than one vendor.

- Clients should always have antivirus software installed.

Figure 25.17 shows a network with three layers of protection. Inbound e-mail is directed to an SMTP-based antivirus system located in the organization's perimeter network. The organization's MX record directs inbound SMTP mail to the SMTP message hygiene system in the perimeter.

The system in the perimeter network could be an Exchange 2007 Edge Transport server or it could be a third-party software package or mail security appliance. In the perimeter, the messages are inspected for viruses (and possibly also spam) and then directed to the Hub Transport server.

FIGURE 25.17

An example of a multilayer message hygiene system

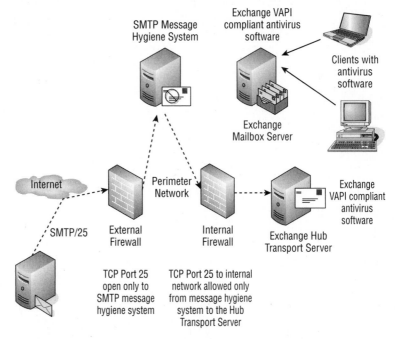

The Hub Transport server inspects the message "in transit" and then passes it on to the Exchange 2007 Mailbox server. The Mailbox server may optionally also have antivirus software that inspects the message for viruses, though both database level and message transport level scanning is probably not necessary in the case of Exchange 2007. This is because all messages are sent through the Hub Transport server.

Clients can then download and view the message, where it may be inspected once again for a virus. In an ideal world, a different scanning engine would be used each step of the way. So the system in the perimeter network would use the vendor's scanning engine, the Hub Transport (and/or the Mailbox) server would use a different solution, and the clients would use a third vendor's solution. Some SMTP scanning systems and Exchange-aware solutions (such as Forefront Security for Exchange) already incorporate multiple scanning engines.

This approach may seem like overkill to some organizations, but it offers a few advantages:

◆ Hostile content can be blocked in the perimeter.

◆ There is an increased probability of detecting hostile content with multiple scanning engines.

◆ Corporate or security policies can be enforced at the perimeter by blocking undesirable file types (including multimedia files and compressed files).

◆ Internet IP addresses do not have direct access via SMTP to the Exchange Hub Transport system. The only SMTP system that can deliver e-mail to Exchange is the system in the perimeter network.

Of course, you have to weigh these advantages with the added complexity of managing more than one antivirus product. Another possible approach with many of the same advantages is to use a third-party managed provider to handle the initial message hygiene inspection.

Figure 25.18 shows how this might work. The organization's DNS MX records are configured to point to the managed provider's SMTP servers, not its own. The managed provider handles the initial message hygiene functions and then forwards the mail to the public IP address of the organization's Hub Transport servers. Then the internal virus scanning software can provide an additional layer of protection.

FIGURE 25.18
Using a third-party message hygiene solution

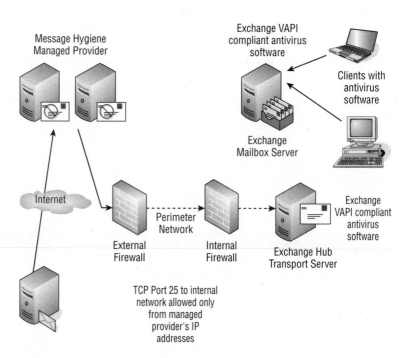

There are a few additional advantages to using a managed provider to provide this initial layer of protection besides just replacing software that you would have to manage:

◆ Managed providers are usually staffed 24×7×365 and can react very quickly to emerging threats.

◆ Managed providers usually use multiple scanning engines for both virus protection and spam detection.

◆ Both malware and spam can be blocked before it ever even reaches your network connection, thus eliminating a burden on your own Internet links.

◆ Your firewall can be configured to accept inbound SMTP only from the managed provider's IP addresses and thus provide better protection for your Hub Transport servers.

If you purchased Exchange 2007 Enterprise Client Access Licenses and you have a Software Assurance agreement with Microsoft, this includes the ability to use Microsoft's Hosted Exchange Filtering service at no additional cost.

Using a Reverse Proxy to Protect Web Services

A lot of organizations expose their Client Access servers directly to the Internet. If the server is properly hardened and security updates are applied as needed, this scenario will work. However, many organizations have policies that state that no internal web server can have Internet connections directed to it. These organizations will often try to locate the Client Access server role in the perimeter network, which is not recommended. Other organizations are just concerned with improving security wherever possible.

In the previous section, "Implementing a Message Hygiene System," I talked about preventing direct SMTP access to the Hub Transport role by using an SMTP relay located in the perimeter network. You can employ very similar protection by using a reverse proxy.

Figure 25.19 shows an organization that has implemented a reverse proxy in its perimeter network. A reverse proxy is similar to a regular proxy server. Inbound HTTPS is directed to the reverse proxy server instead of the Client Access server. Depending on the type of reverse proxy server, some additional security steps may be taken. The reverse proxy server then places the HTTP data back on the network (either as HTTP or as HTTPS) and sends it on to the Client Access server. The internal firewall is configured so that the HTTPS data will be passed through the internal firewall only if it is sent from the reverse proxy server.

FIGURE 25.19
Implementing a reverse proxy in the perimeter network

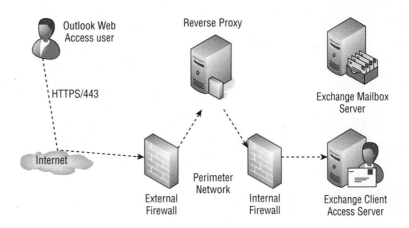

The Client Access server will accept the request, process it, and send the response back to the reverse proxy server. The reverse proxy server then sends the requested data back to the originating client. Depending on the reverse proxy server you are using, you may have some additional security benefits associated with using this solution:

◆ Improved security for all web services, including Outlook Web Access, ActiveSync, Outlook Anywhere, Autodiscover, Availability, and others.

◆ Validation of URL path. The reverse proxy server sends to the Client Access server only those URL paths that are allowed and/or valid.

◆ URLs examined for invalid HTTP requests such as directory traversal attacks or buffer overflow attacks.

◆ Authentication offloaded so that the reverse proxy authenticates the client before ever allowing the client to connect to the Client Access server.

◆ The overhead of SSL offloaded so that the reverse proxy rather than the Client Access server handles SSL encryption and decryption.

A number of different reverse proxy solutions are available that can help you improve the security of your published web applications. Microsoft's ISA Server (www.microsoft.com/isa), Blue Coat SG Appliances (www.bluecoat.com), and Squid Web Proxy (www.squid-cache.org) for Linux are just a few examples.

The example in Figure 25.19 shows one possible configuration that will work with most any reverse proxy solution. However, Microsoft ISA Server can also act as a complete firewall solution. Some organizations deploy ISA Server as their only firewall or use it as an internal firewall. Figure 25.20 shows a configuration where ISA Server is acting as an internal firewall; in this configuration it can also act as a reverse proxy.

FIGURE 25.20
Using ISA Server as an internal firewall and reverse proxy

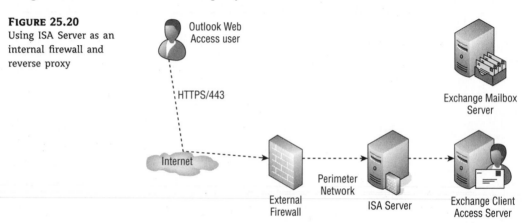

If you are using Microsoft ISA Server, the menus and wizards do not refer to this as a reverse proxy feature but rather as *mail-server publishing*.

Summary

Any Exchange server that either receives e-mail from the Internet or is accessed by remote clients should be deployed with security in mind. The first and most critical step involved in securing an Exchange server is to ensure that the operating system and Exchange server software have recent security fixes and updates.

The Security Configuration Wizard can also be used to further harden an Exchange server by restricting the services that are running on the server as well as customizing the security settings in the Registry and the Windows firewall.

For Internet clients such as Outlook Web Access and Outlook Anywhere, implementing Secure Sockets Layer (SSL) ensures that data and authentication credentials transmitted over the network cannot be intercepted by someone using a protocol analyzer tool.

Protecting your users' mailboxes from malware (viruses, worms, Trojan horses) is the function of your message hygiene system. The Exchange server should be protected by Exchange Server-aware software. Implementing multiple layers of protection such as requiring that all clients have antivirus software and that inbound e-mail is first scanned in the perimeter network can help to ensure the security of the message transport system as well as prevent unwanted content from reaching a user's mailbox.

Finally, additional security can be provided for Client Access servers by putting a reverse proxy system between the users and the Client Access server. The reverse proxy intercepts inbound HTTPS requests and inspects them before passing them on to internal Client Access servers. The reverse proxy can also implement additional security measures.

Chapter 26

Logging, Auditing, and Monitoring

On a day-to-day basis, Exchange Server does not require a lot of direct attention. Once it's set up and configured properly, the server itself can pretty much just sit on a corner of your computer room and run. For the most part, you really just need to leave the server alone. You don't need to regularly reboot the server. You don't need to be performing maintenance on the databases. Very few day-to-day tasks require direct management on the Exchange server.

So what should you be doing? Most everything that I recommend really falls into the "monitoring" category rather than the "direct action" category. Once you have been managing an Exchange organization for a while, I think you will agree that the most critical tasks are simply related to watching Exchange and making sure it continues to perform as you expect and within the boundaries that you have set.

You need to define the expected behavior of your Exchange Server system. These definitions, such as the amount of disk space you are consuming (or expect to be consuming), will need to change over time. Also, over time you may expect the CPU load or memory usage to increase as usage on the Exchange server increases. Understanding how these things are changing is an important part of your monitoring task.

In this chapter you learn to:

- ◆ Perform daily and weekly recommended maintenance
- ◆ Use the Exchange Best Practices Analyzer
- ◆ Handle auditing and logging tasks
- ◆ Track messages
- ◆ Monitor performance
- ◆ Remove content from users' mailboxes

Daily and Weekly Tasks

In the introduction to this chapter, I said that, with Exchange Server, your most important duty is to leave it alone. This brings us to the big question: What *do* you need to do to an Exchange server? This section discusses the five tasks you need to perform, and, best of all, describes a number of tasks that you *don't* need to perform.

The Big Five

There are only five *daily* tasks you need to perform on your Exchange Server. I call these *the big five*. The five most important daily management tasks for Exchange Server are as follows:

◆ Perform and verify daily backups of Exchange data.

◆ Check available disk space.

◆ Confirm that the message hygiene system (antivirus and anti-spam) is running and has up-to-date signatures.

◆ Review the event logs for errors and warnings.

◆ Check the message queues for stalled messages.

Did you notice something about this list? There is really nothing that you are *doing* directly to the Exchange server except running daily backups. Everything else falls into the *monitoring* category.

Unnecessary Tasks

In 11 years of Exchange consulting, I have seen Exchange administrators cook up a lot of tasks that are really unnecessary. In their defense, many of these tasks may have been useful or even contributed to the improved availability of Exchange Server when performed on earlier versions of Exchange. However, with each new version of Exchange, you need to evaluate whether the tasks you routinely performed are still necessary. The following are some tasks that are probably not necessary in your environment.

Offline maintenance and defragmenting databases I commonly find administrators scheduling downtime to perform offline information store integrity checks (using the ISINTEG.EXE utility) and offline compaction/defragmentation (using the ESEUTIL.EXE utility). These tasks are never necessary on an ongoing basis. You only need to run these utilities as part of maintenance if you have recently deleted or moved a large number of mailboxes off the server or you have recently archived or deleted a large amount of mail. These tools are intended for use when repairing a corrupted database.

Reboots Frequent reboots of a Windows 2003 or Windows 2008 server running Exchange Server 2007 should not be necessary. Thanks to a larger addressable memory space, Exchange Server 2007 does not have the memory fragmentation problems that earlier versions had. You should only need to reboot your server when applying critical updates and service packs every few months. If you have a problem with an application that is requiring frequent reboots (more than once every month or two), you should be working with Microsoft or the software vendor to find out why, because this is not normal.

Unnecessary software updates It is sure tempting to go into the Windows Update or Microsoft Update client on a monthly basis and apply every possible update that is available. Some of these updates will be relevant to your environment and possibly necessary, but many of the monthly updates are targeted toward Windows Media Player, Internet Explorer, or fixes relevant to end users' computers. Evaluate each fix and determine if it is necessary for your particular server. If the fix is not required, don't apply it.

Moving databases and logs One administrator that I worked with insisted on moving the Exchange databases and transaction logs to different disk volumes every four months. His logic was that the disks become fragmented and hurt read and write performance. In fact, if the databases are on their own logical volume and the transaction logs are on a separate volume, then disk fragmentation will not be much of an issue.

For servers with lots of databases or servers on which you use Volume Shadow Copy or snapshot software, isolate each database to its own volume or logical unit (LUN).

Spyware and scheduled antivirus scans Are spyware and file-based antivirus software really necessary on a production server? After all, you should not be web surfing or loading new or untested software on your production servers. But, in the real world, accidents do happen. Many administrators don't like installing file-based antivirus scanning software on their Exchange servers. Others do and schedule file system scans to run sometimes two or three times per day. As long as the file-system scanner is configured properly (so that it ignores the Exchange database files, logs, and queues), I have no objection. However, I recommend scheduled scans only once per week to avoid consuming too many server resources.

Running the Exchange Best Practices Analyzer

The Exchange team has developed an excellent tool for helping you to find potential problems and check to see if you are following best practices in your Exchange environment. This tool is called the Exchange Best Practices Analyzer, or just the ExBPA; I mentioned this tool in Chapter 24, "Monitoring Performance," but it deserves another mention here. Originally, the ExBPA tool was a separate tool that you downloaded from Microsoft and then ran on your system. The ExBPA now comes as part of the Exchange Server 2007 software. You can find the ExBPA tool in the Exchange Management Console (EMC) Toolbox work center (see Figure 26.1).

FIGURE 26.1
Exchange Server 2007 Toolbox work center

The Exchange 2007 ExBPA has been completely rewritten to take advantage of the new Windows PowerShell and the Exchange Management Shell extensions to PowerShell.

Exchange programmers, support engineers, consultants, and other specialists have all collaborated on what is the best possible configuration for Exchange Server in different environments. From this collaboration, a consensus of the best configuration is developed and added to the ExBPA database. As new best practices are developed, the database is updated. The ExBPA downloads the latest "best practices" definitions from Microsoft so that each time you run it you are using the most up-to-date information possible.

The ExBPA uses these recommendations and best practices in its database to gather performance and configuration data about your Exchange organization, perform specific tests in your environment, and make recommendations about what might need to be changed.

QUARTERLY BEST PRACTICES ANALYSIS RECOMMENDED

The ExBPA is not a "once-a-week" or even "once-a-month" tool, but you should consider running it about once per quarter. If you are not yet running Exchange Server 2007, you can download the latest tool from www.exbpa.com.

A Sample Best Practices Run

Let's start with an example of what a typical ExBPA run looks like. You can either run the Best Practices Analyzer link in the Toolbox work center or you can run it manually: C:\Program Files\Microsoft\Exchange Server\Bin\exbpa.exe. Anytime you start the ExBPA, it will check to see if there are any updates to the ExBPA database. You can also check for updates once you have launched the ExBPA. Naturally, this requires Internet access.

Checking for Updates...

Please wait while we check for updates.

████████████████████████████ ———— 70%

Estimated time to complete: 0 minutes, 16 seconds

Once the ExBPA is updated, the next step is to go to the Welcome screen (by clicking the Go To Welcome Screen link). Because you are running a new ExBPA scan, choose the Select Options For A New Scan option on the Welcome screen. You will then see the Connect To Active Directory page (shown in Figure 26.2). Figure 26.2 shows this page along with its advanced login options. From this page, you specify the name of the domain controller that you will use for discovery of Exchange- and Active Directory–related information. As long as you are logged on as a user account that is both an Exchange and Active Directory administrator, you do not need to use the advanced login options.

The Connect To Active Directory page also allows you to provide alternate credentials for accessing Active Directory and Exchange. In many organizations, the administrative account will have all of the permissions necessary to perform the scan, but in other organizations the administration roles between Exchange Server and Active Directory are separated.

In order to successfully run the ExBPA against Active Directory, the user account you are using must be a member of each global catalog server's local Administrators group. The ExBPA must confirm configuration values on the global catalogs and therefore will need to connect as an administrator.

For each Exchange server, the account that the ExBPA uses must be a member of that server's local Administrators group and it must have at least View Only administrator permissions to the Exchange organization.

As long as the account you are using has the necessary permissions, you can just click the Connect To The Active Directory link to continue.

Connect to Active Directory

The Exchange Best Practices Analyzer must have read access to Active Directory. By default the tool will use the currently logged-on account, and will automatically find and connect to a suitable global catalog server. The account that you are logged on with will also need administrator or equivalent access to each Exchange server.

If you are running the Exchange Best Practices Analyzer in a different domain or want to specify a different global catalog server for the tool to connect to, enter the fully qualified domain name (FQDN) of the global catalog server here:

Active Directory Server: `HNLDC01`

To run the Exchange Best Practices Analyzer under different accounts, click "Show advanced login options."

⌄ Hide advanced login options

☑ For Active Directory server access, please specify an account for the Exchange Best Practices Analyzer to run under. The account should have computer-level administrator or equivalent permissions to each global catalog server.

User name: `DomainAdmin01`
Password: `•••••••••••`
Domain: `volcanosurfboards.com`

☑ For Exchange server access, please specify an account for the Exchange Best Practices Analyzer to run under. The account should have at least Exchange administrator View Only permissions at the organization level, and be a member of the built-in administrators group on each Exchange server.

User name: `ExchangeAdmin01`
Password: `•••••••••••`
Domain: `volcanosurfboards.com`

▷ Connect to the Active Directory server

The next page in the wizard is the Start A New Best Practices Scan page; this page is shown in Figure 26.3. The first thing to do is specify a descriptive name for this scan because you will probably want to refer back to it in the future. Next, in the Specify The Scope For This Scan box, select the Exchange servers that you want to run the scan against. Figure 26.3 shows a mixed Exchange 2003/Exchange 2007 organization, so you will scan against both of them.

Start a New Best Practices scan

Enter an identifying label for this scan: `15 December BPA Scan`

Specify the scope for this scan:

```
☐ ☑ 🖳 Volcano Surfboards
   ☐ ☑ 🌐 Exchange Administrative Group (FYDIB(
          ☑ 🖥 HNLEX04
          ☐ 🖥 HNLEX05
          ☑ 🖥 HNLSCR01
   ☐ ☑ 🌐 First Administrative Group
          ☑ 🖥 HNLEX01
```

Summary:
Scope is set to 3 server(s), 2 administration group(s), and the organization.

▷ Select all
▷ Unselect all

Select the type of scan to perform:

- ⦿ Health Check
- ○ Permission Check
- ○ Connectivity Test
- ○ Baseline
- ○ Exchange 2007 Readiness Check

Health Check options:
☐ Performance Baseline (2 hours)

Select the speed of the network to adjust estimated time value: `Fast LAN (100 mbps or more) ▼`

This scan will take approximately 6 minutes

▷ Start scanning
▷ Schedule a scan

The Select The Type Of Scan To Perform options allow you to specify what you want checked during this particular scan. The most common is the health check. Here is a list of the options available and what they perform:

EXBPA OPTION	FUNCTION
Health Check	The health check runs a complete scan against the selected servers to look for possible incorrect configuration settings, changes, warnings, and errors.
Permission Check	The permission check verifies that you have the Exchange, Active Directory, and Windows permissions necessary to run the scan you are about to run.
Connectivity Test	The connectivity test checks each of the selected servers and confirms that the permissions are valid to run the ExBPA and that the servers have the necessary connectivity (such as opened ports) between them to function. This test also verifies connectivity to the Active Directory.
Baseline	The baseline scan allows you to run a configuration scan against the selected servers to confirm that they are still configured the same as they were when you originally set baseline values.
Exchange 2007 Readiness Check	The readiness check validates that the Exchange organization is ready for Exchange 2007 to be installed.

If you select Health Check, you see a Health Check Options check box available for running a performance baseline. This runs for two hours and monitors common Exchange performance counters on the selected Exchange servers. The other scan options do not have additional options.

The LAN speed selection allows you to specify your estimated connectivity to the selected servers. This value is merely used to give you an estimate of how long the scan will take and does not affect any of the scan parameters.

Finally, you can click the Start Scanning link or the Schedule A Scan link. You might want to schedule the scan during off hours if you are concerned about network bandwidth or affecting your production environment.

In this example, you are going to run a health check immediately. Now comes the part that requires some patience. In the scan you are running, both servers are on the same LAN and will scan much more quickly than if one of them were on the other side of a WAN link. The progress bar will indicate the estimated time left in the scan, and you can also see which scans have completed and which are still pending. Figure 26.4 shows part of the progress screen and the status for two of the three servers that are being scanned.

FIGURE 26.4
Best Practices Analyzer scanning in progress

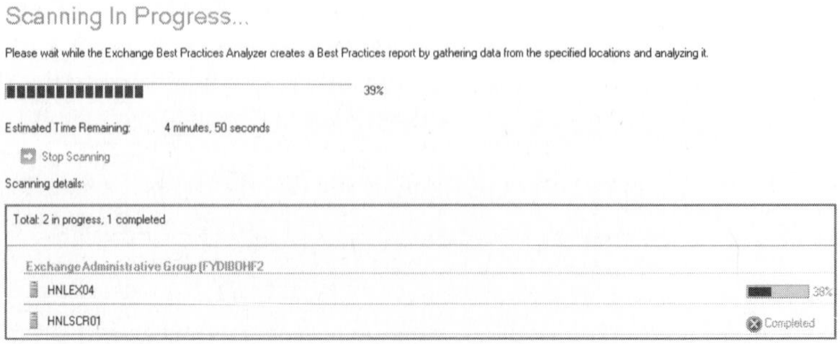

Scanning In Progress...

Please wait while the Exchange Best Practices Analyzer creates a Best Practices report by gathering data from the specified locations and analyzing it.

■■■■■■■■■■■■   39%

Estimated Time Remaining: 4 minutes, 50 seconds

Stop Scanning

Scanning details:

Total: 2 in progress, 1 completed

Exchange Administrative Group [FYDIBOHF2

HNLEX04   39%

HNLSCR01   Completed

In a larger environment, you will notice some servers completing before others. This is due not only to link speeds, but also to the servers' performance and Exchange roles. When the scan is complete, you'll see a "Scanning Completed" message and a View A Report Of This Best Practices Scan link.

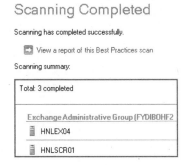

The real meat of the ExBPA is on the View Best Practices Report page. From here you can view the report as a tree view (based on category of listing) or you can view the report based on the ranking of the issues. The List Reports type offers several report property pages and options for viewing the report. The Critical Issues property page shows the things that the ExBPA thinks are the most important. Figure 26.5 shows the Critical Issues page of the list report. Notice that the report has two critical issues listed.

FIGURE 26.5
Viewing the critical issues

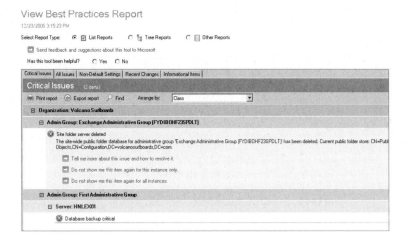

One of the critical issues listed is that one of the Exchange servers shown has not had a recent backup. The other issue reports that a site-wide public folder database has been deleted. As shown in Figure 26.5, if you click the link for an issue, you see more information about the problem.

When you choose to see additional information about a problem, as in Figure 26.5, you see three links. These links are the same for all issues:

Tell Me More About This Issue And How To Resolve It This link opens an external web browser window. The web browser is directed to a link at Microsoft that provides more information about the issue and how to resolve it (if necessary). The resolution to the site folder issue reported by the ExBPA is shown in Figure 26.6.

FIGURE 26.6

Getting advice on problem resolution from the Best Practices Analyzer

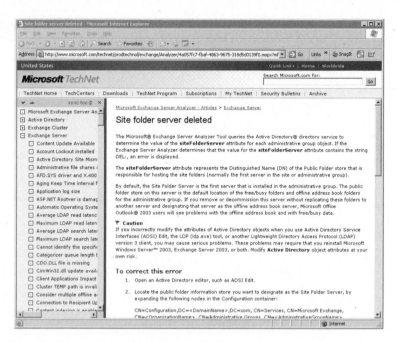

The Tell Me More links will give you excellent information about fine-tuning Exchange. Microsoft has done a good job of writing and presenting some in-depth technical information for Exchange, and I urge you to take advantage of this resource.

Do Not Show Me This Item Again For This Instance Only This link tells the ExBPA not to report this particular issue the next time it runs. This might be useful if you know that the configuration property or item that is being reported is not really relevant to your configuration.

Do Not Show Me This Item Again For All Instances This link tells the ExBPA that it should ignore this issue anytime it is reported for any server or administrative group.

You can expand this report and delve more deeply into the findings and recommendations of the ExBPA by selecting the All Issues tab on the View Best Practices Report page. Despite the fact that the tab is labeled All Issues, it does not contain "all the information" that the ExBPA has collected. All Issues lists anything that the ExBPA finds to be out of the ordinary, not a best practice, or things that are potentially a problem.

Figure 26.7 shows part of an All Issues page. This page has been arranged by the issue severity. You can still see the two critical issues at the top of the page. Below the critical issues are the warnings. Finally, below that are the recommendations based on best practices.

You can export the report to an HTML, CSV, or XML file. The report is also saved to your local user profile directory so you can view it again if you want to. You can find it in the \Application Data\Microsoft\ExBPA folder within your user profile.

If you had chosen to include a performance baseline when you started the scan, the Best Practices Report would include an additional tab called Baseline. A sample is shown in Figure 26.8. This part of the report includes the maximum and averaged values for some of the critical performance counters. When you first configure your Exchange server, you can run a performance baseline report and then periodically run the report again as you start adding mailboxes.

FIGURE 26.7
Viewing the Best Practices All Issues report

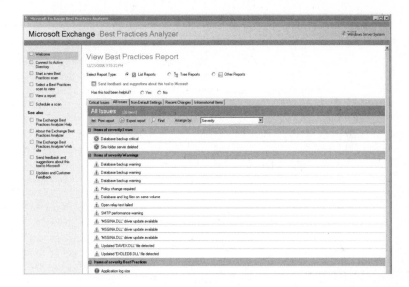

FIGURE 26.8
Including a performance baseline in the Best Practices report

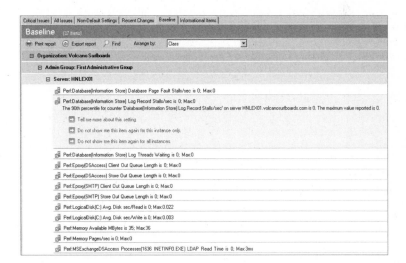

As you can in other parts of an ExBPA report, you can expand any of the items in the report to access links that allow you to see more about a particular setting or to exclude a setting from future reports.

Microsoft's Best Practices vs. Your Best Practices

A common misconception when using the ExBPA is that it is the Exchange team's magic wand. Some administrators believe that you can run it, follow its recommendations blindly, and enter Exchange nirvana. It's not quite that easy.

Although the ExBPA may *help* you on the road to Exchange nirvana, it is certainly not a magic wand. The ExBPA is using a database of best practices that were developed without knowledge of your specific environment. You cannot follow it blindly, and therefore you must review each recommendation and determine if it applies to your environment and how following it might affect your configuration. A recommendation that would dramatically help performance, recoverability, or stability for one environment might actually break something in another.

Look at the report run previously and shown in Figure 26.7. There are a couple of issues reported as warnings that might actually be required functions in your organization. For example, the Database And Log Files On Same Volume warning recommends that for best performance and reliability, the database files be on a separate volume. In general that is a very good recommendation, but if this server has a single RAID 1 or RAID 5 array and supports only 50 or 100 mailboxes, this would not be as critical an issue to resolve. Certainly 100 users would usually not overtax a well-configured server, even if all of the files are on the same disk volume.

Another example of a warning message that might not be relevant is Open Relay Test Failed. The ExBPA attempts to relay mail through each of the SMTP servers that it finds in the organization. This particular SMTP virtual server (on an Exchange 2003 server) is configured to allow relay for certain internal IP addresses only. The warning is worth looking into, but it does not mean that it is something that must be changed.

The ExBPA will report a number of other issues like this to you. It is your job as the Exchange server administrator to research each of them and decide if it is something that must be fixed or changed for your organization.

Auditing and Logging

Both Windows and Exchange Server present you with a lot of options for recording activity that occurs on an Exchange server. Some auditing and logging options are on by default, whereas others must be enabled manually. I will break these up into two broad categories. The first is Windows auditing, which reports on security- and operational-related events that affect the Windows operating system. The second is auditing and logs related to Exchange; I can further break down this category into audit events relating to security and operations and events relating to message transport.

KEEP A FEW WEEKS' WORTH OF LOGS

You never know when you are going to need historical information from logs. Plan to have a few weeks' worth when configuring logs and designing the capacity of your Exchange servers.

This section examines a number of different types of logging and auditing. I will often recommend that you turn on logging and auditing that is not turned on by default. My reasoning is that when you must start troubleshooting a problem or looking into a possible security issue, you will need these logs available to you.

However, keep in mind that each time you increase the amount of logging or auditing that a system is doing, you increase the system overhead (CPU, disk, and memory).

Windows Auditing

Windows auditing can be applied to each server by using the Local Security Policy Editor or by applying the settings centrally using a group policy object (GPO) via Active Directory. This example uses the Local Security Policy Editor. By default, Windows 2003 and Windows 2008 enable success auditing for some event logging categories, but I recommend enabling additional auditing of both success and failures.

When choosing to enable success, failure, or both types of auditing, there are two different philosophies at work. Those that recommend enabling mostly success auditing are usually interested in auditing things that actually happened or things that were successfully done by authorized users. This seems to be the mindset of the people who set the original Windows default auditing values.

Those that recommend enabling mostly failure auditing are usually interested in auditing things that were attempted but failed, such as logon failures or someone trying to run a program that they did not have permission to run.

If you are interested in auditing changes made to users or Exchange objects, you should also enable object access auditing. This auditing level must be enabled for domain controllers, though, because all changes to user objects and Exchange configuration objects are made to the Active Directory.

Finally, there is a third category of event logging, which can best be described as logging done by paranoid control freaks. That is the category into which I sometimes place myself. Not only do I want an audit history of successful events, I also want to be able to audit failures that might help me track down intrusion or unauthorized access attempts.

As you increase the amount of logging that you are doing on any server, you will increase the load that is placed on it. The larger the event logs grow, the more challenging it will become to gather any useful information from them. So keep this in mind. Security-minded organizations with more than a few servers and a few hundred users should consider investing in an event log management system that can collect and analyze event logs centrally.

INCREASING THE SIZE OF EVENT LOGS

If you plan on keeping more than a few hours' worth of information in your security and application logs, you will probably need to increase the overall size of the logs. The default event log file sizes are not sufficient for larger servers. You can configure the size of the event log using the Event Viewer (right-click each event log and select Properties from the pop-up menu). The application event log properties are shown in Figure 26.9. The size of the event log is set in the Maximum Log Size box and must be in multiples of 64KB.

Event log sizes and overwrite settings can be configured using Event Viewer on a server-by-server basis, as just described, or by using an Active Directory group policy object. If you have more than one or two servers, using a GPO is much simpler.

I recommend that you increase the size of your event logs on both your Exchange servers and your domain controllers. Table 26.1 shows the recommended event log sizes for Exchange servers and domain controllers

The recommended sizes shown in Table 26.1 are just estimates and you can tweak them in whatever direction you see necessary. However, for the best performance and accuracy with event logs, I recommend that the combined size of all event logs not exceed 300MB. Even better is to get some type of log archival system that archives Windows logs from all servers to a single point for analysis and review.

TABLE 26.1:   Recommended Maximum Event Log Sizes

EVENT LOG	EXCHANGE SERVER	DOMAIN CONTROLLER
Application	147,456KB	49,152KB
Security	49,152KB	147,456KB
System	49,152KB	49,152KB
PowerShell	16,384KB	N/A
Directory Service	N/A	16,384KB
File Replication Service	N/A	16,384KB
DNS Server	N/A	16,384KB

The Application Properties page (see Figure 26.9, below) includes a setting for controlling the behavior of event logging when the maximum log size is reached. The default is Overwrite Events As Needed. In a security-conscious environment, you may want to set this to either Overwrite Events Older Than 7 Days (you can change the number of days) or Do Not Overwrite Events (Clear Log Manually). If you set either of these two settings and the event log fills up before it is either cleared or the maximum number of days is reached, event logging will stop. That is considered a feature — it is designed to prevent an intruder or evildoer from covering their tracks by generating additional event logging and thus removing evidence of their evil deed.

FIGURE 26.9
Application event log properties

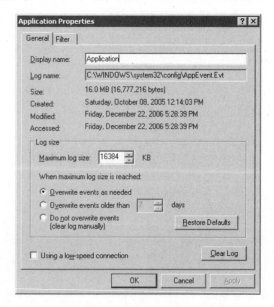

Defining an Audit Policy

Defining an auditing policy for a member server is really simple. Open the Local Security Policy management console program and drill down to the Local Policies ➢ Audit Policies container (shown in Figure 26.10).

FIGURE 26.10

Configuring events to be audited

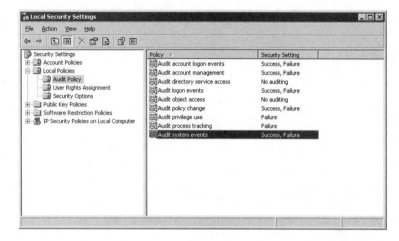

Table 26.2 shows the audit settings that I recommend enabling for a Windows 2003 machine that is functioning as a member server. Anything that is logged by these settings will be logged to the Security event log.

TABLE 26.2:   Auditing Levels for a Windows 2003 Member Server

POLICY	SETTINGS
Audit Account Logon Events	Success and Failure
Audit Account Management	Success and Failure
Audit Directory Service Access	No auditing
Audit Logon Events	Success and Failure
Audit Object Access	No auditing
Audit Policy Change	Success and Failure
Audit Privilege Use	Success and Failure
Audit Process Tracking	Failure
Audit System Events	Success and Failure

To select an audit level, double-click the policy to see the dialog box that allows you to select whether to audit the success or failure of events (Figure 26.11).

FIGURE 26.11
Choosing which
attempts to audit

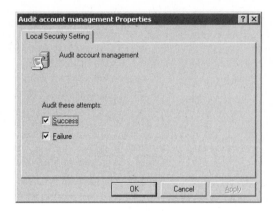

Exchange Diagnostics Logging

Exchange Server has a lot of possible categories for diagnostics logging and troubleshooting. Most of this report information is much more advanced and detailed than you typically need on a day-to-day basis when monitoring Exchange, but there are some diagnostics logging events that I recommend you enable. They help you to monitor some of the common events that you might need to be aware of for either security reasons or operational purposes. Figure 26.12 shows an example of one of these events; in this event you see that a user is logging in to his own mailbox.

FIGURE 26.12
An application event
indicating that a user
is logging in to his own
mailbox

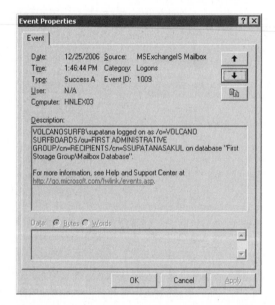

Exchange diagnostics logging information appears in the Application event log. Table 26.3 lists event log services and categories that you should consider enabling.

TABLE 26.3: Recommended Exchange Diagnostics Logging Categories

EVENT CATEGORY	DESCRIPTION
MSExchangeIS\9000 Private\Logons	Audit events relating to mailbox access
MSExchangeIS\9000 Private\Send As	Audit events relating to the use of the Send As permission
MSExchangeIS\9000 Private\Send On Behalf Of	Audit events relating to the use of the Send On Behalf Of permission
MSExchangeIS\9000 Private\Storage Limits	Audit events indicating that mailboxes are exceeding storage limits
MSExchangeIS\9002 System\Move Mailbox	Audit events indicating that a mailbox has been moved
MSExchangeIS\9002 System\Virus Scanning	Audit events relating to virus scanning
MSExchangeMailboxAssistants\ Email_Lifecyle_Assistants	Audit events relating to processing message records management settings
MSExchangeMailboxAssistants\Resource Booking Assistant	Audit events relating to the use of the resource booking assistant

If you are familiar with Exchange 2000/2003, you probably already know that diagnostics logging was set up using the Exchange System Manager. However, Exchange 2007 does not include a graphical user interface for managing diagnostics logging. These must be enabled using the Exchange Management Shell (EMS). Two EMS cmdlets are used to retrieve event logging levels and to set them. They are as follows:

| `Get-EventLogLevel` | Reports on the level of logging of the specified event category or all categories if no category is specified |
| `Set-EventLogLevel` | Configures the diagnostics logging level of the specified logging category |

If you use the `Get-EventLogLevel` cmdlet with no parameters, the output will show you all of the diagnostics logging levels relating to Exchange. Table 26.4 shows the Exchange Server 2007 event logging categories and the default level for each category; I used the `Get-EventLogLevel` cmdlet to generate this list.

TABLE 26.4: Exchange Server 2007 Event Logging Categories

LOGGING CATEGORY	DEFAULT LEVEL
MSExchange ActiveSync\Requests	Lowest
MSExchange ActiveSync\Configuration	Lowest
MSExchange Antispam\General	Lowest
MSExchange Autodiscover\Core	Lowest
MSExchange Autodiscover\Web	Lowest
MSExchange Autodiscover\Provider	Lowest
MSExchange Availability\Availability Service	Lowest
MSExchange Availability\Availability Service General	Lowest
MSExchange Availability\Availability Service Authentication	Lowest
MSExchange Availability\Availability Service Authorization	Lowest
MSExchange Cluster\Move	Lowest
MSExchange Cluster\Upgrade	Lowest
MSExchange Cluster\Action	Lowest
MSExchange Common\General	Lowest
MSExchange Common\Configuration	Lowest
MSExchange Common\Logging	Lowest
MSExchange Extensibility\Transport Address Book	Lowest
MSExchange Extensibility\MExRuntime	Lowest
MSExchange EdgeSync\Synchronization	Lowest
MSExchange EdgeSync\Topology	Lowest
MSExchange EdgeSync\SyncNow	Lowest
MSExchange TransportService\TransportService	Lowest
MSExchange Web Services\Core	Lowest
MSExchange IMAP4\General	Lowest
MSExchange Messaging Policies\Journaling	Lowest

TABLE 26.4:   Exchange Server 2007 Event Logging Categories *(CONTINUED)*

LOGGING CATEGORY	DEFAULT LEVEL
MSExchange Messaging Policies\AttachFilter	Lowest
MSExchange Messaging Policies\AddressRewrite	Lowest
MSExchange Messaging Policies\Rules	Lowest
MSExchange Messaging Policies\Prelicensing	Lowest
MSExchange Anti-spam Update\HygieneUpdate	Lowest
MSExchange Management Application\Shell	Lowest
MSExchange Management Application\Console	Lowest
MSExchange OWA\FormsRegistry	Lowest
MSExchange OWA\Core	Lowest
MSExchange OWA\Configuration	Lowest
MSExchange OWA\Themes	Lowest
MSExchange OWA\SmallIcons	Lowest
MSExchange OWA\Proxy	Lowest
MSExchange OWA\Transcoding	Lowest
MSExchange OWA\ADNotifications	Lowest
MSExchange POP3\General	Lowest
MSExchange Process Manager\ProcessManager	Lowest
MSExchange Repl\Service	Lowest
MSExchange Repl\Exchange VSS Writer	Lowest
MSExchange System Attendant Mailbox\General	Lowest
MSExchange ADAccess\General	Lowest
MSExchange ADAccess\Cache	Lowest
MSExchange ADAccess\Topology	Low
MSExchange ADAccess\Configuration	Lowest

TABLE 26.4: Exchange Server 2007 Event Logging Categories *(CONTINUED)*

LOGGING CATEGORY	DEFAULT LEVEL
MSExchange ADAccess\LDAP	Lowest
MSExchange ADAccess\Validation	Low
MSExchange ADAccess\Recipient Update Service	Lowest
MSExchange ADAccess\Site Update	Lowest
MSExchangeAL\Ldap Operations	Lowest
MSExchangeAL\Service Control	Lowest
MSExchangeAL\Attribute Mapping	Lowest
MSExchangeAL\Account Management	Lowest
MSExchangeAL\Address List Synchronization	Lowest
MSExchangeIS\9000 Private\Transport General	Lowest
MSExchangeIS\9000 Private\General	Lowest
MSExchangeIS\9000 Private\Transport Sending	Lowest
MSExchangeIS\9000 Private\Transport Delivering	Lowest
MSExchangeIS\9000 Private\Transfer Into Gateway	Lowest
MSExchangeIS\9000 Private\Transfer Out Of Gateway	Lowest
MSExchangeIS\9000 Private\MTA Connections	Lowest
MSExchangeIS\9000 Private\Logons	Low
MSExchangeIS\9000 Private\Access Control	Lowest
MSExchangeIS\9000 Private\Send On Behalf Of	Lowest
MSExchangeIS\9000 Private\Send As	Lowest
MSExchangeIS\9000 Private\Rules	Lowest
MSExchangeIS\9000 Private\Storage Limits	Lowest
MSExchangeIS\9000 Private\Background Cleanup	Lowest
MSExchangeIS\9000 Private\DS Synchronization	Lowest
MSExchangeIS\9000 Private\Views	Lowest

TABLE 26.4:   Exchange Server 2007 Event Logging Categories *(CONTINUED)*

LOGGING CATEGORY	DEFAULT LEVEL
MSExchangeIS\9000 Private\Download	Lowest
MSExchangeIS\9000 Private\Local Replication	Lowest
MSExchangeIS\9001 Public\Transport General	Lowest
MSExchangeIS\9001 Public\General	Lowest
MSExchangeIS\9001 Public\Replication DS Updates	Lowest
MSExchangeIS\9001 Public\Replication Incoming Messages	Lowest
MSExchangeIS\9001 Public\Replication Outgoing Messages	Lowest
MSExchangeIS\9001 Public\Replication NDRs	Lowest
MSExchangeIS\9001 Public\Transport Sending	Lowest
MSExchangeIS\9001 Public\Transport Delivering	Lowest
MSExchangeIS\9001 Public\MTA Connections	Lowest
MSExchangeIS\9001 Public\Logons	Lowest
MSExchangeIS\9001 Public\Access Control	Lowest
MSExchangeIS\9001 Public\Send On Behalf Of	Lowest
MSExchangeIS\9001 Public\Send As	Lowest
MSExchangeIS\9001 Public\Rules	Lowest
MSExchangeIS\9001 Public\Storage Limits	Lowest
MSExchangeIS\9001 Public\Replication Site Folders	Lowest
MSExchangeIS\9001 Public\Replication Expiry	Lowest
MSExchangeIS\9001 Public\Replication Conflicts	Lowest
MSExchangeIS\9001 Public\Replication Backfill	Lowest
MSExchangeIS\9001 Public\Background Cleanup	Lowest
MSExchangeIS\9001 Public\Replication Errors	Lowest
MSExchangeIS\9001 Public\DS Synchronization	Lowest

TABLE 26.4: Exchange Server 2007 Event Logging Categories *(CONTINUED)*

LOGGING CATEGORY	DEFAULT LEVEL
MSExchangeIS\9001 Public\Views	Lowest
MSExchangeIS\9001 Public\Replication General	Lowest
MSExchangeIS\9001 Public\Download	Lowest
MSExchangeIS\9001 Public\Local Replication	Lowest
MSExchangeIS\9002 System\Recovery	Lowest
MSExchangeIS\9002 System\General	Lowest
MSExchangeIS\9002 System\Connections	Lowest
MSExchangeIS\9002 System\Table Cache	Lowest
MSExchangeIS\9002 System\Content Engine	Lowest
MSExchangeIS\9002 System\Performance Monitor	Lowest
MSExchangeIS\9002 System\Move Mailbox	Lowest
MSExchangeIS\9002 System\Download	Lowest
MSExchangeIS\9002 System\Virus Scanning	Lowest
MSExchangeIS\9002 System\Exchange Writer	Lowest
MSExchangeIS\9002 System\Backup Restore	Lowest
MSExchangeIS\9002 System\Client Monitoring	Lowest
MSExchangeIS\9002 System\Event History	Lowest
MSExchangeIS\9002 System\Database Storage Engine	Lowest
MSExchangeMailboxAssistants\Service	Lowest
MSExchangeMailboxAssistants\OOF Assistant	Lowest
MSExchangeMailboxAssistants\OOF Library	Lowest
MSExchangeMailboxAssistants\Resource Booking Attendant	Lowest
MSExchangeMailboxAssistants\Email_Lifecycle_Assistant	Low
MSExchangeMailSubmission\General	Lowest
MSExchangeMU\General	Lowest

TABLE 26.4:   Exchange Server 2007 Event Logging Categories *(CONTINUED)*

LOGGING CATEGORY	DEFAULT LEVEL
MSExchangeSA\Clean Mailbox	Lowest
MSExchangeSA\NSPI Proxy	Lowest
MSExchangeSA\RFR Interface	Lowest
MSExchangeSA\OAL Generator	Lowest
MSExchangeSA\Proxy Generation	Lowest
MSExchangeSA\RPC Calls	Lowest
MSExchangeSA\RPC-HTTP Management	Lowest
MSExchangeTransport\SmtpReceive	Lowest
MSExchangeTransport\SmtpSend	Lowest
MSExchangeTransport\DSN	Lowest
MSExchangeTransport\Routing	Lowest
MSExchangeTransport\Logging	Lowest
MSExchangeTransport\Components	Lowest
MSExchangeTransport\RemoteDelivery	Lowest
MSExchangeTransport\Pickup	Lowest
MSExchangeTransport\Categorizer	Lowest
MSExchangeTransport\PoisonMessage	Lowest
MSExchangeTransport\MessageSecurity	Lowest
MSExchangeTransport\TransportService	Lowest
MSExchangeTransport\Exch50	Lowest
MSExchangeTransport\Process	Lowest
MSExchangeTransport\ResourceManager	Lowest
MSExchangeTransport\Configuration	Lowest
MSExchangeTransport\Storage	Lowest
MSExchangeTransport\Agents	Lowest
MSExchangeFDS\General	Lowest
MSExchangeFDS\FileReplication	Lowest

Each diagnostics logging category can be set to one of five levels. Each of the levels will log progressively more information. The levels are as follows:

Lowest (0)
: Lowest is the default level for most categories of Exchange diagnostics logging. When a category is set at this level, you will only see the default information. Depending on the category, that may be no events at all, some informational events, warnings, or only errors.

Low (1)
: Low-level logging reports generic warnings and errors but does not report a significant amount of detail. You should always start logging at the Low level.

Medium (3)
: Medium-level logging reports slightly more detailed information than Low logging.

High (5)
: High-level logging reports detailed support information.

Expert (7)
: Expert-level logging reports information that is usually useful only to Microsoft Customer Support Services. Not all components or programs will report additional information if you set the logging level to Expert.

Any type of ongoing logging should be set to Low; Low is equivalent to minimum logging in Exchange Server 2000/2003. Increase logging levels only if the Low level does not provide you with the information you require to monitor a component or troubleshoot a problem. The level of information you get depends entirely on how much logging the program or component that you are monitoring was designed to report. When you are finished logging a particular category, return the level to Lowest; this reduces overhead on the server.

To adjust the logging level for a particular component (such as information store logons), you use the EMS. Here is an example that would work if you were on the console of the Exchange server in question:

```
Set-EventLogLevel "MSExchangeIS\9000 Private\Logons" -Level Low
```

You can also include the server name as part of the service or component that you are logging such, as this example:

```
Set-EventLogLevel "HNLEX03\MSExchangeIS\9000 Private\Logons" -Level Low
```

Using Message Tracking

All versions of Exchange have had a message tracking facility and Exchange 2007 is no exception. The message tracking features have been nicely expanded in Exchange 2007 and give you access to more details of the message tracking log from the graphical user interface as well as the EMS.

If you have not used the message tracking facility before, you are missing out on a powerful diagnostics tool. When message tracking is enabled, each Exchange component that processes or moves a message within an Exchange organization logs an event that will include information about that message to the current server's message tracking logs.

Information is logged about message submission (SUBMIT), message transmission (SEND), message receipt (RECEIVE), distribution list expansion (EXPAND), and local delivery (DELIVER). From these events, you can track the progress of a message as it moves within your organization.

You can track the progress of a message right up until the point that it leaves your organization, but you cannot track it once it is outside of your organization.

Introducing Message Tracking Logs

Let's first talk about the message tracking logs themselves. Administrators of earlier versions of Exchange will recall that they had to enable message tracking for each server in their organization. In Exchange 2007, message tracking is configured for each Hub Transport server (because that is the server role that actually moves messages around). Message tracking is enabled by default and messages are retained for a maximum of 30 days. You can retrieve information about the message tracking log configuration for each server using the EMS cmdlet `Get-TransportServer`. The following is an example of retrieving the properties relating to message tracking for server HNLEX04. There are quite a few more properties for the Hub Transport server, but we are just interested in those relating to message tracking:

```
Get-TransportServer "HNLEX04" | fl name,*track*
Name                                   : HNLEX03
MessageTrackingLogEnabled              : True
MessageTrackingLogMaxAge               : 30.00:00:00
MessageTrackingLogMaxDirectorySize     : 250MB
MessageTrackingLogMaxFileSize          : 10MB
MessageTrackingLogPath                 : C:\Program Files\Microsoft\
Exchange Server\TransportRoles\Logs\MessageTracking
MessageTrackingLogSubjectLoggingEnabled : True
```

The output of `Get-TransportServer` contains a couple of important pieces of information. Most important is that it is enabled (`MessageTrackingLogEnabled = True`) by default and that the message tracking logs include subject logging (`MessageTrackingLogSubjectLoggingEnabled = True`), but also the following is true:

◆ Message tracking logs are found in the `C:\Program Files\Microsoft\Exchange Server\TransportRoles\Logs\MessageTracking` folder.

◆ Message tracking logs are retained for 30 days. After 30 days they are automatically deleted.

◆ The maximum size of a message tracking log is 10MB.

◆ The maximum amount of space the message tracking logs can consume is 250MB.

For servers with fewer than 500 average users, this is probably sufficient. However, for servers supporting larger numbers of users, you will want to increase the maximum log file size and the maximum amount of space the logs can consume. These can all be changed using the `Set-TransportServer` cmdlet. The following cmdlet will change the maximum log file size to 25MB, change the maximum directory size to 500MB, and change the tracking log folder to `C:\TrackingLogs`:

```
Set-TransportServer "hnlex03" -MessageTrackingLogPath "C:\TrackingLogs"↵
   -MessageTrackingLogMaxFileSize:25MB -MessageTrackingLogMaxDirectorySize:500MB
```

Once you have executed this command, Exchange should automatically start using the new tracking log folder. However, the existing files will not be moved.

DISK PERFORMANCE AND HUB TRANSPORT LOGGING

If your organization is generating thousands of messages per hour, this is placing a larger burden on your Hub Transport servers. Remember that each message sent or received passes through the Hub Transport server and that server's `mail.que` database file.

Though message tracking and protocol logs can be very useful for troubleshooting and analysis, enabling logging also increases the I/O load placed on the disk. For servers that process more than about two thousand messages per hour, put the `mail.que` database on one physical disk and place the log files on a different physical disk drive.

The two thousand messages per hour number is merely an estimate, though, as fewer, but larger-than-average messages per hour may also require disk segmentation.

If you want to implement these settings for all Hub Transport servers, you can use the `Get-TransportServer` and `Set-TransportServer` cmdlets in the same command. The following command will set these settings for all transport servers:

```
Get-TransportServer | Set-TransportServer -MessageTrackingLogPath
"C:\TrackingLogs"↵
-MessageTrackingLogMaxFileSize:25MB -MessageTrackingLogMaxDirectorySize:500MB
```

Tracking a Message

Let's look at the actual message tracking feature. The graphical interface for the message tracking facility is part of the new Exchange Troubleshooting Assistant.

You run the Message Tracking tool from the Toolbox work center of the Exchange Management Console. The Message Tracking portion of the Exchange Troubleshooting Assistant is wizard driven. The first screen in the wizard is the Message Tracking Parameters screen, where you can narrow down the criteria of the message for which you are searching (see Figure 26.13).

FIGURE 26.13
Specifying the criteria for a particular message

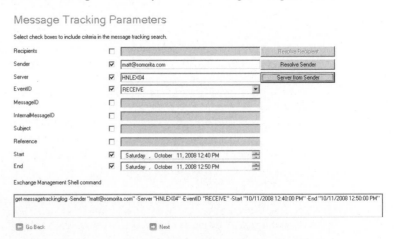

Criteria for searching for a message include the sender, recipient, message ID, and subject. You can narrow the focus of the type of message using the EventID field, which allows you to designate the type of event you are looking for, such as Send, Receive, Submit, Transfer, Expand, DSN, and so on. Finally, you can narrow the focus even further by looking for messages sent only during a specific date and time range.

Once you have specified the criteria you want to use to search for a specific message, click Next and the wizard will find the messages that meet those criteria. Depending on the size of the message tracking logs and the number of servers that the messages will cross, the results might take a minute or two to generate. In a single-server environment, results are generated pretty quickly. A sample output is shown in Figure 26.14 showing the messages that fit the criteria submitted in Figure 26.13.

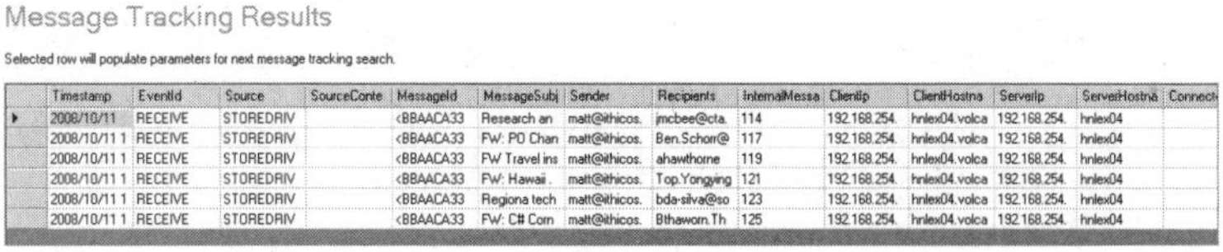

FIGURE 26.14

Viewing the message tracking results

Message Tracking Results

Selected row will populate parameters for next message tracking search.

Timestamp	EventId	Source	SourceConte	MessageId	MessageSubj	Sender	Recipients	InternalMessa	ClientIp	ClientHostna	ServerIp	ServerHostna	Connect
2008/10/11	RECEIVE	STOREDRIV		<BBAACA33	Research an	matt@ithicos.	jmcbee@cta.	114	192.168.254.	hnlex04.volca	192.168.254.	hnlex04	
2008/10/11 1	RECEIVE	STOREDRIV		<BBAACA33	FW: PO Chan	matt@ithicos.	Ben.Schorr@	117	192.168.254.	hnlex04.volca	192.168.254.	hnlex04	
2008/10/11 1	RECEIVE	STOREDRIV		<BBAACA33	FW: Travel ins	matt@ithicos.	ahawthorne	119	192.168.254.	hnlex04.volca	192.168.254.	hnlex04	
2008/10/11 1	RECEIVE	STOREDRIV		<BBAACA33	FW: Hawaii	matt@ithicos.	Top.Yongying	121	192.168.254.	hnlex04.volca	192.168.254.	hnlex04	
2008/10/11 1	RECEIVE	STOREDRIV		<BBAACA33	Regiona tech	matt@ithicos.	bda-silva@so	123	192.168.254.	hnlex04.volca	192.168.254.	hnlex04	
2008/10/11 1	RECEIVE	STOREDRIV		<BBAACA33	FW: C# Com	matt@ithicos.	Bthawom.Th	125	192.168.254.	hnlex04.volca	192.168.254.	hnlex04	

You could have accomplished the same thing with the following EMS command:

```
Get-MessageTrackingLog -Sender "matt@ithicos.com" -Server "HNLEX04"↵
-EventID "RECEIVE" -Start "10/11/2008 12:40:00 PM" -End "10/11/2008 12:50:00 PM"
```

One thing that is a bit annoying about this interface is that the results are not always sorted based on when they occurred. A quick solution to this is to click the Timestamp column to get it to resort; however, the events may still not sort correctly if two events occur during the same second.

If you click one of the events in the message tracking results list and then click Next, the Message Tracking Parameters screen reappears with the specific criteria to track that particular message.

Figure 26.15 shows a modified Message Tracking Parameters screen from which you could track that specific message. You can do so because this screen now includes the message ID; you can pull the message ID from the header of the original message if you have it. Note that the message tracking screen will only show you the logs for the server to which you are currently connected.

Notice at the bottom of the page the EMS command necessary to perform the message tracking using the `Get-MessageTrackingLog` cmdlet. If you select the EventID check box and include SEND in the criteria, you can look for one part of the message trace. Figure 26.16 shows the resulting message track for this particular message. This message was sent by an internal user and was routed through the message transport system and delivered to the Internet. There are only four "hops" because this is a single server system.

The events you are seeing in Figure 26.16 illustrate that the following actions occurred:

1. A message was submitted to the information store.

2. The transport system received the message from the STOREDRIV (store driver).

3. The message went through the message routing system.

4. The message was transmitted via SMTP.

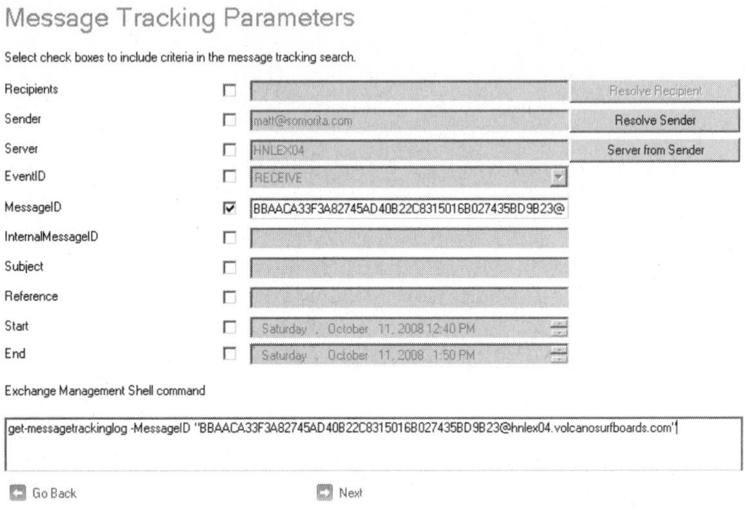

FIGURE 26.15
Tracking a specific event

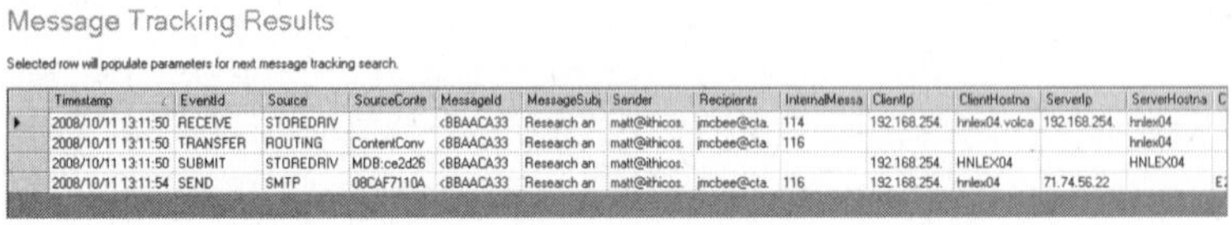

Message Tracking Parameters

Select check boxes to include criteria in the message tracking search.

Recipients	☐	Resolve Recipient
Sender	☐ matt@isomorita.com	Resolve Sender
Server	☐ HNLEX04	Server from Sender
EventID	☐ RECEIVE	
MessageID	☑ BBAACA33F3A82745AD40B22C8315016B027435BD9B23@	
InternalMessageID	☐	
Subject	☐	
Reference	☐	
Start	☐ Saturday , October 11, 2008 12:40 PM	
End	☐ Saturday , October 11, 2008 1:50 PM	

Exchange Management Shell command

```
get-messagetrackinglog -MessageID "BBAACA33F3A82745AD40B22C8315016B027435BD9B23@hnlex04.volcanosurfboards.com"
```

◄ Go Back   ► Next

FIGURE 26.16
Viewing the message
tracking results for a
specific message

Message Tracking Results

Selected row will populate parameters for next message tracking search.

Timestamp	EventId	Source	SourceConte	MessageId	MessageSubj	Sender	Recipients	InternalMessa	ClientIp	ClientHostna	ServerIp	ServerHostna	C
2008/10/11 13:11:50	RECEIVE	STOREDRIV		<BBAACA33	Research an	matt@hicos.	jmcbee@cta.	114	192.168.254.	hnlex04.volca	192.168.254.	hnlex04	
2008/10/11 13:11:50	TRANSFER	ROUTING	ContentConv	<BBAACA33	Research an	matt@hicos.	jmcbee@cta.	116				hnlex04	
2008/10/11 13:11:50	SUBMIT	STOREDRIV	MDB:ce2d26	<BBAACA33	Research an	matt@hicos.			192.168.254.	HNLEX04		HNLEX04	
2008/10/11 13:11:54	SEND	SMTP	08CAF7110A	<BBAACA33	Research an	matt@hicos.	jmcbee@cta.	116	192.168.254.	hnlex04	71.74.56.22		E:

In the following example, I have taken the search criteria shown in Figure 26.15 and used the EMS to track the specific event in which the message was transmitted from the Hub Transport server to a remote server on the Internet:

```
Get-messageTrackingLog -MessageID "BBAACA33F3A82745AD40B22C8315016B0274↵
35BD9B23@hnlex04.volcanosurfboards.com" | Format-List

Timestamp                 : 10/11/2008 1:11:50 PM
ClientIp                  : 192.168.254.24
ClientHostname            : hnlex04.volcanosurfboards.com
ServerIp                  : 192.168.254.24
ServerHostname            : hnlex04
SourceContext             :
ConnectorId               :
Source                    : STOREDRIVER
EventId                   : RECEIVE
InternalMessageId         : 114
MessageId                 : <BBAACA33F3A82745AD40B22C8315016B027435BD9B23@hnlex04
                            .volcanosurfboards.com>
Recipients                : {jmcbee@cta.net}
RecipientStatus           : {}
TotalBytes                : 22223
RecipientCount            : 1
RelatedRecipientAddress   :
Reference                 :
```

```
MessageSubject          : Research and development plans
Sender                  : matt@ithicos.com
ReturnPath              : matt@ithicos.com
MessageInfo             : 04I:

Timestamp               : 10/11/2008 1:11:50 PM
ClientIp                :
ClientHostname          :
ServerIp                :
ServerHostname          : hnlex04
SourceContext           : ContentConversion
ConnectorId             :
Source                  : ROUTING
EventId                 : TRANSFER
InternalMessageId       : 116
MessageId               : <BBAACA33F3A82745AD40B22C8315016B027435BD9B23
@hnlex04.volcanosurfboards.com>
Recipients              : {jmcbee@cta.net}
RecipientStatus         : {}
TotalBytes              : 27585
RecipientCount          : 1
RelatedRecipientAddress :
Reference               : {114}
MessageSubject          : Research and development plans
Sender                  : matt@ithicos.com
ReturnPath              : matt@ithicos.com
MessageInfo             :

Timestamp               : 10/11/2008 1:11:54 PM
ClientIp                : 192.168.254.24
ClientHostname          : hnlex04
ServerIp                : 71.74.56.22
ServerHostname          :
SourceContext           : 08CAF7110A4CD0EB
ConnectorId             : E2K7 Send Connector to Internet
Source                  : SMTP
EventId                 : SEND
InternalMessageId       : 116
MessageId               : <BBAACA33F3A82745AD40B22C8315016B027435BD9B23
@hnlex04volcanosurfboards.com>
Recipients              : {jmcbee@cta.net}
RecipientStatus         : {250 Recipient <jmcbee@cta.net> Ok}
TotalBytes              : 27585
RecipientCount          : 1
RelatedRecipientAddress :
Reference               :
MessageSubject          : Research and development plans
Sender                  : matt@ithicos.com
```

```
ReturnPath                 : matt@ithicos.com
MessageInfo                : 10/11/2008 1:11:50 PM

Timestamp                  : 10/11/2008 1:11:50 PM
ClientIp                   : 192.168.254.24
ClientHostname             : HNLEX04
ServerIp                   :
ServerHostname             : HNLEX04
SourceContext              : MDB:ce2d267f-68e7-431f-aa60-38c2af9ab0d7,
Mailbox:49e3f1e1-ec1b-4dd8-a96f-52b04aec4b2f, Event:2614022,
MessageClass:IPM.Note, CreationTime:2008-10-11T23:11:49. 858Z,
ClientType:OWA
ConnectorId                :
Source                     : STOREDRIVER
EventId                    : SUBMIT
InternalMessageId          :
MessageId                  : <BBAACA33F3A82745AD40B22C8315016B027435BD9B23@hnlex04
                             .volcanosurfboards.com>
Recipients                 : {}
RecipientStatus            : {}
TotalBytes                 :
RecipientCount             :
RelatedRecipientAddress    :
Reference                  :
MessageSubject             : Research and development plans
Sender                     : matt@ithicos.com
ReturnPath                 :
MessageInfo                :
```

Probably the two most relevant properties of this particular event are the `ServerIp` property and the `RecipientStatus` property. The `ServerIp` property tells you the IP address of the remote server to which the message was sent. The `RecipientStatus` property tells you that the message recipient was accepted by the remote server.

I can narrow down the output to a few more useful fields; here is a sample EMS command that narrows down the output of these events to the most useful information:

```
Get-messageTrackingLog -MessageID "BBAACA33F3A82745AD40B22C8315016B0274↩
35BD9B23@hnlex04.volcanosurfboards.com" | ↩
Format-List TimeStamp,EventId,Source*,*IP*
```

```
Timestamp                  : 10/11/2008 1:11:50 PM
EventId                    : RECEIVE
SourceContext              :
Source                     : STOREDRIVER
ClientIp                   : 192.168.254.24
ServerIp                   : 192.168.254.24
Recipients                 : {jmcbee@ithicos.com}
```

```
RecipientStatus       : {}
RecipientCount        : 1
RelatedRecipientAddress :

Timestamp             : 10/11/2008 1:11:50 PM
EventId               : SUBMIT
SourceContext         : MDB:ce2d267f-68e7-431f-aa60-
38c2af9ab0d7, Mailbox:49e3f1e1-ec1b-4dd8-a96f-
52b04aec4b2f, Event:2614022, MessageClass:IPM.Note,
CreationTime:2008-10-11T23:11:49. 858Z, ClientType:OWA
Source                : STOREDRIVER
ClientIp              : 192.168.254.24
ServerIp              :
Recipients            : {}
RecipientStatus       : {}
RecipientCount        :
RelatedRecipientAddress :

Timestamp             : 10/11/2008 1:11:50 PM
EventId               : TRANSFER
SourceContext         : ContentConversion
Source                : ROUTING
ClientIp              :
ServerIp              :
Recipients            : {jmcbee@ithicos.com}
RecipientStatus       : {}
RecipientCount        : 1
RelatedRecipientAddress :

Timestamp             : 10/11/2008 1:11:54 PM
EventId               : SEND
SourceContext         : 08CAF7110A4CD0EB
Source                : SMTP
ClientIp              : 192.168.254.24
ServerIp              : 71.74.56.22
Recipients            : {jmcbee@ithicos.com}
RecipientStatus       : {250 Recipient <jmcbee@ithicos.com> Ok}
RecipientCount        : 1
RelatedRecipientAddress :
```

Introducing Routing, Protocol, and Connectivity Logs

Exchange 2007 provides a lot of options for logging and troubleshooting connectivity problems. Each Hub Transport server has routing logs that can help troubleshoot connectivity and can be configured to track all connectivity to and from that server. Each Send connector or Receive connector can be configured to log inbound or outbound connections. The resulting logs are comma-delimited text files that can be read using any text editor or even imported into a database.

By default, these logs are found in the directory structure shown here:

You can use the `Get-TransportServer` cmdlet to view the locations of the various transport logs:

```
Get-TransportServer hnlex04 | Format-List *path*

ConnectivityLogPath     :
C:\Program Files\Microsoft\Exchange Server\TransportRoles\Logs\Connectivity
MessageTrackingLogPath :
C:\Program Files\Microsoft\Exchange Server\TransportRoles\Logs\MessageTracking
PickupDirectoryPath     :
C:\Program Files\Microsoft\Exchange Server\TransportRoles\Pickup
PipelineTracingPath     :
C:\Program Files\Microsoft\Exchange Server\TransportRoles\Logs\PipelineTracing
ReceiveProtocolLogPath :
C:\Program Files\Microsoft\Exchange Server\TransportRoles\Logs\ProtocolLog\
SmtpReceive
ReplayDirectoryPath     :
C:\Program Files\Microsoft\Exchange Server\TransportRoles\Replay
RootDropDirectoryPath   :
RoutingTableLogPath     :
C:\Program Files\Microsoft\Exchange Server\TransportRoles\Logs\Routing
SendProtocolLogPath     :
C:\Program Files\Microsoft\Exchange Server\TransportRoles\Logs\ProtocolLog\
SmtpSend
```

Configuring Connectivity Logging

Each Hub Transport server can be configured with connectivity logging. The connectivity log contains a record of all communications a particular Hub Transport server handled. This includes inbound and outbound SMTP communication as well as MAPI connections from Mailbox servers. Figure 26.17 shows a sample connectivity log. The names of connectivity log files all start with `CONNECTLOG` followed by the current date.

In this log, you can see the outbound sessions and you can see the MAPI sessions to and from the Mailbox server (named `hnlex04.volcanosurfboards.com` in this log file). One column of interest in this log file is the `direction` column. There are four different characters that you may see in the `direction` column that indicate connections or direction of message flow. They are as follows:

+	A connection is being established either to a remote SMTP system or to a Mailbox server.
–	A connection has been completed or disconnected.
>	A message is being sent outbound to a remote SMTP system.
<	A message is being received from a remote SMTP system.

FIGURE 26.17
Sample connectivity log

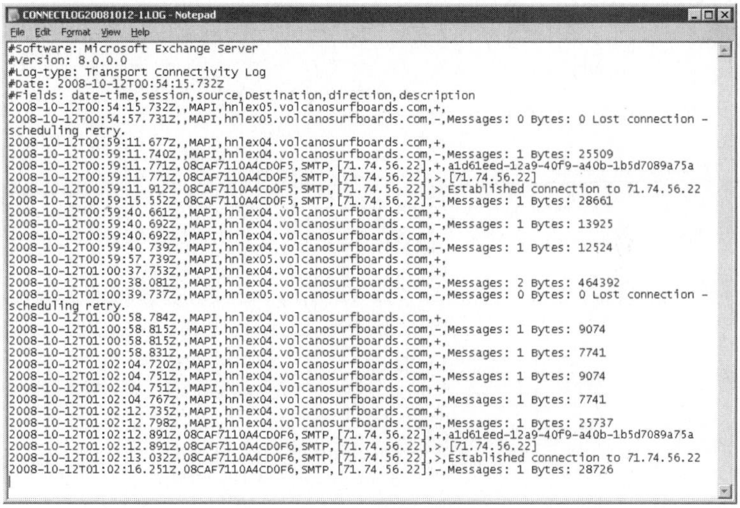

```
CONNECTLOG20081012-1.LOG - Notepad
File Edit Format View Help
#Software: Microsoft Exchange Server
#Version: 8.0.0.0
#Log-type: Transport Connectivity Log
#Date: 2008-10-12T00:54:15.732Z
#Fields: date-time,session,source,Destination,direction,description
2008-10-12T00:54:15.732Z,,MAPI,hnlex05.volcanosurfboards.com,+,
2008-10-12T00:54:57.731Z,,MAPI,hnlex05.volcanosurfboards.com,-,Messages: 0 Bytes: 0 Lost connection -
scheduling retry.
2008-10-12T00:59:11.677Z,,MAPI,hnlex04.volcanosurfboards.com,+,
2008-10-12T00:59:11.740Z,,MAPI,hnlex04.volcanosurfboards.com,-,Messages: 1 Bytes: 25509
2008-10-12T00:59:11.771Z,08CAF7110A4CD0F5,SMTP,[71.74.56.22],+,a1d61eed-12a9-40f9-a40b-1b5d7089a75a
2008-10-12T00:59:11.771Z,08CAF7110A4CD0F5,SMTP,[71.74.56.22],>,[71.74.56.22]
2008-10-12T00:59:11.912Z,08CAF7110A4CD0F5,SMTP,[71.74.56.22],>,Established connection to 71.74.56.22
2008-10-12T00:59:15.552Z,08CAF7110A4CD0F5,SMTP,[71.74.56.22],-,Messages: 1 Bytes: 28661
2008-10-12T00:59:40.661Z,,MAPI,hnlex04.volcanosurfboards.com,+,
2008-10-12T00:59:40.692Z,,MAPI,hnlex04.volcanosurfboards.com,-,Messages: 1 Bytes: 13925
2008-10-12T00:59:40.692Z,,MAPI,hnlex04.volcanosurfboards.com,+,
2008-10-12T00:59:40.739Z,,MAPI,hnlex04.volcanosurfboards.com,-,Messages: 1 Bytes: 12524
2008-10-12T00:59:57.739Z,,MAPI,hnlex05.volcanosurfboards.com,+,
2008-10-12T01:00:37.753Z,,MAPI,hnlex04.volcanosurfboards.com,+,
2008-10-12T01:00:38.081Z,,MAPI,hnlex04.volcanosurfboards.com,-,Messages: 2 Bytes: 464392
2008-10-12T01:00:39.737Z,,MAPI,hnlex05.volcanosurfboards.com,-,Messages: 0 Bytes: 0 Lost connection -
scheduling retry.
2008-10-12T01:00:58.784Z,,MAPI,hnlex04.volcanosurfboards.com,+,
2008-10-12T01:00:58.815Z,,MAPI,hnlex04.volcanosurfboards.com,-,Messages: 1 Bytes: 9074
2008-10-12T01:00:58.815Z,,MAPI,hnlex04.volcanosurfboards.com,+,
2008-10-12T01:00:58.831Z,,MAPI,hnlex04.volcanosurfboards.com,-,Messages: 1 Bytes: 7741
2008-10-12T01:02:04.720Z,,MAPI,hnlex04.volcanosurfboards.com,+,
2008-10-12T01:02:04.751Z,,MAPI,hnlex04.volcanosurfboards.com,-,Messages: 1 Bytes: 9074
2008-10-12T01:02:04.751Z,,MAPI,hnlex04.volcanosurfboards.com,+,
2008-10-12T01:02:04.767Z,,MAPI,hnlex04.volcanosurfboards.com,-,Messages: 1 Bytes: 7741
2008-10-12T01:02:12.735Z,,MAPI,hnlex04.volcanosurfboards.com,+,
2008-10-12T01:02:12.798Z,,MAPI,hnlex04.volcanosurfboards.com,-,Messages: 1 Bytes: 25737
2008-10-12T01:02:12.891Z,08CAF7110A4CD0F6,SMTP,[71.74.56.22],+,a1d61eed-12a9-40f9-a40b-1b5d7089a75a
2008-10-12T01:02:12.891Z,08CAF7110A4CD0F6,SMTP,[71.74.56.22],>,[71.74.56.22]
2008-10-12T01:02:13.032Z,08CAF7110A4CD0F6,SMTP,[71.74.56.22],>,Established connection to 71.74.56.22
2008-10-12T01:02:16.251Z,08CAF7110A4CD0F6,SMTP,[71.74.56.22],-,Messages: 1 Bytes: 28726
```

Another interesting column to know about is the `session-id` column. The session ID is a globally unique identifier that will be the same for an entire SMTP session (it is blank for MAPI sessions). The cool thing about this is that the session ID corresponds to the `session` column in the Send and Receive logs.

Connectivity logging is disabled by default and must be enabled for any Hub Transport server on which you want to view the logs. To enable connectivity logging, you use the `Set-TransportServer` cmdlet. The following is an example for setting connectivity logging on server HNLEX04:

```
Set-TransportServer "HNLEX04" -ConnectivityLogEnabled $True
```

You could use the `Get-TransportServer` and `Set-TransportServer` cmdlets to enable connectivity on all Hub Transport servers as shown here:

```
GetTransportServer | Set-TransportServer "HNLEX03" -ConnectivityLogEnabled $True
```

As with message tracking logs, the connectivity logs are retained by default for 30 days, the maximum size of the log file directory is 250MB, and a maximum log file size is 10MB. The log files are found in the `C:\Program Files\Microsoft\Exchange Server\TransportRoles\Logs\Connectivity` folder.

You can view the connectivity log configuration using the `Get-TransportServer` cmdlet. The following is an example:

```
Get-TransportServer hnlex04 | FL Name,*connectivity*
Name                             : HNLEX03
ConnectivityLogEnabled           : True
ConnectivityLogMaxAge            : 30.00:00:00
ConnectivityLogMaxDirectorySize : 250MB
ConnectivityLogMaxFileSize       : 10MB
ConnectivityLogPath              : C:\Program Files\Microsoft\Exchange Server\
TransportRoles\Logs\Connectivity
```

You update or change this information using the `Set-TransportServer` cmdlet.

Configuring Send and Receive Logging

One big improvement with Exchange 2007 is the ability to narrow the scope of protocol logging to an individual connector only. With Exchange 2000/2003, if you were troubleshooting an SMTP connectivity problem, you had to enable protocol logging for the whole SMTP virtual server. The protocol logs would contain all inbound and outbound SMTP information for all connectors that used that SMTP virtual server.

In Exchange 2007, each Hub Transport server has Send and Receive protocol logs, but these are enabled separately for each Send and Receive connector, not for the entire Hub Transport server. Let's start by looking at the properties of the Send and Receive logs using the `Get-TransportServer` cmdlet. By now, you should be familiar with the properties of these logs because they are almost identical to the properties of the connectivity and message tracking logs.

```
Get-TransportServer "HNLEX04" | Format-List ↵
Name,*sendprotocol*,*receiveprotocol*,*intraorg*
Name       : HNLEX04
SendProtocolLogMaxAge               : 30.00:00:00
SendProtocolLogMaxDirectorySize     : 250MB
SendProtocolLogMaxFileSize          : 10MB
SendProtocolLogPath                 : C:\Program Files\
Microsoft\Exchange Server \TransportRoles\Logs\ProtocolLog\SmtpSend
ReceiveProtocolLogMaxAge            : 30.00:00:00
ReceiveProtocolLogMaxDirectorySize  : 250MB
ReceiveProtocolLogMaxFileSize       : 10MB
ReceiveProtocolLogPath              : C:\Program Files\
Microsoft\Exchange Server\TransportRoles\Logs\ProtocolLog\SmtpReceive
IntraOrgConnectorProtocolLoggingLevel : None
```

By default, these logs are kept for a maximum of 30 days, the maximum log file size is 10MB, and the maximum size of the log file directory is 250MB. The logs are found in separate directories in the `C:\Program Files\Microsoft\Exchange Server\TransportRoles\Logs\ProtocolLog` folder.

The one thing that you may notice is that there is no parameter for enabling or disabling the Send and Receive logs. This is because the actual logging is enabled and disabled on a per-connector basis. For example, I have created a Send connector that delivers mail to the

Internet called E2K7 Send Connector to Internet; on the General property page (shown in Figure 26.18) of that connector, I can enable logging in the Protocol Logging Level drop-down list.

FIGURE 26.18

Enabling protocol logging for a Send connector

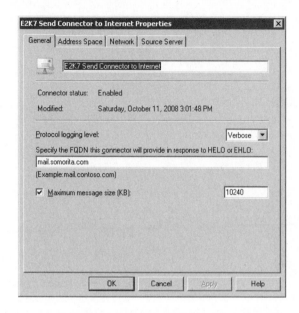

There are two choices for protocol logging on both Send and Receive connectors. The choices are None and Verbose. You can also set the logging level for Send and Receive connectors using the Set-SendConnector and Set-ReceiveConnector cmdlets. Let's first look at an example where a Send connector called E2K7 SMTP to Internet has logging enabled:

```
Get-SendConnector "E2K7 SMTP to Internet" | FL Name,*log*

Name                 : E2K7 SMTP to Internet
ProtocolLoggingLevel : None
```

You can use the Set-SendConnector cmdlet to enable this connector to support logging:

```
Set-SendConnector "E2K7 SMTP to Internet" -ProtocolLoggingLevel Verbose
```

The same format of logging can be used to enable protocol logging for a Receive connector.

One thing you do have to watch out for is whether you have more than one source server configured for the Send connector. When you configure a Send connector, you can specify more than one Hub Transport server to be a source server for the connector. You do this on the Source Server property page of the connector, shown in Figure 26.19.

If you have more than one source server defined, an outbound SMTP message may be processed by any of them. This means that if you are troubleshooting a particular outbound message, you will need to check the Send protocol logs on all of these servers.

Another important point to note when reviewing protocol logs and debugging connectivity problems is that not all communication is logged to the Send protocol logs. All Hub Transport servers have an implicit Send connector that is automatically created but is not visible. This implicit Send connector is used for internal delivery of e-mail between Hub Transport servers, Edge Transport servers, and Exchange 2003 servers. If you want the Hub Transport servers to log internal connectivity, you need to enable this on each Hub Transport server. This is the `IntraOrgConnectorProtocolLoggingLevel` property found on the Hub Transport server's properties page. Here is an example of enabling this type of logging for Hub Transport server HNLEX03:

```
Set-TransportServer "HNLEX03" -IntraOrgConnectorProtocolLoggingLevel Verbose
```

FIGURE 26.19
Defining source servers
for a Send connector

Alternatively, if you want to enable intra-organization logging for all Hub Transport servers, you could use this cmdlet:

```
Get-TransportServer | Set-TransportServer -IntraOrgConnectorProtocolLoggingLevel↩
Verbose
```

Though intra-organization logging may be useful for troubleshooting, you might not want to keep this type of logging enabled all the time. If you need to globally disable intra-organization logging, here is a command that should do the trick:

```
Get-TransportServer | Set-TransportServer -IntraOrgConnectorProtocolLoggingLevel
None
```

Now that you know how to enable and disable Send and Receive protocol logs, let's take a look at an actual log file. The text would not fit nicely here in the text, so Figure 26.20 shows an example of a Send protocol log. Notice that the Send protocol log is much more detailed than the connectivity log.

A lot of the space in both the Send and Receive logs is taken up by the `date-time`, `connector-id`, `session-id`, and `local-endpoint` columns. The real meat of the logs (from a troubleshooting perspective at least) is the information found in the `remote-endpoint` (the IP address of the remote system), `event`, and `data` columns. The `data` column contains the actual data that was sent to the remote system or that was received from the remote system. The `event` column contains a character that helps you to identify what is occurring or the direction of the data. The following information is found in the **event** column:

+	A connection has been established.
–	A connection has been closed.
>	Information is being sent to a remote SMTP system.
<	Information is being received from a remote SMTP system.
*	An informational event has occurred.

FIGURE 26.20

Sample Send protocol log

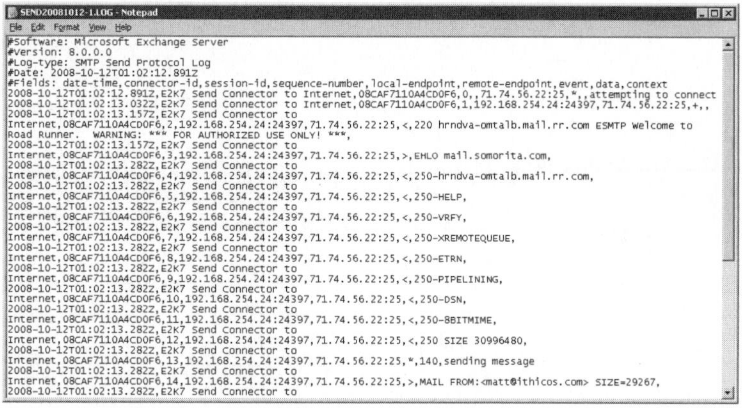

I realize that I have probably tossed a lot of minutiae and detail to you on message tracking, connectivity, and protocol logs, but I think that you will find this information useful.

Viewing the Routing Logs

If you worked much with Exchange Server 2003, you probably worked with the WinRoute utility that allowed you to query the Exchange Server routing engine and display information about known routes and the states of those routes. Exchange Server 2007 does not have a routing engine, but it does maintain logs of the known routes. The log files are written four times a day or when the transport services are restarted; they are found in the following folder:

```
C:\Program Files\Microsoft\Exchange Server\TransportRoles\Logs\Routing
```

However, the log file format is not particularly easy to follow if you open it in a text editor. In Exchange Server 2007 SP1, Microsoft added a new tool to the Exchange Management Console Toolbox work center called the Routing Log Viewer that will allow you to retrieve these logs and to view information such as servers, connectors, address spaces, and Active Directory site information. An example of this is shown in Figure 26.21.

Monitoring

Chapter 24, "Monitoring Performance," talked about monitoring your system. Most of the examples and performance monitor counters discussed were really targeted toward determining

FIGURE 26.21
Using the Routing Log
Viewer

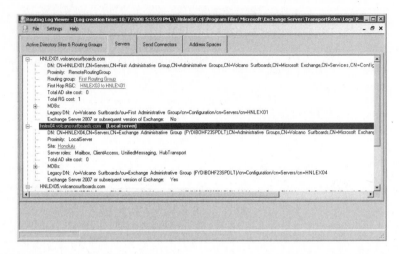

whether it is time to expand the capacity of your system and to help you find bottlenecks. There is certainly overlap between "insufficient capacity" and a "healthy Exchange server," though.

This section looks at some Exchange and Windows tools that you can use to determine whether your server is healthy and processing messages.

Checking Queues

Confirming that e-mail messages are being delivered is one of the most basic and important things that you do when managing an Exchange environment. The Queue Viewer tool is usually your front-line monitoring and troubleshooting tool. Queue Viewer is found in the Toolbox work center of the Exchange Management Console. Figure 26.22 shows the Queue Viewer interface.

FIGURE 26.22
Managing queues on a
Hub Transport server

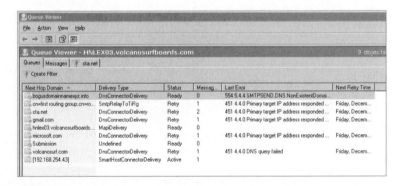

The first thing you need to know about the Queue Viewer is that it communicates with servers that have the Hub Transport role. Because queues are maintained only on the Hub Transport server, there is no reason for it to communicate with another server role. Figure 26.22 shows the Queue Viewer being used to view the queues on server HNLEX03.volcanosurfboards.com; the Microsoft Exchange Transport service must be running on the Hub Transport server. You can use the Connect To Server task in the Actions pane to connect to a different Hub Transport server.

Looking at the queues in Figure 26.22, you can tell a little about the messages that are waiting to be delivered. In this particular environment, server HNLEX03 hosts a Send connector and is responsible for delivery to the Internet. It is also a bridgehead server for a legacy Exchange routing group connector to an Exchange 2000/2003 routing group.

The first column in the Queues listing is the Next Hop Domain column; it shows the destination Internet domain, remote smarthost, remote Hub Transport server, or legacy routing group. The Delivery Type column also shows some interesting information about a particular queue:

DnsConnectorDelivery is a queue for messages that will be sent directly out to the Internet by using DNS to look up the remote domain's MX records.

MapiDelivery is a queue that holds messages queued up for Mailbox servers in the local Active Directory site.

SmartHostConnectorDelivery is a queue that is used to hold messages that are to be delivered to a specific smarthost. The smarthost to be used is specified in the Next Hop Domain column.

SmtpRelaytoRemoteAdSite is the queue that is used to hold messages that are being delivered to a Hub Transport server in another Active Directory site.

SmtpRelayToTiRg is shorthand for SMTP relay to a Titanium routing group. Titanium is the code name for Exchange 2003, but this queue could be a queue to either Exchange 2000 or 2003 routing groups.

SmtpRelayWithinAdSite is the queue that is used to hold messages that must be delivered to another Hub Transport in the same Active Directory site. This other server might be a server that hosts an SMTP connector or an Edge Transport connection.

NonSmtpGatewayDelivery is a queue that holds messages that are queued for delivery to a local, non-SMTP gateway. An example of this type of gateway is the Lotus Notes connector.

SmtpRelayWithinAdSiteToEdge is a queue that holds messages that are queued for delivery to an Edge Transport server.

Undefined is an internal queue that is used to hold messages that have been submitted to the Submission queue but have not been placed in a link queue for delivery to a remote domain, relay, or server.

Unreachable is a queue that holds messages for which a route to the recipient can not be established.

The Status column of the Queue Viewer gives you some indication of what the queue is currently doing. There are four possible status values in the Exchange 2007 Queue Viewer:

Active means that the message transport system is currently servicing this queue and delivering (or attempting to deliver) messages.

Ready means that the queue is currently not servicing any requests but is awaiting the submission of any messages that need to be delivered.

Suspended means that the administrator has placed the queue on hold so that no messages in the queue will be delivered.

Retry means that there has been a problem delivering the messages in this particular queue and that the message transport system will try to deliver the messages again.

Notice the Last Error column in the Queue Viewer; this column can usually give you some helpful troubleshooting information about why messages are not being delivered. I have staged a couple of different potential errors in Figure 26.22 that represent some typical problems. I moved the Last Error column over further to the left and widened it some in this screen capture so that you could see it more clearly. In the default Queue Viewer interface, you may need to scroll to the right to see the Last Error column.

◆ `451 4.4.0 Primary target IP address responded with: "421 4.2.1 Unable to connect." Attempted failover to alternate host, but the attempted failover did not succeed. Either there are no alternate hosts or delivery failed to all alternate hosts.` This message indicates that the remote host did not respond. This could be a connectivity problem or it could be that all of a remote domain's servers are down.

◆ `554 5.4.4 SMTPSEND.DNS.NonExistentDomain.` This error indicates that a user has sent a message to a remote SMTP domain that cannot be resolved in DNS. This may be because the remote domain does not exist or it could be the result of DNS problems. Unlike previous versions of Exchange, within a few minutes Exchange 2007 will issue a non-delivery report to the user.

◆ `451 4.4.0 DNS query failed.` This error indicates that the domain exists but that Mail Exchanger (MX) or address records (A) could not be resolved. Exchange will continue to try to look up address records and deliver the message until the time-out period ends (two days by default).

A common complaint about the Queue Viewer interface is that the Last Error column is difficult to read if there is much text in the column. You can move the mouse pointer over the text and you will see the expanded textual information in that column in much the same way that "fly over" or "mouse over" help works. That still may not be of much help if you need to get a copy of the actual message. That is one place that the EMS cmdlet `Get-Queue` comes in really handy. Here is a example of using the `Get-Queue` cmdlet with no parameters:

```
Get-Queue

Identity            DeliveryType Status MessageCount NextHopDomain
--------            ------------ ------ ------------ -------------
HNLEX03\95          DnsConnec... Retry  2            cta.net
HNLEX03\96          DnsConnec... Retry  1            microsoft.com
HNLEX03\98          SmartHost... Active 1            [192.168.254.43]
HNLEX03\100         DnsConnec... Retry  1            volcanosurf.com
HNLEX03\101         DnsConnec... Retry  1            gmail.com
HNLEX03\102         SmtpRelay... Retry  3            cn=first routing..
HNLEX03\Submission  Undefined    Ready  0            Submission
```

The `Get-Queue` cmdlet outputs the queue identity; that will prove to be really useful in troubleshooting. You can use this queue identity as input for the `Get-Queue` parameter; here is an example for getting all of the information for a particular queue:

```
Get-Queue "hnlex03\95"

Identity            DeliveryType Status MessageCount NextHopDomain
--------            ------------ ------ ------------ -------------
HNLEX03\95          DnsConnec... Retry  2            cta.net
```

You can pipe the output of the Get-Queue cmdlet to the Format-List cmdlet and get the details of the specified queue:

```
Get-Queue "hnlex03\95" | FL

Identity          : HNLEX03\95
DeliveryType      : DnsConnectorDelivery
NextHopDomain     : cta.net
NextHopConnector  : 3fa8724f-689b-4b88-a91c-42b69c77d1f0
Status            : Retry
MessageCount      : 2
LastError         : 451 4.4.0 Primary target IP address responded with: "421 4.2.1
Unable to connect." Attempted failover to alternate host, that did not succeed.
Either there are no alternate host, or delivery failed to all alternate hosts.
LastRetryTime     : 12/30/2006 11:47:03 AM
NextRetryTime     : 12/30/2006 11:57:24 AM
IsValid           : True
ObjectState       : Unchanged
```

When you highlight a particular queue in the Queue Viewer, the Actions pane gives you a number of different options for managing it. These are shown in Figure 26.23.

FIGURE 26.23
Queue Viewer Actions

The following tasks appear in the Actions pane when you select a particular queue:

View Messages allows you to open a new tab in the Queue Viewer. This is the default behavior if you double-click a queue. The View Messages option creates a tab similar to the one shown in Figure 26.24.

Suspend allows you to stop any messages in the specified queue from being delivered. This option will show by default if the queue is not already suspended.

Resume allows you to resume delivery of messages in a queue that has been suspended. This option will appear only if a queue has been suspended.

Retry forces the message transport system to immediately try to deliver the messages in a particular queue.

Remove Messages (With NDR) will delete all of the messages in a particular queue and send the message originator a non-delivery report (NDR) message. This is a nice new capability in Exchange 2007; in previous versions you had to delete messages one at a time.

Remove Messages (Without Sending NDRs) will delete all of the messages in a particular queue but not send a non-delivery report (NDR). As with the preceding task, this is a new capability in Exchange 2007; in previous versions you had to delete messages one at a time.

FIGURE 26.24
Viewing the messages in a specific queue

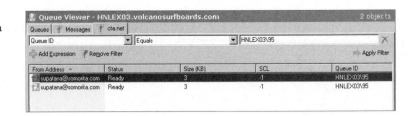

Notice that a filter is automatically created that filters the messages in a specific queue ID.

The Queue Viewer's Messages tab allows you to see all of the messages that are queued for delivery as well as additional information such as the message size, message subject, and the Queue ID and Last Error columns. The Messages tab also allows you to specify a filter based on the sender, Queue ID, Spam Confidence Level (SCL), Size (KB), date received, expiration time, status, or subject. Figure 26.25 shows the Messages property page with a specific sender filter (From Address) applied.

FIGURE 26.25
Viewing and filtering all queued messages

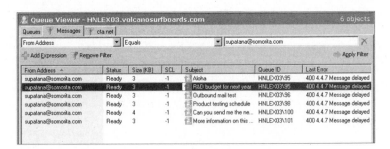

From the Messages tab, you can select one or more messages and suspend, resume, or remove them. There are two remove options: you can remove the message and send an NDR or you can remove the message without sending an NDR. The Properties task on the Actions pane allows you to view more detailed information about the message. The General property page for one of these messages is shown in Figure 26.26.

On the General property page, you can see detailed property information about the selected message. This includes the full text of the Last Error message as well as the identity of the message. The identity of the message can be used with the EMS queue management cmdlets `Get-Message`, `Export-Message`, `Suspend-Message`, `Resume-Message`, and `Remove-Message`. Here is an example of retrieving queued messages using the `Get-Message` cmdlet:

```
Get-Message

Identity          FromAddress       Status  Queue         Subject
--------          -----------       ------  -----         -------
HNLEX03\95\128    supatana@som...   Ready   HNLEX03\95    Aloha
HNLEX03\95\131    supatana@som...   Ready   HNLEX03\95    R&D budget f...
HNLEX03\96\134    supatana@som...   Ready   HNLEX03\96    Outbound mai...
HNLEX03\98\140    supatana@som...   Ready   HNLEX03\98    Product test...
HNLEX03\100\143   supatana@som...   Ready   HNLEX03\100   Can you send...
HNLEX03\101\146   supatana@som...   Ready   HNLEX03\101   More informa...
```

FIGURE 26.26

General properties of a
queued message

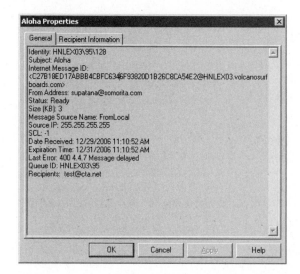

From this listing, you can get the identity of the message you are interested in viewing more information about. If the listing is larger (dozens or hundreds of messages), you could use the Where cmdlet to narrow the search. For example, if you know that the subject includes the word *Aloha*, you could use a search such as this:

```
Get-Message | where {$_.subject -like "Aloha"}

Identity          FromAddress       Status  Queue         Subject
--------          -----------       ------  -----         -------
HNLEX03\95\128    supatana@som...   Ready   HNLEX03\95    Aloha
```

Once you have the message identity, you can use the following command to retrieve more information about the queued message:

```
Get-Message "hnlex03\95\128" -IncludeRecipientInfo | FL

Identity          : HNLEX03\95\128
Subject           : Aloha
```

```
InternetMessageId:<C27B18ED17ABBB4CBFC6346F93820D1B26C8CA54E2
@HNLEX03.volcanosurfboards.com>
FromAddress       : supatana@somorita.com
Status            : Ready
Size              : 3284B
MessageSourceName : FromLocal
SourceIP          : 255.255.255.255
SCL               : -1
DateReceived      : 12/29/2006 11:10:52 AM
ExpirationTime    : 12/31/2006 11:10:52 AM
LastError         : 400 4.4.7 Message delayed
RetryCount        : 0
Queue             : HNLEX03\95
Recipients        : {test@cta.net}
IsValid           : True
ObjectState       : Unchanged
```

Note that this example includes the `-IncludeRecipientInfo` parameter; if this parameter was not included, the Recipients information would be blank.

Monitoring Health

Performance monitoring is one of the more important tasks that administrators need to do for their mail systems. A clear picture of your server's performance may help you to find bottlenecks or performance problems before they affect your users. Yet performance monitoring is something that most Exchange administrators seem to avoid like the plague.

Performance monitoring is not rocket science; it is not even nearly as difficult as most people think (or fear) it is. Often, the challenge to performance monitoring is in knowing which counters and thresholds indicate a possible performance problem. I hope to help you understand that in this chapter, but at the very least I hope to get you started.

If you have not read Chapter 24, you should go back and review the section on performance monitoring. There is quite a bit of overlap between these two chapters, though that chapter focused on counters that might indicate the need to scale additional servers or add additional hardware resources. This chapter focuses more on counters that indicate performance problems and server health.

Using Performance Monitoring Counters

Let's now look at some of the counters that you may find useful when monitoring performance problems or looking for bottlenecks. Before we jump into this discussion, though, here's a review of a few tips for performance monitoring:

◆ Don't sweat spikes in activity. You are interested in average activity over a typical period of time.

◆ Monitor over a few hours rather than a few minutes.

◆ Pick periods of typical activity. If most of your user community arrives at work at 8:00 in the morning and leaves for lunch at 11:30, then monitor during that period of time.

◆ Record performance monitor counter logs. You can analyze them later and refer back to them for historical information.

◆ Avoid performance monitoring immediately after restarting the server. On a mailbox server, a freshly restarted server is in what is called a *cold state operation*; this is when the Exchange server is just beginning to cache frequently used data. The disk I/O profile and CPU usage will be higher than normal.

◆ Performance monitoring is one part science and one part art. Take every counter value that you measure and think about what factors could cause that particular value to be too high (or too low).

MEMORY COUNTERS

Provided you have sufficient memory in your server, it won't usually be a bottleneck for Exchange 2007. I recommend that you have more than just the minimum amount of RAM in your servers. If you suspect memory problems, some counters will prove to be very useful when making this determination. Table 26.5 shows some common performance monitor counters and some recommended values to watch for.

TABLE 26.5: Counters That May Indicate a Shortage of Physical Memory

OBJECT/COUNTER	EXPLANATION\RECOMMENDATION
Memory/Pages/sec	This is the number of pages per second that Windows had to either retrieve from the page file or write to the page file due to a shortage of physical memory. This value should not exceed an average of 10 pages per second during typical activity.
Memory/Available Mbytes	This is the total amount of physical memory that is available to Windows. This value should be greater than 10 percent of the total amount of physical memory in the server.
Process/Working Set	The Working Set counter for each instance of the process running on Windows can give you an idea of how much memory each of the processes running in Windows is allocating.

PROCESSOR COUNTERS

In most cases, the processor subsystem of a server is not usually the bottleneck or the cause of performance problems. Table 26.6 shows some of the common counters that you can use to determine if you need additional CPU capacity.

An example of a performance monitor chart that is analyzing Exchange-related processes is shown in Figure 26.27.

I mentioned in Table 26.5 that the Process object lets you view the usage of specific processes running under Windows. This can be useful if you want to watch the usage of a particular Exchange process. You can add an instance of each Exchange process to a performance monitor chart and see what percentage of the processor each of these processes is using.

DISK COUNTERS

Monitoring disk activity can also help you in determining where possible bottlenecks are within your system. For servers that supported more than a thousand mailboxes in Exchange 2003, disk bottlenecks were a frequent problem, because often the disk subsystem did not have sufficient

I/O capacity to support the number of reads and writes to the disk. Exchange 2007's additional memory capacity has addressed this by allowing for better caching and more efficient disk I/O. But if you do not have sufficient memory, a low memory situation may manifest itself as a disk performance problem. This is due to the fact that when an Exchange server does not have enough RAM to cache frequently used data, it must rely on the disk more frequently.

TABLE 26.6: Counters That May Indicate Insufficient Processor Capacity

OBJECT/COUNTER	EXPLANATION\RECOMMENDATION
Processor/% Processor Time	This is the total percentage of time that the processors are doing useful work (as opposed to running idle threads). You want this to be below 70 percent on a sustained basis. If this value is higher than 70 percent, you may need to add additional processor capacity or split some workload off to another server.
Processor/% Processor Time	The Processor object allows you to select individual programs running under Windows and determine the resources that a particular process is using. In this case, you can isolate the percentage of the CPU that each process is using.

FIGURE 26.27
Monitoring the CPU usage of Exchange-related processes

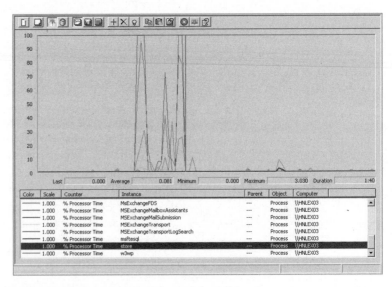

When monitoring disk counters, there are two disk counter objects that you can select: PhysicalDisk and LogicalDisk. Their names are pretty self-explanatory and make it easy to figure out which types of counters they provide. Depending on your system configuration, one or both might be disabled. You can use the diskperf.exe command to determine if the counters are available. Here is an example:

```
C:\>diskperf
Both Logical and Physical Disk Performance counters on this system are automatically
```

```
enabled on demand.
For legacy applications using IOCTL_DISK_PERFORMANCE to retrieve raw counters,
you can use -Y or -N to forcibly enable or disable. No reboot is required.
```

In this case, both the physical and logical disk counters are available.

The physical disk counters are useful when determining which particular physical disks have the greatest load on them, and the logical disk counters are useful if you need to monitor a specific logical disk drive. In a perfect world, each logical disk is on a separate physical disk and the counters will report the same information. When you add performance counters to a chart or report, the physical disk object presents you with instances of the physical disk numbers, and the logical disk object presents you with just the logical drive letters. Figure 26.28 shows the Add Counters dialog box for the PhysicalDisk performance object. If you are looking at the LogicalDisk counter object, there are subtle differences between the physical disk instances and the logical disk instances. The physical disk instances include the disk number as well as the logical disks that are found on particular physical disks. The logical disk instances just include the individual drive letters.

FIGURE 26.28

Choosing counters for a physical disk

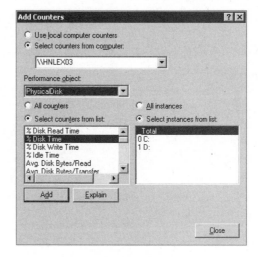

Table 26.7 shows some common disk counters and what to watch out for. I am including just the logical disk counters in this table.

NETWORK COUNTERS

The network is usually not a performance bottleneck for Exchange and Outlook clients if the Exchange server is on a 100Mb/s, full-duplexed, switched network and the network usually has sufficient capacity. Networking problems usually result from improperly configured switches, routers, or virtual LAN components. In some situations, the network adapter or switch port may be misconfigured and either cause network problems or cause the network to function at the lowest possible speed. Table 26.8 shows some counters that are useful in evaluating your network connectivity and determining if there are problems. When selecting counters to monitor, make sure that you select the correct network adapter instance; in some cases the MS TCP Loopback Interface is selected by default.

TABLE 26.7:   Logical Disk Counters That May Be Useful in Determining Disk Bottlenecks

OBJECT/COUNTER	EXPLANATION\RECOMMENDATION
LogicalDisk/% Disk Time	This is the total percentage of time that the disk is spending performing read and write operations. This value should usually be below 50 to 60 percent on a sustained basis. If this value is excessive, you want to look at the LogicalDisk % Read Time and the LogicalDisk % Write Time values to see if you can determine whether the majority of the activity consists of reads or writes.
LogicalDisk/Avg. Disk Queue Length	This is the total number of read and write operations currently queued up and waiting for the disk subsystem to perform. This value should not exceed three or four on a sustained basis.
LogicalDisk/Split IO/Sec	This is the number of times per second that a single I/O operation was split into multiple I/O operations. Though there is no specific number to watch for, a high value may indicate that the disk is fragmented. Ideally, Exchange database and transaction logs are on separate spindles, which reduces the likelihood of fragmentation.

TABLE 26.8:   Common Network Counters That Are Useful for Troubleshooting

OBJECT/COUNTER	EXPLANATION\RECOMMENDATION
Network Interface/Current Bandwidth	This counter will show you the network bandwidth at which the network adapter is configured to operate. The value is in bits, so it might be hard to read.
Network Interface/Bytes Total/sec	This is the total bytes sent and received per second. If you convert this to bits per second and then compare it to the Current Bandwidth counter, it will give you an idea of whether the network or network adapter is nearing its capacity.
Network Interface/Packets Outbound Errors and Network Interface/ Packets Received Errors	These counters show the total number or packets that could not be received or transmitted due to errors. These values should be fairly low and should not be rising while you are looking at them. If these values seem excessive, update the network adapter driver, check for network switch configuration problems, or even possibly replace the cable.
TCPv4/Segments Retransmitted/sec	This counter shows the number of TCP segments that had to be retransmitted because they were not properly received by the remote host. This value should be a very low percentage (less than two to three percent) of the total Segments/sec counter. If this value is excessive, it usually indicates problems with the network infrastructure such as routers or switches dropping packets.

EXCHANGE-SPECIFIC COUNTERS

Now that you have looked at some generic Windows counters for performance monitoring and troubleshooting, let's look at a few counters that Exchange Server provides that might indicate a bottleneck. Table 26.9 shows some counters that may be useful in determining if there are bottlenecks in your environment that affect Exchange servers or users.

TABLE 26.9: Exchange-Specific Counters That Are Helpful in Troubleshooting Problems and Monitoring Performance

OBJECT/COUNTER	EXPLANATION\RECOMMENDATION
MSExchangeIS/RPC Averaged Latency	This counter represents the average latency (in milliseconds) of the last 1,024 RPC packets. This value should be below 50 milliseconds. Higher values indicate that the server is not responding to requests quickly enough or that there are network problems.
Database/Database Cache % Hit	Selecting the Information Store instance of this counter will tell you the percentage of database file page requests that were serviced from memory rather than having to generate read requests to the disk. A low Database Cache % Hit value will cause the disk usage to be higher than it should be. This value should be above 95 percent. If it is not, consider adding more memory.
MSExchange ADAccess Domain Controllers/ LDAP Read Time	This is the time (in milliseconds) that it takes to successfully perform an LDAP search. This value should not be more than 50 milliseconds. Higher values indicate that the selected domain controller is not responding quickly enough due to performance issues of its own or network problems.

Finding the Right Elixir

Depending on your findings when you use Performance Monitor, there may be solutions that let you address performance problems without adding additional hardware. Usually, however, at least some additional hardware needs to be thrown into the mix to improve performance. Let's look at some of the major dependencies of Exchange and how you would address bottlenecks related to Exchange.

PHYSICAL MEMORY

With older versions of Exchange, adding additional memory to an Exchange server was something of a cure-all recommendation. This was true until you reached around 4GB of physical memory. At that point, unless the Windows server was supporting more applications than just Exchange components, adding more memory was just a waste of money. The Exchange 2000/2003 information store service (`store.exe`) could access a maximum of about 1.7GB of physical memory; the other Exchange components together might use another 1GB of memory. Anything over 4GB of RAM was wasted.

With Exchange 2007, adding more memory is once again a cure-all for what ails you. Because Exchange Server 2007 is a 64-bit application, you will find that it has the ability to access far more memory than previous versions of Exchange. Adding additional memory can also reduce demands on the disk subsystem.

The maximum amount of memory that Exchange 2007 can efficiently access and use is 32GB. Beyond this, Exchange reaches a point of diminishing returns where additional memory will not yield sufficient additional performance to be worth the cost, especially given the amount of money necessary to build a server with more than 32GB of RAM. The price of additional memory is coming down, but be careful about going beyond 32GB of memory; this is the maximum amount that Microsoft currently recommends. Some Exchange server roles may actually suffer a performance hit if more than 32GB of RAM is used.

PHYSICAL AND LOGICAL DISKS

If you are finding performance problems relating to your disk subsystem, you have a couple of options available to you. It will depend on the problem you are experiencing, of course, but you should have some low-cost options as well as more expensive options.

◆ If the problem is related to Exchange database reads/writes or transaction log writes, try increasing the amount of physical memory.

◆ If the problem is specific to one physical disk, try distributing the disk I/O to other physical disks. Transaction log writes and database reads/writes should always be split to separate physical disks when possible.

◆ If you're using RAID 5 or RAID 0+1 arrays, add additional disks to the array to allow for additional I/O capacity.

◆ Move one or more server roles to additional hardware. If you have already split server roles on to dedicated server hardware, you may need additional servers handling a specific role.

PROCESSOR CAPACITY

Chapter 4, "Exchange Server 2007 Architecture," talked about having sufficient processor capacity for your servers. The number of processors recommended varies based on the server's roles and, of course, the user profile. Table 26.10 shows Microsoft's processor recommendations for Exchange 2007.

TABLE 26.10:   Processor Recommendations for Exchange 2007

SERVER ROLE	MINIMUM	RECOMMENDED	MAXIMUM
Client Access	1 x processor core	4 x processor cores	4 x processor cores
Combined role	1 x processor core	4 x processor cores	4 x processor cores
Hub Transport	1 x processor core	4 x processor cores	8 x processor cores
Mailbox	1 x processor core	4 x processor cores	8 x processor cores
Unified Messaging	1 x processor core	4 x processor cores	4 x processor cores
Edge Transport	1 x processor core	2 x processor cores	4 x processor cores

Table 26.10 takes into consideration single-core processors, but based on the price and performance of dual-core processors, a dual-core processor might be a better option if you need additional processor capacity.

Note also that Table 26.10 does not take into consideration additional applications that may be running on a particular Exchange server. For example, on a heavily loaded Exchange server, antivirus software can consume quite a bit of both CPU and memory resources. A Hub Transport server that must process dozens or hundreds of transport rules for each message that it handles might also benefit from more cores than the standard recommendation.

You may also have noticed in Table 26.10 that for the combined role server (a server that handles more than one role, such as a server with the Mailbox, Hub Transport, and Client Access server roles), the maximum recommended number of processors is four. The logic behind this (I am assuming) is that once a combined function server gets to the point where it would benefit from more than four processors, the roles should probably be split onto more than one physical machine rather than adding more hardware.

Cleaning Up Unwanted Mailbox Content

I was not quite sure where to put this section of the book because it did not fit well into any particular chapter. So here is where you find information on how to export data out of a mailbox. In the past, we used tools such as ExMerge to remove mail from a mailbox if it was no longer necessary (such as old mail that's archived) or if we had to remove a message that contained a virus.

Exchange 2007 introduces a new Exchange Management Shell cmdlet called `Export-Mailbox` that you can use to remove content from a mailbox or a whole group of mailboxes. `Export-Mailbox` is a lot more efficient and flexible than ExMerge is.

The `Export-Mailbox` wizard allows you to search through one or more mailboxes, and when matching message content is found, it is copied to an alternate mailbox. Optionally, you can specify a parameter that allows you to delete the message from the original location. You can specify a number of different criteria to narrow the scope of the messages for which you are searching. Table 26.11 lists the `Export-Mailbox` parameters along with a description and an example of using each one.

When using the `Export-Mailbox` cmdlet, you must specify a target mailbox and a target folder to which you want to copy or move the messages. The `-TargetMailbox` parameter is used to specify the name of an existing mailbox; the mailbox must exist. You can give this parameter in the form of the Exchange alias, the SMTP address, or the display name of the mailbox. `Export-Mailbox` will also accept as input mail-enabled objects piped from cmdlets such as `Get-Mailbox` and `Get-DistributionGroupMember`. The `-TargetFolder` parameter specifies the name of a folder in the root of the target mailbox. If this folder does not exist, it will be created.

Mail is copied (or moved) to the target folder in the specified target mailbox. A folder structure is created under the specified target folder that includes the recovered data, the mailbox name, and the date of the recovery. An example of this is shown in Figure 26.29. One thing that you may find annoying is that all folders from the source mailbox are created even if there are no messages that meet the search criteria in a particular folder.

Let's start out with a really simple example and look at the output. In this example, you want to export (copy) everything in a mailbox called `supatana` over the date range 01/01/2006 through 12/31/2006. The target mailbox is called `MergeMailbox` and the target folder is `Jan2007Archive`. Here is the cmdlet that will perform this operation:

```
Export-Mailbox supatana -TargetMailbox MergeMailbox -TargetFolder Jan2007Archive↵
-StartDate "01/01/2006" -EndDate "12/31/06"
```

TABLE 26.11: Search Parameters That Can Be Used with the Export-Mailbox Cmdlet

PARAMETER	DESCRIPTION AND EXAMPLE
AllContentKeywords	When AllContentKeywords is used, the command will find the keywords you specify in the message subject, body, and attachments. This parameter should not be used in conjunction with the ContentKeywords and SubjectKeywords parameters. Here is an example of this parameter's formatting: -AllContentKeywords "ILOVEYOU"
AttachmentFilenames	Locates messages with a specific filename or when using wildcards. Here are two examples: -AttachmentFilenames "*.txt" and -AttachmentFilenames "iloveyou.vbs"
ContentKeywords	Content keywords allow you to search for content in the message body and attachment content. If you use ContentKeywords and SubjectKeywords in the same command, the content must match both. Here is an example: -ContentKeywords "secret formula"
EndDate	EndDate specifies the last date that will be used when copying or moving messages out of a mailbox. If a message is dated after the end date but it meets the criteria, it will not be copied or moved. You can optionally use a time with the date if you want to search only to a certain point during a day. Here are some examples: -EndDate "02/01/2007" and -EndDate "02/02/2007 11:30:00"
ExcludeFolders	If you have specific folders that you do not want to include in the search, you can use the ExcludeFolders parameter. Here is an example where you can exclude the Sent Items folder: -ExcludeFolders "\Sent Items"
IncludeFolders	If you have only specific folders that you want to include in your search, you can use the IncludeFolders parameter. For example, if you want to search in only the Inbox folder, here is an example: -IncludeFolders "\Inbox"
PSTFolderPath	PSTFolderPath specifies the path to use when creating a PST file. An example would be: -PSTFolderPath c:\PSTs\Dawne.pst
StartDate	StartDate allows you to specify a starting date for your search. When it's used in conjunction with the EndDate parameter, you can narrow the scope of time you are using to search for messages. You can optionally use a time with the date if you want to search only to a certain point during a day. Here are some examples: -StartDate "01/31/2007" and -StartDate"1/31/2007 11:30:00"
SubjectKeywords	Subject keywords are words found in the subject of a message. Here is an example: -SubjectKeywords "I quit"

FIGURE 26.29

Example of the folder structure created by the Export-Mailbox cmdlet.

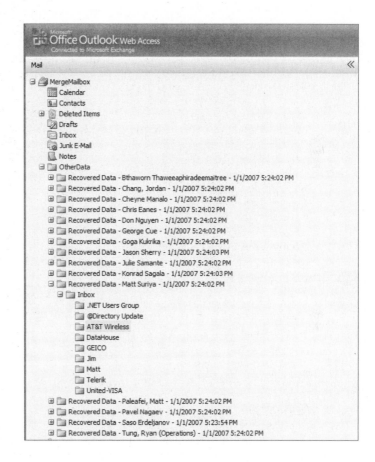

When you kick off the command, you will see a progress bar on the top of the management shell window.

The actual text output of this operation is as follows:

```
Confirm
Are you sure you want to perform this action?
Exporting mailbox content from the mailbox 'Matt Suriya' into the mailbox for
'MergeMailbox (MergeMailbox@somorita.com)' inside folder
'\Jan2007Archive\Recovered Data - Matt Suriya - 1/1/2007 5:40:33 PM'.
 This operation may take a long time to complete.
[Y] Yes  [A] Yes to All  [N] No  [L] No to All  [S] Suspend  [?] Help
(default is "Y"):y
```

```
Identity: volcanosurfboards.com/Somorita Surfboards/
Matt Suriya
DistinguishedName              : CN=Matt Suriya,OU=Somorita Surfboards,
DC=volcanosurfboards,DC=com
DisplayName                    : Matt Suriya
Alias                          : supatana
LegacyExchangeDN               : /o=VOLCANO SURFBOARDS/ou=FIRST
ADMINISTRATIVE GROUP/cn=RECIPIENTS/cn=SSUPATANASAKUL
PrimarySmtpAddress             : supatana@somorita.com
SourceServer                   : HNLEX03.volcanosurfboards.com
SourceDatabase                 : HNLEX03\First Storage Group\Mailbox Database
SourceGlobalCatalog            : HNLDC01
SourceDomainController         :
TargetGlobalCatalog            : HNLDC01
TargetDomainController         :
TargetMailbox                  : volcanosurfboards.com/Users/MergeMailbox
TargetServer                   : HNLEX03.volcanosurfboards.com
TargetDatabase                 : HNLEX03\First Storage Group\Mailbox Database
MailboxSize                    : 198655KB
IsResourceMailbox              : False
SIDUsedInMatch                 :
SMTPProxies                    :
SourceManager                  :
SourceDirectReports            :
SourcePublicDelegates          :
SourcePublicDelegatesBL        :
SourceAltRecipient             :
SourceAltRecipientBL           :
SourceDeliverAndRedirect       :
MatchedTargetNTAccountDN       :
IsMatchedNTAccountMailboxEnabled :
MatchedContactsDNList          :
TargetNTAccountDNToCreate      :
TargetManager                  :
TargetDirectReports            :
TargetPublicDelegates          :
TargetPublicDelegatesBL        :
TargetAltRecipient             :
TargetAltRecipientBL           :
TargetDeliverAndRedirect       :
Options                        : Default
SourceForestCredential         :
TargetForestCredential         :
TargetFolder                   : \Jan2007Archive\Recovered Data -
Matt Suriya - 1/1/2007 5:40:33 PM
RsgMailboxGuid                 :
```

```
RsgMailboxLegacyExchangeDN       :
RsgMailboxDisplayName            :
RsgDatabaseGuid                  :
MoveType                         : Export
MoveStage                        : Completed
StartTime                        : 1/1/2007 5:40:36 PM
EndTime                          : 1/1/2007 5:48:28 PM
StatusCode                       : 0
StatusMessage                    : This mailbox has been exported to the target
user mailbox.
```

The report says that the mailbox was "exported," but that is actually a little misleading. It would be better to say that the mailbox was "copied" because the command did not delete any of the original content from the mailbox. To remove the content after it was copied, you could have used the -DeleteContent parameter in the command.

You may also wonder about all of the properties that don't seem to have values in this output. The Export-Mailbox cmdlet can also be used to move mailboxes from other Exchange organizations and into Exchange 2007, so many of these options are used with migrations from other organizations.

Be careful when using a broad search and copy category. You could easily fill up a transaction log or database disk if you selected all of the mailboxes in your organization!

Let's look at a more useful example. What if a user had sent a message with the subject "Executive Compensation" to everyone in the Viper Pilots group? You can use a combination of two cmdlets to completely remove any message with that subject:

```
Get-DistributionGroupMember "Viper Pilots" | Export-Mailbox↵
-TargetMailbox MergeMailbox -TargetFolder ExecutivesCompMessage↵
-SubjectKeyWords "Executive Compensation" -DeleteContent
```

Exchange Server 2007 SP1 introduced a feature that had been widely requested. This is the ability to import (Import-Mailbox) and export (Export-Mailbox) using a PST file; you use the -PSTFolderPath option of these two cmdlets. There are a few caveats to using this new feature, though. Here are a few "factoids" about this functionality:

◆ You can only run this cmdlet from a 32-bit version of Windows that has the 32-bit version of the management tools installed.

◆ Exchange Server 2007 SP1 does not have the necessary MAPI components to create PST files. Outlook 2003 SP2 (or later) or Outlook 2007 must be installed on the computer.

◆ You must be an Exchange Server administrator on any Exchange server that contains a mailbox you are going to export.

◆ The PST files that are created use Unicode and can be larger than 2GB, though I recommend not letting them get created much larger than that.

If you want to export an entire mailbox to a PST file, you can do so with a command like this:

```
Export-Mailbox Sueko.Miura -PSTFolderPath c:\psts\Sueko.pst
```

Of course, all of the other `Export-Mailbox` options (except for `-TargetMailbox`) work when exporting to PST. For example, here is a command that will allow you to export everything for a specific date range to a PST file.

```
Export-Mailbox Easter.Bruce -StartDate "01/01/07" -EndDate "12/31/08"↵
-PSTFolderPath C:\PSTs\easter.pst
```

Summary

Administrators that run healthy Exchange organizations and provide their users with good availability have something in common. They're attentive to their Exchange server's needs without over-administering the server. Here is the list of the "big five" tasks that I recommend administrators perform daily:

◆ Perform and verify daily Exchange database backups.

◆ Verify that a sufficient amount of disk (and approximately the expected amount of disk space) is available.

◆ Check the Hub Transport server queues to verify that outbound messages are not stalled and queuing up.

◆ Review the event logs for unexpected errors or warnings.

◆ Confirm that your message hygiene software is up-to-date.

Granted these guidelines are just an overview of some basic tasks, but they give you an idea of the types of things you should do on a regular basis. These tasks have a few things in common. Most important, they are more focused on monitoring Exchange and checking to make sure things are done (like daily backups) than on performing any sort of direct action against the Exchange server. Contrary to popular belief, a stable, well-configured Exchange server does not need to be rebooted regularly, nor do databases need any sort of offline maintenance.

Some basic auditing and diagnostics logging categories should be enabled to allow the server to be audited or to get information about daily activity. Periodically, you may need to increase diagnostics logging on other components for troubleshooting and diagnostics. If more in-depth troubleshooting and diagnostics logging are used, they should be disabled or set back to their default values after you are through.

To know what normal behavior is for your server, though, you should do some basic performance monitoring periodically on your Exchange servers. It does not need to be done weekly or even monthly. Perhaps once every three to four months should be sufficient. Look at some of the common Windows and Exchange performance monitor counters to make sure you have not developed any bottlenecks.

Finally, Exchange administrators periodically find themselves faced with the need to remove content from users' mailboxes. This may be viruses, messages with unauthorized content, or just data that needs to be archived. Exchange 2007 provides a powerful new cmdlet called `Export-Mailbox` that serves this purpose.

Appendix

Cool Third-Party Applications for Exchange Server and Outlook Clients

I never appreciated the meaning of *cool* until I started playing with Exchange Server and its clients and some of the fantastic applications that third-party vendors have created to extend the reach of an already great set of products. Here I will tell you about some of my favorite products.

Products are listed by category, along with information on how you can contact the vendors. Some vendors provide live demos or even trial versions of their products that you can download over the Internet.

Though I have tried hard to keep this list of tools and vendors accurate, it is by no means complete and may not even be completely accurate by the time you read it. There is continual change in vendors and ownership of products in our industry.

Most of the vendors here have Exchange Server 2007-specific versions of their products; you should always verify that you have the right version of a product when you are moving from one version of Exchange to another. Contact the vendor for more information.

TEST EVERYTHING!

Remember, I can't be responsible for the performance of these products in your Exchange Server and organizational environments. I recommend that you install and test each product in a lab environment prior to putting it into production.

Administration and Management

Exchange administration and management covers a wide area. The products listed here do the same. Some monitor Exchange servers and connectors, reporting on such things as e-mail loads and network availability. Other products assist in migrating mailboxes and other Exchange objects within an Exchange organization or between Exchange organizations. Still other products help you automate the resource-draining creation of Outlook profiles for Exchange Server. And one product in this section is a substitute for Windows clustered servers.

ChooseFrom for Microsoft Exchange 2007 ChooseFrom allows a user to choose an alternate address for a message to be from rather than their default address. This is useful, for example, when a group of users receive a message sent to the Sales alias and a user wants to reply to that message with the Sales e-mail address rather than his or her own address in the From field. Contact: IVASoft (www.ivasoft.com)

Directory Update Directory Update is a web-based administration tool that allows end users to update their own information in the Active Directory and thus the Exchange address lists.

The administrator specifies which attributes the user can update. Contact: Ithicos Solutions (www.ithicos.com)

EmpowerID Suite The EmpowerID Suite is a web-based account provisioning system that works against Active Directory and ADAM directories. EmpowerID can join attributes from multiple directories. Contact: The Dot Net Factory (www.thedotnetfactory.com)

Exchange Administrator Exchange Administrator is a nice front end for managing the Active Directory side of Exchange Server. It supports the automation of administrative tasks such as mailbox creation. The product is an add-on to NetIQ's Directory and Resource Administrator. Contact: NetIQ (www.netiq.com)

Exchange Migration Wizard The Exchange Migration Wizard is a comprehensive migration tool that will allow you to perform migrations from Exchange 5.5 to Exchange 2007 with minimal disruption to your user community. This tool is part of a fairly comprehensive offering of migration tools from Quest Software. Contact: Quest Software (www.quest.com)

Exchange Migrator Another product from NetIQ, Exchange Migrator simplifies the migration of Exchange objects from one Exchange organization to another. Contact: NetIQ (www.netiq.com)

Exchange POP3 Exchange POP is a gateway that downloads messages from non-Exchange POP3 and IMAP4 mailboxes to Exchange mailboxes. This product is useful for users who receive all or some of their e-mail outside of Exchange, for example, at an ISP. Exchange POP3 includes antivirus and anti-spam screening. See also the product Mail Essentials for Exchange/SMTP in the section "Virus, Spam, and Content Control" later in this appendix. Contact: Kinesphere Corporation (www.exchangepop3.com)

MailShadow MailShadow is one of the truly unique products on the market for Exchange Server. It allows the administrator to select mailboxes and have the content replicated and then synchronized to another server. If the user's mailbox server fails, he/she can be switched over to the backup mailbox. Contact: Cemaphore Systems (www.cemaphore.com)

Message Classification Titus Labs Message Classification is a classification and policy enforcement tool for Outlook and Outlook Web Access that allows customers to manage the classification, distribution, and retention of valuable corporate e-mail. Designed for large enterprises, Message Classification allows users to assign categorization properties to e-mail messages. It includes the ability to require users to assign e-mail classification labels at the desktop before messages are sent, restricting the distribution of sensitive e-mail to authorized recipients only. In addition, it allows users to categorize e-mail for easy storage, search, and retrieval. Contact: Titus Labs (www.titus-labs.com)

Message Manager Message Manager can scan e-mail databases for specific content to find information leaks, track specific messages, and investigate e-mail related to specific employees or subjects. Contact: Intellireach Corp. (www.intellireach.com)

Migration Manager for Exchange Migration Manager for Exchange is a comprehensive solution for seamless, transparent inter-org migrations from Exchange 2000/2003 to Exchange Server 2007. It supports multiple Exchange migration scenarios; one- or two-way synchronization of directory objects; mailboxes and public folders; address updating on migrated messages; and coexistence capabilities. Contact: Quest Software (www.quest.com)

Network E-mail Examiner Network E-mail Examiner is a tool that allows you to search and analyze an Exchange Server database for words and phrases that are not permitted within your organization or performing a legal discovery. At press time, an Exchange 2007 version of this tool has not been announced, but check with the vendor. Contact: Paraben Forensic Tools (www.paraben-forensics.com)

Notes Migrator for Exchange   Quest Notes Migrator for Exchange enables organizations to migrate directly from Lotus Notes to Microsoft Exchange Server 2007 with complete project management and reporting while minimizing impact to users. Contact: Quest Software (www.quest.com)

Profiler   Profiler is a web-based tool that allows a user to update some of their Active Directory/global address list information via a web page. This includes mailbox forwarding. Profiler also allows designated account managers to manage user accounts through a web interface. Contact: Directory Wizards (www.dirwiz.com)

PST Policy Administrator   PST Policy Administrator is software that allows you to keep your users' PST usage in check. The software can also manage PST file content and delete attachments from PST files. Contact: Sherpa Software (www.sherpasoftware.com)

Public Folder Migrator for SharePoint   Public Folder Migrator for SharePoint is a new tool from Quest Software that allows you to perform assessments of migration requirements and to migrate the public folder hierarchy and data into SharePoint sites. It is no secret that public folders are going to be less important in the future. Organizations that get a head start toward moving their public folder content to another platform will be much better prepared for future versions of Exchange. Contact: Quest Software (www.quest.com)

SimpleSync   SimpleSync is a directory synchronization tool that allows you to synchronize user and contact information between multiple directory sources, including Active Directory, Exchange 5.5, and others. Contact: Directory Wizards (www.dirwiz.com)

WebDir   WebDir is a complete web-based account provisioning system that includes delegated administration, Exchange mailbox management, and self-service directory management options. Contact: Imanami (www.imanami.com)

Monitoring and Reporting

Let's face it, our bosses love reports — especially if those reports have colors and graphics! Systems people love monitoring systems that will help them be more proactive in the monitoring of their servers. In this section, I introduce you to a few monitoring and reporting packages that will make your life easier and let you send the boss those spiffy reports.

AppManager for Microsoft Exchange   AppManager for Exchange lets you monitor the health and performance of an entire distributed Exchange system. It can tell you such things as the time it takes to deliver e-mail, where Internet e-mail is being sent, what is making some mailboxes as large as they are, and where offensive e-mail resides on your server. Contact: NetIQ (www.netiq.com)

Argent Exchange Monitor   Argent Exchange Monitor is for small to very large Exchange environments (up to 2,000 Exchange servers). Monitoring includes response-time tracking, SMTP connectivity, top senders and receivers of messages, and mailboxes over storage limits. Contact: Argent Software (www.argent.com)

Promodag Reports   Promodag Reports is an agent-less reporting tool that uses existing Exchange log files such as the message tracking logs to provide extensive usage reports on your Exchange servers. Contact: Promodag (www.promodag.com)

MessageStats   MessageStats is a comprehensive reporting tool for Exchange Server that reports on mailbox usage, top senders, most commonly used domains, and more. Contact: Quest Software (www.quest.com)

OmniAnalyser   OmniAnalyser provides monitoring and reporting solutions for Exchange as well as service metrics that can be used for service-level agreement management. Contact: Hypersoft (www.hypersoft.com)

PowerGUI   PowerGUI is an extensible graphical administrative console for managing systems based on Windows PowerShell. These include Windows OS (XP, 2003, Vista), Exchange 2007, Operations Manager 2007, and other new systems from Microsoft. The tool allows administrators to access and use the rich capabilities of Windows PowerShell in a familiar and intuitive GUI console. Contact: Quest Software (www.quest.com)

Spotlight on Exchange   Spotlight on Exchange and its companion product Spotlight on Active Directory are two of the most "Star Trek"-looking server monitoring tools on the market. These tools monitor server health and report server problems, bottlenecks, and performance in a very slick graphical user interface. Contact: Quest Software (www.quest.com)

Smarts Application Discovery Manager   EMC Smarts Application Discovery Manager is powered by EMC nLayers technology and provides the infrastructure for real-time hands-off dependency-driven change, configuration, incident, and problem management. It works with Exchange, SQL, and Active Directory among other applications. Contact: EMC Corporation (www.emc.com)

Zenprise   Zenprise is a not really a monitoring or reporting tool in the traditional sense but rather a proactive monitoring and diagnostics tool for Exchange. Zenprise scans your Exchange server's configuration, event logs, and services and analyzes Exchange in real time. Its knowledge base of common problems and solutions can provide administrators with knowledge of an impending problem before it affects users. Contact: Zenprise (www.zenprise.com)

Backup, Recovery, and Archiving Software

The key here is support for Exchange Server. Windows Server 2003's own backup program backs up the Exchange mailbox and public databases while they're open and in use. That's really nice, but Windows Server 2003's Backup utility isn't the most full-featured backup product around. Still, the Windows 2003 backup program can work well for small networks, especially if each server is backed up locally. However, Microsoft surprised many Exchange administrators when it announced that Windows Server 2008 would not support streaming backups for Exchange Server 2007, so you will require third-party backup software if you are running Windows Server 2008. For more features, turn to third-party backup solutions that include such features as Windows Server 2003 or 2008's ability to do volume shadow copy backups of Exchange databases.

Organizational requirements, governmental regulations, or just plain diminishing disk-storage resources might require that e-mail be archived. Whether it's to protect employee pension information, to meet the financial requirements of agencies such as the Securities Exchange Commission, or to free up space on Exchange Server disks, e-mail archiving is becoming an important function in IT shops. You can do some archiving with tools built into Exchange Server and Outlook, but third-party add-ons make archiving much easier.

Archive Manager   Archive Manager captures, indexes, and stores messaging data for the purpose of mailbox management, compliance archiving, and knowledge sharing. Powerful search tools allow for retrieval from the archive to support e-discovery. Features mobile access for BlackBerry and Windows Mobile 5 devices as well. Contact: Quest Software (`www.quest.com`)

CA ARCserve Backup   ARCserve has been around for a long time and is a good package. Under the enterprise-oriented hand of Computer Associates, the CA ARCserve Backup suite has become a very strong contender in large system backup. Contact: Computer Associates (`www.cai.com`)

Backup Exec   Like ARCserve, Backup Exec has been around for eons and is a good backup product with nice backup-scheduling capabilities. Also check out Symantec's Remote Storage for Exchange, which archives message attachments to a secondary storage device such as tape and then seamlessly returns the attachment when a user tries to access it. Contact: Symantec (`www.symantec.com`)

Enterprise Archive Solution   Exchange Archive Solution archives Exchange messages so that they can be managed and retrieved as needed. This is a high-powered product that allows for centralized backup while leaving room for local control and end-user recovery of archived messages. Contact: ZANTAZ (`www.zantaz.com`)

Galaxy Backup and Recovery   Galaxy Backup and Recovery for Microsoft Exchange is a very nice product. It has a fine user interface and it allows individual recovery of messages and other Exchange items. Contact: CommVault Systems (`www.commvault.com`)

EmailXtender   EmailXtender is an e-mail archiving application. It runs on a separate server and can archive mail in a variety of server environments, including Exchange, Lotus Notes, and Unix Sendmail. Data is stored in Microsoft SQL Server. Administration includes the ability to set retention parameters and policies for categorization of messages. Contact: EMC Corporation (`www.emc.com`)

Enterprise Vault   Enterprise Vault is one of the industry leaders in Exchange archiving. It runs on a dedicated server and supports Exchange 5.5–2007, Lotus Notes, File Server Archiving, SharePoint Archiving, PST migrations, and many third-party add-ins such as instant messaging, Bloomberg, and fax archiving. Contact: Symantec (`www.symantec.com`)

NearPoint   Mimosa Systems' NearPoint product and associated add-ons approach e-mail archival from a unique perspective. Instead of performing MAPI crawls of the mailboxes at timed intervals, they copy the transaction logs and replay them to the archive. This reduces I/O requirements on the Exchange server and ensures that all mail server data is kept in the archive. Contact: Mimosa Systems (`www.mimosasystems.com`)

NetWorker   Well known for the excellence of its storage products and Unix backup products, EMC also supports the Windows NT 4 and Windows 200x Server environments with its NetWorker backup product. An optional module extends support to Exchange Server. Contact: EMC Corporation (`www.emc.com`)

NetBackup   NetBackup is the industrial-strength enterprise backup product from Symantec, makers of Backup Exec. The product provides centralized control of the backup process and comes in three flavors for different-sized organizations and backup needs. Contact: Symantec (`www.symantec.com`)

Recovery Manager for Exchange   Recovery Manager for Exchange allows administrators to restore, search, and export individual message-level items, including e-mails, appointments, tasks, contacts, and attachments from backups, un-mounted EDB files, and PST files without setting up multiple dedicated Exchange recovery servers. Contact: Quest Software (`www.quest.com`)

Replication Manager EMC Replication Manager manages EMC replication technologies and coordinates the entire replication process, from discovery and configuration to the operation of multiple disk-based replicas. Put the right data in the right place at the right time, on demand or based on user-defined schedules and policies. With Replication Manager, you can automate the discovery of storage arrays, applications, replication technologies, and hosts in the environment; record and catalog all information and activities for replicas; and enable point-and-click copies of information. Contact: EMC Corporation (www.emc.com)

UltraBac UltraBac Software's backup entry sports very nice backup setup and scheduling interfaces. An optional Exchange information store backup module is available. Contact: Ultra-Bac Software (www.ultrabac.com)

Fax Servers

Though Exchange Server 2007 provides good integration for inbound faxing with the Unified Messaging server role, you may have other needs, such as outbound faxing. The cost to implement a full unified messaging solution may also be too high for your organization. Generally, fax servers enable users to send and receive faxes through a central server instead of their own workstations or traditional fax machines. Fax servers that integrate with Exchange Server add a new address type for faxing. To send a message to an e-mail user, you select the user's e-mail address from an Exchange address book. To send a message to a fax user, you select the fax address from an Exchange address book.

FACSys Enterprise FACSys Enterprise operates pretty much like any other connector on an Exchange server, but it sends faxes. The product is managed right inside Exchange System Manager. Contact: emFAST (www.emfast.com)

Faxcom for Exchange Faxcom for Exchange runs as a Windows service. It integrates Exchange recipient information so users can send faxes using their Outlook contacts. Contact: Biscom, Inc. (www.biscom.com)

Faxination Server for Microsoft Exchange Faxination Server for Microsoft Exchange provides full Exchange Server integration and supports a range of languages. It allows for off-hours scheduling and least-cost routing. Contact: Fenestrae, Inc. (www.fenestrae.com)

FAXmaker for Exchange FAXmaker for Exchange runs as a Windows service and allows faxes and GSM phone service SMS messages to be sent from an Outlook client with seamless Exchange Server integration. It includes call cost accounting. Contact: GFI (www.gfi.com)

DM Fax Server DM Fax Server installs and works as a Windows service. It can function as a high-traffic fax server and it can support a range of e-document distribution functions, such as automated faxback. Contact: IMECOM Group (www.imecominc.com)

Genifax Genifax is a sophisticated fax server that works with a wide range of high-end messaging platforms, including Lotus Notes and Exchange Server. Omtool, the product's manufacturer, specializes in the legal and health care industries. Genifax can be expanded to include e-document distribution functionality. Contact: Omtool (www.omtool.com)

msXfax for Exchange Server/SMTP msXfax for Exchange Server/SMTP can be installed on an Exchange or Windows server. It integrates with Active Directory without modifying the schema. Contact: BNS Group (www.bnsgroup.com.au)

RightFax RightFax is an enterprise-level product focusing on e-document delivery. The product is tightly coupled with application solutions from SAP AG. Contact: Captaris, Inc. (www.captaris.com/rightfax)

Replication and High-Availability Software

Exchange Services are now required in many instances to be highly available or recoverable in alternate locations. With these rigorous requirements, organizations are adopting tools to supplement the backup technologies in place and the built-in replication mechanisms available. The goal of these vendors is to provide flexibility and control in how Exchange databases are replicated and how they will be available during a disaster.

MailShadow   MailShadow is one of the truly unique products on the market for Exchange Server. This product allows the administrator to select mailboxes and have the content replicated and then synchronized to another server. If the user's mailbox server fails, they can be switched over to their backup mailbox. Contact: Cemaphore Systems (`www.cemaphore.com`)

NearPoint   Mimosa NearPoint for Microsoft Exchange Server is the industry's most comprehensive information management solution for Microsoft Exchange. It unifies archival, eDiscovery or e-mail discovery, fine-grained and immediate recovery, user self-service access to all historical e-mail, and storage management. The NearPoint software solution comprises Information Management (ILM), e-mail archiving, disaster recovery, data protection, and mailbox extension functions. Contact: Mimosa Systems, Inc. (`www.mimosasystems.com`)

EMC RepliStor   EMC RepliStor is an easy-to-use, out-of-the-box software technology that provides data recovery and protection for Microsoft Windows. RepliStor increases the availability of your data by delivering real-time replicas to one or many locations. You can use data for offline backup protection, disaster recovery, data distribution, and application testing. Contact: EMC Corporation (`www.emc.com`)

RecoverPoint   EMC RecoverPoint (formerly Kashya) is an intelligent data protection and recovery solution that runs on out-of-band appliances located on the network. RecoverPoint provides comprehensive data recovery for storage area network (SAN)-attached devices across the entire data center, including heterogeneous, continuous remote replication and local continuous data protection. You can protect your organization from data loss due to common issues such as server failures, data corruption, software errors, viruses, and end-user errors, as well as from catastrophic events that can bring entire data centers to a standstill. Contact: EMC Corporation (`www.emc.com`)

SRDF Family   The SRDF family of software is a powerful suite of remote storage replication solutions available for disaster recovery and business continuity. It leverages high-end Symmetrix storage architecture to offer unmatched deployment flexibility and massive scalability — so you can meet mixed service-level requirements with minimal operational impact. Regardless of the application and RTO/RPO requirements, SRDF has the capability to meet your needs. Contact: EMC Corporation (`www.emc.com`)

CA XOsoft High Availability Option for Exchange   CA XOsoft High Availability Option for Exchange is an Exchange Server replication tool that provides not only replication services but also automated failover and failback. Contact: CA Xosoft (`www.xosoft.com`)

Network Security Monitors, Scanners, and Intrusion Detectors

I talked about network security monitors and scanners in Chapter 25, "Securing Exchange Server." Scanner products plow through network nodes on an IP-by-IP basis looking for such things as missing service packs and hotfixes, open ports, weak passwords, and potentially dangerous assignments of security privileges, as well as services, applications, and Registry key entries that might threaten security. Security monitors examine system logs for potential security holes and breaches.

Intrusion detectors are sort of intelligent firewalls for networks, servers, and workstations. They can find and thwart internal and external attempts to access resources far beyond the port and protocol level.

LANGuard Security Event Log Monitor LANGuard Monitor combs Windows event logs looking for evidence of internal and external security violations. It provides real-time notifications and reports to system managers. LANGuard also supports systemwide log management, including automated archiving and clearing of event logs. Contact: GFI Software (www.gfi.com)

LANGuard Network Security Scanner LANGuard Scanner looks at network nodes for known security problems. It's fast, and I have found it to be quite accurate. It produces very nice reports in HTTP format. LANGuard can remotely install service packs and hotfixes. Contact: GFI (www.gfi.com)

MonitorMagic MonitorMagic stores its findings in Microsoft SQL Server or Access databases. It comes with a range of very useful preconfigured security and other reports. A web interface is also included. Contact: Advanced Toolware (www.advtoolware.com)

Numara Network Monitor Numara Network Monitor includes features similar to LAN-Guard Monitor. The product also includes performance monitoring based on Windows performance logs and Windows service monitoring with auto restarts. Contact: Numara Software (www.numarasoftware.com)

RealSecure Network Protection Components The RealSecure Network Protection Components suite includes modules for networks, gateways, servers, and workstations. The modules detect attempted internal and external intrusions and stop them in real time. Contact: Internet Security Systems (www.iss.net)

RealSecure Vulnerability Assessment The RealSecure Vulnerability Assessment suite includes components for the Internet, servers, databases, and 802.11b wireless networks. These components scan their targets looking for a range of security threats. This product offers the most comprehensive approach to system security. Contact: Internet Security Systems (www.iss.net)

RETINA Network Security Scanner Like LANGuard, RETINA scans network nodes for known security problems. The program includes an interesting, if not easy-to-validate, artificial intelligence component that tries to get into a network as a hacker might. In my experience, RETINA is fast and quite accurate. Contact: eEye Digital Security (www.eeye.com)

SecureIIS SecureIIS is designed to protect Microsoft's Internet Information Server from external and internal attacks. The product examines traffic coming into IIS and stops packets that pose a threat. It can protect IIS servers with security problems for which Microsoft has not yet issued fixes. Contact: eEye Digital Security (www.eeye.com)

Unified Messaging

Unified messaging, the linking of a variety of messaging tools — pagers, telephones, e-mail clients, fax — has long been a dream of forward-looking communications types. As these products indicate, the tools for accomplishing unified messaging have emerged.

Mitel Networks Messaging Server   Mitel Networks Messaging Server brings together voice, incoming fax, and e-mail messaging. It also supports text-to-speech conversion and is scheduled to support speech-to-text in the near future. Wireless PDAs are supported. Contact: Mitel Networks Corporation (www.mitel.com)

PageMaster/ex   PageMaster/ex allows Exchange Server users to send pages and text messages to pagers. Page recipients appear on Exchange and can be selected from global or personal address lists. Messages can be sent in pager alphanumeric or GMS SMS format. It has a companion product called PageMaster/ol, which will send text messages for Outlook reminders. Contact: OmniTrend Software, Inc. (www.omnitrend.com)

Unified Communications   Avaya's Unified Communications is a high-end product that integrates with Exchange Server or Lotus Notes. It stores voicemail messages inside users' Exchange mailboxes. You can reply to voicemail with e-mail and vice versa. Contact: Avaya, Inc. (www.avaya.com)

Virus, Spam, and Content Control

What scares users more than the boss? Viruses, junk mail, and outgoing messages containing confidential information! These products let you catch mail-borne viruses, spam messages, and messages with sensitive content in their natural habitat: your Exchange server. They automatically download and install virus updates. Most also scan for viruses in real time as messages pass through your Exchange server and can perform scheduled and on-demand scans of information stores for viruses.

Forefront Security for Exchange Server   Forefront Security for Exchange Server (formerly Sybari Antigen) does real-time virus scans and repairs of inbound and outbound messages. It also does scheduled scans and fixes. Forefront supports third-party virus-scan engines for better virus coverage, especially for new viruses. Contact: Microsoft Corporation (www.microsoft.com/forefront)

Clearswift MIMESweeper   MIMESweeper is a suite of content security products that integrate with Exchange. MIMESweeper has been used since Exchange 5.5 and continues to be reliable. Contact: Clearswift Ltd. (www.clearswift.com)

Mail Essentials for Exchange/SMTP   Mail Essentials for Exchange/SMTP is a multi-featured package that does spam control with keyword and black and white lists, addition of disclaimers to outgoing messages, mail archiving, mail monitoring, and automatic replies. It also can download mail from POP3 mailboxes into Exchange mailboxes. Contact: GFI (www.gfi.com)

Mail Security for Exchange/SMTP/Lotus   Mail Security for Exchange/SMTP/Lotus is a comprehensive virus-control package that supports multiple virus-scanning engines. It also does content checking and HTML script checking and blocking. Contact: GFI (www.gfi.com)

Mail Security for Microsoft Exchange   Mail Security for Microsoft Exchange provides full-service virus scanning and cleaning. It also includes spam control features. Contact: Symantec Corporation (www.symantec.com)

MailWise   MailWise isn't a product that's installed on servers or workstations. Rather, it's a third-party service set up to receive mail destined for an SMTP server and quarantine it if it contains viruses or spam. Administrators can then either delete quarantined mail or send it along to its recipient. Contact: MailWise (www.mailwise.com)

MessageScreen   MessageScreen supports virus and spam control as well as detection and prevention of information leaks. Contact: Intellireach Corp. (`www.intellireach.com`)

Panda Security for Business with Exchange   Panda Anti-Virus for Exchange Server does most of the Exchange Server-based virus scanning and cleaning tricks performed by its competitors. Contact: Panda Software (`www.pandasecurity.com`)

Praetor for Microsoft Exchange Server   Praetor for Microsoft Exchange Server includes both antivirus and anti-spam functions. The product includes proprietary technology developed through the analysis of techniques used by spammers. Contact: Computer Mail Services, Inc. (`www.cmsconnect.com`)

ScanMail   Trend ScanMail looks for viruses on an Exchange server, even in encoded and compressed items. The product also does limited spam control. Contact: Trend Micro Inc. (`www.antivirus.com`)

SecurExchange Anti-Virus   SecurExchange Anti-Virus, like most of its competitors, scans e-mail and attachments (including zipped files on an Exchange server) for viruses. Contact: Nemx Software (`www.nemx.com`)

Websense Email Security   Websense Email Security is a comprehensive SMTP scanning package that includes multi-engine virus scanning, high-powered anti-spam control, and very sophisticated content-checking functionality. Contact: Websense, Inc. (`www.websense.com`)

Outlook and Outlook Web Access Add-Ins

There is a huge number of Outlook add-ins available out there in the third-party world. Here are a few extensions and add-ins from third parties that I found particularly useful.

EasyRecovery EmailRepair   EasyRecovery EmailRepair is a software utility that allows you to repair damaged Outlook PST and OST files. Contact: Kroll Ontrack (`www.krollontrack.com`)

MaX Compression   MaX Compression integrates with Outlook, Outlook Web Access, Exchange Server, and SMTP gateways to automatically compress (and optionally decompress) e-mail messages with attachments. If the client has MaX Compression installed, the compression and decompression process is transparent to the end user. Contact: C2C Systems (`www.c2c.com`)

Outlook Web Access for PDA/Outlook Web Access for WAP   Outlook Web Access for PDA and Outlook Web Access for WAP are two extensions for Outlook Web Access that provide a significantly better OWA interface for small screens such as PDA screens or for WAP browser-enabled cell phones. Outlook Web Access for WAP is a nice addition to Exchange Server 2007 since the Outlook Mobile Access feature is no longer supported. Contact: Lee Derbyshire (`www.leederbyshire.com`)

PKZIP for Windows   PKZIP for Windows includes an extension for Outlook that will automatically compress e-mail attachments larger than a certain size. This can dramatically reduce your mail storage requirements and bandwidth necessary to transmit e-mail messages. Contact: PKWare (`www.pkware.com`)

Workflow

The great promise of electronic messaging systems such as Exchange Server lies in their capability to help manage the flow of documents to complete a specific task among the various persons who need to be involved in the task. The products listed here add to Exchange Server's already wide-ranging capabilities in the workflow arena.

80-20 Document Manager   80-20 Document Manager works with Exchange, IBM DB2, and Microsoft SQL Server databases. It enables users to share files with full document-level security, version control, check-in/check-out, and full-text indexing. This product enables serious Exchange-based groupware applications. Contact: 80-20 Software (`www.80-20.com`)

illumio   illumio scans corporate e-mail looking for topic areas and connections based on senders and recipients. It seeks to find sources of organizational expertise and activity. Users can then access the illumio database when embarking on new projects or to enhance ongoing projects. Contact: Tacit Software (`www.tacit.com`)

Index

Note to the Reader: Throughout this index **boldfaced** page numbers indicate primary discussions of a topic. *Italicized* page numbers indicate illustrations.